THE ENGLISH POETS

GENERAL EDITOR: CHRISTOPHER RICKS

Property of
Robert M. Harris
Scottsbluff, Nebraska
25 March 1982

Also available in this series

Robert Browning: The Poems, volume one
Robert Browning: The Ring and the Book
Edmund Spenser: The Faerie Queene
Henry Vaughan: The Complete Poems
William Wordsworth: The Poems, volume one
William Wordsworth: The Poems, volume two
William Wordsworth: The Prelude
Sir Thomas Wyatt: The Complete Poems

Robert Browning:
The Poems

VOLUME TWO

EDITED BY JOHN PETTIGREW

Supplemented and Completed by
THOMAS J. COLLINS

NEW HAVEN AND LONDON
YALE UNIVERSITY PRESS

First published 1981 in the United Kingdom in a paperback edition by Penguin Books Limited in the series Penguin English Poets. First published 1981 in the United States of America by Yale University Press.

Printed in the United States of America.

Library of Congress Cataloging in Publication Data

Browning, Robert, 1812–1889.
Robert Browning, The poems.

(The English poets ; 1–2)
Includes bibliographical references and indexes.
I. Pettigrew, John. II. Series: English poets ; 1–2.
PR4202.P44 1981 821′.8 80–53976
ISBN 0–300–02675–7 (v. 1)
ISBN 0–300–02683–8 (pbk. : v. 1)
ISBN 0–300–02676–5 (v. 2)
ISBN 0–300–02684–6 (pbk. : v. 2)

10 9 8 7 6 5 4 3 2 1

To Pat and Sara

Contents

Preface

This edition, complementing Professor Altick's of *The Ring and the Book* in the Penguin English Poets series, includes the poems that Robert Browning himself collected, those he printed but did not collect, some first published after his death, and some poems and fragments previously unpublished; the important prose essay on Shelley is in the Appendix to Volume I. Except for *Pippa Passes*, the plays that appeared between 1837 and 1846 are excluded, as is the 'transcript' of the *Agamemnon* of Aeschylus. Otherwise completeness has been aimed at. It has not, however, been achieved: among verses still to be added to the canon are some in private hands, some recorded in sales catalogues that seem temporarily to have disappeared, and some verses in letters as yet unpublished (some letters of Browning's sister in the University of Texas are, for example, reported to include recollected snatches of Browning verses, but I was not permitted to see them). Missing also are some unpublished verses in the great Armstrong Browning Library for which permission to print has been refused: an eight-line lyric called 'Magari'; ten comic lines called 'On Andrea del Sarto's "Jupiter and Leda"'; and a translation of *Iliad* xviii, 202–31, the exclusion of which is the more regretted since the lines are a rendering of the same passage translated by Tennyson as 'Achilles Over the Trench'.

The Penguin edition is the first aiming at completeness and newly edited since Browning revised his works for the sixteen-volume collection of 1888–9 (in 1894 a seventeenth volume incorporated the poems in *Asolando*, which appeared on the day Browning died). Three earlier collections lack textual apparatus, and are more reprints than editions: the pioneering 'Florentine' edition (1898) of Charlotte Porter and Helen A. Clarke with extensive introductions and annotation, the 'Centenary' edition (1912) of F. G. Kenyon with brief introductions and no annotation, and the 'Macmillan' edition (1915) with negligible annotation. In progress is the 'Ohio' edition in a projected thirteen volumes, of which four have so far appeared. Edited by a large team, it aims at definitiveness, and has full textual apparatus and limited annotation. Some of the edition's principles and procedures have been challenged, and it is unfortunate that, in the volumes so far published, important manuscript materials have been ignored, and that the text, textual apparatus and annotation are not reliable.

Like these editions, the present one uses as its basic copy-text the collected edition of 1888–9. The first edition of *Asolando* has been used for the poems first published in that volume. Other poems are printed from manuscripts or first printings: for one poem the copy-text is – surely delightfully – a gravestone in the additional burying-ground of Saint Mary's Church, Barnsley, Yorkshire. There is much to be said for printing some of Browning's poems from the first edition, as Professor Altick did with *The Ring and the Book* – the 1833 *Pauline*, for instance, is more interesting, though less satisfactory, than the 1888 *Pauline*. For a collected edition aiming at consistency, however, the 1888–9 edition is as obviously the right basic copy-text as is, say, the Eversley for Tennyson. Browning revised his poems for it, and took pains over what was conceived of as the final text. Carefully planned by a great publisher who wished the edition to honour his friend, it was seen through the press with Browning's usual meticulous attention. 'Authorship has the alteration-itch,' and it is true that Browning's revisions seem often to testify more to a sense of insecurity within the poet than to anything else, and that, in Professor Altick's words, 'concentration on minutiae frequently drifted into a profitless concern with trivia'. Nevertheless, the 1888–9 text is almost invariably better than that of earlier editions. Moreover, Browning gave further attention to the text after the first impression appeared: sales were good, and the poet set about correcting typographical errors and making minor revisions for the second impression that was soon needed. When he left for Italy in 1889, he had revised the first ten volumes (the poems up to, and including, *The Ring and the Book*). He left a record of the over 200 planned alterations, only a few of them verbal ones, in a copy of the first impression of *1888–9* which is now in the British Library; some of the changes are recorded also on papers now in the Brown University Library (full details are given by Philip Kelley and William S. Peterson, 'Browning's Final Revisions', *Browning Institute Studies* I, 1973, 87–118). My collation of the British Museum and Brown University records shows that the poet's instructions were scrupulously followed. The present edition therefore incorporates the wanted changes (they affect the poems up to, and including, those in *Dramatis Personae*; in the few insignificant cases where the two records differ the present text is eclectic).

The texts have been collated with those of textually significant editions, the most important of which are the first editions, the collected editions of 1849, 1863 and 1868, and the second edition of *Dramatis*

Personae. They have been collated also with available manuscripts, the most important of which are those of *Paracelsus* and *Christmas-Eve and Easter-Day* in the Victoria and Albert Museum, *Dramatis Personae* and *Asolando* in the Pierpont Morgan Library in New York, and the volumes published between 1871 and 1887 in the Library of Balliol College, Oxford. Also consulted have been proofsheets (the most interesting of which are the sets of *Red Cotton Night-Cap Country* in the Berg Collection of the New York Public Library), and copies of poems with holograph alterations, like those of the first edition of *Paracelsus* that Browning used in preparing the *Poems* of 1849, which are now in the Berg Collection and the Beinecke Library of Yale University. Between manuscript and first edition, changes are often extensive; it was the poet's general practice to use his proof to make many alterations, especially in punctuation. The present edition also makes use of such fascinating volumes as J. S. Mill's review copy of *Pauline*, which with Mill's detailed comments was returned to Browning, who in turn wrote remarks and notes in it; the copy of *Ferishtah's Fancies* which Browning annotated for Mrs Orr; and the copy of *Sordello* owned by the poet's friend, Alfred Domett, and written in by both Domett and Browning.

Among the notes in the present edition is a generous selection of manuscript and textual variants of a kind not previously available except in the Ohio edition now in progress. As a general rule (to which such works as *Paracelsus*, *Pippa Passes* and 'Gold Hair' are exceptions), Browning's changes are not extensive from one printing to another, but they often can be most illuminating in any number of ways. Browning, incidentally, usually revised his work for the various collected editions using the immediately preceding collected edition for poems previously gathered, and the first or more recent edition otherwise.

The poet's reach for perfect texts inevitably exceeded his grasp as a proofreader, a capacity in which he was no match for, say, Tennyson. His final text is nevertheless a very good one indeed, and it is seldom necessary or desirable to depart from it. The odd spelling mistake ('villany', 'obsidion') and a few typographical errors have been silently corrected. Otherwise the text here – the same principles have been applied in the Notes – differs from copy-text in the following respects only:

(a) Spelling has been generally standardized (both 'gray' and 'grey', 'balk' and 'baulk', 'thro'' and 'through', English and American spellings of words ending in -or and -our, appear in Browning's text, for instance); also standardized is the use of the hyphen in adjectival combinations. Not standardized, however, is the spelling of the preterite or past participle, because sometimes one form seems clearly preferable to the other: in 'The Pied Piper', 'stept' and 'pressed' seem in context superior to 'stepped' and 'prest' in lines 98 and 221. Spellings preferred in Penguin style have normally been used ('gypsy' for 'gipsy', 'tonight' for 'to-night', 'judgement' for 'judgment'), but no change of this kind has been made if it would affect pronunciation ('sty' is substituted for 'stye', but not 'burden' for 'burthen'). Browning felt strongly about his Greek spellings; these have been kept, and inconsistencies in them from one poem to another remain. Not modified, capricious though it often is, is capitalization. The young poet threw capitals around with gay abandon, but after *Dramatis Personae* the older poet reduced their number considerably, and I have judged it best to leave well enough alone. I do not understand, for instance, the 'Man' of 'An Epistle' (line 69), but the use of the capital for 'He' in the last line of that masterpiece may be the most exciting in all literature.

(b) Among extant printers' manuscripts, that of *Paracelsus* gives the only example of a work in which Browning's punctuation was subjected to extensive (and there very much needed!) editorial work by the printer; Browning himself remarked, perhaps accurately, that the printers were responsible for the errors and inadequacies in punctuation in the first edition of *Sordello*. In later years, we know too, others made minor changes in Browning's texts; in a letter of 1889 for instance, the poet thanked his printer's reader for his care, and for his corrections and changes, in preparing *1888–9*. There is, however, a host of evidence to show that the poet had final control over punctuation and that he was deeply concerned about it. In the present edition, then, Browning's punctuation has been only very slightly modified, even, in many cases, when by today's rules it is technically incorrect: Browning often uses, for instance, double punctuation (a parenthesis and a comma, or a colon and a dash) where a modern writer would use single. As Dr Honan has indicated in his *Browning's Characters* (284–91), Browning's punctuation is very much his own, developed during a period when theories of punctuation were coming to be founded on syntactical rather than elocutionary bases. The implication of Dr Honan's penetrating discussion is clear: to interfere much with Browning's punctuation is often to meddle with effects deliberately sought, and to substitute mere technical correctness for demonstrable substantive significance. Penguin style has been followed in the handling of quotation marks: the inverted commas which, especially in the earlier volumes of *1888–9*, in many cases introduced each line of quoted matter, have been deleted. Again, single quotation marks replace Browning's double ones, and double ones consequently replace

Browning's single ones within quotations. In texts printed here from published texts not supervised by Browning and from manuscripts, of which some are very rough drafts, I have tried to use pointing that accords with Browning's practice elsewhere. The odd comma has been supplied in places where Browning, for no apparent reason, departed from his normal rules, and such definite errors as the omission of necessary periods or quotation marks have been corrected. In thirteen instances where question marks are incorrectly placed within quotations in the copy-text, silent transpositions have been made: *Pippa Passes*, i, 171; *Christmas Eve*, 1054, 1056; 'Blougram', 197; 'In a Balcony', 120; 'Rabbi Ben Ezra' 54; *Red Cotton*, 3277; *Aristophanes' Apology*, 5331; 'Of Pacchiarotto', 559; 'Doctor —', 78; 'Cherries', 74; 'Mihrab Shah') 'So, the head aches'), 20; 'Parleying with Dodington', 146. Otherwise Browning's own punctuation is reproduced.

(c) Paragraphing in the present edition often silently departs from that of the copy-text to follow that of the manuscript or first edition, and this for two reasons. Browning generally, though not invariably, preferred not to indent his verse paragraphs, but simply to use a space in the text to mark a new paragraph; consequently both printer and Browning, using an earlier printing for copy, often failed to note the desirable paragraph division when, in the earlier edition, a paragraph had ended at the foot of a page. The second reason is that the spaces between paragraphs in the proofs of first editions often presented the thrifty Browning with irresistible temptation; in would go a new line to fill the gap, and – since Browning worked with page proofs, not galleys – the printer could not without unreasonable expense make a new space. Thus desirable divisions disappeared from first editions and were usually not restored in later printings. No changes in paragraph structure have, however, been made in this edition without manuscript or textual authority.

(d) Browning sometimes used accents to assist readers with pronunciation. These have been retained, and others have been added in accordance with series policy: the *e* of the participial ending has been given a grave accent if the syllable containing it is, for metrical reasons, to be pronounced where in modern usage it would normally be silent; an acute accent is used to indicate a difference in stress from normal stress today (in 'Mílan' and 'illústrate', for example).

(e) Very occasionally a compositor's error led to a reading less satisfactory than that of the copy, a reading that escaped attention. In line 608 of 'Bishop Blougram's Apology', for instance, the 'soil' of first edition and *1863* became the less good 'soul' of *1868*, and the error was perpetuated in *1888–9*; in line 1736 of *Balaustion's Adventure*, all editions have read 'stud', but the manuscript reading is the superior 'steeds'; in line 951 of *Aristophanes' Apology*, all editions have 'Let', but the manuscript reading, 'Set', is better. In this edition 'soil', 'steeds' and 'Set' are printed. Sometimes one cannot be sure whether misprint or authorial revision is involved. In *Prince Hohenstiel-Schwangau*, line 539 has 'leaving' in the first edition and *1888–9*, 'having' in the manuscript: both are acceptable readings, but the latter seems more likely and, if anything, superior, and is printed in this edition. In line 91 of *Pauline* the 'wide' of 1833 became 'wild' in *1868*, a reading retained in *1888–9*; this edition prints 'wide', judging 'wild' an unnoted error and not a revision. In *Sordello* V, 483, both the 'crown' of *1840* and *1863* and the 'crowd' of *1868* and *1888–9* are acceptable, and since Browning made similar revisions elsewhere, a decision is called for: the present edition departs from copy-text to print 'crown'. The present text is generally extremely conservative, and, corrected spelling errors and misprints apart, there is only a handful of readings representing departures from all manuscripts and all editions supervised by Browning: 'grate' is emended to 'gate' in 'Donald', line 234, and 'captive' to 'capture' in 'Flute-Music', line 93, while lines 87–103 of the 'Parleying with Christopher Smart' print revisions, recorded in a late letter to J. T. Nettleship, that Browning proposed to incorporate in his next printing. Except for obvious misprints, the annotation records the few verbal differences between Browning's final text and that of the present edition.

There is no clearly right order in which to print Browning's poems. One does not slavishly follow the order of the final collected edition, especially since it was sometimes determined by a wish to have the volumes approximately equal in size (which is why *Sordello* there precedes *Paracelsus*). Many of Browning's poems cannot be accurately dated, and to attempt to print the poems in the order of composition would involve much bluffing and be misleading. In arranging his own works, Browning reclassified the poems originally printed in *Dramatic Lyrics* (1842), *Dramatic Romances and Lyrics* (1845), and *Men and Women* (1855), but his regroupings, details of which are given in an Appendix to Volume I of this edition, have generally been thought as unprofitable as, say, those of Wordsworth and Arnold. Everything considered, I have judged it best to print poems gathered by the poet in the order in which they first appeared, and in the chronological order of Browning's volumes. Verses that Browning left ungathered or unpublished appear in this edition in a group at the end of the text in an order approximating that of composition.

'There is a crying need for a really good popular edition of Browning's works.' Thus Dr Isobel Armstrong (*Browning Society Notes* II, No. 1, 1972, 20), noting what is certainly true: that 'the twentieth century has created gratuitous difficulty for readers of Browning because editions of his work have been, for the most part, simply appalling'. Comments like Dr Armstrong's are frequent, and so are complaints that Browning scholarship is not yet mature: Browning has been in all probability the worst served of major English poets. The present edition comes reasonably close, I believe, to being textually definitive; annotation is far from being so.

The ideal Browning annotator needs – besides sympathy – to be thoroughly at home with music, art, and seven or eight languages and literatures, to know the Bible and the plays of Euripides and Aristophanes (and Victorian scholarship on them) by heart, to be intimately familiar – for a start – with Keats and Shelley and Donne and Milton and Homer and Anacreon and Alciphron and Herodotus and Thucydides and Horace and Shakespeare and Wanley and Quarles and the *Illustrated London News* and Johnson's *Dictionary* and the fifty-odd – very odd – volumes of the *Biographie Universelle*. He needs to possess an outstanding knowledge of Italian topography and art and the more obscure recesses of Italian history, and to have read all those strange books which, one comes to believe, have had in their long history only one reader – Robert Browning. It would be helpful to have a photographic memory, to have lived an eon or two with faculties unimpaired, and to possess the kind of diligence that would have brought sweat into the brow of Browning's grammarian. Being therefore disqualified hopelessly in every essential respect from annotating Browning, one falls back on others' work and is able to steal much and verify it (the process often involving discrimination between quite irreconcilable scholarly 'facts'). Unfortunately one also finds, especially with the later poems, deserts of vast vacuity in which the planting of the odd signpost, let alone the creation of oases, is far from easy. At any rate, I have not consciously ducked difficulties, with the result that where I have failed, I have reminded myself – and doubtless will others – of Lounsbury's foghorn which proclaims the existence of fog without doing anything to disperse it.

The notes attempt to be concise without being cryptic, to provide important facts (dates, sources, textual details, biographical relevance, etc.) about each poem, and to give the usual kind of help with terms, allusions, words and phrases that may create difficulties for readers. The notes deliberately avoid paraphrase and criticism, but references to much of the best scholarship and criticism are there for readers who want them. While Browning's own notes are in the text itself as he wished them to be, the annotation includes important remarks by the poet in letters or in others' records. The annotation is thin on cross-references between one Browning poem and another simply because with a writer as prolific and repetitious as Browning such annotation can easily swamp other and more important kinds. And of these kinds the most helpful for Browning is unquestionably that which the Penguin English Poets series generally stresses: the linguistic.

The present edition aims to be fully glossed, for Browning is, as Mary Wilson remarked many years ago, a poet who had 'the curiosities of all dictionaries at his fingers' ends' (*Primer on Browning*, 37), and also because Dr Philip Drew is, I believe, right when he declares that 'a fully glossed edition of Browning would encourage many people to read him who are at present deterred by not knowing the meaning of all the words he uses' (*The Poetry of Browning*, 76). Browning is not only among the most prolific of English poets, but the employer of one of the most voluminous of poetic vocabularies: roughly 40,000 words, or about double that of Tennyson or of Shakespeare. With Browning as much as with any poet it would seem true that the *critical* relevance of the *Oxford English Dictionary* is prodigious, and the work indispensable to full understanding. I have stolen liberally from it.

Browning's vast poetic vocabulary, his delight in language of all kinds, familiar and remote, literary and technical and colloquial, his struggle to subdue language to his will – these things create both barriers to understanding, and huge rewards for those who read him in the right spirit. The same is true of the wealth of literary and historical reference, often to people, places, works and events that were scarcely of importance in their own day, let alone part of the stock in trade of literate readers of Browning's time or ours. To have the slightest chance of arriving at anything like understanding of that superb disaster of a poem, *Sordello*, for instance, one must have help (of a kind that this edition seeks to provide) with references to lore that is indeed quaint and curious. The same kind of thing is even more true of a later poem like *Aristophanes' Apology*, which has daunted even leading Browning scholars and which has been called by one of them, Philip Drew, 'the most erudite of Browning's poems and probably the most truly difficult' (*The Poetry of Browning*, 99). In fact *Aristophanes' Apology* is no such thing, and it is very different from *Sordello* and very much easier in every way because the sole real source of difficulty is the apparent erudition. It is otherwise one of the most straightforward of Browning's poems. It will not appeal to readers who are not prepared to be fascinated by such things as the proper method of cooking Copaic eels, the lost plays of Euripides, the curious position adopted by Euripides in writing his plays and the mysterious place in which he is buried, the rival claims of comic and tragic art, the astonishingly fertile mind of the father of comic drama and the grandeur of the old Sophocles. The annotation in this edition strives to help readers willing to give themselves to such interests to overcome – and to feel the joy of overcoming – the surface obstacles to the appreciation of what may well be (as it is for me) the masterpiece of Browning's later years.

For many of Browning's poems the present edition provides the first full glosses; this is perhaps a manifestation of the strange belief generally held until fairly recently that somehow or other the Victorians were close enough to us not to need editing. Inevitably, since some of Browning's later poems have received almost no attention and have, for practical purposes, never been annotated before, there is much that is new in the notes to the present edition. There is also much that is new in the notes to poems that have been treated in detail: in the notes to *Sordello*, for instance, which correct many traditional errors and which attempt to deal with some of the problems about which scholars and critics have been discreetly silent. It is, however, more important to point out that the notes would be even less adequate than they are were it not for the labours of many students of Browning over the years. I have stolen a great deal from many scholars, but I am especially conscious of debts to Paul Turner's recent edition of *Men and Women*, to T. L. Hood's work on Browning's classical sources and that of Elvan Kintner and E. C. McAleer on the letters, to S. W. Holmes on the sources of *Sordello*, to C. N. Jackson and F. M. Tisdel on *Aristophanes' Apology*, to A. B. Crowder and C. C. Watkins on *The Inn Album*, and to W. C. DeVane on the *Parleyings*. And all students of Browning know that while it is easy and true to say that the late Dean DeVane's *Handbook* is out of date on many matters, often wrong on textual matters particularly, and given to confusing conjecture with fact, it remains a work without which the reader of Browning can scarcely function.

Catharine Parr Traill College, Peterborough, Ontario 1976

John Pettigrew was a man of wit, intelligence and humanity. The quality of his work on Browning, represented by this edition, is proof of the loss created by his death. It has been my privilege to see *Browning: The Poems* through the press. My thanks to Pat Pettigrew for allowing me to fulfil his brother's wish.

University of Western Ontario Thomas J. Collins 1981

Acknowledgements

I am deeply grateful to many institutions and individuals:

to the Canada Council for a research grant;

to the authorities and staffs of the Library of Wellesley College, the Houghton and Widener Libraries of Harvard University, the Boston Public Library, the Beinecke Rare Book and Manuscript Library of Yale University, the Henry W. and Albert A. Berg Collection of the New York Public Library, the New York Public Library, the Pierpont Morgan Library, the Carl H. Pforzheimer Library, the Library of Congress, the Folger Shakespeare Library, the Armstrong Browning Library of Baylor University, the Miriam Lutcher Stark Library of the University of Texas, the Henry E. Huntington Library, the Library of Scripps College, the Mills Library of McMaster University, the Robarts Library of the University of Toronto, the Bata Library of Trent University, the Tennyson Research Centre in the City Library of Lincoln, the Cambridge University Library, the Library of King's College, Cambridge, the University of London Library, the British Library, the Library of the Victoria and Albert Museum, the Bodleian Library of Oxford University, the Balliol College Library, the Keats-Shelley House in Rome, the Biblioteca Nazionale in Florence, the Library of the Casa Goldoni in Venice;

to the following for permission to print materials owned by them: the Houghton Library; the Trustees of the Boston Public Library; the Library Board of Cornell University; the Beinecke Rare Book and Manuscript Library; the Pierpont Morgan Library; the Henry W. and Albert A. Berg Collection, the New York Public Library, Astor, Lenox and Tilden Foundations; the Carl and Lily Pforzheimer Foundation, Inc.; the Armstrong Browning Library; the Huntington Library, San Marino, California; the Library of the Victoria and Albert Museum; the British Library; the Master and Fellows of Balliol College, Oxford; the Tennyson Research Centre;

to John Murray for permission to publish materials on which the firm holds the copyright;

and to individuals for help of various kinds: my parents and my brother and sister, Professor F. E. L. Priestley, Professor T. J. Collins, Principal Nancy Sherouse, Professor Robert Chambers, Professor David Glassco, Professor and Mrs James Neufeld, Professor Ian Storey, Professor W. Whitla, and many other friends and former colleagues. My greatest debt is to the General Editor of the series for his encouragement, patience and careful criticism.

Table of Dates

1812	*7 May* Born at Camberwell, suburb of London. Son of Robert Browning, eccentric bibliophile, amateur scholar and bank-clerk, and Sarah Anna Browning (née Wiedemann).
1814	Birth of Sarah Anna (Sarianna), Browning's sister.
c. 1820–26	At the school of Rev. Thomas Ready at Peckham. Most of Browning's education was informal, at his home, where he had professional tutors, his father, and a huge library to guide him.
1826	Discovers Shelley and becomes atheist and vegetarian.
1828	Enters London University, where he remains for almost the entire academic year.
1833	*March* *Pauline* published anonymously; unsold and little noticed.
1834	*March and April* Visits St Petersburg.
1835	*October* *Paracelsus* published.
1836	*May* John Forster's *Life of Strafford* in which Browning had some share, perhaps a large one.
1837	*May* *Strafford* published, and performed five times.
1838	*April–July* First visit to Italy (Venice and surrounding area).
1840	*March* *Sordello* published; becomes notorious for obscurity.
1841	*April* *Bells and Pomegranates I: Pippa Passes.*
1842	*March* *Bells and Pomegranates II: King Victor and King Charles.*
	July 'Essay on Chatterton' published anonymously in *Foreign Quarterly Review.*
	November *Bells and Pomegranates III: Dramatic Lyrics.*
1843	*January* *Bells and Pomegranates IV: The Return of the Druses.*
	February *Bells and Pomegranates V: A Blot in the 'Scutcheon*; performed three times.
1844	*April* *Bells and Pomegranates VI: Colombe's Birthday.*

	Browning's last play for the stage, it was presented successfully in London and Manchester in 1853.
	Autumn Second visit to Italy (Naples, Rome, Florence; return along the Rhine).
1845	*10 January* First letter to Elizabeth Barrett.
	20 May First visit to Wimpole Street.
	November *Bells and Pomegranates VII: Dramatic Romances and Lyrics.*
1846	*April* *Bells and Pomegranates VIII: Luria* and *A Soul's Tragedy.*
	12 September Marriage to Elizabeth Barrett.
	19 September The Brownings leave England for Pisa.
1847	*April* Move to Florence, where Casa Guidi shortly becomes their home for the rest of the marriage.
1849	*January* *Poems* (2 volumes).
	March Son, Robert Wiedemann Barrett Browning ('Penini', 'Pen'), born. Browning's mother dies.
1850	*April* *Christmas-Eve and Easter-Day* published.
1852	'Essay on Shelley' published.
1855	*November* *Men and Women.*
1856	John Kenyon's legacy of £11,000 solves the Brownings' financial problems.
1860	*June* Buys the 'Old Yellow Book'.
1861	*29 June* Death of Elizabeth Barrett Browning.
	August Browning leaves Florence, and never returns.
	October Browning settles in London after a holiday in France.
1863	*The Poetical Works* (3 volumes).
1864	*May* *Dramatis Personae* published.
	Autumn Begins writing *The Ring and the Book.*
1866	Death of Browning's father.
1867	Honorary M.A. from Oxford; Honorary Fellow of Balliol College, Oxford.
1868	*The Poetical Works* (6 volumes).
1868–9	*November–February* *The Ring and the Book.*
1869	*September* Proposal of marriage (by ?, to ?) Lady Ashburton ?
1871	*August* *Balaustion's Adventure.*
	December *Prince Hohenstiel-Schwangau.*
1872	*June* *Fifine at the Fair.*
1873	*May* *Red Cotton Night-Cap Country.*
1875	*April* *Aristophanes' Apology.*

	November *The Inn Album.*
1876	*July* *Pacchiarotto and How He Worked in Distemper.*
1877	*October* *The Agamemnon of Aeschylus.*
1878	*May* *La Saisiaz: Two Poets of Croisic.*
	Revisits Italy, as in most years for the rest of his life.
1879	*April* *Dramatic Idyls.*
	LL.D. from Cambridge.
1880	*June* *Dramatic Idyls: Second Series.*
1881	*October* Founding of the Browning Society.
1882	D.C.L. from Oxford.
1883	*March* *Jocoseria.*
1884	LL.D. from Edinburgh.
	November *Ferishtah's Fancies.*
1886	*September* Death of Browning's friend Joseph Milsand.
1887	*January* *Parleyings with Certain People of Importance in Their Day.*
	October Marriage of Pen Browning and Fannie Coddington.
1888–9	*The Poetical Works* (16 volumes).
1889	*12 December* *Asolando*; Browning dies at Venice later in the day.
	31 December Buried in Poets' Corner, Westminster Abbey.
1903	Death of Sarianna.
1912	Death of Pen at Asolo.
1913	Dispersal of the Browning estates at auction.

Further Reading

Works concerned with a single volume and with a single poem or a handful of poems are listed in the appropriate places in the 'Notes'.

EDITIONS

The sixteen-volume *Poetical Works of Robert Browning*, Smith, Elder, 1888–9, is copy-text for most subsequent editions (a second impression in which all volumes are dated 1889 followed); in 1894 a seventeenth volume appeared, edited by Edward Berdoe, and including *Asolando* and notes. In 1898 Charlotte Porter and Helen A. Clarke published their twelve-volume edition (Crowell). Called the 'Florentine Edition' in one of its forms, it subsequently appeared in various formats with a variety of names. The best edition to date, it includes extensive introductions tending to often useful summary, and annotation of varying bulk, accuracy and usefulness. The ten-volume 'Centenary Edition' of 1912, edited by F. G. Kenyon (Smith, Elder), has brief introductions but no annotation; it is often regarded as the standard edition. In 1914 Smith, Elder published Kenyon's *New Poems by Robert Browning and Elizabeth Barrett Browning;* the new poems were included in the *Complete Poetical Works*, published in 1915 in New York by Macmillan. What are virtual reprints of that edition, one that includes the occasional note, have been published by John Murray since 1929. In progress – four volumes appeared between 1969 and 1973 – is the projected fourteen-volume *The Complete Works of Robert Browning* (the 'Ohio Browning'), published by the Ohio University Press under the general editorship of Roma A. King, Jr. In 1977 Baylor University joined Ohio as joint publisher, and the original editorial board was much altered. The edition is the first to include full textual apparatus, is annotated, and aims at definitiveness. Regrettably, however, the volumes so far published are not definitive: the editorial principles have been challenged, important manuscript materials have been neglected, and the inaccuracy of text, textual apparatus and annotation has been demonstrated (see, for instance, Thomas J. Collins in *Victorian Studies* XIII, 1970, 441–4; John Pettigrew in *Essays in Criticism* XXII,

1972, 436–41 – the same journal printed Roma A. King's reply: XXIV, 1974, 317–19, and Pettigrew's rejoinder: XXV, 1975, 480–83; and Donald H. Reiman in *Victorian Poetry* XII, 1974, 86–96). Extensive problems in the Ohio notes to *Sordello* are detailed in John Pettigrew's posthumously published essay in *The Library* XXXIII, 1978, 162–9. An edition in the Longman Annotated English Poets series, edited by John Woolford, is announced for the future. The unannotated Oxford Standard Authors edition by Ian Jack (1970) includes only the poems published before *The Ring and the Book*.

Among usefully annotated volumes of selections are: Kenneth Allott (ed.), *Browning: Selected Poems*, Oxford University Press, 1967; Joseph E. Baker (ed.), *'Pippa Passes' and Shorter Poems*, Odyssey, 1947; E. K. Brown and J. O. Bailey (eds.), in *Victorian Poetry*, 2nd edn, Ronald, 1962; William Clyde DeVane (ed.), *The Shorter Poems of Robert Browning*, Appleton-Century-Crofts, 1934; Walter E. Houghton and G. Robert Stange (eds.), *Victorian Poetry and Poetics*, 2nd edn, Houghton-Mifflin, 1968; Jacob Korg (ed.), *The Poetry of Robert Browning*, Bobbs-Merrill, 1971; Donald Smalley (ed.), *Poems of Robert Browning*, Houghton-Mifflin, 1956. Browning's so-called *Essay on Shelley* (included here in the Appendix to Volume I) was edited by L. Winstanley in 1911, and by H. F. B. Brett-Smith in 1921. Donald Smalley edited Browning's *Essay on Chatterton*, Harvard University Press, 1948.

BIBLIOGRAPHIES AND REFERENCE WORKS

The standard bibliography is Leslie Nathan Broughton, Clark Sutherland Northup and Robert Brainard Pearsall, *Robert Browning: A Bibliography, 1830–1950*, Cornell University Press, 1953. It is continued by William S. Peterson, *Robert and Elizabeth Barrett Browning: An Annotated Bibliography, 1951–1970*, Browning Institute, 1974, and in the annual bibliographies published in *Browning Institute Studies*, 1973–.

Still of value despite the inclusion of his own forgeries are Thomas J. Wise's *Bibliography* (1897) and *A Browning Library* (1929). Valuable too is the Sotheby, Wilkinson and Hodge sales catalogue, *The Browning Collections* (1913). Expert guidance is available from Park Honan in *The Victorian Poets: A Guide to Research*, ed. Frederic E. Faverty, Harvard University Press, 1968; from Ian Jack in *English Poetry: Select Bibliographical Guides*, ed. A. E. Dyson, Oxford University Press, 1971; and from P. J. Keating in *Robert Browning*, ed. Isobel

Armstrong, Bell, 1974. Also useful are the annual bibliographies in the June issues of *Victorian Studies*, the check lists in *The Browning Newsletter* and *Studies in Browning and His Circle*, and the annual guides in summer issues of *Victorian Poetry*. Warner Barnes compiled the *Catalogue of the Browning Collection at the University of Texas*, 1966. The standard *Concordance* is that of Leslie N. Broughton and Benjamin F. Stelter, 2 volumes, Steckert, 1924–5.

Journals: *Victorian Poetry* and *Victorian Studies* include much Browning material. Three journals are devoted to the Brownings: *Studies in Browning and His Circle* (formerly called *The Browning Newsletter*) appears twice a year from the Armstrong Browning Library of Baylor University, *Browning Institute Studies* is published annually by the Browning Institute of New York, and *Browning Society Notes* is published three times a year by the Browning Society of London.

Handbooks: Still indispensable, despite being dated and often erroneous, is William Clyde DeVane, *A Browning Handbook*, 2nd edn, Appleton-Century-Crofts, 1955. Also important, since it was written by a close friend of Browning, who in a sense gave his blessing to it despite its frequent errors, is Mrs Sutherland Orr's *A Handbook to the Works of Robert Browning*, 6th edn, Bell, 1892. Norton B. Crowell, *A Reader's Guide to Robert Browning*, University of New Mexico Press, 1972, has a misleading title: it focuses on twenty-three better-known poems.

Collections of Critical Essays: Criticism from 1833 to 1891 is collected in Boyd Litzinger and Donald Smalley (eds.), *Browning: The Critical Heritage*, Routledge & Kegan Paul, 1970. Other standard collections are: Boyd Litzinger and K. L. Knickerbocker (eds.), *The Browning Critics*, University of Kentucky Press, 1965; Philip Drew (ed.), *Robert Browning: A Collection of Critical Essays*, Methuen, 1966; Clarence Tracy (ed.), *Browning's Mind and Art*, Oliver & Boyd, 1968; and Isobel Armstrong (ed.), *Robert Browning*, Bell, 1974.

LETTERS

Most of Browning's letters remain unpublished, and Philip Kelley and Ronald Hudson project an edition of the complete letters of Browning and his wife in about forty volumes. Their *Checklist* of Browning correspondence, published in 1978 (Browning Institute and Wedgestone Press), contains 9,789 entries. Many letters have appeared singly or in small gatherings in periodicals, biographies, etc. The most important collections so far are:

W. R. Benét (ed.), *Twenty-Two Unpublished Letters of Elizabeth Barrett Browning and Robert Browning*, United Feature Syndicate, 1935.

Thomas J. Collins (ed.), *The Brownings to the Tennysons*, Baylor Browning Interests, 1971.

Richard Curle (ed.), *Robert Browning and Julia Wedgwood: A Broken Friendship as Revealed in Their Letters*, John Murray and Jonathan Cape, 1937.

David J. De Laura (ed.), 'Ruskin and the Brownings: Twenty-five Unpublished Letters', *Bulletin of John Rylands Library* LIV, 1972, 314–56.

William Clyde DeVane and Kenneth Leslie Knickerbocker (eds.), *New Letters of Robert Browning*, Yale University Press, 1950.

Thurman L. Hood (ed.), *Letters of Robert Browning Collected by Thomas J. Wise*, Yale University Press, 1933.

Gertrude Reese Hudson (ed.), *Browning to His American Friends: Letters Between the Brownings, the Storys, and James Russell Lowell, 1841–1890*, Bowes & Bowes, 1965.

F. G. Kenyon (ed.), *Robert Browning and Alfred Domett*, Smith, Elder, 1906.

Elvan Kintner (ed.), *The Letters of Robert Browning and Elizabeth Barrett, 1845–1846*, 2 volumes, Belknap Press of Harvard University Press, 1969.

Paul Landis (ed.), *Letters of the Brownings to George Barrett*, University of Illinois Press, 1958.

Edward C. McAleer (ed.), *Dearest Isa: Robert Browning's Letters to Isa Blagden*, University of Texas Press, 1951.

Edward C. McAleer (ed.), *Learned Lady: Letters from Robert Browning to Mrs. Thomas FitzGerald 1876–1889*, Carl H. Pforzheimer Library, 1966.

BIOGRAPHIES

W. Hall Griffin and Harry Christopher Minchin, *The Life of Robert Browning*, Methuen, 1910. (A standard Life. The photographs in *1910* make it more useful than the very slightly revised version of 1938.)

William Irvine and Park Honan, *The Book, the Ring, and the Poet: A Biography of Robert Browning*, McGraw-Hill, 1974. (Probably the best biography, it includes valuable criticism.)

John Maynard, *Browning's Youth*, Harvard University Press, 1977. (An invaluable source of information on the early years, containing much new material.)

Betty Miller, *Robert Browning: A Portrait*, John Murray, 1952. (The most widely read Life, it is readable, challenging, often cavalier with facts and Freud.)
Mrs Sutherland Orr, *Life and Letters of Robert Browning*, revised and in part rewritten by F. G. Kenyon, Smith, Elder, 1908. (First published in 1891, the Life is important as the product of a close friend, and for its letters.)
Maisie Ward, *Robert Browning and His World*, 2 volumes, Cassell, 1967, 1969.
Lilian Whiting, *The Brownings: Their Life and Art*, Little, Brown, 1911.

Among other useful biographical sources are the short story of Henry James, 'The Private Life' (1892), with its central character modelled on Browning and James; James's *William Wetmore Story and His Friends*, 2 volumes, 1903; Katherine C. de K. Bronson, 'Browning in Asolo', *Century Magazine* LIX, 1900, 920–31, and 'Browning in Venice', *Cornhill Magazine* LXXXV, 1902, 145–71; Fannie B. Browning, *Some Memories of Robert Browning by His Daughter-in-Law*, Marshall Jones, 1928; E. A. Horsman (ed.), *The Diary of Alfred Domett, 1872–1885*, Oxford University Press, 1953; B. R. Jerman, 'The Death of Robert Browning', *University of Toronto Quarterly* XXXV, 1965, 47–74; William Whitla, 'Browning and the Ashburton Affair', *Browning Society Notes* II, No. 2, 1972, 12–41. Richard D. Altick's contentious 'The Private Life of Robert Browning' and Kenneth L. Knickerbocker's reply in 'A Tentative Apology for Robert Browning' are both included in Litzinger and Knickerbocker, *The Browning Critics*.

GENERAL SCHOLARSHIP AND CRITICISM

Isobel Armstrong, 'Browning and the Grotesque Style', in Isobel Armstrong (ed.), *The Major Victorian Poets: Reconsiderations*, Routledge & Kegan Paul, 1969, 93–123.
Kingsbury Badger, '"See the Christ Stand!": Browning's Religion', *Boston University Studies in English* I, 1955, 53–73. (In Drew, *Robert Browning*, 72–95.)
G. K. Chesterton, *Robert Browning*, Macmillan, 1903.
J. M. Cohen, *Robert Browning*, Longmans, Green, 1952.
Thomas J. Collins, *Robert Browning's Moral-Aesthetic Theory 1833–1855*, University of Nebraska Press, 1967.
Eleanor Cook, *Browning's Lyrics: An Exploration*, University of Toronto Press, 1974.

Norton B. Crowell, *The Convex Glass: The Mind of Robert Browning*, University of New Mexico Press, 1968.
Norton B. Crowell, *The Triple Soul: Browning's Theory of Knowledge*, University of New Mexico Press, 1963.
A. Dwight Culler, 'Monodrama and the Dramatic Monologue', *PMLA* XC, 1975, 366–85.
William Clyde DeVane, 'Browning and the Spirit of Greece', in *Nineteenth-Century Studies*, ed. H. Davis, W. C. DeVane and R. C. Bald, Cornell University Press, 1940, 179–98.
William Clyde DeVane, 'The Virgin and the Dragon', *Yale Review*, new series XXXVII, 1947, 33–46. (In Drew, *Robert Browning*, 96–109, and Litzinger and Knickerbocker, *The Browning Critics*, 181–96.)
Edward Dowden, *Robert Browning*, Dent, 1904.
Philip Drew, *The Poetry of Browning: A Critical Introduction*, Methuen, 1970.
F. R. G. Duckworth, *Browning: Background and Conflict*, Benn, 1931.
Henry Charles Duffin, *Amphibian: A Reconsideration of Browning*, Bowes & Bowes, 1956.
F. J. Furnivall (ed.), *The Browning Society's Papers*, 3 volumes, Browning Society, 1881–91.
Donald S. Hair, *Browning's Experiments with Genre*, University of Toronto Press, 1972.
Park Honan, *Browning's Characters*, Yale University Press, 1961.
Thurman L. Hood, 'Browning's Ancient Classical Sources', *Harvard Studies in Classical Philology* XXXIII, 1922, 79–180.
Ian Jack, *Browning's Major Poetry*, Clarendon Press, 1973.
Henry James, 'Browning in Westminster Abbey' (1890). (In Drew, *Robert Browning*, 11–16.)
E. D. H. Johnson, 'Browning', in his *The Alien Vision of Victorian Poetry*, Princeton University Press, 1952, 71–143.
Henry Jones, *Browning as a Philosophical and Religious Teacher*, Maclehose, 1891.
Roma A. King, Jr, *The Bow and the Lyre: The Art of Robert Browning*, University of Michigan Press, 1957.
Robert Langbaum, *The Poetry of Experience*, Random House, 1957.
Barbara Melchiori, *Browning's Poetry of Reticence*, Oliver & Boyd, 1968.
J. Hillis Miller, 'Robert Browning', in his *The Disappearance of God*, Belknap Press of Harvard University Press, 1963, 81–156.
William S. Peterson, *Interrogating the Oracle: A History of the London Browning Society*, Ohio University Press, 1970.
F. A. Pottle, *Shelley and Browning, A Myth and Some Facts*, Pembroke Press, 1923.

Robert O. Preyer, 'Robert Browning: A Reading of the Early Narratives', *ELH* XXVI, 1959, 531–48. (In Drew, *Robert Browning*, 157–75; and Litzinger and Knickerbocker, *The Browning Critics*, 343–63.)
Robert O. Preyer, 'Two Styles in the Verse of Robert Browning', *ELH* XXXII, 1965, 62–84.
Ralph W. Rader, 'The Dramatic Monologue and Related Lyric Forms', *Critical Inquiry* III, 1976, 131–51.
William O. Raymond, *The Infinite Moment and Other Essays in Robert Browning*, 2nd edn, University of Toronto Press, 1965.
Clyde de L. Ryals, *Browning's Later Poetry: 1871–1889*, Cornell University Press, 1975.
W. David Shaw, *The Dialectical Temper: The Rhetorical Art of Robert Browning*, Cornell University Press, 1968.
C. Willard Smith, *Browning's Star-Imagery: The Study of a Detail in Poetic Design*, Princeton University Press, 1941.
Lionel Stevenson, 'The Pertinacious Victorian Poets', *University of Toronto Quarterly* XXI, 1952, 232–45.
Lionel Stevenson, 'Tennyson, Browning, and a Romantic Fallacy', *University of Toronto Quarterly* XIII, 1944, 175–95.
Arthur Symons, *An Introduction to the Study of Browning*, rev. edn, Dent, 1906.
Michael Timko, 'Ah, Did You Once See Browning Plain?', *Studies in English Literature* VI, 1966, 731–42.
C. R. Tracy, 'Browning's Heresies', *Studies in Philology* XXXIII, 1936, 610–25.
William Whitla, *The Central Truth: The Incarnation in Browning's Poetry*, University of Toronto Press, 1963.

The Poems

Fifine at the Fair

1872

DONE ELVIRE: Vous plaît-il, don Juan, nous éclaircir ces beaux mystères?
DON JUAN: Madame, à vous dire la vérité...
DONE ELVIRE: Ah! que vous savez mal vous défendre pour un homme de cour, et qui doit être accoutumé à ces sortes de choses! J'ai pitié de vous voir la confusion que vous avez. Que ne vous armez-vous le front d'une noble effronterie? Que ne me jurez-vous que vous êtes toujours dans les mêmes sentimens pour moi, que vous m'aimez toujours avec une ardeur sans égale, et que rien n'est capable de vous détacher de moi que la mort?

MOLIÈRE, *Don Juan* I. 3

DONNA ELVIRA: Don Juan, might you please to help one give a guess,
Hold up a candle, clear this fine mysteriousness?
DON JUAN: Madam, if needs I must declare the truth, – in short...
DONNA ELVIRA: Fie, for a man of mode, accustomed at the court
To such a style of thing, how awkwardly my lord
Attempts defence! You move compassion, that's the word –
Dumb-foundered and chap-fallen! Why don't you arm your brow
With noble impudence? Why don't you swear and vow
No sort of change is come to any sentiment
You ever had for me? Affection holds the bent,
You love me now as erst, with passion that makes pale
All ardour else: nor aught in nature can avail
To separate us two, save what, in stopping breath,
May peradventure stop devotion likewise – death!

Prologue

Amphibian

I
The fancy I had today,
Fancy which turned a fear!
I swam far out in the bay,
Since waves laughed warm and clear.

II
I lay and looked at the sun,
The noon-sun looked at me:
Between us two, no one
Live creature, that I could see.

III
Yes! There came floating by
Me, who lay floating too,
Such a strange butterfly!
Creature as dear as new:

IV
Because the membraned wings
So wonderful, so wide,
So sun-suffused, were things
Like soul and naught beside.

V
A handbreadth over head!
All of the sea my own,
It owned the sky instead;
Both of us were alone.

VI
I never shall join its flight,
For, naught buoys flesh in air.
If it touch the sea – good-night!
Death sure and swift waits there.

VII

Can the insect feel the better
For watching the uncouth play
Of limbs that slip the fetter,
Pretend as they were not clay?

VIII

Undoubtedly I rejoice
That the air comports so well
With a creature which had the choice
Of the land once. Who can tell?

IX

What if a certain soul
Which early slipped its sheath,
And has for its home the whole
Of heaven, thus look beneath,

X

Thus watch one who, in the world,
Both lives and likes life's way,
Nor wishes the wings unfurled
That sleep in the worm, they say?

XI

But sometimes when the weather
Is blue, and warm waves tempt
To free oneself of tether,
And try a life exempt

XII

From worldly noise and dust,
In the sphere which overbrims
With passion and thought, – why, just
Unable to fly, one swims!

XIII

By passion and thought upborne,
One smiles to oneself – 'They fare
Scarce better, they need not scorn
Our sea, who live in the air!'

XIV
Emancipate through passion
And thought, with sea for sky,
We substitute, in a fashion,
For heaven – poetry:

XV
Which sea, to all intent,
Gives flesh such noon-disport
As a finer element
Affords the spirit-sort.

XVI
Whatever they are, we seem:
Imagine the thing they know;
All deeds they do, we dream;
Can heaven be else but so?

XVII
And meantime, yonder streak
Meets the horizon's verge;
That is the land, to seek
If we tire or dread the surge:

XVIII
Land the solid and safe –
To welcome again (confess!)
When, high and dry, we chafe
The body, and don the dress.

XIX
Does she look, pity, wonder
At one who mimics flight,
Swims – heaven above, sea under,
Yet always earth in sight?

Fifine at the Fair

I

O trip and skip, Elvire! Link arm in arm with me!
Like husband and like wife, together let us see
The tumbling-troop arrayed, the strollers on their stage,
Drawn up and under arms, and ready to engage.

II

Now, who supposed the night would play us such a prank?
– That what was raw and brown, rough pole and shaven plank?
Mere bit of hoarding, half by trestle propped, half tub,
Would flaunt it forth as brisk as butterfly from grub?
This comes of sun and air, of Autumn afternoon,
And Pornic and Saint Gille, whose feast affords the boon –
This scaffold turned parterre, this flower-bed in full blow,
Bateleurs, baladines! We shall not miss the show!
They pace and promenade; they presently will dance:
What good were else i' the drum and fife? O pleasant land of
France!

III

Who saw them make their entry? At wink of eve, be sure!
They love to steal a march, nor lightly risk the lure.
They keep their treasure hid, nor stale (improvident)
Before the time is ripe, each wonder of their tent –
Yon six-legged sheep, to wit, and he who beats a gong,
Lifts cap and waves salute, exhilarates the throng –
Their ape of many years and much adventure, grim
And grey with pitying fools who find a joke in him.
Or, best, the human beauty, Mimi, Toinette, Fifine,
Tricot fines down if fat, padding plumps up if lean,
Ere, shedding petticoat, modesty, and such toys,
They bounce forth, squalid girls transformed to gamesome
boys.

IV

No, no, thrice, Pornic, no! Perpend the authentic tale!
'Twas not for every Gawain to gaze upon the Grail!
But whoso went his rounds, when flew bat, flitted midge,

Might hear across the dusk, – where both roads join the bridge,
Hard by the little port, – creak a slow caravan,
A chimneyed house on wheels; so shyly-sheathed, began
To broaden out the bud which, bursting unaware,
Now takes away our breath, queen-tulip of the Fair!

V

Yet morning promised much: for, pitched and slung and reared
On terrace 'neath the tower, 'twixt tree and tree appeared
An airy structure; how the pennon from its dome,
Frenetic to be free, makes one red stretch for home!
The home far and away, the distance where lives joy,
The cure, at once and ever, of world and world's annoy;
Since, what lolls full in front, a furlong from the booth,
But ocean-idleness, sky-blue and millpond-smooth?

VI

Frenetic to be free! And, do you know, there beats
Something within my breast, as sensitive? – repeats
The fever of the flag? My heart makes just the same
Passionate stretch, fires up for lawlessness, lays claim
To share the life they lead; losels, who have and use
The hour what way they will, – applaud them or abuse
Society, whereof myself am at the beck,
Whose call obey, and stoop to burden stiffest neck!

VII

Why is it that whene'er a faithful few combine
To cast allegiance off, play truant, nor repine,
Agree to bear the worst, forego the best in store
For us who, left behind, do duty as of yore, –
Why is it that, disgraced, they seem to relish life the more?
– Seem as they said 'We know a secret passing praise
Or blame of such as you! Remain! we go our ways
With something you o'erlooked, forgot or chose to sweep
Clean out of door: our pearl picked from your rubbish-heap.
You care not for your loss, we calculate our gain.
All's right. Are you content? Why, so let things remain!
To the wood then, to the wild: free life, full liberty!'
And when they rendezvous beneath the inclement sky,

House by the hedge, reduced to brute-companionship,
– Misguided ones who gave society the slip,
And find too late how boon a parent they despised,
What ministration spurned, how sweet and civilized –
Then, left alone at last with self-sought wretchedness,
No interloper else! – why is it, can we guess? –
At somebody's expense, goes up so frank a laugh?
As though they held the corn, and left us only chaff
From garners crammed and closed. And we indeed are clever
If we get grain as good, by thrashing straw for ever!

VIII

Still, truants as they are and purpose yet to be,
That nowise needs forbid they venture – as you see –
To cross confine, approach the once familiar roof
O' the kindly race their flight estranged: stand half aloof,
Sidle half up, press near, and proffer wares for sale
– In their phrase – make, in ours, white levy of black mail.
They, of the wild, require some touch of us the tame,
Since clothing, meat and drink, mean money all the same.

IX

If hunger, proverbs say, allures the wolf from wood,
Much more the bird must dare a dash at something good:
Must snatch up, bear away in beak, the trifle-treasure
To wood and wild, and then – O how enjoy at leisure!
Was never tree-built nest, you climbed and took, of bird
(Rare city-visitant, talked of, scarce seen or heard),
But, when you would dissect the structure, piece by piece,
You found, enwreathed amid the country-product – fleece
And feather, thistle-fluffs and bearded windlestraws –
Some shred of foreign silk, unravelling of gauze,
Bit, may be, of brocade, 'mid fur and blow-bell-down:
Filched plainly from mankind, dear tribute paid by town,
Which proved how oft the bird had plucked up heart of grace,
Swooped down at waif and stray, made furtively our place
Pay tax and toll, then borne the booty to enrich
Her paradise i' the waste; the how and why of which,
That is the secret, there the mystery that stings!

X

For, what they traffic in, consists of just the things
We, – proud ones who so scorn dwellers without the pale,
Bateleurs, baladines, white leviers of black mail, –
I say, they sell what we most pique us that we keep!
How comes it, all we hold so dear they count so cheap?

XI

What price should you impose, for instance, on repute,
Good fame, your own good fame and family's to boot?
Stay start of quick moustache, arrest the angry rise
Of eyebrow! All I asked is answered by surprise.
Now tell me: are you worth the cost of a cigar?
Go boldly, enter booth, disburse the coin at bar
Of doorway where presides the master of the troop,
And forthwith you survey his Graces in a group,
Live Picture, picturesque no doubt and close to life:
His sisters, right and left; the Grace in front, his wife.
Next, who is this performs the feat of the Trapeze?
Lo, she is launched, look – fie, the fairy! – how she flees
O'er all those heads thrust back, – mouths, eyes, one gape and
stare, –
No scrap of skirt impedes free passage through the air,
Till, plumb on the other side, she lights and laughs again,
That fairy-form, whereof each muscle, nay, each vein
The curious may inspect, – his daughter that he sells
Each rustic for five sous. Desiderate aught else
O' the vendor? As you leave his show, why, joke the man!
'You cheat: your six-legged sheep, I recollect, began
Both life and trade, last year, trimmed properly and clipt,
As the Twin-headed Babe, and Human Nondescript!'
What does he care? You paid his price, may pass your jest.
So values he repute, good fame, and all the rest!

XII

But try another tack; say: 'I indulge caprice,
Who am Don and Duke, and Knight, beside, o' the Golden
Fleece,
And, never mind how rich. Abandon this career!
Have hearth and home, nor let your womankind appear
Without as multiplied a coating as protects
An onion from the eye! Become, in all respects,

God-fearing householder, subsistent by brain-skill,
Hand-labour; win your bread whatever way you will,
So it be honestly, – and, while I have a purse,
Means shall not lack!' – His thanks will be the roundest curse
That ever rolled from lip.

XIII

Now, what is it? – returns
The question – heartens so this losel that he spurns
All we so prize? I want, put down in black and white,
What compensating joy, unknown and infinite,
Turns lawlessness to law, makes destitution – wealth,
Vice – virtue, and disease of soul and body – health?

XIV

Ah, the slow shake of head, the melancholy smile,
The sigh almost a sob! What's wrong, was right erewhile?
Why are we two at once such ocean-width apart?
Pale fingers press my arm, and sad eyes probe my heart.
Why is the wife in trouble?

XV

This way, this way, Fifine!
Here's she, shall make my thoughts be surer what they mean!
First let me read the signs, portray you past mistake
The gypsy's foreign self, no swarth our sun could bake.
Yet where's a woolly trace degrades the wiry hair?
And note the Greek-nymph nose, and – oh, my Hebrew pair
Of eye and eye – o'erarched by velvet of the mole –
That swim as in a sea, that dip and rise and roll,
Spilling the light around! While either ear is cut
Thin as a dusk-leaved rose carved from a cocoa-nut.
And then, her neck! now, grant you had the power to deck,
Just as your fancy pleased, the bistre-length of neck,
Could lay, to shine against its shade, a moonlike row
Of pearls, each round and white as bubble Cupids blow
Big out of mother's milk, – what pearl-moon would surpass
That string of mock-turquoise, those almandines of glass,
Where girlhood terminates? for with breasts'-birth commence
The boy, and page-costume, till pink and impudence
End admirably all: complete the creature trips

Our way now, brings sunshine upon her spangled hips,
As here she fronts us full, with pose half-frank, half-fierce!

XVI

Words urged in vain, Elvire! You waste your quarte and tierce,
Lunge at a phantom here, try fence in fairy-land.
For me, I own defeat, ask but to understand
The acknowledged victory of whom I call my queen,
Sexless and bloodless sprite: though mischievous and mean,
Yet free and flower-like too, with loveliness for law,
And self-sustainment made morality.

XVII

A flaw
Do you account i' the lily, of lands which travellers know,
That, just as golden gloom supersedes Northern snow
I' the chalice, so, about each pistil, spice is packed, –
Deliriously-drugged scent, in lieu of odour lacked,
With us, by bee and moth, their banquet to enhance
At morn and eve, when dew, the chilly sustenance,
Needs mixture of some chaste and temperate perfume?
I ask, is she in fault who guards such golden gloom,
Such dear and damning scent, by who cares what devices,
And takes the idle life of insects she entices
When, drowned to heart's desire, they satiate the inside
O' the lily, mark her wealth and manifest her pride?

XVIII

But, wiser, we keep off, nor tempt the acrid juice;
Discreet we peer and praise, put rich things to right use.
No flavorous venomed bell, – the rose it is, I wot,
Only the rose, we pluck and place, unwronged a jot,
No worse for homage done by every devotee,
I' the proper loyal throne, on breast where rose should be.
Or if the simpler sweets we have to choose among,
Would taste between our teeth, and give its toy the tongue, –
O gorgeous poison-plague, on thee no hearts are set!
We gather daisy meek, or maiden violet:
I think it is Elvire we love, and not Fifine.

XIX

'How does she make my thoughts be sure of what they mean?'
Judge and be just! Suppose, an age and time long past
Renew for our behoof one pageant more, the last
O' the kind, sick Louis liked to see defile between
Him and the yawning grave, its passage served to screen.
With eye as grey as lead, with cheek as brown as bronze,
Here where we stand, shall sit and suffer Louis Onze:
The while from yonder tent parade forth, not – oh, no –
Bateleurs, baladines! but range themselves a-row
Those well-sung women-worthies whereof loud fame still finds
Some echo linger faint, less in our hearts than minds.

XX

See, Helen! pushed in front o' the world's worst night and storm,
By Lady Venus' hand on shoulder: the sweet form
Shrinkingly prominent, though mighty, like a moon
Outbreaking from a cloud, to put harsh things in tune,
And magically bring mankind to acquiesce
In its own ravage, – call no curse upon, but bless
(Beldame, a moment since) the outbreaking beauty, now,
That casts o'er all the blood a candour from her brow.
See, Cleopatra! bared, the entire and sinuous wealth
O' the shining shape; each orb of indolent ripe health,
Captured, just where it finds a fellow-orb as fine
I' the body: traced about by jewels which outline,
Fire-frame, and keep distinct, perfections – lest they melt
To soft smooth unity ere half their hold be felt:
Yet, o'er that white and wonder, a soul's predominance
I' the head so high and haught – except one thievish glance,
From back of oblong eye, intent to count the slain.
Hush, – O I know, Elvire! Be patient, more remain!
What say you to Saint . . . Pish! Whatever Saint you please,
Cold-pinnacled aloft o' the spire, prays calm the seas
From Pornic Church, and oft at midnight (peasants say)
Goes walking out to save from shipwreck: well she may!
For think how many a year has she been conversant
With naught but winds and rains, sharp courtesy and scant
O' the wintry snow that coats the pent-house of her shrine,
Covers each knee, climbs near, but spares the smile benign
Which seems to say 'I looked for scarce so much from earth!'

She follows, one long thin pure finger in the girth
O' the girdle – whence the folds of garment, eye and eye,
Besprent with fleurs-de-lys, flow down and multiply
Around her feet, – and one, pressed hushingly to lip:
As if, while thus we made her march, some foundering ship
Might miss her from her post, nearer to God half-way
In heaven, and she inquired 'Who that treads earth can pray?
I doubt if even she, the unashamed! though, sure,
She must have stripped herself only to clothe the poor.'

XXI

This time, enough's a feast, not one more form, Elvire!
Provided you allow that, bringing up the rear
O' the bevy I am loth to – by one bird – curtail,
First note may lead to last, an octave crown the scale,
And this feminity be followed – do not flout! –
By – who concludes the masque with curtsey, smile and pout,
Submissive-mutinous? No other than Fifine
Points toe, imposes haunch, and pleads with tambourine!

XXII

'Well, what's the meaning here, what does the masque intend,
Which, unabridged, we saw file past us, with no end
Of fair ones, till Fifine came, closed the catalogue?'

XXIII

Task fancy yet again! Suppose you cast this clog
Of flesh away (that weeps, upbraids, withstands my arm)
And pass to join your peers, paragon charm with charm,
As I shall show you may, – prove best of beauty there!
Yourself confront yourself! This, help me to declare
That yonder-you, who stand beside these, braving each
And blinking none, beat her who lured to Troy-town beach
The purple prows of Greece, – nay, beat Fifine; whose face,
Mark how I will inflame, when seigneur-like I place
I' the tambourine, to spot the strained and piteous blank
Of pleading parchment, see, no less than a whole franc!

XXIV

Ah, do you mark the brown o' the cloud, made bright with fire
Through and through? as, old wiles succeeding to desire,
Quality (you and I) once more compassionate

A hapless infant, doomed (fie on such partial fate!)
To sink the inborn shame, waive privilege of sex,
And posture as you see, support the nods and becks
Of clowns that have their stare, nor always pay its price;
An infant born perchance as sensitive and nice
As any soul of you, proud dames, whom destiny
Keeps uncontaminate from stigma of the sty
She wallows in! You draw back skirts from filth like her
Who, possibly, braves scorn, if, scorned, she minister
To age, want, and disease of parents one or both;
Nay, peradventure, stoops to degradation, loth
That some just-budding sister, the dew yet on the rose,
Should have to share in turn the ignoble trade, – who knows?

XXV

Ay, who indeed! Myself know nothing, but dare guess
That off she trips in haste to hand the booty . . . yes,
'Twixt fold and fold of tent, there looms he, dim-discerned,
The ogre, lord of all those lavish limbs have earned!
– Brute-beast-face, – ravage, scar, scowl and malignancy, –
O' the Strong Man, whom (no doubt, her husband) by-and-by
You shall behold do feats: lift up nor quail beneath
A quintal in each hand, a cart-wheel 'twixt his teeth.
Oh she prefers sheer strength to ineffective grace,
Breeding and culture! seeks the essential in the case!
To him has flown my franc; and welcome, if that squint
O' the diabolic eye so soften through absinthe,
That, for once, tambourine, tunic and tricot 'scape
Their customary curse 'Not half the gain o' the ape!'
Ay, they go in together!

XXVI

Yet still her phantom stays
Opposite, where you stand: as steady 'neath our gaze –
The live Elvire's and mine – though fancy-stuff and mere
Illusion; to be judged, – dream-figures, – without fear
Or favour, those the false, by you and me the true.

XXVII

'What puts it in my head to make yourself judge you?'
Well, it may be, the name of Helen brought to mind
A certain myth I mused in years long left behind:

How she that fled from Greece with Paris whom she loved,
And came to Troy, and there found shelter, and so proved
Such cause of the world's woe, – how she, old stories call
This creature, Helen's self, never saw Troy at all.
Jove had his fancy-fit, must needs take empty air,
Fashion her likeness forth, and set the phantom there
I' the midst for sport, to try conclusions with the blind
And blundering race, the game create for Gods, mankind:
Experiment on these, – establish who would yearn
To give up life for her, who, other-minded, spurn
The best her eyes could smile, – make half the world sublime,
And half absurd, for just a phantom all the time!
Meanwhile true Helen's self sat, safe and far away,
By a great river-side, beneath a purer day,
With solitude around, tranquillity within;
Was able to lean forth, look, listen, through the din
And stir; could estimate the worthlessness or worth
Of Helen who inspired such passion to the earth,
A phantom all the time! That put it in my head,
To make yourself judge you – the phantom-wife instead
O' the tearful true Elvire!

XXVIII

I thank the smile at last
Which thins away the tear! Our sky was overcast,
And something fell; but day clears up: if there chanced rain,
The landscape glistens more. I have not vexed in vain
Elvire: because she knows, now she has stood the test,
How, this and this being good, herself may still be best
O' the beauty in review; because the flesh that claimed
Unduly my regard, she thought, the taste, she blamed
In me, for things extern, was all mistake, she finds, –
Or will find, when I prove that bodies show me minds,
That, through the outward sign, the inward grace allures,
And sparks from heaven transpierce earth's coarsest covertures, –
All by demónstrating the value of Fifine!

XXIX

Partake my confidence! No creature's made so mean
But that, some way, it boasts, could we investigate,
Its supreme worth: fulfils, by ordinance of fate,
Its momentary task, gets glory all its own,

Tastes triumph in the world, pre-eminent, alone.
Where is the single grain of sand, 'mid millions heaped
Confusedly on the beach, but, did we know, has leaped
Or will leap, would we wait, i' the century, some once,
To the very throne of things? – earth's brightest for the nonce,
When sunshine shall impinge on just that grain's facette
Which fronts him fullest, first, returns his ray with jet
Of promptest praise, thanks God best in creation's name!
As firm is my belief, quick sense perceives the same
Self-vindicating flash illústrate every man
And woman of our mass, and prove, throughout the plan,
No detail but, in place allotted it, was prime
And perfect.

XXX

Witness her, kept waiting all this time!
What happy angle makes Fifine reverberate
Sunshine, least sand-grain, she, of shadiest social state?
No adamantine shield, polished like Helen there,
Fit to absorb the sun, regorge him till the glare,
Dazing the universe, draw Troy-ward those blind beaks
Of equal-sided ships rowed by the well-greaved Greeks!
No Asian mirror, like yon Ptolemaic witch
Able to fix sun fast and tame sun down, enrich,
Not burn the world with beams thus flatteringly rolled
About her, head to foot, turned slavish snakes of gold!
And oh, no tinted pane of oriel sanctity,
Does our Fifine afford, such as permits supply
Of lustrous heaven, revealed, far more than mundane sight
Could master, to thy cell, pure Saint! where, else too bright,
So suits thy sense the orb, that, what outside was noon,
Pales, through thy lozenged blue, to meek benefic moon!
What then? does that prevent each dunghill, we may pass
Daily, from boasting too its bit of looking-glass,
Its sherd which, sun-smit, shines, shoots arrowy fire beyond
That satin-muffled mope, your sulky diamond?

XXXI

And now, the mingled ray she shoots, I decompose.
Her antecedents, take for execrable! Gloze
No whit on your premise: let be, there was no worst

Of degradation spared Fifine: ordained from first
To last, in body and soul, for one life-long debauch,
The Pariah of the North, the European Nautch!
This, far from seek to hide, she puts in evidence
Calmly, displays the brand, bids pry without offence
Your finger on the place. You comment 'Fancy us
So operated on, maltreated, mangled thus!
Such torture in our case, had we survived an hour?
Some other sort of flesh and blood must be, with power
Appropriate to the vile, unsensitive, tough-thonged,
In lieu of our fine nerve! Be sure, she was not wronged
Too much: you must not think she winced at prick as we!'
Come, come, that's what you say, or would, were thoughts but free.

XXXII

Well then, thus much confessed, what wonder if there steal
Unchallenged to my heart the force of one appeal
She makes, and justice stamp the sole claim she asserts?
So absolutely good is truth, truth never hurts
The teller, whose worst crime gets somehow grace, avowed.
To me, that silent pose and prayer proclaimed aloud
'Know all of me outside, the rest be emptiness
For such as you! I call attention to my dress,
Coiffure, outlandish features, lithe memorable limbs,
Piquant entreaty, all that eye-glance over-skims.
Does this give pleasure? Then, repay the pleasure, put
Its price i' the tambourine! Do you seek further? Tut!
I'm just my instrument, – sound hollow: mere smooth skin
Stretched o'er gilt framework, I: rub-dub, naught else within –
Always, for such as you! – if I have use elsewhere, –
If certain bells, now mute, can jingle, need you care?
Be it enough, there's truth i' the pleading, which comports
With no word spoken out in cottages or courts,
Since all I plead is "Pay for just the sight you see,
And give no credit to another charm in me!"
Do I say, like your Love? "To praise my face is well,
But, who would know my worth, must search my heart to tell!"
Do I say, like your Wife? "Had I passed in review
The produce of the globe, my man of men were – you!"
Do I say, like your Helen? "Yield yourself up, obey

Implicitly, nor pause to question, to survey
Even the worshipful! prostrate you at my shrine!
Shall you dare controvert what the world counts divine?
Array your private taste, own liking of the sense,
Own longing of the soul, against the impudence
Of history, the blare and bullying of verse?
As if man ever yet saw reason to disburse
The amount of what sense liked, soul longed for, – given, devised
As love, forsooth, – until the price was recognized
As moderate enough by divers fellow-men!
Then, with his warrant safe that these would love too, then,
Sure that particular gain implies a public loss,
And that no smile he buys but proves a slash across
The face, a stab into the side of somebody –
Sure that, along with love's main-purchase, he will buy
Up the whole stock of earth's uncharitableness,
Envy and hatred, – then, decides he to profess
His estimate of one, by love discerned, though dim
To all the world beside: since what's the world to him?"
Do I say, like your Queen of Egypt? "Who foregoes
My cup of witchcraft – fault be on the fool! He knows
Nothing of how I pack my wine-press, turn its winch
Three-times-three, all the time to song and dance, nor flinch
From charming on and on, till at the last I squeeze
Out the exhaustive drop that leaves behind mere lees
And dregs, vapidity, thought essence heretofore!
Sup of my sorcery, old pleasures please no more!
Be great, be good, love, learn, have potency of hand
Or heart or head, – what boots? You die, nor understand
What bliss might be in life: you ate the grapes, but knew
Never the taste of wine, such vintage as I brew!"
Do I say, like your Saint? "An exquisitest touch
Bides in the birth of things: no after-time can much
Enhance that fine, that faint, fugitive first of all!
What colour paints the cup o' the May-rose, like the small
Suspicion of a blush which doubtfully begins?
What sound outwarbles brook, while, at the source, it wins
That moss and stone dispart, allow its bubblings breathe?
What taste excels the fruit, just where sharp flavours sheathe
Their sting, and let encroach the honey that allays?
And so with soul and sense; when sanctity betrays
First fear lest earth below seem real as heaven above,

And holy worship, late, change soon to sinful love –
Where is the plenitude of passion which endures
Comparison with that, I ask of amateurs?"
Do I say, like Elvire' . . .

XXXIII

(Your husband holds you fast
Will have you listen, learn your character at last!)
'Do I say? – like her mixed unrest and discontent,
Reproachfulness and scorn, with that submission blent
So strangely, in the face, by sad smiles and gay tears, –
Quiescence which attacks, rebellion which endears, –
Say? "As you loved me once, could you but love me now!
Years probably have graved their passage on my brow,
Lips turn more rarely red, eyes sparkle less than erst;
Such tribute body pays to time; but, unamerced,
The soul retains, nay, boasts old treasure multiplied.
Though dew-prime flee, – mature at noonday, love defied
Chance, the wind, change, the rain: love, strenuous all the more
For storm, struck deeper root and choicer fruitage bore,
Despite the rocking world; yet truth struck root in vain:
While tenderness bears fruit, you praise, not taste again.
Why? They are yours, which once were hardly yours, might go
To grace another's ground: and then – the hopes we know,
The fears we keep in mind! – when, ours to arbitrate,
Your part was to bow neck, bid fall decree of fate.
Then, O the knotty point – white-night's work to revolve –
What meant that smile, that sigh? Not Solon's self could solve!
Then, O the deep surmise what one word might express,
And if what seemed her 'No' may not have meant her 'Yes!'
Then, such annoy, for cause – calm welcome, such acquist
Of rapture if, refused her arm, hand touched her wrist!
Now, what's a smile to you? Poor candle that lights up
The decent household gloom which sends you out to sup.
A tear? worse! warns that health requires you keep aloof
From nuptial chamber, since rain penetrates the roof!
Soul, body got and gained, inalienably safe
Your own, become despised; more worth has any waif
Or stray from neighbour's pale: pouch that, – 'tis pleasure, pride,
Novelty, property, and larceny beside!
Preposterous thought! to find no value fixed in things,

To covet all you see, hear, dream of, till fate brings
About that, what you want, you gain; then follows change.
Give you the sun to keep, forthwith must fancy range:
A goodly lamp, no doubt, – yet might you catch her hair
And capture, as she frisks, the fen-fire dancing there!
What do I say? at least a meteor's half in heaven;
Provided filth but shine, my husband hankers even
After putridity that's phosphorescent, cribs
The rustic's tallow-rush, makes spoil of urchins' squibs,
In short prefers to me – chaste, temperate, serene –
What sputters green and blue, this fizgig called Fifine!"'

XXXIV

So all your sex mistake! Strange that so plain a fact
Should raise such dire debate! Few families were racked
By torture self-supplied, did Nature grant but this –
That women comprehend mental analysis!

XXXV

Elvire, do you recall when, years ago, our home
The intimation reached, a certain pride of Rome,
Authenticated piece, in the third, last and best
Manner, – whatever fools and connoisseurs contest, –
No particle disturbed by rude restorer's touch,
The palaced picture-pearl, so long eluding clutch
Of creditor, at last, the Rafael might – could we
But come to terms – change lord, pass from the Prince to me?
I think you recollect my fever of a year:
How the Prince would, and how he would not; now, – too dear
That promise was, he made his grandsire so long since,
Rather to boast 'I own a Rafael' than 'am Prince!'
And now, the fancy soothed – if really sell he must
His birthright for a mess of pottage – such a thrust
I' the vitals of the Prince were mollified by balm,
Could he prevail upon his stomach to bear qualm,
And bequeath Liberty (because a purchaser
Was ready with the sum – a trifle!) yes, transfer
His heart at all events to that land where, at least,
Free institutions reign! And so, its price increased
Five-fold (Americans are such importunates!),
Soon must his Rafael start for the United States.
O alternating bursts of hope now, then despair!

At last, the bargain's struck, I'm all but beggared, there
The Rafael faces me, in fine, no dream at all,
My housemate, evermore to glorify my wall.
A week must pass, before heart-palpitations sink,
In gloating o'er my gain, so late I edged the brink
Of doom; a fortnight more, I spent in Paradise:
'Was outline e'er so true, could colouring entice
So calm, did harmony and quiet so avail?
How right, how resolute, the action tells the tale!'
A month, I bid my friends congratulate their best:
'You happy Don!' (to me): 'The blockhead!' (to the rest):
'No doubt he thinks his daub original, poor dupe!'
Then I resume my life: one chamber must not coop
Man's life in, though it boast a marvel like my prize.
Next year, I saunter past with unaverted eyes,
Nay, loll and turn my back: perchance to overlook
With relish, leaf by leaf, Doré's last picture-book.

XXXVI

Imagine that a voice reproached me from its frame:
'Here do I hang, and may! Your Rafael, just the same,
'Tis only you that change: no ecstasies of yore!
No purposed suicide distracts you any more!'
Prompt would my answer meet such frivolous attack:
'You misappropriate sensations. What men lack,
And labour to obtain, is hoped and feared about
After a fashion; what they once obtain, makes doubt,
Expectancy's old fret and fume, henceforward void.
But do they think to hold such havings unalloyed
By novel hopes and fears, of fashion just as new,
To correspond i' the scale? Nowise, I promise you!
Mine you are, therefore mine will be, as fit to cheer
My soul and glad my sense today as this-day-year.
So, any sketch or scrap, pochade, caricature,
Made in a moment, meant a moment to endure,
I snap at, seize, enjoy, then tire of, throw aside,
Find you in your old place. But if a servant cried
'Fire in the gallery!' – methinks, were I engaged
In Doré, elbow-deep, picture-books million-paged
To the four winds would pack, sped by the heartiest curse
Was ever launched from lip, to strew the universe.
Would not I brave the best o' the burning, bear away

Either my perfect piece in safety, or else stay
And share its fate, be made its martyr nor repine?
Inextricably wed, such ashes mixed with mine!'

XXXVII

For which I get the eye, the hand, the heart, the whole
O' the wondrous wife again!

XXXVIII

But no, play out your *rôle*
I' the pageant! 'Tis not fit your phantom leave the stage:
I want you, there, to make you, here, confess you wage
Successful warfare, pique those proud ones, and advance
Claim to . . . equality? nay, but predominance
In *physique* o'er them all, where Helen heads the scene
Closed by its tiniest of tail-tips, pert Fifine.
How ravishingly pure you stand in pale constraint!
My new-created shape, without or touch or taint,
Inviolate of life and worldliness and sin –
Fettered, I hold my flower, her own cup's weight would win
From off the tall slight stalk a-top of which she turns
And trembles, makes appeal to one who roughly earns
Her thanks instead of blame, (did lily only know),
By thus constraining length of lily, letting snow
Of cup-crown, that's her face, look from its guardian stake,
Superb on all that crawls beneath, and mutely make
Defiance, with the mouth's white movements of disdain,
To all that stoops, retires and hovers round again!
How windingly the limbs delay to lead up, reach
Where, crowned, the head waits calm: as if reluctant, each,
That eye should traverse quick such lengths of loveliness,
From feet, which just are found embedded in the dress
Deep swathed about with folds and flowings virginal,
Up to the pleated breasts, rebellious 'neath their pall,
As if the vesture's snow were moulding sleep not death,
Must melt and so release; whereat, from the fine sheath,
The flower-cup-crown starts free, the face is unconcealed,
And what shall now divert me, once the sweet face revealed,
From all I loved so long, so lingeringly left?

XXXIX

Because indeed your face fits into just the cleft
O' the heart of me, Elvire, makes right and whole once more
All that was half itself without you! As before,
My truant finds its place! Doubtlessly sea-shells yearn,
If plundered by sad chance: would pray their pearls return,
Let negligently slip away into the wave!
Never may eyes desist, those eyes so grey and grave,
From their slow sure supply of the effluent soul within!
And, would you humour me? I dare to ask, unpin
The web of that brown hair! O'erwash o' the sudden, but
As promptly, too, disclose, on either side, the jut
Of alabaster brow! So part rich rillets dyed
Deep by the woodland leaf, when down they pour, each side
O' the rock-top, pushed by Spring!

XL

'And where i' the world is all
This wonder, you detail so trippingly, espied?
My mirror would reflect a tall, thin, pale, deep-eyed
Personage, pretty once, it may be, doubtless still
Loving, – a certain grace yet lingers, if you will, –
But all this wonder, where?'

XLI

Why, where but in the sense
And soul of me, Art's judge? Art is my evidence
That something was, is, might be; but no more thing itself,
Than flame is fuel. Once the verse-book laid on shelf,
The picture turned to wall, the music fled from ear, –
Each beauty, born of each, grows clearer and more clear,
Mine henceforth, ever mine!

XLII

But if I would re-trace
Effect, in Art, to cause, – corroborate, erase
What's right or wrong i' the lines, test fancy in my brain
By fact which gave it birth? I re-peruse in vain
The verse, I fail to find that vision of delight
I' the Bazzi's lost-profile, eye-edge so exquisite.
And, music: what? that burst of pillared cloud by day
And pillared fire by night, was product, must we say,

Of modulating just, by enharmonic change, –
The augmented sixth resolved, – from out the straighter range
Of D sharp minor, – leap of disimprisoned thrall, –
Into thy light and life, D major natural?

XLIII

Elvire, will you partake in what I shall impart?
I seem to understand the way heart chooses heart
By help of the outside form, – a reason for our wild
Diversity in choice, – why each grows reconciled
To what is absent, what superfluous in the mask
Of flesh that's meant to yield, – did nature ply her task
As artist should, – precise the features of the soul,
Which, if in any case they found expression, whole
I' the traits, would give a type, undoubtedly display
A novel, true, distinct perfection in its way.
Never shall I believe any two souls were made
Similar; granting, then, each soul of every grade
Was meant to be itself, prove in itself complete
And, in completion, good, – nay, best o' the kind, – as meet
Needs must it be that show on the outside correspond
With inward substance, – flesh, the dress which soul has donned,
Exactly reproduce, – were only justice done
Inside and outside too, – types perfect everyone.
How happens it that here we meet a mystery
Insoluble to man, a plaguy puzzle? Why
Each soul is either made imperfect, and deserves
As rude a face to match, or else a bungler swerves,
And nature, on a soul worth rendering aright,
Works ill, or proves perverse, or, in her own despite,
– Here too much, there too little, – bids each face, more or less,
Retire from beauty, make approach to ugliness?
And yet succeeds the same: since, what is wanting to success,
If somehow every face, no matter how deform,
Evidence, to some one of hearts on earth, that, warm
Beneath the veriest ash, there hides a spark of soul
Which, quickened by love's breath, may yet pervade the whole
O' the grey, and, free again, be fire? – of worth the same,
Howe'er produced, for, great or little, flame is flame.
A mystery, whereof solution is to seek.

XLIV

I find it in the fact that each soul, just as weak
Its own way as its fellow, – departure from design
As flagrant in the flesh, – goes striving to combine
With what shall right the wrong, the under or above
The standard: supplement unloveliness by love.
– Ask Plato else! And this corroborates the sage,
That Art, – which I may style the love of loving, rage
Of knowing, seeing, feeling the absolute truth of things
For truth's sake, whole and sole, not any good, truth brings
The knower, seer, feeler, beside, – instinctive Art
Must fumble for the whole, once fixing on a part
However poor, surpass the fragment, and aspire
To reconstruct thereby the ultimate entire.
Art, working with a will, discards the superflux,
Contributes to defect, toils on till, – *fiat lux*, –
There's the restored, the prime, the individual type!

XLV

Look, for example now! This piece of broken pipe
(Some shipman's solace erst) shall act as crayon; and
What tablet better serves my purpose than the sand?
– Smooth slab whereon I draw, no matter with what skill,
A face, and yet another, and yet another still.
There lie my three prime types of beauty!

XLVI

Laugh your best!
'Exaggeration and absurdity?' Confessed!
Yet, what may that face mean, no matter for its nose,
A yard long, or its chin, a foot short?

XLVII

'You suppose,
Horror?' Exactly! What's the odds if, more or less
By yard or foot, the features do manage to express
Such meaning in the main? Where I of Gérôme's force,
Nor feeble as you see, quick should my crayon course
O'er outline, curb, excite, till, – so completion speeds
With Gérôme well at work, – observe how brow recedes,
Head shudders back on spine, as if one haled the hair,
Would have the full-face front what pin-point eye's sharp stare

Announces; mouth agape to drink the flowing fate,
While chin protrudes to meet the burst o' the wave: elate
Almost, spurred on to brave necessity, expend
All life left, in one flash, as fire does at its end.
Retrenchment and addition effect a masterpiece,
Not change i' the motive: here diminish, there increase –
And who wants Horror, has it.

XLVIII

Who wants some other show
Of soul, may seek elsewhere – this second of the row?
What does it give for germ, monadic mere intent
Of mind in face, faint first of meanings ever meant?
Why, possibly, a grin, that, strengthened, grows a laugh;
That, softened, leaves a smile; that, tempered, bids you quaff
At such a magic cup as English Reynolds once
Compounded: for the witch pulls out of you response
Like Garrick's to Thalia, however due may be
Your homage claimed by that stiff-stoled Melpomene!

XLIX

And just this one face more! Pardon the bold pretence!
May there not lurk some hint, struggle toward evidence
In that compressed mouth, those strained nostrils, steadfast eyes
Of utter passion, absolute self-sacrifice,
Which, – could I but subdue the wild grotesque, refine
That bulge of brow, make blunt that nose's aquiline,
And let, although compressed, a point of pulp appear
I' the mouth, – would give at last the portrait of Elvire?

L

Well, and if so succeed hand-practice on awry
Preposterous art-mistake, shall soul-proficiency
Despair, – when exercised on nature, which at worst
Always implies success, however crossed and curst
By failure, – such as art would emulate in vain?
Shall any soul despair of setting free again
Trait after trait, until the type as wholly start
Forth, visible to sense, as that minutest part,
(Whate'er the chance) which first arresting eye, warned soul
That, under wrong enough and ravage, lay the whole
O' the loveliness it 'loved' – I take the accepted phrase?

LI

So I account for tastes: each chooses, none gainsays
The fancy of his fellow, a paradise for him,
A hell for all beside. You can but crown the brim
O' the cup; if it be full, what matters less or more?
Let each, i' the world, amend his love, as I, o' the shore,
My sketch, and the result as undisputed be!
Their handiwork to them, and my Elvire to me:
– Result more beautiful than beauty's self, when lo,
What was my Rafael turns my Michelagnolo!

LII

For, we two boast, beside our pearl, a diamond.
I' the palace-gallery, the corridor beyond,
Upheaves itself a marble, a magnitude man-shaped
As snow might be. One hand, – the Master's, – smoothed and scraped
That mass, he hammered on and hewed at, till he hurled
Life out of death, and left a challenge: for the world,
Death still, – since who shall dare, close to the image, say
If this be purposed Art, or mere mimetic play
Of Nature? – wont to deal with crag or cloud, as stuff
To fashion novel forms, like forms we know, enough
For recognition, but enough unlike the same,
To leave no hope ourselves may profit by her game;
Death therefore to the world. Step back a pace or two!
And then, who dares dispute the gradual birth its due
Of breathing life, or breathless immortality,
Where out she stands, and yet stops short, half bold, half shy,
Hesitates on the threshold of things, since partly blent
With stuff she needs must quit, her native element
I' the mind o' the Master, – what's the creature, dear-divine
Yet earthly-awful too, so manly-feminine,
Pretends this white advance? What startling brain-escape
Of Michelagnolo takes elemental shape?
I think he meant the daughter of the old man o' the sea,
Emerging from her wave, goddess Eidotheé –
She who, in elvish sport, spite with benevolence
Mixed Mab-wise up, must needs instruct the Hero whence
Salvation dawns o'er that mad misery of his isle.
Yes, she imparts to him, by what a pranksome wile
He may surprise her sire, asleep beneath a rock,

When he has told their tale, amid his web-foot flock
Of sea-beasts, 'fine fat seals with bitter breath!' laughs she
At whom she likes to save, no less: Eidotheé,
Whom you shall never face evolved, in earth, in air,
In wave; but, manifest i' the soul's domain, why, there
She ravishingly moves to meet you, all through aid
O' the soul! Bid shine what should, dismiss into the shade
What should not be, – and there triumphs the paramount
Emprise o' the Master! But, attempt to make account
Of what the sense, without soul's help, perceives? I bought
That work – (despite plain proof, whose hand it was had wrought
I' the rough: I think we trace the tool of triple tooth,
Here, there and everywhere) – bought dearly that uncouth
Unwieldy bulk, for just ten dollars – 'Bulk, would fetch –
Converted into lime – some five pauls!' grinned a wretch,
Who, bound on business, paused to hear the bargaining,
And would have pitied me 'but for the fun o' the thing!'

LIII

Shall such a wretch be – you? Must – while I show Elvire
Shaming all other forms, seen as I see her here
I' the soul, – this other-you perversely look outside,
And ask me, 'Where i' the world is charm to be descried
I' the tall thin personage, with paled eye, pensive face,
Any amount of love, and some remains of grace?'
See yourself in my soul!

LIV

And what a world for each
Must somehow be i' the soul, – accept that mode of speech, –
Whether an aura gird the soul, wherein it seems
To float and move, a belt of all the glints and gleams
It struck from out that world, its weaklier fellows found
So dead and cold; or whether these not so much surround,
As pass into the soul itself, add worth to worth,
As wine enriches blood, and straightway send it forth,
Conquering and to conquer, through all eternity,
That's battle without end.

LV

I search but cannot see
What purpose serves the soul that strives, or world it tries
Conclusions with, unless the fruit of victories
Stay, one and all, stored up and guaranteed its own
For ever, by some mode whereby shall be made known
The gain of every life. Death reads the title clear –
What each soul for itself conquered from out things here:
Since, in the seeing soul, all worth lies, I assert, –
And naught i' the world, which, save for soul that sees, inert
Was, is, and would be ever, – stuff for transmuting, – null
And void until man's breath evoke the beautiful –
But, touched aright, prompt yields each particle its tongue
Of elemental flame, – no matter whence flame sprung
From gums and spice, or else from straw and rottenness,
So long as soul has power to make them burn, express
What lights and warms henceforth, leaves only ash behind,
Howe'er the chance: if soul be privileged to find
Food so soon that, by first snatch of eye, suck of breath,
It can absorb pure life: or, rather, meeting death
I' the shape of ugliness, by fortunate recoil
So put on its resource, it find therein a foil
For a new birth of life, the challenged soul's response
To ugliness and death, – creation for the nonce.

LVI

I gather heart through just such conquests of the soul,
Through evocation out of that which, on the whole,
Was rough, ungainly, partial accomplishment, at best,
And – what, at worst, save failure to spit at and detest? –
– Through transference of all, achieved in visible things,
To where, secured from wrong, rest soul's imaginings –
Through ardour to bring help just where completion halts,
Do justice to the purpose, ignore the slips and faults –
And, last, through waging with deformity a fight
Which wrings thence, at the end, precise its opposite.
I praise the loyalty o' the scholar, – stung by taunt
Of fools 'Does this evince thy Master men so vaunt?
Did he then perpetrate the plain abortion here?'
Who cries 'His work am I! full fraught by him, I clear
His fame from each result of accident and time,
Myself restore his work to its fresh morning-prime,

Not daring touch the mass of marble, fools deride,
But putting my idea in plaster by its side,
His, since mine; I, he made, vindicate who made me!'

LVII

For, you must know, I too achieved Eidotheé,
In silence and by night – dared justify the lines
Plain to my soul, although, to sense, that triple-tine's
Achievement halt half-way, break down, or leave a blank.
If she stood forth at last, the Master was to thank!
Yet may there not have smiled approval in his eyes –
That one at least was left who, born to recognize
Perfection in the piece imperfect, worked, that night,
In silence, such his faith, until the apposite
Design was out of him, truth palpable once more?
And then, – for at one blow, its fragments strewed the floor, –
Recalled the same to live within his soul as heretofore.

LVIII

And, even as I hold and have Eidotheé,
I say, I cannot think that gain, – which would not be
Except a special soul had gained it, – that such gain
Can ever be estranged, do aught but appertain
Immortally, by right firm, indefeasible,
To who performed the feat, through God's grace and man's will!
Gain, never shared by those who practised with earth's stuff,
And spoiled whate'er they touched, leaving its roughness rough,
Its blankness bare, and, when the ugliness opposed,
Either struck work or laughed 'He doted or he dozed!'

LIX

While, oh, how all the more will love become intense
Hereafter, when 'to love' means yearning to dispense,
Each soul, its own amount of gain through its own mode
Of practising with life, upon some soul which owed
Its treasure, all diverse and yet in worth the same,
To new work and changed way! Things furnish you rose-flame,
Which burn up red, green, blue, nay, yellow more than needs,
For me, I nowise doubt; why doubt a time succeeds
When each one may impart, and each receive, both share
The chemic secret, learn, – where I lit force, why there
You drew forth lambent pity, – where I found only food

For self-indulgence, you still blew a spark at brood
I' the greyest ember, stopped not till self-sacrifice imbued
Heaven's face with flame? What joy, when each may supplement
The other, changing each as changed, till, wholly blent,
Our old things shall be new, and, what we both ignite,
Fuse, lose the varicolor in achromatic white!
Exemplifying law, apparent even now
In the eternal progress, – love's law, which I avow
And thus would formulate: each soul lives, longs and works
For itself, by itself, – because a lodestar lurks,
An other than itself, – in whatsoe'er the niche
Of mistiest heaven it hide, whoe'er the Glumdalclich
May grasp the Gulliver: or it, or he, or she –
Theosutos e broteios eper kekramene, –
(For fun's sake, where the phrase has fastened, leave it fixed!
So soft it says, – 'God, man, or both together mixed'!)
This, guessed at through the flesh, by parts which prove the
whole,
This constitutes the soul discernible by soul
– Elvire, by me!

LX

'And then' – (pray you, permit remain
This hand upon my arm! – your cheek dried, if you deign,
Choosing my shoulder) – 'then' – (Stand up for, boldly state
The objection in its length and breadth!) 'you abdicate,
With boast yet on your lip, soul's empire, and accept
The rule of sense; the Man, from monarch's throne has stept –
Leapt, rather, at one bound, to base, and there lies, Brute.
You talk of soul, – how soul, in search of soul to suit,
Must needs review the sex, the army, rank and file
Of womankind, report no face nor form so vile
But that a certain worth, by certain signs, may thence
Evolve itself and stand confessed – to soul – by sense.
Sense? Oh, the loyal bee endeavours for the hive!
Disinterested hunts the flower-field through, alive
Not one mean moment, no, – suppose on flower he light, –
To his peculiar drop, petal-dew perquisite,
Matter-of-course snatched snack: unless he taste, how try?
This, light on tongue-tip laid, allows him pack his thigh,
Transport all he counts prize, provision for the comb,
Food for the future day, – a banquet, but at home!

Soul? Ere you reach Fifine's, some flesh may be to pass!
That bombèd brow, that eye, a kindling chrysopras,
Beneath its stiff black lash, inquisitive how speeds
Each functionary limb, how play of foot succeeds,
And how you let escape or duly sympathize
With gastroknemian grace, – true, your soul tastes and tries,
And trifles time with these, but, fear not, will arrive
At essence in the core, bring honey home to hive,
Brain-stock and heart-stuff both – to strike objectors dumb –
Since only soul affords the soul fit pabulum!
Be frank for charity! Who is it you deceive –
Yourself or me or God, with all this make-believe?'

LXI

And frank I will respond as you interrogate.
Ah, Music, wouldst thou help! Words struggle with the weight
So feebly of the False, thick element between
Our soul, the True, and Truth! which, but that intervene
False shows of things, were reached as easily by thought
Reducible to word, as now by yearnings wrought
Up with thy fine free force, oh Music, that canst thrid,
Electrically win a passage through the lid
Of earthly sepulchre, our words may push against,
Hardly transpierce as thou! Not dissipate, thou deign'st,
So much as tricksily elude what words attempt
To heave away, i' the mass, and let the soul, exempt
From all that vapoury obstruction, view, instead
Of glimmer underneath, a glory overhead.
Not feebly, like our phrase, against the barrier go
In suspirative swell the authentic notes I know,
By help whereof, I would our souls were found without
The pale, above the dense and dim which breeds the doubt!
But Music, dumb for you, withdraws her help from me;
And, since to weary words recourse again must be,
At least permit they rest their burthen here and there,
Music-like: cover space! My answer, – need you care
If it exceed the bounds, reply to questioning
You never meant should plague? Once fairly on the wing,
Let me flap far and wide!

LXII

For this is just the time,
The place, the mood in you and me, when all things chime.
Clash forth life's common chord, whence, list how there ascend
Harmonics far and faint, till our perception end, –
Reverberated notes whence we construct the scale
Embracing what we know and feel and are! How fail
To find or, better, lose your question, in this quick
Reply which nature yields, ample and catholic?
For, arm in arm, we two have reached, nay, passed, you see,
The village-precinct; sun sets mild on Sainte Marie –
We only catch the spire, and yet I seem to know
What's hid i' the turn o' the hill: how all the graves must glow
Soberly, as each warms its little iron cross,
Flourished about with gold, and graced (if private loss
Be fresh) with stiff rope-wreath of yellow crisp bead-blooms
Which tempt down birds to pay their supper, 'mid the tombs,
With prattle good as song, amuse the dead awhile,
If couched they hear beneath the matted camomile!

LXIII

Bid them good-bye before last friend has sung and supped!
Because we pick our path and need our eyes, – abrupt
Descent enough, – but here's the beach, and there's the bay,
And, opposite, the streak of Île Noirmoutier.
Thither the waters tend; they freshen as they haste,
At feel o' the night-wind, though, by cliff and cliff embraced,
This breadth of blue retains its self-possession still;
As you and I intend to do, who take our fill
Of sights and sounds – soft sound, the countless hum and skip
Of insects we disturb, and that good fellowship
Of rabbits our foot-fall sends huddling, each to hide
He best knows how and where; and what whirred past, wings wide?
That was an owl, their young may justlier apprehend!
Though you refuse to speak, your beating heart, my friend,
I feel against my arm, – though your bent head forbids
A look into your eyes, yet, on my cheek, their lids
That ope and shut, soft send a silken thrill the same.
Well, out of all and each these nothings, comes – what came
Often enough before, the something that would aim

Once more at the old mark: the impulse to at last
Succeed where hitherto was failure in the past,
And yet again essay the adventure. Clearlier sings
No bird to its couched corpse 'Into the truth of things –
Out of their falseness rise, and reach thou, and remain!'

LXIV

'That rise into the true out of the false – explain?'
May an example serve? In yonder bay I bathed,
This sunny morning: swam my best, then hung, half swathed
With chill, and half with warmth, i' the channel's midmost deep:
You know how one – not treads, but stands in water? Keep
Body and limbs below, hold head back, uplift chin,
And, for the rest, leave care! If brow, eyes, mouth, should win
Their freedom, – excellent! If they must brook the surge,
No matter though they sink, let but the nose emerge.
So, all of me in brine lay soaking: did I care
One jot? I kept alive by man's due breath of air
I' the nostrils, high and dry. At times, o'er these would run
The ripple, even wash the wavelet, – morning's sun
Tempted advance, no doubt: and always flash of froth,
Fish-outbreak, bubbling by, would find me nothing loth
To rise and look around; then all was overswept
With dark and death at once. But trust the old adept!
Back went again the head, a merest motion made,
Fin-fashion, either hand, and nostril soon conveyed
Assurance light and life were still in reach as erst:
Always the last and, – wait and watch, – sometimes the first.
Try to ascend breast-high? wave arms wide free of tether?
Be in the air and leave the water altogether?
Under went all again, till I resigned myself
To only breathe the air, that's footed by an elf,
And only swim the water, that's native to a fish.
But there is no denying that, ere I curbed my wish,
And schooled my restive arms, salt entered mouth and eyes
Often enough – sun, sky, and air so tantalize!
Still, the adept swims, this accorded, that denied;
Can always breathe, sometimes see and be satisfied!

LXV

I liken to this play o' the body, – fruitless strife
To slip the sea and hold the heaven, – my spirit's life

'Twixt false, whence it would break, and true, where it would bide.
I move in, yet resist, am upborne every side
By what I beat against, an element too gross
To live in, did not soul duly obtain her dose
Of life-breath, and inhale from truth's pure plenitude
Above her, snatch and gain enough to just illude
With hope that some brave bound may baffle evermore
The obstructing medium, make who swam henceforward soar:
– Gain scarcely snatched when, foiled by the very effort, sowse,
Underneath ducks the soul, her truthward yearnings dowse
Deeper in falsehood! ay, but fitted less and less
To bear in nose and mouth old briny bitterness
Proved alien more and more: since each experience proves
Air – the essential good, not sea, wherein who moves
Must thence, in the act, escape, apart from will or wish.
Move a mere hand to take waterweed, jelly-fish,
Upward you tend! And yet our business with the sea
Is not with air, but just o' the water, watery:
We must endure the false, no particle of which
Do we acquaint us with, but up we mount a pitch
Above it, find our head reach truth, while hands explore
The false below: so much while here we bathe, – no more!

LXVI

Now, there is one prime point (hear and be edified!)
One truth more true for me than any truth beside –
To-wit, that I am I, who have the power to swim,
The skill to understand the law whereby each limb
May bear to keep immersed, since, in return, made sure
That its mere movement lifts head clean through coverture.
By practice with the false, I reach the true? Why, thence
It follows, that the more I gain self-confidence,
Get proof I know the trick, can float, sink, rise, at will,
The better I submit to what I have the skill
To conquer in my turn, even now, and by and by
Leave wholly for the land, and there laugh, shake me dry
To last drop, saturate with noonday – no need more
Of wet and fret, plagued once: on Pornic's placid shore,
Abundant air to breathe, sufficient sun to feel!
Meantime I buoy myself: no whit my senses reel
When over me there breaks a billow; nor, elate

Too much by some brief taste, I quaff intemperate
The air, o'ertop breast-high the wave-environment.
Full well I know the thing I grasp, as if intent
To hold, – my wandering wave, – will not be grasped at all:
The solid-seeming grasped, the handful great or small
Must go to nothing, glide through fingers fast enough;
But none the less, to treat liquidity as stuff –
Though failure – certainly succeeds beyond its aim,
Sends head above, past thing that hands miss, all the same.

LXVII

So with this wash o' the world, wherein life-long we drift;
We push and paddle through the foam by making shift
To breathe above at whiles when, after deepest duck
Down underneath the show, we put forth hand and pluck
At what seems somehow like reality – a soul.
I catch at this and that, to capture and control,
Presume I hold a prize, discover that my pains
Are run to naught: my hands are balked, my head regains
The surface where I breathe and look about, a space.
The soul that helped me mount? Swallowed up in the race
O' the tide, come who knows whence, gone gaily who knows where!
I thought the prize was mine; I flattered myself there.
It did its duty, though: I felt it, it felt me,
Or, where I look about and breathe, I should not be.
The main point is – the false fluidity was bound
Acknowledge that it frothed o'er substance, nowise found
Fluid, but firm and true. Man, outcast, 'howls,' – at rods? –
If 'sent in playful spray a-shivering to his gods!'
Childishest childe, man makes thereby no bad exchange.
Stay with the flat-fish, thou! We like the upper range
Where the 'gods' live, perchance the daemons also dwell:
Where operates a Power, which every throb and swell
Of human heart invites that human soul approach,
'Sent' near and nearer still, however 'spray' encroach
On 'shivering' flesh below, to altitudes, which gained,
Evil proves good, wrong right, obscurity explained,
And 'howling' childishness. Whose howl have we to thank,
If all the dogs 'gan bark and puppies whine, till sank
Each yelper's tail 'twixt legs? for Huntsman Commonsense
Came to the rescue, bade prompt thwack of thong dispense

Quiet i' the kennel; taught that ocean might be blue,
And rolling and much more, and yet the soul have, too,
Its touch of God's own flame, which He may so expand
'Who measured the waters i' the hollow of His hand'
That ocean's self shall dry, turn dew-drop in respect
Of all-triumphant fire, matter with intellect
Once fairly matched; bade him who egged on hounds to bay,
Go curse, i' the poultry yard, his kind: 'there let him lay'
The swan's one addled egg: which yet shall put to use,
Rub breast-bone warm against, so many a sterile goose!

LXVIII

No, I want sky not sea, prefer the larks to shrimps,
And never dive so deep but that I get a glimpse
O' the blue above, a breath of the air around. Elvire,
I seize – by catching at the melted beryl here,
The tawny hair that just has trickled off, – Fifine!
Did not we two trip forth to just enjoy the scene,
The tumbling-troop arrayed, the strollers on their stage,
Drawn up and under arms, and ready to engage –
Dabble, and there an end, with foam and froth o'er face,
Till suddenly Fifine suggested change of place?
Now we taste aether, scorn the wave, and interchange apace
No ordinary thoughts, but such as evidence
The cultivated mind in both. On what pretence
Are you and I to sneer at who lent help to hand,
And gave the lucky lift?

LXIX

Still sour? I understand!
One ugly circumstance discredits my fair plan –
That Woman does the work: I waive the help of Man.
'Why should experiment be tried with only waves,
When solid spars float round? Still some Thalassia saves
Too pertinaciously, as though no Triton, bluff
As e'er blew brine from conch, were free to help enough!
Surely, to recognize a man, his mates serve best!
Why is there not the same or greater interest
In the strong spouse as in the pretty partner, pray,
Were recognition just your object, as you say,
Amid this element o' the false?'

LXX

We come to terms.
I need to be proved true; and nothing so confirms
One's faith in the prime point that one's alive, not dead,
In all Descents to Hell whereof I ever read,
As when a phantom there, male enemy or friend,
Or merely stranger-shade, is struck, is forced suspend
His passage: 'You that breathe, along with us the ghosts?'
Here, why must it be still a woman that accosts?

LXXI

Because, one woman's worth, in that respect, such hairy hosts
Of the other sex and sort! Men? Say you have the power
To make them yours, rule men, throughout life's little hour,
According to the phrase; what follows? Men, you make,
By ruling them, your own: each man for his own sake
Accepts you as his guide, avails him of what worth
He apprehends in you to sublimate his earth
With fire: content, if so you convoy him through night,
That you shall play the sun, and he, the satellite,
Pilfer your light and heat and virtue, starry pelf,
While, caught up by your course, he turns upon himself.
Women rush into you, and there remain absorbed.
Beside, 'tis only men completely formed, full-orbed,
Are fit to follow track, keep pace, illústrate so
The leader: any sort of woman may bestow
Her atom on the star, or clod she counts for such, –
Each little making less bigger by just that much.
Women grow you, while men depend on you at best.
And what dependence! Bring and put him to the test,
Your specimen disciple, a handbreadth separate
From you, he almost seemed to touch before! Abate
Complacency you will, I judge, at what's divulged!
Some flabbiness you fixed, some vacancy outbulged,
Some – much – nay, all, perhaps, the outward man's your work:
But, inside man? – find him, wherever he may lurk,
And where's a touch of you in his true self?

LXXII

I wish
Some wind would waft this way a glassy bubble-fish
O' the kind the sea inflates, and show you, once detached

From wave . . . or no, the event is better told than watched:
Still may the thing float free, globose and opaline
All over, save where just the amethysts combine
To blue their best, rim-round the sea-flower with a tinge
Earth's violet never knew! Well, 'neath that gem-tipped fringe,
A head lurks – of a kind – that acts as stomach too;
Then comes the emptiness which out the water blew
So big and belly-like, but, dry of water drained,
Withers away nine-tenths. Ah, but a tenth remained!
That was the creature's self: no more akin to sea,
Poor rudimental head and stomach, you agree,
Than sea's akin to sun who yonder dips his edge.

LXXIII

But take the rill which ends a race o'er yonder ledge
O' the fissured cliff, to find its fate in smoke below!
Disengage that, and ask – what news of life, you know
It led, that long lone way, through pasture, plain and waste?
All's gone to give the sea! no touch of earth, no taste
Of air, reserved to tell how rushes used to bring
The butterfly and bee, and fisher-bird that's king
O' the purple kind, about the snow-soft silver-sweet
Infant of mist and dew; only these atoms fleet,
Embittered evermore, to make the sea one drop
More big thereby – if thought keep count where sense must stop.

LXXIV

The full-blown ingrate, mere recipient of the brine,
That takes all and gives naught, is Man; the feminine
Rillet that, giving all and taking naught in turn,
Goes headlong to her death i' the sea, without concern
For the old inland life, snow-soft and silver-clear,
That's woman – typified from Fifine to Elvire.

LXXV

Then, how diverse the modes prescribed to who would deal
With either kind of creature! 'Tis Man, you seek to seal
Your very own? Resolve, for first step, to discard
Nine-tenths of what you are! To make, you must be marred, –
To raise your race, must stoop, – to teach them aught, must learn
Ignorance, meet half-way what most you hope to spurn
I' the sequel. Change yourself, dissimulate the thought

And vulgarize the word, and see the deed be brought
To look like nothing done with any such intent
As teach men – though perchance it teach, by accident!
So may you master men: assured that if you show
One point of mastery, departure from the low
And level, – head or heart-revolt at long disguise,
Immurement, stifling soul in mediocrities, –
If inadvertently a gesture, much more, word
Reveal the hunter no companion for the herd,
His chance of capture's gone. Success means, they may snuff,
Examine, and report, – a brother, sure enough,
Disports him in brute-guise; for skin is truly skin,
Horns, hoofs are hoofs and horns, and all, outside and in,
Is veritable beast, whom fellow-beasts resigned
May follow, made a prize in honest pride, behind
One of themselves and not creation's upstart lord!
Well, there's your prize i' the pound – much joy may it afford
My Indian! Make survey and tell me, – was it worth
You acted part so well, went all-fours upon earth
The live-long day, brayed, belled, and all to bring to pass
That stags should deign eat hay when winter stints them grass?

LXXVI

So much for men, and how disguise may make them mind
Their master. But you have to deal with womankind?
Abandon stratagem for strategy! Cast quite
The vile disguise away, try truth clean-opposite
Such creep-and-crawl, stand forth all man and, might it chance,
Somewhat of angel too! – whate'er inheritance,
Actual on earth, in heaven prospective, be your boast,
Lay claim to! Your best self revealed at uttermost, –
That's the wise way o' the strong! And e'en should falsehood tempt
The weaker sort to swerve, – at least the lie's exempt
From slur, that's loathlier still, of aiming to debase
Rather than elevate its object. Mimic grace,
Not make deformity your mask! Be sick by stealth,
Nor traffic with disease – malingering in health!
No more of: 'Countrymen, I boast me one like you –
My lot, the common strength, the common weakness too!
I think the thoughts you think; and if I have the knack
Of fitting thoughts to words, you peradventure lack,

Envy me not the chance, yourselves more fortunate!
Many the loaded ship self-sunk through treasure-freight,
Many the pregnant brain brought never child to birth,
Many the great heart broke beneath its girdle-girth!
Be mine the privilege to supplement defect,
Give dumbness voice, and let the labouring intellect
Find utterance in word, or possibly in deed!
What though I seem to go before? 'tis you that lead!
I follow what I see so plain – the general mind
Projected pillar-wise, flame kindled by the kind,
Which dwarfs the unit – me – to insignificance!
Halt you, I stop forthwith, – proceed, I too advance!'

LXXVII

Ay, that's the way to take with men you wish to lead,
Instruct and benefit. Small prospect you succeed
With women so! Be all that's great and good and wise,
August, sublime – swell out your frog the right ox-size –
He's buoyed like a balloon, to soar, not burst, you'll see!
The more you prove yourself, less fear the prize will flee
The captor. Here you start after no pompous stag
Who condescends be snared, with toss of horn, and brag
Of bray, and ramp of hoof; you have not to subdue
The foe through letting him imagine he snares you!
'Tis rather with . . .

LXXVIII

Ah, thanks! quick – where the dipping disk
Shows red against the rise and fall o' the fin! there frisk
In shoal the – porpoises? Dolphins, they shall and must
Cut through the freshening clear – dolphins, my instance just!
'Tis fable, therefore truth: who has to do with these,
Needs never practise trick of going hands and knees
As beasts require. Art fain the fish to captivate?
Gather thy greatness round, Arion! Stand in state,
As when the banqueting thrilled conscious – like a rose
Throughout its hundred leaves at that approach it knows
Of music in the bird – while Corinth grew one breast
A-throb for song and thee; nay, Periander pressed
The Methymnaean hand, and felt a king indeed, and guessed
How Phoebus' self might give that great mouth of the gods

Such a magnificence of song! The pillar nods,
Rocks roof, and trembles door, gigantic, post and jamb,
As harp and voice rend air – the shattering dithyramb!
So stand thou, and assume the robe that tingles yet
With triumph; strike the harp, whose every golden fret
Still smoulders with the flame, was late at fingers' end –
So, standing on the bench o' the ship, let voice expend
Thy soul, sing, unalloyed by meaner mode, thine own,
The Orthian lay; then leap from music's lofty throne,
Into the lowest surge, make fearlessly thy launch!
Whatever storm may threat, some dolphin will be staunch!
Whatever roughness rage, some exquisite sea-thing
Will surely rise to save, will bear – palpitating –
One proud humility of love beneath its load –
Stem tide, part wave, till both roll on, thy jewelled road
Of triumph, and the grim o' the gulph grow wonder-white
I' the phosphorescent wake; and still the exquisite
Sea-thing stems on, saves still, palpitatingly thus,
Lands safe at length its load of love at Taenarus,
True woman-creature!

LXXIX

Man? Ah, would you prove what power
Marks man, – what fruit his tree may yield, beyond the sour
And stinted crab, he calls love-apple, which remains
After you toil and moil your utmost, – all, love gains
By lavishing manure? – try quite the other plan!
And, to obtain the strong true product of a man,
Set him to hate a little! Leave cherishing his root,
And rather prune his branch, nip off the pettiest shoot
Superfluous on his bough! I promise, you shall learn
By what grace came the goat, of all beasts else, to earn
Such favour with the god o' the grape: 'twas only he
Who, browsing on its tops, first stung fertility
Into the stock's heart, stayed much growth of tendril-twine,
Some faintish flower, perhaps, but gained the indignant wine,
Wrath of the red press! Catch the puniest of the kind –
Man-animalcule, starved body, stunted mind,
And, as you nip the blotch 'twixt thumb and finger-nail,
Admire how heaven above and earth below avail
No jot to soothe the mite, sore at God's prime offence
In making mites at all, – coax from its impotence

One virile drop of thought, or word, or deed, by strain
To propagate for once – which nature rendered vain,
Who lets first failure stay, yet cares not to record
Mistake that seems to cast opprobrium on the Lord!
Such were the gain from love's best pains! But let the elf
Be touched with hate, because some real man bears himself
Manlike in body and soul, and, since he lives, must thwart
And furify and set a-fizz this counterpart
O' the pismire that's surprised to effervescence, if,
By chance, black bottle come in contact with chalk cliff,
Acid with alkali! Then thrice the bulk, out blows
Our insect, does its kind, and cuckoo-spits some rose!

LXXX

No – 'tis ungainly work, the ruling men, at best!
The graceful instinct's right: 'tis women stand confessed
Auxiliary, the gain that never goes away,
Takes nothing and gives all: Elvire, Fifine, 'tis they
Convince, – if little, much, no matter! – one degree
The more, at least, convince unreasonable me
That I am, anyhow, a truth, though all else seem
And be not: if I dream, at least I know I dream.
The falsity, beside, is fleeting: I can stand
Still, and let truth come back, – your steadying touch of hand
Assists me to remain self-centred, fixed amid
All on the move. Believe in me, at once you bid
Myself believe that, since one soul has disengaged
Mine from the shows of things, so much is fact: I waged
No foolish warfare, then, with shades, myself a shade,
Here in the world – may hope my pains will be repaid!
How false things are, I judge: how changeable, I learn
When, where and how it is I shall see truth return,
That I expect to know, because Fifine knows me! –
How much more, if Elvire!

LXXXI

'And why not, only she?
Since there can be for each, one Best, no more, such Best,
For body and mind of him, abolishes the rest
O' the simply Good and Better. You please select Elvire
To give you this belief in truth, dispel the fear
Yourself are, after all, as false as what surrounds;

And why not be content? When we two watched the rounds
The boatman made, 'twixt shoal and sandbank, yesterday,
As, at dead slack of tide, he chose to push his way,
With oar and pole, across the creek, and reach the isle
After a world of pains – my word provoked your smile,
Yet none the less deserved reply: " 'Twere wiser wait
The turn o' the tide, and find conveyance for his freight –
How easily – within the ship to purpose moored,
Managed by sails, not oars! But no, – the man's allured
By liking for the new and hard in his exploit!
First come shall serve! He makes, – courageous and adroit, –
The merest willow-leaf of boat do duty, bear
His merchandise across: once over, needs he care
If folk arrive by ship, six hours hence, fresh and gay?"
No: he scorns commonplace, affects the unusual way;
And good Elvire is moored, with not a breath to flap
The yards of her, no lift of ripple to o'erlap
Keel, much less, prow. What care? since here's a cockle-shell,
Fifine, that's taut and crank, and carries just as well
Such seamanship as yours!'

LXXXII

Alack, our life is lent,
From first to last, the whole, for this experiment
Of proving what I say – that we ourselves are true!
I would there were one voyage, and then no more to do
But tread the firmland, tempt the uncertain sea no more.
I would we might dispense with change of shore for shore
To evidence our skill, demónstrate – in no dream
It was, we tided o'er the trouble of the stream.
I would the steady voyage, and not the fitful trip, –
Elvire, and not Fifine, – might test our seamanship.
But why expend one's breath to tell you, change of boat
Means change of tactics too? Come see the same afloat
Tomorrow, all the change, new stowage fore and aft
O' the cargo; then, to cross requires new sailor-craft!
Today, one step from stern to bow keeps boat in trim:
Tomorrow, some big stone, – or woe to boat and him! –
Must ballast both. That man stands for Mind, paramount
Throughout the adventure: ay, howe'er you make account,
'Tis mind that navigates, – skips over, twists between
The bales i' the boat, – now gives importance to the mean,

And now abates the pride of life, accepts all fact,
Discards all fiction, – steers Fifinc, and cries, i' the act,
'Thou art so bad, and yet so delicate a brown!
Wouldst tell no end of lies: I talk to smile or frown!
Wouldst rob me: do men blame a squirrel, lithe and sly,
For pilfering the nut she adds to hoard?' Nor I.
Elvire is true, as truth, honesty's self, alack!
The worse! too safe the ship, the transport there and back
Too certain! one may loll and lounge and leave the helm,
Let wind and tide do work: no fear that waves o'er-whelm
The steady-going bark, as sure to feel her way
Blindfold across, reach land, next year as yesterday!
How can I but suspect, the true feat were to slip
Down side, transfer myself to cockle-shell from ship,
And try if, trusting to sea-tracklessness, I class
With those around whose breast grew oak and triple brass:
Who dreaded no degree of death, but, with dry eyes,
Surveyed the turgid main and its monstrosities –
And rendered futile so, the prudent Power's decree
Of separate earth and disassociating sea;
Since, how is it observed, if impious vessels leap
Across, and tempt a thing they should not touch – the deep?
(See Horace to the boat, wherein, for Athens bound,
When Virgil must embark – Jove keep him safe and sound! –
The poet bade his friend start on the watery road,
Much reassured by this so comfortable ode.)

LXXXIII

Then, never grudge my poor Fifine her compliment!
The rakish craft could slip her moorings in the tent,
And, hoisting every stitch of spangled canvas, steer
Through divers rocks and shoals, – in fine, deposit here
Your Virgil of a spouse, in Attica: yea, thrid
The mob of men, select the special virtue hid
In him, forsooth, and say – or rather, smile so sweet,
'Of all the multitude, you – I prefer to cheat!
Are you for Athens bound? I can perform the trip,
Shove little pinnace off, while yon superior ship,
The Elvire, refits in port!' So, off we push from beach
Of Pornic town, and lo, ere eye can wink, we reach
The Long Walls, and I prove that Athens is no dream,
For there the temples rise! they are, they nowise seem!

Earth is not all one lie, this truth attests me true!
Thanks therefore to Fifine! Elvire, I'm back with you!
Share in the memories! Embark I trust we shall
Together some fine day, and so, for good and all,
Bid Pornic Town adieu, – then, just the strait to cross,
And we reach harbour, safe, in Iostephanos!

LXXXIV

How quickly night comes! Lo, already 'tis the land
Turns sea-like; overcrept by grey, the plains expand,
Assume significance; while ocean dwindles, shrinks
Into a pettier bound: its plash and plaint, methinks,
Six steps away, how both retire, as if their part
Were played, another force were free to prove her art,
Protagonist in turn! Are you unterrified?
All false, all fleeting too! And nowhere things abide,
And everywhere we strain that things should stay, – the one
Truth, that ourselves are true!

LXXXV

A word, and I have done.
Is it not just our hate of falsehood, fleetingness,
And the mere part, things play, that constitutes express
The inmost charm of this Fifine and all her tribe?
Actors! We also act, but only they inscribe
Their style and title so, and preface, only they,
Performance with 'A lie is all we do or say.'
Wherein but there can be the attraction, Falsehood's bribe,
That wins so surely o'er to Fifine and her tribe
The liking, nay the love of who hate Falsehood most,
Except that these alone of mankind make their boast
'Frankly, we simulate!' To feign, means – to have grace
And so get gratitude! This ruler of the race,
Crowned, sceptred, stoled to suit, – 'tis not that you detect
The cobbler in the king, but that he makes effect
By seeming the reverse of what you know to be
The man, the mind, whole form, fashion and quality.
Mistake his false for true, one minute, – there's an end
Of the admiration! Truth, we grieve at or rejoice:
'Tis only falsehood, plain in gesture, look and voice,
That brings the praise desired, since profit comes thereby.
The histrionic truth is in the natural lie.

Because the man who wept the tears was, all the time,
Happy enough; because the other man, a-grime
With guilt, was, at the least, as white as I and you;
Because the timid type of bashful maidhood, who
Starts at her own pure shade, already numbers seven
Born babes and, in a month, will turn their odd to even;
Because the saucy prince would prove, could you unfurl
Some yards of wrap, a meek and meritorious girl –
Precisely as you see success attained by each
O' the mimes, do you approve, not foolishly impeach
The falsehood!

LXXXVI

That's the first o' the truths found: all things, slow
Or quick i' the passage, come at last to that, you know!
Each has a false outside, whereby a truth is forced
To issue from within: truth, falsehood, are divorced
By the excepted eye, at the rare season, for
The happy moment. Life means – learning to abhor
The false, and love the true, truth treasured snatch by snatch,
Waifs counted at their worth. And when with strays they match
I' the parti-coloured world, – when, under foul, shines fair,
And truth, displayed i' the point, flashes forth everywhere
I' the circle, manifest to soul, though hid from sense,
And no obstruction more affects this confidence, –
When faith is ripe for sight, – why, reasonably, then
Comes the great clearing-up. Wait threescore years and ten!

LXXXVII

Therefore I prize stage-play, the honest cheating; thence
The impulse pricked, when fife and drum bade Fair commence,
To bid you trip and skip, link arm in arm with me,
Like husband and like wife, and so together see
The tumbling-troop arrayed, the strollers on their stage
Drawn up and under arms, and ready to engage.
And if I started thence upon abstruser themes...
Well, 'twas a dream, pricked too!

LXXXVIII

A poet never dreams:
We prose-folk always do: we miss the proper duct
For thoughts on things unseen, which stagnate and obstruct

The system, therefore; mind, sound in a body sane,
Keeps thoughts apart from facts, and to one flowing vein
Confines its sense of that which is not, but might be,
And leaves the rest alone. What ghosts do poets see?
What daemons fear? what man or thing misapprehend?
Unchoked, the channel's flush, the fancy's free to spend
Its special self aright in manner, time and place.
Never believe that who create the busy race
O' the brain, bring poetry to birth, such act performed,
Feel trouble them, the same, such residue as warmed
My prosy blood, this morn, – intrusive fancies, meant
For outbreak and escape by quite another vent!
Whence follows that, asleep, my dreamings oft exceed
The bound. But you shall hear.

LXXXIX

I smoked. The webs o' the weed,
With many a break i' the mesh, were floating to re-form
Cupola-wise above: chased thither by soft warm
Inflow of air without; since I – of mind to muse, to clench
The gain of soul and body, got by their noon-day drench
In sun and sea, – had flung both frames o' the window wide,
To soak my body still and let soul soar beside.
In came the country sounds and sights and smells – that fine
Sharp needle in the nose from our fermenting wine!
In came a dragon-fly with whir and stir, then out,
Off and away: in came, – kept coming, rather, – pout
Succeeding smile, and take-away still close on give, –
One loose long creeper-branch, tremblingly sensitive
To risks which blooms and leaves, – each leaf tongue-broad, each bloom
Mid-finger-deep, – must run by prying in the room
Of one who loves and grasps and spoils and speculates.
All so far plain enough to sight and sense: but, weights,
Measures and numbers, – ah, could one apply such test
To other visitants that came at no request
Of who kept open house, – to fancies manifold
From this four-cornered world, the memories new and old,
The antenatal prime experience – what know I? –
The initiatory love preparing us to die –

Such were a crowd to count, a sight to see, a prize
To turn to profit, were but fleshly ears and eyes
Able to cope with those o' the spirit!

XC

Therefore, – since
Thought hankers after speech, while no speech may evince
Feeling like music, – mine, o'erburthened with each gift
From every visitant, at last resolved to shift
Its burthen to the back of some musician dead
And gone, who feeling once what I feel now, instead
Of words, sought sounds, and saved for ever, in the same,
Truth that escapes prose, – nay, puts poetry to shame.
I read the note, I strike the key, I bid *record*
The instrument – thanks greet the veritable word!
And not in vain I urge: 'O dead and gone away,
Assist who struggles yet, thy strength become my stay,
Thy record serve as well to register – I felt
And knew thus much of truth! With me, must knowledge melt
Into surmise and doubt and disbelief, unless
Thy music reassure – I gave no idle guess,
But gained a certitude I yet may hardly keep!
What care? since round is piled a monumental heap
Of music that conserves the assurance, thou as well
Wast certain of the same! thou, master of the spell,
Mad'st moonbeams marble, didst *record* what other men
Feel only to forget!' Who was it helped me, then?
What master's work first came responsive to my call,
Found my eye, fixed my choice?

XCI

Why, Schumann's 'Carnival!'
My choice chimed in, you see, exactly with the sounds
And sights of yestereve when, going on my rounds,
Where both roads join the bridge, I heard across the dusk
Creak a slow caravan, and saw arrive the husk
O' the spice-nut, which peeled off this morning, and displayed,
'Twixt tree and tree, a tent whence the red pennon made
Its vivid reach for home and ocean-idleness –
And where, my heart surmised, at that same moment, – yes, –
Tugging her *tricot* on, – yet tenderly, lest stitch

Announce the crack of doom, reveal disaster which
Our Pornic's modest stock of merceries in vain
Were ransacked to retrieve, – there, cautiously a-strain,
(My heart surmised) must crouch in that tent's corner, curved
Like Spring-month's russet moon, some girl by fate reserved
To give me once again the electric snap and spark
Which prove, when finger finds out finger in the dark
O' the world, there's fire and life and truth there, link but hands
And pass the secret on. Lo, link by link, expands
The circle, lengthens out the chain, till one embrace
Of high with low is found uniting the whole race,
Not simply you and me and our Fifine, but all
The world: the Fair expands into the Carnival,
And Carnival again to . . . ah, but that's my dream!

XCII

I somehow played the piece: remarked on each old theme
I' the new dress; saw how food o' the soul, the stuff that's made
To furnish man with thought and feeling, is purveyed
Substantially the same from age to age, with change
Of the outside only for successive feasters. Range
The banquet-room o' the world, from the dim farthest head
O' the table, to its foot, for you and me bespread,
This merry morn, we find sufficient fare, I trow.
But, novel? Scrape away the sauce; and taste, below,
The verity o' the viand, – you shall perceive there went
To board-head just the dish which other condiment
Makes palatable now: guests came, sat down, fell-to,
Rose up, wiped mouth, went way, – lived, died, – and never knew
That generations yet should, seeking sustenance,
Still find the selfsame fare, with somewhat to enhance
Its flavour, in the kind of cooking. As with hates
And loves and fears and hopes, so with what emulates
The same, expresses hates, loves, fears and hopes in Art:
The forms, the themes – no one without its counterpart
Ages ago; no one but, mumbled the due time
I' the mouth of the eater, needs be cooked again in rhyme,
Dished up anew in paint, sauce-smothered fresh in sound,
To suit the wisdom-tooth, just cut, of the age, that's found
With gums obtuse to gust and smack which relished so
The meat o' the meal folk made some fifty years ago.
But don't suppose the new was able to efface

The old without a struggle, a pang! The commonplace
Still clung about his heart, long after all the rest
O' the natural man, at eye and ear, was caught, confessed
The charm of change, although wry lip and wrinkled nose
Owned ancient virtue more conducive to repose
Than modern nothings roused to somethings by some shred
Of pungency, perchance garlic in amber's stead.
And so on, till one day, another age, by due
Rotation, pries, sniffs, smacks, discovers old is new,
And sauce, our sires pronounced insipid, proves again
Sole piquant, may resume its titillating reign –
With music, most of all the arts, since change is there
The law, and not the lapse: the precious means the rare,
And not the absolute in all good save surprise.
So I remarked upon our Schumann's victories
Over the commonplace, how faded phrase grew fine,
And palled perfection – piqued, upstartled by that brine,
His pickle – bit the mouth and burnt the tongue aright,
Beyond the merely good no longer exquisite:
Then took things as I found, and thanked without demur
The pretty piece – played through that movement, you prefer,
Where dance and shuffle past, – he scolding while she pouts,
She canting while he calms, – in those eternal bouts
Of age, the dog – with youth, the cat – by rose-festoon
Tied teasingly enough – Columbine, Pantaloon:
She, toe-tips and *staccato*, – *legato* shakes his poll
And shambles in pursuit, the senior. *Fi la folle!*
Lie to him! get his gold and pay its price! begin
Your trade betimes, nor wait till you've wed Harlequin
And need, at the week's end, to play the duteous wife,
And swear you still love slaps and leapings more than life!
Pretty! I say.

XCIII

And so, I somehow-nohow played
The whole o' the pretty piece; and then . . . whatever weighed
My eyes down, furled the films about my wits? suppose,
The morning-bath, – the sweet monotony of those
Three keys, flat, flat and flat, never a sharp at all, –
Or else the brain's fatigue, forced even here to fall
Into the same old track, and recognize the shift
From old to new, and back to old again, and, – swift

Or slow, no matter, – still the certainty of change,
Conviction we shall find the false, where'er we range,
In art no less than nature: or what if wrist were numb,
And over-tense the muscle, abductor of the thumb,
Taxed by those tenths' and twelfths' unconscionable stretch?
Howe'er it came to pass, I soon was far to fetch –
Gone off in company with Music!

XCIV

Whither bound
Except for Venice? She it was, by instinct found
Carnival-country proper, who far below the perch
Where I was pinnacled, showed, opposite, Mark's Church,
And, underneath, Mark's Square, with those two lines of street,
Procuratié-sides, each leading to my feet –
Since from above I gazed, however I got there.

XCV

And what I gazed upon was a prodigious Fair,
Concourse immense of men and women, crowned or casqued,
Turbaned or tiared, wreathed, plumed, hatted or wigged, but
masked –
Always masked, – only, how? No face-shape, beast or bird,
Nay, fish and reptile even, but someone had preferred,
From out its frontispiece, feathered or scaled or curled,
To make the vizard whence himself should view the world,
And where the world believed himself was manifest.
Yet when you came to look, mixed up among the rest
More funnily by far, were masks to imitate
Humanity's mishap: the wrinkled brow, bald pate
And rheumy eyes of Age, peaked chin and parchment chap,
Were signs of day-work done, and wage-time near, – mishap
Merely; but, Age reduced to simple greed and guile,
Worn apathetic else as some smooth slab, erewhile
A clear-cut man-at-arms i' the pavement, till foot's tread
Effaced the sculpture, left the stone you saw instead, –
Was not that terrible beyond the mere uncouth?
Well, and perhaps the next revolting you was Youth,
Stark ignorance and crude conceit, half smirk, half stare
On that frank fool-face, gay beneath its head of hair
Which covers nothing.

XCVI

These, you are to understand,
Were the mere hard and sharp distinctions. On each hand,
I soon became aware, flocked the infinitude
Of passions, loves and hates, man pampers till his mood
Becomes himself, the whole sole face we name him by,
Nor want denotement else, if age or youth supply
The rest of him: old, young, – classed creature: in the main
A love, a hate, a hope, a fear, each soul a-strain
Some one way through the flesh – the face, an evidence
O' the soul at work inside; and, all the more intense,
So much the more grotesque.

XCVII

'Why should each soul be tasked
Some one way, by one love or else one hate?' I asked,
When it occurred to me, from all these sights beneath
There rose not any sound: a crowd, yet dumb as death!

XCVIII

Soon I knew why. (Propose a riddle, and 'tis solved
Forthwith – in dream!) They spoke; but, – since on me devolved
To see, and understand by sight, – the vulgar speech
Might be dispensed with. 'He who cannot see, must reach
As best he may the truth of men by help of words
They please to speak, must fare at will of who affords
The banquet,' – so I thought. 'Who sees not, hears and so
Gets to believe; myself it is that, seeing, know,
And, knowing, can dispense with voice and vanity
Of speech. What hinders then, that, drawing closer, I
Put privilege to use, see and know better still
These *simulacra*, taste the profit of my skill,
Down in the midst?'

XCIX

And plumb I pitched into the square –
A groundling like the rest. What think you happened there?
Precise the contrary of what one would expect!
For, – whereas so much more monstrosities deflect
From nature and the type, as you the more approach
Their precinct, – here, I found brutality encroach
Less on the human, lie the lightlier as I looked

The nearlier on these faces that seemed but now so crooked
And clawed away from God's prime purpose. They diverged
A little from the type, but somehow rather urged
To pity than disgust: the prominent, before,
Now dwindled into mere distinctness, nothing more.
Still, at first sight, stood forth undoubtedly the fact
Some deviation was: in no one case there lacked
The certain sign and mark, – say hint, say, trick of lip
Or twist of nose, – that proved a fault in workmanship,
Change in the prime design, some hesitancy here
And there, which checked the man and let the beast appear;
But that was all.

C

All: yet enough to bid each tongue
Lie in abeyance still. They talked, themselves among,
Of themselves, to themselves; I saw the mouths at play,
The gesture that enforced, the eye that strove to say
The same thing as the voice, and seldom gained its point
– That this was so, I saw; but all seemed out of joint
I' the vocal medium 'twixt the world and me. I gained
Knowledge by notice, not by giving ear, – attained
To truth by what men seemed, not said: to me one glance
Was worth whole histories of noisy utterance,
– At least, to me in dream.

CI

And presently I found
That, just as ugliness had withered, so unwound
Itself, and perished off, repugnance to what wrong
Might linger yet i' the make of man. My will was strong
I' the matter; I could pick and choose, project my weight:
(Remember how we saw the boatman trim his freight!)
Determine to observe, or manage to escape,
Or make divergency assume another shape
By shift of point of sight in me the observer: thus
Corrected, added to, subtracted from, – discuss
Each variant quality, and brute-beast touch was turned
Into mankind's safeguard! Force, guile, were arms which earned
My praise, not blame at all: for we must learn to live,
Case-hardened at all points, not bare and sensitive,
But plated for defence, nay, furnished for attack,

With spikes at the due place, that neither front nor back
May suffer in that squeeze with nature, we find – life.
Are we not here to learn the good of peace through strife,
Of love through hate, and reach knowledge by ignorance?
Why, those are helps thereto, which late we eyed askance,
And nicknamed unaware! Just so, a sword we call
Superfluous, and cry out against, at festival:
Wear it in time of war, its clink and clatter grate
O' the ear to purpose then!

CII

I found, one must abate
One's scorn of the soul's casing, distinct from the soul's self –
Which is the centre-drop: whereas the pride in pelf,
The lust to seem the thing it cannot be, the greed
For praise, and all the rest seen outside, – these indeed
Are the hard polished cold crystal environment
Of those strange orbs unearthed i' the Druid temple, meant
For divination (so the learned please to think)
Wherein you may admire one dew-drop roll and wink,
All unaffected by – quite alien to – what sealed
And saved it long ago: though how it got congealed
I shall not give a guess, nor how, by power occult,
The solid surface-shield was outcome and result
Of simple dew at work to save itself amid
The unwatery force around; protected thus, dew slid
Safe through all opposites, impatient to absorb
Its spot of life, and last for ever in the orb
We, now, from hand to hand pass with impunity.

CIII

And the delight wherewith I watch this crowd must be
Akin to that which crowns the chemist when he winds
Thread up and up, till clue be fairly clutched, – unbinds
The composite, ties fast the simple to its mate,
And, tracing each effect back to its cause, elate,
Constructs in fancy, from the fewest primitives,
The complex and complete, all diverse life, that lives
Not only in beast, bird, fish, reptile, insect, but
The very plants and earths and ores. Just so I glut
My hunger both to be and know the thing I am,
By contrast with the thing I am not; so, through sham

And outside, I arrive at inmost real, probe
And prove how the nude form obtained the chequered robe.

CIV

– Experience, I am glad to master soon or late,
Here, there and everywhere i' the world, without debate!
Only, in Venice why? What reason for Mark's Square
Rather than Timbuctoo?

CV

And I became aware,
Scarcely the word escaped my lips, that swift ensued
In silence and by stealth, and yet with certitude,
A formidable change of the amphitheatre
Which held the Carnival; although the human stir
Continued just the same amid that shift of scene.

CVI

For as on edifice of cloud i' the grey and green
Of evening, – built about some glory of the west,
To barricade the sun's departure, – manifest,
He plays, pre-eminently gold, gilds vapour, crag and crest,
Which bend in rapt suspense above the act and deed
They cluster round and keep their very own, nor heed
The world at watch; while we, breathlessly at the base
O' the castellated bulk, note momently the mace
Of night fall here, fall there, bring change with every blow,
Alike to sharpened shaft and broadened portico
I' the structure: heights and depths, beneath the leaden stress,
Crumble and melt and mix together, coalesce
Re-form, but sadder still, subdued yet more and more
By every fresh defeat, till wearied eyes need pore
No longer on the dull impoverished decadence
Of all that pomp of pile in towering evidence
So lately: –

CVII

Even thus nor otherwise, meseemed
That if I fixed my gaze awhile on what I dreamed
Was Venice' Square, Mark's Church, the scheme was straight unschemed,
A subtle something had its way within the heart

Of each and every house I watched, with counterpart
Of tremor through the front and outward face, until
Mutation was at end; impassive and stock-still
Stood now the ancient house, grown – new, is scarce the phrase,
Since older, in a sense, – altered to . . . what i' the ways,
Ourselves are wont to see, coerced by city, town
Or village, anywhere i' the world, pace up or down
Europe! In all the maze, no single tenement
I saw, but I could claim acquaintance with.

CVIII

There went
Conviction to my soul, that what I took of late
For Venice was the world; its Carnival – the state
Of mankind, masquerade in life-long permanence
For all time, and no one particular feast-day. Whence
'Twas easy to infer what meant my late disgust
At the brute-pageant, each grotesque of greed and lust
And idle hate, and love as impotent for good –
When from my pride of place I passed the interlude
In critical review; and what, the wonder that ensued
When, from such pinnacled pre-eminence, I found
Somehow the proper goal for wisdom was the ground
And not the sky, – so, slid sagaciously betimes
Down heaven's baluster-rope, to reach the mob of mimes
And mummers; whereby came discovery there was just
Enough and not too much of hate, love, greed and lust,
Could one discerningly but hold the balance, shift
The weight from scale to scale, do justice to the drift
Of nature, and explain the glories by the shames
Mixed up in man, one stuff miscalled by different names
According to what stage i' the process turned his rough,
Even as I gazed, to smooth – only get close enough!
– What was all this except the lesson of a life?

CIX

And – consequent upon the learning how from strife
Grew peace – from evil, good – came knowledge that, to get
Acquaintance with the way o' the world, we must nor fret
Nor fume, on altitudes of self-sufficiency,
But bid a frank farewell to what – we think – should be,
And, with as good a grace, welcome what is – we find.

CX

Is – for the hour, observe! Since something to my mind
Suggested soon the fancy, nay, certitude that change,
Never suspending touch, continued to derange
What architecture, we, walled up within the cirque
O' the world, consider fixed as fate, not fairy-work.
For those were temples, sure, which tremblingly grew blank
From bright, then broke afresh in triumph, – ah, but sank
As soon, for liquid change through artery and vein
O' the very marble wound its way! And first a stain
Would startle and offend amid the glory; next,
Spot swift succeeded spot, but found me less perplexed
By portents; then as 'twere a sleepiness soft stole
Over the stately fane, and shadow sucked the whole
Façade into itself, made uniformly earth
What was a piece of heaven; till, lo, a second birth,
And the veil broke away because of something new
Inside, that pushed to gain an outlet, paused in view
At last, and proved a growth of stone or brick or wood
Which, alien to the aim o' the Builder, somehow stood
The test, could satisfy, if not the early race
For whom he built, at least our present populace,
Who must not bear the blame for what, blamed, proves mishap
Of the Artist: his work gone, another fills the gap,
Serves the prime purpose so. Undoubtedly there spreads
Building around, above, which makes men lift their heads
To look at, or look through, or look – for aught I care –
Over: if only up, it is, not down, they stare,
'Commercing with the skies,' and not the pavement in the Square.

CXI

But are they only temples that subdivide, collapse,
And tower again, transformed? Academies, perhaps!
Domes where dwells Learning, seats of Science, bower and hall
Which house Philosophy – do these, too, rise and fall,
Based though foundations be on steadfast mother-earth,
With no chimeric claim to supermundane birth,
No boast that, dropped from cloud, they did not grow from ground?
Why, these fare worst of all! these vanish and are found
Nowhere, by who tasks eye some twice within his term
Of threescore years and ten, for tidings what each germ

Has burgeoned out into, whereof the promise stunned
His ear with such acclaim, – praise-payment to refund
The praisers, never doubt, some twice before they die
Whose days are long i' the land.

CXII

Alack, Philosophy!
Despite the chop and change, diminished or increased,
Patched-up and plastered-o'er, Religion stands at least
I' the temple-type. But thou? Here gape I, all agog
These thirty years, to learn how tadpole turns to frog;
And thrice at least have gazed with mild astonishment,
As, skyward up and up, some fire-new fabric sent
Its challenge to mankind that, clustered underneath
To hear the word, they straight believe, ay, in the teeth
O' the Past, clap hands and hail triumphant Truth's outbreak –
Tadpole-frog-theory propounded past mistake!
In vain! A something ails the edifice, it bends,
It bows, it buries . . . Haste! cry 'Heads below' to friends –
But have no fear they find, when smother shall subside,
Some substitution perk with unabated pride
I' the predecessor's place!

CXIII

No, – the one voice which failed
Never, the preachment's coign of vantage nothing ailed, –
That had the luck to lodge i' the house not made with hands!
And all it preached was this: 'Truth builds upon the sands,
Though stationed on a rock: and so her work decays,
And so she builds afresh, with like result. Naught stays
But just the fact that Truth not only is, but fain
Would have men know she needs must be, by each so plain
Attempt to visibly inhabit where they dwell.'
Her works are work, while she is she; that work does well
Which lasts mankind their life-time through, and lets believe
One generation more, that, though sand run through sieve,
Yet earth now reached is rock, and what we moderns find
Erected here is Truth, who, 'stablished to her mind
I' the fullness of the days, will never change in show
More than in substance erst: men thought they knew; we know!

CXIV

Do you, my generation? Well, let the blocks prove mist
I' the main enclosure, – church and college, if they list,
Be something for a time, and everything anon,
And anything awhile, as fit is off or on,
Till they grow nothing, soon to reappear no less
As something, – shape reshaped, till out of shapelessness
Come shape again as sure! no doubt, or round or square
Or polygon its front, some building will be there,
Do duty in that nook o' the wall o' the world where once
The Architect saw fit precisely to ensconce
College or church, and bid such bulwark guard the line
O' the barrier round about, humanity's confine.

CXV

Leave watching change at work i' the greater scale, on these
The main supports, and turn to their interstices
Filled up by fabrics too, less costly and less rare,
Yet of importance, yet essential to the Fair
They help to circumscribe, instruct and regulate!
See, where each booth-front boasts, in letters small or great,
Its specialty, proclaims its privilege to stop
A breach, beside the best!

CXVI

Here History keeps shop,
Tells how past deeds were done, so and not otherwise:
'Man! hold truth evermore! forget the early lies!'
There sits Morality, demure behind her stall,
Dealing out life and death: 'This is the thing to call
Right, and this other, wrong; thus think, thus do, thus say,
Thus joy, thus suffer! – not today as yesterday –
Yesterday's doctrine dead, this only shall endure!
Obey its voice and live!' – enjoins the dame demure.
While Art gives flag to breeze, bids drum beat, trumpet blow,
Inviting eye and ear to yonder raree-show.
Up goes the canvas, hauled to height of pole. I think,
We know the way – long lost, late learned – to paint! A wink
Of eye, and lo, the pose! the statue on its plinth!
How could we moderns miss the heart o' the labyrinth
Perversely all these years, permit the Greek seclude
His secret till today? And here's another feud

Now happily composed: inspect this quartet-score!
Got long past melody, no word has Music more
To say to mortal man! But is the bard to be
Behindhand? Here's his book, and now perhaps you see
At length what poetry can do!

CXVII

Why, that's stability
Itself, that change on change we sorrowfully saw
Creep o'er the prouder piles! We acquiesced in law
When the fine gold grew dim i' the temple, when the brass
Which pillared that so brave abode where Knowledge was,
Bowed and resigned the trust; but, bear all this caprice,
Harlequinade where swift to birth succeeds decease
Of hue at every turn o' the tinsel-flag which flames
While Art holds booth in Fair? Such glories chased by shames
Like these, distract beyond the solemn and august
Procedure to decay, evanishment in dust,
Of those marmoreal domes, – above vicissitude,
We used to hope!

CXVIII

'So, all is change, in fine,' pursued
The preachment to a pause. When – 'All is permanence!'
Returned a voice. Within? without? No matter whence
The explanation came: for, understand, I ought
To simply say – 'I saw,' each thing I say 'I thought.'
Since ever as, unrolled, the strange scene-picture grew
Before me, sight flashed first, though mental comment too
Would follow in a trice, come hobblingly to halt.

CXIX

So, what did I see next but, – much as when the vault
I' the west, – wherein we watch the vapoury manifold
Transfiguration, – tired turns blaze to black, – behold,
Peak reconciled to base, dark ending feud with bright,
The multiform subsides, becomes the definite.
Contrasting life and strife, where battle they i' the blank
Severity of peace in death, for which we thank
One wind that comes to quell the concourse, drive at last
Things to a shape which suits the close of things, and cast
Palpably o'er vexed earth heaven's mantle of repose?

CXX

Just so, in Venice' Square, that things were at the close
Was signalled to my sense; for I perceived arrest
O' the change all round about. As if some impulse pressed
Each gently into each, what was distinctness, late,
Grew vague, and, line from line no longer separate,
No matter what its style, edifice . . . shall I say,
Died into edifice? I find no simpler way
Of saying how, without or dash or shock or trace
Of violence, I found unity in the place
Of temple, tower, – nay, hall and house and hut, – one blank
Severity of peace in death; to which they sank
Resigned enough, till . . . ah, conjecture, I beseech,
What special blank did they agree to, all and each?
What common shape was that wherein they mutely merged
Likes and dislikes of form, so plain before?

CXXI

I urged
Your step this way, prolonged our path of enterprise
To where we stand at last, in order that your eyes
Might see the very thing, and save my tongue describe
The Druid monument which fronts you. Could I bribe
Nature to come in aid, illústrate what I mean,
What wants there she should lend to solemnize the scene?

CXXII

How does it strike you, this construction gaunt and grey –
Sole object, these piled stones, that gleam unground-away
By twilight's hungry jaw, which champs fine all beside
I' the solitary waste we grope through? Oh, no guide
Need we to grope our way and reach the monstrous door
Of granite! Take my word, the deeper you explore
That caverned passage, filled with fancies to the brim,
The less will you approve the adventure! such a grim
Bar-sinister soon blocks abrupt your path, and ends
All with a cold dread shape, – shape whereon Learning spends
Labour, and leaves the text obscurer for the gloss,
While Ignorance reads right – recoiling from that Cross!
Whence came the mass and mass, strange quality of stone
Unquarried anywhere i' the region round? Unknown!
Just as unknown, how such enormity could be

Conveyed by land, or else transported over sea,
And laid in order, so, precisely each on each,
As you and I would build a grotto where the beach
Sheds shell – to last an hour: this building lasts from age
To age the same. But why?

CXXIII

Ask Learning! I engage
You get a prosy wherefore, shall help you to advance
In knowledge just as much as helps you Ignorance
Surmising, in the mouth of peasant-lad or lass,
'I heard my father say he understood it was
A building, people built as soon as earth was made
Almost, because they might forget (they were afraid)
Earth did not make itself, but came of Somebody.
They laboured that their work might last, and show thereby
He stays, while we and earth, and all things come and go.
Come whence? Go whither? That, when come and gone, we know
Perhaps, but not while earth and all things need our best
Attention: we must wait and die to know the rest.
Ask, if that's true, what use in setting up the pile?
To make one fear and hope: remind us, all the while
We come and go, outside there's Somebody that stays;
A circumstance which ought to make us mind our ways,
Because, – whatever end we answer by this life, –
Next time, best chance must be for who, with toil and strife,
Manages now to live most like what he was meant
Become: since who succeeds so far, 'tis evident,
Stands foremost on the file; who fails, has less to hope
From new promotion. That's the rule – with even a rope
Of mushrooms, like this rope I dangle! those that grew
Greatest and roundest, all in life they had to do,
Gain a reward, a grace they never dreamed, I think;
Since, outside white as milk and inside black as ink,
They go to the Great House to make a dainty dish
For Don and Donna; while this basket-load, I wish
Well off my arm, it breaks, – no starveling of the heap
But had his share of dew, his proper length of sleep
I' the sunshine: yet, of all, the outcome is – this queer
Cribbed quantity of dwarfs which burthen basket here
Till I reach home; 'tis there that, having run their rigs,

They end their earthly race, are flung as food for pigs.
Any more use I see? Well, you must know, there lies
Something, the Curé says, that points to mysteries
Above our grasp: a huge stone pillar, once upright,
Now laid at length, half-lost – discreetly shunning sight
I' the bush and briar, because of stories in the air –
Hints what it signified, and why was stationed there,
Once on a time. In vain the Curé tasked his lungs –
Showed, in a preachment, how, at bottom of the rungs
O' the ladder, Jacob saw, where heavenly angels stept
Up and down, lay a stone which served him, while he slept,
For pillow; when he woke, he set the same upright
As pillar, and a-top poured oil: things requisite
To instruct posterity, there mounts from floor to roof,
A staircase, earth to heaven; and also put in proof,
When we have scaled the sky, we well may let alone
What raised us from the ground, and, – paying to the stone
Proper respect, of course, – take staff and go our way,
Leaving the Pagan night for Christian break of day.
"For," preached he, "what they dreamed, these Pagans wide-awake
We Christians may behold. How strange, then, were mistake
Did anybody style the stone, – because of drop
Remaining there from oil which Jacob poured a-top, –
Itself the Gate of Heaven, itself the end, and not
The means thereto!" Thus preached the Curé, and no jot
The more persuaded people but that, what once a thing
Meant and had right to mean, it still must mean. So cling
Folk somehow to the prime authoritative speech,
And so distrust report, it seems as they could reach
Far better the arch-word, whereon their fate depends,
Through rude charactery, than all the grace it lends,
That lettering of your scribes! who flourish pen apace
And ornament the text, they say – we say, efface.
Hence, when the earth began its life afresh in May,
And fruit-trees bloomed, and waves would wanton, and the bay
Ruffle its wealth of weed, and stranger-birds arrive,
And beasts take each a mate, – folk, too, found sensitive,
Surmised the old grey stone upright there, through such tracts
Of solitariness and silence, kept the facts
Entrusted it, could deal out doctrine, did it please:
No fresh and frothy draught, but liquor on the lees,

Strong, savage and sincere: first bleedings from a vine
Whereof the product now do Curés so refine
To insipidity, that, when heart sinks, we strive
And strike from the old stone the old restorative.
"Which is?" – why, go and ask our grandames how they used
To dance around it, till the Curé disabused
Their ignorance, and bade the parish in a band
Lay flat the obtrusive thing that cumbered so the land!
And there, accordingly, in bush and briar it – "bides
Its time to rise again!" (so somebody derides,
That's pert from Paris) "since, yon spire, you keep erect
Yonder, and pray beneath, is nothing, I suspect,
But just the symbol's self, expressed in slate for rock,
Art's smooth for Nature's rough, new chip from the old block!"
There, sir, my say is said! Thanks, and Saint Gille increase
The wealth bestowed so well!' – wherewith he pockets piece,
Doffs cap, and takes the road. I leave in Learning's clutch
More money for his book, but scarcely gain as much.

CXXIV

To this it was, this same primeval monument,
That, in my dream, I saw building with building blent
Fall: each on each they fast and founderingly went
Confusion-ward; but thence again subsided fast,
Became the mound you see. Magnificently massed
Indeed, those mammoth-stones, piled by the Protoplast
Temple-wise in my dream! beyond compare with fanes
Which, solid-looking late, had left no least remains
I' the bald and blank, now sole usurper of the plains
Of heaven, diversified and beautiful before.
And yet simplicity appeared to speak no more
Nor less to me than spoke the compound. At the core,
One and no other word, as in the crust of late,
Whispered, which, audible through the transition-state,
Was no loud utterance in even the ultimate
Disposure. For as some imperial chord subsists,
Steadily underlies the accidental mists
Of music springing thence, that run their mazy race
Around, and sink, absorbed, back to the triad base, –
So, out of that one word, each variant rose and fell
And left the same 'All's change, but permanence as well.'
– Grave note whence – list aloft! – harmonics sound, that mean:

'Truth inside, and outside, truth also; and between
Each, falsehood that is change, as truth is permanence.
The individual soul works through the shows of sense,
(Which, ever proving false, still promise to be true)
Up to an outer soul as individual too;
And, through the fleeting, lives to die into the fixed,
And reach at length "God, man, or both together mixed,"
Transparent through the flesh, by parts which prove a whole,
By hints which make the soul discernible by soul –
Let only soul look up, not down, not hate but love,
As truth successively takes shape, one grade above
Its last presentment, tempts as it were truth indeed
Revealed this time; so tempts, till we attain to read
The signs aright, and learn, by failure, truth is forced
To manifest itself through falsehood; whence divorced
By the excepted eye, at the rare season, for
The happy moment, truth instructs us to abhor
The false, and prize the true, obtainable thereby.
Then do we understand the value of a lie;
Its purpose served, its truth once safe deposited.
Each lie, superfluous now, leaves, in the singer's stead,
The indubitable song; the historic personage
Put by, leaves prominent the impulse of his age;
Truth sets aside speech, act, time, place, indeed, but brings
Nakedly forward now the principle of things
Highest and least.'

CXXV

Wherewith change ends. What change to dread
When, disengaged at last from every veil, instead
Of type remains the truth? once – falsehood: but anon
Theosuton e broteion eper kekramenon,
Something as true as soul is true, though veils between
Prove false and fleet away. As I mean, did he mean,
The poet whose bird-phrase sits, singing in my ear
A mystery not unlike? What through the dark and drear
Brought comfort to the Titan? Emerging from the lymph,
'God, man, or mixture' proved only to be a nymph:
'From whom the clink on clink of metal' (money, judged
Abundant in my purse) 'struck' (bumped at, till it budged)
'The modesty, her soul's habitual resident'

(Where late the sisterhood were lively in their tent)
'As out of wingèd car' (that caravan on wheels)
'Impulsively she rushed, no slippers to her heels,'
And 'Fear not, friends we flock!' soft smiled the sea-Fifine –
Primitive of the veils (if he meant what I mean)
The poet's Titan learned to lift, ere 'Three-formed Fate,
Moirai Trimorphoi' stood unmasked the Ultimate.

CXXVI

Enough o' the dream! You see how poetry turns prose.
Announcing wonder-work, I dwindle at the close
Down to mere commonplace old facts which everybody knows.
So dreaming disappoints! The fresh and strange at first,
Soon wears to trite and tame, nor warrants the outburst
Of heart with which we hail those heights, at very brink
Of heaven, whereto one least of lifts would lead, we think,
But wherefrom quick decline conducts our step, we find,
To homely earth, old facts familiar left behind.
Did not this monument, for instance, long ago
Say all it had to say, show all it had to show,
Nor promise to do duty more in dream?

CXXVII

Awaking so,
What if we, homeward-bound, all peace and some fatigue,
Trudge, soberly complete our tramp of near a league,
Last little mile which makes the circuit just, Elvire?
We end where we began; that consequence is clear.
All peace and some fatigue, wherever we were nursed
To life, we bosom us on death, find last is first
And thenceforth final too.

CXXVIII

'Why final? Why the more
Worth credence now than when such truth proved false before?'
Because a novel point impresses now: each lie
Redounded to the praise of man, was victory
Man's nature had both right to get, and might to gain,
And by no means implied submission to the reign
Of other quite as real a nature, that saw fit
To have its way with man, not man his way with it.
This time, acknowledgement and acquiescence quell

Their contrary in man; promotion proves as well
Defeat: and Truth, unlike the False with Truth's outside,
Neither plumes up his will nor puffs him out with pride.
I fancy, there must lurk some cogency i' the claim,
Man, such abatement made, submits to, all the same.
Soul finds no triumph, here, to register like Sense
With whom 'tis ask and have, – the want, the evidence
That the thing wanted, soon or late, will be supplied.
This indeed plumes up will; this, sure, puffs out with pride,
When, reading records right, man's instincts still attest
Promotion comes to Sense because Sense likes it best;
For bodies sprouted legs, through a desire to run:
While hands, when fain to filch, got fingers one by one,
And nature, that's ourself, accommodative brings
To bear that, tired of legs which walk, we now bud wings
Since of a mind to fly. Such savour in the nose
Of Sense, would stimulate Soul sweetly, I suppose,
Soul with its proper itch of instinct, prompting clear
To recognize soul's self Soul's only master here
Alike from first to last. But, if time's pressure, light's
Or rather, dark's approach, wrest thoroughly the rights
Of rule away, and bid the soul submissive bear
Another soul than it play master everywhere
In great and small, – this time, I fancy, none disputes
There's something in the fact that such conclusion suits
Nowise the pride of man, nor yet chimes in with attributes
Conspicuous in the lord of nature. He receives
And not demands – not first likes faith and then believes.

CXXIX

And as with the last essence so with its first faint type.
Inconstancy means raw, 'tis faith alone means ripe
I' the soul which runs its round: no matter how it range
From Helen to Fifine, Elvire bids back the change
To permanence. Here, too, love ends where love began.
Such ending looks like law, because the natural man
Inclines the other way, feels lordlier free than bound.
Poor pabulum for pride when the first love is found
Last also! and, so far from realizing gain,
Each step aside just proves divergency in vain.
The wanderer brings home no profit from his quest
Beyond the sad surmise that keeping house were best

Could life begin anew. His problem posed aright
Was – 'From the given point evolve the infinite!'
Not – 'Spend thyself in space, endeavouring to joint
Together, and so make infinite, point and point:
Fix into one Elvire a Fair-ful of Fifines!'
Fifine, the foam-flake, she: Elvire, the sea's self, means
Capacity at need to shower how many such!
And yet we left her calm profundity, to clutch
Foam-flutter, bell on bell, that, bursting at a touch,
Blistered us for our pains. But wise, we want no more
O' the fickle element. Enough of foam and roar!
Land-locked, we live and die henceforth: for here's the
villa-door.

CXXX

How pallidly you pause o' the threshold! Hardly night,
Which drapes you, ought to make real flesh and blood so white!
Touch me, and so appear alive to all intents!
Will the saint vanish from the sinner that repents?
Suppose you are a ghost! A memory, a hope,
A fear, a conscience! Quick! Give back the hand I grope
I' the dusk for!

CXXXI

That is well. Our double horoscope
I cast, while you concur. Discard that simile
O' the fickle element! Elvire is land not sea –
The solid land, the safe. All these word-bubbles came
O' the sea, and bite like salt. The unlucky bath's to blame.
This hand of yours on heart of mine, no more the bay
I beat, nor bask beneath the blue! In Pornic, say,
The Mayor shall catalogue me duly domiciled,
Contributable, good-companion of the guild
And mystery of marriage. I stickle for the town,
And not this tower apart; because, though, half-way down,
Its mullions wink o'erwebbed with bloomy greenness, yet
Who mounts to staircase top may tempt the parapet,
And sudden there's the sea! No memories to arouse,
No fancies to delude! Our honest civic house
Of the earth be earthy too! – or graced perchance with shell
Made prize of long ago, picked haply where the swell
Menaced a little once – or seaweed-branch that yet

Dampens and softens, notes a freak of wind, a fret
Of wave: though, why on earth should sea-change mend or mar
The calm contemplative householders that we are?
So shall the seasons fleet, while our two selves abide:
E'en past astonishment how sunrise and springtide
Could tempt one forth to swim; the more if time appoints
That swimming grow a task for one's rheumatic joints.
Such honest civic house, behold, I constitute
Our villa! Be but flesh and blood, and smile to boot!
Enter for good and all! then fate bolt fast the door,
Shut you and me inside, never to wander more!

CXXXII

Only, – you do not use to apprehend attack!
No doubt, the way I march, one idle arm, thrown slack
Behind me, leaves the open hand defenceless at the back,
Should an impertinent on tiptoe steal, and stuff
– Whatever can it be? A letter sure enough,
Pushed betwixt palm and glove! That largess of a franc?
Perhaps inconsciously, – to better help the blank
O' the nest, her tambourine, and, laying egg, persuade
A family to follow, the nest-egg that I laid
May have contained, – but just to foil suspicious folk, –
Between two silver whites a yellow double yolk!
Oh, threaten no farewell! five minutes shall suffice
To clear the matter up. I go, and in a trice
Return; five minutes past, expect me! If in vain –
Why, slip from flesh and blood, and play the ghost again!

Epilogue

The Householder

I

Savage I was sitting in my house, late, lone:
  Dreary, weary with the long day's work:
Head of me, heart of me, stupid as a stone:
  Tongue-tied now, now blaspheming like a Turk;
When, in a moment, just a knock, call, cry,
  Half a pang and all a rapture, there again were we! –

'What, and is it really you again?' quoth I:
  'I again, what else did you expect?' quoth She.

II

'Never mind, hie away from this old house –
  Every crumbling brick embrowned with sin and shame!
Quick, in its corners ere certain shapes arouse!
  Let them – every devil of the night – lay claim,
Make and mend, or rap and rend, for me! Good-bye!
  God be their guard from disturbance at their glee,
Till, crash, comes down the carcass in a heap!' quoth I:
  'Nay, but there's a decency required!' quoth She.

III

'Ah, but if you knew how time has dragged, days, nights!
  All the neighbour-talk with man and maid – such men!
All the fuss and trouble of street-sounds, window-sights:
  All the worry of flapping door and echoing roof; and then,
All the fancies . . . Who were they had leave, dared try
  Darker arts that almost struck despair in me?
If you knew but how I dwelt down here!' quoth I:
  'And was I so better off up there?' quoth She.

IV

'Help and get it over! *Reunited to his wife*
  (How draw up the paper lets the parish-people know?)
Lies M., or N., departed from this life,
  Day the this or that, month and year the so and so.
What i' the way of final flourish? Prose, verse? Try!
  Affliction sore long time he bore, or, what is it to be?
Till God did please to grant him ease. Do end!' quoth I:
  'I end with – Love is all and Death is naught!' quoth She.

Red Cotton Night-Cap Country
or
Turf and Towers

1873

To Miss Thackeray

Red Cotton Night-Cap Country

I

And so, here happily we meet, fair friend!
Again once more, as if the years rolled back
And this our meeting-place were just that Rome
Out in the champaign, say, o'er-rioted
By verdure, ravage, and gay winds that war
Against strong sunshine settled to his sleep;
Or on the Paris Boulevard, might it prove,
You and I came together saunteringly,
Bound for some shop-front in the Place Vendôme –
Gold-smithy and Golconda mine, that makes
'The Firm-Miranda' blazed about the world –
Or, what if it were London, where my toe
Trespassed upon your flounce? 'Small blame,' you smile,
Seeing the Staircase Party in the Square
Was Small and Early, and you broke no rib.

Even as we met where we have met so oft,
Now meet we on this unpretending beach
Below the little village: little, ay!
But pleasant, may my gratitude subjoin?
Meek, hitherto un-Murrayed bathing-place,
Best loved of sea-coast-nook-ful Normandy!
That, just behind you, is mine own hired house:
With right of pathway through the field in front,
No prejudice to all its growth unsheaved
Of emerald luzern bursting into blue.
Be sure I keep the path that hugs the wall,
Of mornings, as I pad from door to gate!
Yon yellow – what if not wild-mustard flower? –
Of that, my naked sole makes lawful prize,
Bruising the acrid aromatics out,
Till, what they preface, good salt savours sting
From, first, the sifted sands, then sands in slab,
Smooth save for pipy wreath-work of the worm:
(Granite and mussel-shell are ground alike
To glittering paste, – the live worm troubles yet.)
Then, dry and moist, the varech limit-line,
Burnt cinder-black, with brown uncrumpled swathe
Of berried softness, sea-swoln thrice its size;

And, lo, the wave protrudes a lip at last,
And flecks my foot with froth, nor tempts in vain.

Such is Saint-Rambert, wilder very much
Than Joyeux, that famed Joyous-Gard of yours,
Some five miles farther down; much homelier too –
Right for me, – right for you the fine and fair!
Only, I could endure a transfer – wrought
By angels famed still, through our countryside,
For weights they fetched and carried in old time
When nothing like the need was – transfer, just
Of Joyeux church, exchanged for yonder prig,
Our brand-new stone cream-coloured masterpiece.

Well – and you know, and not since this one year,
The quiet seaside country? So do I:
Who like it, in a manner, just because
Nothing is prominently likable
To vulgar eye without a soul behind,
Which, breaking surface, brings before the ball
Of sight, a beauty buried everywhere.
If we have souls, know how to see and use,
One place performs, like any other place,
The proper service every place on earth
Was framed to furnish man with: serves alike
To give him note that, through the place he sees,
A place is signified he never saw,
But, if he lack not soul, may learn to know.
Earth's ugliest walled and ceiled imprisonment
May suffer, through its single rent in roof,
Admittance of a cataract of light
Beyond attainment through earth's palace-panes
Pinholed athwart their windowed filagree
By twinklings sobered from the sun outside.
Doubtless the High Street of our village here
Imposes hardly as Rome's Corso could:
And our projected race for sailing-boats
Next Sunday, when we celebrate our Saint,
Falls very short of that attractiveness,
That artistry in festive spectacle,
Paris ensures you when she welcomes back
(When shall it be?) the Assembly from Versailles;

While the best fashion and intelligence
Collected at the counter of our Mayor
(Dry goods he deals in, grocery beside)
What time the post-bag brings the news from Vire, –
I fear me much, it scarce would hold its own,
That circle, that assorted sense and wit,
With Five o'clock Tea in a house we know.

Still, 'tis the check that gives the leap its lift.
The nullity of cultivated souls,
Even advantaged by their news from Vire,
Only conduces to enforce the truth
That, thirty paces off, this natural blue
Broods o'er a bag of secrets, all unbroached,
Beneath the bosom of the placid deep,
Since first the Post Director sealed them safe;
And formidable I perceive this fact –
Little Saint-Rambert touches the great sea.
From London, Paris, Rome, where men are men,
Not mice, and mice not Mayors presumably,
Thought scarce may leap so fast, alight so far.
But this is a pretence, you understand,

Disparagement in play, to parry thrust
Of possible objector: nullity
And ugliness, the taunt be his, not mine
Nor yours, – I think we know the world too well!
Did you walk hither, jog it by the plain,
Or jaunt it by the highway, braving bruise
From springless and uncushioned vehicle?
Much, was there not, in place and people both,
To lend an eye to? and what eye like yours –
The learned eye is still the loving one!
Our land: its quietude, productiveness,
Its length and breadth of grain-crop, meadow-ground,
Its orchards in the pasture, farms a-field
And hamlets on the road-edge, naught you missed
Of one and all the sweet rusticities!
From stalwart strider by the wagon-side,
Brightening the acre with his purple blouse,
To those dark-featured comely women-folk,
Healthy and tall, at work, and work indeed,

On every cottage door-step, plying brisk
Bobbins that bob you ladies out such lace!
Oh, you observed! and how that nimble play
Of finger formed the sole exception, bobbed
The one disturbance to the peace of things,
Where nobody esteems it worth his while,
If time upon the clock-face goes asleep,
To give the rusted hands a helpful push.
Nobody lifts an energetic thumb
And index to remove some dead and gone
Notice which, posted on the barn, repeats
For truth what two years' passage made a lie.
Still is for sale, next June, that same château
With all its immobilities, – were sold
Duly next June behind the last but last,
And, woe's me, still placards the Emperor
His confidence in war he means to wage,
God aiding and the rural populace.
No: rain and wind must rub the rags away
And let the lazy land untroubled snore.

Ah, in good truth? and did the drowsihead
So suit, so soothe the learned loving eye,
That you were minded to confer a crown,
(Does not the poppy boast such?) – call the land
By one slow hither-thither stretching, fast
Subsiding-into-slumber sort of name,
Symbolic of the place and people too,
'*White Cotton Night-cap Country?*' Excellent!
For they do, all, dear women young and old,
Upon the heads of them bear notably
This badge of soul and body in repose;
Nor its fine thimble fits the acorn-top,
Keeps woolly ward above that oval brown,
Its placid feature, more than muffler makes
A safeguard, circumvents intelligence
In – what shall evermore be named and famed,
If happy nomenclature aught avail,
'*White Cotton Night-cap Country.*'

Do I hear –
Oh, better, very best of all the news –
You mean to catch and cage the wingèd word,
And make it breed and multiply at home
Till Norman idlesse stock our England too?
Normandy shown minute yet magnified
In one of those small books, the truly great,
We never know enough, yet know so well?
How I foresee the cursive diamond-dints, –
Composite pen that plays the pencil too, –
As, touch the page and up the glamour goes,
And filmily o'er grain-crop, meadow-ground,
O'er orchard in the pasture, farm a-field
And hamlet on the road-edge, floats and forms
And falls, at lazy last of all, the Cap
That crowns the country! we, awake outside,
Farther than ever from the imminence
Of what cool comfort, what close coverture
Your magic, deftly weaving, shall surround
The unconscious captives with. Be theirs to drowse
Trammeled, and ours to watch the trammel-trick!
Ours be it, as we con the book of books,
To wonder how is winking possible!

All hail, 'White Cotton Night-cap Country,' then!
And yet, as on the beach you promise book, –
On beach, mere razor-edge 'twixt earth and sea,
I stand at such a distance from the world
That 'tis the whole world which obtains regard,
Rather than any part, though part presumed
A perfect little province in itself,
When wayfare made acquaintance first therewith.
So standing, therefore, on this edge of things,
What if the backward glance I gave, return
Loaded with other spoils of vagrancy
Than I dispatched it for, till I propose
The question – puzzled by the sudden store
Officious fancy plumps beneath my nose –
'Which sort of Night-cap have you glorified?'

You would be gracious to my ignorance:
'What other Night-cap than the normal one? –
Old honest guardian of man's head and hair
In its elastic yet continuous, soft,
No less persisting, circumambient gripe, –
Night's notice, life is respited from day!
Its form and fashion vary, suiting so
Each seasonable want of youth and age.
In infancy, the rosy naked ball
Of brain, and that faint golden fluff it bears,
Are smothered from disaster, – nurses know
By what foam-fabric; but when youth succeeds,
The sterling value of the article
Discards adornment, cap is cap henceforth
Unfeathered by the futile row on row.
Manhooe strains hard a sturdy stocking-stuff
O'er well-deserving head and ears: the cone
Is tassel-tipt, commendably takes pride,
Announcing workday done and wages pouched,
And liberty obtained to sleep, nay, snore.
Unwise, he peradventure shall essay
The sweets of independency for once –
Waive its advantage on his wedding-night:
Fool, only to resume it, night the next,
And never part companionship again.
Since, with advancing years, night's solace soon
Intrudes upon the daybreak dubious life
Persuades it to appear the thing it is,
Half-sleep; and so, encroaching more and more,
It lingers long past the abstemious meal
Of morning, and, as prompt to serve, precedes
The supper-summons, gruel grown a feast.
Finally, when the last sleep finds the eye
So tired it cannot even shut itself,
Does not a kind domestic hand unite
Friend to friend, lid from lid to part no more,
Consigned alike to that receptacle
So bleak without, so warm and white within?

'Night-caps, night's comfort of the human race:
Their usage may be growing obsolete,
Still, in the main, the institution stays.

And though yourself may possibly have lived,
And probably will die, undignified –
The Never-night-capped – more experienced folk
Laugh you back answer – What should Night-cap be
Save Night-cap pure and simple? Sorts of such?
Take cotton for the medium, cast an eye
This side to comfort, lambswool or the like,
That side to frilly cambric costliness,
And all between proves Night-cap proper.' Add
'Fiddle!' and I confess the argument.

Only, your ignoramus here again
Proceeds as tardily to recognize
Distinctions: ask him what a fiddle means,
And 'Just a fiddle' seems the apt reply.
Yet, is not there, while we two pace the beach,
This blessed moment, at your Kensington,
A special Fiddle-Show and rare array
Of all the sorts were ever set to cheek,
'Stablished on clavicle, sawn bow-hand-wise,
Or touched lute-fashion and forefinger-plucked?
I doubt not there be duly catalogued
Achievements all and some of Italy,
Guarnerius, Straduarius, – old and new,
Augustly rude, refined to finicking,
This mammoth with his belly full of blare,
That mouse of music – inch-long silvery wheeze.
And here a specimen has effloresced
Into the scroll-head, there subsides supreme,
And with the tail-piece satisfies mankind.
Why should I speak of woods, grains, stains and streaks,
The topaz varnish or the ruby gum?
We preferably pause where tickets teach
'Over this sample would Corelli croon,
Grieving, by minors, like the cushat-dove,
Most dulcet Giga, dreamiest Saraband.'
'From this did Paganini comb the fierce
Electric sparks, or to tenuity
Pull forth the inmost wailing of the wire –
No cat-gut could swoon out so much of soul!'

Three hundred violin-varieties
Exposed to public view! And dare I doubt
Some future enterprise shall give the world
Quite as remarkable a Night-cap-show?
Methinks, we, arm-in-arm, that festal day,
Pace the long range of relics shrined aright,
Framed, glazed, each cushioned curiosity,
And so begin to smile and to inspect:
'Pope's sickly head-sustainment, damped with dews
Wrung from the all-unfair fight: such a frame –
Though doctor and the devil helped their best –
Fought such a world that, waiving doctor's help,
Had the mean devil at its service too!
Voltaire's imperial velvet! Hogarth eyed
The thumb-nail record of some alley-phyz,
Then chucklingly clapped yonder cosiness
On pate, and painted with true flesh and blood!
Poor hectic Cowper's soothing sarsnet-stripe!'
And so we profit by the catalogue,
Somehow our smile subsiding more and more,
Till we decline into . . . but no! shut eyes
And hurry past the shame uncoffined here,
The hangman's toilet! If we needs must trench,
For science' sake which craves completeness still,
On the sad confine, not the district's self,
The object that shall close review may be . . .

Well, it is French, and here are we in France:
It is historic, and we live to learn,
And try to learn by reading story-books.
It is an incident of 'Ninety-two,
And, twelve months since, the Commune had the sway.
Therefore resolve that, after all the Whites
Presented you, a solitary Red
Shall pain us both, a minute and no more!
Do not you see poor Louis pushed to front
Of palace-window, in persuasion's name,
A spectacle above the howling mob
Who tasted, as it were, with tiger-smack,
The outstart, the first spirt of blood on brow,
The Phrygian symbol, the new crown of thorns,
The Cap of Freedom? See the feeble mirth

At odds with that half-purpose to be strong
And merely patient under misery!
And note the ejaculation, ground so hard
Between his teeth, that only God could hear,
As the lean pale proud insignificance
With the sharp-featured liver-worried stare
Out of the two grey points that did him stead
And passed their eagle-owner to the front
Better than his mob-elbowed undersize, –
The Corsican lieutenant commented
'Had I but one good regiment of my own,
How soon should volleys to the due amount
Lay stiff upon the street-flags this *canaille!*
As for the droll there, he that plays the king
And screws out smile with a Red night-cap on,
He's done for! Somebody must take his place.'
White Cotton Night-cap Country: excellent!
Why not Red Cotton Night-cap Country too?

'Why not say swans are black and blackbirds white,
Because the instances exist?' you ask.
'Enough that white, not red, predominates,
Is normal, typical, in cleric phrase
Quod semel, semper, et ubique.' Here,
Applying such a name to such a land,
Especially you find inopportune,
Impertinent, my scruple whether white
Or red describes the local colour best.
'Let be' (you say), 'the universe at large
Supplied us with exceptions to the rule,
So manifold, they bore no passing-by, –
Little Saint-Rambert has conserved at least
The pure tradition: white from head to heel,
Where is a hint of the ungracious hue?
See, we have traversed with hop, step and jump,
From heel to head, the main-street in a trice,
Measured the garment (help my metaphor!)
Not merely criticized the cap, forsooth;
And were you pricked by that collecting-itch,
That pruriency for writing o'er your reds
"Rare, rarer, rarest, not rare but unique," –
The shelf, Saint-Rambert, of your cabinet,

Unlabelled, – virginal, no Rahab-thread
For blushing token of the spy's success, –
Would taunt with vacancy, I undertake!
What, yonder is your best apology,
Pretence at most approach to naughtiness,
Impingement of the ruddy on the blank?
This is the criminal Saint-Rambertese
Who smuggled in tobacco, half-a-pound!
The Octroi found it out and fined the wretch.
This other is the culprit who dispatched
A hare, he thought a hedgehog (clods obstruct),
Unfurnished with Permission for the Chase!
As to the womankind – renounce from those
The hope of getting a companion-tinge,
First faint touch promising romantic fault!'

Enough: there stands Red Cotton Night-cap shelf –
A cavern's ostentatious vacancy –
My contribution to the show; while yours –
Whites heap your row of pegs from every hedge
Outside, and house inside Saint-Rambert here –
We soon have come to end of. See, the church
With its white steeple gives your challenge point,
Perks as it were the night-cap of the town,
Starchedly warrants all beneath is matched
By all above, one snowy innocence!

You put me on my mettle. British maid
And British man, suppose we have it out
Here in the fields, decide the question so?
Then, British fashion, shake hands hard again,
Go home together, friends the more confirmed
That one of us – assuredly myself –
Looks puffy about eye, and pink at nose?
Which 'pink' reminds me that the arduousness
We both acknowledge in the enterprise,
Claims, counts upon a large and liberal
Acceptance of as good as victory
In whatsoever just escapes defeat.
You must be generous, strain point, and call
Victory, any the least flush of pink
Made prize of, labelled scarlet for the nonce –

Faintest pretension to be wrong and red
And picturesque, that varies by a splotch
The righteous flat of insipidity.

Quick to the quest, then – forward, the firm foot!
Onward, the quarry-overtaking eye!
For, what is this, by way of march-tune, makes
The musicalest buzzing at my ear
By reassurance of that promise old
Though sins are scarlet they shall be as wool?
Whence – what fantastic hope do I deduce?
I am no Liebig: when the dyer dyes
A texture, can the red dye prime the white?
And if we washed well, wrung the texture hard,
Would we arrive, here, there and everywhere,
At a fierce ground beneath the surface meek?

I take the first chance, rub to threads what rag
Shall flutter snowily in sight. For see!
Already these few yards upon the rise,
Our back to brave Saint-Rambert, how we reach
The open, at a dozen steps or strides!
Turn round and look about, a breathing-while!
There lie, outspread at equidistance, thorpes
And villages and towns along the coast,
Distinguishable, each and all alike,
By white persistent Night-cap, spire on spire.
Take the left: yonder town is – what say you
If I say 'Londres'? Ay, the mother-mouse
(Reversing fable, as truth can and will)
Which gave our mountain of a London birth!
This is the Conqueror's country, bear in mind,
And Londres-district blooms with London-pride.
Turn round: La Roche, to right, where oysters thrive:
Monlieu – the lighthouse is a telegraph;
This, full in front, Saint-Rambert; then succeeds
Villeneuve, and Pons the Young with Pons the Old,
And – ere faith points to Joyeux, out of sight,
A little nearer – oh, La Ravissante!

There now is something like a Night-cap spire,
Donned by no ordinary Notre-Dame
For, one of the three safety-guards of France,
You front now, lady! Nothing intercepts
The privilege, by crow-flight, two miles far.
She and her sisters Lourdes and La Salette
Are at this moment hailed the cynosure
Of poor dear France, such waves have buffeted
Since she eschewed infallibility
And chose to steer by the vague compass-box.
This same midsummer month, a week ago,
Was not the memorable day observed
For reinstatement of the misused Three
In old supremacy for evermore?
Did not the faithful flock in pilgrimage
By railway, diligence and steamer – nay
On foot with staff and scrip, to see the sights
Assured them? And I say best sight was here:
And nothing justified the rival Two
In their pretension to equality;
Our folk laid out their ticket-money best,
And wiseliest, if they walked, wore shoe away;
Not who went farther only to fare worse.
For, what was seen at Lourdes and La Salette
Except a couple of the common cures
Such as all three can boast of, any day?
While here it was, here and by no means there,
That the Pope's self sent two great real gold crowns
As thick with jewelry as thick could stick,
His present to the Virgin and her Babe –
Provided for – who knows not? – by that fund,
Count Alessandro Sforza's legacy,
Which goes to crown some Virgin every year.
But this year, poor Pope was in prison-house,
And money had to go for something else;
And therefore, though their present seemed the Pope's,
The faithful of our province raised the sum
Preached and prayed out of – nowise purse alone.
Gentle and simple paid in kind, not cash,
The most part: the great lady gave her brooch,
The peasant-girl her hair-pin; 'twas the rough
Bluff farmer mainly who, – admonished well

By wife to care lest his new colewort-crop
Stray sorrowfully sparse like last year's seed, –
Lugged from reluctant pouch the fifty-franc,
And had the Curé's hope that rain would cease.
And so, the sum in evidence at length,
Next step was to obtain the donative
By the spontaneous bounty of the Pope –
No easy matter, since his Holiness
Had turned a deaf ear, long and long ago,
To much entreaty on our Bishop's part,
Commendably we boast. 'But no,' quoth he,
'Image and image needs must take their turn:
Here stand a dozen as importunate.'
Well, we were patient; but the cup ran o'er
When – who was it pressed in and took the prize
But our own offset, set far off indeed
To grow by help of our especial name,
She of the Ravissante – in Martinique!
'What?' cried our patience at the boiling-point,
'The daughter crowned, the mother's head goes bare?
Bishop of Raimbaux!' – that's our diocese –
'Thou hast a summons to repair to Rome,
Be efficacious at the Council there:
Now is the time or never! Right our wrong!
Hie thee away, thou valued Morillon,
And have the promise, thou who hast the vote!'
So said, so done, so followed in due course
(To cut the story short) this festival,
This famous Twenty-second, seven days since.

Oh, but you heard at Joyeux! Pilgrimage,
Concourse, procession with, to head the host,
Cardinal Mirecourt, quenching lesser lights:
The leafy street-length through, decked end to end
With August-strippage, and adorned with flags
That would have waved right well but that it rained
Just this picked day, by some perversity.
And so were placed, on Mother and on Babe,
The pair of crowns: the Mother's, you must see!
Miranda, the great Paris goldsmith, made
The marvel, – he's a neighbour: that's his park
Before you, tree-topped wall we walk toward.

His shop it was turned out the masterpiece,
Probably at his own expenditure;
Anyhow, his was the munificence
Contributed the central and supreme
Splendour that crowns the crown itself, The Stone.
Not even Paris, ransacked, could supply
That gem: he had to forage in New York,
This jeweller, and country-gentleman,
And most undoubted devotee beside!
Worthily wived, too: since his wife it was
Bestowed 'with friendly hand' – befitting phrase!
The lace which trims the coronation-robe –
Stiff wear – a mint of wealth on the brocade.

Do go and see what I saw yesterday!
And, for that matter, see in fancy still,
Since . . .

There now! Even for unthankful me,
Who stuck to my devotions at high-tide
That festal morning, never had a mind
To trudge the little league and join the crowd –
Even for me is miracle vouchsafed!
How pointless proves the sneer at miracles!
As if, contrariwise to all we want
And reasonably look to find, they graced
Merely those graced-before, grace helps no whit,
Unless, made whole, they need physician still.
I – sceptical in every inch of me –
Did I deserve that, from the liquid name
'Miranda,' – faceted as lovelily
As his own gift, the gem, – a shaft should shine,
Bear me along, another Abaris,
Nor let me light till, lo, the Red is reached,
And yonder lies in luminosity!

Look, lady! where I bade you glance but now!
Next habitation, though two miles away, –
No tenement for man or beast between, –
That, park and domicile, is country-seat
Of this same good Miranda! I accept

The augury. Or there, or nowhere else,
Will I establish that a Night-cap gleams
Of visionary Red, not White for once!
'Heaven' saith the sage 'is with us, here inside
Each man:' 'Hell also,' simpleness subjoins,
By White and Red describing human flesh.

And yet as we continue, quicken pace,
Approach the object which determines me
Victorious or defeated, more forlorn
My chance seems, – that is certainty at least.
Halt midway, reconnoitre! Either side
The path we traverse (turn and see) stretch fields
Without a hedge: one level, scallop-striped
With bands of beet and turnip and luzern,
Limited only by each colour's end,
Shelves down, – we stand upon an eminence, –
To where the earth-shell scallops out the sea,
A sweep of semicircle; and at edge –
Just as the milk-white incrustations stud
At intervals some shell-extremity,
So do the little growths attract us here,
Towns with each name I told you: say, they touch
The sea, and the sea them, and all is said,
So sleeps and sets to slumber that broad blue!
The people are as peaceful as the place.
This, that I call 'the path' is road, highway;
But has there passed us by a market-cart,
Man, woman, child, or dog to wag a tail?
True, I saw weeders stooping in a field;
But – formidably white the Cap's extent!

Round again! Come, appearance promises!
The boundary, the park-wall, ancient brick,
Upholds a second wall of tree-heads high
Which overlean its top, a solid green.
That surely ought to shut in mysteries!
A jeweller – no unsuggestive craft!
Trade that admits of much romance, indeed.
For, whom but goldsmiths used old monarchs pledge
Regalia to, or seek a ransom from,

Or pray to furnish dowry, at a pinch,
According to authentic story-books?
Why, such have revolutionized this land
With diamond-necklace-dealing! not to speak
Of families turned upside-down, because
The gay wives went and pawned clandestinely
Jewels, and figured, till found out, with paste,
Or else redeemed them – how, is horrible!
Then there are those enormous criminals
That love their ware and cannot lose their love,
And murder you to get your purchase back.
Others go courting after such a stone,
Make it their mistress, marry for their wife,
And find out, some day, it was false the while,
As ever wife or mistress, man too fond
Has named his Pilgrim, Hermit, Ace of Hearts.

Beside – what style of edifice begins
To grow in sight at last and top the scene?
That grey roof, with the range of *lucarnes,* four
I count, and that erection in the midst –
Clock-house, or chapel-spire, or what, above?
Conventual, that, beyond manorial, sure!
And reason good; for Clairvaux, such its name,
Was built of old to be a Priory,
Dependence on that Abbey-for-the-Males
Our Conqueror founded in world-famous Caen,
And where his body sought the sepulture
It was not to retain: you know the tale.
Such Priory was Clairvaux, prosperous
Hundreds of years; but nothing lasts below,
And when the Red Cap pushed the Crown aside,
The Priory became, like all its peers,
A National Domain: which, bought and sold
And resold, needs must change, with ownership,
Both outside show and inside use; at length
The messuage, three-and-twenty years ago,
Became the purchase of rewarded worth
Impersonate in Father – I must stoop
To French phrase for precision's sake, I fear –
Father Miranda, goldsmith of renown:
By birth a Madrilene, by domicile

And sojourning accepted French at last.
His energy it was which, trade transferred
To Paris, throve as with a golden thumb,
Established in the Place Vendôme. He bought
Not building only, but belongings far
And wide, at Gonthier there, Monlieu, Villeneuve,
A plentiful estate: which, twelve years since,
Passed, at the good man's natural demise,
To Son and Heir Miranda – Clairvaux here,
The Paris shop, the mansion – not to say
Palatial residence on Quai Rousseau,
With money, movables, a mine of wealth –
And young Léonce Miranda got it all.

Ah, but – whose might the transformation be?
Were you prepared for this, now? As we talked,
We walked, we entered the half-privacy,
The partly-guarded precinct: passed beside
The little paled-off islet, trees and turf,
Then found us in the main ash-avenue
Under the blessing of its branchage-roof.
Till, on emergence, what affronts our gaze?
Priory – Conqueror – Abbey-for-the-Males –
Hey, presto, pass, who conjured all away?
Look through the railwork of the gate: a park
– Yes, but *à l'Anglaise,* as they compliment!
Grass like green velvet, gravel-walks like gold,
Bosses of shrubs, embosomings of flowers,
Lead you – through sprinkled trees of tiny breed
Disporting, within reach of coverture,
By some habitual acquiescent oak
Or elm, that thinks, and lets the youngsters laugh –
Lead, lift at last your soul that walks the air,
Up to the house-front, or its back perhaps –
Whether façade or no, one coquetry
Of coloured brick and carved stone! Stucco? Well,
The daintiness is cheery, that I know,
And all the sportive floral framework fits
The lightsome purpose of the architect.
Those *lucarnes* which I called conventual, late,
Those are the outlets in the *mansarde*-roof;
And, underneath, what long light elegance

Of windows here suggests how brave inside
Lurk eyeballed gems they play the eyelids to!
Festive arrangements look through such, be sure!
And now the tower a-top, I took for clock's
Or bell's abode, turns out a quaint device,
Pillared and temple-treated Belvedere –
Pavilion safe within its railed-about
Sublimity of area – whence what stretch
Of sea and land, throughout the seasons' change,
Must greet the solitary! Or suppose
– If what the husband likes, the wife likes too –
The happy pair of students cloistered high,
Alone in April kiss when Spring arrives!
Or no, he mounts there by himself to meet
Winds, welcome wafts of sea-smell, first white bird
That flaps thus far to taste the land again,
And all the promise of the youthful year;
Then he descends, unbosoms straight his store
Of blessings in the bud, and both embrace,
Husband and wife, since earth is Paradise,
And man at peace with God. You see it all?

Let us complete our survey, go right round
The place: for here, it may be, we surprise
The Priory, – these solid walls, big barns,
Grey orchard-grounds, huge four-square stores for stock,
Betoken where the Church was busy once.
Soon must we come upon the Chapel's self.
No doubt next turn will treat us to . . . Aha,
Again our expectation proves at fault!
Still the bright graceful modern – not to say
Modish adornment, meets us: *Parc Anglais*,
Tree-sprinkle, shrub-embossment as before.
See, the sun splits on yonder bauble world
Of silvered glass concentrating, every side,
All the adjacent wonder, made minute
And touched grotesque by ball-convexity!
Just so, a sense that something is amiss,
Something is out of sorts in the display,
Affects us, past denial, everywhere.
The right erection for the Fields, the Wood,
(Fields – but *Elysées,* wood – but *de Boulogne*)

Is peradventure wrong for wood and fields
When Vire, not Paris, plays the Capital.

So may a good man have deficient taste;
Since Son and Heir Miranda, he it was
Who, six years now elapsed, achieved the work
And truly made a wilderness to smile.
Here did their domesticity reside,
A happy husband and as happy wife,
Till . . . how can I in conscience longer keep
My little secret that the man is dead
I, for artistic purpose, talk about
As if he lived still? No, these two years now,
Has he been dead. You ought to sympathize,
Not mock the sturdy effort to redeem
My pledge, and wring you out some tragedy
From even such a perfect commonplace!
Suppose I boast the death of such desert
My tragic bit of Red? Who contravenes
Assertion that a tragedy exists
In any stoppage of benevolence,
Utility, devotion above all?
Benevolent? There never was his like:
For poverty, he had an open hand
. . . Or stop – I use the wrong expression here –
An open purse, then, ever at appeal;
So that the unreflecting rather taxed
Profusion than penuriousness in alms.
One, in his day and generation, deemed
Of use to the community? I trust
Clairvaux thus renovated, regalized,
Paris expounded thus to Normandy,
Answers that question. Was the man devout?
After a life – one mere munificence
To Church and all things churchly, men or mice, –
Dying, his last bequeathment gave land, goods,
Cash, every stick and stiver, to the Church,
And notably to that church yonder, that
Belovèd of his soul, La Ravissante –
Wherefrom, the latest of his gifts, the Stone
Gratefully bore me as on arrow-flash
To Clairvaux, as I told you.

'Ay, to find
Your Red desiderated article,
Where every scratch and scrape provokes my White
To all the more superb a prominence!
Why, 'tis the story served up fresh again –
How it befell the restive prophet old
Who came and tried to curse, but blessed the land.
Come, your last chance! he disinherited
Children: he made his widow mourn too much
By this endowment of the other Bride –
Nor understood that gold and jewelry
Adorn her in a figure, not a fact.
You make that White, I want, so very white,
'Tis I say now – some trace of Red should be
Somewhere in this Miranda-sanctitude!'

Not here, at all events, sweet mocking friend!
For he was childless; and what heirs he had
Were an uncertain sort of Cousinry
Scarce claiming kindred so as to withhold
The donor's purpose though fantastical:
Heirs, for that matter, wanting no increase
Of wealth, since rich already as himself;
Heirs that had taken trouble off his hands,
Bought that productive goldsmith-business he,
With abnegation wise as rare, renounced
Precisely at a time of life when youth,
Nigh on departure, bids mid-age discard
Life's other loves and likings in a pack,
To keep, in lucre, comfort worth them all.
This Cousinry are they who boast the shop
Of 'Firm-Miranda, London and New York.'
Cousins are an unconscionable kind;
But these – pretension surely on their part
To share inheritance were too absurd!

'Remains then, he dealt wrongly by his wife,
Despoiled her somehow by such testament?'
Farther than ever from the mark, fair friend!
The man's love for his wife exceeded bounds
Rather than failed the limit. 'Twas to live
Hers and hers only, to abolish earth

Outside – since Paris holds the pick of earth –
He turned his back, shut eyes, stopped ears to all
Delicious Paris tempts her children with,
And fled away to this far solitude –
She peopling solitude sufficiently!
She, partner in each heavenward flight sublime,
Was, with each condescension to the ground,
Duly associate also: hand in hand,
. . . Or side by side, I say by preference –
On every good work sidelingly they went.
Hers was the instigation – none but she
Willed that, if death should summon first her lord,
Though she, sad relict, must drag residue
Of days encumbered by this load of wealth –
(Submitted to with something of a grace
So long as her surviving vigilance
Might worthily administer, convert
Wealth to God's glory and the good of man,
Give, as in life, so now in death, effect
To cherished purpose) – yet she begged and prayed
That, when no longer she could supervise
The House, it should become a Hospital:
For the support whereof, lands, goods and cash
Alike will go, in happy guardianship,
To yonder church, La Ravissante: who debt
To God and man undoubtedly will pay.

'Not of the world, your heroine!'

Do you know
I saw her yesterday – set eyes upon
The veritable personage, no dream?
I in the morning strolled this way, as oft,
And stood at entry of the avenue.
When, out from that first garden-gate, we gazed
Upon and through, a small procession swept –
Madame Miranda with attendants five.
First, of herself: she wore a soft and white
Engaging dress, with velvet stripes and squares
Severely black, yet scarce discouraging:
Fresh Paris-manufacture! (Vire's would do?
I doubt it, but confess my ignorance.)

Her figure? somewhat small and darlinglike.
Her face? well, singularly colourless,
For first thing: which scarce suits a blonde, you know.
Pretty you would not call her: though perhaps
Attaining to the ends of prettiness
And somewhat more, suppose enough of soul.
Then she is forty full: you cannot judge
What beauty was her portion at eighteen,
The age she married at. So, colourless
I stick to, and if featureless I add,
Your notion grows completer: for, although
I noticed that her nose was aquiline,
The whole effect amounts with me to – blank!
I never saw what I could less describe.
The eyes, for instance, unforgettable
Which ought to be, are out of mind as sight.

Yet is there not conceivably a face,
A set of wax-like features, blank at first,
Which, as you bendingly grow warm above,
Begins to take impressment from your breath?
Which, as your will itself were plastic here
Nor needed exercise of handicraft,
From formless moulds itself to correspond
With all you think and feel and are – in fine
Grows a new revelation of yourself,
Who know now for the first time what you want?
Here has been something that could wait awhile,
Learn your requirement, nor take shape before,
But, by adopting it, make palpable
Your right to an importance of your own,
Companions somehow were so slow to see!
– Far delicater solace to conceit
Than should some absolute and final face,
Fit representative of soul inside,
Summon you to surrender – in no way
Your breath's impressment, nor, in stranger's guise,
Yourself – or why of force to challenge you?
Why should your soul's reflection rule your soul?
('You' means not you, nor me, nor anyone
Framed, for a reason I shall keep suppressed,

To rather want a master than a slave:
The slavish still aspires to dominate!)
So, all I say is, that the face, to me
One blur of blank, might flash significance
To who had seen his soul reflected there
By that symmetric silvery phantom-like
Figure, with other five processional.
The first, a black-dressed matron – maybe, maid –
Mature, and dragonish of aspect, – marched;
Then four came tripping in a joyous flock,
Two giant goats and two prodigious sheep
Pure as the arctic fox that suits the snow
Tripped, trotted, turned the march to merriment,
But ambled at their mistress' heel – for why?
A rod of guidance marked the *Châtelaine*,
And ever and anon would sceptre wave,
And silky subject leave meandering.
Nay, one great naked sheep-face stopped to ask
Who was the stranger, snuffed inquisitive
My hand that made acquaintance with its nose,
Examined why the hand – of man at least –
Patted so lightly, warmly, so like life!
Are they such silly natures after all?
And thus accompanied, the paled-off space,
Isleted shrubs and verdure, gained the group;
Till, as I gave a furtive glance, and saw
Her back-hair was a block of solid gold,
The gate shut out my harmless question – Hair
So young and yellow, crowning sanctity,
And claiming solitude . . . can hair be false?

'Shut in the hair and with it your last hope
Yellow might on inspection pass for Red! –
Red, Red, where is the tinge of promised Red
In this old tale of town and country life,
This rise and progress of a family?
First comes the bustling man of enterprise,
The fortune-founding father, rightly rough,
As who must grub and grab, play pioneer.
Then, with a light and airy step, succeeds
The son, surveys the fabric of his sire

And enters home, unsmirched from top to toe.
Polish and education qualify
Their fortunate possessor to confine
His occupancy to the first-floor suite
Rather than keep exploring needlessly
Where dwelt his sire content with cellarage:
Industry bustles underneath, no doubt,
And supervisors should not sit too close.
Next, rooms built, there's the furniture to buy,
And what adornment like a worthy wife?
In comes she like some foreign cabinet,
Purchased indeed, but purifying quick
What space receives it from all traffic-taint.
She tells of other habits, palace-life;
Royalty may have pried into those depths
Of sandal-wooded drawer, and set a-creak
That pygmy portal pranked with lazuli.
More fit by far the ignoble we replace
By objects suited to such visitant
Than that we desecrate her dignity
By neighbourhood of vulgar table, chair,
Which haply helped old age to smoke and doze.
The end is, an exchange of city-stir
And too intrusive burgess-fellowship,
For rural isolated elegance,
Careless simplicity, how preferable!
There one may fairly throw behind one's back
The used-up worn-out Past, we want away,
And make a fresh beginning of stale life.
"In just the place" – does anyone object? –
"Where aboriginal gentility
Will scout the upstart, twit him with each trick
Of townish trade-mark that stamps word and deed,
And most of all resent that here town-dross
He daubs with money-colour to deceive!"
Rashly objected! Is there not the Church
To intercede and bring benefic truce
At outset? She it is shall equalize
The labourers i' the vineyard, last as first.
Pay court to her, she stops impertinence.
"Duke, once your sires crusaded it, we know:
Our friend the newcomer observes, no less,

Your chapel, rich with their emblazonry,
Wants roofing – might he but supply the means!
Marquise, you gave the honour of your name,
Titular patronage, abundant will
To what should be an Orphan Institute:
Gave everything but funds, in brief; and these,
Our friend, the lady newly resident,
Proposes to contribute, by your leave!"
Brothers and sisters lie they in thy lap,
Thou none-excluding, all-collecting Church!
Sure, one has half a foot i' the hierarchy
Of birth, when "Nay, my dear," laughs out the Duke,
"I'm the crown's cushion-carrier, but the crown –
Who gave its central glory, I or you?"
When Marquise jokes "My quest, forsooth? Each doit
I scrape together goes for Peter-pence
To purvey bread and water in his bonds
For Peter's self imprisoned – Lord, how long?
Yours, yours alone the bounty, dear my dame,
You plumped the purse which, poured into the plate,
Made the Archbishop open brows so broad!
And if you really mean to give that length
Of lovely lace to edge the robe!" ... Ah, friends,
Gem better serves so than by calling crowd
Round shop-front to admire the million's-worth!
Lace gets more homage than from *lorgnette*-stare,
And comment coarse to match, (should one display
One's robe a trifle o'er the *baignoire*-edge,)
"Well may she line her slippers with the like,
If minded so! their shop it was produced
That wonderful *parure*, the other day,
Whereof the Baron said it beggared him."
And so the paired Mirandas built their house,
Enjoyed their fortune, sighed for family,
Found friends would serve their purpose quite as well,
And come, at need, from Paris – anyhow,
With evident alacrity, from Vire –
Endeavour at the chase, at least succeed
In smoking, eating, drinking, laughing, and
Preferring country, oh so much to town!
Thus lived the husband; though his wife would sigh
In confidence, when Countesses were kind,

"Cut off from Paris and society!"
White, White, I once more round you in the ears!
Though you have marked it, in a corner, yours
Henceforth, – Red-lettered "Failure" very plain,
I shall acknowledge, on the snowy hem
Of ordinary Night-cap! Come, enough!
We have gone round its cotton vastitude,
Or half-round, for the end's consistent still,
A *cul-de-sac* with stoppage at the sea.
Here we return upon our steps. One look
May bid good morning – properly good night –
To civic bliss, Miranda and his mate!
Are we to rise and go?'

No, sit and stay!
Now comes my moment, with the thrilling throw
Of curtain from each side a shrouded case.
Don't the rings shriek an ominous 'Ha! ha!
So you take Human Nature upon trust?'
List but with like trust to an incident
Which speedily shall make quite Red enough
Burn out of yonder spotless napery!

Sit on the little mound here, whence you seize
The whole of the gay front sun-satisfied,
One laugh of colour and embellishment!
Because it was there, – past those laurustines,
On that smooth gravel-sweep 'twixt flowers and sward, –
There tragic death befell; and not one grace
Outspread before you but is registered
In that sinístrous coil these last two years
Were occupied in winding smooth again.

'True?' Well, at least it was concluded so,
Sworn to be truth, allowed by Law as such
(With my concurrence, if it matter here)
A month ago: at Vire they tried the case.

II

Monsieur Léonce Miranda, then, . . . but stay!
Permit me a preliminary word,
And, after, all shall go so straight to end!

Have you, the travelled lady, found yourself
Inside a ruin, fane or bath or cirque,
Renowned in story, dear through youthful dream?
If not, – imagination serves as well.
Try fancy-land, go back a thousand years,
Or forward, half the number, and confront
Some work of art gnawn hollow by Time's tooth, –
Hellenic temple, Roman theatre,
Gothic cathedral, Gallic Tuileries,
But ruined, one and whichsoe'er you like.
Obstructions choke what still remains intact,
Yet proffer change that's picturesque in turn;
Since little life begins where great life ends,
And vegetation soon amalgamates,
Smooths novel shape from out the shapeless old,
Till broken column, battered cornice block
The centre with a bulk half weeds and flowers,
Half relics you devoutly recognize.
Devoutly recognizing, – hark, a voice
Not to be disregarded! 'Man worked here
Once on a time; here needs again to work;
Ruins obstruct, which man must remedy.'
Would you demur 'Let Time fulfil his task,
And, till the scythe-sweep find no obstacle,
Let man be patient'?

The reply were prompt:
'Glisteningly beneath the May-night moon,
Herbage and floral coverture bedeck
Yon splintered mass amidst the solitude:
Wolves occupy the background, or some snake
Glides by at distance; picturesque enough!
Therefore, preserve it? Nay, pour daylight in, –
The mound proves swarming with humanity.
There never was a thorough solitude,
Now you look nearer: mortal busy life
First of all brought the crumblings down on pate,
Which trip man's foot still, plague his passage much,
And prove – what seems to you so picturesque
To him is . . . but experiment yourself
On how conducive to a happy home
Will be the circumstance your bed for base

Boasts tessellated pavement, – equally
Affected by the scorpion for his nest, –
While what o'erroofs bed is an architrave,
Marble, and not unlikely to crush man
To mummy, should its venerable prop,
Some fig-tree-stump, play traitor underneath.
Be wise! Decide! For conservation's sake,
Clear the arena forthwith! lest the tread
Of too-much-tried impatience trample out
Solid and unsubstantial to one blank
Mud-mixture, picturesque to nobody, –
And, task done, quarrel with the parts intact
Whence came the filtered fine dust, whence the crash
Bides but its time to follow. Quick conclude
Removal, time effects so tardily,
Of what is plain obstruction; rubbish cleared,
Let partial-ruin stand while ruin may,
And serve world's use, since use is manifold.
Repair wreck, stanchion wall to heart's content,
But never think of renovation pure
And simple, which involves creation too.
Transform and welcome! Yon tall tower may help
(Though built to be a belfry and naught else)
Some Father Secchi to tick Venus off
In transit: never bring there bell again,
To damage him aloft, brain us below,
When new vibrations bury both in brick!'

Monsieur Léonce Miranda, furnishing
The application at his cost, poor soul!
Was instanced how, – because the world lay strewn
With ravage of opinions in his path,
And neither he, nor any friendly wit,
Knew and could teach him which was firm, which frail,
In his adventure to walk straight through life
The partial-ruin, – in such enterprise,
He straggled into rubbish, struggled on,
And stumbled out again observably.
'Yon buttress still can back me up,' he judged:
And at a touch down came both he and it.
'A certain statue, I was warned against,

Now, by good fortune, lies well under foot,
And cannot tempt to folly any more':
So, lifting eye, aloft since safety lay,
What did he light on? the Idalian shape,
The undeposed, erectly Victrix still!
'These steps ascend the labyrinthine stair
Whence, darkling and on all-fours, out I stand
Exalt and safe, and bid low earth adieu –
For so instructs "Advice to who would climb"':
And all at once the climbing landed him
– Where, is my story.

Take its moral first.
Do you advise a climber? Have respect
To the poor head, with more or less of brains
To spill, should breakage follow your advice!
Head-break to him will be heart-break to you
For having preached 'Disturb no ruins here!
Are not they crumbling of their own accord?
Meantime, let poets, painters keep a prize!
Beside, a sage pedestrian picks his way.'
A sage pedestrian – such as you and I!
What if there trip, in merry carelessness,
And come to grief, a weak and foolish child?
Be cautious how you counsel climbing, then!

Are you adventurous and climb yourself?
Plant the foot warily, accept a staff,
Stamp only where you probe the standing-point,
Move forward, well assured that move you may:
Where you mistrust advance, stop short, there stick!
This makes advancing slow and difficult?
Hear what comes of the endeavour of brisk youth
To foot it fast and easy! Keep this same
Notion of outside mound and inside mash,
Towers yet intact round turfy rottenness,
Symbolic partial-ravage, – keep in mind!
Here fortune placed his feet who first of all
Found no incumbrance, till head found . . . But hear!

This son and heir then of the jeweller,
Monsieur Léonce Miranda, at his birth,
Mixed the Castilian passionate blind blood
With answerable gush, his mother's gift,
Of spirit, French and critical and cold.
Such mixture makes a battle in the brain,
Ending as faith or doubt gets uppermost;
Then will has way a moment, but no more:
So nicely-balanced are the adverse strengths,
That victory entails reverse next time.
The tactics of the two are different
And equalize the odds: for blood comes first,
Surrounding life with undisputed faith.
But presently, a new antagonist,
By scarce-suspected passage in the dark,
Steals spirit, fingers at each crevice found
Athwart faith's stronghold, fronts the astonished man:
'Such pains to keep me far, yet here stand I,
Your doubt inside the faith-defence of you!'

With faith it was friends bulwarked him about
From infancy to boyhood; so, by youth,
He stood impenetrably circuited,
Heaven-high and low as hell: what lacked he thus,
Guarded against aggression, storm or sap?
What foe would dare approach? Historic Doubt?
Ay, were there some half-knowledge to attack!
Batter doubt's best, sheer ignorance will beat.
Acumen metaphysic? – drills its way
Through what, I wonder! A thick feather-bed
Of thoughtlessness, no operating tool –
Framed to transpierce the flint-stone – fumbles at,
With chance of finding an impediment!
This Ravissante, now: when he saw the church
For the first time, and to his dying-day,
His firm belief was that the name fell fit
From the Delivering Virgin, niched and known;
As if there wanted records to attest
The appellation was a pleasantry,
A pious rendering of Rare Vissante,
The proper name which erst our province bore.
He would have told you that Saint Aldabert

Founded the church, (Heaven early favoured France,)
About the second century from Christ;
Though the true man was Bishop of Raimbaux,
Eleventh in succession, Eldobert,
Who flourished after some six hundred years.
He it was brought the image 'from afar,'
(Made out of stone the place produces still)
'Infantine Art divinely artless,' (Art
In the decrepitude of Decadence,)
And set it up a-working miracles
Until the Northmen's fury laid it low,
Not long, however: an egregious sheep,
Zealous with scratching hoof and routing horn,
Unearthed the image in good Mailleville's time,
Count of the country. 'If the tale be false,
Why stands it carved above the portal plain?'
Monsieur Léonce Miranda used to ask.
To Londres went the prize in solemn pomp,
But, liking old abode and loathing new,
Was borne – this time, by angels – back again.
And, reinaugurated, miracle
Succeeded miracle, a lengthy list,
Until indeed the culmination came –
Archbishop Chaumont prayed a prayer and vowed
A vow – gained prayer and paid vow properly –
For the conversion of Prince Vertgalant.
These facts, sucked in along with mother's-milk,
Monsieur Léonce Miranda would dispute
As soon as that his hands were flesh and bone,
Milk-nourished two-and-twenty years before.

So fortified by blind Castilian blood,
What say you to the chances of French cold
Critical spirit, should Voltaire besiege
'Alp, Apennine, and fortified redoubt'?
Ay, would such spirit please to play faith's game
Faith's way, attack where faith defends so well!
But then it shifts, tries other strategy.
Coldness grows warmth, the critical becomes
Unquestioning acceptance. 'Share and share
Alike in facts, to truth add other truth!
Why with old truth needs new truth disagree?'

Thus doubt was found invading faith, this time,
By help of not the spirit but the flesh:
Fat Rabelais chuckled, where faith lay in wait
For lean Voltaire's grimace – French, either foe.
Accordingly, while round about our friend
Ran faith without a break which learned eye
Could find at two-and-twenty years of age,
The twenty-two-years-old frank footstep soon
Assured itself there spread a standing-space
Flowery and comfortable, nowise rock
Nor pebble-pavement roughed for champion's tread
Who scorns discomfort, pacing at his post.
Tall, long-limbed, shoulder right and shoulder left,
And 'twixt *acromia* such a latitude,
Black heaps of hair on head, and blacker bush
O'er-rioting chin, cheek and throat and chest, –
His brown meridional temperament
Told him – or rather pricked into his sense
Plainer than language – 'Pleasant station here!
Youth, strength, and lustihood can sleep on turf
Yet pace the stony platform afterward:
First signal of a foe and up they start!
Saint Eldobert, at all such vanity,
Nay – sinfulness, had shaken head austere.
Had he? But did Prince Vertgalant? And yet,
After how long a slumber, of what sort,
Was it, he stretched octogenary joints
And, nigh on Day-of-Judgement trumpet-blast,
Jumped up and manned wall, brisk as any bee?'

Nor Rabelais nor Voltaire, but Sganarelle,
You comprehend, was pushing through the chink!
That stager in the saint's correct costume,
Who ever has his speech in readiness
For thickhead juvenility at fault:
'Go pace yon platform and play sentinel!
You won't? The worse! but still a worse might hap.
Stay then, provided that you keep in sight
The battlement, one bold leap lands you by!
Resolve not desperately "Wall or turf,
Choose this, choose that, but no alternative!"

No! Earth left once were left for good and all:
"With Heaven you may accommodate yourself."'

Saint Eldobert – I much approve his mode;
With sinner Vertgalant I sympathize;
But histrionic Sganarelle, who prompts
While pulling back, refuses yet concedes, –
Whether he preach in chair, or print in book,
Or whisper due sustainment to weak flesh,
Counting his sham beads threaded on a lie –
Surely, one should bid pack that mountebank!
Surely, he must have momentary fits
Of self-sufficient stage-forgetfulness,
Escapings of the actor-lassitude
When he allows the grace to show the grin,
Which ought to let even thickheads recognize
(Through all the busy and benefic part, –
Bridge-building, or rock-riving, or good clean
Transport of church and congregation both
From this to that place with no harm at all,)
The Devil, that old stager, at his trick
Of general utility, who leads
Downward, perhaps, but fiddles all the way!

Therefore, no sooner does our candidate
For saintship spotlessly emerge soul-cleansed
From First Communion to mount guard at post,
Paris-proof, top to toe, than up there starts
The Spirit of the Boulevard – you know Who –
With jocund 'So, a structure fixed as fate,
Faith's tower joins on to tower, no ring more round,
Full fifty years at distance, too, from youth!
Once reach that precinct and there fight your best,
As looking back you wonder what has come
Of daisy-dappled turf you danced across!
Few flowers that played with youth shall pester age,
However age esteem the courtesy;
And Eldobert was something past his prime,
Stocked Caen with churches ere he tried hand here.
Saint-Sauveur, Notre-Dame, Saint-Pierre, Saint-Jean
Attest his handiwork commenced betimes.

He probably would preach that turf is mud.
Suppose it mud, through mud one picks a way,
And when, clay-clogged, the struggler steps to stone,
He uncakes shoe, arrives in manlier guise
Than carried pick-a-back by Eldobert
Big-baby-fashion, lest his leathers leak!
All that parade about Prince Vertgalant
Amounts to – your Castilian helps enough –
Inveni ovem quae perierat:
But ask the pretty votive statue-thing
What the lost sheep's meantime amusements were
Till the Archbishop found him! That stays blank:
They washed the fleece well and forgot the rest.
Make haste, since time flies, to determine, though!'

Thus opportunely took up parable, –
Admonishing Miranda just emerged
Pure from The Ravissante and Paris-proof, –
Saint Sganarelle: then slipped aside, changed mask,
And made re-entry as a gentleman
Born of the Boulevard, with another speech
I spare you.

So, the year or two revolved,
And ever the young man was dutiful
To altar and to hearth: had confidence
In the whole Ravissantish history.
Voltaire? Who ought to know so much of him, –
Old sciolist, whom only boys think sage, –
As one whose father's house upon the Quai
Neighboured the very house where that Voltaire
Died mad and raving, not without a burst
Of squibs and crackers too significant?
Father and mother hailed their best of sons,
Type of obedience, domesticity,
Never such an example inside doors!
Outside, as well not keep too close a watch;
Youth must be left to some discretion there.
And what discretion proved, I find deposed
At Vire, confirmed by his own words: to wit,
How, with the sprightliness of twenty-five,
Five – and not twenty, for he gave their names

With laudable precision – were the few
Appointed by him unto mistress-ship;
While, meritoriously the whole long week
A votary of commerce only, week
Ended, 'at shut of shop on Saturday,
Do I, as is my wont, get drunk,' he writes
In airy record to a confidant.
'Bragging and lies!' replied the apologist:
'And do I lose by that?' laughed Somebody
At the Court-edge a-tiptoe, 'mid the crowd,
In his own clothes, a-listening to men's Law.

Thus while, prospectively a combatant,
The volunteer bent brows, clenched jaws, and fierce
Whistled the march-tune 'Warrior to the wall!'
Something like flowery laughters round his feet
Tangled him of a sudden with 'Sleep first!'
And fairly flat upon the turf sprawled he
And let strange creatures make his mouth their home.

Anyhow, 'tis the nature of the soul
To seek a show of durability,
Nor, changing, plainly be the slave of change.
Outside the turf, the towers: but, round the turf,
A tent may rise, a temporary shroud,
Mock-faith to suit a mimic dwelling-place:
Tent which, while screening jollity inside
From the external circuit – evermore
A menace to who lags when he should march –
Yet stands a-tremble, ready to collapse
At touch of foot: turf is acknowledged grass,
And grass, though pillowy, held contemptible
Compared with solid rock, the rampired ridge.
To truth a pretty homage thus we pay
By testifying – what we dally with,
Falsehood, (which, never fear we take for truth!)
We may enjoy, but then – how we despise!

Accordingly, on weighty business bound,
Monsieur Léonce Miranda stooped to play,
But, with experience, soon reduced the game
To principles, and thenceforth played by rule:

Rule, dignifying sport as sport, proclaimed
No less that sport was sport and nothing more.
He understood the worth of womankind, –
To furnish man – provisionally – sport:
Sport transitive – such earth's amusements are:
But, seeing that amusements pall by use,
Variety therein is requisite.
And since the serious work of life were wronged
Should we bestow importance on our play,
It follows, in such womankind-pursuit,
Cheating is lawful chase. We have to spend
An hour – they want a lifetime thrown away:
We seek to tickle sense – they ask for soul,
As if soul had no higher ends to serve!
A stag-hunt gives the royal creature law:
Bat-fowling is all fair with birds at roost,
The lantern and the clapnet suit the hedge.
Which must explain why, bent on Boulevard game,
Monsieur Léonce Miranda decently
Was prudent in his pleasure – passed himself
Off on the fragile fair about his path
As the gay devil rich in mere good looks,
Youth, hope – what matter though the purse be void?
'If I were only young Miranda, now,
Instead of a poor clerkly drudge at desk
All day, poor artist vainly bruising brush
On palette, poor musician scraping gut
With horsehair teased that no harmonics come!
Then would I love with liberality,
Then would I pay! – who now shall be repaid,
Repaid alike for present pain and past,
If Mademoiselle permit the contre-danse,
Sing "Gay in garret youth at twenty lives,"
And afterward accept a lemonade!'

Such sweet facilities of intercourse
Afford the Winter-Garden and Mabille!
'Oh, I unite' – runs on the confidence,
Poor fellow, that was read in open Court,
– 'Amusement with discretion: never fear
My *escapades* cost more than market-price!

No durably-attached Miranda-dupe,
Sucked dry of substance by two clinging lips,
Promising marriage, and performing it!
Trust me, I know the world, and know myself,
And know where duty takes me – in good time!'

Thus fortified and realistic, then,
At all points thus against illusion armed,
He wisely did New Year inaugurate
By playing truant to the favoured five:
And sat installed at 'The Varieties,' –
Playhouse appropriately named, – to note
(Prying amid the turf that's flowery there)
What primrose, firstling of the year, might push
The snows aside to deck his button-hole –
Unnoticed by that outline sad, severe,
(Though fifty good long years removed from youth)
That tower and tower, – our image, bear in mind!

No sooner was he seated than, behold,
Out burst a polyanthus! He was 'ware
Of a young woman niched in neighbourhood;
And ere one moment flitted, fast was he
Found captive to the beauty evermore,
For life, for death, for heaven, for hell, her own.
Philosophy, bewail thy fate! Adieu,
Youth realistic and illusion-proof!
Monsieur Léonce Miranda, – hero late
Who 'understood the worth of womankind,'
'Who found therein – provisionally – sport,' –
Felt, in the flitting of a moment, fool
Was he, and folly all that seemed so wise,
And the best proof of wisdom's birth would be
That he made all endeavour, body, soul,
By any means, at any sacrifice
Of labour, wealth, repute, and (– well, the time
For choosing between heaven on earth, and heaven
In heaven, was not at hand immediately –)
Made all endeavour, without loss incurred
Of one least minute, to obtain her love.
'Sport transitive?' 'Variety required?'

'In loving were a lifetime thrown away?'
How singularly may young men mistake!
The fault must be repaired with energy.

Monsieur Léonce Miranda ate her up
With eye-devouring; when the unconscious fair
Passed from the close-packed hall, he pressed behind;
She mounted vehicle, he did the same,
Coach stopped, and cab fast followed, at one door –
Good house in unexceptionable street.
Out stepped the lady, – never think, alone!
A mother was not wanting to the maid,
Or, may be, wife, or widow, might one say?
Out stepped and properly down flung himself
Monsieur Léonce Miranda at her feet –
And never left them after, so to speak,
For twenty years, till his last hour of life,
When he released them, as precipitate.
Love proffered and accepted then and there!
Such potency in word and look has truth.

Truth I say, truth I mean: this love was true,
And the rest happened by due consequence.
By which we are to learn that there exists
A falsish false, for truth's inside the same,
And truth that's only half true, falsish truth.
The better for both parties! folk may taunt
That half your rock-built wall is rubble-heap:
Answer them, half their flowery turf is stones!
Our friend had hitherto been decking coat
If not with stones, with weeds that stones befit,
With dandelions – 'primrose-buds,' smirked he;
This proved a polyanthus on his breast,
Prize-lawful or prize-lawless, flower the same.
So with his other instance of mistake:
Was Christianity the Ravissante?

And what a flower of flowers he chanced on now!
To primrose, polyanthus I prefer
As illustration, from the fancy-fact
That out of simple came the composite
By culture: that the florist bedded thick

His primrose-root in ruddle, bullock's blood,
Ochre and devils'-dung, for aught I know,
Until the pale and pure grew fiery-fine,
Ruby and topaz, rightly named anew.
This lady was no product of the plain;
Social manure had raised a rarity.

Clara de Millefleurs (note the happy name)
Blazed in the full-blown glory of her Spring.
Peerlessly perfect, form and face: for both –
'Imagine what, at seventeen, may have proved
Miss Pages, the actress: Pages herself, my dear!'
Noble she was, the name denotes: and rich?
'The apartment in this Coliseum Street,
Furnished, my dear, with such an elegance,
Testifies wealth, my dear, sufficiently!
What quality, what style and title, eh?
Well now, waive nonsense, you and I are boys
No longer: somewhere must a screw be slack!
Don't fancy, Duchesses descend at door
From carriage-step to stranger prostrate stretched,
And bid him take heart, and deliver mind,
March in and make himself at ease forthwith, –
However broad his chest and black his beard,
And comely his belongings, – all through love
Protested in a world of ways save one
Hinting at marriage!' – marriage which yet means
Only the obvious method, easiest help
To satisfaction of love's first demand,
That love endure eternally: 'my dear,
Somewhere or other must a screw be slack!'

Truth is the proper policy: from truth –
Whate'er the force wherewith you fling your speech, –
Be sure that speech will lift you, by rebound,
Somewhere above the lowness of a lie!
Monsieur Léonce Miranda heard too true
A tale – perhaps I may subjoin, too trite!

As the meek martyr takes her statued stand
Above our pity, claims our worship just
Because of what she puts in evidence,

Signal of suffering, badge of torture borne
In days gone by, shame then but glory now,
Barb, in the breast, turned aureole for the front!
So, half timidity, composure half,
Clara de Millefleurs told her martyrdom.

Of poor though noble parentage, deprived
Too early of a father's guardianship,
What wonder if the prodigality
Of nature in the girl, whose mental gifts
Matched her external dowry, form and face –
If these suggested a too prompt resource
To the resourceless mother? 'Try the Stage
And so escape starvation! Prejudice
Defames Mimetic Art: be yours to prove
That gold and dross may meet and never mix,
Purity plunge in pitch yet soil no plume!'

All was prepared in London – (you conceive
The natural shrinking from publicity
In Paris, where the name excites remark)
London was ready for the grand *début*;
When some perverse ill-fortune, incident
To art mimetic, some malicious thrust
Of Jealousy who sidles 'twixt the scenes
Or pops up sudden from the prompter's hole, –
Somehow the brilliant bubble burst in suds.
Want followed: in a foreign land, the pair!
O hurry over the catastrophe –
Mother too sorely tempted, daughter tried
Scarcely so much as circumvented, say!
Caged unsuspecting artless innocence!

Monsieur Léonce Miranda tell the rest! –
The rather that he told it in a style
To puzzle Court Guide students, much more me.
'Brief, she became the favourite of Lord N.,
An aged but illustrious Duke, thereby
Breaking the heart of his competitor
The Prince of O. Behold her palaced straight
In splendour, clothed in diamonds' (phrase how fit!),

'Giving tone to the City by the Thames!
Lord N., the aged but illustrious Duke,
Was even on the point of wedding her,
Giving his name to her' (why not to us?)
'But that her better angel interposed.
She fled from such a fate to Paris back,
A fortnight since: conceive Lord N.'s despair!
Duke as he is, there's no invading France.
He must restrict pursuit to postal plague
Of writing letters daily, duly read
As darlingly she hands them to myself,
The privileged supplanter, who therewith
Light a cigar and see abundant blue' –
(Either of heaven or else Havana-smoke.)
'Think! she, who helped herself to diamonds late,
In passion of disinterestedness
Now – will accept no tribute of my love
Beyond a paltry ring, three Louis'-worth!
Little she knows I have the rummaging
Of old Papa's shop in the Place Vendôme!'

So wrote entrancedly to confidant
Monsieur Léonce Miranda. Surely now,
If Heaven, that sees all, understands no less,
It finds temptation pardonable here,
It mitigates the promised punishment,
It recognizes that to tarry just
An April hour amid such dainty turf
Means no rebellion against task imposed
Of journey to the distant wall one day?
Monsieur Léonce Miranda puts the case!
Love, he is purposed to renounce, abjure;
But meanwhile, is the case a common one?
Is it the vulgar sin, none hates as he?

Which question, put directly to 'his dear'
(His brother – I will tell you in a trice)
Was doubtless meant, by due meandering,
To reach, to fall not unobserved before
The auditory cavern 'neath the cope
Of Her, the placable, the Ravissante.

But here's the drawback, that the image smiles,
Smiles on, smiles ever, says to supplicant
'Ay, ay, ay' – like some kindly weathercock
Which, stuck fast at Set Fair, Favonian Breeze,
Still warrants you from rain, though Auster's lead
Bring down the sky above your cloakless mirth.
Had he proposed this question to, nor 'dear'
Nor Ravissante, but prompt to the Police,
The Commissary of his Quarter, now –
There had been shaggy eyebrows elevate
With twinkling apprehension in each orb
Beneath, and when the sudden shut of mouth
Relaxed, – lip pressing lip, lest out should plump
The pride of knowledge in too frank a flow, –
Then, fact on fact forthcoming, dose were dealt
Of truth remedial in sufficiency
To save a chicken threatened with the pip,
Head-staggers and a tumble from its perch.

Alack, it was the lady's self that made
The revelation, after certain days
– Nor so unwisely! As the hashish-man
Prepares a novice to receive his drug,
Adroitly hides the soil with sudden spread
Of carpet ere he seats his customer:
Then shows him how to smoke himself about
With Paradise; and only when, at puff
Of pipe, the Houri dances round the brain
Of dreamer, does he judge no need is now
For circumspection and punctiliousness;
He may resume the serviceable scrap
That made the votary unaware of muck.
Just thus the lady, when her brewage – love –
Was well a-fume about the novice-brain,
Saw she might boldly pluck from underneath
Her lover the preliminary lie.

Clara de Millefleurs, of the noble race,
Was Lucie Steiner, child to Dominique
And Magdalen Commercy; born at Sierck,
About the bottom of the Social Couch.
The father having come and gone again,

The mother and the daughter found their way
To Paris, and professed mode-merchandise,
Were milliners, we English roughlier say;
And soon a fellow-lodger in the house,
Monsieur Ulysse Muhlhausen, young and smart,
Tailor by trade, perceived his housemate's youth,
Smartness, and beauty over and above.
Courtship was brief, and marriage followed quick,
And quicklier – impecuniosity.
The young pair quitted Paris to reside
At London: which repaid the compliment
But scurvily, since not a whit the more
Trade prospered by the Thames than by the Seine.
Failing all other, as a last resource,
'He would have trafficked in his wife,' – she said.
If for that cause they quarrelled, 'twas, I fear,
Rather from reclamation of her rights
To wifely independence, than as wronged
Otherwise by the course of life proposed:
Since, on escape to Paris back again
From horror and the husband, – ill-exchanged
For safe maternal home recovered thus, –
I find her domiciled and dominant
In that apartment, Coliseum Street,
Where all the splendid magic met and mazed
Monsieur Léonce Miranda's venturous eye.
Only, the same was furnished at the cost
Of someone notable in days long since,
Carlino Centofanti: he it was
Found entertaining unawares – if not
An angel, yet a youth in search of one.

Why this revealment after reticence?
Wherefore, beginning 'Millefleurs,' end at all
Steiner, Muhlhausen, and the ugly rest?
Because the unsocial purse-comptrolling wight,
Carlino Centofanti, – made aware
By misadventure that his bounty, crumbs
From table, comforted a visitant, –
Took churlish leave, and left, too, debts to pay.
Loaded with debts, the lady needs must bring
Her soul to bear assistance from a friend

Beside that paltry ring, three Louis'-worth;
And therefore might the little circumstance
That Monsieur Léonce had the rummaging
Of old Papa's shop in the Place Vendôme
Pass, perhaps, not so unobservably.

Frail shadow of a woman in the flesh,
These very eyes of mine saw yesterday,
Would I re-tell this story of your woes,
Would I have heart to do you detriment
By pinning all this shame and sorrow plain
To that poor *chignon*, – staying with me still,
Though form and face have well-nigh faded now, –
But that men read it, rough in brutal print,
As two years since some functionary's voice
Rattled all this – and more by very much –
Into the ear of vulgar Court and crowd?
Whence, by reverberation, rumblings grew
To what had proved a week-long roar in France,
Had not the dreadful cannonry drowned all.
Was, now, the answer of your advocate
More than just this? 'The shame fell long ago,
The sorrow keeps increasing: God forbid
We judge man by the faults of youth in age!'
Permit me the expression of a hope
Your youth proceeded like your avenue,
Stepping by bush, and tree, and taller tree,
Until, columnar, at the house they end.
So might your creeping youth columnar rise
And reach, by year and year, symmetrical,
To where all shade stops short, shade's service done.
Bushes on either side, and boughs above,
Darken, deform the path else sun would streak;
And, cornered half-way somewhere, I suspect
Stagnation and a horse-pond: hurry past!
For here's the house, the happy half-and-half
Existence – such as stands for happiness
True and entire, howe'er the squeamish talk!
Twenty years long, you may have loved this man;
He must have loved you; that's a pleasant life,
Whatever was your right to lead the same.

The white domestic pigeon pairs secure,
Nay, does mere duty by bestowing egg
In authorized compartment, warm and safe,
Boarding about, and gilded spire above,
Hoisted on pole, to dogs' and cats' despair!
But I have spied a veriest trap of twigs
On tree-top, every straw a thievery,
Where the wild dove – despite the fowler's snare,
The sportsman's shot, the urchin's stone, – crooned gay,
And solely gave her heart to what she hatched,
Nor minded a malignant world below.
I throw first stone forsooth? 'Tis mere assault
Of playful sugarplum against your cheek,
Which, if it makes cheek tingle, wipes off rouge!
You, my worst woman? Ah, that touches pride,
Puts on his mettle the exhibitor
Of Night-caps, if you taunt him 'This, no doubt, –
Now we have got to Female-garniture, –
Crowns your collection, Reddest of the row!'
O unimaginative ignorance
Of what dye's depth keeps best apart from worst
In womankind! – how heaven's own pure may seem
To blush aurorally beside such blanched
Divineness as the women-wreaths named White:
While hell, eruptive and fuliginous,
Sickens to very pallor as I point
Her place to a Red clout called woman too!
Hail, heads that ever had such glory once
Touch you a moment, like God's cloven tongues
Of fire! your lambent aureoles lost may leave
You marked yet, dear beyond true diadems:
And hold, each foot, nor spurn, to man's disgrace,
What other twist of fetid rag may fall!
Let slink into the sewer the cupping-cloth!

Lucie, much solaced, I re-finger you,
The medium article; if ruddy-marked
With iron-mould, your cambric, – clean at least
From poison-speck of rot and purulence.
Lucie Muhlhausen said – 'Such thing am I:
Love me, or love me not!' Miranda said
'I do love, more than ever, most for this.'

The revelation of the very truth
Proved the concluding necessary shake
Which bids the tardy mixture crystallize
Or else stay ever liquid: shoot up shaft,
Durably diamond, or evaporate –
Sluggish solution through a minute's slip.
Monsieur Léonce Miranda took his soul
In both his hands, as if it were a vase,
To see what came of the convulsion there,
And found, amid subsidence, love new-born
So sparklingly resplendent, old was new.
'Whatever be my lady's present, past,
Or future, this is certain of my soul,
I love her: in despite of all I know,
Defiance of the much I have to fear,
I venture happiness on what I hope,
And love her from this day for evermore:
No prejudice to old profound respect
For certain Powers! I trust they bear in mind
A most peculiar case, and straighten out
What's crooked there, before we close accounts.
Renounce the world for them – some day I will:
Meantime, to me let her become the world!'

Thus mutely might our friend soliloquize
Over the tradesmen's bills, his Clara's gift –
In the apartment, Coliseum Street,
Carlino Centofanti's legacy,
Provided rent and taxes were discharged –
In face of Steiner now, De Millefleurs once,
The tailor's wife and runaway confessed.

On such a lady if election light,
(According to a social prejudice)
If henceforth 'all the world' she constitute
For any lover, – needs must he renounce
Our world in ordinary, walked about
By couples loving as its laws prescribe, –
Renunciation sometimes difficult.
But, in this instance, time and place and thing
Combined to simplify experiment,

And make Miranda, in the current phrase,
Master the situation passably.

For first facility, his brother died –
Who was, I should have told you, confidant,
Adviser, referee and substitute,
All from a distance: but I knew how soon
This younger brother, lost in Portugal,
Had to depart and leave our friend at large.
Cut off abruptly from companionship
With brother-soul of bulk about as big,
(Obvious recipient – by intelligence
And sympathy, poor little pair of souls –
Of much affection and some foolishness)
Monsieur Léonce Miranda, meant to lean
By nature, needs must shift the leaning-place
To his love's bosom from his brother's neck,
Or fall flat unrelieved of freight sublime.

Next died the lord of the Aladdin's cave,
Master o' the mint and keeper of the keys
Of chests chokeful with gold and silver changed
By Art to forms where wealth forgot itself,
And caskets where reposed each pullet-egg
Of diamond, slipping flame from fifty slants.
In short, the father of the family
Took his departure also from our scene,
Leaving a fat succession to his heir
Monsieur Léonce Miranda, – 'fortunate
If ever man was, in a father's death,'
(So commented the world, – not he, too kind,
Could that be, rather than scarce kind enough)
Indisputably fortunate so far,
That little of incumbrance in his path,
Which money kicks aside, would lie there long.

And finally, a rough but wholesome shock,
An accident which comes to kill or cure,
A jerk which mends a dislocated joint!
Such happy chance, at cost of twinge, no doubt,
Into the socket back again put truth,

And stopped the limb from longer dragging lie.
For love suggested 'Better shamble on,
And bear your lameness with what grace you may!'
And but for this rude wholesome accident,
Continuance of disguise and subterfuge,
Retention of first falsehood as to name
And nature in the lady, might have proved
Too necessary for abandonment.
Monsieur Léonce Miranda probably
Had else been loth to cast the mask aside,
So politic, so self-preservative,
Therefore so pardonable – though so wrong!
For see the bugbear in the background! Breathe
But ugly name, and wind is sure to waft
The husband news of the wife's whereabout:
From where he lies perdue in London town,
Forth steps the needy tailor on the stage,
Deity-like from dusk machine of fog,
And claims his consort, or his consort's worth
In rubies which her price is far above.
Hard to propitiate, harder to oppose, –
Who but the man's self came to banish fear,
A pleasant apparition, such as shocks
A moment, tells a tale, then goes for good!

Monsieur Ulysse Muhlhausen proved no less
Nor more than 'Gustave,' lodging opposite
Monsieur Léonce Miranda's diamond-cave
And ruby-mine, and lacking little thence
Save that its gnome would keep the captive safe,
Never return his Clara to his arms.
For why? He was become the man in vogue,
The indispensable to who went clothed
Nor cared encounter Paris-fashion's blame, –
Such miracle could London absence work.
Rolling in riches – so translate 'the vogue' –
Rather his object was to keep off claw
Should griffin scent the gold, should wife lay claim
To lawful portion at a future day,
Than tempt his partner from her private spoils.
Best forage each for each, nor coupled hunt!

Pursuantly, one morning, – knock at door
With knuckle, dry authoritative cough,
And easy stamp of foot, broke startlingly
On household slumber, Coliseum Street:
'Admittance in the name of Law!' In marched
The Commissary and subordinate.
One glance sufficed them. 'A marital pair:
We certify, and bid good morning, sir!
Madame, a thousand pardons!' Whereupon
Monsieur Ulysse Muhlhausen, otherwise
Called 'Gustave' for conveniency of trade,
Deposing in due form complaint of wrong,
Made his demand of remedy – divorce
From bed, board, share of name, and part in goods.
Monsieur Léonce Miranda owned his fault,
Protested his pure ignorance, from first
To last, of rights infringed in 'Gustave's' case:
Submitted him to judgement. Law decreed
'Body and goods be henceforth separate!'
And thereupon each party took its way,
This right, this left, rejoicing, to abide
Estranged yet amicable, opposites
In life as in respective dwelling-place.
Still does one read on his establishment
Huge-lettered 'Gustave,' – gold out-glittering
'Miranda, goldsmith,' just across the street –
'A first-rate hand at riding-habits' – say
The instructed – 'special cut of chamber-robes.'

Thus by a rude in seeming – rightlier judged
Beneficent surprise, publicity
Stopped further fear and trembling, and what tale
Cowardice thinks a covert: one bold splash
Into the mid-shame, and the shiver ends,
Though cramp and drowning may begin perhaps.

To cite just one more point which crowned success:
Madame, Miranda's mother, most of all
An obstacle to his projected life
In licence, as a daughter of the Church,
Duteous, exemplary, severe by right –
Moreover one most thoroughly beloved

Without a rival till the other sort
Possessed her son, – first storm of anger spent,
She seemed, though grumblingly and grudgingly,
To let be what needs must be, acquiesce.
'With Heaven – accommodation possible!'
Saint Sganarelle had preached with such effect,
She saw now mitigating circumstance.
'The erring one was most unfortunate,
No question: but worse Magdalens repent.
Were Clara free, did only Law allow,
What fitter choice in marriage could have made
Léonce or anybody?' 'Tis alleged
And evidenced, I find, by advocate
'Never did she consider such a tie
As baleful, springe to snap whate'er the cost.'
And when the couple were in safety once
At Clairvaux, motherly, considerate,
She shrank not from advice. 'Since safe you be,
Safely abide! for winter, I know well,
Is troublesome in a cold country-house.
I recommend the south room, that we styled,
Your sire and I, the winter-chamber.'

Chance
Or purpose, – who can read the mystery? –
Combined, I say, to bid 'Entrench yourself,
Monsieur Léonce Miranda, on this turf,
About this flower, so firmly that, as tent
Rises on every side around you both,
The question shall become, – Which arrogates
Stability, this tent or those far towers?
May not the temporary structure suit
The stable circuit, co-exist in peace? –
Always until the proper time, no fear!
"Lay flat your tent!" is easier said than done.'

So, with the best of auspices, betook
Themselves Léonce Miranda and his bride –
Provisionary – to their Clairvaux house,
Never to leave it – till the proper time.

I told you what was Clairvaux-Priory
Ere the improper time: an old demesne
With memories, – relic half, and ruin whole, –
The very place, then, to repair the wits
Worn out with Paris-traffic, when its lord,
Miranda's father, took his month of ease
Purchased by industry. What contrast here!
Repose, and solitude, and healthy ways.
That ticking at the back of head, he took
For motion of an inmate, stopped at once,
Proved nothing but the pavement's rattle left
Behind at Paris: here was holiday.
Welcome the quaint succeeding to the spruce,
The large and lumbersome and – might he breathe
In whisper to his own ear – dignified
And gentry-fashioned old-style haunts of sleep!
Palatial gloomy chambers for parade,
And passage-lengths of lost significance,
Never constructed as receptacle,
At his odd hours, for him their actual lord
By dint of diamond-dealing, goldsmithry.
Therefore Miranda's father chopped and changed
Nor roof-tile nor yet floor-brick, undismayed
By rains a-top or rats at bottom there.
Such contrast is so piquant for a month!
But now arrived quite other occupants
Whose cry was 'Permanency, – life and death
Here, here, not elsewhere, change is all we dread!'
Their dwelling-place must be adapted, then,
To inmates, no mere truants from the town,
No temporary sojourners, forsooth,
At Clairvaux: change it into Paradise!

Fair friend, – who listen and let talk, alas! –
You would, in even such a state of things,
Pronounce, – or am I wrong? – for bidding stay
The old-world inconvenience, fresh as found.
All folk of individuality
Prefer to be reminded now and then,
Though at the cost of vulgar cosiness,
That the shell-outside only harbours man
The vital and progressive, meant to build,

When build he may, with quite a difference,
Some time, in that far land we dream about,
Where every man is his own architect.
But then the couple here in question, each
At one in project for a happy life,
Were by no acceptation of the word
So individual that they must aspire
To architecture all-appropriate
And, therefore, in this world impossible:
They needed house to suit the circumstance,
Proprietors, not tenants for a term.
Despite a certain marking, here and there,
Of fleecy black or white distinguishment,
These vulgar sheep wore the flock's uniform.
They love the country, *they* renounce the town?
They gave a kick, as our Italians say,
To Paris ere it turned and kicked themselves!
Acquaintances might prove too hard to seek,
Or the reverse of hard to find, perchance,
Since Monsieur Gustave's apparition there.
And let me call remark upon the list
Of notabilities invoked, in Court
At Vire, to witness, by their phrases culled
From correspondence, what was the esteem
Of those we pay respect to, for 'the pair
Whereof they knew the inner life,' 'tis said.
Three, and three only, answered the appeal.
First, Monsieur Vaillant, music-publisher,
'Begs Madame will accept civilities.'
Next, Alexandre Dumas, – sire, not son, –
'Sends compliments to Madame and to you.'
And last – but now prepare for England's voice!
I will not mar nor make – here's word for word –
'A rich proprietor of Paris, he
To whom belonged that beauteous *Bagatelle*
Close to the wood of Boulogne, Hertford hight,
Assures of homages and compliments
Affectionate' – not now Miranda but
'Madame Muhlhausen.' (Was this friend, the Duke
Redoubtable in rivalry before?)
Such was the evidence when evidence
Was wanted, then if ever, to the worth

Whereat acquaintances in Paris prized
Monsieur Léonce Miranda's household charm.

No wonder, then, his impulse was to live,
In Norman solitude, the Paris life:
Surround himself with Art transported thence,
And nature like those famed Elysian Fields:
Then, warm up the right colour out of both,
By Boulevard friendships tempted to come taste
How Paris lived again in little there.

Monsieur Léonce Miranda practised Art.
Do let a man for once live as man likes!
Politics? Spend your life, to spare the world's:
Improve each unit by some particle
Of joy the more, deteriorate the orb
Entire, your own: poor profit, dismal loss!
Write books, paint pictures, or make music – since
Your nature leans to such life-exercise!
Ay, but such exercise begins too soon,
Concludes too late, demands life whole and sole
Artistry being battle with the age
It lives in! Half life, – silence, while you learn
What has been done; the other half, – attempt
At speech, amid world's wail of wonderment –
'Here's something done was never done before!'
To be the very breath that moves the age
Means not to have breath drive you bubble-like
Before it – but yourself to blow: that's strain;
Strain's worry through the life-time, till there's peace;
We know where peace expects the artist-soul.

Monsieur Léonce Miranda knew as much.
Therefore in Art he nowise cared to be
Creative; but creation, that had birth
In storminess long years before was born
Monsieur Léonce Miranda, – Art, enjoyed
Like fleshly objects of the chace that tempt
In cookery, not in capture – these might feast
The dilettante, furnish tavern-fare
Open to all with purses open too.
To sit free and take tribute *seigneur*-like –

Now, not too lavish of acknowledgement,
Now, self-indulgently profuse of pay,
Always Art's *seigneur*, not Art's serving-man
Whate'er the style and title and degree, –
That is the quiet life and easy death
Monsieur Léonce Miranda would approve
Wholly – provided (back I go again
To the first simile) that while glasses clink,
And viands steam, and banqueting laughs high,
All that's outside the temporary tent,
The dim grim outline of the circuit-wall,
Forgets to menace 'Soon or late will drop
Pavilion, soon or late you needs must march,
And laggards will be sorry they were slack!
Always – unless excuse sound plausible!'

Monsieur Léonce Miranda knew as much:
Whence his determination just to paint
So creditably as might help the eye
To comprehend how painter's eye grew dim
Ere it produced L'Ingegno's piece of work –
So to become musician that his ear
Should judge, by its own tickling and turmoil,
Who made the Solemn Mass might well die deaf –
So cultivate a literary knack
That, by experience how it wiles the time,
He might imagine how a poet, rapt
In rhyming wholly, grew so poor at last
By carelessness about his banker's-book,
That the Sieur Boileau (to provoke our smile)
Began abruptly, – when he paid devoir
To Louis Quatorze as he dined in state, –
'Sire, send a drop of broth to Pierre Corneille
Now dying and in want of sustenance!'
– I say, these half-hour playings at life's toil,
Diversified by billiards, riding, sport –
With now and then a visitor – Dumas,
Hertford – to check no aspiration's flight –
While Clara, like a diamond in the dark,
Should extract shining from what else were shade,
And multiply chance rays a million-fold, –
How could he doubt that all offence outside, –

Wrong to the towers, which, pillowed on the turf,
He thus shut eyes to, – were as good as gone?

So, down went Clairvaux-Priory to dust,
And up there rose, in lieu, yon structure gay
Above the Norman ghosts: and where the stretch
Of barren country girdled house about,
Behold the Park, the English preference!
Thus made undoubtedly a desert smile
Monsieur Léonce Miranda.

Ay, but she?
One should not so merge soul in soul, you think?
And I think: only, let us wait, nor want
Two things at once – her turn will come in time.
A cork-float danced upon the tide, we saw,
This morning, blinding-bright with briny dews:
There was no disengaging soaked from sound,
Earth-product from the sister-element.
But when we turn, the tide will turn, I think,
And bare on beach will lie exposed the buoy:
A very proper time to try, with foot
And even finger, which was buoying wave,
Which merely buoyant substance, – power to lift,
And power to be sent skyward passively.
Meanwhile, no separation of the pair!

III

And so slipt pleasantly away five years
Of Paradisiac dream; till, as there flit
Premonitory symptoms, pricks of pain,
Because the dreamer has to start awake
And find disease dwelt active all the while
In head or stomach through his night-long sleep, –
So happened here disturbance to content.

Monsieur Léonce Miranda's last of cares,
Ere he composed himself, had been to make
Provision that, while sleeping safe he lay,
Somebody else should, dragon-like, let fall
Never a lid, coiled round the apple-stem,
But watch the precious fruitage. Somebody

Kept shop, in short, played Paris-substitute.
Himself, shrewd, well-trained, early-exercised,
Could take in, at an eye-glance, luck or loss –
Know commerce throve, though lazily uplift
On elbow merely: leave his bed, forsooth?
Such active service was the substitute's.

But one October morning, at first drop
Of appled gold, first summons to be grave
Because rough Autumn's play turns earnest now,
Monsieur Léonce Miranda was required
In Paris to take counsel, face to face,
With Madame-mother: and be rated, too,
Roundly at certain items of expense
Whereat the government provisional,
The Paris substitute and shopkeeper,
Shook head, and talked of funds inadequate:
Oh, in the long run, – not if remedy
Occurred betimes! Else, – tap the generous bole
Too near the quick, – it withers to the root –
Leafy, prolific, golden apple-tree,
'Miranda,' sturdy in the Place Vendôme!

'What is this reckless life you lead?' began
Her greeting she whom most he feared and loved,
Madame Miranda. 'Luxury, extravagance
Sardanapalus' self might emulate, –
Did your good father's money go for this?
Where are the fruits of education, where
The morals which at first distinguished you,
The faith which promised to adorn your age?
And why such wastefulness outbreaking now,
When heretofore you loved economy?
Explain this pulling-down and building-up
Poor Clairvaux, which your father bought because
Clairvaux he found it, and so left to you,
Not a gilt-gingerbread big baby-house!
True, we could somehow shake head and shut eye
To what was past prevention on our part –
This reprehensible illicit bond:
We, in a manner, winking, watched consort
Our modest well-conducted pious son

With Dalilah: we thought the smoking flax
Would smoulder soon away and end in snuff.
Is spark to strengthen, prove consuming fire?
No lawful family calls Clairvaux 'home' –
Why play that fool of Scripture whom the voice
Admonished 'Whose tonight shall be those things
Provided for thy morning jollity?"
To take one specimen of pure caprice
Out of the heap conspicuous in the plan, –
Puzzle of change, I call it, – titled big
"Clairvaux Restored": what means this Belvedere?
This Tower, stuck like a fool's-cap on the roof –
Do you intend to soar to heaven from thence?
Tower, truly! Better had you planted turf –
More fitly would you dig yourself a hole
Beneath it for the final journey's help!
O we poor parents – could we prophesy!'

Léonce was found affectionate enough
To man, to woman, child, bird, beast, alike;
But all affection, all one fire of heart
Flaming toward Madame-mother. Had she posed
The question plainly at the outset 'Choose!
Cut clean in half your all-the-world of love,
The mother and the mistress: then resolve,
Take me or take her, throw away the one!' –
He might have made the choice and marred my tale.
But, much I apprehend, the problem put
Was 'Keep both halves, yet do no detriment
To either! Prize each opposite in turn!'
Hence, while he prized at worth the Clairvaux-life
With all its tolerated naughtiness,
He, visiting in fancy Quai Rousseau,
Saw, cornered in the cosiest nook of all
That range of rooms through number Thirty-three,
The lady-mother bent o'er her *bézique*;
While Monsieur Curé This, and Sister That –
Superior of no matter what good House –
Did duty for Duke Hertford and Dumas,
Nay – at his mother's age – for Clara's self.
At Quai Rousseau, things comfortable thus,
Why should poor Clairvaux prove so troublesome?

She played at cards, he built a Belvedere.
But here's the difference: she had reached the Towers
And there took pastime: he was still on Turf –
Though fully minded that, when once he marched,
No sportive fancy should distract him more.

In brief, the man was angry with himself,
With her, with all the world and much beside:
And so the unseemly words were interchanged
Which crystallize what else evaporates,
And make mere misty petulance grow hard
And sharp inside each softness, heart and soul.
Monsieur Léonce Miranda flung at last
Out of doors, fever-flushed: and there the Seine
Rolled at his feet, obsequious remedy
For fever, in a cold Autumnal flow.
'Go and be rid of memory in a bath!'
Craftily whispered Who besets the ear
On such occasions.

                                        Done as soon as dreamed.
Back shivers poor Léonce to bed – where else?
And there he lies a month 'twixt life and death,
Raving. 'Remorse of conscience!' friends opine.

'Sirs, it may partly prove so,' represents
Beaumont – (the family physician, he
Whom last year's Commune murdered, do you mind?)
Beaumont reports 'There is some active cause,
More than mere pungency of quarrel past, –
Cause that keeps adding other food to fire.
I hear the words and know the signs, I say!
Dear Madame, you have read the Book of Saints,
How Antony was tempted? As for me,
Poor heathen, 'tis by pictures I am taught.
I say then, I see standing here, – between
Me and my patient, and that crucifix
You very properly would interpose, –
A certain woman-shape, one white appeal
"Will you leave me, then, me, me, me for her?"
Since cold Seine could not quench this flame, since flare
Of fever does not redden it away, –

Be rational, indulgent, mute – should chance
Come to the rescue – Providence, I mean –
The while I blister and phlebotomize!'

Well, somehow rescued by whatever power,
At month's end, back again conveyed himself
Monsieur Léonce Miranda, worn to rags,
Nay, tinder: stuff irreparably spoiled,
Though kindly hand should stitch and patch its best.
Clairvaux in Autumn is restorative.
A friend stitched on, patched ever. All the same,
Clairvaux looked greyer than a month ago.
Unglossed was shrubbery, unglorified
Each copse, so wealthy once; the garden-plots,
The orchard-walks showed dearth and dreariness.
The sea lay out at distance crammed by cloud
Into a leaden wedge; and sorrowful
Sulked field and pasture with persistent rain.
Nobody came so far from Paris now:
Friends did their duty by an invalid
Whose convalescence claimed entire repose.
Only a single ministrant was staunch
At quiet reparation of the stuff –
Monsieur Léonce Miranda, worn to rags:
But she was Clara and the world beside.

Another month, the year packed up his plagues
And sullenly departed, pedlar-like,
As apprehensive old-world ware might show
To disadvantage when the new-comer,
Merchant of novelties, young 'Sixty-eight,
With brand-new bargains, whistled o'er the lea.
Things brightened somewhat o'er the Christmas hearth,
As Clara plied assiduously her task.

'Words are but words and wind. Why let the wind
Sing in your ear, bite, sounding, to your brain?
Old folk and young folk, still at odds, of course!
Age quarrels because spring puts forth a leaf
While winter has a mind that boughs stay bare;
Or rather – worse than quarrel – age descries
Propriety in preaching life to death.

"Enjoy nor youth, nor Clairvaux, nor poor me?"
Dear Madame, you enjoy your age, 'tis thought!
Your number Thirty-three on Quai Rousseau
Cost fifty times the price of Clairvaux, tipped
Even with our prodigious Belvedere;
You entertain the Curé, – we, Dumas:
We play charades, while you prefer *bézique*:
Do lead your own life and let ours alone!
Cross Old Year shall have done his worst, my friend!
Here comes gay New Year with a gift, no doubt.
Look up and let in light that longs to shine –
One flash of light, and where will darkness hide?
Your cold makes me too cold, love! Keep me warm!'

Whereat Léonce Miranda raised his head
From his two white thin hands, and forced a smile,
And spoke: 'I do look up, and see your light
Above me! Let New Year contribute warmth –
I shall refuse no fuel that may blaze.'

Nor did he. Three days after, just a spark
From Paris, answered by a snap at Caen
Or whither reached the telegraphic wire:
'Quickly to Paris! On arrival, learn
Why you are wanted!' Curt and critical!

Off starts Léonce, one fear from head to foot;
Caen, Rouen, Paris, as the railway helps;
Then come the Quai and Number Thirty-three.
'What is the matter, concierge?' – a grimace!
He mounts the staircase, makes for the main seat
Of dreadful mystery which draws him there –
Bursts in upon a bedroom known too well –
There lies all left now of the mother once.
Tapers define the stretch of rigid white,
Nor want there ghastly velvets of the grave.
A blackness sits on either side at watch,
Sisters, good souls but frightful all the same,
Silent: a priest is spokesman for his corpse.
'Dead, through Léonce Miranda! stricken down
Without a minute's warning, yesterday!
What did she say to you, and you to her,

Two months ago? This is the consequence!
The doctors have their name for the disease;
I, you, and God say – heart-break, nothing more!'
Monsieur Léonce Miranda, like a stone
Fell at the bedfoot and found respite so,
While the priest went to tell the company.
What follows you are free to disbelieve.

It may be true or false that this good priest
Had taken his instructions, – who shall blame? –
From quite another quarter than, perchance,
Monsieur Léonce Miranda might suppose
Would offer solace in such pressing need.
All he remembered of his kith and kin
Was they were worthily his substitutes
In commerce, did their work and drew their pay.
But *they* remembered, in addition, this –
They fairly might expect inheritance,
As nearest kin, called Family by law
And gospel both. Now, since Miranda's life
Showed nothing like abatement of distaste
For conjugality, but preference
Continued and confirmed of that smooth chain
Which slips and leaves no knot behind, no heir –
Presumption was, the man, become mature,
Would at a calculable day discard
His old and outworn . . . what we blush to name,
And make society the just amends;
Scarce by a new attachment – Heaven forbid!
Still less by lawful marriage: that's reserved
For those who make a proper choice at first –
Not try both courses and would grasp in age
The very treasure youth preferred to spurn.
No! putting decently such thought aside,
The penitent must rather give his powers
To such a reparation of the past
As, edifying kindred, makes them rich.
Now, how would it enrich prospectively
The Cousins, if he lavished such expense
On Clairvaux? – pretty as a toy, but then
As toy, so much productive and no more!
If all the outcome of the goldsmith's shop

Went to gild Clairvaux, where remain the funds
For Cousinry to spread out lap and take?
This must be thought of and provided for.
I give it you as mere conjecture, mind!

To help explain the wholesome unannounced
Intelligence, the shock that startled guilt,
The scenic show, much yellow, black and white
By taper-shine, the nuns – portentous pair,
And, more than all, the priest's admonishment –
'No flattery of self! You murdered her!
The grey lips, silent now, reprove by mine.
You wasted all your living, rioted
In harlotry – she warned and I repeat!
No warning had she, for she needed none:
If this should be the last yourself receive?'

Done for the best, no doubt, though clumsily, –
Such, and so startling, the reception here,
You hardly wonder if down fell at once
The tawdry tent, pictorial, musical,
Poetical, besprent with hearts and darts;
Its cobweb-work, betinselled stitchery,
Lay dust about our sleeper on the turf,
And showed the outer towers distinct and dread.

Senseless he fell, and long he lay, and much
Seemed salutary in his punishment
To planners and performers of the piece.
When pain ends, pardon prompt may operate.
There was a good attendance close at hand,
Waiting the issue in the great saloon,
Cousins with consolation and advice.

All things thus happily performed to point,
No wonder at success commensurate.
Once swooning stopped, once anguish subsequent
Raved out, – a sudden resolution chilled
His blood and changed his swimming eyes to stone,
As the poor fellow raised himself upright,
Collected strength, looked, once for all, his look,
Then, turning, put officious help aside

And passed from out the chamber. 'For affairs!'
So he announced himself to the saloon:
'We owe a duty to the living too!' –
Monsieur Léonce Miranda tried to smile.

How did the hearts of Cousinry rejoice
At their stray sheep returning thus to fold,
As, with a dignity, precision, sense,
All unsuspected in the man before,
Monsieur Léonce Miranda made minute
Detail of his intended scheme of life
Thenceforward and for ever. 'Vanity
Was ended: its redemption must begin –
And, certain, would continue; but since life
Was awfully uncertain – witness here! –
Behoved him lose no moment but discharge
Immediate burthen of the world's affairs
On backs that kindly volunteered to crouch.
Cousins, with easier conscience, blamelessly
Might carry on the goldsmith's trade, in brief,
Uninterfered with by its lord who late
Was used to supervise and take due tithe.
A stipend now sufficed his natural need:
Themselves should fix what sum allows man live.
But half a dozen words concisely plain
Might, first of all, make sure that, on demise,
Monsieur Léonce Miranda's property
Passed by bequeathment, every particle,
To the right heirs, the cousins of his heart.
As for that woman – they would understand!
This was a step must take her by surprise.
It were too cruel did he snatch away
Decent subsistence. She was young, and fair,
And . . . and attractive! Means must be supplied
To save her from herself, and from the world,
And . . . from anxieties might haunt him else
When he were fain have other thoughts in mind.'

It was a sight to melt a stone, that thaw
Of rigid disapproval into dew
Of sympathy, as each extended palm
Of cousin hasted to enclose those five

Cold fingers, tendered so mistrustfully,
Despairingly of condonation now!
You would have thought, – at every fervent shake,
In reassurance of those timid tips, –
The penitent had squeezed, considerate,
By way of fee into physician's hand
For physicking his soul, some diamond knob.

And now let pass a week. Once more behold
The same assemblage in the same saloon,
Waiting the entry of protagonist
Monsieur Léonce Miranda. 'Just a week
Since the death-day, – was ever man transformed
Like this man?' questioned cousin of his mate.

Last seal to the repentance had been set
Three days before, at Sceaux in neighbourhood
Of Paris, where they laid with funeral pomp
Mother by father. Let me spare the rest:
How the poor fellow, in his misery,
Buried hot face and bosom, where heaped snow
Offered assistance, at the grave's black edge,
And there lay, till uprooted by main force
From where he prayed to grow and ne'er again
Walk earth unworthily as heretofore.
It is not with impunity priests teach
The doctrine he was dosed with from his youth –
'Pain to the body – profit to the soul;
Corporeal pleasure – so much woe to pay
When disembodied spirit gives account.'

However, woe had done its worst, this time.
Three days allow subsidence of much grief.
Already, regular and equable,
Forward went purpose to effect. At once
The testament was written, signed and sealed.
Disposure of the commerce – that took time,
And would not suffer by a week's delay;
But the immediate, the imperious need,
The call demanding of the Cousinry
Co-operation, what convened them thus,

Was – how and when should deputation march
To Coliseum Street, the old abode
Of wickedness, and there acquaint – oh, shame!
Her, its old inmate, who had followed up
And lay in wait in the old haunt for prey –
That they had rescued, they possessed Léonce,
Whose loathing at recapture equalled theirs –
Upbraid that sinner with her sinfulness,
Impart the fellow-sinner's firm resolve
Never to set eyes on her face again:
Then, after stipulations strict but just,
Hand her the first instalment, – moderate
Enough, no question, – of her salary:
Admonish for the future, and so end. –
All which good purposes, decided on
Sufficiently, were waiting full effect
When presently the culprit should appear.

Somehow appearance was delayed too long;
Chatting and chirping sunk inconsciously
To silence, nay, uneasiness, at length
Alarm, till – anything for certitude! –
A peeper was commissioned to explore,
At keyhole, what the laggard's task might be –
What caused so palpable a disrespect!

Back came the tiptoe cousin from his quest.
'Monsieur Léonce was busy,' he believed,
'Contemplating – those love-letters, perhaps,
He always carried, as if precious stones,
About with him. He read, one after one,
Some sort of letters. But his back was turned.
The empty coffer open at his side,
He leant on elbow by the mantelpiece
Before the hearth-fire; big and blazing too.'

'Better he shovelled them all in at once,
And burned the rubbish!' was a cousin's quip,
Warming his own hands at the fire the while.
I told you, snow had fallen outside, I think.

When suddenly a cry, a host of cries,
Screams, hubbub and confusion thrilled the room.
All by a common impulse rushed thence, reached
The late death-chamber, tricked with trappings still,
Skulls, cross-bones, and such moral broidery.
Madame Muhlhausen might have played the witch,
Dropped down the chimney and appalled Léonce
By some proposal 'Parting touch of hand!'
If she but touched his foolish hand, you know!!

Something had happened quite contrariwise.
Monsieur Léonce Miranda, one by one,
Had read the letters and the love they held,
And, that task finished, had required his soul
To answer frankly what the prospect seemed
Of his own love's departure – pledged to part!
Then, answer being unmistakable,
He had replaced the letters quietly,
Shut coffer, and so, grasping either side
By its convenient handle, plunged the whole –
Letters and coffer and both hands to boot,
Into the burning grate and held them there.
'Burn, burn and purify my past!' said he,
Calmly, as if he felt no pain at all.

In vain they pulled him from the torture-place:
The strong man, with the soul of tenfold strength,
Broke from their clutch: and there again smiled he,
The miserable hands re-bathed in fire –
Constant to that ejaculation 'Burn,
Burn, purify!' And when, combining force,
They fairly dragged the victim out of reach
Of further harm, he had no hands to hurt –
Two horrible remains of right and left,
'Whereof the bones, phalanges formerly,
Carbonized, were still crackling with the flame,'
Said Beaumont. And he fought them all the while:
'Why am I hindered when I would be pure?
Why leave the sacrifice still incomplete?
She holds me, I must have more hands to burn!'
They were the stronger, though, and bound him fast.

Beaumont was in attendance presently.
'What did I tell you? Preachment to the deaf!
I wish he had been deafer when they preached,
Those priests! But wait till next Republic comes!'

As for Léonce, a single sentiment
Possessed his soul and occupied his tongue –
Absolute satisfaction at the deed.
Never he varied, 'tis observable,
Nor in the stage of agonies (which proved
Absent without leave, – science seemed to think)
Nor yet in those three months' febricity
Which followed, – never did he vary tale –
Remaining happy beyond utterance.
'Ineffable beatitude' – I quote
The words, I cannot give the smile – 'such bliss
Abolished pain! Pain might or might not be:
He felt in heaven, where flesh desists to fret.
Purified now and henceforth, all the past
Reduced to ashes with the flesh defiled!
Why all those anxious faces round his bed?
What was to pity in their patient, pray,
When doctor came and went, and Cousins watched?
– Kindness, but in pure waste!' he said and smiled.
And if a trouble would at times disturb
The ambrosial mood, it came from other source
Than the corporeal transitory pang.
'If sacrifice be incomplete!' cried he –
'If ashes have not sunk reduced to dust,
To nullity! If atoms coalesce
Till something grow, grow, get to be a shape
I hate, I hoped to burn away from me!
She is my body, she and I are one,
Yet, all the same, there, there at bed-foot stands
The woman wound about my flesh and blood,
There, the arms open, the more wonderful,
The whiter for the burning... Vanish thou!
Avaunt, fiend's self found in the form I wore!'

'Whereat,' said Beaumont, 'since his hands were gone,
The patient in a frenzy kicked and kicked
To keep off some imagined visitant.

So will it prove as long as priests may preach
Spiritual terrors!' groaned the evidence
Of Beaumont that his patient was stark mad –
Produced in time and place: of which anon.
'Mad, or why thus insensible to pain?
Body and soul are one thing, with two names
For more or less elaborated stuff.'

Such is the new *Religio Medici.*
Though antiquated faith held otherwise,
Explained that body is not soul, but just
Soul's servant: that, if soul be satisfied,
Possess already joy or pain enough,
It uses to ignore, as master may,
What increase, joy or pain, its servant brings –
Superfluous contribution: soul, once served,
Has naught to do with body's service more.
Each, speculated on exclusively,
As if its office were the only one,
Body or soul, either shows service paid
In joy and pain, that's blind and objectless –
A servant's toiling for no master's good –
Or else shows good received and put to use,
As if within soul's self grew joy and pain,
Nor needed body for a ministrant.
I note these old unscientific ways:
Poor Beaumont cannot: for the Commune ruled
Next year, and ere they shot his priests, shot him.

Monsieur Léonce Miranda raved himself
To rest; lay three long months in bliss or bale,
Inactive, anyhow: more need that heirs,
His natural protectors, should assume
The management, bestir their cousinship,
And carry out that purpose of reform
Such tragic work now made imperative.
A deputation, with austerity,
Nay, sterness, bore her sentence to the fiend
Aforesaid, – she at watch for turn of wheel
And fortune's favour, Street – you know the name.

A certain roughness seemed appropriate: 'You –
Steiner, Muhlhausen, whatsoe'er your name,
Cause whole and sole of this catastrophe!' –
And so forth, introduced the embassage.

'Monsieur Léonce Miranda was divorced
Once and for ever from his – ugly word.
Himself had gone for good to Portugal:
They came empowered to act and stipulate.
Hold! no discussion! Terms were settled now:
So much of present and prospective pay,
But also – good engagement in plain terms
She never seek renewal of the past!'

This little harmless tale produced effect.
Madame Muhlhausen owned her sentence just,
Its execution gentle. 'Stern their phrase,
These kinsfolk with a right she recognized –
But kind its import probably, which now
Her agitation, her bewilderment
Rendered too hard to understand, perhaps.
Let them accord the natural delay,
And she would ponder and decide. Meantime,
So far was she from wish to follow friend
Who fled her, that she would not budge from place –
Now that her friend was fled to Portugal, –
Never! *She* leave this Coliseum Street?
No, not a footstep!' she assured them.

So –
They saw they might have left that tale untold
When, after some weeks more were gone to waste,
Recovery seemed incontestable,
And the poor mutilated figure, once
The gay and glancing fortunate young spark,
Miranda, humble and obedient took
The doctor's counsel, issued sad and slow
From precincts of the sick-room, tottered down,
And out, and into carriage for fresh air,
And so drove straight to Coliseum Street,
And tottered upstairs, knocked, and in a trice
Was clasped in the embrace of whom you know –

With much asseveration, I omit,
Of constancy henceforth till life should end.
When all this happened, – 'What reward,' cried she,
'For judging her Miranda by herself!
For never having entertained a thought
Of breaking promise, leaving home forsooth,
To follow who was fled to Portugal!
As if she thought they spoke a word of truth!
She knew what love was, knew that he loved her;
The Cousinry knew nothing of the kind.'

I will not scandalize you and recount
How matters made the morning pass away.
Not one reproach, not one acknowledgement,
One explanation: all was understood!
Matters at end, the home-uneasiness
Cousins were feeling at this jaunt prolonged
Was ended also by the entry of –
Not simply him whose exit had been made
By mild command of doctor 'Out with you!
I warrant we receive another man!'
But – would that I could say, the married pair!

And, quite another man assuredly,
Monsieur Léonce Miranda took on him
Forthwith to bid the trio, priest and nuns,
Constant in their attendance all this while,
Take his thanks and their own departure too;
Politely but emphatically. Next,
The Cousins were dismissed: 'No protest, pray!
Whatever I engaged to do is done,
Or shall be – I but follow your advice:
Love I abjure; the lady, you behold,
Is changed as I myself; her sex is changed:
This is my Brother – He will tend me now,
Be all my world henceforth as brother should.
Gentlemen, of a kinship I revere,
Your interest in trade is laudable;
I purpose to indulge it: manage mine,
My goldsmith-business in the Place Vendôme,
Wholly – through purchase at the price adjudged
By experts I shall have assistance from.

If, in conformity with sage advice,
I leave a busy world of interests
I own myself unfit for – yours the care
That any world of other aims, wherein
I hope to dwell, be easy of access
Through ministration of the moneys due,
As we determine, with all proper speed,
Since I leave Paris to repair my health.
Say farewell to our Cousins, Brother mine!'

And, all submissiveness, as brother might,
The lady curtseyed gracefully, and dropt
More than mere curtsey, a concluding phrase
So silver-soft, yet penetrative too,
That none of it escaped the favoured ears:
'Had I but credited one syllable,
I should today be lying stretched on straw,
The produce of your miserable *rente*!
Whereas, I hold him – do you comprehend?'
Cousin regarded cousin, turned up eye,
And took departure, as our Tuscans laugh,
Each with his added palm-breadth of long nose, –
Curtailed but imperceptibly, next week,
When transfer was accomplished, and the trade
In Paris did indeed become their own,
But bought by them and sold by him on terms
'Twixt man and man, – might serve 'twixt wolf and wolf,
Substitute 'bit and clawed' for 'signed and sealed' –
Our ordinary business-terms, in short.

Another week, and Clairvaux broke in bloom
At end of April, to receive again
Monsieur Léonce Miranda, gentleman,
Ex-jeweller and goldsmith: never more, –
According to the purpose he professed, –
To quit this paradise, his property,
This Clara, his companion: so it proved.

The Cousins, each with elongated nose,
Discussed their bargain, reconciled them soon
To hard necessity, disbursed the cash,
And hastened to subjoin, wherever type

Proclaimed 'Miranda' to the public, 'Called
Now Firm-Miranda.' There, a colony,
They flourish underneath the name that still
Maintains the old repute, I understand.
They built their Clairvaux, dream-Château, in Spain,
Perhaps – but Place Vendôme is waking worth:
Oh, they lost little! – only, man and man
Hardly conclude transactions of the kind
As cousin should with cousin, – cousins think.
For the rest, all was honourably done,
So, ere buds break to blossom, let us breathe!
Never suppose there was one particle
Of recrudescence – wound, half-healed before,
Set freshly running – sin, repressed as such,
New loosened as necessity of life!
In all this revocation and resolve,
Far be sin's self-indulgence from your thought!
The man had simply made discovery,
By process I respect if not admire,
That what was, was: – that turf, his feet had touched,
Felt solid just as much as yonder towers
He saw with eyes, but did not stand upon,
And could not, if he would, reach in a leap.
People had told him flowery turf was false
To footstep, tired the traveller soon, beside:
That was untrue. They told him 'One fair stride
Plants on safe platform and secures man rest.'
That was untrue. Some varied the advice:
'Neither was solid, towers no more than turf.'
Double assertion, therefore twice as false.
'I like these amateurs' – our friend had laughed,
Could he turn what he felt to what he thought,
And, that again, to what he put in words:
'I like their pretty trial, proof of paste
Or precious stone, by delicate approach
Of eye askance, fine feel of finger-tip,
Or touch of tongue inquisitive for cold.
I tried my jewels in a crucible:
Fierce fire has felt them, licked them, left them sound.
Don't tell me that my earthly love is sham,
My heavenly fear a clever counterfeit!
Each may oppose each, yet be true alike!'

To build up, independent of the towers,
A durable pavilion o'er the turf,
Had issued in disaster. 'What remained
Except, by tunnel, or else gallery,
To keep communication 'twixt the two,
Unite the opposites, both near and far,
And never try complete abandonment
Of one or other?' so he thought, not said.

And to such engineering feat, I say,
Monsieur Léonce Miranda saw the means
Precisely in this revocation prompt
Of just those benefits of worldly wealth
Conferred upon his Cousinry – all but!

This Clairvaux – you would know, were you at top
Of yonder crowning grace, its Belvedere –
Is situate in one angle-niche of three
At equidistance from Saint-Rambert – there
Behind you, and The Ravissante, beside –
There: steeple, steeple, and this Clairvaux-top,
(A sort of steeple) constitute a trine,
With not a tenement to break each side,
Two miles or so in length, if eye can judge.

Now, this is native land of miracle.
O why, why, why, from all recorded time,
Was miracle not wrought once, only once,
To help whoever wanted help indeed?
If on the day when Spring's green girlishness
Grew nubile and she trembled into May,
And our Miranda climbed to clasp the Spring
A-tiptoe o'er the sea, those wafts of warmth,
Those cloudlets scudding under the bare blue,
And all that new sun, that fresh hope about
His airy place of observation, – friend,
Feel with me that if just then, just for once,
Some angel, – such as the authentic pen
Yonder records a daily visitant
Of ploughman Claude, rheumatic in the joints,
And spinster Jeanne, with megrim troubled sore, –
If such an angel, with naught else to do,

Had taken station on the pinnacle
And simply said 'Léonce, look straight before!
Neither to right hand nor to left: for why?
Being a stupid soul, you want a guide
To turn the goodness in you to account
And make stupidity submit itself.
Go to Saint-Rambert! Straightway get such guide!
There stands a man of men. You, jeweller,
Must needs have heard how once the biggest block
Of diamond now in Europe lay exposed
'Mid specimens of stone and earth and ore,
On huckster's stall, – Navona names the Square,
And Rome the city for the incident, –
Labelled "quartz-crystal, price one halfpenny."
Haste and secure that ha'p'worth, on your life!
That man will read you rightly head to foot,
Mark the brown face of you, the bushy beard,
The breadth 'twixt shoulderblades, and through each black
Castilian orbit, see into your soul.
Talk to him for five minutes – nonsense, sense,
No matter what – describe your horse, your hound, –
Give your opinion of the policy
Of Monsieur Rouher, – will he succour Rome?
Your estimate of what may outcome be
From Ecumenical Assemblage there!
After which samples of intelligence,
Rapidly run through those events you call
Your past life, tell what once you tried to do,
What you intend on doing this next May!
There he stands, reads an English newspaper,
Stock-still, and now, again upon the move,
Paces the beach to taste the Spring, like you,
Since both are human beings in God's eye.
He will have understood you, I engage.
Endeavour, for your part, to understand
He knows more, and loves better, than the world
That never heard his name, and never may.
He will have recognized, ere breath be spent
And speech at end, how much that's good in man,
And generous, and self-devoting, makes
Monsieur Léonce Miranda worth his help;
While sounding to the bottom ignorance

Historical and philosophical
And moral and religious, all one couch
Of crassitude, a portent of its kind.
Then, just as he would pityingly teach
Your body to repair maltreatment, give
Advice that you should make those stumps to stir
With artificial hands of caoutchouc,
So would he soon supply your crippled soul
With crutches, from his own intelligence,
Able to help you onward in the path
Of rectitude whereto your face is set,
And counsel justice – to yourself, the first,
To your associate, very like a wife
Or something better, – to the world at large,
Friends, strangers, horses, hounds and Cousinry –
All which amount of justice will include
Justice to God. Go and consult his voice!'
Since angel would not say this simple truth,
What hinders that my heart relieve itself,
Milsand, who makest warm my wintry world,
And wise my heaven, if there we consort too?

Monsieur Léonce Miranda turned, alas,
Or was turned, by no angel, t' other way,
And got him guidance of The Ravissante.

Now, into the originals of faith,
Yours, mine, Miranda's, no inquiry here!
Of faith, as apprehended by mankind,
The causes, were they caught and catalogued,
Would too distract, too desperately foil
Inquirer. How may analyst reduce
Quantities to exact their opposites,
Value to zero, then bring zero back
To value of supreme preponderance
How substitute thing meant for thing expressed?
Detect the wire-thread through that fluffy silk
Men call their rope, their real compulsive power?
Suppose effected such anatomy,
And demonstration made of what belief
Has moved believer – were the consequence
Reward at all? would each man straight deducc,

From proved reality of cause, effect
Conformable – believe and unbelieve
According to your True thus disengaged
From all his heap of False called reason first?

No: hand once used to hold a soft thick twist,
Cannot now grope its way by wire alone:
Childhood may catch the knack, scarce Youth, not Age!
That's the reply rewards you. Just as well
Demonstrate to yon peasant in the blouse
That, had he justified the true intent
Of Nature who composed him thus and thus,
Weakly or strongly, here he would not stand
Struggling with uncongenial earth and sky,
But elsewhere tread the surface of the globe,
Since one meridian suits the faulty lungs,
Another bids the sluggish liver work.
'Here I was born, for better or for worse:
I did not choose a climate for myself;
Admit, my life were healthy, led elsewhere,'
(He answers) 'how am I to migrate, pray?'

Therefore the course to take is – spare your pains,
And trouble uselessly with discontent
Nor soul nor body, by parading proof
That neither haply had known ailment, placed
Precisely where the circumstance forbade
Their lot should fall to either of the pair.
But try and, what you find wrong, remedy,
Accepting the conditions: never ask
'How came you to be born here with those lungs,
That liver?' But bid asthma smoke a pipe,
Stramonium, just as if no Tropics were,
And ply with calomel the sluggish duct,
Nor taunt 'The born Norwegian breeds no bile!'
And as with body, so proceed with soul:
Nor less discerningly, where faith you found,
However foolish and fantastic, grudge
To play the doctor and amend mistake,
Because a wisdom were conceivable
Whence faith had sprung robust above disease.
Far beyond human help, that source of things!

Since, in the first stage, so to speak, – first stare
Of apprehension at the invisible, –
Begins divergency of mind from mind,
Superior from inferior: leave this first!
Little you change there! What comes afterward –
From apprehended thing, each inference
With practicality concerning life,
This you may test and try, confirm the right
Or contravene the wrong which reasons there.
The offspring of the sickly faith must prove
Sickly act also: stop a monster-birth!
When water's in the cup and not the cloud,
Then is the proper time for chemic test:
Belief permits your skill to operate
When, drop by drop condensed from misty heaven,
'Tis wrung out, lies a bowlful in the fleece.
How dew by spoonfuls came, let Gideon say:
What purpose water serves, your word or two
May teach him, should he fancy it lights fire.

Concerning, then, our vaporous Ravissante –
How fable first precipitated faith –
Silence you get upon such point from me.
But when I see come posting to the pair
At Clairvaux, for the cure of soul-disease,
This Father of the Mission, Parish-priest,
This Mother of the Convent, Nun I know –
They practise in that second stage of things;
They boast no fresh distillery of faith;
'Tis dogma in the bottle, bright and old,
They bring; and I pretend to pharmacy.
They undertake the cure with all my heart!
He trusts them, and they surely trust themselves.
I ask no better. Never mind the cause,
Fons et origo of the malady:
Apply the drug with courage! Here's our case.
Monsieur Léonce Miranda asks of God,
– May a man, living in illicit tie,
Continue, by connivance of the Church,
No matter what amends he please to make
Short of forthwith relinquishing the sin?
Physicians, what do you propose for cure?

Father and Mother of the Ravissante,
Read your own records, and you find prescribed
As follows, when a couple out of sorts
Rather than gravely suffering, sought your skill
And thereby got their health again. Perpend!

Two and a half good centuries ago,
Luc de la Maison Rouge, a nobleman
Of Claise (the river gives this country name),
And, just as noblewoman, Maude his wife,
Having been married many happy years
Spent in God's honour and man's service too,
Conceived, while yet in flower of youth and hope,
The project of departing each from each
Forever, and dissolving marriage-bonds
That both might enter a religious life.
Needing, before they came to such resolve,
Divine illumination, – course was clear, –
They visited your church in pilgrimage,
On Christmas morn: communicating straight,
They heard three Masses proper for the day,
'It is incredible with what effect' –
Quoth the Cistercian monk I copy from –
And, next day, came, again communicants,
Again heard Masses manifold, but now
With added thanks to Christ for special grace
And consolation granted: in the night,
Had been divorce from marriage, manifest
By signs and tokens. So, they made great gifts,
Left money for more Masses, and returned
Homeward rejoicing – he, to take the rules,
As Brother Dionysius, Capucin;
She, to become first postulant, then nun
According to the rules of Benedict,
Sister Scolastica: so ended they,
And so do I – not end nor yet commence
One note or comment. What was done was done.

Now, Father of the Mission, here's your case!
And, Mother of the Convent, here's its cure!
If separation was permissible,
And that decree of Christ 'What God hath joined

Let no man put asunder' nullified
Because a couple, blameless in the world,
Had the conceit that, still more blamelessly,
Out of the world, by breach of marriage-vow,
Their life was like to pass, – you oracles
Of God, – since holy Paul says such you are, –
Hesitate, not one moment, to pronounce
When questioned by the pair now needing help
'Each from the other go, you guilty ones,
Preliminary to your least approach
Nearer the Power that thus could strain a point
In favour of a pair of innocents
Who thought their wedded hands not clean enough
To touch and leave unsullied their souls' snow!
Are not your hands found filthy by the world,
Mere human law and custom? Not a step
Nearer till hands be washed and purified!'

What they did say is immaterial, since
Certainly it was nothing of the kind.
There was no washing hands of him (alack,
You take me? – in the figurative sense!),
But, somehow, gloves were drawn o'er dirt and all,
And practice with the Church procured thereby.
Seeing that, – all remonstrance proved in vain,
Persuasives tried and terrors put to use,
I nowise question, – still the guilty pair
Only embraced the closelier, obstinate, –
Father and Mother went from Clairvaux back
Their weary way, with heaviness of heart,
I grant you, but each palm well crossed with coin,
And nothing like a smutch perceptible.
Monsieur Léonce Miranda might compound
For sin? – no, surely! but by gifts – prepare
His soul the better for contrition, say!
Gift followed upon gift, at all events.
Good counsel was rejected, on one part:
Hard money, on the other – may we hope
Was unreflectingly consigned to purse?

Two years did this experiment engage
Monsieur Léonce Miranda: how, by gifts
To God and to God's poor, a man might stay
In sin and yet stave off sin's punishment.
No salve could be conceived more nicely mixed
For this man's nature: generosity, –
Susceptibility to human ills,
Corporeal, mental, – self-devotedness
Made up Miranda – whether strong or weak
Elsewhere, may be inquired another time.
In mercy he was strong, at all events.
Enough! he could not see a beast in pain,
Much less a man, without the will to aid;
And where the will was, oft the means were too,
Since that good bargain with the Cousinry.

The news flew fast about the countryside
That, with the kind man, it was ask and have;
And ask and have they did. To instance you: –
A mob of beggars at The Ravissante
Clung to his skirts one day, and cried 'We thirst!'
Forthwith he bade a cask of wine be broached
To satisfy all comers, till, dead-drunk
So satisfied, they strewed the holy place.
For this was grown religious and a rite:
Such slips of judgement, gifts irregular,
Showed but as spillings of the golden grist
On either side the hopper, through blind zeal;
Steadily the main stream went pouring on
From mill to mouth of sack – held wide and close
By Father of the Mission, Parish-priest,
And Mother of the Convent, Nun I know,
With such effect that, in the sequel, proof
Was tendered to the Court at Vire, last month,
That in these same two years, expenditure
At quiet Clairvaux rose to the amount
Of Forty Thousand English Pounds: whereof
A trifle went, no inappropriate close
Of bounty, to supply the Virgin's crown
With that stupendous jewel from New York,
Now blazing as befits the Star of Sea.

Such signs of grace, outward and visible,
I rather give you, for your sake and mine,
Than put in evidence the inward strife,
Spiritual effort to compound for fault
By payment of devotion – thank the phrase!
That payment was as punctual, do not doubt,
As its far easier fellow. Yesterday
I trudged the distance from The Ravissante
To Clairvaux, with my two feet: but our friend,
The more to edify the country-folk,
Was wont to make that journey on both knees.
'Maliciously perverted incident!'
Snarled the retort, when this was told at Vire:
'The man paid mere devotion as he passed,
Knelt decently at just each wayside shrine!'
Alas, my lawyer, I trudged yesterday –
On my two feet, and with both eyes wide ope, –
The distance, and could find no shrine at all!
According to his lights, I praise the man.

Enough! incessant was devotion, say –
With her, you know of, praying at his side.
Still, there be relaxations of the tense;
Or life indemnifies itself for strain,
Or finds its very strain grow feebleness.
Monsieur Léonce Miranda's days were passed
Much as of old, in simple work and play.
His first endeavour, on recovery
From that sad ineffectual sacrifice,
Had been to set about repairing loss:
Never admitting, loss was to repair.
No word at any time escaped his lips
– Betrayed a lurking presence, in his heart,
Of sorrow; no regret for mischief done –
Punishment suffered, he would rather say.
Good-tempered schoolboy-fashion, he preferred
To laugh away his flogging, fair price paid
For pleasure out of bounds: if needs must be,
Get pleasure and get flogged a second time!
A sullen subject would have nursed the scars
And made excuse, for throwing grammar by,
That bench was grown uneasy to the seat.

No: this poor fellow cheerfully got hands
Fit for his stumps, and what hands failed to do,
The other members did in their degree –
Unwonted service. With his mouth alone
He wrote, nay, painted pictures – think of that!
He played on a piano pedal-keyed,
Kicked out – if it was Bach's – good music thence.
He rode, that's readily conceivable,
But then he shot and never missed his bird,
With other feats as dexterous: I infer
He was not ignorant what hands are worth,
When he resolved on ruining his own.

So the two years passed somehow – who shall say
Foolishly, – as one estimates mankind,
The work they do, the play they leave undone? –
Two whole years spent in that experiment
I told you of, at Clairvaux all the time,
From April on to April: why that month
More than another, notable in life?
Does the awakening of the year arouse
Man to new projects, nerve him for fresh feats
Of what proves, for the most part of mankind
Playing or working, novel folly too?
At any rate, I see no slightest sign
Of folly (let me tell you in advance)
Nothing but wisdom meets me manifest
In the procedure of the Twentieth Day
Of April, 'Seventy, – folly's year in France.

It was delightful Spring, and out of doors
Temptation to adventure. Walk or ride?
There was a wild young horse to exercise,
And teach the way to go and pace to keep:
Monsieur Léonce Miranda chose to ride.
So, while they clapped soft saddle straight on back,
And bitted jaw to satisfaction, – since
The partner of his days must stay at home,
Teased by some trifling legacy of March
To throat or shoulder, – visit duly paid
And 'farewell' given and received again, –
As chamber-door considerately closed

Behind him, still five minutes were to spend.
How better, than by clearing, two and two,
The staircase-steps and coming out aloft
Upon the platform yonder (raise your eyes!)
And tasting, just as those two years before,
Spring's bright advance upon the tower a-top,
The feature of the front, the Belvedere?

Look at it for a moment while I breathe.

IV

Ready to hear the rest? How good you are!

Now for this Twentieth splendid day of Spring,
All in a tale, – sun, wind, sky, earth and sea, –
To bid man 'Up, be doing!' Mount the stair,
Monsieur Léonce Miranda mounts so brisk,
And look – ere his elastic foot arrive –
Your longest, far and wide, o'er fronting space.
Yon white streak – Havre lighthouse! Name and name,
How the mind runs from each to each relay,
Town after town, till Paris' self be touched,
Superlatively big with life and death
To all the world, that very day perhaps!
He who stepped out upon the platform here,
Pinnacled over the expanse, gave thought
Neither to Rouher nor Ollivier, Roon
Nor Bismarck, Emperor nor King, but just
To steeple, church, and shrine, The Ravissante!

He saw Her, whom myself saw, but when Spring
Was passing into Fall: not robed and crowned
As, thanks to him, and her you know about,
She stands at present; but She smiled the same.
Thither he turned – to never turn away.

He thought . . .

(Suppose I should prefer 'He said'?
Along with every act – and speech is act –
There go, a multitude impalpable
To ordinary human faculty,

The thoughts which give the act significance.
Who is a poet needs must apprehend
Alike both speech and thoughts which prompt to speak.
Part these, and thought withdraws to poetry:
Speech is reported in the newspaper.)

He said, then, probably no word at all,
But thought as follows – in a minute's space –
One particle of ore beats out such leaf!

'This Spring-morn I am forty-three years old:
In prime of life, perfection of estate
Bodily, mental, nay, material too, –
My whole of worldly fortunes reach their height.
Body and soul alike on eminence:
It is not probable I ever raise
Soul above standard by increase of worth,
Nor reasonably may expect to lift
Body beyond the present altitude.

'Behold me, Lady called The Ravissante!
Such as I am, I – gave myself to you
So long since, that I cannot say "I give."
All my belongings, what is summed in life,
I have submitted wholly – as man might,
At least, as *I* might, who am weak, not strong, –
Wholly, then, to your rule and governance,
So far as I had strength. My weakness was –
I felt a fascination, at each point
And pore of me, a Power as absolute
Claiming that soul should recognize her sway.
O you were no whit clearlier Queen, I see,
Throughout the life that rolls out ribbon-like
Its shot-silk length behind me, than the strange
Mystery – how shall I denominate
The unrobed One? Robed you go and crowned as well,
Named by the nations: she is hard to name,
Though you have spelt out certain characters
Obscure upon what fillet binds her brow,
Lust of the flesh, lust of the eye, life's pride.
"So call her, and contemn the enchantress!" – "Crush
The despot, and recover liberty!" –

Cried despot and enchantress at each ear.
You were conspicuous and pre-eminent,
Authoritative and imperial, – you
Spoke first, claimed homage: did I hesitate?
Born for no mastery, but servitude,
Men cannot serve two masters, says the Book;
Master should measure strength with master, then,
Before on servant is imposed a task.
You spoke first, promised best, and threatened most;
The other never threatened, promised, spoke
A single word, but, when your part was done,
Lifted a finger, and I, prostrate, knew
Films were about me, though you stood aloof
Smiling or frowning "Where is power like mine
To punish or reward thee? Rise, thou fool!
Will to be free, and, lo, I lift thee loose!"
Did I not will, and could I rise a whit?
Lay I, at any time, content to lie?
"To lie, at all events, brings pleasure: make
Amends by undemanded pain!" I said.
Did not you prompt me? "Purchase now by pain
Pleasure hereafter in the world to come!"
I could not pluck my heart out, as you bade
Unbidden, I burned off my hands at least.
My soul retained its treasure; but my purse
Lightened itself with much alacrity.
Well, where is the reward? what promised fruit
Of sacrifice in peace, content? what sense
Of added strength to bear or to forbear?
What influx of new light assists me now
Even to guess you recognize a gain
In what was loss enough to mortal me?
But she, the less authoritative voice,
Oh, how distinct enunciating, how
Plain dealing! Gain she gave was gain indeed!
That, you deny: that, you contemptuous call
Acorns, swine's food not man's meat! "Spurn the draff!"
Ay, but those life-tree apples I prefer,
Am I to die of hunger till they drop?
Husks keep flesh from starvation, anyhow.
Give those life-apples! – one, worth woods of oak,
Worth acorns by the wagon-load, – one shoot

Through heart and brain, assurance bright and brief
That you, my Lady, my own Ravissante,
Feel, through my famine, served and satisfied,
Own me, your starveling, soldier of a sort!
Your soldier! do I read my title clear
Even to call myself your friend, not foe?
What is the pact between us but a truce?
At best I shall have staved off enmity,
Obtained a respite, ransomed me from wrath.
I pay, instalment by instalment, life,
Earth's tribute-money, pleasures great and small,
Whereof should at the last one penny piece
Fall short, the whole heap becomes forfeiture.
You find in me deficient soldiership:
Want the whole life or none. I grudge that whole,
Because I am not sure of recompense:
Because I want faith. Whose the fault? I ask.
If insufficient faith have done thus much,
Contributed thus much of sacrifice,
More would move mountains, you are warrant. Well,
Grant, you, the grace, I give the gratitude!
And what were easier? "Ask and have" folk call
Miranda's method: "Have, nor need to ask!"
So do they formulate your quality
Superlative beyond my human grace.
The Ravissante, you ravish men away
From puny aches and petty pains, assuaged
By man's own art with small expenditure
Of pill or potion, unless, put to shame,
Nature is roused and sets things right herself.
Your miracles are grown our commonplace;
No day but pilgrim hobbles his last mile,
Kneels down and rises up, flings crutch away,
Or else appends it to the reverend heap
Beneath you, votive cripple-carpentry.
Some few meet failure – oh, they wanted faith,
And may betake themselves to La Salette,
Or seek Lourdes, so that hence the scandal limp!
The many get their grace and go their way
Rejoicing, with a tale to tell, – most like,
A staff to borrow, since the crutch is gone,

Should the first telling happen at my house,
And teller wet his whistle with my wine.
I tell this to a doctor and he laughs:
"Give me permission to cry – Out of bed,
You loth rheumatic sluggard! Cheat yon chair
Of laziness, its gouty occupant! –
You should see miracles performed. But now,
I give advice, and take as fee ten francs,
And do as much as does your Ravissante.
Send her that case of cancer to be cured
I have refused to treat for any fee,
Bring back my would-be patient sound and whole,
And see me laugh on t' other side my mouth!"
Can he be right, and are you hampered thus?
Such pettiness restricts a miracle
Wrought by the Great Physician, who hears prayer,
Visibly seated in your mother-lap!
He, out of nothing, made sky, earth, and sea,
And all that in them is – man, beast, bird, fish,
Down to this insect on my parapet.
Look how the marvel of a minim crawls!
Were I to kneel among the halt and maimed,
And pray "Who mad'st the insect with ten legs,
Make me one finger grow where ten were once!"
The very priests would thrust me out of church.
"What folly does the madman dare expect?
No faith obtains – in this late age, at least –
Such cure as that! We ease rheumatics, though!"

'Ay, bring the early ages back again,
What prodigy were unattainable?
I read your annals. Here came Louis Onze,
Gave thrice the sum he ever gave before
At one time, some three hundred crowns, to wit –
On pilgrimage to pray for – health, he found?
Did he? I do not read it in Commines.
Here sent poor joyous Marie-Antoinette
To thank you that a Dauphin dignified
Her motherhood – called Duke of Normandy
And Martyr of the Temple, much the same
As if no robe of hers had dressed you rich;

No silver lamps, she gave, illume your shrine!
Here, following example, fifty years
Ago, in gratitude for birth again
Of yet another destined King of France,
Did not the Duchess fashion with her hands,
And frame in gold and crystal, and present
A bouquet made of artificial flowers?
And was he King of France, and is not he
Still Count of Chambord?

'Such the days of faith,
And such their produce to encourage mine!
What now, if I too count without my host?
I too have given money, ornament,
And "artificial flowers" – which, when I plucked,
Seemed rooting at my heart and real enough:
What if I gain thereby nor health of mind,
Nor youth renewed which perished in its prime,
Burnt to a cinder 'twixt the red-hot bars,
Nor gain to see my second baby-hope
Of managing to live on terms with both
Opposing potentates, the Power and you,
Crowned with success? I dawdle out my days
In exile here at Clairvaux, with mock love,
That gives – while whispering "Would I dared refuse!" –
What the loud voice declares my heart's free gift:
Mock worship, mock superiority
O'er those I style the world's benighted ones,
That irreligious sort I pity so,
Dumas and even Hertford who is Duke.

'Impiety? Not if I know myself!
Not if you know the heart and soul I bare,
I bid you cut, hack, slash, anatomize,
Till peccant part be found and flung away!
Demonstrate where I need more faith! Describe
What act shall evidence sufficiency
Of faith, your warrant for such exercise
Of power, in my behalf, as all the world
Except poor praying me declares profuse?
Poor me? It is that world, not me alone,

That world which prates of fixed laws and the like,
I fain would save, poor world so ignorant!
And your part were – what easy miracle?
Oh, Lady, could I make your want like mine!'

Then his face grew one luminosity.

'Simple, sufficient! Happiness at height!
I solve the riddle, I persuade mankind.
I have been just the simpleton who stands –
Summoned to claim his patrimonial rights –
At shilly-shally, may he knock or no
At his own door in his own house and home
Whereof he holds the very title-deeds!
Here is my title to this property,
This power you hold for profit of myself
And all the world at need – which need is now!

'My title – let me hear who controverts!
Count Mailleville built yon church. Why did he so?
Because he found your image. How came that?
His shepherd told him that a certain sheep
Was wont to scratch with hoof and scrape with horn
At ground where once the Danes had razed a church.
Thither he went, and there he dug, and thence
He disinterred the image he conveyed
In pomp to Londres yonder, his domain.
You liked the old place better than the new.
The Count might surely have divined as much:
He did not; someone might have spoke a word:
No one did. A mere dream had warned enough
That back again in pomp you best were borne:
No dream warned, and no need of convoy was;
An angel caught you up and clapped you down –
No mighty task, you stand one *mètre* high,
And people carry you about at times.
Why, then, did you despise the simple course?
Because you are the Queen of Angels: when
You front us in a picture, there flock they,
Angels around you, here and everywhere.

'Therefore, to prove indubitable faith,
Those angels that acknowledge you their queen,
I summon them to bear me to your feet
From Clairvaux through the air, an easy trip!
Faith without flaw! I trust your potency,
Benevolence, your will to save the world –
By such a simplest of procedures, too!
Not even by affording angel-help,
Unless it please you: there's a simpler mode:
Only suspend the law of gravity,
And, while at back, permitted to propel,
The air helps onwards, let the air in front
Cease to oppose my passage through the midst!

'Thus I bestride the railing, leg o'er leg,
Thus, lo, I stand, a single inch away,
At dizzy edge of death, – no touch of fear,
As safe on tower above as turf below!
Your smile enswathes me in beatitude,
You lift along the votary – who vaults,
Who, in the twinkling of an eye, revives,
Dropt safely in the space before the church –
How crowded, since this morn is market-day!
I shall not need to speak. The news will run
Like wild-fire. "Thousands saw Miranda's flight!"
'Tis telegraphed to Paris in a trice.
The Boulevard is one buzz "Do you believe?
Well, this time, thousands saw Miranda's flight:
You know him, goldsmith in the Place Vendôme."
In goes the Empress to the Emperor:
"Now – will you hesitate to make disgorge
Your wicked King of Italy his gains,
Give the Legations to the Pope once more?"
Which done, – why, grace goes back to operate,
They themselves set a good example first,
Resign the empire twenty years usurped,
And Henry, the Desired One, reigns o'er France!
Regenerated France makes all things new!
My house no longer stands on Quai Rousseau
But Quai rechristened Alacoque: a quai
Where Renan burns his book, and Veuillot burns
Renan beside, since Veuillot rules the roast,

Re-edits now indeed "The Universe."
O blessing, O superlatively big
With blessedness beyond all blessing dreamed
By man! for just that promise has effect,
"Old things shall pass away and all be new!"
Then, for a culminating mercy-feat,
Wherefore should I dare dream impossible
That I too have my portion in the change?
My past with all its sorrow, sin and shame,
Becomes a blank, a nothing! There she stands,
Clara de Millefleurs, all deodorized,
Twenty years' stain wiped off her innocence!
There never was Muhlhausen, nor at all
Duke Hertford: naught that was, remains, except
The beauty, – yes, the beauty is unchanged!
Well, and the soul too, that must keep the same!
And so the trembling little virgin hand
Melts into mine, that's back again, of course!
– Think not I care about my poor old self!
I only want my hand for that one use,
To take her hand, and say "I marry you –
Men, women, angels, you behold my wife!
There is no secret, nothing wicked here,
Nothing she does not wish the world to know!"
None of your married women have the right
To mutter "Yes, indeed, she beats us all
In beauty, – but our lives are pure at least!"
Bear witness, for our marriage is no thing
Done in a corner! 'Tis the Ravissante
Repairs the wrong of Paris. See, She smiles,
She beckons, She bids "Hither, both of you!"
And may we kneel? And will you bless us both?
And may I worship you, and yet love her?
Then!' –
                    A sublime spring from the balustrade
About the tower so often talked about,
A flash in middle air, and stone-dead lay
Monsieur Léonce Miranda on the turf.

A gardener who watched, at work the while
Dibbling a flower-bed for geranium-shoots,
Saw the catastrophe, and, straightening back,

Stood up and shook his brows. 'Poor soul, poor soul!
Just what I prophesied the end would be!
Ugh – the Red Night-cap!' (as he raised the head)
'This must be what he meant by those strange words
While I was weeding larkspurs yesterday,
"Angels would take him!" Mad!'

No! sane, I say.
Such being the conditions of his life,
Such end of life was not irrational.
Hold a belief, you only half-believe,
With all-momentous issues either way, –
And I advise you imitate this leap,
Put faith to proof, be cured or killed at once!
Call you men, killed through cutting cancer out,
The worse for such an act of bravery?
That's more than *I* know. In my estimate,
Better lie prostrate on his turf at peace,
Than, wistful, eye, from out the tent, the tower,
Racked with a doubt 'Will going on bare knees
All the way to The Ravissante and back,
Saying my Ave Mary all the time,
Somewhat excuse if I postpone my march?
– Make due amends for that one kiss I gave
In gratitude to her who held me out
Superior Fricquot's sermon, hot from press,
A-spread with hands so sinful yet so smooth?'

And now, sincerely do I pray she stand,
Clara, with interposing sweep of robe,
Between us and this horror! Any screen
Turns white by contrast with the tragic pall;
And her dubiety distracts at least,
As well as snow, from such decided black.
With womanhood, at least, we have to do:
Ending with Clara – is the word too kind?

Let pass the shock! There's poignancy enough
When what one parted with, a minute since,
Alive and happy, is returned a wreck –
All that was, all that seemed about to be,
Razed out and ruined now for evermore,

Because a straw descended on this scale
Rather than that, made death o'erbalance life.
But think of cage-mates in captivity,
Inured to day-long, night-long vigilance
Each of the other's tread and angry turn
If behind prison-bars the jailer knocked:
These whom society shut out, and thus
Penned in, to settle down and regulate
By the strange law, the solitary life –
When death divorces such a fellowship,
Theirs may pair off with that prodigious woe
Imagined of a ghastly brotherhood –
One watcher left in lighthouse out at sea
With leagues of surf between the land and him
Alive with his dead partner on the rock;
One galley-slave, whom curse and blow compel
To labour on, ply oar – beside his chain,
Encumbered with a corpse-companion now.
Such these: although, no prisoners, self-entrenched
They kept the world off from their barricade.

Memory, gratitude was poignant, sure,
Though pride brought consolation of a kind.
Twenty years long had Clara been – of whom
The rival, nay, the victor, past dispute?
What if in turn The Ravissante at length
Proved victor – which was doubtful – anyhow,
Here lay the inconstant with, conspicuous too,
The fruit of his good fortune!

'Has he gained
By leaving me?' she might soliloquize:
'All love could do, I did for him. I learned
By heart his nature, what he loved and loathed,
Leaned to with liking, turned from with distaste.
No matter what his least velleity,
I was determined he should want no wish,
And in conformity administered
To his requirement; most of joy I mixed
With least of sorrow in life's daily draught,
Twenty years long, life's proper average.
And when he got to quarrel with my cup,

Would needs outsweeten honey, and discard
That gall-drop we require lest nectar cloy, –
I did not call him fool, and vex my friend,
But quietly allowed experiment,
Encouraged him to spice his drink, and now
Grate *lignum vitae*, now bruise so-called grains
Of Paradise, and pour now, for perfume,
Distilment rare, the rose of Jericho,
Holy-thorn, passion-flower, and what know I?
Till beverage obtained the fancied smack.
'Twas wild-flower-wine that neither helped nor harmed
Who sipped and held it for restorative –
What harm? But here has he been through the hedge
Straying in search of simples, while my back
Was turned a minute, and he finds a prize,
Monkshood and belladonna! O my child,
My truant little boy, despite the beard,
The body two feet broad and six feet long,
And what the calendar counts middle age –
You wanted, did you, to enjoy a flight?
Why not have taken into confidence
Me, that was mother to you? – never mind
What mock disguise of mistress held you mine!
Had you come laughing, crying, with request,
"Make me fly, mother!" I had run upstairs
And held you tight the while I danced you high
In air from tower-top, singing "Off we go
(On pilgrimage to Lourdes some day next month)
And swift we soar (to Rome with Peter-pence)
And low we light (at Paris where we pick
Another jewel from our store of stones
And send it for a present to the Pope)!"
So, dropt indeed you were, but on my knees,
Rolling and crowing, not a whit the worse
For journey to your Ravissante and back.
Now, no more Clairvaux – which I made you build,
And think an inspiration of your own –
No more fine house, trim garden, pretty park,
Nothing I used to busy you about,
And make believe you worked for my surprise!
What weariness to me will work become
Now that I need not seem surprised again!

This boudoir, for example, with the doves
(My stupid maid has damaged, dusting one)
Embossed in stucco o'er the looking-glass
Beside the toilet-table! dear – dear me!'

Here she looked up from her absorbing grief,
And round her, crow-like grouped, the Cousinry,
(She grew aware) sat witnesses at watch.
For, two days had elapsed since fate befell
The courser in the meadow, stretched so stark.
They did not cluster on the tree-tops, close
Their sooty ranks, caw and confabulate
For nothing: but, like calm determined crows,
They came to take possession of their corpse.
And who shall blame them? Had not they the right?

One spoke. 'They would be gentle, not austere.
They understood and were compassionate.
Madame Muhlhausen lay too abject now
For aught but the sincerest pity; still,
Since plain speech salves the wound it seems to make,
They must speak plainly – circumstances spoke!
Sin had conceived and brought forth death indeed.
As the commencement so the close of things:
Just what might be expected all along!
Monsieur Léonce Miranda launched his youth
Into a cesspool of debauchery,
And if he thence emerged all dripping slime,
Where was the change except from thin to thick,
One warm rich mud-bath, Madame? – you, in place
Of Paris-drainage and distilment, you
He never needed budge from, boiled to rags!
True, some good instinct left the natural man,
Some touch of that deep dye wherewith imbued
By education, in his happier day,
The hopeful offspring of high parentage
Was fleece-marked moral and religious sheep, –
Some ruddle, faint remainder, (we admit)
Stuck to Miranda, rubbed he ne'er so rude
Against the goatly coarseness: to the last,
Moral he styled himself, religious too!
Which means – what ineradicable good

You found, you never left till good's self proved
Perversion and distortion, nursed to growth
So monstrous, that the tree-stock, dead and dry,
Were seemlier far than such a heap grotesque
Of fungous flourishing excrescence. Here
Sap-like affection, meant for family,
Stole off to feed one sucker fat – yourself;
While branchage, trained religiously aloft
To rear its head in reverence to the sun,
Was pulled down earthward, pegged and picketed,
By topiary contrivance, till the tree
Became an arbour where, at vulgar ease,
Sat superstition grinning through the loops.
Still, nature is too strong or else too weak
For cockney treatment: either, tree springs back
To pristine shape, or else degraded droops,
And turns to touchwood at the heart. So here –
Body and mind, at last the man gave way.
His body – there it lies, what part was left
Unmutilated! for, the strife commenced
Two years ago, when, both hands burnt to ash,
– A branch broke loose, by loss of what choice twigs!
As for his mind – behold our register
Of all its moods, from the incipient mad,
Nay, mere erratic, to the stark insane,
Absolute idiocy or what is worse!
All have we catalogued – extravagance
In worldly matters, luxury absurd,
And zeal as crazed in its expenditure
Of nonsense called devotion. Don't we know
– We Cousins, bound in duty to our kin, –
What mummeries were practised by you two
At Clairvaux? Not a servant got discharge
But came and told his grievance, testified
To acts which turn religion to a farce.
And as the private mock, so patent – see –
The public scandal! Ask the neighbourhood –
Or rather, since we asked them long ago,
Read what they answer, depositions down,
Signed, sealed and sworn to! Brief, the man was mad.
We are his heirs and claim our heritage.
Madame Muhlhausen, – whom good taste forbids

We qualify as do these documents, –
Fear not lest justice stifle mercy's prayer!
True, had you lent a willing ear at first,
Had you obeyed our call two years ago,
Restrained a certain insolence of eye,
A volubility of tongue, that time,
Your prospects had been none the worse, perhaps.
Still, fear not but a decent competence
Shall smooth the way for your declining age!
What we propose, then ...'

Clara dried her eyes,
Sat up, surveyed the consistory, spoke
After due pause, with something of a smile.

'Gentlemen, kinsfolk of my friend defunct,
In thus addressing me – of all the world! –
You much misapprehend what part I play.
I claim no property you speak about.
You might as well address the park-keeper,
Harangue him on some plan advisable
For covering the park with cottage-plots.
He is the servant, no proprietor,
His business is to see the sward kept trim,
Untrespassed over by the indiscreet:
Beyond that, he refers you to myself –
Another servant of another kind –
Who again – quite as limited in act –
Refer you, with your projects, – can I else?
To who in mastery is ultimate,
The Church. The Church is sole administrant,
Since sole possessor of what worldly wealth
Monsieur Léonce Miranda late possessed.
Often enough has he attempted, nay,
Forced me, well-nigh, to occupy the post
You seemingly suppose I fill, – receive
As gift the wealth entrusted me as grace.
This – for quite other reasons than appear
So cogent to your perspicacity –
This I refused; and, firm as you could wish,
Still was my answer "We two understand
Each one the other. I am intimate

– As how can be mere fools and knaves – or, say,
Even your Cousins? – with your love to me,
Devotion to the Church. Would Providence
Appoint, and make me certain of the same,
That I survive you (which is little like,
Seeing you hardly overpass my age
And more than match me in abundant health)
In such case, certainly I would accept
Your bounty: better I than alien hearts
Should execute your planned benevolence
To man, your proposed largess to the Church.
But though I be survivor, – weakly frame,
With only woman's wit to make amends, –
When I shall die, or while I am alive,
Cannot you figure me an easy mark
For hypocritical rapacity,
Kith, kin and generation, couching low
Ever on the alert to pounce on prey?
Far be it I should say they profited
By that first frenzy-fit themselves induced, –
Cold-blooded scenical buffoons at sport
With horror and damnation o'er a grave:
That were too shocking – I absolve them there!
Nor did they seize the moment of your swoon
To rifle pocket, wring a paper thence,
Their Cousinly dictation, and enrich
Thereby each mother's son as heart could wish,
Had nobody supplied a codicil.
But when the pain, poor friend! had prostrated
Your body, though your soul was right once more,
I fear they turned your weakness to account!
Why else to me, who agonizing watched,
Sneak, cap in hand, now bribe me to forsake
My maimed Léonce, now bully, cap on head,
The impudent pretension to assuage
Such sorrows as demanded Cousins' care? –
For you rejected, hated, fled me, far
In foreign lands you laughed at me! – they judged.
And, think you, will the unkind ones hesitate
To try conclusions with my helplessness, –
To pounce on and misuse your derelict,
Helped by advantage that bereavement lends

Folk, who, while yet you lived, played tricks like these?
You only have to die, and they detect,
In all you said and did, insanity!
Your faith was fetish-worship, your regard
For Christ's prime precept which endows the poor
And strips the rich, a craze from first to last!
They so would limn your likeness, paint your life,
That if it ended by some accident, –
For instance, if, attempting to arrange
The plants below that dangerous Belvedere
I cannot warn you from sufficiently,
You lost your balance and fell headlong – fine
Occasion, such, for crying *Suicide!*
Non compos mentis, naturally next,
Hands over Clairvaux to a Cousin-tribe
Who nor like me nor love The Ravissante:
Therefore be ruled by both! Life-interest
In Clairvaux, – conservation, guardianship
Of earthly good for heavenly purpose, – give
Such and no other proof of confidence!
Let Clara represent the Ravissante!"
– To whom accordingly, he then and there
Bequeathed each stick and stone, by testament
In holograph, mouth managing the quill:
Go, see the same in Londres, if you doubt!'

Then smile grew laugh, as sudden up she stood
And out she spoke: intemperate the speech!

'And now, sirs, for your special courtesy,
Your candle held up to the character
Of Lucie Steiner, whom you qualify
As coming short of perfect womanhood.
Yes, kindly critics, truth for once you tell!
True is it that through childhood, poverty,
Sloth, pressure of temptation, I succumbed,
And, ere I found what honour meant, lost mine.
So was the sheep lost, which the Shepherd found
And never lost again. My friend found me;
Or better say, the Shepherd found us both –
Since he, my friend, was much in the same mire
When first we made acquaintance. Each helped each, –

A two-fold extrication from the slough;
And, saving me, he saved himself. Since then,
Unsmirched we kept our cleanliness of coat.
It is his perfect constancy, you call
My friend's main fault – he never left his love!
While as for me, I dare your worst, impute
One breach of loving bond, these twenty years,
To me whom only cobwebs bound, you count!
"He was religiously disposed in youth!"
That may be, though we did not meet at church.
Under my teaching did he, like you scamps,
Become Voltairian – fools who mock his faith?
"Infirm of body!" I am silent there:
Even yourselves acknowledge service done,
Whatever motive your own souls supply
As inspiration. Love made labour light.'

Then laugh grew frown, and frown grew terrible.
Do recollect what sort of person shrieked –
'Such was I, saint or sinner, what you please:
And who is it casts stone at me but you?
By your own showing, sirs, you bought and sold,
Took what advantage bargain promised bag,
Abundantly did business, and with whom?
The man whom you pronounce imbecile, push
Indignantly aside if he presume
To settle his affairs like other folk!
How is it you have stepped into his shoes
And stand there, bold as brass, "Miranda, late,
Now, Firm-Miranda"? Sane, he signed away
That little birthright, did he? Hence to trade!
I know and he knew who 'twas dipped and ducked,
Trucked and played the parasite in vain,
As now one, now the other, here you cringed,
Were feasted, took our presents, you – those drops
Just for your wife's adornment! you – that spray
Exactly suiting, as most diamonds would,
Your daughter on her marriage! No word then
Of somebody the wanton! Hence, I say,
Subscribers to the *Siècle*, every snob –
For here the post brings me the *Univers*!
Home and make money in the Place Vendôme,

Sully yourselves no longer by my sight,
And, when next Schneider wants a new *parure*,
Be careful lest you stick there by mischance
That stone beyond compare entrusted you
To kindle faith with, when, Miranda's gift,
Crowning the very crown, the Ravissante
Shall claim it! As to Clairvaux – talk to Her!
She answers by the Chapter of Raimbaux!'
Vituperative, truly! All this wrath
Because the man's relations thought him mad!
Whereat, I hope you see the Cousinry
Turn each to other, blankly dolorous,
Consult a moment, more by shrug and shrug
Than mere man's language, – finally conclude
To leave the reprobate untroubled now
In her unholy triumph, till the Law
Shall right the injured ones; for gentlemen
Allow the female sex, this sort at least,
Its privilege. So, simply 'Cockatrice!' –
'Jezebel!' – 'Queen of the Camellias!' – cried
Cousin to cousin, as yon hinge a-creak
Shut out the party, and the gate returned
To custody of Clairvaux. 'Pretty place!
What say you, when it proves our property,
To trying a concurrence with La Roche,
And laying down a rival oyster-bed?
Where the park ends, the sea begins, you know.'
So took they comfort till they came to Vire.

But I would linger, fain to snatch a look
At Clara as she stands in pride of place,
Somewhat more satisfying than my glance
So furtive, so near futile, yesterday,
Because one must be courteous. Of the masks
That figure in this little history,
She only has a claim to my respect,
And one-eyed, in her French phrase, rules the blind.
Miranda hardly did his best with life:
He might have opened eye, exerted brain,
Attained conception as to right and law
In certain points respecting intercourse
Of man with woman – love, one likes to say;

Which knowledge had dealt rudely with the claim
Of Clara to play representative
And from perdition rescue soul, forsooth!
Also, the sense of him should have sufficed
For building up some better theory
Of how God operates in heaven and earth,
Than would establish Him participant
In doings yonder at the Ravissante.
The heart was wise according to its lights
And limits; but the head refused more sun,
And shrank into its mew and craved less space.
Clara, I hold the happier specimen, –
It may be, through that artist-preference
For work complete, inferiorly proposed,
To incompletion, though it aim aright.
Morally, no! Aspire, break bounds! I say,
Endeavour to be good, and better still,
And best! Success is naught, endeavour's all.
But intellect adjusts the means to ends,
Tries the low thing, and leaves it done, at least;
No prejudice to high thing, intellect
Would do and will do, only give the means.
Miranda, in my picture-gallery,
Presents a Blake; be Clara – Meissonier!
Merely considered so by artist, mind!
For, break through Art and rise to poetry,
Being Art to tremble nearer, touch enough
The verge of vastness to inform our soul
What orb makes transit through the dark above,
And there's the triumph! – there the incomplete,
More than completion, matches the immense, –
Then, Michelagnolo against the world!
With this proviso, let me study her
Approvingly, the finished little piece!
Born, bred, with just one instinct, – that of growth, –
Her quality was, caterpillar-like,
To all-unerringly select a leaf
And without intermission feed her fill,
Become the Painted-peacock, or belike
The Brimstone-wing, when time of year should suit;
And 'tis a sign (say entomologists)

Of sickness, when the creature stops its meal
One minute, either to look up at heaven,
Or turn aside for change of aliment.
No doubt there was a certain ugliness
In the beginning, as the grub grew worm:
She could not find the proper plant at once,
But crawled and fumbled through a whole parterre.
Husband Muhlhausen served for stuff not long:
Then came confusion of the slimy track
From London, 'where she gave the tone awhile,'
To Paris: let the stalks start up again,
Now she is off them, all the greener they!
But, settled on Miranda, how she sucked,
Assimilated juices, took the tint,
Mimicked the form and texture of her food!
Was he for pastime? Who so frolic-fond
As Clara? Had he a devotion-fit?
Clara grew serious with like qualm, be sure!
In health and strength he, – healthy too and strong,
She danced, rode, drove, took pistol-practice, fished,
Nay, 'managed sea-skiff with consummate skill.'
In pain and weakness, he, – she patient watched
And wiled the slow drip-dropping hours away.
She bound again the broken self-respect,
She picked out the true meaning from mistake,
Praised effort in each stumble, laughed 'Well-climbed!'
When others groaned 'None ever grovelled so!'
'Rise, you have gained experience!' was her word:
'Lie satisfied, the ground is just your place!'
They thought appropriate counsel. 'Live, not die,
And take my full life to eke out your own:
That shall repay me and with interest!
Write! – is your mouth not clever as my hand?
Paint! – the last Exposition warrants me,
Plenty of people must ply brush with toes.
And as for music – look, what folk nickname
A lyre, those ancients played to ravishment, –
Over the *pendule*, see, Apollo grasps
A three-stringed gimcrack which no Liszt could coax
Such music from as jew's-harp makes today!
Do your endeavour like a man, and leave

The rest to "fortune who assists the bold" –
Learn, you, the Latin which you taught me first,
You clever creature – clever, yes, I say!'

If he smiled 'Let us love, love's wrong comes right,
Shows reason last of all! Necessity
Must meanwhile serve for plea – so, mind not much
Old Fricquot's menace!' – back she smiled 'Who minds?'
If he sighed 'Ah, but She is strict, they say,
For all Her mercy at the Ravissante,
She scarce will be put off so!' – straight a sigh
Returned 'My lace must go to trim Her gown!'
I nowise doubt she inwardly believed
Smiling and sighing had the same effect
Upon the venerated image. What
She did believe in, I as little doubt,
Was – Clara's self's own birthright to sustain
Existence, grow from grub to butterfly,
Upon unlimited Miranda-leaf;
In which prime article of faith confirmed,
According to capacity, she fed
On and on till the leaf was eaten up
That April morning. Even then, I praise
Her forethought which prevented leafless stalk
Bestowing any hoarded succulence
On earwig and blackbeetle squat beneath
Clairvaux, that stalk whereto her hermitage
She tacked by golden throw of silk, so fine,
So anything but feeble, that her sleep
Inside it, through last winter, two years long,
Recked little of the storm and strife without.
'But – loved him?' Friend, I do not praise her love!
True love works never for the loved one so,
Nor spares skin-surface, smoothening truth away.
Love bids touch truth, endure truth, and embrace
Truth, though, embracing truth, love crush itself.
'Worship not me but God!' the angels urge:
That is love's grandeur: still, in pettier love
The nice eye can distinguish grade and grade.
Shall mine degrade the velvet green and puce
Of caterpillar, palmer-worm – or what –

Ball in and out of ball, each ball with brush
Of Venus' eye-fringe round the turquoise egg
That nestles soft, – compare such paragon
With any scarabaeus of the brood
Which, born to fly, keeps wing in wing-case, walks
Persistently a-trundling dung on earth?
Egypt may venerate such hierophants,
Not I – the couple yonder, Father Priest
And Mother Nun, who came and went and came,
Beset this Clairvaux, trundled money-muck
To midden and the main heap oft enough,
But never bade unshut from sheath the gauze,
Nor showed that, who would fly, must let fall filth,
And warn 'Your jewel, brother, is a blotch:
Sister, your lace trails ordure! Leave your sins,
And so best gift with Crown and grace with Robe!'

The superstition is extinct, you hope?
It were, with my good will! Suppose it so,
Bethink you likewise of the latest use
Whereto a Night-cap is convertible,
And draw your very thickest, thread and thrum,
O'er such a decomposing face of things,
Once so alive, it seemed immortal too!

This happened two years since. The Cousinry
Returned to Paris, called in help from Law,
And in due form proceeded to dispute
Monsieur Léonce Miranda's competence,
Being insane, to make a valid Will.

Much testimony volunteered itself;
The issue hardly could be doubtful – but
For that sad 'Seventy which must intervene,
Provide poor France with other work to mind
Than settling lawsuits, even for the sake
Of such a party as the Ravissante.
It only was this Summer that the case
Could come and be disposed of, two weeks since,
At Vire – Tribunal Civil – Chamber First.

Here, issued with all regularity,
I hold the judgement – just, inevitable,
Nowise to be contested by what few
Can judge the judges; sum and substance, thus –

'Inasmuch as we find, the Cousinry,
During that very period when they take
Monsieur Léonce Miranda for stark mad,
Considered him to be quite sane enough
For doing much important business with –
Nor showed suspicion of his competence
Until, by turning of the tables, loss
Instead of gain accrued to them thereby, –
Plea of incompetence we set aside.

– 'The rather, that the dispositions, sought
To be impugned, are natural and right,
Nor jar with any reasonable claim
Of kindred, friendship or acquaintance here.
Nobody is despoiled, none overlooked;
Since the testator leaves his property
To just that person whom, of all the world,
He counted he was most indebted to.
In mere discharge, then, of conspicuous debt,
Madame Muhlhausen has priority,
Enjoys the usufruct of Clairvaux.

'Next,
Such debt discharged, such life determining,
Such earthly interest provided for,
Monsieur Léonce Miranda may bequeath,
In absence of more fit recipient, fund
And usufruct together to the Church
Whereof he was a special devotee.

'– Which disposition, being consonant
With a long series of such acts and deeds
Notorious in his life-time, needs must stand,
Unprejudiced by eccentricity
Nowise amounting to distemper: since,
In every instance signalized as such,
We recognize no overleaping bounds,

No straying out of the permissible:
Duty to the Religion of the Land, –
Neither excessive nor inordinate.

'The minor accusations are dismissed;
They prove mere freak and fancy, boyish mood
In age mature of simple kindly man.
Exuberant in generosities
To all the world: no fact confirms the fear
He meditated mischief to himself
That morning when he met the accident
Which ended fatally. The case is closed.'

How otherwise? So, when I grazed the skirts,
And had the glimpse of who made, yesterday, –
Woman and retinue of goats and sheep, –
The sombre path one whiteness, vision-like,
As out of gate, and in at gate again,
They wavered, – she was lady there for life:
And, after life – I hope, a white success
Of some sort, wheresoever life resume
School interrupted by vacation – death;
Seeing that home she goes with prize in hand,
Confirmed the Châtelaine of Clairvaux.

True,
Such prize fades soon to insignificance.
Though she have eaten her Miranda up,
And spun a cradle-cone through which she pricks
Her passage, and proves Peacock-butterfly
This Autumn – wait a little week of cold!
Peacock and death's-head-moth end much the same.
And could she still continue spinning, – sure,
Cradle would soon crave shroud for substitute,
And o'er this life of hers distaste would drop
Red-cotton-Night-cap-wise.

How say you, friend?
Have I redeemed my promise? Smile assent
Through the dark Winter-gloom between us both!

Already, months ago and miles away,
I just as good as told you, in a flash,
The while we paced the sands before my house,
All this poor story – truth and nothing else.
Accept that moment's flashing, amplified,
Impalpability reduced to speech,
Conception proved by birth, – no other change!
Can what Saint-Rambert flashed me in a thought,
Good gloomy London make a poem of?
Such ought to be whatever dares precede,
Play ruddy herald-star to your white blaze
About to bring us day. How fail imbibe
Some foretaste of effulgence? Sun shall wax,
And star shall wane: what matter, so star tell
The drowsy world to start awake, rub eyes,
And stand all ready for morn's joy a-blush?

23 January 1873

Aristophanes' Apology: including a Transcript from Euripides: being the Last Adventure of Balaustion

PERSONS IN THE
TRANSCRIBED PLAY OF 'HERAKLES'

Amphitruon
Megara
Lukos
Herakles
Iris
Lutta (Madness)
Messenger
Theseus
Choros of Aged Thebans

οὐκ ἔσθω κενέβρει᾽· ὁπόταν δὲ θύῃς τι, κάλει με.

I eat no carrion; when you sacrifice
Some cleanly creature – call me for a slice!

Aristophanes' Apology

Wind, wave, and bark, bear Euthukles and me,
Balaustion, from – not sorrow but despair,
Not memory but the present and its pang!
Athenai, live thou hearted in my heart:
Never, while I live, may I see thee more,
Never again may these repugnant orbs
Ache themselves blind before the hideous pomp,
The ghastly mirth which mocked thine overthrow
– Death's entry, Haides' outrage!
Doomed to die, –
Fire should have flung a passion of embrace
About thee till, resplendently inarmed,
(Temple by temple folded to his breast,
All thy white wonder fainting out in ash)
Lightly some vaporous sigh of soul escaped,
And so the Immortals bade Athenai back!
Or earth might sunder and absorb thee, save,
Buried below Olumpos and its gods,
Akropolis to dominate her realm
For Koré, and console the ghosts; or, sea,
What if thy watery plural vastitude,
Rolling unanimous advance, had rushed,
Might upon might, a moment, – stood, one stare,
Sea-face to city-face, thy glaucous wave
Glassing that marbled last magnificence, –
Till fate's pale tremulous foam-flower tipped the grey,
And when wave broke and overswarmed and, sucked
To bounds back, multitudinously ceased,
Let land again breathe unconfused with sea,
Attiké was, Athenai was not now!

Such end I could have borne, for I had shared.
But this which, glanced at, aches within my orbs
To blinding, – bear me thence, bark, wind and wave!
Me, Euthukles, and, hearted in each heart,
Athenai, undisgraced as Pallas' self,
Bear to my birthplace, Helios' island-bride,
Zeus' darling: thither speed us, homeward-bound.

Wafted already twelve hours' sail away
From horror, nearer by one sunset Rhodes!

Why should despair be? Since, distinct above
Man's wickedness and folly, flies the wind
And floats the cloud, free transport for our soul
Out of its fleshly durance dim and low, –
Since disembodied soul anticipates
(Thought-borne as now, in rapturous unrestraint)
Above all crowding, crystal silentness,
Above all noise, a silver solitude: –
Surely, where thought so bears soul, soul in time
May permanently bide, 'assert the wise,'
There live in peace, there work in hope once more –
O nothing doubt, Philemon! Greed and strife,
Hatred and cark and care, what place have they
In yon blue liberality of heaven?
How the sea helps! How rose-smit earth will rise
Breast-high thence, some bright morning, and be Rhodes!
Heaven, earth and sea, my warrant – in their name,
Believe – o'er falsehood, truth is surely sphered,
O'er ugliness beams beauty, o'er this world
Extends that realm where, 'as the wise assert,'
Philemon, thou shalt see Euripides
Clearer than mortal sense perceived the man!

A sunset nearer Rhodes, by twelve hours' sweep
Of surge secured from horror? Rather say,
Quieted out of weakness into strength.
I dare invite, survey the scene my sense
Staggered to apprehend: for, disinvolved
From the mere outside anguish and contempt,
Slowly a justice centred in a doom
Reveals itself. Ay, pride succumbed to pride,
Oppression met the oppressor and was matched.
Athenai's vaunt braved Sparté's violence
Till, in the shock, prone fell Peiraius, low
Rampart and bulwark lay, as, – timing stroke
Of hammer, axe, and beam hoist, poised and swung, –
The very flute-girls blew their laughing best,
In dance about the conqueror while he bade
Music and merriment help enginery

Batter down, break to pieces all the trust
Of citizens once, slaves now. See what walls
Play substitute for the long double range
Themistoklean, heralding a guest
From harbour on to citadel! Each side
Their senseless walls demolished stone by stone,
See, – outer walls as stonelike, – heads and hearts, –
Athenai's terror-stricken populace!
Prattlers, tongue-tied in crouching abjectness, –
Braggarts, who wring hands wont to flourish swords –
Sophist and rhetorician, demagogue,
(Argument dumb, authority a jest)
Dikast and heliast, pleader, litigant,
Quack-priest, sham-prophecy-retailer, scout
O' the customs, sycophant, whate'er the style,
Altar-scrap-snatcher, pimp and parasite, –
Rivalities at truce now each with each,
Stupefied mud-banks, – such an use they serve!
While the one order which performs exact
To promise, functions faithful last as first,
What is it but the city's lyric troop,
Chantress and psaltress, flute-girl, dancing-girl?
Athenai's harlotry takes laughing care
Their patron miss no pipings, late she loved,
But deathward tread at least the kordax-step.

Die then, who pulled such glory on your heads!
There let it grind to powder! Perikles!
The living are the dead now: death be life!
Why should the sunset yonder waste its wealth?
Prove thee Olympian! If my heart supply
Inviolate the structure, – true to type,
Build me some spirit-place no flesh shall find,
As Pheidias may inspire thee: slab on slab,
Renew Athenai, quarry out the cloud,
Convert to gold yon west extravagance!
'Neath Propulaia, from Akropolis
By vapoury grade and grade, gold all the way,
Step to thy snow-Pnux, mount thy Bema-cloud,
Thunder and lighten thence a Hellas through
That shall be better and more beautiful
And too august for Spartè's foot to spurn!

Chasmed in the crag, again our Theatre
Predominates, one purple: Staghunt-month,
Brings it not Dionusia? Hail, the Three!
Aischulos, Sophokles, Euripides
Compete, gain prize or lose prize, godlike still.
Nay, lest they lack the old god-exercise –
Their noble want the unworthy, – as of old,
(How otherwise should patience crown their might?)
What if each find his ape promoted man,
His censor raised for antic service still?
Some new Hermippos to pelt Perikles,
Kratinos to swear Pheidias robbed a shrine,
Eruxis – I suspect, Euripides,
No brow will ache because with mop and mow
He gibes my poet! There's a dog-faced dwarf
That gets to godship somehow, yet retains
His apehood in the Egyptian hierarchy,
More decent, indecorous just enough:
Why should not dog-ape, graced in due degree,
Grow Momos as thou Zeus? Or didst thou sigh
Rightly with thy Makaria? 'After life,
Better no sentiency than turbulence;
Death cures the low contention.' Be it so!
Yet progress means contention, to my mind.

Euthukles, who, except for love that speaks,
Art silent by my side while words of mine
Provoke that foe from which escape is vain
Henceforward, wake Athenai's fate and fall, –
Memories asleep as, at the altar-foot
Those Furies in the Oresteian song, –
Do I amiss who, wanting strength, use craft,
Advance upon the foe I cannot fly,
Nor feign a snake is dormant though it gnaw?
That fate and fall, once bedded in our brain,
Roots itself past upwrenching; but coaxed forth,
Encouraged out to practise fork and fang, –
Perhaps, when satiate with prompt sustenance,
It may pine, likelier die than if left swell
In peace by our pretension to ignore,
[illegible] pricked to threefold fury, should our stamp
[illegible] ise and not brain the pest.

A middle course!
What hinders that we treat this tragic theme
As the Three taught when either woke some woe,
– How Klutaimnestra hated, what the pride
Of Iokasté, why Medeia clove
Nature asunder. Small rebuked by large,
We felt our puny hates refine to air,
Our poor prides sink, prevent the humbling hand,
Our petty passions purify their tide.
So, Euthukles, permit the tragedy
To re-enact itself, this voyage through,
Till sunsets end and sunrise brighten Rhodes!
Majestic on the stage of memory,
Peplosed and kothorned, let Athenai fall
Once more, nay, oft again till life conclude,
Lent for the lesson: Choros, I and thou!
What else in life seems piteous any more
After such pity, or proves terrible
Beside such terror?

Still – since Phrunichos
Offended, by too premature a touch
Of that Milesian smart-place freshly frayed –
(Ah, my poor people, whose prompt remedy
Was – fine the poet, not reform thyself!)
Beware precipitate approach! Rehearse
Rather the prologue, well a year away,
Than the main misery, a sunset old.
What else but fitting prologue to the piece
Style an adventure, stranger than my first
By so much as the issue it enwombed
Lurked big beyond Balaustion's littleness?
Second supreme adventure! O that Spring,
That eve I told the earlier to my friends!
Where are the four now, with each red-ripe mouth
Crumpled so close, no quickest breath it fetched
Could disengage the lip-flower furled to bud
For fear Admetos, – shivering head and foot,
As with sick soul and blind averted face
He trusted hand forth to obey his friend, –
Should find no wife in her cold hand's response,
Nor see the disenshrouded statue start

Alkestis, live the life and love the love!
I wonder, does the streamlet ripple still,
Outsmoothing galingale and watermint
Its mat-floor? while at brim, 'twixt sedge and sedge,
What bubblings past Baccheion, broadened much,
Pricked by the reed and fretted by the fly,
Oared by the boatman-spider's pair of arms!
Lenaia was a gladsome month ago –
Euripides had taught 'Andromedé':
Next month, would teach 'Kresphontes' – which same month
Someone from Phokis, who companioned me
Since all that happened on those temple-steps,
Would marry me and turn Athenian too.
Now! if next year the masters let the slaves
Do Bacchic service and restore mankind
That trilogy whereof, 'tis noised, one play
Presents the Bacchai, – no Euripides
Will teach the choros, nor shall we be tinged
By any such grand sunset of his soul,
Exiles from dead Athenai, – not the live
That's in the cloud there with the new-born star!

Speak to the infinite intelligence,
Sing to the everlasting sympathy!
Winds belly sail, and drench of dancing brine
Buffet our boat-side, so the prore bound free!
Condense our voyage into one great day
Made up of sunset-closes: eve by eve,
Resume that memorable night-discourse
When, – like some meteor-brilliance, fire and filth,
Or say, his own Amphitheos, deity
And dung, who, bound on the gods' embassage,
Got men's acknowledgement in kick and cuff –
We made acquaintance with a visitor
Ominous, apparitional, who went
Strange as he came, but shall not pass away.
Let us attempt that memorable talk,
Clothe the adventure's every incident
With due expression: may not looks be told,
Gesture made speak, and speech so amplified
That words find blood-warmth which, cold-writ, they lose?

Recall the night we heard the news from Thrace,
One year ago, Athenai still herself.

We two were sitting silent in the house,
Yet cheerless hardly. Euthukles, forgive!
I somehow speak to unseen auditors.
Not *you*, but – Euthukles had entered, grave,
Grand, may I say, as who brings laurel-branch
And message from the tripod: such it proved.

He first removed the garland from his brow,
Then took my hand and looked into my face.

'Speak good words!' much misgiving faltered I.

'Good words, the best, Balaustion! He is crowned,
Gone with his Attic ivy home to feast,
Since Aischulos required companionship.
Pour a libation for Euripides!'

When we had sat the heavier silence out –
'Dead and triumphant still!' began reply
To my eye's question. 'As he willed he worked:
And, as he worked, he wanted not, be sure,
Triumph his whole life through, submitting work
To work's right judges, never to the wrong –
To competency, not ineptitude.
When he had run life's proper race and worked
Quite to the stade's end, there remained to try
The stade's turn, should strength dare the double course
Half the diaulos reached, the hundred plays
Accomplished, force in its rebound sufficed
To lift along the athlete and ensure
A second wreath, proposed by fools for first,
The statist's olive as the poet's bay.
Wiselier, he suffered not a twofold aim
Retard his pace, confuse his sight; at once
Poet and statist; though the multitude
Girded him ever "All thine aim thine art?
The idle poet only? No regard
For civic duty, public service, here?
We drop our ballot-bean for Sophokles!

Not only could he write 'Antigoné,'
But – since (we argued) whoso penned that piece
Might just as well conduct a squadron, – straight
Good-naturedly he took on him command,
Got laughed at, and went back to making plays,
Having allowed us our experiment
Respecting the fit use of faculty."
No whit the more did athlete slacken pace.
Soon the jeers grew: "Cold hater of his kind,
A sea-cave suits him, not the vulgar hearth!
What need of tongue-talk, with a bookish store
Would stock ten cities?" Shadow of an ass!
No whit the worse did athlete touch the mark
And, at the turning-point, consign his scorn
O' the scorners to that final trilogy
"Hupsipule," "Phoinissai," and the Match
Of Life Contemplative with Active Life,
Zethos against Amphion. Ended so?
Nowise! – began again; for heroes rest
Dropping shield's oval o'er the entire man,
And he who thus took Contemplation's prize
Turned stade-point but to face Activity.
Out of all shadowy hands extending help
For life's decline pledged to youth's labour still,
Whatever renovation flatter age, –
Society with pastime, solitude
With peace, – he chose the hand that gave the heart,
Bade Macedonian Archelaos take
The leavings of Athenai, ash once flame.
For fifty politicians' frosty work,
One poet's ash proved ample and to spare:
He propped the state and filled the treasury,
Counselled the king as might a meaner soul,
Furnished the friend with what shall stand in stead
Of crown and sceptre, star his name about
When these are dust; for him, Euripides
Last the old hand on the old phorminx flung,
Clashed thence Alkmaion, maddened Pentheus up;
Then music sighed itself away, one moan
Iphigeneia made by Aulis' strand;
With her and music died Euripides.

'The poet-friend who followed him to Thrace,
Agathon, writes thus much: the merchant-ship
Moreover brings a message from the king
To young Euripides, who went on board
This morning at Mounuchia: all is true.'

I said 'Thank Zeus for the great news and good!'

'Nay, the report is running in brief fire
Through the town's stubbly furrow,' he resumed:
– 'Entertains brightly what their favourite styles
"The City of Gapers" for a week perhaps,
Supplants three luminous tales, but yesterday
Pronounced sufficient lamps to last the month:
How Glauketes, outbidding Morsimos,
Paid market-price for one Kopaic eel
A thousand drachmai, and then cooked his prize
Not proper conger-fashion but in oil
And nettles, as man fries the foam-fish-kind;
How all the captains of the triremes, late
Victors at Arginousai, on return
Will, for reward, be straightway put to death;
How Mikon wagered a Thessalian mime
Trained him by Lais, looked on as complete,
Against Leogoras' blood-mare koppa-marked,
Valued six talents, – swore, accomplished so,
The girl could swallow at a draught, nor breathe,
A choinix of unmixed Mendesian wine;
And having lost the match will – dine on herbs!
Three stories late a-flame, at once extinct,
Outblazed by just "Euripides is dead!"

'I met the concourse from the Theatre,
The audience flocking homeward: victory
Again awarded Aristophanes
Precisely for his old play chopped and changed
"The Female Celebrators of the Feast" –
That Thesmophoria, tried a second time.
"Never such full success!" – assured the folk,
Who yet stopped praising to have word of mouth
With "Euthukles, the bard's own intimate,
Balaustion's husband, the right man to ask."

'"Dead, yes, but how dead, may acquaintance know?
You were the couple constant at his cave:
Tell us now, is it true that women, moved
By reason of his liking Krateros ..."

'I answered "He was loved by Sokrates."

'"Nay," said another, "envy did the work!
For, emulating poets of the place,
One Arridaios, one Krateues, both
Established in the royal favour, these ..."

'Protagoras instructed him,' said I.

'"*Phu*," whistled Comic Platon," hear the fact!
'Twas well said of your friend by Sophokles
'He hate our women? In his verse, belike:
But when it comes to prose-work, – ha, ha, ha!'
New climes don't change old manners: so, it chanced,
Pursuing an intrigue one moonless night
With Arethousian Nikodikos' wife,
(Come now, his years were simply seventy-five)
Crossing the palace-court, what haps he on
But Archelaos' pack of hungry hounds?
Who tore him piecemeal ere his cry brought help."

'I asked: Did not you write "The Festivals"?
You best know what dog tore him when alive.
You others, who now make a ring to hear,
Have not you just enjoyed a second treat,
Proclaimed that ne'er was play more worthy prize
Than this, myself assisted at, last year,
And gave its worth to, – spitting on the same?
Appraise no poetry, – price cuttlefish,
Or that seaweed-alphestes, scorpion-sort,
Much famed for mixing mud with fantasy
On midnights! I interpret no foul dreams.'

If so said Euthukles, so could not I,
Balaustion, say. After 'Lusistraté'
No more for me of 'people's privilege,'
No witnessing 'the Grand old Comedy

Coëval with our freedom, which, curtailed,
Were freedom's deathblow: relic of the past,
When Virtue laughingly told truth to Vice,
Uncensured, since the stern mouth, stuffed with flowers,
Through poetry breathed satire, perfumed blast
Which sense snuffed up while searched unto the bone!'
I was a stranger: 'For first joy,' urged friends,
'Go hear our Comedy, some patriot piece
That plies the selfish advocates of war
With argument so unevadable
That crash fall Kleons whom the finer play
Of reason, tickling, deeper wounds no whit
Than would a spear-thrust from a savory-stalk!
No: you hear knave and fool told crime and fault,
And see each scourged his quantity of stripes.
"Rough dealing, awkward language," whine our fops:
The world's too squeamish now to bear plain words
Concerning deeds it acts with gust enough:
But, thanks to wine-lees and democracy,
We've still our stage where truth calls spade a spade!
Ashamed? Phuromachos' decree provides
The sex may sit discreetly, witness all,
Sorted, the good with good, the gay with gay,
Themselves unseen, no need to force a blush.
A Rhodian wife and ignorant so long?
Go hear next play!'
I heard 'Lusistraté.'
Waves, said to wash pollution from the world,
Take that plague-memory, cure that pustule caught
As, past escape, I sat and saw the piece
By one appalled at Phaidra's fate, – the chaste,
Whom, because chaste, the wicked goddess chained
To that same serpent of unchastity
She loathed most, and who, coiled so, died distraught
Rather than make submission, loose one limb
Love-wards, at lambency of honeyed tongue,
Or torture of the scales which scraped her snow
– I say, the piece by him who charged this piece
(Because Euripides shrank not to teach,
If gods be strong and wicked, man, though weak,
May prove their match by willing to be good)
With infamies the Scythian's whip should cure –

'Such outrage done the public – Phaidra named!
Such purpose to corrupt ingenuous youth,
Such insult cast on female character!' –
Why, when I saw that bestiality –
So beyond all brute-beast imagining,
That when, to point the moral at the close,
Poor Salabaccho, just to show how fair
Was 'Reconciliation,' stripped her charms,
That exhibition simply bade us breathe,
Seemed something healthy and commendable
After obscenity grotesqued so much
It slunk away revolted at itself.
Henceforth I had my answer when our sage
Pattern-proposing seniors pleaded grave
'You fail to fathom here the deep design!
All's acted in the interest of truth,
Religion, and those manners old and dear
Which made our city great when citizens
Like Aristeides and like Miltiades
Wore each a golden tettix in his hair.'
What do they wear now under – Kleophon?

Well, for such reasons, – I am out of breath,
But loathsomeness we needs must hurry past, –
I did not go to see, nor then nor now,
The 'Thesmophoriazousai.' But, since males
Choose to brave first, blame afterward, nor brand
Without fair taste of what they stigmatize,
Euthukles had not missed the first display,
Original portrait of Euripides
By 'Virtue laughingly reproving Vice':
'Virtue,' – the author, Aristophanes,
Who mixed an image out of his own depths,
Ticketed as I tell you. Oh, this time
No more pretension to recondite worth!
No joke in aid of Peace, no demagogue
Pun-pelleted from Pnux, no kordax-dance
Overt helped covertly the Ancient Faith!
All now was muck, home-produce, honestman
The author's soul secreted to a play
Which gained the prize that day we heard the death.

I thought 'How thoroughly death alters things!
Where is the wrong now, done our dead and great?
How natural seems grandeur in relief,
Cliff-base with frothy spites against its calm!'

Euthukles interposed – he read my thought –

'O'er them, too, in a moment came the change.
The crowd's enthusiastic, to a man:
Since, rake as such may please the ordure-heap
Because of certain sparkles presumed ore,
At first flash of true lightning overhead,
They look up, nor resume their search too soon.
The insect-scattering sign is evident,
And nowhere winks a fire-fly rival now,
Nor bustles any beetle of the brood
With trundled dung-ball meant to menace heaven.
Contrariwise, the cry is "Honour him!"
"A statue in the theatre!" wants one;
Another "Bring the poet's body back,
Bury him in Peiraius: o'er his tomb
Let Alkamenes carve the music-witch,
The songstress-seiren, meed of melody:
Thoukudides invent his epitaph!"
Tonight the whole town pays its tribute thus.'

Our tribute should not be the same, my friend!
Statue? Within our heart he stood, he stands!
As for the vest outgrown now by the form,
Low flesh that clothed high soul, – a vesture's fate –
Why, let it fade, mix with the elements
There where it, falling, freed Euripides!
But for the soul that's tutelary now
Till time end, o'er the world to teach and bless –
How better hail its freedom than by first
Singing, we two, its own song back again,
Up to that face from which flowed beauty – face
Now abler to see triumph and take love
Than when it glorified Athenai once?

The sweet and strange 'Alkestis,' which saved me,
Secured me – you, ends nowise, to my mind,
In pardon of Admetos. Hearts are fain
To follow cheerful weary Herakles
Striding away from the huge gratitude,
Club shouldered, lion-fleece round loin and flank,
Bound on the next new labour 'height o'er height
Ever surmounting, – destiny's decree!'
Thither He helps us: that's the story's end;
He smiling said so, when I told him mine –
My great adventure, how Alkestis helped.
Afterward, when the time for parting fell,
He gave me, with two other precious gifts,
This third and best, consúmmating the grace,
'Herakles,' writ by his own hand, each line.

'If it have worth, reward is still to seek.
Somebody, I forgot who, gained the prize
And proved arch-poet: time must show!' he smiled:
'Take this, and, when the noise tires out, judge me –
Some day, not slow to dawn, when somebody –
Who? I forget – proves nobody at all!'

Is not that day come? What if you and I
Re-sing the song, inaugurate the fame?
We have not waited to acquaint ourselves
With song and subject; we can prologize
How, at Eurustheus' bidding, – hate strained hard, –
Herakles had departed, one time more,
On his last labour, worst of all the twelve;
Descended into Haides, thence to drag
The triple-headed hound, which sun should see
Spite of the god whose darkness whelped the Fear.
Down went the hero, 'back – how should he come?'
So laughed King Lukos, an old enemy,
Who judged that absence testified defeat
Of the land's loved one, – since he saved the land
And for that service wedded Megara
Daughter of Thebai, realm her child should rule.
Ambition, greed and malice seized their prey,
The Heracleian House, defenceless left,
Father and wife and child, to trample out

Trace of its hearth-fire: since extreme old age
Wakes pity, woman's wrong wins championship,
And child may grow up man and take revenge.
Hence see we that, from out their palace-home
Hunted, for last resource they cluster now
Couched on the cold ground, hapless supplicants
About their courtyard altar, – Household Zeus
It is, the Three in funeral garb beseech,
Delaying death so, till deliverance come –
When did it ever? – from the deep and dark.
And thus breaks silence old Amphitruon's voice . . .
Say I not true thus far, my Euthukles?

Suddenly, torch-light! knocking at the door,
Lord, quick, 'Admittance for the revels' lord!'
Some unintelligible Komos-cry –
Raw-flesh red, no cap upon his head,
Dionusos, Bacchos, Phales, Iacchos,
In let him reel with the kid-skin at his heel,
Where it buries in the spread of the bushy myrtle-bed!
(Our Rhodian Jackdaw-song was sense to that!)
Then laughter, outbursts ruder and more rude,
Through which, with silver point, a fluting pierced,
And ever 'Open, open, Bacchos bids!'

But at last – one authoritative word,
One name of an immense significance:
For Euthukles rose up, threw wide the door.

There trooped the Choros of the Comedy
Crowned and triumphant; first, those flushed Fifteen
Men that wore women's garb, grotesque disguise.
Then marched the Three, – who played Mnesilochos,
Who, Toxotes, and who, robed right, masked rare,
Monkeyed our Great and Dead to heart's content
That morning in Athenai. Masks were down
And robes doffed now; the sole disguise was drink.

Mixing with these – I know not what gay crowd,
Girl-dancers, flute-boys, and pre-eminent
Among them, – doubtless draped with such reserve
As stopped fear of the fifty-drachma fine

(Beside one's name on public fig-tree nailed)
Which women pay who in the streets walk bare, –
Behold Elaphion of the Persic dance!
Who lately had frisked fawn-foot, and the rest,
– All for the Patriot Cause, the Antique Faith,
The Conservation of True Poesy –
Could I but penetrate the deep design!
Elaphion, more Peiraius-known as 'Phaps,'
Tripped at the head of the whole banquet-band
Who came in front now, as the first fell back;
And foremost – the authoritative voice,
The revels-leader, he who gained the prize,
And got the glory of the Archon's feast –
There stood in person Aristophanes.

And no ignoble presence! On the bulge
Of the clear baldness, – all his head one brow, –
True, the veins swelled, blue network, and there surged
A red from cheek to temple, – then retired
As if the dark-leaved chaplet damped a flame, –
Was never nursed by temperance or health.
But huge the eyeballs rolled black native fire,
Imperiously triumphant: nostrils wide
Waited their incense; while the pursed mouth's pout
Aggressive, while the beak supreme above,
While the head, face, nay, pillared throat thrown back,
Beard whitening under like a vinous foam,
These made a glory, of such insolence –
I thought, – such domineering deity
Hephaistos might have carved to cut the brine
For his gay brother's prow, imbrue that path
Which, purpling, recognized the conqueror.
Impudent and majestic: drunk, perhaps,
But that's religion; sense too plainly snuffed:
Still, sensuality was grown a rite.

What I had disbelieved most proved most true.
There was a mind here, mind a-wantoning
At ease of undisputed mastery
Over the body's brood, those appetites.
Oh but he grasped them grandly, as the god
His either struggling handful, – hurtless snakes

Held deep down, strained hard off from side and side!
Mastery his, theirs simply servitude,
So well could firm fist help intrepid eye.
Fawning and fulsome, had they licked and hissed?
At mandate of one muscle, order reigned.
They had been wreathing much familiar now
About him on his entry; but a squeeze
Choked down the pests to place: their lord stood free.

Forward he stepped: I rose and fronted him.

'Hail, house, the friendly to Euripides!'
(So he began) 'Hail, each inhabitant!
You, lady? What, the Rhodian? Form and face,
Victory's self upsoaring to receive
The poet? Right they named you . . . some rich name,
Vowel-buds thorned about with consonants,
Fragrant, felicitous, rose-glow enriched
By the Isle's unguent: some diminished end
In *ion*, Kallistion? delicater still,
Kubelion or Melittion, – or, suppose
(Less vulgar love than bee or violet)
Phibalion, for the mouth split red-fig-wise,
Korakinidion for the coal-black hair,
Nettarion, Phabion for the darlingness?
But no, it was some fruit-flower, Rhoidion . . . ha,
We near the balsam-bloom – Balaustion! Thanks,
Rhodes! Folk have called me Rhodian, do you know?
Not fools so far! Because, if Helios wived,
As Pindaros sings somewhere prettily,
Here blooms his offspring, earth-flesh with sun-fire,
Rhodes' blood and Helios' gold. My phorminx, boy!
Why does the boy hang back and balk an ode
Tiptoe at spread of wing? But like enough,
Sunshine frays torchlight. Witness whom you scare,
Superb Balaustion! Look outside the house!
Pho, you have quenched my Komos by first frown
Struck dead all joyance: not a fluting puffs
From idle cheekband! Ah, my Choros too?
You've eaten cuckoo-apple? Dumb, you dogs?
So much good Thasian wasted on your throats
And out of them not one *Threttanelo?*

Neblaretai! Because this earth-and-sun
Product looks wormwood and all bitter herbs?
Well, do I blench, though me she hates the most
Of mortals? By the cabbage, off they slink!
You, too, my Chrusomelolonthion-Phaps,
Girl-goldling-beetle-beauty? You, abashed,
Who late, supremely unabashable,
Propped up my play at that important point
When Artamouxia tricks the Toxotes?
Ha, ha, – thank Hermes for the lucky throw, –
We came last comedy of the whole seven,
So went all fresh to judgement well-disposed
For who should fatly feast them, eye and ear,
We two between us! What, you fail your friend?
Away then, free me of your cowardice!
Go, get you the goat's breakfast! Fare afield,
Ye circumcised of Egypt, pigs to sow,
Back to the Priest's or forward to the crows,
So you but rid me of such company!
Once left alone, I can protect myself
From statuesque Balaustion pedestalled
On much disapprobation and mistake!
She dares not beat the sacred brow, beside!
Bacchos' equipment, ivy safeguards well
As Phoibos' bay.

'They take me at my word!
One comfort is, I shall not want them long,
The Archon's cry creaks, creaks, "Curtail expense!"
The war wants money, year the twenty-sixth!
Cut down our Choros number, clip costume,
Save birds' wings, beetles' armour, spend the cash
In three-crest skull-caps, three days' salt-fish-slice,
Three-banked-ships for these sham-ambassadors,
And what not: any cost but Comedy's!
"No Choros" – soon will follow; what care I?
Archinos and Agurrhios, scrape your flint,
Flay your dead dog, and curry favour so!
Choros in rags, with loss of leather next,
We lose the boys' vote, lose the song and dance,
Lose my Elaphion! Still, the actor stays.
Save but my acting, and the baldhead bard

Kudathenaian and Pandionid,
Son of Philippos, Aristophanes
Surmounts his rivals now as heretofore,
Though stinted to mere sober prosy verse –
"Manners and men," so squeamish gets the world!
No more "Step forward, strip for anapaests!"
No calling naughty people by their names,
No tickling audience into gratitude
With chick-peas, barley-groats and nuts and plums,
No setting Salabaccho . . .'

As I turned –

'True, lady, I am tolerably drunk:
The proper inspiration! Otherwise, –
Phrunichos, Choirilos! – had Aischulos
So foiled you at the goat-song? Drink's a god.
How else did that old doting driveller
Kratinos foil me, match my masterpiece
The "Clouds"? I swallowed cloud-distilment – dew
Undimmed by any grape-blush, knit my brow
And gnawed my style and laughed my learnedest;
While he worked at his "Willow-wicker-flask,"
Swigging at that same flask by which he swore,
Till, sing and empty, sing and fill again,
Somehow result was – what it should not be
Next time, I promised him and kept my word!
Hence, brimful now of Thasian . . . I'll be bound,
Mendesian, merely: triumph-night, you know,
The High Priest entertains the conqueror,
And, since war worsens all things, stingily
The rascal starves whom he is bound to stuff,
Choros and actors and their lord and king
The poet; supper, still he needs must spread –
And this time all was conscientious fare:
He knew his man, his match, his master – made
Amends, spared neither fish, flesh, fowl nor wine:
So merriment increased, I promise you,
Till – something happened.'

Here he strangely paused.

'After that, – well, it either was the cup
To the Good Genius, our concluding pledge,
That wrought me mischief, decently unmixed, –
Or, what if, when *that* happened, need arose
Of new libation? Did you only know
What happened! Little wonder I am drunk.'

Euthukles, o'er the boat-side, quick, what change,
Watch, in the water! But a second since,
It laughed a ripply spread of sun and sea,
Ray fused with wave, to never disunite.
Now, sudden all the surface, hard and black,
Lies a quenched light, dead motion: what the cause?
Look up and lo, the menace of a cloud
Has solemnized the sparkling, spoiled the sport!
Just so, some overshadow, some new care
Stopped all the mirth and mocking on his face
And left there only such a dark surmise
– No wonder if the revel disappeared,
So did his face shed silence every side!
I recognized a new man fronting me.

'So!' he smiled, piercing to my thought at once,
'You see myself? Balaustion's fixed regard
Can strip the proper Aristophanes
Of what our sophists, in their jargon, style
His accidents? My soul sped forth but now
To meet your hostile survey, – soul unseen,
Yet veritably cinct for soul-defence
With satyr sportive quips, cranks, boss and spike,
Just as my visible body paced the street,
Environed by a boon companionship
Your apparition also puts to flight.
Well, what care I if, unaccoutred twice,
I front my foe – no comicality
Round soul, and body-guard in banishment?
Thank your eyes' searching, undisguised I stand:
The merest female child may question me.
Spare not, speak bold, Balaustion!'

I did speak:

'Bold speech be – welcome to this honoured hearth,
Good Genius! Glory of the poet, glow
O' the humorist who castigates his kind,
Suave summer-lightning lambency which plays
On stag-horned tree, misshapen crag askew,
Then vanishes with unvindictive smile
After a moment's laying black earth bare.
Splendour of wit that springs a thunderball –
Satire – to burn and purify the world,
True aim, fair purpose: just wit justly strikes
Injustice, – right, as rightly quells the wrong,
Finds out in knaves', fools', cowards' armoury
The tricky tinselled place fire flashes through,
No damage else, sagacious of true ore;
Wit, learned in the laurel, leaves each wreath
O'er lyric shell or tragic barbiton, –
Though alien gauds be singed, – undesecrate,
The genuine solace of the sacred brow.
Ay, and how pulses flame a patriot-star
Steadfast athwart our country's night of things,
To beacon, would she trust no meteor-blaze,
Athenai from the rock she steers for straight!
O light, light, light, I hail light everywhere,
No matter for the murk that was, – perchance,
That will be, – certes, never should have been
Such orb's associate!

'Aristophanes!
"The merest female child may question you?"
Once, in my Rhodes, a portent of the wave
Appalled our coast: for many a darkened day,
Intolerable mystery and fear.
Who snatched a furtive glance through crannied peak,
Could but report of snake-scale, lizard-limb, –
So swam what, making whirlpools as it went,
Madded the brine with wrath or monstrous sport.
" 'Tis Tuphon, loose, unmanacled from mount,"
Declared the priests, "no way appeasable
Unless perchance by virgin-sacrifice!"
Thus grew the terror and o'erhung the doom –
Until one eve a certain female-child
Strayed in safe ignorance to seacoast edge,

And there sat down and sang to please herself.
When all at once, large-looming from his wave,
Out leaned, chin hand-propped, pensive on the ledge,
A sea-worn face, sad as mortality,
Divine with yearning after fellowship.
He rose but breast-high. So much god she saw;
So much she sees now, and does reverence!'

Ah, but there followed tail-splash, frisk of fin!
Let cloud pass, the sea's ready laugh outbreaks.
No very godlike trace retained the mouth
Which mocked with –

'So, He taught you tragedy!
I always asked "Why may not women act?"
Nay, wear the comic visor just as well;
Or, better, quite cast off the face-disguise
And voice-distortion, simply look and speak,
Real women playing women as men – men!
I shall not wonder if things come to that,
Some day when I am distant far enough.
Do you conceive the quite new Comedy
When laws allow? laws only let girls dance,
Pipe, posture, – above all, Elaphionize,
Provided they keep decent – that is, dumb.
Ay, and, conceiving, I would execute,
Had I but two lives: one were overworked!
How penetrate encrusted prejudice,
Pierce ignorance three generations thick
Since first Sousarion crossed our boundary?
He battered with a big Megaric stone;
Chionides felled oak and rough-hewed thence
This club I wield now, having spent my life
In planing knobs and sticking studs to shine;
Somebody else must try mere polished steel!'

Emboldened by the sober mood's return,
'Meanwhile,' said I, 'since planed and studded club
Once more has pashed competitors to dust,
And poet proves triumphant with that play
Euthukles found last year unfortunate, –
Does triumph spring from smoothness still more smoothed,

Fresh studs sown thick and threefold? In plain words,
Have you exchanged brute-blows, – which teach the brute
Man may surpass him in brutality, –
For human fighting, or true god-like force
Which breathes persuasion nor needs fight at all?
Have you essayed attacking ignorance,
Convicting folly, by their opposites,
Knowledge and wisdom? not by yours for ours,
Fresh ignorance and folly, new for old,
Greater for less, your crime for our mistake!
If so success at last have crowned desert,
Bringing surprise (dashed haply by concern
At your discovery such wild waste of strength
– And what strength! – went so long to keep in vogue
Such warfare – and what warfare! – shamed so fast,
So soon made obsolete, as fell their foe
By the first arrow native to the orb,
First onslaught worthy Aristophanes) –
Was this conviction's entry that same strange
"Something that happened" to confound your feast?'

'Ah, did he witness then my play that failed,
First "Thesmophoriazousai"? Well and good!
But did he also see, – your Euthukles, –
My "Grasshoppers" which followed and failed too,
Three months since, at the "Little-in-the-Fields"?'

'To say that he did see that First – should say
He never cared to see its following.'

'There happens to be reason why I wrote
First play and second also. Ask the cause!
I warrant you receive ere talk be done,
Fit answer, authorizing either act.
But here's the point: as Euthukles made vow
Never again to taste my quality,
So I was minded next experiment
Should tickle palate – yea, of Euthukles!
Not by such utter change, such absolute
A topsy-turvy of stage-habitude
As you and he want, – Comedy built fresh,
By novel brick and mortar, base to roof, –

No, for I stand too near and look too close!
Pleasure and pastime yours, spectators brave,
Should I turn art's fixed fabric upside down!
Little you guess how such tough work tasks soul!
Not overtasks, though: give fit strength fair play,
And strength's a demiourgos! Art renewed?
Ay, in some closet where strength shuts out – first
The friendly faces, sympathetic cheer:
"More of the old provision none supplies
So bounteously as thou, – our love, our pride,
Our author of the many a perfect piece!
Stick to that standard, change were decadence!"
Next, the unfriendly: "This time, strain will tire,
He's fresh, Ameipsias thy antagonist!"
– Or better, in some Salaminian cave
Where sky and sea and solitude make earth
And man and noise one insignificance,
Let strength propose itself, – behind the world, –
Sole prize worth winning, work that satisfies
Strength it has dared and done strength's uttermost!
After which, – clap-to closet and quit cave, –
Strength may conclude in Archelaos' court,
And yet esteem the silken company
So much sky-scud, sea-froth, earth-thistledown,
For aught their praise or blame should joy or grieve.
Strength amid crowds as late in solitude
May lead the still life, ply the wordless task:
Then only, when seems need to move or speak,
Moving – for due respect, when statesmen pass,
(Strength, in the closet, watched how spiders spin)
Speaking – when fashion shows intelligence,
(Strength, in the cave, oft whistled to the gulls)
In short, has learnt first, practised afterwards!
Despise the world and reverence yourself, –
Why, you may unmake things and remake things,
And throw behind you, unconcerned enough,
What's made or marred: "you teach men, are not taught!"
So marches off the stage Euripides!

'No such thin fare feeds flesh and blood like mine
No such faint fume of fancy sates my soul,
No such seclusion, closet, cave or court,

Suits either: give me Iostephanos
Worth making happy what coarse way she will –
O happy-maker, when her cries increase
About the favourite! "Aristophanes!
More grist to mill, here's Kleophon to grind!
He's for refusing peace, though Sparté cede
Even Dekeleia! Here's Kleonumos
Declaring – though he threw away his shield,
He'll thrash you till you lay your lyre aside!
Orestes bids mind where you walk of nights –
He wants your cloak as you his cudgelling:
Here's, finally, Melanthios fat with fish,
The gormandizer-spendthrift-dramatist!
So, bustle! Pounce on opportunity!
Set fun a-screaming in Parabasis,
Find food for folk agape at either end,
Mad for amusement! Times grow better too,
And should they worsen, why, who laughs, forgets.
In no case, venture boy-experiments!
Old wine's the wine: new poetry drinks raw:
Two plays a season is your pledge, beside;
So, give us 'Wasps' again, grown hornets now!"'

Then he changed.
'Do you so detect in me –
Brow-bald, chin-bearded, me, curved cheek, carved lip,
Or where soul sits and reigns in either eye –
What suits the – stigma, I say, – style say you,
Of "Wine-lees-poet"? Bravest of buffoons,
Less blunt than Telekleides, less obscene
Than Murtilos, Hermippos: quite a match
In elegance for Eupolis himself,
Yet pungent as Kratinos at his best?
Graced with traditional immunity
Ever since, much about my grandsire's time,
Some funny village-man in Megara,
Lout-lord and clown-king, used a privilege,
As due religious drinking-bouts came round,
To daub his phyz, – no, that was afterward, –
He merely mounted cart with mates of choice
And traversed country, taking house by house,
At night, – because of danger in the freak, –

Then hollaed "Skin-flint starves his labourers!
Clench-fist stows figs away, cheats government!
Such an one likes to kiss his neighbour's wife,
And beat his own; while such another . . . Boh!"
Soon came the broad day, circumstantial tale,
Dancing and verse, and there's our Comedy,
There's Mullos, there's Euetes, there's the stock
I shall be proud to graft my powers upon!
Protected? Punished quite as certainly
When Archons pleased to lay down each his law, –
Your Morucheides-Surakosios sort, –
Each season, "No more naming citizens,
Only abuse the vice, the vicious spare!
Observe, henceforth no Areopagite
Demean his rank by writing Comedy!"
(They one and all could write the "Clouds" of course.)
"Needs must we nick expenditure, allow
Comedy half a choros, supper – none,
Times being hard, while applicants increase
For, what costs cash, the Tragic Trilogy."
Lofty Tragedians! How they lounge aloof
Each with his Triad, three plays to my one,
Not counting the contemptuous fourth, the frank
Concession to mere mortal levity,
Satyric pittance tossed our beggar-world!
Your proud Euripides from first to last
Doled out some five such, never deigned us more!
And these – what curds and whey for marrowy wine!
That same "Alkestis" you so rave about
Passed muster with him for a Satyr-play,
The prig! – why trifle time with toys and skits
When he could stuff four ragbags sausage-wise
With sophistry, with bookish odds and ends,
Sokrates, meteors, moonshine, "Life's not Life,"
"The tongue swore, but unsworn the mind remains,"
And fifty such concoctions, crab-tree-fruit
Digested while, head low and heels in heaven,
He lay, let Comics laugh – for privilege!
Looked puzzled on, or pityingly off,
But never dreamed of paying gibe by jeer,
Buffet by blow: plenty of proverb-pokes
At vice and folly, wicked kings, mad mobs!

No sign of wincing at my Comic lash,
No protest against infamous abuse,
Malignant censure, – naught to prove I scourged
With tougher thong than leek-and-onion-plait!
If ever he glanced gloom, aggrieved at all,
The aggriever must be – Aischulos perhaps:
Or Sophokles he'd take exception to.
– Do you detect in me – in me, I ask,
The man like to accept this measurement
Of faculty, contentedly sit classed
Mere Comic Poet – since I wrote "The Birds"?'

I thought there might lurk truth in jest's disguise.

'Thanks!' he resumed, so quick to construe smile!
'I answered – in my mind – these gapers thus:
Since old wine's ripe and new verse raw, you judge –
What if I vary vintage-mode and mix
Blossom with must, give nosegay to the brew,
Fining, refining, gently, surely, till
The educated taste turns unawares
From customary dregs to draught divine?
Then answered – with my lips: More "Wasps" you want?
Come next year and I give you "Grasshoppers"!
And "Grasshoppers" I gave them, – last month's play.
They formed the Choros. Alkibiades,
No longer Triphales but Trilophos,
(Whom I called Darling-of-the-Summertime,
Born to be nothing else but beautiful
And brave, to eat, drink, love his life away)
Persuades the Tettix (our Autochthon-brood,
That sip the dew and sing on olive-branch
Above the ant-and-emmet populace)
To summon all who meadow, hill and dale
Inhabit – bee, wasp, woodlouse, dragonfly –
To band themselves against red nipper-nose
Stagbeetle, huge Taügetan (you guess –
Sparté) Athenai needs must battle with,
Because her sons are grown effeminate
To that degree – so morbifies their flesh
The poison-drama of Euripides,
Morals and music – there's no antidote

Occurs save warfare which inspirits blood,
And brings us back perchance the blessed time
When (Choros takes up tale) our commonalty
Firm in primeval virtue, antique faith,
Ere earwig-sophist plagued or pismire-sage,
Cockered no noddle up with A, b, g,
Book-learning, logic-chopping, and the moon,
But just employed their brains on "*Ruppapai,*
Row, boys, munch barley-bread, and take your ease –
Mindful, however, of the tier beneath!"
Ah, golden epoch! while the nobler sort
(Such needs must study, no contesting that!)
Wore no long curls but used to crop their hair,
Gathered the tunic well about the ham,
Remembering 'twas soft sand they used for seat
At school-time, while – mark this – the lesson long,
No learner ever dared to cross his legs!
Then, if you bade him take the myrtle-bough
And sing for supper – 'twas some grave romaunt
How man of Mitulené, wondrous wise,
Jumped into hedge, by mortals quickset called,
And there, anticipating Oidipous,
Scratched out his eyes and scratched them in again.
None of your Phaidras, Augés, Kanakés,
To mincing music, turn, trill, tweedle-trash,
Whence comes that Marathon is obsolete!
Next, my Antistrophé was – praise of Peace:
Ah, could our people know what Peace implies!
Home to the farm and furrow! Grub one's vine,
Romp with one's Thratta, pretty serving-girl,
When wifie's busy bathing! Eat and drink,
And drink and eat, what else is good in life?
Slice hare, toss pancake, gaily gurgle down
The Thasian grape in celebration due
Of Bacchos! Welcome, dear domestic rite,
When wife and sons and daughters, Thratta too,
Pour peasoup as we chant delectably
In Bacchos reels, his tunic at his heels!
Enough, you comprehend, – I do at least!
Then, – be but patient, – the Parabasis!
Pray! For in that I also pushed reform.

None of the self-laudation, vulgar brag,
Vainglorious rivals cultivate so much!
No! If some merest word in Art's defence
Justice demanded of me, – never fear!
Claim was preferred, but dignifiedly.
A cricket asked a locust (winged, you know)
What he had seen most rare in foreign parts?
"I have flown far," chirped he, "North, East, South, West,
And nowhere heard of poet worth a fig
If matched with Bald-head here, Aigina's boast,
Who in this play bids rivalry despair
Past, present, and to come, so marvellous
His Tragic, Comic, Lyric excellence!
Whereof the fit reward were (not to speak
Of dinner every day at public cost
I' the Prutaneion) supper with yourselves,
My Public, best dish offered bravest bard!"
No more! no sort of sin against good taste!
Then, satire, – Oh, a plain necessity!
But I won't tell you: for – could I dispense
With one more gird at old Ariphrades?
How scorpion-like he feeds on human flesh –
Ever finds out some novel infamy
Unutterable, inconceivable,
Which all the greater need was to describe
Minutely, each tail-twist at ink-shed time...

'Now, what's your gesture caused by? What you loathe,
Don't I loathe doubly, else why take such pains
To tell it you? But keep your prejudice!
My audience justified you! Housebreakers!
This pattern-purity was played and failed
Last Rural Dionusia – failed! for why?
Ameipsias followed with the genuine stuff.
He had been mindful to engage the Four –
Karkinos and his dwarf-crab-family –
Father and sons, they whirled like spinning-tops,
Choros gigantically poked his fun,
The boys' frank laugh relaxed the seniors' brow,
The skies re-echoed victory's acclaim,
Ameipsias gained his due, I got my dose

Of wisdom for the future. Purity?
No more of that next month, Athenai mine!
Contrive new cut of robe who will, – I patch
The old exomis, add no purple sleeve!
The Thesmophoriazousai, smartened up
With certain plaits, shall please, I promise you!

'Yes, I took up the play that failed last year,
And re-arranged things; threw adroitly in, –
No Parachoregema, – men to match
My women there already; and when these
(I had a hit at Aristullos here,
His plan how womankind should rule the roast)
Drove men to plough – "A-field, ye cribbed of cape!"
Men showed themselves exempt from service straight
Stupendously, till all the boys cried "Brave!"
Then for the elders, I bethought me too,
Improved upon Mnesilochos' release
From the old bowman, board and binding-strap:
I made his son-in-law Euripides
Engage to put both shrewish wives away –
"Gravity" one, the other "Sophist-lore" –
And mate with the Bald Bard's hetairai twain –
"Goodhumour" and "Indulgence": on they tripped,
Murrhiné, Akalanthis, – "beautiful
Their whole belongings" – crowd joined choros there!
And while the Toxotes wound up his part
By shower of nuts and sweetmeats on the mob,
The woman-choros celebrated New
Kalligeneia, the frank last-day rite.
Brief, I was chairèd and caressed and crowned
And the whole theatre broke out a-roar,
Echoed my admonition – choros-cap –
Rivals of mine, your hands to your faces!
Summon no more the Muses, the Graces,
Since here by my side they have chosen their places!

'And so we all flocked merrily to feast,
I, my choragos, choros, actors, mutes
And flutes aforesaid, friends in crowd, no fear,
At the Priest's supper; and hilarity
Grew none the less that, early in the piece,

Ran a report, from row to row close-packed,
Of messenger's arrival at the Port
With weighty tidings, "Of Lusandros' flight,"
Opined one; "That Euboia penitent
Sends the Confederation fifty ships,"
Preferred another; while "The Great King's Eye
Has brought a present for Elaphion here,
That rarest peacock Kompolakuthes!"
Such was the supposition of a third.
"No matter what the news," friend Strattis laughed,
"It won't be worse for waiting: while each click
Of the klepsudra sets a-shaking grave
Resentment in our shark's-head, boiled and spoiled
By this time: dished in Sphettian vinegar,
Silphion and honey, served with cock's-brain-sauce!
So, swift to supper, Poet! No mistake,
This play; nor, like the unflavoured 'Grasshoppers,'
Salt without thyme!" Right merrily we supped,
Till – something happened.

'Out it shall, at last!

'Mirth drew to ending, for the cup was crowned
To the Triumphant! "Kleonclapper erst,
Now, Plier of a scourge Euripides
Fairly turns tail from, flying Attiké
For Makedonia's rocks and frosts and bears,
Where, furry grown, he growls to match the squeak
Of girl-voiced, crocus-vested Agathon!
Ha ha, he he!" When suddenly a knock –
Sharp, solitary, cold, authoritative.

'"*Babaiax!* Sokrates a-passing by,
A-peering in for Aristullos' sake,
To put a question touching Comic Law?"

'No! Enters an old pale-swathed majesty,
Makes slow mute passage through two ranks as mute,
(Strattis stood up with all the rest, the sneak!)
Grey brow still bent on ground, upraised at length
When, our Priest reached, full-front the vision paused.

'"Priest!" – the deep tone succeeded the fixed gaze –
"Thou carest that thy god have spectacle
Decent and seemly; wherefore I announce
That, since Euripides is dead today,
My Choros, at the Greater Feast, next month,
Shall, clothed in black, appear ungarlanded!"

'Then the grey brow sank low, and Sophokles
Re-swathed him, sweeping doorward: mutely passed
'Twixt rows as mute, to mingle possibly
With certain gods who convoy age to port;
And night resumed him.

'When our stupor broke,
Chirpings took courage, and grew audible.

'"Dead – so one speaks now of Euripides!
Ungarlanded dance Choros, did he say?
I guess the reason: in extreme old age
No doubt such have the gods for visitants.
Why did he dedicate to Herakles
An altar else, but that the god, turned Judge,
Told him in dream who took the crown of gold?
He who restored Akropolis the theft,
Himself may feel perhaps a timely twinge
At thought of certain other crowns he filched
From – who now visits Herakles the Judge.
Instance "Medeia"! that play yielded palm
To Sophokles; and he again – to whom?
Euphorion! Why? Ask Herakles the Judge!"

'"Ungarlanded, just means – economy!
Suppress robes, chaplets, everything suppress
Except the poet's present! An old tale
Put capitally by Trugaios – eh?
– News from the world of transformation strange!
How Sophokles is grown Simonides,
And, – aged, rotten, – all the same, for greed
Would venture on a hurdle out to sea! –"
So jokes Philonides. Kallistratos
Retorts – "Mistake! Instead of stinginess,
The fact is, in extreme decrepitude,

He has discarded poet and turned priest,
Priest of Half-Hero Alkon: visited
In his own house too by Asklepios' self,
So he avers. Meanwhile, his own estate
Lies fallow; Iophon's the manager, –
Nay, touches up a play, brings out the same,
Asserts true sonship. See to what you sink
After your dozen-dozen prodigies!
Looking so old – Euripides seems young,
Born ten years later."

'"Just his tricky style!
Since, stealing first away, he wins first word
Out of good-natured rival Sophokles,
Procures himself no bad panegyric.
Had fate willed otherwise, himself were taxed
To pay survivor's-tribute, – harder squeezed
From anybody beaten first to last,
Than one who, steadily a conqueror,
Finds that his magnanimity is tasked
To merely make pretence and – beat itself!"

'So chirped the feasters though suppressedly.

'But I – what else do you suppose? – had pierced
Quite through friends' outside-straining, foes' mock-praise,
And reached conviction hearted under all.
Death's rapid line had closed a life's account,
And cut off, left unalterably clear
The summed-up value of Euripides.

'Well, it might be the Thasian! Certainly
There sang suggestive music in my ears;
And, through – what sophists style – the wall of sense
My eyes pierced: death seemed life and life seemed death,
Envisaged that way, now, which I, before,
Conceived was just a moonstruck mood. Quite plain
There re-insisted, – ay, each prim stiff phrase
Of each old play, my still-new laughing-stock,
Had meaning, well worth poet's pains to state,
Should life prove half true life's term, – death, the rest.

'As for the other question, late so large
Now all at once so little, – he or I,
Which better comprehended playwright craft, –
There, too, old admonition took fresh point.
As clear recurred our last word-interchange
Two years since, when I tried with "Ploutos." "Vain!"
Saluted me the cold grave-bearded bard –
"Vain, this late trial, Aristophanes!
None balks the genius with impunity!
You know what kind's the nobler, what makes grave
Or what makes grin; there's yet a nobler still,
Possibly, – what makes wise, not grave, – and glad,
Not grinning: whereby laughter joins with tears,
Tragic and Comic Poet prove one power,
And Aristophanes becomes our Fourth –
Nay, greatest! Never needs the Art stand still,
But those Art leans on lag, and none like you,
Her strongest of supports, whose step aside
Undoes the march: defection checks advance
Too late adventured! See the 'Ploutos' here!
This step decides your foot from old to new –
Proves you relinquish song and dance and jest,
Discard the beast, and, rising from all-fours,
Fain would paint, manlike, actual human life,
Make veritable men think, say and do.
Here's the conception: which to execute,
Where's force? Spent! Ere the race began, was breath
O' the runner squandered on each friendly fool –
Wit-fireworks fizzed off while day craved no flame:
How should the night receive her due of fire
Flared out in Wasps and Horses, Clouds and Birds,
Prodigiously a-crackle? Rest content!
The new adventure for the novel man
Born to that next success myself foresee
In right of where I reach before I rest.
At end of a long course, straight all the way,
Well may there tremble somewhat into ken
The untrod path, clouds veiled from earlier gaze!
None may live two lives: I have lived mine through,
Die where I first stand still. You retrograde.
I leave my life's work. *I* compete with you,
My last with your last, my 'Antiope' –

'Phoinissai' – with this 'Ploutos'? No, I think!
Ever shall 'great and awful Victory
Accompany my life' – in Maketis
If not Athenai. Take my farewell, friend!
Friend, – for from no consummate excellence
Like yours, whatever fault may countervail,
Do I profess estrangement: murk the marsh,
Yet where a solitary marble block
Blanches the gloom, there let the eagle perch!
You show – what splinters of Pentelikos,
Islanded by what ordure! Eagles fly,
Rest on the right place, thence depart as free;
But 'ware man's footstep, would it traverse mire
Untainted! Mire is safe for worms that crawl."

'Balaustion! Here are very many words,
All to portray one moment's rush of thought, –
And much they do it! Still, you understand.
The Archon, the Feast-master, read their sum
And substance, judged the banquet-glow extinct,
So rose, discreetly if abruptly, crowned
The parting cup, – "To the Good Genius, then!"

'Up starts young Strattis for a final flash:
"Ay the Good Genius! To the Comic Muse,
She who evolves superiority,
Triumph and joy from sorrow, unsuccess
And all that's incomplete in human life;
Who proves such actual failure transient wrong,
Since out of body uncouth, halt and maimed –
Since out of soul grotesque, corrupt or blank –
Fancy, uplifted by the Muse, can flit
To soul and body, reinstate them Man:
Beside which perfect man, how clear we see
Divergency from type was earth's effect!
Escaping whence by laughter, – Fancy's feat, –
We right man's wrong, establish true for false, –
Above misshapen body, uncouth soul,
Reach the fine form, the clear intelligence –
Above unseemliness, reach decent law, –
By laughter: attestation of the Muse
That low-and-ugsome is not signed and sealed

Incontrovertibly man's portion here,
Or, if here, – why, still high-and-fair exists
In that ethereal realm where laughs our soul
Lift by the Muse. Hail thou her ministrant!
Hail who accepted no deformity
In man as normal and remediless,
But rather pushed it to such gross extreme
That, outraged, we protest by eye's recoil
The opposite proves somewhere rule and law!
Hail who implied, by limning Lamachos,
Plenty and pastime wait on peace, not war!
Philokleon – better bear a wrong than plead,
Play the litigious fool to stuff the mouth
Of dikast with the due three-obol fee!
The Paphlagonian – stick to the old sway
Of few and wise, not rabble-government!
Trugaios, Pisthetairos, Strepsiades, –
Why multiply examples? Hail, in fine,
The hero of each painted monster – so
Suggesting the unpictured perfect shape!
Pour out! A laugh to Aristophanes!"

'"Stay, my fine Strattis" – and I stopped applause –
"To the Good Genius – but the Tragic Muse!
She who instructs her poet, bids man's soul
Play man's part merely nor attempt the gods'
Ill-guessed of! Task humanity to height,
Put passion to prime use, urge will, unshamed
When will's last effort breaks in impotence!
No power forego, elude: no weakness, – plied
Fairly by power and will, – renounce, deny!
Acknowledge, in such miscalled weakness strength
Latent: and substitute thus things for words!
Make man run life's race fairly, – legs and feet,
Craving no false wings to o'erfly its length!
Trust on, trust ever, trust to end – in truth!
By truth of extreme passion, utmost will,
Shame back all false display of either force –
Barrier about such strenuous heat and glow,
That cowardice shall shirk contending, – cant,
Pretension, shrivel at truth's first approach!
Pour to the Tragic Muse's ministrant

Who, as he pictured pure Hippolutos,
Abolished our earth's blot Ariphrades;
Who, as he drew Bellerophon the bold,
Proclaimed Kleonumos incredible;
Who, as his Theseus towered up man once more,
Made Alkibiades shrink boy again!
A tear – no woman's tribute, weak exchange
For action, water spent and heart's-blood saved –
No man's regret for greatness gone, ungraced
Perchance by even that poor meed, man's praise –
But some god's superabundance of desire,
Yearning of will to 'scape necessity, –
Love's overbrimming for self-sacrifice,
Whence good might be, which never else may be,
By power displayed, forbidden this strait sphere, –
Effort expressible one only way –
Such tear from me fall to Euripides!"

'The Thasian! – All, the Thasian, I account!

'Whereupon outburst the whole company
Into applause and – laughter, would you think?

'"The unrivalled one! How, never at a loss,
He turns the Tragic on its Comic side
Else imperceptible! Here's death itself –
Death of a rival, of an enemy, –
Scarce seen as Comic till the master-touch
Made it acknowledge Aristophanes!
Lo, that Euripidean laurel-tree
Struck to the heart by lightning! Sokrates
Would question us, with buzz of how and why,
Wherefore the berry's virtue, the bloom's vice,
Till we all wished him quiet with his friend;
Agathon would compose an elegy,
Lyric bewailment fit to move a stone,
And, stones responsive, we might wince, 'tis like;
Nay, with most cause of all to weep the least,
Sophokles ordains mourning for his sake
While we confess to a remorseful twinge: –
Suddenly, who but Aristophanes,
Prompt to the rescue, puts forth solemn hand,

Singles us out the tragic tree's best branch,
Persuades it groundward and, at tip, appends,
For votive-visor, Faun's goat-grinning face!
Back it flies, evermore with jest a-top,
And we recover the true mood, and laugh!"

'I felt as when some Nikias, – ninny-like
Troubled by sunspot-portent, moon-eclipse, –
At fault a little, sees no choice but sound
Retreat from foeman; and his troops mistake
The signal, and hail onset in the blast,
And at their joyous answer, *alalé*,
Back the old courage brings the scattered wits;
He wonders what his doubt meant, quick confirms
The happy error, blows the charge amain.
So I repaired things.

'Both be praised' thanked I.
'You who have laughed with Aristophanes,
You who wept rather with the Lord of Tears!
Priest, do thou, president alike o'er each,
Tragic and Comic function of the god,
Help with libation to the blended twain!
Either of which who serving, only serves –
Proclaims himself disqualified to pour
To that Good Genius – complex Poetry,
Uniting each god-grace, including both:
Which, operant for body as for soul,
Masters alike the laughter and the tears,
Supreme in lowliest earth, sublimest sky.
Who dares disjoin these, – whether he ignores
Body or soul, whichever half destroys, –
Maims the else perfect manhood, perpetrates
Again the inexpiable crime we curse –
Hacks at the Hermai, halves each guardian shape
Combining, nowise vainly, prominence
Of august head and enthroned intellect,
With homelier symbol of asserted sense, –
Nature's prime impulse, earthly appetite.
For, when our folly ventures on the freak,
Would fain abolish joy and fruitfulness,
Mutilate nature – what avails the Head

Left solitarily predominant, –
Unbodied soul, – not Hermes, both in one?
I, no more than our City, acquiesce
In such a desecration, but defend
Man's double nature – ay, wert thou its foe!
Could I once more, thou cold Euripides,
Encounter thee, in naught would I abate
My warfare, nor subdue my worst attack
On thee whose life-work preached "Raise soul, sink sense!
Evirate Hermes!" – would avenge the god,
And justify myself. Once face to face,
Thou, the argute and tricksy, shouldst not wrap,
As thine old fashion was, in silent scorn
The breast that quickened at the sting of truth,
Nor turn from me, as, if the tale be true,
From Lais when she met thee in thy walks,
And questioned why she had no rights as thou:
Not so shouldst thou betake thee, be assured,
To book and pencil, deign me no reply!
I would extract an answer from those lips
So closed and cold, were mine the garden-chance!
Gone from the world! Does none remain to take
Thy part and ply me with thy sophist-skill?
No sun makes proof of his whole potency
For gold and purple in that orb we view:
The apparent orb does little but leave blind
The audacious, and confused the worshipping;
But, close on orb's departure, must succeed
The serviceable cloud, – must intervene,
Induce expenditure of rose and blue,
Reveal what lay in him was lost to us.
So, friends, what hinders, as we homeward go,
If, privileged by triumph gained today,
We clasp that cloud our sun left saturate,
The Rhodian rosy with Euripides?
Not of my audience on my triumph-day,
She nor her husband! After the night's news
Neither will sleep but watch; I know the mood.
Accompany! my crown declares my right!

'And here you stand with those warm golden eyes!

'In honest language, I am scarce too sure
Whether I really felt, indeed expressed
Then, in that presence, things I now repeat:
Nor half, nor any one word, – will that do?
May be, such eyes must strike conviction, turn
One's nature bottom upwards, show the base –
The live rock latent under wave and foam:
Superimposure these! Yet solid stuff
Will ever and anon, obeying star,
(And what star reaches rock-nerve like an eye?)
Swim up to surface, spout or mud or flame,
And find no more to do than sink as fast.

'Anyhow, I have followed happily
The impulse, pledged my Genius with effect,
Since, come to see you, I am shown – myself!'

I answered:

'One of us declared for both
"Welcome the glory of Aristophanes."
The other adds: and, – if that glory last,
Nor marsh-born vapour creep to veil the same, –
Once entered, share in our solemnity!
Commemorate, as we, Euripides!'

'What?' he looked round, 'I darken the bright house?
Profane the temple of your deity?
That's true! Else wherefore does he stand portrayed?
What Rhodian paint and pencil saved so much,
Beard, freckled face, brow – all but breath, I hope!
Come, that's unfair: myself am somebody,
Yet my pictorial fame's just potter's-work, –
I merely figure on men's drinking-mugs!
I and the Flat-nose, Sophroniskos' son,
Oft make a pair. But what's this lies below?
His table-book and graver, playwright's tool!
And lo, the sweet psalterion, strung and screwed,
Whereon he tried those *le-é-é-é-és*
And *ke-é-é-é-és* and turns and trills,
Lovely lark's tirra-lirra, lad's delight!
Aischulos' bronze-throat eagle-bark at blood

Has somehow spoiled my taste for twitterings!
With . . . what, and did he leave you "Herakles"?
The "Frenzied Hero," one unfractured sheet,
No pine-wood tablets smeared with treacherous wax –
Papuros perfect as e'er tempted pen!
This sacred twist of bay-leaves dead and sere
Must be that crown the fine work failed to catch, –
No wonder! This might crown "Antiope."
"Herakles" triumph? In your heart perhaps!
But elsewhere? Come now, I'll explain the case,
Show you the main mistake. Give me the sheet!'

I interrupted:

'Aristophanes!
The stranger-woman sues in her abode –
"Be honoured as our guest!" But, call it – shrine,
Then "No dishonour to the Daimon!" bids
The priestess "or expect dishonour's due!"
You enter fresh from your worst infamy,
Last instance of long outrage; yet I pause,
Withhold the word a-tremble on my lip,
Incline me, rather, yearn to reverence, –
So you but suffer that I see the blaze
And not the bolt, – the splendid fancy-fling,
Not the cold iron malice, the launched lie
Whence heavenly fire has withered; impotent,
Yet execrable, leave it 'neath the look
Of yon impassive presence! What he scorned,
His life long, need I touch, offend my foot,
To prove that malice missed its mark, that lie
Cumbers the ground, returns to whence it came?
I marvel, I deplore, – the rest be mute!
But, throw off hate's celestiality, –
Show me, apart from song-flash and wit-flame,
A mere man's hand ignobly clenched against
Yon supreme calmness, – and I interpose,
Such as you see me! Silk breaks lightning's blow!'

He seemed to scarce so much as notice me,
Aught had I spoken, save the final phrase:
Arrested there.

'Euripides grown calm!
Calmness supreme means dead and therefore safe,'
He muttered; then more audibly began –

'Dead! Such must die! Could people comprehend!
There's the unfairness of it! So obtuse
Are all: from Solon downward with his saw
"Let none revile the dead, – no, though the son,
Nay, far descendant, should revile thyself!" –
To him who made Elektra, in the act
Of wreaking vengeance on her worst of foes,
Scruple to blame, since speech that blames insults
Too much the very villain life-released.
Now, *I* say, only after death, begins
That formidable claim, – immunity
Of faultiness from fault's due punishment!
The living, who defame me, – why, they live:
Fools, – I best prove them foolish by their life,
Will they but work on, lay their work by mine,
And wait a little, one Olympiad, say!
Then – where's the vital force, mine froze beside?
The sturdy fibre, shamed my brittle stuff?
The school-correctness, sure of wise award
When my vagaries cease to tickle taste?
Where's censure that must sink me, judgement big
Awaiting just the word posterity
Pants to pronounce? Time's wave breaks, buries – *whom*,
Fools, when myself confronts you four years hence?
But die, ere next Lenaia, – safely so
You 'scape me, slink with all your ignorance,
Stupidity and malice, to that hole
O'er which survivors croak "Respect the dead!"
Ay, for I needs must! But allow me clutch
Only a carrion-handful, lend it sense,
(Mine, not its own, or could it answer me?)
And question "You, I pluck from hiding-place,
Whose cant was, certain years ago, my 'Clouds'
Might last until the swallows came with Spring –
Whose chatter, 'Birds' are unintelligible,
Mere psychologic puzzling: poetry?
List, the true lay to rock a cradle with!

O man of Mitulené, wondrous wise!"
– Would not I rub each face in its own filth
To tune of "Now that years have come and gone,
How does the fact stand? What's demonstrable
By time, that tries things? – your own test, not mine
Who think men are, were, ever will be fools,
Though somehow fools confute fools, – as these, you!
Don't mumble to the sheepish twos and threes
You cornered and called 'audience'! Face this *me*
Who know, and can, and – helped by fifty years –
Do pulverize you pygmies, then as now!"

'Ay, now as then, I pulverize the brood,
Balaustion! Mindful, from the first, where foe
Would hide head safe when hand had flung its stone,
I did not turn cheek and take pleasantry,
But flogged while skin could purple and flesh start,
To teach fools whom they tried conclusions with.
First face a-splutter at me got such splotch
Of prompt slab mud as, filling mouth to maw,
Made its concern thenceforward not so much
To criticize me as go cleanse itself.
The only drawback to which huge delight, –
(He saw it, how he saw it, that calm cold
Sagacity you call Euripides!)
– Why, 'tis that, make a muckheap of a man,
There, pillared by your prowess, he remains,
Immortally immerded. Not so he!
Men pelted him but got no pellet back.
He reasoned, I'll engage, – "Acquaint the world
Certain minuteness butted at my knee?
Dogface Eruxis, the small satirist, –
What better would the manikin desire
Than to strut forth on tiptoe, notable
As who, so far up, fouled me in the flank?"
So dealt he with the dwarfs: we giants, too,
Why must we emulate their pin-point play?
Render imperishable – impotence,
For mud throw mountains? Zeus, by mud unreached,
Well, 'twas no dwarf he heaved Olumpos at!'

My heart burned up within me to my tongue.

'And why must men remember, ages hence,
Who it was rolled down rocks, but refuse too –
Strattis might steal from! mixture-monument,
Recording what? "I, Aristophanes,
Who boast me much inventive in my art,
Against Euripides thus volleyed muck
Because, in art, he too extended bounds.
I – patriot, loving peace and hating war, –
Choosing the rule of few, but wise and good,
Rather than mob-dictature, fools and knaves
However multiplied their mastery, –
Despising most of all the demagogue,
(Noisome air-bubble, buoyed up, borne along
By kindred breath of knave and fool below,
Whose hearts swell proudly as each puffing face
Grows big, reflected in that glassy ball,
Vacuity, just bellied out to break
And righteously bespatter friends the first) –
I loathing, – beyond less puissant speech
Than my own god-grand language to declare, –
The fawning, cozenage and calumny
Wherewith such favourite feeds the populace
That fan and set him flying for reward: –
I who, detecting what vice underlies
Thought's superstructure, – fancy's sludge and slime
'Twixt fact's sound floor and thought's mere surface-growth
Of hopes and fears which root no deeplier down
Than where all such mere fungi breed and bloat –
Namely, man's misconception of the God: –
I, loving, hating, wishful from my soul
That truth should triumph, falsehood have defeat,
– Why, all my soul's supremacy of power
Did I pour out in volley just on him
Who, his whole life long, championed every cause
I called my heart's cause, loving as I loved,
Hating my hates, spurned falsehood, championed truth, –
Championed truth not by flagellating foe
With simple rose and lily, gibe and jeer,
Sly wink of boon-companion o'er his bowze
Who, while he blames the liquor, smacks the lip,
Blames, doubtless, but leers condonation too, –

No, the balled fist broke brow like thunderbolt,
Battered till brain flew! Seeing which descent,
None questioned that was first acquaintanceship,
The avenger's with the vice he crashed through bone.
Still, he displeased me; and I turned from foe
To fellow-fighter, flung much stone, more mud, –
But missed him, since he lives aloof, I see."
Pah! stop more shame, deep-cutting glory through,
Nor add, this poet, learned, – found no taunt
Tell like "That other poet studies books!"
Wise, – cried "At each attempt to move our hearts,
He uses the mere phrase of daily life!"
Witty, – "His mother was a herb-woman!"
Veracious, honest, loyal, fair and good, –
"It was Kephisophon who helped him write!"

'Whence, – O the tragic end of comedy! –
Balaustion pities Aristophanes.
For, who believed him? Those who laughed so loud?
They heard him call the sun Sicilian cheese!
Had he called true cheese – curd, would muscle move?
What made them laugh but the enormous lie?
"Kephisophon wrote 'Herakles'? ha, ha,
What can have stirred the wine-dregs, soured the soul
And set a-lying Aristophanes?
Some accident at which he took offence!
The Tragic Master in a moody muse
Passed him unhailing, and it hurts – it hurts!
Beside, there's licence for the Wine-lees-song!"'

Blood burnt the cheek-bone, each black eye flashed fierce.

'But this exceeds our licence! Stay awhile –
That's the solution! both are foreigners,
The fresh-come Rhodian lady and her spouse
The man of Phokis: newly resident,
Nowise instructed – that explains it all!
No born and bred Athenian but would smile,
Unless frown seemed more fit for ignorance.
These strangers have a privilege!

'You blame'
(Presently he resumed with milder mien)
'Both theory and practice – Comedy:
Blame her from altitudes the Tragic friend
Rose to, and upraised friends along with him,
No matter how. Once there, all's cold and fine,
Passionless, rational; our world beneath
Shows (should you condescend to grace so much
As glance at poor Athenai) grimly gross –
A population which, mere flesh and blood,
Eats, drinks and kisses, falls to fisticuffs,
Then hugs as hugely: speaks too as it acts,
Prodigiously talks nonsense, – townsmen needs
Must parley in their town's vernacular.
Such world has, of two courses, one to choose:
Unworld itself, – or else go blackening off
To its crow-kindred, leave philosophy
Her heights serene, fit perch for owls like you.
Now, since the world demurs to either course,
Permit me, – in default of boy or girl,
So they be reared Athenian, good and true, –
To praise what you most blame! Hear Art's defence!
I'll prove our institution, Comedy,
Coëval with the birth of freedom, matched
So nice with our Republic, that its growth
Measures each greatness, just as its decline
Would signalize the downfall of the pair.
Our Art began when Bacchos . . . never mind!
You and your master don't acknowledge gods:
"They are not, no, they are not!" well, – began
When the rude instinct of our race outspoke,
Found, – on recurrence of festivity
Occasioned by black mother-earth's good will
To children, as they took her vintage-gifts, –
Found – not the least of many benefits –
That wine unlocked the stiffest lip, and loosed
The tongue late dry and reticent of joke,
Through custom's gripe which gladness thrusts aside.
So, emulating liberalities,
Heaven joined with earth for that god's day at least,
Renewed man's privilege, grown obsolete,
Of telling truth nor dreading punishment.

Whereon the joyous band disguised their forms
With skins, beast-fashion, daubed each phyz with dregs,
Then hollaed "Neighbour, you are fool, you – knave,
You – hard to serve, you – stingy to reward!"
The guiltless crowed, the guilty sunk their crest,
And good folk gained thereby, 'twas evident.
Whence, by degrees, a birth of happier thought,
The notion came – not simply this to say,
But this to do – prove, put in evidence,
And act the fool, the knave, the harsh, the hunks,
Who *did* prate, cheat, shake fist, draw purse-string tight,
As crowd might see, which only heard before.

'So played the Poet, with his man of parts;
And all the others, found unqualified
To mount cart and be persons, made the mob,
Joined choros, fortified their fellows' fun,
Anticipated the community,
Gave judgement which the public ratified.
Suiting rough weapon doubtless to plain truth,
They flung, for word-artillery, why – filth;
Still, folk who wiped the unsavoury salute
From visage, would prefer the mess to wit –
Steel, poked through midriff with a civil speech,
As now the way is: then, the kindlier mode
Was – drub not stab, ribroast not scarify!
So did Sousarion introduce, and so
Did I, acceding, find the Comic Art:
Club, – if I call it, – notice what's implied!
An engine proper for rough chastisement,
No downright slaying: with impunity –
Provided crabtree, steeped in oily joke,
Deal only such a bruise as laughter cures.
I kept the gained advantage: stickled still
For club-law – stout fun and allowanced thumps:
Knocked in each knob a crevice to hold joke
As fig-leaf holds the fat-fry.

'Next, whom thrash?
Only the coarse fool and the clownish knave?
Higher, more artificial, composite
Offence should prove my prowess, eye and arm!

Not who robs hen-roost, tells of untaxed figs,
Spends all his substance on stewed ellops-fish,
Or gives a pheasant to his neighbour's wife:
No! strike malpractice that affects the State,
The common weal – intriguer or poltroon,
Venality, corruption, what care I
If shrewd or witless merely? – so the thing
Lay sap to aught that made Athenai bright
And happy, change her customs, lead astray
Youth or age, play the demagogue at Pnux,
The sophist in Palaistra, or – what's worst,
As widest mischief, – from the Theatre
Preach innovation, bring contempt on oaths,
Adorn licentiousness, despise the Cult.
Are such to be my game? Why, then there wants
Quite other cunning than a cudgel-sweep!
Grasp the old stout stock, but new tip with steel
Each boss, if I would bray – no callous hide
Simply, but Lamachos in coat of proof,
Or Kleon cased about with impudence!
Shaft pushed no worse while point pierced sparkling so
That none smiled "Sportive, what seems savagest,
– Innocuous anger, spiteless rustic mirth!"
Yet spiteless in a sort, considered well,
Since I pursued my warfare till each wound
Went through the mere man, reached the principle
Worth purging from Athenai. Lamachos?
No, I attacked war's representative;
Kleon? No, flattery of the populace;
Sokrates? No, but that pernicious seed
Of sophists whereby hopeful youth is taught
To jabber argument, chop logic, pore
On sun and moon, and worship Whirligig.
O your tragedian, with the lofty grace,
Aims at no other and effects as much?
Candidly: what's a polished period worth,
Filed curt sententiousness of loaded line,
When he who deals out doctrine, primly steps
From just that selfsame moon he maunders of,
And, blood-thinned by his pallid nutriment,
Proposes to rich earth-blood – purity?
In me, 'twas equal-balanced flesh rebuked

Excess alike in stuff-guts Glauketes
Or starveling Chairephon; I challenged both, –
Strong understander of our common life,
I urged sustainment of humanity.
Whereas when your tragedian cries up Peace –
He's silent as to cheesecakes Peace may chew;
Seeing through rabble-rule, he shuts his eye
To what were better done than crowding Pnux –
That's – dance "*Threttanelo*, the Kuklops drunk!"

'My power has hardly need to vaunt itself!
Opposers peep and mutter, or speak plain:
"No naming names in Comedy!" votes one,
"Nor vilifying live folk!" legislates
Another, "urge amendment on the dead!"
"Don't throw away hard cash," supplies a third,
"But crib from actor's dresses, choros-treats!"
Then Kleon did his best to bully me:
Called me before the Law Court: "Such a play
Satirized citizens with strangers there,
Such other," – why, its fault was in myself!
I was, this time, the stranger, privileged
To act no play at all, – Egyptian, I –
Rhodian or Kameirensian, Aiginete,
Lindian, or any foreigner he liked –
Because I can't write Attic, probably!
Go ask my rivals, – how they roughed my fleece,
And how, shorn pink themselves, the huddled sheep
Shiver at distance from the snapping shears!
Why must they needs provoke me?

'All the same,
No matter for my triumph, I foretell
Subsidence of the day-star: quench his beams
No Aias e'er was equal to the feat
By throw of shield, tough-hided seven times seven,
'Twixt sky and earth! 'tis dullards soft and sure
Who breathe against his brightest, here a sigh
And there a "So let be, we pardon you!"
Till the minute mist hangs a block, has tamed
Noonblaze to "twilight mild and equable,"
Vote the old women spinning out of doors.

Give me the earth-spasm, when the lion ramped
And the bull gendered in the brave gold flare!
O you shall have amusement, – better still,
Instruction! no more horse-play, naming names,
Taxing the fancy when plain sense will serve!
Thearion, now, my friend who bakes you bread,
What's worthier limning than his household life?
His whims and ways, his quarrels with the spouse,
And how the son, instead of learning knead
Kilikian loaves, brings heart-break on his sire
By buying horseflesh branded *San*, each flank,
From shrewd Menippos who imports the ware:
While pretty daughter Kepphé too much haunts
The shop of Sporgilos the barber! brave!
Out with Thearion's meal-tub politics
In lieu of Pisthetairos, Strepsiades!
That's your exchange? O Muse of Megara!
Advise the fools "*Feed babe on weasel-lap*
For wild-boar's marrow, Cheiron's hero-pap,
And rear, for man – Ariphrades, mayhap!"
Yes, my Balaustion, yes, my Euthukles,
That's *your* exchange, – who, foreigners in fact
And fancy, would impose your squeamishness
On sturdy health, and substitute such brat
For the right offspring of us Rocky Ones,
Because babe kicks the cradle, – crows, not mewls!

'Which brings me to the prime fault, poison-speck
Whence all the plague springs – that first feud of all
'Twixt me and you and your Euripides.
"Unworld the world" frowns he, my opposite.
I cry "Life!" "Death," he groans, "our better Life!"
Despise what is – the good and graspable,
Prefer the out of sight and in at mind,
To village-joy, the well-side violet-patch,
The jolly club-feast when our field's in soak,
Roast thrushes, hare-soup, pea-soup, deep washed down
With Peparethian; the prompt paying off
That black-eyed brown-skinned country-flavoured wench
We caught among our brushwood foraging:
On these look fig-juice, curdle up life's cream,
And fall to magnifying misery!

Or, if you condescend to happiness,
Why, talk, talk, talk about the empty name
While thing's self lies neglected 'neath your nose!
I need particular discourtesy
And private insult from Euripides
To render contest with him credible?
Say, all of me is outraged! one stretched sense,
I represent the whole Republic, – gods,
Heroes, priests, legislators, poets, – prone,
And pummelled into insignificance,
If will in him were matched with power of stroke.
For see what he has changed or hoped to change!
How few years since, when he began the fight,
Did there beat life indeed Athenai through!
Plenty and peace, then! Hellas thundersmote
The Persian. He himself had birth, you say,
That morn salvation broke at Salamis,
And heroes still walked earth. Themistokles –
Surely his mere back-stretch of hand could still
Find, not so lost in dark, Odusseus? – he
Holding as surely on to Herakles, –
Who touched Zeus, link by link, the unruptured chain!
Were poets absent? Aischulos might hail –
With Pindaros, Theognis, – whom for sire?
Homeros' self, departed yesterday!
While Hellas, saved and sung to, then and thus, –
Ah, people, – ah, lost antique liberty!
We lived, ourselves, undoubted lords of earth:
Wherever olives flourish, corn yields crop
To constitute our title – ours such land!
Outside of oil and breadstuff, – barbarism!
What need of conquest? Let barbarians starve!
Devote our whole strength to our sole defence,
Content with peerless native products, home,
Beauty profuse in earth's mere sights and sounds,
Such men, such women, and such gods their guard!
The gods? he worshipped best who feared them most,
And left their nature uninquired into,
– Nature? their very names! pay reverence,
Do sacrifice for our part, theirs would be
To prove benignantest of playfellows.
With kindly humanism they countenanced

Our emulation of divine escapes
Through sense and soul: soul, sense are made to use;
Use each, acknowledging its god the while!
Crush grape, dance, drink, indulge, for Bacchos' sake!
'Tis Aphrodité's feast-day – frisk and fling,
Provided we observe our oaths, and house
Duly the stranger: Zeus takes umbrage else!
Ah, the great time – had I been there to taste!
Perikles, right Olumpian, – occupied
As yet with getting an Olumpos reared
Marble and gold above Akropolis, –
Wisely so spends what thrifty fools amassed
For cut-throat projects. Who carves Promachos?
Who writes the "Oresteia"?

'Ah, the time!
For, all at once, a cloud has blanched the blue,
A cold wind creeps through the close vineyard-rank,
The olive-leaves curl, violets crisp and close
Like a nymph's wrinkling at the bath's first splash
On breast. (Your pardon!) There's a restless change,
Deterioration. Larks and nightingales
Are silenced, here and there a gorcrow grim
Flaps past, as scenting opportunity.
Where Kimon passaged to the Boulé once,
A starveling crew, unkempt, unshorn, unwashed,
Occupy altar-base and temple-step,
Are minded to indoctrinate our youth!
How call these carrion kill-joys that intrude?
"Wise men," their nomenclature! Prodikos –
Who scarce could, unassisted, pick his steps
From way Theseia to the Tripods' way, –
This empty noddle comprehends the sun, –
How he's Aigina's bigness, wheels no whit
His way from east to west, nor wants a steed!
And here's Protagoras sets wrongheads right,
Explains what virtue, vice, truth, falsehood mean,
Makes all we seemed to know prove ignorance
Yet knowledge also, since, on either side
Of any question, something is to say,
Nothing to 'stablish, all things to disturb!
And shall youth go and play at kottabos,

Leaving unsettled whether moon-spots breed?
Or dare keep Choes ere the problem's solved –
Why should I like my wife who dislikes me?
"But sure the gods permit this, censure that?"
So tell them! straight the answer's in your teeth:
"You relegate these points, then, to the gods?
What and where are they?" What my sire supposed,
And where yon cloud conceals them! "Till they 'scape
And scramble down to Leda, as a swan,
Europa, as a bull! why not as – ass
To somebody? Your sire was Zeus perhaps!
Either – away with such ineptitude!
Or, wanting energy to break your bonds,
Stick to the good old stories, think the rain
Is – Zeus distilling pickle through a sieve!
Think thunder's thrown to break Theoros' head
For breaking oaths first! Meanwhile let ourselves
Instruct your progeny you prate like fools
Of father Zeus, who's but the atmosphere,
Brother Poseidon, otherwise called – sea,
And son Hephaistos – fire and nothing else!
Over which nothings there's a something still,
'Necessity,' that rules the universe
And cares as much about your Choes-feast
Performed or intermitted, as you care
Whether gnats sound their trump from head or tail!"
When, stupefied at such philosophy,
We cry – Arrest the madmen, governor!
Pound hemlock and pour bull's-blood, Perikles! –
Would you believe? The Olumpian bends his brow,
Scarce pauses from his building! "Say they thus?
Then, they say wisely. Anaxagoras,
I had not known how simple proves eclipse
But for thy teaching! Go, fools, learn like me!"

'Well, Zeus nods: man must reconcile himself,
So, let the Charon's-company harangue,
And Anaxagoras be – as we wish!
A comfort is in nature: while grass grows
And water runs, and sesame pricks tongue,
And honey from Brilesian hollow melts
On mouth, and Bacchis' flavorous lip beats both,

You will not be untaught life's use, young man?
Pho! My young man just proves that panniered ass
Said to have borne Youth strapped on his stout back,
With whom a serpent bargained, bade him swap
The priceless boon for – water to quench thirst!
What's youth to my young man? In love with age,
He Spartanizes, argues, fasts and frowns,
Denies the plainest rules of life, long since
Proved sound; sets all authority aside,
Must simply recommence things, learn ere act,
And think out thoroughly how youth should pass –
Just as if youth stops passing, all the same!

'One last resource is left us – poetry!
Vindicate nature, prove Plataian help,
Turn out, a thousand strong, all right and tight,
To save Sense, poet! Bang the sophist-brood
Would cheat man out of wholesome sustenance
By swearing wine is water, honey – gall,
Saperdion – the Empousa! Panic-smit,
Our juveniles abstain from Sense and starve:
Be yours to disenchant them! Change things back!
Or better, strain a point the other way
And handsomely exaggerate wronged truth!
Lend wine a glory never gained from grape,
Help honey with a snatch of him we style
The Muses' Bee, bay-bloom-fed Sophokles,
And give Saperdion a Kimberic robe!

'"I, his successor," gruff the answer grunts,
"Incline to poetize philosophy,
Extend it rather than restrain; as thus –
Are heroes men? No more, and scarce as much,
Shall mine be represented. Are men poor?
Behold them ragged, sick, lame, halt and blind!
Do they use speech? Ay, street-terms, market-phrase!
Having thus drawn sky earthwards, what comes next
But dare the opposite, lift earth to sky?
Mere puppets once, I now make womankind,
For thinking, saying, doing, match the male.
Lift earth? I drop to, dally with, earth's dung!
– Recognize in the very slave – man's mate,

Declare him brave and honest, kind and true,
And reasonable as his lord, in brief.
I paint men as they are – so runs my boast –
Not as they should be: paint – what's part of man
– Women and slaves – not as, to please your pride,
They should be, but your equals, as they are.
O and the Gods! Instead of abject mien,
Submissive whisper, while my Choros cants
'Zeus, – with thy cubit's length of attributes, –
May I, the ephemeral, ne'er scrutinize
Who made the heaven and earth and all things there!'
Myself shall say" . . . Ay, Herakles may help!
Give me, – I want the very words, – attend!'

He read. Then 'Murder's out, – "There are no Gods,"
Mån has no master, owns, by consequence,
No right, no wrong, except to please or plague
His nature: what man likes be man's sole law!
Still, since he likes Saperdion, honey, figs,
Man may reach freedom by your roundabout.
"Never believe yourselves the freer thence!
There are no gods, but there's 'Necessity,' –
Duty enjoined you, fact in figment's place,
Throned on no mountain, native to the mind!
Therefore deny yourselves Saperdion, figs
And honey, for the sake of – what I dream,
A-sitting with my legs up!"

'Infamy!
The poet casts in calm his lot with these
Assailants of Apollon! Sworn to serve
Each Grace, the Furies call him minister –
He, who was born for just that roseate world
Renounced so madly, where what's false is fact,
Where he makes beauty out of ugliness,
Where he lives, life itself disguised for him
As immortality – so works the spell,
The enthusiastic mood which marks a man
Muse-mad, dream-drunken, wrapt around by verse,
Encircled with poetic atmosphere,
As lark emballed by its own crystal song,
Or rose enmisted by that scent it makes!

No, this were unreality! the real
He wants, not falsehood, – truth alone he seeks,
Truth, for all beauty! Beauty, in all truth –
That's certain somehow! Must the eagle lilt
Lark-like, needs fir-tree blossom rose-like? No!
Strength and utility charm more than grace,
And what's most ugly proves most beautiful.
So much assistance from Euripides!

'Whereupon I betake me, since needs must,
To a concluding – "Go and feed the crows!"
Do! Spoil your art as you renounce your life,
Poetize your so precious system, do,
Degrade the hero, nullify the god,
Exhibit women, slaves and men as peers, –
Your castigation follows prompt enough!
When all's concocted upstairs, heels o'er head,
Down must submissive drop the masterpiece
For public praise or blame: so, praise away,
Friend Socrates, wife's-friend Kephisophon!
Boast innovations, cramp phrase, uncouth song,
Hard matter and harsh manner, gods, men, slaves
And women jumbled to a laughing-stock
Which Hellas shall hold sides at lest she split!
Hellas, on these, shall have her word to say!

'She has it and she says it – there's the curse! –
She finds he makes the shag-rag hero-race,
The noble slaves, wise women, move as much
Pity and terror as true tragic types:
Applauds inventiveness – the plot so new,
The turn and trick subsidiary so strange!
She relishes that homely phrase of life,
That common town-talk, more than trumpet-blasts:
Accords him right to chop and change a myth:
What better right had he, who told the tale
In the first instance, to embellish fact?
This last may disembellish yet improve!
Both find a block: this man carves back to bull
What first his predecessor cut to sphinx:
Such genuine actual roarer, nature's brute,
Intelligible to our time, was sure

The old-world artist's purpose, had he worked
To mind; this both means and makes the thing!
If, past dispute, the verse slips oily-bathed
In unctuous music – say, effeminate –
We also say, like Kuthereia's self,
A lulling effluence which enswathes some isle
Where hides a nymph, not seen but felt the more.
That's Hellas' verdict!

'Does Euripides
Even so far absolved, remain content?
Nowise! His task is to refine, refine,
Divide, distinguish, subtilize away
Whatever seemed a solid planting-place
For foot-fall, – not in that phantasmal sphere
Proper to poet, but on vulgar earth
Where people used to tread with confidence.
There's left no longer one plain positive
Enunciation incontestable
Of what is good, right, decent here on earth.
Nobody now can say "this plot is mine,
Though but a plethron square, – my duty!" – "Yours?
Mine, or at least not yours," snaps somebody!
And, whether the dispute be parent-right
Or children's service, husband's privilege
Or wife's submission, there's a snarling straight,
Smart passage of opposing "yea" and "nay,"
"Should," "should not," till, howe'er the contest end,
Spectators go off sighing – Clever thrust!
Why was I so much hurried to pay debt,
Attend my mother, sacrifice an ox,
And set my name down "for a trireme, good"?
Something I might have urged on t'other side!
No doubt, Kresphontes or Bellerophon
We don't meet every day; but Stab-and-stitch
The tailor – ere I turn the drachmas o'er
I owe him for a chiton, as he thinks,
I'll pose the blockhead with an argument!

'So has he triumphed, your Euripides!
Oh, I concede, he rarely gained a prize:
That's quite another matter! cause for that!

Still, when 'twas got by Ions, Iophons,
Off he would pace confoundedly superb,
Supreme, no smile at movement on his mouth
Till Sokrates winked, whispered: out it broke!
And Aristullos jotted down the jest,
While Iophons or Ions, bay on brow,
Looked queerly, and the foreigners – like you –
Asked o'er the border with a puzzled smile
– "And so, you value Ions, Iophons,
Euphorions! How about Euripides?"
(Eh, brave bard's-champion? Does the anger boil?
Keep within bounds a moment, – eye and lip
Shall loose their doom on me, their fiery worst!)
What strangers? Archelaos heads the file!
He sympathizes, he concerns himself,
He pens epistle, each successless play:
"Athenai sinks effete; there's younger blood
In Makedonia. Visit where I rule!
Do honour to me and take gratitude!
Live the guest's life, or work the poet's way,
Which also means the statesman's: he who wrote
'Erechtheus' may seem rawly politic
At home where Kleophon is ripe; but here
My council-board permits him choice of seats."

'Now this was operating, – what should prove
A poison-tree, had flowered far on to fruit
For many a year, – when I was moved, first man,
To dare the adventure, down with root and branch.
So, from its sheath I drew my Comic steel,
And dared what I am now to justify.
A serious question first, though!

'Once again!
Do you believe, when I aspired in youth,
I made no estimate of power at all,
Nor paused long, nor considered much, what class
Of fighters I might claim to join, beside
That class wherewith I cast in company?
Say, you – profuse of praise no less than blame–
Could not I have competed – franker phrase

Might trulier correspond to meaning – still,
Competed with your Tragic paragon?
Suppose me minded simply to make verse,
To fabricate, parade resplendent arms,
Flourish and sparkle out a Trilogy, –
Where was the hindrance? But my soul bade "Fight!
Leave flourishing for mock-foe, pleasure-time;
Prove arms efficient on real heads and hearts!"
How? With degeneracy sapping fast
The Marathonian muscle, nerved of old
To maul the Mede, now strung at best to help
– How did I fable? – War and Hubbub mash
To mincemeat Fatherland and Brotherhood,
Pound in their mortar Hellas, State by State,
That greed might gorge, the while frivolity
Rubbed hands and smacked lips o'er the dainty dish!
Authority, experience – pushed aside
By any upstart who pleads throng and press
O' the people! "Think, say, do thus!" Wherefore, pray?
"We are the people: who impugns our right
Of choosing Kleon that tans hide so well,
Huperbolos that turns out lamps so trim,
Hemp-seller Eukrates or Lusikles
Sheep-dealer, Kephalos the potter's son,
Diitriphes who weaves the willow-work
To go round bottles, and Nausikudes
The meal-man? Such we choose and more, their mates,
To think and say and do in our behalf!"
While sophistry wagged tongue, emboldened still,
Found matter to propose, contest, defend,
'Stablish, turn topsy-turvy, – all the same,
No matter what, provided the result
Were something new in place of something old, –
Set wagging by pure insolence of soul
Which needs must pry into, have warrant for
Each right, each privilege good policy
Protects from curious eye and prating mouth!
Everywhere lust to shape the world anew,
Spurn this Athenai as we find her, build
A new impossible Cloudcuckooburg
For feather-headed birds, once solid men,

Where rules, discarding jolly habitude,
Nourished on myrtle-berries and stray ants,
King Tereus who, turned Hoopoe Triple-Crest,
Shall terrify and bring the gods to terms!

'Where was I? Oh! Things ailing thus – I ask,
What cure? Cut, thrust, hack, hew at heap-on-heaped
Abomination with the exquisite
Palaistra-tool of polished Tragedy?
Erechtheus shall harangue Amphiktuon,
And incidentally drop word of weight
On justice, righteousness, so turn aside
The audience from attacking Sicily! –
The more that Choros, after he recounts
How Phrixos rode the ram, the far-famed Fleece,
Shall add – at last fall of grave dancing-foot –
"Aggression never yet was helped by Zeus!"
That helps or hinders Alkibiades?
As well expect, should Pheidias carve Zeus' self
And set him up, some half a mile away,
His frown would frighten sparrows from your field!
Eagles may recognize their lord, belike,
But as for vulgar sparrows, – change the god,
And plant some big Priapos with a pole!
I wield the Comic weapon rather – hate!
Hate! honest, earnest and directest hate –
Warfare wherein I close with enemy,
Call him one name and fifty epithets,
Remind you his great-grandfather sold bran,
Describe the new exomion, sleeveless coat
He knocked me down last night and robbed me of,
Protest he voted for a tax on air!
And all this hate – if I write Comedy –
Finds tolerance, most like – applause, perhaps
True veneration; for I praise the god
Present in person of his minister,
And pay – the wilder my extravagance –
The more appropriate worship to the Power
Adulterous, night-roaming, and the rest:
Otherwise, – that originative force
Of nature, impulse stirring death to life,
Which, underlying law, seems lawlessness,

Yet is the outbreak which, ere order be,
Must thrill creation through, warm stocks and stones,
Phales Iacchos.

'Comedy for me!
Why not for you, my Tragic masters? Sneaks
Whose art is mere desertion of a trust!
Such weapons lay to hand, the ready club,
The clay-ball, on the ground a stone to snatch, –
Arms fit to bruise the boar's neck, break the chine
O' the wolf, – and you must impiously – despise?
No, I'll say, furtively let fall that trust
Consigned you! 'Twas not "take or leave alone,"
But "take and, wielding, recognize your god
In his prime attributes!" And though full soon
You sneaked, subsided into poetry,
Nor met your due reward, still, – heroize
And speechify and sing-song and forego
Far as you may your function, – still its pact
Endures, one piece of early homage still
Exacted of you; after your three bouts
At hoity-toity, great men with long words,
And so forth, – at the end, must tack itself
The genuine sample, the Satyric Play,
Concession, with its wood-boys' fun and freak,
To the true taste of the mere multitude.
Yet, there again! What does your Still-at-itch,
Always-the-innovator? Shrugs and shirks!
Out of his fifty Trilogies, some five
Are somehow suited: Satyrs dance and sing,
Try merriment, a grimly prank or two,
Sour joke squeezed through pursed lips and teeth on edge,
Then quick on top of toe to pastoral sport,
Goat-tending and sheep-herding, cheese and cream,
Soft grass and silver rillets, country-fare –
When throats were promised Thasian! Five such feats, –
Then frankly off he threw the yoke; next Droll,
Next festive drama, covenanted fun,
Decent reversion to indecency,
Proved – your "Alkestis"! There's quite fun enough,
Herakles drunk! From out fate's blackening wave
Calamitous, just zigzags some shot star,

Poor promise of faint joy, and turns the laugh
On dupes whose fears and tears were all in waste!

'For which sufficient reasons, in truth's name,
I closed with whom you count the Meaner Muse,
Classed me with Comic Poets who should weld
Dark with bright metal, show their blade may keep
Its adamantine birthright though a-blaze
With poetry, the gold, and wit, the gem,
And strike mere gold, unstiffened out by steel,
Or gem, no iron joints its strength around,
From hand of – posturer, not combatant!

'Such was my purpose: it succeeds, I say!
Have not we beaten Kallikratidas,
Not humbled Sparté? Peace awaits our word,
Spite of Theramenes, and fools his like.
Since my previsions, – warranted too well
By the long war now waged and worn to end –
Had spared such heritage of misery,
My after-counsels scarce need fear repulse.
Athenai, taught prosperity has wings,
Cages the glad recapture. Demos, see,
From folly's premature decrepitude
Boiled young again, emerges from the stew
Of twenty-five years' trouble, sits and sways,
One brilliance and one balsam, – sways and sits
Monarch of Hellas! ay and, sage again,
No longer jeopardizes chieftainship,
No longer loves the brutish demagogue
Appointed by a bestial multitude
But seeks out sound advisers. Who are they?
Ourselves, of parentage proved wise and good!
To such may hap strains thwarting quality,
(As where shall want its flaw mere human stuff?)
Still, the right grain is proper to right race;
What's contrary, call curious accident!
Hold by the usual! Orchard-grafted tree,
Not wilding, race-horse-sired, not rouncey-born,
Aristocrat, no sausage-selling snob!
Nay, why not Alkibiades, come back
Filled by the Genius, freed of petulance,

Frailty, – mere youthfulness that's all at fault, –
Advanced to Perikles and something more?
– Being at least our duly born and bred, –
Curse on what chaunoprockt first gained his ear
And got his . . . well, once true man in right place,
Our commonalty soon content themselves
With doing just what they are born to do,
Eat, drink, make merry, mind their own affairs
And leave state-business to the larger brain.
I do not stickle for their punishment;
But certain culprits have a cloak to twitch,
A purse to pay the piper: flog, say I,
Your fine fantastics, paragons of parts,
Who choose to play the important! Far from side
With us, their natural supports, allies, –
And, best by brain, help who are best by birth
To fortify each weak point in the wall
Built broad and wide and deep for permanence
Between what's high and low, what's rare and vile, –
They cast their lot perversely in with low
And vile, lay flat the barrier, lift the mob
To dizzy heights where Privilege stood firm.
And then, simplicity become conceit, –
Woman, slave, common soldier, artisan,
Crazy with new-found worth, new-fangled claims, –
These must be taught next how to use their heads
And hands in driving man's right to mob's rule!
What fellows thus inflame the multitude?
Your Sokrates, still crying "Understand!"
Your Aristullos, – "Argue!" Last and worst,
Should, by good fortune, mob still hesitate,
Remember there's degree in heaven and earth,
Cry "Aischulos enjoined us fear the gods,
And Sophokles advised respect the kings!"
Why, your Euripides informs them – "Gods?
They are not! Kings? They are, but . . . do not I,
In 'Suppliants,' make my Theseus, – yours, no more, –
Fire up at insult of who styles him King?
Play off that Herald, I despise the most,
As patronizing kings' prerogative
Against a Theseus proud to dare no step
Till he consult the people?"

'Such as these –
Ah, you expect I am for strangling straight?
Nowise, Balaustion! All my roundabout
Ends at beginning, with my own defence.
I dose each culprit just with – Comedy.
Let each be doctored in exact the mode
Himself prescribes: by words, the word-monger –
My words to his words, – my lies, if you like,
To his lies. Sokrates I nickname thief,
Quack, necromancer; Aristullos, – say,
Male Kirké who bewitches and bewrays
And changes folk to swine; Euripides, –
Well, I acknowledge! Every word is false,
Looked close at; but stand distant and stare through,
All's absolute indubitable truth
Behind lies, truth which only lies declare!
For come, concede me truth's in thing not word,
Meaning not manner! Love smiles "rogue" and "wretch"
When "sweet" and "dear" seem vapid: Hate adopts
Love's "sweet" and "dear" when "rogue" and "wretch" fall flat:
Love, Hate – are truths, then, each, in sense not sound.
Further: if Love, remaining Love, fell back
On "sweet" and "dear," – if Hate, though Hate the same,
Dropped down to "rogue" and "wretch," – each phrase were false.
Good! and now grant I hate no matter whom
With reason: I must therefore fight my foe,
Finish the mischief which made enmity.
How? By employing means to most hurt him
Who much harmed me. What way did he do harm?
Through word or deed? Through word? with word, wage war!
Word with myself directly? As direct
Reply shall follow: word to you, the wise,
Whence indirectly came the harm to me?
What wisdom I can muster waits on such.
Word to the populace which, misconceived
By ignorance and incapacity,
Ends in no such effect as follows cause
When I, or you the wise, are reasoned with,
So damages what I and you hold dear?
In that event, I ply the populace

With just such word as leavens their whole lump
To the right ferment for my purpose. *They*
Arbitrate properly between us both?
They weigh my answer with his argument,
Match quip with quibble, wit with eloquence?
All they attain to understand is – blank!
Two adversaries differ: which is right
And which is wrong, none takes on him to say,
Since both are unintelligible. Pooh!
Swear my foe's mother vended herbs she stole,
They fall a-laughing! Add, – his household drudge
Of all-work justifies that office well,
Kisses the wife, composing him the play, –
They grin at whom they gaped in wonderment,
And go off – "Was he such a sorry scrub?
This other seems to know! we praised too fast!"
Why then, my lies have done the work of truth,
Since "scrub," improper designation, means
Exactly what the proper argument
– Had such been comprehensible – proposed
To proper audience – were I graced with such –
Would properly result in; so your friend
Gets an impartial verdict on his verse
"The tongue swears, but the soul remains unsworn!"

'There, my Balaustion! All is summed and said.
No other cause of quarrel with yourself!
Euripides and Aristophanes
Differ: he needs must round our difference
Into the mob's ear; with the mob I plead.
You angrily start forward "This to me?"
No speck of this on you the thrice refined!
Could parley be restricted to us two,
My first of duties were to clear up doubt
As to our true divergence each from each.
Does my opinion so diverge from yours?
Probably less than little – not at all!
To know a matter, for my very self
And intimates – that's one thing; to imply
By "knowledge" – loosing whatsoe'er I know
Among the vulgar who, by mere mistake,
May brain themselves and me in consequence, –

That's quite another. "O the daring flight!
This only bard maintains the exalted brow,
Nor grovels in the slime nor fears the gods!"
Did *I* fear – *I* play superstitious fool,
Who, with the due proviso, introduced,
Active and passive, their whole company
As creatures too absurd for scorn itself?
Zeus? I have styled him – "slave, mere thrashing-block!"
I'll tell you: in my very next of plays,
At Bacchos' feast, in Bacchos' honour, full
In front of Bacchos' representative,
I mean to make main-actor – Bacchos' self!
Forth shall he strut, apparent, first to last,
A blockhead, coward, braggart, liar, thief,
Demónstrated all these by his own mere
Xanthias the man-slave: such man shows such god
Shamed to brute-beastship by comparison!
And when ears have their fill of his abuse,
And eyes are sated with his pummelling, –
My Choros taking care, by, all the while,
Singing his glory, that men recognize
A god in the abused and pummelled beast, –
Then, should one ear be stopped of auditor,
Should one spectator shut revolted eye, –
Why, the Priest's self will first raise outraged voice
"Back, thou barbarian, thou ineptitude!
Does not most license hallow best our day,
And least decorum prove its strictest rite?
Since Bacchos bids his followers play the fool,
And there's no fooling like a majesty
Mocked at, – who mocks the god, obeys the law –
Law which, impute but indiscretion to,
And . . . why, the spirit of Euripides
Is evidently active in the world!"
Do I stop here? No! feat of flightier force!
See Hermes! what commotion raged, – reflect! –
When imaged god alone got injury
By drunkards' frolic! How Athenai stared
Aghast, then fell to frenzy, fit on fit, –
Ever the last the longest! At this hour,
The craze abates a little; so, my Play
Shall have up Hermes: and a Karion, slave,

(Since there's no getting lower) calls our friend
The profitable god, we honour so,
Whatever contumely fouls the mouth –
Bids him go earn more honest livelihood
By washing tripe in well-trough – wash he does,
Duly obedient! Have I dared my best?
Asklepios, answer! – deity in vogue,
Who visits Sophokles familiarly,
If you believe the old man, – at his age,
Living is dreaming, and strange guests haunt door
Of house, belike, peep through and tap at times
When a friend yawns there, waiting to be fetched, –
At any rate, to memorize the fact,
He has spent money, set an altar up
In the god's temple, now in much repute.
That temple-service trust me to describe –
Cheaters and choused, the god, his brace of girls,
Their snake, and how they manage to snap gifts
"And consecrate the same into a bag,"
For whimsies done away with in the dark!
As if, a stone's throw from that theatre
Whereon I thus unmask their dupery,
The thing were not religious and august!

'Of Sophokles himself – nor word nor sign
Beyond a harmless parody or so!
He founds no anti-school, upsets no faith,
But, living, lets live, the good easy soul
Who, – if he saves his cash, unpoetlike,
Loves wine and – never mind what other sport,
Boasts for his father just a sword-blade-smith,
Proves but queer captain when the people claim,
For one who conquered with "Antigone,"
The right to undertake a squadron's charge, –
And needs the son's help now to finish plays,
Seeing his dotage calls for governance
And Iophon to share his property, –
Why, of all this, reported true, I breathe
Not one word – true or false, I like the man.
Sophokles lives and lets live: long live he!
Otherwise, – sharp the scourge and hard the blow!

'And what's my teaching but – accept the old,
Contest the strange! acknowledge work that's done,
Misdoubt men who have still their work to do!
Religions, laws and customs, poetries,
Are old? So much achieved victorious truth!
Each work was product of a life-time, wrung
From each man by an adverse world: for why?
He worked, destroying other older work
Which the world loved and so was loth to lose.
Whom the world beat in battle – dust and ash!
Who beat the world, left work in evidence,
And wears its crown till new men live new lives,
And fight new fights, and triumph in their turn.
I mean to show you on the stage: you'll see
My Just Judge only venture to decide
Between two suitors, which is god, which man,
By thrashing both of them as flesh can bear.
You shall agree, – whichever bellows first,
He's human; who holds longest out, divine:
That is the only equitable test.
Cruelty? Pray, who pricked them on to court
My thong's award? Must they needs dominate?
Then I – rebel. Their instinct grasps the new?
Mine bids retain the old: a fight must be,
And which is stronger the event will show.
O but the pain! Your proved divinity
Still smarts all reddened? And the rightlier served!
Was not some man's-flesh in him, after all?
Do let us lack no frank acknowledgement
There's nature common to both gods and men!
All of them – spirit? What so winced was clay.
Away pretence to some exclusive sphere
Cloud-nourishing a sole selected few
Fume-fed with self-superiority!
I stand up for the common coarse-as-clay
Existence, – stamp and ramp with heel and hoof
On solid vulgar life, you fools disown.
Make haste from your unreal eminence,
And measure lengths with me upon that ground
Whence this mud-pellet sings and summons you!
I know the soul, too, how the spark ascends
And how it drops apace and dies away.

I am your poet-peer, man thrice your match.
I too can lead an airy life when dead,
Fly like Kinesias when I'm cloudward bound;
But here, no death shall mix with life it mars.

'So, my old enemy who caused the fight,
Own I have beaten you, Euripides!
Or, – if your advocate would contravene, –
Help him, Balaustion! Use the rosy strength!
I have not done my utmost, – treated you
As I might Aristullos, mint-perfumed, –
Still, let the whole rage burst in brave attack!
Don't pay the poor ambiguous compliment
Of fearing any pearl-white knuckled fist
Will damage this broad buttress of a brow!
Fancy yourself my Aristonumos,
Ameipsias or Sannurion: punch and pound!
Three cuckoos who cry "cuckoo"! much I care!
They boil a stone! *Neblaretai! Rattei!*'

Cannot your task have end here, Euthukles?
Day by day glides our galley on its path:
Still sunrise and still sunset, Rhodes half-reached,
And still, my patient scribe! no sunset's peace
Descends more punctual than that brow's incline
O'er tablets which your serviceable hand
Prepares to trace. Why treasure up, forsooth,
These relics of a night that make me rich,
But, half-remembered merely, leave so poor
Each stranger to Athenai and her past?
For – how remembered! As some greedy hind
Persuades a honeycomb, beyond the due,
To yield its hoarding, – heedless what alloy
Of the poor bee's own substance taints the gold
Which, unforced, yields few drops, but purity, –
So would you fain relieve of load this brain,
Though the hived thoughts must bring away, with strength,
What words and weakness, strength's receptacle –
Wax from the store! Yet, – aching soothed away, –
Accept the compound! No suspected scent

But proves some rose was rifled, though its ghost
Scarce lingers with what promised musk and myrrh.
No need of farther squeezing. What remains
Can only be Balaustion, just her speech.

Ah, but – because speech serves a purpose still! –

He ended with that flourish. I replied,

Fancy myself your Aristonumos?
Advise me, rather, to remain myself,
Balaustion, – mindful what mere mouse confronts
The forest-monarch Aristophanes!
I who, a woman, claim no quality
Beside the love of all things lovable
Created by a power pre-eminent
In knowledge, as in love I stand perchance,
– You, the consummately-creative! How
Should I, then, dare deny submissive trust
To any process aiming at result
Such as you say your songs are pregnant with?
Result, all judge: means, let none scrutinize
Save those aware how glory best is gained
By daring means to end, ashamed of shame,
Constant in faith that only good works good,
While evil yields no fruit but impotence!
Graced with such plain good, I accept the means.
Nay, if result itself in turn become
Means, – who shall say? – to ends still loftier yet, –
Though still the good prove hard to understand,
The bad still seemingly predominate, –
Never may I forget which order bears
The burden, toils to win the great reward,
And finds, in failure, the grave punishment,
So, meantime, claims of me a faith I yield!
Moreover, a mere woman, I recoil
From what may prove man's-work permissible,
Imperative. Rough strokes surprise: what then?
Some lusty armsweep needs must cause the crash
Of thorn and bramble, ere those shrubs, those flowers,

We fain would have earth yield exclusively,
Are sown, matured and garlanded for boys
And girls, who know not how the growth was gained.
Finally, am I not a foreigner?
No born and bred Athenian, – isled about,
I scarce can drink, like you, at every breath,
Just some particular doctrine which may best
Explain the strange thing I revolt against –
How – by involvement, who may extricate? –
Religion perks up through impiety,
Law leers with licence, folly wise-like frowns,
The seemly lurks inside the abominable.
But opposites, – each neutralizes each
Haply by mixture: what should promise death,
May haply give the good ingredient force,
Disperse in fume the antagonistic ill.
This institution, therefore, – Comedy, –
By origin, a rite, – by exercise,
Proved an achievement tasking poet's power
To utmost, eking legislation out
Beyond the legislator's faculty,
Playing the censor where the moralist
Declines his function, far too dignified
For dealing with minute absurdities:
By efficacy, – virtue's guard, the scourge
Of vice, each folly's fly-flap, arm in aid
Of all that's righteous, customary, sound
And wholesome; sanctioned therefore, – better say,
Prescribed for fit acceptance of this age
By, not alone the long recorded roll
Of earlier triumphs but, success today –
(The multitude as prompt recipient still
Of good gay teaching from that monitor
They crowned this morning – Aristophanes –
As when Sousarion's car first traversed street) –
This product of Athenai – *I* dispute,
Impugn? There's just one only circumstance
Explains that! I, poor critic, see, hear, feel;
But eyes, ears, senses prove me – foreigner!
Who shall gainsay that the raw new-come guest
Blames oft, too sensitive? On every side
Of – larger than your stage – life's spectacle,

Convention here permits and there forbids
Impulse and action, nor alleges more
Than some mysterious 'So do all, and so
Does no one': which the hasty stranger blames
Because, who bends the head unquestioning,
Transgresses, turns to wrong what else were right,
By failure of a reference to law
Beyond convention; blames unjustly, too –
As if, through that defect, all gained were lost
And slave-brand set on brow indelibly; –
Blames unobservant or experienceless
That men, like trees, if stout and sound and sane,
Show stem no more affected at the root
By bough's exceptional submissive dip
Of leaf and bell, light danced at end of spray
To windy fitfulness in wayward sport –
No more lie prostrate – than low files of flower
Which, when the blast goes by, unruffled raise
Each head again o'er ruder meadow-wreck
Of thorn and thistle that refractory
Demurred to cower at passing wind's caprice.
Why shall not guest extend like charity,
Conceive how, – even when astounded most
That natives seem to acquiesce in muck
Changed by prescription, they affirm, to gold, –
Such may still bring to test, still bear away
Safely and surely much of good and true
Though latent ore, themselves unspecked, unspoiled?
Fresh bathed i' the ice-brook, any hand may pass
A placid moment through the lamp's fierce flame:
And who has read your 'Lemnians,' seen 'The Hours,'
Heard 'Female-Playhouse-seat-Preoccupants,'
May feel no worse effect than, once a year,
Those who leave decent vesture, dress in rags
And play the mendicant, conform thereby
To country's rite, and then, no beggar-taint
Retained, don vesture due next morrow-day.
What if I share the stranger's weakness then?
Well, could I also show his strength, his sense
Untutored, ay! – but then untampered with!

I fancy, though the world seems old enough,
Though Hellas be the sole unbarbarous land,
Years may conduct to such extreme of age,
And outside Hellas so isles new may lurk,
That haply, – when and where remain a dream! –
In fresh days when no Hellas fills the world,
In novel lands as strange where, all the same,
Their men and women yet behold, as we,
Blue heaven, black earth, and love, hate, hope and fear,
Over again, unhelped by Attiké –
Haply some philanthropic god steers bark,
Gift-laden, to the lonely ignorance
Islanded, say, where mist and snow mass hard
To metal – ay, those Kassiterides!
Then asks: 'Ye apprehend the human form.
What of this statue, made to Pheidias' mind,
This picture, as it pleased our Zeuxis paint?
Ye too feel truth, love beauty: judge of these!'
Such strangers may judge feebly, stranger-like:
'Each hair too indistinct – for, see our own!
Hands, not skin-coloured as these hands we have,
And lo, the want of due decorum here!
A citizen, arrayed in civic garb,
Just as he walked your streets apparently,
Yet wears no sword by side, adventures thus,
In thronged Athenai! foolish painter's-freak!
While here's his brother-sculptor found at fault
Still more egregiously, who shames the world,
Shows wrestler, wrestling at the public games,
Atrociously exposed from head to foot!'
Sure, the Immortal would impart at once
Our slow-stored knowledge, how small truths suppressed
Conduce to the far greater truth's display, –
Would replace simple by instructed sense,
And teach them how Athenai first so tamed
The natural fierceness that her progeny
Discarded arms nor feared the beast in man:
Wherefore at games, where earth's wise gratitude,
Proved by responsive culture, claimed the prize
For man's mind, body, each in excellence, –
When mind had bared itself, came body's turn,
And only irreligion grudged the gods

One naked glory of their master-work
Where all is glorious rightly understood, –
The human frame; enough that man mistakes:
Let him not think the gods mistaken too!

But, peradventure, if the stranger's eye
Detected . . . Ah, too high my fancy-flight!
Pheidias, forgive, and Zeuxis bear with me –
How on your faultless should I fasten fault
Of my own framing, even? Only say, –
Suppose the impossible were realized,
And some as patent incongruity,
Unseemliness, – of no more warrant, there
And then, than now and here, whate'er the time
And place, – I say, the Immortal – who can doubt? –
Would never shrink, but own 'The blot escaped
Our artist: thus he shows humanity.'

May stranger tax one peccant part in thee,
Poet, three-parts divine? May I proceed?

'Comedy is prescription and a rite.'
Since when? No growth of the blind antique time,
'It rose in Attiké with liberty;
When freedom falls, it too will fall.' Scarce so!
Your games, – the Olympian, Zeus gave birth to these;
Your Pythian, – these were Phoibos' institute.
Isthmian, Nemeian, – Theseus, Herakles
Appointed each, the boys and barbers say!
Earth's day is growing late: where's Comedy?
'Oh, that commenced an age since, – two, belike, –
In Megara, whence here they brought the thing!'
Or I misunderstand, or here's the fact –
Your grandsire could recall that rustic song,
How suchanone was thief, and miser such
And how, – immunity from chastisement
Once promised to bold singers of the same
By daylight on the drunkard's holiday, –
The clever fellow of the joyous troop
Tried acting what before he sang about,
Acted and stole, or hoarded, acting too:
While his companions ranged a-row, closed up

For Choros, – bade the general rabblement
Sit, see, hear, laugh, – not join the dance themselves.
Soon, the same clever fellow found a mate,
And these two did the whole stage-mimicking,
Still closer in approach to Tragedy, –
So led the way to Aristophanes,
Whose grandsire saw Sousarion, and whose sire –
Chionides; yourself wrote 'Banqueters'
When Aischulos had made 'Prometheus,' nay,
All of the marvels; Sophokles, – I'll cite,
'Oidipous' – and Euripides – I bend
The head – 'Medeia' henceforth awed the world!
'Banqueters,' 'Babylonians' – next come you!
Surely the great days that left Hellas free
Happened before such advent of huge help,
Eighty-years-late assistance? Marathon,
Plataia, Salamis were fought, I think,
Before new educators stood reproved,
Or foreign legates blushed, excepted to!
Where did the helpful rite pretend its rise?
Did it break forth, as gifts divine are wont,
Plainly authentic, incontestably
Adequate to the helpful ordinance?
Founts, dowered with virtue, pulse out pure from source;
'Tis there we taste the god's benign intent:
Not when, – fatigued away by journey, foul
With brutish trampling, – crystal sinks to slime,
And lymph forgets the first salubriousness.
Sprang Comedy to light thus crystal-pure?
'Nowise!' yourself protest with vehemence;
'Gross, bestial, did the clowns' diversion break;
Every successor paddled in the slush;
Nay, my contemporaries one and all
Gay played the mudlark till I joined their game;
Then was I first to change buffoonery
For wit, and stupid filth for cleanly sense,
Transforming pointless joke to purpose fine,
Transfusing rude enforcement of home-law –
"Drop knave's-tricks, deal more neighbour-like, ye boors!" –
With such new glory of poetic breath
As, lifting application far past use
O' the present, launched it o'er men's lowly heads

To future time, when high and low alike
Are dead and done with, while my airy power
Flies disengaged, as vapour from what stuff
It – say not, dwelt in – fitlier, dallied with
To forward work, which done, – deliverance brave, –
It soars away, and mud subsides to dust.
Say then, myself invented Comedy!'

So mouths full many a famed Parabasis!
Agreed! No more, then, of prescriptive use,
Authorization by antiquity,
For what offends our judgement! 'Tis your work,
Performed your way: not work delivered you
Intact, intact producible in turn.
Everywhere have you altered old to new –
Your will, your warrant: therefore, work must stand
Or stumble by intrinsic worth. What worth?
Its aim and object! Peace you advocate,
And war would fain abolish from the land:
Support religion, lash irreverence,
Yet laughingly administer rebuke
To superstitious folly, – equal fault!
While innovating rashness, lust of change,
New laws, new habits, manners, men and things,
Make your main quarry, – 'oldest' meaning 'best.'
You check the fretful litigation-itch,
Withstand mob-rule, expose mob-flattery,
Punish mob-favourites; most of all press hard
On sophists who assist the demagogue,
And poets their accomplices in crime.
Such your main quarry: by the way, you strike
Ignobler game, mere miscreants, snob or scamp,
Cowardly, gluttonous, effeminate:
Still with a bolt to spare when dramatist
Proves haply unproficient in his art.
Such aims – alone, no matter for the means –
Declare the unexampled excellence
Of their first author – Aristophanes!

Whereat – Euripides, oh, not thyself –
Augustlier than the need! – thy century
Of subjects dreamed and dared and done, before

'Banqueters' gave dark earth enlightenment,
Or 'Babylonians' played Prometheus here, –
These let me summon to defend thy cause!
Lo, as indignantly took life and shape
Labour by labour, all of Herakles, –
Palpably fronting some o'erbold pretence
'Eurustheus slew the monsters, purged the world!'
So shall each poem pass you and imprint
Shame on the strange assurance. *You* praised Peace?
Sing him full-face, Kresphontes! 'Peace' the theme?
'Peace, in whom depths of wealth lie, – of the blest
Immortals beauteousest, –
Come! for the heart within me dies away,
So long dost thou delay!
O I have feared lest old age, much annoy,
Conquer me, quite outstrip the tardy joy,
Thy gracious triumph-season I would see,
The song, the dance, the sport, profuse of crowns to be.
But come! for my sake, goddess great and dear,
Come to the city here!
Hateful Sedition drive thou from our homes,
With Her who madly roams
Rejoicing in the steel against the life
That's whetted – banish Strife!'

Shall I proceed? No need of next and next!
That were too easy, play so presses play,
Trooping tumultuous, each with instance apt,
Each eager to confute the idle boast.
What virtue but stands forth panegyrized,
What vice, unburned by stigma, in the books
Which bettered Hellas, – beyond graven gold
Or gem-indenture, sung by Phoibos' self
And saved in Kunthia's mountain treasure-house –
Ere you, man, moralist, were youth or boy?
– Not praise which, in the proffer, mocks the praised
By sly admixture of the blameworthy
And enforced coupling of base fellowship, –
Not blame which gloats the while it frowning laughs,
'Allow one glance on horrors – laughable!' –
This man's entire of heart and soul, discharged
Its love or hate, each unalloyed by each,

On objects worthy either; earnestness,
Attribute him, and power! but novelty?
Nor his nor yours a doctrine – all the world's!
What man of full-grown sense and sanity
Holds other than the truth, – wide Hellas through, –
Though truth, he acts, discredit truth he holds?
What imbecile has dared to formulate
'Love war, hate peace, become a litigant!' –
And so preach on, reverse each rule of right
Because he quarrels, combats, goes to law?
No, for his comment runs, with smile or sigh
According to heart's temper, 'Peace were best,
Except occasions when we put aside
Peace, and bid all the blessings in her gift
Quick join the crows, for sake of Marathon!'

'Nay,' you reply; for one, whose mind withstands
His heart, and, loving peace, for conscience' sake
Wants war, – you find a crowd of hypocrites
Whose conscience means ambition, grudge and greed.
On such, reproof, sonorous doctrine, melts
Distilled like universal but thin dew
Which all too sparsely covers country: dear,
No doubt, to universal crop and clown,
Still, each bedewed keeps his own head-gear dry
With upthrust *skiadeion*, shakes adroit
The droppings to his neighbour. No! collect
All of the moisture, leave unhurt the heads
Which nowise need a washing, save and store
And dash the whole condensed to one fierce spout
On some one evildoer, sheltered close, –
The fool supposed, – till you beat guard away,
And showed your audience, not that war was wrong,
But Lamachos absurd, – case, crests and all, –
Not that democracy was blind of choice,
But Kleon and Huperbolos were shams:
Not superstition vile, but Nikias crazed, –
The concrete for the abstract; that's the way!
What matters Choros crying 'Hence, impure!'
You cried 'Ariphrades does thus and thus!'
Now, earnestness seems never earnest more
Than when it dons for garb – indifference;

So there's much laughing: but, compensative,
When frowning follows laughter, then indeed
Scout innuendo, sarcasm, irony! –
Wit's polished warfare glancing at first graze
From off hard headpiece, coarsely-coated brain
O' the commonalty – whom, unless you prick
To purpose, what avails that finer pates
Succumb to simple scratching? Those – not these –
'Tis Multitude, which, moved, fines Lamachos,
Banishes Kleon and burns Sokrates,
House over head, or, better, poisons him.
Therefore in dealing with King Multitude,
Club-drub the callous numskulls! In and in
Beat this essential consequential fact
That here they have a hater of the three,
Who hates in word, phrase, nickname, epithet
And illustration, beyond doubt at all!
And similarly, would you win assent
To – Peace, suppose? You tickle the tough hide
With good plain pleasure her concomitant –
And, past mistake again, exhibit Peace –
Peace, vintager and festive, cheesecake-time,
Hare-slice-and-peasoup-season, household joy:
Theoria's beautiful belongings match
Opora's lavish condescendings: brief,
Since here the people are to judge, you press
Such argument as people understand:
If with exaggeration – what care you?

Have I misunderstood you in the main?
No! then must answer be, such argument,
Such policy, no matter what good love
Or hate it help, in practice proves absurd,
Useless and null: henceforward intercepts
Sober effective blow at what you blame,
And renders nugatory rightful praise
Of thing or person. The coarse brush has daubed –
What room for the fine limner's pencil-mark?
Blame? You curse, rather, till who blames must blush –
Lean to apology or praise, more like!
Does garment, simpered o'er as white, prove grey?
'Black, blacker than Acharnian charcoal, black

Beyond Kimmerian, Stugian blackness black,'
You bawl, till men sigh 'nearer snowiness!'
What follows? What one faint-rewarding fall
Of foe belaboured ne'er so lustily?
Laugh Lamachos from out the people's heart?
He died, commanding, 'hero,' say yourself!
Gibe Nikias into privacy? – nay, shake
Kleon a little from his arrogance
By cutting him to shoe-sole-shreds? I think,
He ruled his life long and, when time was ripe,
Died fighting for amusement, – good tough hide!
Sokrates still goes up and down the streets,
And Aristullos puts his speech in book,
When both should be abolished long ago.
Nay, wretchedest of rags, Ariphrades –
You have been fouling that redoubtable
Harp-player, twenty years, with what effect?
Still he strums on, strums ever cheerily,
And earns his wage, – 'Who minds a joke?' men say.
No, friend! The statues stand – mudstained at most –
Titan or pygmy: what achieves their fall
Will be, long after mud is flung and spent,
Some clear thin spirit-thrust of lightning – truth!

Your praise, then – honey-smearing helps your friend,
More than blame's ordure-smirch hurts foe, perhaps?
Peace, now, misunderstood, ne'er prized enough,
You have interpreted to ignorance
Till ignorance opes eye, bat-blind before,
And for the first time knows Peace means the power
On maw of pan-cake, cheese-cake, barley-cake,
No stop nor stint to stuffing. While, in camp,
Who fights chews rancid tunny, onions raw,
Peace sits at cosy feast with lamp and fire,
Complaisant smooth-sleeked flute-girls giggling gay.
How thick and fast the snow falls, freezing War
Who shrugs, campaigns it, and may break a shin
Or twist an ankle! come, who hesitates
To give Peace, over War, the preference?
Ah, friend – had this indubitable fact
Haply occurred to poor Leonidas,
How had he turned tail on Thermopulai!

It cannot be that even his few wits
Were addled to the point that, so advised,
Preposterous he had answered – 'Cakes are prime,
Hearth-sides are snug, sleek dancing-girls have worth,
And yet – for country's sake, to save our gods
Their temples, save our ancestors their tombs,
Save wife and child and home and liberty, –
I would chew sliced-salt-fish, bear snow – nay, starve,
If need were, – and by much prefer the choice!'
Why, friend, your genuine hero, all the while,
Has been – who served precisely for your butt –
Kleonumos that, wise, cast shield away
On battle-ground; cried 'Cake my buckler be,
Embossed with cream-clot! peace, not war, I choose,
Holding with Dikaiopolis!' Comedy
Shall triumph, Dikaiopolis win assent,
When Miltiades shall next shirk Marathon,
Themistokles swap Salamis for – cake,
And Kimon grunt 'Peace, grant me dancing-girls!'
But sooner, hardly! twenty-five years since,
The war began, – such pleas for Peace have reached
A reasonable age. The end shows all.

And so with all the rest you advocate!
'Wise folk leave litigation! 'ware the wasps!
Whoso loves law and lawyers, heliast-like,
Wants hemlock!' None shows that so funnily.
But, once cure madness, how comports himself
Your sane exemplar, what's our gain thereby?
Philokleon turns Bdelukleon! just this change, –
New sanity gets straightway drunk as sow,
Cheats baker-wives, brawls, kicks, cuffs, curses folk,
Parades a shameless flute-girl, bandies filth
With his own son who cured his father's cold
By making him catch fever – funnily!
But as for curing love of lawsuits – faugh!

And how does new improve upon the old
– Your boast – in even abusing? Rough, may be –
Still, honest was the old mode. 'Call thief – thief!'
But never call thief even – murderer!
Much less call fop and fribble, worse one whit

Than fribble and fop! Spare neither! beat your brains
For adequate invective, – cut the life
Clean out each quality, – but load your lash
With no least lie, or we pluck scourge from hand!
Does poet want a whipping, write bad verse,
Inculcate foul deeds? There's the fault to flog!
You vow 'The rascal cannot read nor write,
Spends more in buying fish than Morsimos,
Somebody helps his Muse and courts his wife,
His uncle deals in crockery, and last, –
Himself's a stranger!' That's the cap and crown
Of stinging-nettle, that's the master-stroke!
What poet-rival, – after 'housebreaker,'
'Fish-gorging,' 'midnight footpad' and so forth, –
Proves not, beside, 'a stranger'? Chased from charge
To charge, and, lie by lie, laughed out of court, –
Lo, wit's sure refuge, satire's grand resource –
All, from Kratinos downward – 'strangers' they!
Pity the trick's too facile! None so raw
Among your playmates but have caught the ball
And sent it back as briskly to – yourself!
You too, my Attic, are styled 'stranger' – Rhodes,
Aigina, Lindos or Kameiros, – nay,
'Twas Egypt reared, if Eupolis be right,
Who wrote the comedy (Kratinos vows)
Kratinos helped a little! Kleon's self
Was nigh promoted Comic, when he haled
My poet into court, and o'er the coals
Hauled and re-hauled 'the stranger, – insolent,
Who brought out plays, usurped our privilege!'
Why must you Comics one and all take stand
On lower ground than truth from first to last?
Why all agree to let folk disbelieve,
So laughter but reward a funny lie?
Repel such onslaughts – answer, sad and grave,
Your fancy-fleerings – who would stoop so low?
Your own adherents whisper, – when disgust
Too menacingly thrills Logeion through
At – Perikles invents this present war
Because men robbed his mistress of three maids –
Or – Sokrates wants burning, house o'er head, –
'What, so obtuse, not read between the lines?

Our poet means no mischief! All should know –
Ribaldry here implies a compliment!
He deals with things, not men, – his men are things –
Each represents a class, plays figure-head
And names the ship: no meaner than the first
Would serve; he styles a trireme "Sokrates" –
Fears "Sokrates" may prove unseaworthy
(That's merely – "Sophists are the bane of boys")
Rat-riddled ("they are capable of theft"),
Rotten or whatsoe'er shows ship-disease,
("They war with gods and worship whirligig").
You never took the joke for earnest? scarce
Supposed mere figure-head meant entire ship,
And Sokrates – the whole fraternity?'

This then is Comedy, our sacred song,
Censor of vice, and virtue's guard as sure:
Manners-instructing, morals' stop-estray,
Which, born a twin with public liberty,
Thrives with its welfare, dwindles with its wane!
Liberty? what so exquisitely framed
And fitted to suck dry its life of life
To last faint fibre? – since that life is truth.
You who profess your indignation swells
At sophistry, when specious words confuse
Deeds right and wrong, distinct before, you say –
(Though all that's done is – dare veracity,
Show that the true conception of each deed
Affirmed, in vulgar parlance, 'wrong' or 'right,'
Proves to be neither, as the hasty hold,
But, change your side, shoots light, where dark alone
Was apprehended by the vulgar sense)
You who put sophistry to shame, and shout
'There's but a single side to man and thing;
A side so much more big than thing or man
Possibly can be, that – believe 'tis true?
Such were too marvellous simplicity!' –
Confess, those sophists whom yourself depict,
(– Abide by your own painting!) what they teach,
They wish at least their pupil to believe,
And, what believe, to practise! Did *you* wish
Hellas should haste, as taught, with torch in hand,

And fire the horrid Speculation-shop?
Straight the shop's master rose and showed the mob
What man was your so monstrous Sokrates;
Himself received amusement, why not they?
Just as did Kleon first play magistrate
And bid you put your birth in evidence –
Since no unbadged buffoon is licensed here
To shame us all when foreign guests may mock –
Then, – birth established, fooling licensed you, –
He, duty done, resumed mere auditor,
Laughed with the loudest at his Lamia-shape,
Kukloboros-roaring, and the camel-rest.
Nay, Aristullos, – once your volley spent
On the male-Kirké and her swinish crew, –
PLATON, – so others call the youth we love, –
Sends your performance to the curious king –
'Do you desire to know Athenai's knack
At turning seriousness to pleasantry?
Read this! One Aristullos means myself.
The author is indeed a merry grig!'
Nay, it would seem as if yourself were bent
On laying down the law 'Tell lies I must –
Aforethought and of purpose, no mistake!'
When forth yourself step, tell us from the stage
'Here you behold the King of Comedy –
Me, who, the first, have purged my every piece
From each and all my predecessors' filth,
Abjured those satyr-adjuncts sewn to bid
The boys laugh, satyr-jokes whereof not one
Least sample but would make my hair turn grey
Beyond a twelvemonth's ravage! I renounce
Mountebank-claptrap, such as firework-fizz
And torchflare, or else nuts and barleycorns
Scattered among the crowd, to scramble for
And stop their mouths with; no such stuff shames me!
Who, – what's more serious, – know both when to strike
And when to stay my hand: once dead, my foe,
Why, done, my fighting! *I* attack a corpse?
I spare the corpse-like even! punish age?
I pity from my soul that sad effete
Toothless old mumbler called Kratinos! once
My rival, – now, alack, the dotard slinks

Ragged and hungry to what hole's his home;
Ay, slinks through byways where no passenger
Flings him a bone to pick. You formerly
Adored the Muses' darling: dotard now,
Why, he may starve! O mob most mutable!'
So you harangued in person; while, – to point
Precisely out, these were but lies you launched, –
Prompt, a play followed primed with satyr-frisks,
No spice spared of the stomach-turning stew,
Full-fraught with torch-display, and barley-throw,
And Kleon, dead enough, bedaubed afresh;
While daft Kratinos – home to hole trudged he,
Wrung dry his wit to the last vinous dregs,
Decanted them to 'Bottle,' – beat, next year, –
'Bottle' and dregs – your best of 'Clouds' and dew!
Where, Comic King, may keenest eye detect
Improvement on your predecessors' work
Except in lying more audaciously?

Why – genius! That's the grandeur, that's the gold –
That's *you* – superlatively true to touch –
Gold, leaf or lump – gold, anyhow the mass
Takes manufacture and proves Pallas' casque
Or, at your choice, simply a cask to keep
Corruption from decay. Your rivals' hoard
May ooze forth, lacking such preservative:
Yours cannot – gold plays guardian far too well!
Genius, I call *you*: dross, your rivals share;
Ay, share and share alike, too! says the world,
However you pretend supremacy
In aught beside that gold, your very own.
Satire? 'Kratinos for our satirist!'
The world cries. Elegance? 'Who elegant
As Eupolis?' resounds as noisily.
Artistic fancy? Choros-creatures quaint?
Magnes invented 'Birds' and 'Frogs' enough,
Archippos punned, Hegemon parodied
To heart's content, before you stepped on stage.
Moral invective? Eupolis exposed
'That prating beggar, he who stole the cup,'
Before your 'Clouds' rained grime on Sokrates;
Nay, what beat 'Clouds' but 'Konnos,' muck for mud?

Courage? How long before, well-masked, you poured
Abuse on Eukrates and Lusikles,
Did Telekleides and Hermippos pelt
Their Perikles and Kumon? standing forth,
Bareheaded, not safe crouched behind a name, –
Philonides or else Kallistratos,
Put forth, when danger threatened, – mask for face,
To bear the brunt, – if blame fell, take the blame, –
If praise . . . why, frank laughed Aristophanes
'They write such rare stuff? No, I promise you!'

Rather, I see all true improvements, made
Or making, go against you – tooth and nail
Contended with; 'tis still Morucheides,
'Tis Euthumenes, Surakosios, nay,
Argurrhios and Kinesias, – common sense
And public shame, these only cleanse your sty!
Coerced, prohibited, – you grin and bear,
And, soon as may be, hug to heart again
The banished nastiness too dear to drop!
Krates could teach and practise festive song
Yet scorn scurrility; as gay and good,
Pherekrates could follow. *Who* loosed hold,
Must let fall rose-wreath, stoop to muck once more?
Did your particular self advance in aught,
Task the sad genius – steady slave the while –
To further – say, the patriotic aim?
No, there's deterioration manifest
Year by year, play by play! survey them all,
From that boy's-triumph when 'Acharnes' dawned,
To 'Thesmophoriazousai,' – this man's-shame!
There, truly, patriot zeal so prominent
Allowed friends' plea perhaps: the baser stuff
Was but the nobler spirit's vehicle.
Who would imprison, unvolatilize
A violet's perfume, blends with fatty oils
Essence too fugitive in flower alone;
So, calling unguent – violet, call the play –
Obscenity impregnated with 'Peace'!
But here's the boy grown bald, and here's the play
With twenty years' experience: where's one spice
Of odour in the hog's-lard? what pretends

To aught except a grease-pot's quality?
Friend, sophist-hating! know, – worst sophistry
Is when man's own soul plays its own self false,
Reasons a vice into a virtue, pleads
'I detail sin to shame its author' – not
'I shame Ariphrades for sin's display'!
'I show Opora to commend Sweet Home' –
Not 'I show Bacchis for the striplings' sake!'

Yet all the same – O genius and O gold –
Had genius ne'er diverted gold from use
Worthy the temple, to do copper's work
And coat a swine's trough – which abundantly
Might furnish Phoibos' tripod, Pallas' throne!
Had you, I dream, discarding all the base,
The brutish, spurned alone convention's watch
And ward against invading decency
Disguised as license, law in lawlessness,
And so, re-ordinating outworn rule,
Made Comedy and Tragedy combine,
Prove some new Both-yet-neither, all one bard,
Euripides with Aristophanes
Coöperant! this, reproducing Now
As that gave Then existence: Life today,
This, as that other – Life dead long ago!
The mob decrees such feat no crown, perchance,
But – why call crowning the reward of quest?
Tell him, my other poet, – where thou walk'st
Some rarer world than e'er Ilissos washed!

But dream goes idly in the air. To earth!
Earth's question just amounts to – which succeeds,
Which fails of two life-long antagonists?
Suppose my charges all mistake! assume
Your end, despite ambiguous means, the best –
The only! you and he, a patriot-pair,
Have striven alike for one result – say, Peace!
You spoke your best straight to the arbiters –
Our people: have you made them end this war
By dint of laughter and abuse and lies
And postures of Opora? Sadly – No!
This war, despite your twenty-five years' work,

May yet endure until Athenai falls,
And freedom falls with her. So much for you!
Now, the antagonist Euripides –
Has he succeeded better? Who shall say?
He spoke quite o'er the heads of Kleon's crowd
To a dim future, and if there he fail,
Why, you are fellows in adversity.
But that's unlike the fate of wise words launched
By music on their voyage. Hail, Depart,
Arrive, Glad Welcome! Not my single wish –
Yours also wafts the white sail on its way,
Your nature too is kingly. All beside
I call pretension – no true potentate,
Whatever intermediary be crowned,
Zeus or Poseidon, where the vulgar sky
Lacks not Triballos to complete the group.
I recognize, – behind such phantom-crew, –
Necessity, Creation, Poet's Power,
Else never had I dared approach, appeal
To poetry, power, Aristophanes!
But I trust truth's inherent kingliness,
Trust who, by reason of much truth, shall reign
More or less royally – may prayer but push
His sway past limit, purge the false from true!
Nor, even so, had boldness nerved my tongue
But that the other king stands suddenly,
In all the grand investiture of death,
Bowing your knee beside my lowly head –
Equals one moment!

Now, arise and go!
Both have done homage to Euripides!

Silence pursued the words: till he broke out –

'Scarce so! This constitutes, I may believe,
Sufficient homage done by who defames
Your poet's foe, since you account me such;
But homage-proper, – pay it by defence
Of him, direct defence and not oblique,
Not by mere mild admonishment of me!'

Defence? The best, the only! I replied.
A story goes – When Sophokles, last year,
Cited before tribunal by his son
(A poet – to complete the parallel)
Was certified unsound of intellect,
And claimed as only fit for tutelage,
Since old and doting and incompetent
To carry on this world's work, – the defence
Consisted just in his reciting (calm
As the verse bore, which sets our heart a-swell
And voice a-heaving too tempestuously)
That choros-chant 'The station of the steed,
Stranger! thou comest to, – Kolonos white!'
Then he looked round and all revolt was dead.
You know the one adventure of my life –
What made Euripides Balaustion's friend.
When I last saw him, as he bade farewell,
'I sang another "Herakles,"' smiled he;
'It gained no prize: your love be prize I gain!
Take it – the tablets also where I traced
The story first with stulos pendent still –
Nay, the psalterion may complete the gift,
So, should you croon the ode bewailing Age,
Yourself shall modulate – same notes, same strings –
With the old friend who loved Balaustion once.'
There they lie! When you broke our solitude,
We were about to honour him once more
By reading the consummate Tragedy.
Night is advanced; I have small mind to sleep;
May I go on, and read, – so make defence,
So test true godship? You affirm, not I,
– Beating the god, affords such test: *I* hold
That when rash hands but touch divinity,
The chains drop off, the prison-walls dispart,
And – fire – he fronts mad Pentheus! Dare we try?

Accordingly I read the perfect piece.

AMPHITRUON: Zeus' Couchmate, – who of mortals knows not me,
Argive Amphitruon whom Alkaios sired
Of old, as Perseus him, I – Herakles?
My home, this Thebai where the earth-born spike
Of Sown-ones burgeoned: Ares saved from these
A handful of their seed that stocks today
With children's children Thebai, Kadmos built.
Of these had Kreon birth, Menoikeus' child,
King of the country, – Kreon that became
The father of this woman, Megara,
Whom, when time was, Kadmeians one and all
Pealed praise to, marriage-songs with fluted help,
While to my dwelling that grand Herakles
Bore her, his bride. But, leaving Thebes – where I
Abode perforce – this Megara and those
Her kinsmen, the desire possessed my son
Rather to dwell in Argos, that walled work,
Kuklopian city, which I fly, myself,
Because I slew Elektruon. Seeking so
To ease away my hardships and once more
Inhabit his own land, for my return
Heavy the price he pays Eurustheus there –
The letting in of light on this choked world!
Either he promised, vanquished by the goad
Of Heré, or because fate willed it thus.
The other labours – why, he toiled them through;
But for this last one – down by Tainaros,
Its mouth, to Haides' realm descended he
To drag into the light the three-shaped hound
Of Hell: whence Herakles returns no more.
Now, there's an old-world tale, Kadmeians have,
How Dirké's husband was a Lukos once,
Holding the seven-towered city here in sway
Before they ruled the land, white-steeded pair,
The twins Amphion, Zethos, born to Zeus.
This Lukos' son, – named like his father too,
No born Kadmeian but Euboia's gift, –
Comes and kills Kreon, lords it o'er the land,

Falling upon our town sedition-sick.
To us, akin to Kreon, just that bond
Becomes the worst of evils, seemingly;
For, since my son is in the earth's abysms,
This man of valour, Lukos, lord and king,
Seeks now to slay these sons of Herakles,
And slay his wife as well, – by murder thus
Thinking to stamp out murder, – slay too me,
(If me 'tis fit you count among men still, –
Useless old age) and all for fear lest these,
Grown men one day, exact due punishment
Of bloodshed and their mother's father's fate.
I therefore, since he leaves me in these domes,
The children's household guardian, – left, when earth's
Dark dread he underwent, that son of mine, –
I, with their mother, lest his boys should die,
Sit at this altar of the saviour Zeus
Which, glory of triumphant spear, he raised
Conquering – my nobly-born! – the Minuai.
Here do we guard our station, destitute
Of all things, drink, food, raiment, on bare ground
Couched side by side: sealed out of house and home
Sit we in a resourcelessness of help.
Our friends – why, some are no true friends, I see!
The rest, that are true, want the means to aid.
So operates in man adversity:
Whereof may never anybody – no,
Though half of him should really wish me well, –
Happen to taste! a friend-test faultless, that!
MEGARA: Old man, who erst didst raze the Taphian town,
Illustriously, the army-leader, thou,
Of speared Kadmeians – how gods play men false!
I, now, missed nowise fortune in my sire,
Who, for his wealth, was boasted mighty once,
Having supreme rule, – for the love of which
Leap the long lances forth at favoured breasts, –
And having children too: and me he gave
Thy son, his house with that of Herakles
Uniting by the far-famed marriage-bed.
And now these things are dead and flown away,
While thou and I await our death, old man,
These Herakleian boys too, whom – my chicks –

I save beneath my wings like brooding bird.
But one or other falls to questioning
'O mother,' cries he, 'where in all the world
Is father gone to? What's he doing? when
Will he come back?' At fault through tender years,
They seek their sire. For me, I put them off,
Telling them stories; at each creak of doors,
All wonder 'Does he come?' – and all a-foot
Make for the fall before the parent knee.
Now then, what hope, what method of escape
Facilitatest thou? – for, thee, old man,
I look to, – since we may not leave by stealth
The limits of the land, and guards, more strong
Than we, are at the outlets: nor in friends
Remain to us the hopes of safety more.
Therefore, whatever thy decision be,
Impart it for the common good of all!
Lest now should prove the proper time to die,
Though, being weak, we spin it out and live.

AMPHITRUON: Daughter, it scarce is easy, do one's best,
To blurt out counsel, things at such a pass.

MEGARA: You want some sorrow more, or so love life?

AMPHITRUON: I both enjoy life, and love hopes beside.

MEGARA: And I; but hope against hope – no, old man!

AMPHITRUON: In these delayings of an ill lurks cure.

MEGARA: But bitter is the meantime, and it bites.

AMPHITRUON: O there may be a run before the wind
From out these present ills, for me and thee,
Daughter, and yet may come my son, thy spouse!
But hush! and from the children take away
Their founts a-flow with tears, and talk them calm,
Steal them by stories – sad theft, all the same!
For, human troubles – they grow weary too;
Neither the wind-blasts always have their strength,
Nor happy men keep happy to the end:
Since all things change – their natures part in twain;
And that man's bravest, therefore, who hopes on,
Hopes ever: to despair is coward-like.

CHOROS: These domes that over-roof,
This long-used couch, I come to, having made
A staff my prop, that song may put to proof
The swan-like power, age-whitened, – poet's aid

Of sobbed-forth dirges – words that stand aloof
From action now: such am I – just a shade
With night for all its face, a mere night-dream –
And words that tremble too: howe'er they seem,
Devoted words, I deem.

O, of a father ye unfathered ones,
O thou old man, and thou whose groaning stuns –
Unhappy mother – only us above,
Nor reaches him below in Haides' realm, thy love!
– (Faint not too soon, urge forward foot and limb
Way-weary, nor lose courage – as some horse
Yoked to the car whose weight recoils on him
Just at the rock-ridge that concludes his course!
Take by the hand, the peplos, anyone
Whose foothold fails him, printless and fordone!
Agèd, assist along me agèd too,
Who, – mate with thee in toils when life was new,
And shields and spears first made acquaintanceship, –
Stood by thyself and proved no bastard-slip
Of fatherland when loftiest glory grew.) –
See now, how like the sire's
Each eyeball fiercely fires!
What though ill-fortune have not left his race?
Neither is gone the grand paternal grace!
Hellas! O what – what combatants, destroyed
In these, wilt thou one day seek – seek, and find all void!

Pause! for I see the ruler of this land,
Lukos, now passing through the palace-gate.
LUKOS: The Herakleian couple – father, wife –
If needs I must, I question: 'must' forsooth?
Being your master – all I please, I ask.
To what time do you seek to spin out life?
What hope, what help see, so as not to die?
Is it you trust the sire of these, that's sunk
In Haides, will return? How past the pitch,
Suppose you have to die, you pile the woe –
Thou, casting, Hellas through, thy empty vaunts
As though Zeus helped thee to a god for son;
And thou, that thou wast styled our best man's wife!
Where was the awful in his work wound up,

If he did quell and quench the marshy snake
Or the Nemeian monster whom he snared
And – says, by throttlings of his arm, he slew?
With these do you outwrestle me? Such feats
Shall save from death the sons of Herakles
Who got praise, being naught, for bravery
In wild-beast-battle, otherwise a blank?
No man to throw on left arm buckler's weight,
Not he, nor get in spear's reach! bow he bore –
True coward's-weapon: shoot first and then fly!
No bow-and-arrow proves a man is brave,
But who keeps rank, – stands, one unwinking stare
As, ploughing up, the darts come, – brave is he.
My action has no impudence, old man!
Providence, rather: for I own I slew
Kreon, this woman's sire, and have his seat.
Nowise I wish, then, to leave, these grown up,
Avengers on me, payment for my deeds.

AMPHITRUON: As to the part of Zeus in his own child,
Let Zeus defend that! As to mine, 'tis me
The care concerns to show by argument
The folly of this fellow, – Herakles,
Whom I stand up for! since to hear thee styled –
Cowardly – that is unendurable.
First then, the infamous (for I account
Amongst the words denied to human speech,
Timidity ascribed thee, Herakles!)
This I must put from thee, with gods in proof.
Zeus' thunder I appeal to, those four steeds
Whereof he also was the charioteer
When, having shot down the earth's Giant-growth –
(Never shaft flew but found and fitted flank)
Triumph he sang in common with the gods.
The Kentaur-race, four-footed insolence –
Go ask at Pholoé, vilest thou of kings,
Whom they would pick out and pronounce best man,
If not my son, 'the seeming-brave,' say'st thou!
But Dirphus, thy Abantid mother-town,
Question her, and she would not praise, I think!
For there's no spot, where having done some good,
Thy country thou mightst call to witness worth.
Now, that all-wise invention, archer's-gear,

Thou blamest: hear my teaching and grow sage!
A man in armour is his armour's slave,
And, mixed with rank and file that want to run,
He dies because his neighbours have lost heart.
Then, should he break his spear, no way remains
Of warding death off, – gone that body-guard,
His one and only; while, whatever folk
Have the true bow-hand, – here's the one main good, –
Though he have sent ten thousand shafts abroad,
Others remain wherewith the archer saves
His limbs and life, too, – stands afar and wards
Away from flesh the foe that vainly stares
Hurt by the viewless arrow, while himself
Offers no full front to those opposite,
But keeps in thorough cover: there's the point
That's capital in combat – damage foe,
Yet keep a safe skin – foe not out of reach
As you are! Thus my words contrast with thine,
And such, in judging facts, our difference.
These children, now, why dost thou seek to slay?
What have they done thee? In a single point
I count thee wise – if, being base thyself,
Thou dread'st the progeny of nobleness.
Yet this bears hard upon us, all the same,
If we must die – because of fear in thee –
A death 'twere fit thou suffer at our hands,
Thy betters, did Zeus rightly judge us all.
If therefore thou art bent on sceptre-sway,
Thyself, here – suffer us to leave the land,
Fugitives! nothing do by violence,
Or violence thyself shalt undergo
When the god's gale may chance to change for thee!
Alas, O land of Kadmos, – for 'tis thee
I mean to close with, dealing out the due
Revilement, – in such sort dost thou defend
Herakles and his children? Herakles
Who, coming, one to all the world, against
The Minuai, fought them and left Thebes an eye
Unblinded henceforth to front freedom with!
Neither do I praise Hellas, nor shall brook
Ever to keep in silence that I count
Towards my son, craven of cravens – her

Whom it behoved go bring the young ones here
Fire, spears, arms – in exchange for seas made safe,
And cleansings of the land – his labour's price.
But fire, spears, arms, – O children, neither Thebes
Nor Hellas has them for you! 'Tis myself,
A feeble friend, ye look to: nothing now
But a tongue's murmur, for the strength is gone
We had once, and with age are limbs a-shake
And force a-flicker! Were I only young,
Still with the mastery o'er bone and thew,
Grasping first spear that came, the yellow locks
Of this insulter would I bloody so –
Should send him skipping o'er the Atlantic bounds
Out of my arm's reach through poltroonery!
CHOROS: Have not the really good folk starting-points
For speech to purpose, – though rare talkers they?
LUKOS: Say thou against us words thou towerest with!
I, for thy words, will deal thee blows, their due.
Go, some to Helikon, to Parnasos
Some, and the clefts there! Bid the woodmen fell
Oak-trunks, and, when the same are brought inside
The city, pile the altar round with logs,
Then fire it, burn the bodies of them all,
That they may learn thereby, no dead man rules
The land here, but 'tis I, by acts like these!
As for you, old sirs, who are set against
My judgements, you shall groan for – not alone
The Herakleian children, but the fate
Of your own house beside, when faring ill
By any chance: and you shall recollect
Slaves are you of a tyranny that's mine!
CHOROS: O progeny of earth, – whom Ares sowed
When he laid waste the dragon's greedy jaw –
Will ye not lift the staves, right-hand supports,
And bloody this man's irreligious head?
Who, being no Kadmeian, rules, – the wretch, –
Our easy youth: an interloper too!
But not of me, at least, shalt thou enjoy
Thy lordship ever; nor my labour's fruit, –
Hand worked so hard for, – have! A curse with thee,
Whence thou didst come, there go and tyrannize!
For never while I live shalt thou destroy

The Herakleian children: not so deep
Hides he below ground, leaving thee their lord!
But we bear both of you in mind, – that thou,
The land's destroyer, dost possess the land,
While he who saved it, loses every right.
I play the busybody – for I serve
My dead friends when they need friends' service most?
O right-hand, how thou yearnest to snatch spear
And serve indeed! in weakness dies the wish,
Or I had stayed thee calling me a slave,
And nobly drawn my breath at home in Thebes
Where thou exultest! – city that's insane,
Sick through sedition and bad government,
Else never had she gained for master – thee!

MEGARA: Old friends, I praise you: since a righteous wrath
For friend's sake well becomes a friend. But no!
On our account in anger with your lord,
Suffer no injury! Hear my advice,
Amphitruon, if I seem to speak aright.
O yes, I love my children! how not love
What I brought forth, what toiled for? and to die –
Sad I esteem too; still, the fated way
Who stiffens him against, that man I count
Poor creature; us, who are of other mood,
Since we must die, behoves us meet our death
Not burnt to cinders, giving foes the laugh –
To me, worse ill than dying, that! We owe
Our houses many a brave deed, now to pay.
Thee, indeed, gloriously men estimate
For spear-work, so that unendurable
Were it that thou shouldst die a death of shame.
And for my glorious husband, where wants he
A witness that he would not save his boys
If touched in their good fame thereby? Since birth
Bears ill with baseness done for children's sake,
My husband needs must be my pattern here.
See now thy hope – how much I count thereon!
Thou thinkest that thy son will come to light:
And, of the dead, who came from Haides back?
But we with talk this man might mollify:
Never! Of all foes, fly the foolish one!
Wise, well-bred people, make concession to!

Sooner you meet respect by speaking soft.
Already it was in my mind – perchance
We might beg off these children's banishment;
But even that is sad, involving them
In safety, ay – and piteous poverty!
Since the host's visage for the flying friend
Has, only one day, the sweet look, 'tis said.
Dare with us death, which waits thee, dared or no!
We call on thine ancestral worth, old man!
For who outlabours what the gods appoint
Shows energy, but energy gone mad.
Since what must – none e'er makes what must not be.

CHOROS: Had anyone, while yet my arms were strong,
Been scorning thee, he easily had ceased.
But we are naught, now; thine henceforth to see –
Amphitruon, how to push aside these fates!

AMPHITRUON: Nor cowardice nor a desire of life
Stops me from dying: but I seek to save
My son his children. Vain! I set my heart,
It seems, upon impossibility.
See, it is ready for the sword, this throat
To pierce, divide, dash down from precipice!
But one grace grant us, king, we supplicate!
Slay me and this unhappy one before
The children, lest we see them – impious sight! –
Gasping the soul forth, calling all the while
On mother and on father's father! Else,
Do as thy heart inclines thee! No resource
Have we from death, and we resign ourselves.

MEGARA: And I too supplicate: add grace to grace,
And, though but one man, doubly serve us both!
Let me bestow adornment of the dead
Upon these children! Throw the palace wide!
For now we are shut out. Thence these shall share
At least so much of wealth was once their sire's!

LUKOS: These things shall be. Withdraw the bolts, I bid
My servants! Enter and adorn yourselves!
I grudge no peploi; but when these ye wind
About your bodies, – that adornment done, –
Then I shall come and give you to the grave.

MEGARA: O children, follow this unhappy foot,
Your mother's, into your ancestral home,

Where others have the power, are lords in truth,
Although the empty name is left us yet!
AMPHITRUON: O Zeus, in vain I had thee marriage-mate,
In vain I called thee father of my child!
Thou wast less friendly far than thou didst seem.
I, the mere man, o'ermatch in virtue thee
The mighty god: for I have not betrayed
The Herakleian children, – whereas thou
Hadst wit enough to come clandestinely
Into the chamber, take what no man gave,
Another's place; and when it comes to help
Thy loved ones, there thou lackest wit indeed!
Thou art some stupid god or born unjust.
CHOROS: Even a dirge, can Phoibos suit
In song to music jubilant
For all its sorrow: making shoot
His golden plectron o'er the lute,
Melodious ministrant.
And I, too, am of mind to raise,
Despite the imminence of doom,
A song of joy, outpour my praise
To him – what is it rumour says? –
Whether – now buried in the ghostly gloom
Below ground, – he was child of Zeus indeed,
Or mere Amphitruon's mortal seed –
To him I weave the wreath of song, his labour's meed.
For, is my hero perished in the feat?
The virtues of brave toils, in death complete,
These save the dead in song, – their glory-garland meet!

First, then, he made the wood
Of Zeus a solitude,
Slaying its lion-tenant; and he spread
The tawniness behind – his yellow head
Enmuffled by the brute's, backed by that grin of dread.
The mountain-roving savage Kentaur-race
He strewed with deadly bow about their place,
Slaying with winged shafts: Peneios knew,
Beauteously-eddying, and the long tracts too
Of pasture trampled fruitless, and as well
Those desolated haunts Mount Pelion under,
And, grassy up to Homolé, each dell

Whence, having filled their hands with pine-tree plunder,
Horse-like was wont to prance from, and subdue
The land of Thessaly, that bestial crew.
The golden-headed spot-backed stag he slew,
That robber of the rustics: glorified
Therewith the goddess who in hunter's pride
Slaughters the game along Oinoé's side.
And, yoked abreast, he brought the chariot-breed
To pace submissive to the bit, each steed
That in the bloody cribs of Diomede
Champed and, unbridled, hurried down that gore
For grain, exultant the dread feast before –
Of man's flesh: hideous feeders they of yore!
All as he crossed the Hebros' silver-flow
Accomplished he such labour, toiling so
For Mukenaian tyrant; ay, and more –
He crossed the Melian shore
And, by the sources of Amauros, shot
To death that strangers'-pest
Kuknos, who dwelt in Amphanaia: not
Of fame for good to guest!

And next, to the melodious maids he came,
Inside the Hesperian court-yard: hand must aim
At plucking gold fruit from the appled leaves,
Now he had killed the dragon, backed like flame,
Who guards the unapproachable he weaves
Himself all round, one spire about the same.
And into those sea-troughs of ocean dived
The hero, and for mortals calm contrived,
Whatever oars should follow in his wake.
And under heaven's mid-seat his hands thrust he,
At home with Atlas: and, for valour's sake,
Held the gods up their star-faced mansionry.

Also, the rider-host of Amazons
About Maiotis many-streamed, he went
To conquer through the billowy Euxin once,
Having collected what an armament
Of friends from Hellas, all on conquest bent
Of that gold-garnished cloak, dread girdle-chase!
So Hellas gained the girl's barbarian grace

And at Mukenai saves the trophy still –
Go wonder there, who will!

And the ten thousand-headed hound
Of many a murder, the Lernaian snake
He burned out, head by head, and cast around
His darts a poison thence, – darts soon to slake
Their rage in that three-bodied herdsman's gore
Of Erutheia. Many a running more
He made for triumph and felicity,
And, last of toils, to Haides, never dry
Of tears, he sailed: and there he, luckless, ends
His life completely, nor returns again.
The house and home are desolate of friends,
And where the children's life-path leads them, plain
I see, – no step retraceable, no god
Availing, and no law to help the lost!
The oar of Charon marks their period,
Waits to end all. Thy hands, these roofs accost! –
To thee, though absent, look their uttermost!

But if in youth and strength I flourished still,
Still shook the spear in fight, did power match will
In these Kadmeian co-mates of my age,
They would, – and I, – when warfare was to wage,
Stand by these children; but I am bereft
Of youth now, lone of that good genius left!

But hist, desist! for here come these, –
Draped as the dead go, under and over, –
Children long since, – now hard to discover, –
Of the once so potent Herakles!
And the loved wife dragging, in one tether
About her feet, the boys together;
And the hero's aged sire comes last!
Unhappy that I am! Of tears which rise, –
How am I all unable to hold fast,
Longer, the agèd fountains of these eyes!

MEGARA: Be it so! Who is priest, who butcher here
Of these ill-fated ones, or stops the breath
Of me, the miserable? Ready, see,
The sacrifice – to lead where Haides lives!

O children, we are led – no lovely team
Of corpses – age, youth, motherhood, all mixed!
O sad fate of myself and these my sons
Whom with these eyes I look at, this last time!
I, indeed, bore you: but for enemies
I brought you up to be a laughing-stock,
Matter for merriment, destruction-stuff!
Woe's me!
Strangely indeed my hopes have struck me down
From what I used to hope about you once –
The expectation from your father's talk!
For thee, now, thy dead sire dealt Argos to:
Thou wast to have Eurustheus' house one day,
And rule Pelasgia where the fine fruits grow;
And, for a stole of state, he wrapped about
Thy head with that the lion-monster bore,
That which himself went wearing armour-wise.
And thou wast King of Thebes – such chariots there!
Those plains I had for portion – all for thee,
As thou hadst coaxed them out of who gave birth
To thee, his boy: and into thy right hand
He thrust the guardian-club of Daidalos, –
Poor guardian proves the gift that plays thee false!
And upon thee he promised to bestow
Oichalia – what, with those far-shooting shafts,
He ravaged once; and so, since three you were,
With threefold kingdoms did he build you up
To very towers, your father, – proud enough
Prognosticating, from your manliness
In boyhood, what the manhood's self would be.
For my part, I was picking out for you
Brides, suiting each with his alliance – this
From Athens, this from Sparté, this from Thebes –
Whence, suited – as stern-cables steady ship –
You might have hold on life gods bless. All gone!
Fortune turns round and gives us – you, the Fates
Instead of brides – me, tears for nuptial baths,
Unhappy in my hoping! And the sire
Of your sire – he prepares the marriage-feast
Befitting Haides who plays father now –
Bitter relationship! Oh me! which first –
Which last of you shall I to bosom fold?

To whom shall I fit close, his mouth to mine?
Of whom shall I lay hold and ne'er let go?
How would I gather, like the brown-winged bee,
The groans from all, and, gathered into one,
Give them you back again, a crowded tear!
Dearest, if any voice be heard of men
Dungeoned in Haides, thee – to thee I speak!
Here is thy father dying, and thy boys!
And I too perish, famed as fortunate
By mortals once, through thee! Assist them! Come!
But come! though just a shade, appear to me!
For, coming, thy ghost-grandeur would suffice,
Such cowards are they in thy presence, these
Who kill thy children now thy back is turned!

AMPHITRUON: Ay, daughter, bid the powers below assist!
But I will rather, raising hand to heaven,
Call thee to help, O Zeus, if thy intent
Be, to these children, helpful anyway,
Since soon thou wilt be valueless enough!
And yet thou hast been called and called; in vain
I labour: for we needs must die, it seems.
Well, agèd brothers – life's a little thing!
Such as it is, then, pass life pleasantly
From day to night, nor once grieve all the while!
Since Time concerns him not about our hopes, –
To save them, – but his own work done, flies off.
Witness myself, looked up to among men,
Doing noteworthy deeds: when here comes fate
Lifts me away, like feather skyward borne,
In one day! Riches then and glory, – whom
These are found constant to, I know not. Friends,
Farewell! the man who loved you all so much,
Now, this last time, my mates, ye look upon!

MEGARA: Ha!
O father, do I see my dearest? Speak!

AMPHITRUON: No more than thou canst, daughter – dumb like thee!

MEGARA: Is this he whom we heard was under ground?

AMPHITRUON: Unless at least some dream in day we see!

MEGARA: What do I say? what dreams insanely view?
This is no other than thy son, old sire!
Here children! hang to these paternal robes,

Quick, haste, hold hard on him, since here's your true
Zeus that can save – and every whit as well!
HERAKLES: O hail, my palace, my hearth's propula, –
How glad I see thee as I come to light!
Ha, what means this? My children I behold
Before the house in garments of the grave,
Chapleted, and, amid a crowd of men,
My very wife – my father weeping too,
Whatever the misfortune! Come, best take
My station nearer these and learn it all!
Wife, what new sorrow has approached our home?
MEGARA: O dearest! light flashed on thy father now!
Art thou come? art thou saved and dost thou fall
On friends in their supreme extremity?
HERAKLES: How say'st thou? Father! what's the trouble here?
MEGARA: Undone are we! – but thou, old man, forgive
If first I snatch what thou shouldst say to him!
For somehow womanhood wakes pity more.
Here are my children killed and I undone!
HERAKLES: Apollon, with what preludes speech begins!
MEGARA: Dead are my brothers and old father too.
HERAKLES: How say'st thou? – doing what? – by spear-stroke whence?
MEGARA: Lukos destroyed them – the land's noble king!
HERAKLES: Met them in arms? or through the land's disease?
MEGARA: Sedition: and he sways seven-gated Thebes.
HERAKLES: Why then came fear on the old man and thee?
MEGARA: He meant to kill thy father, me, our boys.
HERAKLES: How say'st thou? Fearing what from orphanage?
MEGARA: Lest they should some day pay back Kreon's death.
HERAKLES: And why trick out the boys corpse-fashion thus?
MEGARA: These wraps of death we have already donned.
HERAKLES: And you had died through violence? Woe's me!
MEGARA: Left bare of friends: and thou wast dead, we heard.
HERAKLES: And whence came on you this faintheartedness?
MEGARA: The heralds of Eurustheus brought the news.
HERAKLES: And why was it you left my house and hearth?
MEGARA: Forced thence; thy father – from his very couch!
HERAKLES: And no shame at insulting the old man?
MEGARA: Shame, truly! no near neighbours *he* and Shame!
HERAKLES: And so much, in my absence, lacked I friends?
MEGARA: Friends, – are there any to a luckless man?

HERAKLES: The Minuai-war I waged, – they spat forth these?
MEGARA: Friendless, – again I tell thee, – is ill-luck.
HERAKLES: Will not you cast these hell-wraps from your hair
And look on light again, and with your eyes
Taste the sweet change from nether dark to day?
While I – for now there needs my handiwork –
First I shall go, demolish the abodes
Of these new lordships; next hew off the head
Accurst and toss it for the dogs to trail.
Then, such of the Kadmeians as I find
Were craven though they owed me gratitude, –
Some I intend to handle with this club
Renowned for conquest; and with wingèd shafts
Scatter the others, fill Ismenos full
With bloody corpses, – Dirké's flow so white
Shall be incarnadined. For, whom, I pray,
Behoves me rather help than wife and child
And aged father? Farewell, 'Labours' mine!
Vainly I wrought them: my true work lay here!
My business is to die defending these, –
If for their father's sake they meant to die.
Or how shall we call brave the battling it
With snake and lion, as Eurustheus bade,
If yet I must not labour death away
From my own children? 'Conquering Herakles'
Folk will not call me as they used, I think!
The right thing is for parents to assist
Children, old age, the partner of the couch.
AMPHITRUON: True, son! thy duty is – be friend to friends
And foe to foes; yet – no more haste than needs!
HERAKLES: Why, father, what is over-hasty here?
AMPHITRUON: Many a pauper, – seeming to be rich,
As the word goes, – the king calls partisan.
Such made a riot, ruined Thebes to rob
Their neighbour: for, what good they had at home
Was spent and gone – flew off through idleness.
You came to trouble Thebes, they saw: since seen,
Beware lest, raising foes, a multitude,
You stumble where you apprehend no harm.
HERAKLES: If all Thebes saw me, not a whit care I.
But seeing as I did a certain bird
Not in the lucky seats, I knew some woe

Was fallen upon the house: so, purposely,
By stealth I made my way into the land.
AMPHITRUON: And now, advancing, hail the hearth with praise
And give the ancestral home thine eye to see!
For he himself will come, thy wife and sons
To drag-forth – slaughter – slay me too, – this king!
But, here remaining, all succeeds with thee –
Gain lost by no false step. So, this thy town
Disturb not, son, ere thou right matters here!
HERAKLES: Thus will I do, for thou say'st well; my home
Let me first enter! Since at the due time
Returning from the unsunned depths where dwells
Haides' wife Koré, let me not affront
Those gods beneath my roof I first should hail!
AMPHITRUON: For didst thou really visit Haides, son?
HERAKLES: Ay – dragged to light, too, his three-headed beast.
AMPHITRUON: By fight didst conquer, or through Koré's gift?
HERAKLES: Fight: well for me, I saw the Orgies first!
AMPHITRUON: And is he in Eurustheus' house, the brute?
HERAKLES: Chthonia's grove, Hermion's city, hold him now.
AMPHITRUON: Does not Eurustheus know thee back on earth?
HERAKLES: No: I would come first and see matters here.
AMPHITRUON: But how wast thou below ground such a time?
HERAKLES: I stopped, from Haides, bringing Theseus up.
AMPHITRUON: And where is he? – bound o'er the plain for home?
HERAKLES: Gone glad to Athens – Haides' fugitive!
But, up, boys! follow father into house!
There's a far better going-in for you
Truly, than going-out was! Nay, take heart,
And let the eyes no longer run and run!
And thou, O wife, my own, collect thy soul
Nor tremble now! Leave grasping, all of you,
My garments! I'm not winged, nor fly from friends!
Ah, –
No letting go for these, who all the more
Hang to my garments! Did you foot indeed
The razor's edge? Why, then I'll carry them –
Take with my hands these small craft up, and tow
Just as a ship would. There! don't fear I shirk
My children's service! this way, men are men,
No difference! best and worst, they love their boys

After one fashion: wealth they differ in –
Some have it, others not; but each and all
Combine to form the children-loving race.
CHOROS: Youth is a pleasant burthen to me;
But age on my head, more heavily
Than the crags of Aitna, weighs and weighs,
And darkening cloaks the lids and intercepts the rays.
Never be mine the preference
Of an Asian empire's wealth, nor yet
Of a house all gold, to youth, to youth
That's beauty, whatever the gods dispense!
Whether in wealth we joy, or fret
Paupers, – of all God's gifts most beautiful, in truth!

But miserable murderous age I hate!
Let it go to wreck, the waves adown,
Nor ever by rights plague tower or town
Where mortals bide, but still elate
With wings, on ether, precipitate,
Wander them round – nor wait!

But if the gods, to man's degree,
Had wit and wisdom, they would bring
Mankind a twofold youth, to be
Their virtue's sign-mark, all should see,
In those with whom life's winter thus grew spring.
For when they died, into the sun once more
Would they have traversed twice life's race-course o'er;
While ignobility had simply run
Existence through, nor second life begun.
And so might we discern both bad and good
As surely as the starry multitude
Is numbered by the sailors, one and one.
But now the gods by no apparent line
Limit the worthy and the base define;
Only, a certain period rounds, and so
Brings man more wealth, – but youthful vigour, no!

Well! I am not to pause
Mingling together – wine and wine in cup –
The Graces with the Muses up –
Most dulcet marriage: loosed from music's laws,

No life for me!
But where the wreaths abound, there ever may I be!
And still, an aged bard, I shout Mnemosuné –
Still chant of Herakles the triumph-chant,
Companioned by the seven-stringed tortoise-shell
And Libuan flute, and Bromios' self as well,
God of the grape, with man participant!
Not yet will we arrest their glad advance –
The Muses who so long have led me forth to dance!
A paian – hymn the Delian girls indeed,
Weaving a beauteous measure in and out
His temple-gates, Latona's goodly seed;
And paians – I too, these thy domes about,
From these grey cheeks, my king, will swan-like shout –
Old songster! Ay, in song it starts off brave –
'Zeus' son is he!' and yet, such grace of birth
Surpassing far, to man his labours gave
Existence, one calm flow without a wave,
Having destroyed the beasts, the terrors of the earth.
LUKOS: From out the house Amphitruon comes – in time!
For 'tis a long while now since ye bedecked
Your bodies with the dead-folk's finery.
But quick! the boys and wife of Herakles –
Bid them appear outside this house, keep pact
To die, and need no bidding but your own!
AMPHITRUON: King! you press hard on me sore-pressed
enough,
And give me scorn – beside my dead ones here.
Meet in such matters were it, though you reign,
To temper zeal with moderation. Since
You do impose on us the need to die –
Needs must we love our lot, obey your will.
LUKOS: Where's Megara, then? Alkmené's grandsons, where?
AMPHITRUON: She, I think, – as one figures from outside, –
LUKOS: Well, this same thinking, – what affords its ground?
AMPHITRUON: – Sits suppliant on the holy altar-steps, –
LUKOS: Idly indeed a suppliant to save life!
AMPHITRUON: – And calls on her dead husband, vainly too!
LUKOS: For he's not come, nor ever will arrive.
AMPHITRUON: Never – at least, if no god raise him up.
LUKOS: Go to her, and conduct her from the house!
AMPHITRUON: I should partake the murder, doing that.

LUKOS: We, – since thou hast a scruple in the case, –
Outside of fears, we shall march forth these lads,
Mother and all. Here, follow me, my folk –
And gladly so remove what stops our toils!
AMPHITRUON: Thou – go then! March where needs must! What remains –
Perhaps concerns another. Doing ill,
Expect some ill be done thee!
Ha, old friends!
On he strides beautifully! in the toils
O' the net, where swords spring forth, will he be fast –
Minded to kill his neighbours – the arch-knave!
I go, too – I must see the falling corpse!
For he has sweets to give – a dying man,
Your foe, that pays the price of deeds he did.
CHOROS; Troubles are over! He the great king once
Turns the point, tends for Haides, goal of life!
O justice, and the gods' back-flowing fate!
AMPHITRUON: Thou art come, late indeed, where death pays crime –
These insults heaped on better than thyself!
CHOROS: Joy gives this outburst to my tears! Again
Come round those deeds, his doing, which of old
He never dreamed himself was to endure –
King of the country! But enough, old man!
Indoors, now, let us see how matters stand –
If somebody be faring as I wish!
LUKOS: Ah me – me!
CHOROS: This strikes the keynote – music to my mind,
Merry i' the household! Death takes up the tune!
The king gives voice, groans murder's prelude well!
LUKOS: O, all the land of Kadmos! slain by guile!
CHOROS: Ay, for who slew first? Paying back thy due,
Resign thee! make, for deeds done, mere amends!
Who was it grazed the gods through lawlessness –
Mortal himself, threw up his fool's-conceit
Against the blessed heavenly ones – as though
Gods had no power? Old friends, the impious man
Exists not any more! The house is mute.
Turn we to song and dance! For, those I love,
Those I wish well to, well fare they, to wish!

Dances, dances and banqueting
To Thebes, the sacred city through,
Are a care! for, change and change
Of tears to laughter, old to new,
Our lays, glad birth, they bring, they bring!
He is gone and past, the mighty king!
And the old one reigns, returned – O strange!
From the Acherontian harbour too!
Advent of hope, beyond thought's widest range!
To the gods, the gods, are crimes a care,
And they watch our virtue, well aware
That gold and that prosperity drive man
Out of his mind – those charioteers who hale
Might-without-right behind them: face who can
Fortune's reverse which time prepares, nor quail?
– He who evades law and in lawlessness
Delights him, – he has broken down his trust –
The chariot, riches haled – now blackening in the dust!

Ismenos, go thou garlanded!
Break into dance, ye ways, the polished bed
O' the seven-gated city! Dirké, thou
Fair-flowing, with the Asopiad sisters all,
Leave your sire's stream, attend the festival
Of Herakles, one choir of nymphs, sing triumph now!
O woody rock of Puthios and each home
O' the Helikonian Muses, ye shall come
With joyous shouting to my walls, my town
Where saw the light that Spartan race, those 'Sown,'
Brazen-shield-bearing chiefs, whereof the band
With children's children renovates our land,
To Thebes a sacred light!
O combination of the marriage rite –
Bed of the mortal-born and Zeus, who couched
Beside the nymph of Perseus' progeny!
For credible, past hope, becomes to me
That nuptial story long ago avouched,
O Zeus! and time has turned the dark to bright,
And made one blaze of truth the Herakleidan might –
His, who emerged from earth's pavilion, left
Plouton's abode, the nether palace-cleft.

Thou wast the lord that nature gave me – not
That baseness born and bred – my king, by lot!
– Baseness made plain to all, who now regard
The match of sword with sword in fight, –
If to the gods the Just and Right
Still pleasing be, still claim the palm's award.

Horror!
Are we come to the self-same passion of fear,
Old friends? – such a phantasm fronts me here
Visible over the palace-roof!
In flight, in flight, the laggard limb
Bestir! and haste aloof
From that on the roof there – grand and grim!
O Paian, king!
Be thou my safeguard from the woeful thing!

IRIS: Courage, old men! beholding here – Night's birth –
Madness, and me the handmaid of the gods,
Iris: since to your town we come, no plague –
Wage war against the house of but one man
From Zeus and from Alkmené sprung, they say.
Now, till he made an end of bitter toils,
Fate kept him safe, nor did his father Zeus
Let us once hurt him, Heré nor myself.
But, since he has toiled through Eurustheus' task,
Heré desires to fix fresh blood on him –
Slaying his children: I desire it too.

Up then, collecting the unsoftened heart,
Unwedded virgin of black Night! Drive, drag
Frenzy upon the man here – whirls of brain
Big with child-murder, while his feet leap gay!
Let go the bloody cable its whole length!
So that, – when o'er the Acherousian ford
He has sent floating, by self-homicide,
His beautiful boy-garland, – he may know
First, Heré's anger, what it is to him,
And then learn mine. The gods are vile indeed
And mortal matters vast, if he 'scape free!

MADNESS: Certes, from well-born sire and mother too
Had I my birth, whose blood is Night's and Heaven's;

But here's my glory, – not to grudge the good!
Nor love I raids against the friends of man.
I wish, then, to persuade, – before I see
You stumbling, you and Heré! trust my words!
This man, the house of whom ye hound me to,
Is not unfamed on earth nor gods among;
Since, having quelled waste land and savage sea,
He alone raised again the falling rights
Of gods – gone ruinous through impious men.
Desire no mighty mischief, I advise!
IRIS: Give thou no thought to Heré's faulty schemes!
MADNESS: Changing her step from faulty to fault-free!
IRIS: Not to be wise, did Zeus' wife send thee here.
MADNESS: Sun, thee I cite to witness – doing what I loathe to do!
But since indeed to Heré and thyself I must subserve,
And follow you quick, with a whizz, as the hounds a-hunt with the huntsman,
– Go I will! and neither the sea, as it groans with its waves so furiously,
Nor earthquake, no, nor the bolt of thunder gasping out heaven's labour-throe,
Shall cover the ground as I, at a bound, rush into the bosom of Herakles!
And home I scatter, and house I batter,
Having first of all made the children fall, –
And he who felled them is never to know
He gave birth to each child that received the blow,
Till the Madness, I am, have let him go!

Ha, behold! already he rocks his head – he is off from the starting-place!
Not a word, as he rolls his frightful orbs, from their sockets wrenched in the ghastly race!
And the breathings of him he tempers and times no more than a bull in act to toss,
And hideously he bellows invoking the Keres, daughters of Tartaros.
Ay, and I soon will dance thee madder, and pipe thee quite out of thy mind with fear!
So, up with the famous foot, thou Iris, march to Olumpos, leave me here!

Me and mine, who now combine, in the dreadful shape no
mortal sees,
And now are about to pass, from without, inside of the home
of Herakles!

CHOROS: Ototototoi, – groan!
Away is mown
Thy flower, Zeus' offspring, City!
Unhappy Hellas, who dost cast (the pity!)
Who worked thee all the good,
Away from thee, – destroyest in a mood
Of madness him, to death whom pipings dance!
There goes she, in her chariot, – groans, her brood, –
And gives her team the goad, as though adrift
For doom, Night's Gorgon, Madness, she whose glance
Turns man to marble! with what hissings lift
Their hundred heads the snakes, her head's inheritance!
Quick has the god changed fortune: through their sire
Quick will the children, that he saved, expire!
O miserable me! O Zeus! thy child –
Childless himself – soon vengeance, hunger-wild,
Craving for punishment, will lay how low –
Loaded with many a woe!

O palace-roofs! your courts about,
A measure begins all unrejoiced
By the tympanies and the thyrsos hoist
Of the Bromian revel-rout!
O ye domes! and the measure proceeds
For blood, not such as the cluster bleeds
Of the Dionusian pouring-out!

Break forth, fly, children! fatal this –
Fatal the lay that is piped, I wis!
Ay, for he hunts a children-chase –
Never shall Madness lead her revel
And leave no trace in the dwelling-place!
Ai ai, because of the evil!
Ai ai, the old man – how I groan
For the father, and not the father alone!
She who was nurse of his children, – small
Her gain that they ever were born at all!

See! See!
A whirlwind shakes hither and thither
The house – the roof falls in together!
Ha, ha, what dost thou, son of Zeus?
A trouble of Tartaros broke loose,
Such as once Pallas on the Titan thundered,
Thou sendest on thy domes, roof-shattered and wall-sundered!
MESSENGER: O bodies white with age! –
CHOROS: What cry, to me –
What, dost thou call with?
MESSENGER: There's a curse indoors.
CHOROS: I shall not bring a prophet: you suffice.
MESSENGER: Dead are the children.
CHOROS: Ai ai!
MESSENGER: Groan! for, groans
Suit well the subject. Dire the children's death,
Dire too the parent's hands that dealt the fate.
No one could tell worse woe than we have borne.
CHOROS: How dost thou that same curse – curse, cause for groan –
The father's on the children, make appear?
Tell in what matter they were hurled from heaven
Against the house – these evils; and recount
The children's hapless fate, O Messenger!
MESSENGER: The victims were before the hearth of Zeus,
A household-expiation: since the king
O' the country, Herakles had killed and cast
From out the dwelling; and a beauteous choir
Of boys stood by his sire, too, and his wife.
And now the basket had been carried round
The altar in a circle, and we used
The consecrated speech. Alkmené's son, –
Just as he was about, in his right hand,
To bear the torch, that he might dip into
The cleansing-water, – came to a stand-still;
And, as their father yet delayed, his boys
Had their eyes on him. But he was himself
No longer: lost in rollings of the eyes;
Out-thrusting eyes – their very roots – like blood!
Froth he dropped down his bushy-bearded cheek,
And said – together with a madman's laugh –
'Father! why sacrifice, before I slay

Eurustheus? why have twice the lustral fire,
And double pains, when 'tis permitted me
To end, with one good hand-sweep, matters here?
Then, – when I hither bring Eurustheus' head, –
Then for these just slain, wash hands once for all!
Now, – cast drink-offerings forth, throw baskets down!
Who gives me bow and arrows, who my club?
I go to that Mukenai. One must match
Crowbars and mattocks, so that – those sunk stones
The Kuklops squared with picks and plumb-line red –
I, with my bent steel, may o'ertumble town.'
Which said, he goes and – with no car to have –
Affirms he has one! mounts the chariot-board,
And strikes, as having really goad in hand!
And two ways laughed the servants – laugh with awe;
And one said, as each met the other's stare,
'Playing us boys' tricks? or is master mad?'
But up he climbs, and down along the roof,
And, dropping into the men's place, maintains
He's come to Nisos' city, when he's come
Only inside his own house! then reclines
On floor, for couch, and, as arrived indeed,
Makes himself supper; goes through some brief stay
Then says he's traversing the forest-flats
Of Isthmos; thereupon lays body bare
Of bucklings, and begins a contest with
– No one! and is proclaimed the conqueror –
He by himself – having called out to hear
– Nobody! Then, if you will take his word,
Blaring against Eurustheus horribly,
He's at Mukenai. But his father laid
Hold of the strong hand and addressed him thus:
'O son, what ails thee? Of what sort is this
Extravagance? Has not some murder-craze,
Bred of those corpses thou didst just dispatch,
Danced thee drunk?' But he, – taking him to crouch,
Eurustheus' sire, that apprehensive touched
His hand, a suppliant, – pushes him aside,
Gets ready quiver, and bends bow against
His children – thinking them Eurustheus' boys
He means to slay. They, horrified with fear,
Rushed here and there, – this child, into the robes

O' the wretched mother – this, beneath the shade
O' the column, – and this other, like a bird,
Cowered at the altar-foot. The mother shrieks
'Parent – what dost thou? – kill thy children?' So
Shriek the old sire and crowd of servitors.
But he, outwinding him, as round about
The column ran the boy, – a horrid whirl
O' the lathe his foot described! – stands opposite,
Strikes through the liver; and supine the boy
Bedews the stone shafts, breathing out his life.
But 'Victory!' he shouted – boasted thus:
'Well, this one nestling of Eurustheus – dead –
Falls by me, pays back the paternal hate!'
Then bends bow on another who was crouched
At base of altar – overlooked, he thought –
And now prevents him, falls at father's knee,
Throwing up hand to beard and cheek above.
'O dearest!' cries he; 'father, kill me not!
Yours I am – your boy: not Eurustheus' boy
You kill now!' But he, rolling the wild eye
Of Gorgon, – as the boy stood all too close
For deadly bowshot, – mimicry of smith
Who batters red-hot iron, – hand o'er head
Heaving his club, on the boy's yellow hair
Hurls it and breaks the bone. This second caught, –
He goes, would slay the third, one sacrifice
He and the couple; but, beforehand here,
The miserable mother catches up,
Carries him inside house and bars the gate.
Then he, as he were at those Kuklops' work,
Digs at, heaves doors up, wrenches doorposts out,
Lays wife and child low with the selfsame shaft.
And this done, at the old man's death he drives;
But there came, as it seemed to us who saw,
A statue – Pallas with the crested head,
Swinging her spear – and threw a stone which smote
Herakles' breast and stayed his slaughter-rage,
And sent him safe to sleep. He falls to ground –
Striking against the column with his back –
Column which, with the falling of the roof,
Broken in two, lay by the altar-base.
And we, foot-free now from our several flights,

Along with the old man, we fastened bonds
Of rope-noose to the column, so that he,
Ceasing from sleep, might not go adding deeds
To deeds done. And he sleeps a sleep, poor wretch,
No gift of any god! since he has slain
Children and wife. For me, I do not know
What mortal has more misery to bear.

CHOROS: A murder there was which Argolis
Holds in remembrance, Hellas through,
As, at that time, best and famousest:
Of those, the daughters of Danaos slew.
A murder indeed was that! but this
Outstrips it, straight to the goal has pressed.
I am able to speak of a murder done
To the hapless Zeus-born offspring, too –
Prokné's son, who had but one –
Or a sacrifice to the Muses, say
Rather, who Itus sing alway,
Her single child. But thou, the sire
Of children three – O thou consuming fire! –
In one outrageous fate hast made them all expire.
And this outrageous fate –
What groan, or wail, or dead-men's dirge,
Or choric dance of Haides shall I urge
The Muse to celebrate?

Woe! woe! behold!
The portalled palace lies unrolled,
This way and that way, each prodigious fold!
Alas for me! these children, see,
Stretched, hapless group, before their father – he
The all-unhappy, who lies sleeping out
The murder of his sons, a dreadful sleep!
And bonds, see, all about, –
Rope-tangle, ties and tether, – these
Tightenings around the body of Herakles
To the stone columns of the house made fast!

But – like a bird that grieves
For callow nestlings some rude hand bereaves –
See, here, a bitter journey overpast,
The old man – all too late – is here at last!

AMPHITRUON: Silently, silently, aged Kadmeians!
Will ye not suffer my son, diffused
Yonder, to slide from his sorrows in sleep?
CHOROS: And thee, old man, do I, groaning, weep,
And the children too, and the head there – used
Of old to the wreaths and paians!
AMPHITRUON: Farther away! Nor beat the breast,
Nor wail aloud, nor rouse from rest
The slumberer – asleep, so best!
CHOROS: Ah me – what a slaughter!
AMPHITRUON: Refrain – refrain!
Ye will prove my perdition.
CHOROS: Unlike water,
Bloodshed rises from earth again.
AMPHITRUON: Do I bid you bate your breath, in vain –
Ye elders? Lament in a softer strain!
Lest he rouse himself, burst every chain,
And bury the city in ravage – bray
Father and house to dust away!
CHOROS: I cannot forbear – I cannot forbear!
AMPHITRUON: Hush! I will learn his breathings: there!
I will lay my ears close.
CHOROS: What, he sleeps?
AMPHITRUON: Ay, – sleeps! A horror of slumber keeps
The man who has piled
On wife and child
Death and death, as he shot them down
With clang o' the bow.
CHOROS: Wail –
AMPHITRUON: Even so!
CHOROS: – The fate of the children –
AMPHITRUON: Triple woe!
CHOROS: – Old man, the fate of thy son!
AMPHITRUON: Hush, hush! Have done!
He is turning about!
He is breaking out!
Away! I steal
And my body conceal,
Before he arouse,
In the depths of the house.
CHOROS: Courage! The Night
Maintains her right

On the lids of thy son there, sealed from sight!
AMPHITRUON: See, see! To leave the light
And, wretch that I am, bear one last ill,
I do not avoid; but if he kill
Me his own father, and devise
Beyond the present miseries
A misery more ghastly still –
And to haunt him, over and above
Those here who, as they used to love,
Now hate him, what if he have with these
My murder, the worst of Erinues?
CHOROS: Then was the time to die, for thee,
When ready to wreak in the full degree
Vengeance on those
Thy consort's foes
Who murdered her brothers! glad, life's close,
With the Taphioi down,
And sacked their town
Clustered about with a wash of sea!
AMPHITRUON: To flight – to flight!
Away from the house, troop off, old men!
Save yourselves out of the maniac's sight!
He is rousing himself right up: and then,
Murder on murder heaping anew,
He will revel in blood your city through!
CHOROS: O Zeus, why hast, with such unmeasured hate,
Hated thy son, whelmed in this sea of woes?
HERAKLES: Ha, –
In breath indeed I am – see things I ought –
Aether, and earth, and these the sunbeam-shafts!
But then – some billow and strange whirl of sense
I have fallen into! and breathings hot I breathe –
Smoked upwards, not the steady work from lungs.
See now! Why bound, – at moorings like a ship, –
About my young breast and young arm, to this
Stone piece of carved work broke in half, do I
Sit, have my rest in corpses' neighbourhood?
Strewn on the ground are winged darts, and bow
Which played my brother-shieldman, held in hand, –
Guarded my side, and got my guardianship!
I cannot have gone back to Haides – twice
Begun Eurustheus' race I ended thence?

But I nor see the Sisupheian stone,
Nor Plouton, nor Demeter's sceptred maid!
I am struck witless sure! Where can I be?
Ho there! what friend of mine is near or far –
Some one to cure me of bewilderment?
For naught familiar do I recognize.

AMPHITRUON: Old friends, shall I go close to these my woes?
CHOROS: Ay, and let me too, – nor desert your ills!
HERAKLES: Father, why weepest thou, and buriest up
Thine eyes, aloof so from thy much-loved son?
AMPHITRUON: O child! – for, faring badly, mine thou art!
HERAKLES: Do I fare somehow ill, that tears should flow?
AMPHITRUON: Ill, – would cause any god who bore, to groan!
HERAKLES: That's boasting, truly! still, you state no hap.
AMPHITRUON: For, thyself seest – if in thy wits again.
HERAKLES: Heyday! How riddlingly that hint returns!
AMPHITRUON: Well, I am trying – art thou sane and sound!
HERAKLES: Say if thou lay'st aught strange to my life's charge!
AMPHITRUON: If thou no more art Haides-drunk, – I tell!
HERAKLES: I bring to mind no drunkenness of soul.
AMPHITRUON: Shall I unbind my son, old men, or what?
HERAKLES: And who was binder, tell! – not *that*, my deed!
AMPHITRUON: Mind that much of misfortune – pass the rest!
HERAKLES: Enough! from silence, I nor learn nor wish.
AMPHITRUON: O Zeus, dost witness here throned Heré's work?
HERAKLES: But have I had to bear aught hostile thence?
AMPHITRUON: Let be the goddess – bury thine own guilt!
HERAKLES: Undone! What is the sorrow thou wilt say?
AMPHITRUON: Look! See the ruins of thy children here!
HERAKLES: Ah me! What sight do wretched I behold?
AMPHITRUON: Unfair fight, son, this fight thou fastenedst
On thine own children!
HERAKLES: What fight? Who slew these?
AMPHITRUON: Thou and thy bow, and who of gods was cause.
HERAKLES: How say'st? What did I? Ill-announcing sire!
AMPHITRUON: – Go mad! Thou askest a sad clearing up.
HERAKLES: And am I also murderer of my wife?
AMPHITRUON: All the work here was just one hand's work – thine!
HERAKLES: Ai ai – for groans encompass me – a cloud!
AMPHITRUON: For these deeds' sake do I begroan thy fate.
HERAKLES: Did I break up my house or dance it down?

AMPHITRUON: I know just one thing – all's a woe with thee.
HERAKLES: But where did the craze catch me? where destroy?
AMPHITRUON: When thou didst cleanse hands at the altar-
flame.
HERAKLES: Ah me! why is it then I save my life –
Proved murderer of my dearest ones, my boys?
Shall not I rush to the rock-level's leap,
Or, darting sword through breast and all, become
My children's blood-avenger? or, this flesh
Burning away with fire, so thrust away
The infamy, which waits me there, from life?

Ah but, – a hindrance to my purposed death,
Theseus arrives, my friend and kinsman, here!
Eyes will be on me! my child-murder-plague
In evidence before friends loved so much!
O me, what shall I do? Where, taking wing
Or gliding underground, shall I seek out
A solitariness from misery?
I will pull night upon my muffled head!
Let this wretch here content him with his curse
Of blood: I would pollute no innocents.
THESEUS: I come, – with others who await beside
Asopos' stream, the armed Athenian youth, –
Bring thy son, old man, spear's fight-fellowship!
For a bruit reached the Erechtheidai's town
That, having seized the sceptre of this realm,
Lukos prepares you battle-violence.
So, paying good back, – Herakles began,
Saving me down there, – I have come, old man,
If aught, of my hand or my friends', you want.
What's here? Why all these corpses on the ground?
Am I perhaps behindhand – come too late
For newer ill? Who killed these children now?
Whose wife was she, this woman I behold?
Boys, at least, take no stand in reach of spear!
Some other woe than war, I chance upon.
AMPHITRUON: O thou, who sway'st the olive-bearing height! –
THESEUS: Why hail'st thou me with woeful prelude thus?
AMPHITRUON: Dire sufferings have we suffered from the gods.
THESEUS: These boys, – who are they thou art weeping o'er?
AMPHITRUON: He gave them birth, indeed, my hapless son!

Begot, but killed them – dared their bloody death.
THESEUS: Speak no such horror!
AMPHITRUON: Would I might obey!
THESEUS: O teller of dread tidings!
AMPHITRUON: Lost are we –
Lost – flown away from life!
THESEUS: What sayest thou?
What did he?
AMPHITRUON: Erring through a frenzy-fit,
He did all, with the arrows dipt in dye
Of hundred-headed Hudra.
THESEUS: Heré's strife!
But who is this among the dead, old man?
AMPHITRUON: Mine, mine, this progeny – the labour-plagued,
Who went with gods once to Phlegruia's plain,
And in the giant-slaying war bore shield.
THESEUS: Woe – woe! What man was born mischanceful thus!
AMPHITRUON: Thou couldst not know another mortal man
Toil-weary, more outworn by wanderings.
THESEUS: And why i' the peploi hides he his sad head?
AMPHITRUON: Not daring meet thine eye, thy friendliness
And kinship, – nor that children's-blood about.
THESEUS: But *I* come to who shared my woe with me!
Uncover him!
AMPHITRUON: O child, put from thine eyes
The peplos, throw it off, show face to sun!
Woe's weight well matched contends with tears in thee.
I supplicate thee, falling at thy cheek
And knee and hand, and shedding this old tear!
O son, remit the savage lion's mood,
Since to a bloody, an unholy race
Art thou led forth, if thou be resolute
To go on adding ill to ill, my child!
THESEUS: Let me speak! Thee, who sittest – seated woe –
I call upon to show thy friends thine eye!
For there's no darkness has a cloud so black
May hide thy misery thus absolute.
Why, waving hand, dost sign me – murder's done?
Lest a pollution strike me, from thy speech?
Naught care I to – with thee, at least – fare ill:
For I had joy once! *Then*, – soul rises to, –
When thou didst save me from the dead to light!

Friends' gratitude that tastes old age, I loathe,
And him who likes to share when things look fine,
But, sail along with friends in trouble – no!
Arise, uncover thine unhappy head!
Look on us! Every man of the right race
Bears what, at least, the gods inflict, nor shrinks.
HERAKLES: Theseus, hast seen this match – my boys with me?
THESEUS: I heard of, now I see the ills thou sign'st.
HERAKLES: Why then hast thou displayed my head to sun?
THESEUS: Why? mortals bring no plague on aught divine.
HERAKLES: Fly, O unhappy, this my impious plague!
THESEUS: No plague of vengeance flits to friends from friends.
HERAKLES: I praise thee. But I helped thee, – that is truth.
THESEUS: And I, advantaged then, now pity thee.
HERAKLES: – The pitiable, – my children's murderer!
THESEUS: I mourn for thy sake, in this altered lot.
HERAKLES: Hast thou found others in still greater woe?
THESEUS: Thou, from earth, touchest heaven, one huge distress!
HERAKLES: Accordingly, I am prepared to die.
THESEUS: Think'st thou thy threats at all import the gods?
HERAKLES: Gods please themselves: to gods I give their like.
THESEUS: Shut thy mouth, lest big words bring bigger woe!
HERAKLES: I am full fraught with ills – no stowing more!
THESEUS: Thou wilt do – what, then? Whither moody borne?
HERAKLES: Dying, I go below earth whence I came.
THESEUS: Thou hast used words of – what man turns up first!
HERAKLES: While thou, being outside sorrow, schoolest me.
THESEUS: The much-enduring Herakles talks thus? –
HERAKLES: Not the so much-enduring: measure's past.
THESEUS: – Mainstay to mortals, and their mighty friend?
HERAKLES: They nowise profit me: but Heré rules.
THESEUS: Hellas forbids thou shouldst ineptly die.
HERAKLES: But hear, then, how I strive by arguments
Against thy teachings! I will ope thee out
My life – past, present – as unlivable.
First, I was born of this man, who had slain
His mother's aged sire, and, sullied so,
Married Alkmené, she who gave me birth.
Now, when the basis of a family
Is not laid right, what follows needs must fall;
And Zeus, whoever Zeus is, formed me foe
To Heré (take not thou offence, old man!

Since father, in Zeus' stead, account I thee),
And, while I was at suck yet, frightful snakes
She introduced among my swaddling-clothes, –
That bedfellow of Zeus! – to end me so.
But when I gained the youthful garb of flesh,
The labours I endured – what need to tell?
What lions ever, or three-bodied brutes,
Tuphons or giants, or the four-legg'd swarms
Of Kentaur-battle, did not I end out?
And that hound, headed all about with heads
Which cropped up twice, the Hudra, having slain –
I both went through a myriad other toils
In full drove, and arrived among the dead
To convoy, as Eurustheus bade, to light
Haides' three-headed dog and doorkeeper.
But then I, – wretch, – dared this last labour – see!
Slew my sons, keystone-coped my house with ills.
To such a strait I come! nor my dear Thebes
Dare I inhabit: and, suppose I stay?
Into what fane or festival of friends
Am I to go? My curse scarce courts accost!
Shall I seek Argos? How, if fled from home?
But say – I hurry to some other town!
And there they eye me, as notorious now, –
Kept by sharp tongue-taunts under lock and key –
'Is not this he, Zeus' son, who murdered once
Children and wife? Let him go rot elsewhere!'
To any man renowned as happy once,
Reverses are a grave thing; but to whom
Evil is old acquaintance there's no hurt
To speak of, he and misery are twins.
To this degree of woe I think to come:
For earth will utter voice forbidding me
To touch the ground, and sea – to pierce the wave,
The river-springs – to drink, and I shall play
Ixion's part quite out, the chained and wheeled!
And best of all will be, if so I 'scape
Sight from one man of those Hellenes, – once
I lived among, felicitous and rich!
Why ought I then to live? What gain accrues
From good-for-nothing, wicked life I lead?
In fine, let Zeus' brave consort dance and sing,

Stamp foot, the Olumpian Zeus' own sandal-trick!
What she has willed, that brings her will to pass –
The foremost man of Hellas pedestalled,
Up, over, and down whirling! Who would pray
To such a goddess? – that, begrudging Zeus
Because he loved a woman, ruins me –
Lover of Hellas, faultless of the wrong!

THESEUS: This strife is from no other of the gods
Than Zeus' wife; rightly apprehend, as well,
Why, to no death – thou meditatest now –
I would persuade thee, but to bear thy woes!
None, none of mortals boasts a fate unmixed,
Nor gods – if poets' teaching be not false.
Have not they joined in wedlock against law
With one another? not, for sake of rule,
Branded their sires in bondage? Yet they house,
All the same, in Olumpos, carry heads
High there, notorious sinners though they be!
What wilt thou say, then, if thou, mortal-born,
Bearest outrageously fate gods endure?
Leave Thebes, now, pay obedience to the law
And follow me to Pallas' citadel!
There, when thy hands are purified from stain,
House will I give thee, and goods shared alike.
What gifts I hold too from the citizens
For saving twice seven children, when I slew
The Knosian bull, these also give I thee.
And everywhere about the land are plots
Apportioned me: these, named by thine own name,
Shall be henceforward styled by all men – thine,
Thy life long; but at death, when Haides-bound,
All Athens shall uphold the honoured one
With sacrifices, and huge marble heaps:
For that's a fair crown our Hellenes grant
Their people – glory, should they help the brave!
And I repay thee back this grace for thine
That saved me, now that thou art lorn of friends –
Since, when the gods give honour, friends may flit:
For, a god's help suffices, if he please.

HERAKLES: Ah me, these words are foreign to my woes!
I neither fancy gods love lawless beds,
Nor, that with chains they bind each other's hands,

Have I judged worthy faith, at any time;
Nor shall I be persuaded – one is born
His fellows' master! since God stands in need –
If he is really God – of naught at all.
These are the poets' pitiful conceits!
But this it was I pondered, though woe-whelmed –
'Take heed lest thou be taxed with cowardice
Somehow in leaving thus the light of day!'
For whoso cannot make a stand against
These same misfortunes, neither could withstand
A mere man's dart, oppose death, strength to strength.
Therefore unto thy city I will go
And have the grace of thy ten thousand gifts.
There! I have tasted of ten thousand toils
As truly – never waived a single one,
Nor let these runnings drop from out my eyes:
Nor ever thought it would have come to this –
That I from out my eyes do drop tears. Well!
At present, as it seems, one bows to fate.
So be it! Old man, thou seest my exile –
Seest, too, me – my children's murderer!
These give thou to the tomb, and deck the dead,
Doing them honour with thy tears – since me
Law does not sanction. Propping on her breast,
And giving them into their mother's arms,
– Re-institute the sad community
Which I, unhappy, brought to nothingness –
Not by my will! And, when earth hides the dead,
Live in this city! – sad, but, all the same,
Force thy soul to bear woe along with me!
O children, who begat and gave you birth –
Your father – has destroyed you! naught you gain
By those fair deeds of mine I laid you up,
As by main-force I laboured glory out
To give you, – that fine gift of fatherhood!
And thee, too, O my poor one, I destroyed,
Not rendering like for like, as when thou kept'st
My marriage-bed inviolate, – those long
Household-seclusions draining to the dregs
Inside my house! O me, my wife, my boys –
And – O myself, how, miserably moved,
Am I disyoked now from both boys and wife!

O bitter those delights of kisses now –
And bitter these my weapons' fellowship!
For I am doubtful whether shall I keep
Or cast away these arrows which will clang
Ever such words out, as they knock my side –
'Us – thou didst murder wife and children with!
Us – child-destroyers – still thou keepest thine!'
Ha, shall I bear them in my arms, then? What
Say for excuse? Yet, naked of my darts
Wherewith I did my bravest, Hellas through,
Throwing myself beneath foot to my foes,
Shall I die basely? No! relinquishment
Of these must never be, – companions once,
We sorrowfully must observe the pact.
In just one thing, co-operate with me
Thy sad friend, Theseus! Go along with him
To Argos, and in concert get arranged
The price my due for bringing there the Hound!
O land of Kadmos, Theban people all,
Shear off your locks, lament one wide lament,
Go to my children's grave and, in one strain,
Lament the whole of us – my dead and me –
Since all together are fordone and lost,
Smitten by Heré's single stroke of fate!

THESEUS: Rise up now from thy dead ones! Tears enough,
Poor friend!

HERAKLES: I cannot: for my limbs are fixed.

THESEUS: Ay: even these strong men fate overthrows.

HERAKLES: Woe!
Here might I grow a stone, nor mind woes more!

THESEUS: Cease! Give thy hand to friendly helpmate now!

HERAKLES: Nay, but I wipe off blood upon thy robes.

THESEUS: Squeeze out and spare no drop! I take it all!

HERAKLES: Of sons bereaved, I have thee like my son.

THESEUS: Give to my neck thy hand! 'tis I will lead.

HERAKLES: Yoke-fellows friendly – one heart-broken, though!
O father, such a man we need for friend!

AMPHITRUON: Certes the land that bred him boasts good sons.

HERAKLES: Turn me round, Theseus – to behold my boys!

THESEUS: What? will the having such a love-charm soothe?

HERAKLES: I want it; and to press my father's breast.

AMPHITRUON: See here, O son! for, what I love thou seek'st.

THESEUS: Strange! Of thy labours no more memory?
HERAKLES: All those were less than these, those ills I bore.
THESEUS: Who sees thee grow a woman, – will not praise.
HERAKLES: I live low to thee? Not so once, I think.
THESEUS: Too low by far! 'Famed Herakles' – where's he?
HERAKLES: Down amid evils, of what kind wast *thou*?
THESEUS: As far as courage – least of all mankind!
HERAKLES: How say'st, then, *I* in evils shrink to naught?
THESEUS: Forward!
HERAKLES: Farewell, old father!
AMPHITRUON: Thou too, son!
HERAKLES: Bury the boys as I enjoined!
AMPHITRUON: And *me* –
Who will be found to bury now, my child?
HERAKLES: Myself.
AMPHITRUON: When, coming?
HERAKLES: When thy task is done.
AMPHITRUON: How?
HERAKLES: I will have thee carried forth from Thebes
To Athens. But bear in the children, earth
Is burthened by! Myself, – who with these shames
Have cast away my house, – a ruined hulk,
I follow – trailed by Theseus – on my way;
And whoso rather would have wealth and strength
Than good friends, reasons foolishly therein.
CHOROS: And we depart, with sorrow at heart,
Sobs that increase with tears that start;
The greatest of all our friends of yore
We have lost for evermore!

When the long silence ended, – 'Our best friend –
Lost, our best friend!' he muttered musingly.

Then, 'Lachares the sculptor' (half aloud)
'Sinned he or sinned he not? "Outrageous sin!"
Shuddered our elders, "Pallas should be clothed:
He carved her naked." "But more beautiful!"
Answers this generation: "Wisdom formed
For love not fear!" And there the statue stands,
Entraps the eye severer art repels.

Moreover, Pallas wields the thunderbolt
Yet has not struck the artist all this while.
Pheidias and Aischulos? Euripides
And Lachares? But youth will have its way.
The ripe man ought to be as old as young –
As young as old. I too have youth at need.
Much may be said for stripping wisdom bare.

'And who's "our best friend"? You play kottabos;
Here's the last mode of playing. Take a sphere
With orifices at due interval,
Through topmost one of which, a throw adroit
Sends wine from cup, clean passage, from outside
To where, in hollow midst, a manikin
Suspended ever bobs with head erect
Right underneath whatever hole's a-top
When you set orb a-rolling: plumb, he gets
Ever this benediction of the splash.
An other-fashioned orb presents him fixed:
Of all the outlets, he fronts only one,
And only when that one, – and rare the chance, –
Comes uppermost, does he turn upward too:
He can't turn all sides with the turning orb.
Inside this sphere of life, – all objects, sense
And soul perceive, – Euripides hangs fixed,
Gets knowledge through the single aperture
Of High and Right: with visage fronting these
He waits the wine thence ere he operate,
Work in the world and write a tragedy.
When that hole happens to revolve to point,
In drops the knowledge, waiting meets reward.
But, duly in rotation, Low and Wrong –
When these enjoy the moment's altitude,
His heels are found just where his head should be!
No knowledge that way! *I* am movable, –
To slightest shift of orb make prompt response,
Face Low and Wrong and Weak and all the rest,
And still drink knowledge, wine-drenched every turn, –
Equally favoured by their opposites.
Little and Bad exist, are natural:
Then let me know them, and be twice as great
As he who only knows one phase of life!

So doubly shall I prove "best friend of man,"
If I report the whole truth – Vice, perceived
While he shut eyes to all but Virtue there.
Man's made of both: and both must be of use
To somebody: if not to him, to me.
While, as to your imaginary Third
Who, stationed (by mechanics past my guess)
So as to take in every side at once,
And not successively, – may reconcile
The High and Low in tragi-comic verse, –
He shall be hailed superior to us both
When born – in the Tin-islands! Meantime, here
In bright Athenai, I contest the claim,
Call myself Iostephanos' "best friend,"
Who took my own course, worked as I descried
Ordainment, stuck to my first faculty.

'For listen! There's no failure breaks the heart,
Whate'er be man's endeavour in this world,
Like the rash poet's when he – nowise fails
By poetizing badly, – Zeus or makes
Or mars a man, so – at it, merrily!
But when, – made man, – much like myself, – equipt
For such and such achievement, – rash he turns
Out of the straight path, bent on snatch of feat
From – who's the appointed fellow born thereto, –
Crows take him! – in your Kassiterides?
Half-doing his work, leaving mine untouched,
That were the failure. Here I stand, heart-whole,
No Thamuris!

'Well thought of, Thamuris!
Has zeal, pray, for "best friend" Euripides
Allowed you to observe the honour done
His elder rival, in our Poikilé?
You don't know? Once and only once, trod stage,
Sang and touched lyre in person, in his youth,
Our Sophokles, – youth, beauty, dedicate
To Thamuris who named the tragedy.
The voice of him was weak; face, limbs and lyre,
These were worth saving: Thamuris stands yet

Perfect as painting helps in such a case.
At least you know the story, for "best friend"
Enriched his "Rhesos" from the Blind Bard's store;
So haste and see the work, and lay to heart
What it was struck me when I eyed the piece!
Here stands a poet punished for rash strife
With Powers above his power, who see with sight
Beyond his vision, sing accordingly
A song, which he must needs dare emulate.
Poet, remain the man nor ape the Muse!

'But – lend me the psalterion! Nay, for once –
Once let my hand fall where the other's lay!
I see it, just as I were Sophokles,
That sunrise and combustion of the east!'

And then he sang – are these unlike the words?

Thamuris marching, – lyre and song of Thrace –
(Perpend the first, the worst of woes that were
Allotted lyre and song, ye poet-race!)

Thamuris from Oichalia, feasted there
By kingly Eurutos of late, now bound
For Dorion at the uprise broad and bare

Of Mount Pangaios (ore with earth enwound
Glittered beneath his footstep) – marching gay
And glad, Thessalia through, came, robed and crowned,

From triumph on to triumph, 'mid a ray
Of early morn, – came, saw and knew the spot
Assigned him for his worst of woes, that day.

Balura – happier while its name was not –
Met him, but nowise menaced; slipt aside,
Obsequious river to pursue its lot

Of solacing the valley – say, some wide
Thick busy human cluster, house and home,
Embanked for peace, or thrift that thanks the tide.

Thamuris, marching, laughed 'Each flake of foam'
(As sparklingly the ripple raced him by)
'Mocks slower clouds adrift in the blue dome!'

For Autumn was the season; red the sky
Held morn's conclusive signet of the sun
To break the mists up, bid them blaze and die.

Morn had the mastery as, one by one
All pomps produced themselves along the tract
From earth's far ending to near heaven begun.

Was there a ravaged tree? it laughed compact
With gold, a leaf-ball crisp, high-brandished now,
Tempting to onset frost which late attacked.

Was there a wizened shrub, a starveling bough,
A fleecy thistle filched from by the wind,
A weed, Pan's trampling hoof would disallow?

Each, with a glory and a rapture twined
About it, joined the rush of air and light
And force: the world was of one joyous mind.

Say not the birds flew! they forebore their right –
Swam, revelling onward in the roll of things.
Say not the beasts' mirth bounded! that was flight –

How could the creatures leap, no lift of wings?
Such earth's community of purpose, such
The ease of earth's fulfilled imaginings, –

So did the near and far appear to touch
I' the moment's transport, – that an interchange
Of function, far with near, seemed scarce too much;

And had the rooted plant aspired to range
With the snake's license, while the insect yearned
To glow fixed as the flower, it were not strange –

No more than if the fluttery tree-top turned
To actual music, sang itself aloft;
Or if the wind, impassioned chantress, earned

The right to soar embodied in some soft
Fine form all fit for cloud-companionship,
And, blissful, once touch beauty chased so oft.

Thamuris, marching, let no fancy slip
Born of the fiery transport; lyre and song
Were his, to smite with hand and launch from lip –

Peerless recorded, since the list grew long
Of poets (saith Homeros) free to stand
Pedestalled 'mid the Muses' temple-throng,

A statued service, laurelled, lyre in hand,
(Ay, for we see them) – Thamuris of Thrace
Predominating foremost of the band.

Therefore the morn-ray that enriched his face,
If it gave lambent chill, took flame again
From flush of pride; he saw, he knew the place.

What wind arrived with all the rhythms from plain,
Hill, dale, and that rough wildwood interspersed?
Compounding these to one consummate strain,

It reached him, music; but his own outburst
Of victory concluded the account,
And that grew song which was mere music erst.

'Be my Parnassos, thou Pangaian mount!
And turn thee, river, nameless hitherto!
Famed shalt thou vie with famed Pieria's fount!

'Here I await the end of this ado:
Which wins – Earth's poet or the Heavenly Muse.'...

But song broke up in laughter. 'Tell the rest
Who may! *I* have not spurned the common life,
Nor vaunted mine a lyre to match the Muse

Who sings for gods, not men! Accordingly,
I shall not decorate her vestibule –
Mute marble, blind the eyes and quenched the brain,
Loose in the hand a bright, a broken lyre!
– Not Thamuris but Aristophanes!

'There! I have sung content back to myself,
And started subject for a play beside.
My next performance shall content you both.
Did "Prelude-Battle" maul "best friend" too much?
Then "Main-Fight" be my next song, fairness' self!
Its subject – Contest for the Tragic Crown.
Ay, you shall hear none else but Aischulos
Lay down the law of Tragedy, and prove
"Best friend" a stray-away, – no praise denied
His manifold deservings, never fear –
Nor word more of the old fun! Death defends.
Sound admonition has its due effect.
Oh, you have uttered weighty words, believe!
Such as shall bear abundant fruit, next year,
In judgement, regular, legitimate.
Let Bacchos' self preside in person! Ay –
For there's a buzz about those "Bacchanals"
Rumour attributes to your great and dead
For final effort: just the prodigy
Great dead men leave, to lay survivors low!
– Until we make acquaintance with our fate
And find, fate's worst done, we, the same, survive
Perchance to honour more the patron-god,
Fitlier inaugurate a festal year.
Now that the cloud has broken, sky laughs blue,
Earth blossoms youthfully. Athenai breathes.
After a twenty-six years' wintry blank
Struck from her life, – war-madness, one long swoon,
She wakes up: Arginousai bids good cheer.
We have disposed of Kallikratidas;
Once more will Sparté sue for terms, – who knows?
Cede Dekeleia, as the rumour runs:
Terms which Athenai, of right mind again,
Accepts – she can no other. Peace declared,
Have my long labours borne their fruit or no?

Grinned coarse buffoonery so oft in vain?
Enough – it simply saved you. Saved ones, praise
Theoria's beauty and Opora's breadth!
Nor, when Peace realizes promised bliss,
Forget the Bald Bard, Envy! but go burst
As the cup goes round and the cates abound,
Collops of hare with roast spinks rare!
Confess my pipings, dancings, posings served
A purpose: guttlings, guzzlings, had their use!
Say whether light Muse, Rosy-finger-tips,
Or "best friend's" heavy-hand, Melpomené,
Touched lyre to purpose, played Amphion's part,
And built Athenai to the skies once more!
Farewell, brave couple! Next year, welcome me!'

No doubt, in what he said that night, sincere!
One story he referred to, false or fact,
Was not without adaptability.
They do say – Lais the Corinthian once
Chancing to see Euripides (who paced
Composing in a garden, tablet-book
In left hand, with appended stulos prompt)
'Answer me,' she began, 'O Poet, – this!
What didst intend by writing in thy play
Go hang, thou filthy doer?' Struck on heap,
Euripides, at the audacious speech –
'Well now,' quoth he, 'thyself art just the one
I should imagine fit for deeds of filth!'
She laughingly retorted his own line
'What's filth, – unless who does it, thinks it so?'

So might he doubtless think. 'Farewell,' said we.

And he was gone, lost in the morning-grey
Rose-streaked and gold to eastward. Did we dream?
Could the poor twelve-hours hold this argument
We render durable from fugitive,
As duly at each sunset's droop of sail,
Delay of oar, submission to sea-might,

I still remember, you as duly dint
Remembrance, with the punctual rapid style,
Into – what calm cold page!

Thus soul escapes
From eloquence made captive: thus mere words
– Ah, would the lifeless body stay! But no:
Change upon change till, – who may recognize
What did soul service, in the dusty heap?
What energy of Aristophanes
Inflames the wreck Balaustion saves to show?
Ashes be evidence how fire – with smoke –
All night went lamping on! But morn must rise.
The poet – I shall say – burned up and, blank
Smouldered this ash, now white and cold enough.

Nay, Euthukles! for best, though mine it be,
Comes yet. Write on, write ever, wrong no word!

Add, first, – he gone, if jollity went too,
Some of the graver mood, which mixed and marred,
Departed likewise. Sight of narrow scope
Has this meek consolation: neither ills
We dread, nor joys we dare anticipate,
Perform to promise. Each soul sows a seed –
Euripides and Aristophanes;
Seed bears crop, scarce within our little lives;
But germinates, – perhaps enough to judge, –
Next year?

Whereas, next year brought harvest-time!
For, next year came, and went not, but is now,
Still now, while you and I are bound for Rhodes
That's all but reached – and harvest has it brought,
Dire as the homicidal dragon-crop.
Sophokles had dismissal ere it dawned,
Happy as ever; though men mournfully
Plausive, – when only soul could triumph now,
And Iophon produced his father's play, –
Crowned the consummate song where Oidipous
Dared the descent 'mid earthquake-thundering,
And hardly Theseus' hands availed to guard

Eyes from the horror, as their grove disgorged
Its dread ones, while each daughter sank to ground.

Then Aristophanes, on heel of that,
Triumphant also, followed with his 'Frogs':
Produced at next Lenaia, – three months since, –
The promised 'Main-Fight', loyal, license-free!
As if the poet, primed with Thasian juice,
(Himself swore – wine that conquers every kind
For long abiding in the head) could fix
Thenceforward any object in its truth,
Through eyeballs bathed by mere Castalian dew,
Nor miss the borrowed medium, – vinous drop
That colours all to the right crimson pitch
When mirth grows mockery, censure takes the tinge
Of malice!

All was Aristophanes:
There blazed the glory, there shot black the shame.
Ay, Bacchos did stand forth, the Tragic God
In person! and when duly dragged through mire, –
Having lied, filched, played fool, proved coward, flung
The boys their dose of fit indecency,
And finally got trounced to heart's content,
At his own feast, in his own theatre
(– Oh never fear! 'Twas consecrated sport,
Exact tradition, warranted no whit
Offensive to instructed taste, – indeed,
Essential to Athenai's liberty,
Could the poor stranger understand!) why, then –
He was pronounced the rarely-qualified
To rate the work, adjust the claims to worth,
Of Aischulos (of whom, in other mood,
This same appreciative poet pleased
To say 'He's all one stiff and gluey piece
Of back of swine's neck!') – and of Chatterbox
Who, 'twisting words like wool,' usurped his seat
In Plouton's realm: 'the arch-rogue, liar, scamp
That lives by snatching-up of altar-orts,'
– Who failed to recognize Euripides?

Then came a contest for supremacy –
Crammed full of genius, wit and fun and freak.
No spice of undue spite to spoil the dish
Of all sorts, – for the Mystics matched the Frogs
In poetry, no Seiren sang so sweet! –
Till, pressed into the service (how dispense
With Phaps-Elaphion and free foot-display?)
The Muse of dead Euripides danced frank,
Rattled her bits of tile, made all too plain
How baby-work like 'Herakles' had birth!
Last, Bacchos, – candidly disclaiming brains
Able to follow finer argument, –
Confessed himself much moved by three main facts:
First, – if you stick a 'Lost his flask of oil'
At pause of period, you perplex the sense –
Were it the Elegy for Marathon!
Next, if you weigh two verses, 'car' – the word,
Will outweigh 'club' – the word, in each packed line!
And – last, worst fact of all! – in rivalry
The younger poet dared to improvise
Laudation less distinct of – Triphales?
(Nay, that served when ourself abused the youth!)
Pheidippides? (nor that's appropriate now!)
Then, – Alkibiades, our city's hope,
Since times change and we Comics should change too!
These three main facts, well weighed, drew judgement down,
Conclusively assigned the wretch his fate –
'Fate due' admonished the sage Mystic choir,
'To sitting, prate-apace, with Sokrates,
Neglecting music and each tragic aid!'
– All wound-up by a wish 'We soon may cease
From certain griefs, and warfare, worst of them!'
– Since, deaf to Comedy's persistent voice,
War still raged, still was like to rage. In vain
Had Sparté cried once more 'But grant us Peace
We give you Dekeleia back!' Too shrewd
Was Kleophon to let escape, forsooth,
The enemy – at final gasp, besides!

So, Aristophanes obtained the prize,
And so Athenai felt she had a friend
Far better than her 'best friend,' lost last year;

And so, such fame had 'Frogs' that, when came round
This present year, those Frogs croaked gay again
At the great Feast, Elaphebolion-month.
Only – there happened Aigispotamoi!

And, in the midst of the frog-merriment,
Plump o' the sudden, pounces stern King Stork
On the light-hearted people of the marsh!
Spartan Lusandros swooped precipitate,
Ended Athenai, rowed her sacred bay
With oars which brought a hundred triremes back
Captive!

And first word of the conqueror
Was 'Down with those Long Walls, Peiraius' pride!
Destroy, yourselves, your bulwarks! Peace needs none!'
And 'We obey' they shuddered in their dream.

But, at next quick imposure of decree –
'No longer democratic government!
Henceforth such oligarchy as ourselves
Please to appoint you!' – then the horror stung
Dreamers awake; they started up a-stare
At the half-helot captain and his crew
– Spartans, 'men used to let their hair grow long,
To fast, be dirty, and just – Socratize' –
Whose word was 'Trample on Themistokles!'

So, as the way is with much misery,
The heads swam, hands refused their office, hearts
Sunk as they stood in stupor. 'Wreck the Walls?
Ruin Peiraius? – with our Pallas armed
For interference? – Herakles apprised,
And Theseus hasting? Lay the Long Walls low?'

Three days they stood, stared, – stonier than their walls.

Whereupon, sleep who might, Lusandros woke:
Saw the prostration of his enemy,
Utter and absolute beyond belief,
Past hope of hatred even. I surmise
He also probably saw fade in fume

Certain fears, bred of Bakis-prophecy,
Nor apprehended any more that gods
And heroes, – fire, must glow forth, guard the ground
Where prone, by sober day-dawn, corpse-like lay
Powerless Athenai, late predominant
Lady of Hellas, – Sparté's slave-prize now!
Where should a menace lurk in those slack limbs?
What was to move his circumspection? Why
Demolish just Peiraius?

'Stay!' bade he:
'Already promise-breakers? True to type,
Athenians! past and present and to come –
The fickle and the false! No stone dislodged,
No implement applied, yet three days' grace
Expire! Forbearance is no longer-lived.
By breaking promise, terms of peace you break –
Too gently framed for falsehood, fickleness!
All must be reconsidered – yours the fault!'

Wherewith, he called a council of allies.
Pent-up resentment used its privilege, –
Outburst at ending: this the summed result.

'Because we would avenge no transient wrong
But an eternity of insolence,
Aggression, – folly, no disasters mend,
Pride, no reverses teach humility, –
Because too plainly were all punishment,
Such as comports with less obdurate crime,
Evadable by falsehood, fickleness –
Experience proves the true Athenian type, –
Therefore, 'tis need we dig deep down into
The root of evil; lop nor bole nor branch.
Look up, look round and see, on every side,
What nurtured the rank tree to noisome fruit!
We who live hutted (so they laugh) not housed,
Build barns for temples, prize mud-monuments,
Nor show the sneering stranger aught but – men, –
Spartans take insult of Athenians just
Because they boast Akropolis to mount,

And Propulaia to make entry by,
Through a mad maze of marble arrogance
Such as you see – such as let none see more!
Abolish the detested luxury!
Leave not one stone upon another, raze
Athenai to the rock! Let hill and plain
Become a waste, a grassy pasture-ground
Where sheep may wander, grazing goats depend
From shapeless crags once columns! so at last
Shall peace inhabit there, and peace enough.'

Whereon, a shout approved 'Such peace bestow!'

Then did a Man of Phokis rise – O heart!
Rise – when no bolt of Zeus disparted sky,
No omen-bird from Pallas scared the crew,
Rise – when mere human argument could stem
No foam-fringe of the passion surging fierce,
Baffle no wrath-wave that o'er barrier broke –
Who was the Man of Phokis rose and flung
A flower i' the way of that fierce foot's advance,
Which – stop for? – nay, had stamped down sword's assault!
Could it be *He* stayed Sparté with the snatch
'Daughter of Agamemnon, late my liege,
Elektra, palaced once, a visitant
To thy poor rustic dwelling, now I come?'

Ay, facing fury of revenge, and lust
Of hate, and malice moaning to appease
Hunger on prey presumptuous, prostrate now –
Full in the hideous faces – last resource,
You flung that choric flower, my Euthukles!

And see, as through some pinhole, should the wind
Wedgingly pierce but once, in with a rush
Hurries the whole wild weather, rends to rags
The weak sail stretched against the outside storm –
So did the power of that triumphant play
Pour in, and oversweep the assembled foe!
Triumphant play, wherein our poet first
Dared bring the grandeur of the Tragic Two

Down to the level of our common life,
Close to the beating of our common heart.
Elektra? 'Twas Athenai, Sparté's ice
Thawed to, while that sad portraiture appealed –
Agamemnonian lady, lost by fault
Of her own kindred, cast from house and home,
Despoiled of all the brave inheritance,
Dowered humbly as befits a herdsman's mate,
Partaker of his cottage, clothed in rags,
Patient performer of the poorest chares,
Yet mindful, all the while, of glory past
When she walked darling of Mukenai, dear
Beyond Orestes to the King of Men!

So, because Greeks are Greeks, though Sparté's brood,
And hearts are hearts, though in Lusandros' breast,
And poetry is power, and Euthukles
Had faith therein to, full-face, fling the same –
Sudden, the ice-thaw! The assembled foe,
Heaving and swaying with strange friendliness,
Cried 'Reverence Elektra!' – cried 'Abstain
Like that chaste Herdsman, nor dare violate
The sanctity of such reverse! Let stand
Athenai!'

Mindful of that story's close,
Perchance, and how, – when he, the Herdsman chaste,
Needs apprehend no break of tranquil sleep, –
All in due time, a stranger, dark, disguised,
Knocks at the door: with searching glance, notes keen,
Knows quick, through mean attire and disrespect,
The ravaged princess! Ay, right on, the clutch
Of guiding retribution has in charge
The author of the outrage! While one hand,
Elektra's, pulls the door behind, made fast
On fate, – the other strains, prepared to push
The victim-queen, should she make frightened pause
Before that serpentining blood which steals
Out of the darkness where, a pace beyond,
Above the slain Aigisthos, bides his blow
Dreadful Orestes!

Klutaimnestra, wise
This time, forbore; Elektra held her own;
Saved was Athenai through Euripides,
Through Euthukles, through – more than ever – me,
Balaustion, me, who, Wild-pomegranate-flower,
Felt my fruit triumph, and fade proudly so!

But next day, as ungracious minds are wont,
The Spartan, late surprised into a grace,
Grew sudden sober at the enormity,
And grudged, by daybreak, midnight's easy gift;
Splenetically must repay its cost
By due increase of rigour, doglike snatch
At aught still left dog to concede like man.
Rough sea, at flow of tide, may lip, perchance,
Smoothly the land-line reached as for repose –
Lie indolent in all unquestioned sway;
But ebbing, when needs must, all thwart and loth,
Sea claws at sand relinquished strugglingly.
So, harsh Lusandros – pinioned to inflict
The lesser penalty alone – spoke harsh,
As minded to embitter scathe by scorn.

'Athenai's self be saved then, thank the Lyre!
If Tragedy withdraws her presence – quick,
If Comedy replace her, – what more just?
Let Comedy do service, frisk away,
Dance off stage these indomitable stones,
Long Walls, Peiraian bulwarks! Hew and heave,
Pick at, pound into dust each dear defence!
Not to the Kommos – *eleleleleu*
With breast bethumped, as Tragic lyre prefers,
But Comedy shall sound the flute, and crow
At kordax-end – the hearty slapping-dance!
Collect those flute-girls – trash who flattered ear
With whistlings and fed eye with caper-cuts
While we Lakonians supped black broth or crunched
Sea-urchin, conchs and all, unpricked – coarse brutes!
Command they lead off step, time steady stroke
To spade and pickaxe, till demolished lie
Athenai's pride in powder!'

Done that day –
That sixteenth famed day of Munuchion-month!
The day when Hellas fought at Salamis,
The very day Euripides was born,
Those flute-girls – Phaps-Elaphion at their head –
Did blow their best, did dance their worst, the while
Sparté pulled down the walls, wrecked wide the works,
Laid low each merest molehill of defence,
And so the Power, Athenai, passed away!

We would not see its passing. Ere I knew
The issue of their counsels, – crouching low
And shrouded by my peplos, – I conceived,
Despite the shut eyes, the stopped ears, – by count
Only of heart-beats, telling the slow time, –
Athenai's doom was signed and signified
In that assembly, – ay, but knew there watched
One who would dare and do, nor bate at all
The stranger's licensed duty, – speak the word
Allowed the Man from Phokis! Naught remained
But urge departure, flee the sights and sounds,
Hideous exultings, wailings worth contempt,
And press to other earth, new heaven, by sea
That somehow ever prompts to 'scape despair.

Help rose to heart's wish; at the harbour-side,
The old grey mariner did reverence
To who had saved his ship, still weather-tight
As when with prow gay-garlanded she praised
The hospitable port and pushed to sea.
'Convoy Balaustion back to Rhodes, for sake
Of her and her Euripides!' laughed he.

Rhodes, – shall it not be there, my Euthukles,
Till this brief trouble of a life-time end,
That solitude – two make so populous! –
For food finds memories of the past suffice,
May be, anticipations, – hope so swells, –
Of some great future we, familiar once
With who so taught, should hail and entertain?
He lies now in the little valley, laughed
And moaned about by those mysterious streams,

Boiling and freezing, like the love and hate
Which helped or harmed him through his earthly course.
They mix in Arethousa by his grave.
The warm spring, traveller, dip thine arms into,
Brighten thy brow with! Life detests black cold.

I sent the tablets, the psalterion, so
Rewarded Sicily; the tyrant there
Bestowed them worthily in Phoibos' shrine.
A gold-graved writing tells – 'I also loved
The poet, Free Athenai cheaply prized –
King Dionusios, – Archelaos-like!'

And see if young Philemon, – sure one day
To do good service and be loved himself, –
If he too have not made a votive verse!
'Grant, in good sooth, our great dead, all the same,
Retain their sense, as certain wise men say,
I'd hang myself – to see Euripides!'
Hands off, Philemon! nowise hang thyself,
But pen the prime plays, labour the right life,
And die at good old age as grand men use, –
Keeping thee, with that great thought, warm the while, –
That he does live, Philemon! Ay, most sure!
'He lives!' hark, – waves say, winds sing out the same,
And yonder dares the citied ridge of Rhodes
Its headlong plunge from sky to sea, disparts
North bay from south, – each guarded calm, that guest
May enter gladly, blow what wind there will, –
Boiled round with breakers, to no other cry!
All in one choros, – what the master-word
They take up? – hark! 'There are no gods, no gods!
Glory to God – who saves Euripides!'

The Inn Album

1875

The Inn Album

I

'That oblong book's the Album; hand it here!
Exactly! page on page of gratitude
For breakfast, dinner, supper, and the view!
I praise these poets: they leave margin-space;
Each stanza seems to gather skirts around,
And primly, trimly, keep the foot's confine,
Modest and maidlike; lubber prose o'ersprawls
And straddling stops the path from left to right.
Since I want space to do my cipher-work,
Which poem spares a corner? What comes first?
"*Hail, calm acclivity, salubrious spot!*"
(Open the window, we burn daylight, boy!)
Or see – succincter beauty, brief and bold –
"*If a fellow can dine On rumpsteaks and port wine,*
He needs not despair Of dining well here –"
"*Here!*" I myself could find a better rhyme!
That bard's a Browning; he neglects the form:
But ah, the sense, ye gods, the weighty sense!
Still, I prefer this classic. Ay, throw wide!
I'll quench the bits of candle yet unburnt.
A minute's fresh air, then to cipher-work!
Three little columns hold the whole account:
Écarté, after which Blind Hookey, then
Cutting-the-Pack, five hundred pounds the cut.
'Tis easy reckoning: I have lost, I think.'

Two personages occupy this room
Shabby-genteel, that's parlour to the inn
Perched on a view-commanding eminence;
– Inn which may be a veritable house
Where somebody once lived and pleased good taste
Till tourists found his coign of vantage out,
And fingered blunt the individual mark
And vulgarized things comfortably smooth.
On a sprig-pattern-papered wall there brays
Complaint to sky Sir Edwin's dripping stag;
His couchant coast-guard creature corresponds;
They face the Huguenot and Light o' the World.
Grim o'er the mirror on the mantelpiece,
Varnished and coffined, *Salmo ferox* glares

– Possibly at the List of Wines which, framed
And glazed, hangs somewhat prominent on peg.

So much describes the stuffy little room –
Vulgar flat smooth respectability:
Not so the burst of landscape surging in,
Sunrise and all, as he who of the pair
Is, plain enough, the younger personage
Draws sharp the shrieking curtain, sends aloft
The sash, spreads wide and fastens back to wall
Shutter and shutter, shows you England's best.
He leans into a living glory-bath
Of air and light where seems to float and move
The wooded watered country, hill and dale
And steel-bright thread of stream, a-smoke with mist,
A-sparkle with May morning, diamond drift
O' the sun-touched dew. Except the red-roofed patch
Of half a dozen dwellings that, crept close
For hill-side shelter, make the village-clump,
This inn is perched above to dominate –
Except such sign of human neighbourhood,
(And this surmised rather than sensible)
There's nothing to disturb absolute peace,
The reign of English nature – which means art
And civilized existence. Wildness' self
Is just the cultured triumph. Presently
Deep solitude, be sure, reveals a Place
That knows the right way to defend itself:
Silence hems round a burning spot of life.
Now, where a Place burns, must a village brood,
And where a village broods, an inn should boast –
Close and convenient: here you have them both.
This inn, the Something-arms – the family's –
(Don't trouble Guillim: heralds leave out half!)
Is dear to lovers of the picturesque,
And epics have been planned here; but who plan
Take holy orders and find work to do.
Painters are more productive, stop a week,
Declare the prospect quite a Corot, – ay,
For tender sentiment, – themselves incline
Rather to handsweep large and liberal;

Then go, but not without success achieved
– Haply some pencil-drawing, oak or beech,
Ferns at the base and ivies up the bole,
On this a slug, on that a butterfly.
Nay, he who hooked the *salmo* pendent here,
Also exhibited, this same May-month,
'*Foxgloves: a study*' – so inspires the scene,
The air, which now the younger personage
Inflates him with till lungs o'erfraught are fain
Sigh forth a satisfaction might bestir
Even those tufts of tree-tops to the South
I' the distance where the green dies off to grey,
Which, easy of conjecture, front the Place;
He eyes them, elbows wide, each hand to cheek.

His fellow, the much older – either say
A youngish-old man or man oldish-young –
Sits at the table: wicks are noisome-deep
In wax, to detriment of plated ware;
Above – piled, strewn – is store of playing-cards,
Counters and all that's proper for a game.
He sets down, rubs out figures in the book,
Adds and subtracts, puts back here, carries there,
Until the summed-up satisfaction stands
Apparent, and he pauses o'er the work:
Soothes what of brain was busy under brow,
By passage of the hard palm, curing so
Wrinkle and crowfoot for a second's space;
Then lays down book and laughs out. No mistake,
Such the sum-total – ask Colenso else!

Roused by which laugh, the other turns, laughs too –
The youth, the good strong fellow, rough perhaps.

'Well, what's the damage – three, or four, or five?
How many figures in a row? Hand here!
Come now, there's one expense all yours not mine –
Scribbling the people's Album over, leaf
The first and foremost too! You think, perhaps,
They'll only charge you for a brand-new book
Nor estimate the literary loss?

Wait till the small account comes! "*To one night's*
Lodging," – for "beds," they can't say, – "*pound or so;*
Dinner, Apollinaris, – what they please,
Attendance not included"; last looms large
"*Defacement of our Album, late enriched*
With" – let's see what! Here, at the window, though!
Ay, breathe the morning and forgive your luck!
Fine enough country for a fool like me
To own, as next month I suppose I shall!
Eh? True fool's-fortune! so console yourself.
Let's see, however – hand the book, I say!
Well, you've improved the classic by romance.
Queer reading! Verse with parenthetic prose –
"*Hail, calm acclivity, salubrious spot!*"
(Three-two fives) "*life how profitably spent*"
(Five-nought, five-nine fives) "*yonder humble cot,*"
(More and more noughts and fives) "*in mild content;*
And did my feelings find the natural vent
In friendship and in love, how blest my lot!"
Then follow the dread figures – five! "*Content!*"
That's apposite! Are you content as he –
Simpkin the sonneteer? *Ten thousand pounds*
Give point to his effusion – by so much
Leave me the richer and the poorer you
After our night's play; who's content the most,
I, you, or Simpkin?'
So the polished snob.
The elder man, refinement every inch
From brow to boot-end, quietly replies:

'Simpkin's no name I know. I had my whim.'

'Ay, had you! And such things make friendship thick.
Intimates I may boast we were; henceforth,
Friends – shall it not be? – who discard reserve,
Use plain words, put each dot upon each i,
Till death us twain do part? The bargain's struck!
Old fellow, if you fancy – (to begin –)
I failed to penetrate your scheme last week,
You wrong your poor disciple. Oh, no airs!
Because you happen to be twice my age
And twenty times my master, must perforce

No blink of daylight struggle through the web
There's no unwinding? You entoil my legs,
And welcome, for I like it: blind me, – no!
A very pretty piece of shuttle-work
Was that – your mere chance question at the club –
"*Do you go anywhere this Whitsuntide?*
I'm off for Paris, there's the Opera – there's
The Salon, there's a china-sale, – beside
Chantilly; and, for good companionship,
There's Such-and-such and So-and-so. Suppose
We start together?" "*No such holiday!*"
I told you: "*Paris and the rest be hanged!*
Why plague me who am pledged to home-delights?
I'm the engaged now; through whose fault but yours?
On duty. As you well know. Don't I drowse
The week away down with the Aunt and Niece?
No help: it's leisure, loneliness and love.
Wish I could take you; but fame travels fast, –
A man of much newspaper-paragraph
You scare domestic circles; and beside
Would not you like your lot, that second taste
Of nature and approval of the grounds!
You might walk early or lie late, so shirk
Week-day devotions: but stay Sunday o'er,
And morning church is obligatory:
No mundane garb permissible, or dread
The butler's privileged monition! No!
Pack off to Paris, nor wipe tear away!"
Whereon how artlessly the happy flash
Followed, by inspiration! "'*Tell you what –*
Let's turn their flank, try things on t'other side!
Inns for my money! Liberty's the life!
We'll lie in hiding: there's the crow-nest nook,
The tourist's joy, the Inn they rave about,
Inn that's out – out of sight and out of mind
And out of mischief to all four of us –
Aunt and niece, you and me. At night arrive;
At morn, find time for just a Pisgah-view
Of my friend's Land of Promise; then depart.
And while I'm whizzing onward by first train,
Bound for our own place (since my Brother sulks
And says I shun him like the plague) yourself –

Why, you have stepped thence, start from platform, gay
Despite the sleepless journey, – love lends wings, –
Hug aunt and niece who, none the wiser, wait
The faithful advent! Eh?" "With all my heart,"
Said I to you; said I to mine own self:
"Does he believe I fail to comprehend
He wants just one more final friendly snack
At friend's exchequer ere friend runs to earth,
Marries, renounces yielding friends such sport?"
And did I spoil sport, pull face grim, – nay, grave?
Your pupil does you better credit! No!
I parleyed with my pass-book, – rubbed my pair
At the big balance in my banker's hands, –
Folded a cheque cigar-case-shape, – just wants
Filling and signing, – and took train, resolved
To execute myself with decency
And let you win – if not Ten thousand quite,
Something by way of wind-up-farewell burst
Of firework-nosegay! Where's your fortune fled?
Or is not fortune constant after all?
You lose ten thousand pounds: had I lost half
Or half that, I should bite my lips, I think.
You man of marble! Strut and stretch my best
On tiptoe, I shall never reach your height.
How does the loss feel! Just one lesson more!'

The more refined man smiles a frown away.

'The lesson shall be – only boys like you
Put such a question at the present stage.
I had a ball lodge in my shoulder once,
And, full five minutes, never guessed the fact;
Next day, I felt decidedly: and still,
At twelve years' distance, when I lift my arm
A twinge reminds me of the surgeon's probe.
Ask me, this day month, how I feel my luck!
And meantime please to stop impertinence,
For – don't I know its object? All this chaff
Covers the corn, this preface leads to speech,
This boy stands forth a hero. "*There, my lord!*
Our play was true play, fun not earnest! I
Empty your purse, inside out, while my poke

Bulges to bursting? You can badly spare
A doit, confess now, Duke though brother be!
While I'm gold-daubed so thickly, spangles drop
And show my father's warehouse-apron: pshaw!
Enough! We've had a palpitating night!
Good morning! Breakfast and forget our dreams!
My mouth's shut, mind! I tell nor man nor mouse."
There, see! He don't deny it! Thanks, my boy!
Hero and welcome – only, not on me
Make trial of your 'prentice-hand! Enough!
We've played, I've lost and owe ten thousand pounds,
Whereof I muster, at the moment, – well,
What's for the bill here and the back to town.
Still, I've my little character to keep:
You may expect your money at month's end.'

The young man at the window turns round quick –
A clumsy giant handsome creature; grasps
In his large red the little lean white hand
Of the other, looks him in the sallow face.

'I say now – is it right to so mistake
A fellow, force him in mere self-defence
To spout like Mister *Mild Acclivity*
In album-language? You know well enough
Whether I like you – *like's* no album-word
Anyhow: point me to one soul beside
In the wide world I care one straw about!
I first set eyes on you a year ago;
Since when you've done me good – I'll stick to it –
More than I got in the whole twenty-five
That make my life up, Oxford years and all –
Throw in the three I fooled away abroad,
Seeing myself and nobody more sage
Until I met you, and you made me man
Such as the sort is and the fates allow.
I do think, since we two kept company,
I've learnt to know a little – all through you!
It's nature if I like you. Taunt away!
As if I need you teaching me my place –
The snob I am, the Duke your brother is,
When just the good you did was – teaching me

My own trade, how a snob and millionaire
May lead his life and let the Duke's alone,
Clap wings, free jackdaw, on his steeple-perch,
Burnish his black to gold in sun and air,
Nor pick up stray plumes, strive to match in strut
Regular peacocks who can't fly an inch
Over the courtyard-paling. Head and heart
(That's album-style) are older than you know,
For all your knowledge: boy, perhaps – ay, boy
Had his adventure, just as he were man –
His ball-experience in the shoulder-blade,
His bit of life-long ache to recognize,
Although he bears it cheerily about,
Because you came and clapped him on the back,
Advised him "*Walk and wear the aching off!*"
Why, I was minded to sit down for life
Just in Dalmatia, build a sea-side tower
High on a rock, and so expend my days
Pursuing chemistry or botany
Or, very like, astronomy because
I noticed stars shone when I passed the place:
Letting my cash accumulate the while
In England – to lay out in lump at last
As Ruskin should direct me! All or some
Of which should I have done or tried to do,
And preciously repented, one fine day,
Had you discovered Timon, climbed his rock
And scaled his tower, some ten years thence, suppose,
And coaxed his story from him! Don't I see
The pair conversing! It's a novel writ
Already, I'll be bound, – our dialogue!
"*What?*" *cried the elder and yet youthful man –*
So did the eye flash 'neath the lordly front,
And the imposing presence swell with scorn,
As the haught high-bred bearing and dispose
Contrasted with his interlocutor
The flabby low-born who, of bulk before,
Had steadily increased, one stone per week,
Since his abstention from horse-exercise: –
"*What? you, as rich as Rothschild, left, you say,*
London the very year you came of age,
Because your father manufactured goods –

Commission-agent hight of Manchester –
Partly, and partly through a baby case
Of disappointment I've pumped out at last –
And here you spend life's prime in gaining flesh
And giving science one more asteroid?"
Brief, my dear fellow, you instructed me,
At Alfred's and not Istria! proved a snob
May turn a million to account although
His brother be no Duke, and see good days
Without the girl he lost and someone gained.
The end is, after one year's tutelage,
Having, by your help, touched society,
Polo, Tent-pegging, Hurlingham, the Rink –
I leave all these delights, by your advice,
And marry my young pretty cousin here
Whose place, whose oaks ancestral you behold.
(Her father was in partnership with mine –
Does not his purchase look a pedigree?)
My million will be tails and tassels smart
To this plump-bodied kite, this house and land
Which, set a-soaring, pulls me, soft as sleep,
Along life's pleasant meadow, – arm left free
To lock a friend's in, – whose but yours, old boy?
Arm in arm glide we over rough and smooth,
While hand, to pocket held, saves cash from cards.
Now, if you don't esteem ten thousand pounds
(– Which I shall probably discover snug
Hid somewhere in the column-corner capped
With "*Credit,*" based on "*Balance,*" – which, I swear,
By this time next month I shall quite forget
Whether I lost or won – ten thousand pounds,
Which at this instant I would give . . . let's see,
For Galopin – nay, for that Gainsborough
Sir Richard won't sell, and, if bought by me,
Would get my glance and praise some twice a year, –)
Well, if you don't esteem that price dirt-cheap
For teaching me Dalmatia was mistake –
Why then, my last illusion-bubble breaks,
My one discovered phoenix proves a goose,
My cleverest of all companions – oh,
Was worth nor ten pence nor ten thousand pounds!
Come! Be yourself again! So endeth here

The morning's lesson! Never while life lasts
Do I touch card again. To breakfast now!
To bed – I can't say, since you needs must start
For station early – oh, the down-train still,
First plan and best plan – townward trip be hanged!
You're due at your big brother's – pay that debt,
Then owe me not a farthing! Order eggs –
And who knows but there's trout obtainable?'

The fine man looks well-nigh malignant: then –

'Sir, please subdue your manner! Debts are debts:
I pay mine – debts of this sort – certainly.
What do I care how you regard your gains,
Want them or want them not? The thing *I* want
Is – not to have a story circulate
From club to club – how, bent on clearing out
Young So-and-so, young So-and-so cleaned me,
Then set the empty kennel flush again,
Ignored advantage and forgave his friend –
For why? There was no wringing blood from stone!
Oh, don't be savage! You would hold your tongue,
Bite it in two, as man may; but those small
Hours in the smoking-room, when instance apt
Rises to tongue's root, tingles on to tip,
And the thinned company consists of six
Capital well-known fellows one may trust!
Next week, it's in the "World." No, thank you much.
I owe ten thousand pounds: I'll pay them!'

'Now, –
This becomes funny. You've made friends with me:
I can't help knowing of the ways and means!
Or stay! they say your brother closets up
Correggio's long-lost Leda: if he means
To give you that, and if you give it me . . .'

'*I* polished snob off to aristocrat?
You compliment me! father's apron still
Sticks out from son's court-vesture; still silk purse
Roughs finger with some bristle sow-ear-born!
Well, neither I nor you mean harm at heart!

I owe you and shall pay you: which premised,
Why should what follows sound like flattery?
The fact is – you do compliment too much
Your humble master, as I own I am;
You owe me no such thanks as you protest.
The polisher needs precious stone no less
Than precious stone needs polisher: believe
I struck no tint from out you but I found
Snug lying first 'neath surface hair-breadth-deep!
Beside, I liked the exercise: with skill
Goes love to show skill for skill's sake. You see,
I'm old and understand things: too absurd
It were you pitched and tossed away your life,
As diamond were Scotch-pebble! all the more,
That I myself misused a stone of price.
Born and bred clever – people used to say
Clever as most men, if not something more –
Yet here I stand a failure, cut awry
Or left opaque, – no brilliant named and known.
Whate'er my inner stuff, my outside's blank;
I'm nobody – or rather, look that same –
I'm – who I am – and know it; but I hold
What in my hand out for the world to see?
What ministry, what mission, or what book
– I'll say, book even? Not a sign of these!
I began – laughing – "*All these when I like!*"
I end with – well, you've hit it! – "*This boy's cheque*
For just as many thousands as he'll spare!"
The first – I could, and would not; your spare cash
I would, and could not: have no scruple, pray,
But, as I hoped to pocket yours, pouch mine
– When you are able!'
'Which is – when to be?
I've heard, great characters require a fall
Of fortune to show greatness by uprise:
They touch the ground to jollily rebound,
Add to the Album! Let a fellow share
Your secret of superiority!
I know, my banker makes the money breed
Money; I eat and sleep, he simply takes
The dividends and cuts the coupons off,
Sells out, buys in, keeps doubling, tripling cash,

While I do nothing but receive and spend.
But you, spontaneous generator, hatch
A wind-egg; cluck, and forth struts Capital
As Interest to me from egg of gold.
I am grown curious: pay me by all means!
How will you make the money?'
'Mind your own –
Not my affair. Enough: or money, or
Money's worth, as the case may be, expect
Ere month's end, – keep but patient for a month!
Who's for a stroll to station? Ten's the time;
Your man, with my things, follow in the trap;
At stoppage of the down-train, play the arrived
On platform, and you'll show the due fatigue
Of the night-journey, – not much sleep, – perhaps,
Your thoughts were on before you – yes, indeed,
You join them, being happily awake
With thought's sole object as she smiling sits
At breakfast-table. I shall dodge meantime
In and out station-precinct, wile away
The hour till up my engine pants and smokes.
No doubt, she goes to fetch you. Never fear!
She gets no glance at me, who shame such saints!'

II

So, they ring bell, give orders, pay, depart
Amid profuse acknowledgement from host
Who well knows what may bring the younger back.
They light cigar, descend in twenty steps
The '*calm acclivity*,' inhale – beyond
Tobacco's balm – the better smoke of turf
And wood fire, – cottages at cookery
I' the morning, – reach the main road straitening on
'Twixt wood and wood, two black walls full of night
Slow to disperse, though mists thin fast before
The advancing foot, and leave the flint-dust fine
Each speck with its fire-sparkle. Presently
The road's end with the sky's beginning mix
In one magnificence of glare, due East,
So high the sun rides, – May's the merry month.

They slacken pace: the younger stops abrupt,
Discards cigar, looks his friend full in face.

'All right; the station comes in view at end;
Five minutes from the beech-clump, there you are!
I say: let's halt, let's borrow yonder gate
Of its two magpies, sit and have a talk!
Do let a fellow speak a moment! More
I think about and less I like the thing –
No, you must let me! Now, be good for once!
Ten thousand pounds be done for, dead and damned!
We played for love, not hate: yes, hate! I hate
Thinking you beg or borrow or reduce
To strychnine some poor devil of a lord
Licked at Unlimited Loo. I had the cash
To lose – you knew that! – lose and none the less
Whistle tomorrow: it's not every chap
Affords to take his punishment so well!
Now, don't be angry with a friend whose fault
Is that he thinks – upon my soul, I do –
Your head the best head going. Oh, one sees
Names in the newspaper – great this, great that,
Gladstone, Carlyle, the Laureate: – much I care!
Others have their opinion, I keep mine:
Which means – by right you ought to have the things
I want a head for. Here's a pretty place,
My cousin's place, and presently my place,
Not yours! I'll tell you how it strikes a man.
My cousin's fond of music and of course
Plays the piano (it won't be for long!)
A brand-new bore she calls a "*semi-grand,*"
Rosewood and pearl, that blocks the drawing-room,
And cost no end of money. Twice a week
Down comes Herr Somebody and seats himself,
Sets to work teaching – with his teeth on edge –
I've watched the rascal. "*Does he play first-rate?*"
I ask: "*I rather think so,*" answers she –
"*He's What's-his-Name!*" – "*Why give you lessons then?*" –
"*I pay three guineas and the train beside.*" –
"*This instrument, has he one such at home?*" –
"*He? Has to practise on a table-top,*
When he can't hire the proper thing." – "*I see!*

You've the piano, he the skill, and God
The distribution of such gifts." So here:
After your teaching, I shall sit and strum
Polkas on this piano of a Place
You'd make resound with *Rule Britannia!*'

'Thanks!
I don't say but this pretty cousin's place,
Appendaged with your million, tempts my hand
As key-board I might touch with some effect.'

'Then, why not have obtained the like? House, land,
Money, are things obtainable, you see,
By clever head-work: ask my father else!
You, who teach me, why not have learned, yourself?
Played like Herr Somebody with power to thump
And flourish and the rest, not bend demure
Pointing out blunders – "*Sharp, not natural!*
Permit me – on the black key use the thumb!"
There's some fatality, I'm sure! You say
"*Marry the cousin, that's your proper move!*"
And I do use the thumb and hit the sharp:
You should have listened to your own head's hint,
As I to you! The puzzle's past my power,
How you have managed – with such stuff, such means –
Not to be rich nor great nor happy man:
Of which three good things where's a sign at all?
Just look at Dizzy! Come, – what tripped your heels?
Instruct a goose that boasts wings and can't fly!
I wager I have guessed it! – never found
The old solution of the riddle fail!
"*Who was the woman?*" I don't ask, but – "*Where*
I' the path of life stood she who tripped you?"'

'Goose
You truly are! I own to fifty years.
Why don't I interpose and cut out – you?
Compete with five-and-twenty? Age, my boy!'

'Old man, no nonsense! – even to a boy
That's ripe at least for rationality
Rapped into him, as may be mine was, once!

I've had my small adventure lesson me
Over the knuckles! – likely, I forget
The sort of figure youth cuts now and then,
Competing with old shoulders but young head
Despite the fifty grizzling years!'

'Aha?
Then that means – just the bullet in the blade
Which brought Dalmatia on the brain, – that, too,
Came of a fatal creature? Can't pretend
Now for the first time to surmise as much!
Make a clean breast! Recount! a secret's safe
'Twixt you, me and the gate-post!'

'– Can't pretend,
Neither, to never have surmised your wish!
It's no use, – case of unextracted ball –
Winces at finger-touching. Let things be!'

'Ah, if you love your love still! I hate mine.'

'I can't hate.'

'I won't teach you; and won't tell
You, therefore, what you please to ask of me:
As if I, also, may not have my ache!'

'My sort of ache? No, no! and yet – perhaps!
All comes of thinking you superior still.
But live and learn! I say! Time's up! Good jump!
You old, indeed! I fancy there's a cut
Across the wood, a grass path: shall we try?
It's venturesome, however!'

'Stop, my boy!
Don't think I'm stingy of experience! Life
– It's like this wood we leave. Should you and I
Go wandering about there, though the gaps
We went in and came out by were opposed
As the two poles, still, somehow, all the same,
By nightfall we should probably have chanced
On much the same main points of interest –

Both of us measured girth of mossy trunk,
Stript ivy from its strangled prey, clapped hands
At squirrel, sent a fir-cone after crow,
And so forth, – never mind what time betwixt.
So in our lives; allow I entered mine
Another way than you: 'tis possible
I ended just by knocking head against
That plaguy low-hung branch yourself began
By getting bump from; as at last you too
May stumble o'er that stump which first of all
Bade me walk circumspectly. Head and feet
Are vulnerable both, and I, foot-sure,
Forgot that ducking down saves brow from bruise.
I, early old, played young man four years since
And failed confoundedly: so, hate alike
Failure and who caused failure, – curse her cant!'

'Oh, I see! You, though somewhat past the prime,
Were taken with a rosebud beauty! Ah –
But how should chits distinguish? She admired
Your marvel of a mind, I'll undertake!
But as to body . . . nay, I mean . . . that is,
When years have told on face and figure . . .'

'Thanks,
Mister *Sufficiently-Instructed!* Such
No doubt was bound to be the consequence
To suit your self-complacency: she liked
My head enough, but loved some heart beneath
Some head with plenty of brown hair a-top
After my young friend's fashion! What becomes
Of that fine speech you made a minute since
About the man of middle age you found
A formidable peer at twenty-one?
So much for your mock-modesty! and yet
I back your first against this second sprout
Of observation, insight, what you please.
My middle age, Sir, had too much success!
It's odd: my case occurred four years ago –
I finished just while you commenced that turn
I' the wood of life that takes us to the wealth

Of honeysuckle, heaped for who can reach.
Now, I don't boast: it's bad style, and beside,
The feat proves easier than it looks: I plucked
Full many a flower unnamed in that bouquet
(Mostly of peonies and poppies, though!)
Good nature sticks into my button-hole.
Therefore it was with nose in want of snuff
Rather than Ess or Psidium, that I chanced
On what – so far from "*rosebud beauty*" . . . Well –
She's dead: at least you never heard her name;
She was no courtly creature, had nor birth
Nor breeding – mere fine-lady-breeding; but
Oh, such a wonder of a woman! Grand
As a Greek statue! Stick fine clothes on that,
Style that a Duchess or a Queen, – you know,
Artists would make an outcry: all the more,
That she had just a statue's sleepy grace
Which broods o'er its own beauty. Nay, her fault
(Don't laugh!) was just perfection: for suppose
Only the little flaw, and I had peeped
Inside it, learned what soul inside was like.
At Rome some tourist raised the grit beneath
A Venus' forehead with his whittling-knife –
I wish, – now, – I had played that brute, brought blood
To surface from the depths I fancied chalk!
As it was, her mere face surprised so much
That I stopped short there, struck on heap, as stares
The cockney stranger at a certain bust
With drooped eyes, – she's the thing I have in mind, –
Down at my Brother's. All sufficient prize –
Such outside! Now, – confound me for a prig! –
Who cares? I'll make a clean breast once for all!
Beside, you've heard the gossip. My life long
I've been a woman-liker, – liking means
Loving and so on. There's a lengthy list
By this time I shall have to answer for –
So say the good folk: and they don't guess half –
For the worst is, let once collecting-itch
Possess you, and, with perspicacity,
Keeps growing such a greediness that theft
Follows at no long distance, – there's the fact!

I knew that on my Leporello-list
Might figure this, that, and the other name
Of feminine desirability,
But if I happened to desire inscribe,
Along with these, the only Beautiful –
Here was the unique specimen to snatch
Or now or never. "Beautiful" I said –
"Beautiful" say in cold blood, – boiling then
To tune of "*Haste, secure whate'er the cost*
This rarity, die in the act, be damned,
So you complete collection, crown your list!"
It seemed as though the whole world, once aroused
By the first notice of such wonder's birth,
Would break bounds to contest my prize with me
The first discoverer, should she but emerge
From that safe den of darkness where she dozed
Till I stole in, that country-parsonage
Where, country-parson's daughter, motherless,
Brotherless, sisterless, for eighteen years
She had been vegetating lily-like.
Her father was my brother's tutor, got
The living that way: him I chanced to see –
Her I saw – her the world would grow one eye
To see, I felt no sort of doubt at all!
"*Secure her!*" cried the devil: "*afterward*
Arrange for the disposal of the prize!"
The devil's doing! yet I seem to think –
Now, when all's done, – think with "*a head reposed*"
In French phrase – hope I think I meant to do
All requisite for such a rarity
When I should be at leisure, have due time
To learn requirement. But in evil day –
Bless me, at week's end, long as any year,
The father must begin "*Young Somebody,*
Much recommended – for I break a rule –
Comes here to read, next Long Vacation." "*Young!*"
That did it. Had the epithet been "*rich,*"
"*Noble,*" "*a genius,*" even "*handsome,*" – but
– "*Young*"!'

'I say – just a word! I want to know –
You are not married?'

'I?'

'Nor ever were?'

'Never! Why?'

'Oh, then – never mind! Go on!
I had a reason for the question.'

'Come, –
You could not be the young man?'

'No, indeed!
Certainly – if you never married her!'

'That I did not: and there's the curse, you'll see!
Nay, all of it's one curse, my life's mistake
Which, nourished with manure that's warranted
To make the plant bear wisdom, blew out full
In folly beyond field-flower-foolishness!
The lies I used to tell my womankind,
Knowing they disbelieved me all the time
Though they required my lies, their decent due,
This woman – not so much believed, I'll say,
As just anticipated from my mouth:
Since being true, devoted, constant – she
Found constancy, devotion, truth, the plain
And easy commonplace of character.
No mock-heroics but seemed natural
To her who underneath the face, I knew
Was fairness' self, possessed a heart, I judged
Must correspond in folly just as far
Beyond the common, – and a mind to match, –
Not made to puzzle conjurers like me
Who, therein, proved the fool who fronts you, Sir,
And begs leave to cut short the ugly rest!
"*Trust me!*" I said: she trusted. "*Marry me!*"
Or rather, "*We are married: when, the rite?*"
That brought on the collector's next-day qualm
At counting acquisition's cost. There lay
My marvel, there my purse more light by much
Because of its late lie-expenditure:

Ill-judged such moment to make fresh demand –
To cage as well as catch my rarity!
So, I began explaining. At first word
Outbroke the horror. "*Then, my truths were lies!*"
I tell you, such an outbreak, such new strange
All-unsuspected revelation – soul
As supernaturally grand as face
Was fair beyond example – that at once
Either I lost – or, if it please you, found
My senses, – stammered somehow – "*Jest! and now,*
Earnest! Forget all else but – heart has loved,
Does love, shall love you ever! take the hand!"
Not she! no marriage for superb disdain,
Contempt incarnate!'

'Yes, it's different, –
It's only like in being four years since.
I see now!'

'Well, what did disdain do next,
Think you?'

'That's past me: did not marry you! –
That's the main thing I care for, I suppose.
Turned nun, or what?'

'Why, married in a month
Some parson, some smug crop-haired smooth-chinned sort
Of curate-creature, I suspect, – dived down,
Down, deeper still, and came up somewhere else –
I don't know where – I've not tried much to know, –
In short, she's happy: what the clodpoles call
"Countrified" with a vengeance! leads the life
Respectable and all that drives you mad:
Still – where, I don't know, and that's best for both.'

'Well, that she did not like you, I conceive.
But why should you hate her, I want to know?'

'My good young friend, – because or her or else
Malicious Providence I have to hate.
For, what I tell you proved the turning-point

Of my whole life and fortune toward success
Or failure. If I drown, I lay the fault
Much on myself who caught at reed not rope,
But more on reed which, with a packthread's pith,
Had buoyed me till the minute's cramp could thaw
And I strike out afresh and so be saved.
It's easy saying – I had sunk before,
Disqualified myself by idle days
And busy nights, long since, from holding hard
On cable, even, had fate cast me such!
You boys don't know how many times men fail
Perforce o' the little to succeed i' the large,
Husband their strength, let slip the petty prey,
Collect the whole power for the final pounce.
My fault was the mistaking man's main prize
For intermediate boy's diversion; clap
Of boyish hands here frightened game away
Which, once gone, goes for ever. Oh, at first
I took the anger easily, nor much
Minded the anguish – having learned that storms
Subside, and teapot-tempests are akin.
Time would arrange things, mend whate'er might be
Somewhat amiss; precipitation, eh?
Reason and rhyme prompt – reparation! Tiffs
End properly in marriage and a dance!
I said "We'll marry, make the past a blank" –
And never was such damnable mistake!
That interview, that laying bare my soul,
As it was first, so was it last chance – one
And only. Did I write? Back letter came
Unopened as it went. Inexorable
She fled, I don't know where, consoled herself
With the smug curate-creature: chop and change!
Sure am I, when she told her shaveling all
His Magdalen's adventure, tears were shed,
Forgiveness evangelically shown,
"Loose hair and lifted eye," – as someone says.
And now, he's worshipped for his pains, the sneak!'

'Well, but your turning-point of life, – what's here
To hinder you contesting Finsbury
With Orton, next election? I don't see ...'

'Not you! But *I* see. Slowly, surely, creeps
Day by day o'er me the conviction – here
Was life's prize grasped at, gained, and then let go!
– That with her – may be, for her – I had felt
Ice in me melt, grow steam, drive to effect
Any or all the fancies sluggish here
I' the head that needs the hand she would not take
And I shall never lift now. Lo, your wood –
Its turnings which I likened life to! Well, –
There she stands, ending every avenue,
Her visionary presence on each goal
I might have gained had we kept side by side!
Still string nerve and strike foot? Her frown forbids:
The steam congeals once more: I'm old again!
Therefore I hate myself – but how much worse
Do not I hate who would not understand,
Let me repair things – no, but sent a-slide
My folly falteringly, stumblingly
Down, down and deeper down until I drop
Upon – the need of your ten thousand pounds
And consequently loss of mine! I lose
Character, cash, nay, common-sense itself
Recounting such a lengthy cock-and-bull
Adventure – lose my temper in the act . . .'

'And lose beside, – if I may supplement
The list of losses, – train and ten-o'clock!
Hark, pant and puff, there travels the swart sign!
So much the better! You're my captive now!
I'm glad you trust a fellow: friends grow thick
This way – that's twice said; we were thickish, though,
Even last night, and, ere night comes again,
I prophesy good luck to both of us!
For see now! – back to "*balmy eminence*"
Or "*calm acclivity,*" or what's the word!
Bestow you there an hour, concoct at ease
A sonnet for the Album, while I put
Bold face on, best foot forward, make for house,
March in to aunt and niece, and tell the truth –
(Even white-lying goes against my taste
After your little story). Oh, the niece

Is rationality itself! The aunt –
If she's amenable to reason too –
Why, you stopped short to pay her due respect,
And let the Duke wait (I'll work well the Duke).
If she grows gracious, I return for you;
If thunder's in the air, why – bear your doom,
Dine on rump-steaks and port, and shake the dust
Of aunty from your shoes as off you go
By evening-train, nor give the thing a thought
How you shall pay me – that's as sure as fate,
Old fellow! Off with you, face left about!
Yonder's the path I have to pad. You see,
I'm in good spirits, God knows why! Perhaps
Because the woman did not marry you
– Who look so hard at me, – and have the right,
One must be fair and own.'

The two stand still

Under an oak.

'Look here!' resumes the youth.
'I never quite knew how I came to like
You – so much – whom I ought not court at all:
Nor how you had a leaning just to me
Who am assuredly not worth your pains.
For there must needs be plenty such as you
Somewhere about, – although I can't say where, –
Able and willing to teach all you know;
While – how can you have missed a score like me
With money and no wit, precisely each
A pupil for your purpose, were it – ease
Fool's poke of tutor's *honorarium*-fee?
And yet, howe'er it came about, I felt
At once my master: you as prompt descried
Your man, I warrant, so was bargain struck.
Now, these same lines of liking, loving, run
Sometimes so close together they converge –
Life's great adventures – you know what I mean –
In people. Do you know, as you advanced,
It got to be uncommonly like fact
We two had fallen in with – liked and loved
Just the same woman in our different ways?

I began life – poor groundling as I prove –
Winged and ambitious to fly high: why not?
There's something in "Don Quixote" to the point,
My shrewd old father used to quote and praise –
"*Am I born man?*" asks Sancho: "*being man,*
By possibility I may be Pope!"
So, Pope I meant to make myself, by step
And step, whereof the first should be to find
A perfect woman; and I tell you this –
If what I fixed on, in the order due
Of undertakings, as next step, had first
Of all disposed itself to suit my tread,
And I had been, the day I came of age,
Returned at head of poll for Westminster
– Nay, and moreover summoned by the Queen
At week's end, when my maiden-speech bore fruit,
To form and head a Tory ministry –
It would not have seemed stranger, no, nor been
More strange to me, as now I estimate,
Than what did happen – sober truth, no dream.
I saw my wonder of a woman, – laugh,
I'm past that! – in Commemoration-week.
A plenty have I seen since, fair and foul, –
With eyes, too, helped by your sagacious wink;
But one to match that marvel – no least trace,
Least touch of kinship and community!
The end was – I did somehow state the fact,
Did, with no matter what imperfect words,
One way or other give to understand
That woman, soul and body were her slave
Would she but take, but try them – any test
Of will, and some poor test of power beside:
So did the strings within my brain grow tense
And capable of . . . hang similitudes!
She answered kindly but beyond appeal.
"*No sort of hope for me, who came too late.*
She was another's. Love went – mine to her,
Hers just as loyally to someone else."
Of course! I might expect it! Nature's law –
Given the peerless woman, certainly
Somewhere shall be the peerless man to match!
I acquiesced at once, submitted me

In something of a stupor, went my way.
I fancy there had been some talk before
Of somebody – her father or the like –
To coach me in the holidays, – that's how
I came to get the sight and speech of her, –
But I had sense enough to break off sharp,
Save both of us the pain.'

'Quite right there!'

'Eh?

Quite wrong, it happens! Now comes worst of all!
Yes, I did sulk aloof and let alone
The lovers – *I* disturb the angel-mates?'

'Seraph paired off with cherub!'

'Thank you! While

I never plucked up courage to inquire
Who he was, even, – certain-sure of this,
That nobody I knew of had blue wings
And wore a star-crown as he needs must do, –
Some little lady, – plainish, pock-marked girl, –
Finds out my secret in my woeful face,
Comes up to me at the Apollo Ball,
And pityingly pours her wine and oil
This way into the wound: "*Dear f-f-friend,*
Why waste affection thus on – must I say,
A somewhat worthless object? Who's her choice –
Irrevocable as deliberate –
Out of the wide world? I shall name no names –
But there's a person in society,
Who, blessed with rank and talent, has grown grey
In idleness and sin of every sort
Except hypocrisy: he's thrice her age,
A by-word for 'successes with the sex'
As the French say – and, as we ought to say,
Consummately a liar and a rogue,
Since – show me where's the woman won without
The help of this one lie which she believes –
That – never mind how things have come to pass,
And let who loves have loved a thousand times –

All the same he now loves her only, loves
Her ever! if by 'won' you just mean 'sold,'
That's quite another compact. Well, this scamp,
Continuing descent from bad to worse,
Must leave his fine and fashionable prey
(Who – fathered, brothered, husbanded, – are hedged
About with thorny danger) and apply
His arts to this poor country ignorance
Who sees forthwith in the first rag of man
Her model hero! Why continue waste
On such a woman treasures of a heart
Would yet find solace, – yes, my f-f-friend –
In some congenial – fiddle-diddle-dee?"'

'Pray, is the pleasant gentleman described
Exact the portrait which my "*f-f-friends*"
Recognize as so like? 'Tis evident
You half surmised the sweet original
Could be no other than myself, just now!
Your stop and start were flattering!'

'Of course
Caricature's allowed for in a sketch!
The longish nose becomes a foot in length,
The swarthy cheek gets copper-coloured, – still,
Prominent beak and dark-hued skin are facts:
And "*parson's daughter*" – "*young man coachable*" –
"*Elderly party*" – "*four years since*" – were facts
To fasten on, a moment! Marriage, though –
That made the difference, I hope.'

'All right!
I never married; wish I had – and then
Unwish it: people kill their wives, sometimes!
I hate my mistress, but I'm murder-free.
In your case, where's the grievance? You came last,
The earlier bird picked up the worm. Suppose
You, in the glory of your twenty-one,
Had happened to precede myself! 'tis odds
But this gigantic juvenility,
This offering of a big arm's bony hand –
I'd rather shake than feel shake me, I know –

Had moved *my* dainty mistress to admire
An altogether new Ideal – deem
Idolatry less due to life's decline
Productive of experience, powers mature
By dint of usage, the made man – no boy
That's all to make! I was the earlier bird –
And what I found, I let fall; what you missed
Who is the fool that blames you for?'

'Myself –
For nothing, everything! For finding out
She, whom I worshipped, was a worshipper
In turn of... but why stir up settled mud?
She married him – the fifty-years-old rake –
How you have teased the talk from me! At last
My secret's told you. I inquired no more,
Nay, stopped ears when informants unshut mouth;
Enough that she and he live, deuce take where,
Married and happy, or else miserable –
It's "Cut-the-pack"; she turned up ace or knave,
And I left Oxford, England, dug my hole
Out in Dalmatia, till you drew me thence
Badger-like, – "*Back to London*" was the word –
"*Do things, a many, there, you fancy hard,*
I'll undertake are easy!" – the advice.
I took it, had my twelvemonth's fling with you –
(Little hand holding large hand pretty tight
For all its delicacy – eh, my lord?),
Until when, t'other day, I got a turn
Somehow and gave up tired: and "*Rest!*" bade you,
"*Marry your cousin, double your estate,*
And take your ease by all means!" So, I loll
On this the springy sofa, mine next month –
Or should loll, but that you must needs beat rough
The very down you spread me out so smooth.
I wish this confidence were still to make!
Ten thousand pounds? You owe me twice the sum
For stirring up the black depths! There's repose
Or, at least, silence when misfortune seems
All that one has to bear; but folly – yes,
Folly, it all was! Fool to be so meek,
So humble, – such a coward rather say!

Fool, to adore the adorer of a fool!
Not to have faced him, tried (a useful hint)
My big and bony, here, against the bunch
Of lily-coloured five with signet-ring,
Most like, for little-finger's sole defence –
Much as you flaunt the blazon there! I grind
My teeth, that bite my very heart, to think –
To know I might have made that woman mine
But for the folly of the coward – know –
Or what's the good of my apprenticeship
This twelvemonth to a master in the art?
Mine – had she been mine – just one moment mine
For honour, for dishonour – anyhow,
So that my life, instead of stagnant . . . Well,
You've poked and proved stagnation is not sleep –
Hang you!'

'Hang *you* for an ungrateful goose!
All this means – I who since I knew you first
Have helped you to conceit yourself this cock
O' the dunghill with all hens to pick and choose –
Ought to have helped you when shell first was chipped
By chick that wanted prompting "*Use the spur!*"
While I was elsewhere putting mine to use.
As well might I blame you who kept aloof,
Seeing you could not guess I was alive,
Never advised me "*Do as I have done –*
Reverence such a jewel as your luck
Has scratched up to enrich unworthiness!"
As your behaviour was should mine have been,
– Faults which we both, too late, are sorry for:
Opposite ages, each with its mistake!
"*If youth but would – if age but could,*" you know.
Don't let us quarrel. Come, we're – young and old –
Neither so badly off. Go you your way,
Cut to the Cousin! I'll to Inn, await
The issue of diplomacy with Aunt,
And wait my hour on "*calm acclivity*"
In rumination manifold – perhaps
About ten thousand pounds I have to pay!'

III

Now, as the elder lights the fresh cigar
Conducive to resource, and saunteringly
Betakes him to the left-hand backward path, –
While, much sedate, the younger strides away
To right and makes for – islanded in lawn
And edged with shrubbery – the brilliant bit
Of Barry's building that's the Place, – a pair
Of women, at this nick of time, one young,
One very young, are ushered with due pomp
Into the same Inn-parlour – '*disengaged*
Entirely now!' the obsequious landlord smiles,
'*Since the late occupants – whereof but one*
Was quite a stranger' – (smile enforced by bow)
'*Left, a full two hours since, to catch the train,*
Probably for the stranger's sake!' (Bow, smile,
And backing out from door soft-closed behind.)

Woman and girl, the two, alone inside,
Begin their talk: the girl, with sparkling eyes –

'Oh, I forewent him purposely! but you,
Who joined at – journeyed from the Junction here –
I wonder how he failed your notice. Few
Stop at our station: fellow-passengers
Assuredly you were – I saw indeed
His servant, therefore he arrived all right.
I wanted, you know why, to have you safe
Inside here first of all, so dodged about
The dark end of the platform; that's his way –
To swing from station straight to avenue
And stride the half a mile for exercise.
I fancied you might notice the huge boy.
He soon gets o'er the distance; at the house
He'll hear I went to meet him and have missed;
He'll wait. No minute of the hour's too much
Meantime for our preliminary talk:
First word of which must be – O good beyond
Expression of all goodness – you to come!'

The elder, the superb one, answers slow.

'There was no helping that. You called for me,
Cried, rather: and my old heart answered you.
Still, thank me! since the effort breaks a vow –
At least, a promise to myself.'

'I know!
How selfish get you happy folk to be!
If I should love my husband, must I needs
Sacrifice straightway all the world to him,
As you do? Must I never dare leave house
On this dread Arctic expedition, out
And in again, six mortal hours, though you,
You even, my own friend for evermore,
Adjure me – fast your friend till rude love pushed
Poor friendship from her vantage – just to grant
The quarter of a whole day's company
And counsel? This makes counsel so much more
Need and necessity. For here's my block
Of stumbling: in the face of happiness
So absolute, fear chills me. If such change
In heart be but love's easy consequence,
Do I love? If to marry mean – let go
All I now live for, should my marriage be?'

The other never once has ceased to gaze
On the great elm-tree in the open, posed
Placidly full in front, smooth bole, broad branch,
And leafage, one green plenitude of May.
The gathered thought runs into speech at last.

'O you exceeding beauty, bosomful
Of lights and shades, murmurs and silences,
Sun-warmth, dew-coolness, – squirrel, bee and bird,
High, higher, highest, till the blue proclaims
"*Leave earth, there's nothing better till next step
Heavenward!*" – so, off flies what has wings to help!'

And henceforth they alternate. Says the girl –

'That's saved then: marriage spares the early taste.'

'Four years now, since my eye took note of tree!'

'If I had seen no other tree but this
My life long, while yourself came straight, you said,
From tree which overstretched you and was just
One fairy tent with pitcher-leaves that held
Wine, and a flowery wealth of suns and moons,
And magic fruits whereon the angels feed –
I looking out of window on a tree
Like yonder – otherwise well-known, much-liked,
Yet just an English ordinary elm –
What marvel if you cured me of conceit
My elm's bird-bee-and-squirrel tenantry
Was quite the proud possession I supposed?
And there is evidence you tell me true.
The fairy marriage-tree reports itself
Good guardian of the perfect face and form,
Fruits of four years' protection! Married friend,
You are more beautiful than ever!'

'Yes:
I think that likely. I could well dispense
With all thought fair in feature, mine or no,
Leave but enough of face to know me by –
With all found fresh in youth except such strength
As lets a life-long labour earn repose
Death sells at just that price, they say; and so,
Possibly, what I care not for, I keep.'

'How you must know he loves you! Chill, before,
Fear sinks to freezing. Could I sacrifice –
Assured my lover simply loves my soul –
One nose-breadth of fair feature? No, indeed!
Your own love . . .'

'The preliminary hour –
Don't waste it!'

'But I can't begin at once!
The angel's self that comes to hear me speak
Drives away all the care about the speech.
What an angelic mystery you are –
Now – that is certain! when I knew you first,
No break of halo and no bud of wing!

I thought I knew you, saw you, round and through,
Like a glass ball; suddenly, four years since,
You vanished, how and whither? Mystery!
Wherefore? No mystery at all: you loved,
Were loved again, and left the world of course:
Who would not? Lapped four years in fairyland,
Out comes, by no less wonderful a chance,
The changeling, touched athwart her trellised bliss
Of blush-rose bower by just the old friend's voice
That's now struck dumb at her own potency.
I talk of my small fortunes? Tell me yours
Rather! The fool I ever was – I am,
You see that: the true friend you ever had,
You have, you also recognize. Perhaps,
Giving you all the love of all my heart,
Nature, that's niggard in me, has denied
The after-birth of love there's someone claims
– This huge boy, swinging up the avenue;
And I want counsel: is defect in me,
Or him who has no right to raise the love?
My cousin asks my hand: he's young enough,
Handsome, – my maid thinks, – manly's more the word:
He asked my leave to "*drop*" the elm-tree there,
Some morning before breakfast. Gentleness
Goes with the strength, of course. He's honest too,
Limpidly truthful. For ability –
All's in the rough yet. His first taste of life
Seems to have somehow gone against the tongue:
He travelled, tried things – came back, tried still more –
He says he's sick of all. He's fond of me
After a certain careless-earnest way
I like: the iron's crude, – no polished steel
Somebody forged before me. I am rich –
That's not the reason, he's far richer: no,
Nor is it that he thinks me pretty, – frank
Undoubtedly on that point! He saw once
The pink of face-perfection – oh, not you –
Content yourself, my beauty! – for she proved
So thoroughly a cheat, his charmer . . . nay,
He runs into extremes, I'll say at once,
Lest you say! Well, I understand he wants

Someone to serve, something to do: and both
Requisites so abound in me and mine
That here's the obstacle which stops consent:
The smoothness is too smooth, and I mistrust
The unseen cat beneath the counterpane.
Therefore I thought "*Would she but judge for me,*
Who, judging for herself succeeded so!"
Do I love him, does he love me, do both
Mistake for knowledge – easy ignorance?
Appeal to its proficient in each art!
I got rough-smooth through a piano-piece,
Rattled away last week till tutor came,
Heard me to end, then grunted "*Ach, mein Gott!*
Sagen Sie 'easy'? Every note is wrong.
All thumped mit wrist: we'll trouble fingers now.
The Fräulein will please roll up Raff again
And exercise at Czerny for one month!"
Am I to roll up cousin, exercise
At Trollope's novels for one month? Pronounce!'

'Now, place each in the right position first,
Adviser and advised one! I perhaps
Am three – nay, four years older; am, beside,
A wife: advantages – to balance which,
You have a full fresh joyous sense of life
That finds you out life's fit food everywhere,
Detects enjoyment where I, slow and dull,
Fumble at fault. Already, these four years,
Your merest glimpses at the world without
Have shown you more than ever met my gaze;
And now, by joyance you inspire joy, – learn
While you profess to teach, and teach, although
Avowedly a learner. I am dazed
Like any owl by sunshine which just sets
The sparrow preening plumage! Here's to spy
– Your cousin! You have scanned him all your life,
Little or much; I never saw his face.
You have determined on a marriage – used
Deliberation therefore – I'll believe
No otherwise, with opportunity
For judgement so abounding! Here stand I –

Summoned to give my sentence, for a whim,
(Well, at first cloud-fleck thrown athwart your blue)
Judge what is strangeness' self to me, – say "*Wed!*"
Or "*Wed not!*" whom you promise I shall judge
Presently, at propitious lunch-time, just
While he carves chicken! Sends he leg for wing?
That revelation into character
And conduct must suffice me! Quite as well
Consult with yonder solitary crow
That eyes us from your elm-top!'

'Still the same!
Do you remember, at the library
We saw together somewhere, those two books
Somebody said were noticeworthy? One
Lay wide on table, sprawled its painted leaves
For all the world's inspection; shut on shelf
Reclined the other volume, closed, clasped, locked –
Clear to be let alone. Which page had we
Preferred the turning over of? You were,
Are, ever will be the locked lady, hold
Inside you secrets written, – soul-absorbed,
My ink upon your blotting-paper. *I* –
What trace of you have I to show in turn?
Delicate secrets! No one juvenile
Ever essayed at croquet and performed
Superiorly but I confided you
The sort of hat he wore and hair it held.
While you? One day a calm note comes by post:
"*I am just married, you may like to hear.*"
Most men would hate you, or they ought; we love
What we fear, – *I* do! "*Cold*" I shall expect
My cousin calls you. I – dislike not him,
But (if I comprehend what loving means)
Love you immeasurably more – more – more
Than even he who, loving you his wife,
Would turn up nose at who impertinent,
Frivolous, forward – *loves* that excellence
Of all the earth he bows in worship to!
And who's this paragon of privilege?
Simply a country parson: his the charm
That worked the miracle! Oh, too absurd

But that you stand before me as you stand!
Such beauty does prove something, everything!
Beauty's the prize-flower which dispenses eye
From peering into what has nourished root –
Dew or manure: the plant best knows its place.
Enough, from teaching youth and tending age
And hearing sermons, – haply writing tracts, –
From such strange love-besprinkled compost, lo,
Out blows this triumph! Therefore love's the soil
Plants find or fail of. You, with wit to find,
Exercise wit on the old friend's behalf,
Keep me from failure! Scan and scrutinize
This cousin! Surely he's as worth your pains
To study as my elm-tree, crow and all,
You still keep staring at. I read your thoughts.'

'At last?'

'At first! "*Would, tree, a-top of thee*
I wingèd were, like crow perched moveless there,
And so could straightway soar, escape this bore,
Back to my nest where broods whom I love best –
The parson o'er his parish – garish – rarish –"
Oh I could bring the rhyme in if I tried:
The Album here inspires me! Quite apart
From lyrical expression, have I read
The stare aright, and sings not soul just so?'

'Or rather *so?* "*Cool comfortable elm*
That men make coffins out of, – none for me
At thy expense, so thou permit I glide
Under thy ferny feet, and there sleep, sleep,
Nor dread awaking though in heaven itself!"'

The younger looks with face struck sudden white.
The elder answers its inquiry.

'Dear,
You are a guesser, not a "*clairvoyante.*"
I'll so far open you the locked and shelved
Volume, my soul, that you desire to see,
As let you profit by the title-page —'

'Paradise Lost?'

'Inferno! – All which comes
Of tempting me to break my vow. Stop here!
Friend, whom I love the best in the whole world,
Come at your call, be sure that I will do
All your requirement – see and say my mind.
It may be that by sad apprenticeship
I have a keener sense: I'll task the same.
Only indulge me – here let sight and speech
Happen – this Inn is neutral ground, you know!
I cannot visit the old house and home,
Encounter the old sociality
Abjured for ever. Peril quite enough
In even this first – last, I pray it prove –
Renunciation of my solitude!
Back, you, to house and cousin! Leave me here,
Who want no entertainment, carry still
My occupation with me. While I watch
The shadow inching round those ferny feet,
Tell him "*A school-friend wants a word with me*
Up at the inn: time, tide and train won't wait:
I must go see her – on and off again –
You'll keep me company?" Ten minutes' talk,
With you in presence, ten more afterward
With who, alone, convoys me station-bound,
And I see clearly – and say honestly
Tomorrow: pen shall play tongue's part, you know.
Go – quick! for I have made our hand-in-hand
Return impossible. So scared you look, –
If cousin does not greet you with "*What ghost*
Has crossed your path?" I set him down obtuse.'

And after one more look, with face still white,
The younger does go, while the elder stands
Occupied by the elm at window there.

IV

Occupied by the elm; and, as its shade
Has crept clock-hand-wise till it ticks at fern
Five inches further to the South, the door
Opens abruptly, someone enters sharp,

The elder man returned to wait the youth:
Never observes the room's new occupant,
Throws hat on table, stoops quick, elbow-propped
Over the Album wide there, bends down brow
A cogitative minute, whistles shrill,
Then, – with a cheery-hopeless laugh-and-lose
Air of defiance to fate visibly
Casting the toils about him, – mouths once more
'Hail, calm acclivity, salubrious spot!'
Then clasps-to cover, sends book spinning off
T'other side table, looks up, starts erect
Full-face with her who, – roused from that abstruse
Question, *'Will next tick tip the fern or no?'*, –
Fronts him as fully.

All her languor breaks,
Away withers at once the weariness
From the black-blooded brow, anger and hate
Convulse. Speech follows slowlier, but at last –

'You here! I felt, I knew it would befall!
Knew, by some subtle undivinable
Trick of the trickster, I should, silly-sooth,
Late or soon, somehow be allured to leave
Safe hiding and come take of him arrears,
My torment due on four years' respite! Time
To pluck the bird's healed breast of down o'er wound!
Have your success! Be satisfied this sole
Seeing you has undone all heaven could do
These four years, puts me back to you and hell!
What will next trick be, next success? No doubt
When I shall think to glide into the grave,
There will you wait disguised as beckoning Death,
And catch and capture me for evermore!
But, God, though I am nothing, be thou all!
Contest him for me! Strive, for he is strong!'

Already his surprise dies palely out
In laugh of acquiescing impotence.
He neither gasps nor hisses: calm and plain –

'I also felt and knew – but otherwise!
You out of hand and sight and care of me
These four years, whom I felt, knew, all the while...
Oh, it's no superstition! It's a gift
O' the gamester that he snuffs the unseen powers
Which help or harm him. Well I knew what lurked,
Lay perdue paralysing me, – drugged, drowsed
And damnified my soul and body both!
Down and down, see where you have dragged me to,
You and your malice! I was, four years since,
– Well, a poor creature! I become a knave.
I squandered my own pence: I plump my purse
With other people's pounds. I practised play
Because I liked it: play turns labour now
Because there's profit also in the sport.
I gamed with men of equal age and craft:
I steal here with a boy as green as grass
Whom I have tightened hold on slow and sure
This long while, just to bring about today
When the boy beats me hollow, buries me
In ruin who was sure to beggar him.
O time indeed I should look up and laugh
"*Surely she closes on me!*" Here you stand!'

And stand she does: while volubility,
With him, keeps on the increase, for his tongue
After long locking-up is loosed for once.

'Certain the taunt is happy!' he resumes:
'So, I it was allured you – only I
– I, and none other – to this spectacle –
Your triumph, my despair – you woman-fiend
That front me! Well, I have my wish, then! See
The low wide brow oppressed by sweeps of hair
Darker and darker as they coil and swathe
The crowned corpse-wanness whence the eyes burn black
Not asleep now! not pin-points dwarfed beneath
Either great bridging eyebrow – poor blank beads –
Babies, I've pleased to pity in my time:
How they protrude and glow immense with hate!
The long triumphant nose attains – retains
Just the perfection; and there's scarlet-skein

My ancient enemy, her lip and lip,
Sense-free, sense-frighting lips clenched cold and bold
Because of chin, that based resolve beneath!
Then the columnar neck completes the whole
Greek-sculpture-baffling body! Do I see?
Can I observe? You wait next word to come?
Well, wait and want! since no one blight I bid
Consume one least perfection. Each and all,
As they are rightly shocking now to me,
So may they still continue! Value them?
Ay, as the vendor knows the money-worth
Of his Greek statue, fools aspire to buy,
And he to see the back of! Let us laugh!
You have absolved me from my sin at least!
You stand stout, strong, in the rude health of hate,
No touch of the tame timid nullity
My cowardice, forsooth, has practised on!
Ay, while you seemed to hint some fine fifth act
Of tragedy should freeze blood, end the farce,
I never doubted all was joke. I kept,
May be, an eye alert on paragraphs,
Newspaper-notice, – let no inquest slip,
Accident, disappearance: sound and safe
Were you, my victim, not of mind to die!
So, my worst fancy that could spoil the smooth
Of pillow, and arrest descent of sleep
Was "*Into what dim hole can she have dived,*
She and her wrongs, her woe that's wearing flesh
And blood away?" Whereas, see, sorrow swells!
Or, fattened, fulsome, have you fed on me,
Sucked out my substance? How much gloss, I pray,
O'erbloomed those hair-swathes when there crept from you
To me that craze, else unaccountable,
Which urged me to contest our county-seat
With whom but my own brother's nominee?
Did that mouth's pulp glow ruby from carmine
While I misused my moment, pushed, – one word, –
One hair's breadth more of gesture, – idiot-like
Past passion, floundered on to the grotesque,
And lost the heiress in a grin? At least,
You made no such mistake! You tickled fish,
Landed your prize the true artistic way!

How did the smug young curate rise to tune
Of "*Friend, a fatal fact divides us. Love*
Suits me no longer. I have suffered shame,
Betrayal: past is past; the future – yours –
Shall never be contaminate by mine.
I might have spared me this confession, not
– Oh, never by some hideousest of lies,
Easy, impenetrable! No! but say,
By just the quiet answer – 'I am cold.'
Falsehood avaunt, each shadow of thee, hence!
Had happier fortune willed . . . but dreams are vain.
Now, leave me – yes, for pity's sake!" Aha,
Who fails to see the curate as his face
Reddened and whitened, wanted handkerchief
At wrinkling brow and twinkling eye, until
Out burst the proper "*Angel, whom the fiend*
Has thought to smirch, – thy whiteness, at one wipe
Of holy cambric, shall disgrace the swan!
Mine be the task" . . . and so forth! Fool? not he!
Cunning in flavours, rather! What but sour
Suspected makes the sweetness doubly sweet,
And what stings love from faint to flamboyant
But the fear-sprinkle? Even horror helps –
"*Love's flame in me by such recited wrong*
Drenched, quenched, indeed? It burns the fiercelier thence!"
Why, I have known men never love their wives
Till somebody – myself, suppose – had "*drenched*
And quenched love," so the blockheads whined: as if
The fluid fire that lifts the torpid limb
Were a wrong done to palsy. But I thrilled
No palsied person: half my age, or less,
The curate was, I'll wager: o'er young blood
Your beauty triumphed! Eh, but – was it *he*?
Then, it *was* he, I heard of! None beside!
How frank you were about the audacious boy
Who fell upon you like a thunderbolt –
Passion and protestation! He it was
Reserved *in petto!* Ay, and "*rich*" beside –
"*Rich*" – how supremely did disdain curl nose!
All that I heard was – "*wedded to a priest*";
Informants sunk youth, riches and the rest.
And so my lawless love disparted loves,

That loves might come together with a rush!
Surely this last achievement sucked me dry:
Indeed, that way my wits went. Mistress-queen,
Be merciful and let your subject slink
Into dark safety! He's a beggar, see –
Do not turn back his ship, Australia-bound,
And bid her land him right amid some crowd
Of creditors, assembled by your curse!
Don't cause the very rope to crack (you can!)
Whereon he spends his last (friend's) sixpence, just
The moment when he hoped to hang himself!
Be satisfied you beat him!'

She replies –

'Beat him! I do. To all that you confess
Of abject failure, I extend belief.
Your very face confirms it: God is just!
Let my face – fix your eyes! – in turn confirm
What I shall say. All-abject's but half truth;
Add to all-abject knave as perfect fool!
So is it you probed human nature, *so*
Prognosticated of me? Lay these words
To heart then, or where God meant heart should lurk!
That moment when you first revealed yourself,
My simple impulse prompted – end forthwith
The ruin of a life uprooted thus
To surely perish! How should such spoiled tree
Henceforward balk the wind of its worst sport,
Fail to go falling deeper, falling down
From sin to sin until some depth were reached
Doomed to the weakest by the wickedest
Of weak and wicked human kind? But when,
That self-display made absolute, – behold
A new revealment! – round you pleased to veer,
Propose me what should prompt annul the past,
Make me "*amends by marriage*" – in your phrase,
Incorporate me henceforth, body and soul,
With soul and body which mere brushing past
Brought leprosy upon me – "*marry*" these!
Why, then despair broke, re-assurance dawned,
Clear-sighted was I that who hurled contempt

As I – thank God! – at the contemptible,
Was scarce an utter weakling. Rent away
By treason from my rightful pride of place,
I was not destined to the shame below.
A cleft had caught me: I might perish there,
But thence to be dislodged and whirled at last
Where the black torrent sweeps the sewage – no!
"*Bare breast be on hard rock,*" laughed out my soul
In gratitude, "*howe'er rock's grip may grind!*
The plain rough wretched holdfast shall suffice
This wreck of me!" The wind, – I broke in bloom
At passage of, – which stripped me bole and branch,
Twisted me up and tossed me here, – turns back,
And, playful ever, would replant the spoil?
Be satisfied, not one least leaf that's mine
Shall henceforth help wind's sport to exercise!
Rather I give such remnant to the rock
Which never dreamed a straw would settle there.
Rock may not thank me, may not feel my breast,
Even: enough that *I* feel, hard and cold,
Its safety my salvation. Safe and saved,
I lived, live. When the tempter shall persuade
His prey to slip down, slide off, trust the wind, –
Now that I know if God or Satan be
Prince of the Power of the Air, – then, then, indeed,
Let my life end and degradation too!'

'Good!' he smiles, 'true Lord Byron! "*Tree and rock*":
"*Rock*" – there's advancement! He's at first a youth,
Rich, worthless therefore; next he grows a priest:
Youth, riches prove a notable resource,
When to leave me for their possessor gluts
Malice abundantly; and now, last change,
The young rich parson represents a rock
– Bloodstone, no doubt. He's Evangelical?
Your Ritualists prefer the Church for spouse!'

She speaks.

'I have a story to relate.
There was a parish-priest, my father knew,
Elderly, poor: I used to pity him

Before I learned what woes are pity-worth.
Elderly was grown old now, scanty means
Were straitening fast to poverty, beside
The ailments which await in such a case.
Limited every way, a perfect man
Within the bounds built up and up since birth
Breast-high about him till the outside world
Was blank save o'erhead one blue bit of sky –
Faith: he had faith in dogma, small or great,
As in the fact that if he clave his skull
He'd find a brain there: who proves such a fact
No falsehood by experiment at price
Of soul and body? The one rule of life
Delivered him in childhood was "*Obey!*
Labour!" He had obeyed and laboured – tame,
True to the mill-track blinked on from above.
Some scholarship he may have gained in youth:
Gone – dropt or flung behind. Some blossom-flake,
Spring's boon, descends on every vernal head,
I used to think; but January joins
December, as his year had known no May
Trouble its snow-deposit, – cold and old!
I heard it was his will to take a wife,
A helpmate. Duty bade him tend and teach –
How? with experience null, nor sympathy
Abundant, – while himself worked dogma dead,
Who would play ministrant to sickness, age,
Womankind, childhood? These demand a wife.
Supply the want, then! theirs the wife; for him –
No coarsest sample of the proper sex
But would have served his purpose equally
With God's own angel, – let but knowledge match
Her coarseness: zeal does only half the work.
I saw this – knew the purblind honest drudge
Was wearing out his simple blameless life,
And wanted help beneath a burthen – borne
To treasure-house or dust-heap, what cared I?
Partner he needed: I proposed myself,
Nor much surprised him – duty was so clear!
Gratitude? What for? Gain of Paradise –
Escape, perhaps, from the dire penalty
Of who hides talent in a napkin? No:

His scruple was – should I be strong enough
– In body? since of weakness in the mind,
Weariness in the heart – no fear of these!
He took me as these Arctic voyagers
Take an aspirant to their toil and pain:
Can he endure them? – that's the point, and not
– Will he? Who would not, rather! Whereupon,
I pleaded far more earnestly for leave
To give myself away, than you to gain
What you called priceless till you gained the heart
And soul and body! which, as beggars serve
Extorted alms, you straightway spat upon.
Not so my husband, – for I gained my suit,
And had my value put at once to proof.
Ask him! These four years I have died away
In village-life. The village? Ugliness
At best and filthiness at worst, inside.
Outside, sterility – earth sown with salt
Or what keeps even grass from growing fresh.
The life? I teach the poor and learn, myself,
That commonplace to such stupidity
Is all-recondite. Being brutalized
Their true need is brute-language, cheery grunts
And kindly cluckings, no articulate
Nonsense that's elsewhere knowledge. Tend the sick,
Sickened myself at pig-perversity,
Cat-craft, dog-snarling, – may be, snapping . . .'

'Brief:

You eat that root of bitterness called Man
– Raw: I prefer it cooked, with social sauce!
So, he was not the rich youth after all!
Well, I mistook. But somewhere needs must be
The compensation. If not young nor rich . . .'

'You interrupt.'

'Because you've daubed enough
Bistre for background. Play the artist now,
Produce your figure well-relieved in front!
The contrast – do not I anticipate?

Though neither rich nor young – what then? 'Tis all
Forgotten, all this ignobility,
In the dear home, the darling word, the smile,
The something sweeter . . .'

'Yes, you interrupt.
I have my purpose and proceed. Who lives
With beasts assumes beast-nature, look and voice,
And, much more, thought, for beasts think. Selfishness
In us met selfishness in them, deserved
Such answer as it gained. My husband, bent
On saving his own soul by saving theirs, –
They, bent on being saved if saving soul
Included body's getting bread and cheese
Somehow in life and somehow after death, –
Both parties were alike in the same boat,
One danger, therefore one equality.
Safety induces culture: culture seeks
To institute, extend and multiply
The difference between safe man and man,
Able to live alone now; progress means
What but abandonment of fellowship?
We were in common danger, still stuck close.
No new books, – were the old ones mastered yet?
No pictures and no music: these divert
– What from? the staving danger off! You paint
The waterspout above, you set to words
The roaring of the tempest round you? Thanks!
Amusement? Talk at end of the tired day
Of the more tiresome morrow! I transcribed
The page on page of sermon-scrawlings – stopped
Intellect's eye and ear to sense and sound –
Vainly: the sound and sense would penetrate
To brain and plague there in despite of me
Maddened to know more moral good were done
Had we two simply sallied forth and preached
I' the "*Green*" they call their grimy, – I with twang
Of long-disused guitar, – with cut and slash
Of much-misvalued horsewhip he, – to bid
The peaceable come dance, the peace-breaker
Pay in his person! Whereas – Heaven and Hell,

Excite with that, restrain with this! So dealt
His drugs my husband; as he dosed himself,
He drenched his cattle: and, for all my part
Was just to dub the mortar, never fear
But drugs, hand pestled at, have poisoned nose!
Heaven he let pass, left wisely undescribed:
As applicable therefore to the sleep
I want, that knows no waking – as to what's
Conceived of as the proper prize to tempt
Souls less world-weary: there, no fault to find!
But Hell he made explicit. After death,
Life: man created new, ingeniously
Perfect for a vindictive purpose now
That man, first fashioned in beneficence,
Was proved a failure; intellect at length
Replacing old obtuseness, memory
Made mindful of delinquent's bygone deeds
Now that remorse was vain, which life-long lay
Dormant when lesson might be laid to heart;
New gift of observation up and down
And round man's self, new power to apprehend
Each necessary consequence of act
In man for well or ill – things obsolete –
Just granted to supplant the idiocy
Man's only guide while act was yet to choose,
With ill or well momentously its fruit;
A faculty of immense suffering
Conferred on mind and body, – mind, erewhile
Unvisited by one compunctious dream
During sin's drunken slumber, startled up,
Stung through and through by sin's significance
Now that the holy was abolished – just
As body which, alive, broke down beneath
Knowledge, lay helpless in the path to good,
Failed to accomplish aught legitimate,
Achieve aught worthy, – which grew old in youth,
And at its longest fell a cut-down flower, –
Dying, this too revived by miracle
To bear no end of burthen now that back
Supported torture to no use at all,
And live imperishably potent – since
Life's potency was impotent to ward

One plague off which made earth a hell before.
This doctrine, which one healthy view of things,
One sane sight of the general ordinance –
Nature, – and its particular object, – man, –
Which one mere eye-cast at the character
Of Who made these and gave man sense to boot,
Had dissipated once and evermore, –
This doctrine I have dosed our flock withal.
Why? Because none believed it. *They* desire
Such Heaven and dread such Hell, whom every day
The alehouse tempts from one, a dog-fight bids
Defy the other? All the harm is done
Ourselves – done my poor husband who in youth
Perhaps read Dickens, done myself who still
Could play both Bach and Brahms. Such life I lead –
Thanks to you, knave! You learn its quality –
Thanks to me, fool!'

He eyes her earnestly,
But she continues.

'– Life which, thanks once more
To you, arch-knave as exquisitest fool,
I acquiescingly – I gratefully
Take back again to heart! and hence this speech
Which yesterday had spared you. Four years long
Life – I began to find intolerable,
Only this moment. Ere your entry just,
The leap of heart which answered, spite of me,
A friend's first summons, first provocative,
Authoritative, nay, compulsive call
To quit, though for a single day, my house
Of bondage – made return seem horrible.
I heard again a human lucid laugh
All trust, no fear; again saw earth pursue
Its narrow busy way amid small cares,
Smaller contentments, much weeds, some few flowers, –
Never suspicious of a thunderbolt
Avenging presently each daisy's death.
I recognized the beech-tree, knew the thrush
Repeated his old music-phrase, – all right,
How wrong was I, then! But your entry broke

Illusion, bade me back to bounds at once.
I honestly submit my soul: which sprang
At love, and losing love lies signed and sealed
"*Failure.*" No love more? then, no beauty more
Which tends to breed love! Purify my powers,
Effortless till some other world procure
Some other chance of prize! or, if none be, –
Nor second world nor chance, – undesecrate
Die then this aftergrowth of heart, surmised
Where May's precipitation left June blank!
Better have failed in the high aim, as I,
Than vulgarly in the low aim succeed
As, God be thanked, I do not! Ugliness
Had I called beauty, falsehood – truth, and you
– My lover! No – this earth's unchanged for me,
By his enchantment whom God made the Prince
O' the Power o' the Air, into a Heaven: there is
Heaven, since there is Heaven's simulation – earth.
I sit possessed in patience; prison-roof
Shall break one day and Heaven beam overhead.'

His smile is done with; he speaks bitterly.

'Take my congratulations, and permit
I wish myself had proved as teachable!
– Or, no! until you taught me, could I learn
A lesson from experience ne'er till now
Conceded? Please you listen while I show
How thoroughly you estimate my worth
And yours – the immeasurably superior! I
Believed at least in one thing, first to last, –
Your love to me: I was the vile and you
The precious; I abused you, I betrayed,
But doubted – never! Why else go my way
Judas-like plodding to this Potter's Field
Where fate now finds me? What has dinned my ear
And dogged my step? The spectre with the shriek
"*Such she was, such were you, whose punishment
Is just!*" And such she was not, all the while!
She never owned a love to outrage, faith
To pay with falsehood! For, my heart knows this –

Love once and you love always. Why, it's down
Here in the Album: every lover knows
Love may use hate but – turn to hate, itself –
Turn even to indifference – no, indeed!
Well, I have been spell-bound, deluded like
The witless negro by the Obeah-man
Who bids him wither: so, his eye grows dim,
His arm slack, arrow misses aim and spear
Goes wandering wide, – and all the woe because
He proved untrue to Fetish, who, he finds,
Was just a feather-phantom! I wronged love,
Am ruined, – and there was no love to wrong!'

'No love? Ah, dead love! I invoke thy ghost
To show the murderer where thy heart poured life
At summons of the stroke he doubts was dealt
On pasteboard and pretence! Not love, my love?
I changed for you the very laws of life:
Made you the standard of all right, all fair.
No genius but you could have been, no sage,
No sufferer – which is grandest – for the truth!
My hero – where the heroic only hid
To burst from hiding, brighten earth one day!
Age and decline were man's maturity;
Face, form were nature's type: more grace, more strength,
What had they been but just superfluous gauds,
Lawless divergence? I have danced through day
On tiptoe at the music of a word,
Have wondered where was darkness gone as night
Burst out in stars at brilliance of a smile!
Lonely, I placed the chair to help me seat
Your fancied presence; in companionship,
I kept my finger constant to your glove
Glued to my breast; then – where was all the world?
I schemed – not dreamed – how I might die some death
Should save your finger aching! Who creates
Destroys, he only: I had laughed to scorn
Whatever angel tried to shake my faith
And make you seem unworthy: you yourself
Only could do that! With a touch 'twas done.
"*Give me all, trust me wholly!*" At the word,

I did give, I did trust – and thereupon
The touch did follow. Ah, the quiet smile,
The masterfully-folded arm in arm,
As trick obtained its triumph one time more!
In turn, my soul too triumphs in defeat:
Treason like faith moves mountains: love is gone!'

He paces to and fro, stops, stands quite close
And calls her by her name. Then –

'God forgives:
Forgive you, delegate of God, brought near
As never priests could bring him to this soul
That prays you both – forgive me! I abase –
Know myself mad and monstrous utterly
In all I did that moment; but as God
Gives me this knowledge – heart to feel and tongue
To testify – so be you gracious too!
Judge no man by the solitary work
Of – well, they do say and I can believe –
The devil in him: his, the moment, – mine
The life – your life!'

He names her name again.

'You were just – merciful as just, you were
In giving me no respite: punishment
Followed offending. Sane and sound once more,
The patient thanks decision, promptitude,
Which flung him prone and fastened him from hurt,
Haply to others, surely to himself.
I wake and would not you had spared one pang.
All's well that ends well!'

Yet again her name.

'Had *you* no fault? Why must you change, forsooth,
Parts, why reverse positions, spoil the play?
Why did your nobleness look up to me,
Not down on the ignoble thing confessed?
Was it your part to stoop, or lift the low?

Wherefore did God exalt you? Who would teach
The brute man's tameness and intelligence
Must never drop the dominating eye:
Wink – and what wonder if the mad fit break,
Followed by stripes and fasting? Sound and sane,
My life, chastised now, couches at your foot.
Accept, redeem me! Do your eyes ask "*How?*"
I stand here penniless, a beggar; talk
What idle trash I may, this final blow
Of fortune fells me. *I* disburse, indeed,
This boy his winnings? when each bubble-scheme
That danced athwart my brain, a minute since,
The worse the better, – of repairing straight
My misadventure by fresh enterprise,
Capture of other boys in foolishness
His fellows, – when these fancies fade away
At first sight of the lost so long, the found
So late, the lady of my life, before
Whose presence I, the lost, am also found
Incapable of one least touch of mean
Expedient, I who teemed with plot and wile –
That family of snakes your eye bids flee!
Listen! Our troublesomest dreams die off
In daylight: I awake, and dream is – where?
I rouse up from the past: one touch dispels
England and all here. I secured long since
A certain refuge, solitary home
To hide in, should the head strike work one day,
The hand forget its cunning, or perhaps
Society grow savage, – there to end
My life's remainder, which, say what fools will,
Is or should be the best of life, – its fruit,
All tends to, root and stem and leaf and flower.
Come with me, love, loved once, loved only, come,
Blend loves there! Let this parenthetic doubt
Of love, in me, have been the trial-test
Appointed to all flesh at some one stage
Of soul's achievement, – when the strong man doubts
His strength, the good man whether goodness be,
The artist in the dark seeks, fails to find
Vocation, and the saint forswears his shrine.
What if the lover may elude, no more

Than these, probative dark, must search the sky
Vainly for love, his soul's star? But the orb
Breaks from eclipse: I breathe again: I love!
Tempted, I fell; but fallen – fallen lie
Here at your feet, see! Leave this poor pretence
Of union with a nature and its needs
Repugnant to your needs and nature! Nay,
False, beyond falsity you reprehend
In me, is such mock marriage with such mere
Man-mask as – whom you witless wrong, beside,
By that expenditure of heart and brain
He recks no more of than would yonder tree
If watered with your life-blood: rains and dews
Answer its ends sufficiently, while me
One drop saves – sends to flower and fruit at last
The laggard virtue in the soul which else
Cumbers the ground! Quicken me! Call me yours –
Yours and the world's – yours and the world's and God's!
Yes, for you can, you only! Think! Confirm
Your instinct! Say, a minute since, I seemed
The castaway you count me, – all the more
Apparent shall the angelic potency
Lift me from out perdition's deep of deeps
To light and life and love! – that's love for you –
Love that already dares match might with yours.
You loved one worthy, – in your estimate, –
When time was; you descried the unworthy taint,
And where was love then? No such test could e'er
Try my love: but you hate me and revile;
Hatred, revilement – had you these to bear
Would you, as I do, nor revile, nor hate,
But simply love on, love the more, perchance?
Abide by your own proof! "*Your love was love:*
Its ghost knows no forgetting!" Heart of mine,
Would that I dared remember! Too unwise
Were he who lost a treasure, did himself
Enlarge upon the sparkling catalogue
Of gems to her his queen who trusted late
The keeper of her caskets! Can it be
That I, custodian of such relic still
As your contempt permits me to retain,
All I dare hug to breast is – "*How your glove*

Burst and displayed the long thin lily-streak!"
What may have followed – that is forfeit now!
I hope the proud man has grown humble. True –
One grace of humbleness absents itself –
Silence! yet love lies deeper than all words,
And not the spoken but the speechless love
Waits answer ere I rise and go my way.'

Whereupon, yet one other time the name.

To end she looks the large deliberate look,
Even prolongs it somewhat; then the soul
Bursts forth in a clear laugh that lengthens on,
On, till – thinned, softened, silvered, one might say
The bitter runnel hides itself in sand,
Moistens the hard grey grimly comic speech.

'Ay – give the baffled angler even yet
His supreme triumph as he hales to shore
A second time the fish once 'scaped from hook:
So artfully has new bait hidden old
Blood-imbrued iron! Ay, no barb's beneath
The gilded minnow here! You bid break trust,
This time, with who trusts me, – not simply bid
Me trust you, me who ruined but myself,
In trusting but myself! Since, thanks to you,
I know the feel of sin and shame, – be sure,
I shall obey you and impose them both
On one who happens to be ignorant
Although my husband – for the lure is love,
Your love! Try other tackle, fisher-friend!
Repentance, expiation, hopes and fears,
What you had been, may yet be, would I but
Prove helpmate to my hero – one and all
These silks and worsteds round the hook seduce
Hardly the late torn throat and mangled tongue.
Pack up, I pray, the whole assortment prompt!
Who wonders at variety of wile
In the Arch-cheat? You are the Adversary!
Your fate is of your choosing: have your choice!
Wander the world, – God has some end to serve
Ere he suppress you! He waits: I endure,

But interpose no finger-tip, forsooth,
To stop your passage to the pit. Enough
That I am stable, uninvolved by you
In the rush downwards: free I gaze and fixed;
Your smiles, your tears, prayers, curses move alike
My crowned contempt. You kneel? Prostrate yourself!
To earth, and would the whole world saw you there!'

Whereupon – 'All right!' carelessly begins
Somebody from outside, who mounts the stair,
And sends his voice for herald of approach:
Half in half out the doorway as the door
Gives way to push.

'Old fellow, all's no good!
The train's your portion! Lay the blame on me!
I'm no diplomatist, and Bismarck's self
Had hardly braved the awful Aunt at broach
Of proposition – so has world-repute
Preceded the illustrious stranger! Ah! –'

Quick the voice changes to astonishment,
Then horror, as the youth stops, sees, and knows.

The man who knelt starts up from kneeling, stands
Moving no muscle, and confronts the stare.

One great red outbreak buries – throat and brow –
The lady's proud pale queenliness of scorn:
Then her great eyes that turned so quick, become
Intenser: quail at gaze, not they indeed!

V

It is the young man shatters silence first.

'Well, my lord – for indeed my lord you are,
I little guessed how rightly – this last proof
Of lordship-paramount confounds too much
My simple head-piece! Let's see how we stand
Each to the other! how we stood i' the game
Of life an hour ago, – the magpies, stile
And oak-tree witnessed. Truth exchanged for truth –

My lord confessed his four-years-old affair –
How he seduced and then forsook the girl
Who married somebody and left him sad.
My pitiful experience was – I loved
A girl whose gown's hem had I dared to touch
My finger would have failed me, palsy-fixed.
She left me, sad enough, to marry – whom?
A better man, – then possibly not you!
How does the game stand? Who is who and what
Is what, o' the board now, since an hour went by?
My lord's "*seduced, forsaken, sacrificed,*"
Starts up, my lord's familiar instrument,
Associate and accomplice, mistress-slave –
Shares his adventure, follows on the sly!
– Ay, and since "bag and baggage" is a phrase –
Baggage lay hid in carpet-bag belike,
Was but unpadlocked when occasion came
For holding council, since my back was turned,
On how invent ten thousand pounds which, paid,
Would lure the winner to lose twenty more,
Beside refunding these! Why else allow
The fool to gain them? So displays herself
The lady whom my heart believed – oh, laugh!
Noble and pure: whom my heart loved at once,
And who at once did speak truth when she said
"*I am not mine now but another's*" – thus
Being that other's! Devil's-marriage, eh?
"*My lie weds thine till lucre us do part?*"
But pity me the snobbish simpleton,
You two aristocratic tip-top swells
At swindling! Quits, I cry! Decamp content
With skin I'm peeled of: do not strip bones bare –
As that you could, I have no doubt at all!
O you two rare ones! Male and female, Sir!
The male there smirked, this morning, "*Come, my boy –*
Out with it! You've been crossed in love, I think:
I recognize the lover's hangdog look;
Make a clean breast and match my confidence,
For, I'll be frank, I too have had my fling,
Am punished for my fault, and smart enough!
Where now the victim hides her head, God knows!"
Here loomed her head life-large, the devil knew!

Look out, Salvini! Here's your man, your match!
He and I sat applauding, stall by stall,
Last Monday – "*Here's Othello*" was our word,
"*But where's Iago?*" Where? Why, there! And now
The fellow-artist, female specimen –
Oh, lady, you must needs describe yourself!
He's great in art, but you – how greater still
– (If I can rightly, out of all I learned,
Apply one bit of Latin that assures
"*Art means just art's concealment*") – tower yourself!
For he stands plainly visible henceforth –
Liar and scamp: while you, in artistry
Prove so consummate – or I prove perhaps
So absolute an ass – that – either way –
You still do seem to me who worshipped you
And see you take the homage of this man
Your master, who played slave and knelt, no doubt,
Before a mistress in his very craft...
Well, take the fact, I nor believe my eyes,
Nor trust my understanding! Still you seem
Noble and pure as when we had the talk
Under the tower, beneath the trees, that day.
And there's the key explains the secret: down
He knelt to ask your leave to rise a grade
I' the mystery of humbug: well he may!
For how you beat him! Half an hour ago,
I held your master for my best of friends;
And now I hate him! Four years since, you seemed
My heart's one love: well, and you so remain!
What's he to you in craft?'

She looks him through.

'My friend, 'tis just that friendship have its turn –
Interrogate thus me whom one, of foes
The worst, has questioned and is answered by.
Take you as frank an answer! answers both
Begin alike so far, divergent soon
World-wide – I own superiority
Over you, over him. As him I searched,
So do you stand seen through and through by me
Who, this time, proud, report your crystal shrines

A dewdrop, plain as amber prisons round
A spider in the hollow heart his house!
Nowise are you that thing my fancy feared
When out you stepped on me, a minute since,
– This man's confederate! no, you step not thus
Obsequiously at beck and call to help
At need some second scheme, and supplement
Guile by force, use my shame to pinion me
From struggle and escape! I fancied that!
Forgive me! Only by strange chance, – most strange
In even this strange world, – you enter now,
Obtain your knowledge. Me you have not wronged
Who never wronged you – least of all, my friend,
That day beneath the College tower and trees,
When I refused to say, – "*not friend but, love!*"
Had I been found as free as air when first
We met, I scarcely could have loved you. No –
For where was that in you which claimed return
Of love? My eyes were all too weak to probe
This other's seeming, but that seeming loved
The soul in me, and lied – I know too late!
While your truth was truth: and I knew at once
My power was just my beauty – bear the word –
As I must bear, of all my qualities,
To name the poorest one that serves my soul
And simulates myself! So much in me
You loved, I know: the something that's beneath
Heard not your call, – uncalled, no answer comes!
For, since in every love, or soon or late
Soul must awake and seek out soul for soul,
Yours, overlooking mine then, would, some day,
Take flight to find some other; so it proved –
Missing me, you were ready for this man.
I apprehend the whole relation: his –
The soul wherein you saw your type of worth
At once, true object of your tribute. Well
Might I refuse such half-heart's homage! Love
Divining, had assured you I no more
Stand his participant in infamy
Than you – I need no love to recognize
As simply dupe and nowise fellow-cheat!
Therefore accept one last friend's-word, – your friend's,

All men's friend, save a felon's. Ravel out
The bad embroilment howsoe'er you may,
Distribute as it please you praise or blame
To me – so you but fling this mockery far –
Renounce this rag-and-feather hero-sham,
This poodle clipt to pattern, lion-like!
Throw him his thousands back, and lay to heart
The lesson I was sent, – if man discerned
Ever God's message, – just to teach. I judge –
To far another issue than could dream
Your cousin, – younger, fairer, as befits –
Who summoned me to judgement's exercise.
I find you, save in folly, innocent.
And in my verdict lies your fate; at choice
Of mine your cousin takes or leaves you. "*Take!*"
I bid her – for you tremble back to truth.
She turns the scale, – one touch of the pure hand
Shall so press down, emprison past relapse
Farther vibration 'twixt veracity –
That's honest solid earth – and falsehood, theft
And air, that's one illusive emptiness!
That reptile capture you? I conquered him:
You saw him cower before me. Have no fear
He shall offend you farther! Spare to spurn –
Safe let him slink hence till some subtler Eve
Than I, anticipate the snake – bruise head
Ere he bruise heel – or, warier than the first,
Some Adam purge earth's garden of its pest
Before the slaver spoil the Tree of Life!

'You! Leave this youth, as he leaves you, as I
Leave each! There's caution surely extant yet
Though conscience in you were too vain a claim.
Hence quickly! Keep the cash but leave unsoiled
The heart I rescue and would lay to heal
Beside another's! Never let her know
How near came taint of your companionship!'

'Ah' – draws a long breath with a new strange look
The man she interpellates – soul a-stir
Under its covert, as, beneath the dust,

A coppery sparkle all at once denotes
The hid snake has conceived a purpose.

'Ah –
Innocence should be crowned with ignorance?
Desirable indeed, but difficult!
As if yourself, now, had not glorified
Your helpmate by imparting him a hint
Of how a monster made the victim bleed
Ere crook and courage saved her – hint, I say, –
Not the whole horror, – that were needless risk, –
But just such inkling, fancy of the fact,
As should suffice to qualify henceforth
The shepherd, when another lamb would stray,
For warning "*Ware the wolf!*" No doubt at all,
Silence is generosity, – keeps wolf
Unhunted by flock's warder! Excellent,
Did – generous to me, mean – just to him!
But, screening the deceiver, lamb were found
Outraging the deceitless! So, – he knows!
And yet, unharmed I breathe – perchance, repent –
Thanks to the mercifully-politic!'

'Ignorance is not innocence but sin –
Witness yourself ignore what after-pangs
Pursue the plague-infected. Merciful
Am I? Perhaps! The more contempt, the less
Hatred; and who so worthy of contempt
As you that rest assured I cooled the spot
I could not cure, by poisoning, forsooth,
Whose hand I pressed there? Understand for once
That, sick, of all the pains corroding me
This burnt the last and nowise least – the need
Of simulating soundness. I resolved –
No matter how the struggle tasked weak flesh –
To hide the truth away as in a grave
From – most of all – my husband: he nor knows
Nor ever shall be made to know your part,
My part, the devil's part, – I trust, God's part
In the foul matter. Saved, I yearn to save
And not destroy: and what destruction like

The abolishing of faith in him, that's faith
In me as pure and true? Acquaint some child
Who takes yon tree into his confidence,
That, where he sleeps now, was a murder done,
And that the grass which grows so thick, he thinks,
Only to pillow him is product just
Of what lies festering beneath! 'Tis God
Must bear such secrets and disclose them. Man?
The miserable thing I have become
By dread acquaintance with my secret – *you* –
That thing had he become by learning *me* –
The miserable, whom his ignorance
Would wrongly call the wicked: ignorance
Being, I hold, sin ever, small or great.
No, he knows nothing!'

'He and I alike
Are bound to you for such discreetness, then.
What if our talk should terminate awhile?
Here is a gentleman to satisfy,
Settle accounts with, pay ten thousand pounds
Before we part – as, by his face, I fear,
Results from your appearance on the scene.
Grant me a minute's parley with my friend
Which scarce admits of a third personage!
The room from which you made your entry first
So opportunely – still untenanted –
What if you please return there? Just a word
To my young friend first – then, a word to you,
And you depart to fan away each fly
From who, grass-pillowed, sleeps so sound at home!'

'So the old truth comes back! A wholesome change, –
At last the altered eye, the rightful tone!
But even to the truth that drops disguise
And stands forth grinning malice which but now
Whined so contritely – I refuse assent
Just as to malice. I, once gone, come back?
No, my lord! I enjoy the privilege
Of being absolutely loosed from you
Too much – the knowledge that your power is null
Which was omnipotence. A word of mouth,

A wink of eye would have detained me once,
Body and soul your slave; and now, thank God,
Your fawningest of prayers, your frightfulest
Of curses – neither would avail to turn
My footstep for a moment!'

'Prayer, then, tries
No such adventure. Let us cast about
For something novel in expedient: take
Command, – what say you? I profess myself
One fertile in resource. Commanding, then,
I bid – not only wait there, but return
Here, where I want you! Disobey and – good!
On your own head the peril!'

'Come!' breaks in
The boy with his good glowing face. 'Shut up!
None of this sort of thing while I stand here
– Not to stand that! No bullying, I beg!
I also am to leave you presently
And never more set eyes upon your face –
You won't mind that much; but – I tell you frank –
I do mind having to remember this
For your last word and deed – my friend who were!
Bully a woman you have ruined, eh?
Do you know, – I give credit all at once
To all those stories everybody told
And nobody but I would disbelieve:
They all seem likely now, – nay, certain, sure!
I dare say you did cheat at cards that night
The row was at the Club: "*sauter la coupe*" –
That was your "cut," for which your friends "cut" you
While I, the booby, "cut" – acquaintanceship
With who so much as laughed when I said "*luck!*"
I dare say you had bets against the horse
They doctored at the Derby; little doubt,
That fellow with the sister found you shirk
His challenge and did kick you like a ball,
Just as the story went about! Enough:
It only serves to show how well advised,
Madam, you were in bidding such a fool
As I, go hang. You see how the mere sight

And sound of you suffice to tumble down
Conviction topsy-turvy: no, – that's false, –
There's no unknowing what one knows; and yet
Such is my folly that, in gratitude
For . . . well, I'm stupid; but you seemed to wish
I should know gently what I know, should slip
Softly from old to new, not break my neck
Between beliefs of what you were and are.
Well then, for just the sake of such a wish
To cut no worse a figure than needs must
In even eyes like mine, I'd sacrifice
Body and soul! But don't think danger – pray! –
Menaces either! He do harm to us?
Let me say "us" this one time! You'd allow
I lent perhaps my hand to rid your ear
Of some cur's yelping – hand that's fortified,
Into the bargain, with a horsewhip? Oh,
One crack and you shall see how curs decamp!
My lord, you know your losses and my gains.
Pay me my money at the proper time!
If cash be not forthcoming, – well, yourself
Have taught me, and tried often, I'll engage,
The proper course: I post you at the Club,
Pillory the defaulter. Crack, today,
Shall, slash, tomorrow, slice through flesh and bone!
There, Madam, you need mind no cur, I think!'

'Ah, what a gain to have an apt no less
Than grateful scholar! Nay, he brings to mind
My knowledge till he puts me to the blush,
So long has it lain rusty! Post my name!
That were indeed a wheal from whipcord! Whew!
I wonder now if I could rummage out
– Just to match weapons – some old scorpion-scourge!
Madam, you hear my pupil, may applaud
His triumph o'er the master. I – no more
Bully, since I'm forbidden: but entreat –
Wait and return – for my sake, no! but just
To save your own defender, should he chance
Get thwacked through awkward flourish of his thong.
And what if – since all waiting's weary work –
I help the time pass 'twixt your exit now

And entry then? for – pastime proper – here's
The very thing, the Album, verse and prose
To make the laughing minutes launch away!
Each of us must contribute. I'll begin –
"*Hail, calm acclivity, salubrious spot!*"
I'm confident I beat the bard, – for why?
My young friend owns me an Iago – him
Confessed, among the other qualities,
A ready rhymer. Oh, he rhymed! Here goes!
– Something to end with "*horsewhip!*" No, that rhyme
Beats me; there's "*cowslip,*" "*boltsprit,*" nothing else!
So, Tennyson take my benison, – verse for bard,
Prose suits the gambler's book best! Dared and done!'

Wherewith he dips pen, writes a line or two,
Closes and clasps the cover, gives the book,
Bowing the while, to her who hesitates,
Turns half away, turns round again, at last
Takes it as you touch carrion, then retires.
The door shuts fast the couple.

VI

With a change
Of his whole manner, opens out at once
The Adversary.

'Now, my friend, for you!
You who, protected late, aggressive grown,
Brandish, it seems, a weapon I must 'ware!
Plain speech in me becomes respectable
Henceforth, because courageous; plainly, then –
(Have lash well loose, hold handle tight and light!)
Throughout my life's experience, you indulged
Yourself and friend by passing in review
So courteously but now, I vainly search
To find one record of a specimen
So perfect of the pure and simple fool
As this you furnish me. Ingratitude
I lump with folly, – all's one lot, – so – fool!
Did I seek you or you seek me? Seek? sneak
For service to, and service you would style –
And did style – godlike, scarce an hour ago!

Fool, there again, yet not precisely there
First-rate in folly: since the hand you kissed
Did pick you from the kennel, did plant firm
Your footstep on the pathway, did persuade
Your awkward shamble to true gait and pace,
Fit for the world you walk in. Once a-strut
On that firm pavement which your cowardice
Was for renouncing as a pitfall, next
Came need to clear your brains of their conceit
They cleverly could distinguish who was who,
Whatever folk might tramp the thoroughfare.
Men, now – familiarly you read them off,
Each phyz at first sight! O you had an eye!
Who couched it? made you disappoint each fox
Eager to strip my gosling of his fluff
So golden as he cackled "Goose trusts lamb?"
"*Ay, but I saved you – wolf defeated fox –*
Wanting to pick your bones myself!" then, wolf
Has got the worst of it with goose for once.
I, penniless, pay you ten thousand pounds
(– No gesture, pray! I pay ere I depart.)
And how you turn advantage to account
Here's the example. Have I proved so wrong
In my peremptory "*debt must be discharged?*"
O you laughed lovelily, were loth to leave
The old friend out at elbows – pooh, a thing
Not to be thought of! I must keep my cash,
And you forget your generosity!
Ha ha, I took your measure when I laughed
My laugh to that! First quarrel – nay, first faint
Pretence at taking umbrage – "*Down with debt,*
Both interest and principal! – The Club,
Exposure and expulsion! – stamp me out!"
That's the magnanimous magnificent
Renunciation of advantage! Well,
But whence and why did you take umbrage, Sir?
Because your master, having made you know
Somewhat of men, was minded to advance,
Expound you women, still a mystery!
My pupil pottered with a cloud on brow,
A clod in breast: had loved, and vainly loved:
Whence blight and blackness, just for all the world

As Byron used to teach us boys. Thought I –
"*Quick rid him of that rubbish! Clear the cloud,*
And set the heart a-pulsing!" – heart, this time:
'Twas nothing but the head I doctored late
For ignorance of Man; now heart's to dose,
Palsied by over-palpitation due
To Woman-worship – so, to work at once
On first avowal of the patient's ache!
This morning you described your malady, –
How you dared love a piece of virtue – lost
To reason, as the upshot showed: for scorn
Fitly repaid your stupid arrogance;
And, parting, you went two ways, she resumed
Her path – perfection, while forlorn you paced
The world that's made for beasts like you and me.
My remedy was – tell the fool the truth!
Your paragon of purity had plumped
Into these arms at their first outspread – "*fallen*
My victim," she prefers to turn the phrase –
And, in exchange for that frank confidence,
Asked for my whole life present and to come –
Marriage: a thing uncovenanted for,
Never so much as put in question. Life –
Implied by marriage – throw that trifle in
And round the bargain off, no otherwise
Than if, when we played cards, because you won
My money you should also want my head!
That, I demurred to: we but played "*for love*" –
She won my love; had she proposed for stakes
"*Marriage,*" – why, that's for whist, a wiser game.
Whereat she raved at me, as losers will,
And went her way. So far the story's known,
The remedy's applied, no farther: which
Here's the sick man's first *honorarium* for –
Posting his medicine-monger at the Club!
That being, Sir, the whole you mean my fee –
In gratitude for such munificence
I'm bound in common honesty to spare
No droplet of the draught: so, – pinch your nose,
Pull no wry faces! – drain it to the dregs!
I say "*She went off*" – "*went off,*" you subjoin,
"*Since not to wedded bliss, as I supposed,*

Sure to some convent: solitude and peace
Help her to hide the shame from mortal view,
With prayer and fasting." No, my sapient Sir!
Far wiselier, straightway she betook herself
To a prize-portent from the donkey-show
Of leathern long-ears that compete for palm
In clerical absurdity: since he,
Good ass, nor practises the shaving-trick,
The candle-crotchet, nonsense which repays
When you've young ladies congregant, – but schools
The poor, – toils, moils and grinds the mill nor means
To stop and munch one thistle in this life
Till next life smother him with roses: just
The parson for her purpose! Him she stroked
Over the muzzle; into mouth with bit,
And on to back with saddle, – there he stood,
The serviceable beast who heard, believed
And meekly bowed him to the burden, – borne
Off in a canter to seclusion – ay,
The lady's lost! But had a friend of mine
– While friend he was – imparted his sad case
To sympathizing counsellor, full soon
One cloud at least had vanished from his brow.
"*Don't fear!*" had followed reassuringly –
"*The lost will in due time turn up again,*
Probably just when, weary of the world,
You think of nothing less than settling-down
To country life and golden days, beside
A dearest best and brightest virtuousest
Wife: who needs no more hope to hold her own
Against the naughty-and-repentant – no,
Than water-gruel against Roman punch!"
And as I prophesied, it proves! My youth, –
Just at the happy moment when, subdued
To spooniness, he finds that youth fleets fast,
That town-life tires, that men should drop boys'-play
That property, position have, no doubt,
Their exigency with their privilege,
And if the wealthy wed with wealth, how dire
The double duty! – in, behold, there beams
Our long-lost lady, form and face complete!
And where's my moralizing pupil now,

Had not his master missed a train by chance?
But, by your side instead of whirled away,
How have I spoiled scene, stopped catastrophe,
Struck flat the stage-effect I know by heart!
Sudden and strange the meeting – improvised?
Bless you, the last event she hoped or dreamed!
But rude sharp stroke will crush out fire from flint –
Assuredly from flesh. "*'Tis you?*" "*Myself.*"
"*Changed?*" "*Changeless.*" "*Then, what's earth to me?*" "*To me
What's heaven?*" "*So, – thine!*" "*And thine!*" "*And likewise
mine!*"
Had laughed "*Amen*" the devil, but for me
Whose intermeddling hinders this hot haste,
And bids you, ere concluding contract, pause –
Ponder one lesson more, then sign and seal
At leisure and at pleasure, – lesson's price
Being, if you have skill to estimate,
– How say you? – I'm discharged my debt in full!
Since paid you stand, to farthing uttermost,
Unless I fare like that black majesty
A friend of mine had visit from last Spring.
Coasting along the Cape-side, he's becalmed
Off an uncharted bay, a novel town
Untouched at by the trader: here's a chance!
Out paddles straight the king in his canoe,
Comes over bulwark, says he means to buy
Ship's cargo – being rich and having brought
A treasure ample for the purpose. See!
Four dragons, stalwart blackies, guard the same
Wrapped round and round: its hulls, a multitude, –
Palm-leaf and cocoa-mat and goat's-hair cloth
All duly braced about with bark and board, –
Suggest how brave, 'neath coat, must kernel be!
At length the peeling is accomplished, plain
The casket opens out its core, and lo
– A brand-new British silver sixpence – bid
That's ample for the Bank, – thinks majesty!
You are the Captain; call my sixpence cracked
Or copper; "*what I've said is calumny;
The lady's spotless!*" Then, I'll prove my words,
Or make you prove them true as truth – yourself,
Here, on the instant! I'll not mince my speech,

Things at this issue. When she enters, then,
Make love to her! No talk of marriage now –
The point-blank bare proposal! Pick no phrase –
Prevent all misconception! Soon you'll see
How different the tactics when she deals
With an instructed man, no longer boy
Who blushes like a booby. Woman's wit!
Man, since you have instruction, blush no more!
Such your five minutes' profit by my pains,
'Tis simply now – demand and be possessed!
Which means – you may possess – may strip the tree
Of fruit desirable to make one wise.
More I nor wish nor want: your act's your act,
My teaching is but – there's the fruit to pluck
Or let alone at pleasure. Next advance
In knowledge were beyond you! Don't expect
I bid a novice – pluck, suck, send sky-high
Such fruit, once taught that neither crab nor sloe
Falls readier prey to who but robs a hedge,
Than this gold apple to my Hercules.
Were you no novice but proficient – then,
Then, truly, I might prompt you – Touch and taste,
Try flavour and be tired as soon as I!
Toss on the prize to greedy mouths agape,
Betake yours, sobered as the satiate grow,
To wise man's solid meal of house and land,
Consols and cousin! but my boy, my boy,
Such lore's above you!

Here's the lady back!
So, Madam, you have conned the Album-page
And come to thank its last contributor?
How kind and condescending! I retire
A moment, lest I spoil the interview,
And mar my own endeavour to make friends –
You with him, him with you, and both with me!
If I succeed – permit me to inquire
Five minutes hence! Friends bid good-bye, you know.'
And out he goes.

VII

She, face, form, bearing, one
Superb composure –

'He has told you all?
Yes, he has told you all, your silence says –
What gives him, as he thinks the mastery
Over my body and my soul! – has told
That instance, even, of their servitude
He now exacts of me? A silent blush!
That's well, though better would white ignorance
Beseem your brow, undesecrate before –
Ay, when I left you! I too learn at last
– Hideously learned as I seemed so late –
What sin may swell to. Yes, – I needed learn
That, when my prophet's rod became the snake
I fled from, it would, one day, swallow up
– Incorporate whatever serpentine
Falsehood and treason and unmanliness
Beslime earth's pavement: such the power of Hell,
And so beginning, ends no otherwise
The Adversary! I was ignorant,
Blameworthy – if you will; but blame I take
Nowise upon me as I ask myself
– *You* – how can you, whose soul I seemed to read
The limpid eyes through, have declined so deep
Even with him for consort? I revolve
Much memory, pry into the looks and words
Of that day's walk beneath the College wall,
And nowhere can distinguish, in what gleams
Only pure marble through my dusky past,
A dubious cranny where such poison-seed
Might harbour, nourish what should yield today
This dread ingredient for the cup I drink.
Do not I recognize and honour truth
In seeming? – take your truth and for return,
Give you my truth, a no less precious gift?
You loved me: I believed you. I replied
– How could I other? "*I was not my own,*"
– No longer had the eyes to see, the ears
To hear, the mind to judge, since heart and soul
Now were another's. My own right in me,

For well or ill, consigned away – my face
Fronted the honest path, deflection whence
Had shamed me in the furtive backward look
At the late bargain – fit such chapman's phrase! –
As though – less hasty and more provident –
Waiting had brought advantage. Not for me
The chapman's chance! Yet while thus much was true,
I spared you – as I knew you then – one more
Concluding word which, truth no less, seemed best
Buried away for ever. Take it now
Its power to pain is past! Four years – that day –
Those limes that make the College avenue!
I would that – friend and foe – by miracle,
I had, that moment, seen into the heart
Of either, as I now am taught to see!
I do believe I should have straight assumed
My proper function, and sustained a soul,
Nor aimed at being just sustained myself
By some man's soul – the weaker woman's-want!
So had I missed the momentary thrill
Of finding me in presence of a god,
But gained the god's own feeling when he gives
Such thrill to what turns life from death before.
"*Gods many and Lords many,*" says the Book:
You would have yielded up your soul to me
– Not to the false god who has burned its clay
In his own image. I had shed my love
Like Spring dew on the clod all flowery thence,
Not sent up a wild vapour to the sun
That drinks and then disperses. Both of us
Blameworthy, – I first meet my punishment –
And not so hard to bear. I breathe again!
Forth from those arms' enwinding leprosy
At last I struggle – uncontaminate:
Why must I leave *you* pressing to the breast
That's all one plague-spot? Did you love me once?
Then take love's last and best return! I think,
Womanliness means only motherhood;
All love begins and ends there, – roams enough,
But, having run the circle, rests at home.
Why is your expiation yet to make?
Pull shame with your own hands from your own head

Now, – never wait the slow envelopment
Submitted to by unelastic age!
One fierce throe frees the sapling: flake on flake
Lull till they leave the oak snow-stupefied.
Your heart retains its vital warmth – or why
That blushing reassurance? Blush, young blood!
Break from beneath this icy premature
Captivity of wickedness – I warn
Back, in God's name! No fresh encroachment here!
This May breaks all to bud – no Winter now!
Friend, we are both forgiven! Sin no more!
I am past sin now, so shall you become!
Meanwhile I testify that, lying once,
My foe lied ever, most lied last of all.
He, waking, whispered to your sense asleep
The wicked counsel, – and assent might seem;
But, roused, your healthy indignation breaks
The idle dream-pact. You would die – not dare
Confirm your dream-resolve, – nay, find the word
That fits the deed to bear the light of day!
Say I have justly judged you! then farewell
To blushing – nay, it ends in smiles, not tears!
Why tears now? I have justly judged, thank God!'

He does blush boy-like, but the man speaks out,
– Makes the due effort to surmount himself.

'I don't know what he wrote – how should I? Nor
How he could read my purpose which, it seems,
He chose to somehow write – mistakenly
Or else for mischief's sake. I scarce believe
My purpose put before you fair and plain
Would need annoy so much; but there's my luck –
From first to last I blunder. Still, one more
Turn at the target, try to speak my thought!
Since he could guess my purpose, won't you read
Right what he set down wrong? He said – let's think!
Ay, so! – he did begin by telling heaps
Of tales about you. Now, you see – suppose
Anyone told me – my own mother died
Before I knew her – told me – to his cost! –
Such tales about my own dead mother: why,

You would not wonder surely if I knew,
By nothing but my own heart's help, he lied,
Would you? No reason's wanted in the case.
So with you! In they burnt on me, his tales,
Much as when madhouse-inmates crowd around,
Make captive any visitor and scream
All sorts of stories of their keeper – he's
Both dwarf and giant, vulture, wolf, dog, cat,
Serpent and scorpion, yet man all the same;
Sane people soon see through the gibberish!
I just made out, you somehow lived somewhere
A life of shame – I can't distinguish more –
Married or single – how, don't matter much:
Shame which himself had caused – that point was clear,
That fact confessed – that thing to hold and keep.
Oh, and he added some absurdity
– That you were here to make me – ha, ha, ha! –
Still love you, still of mind to die for you,
Ha, ha – as if that needed mighty pains!
Now, foolish as . . . but never mind myself
– What I am, what I am not, in the eye
Of the world, is what I never cared for much.
Fool then or no fool, not one single word
In the whole string of lies did I believe,
But this – this only – if I choke, who cares? –
I believe somehow in your purity
Perfect as ever! Else what use is God?
He is God, and work miracles He can!
Then, what shall I do? Quite as clear, my course!
They've got a thing they call their Labyrinth
I' the garden yonder: and my cousin played
A pretty trick once, led and lost me deep
Inside the briery maze of hedge round hedge;
And there might I be staying now, stock-still,
But that I laughing bade eyes follow nose
And so straight pushed my path through let and stop
And soon was out in the open, face all scratched,
But well behind my back the prison-bars
In sorry plight enough, I promise you!
So here: I won my way to truth through lies –
Said, as I saw light, – if her shame be shame
I'll rescue and redeem her, – shame's no shame?

Then, I'll avenge, protect – redeem myself
The stupidest of sinners! Here I stand!
Dear, – let me once dare call you so, – you said
Thus ought you to have done, four years ago,
Such things and such! Ay, dear, and what ought I?
You were revealed to me: where's gratitude,
Where's memory even, where the gain of you
Discernible in my low after-life
Of fancied consolation? why, no horse
Once fed on corn, will, missing corn, go munch
Mere thistles like a donkey! I missed you,
And in your place found – him, made him my love,
Ay, did I, – by this token, that he taught
So much beast-nature that I meant... God knows
Whether I bow me to the dust enough!...
To marry – yes, my cousin here! I hope
That was a master-stroke! Take heart of hers,
And give her hand of mine with no more heart
Than now you see upon this brow I strike!
What atom of a heart do I retain
Not all yours? Dear, you know it! Easily
May she accord me pardon when I place
My brow beneath her foot, if foot so deign,
Since uttermost indignity is spared –
Mere marriage and no love! And all this time
Not one word to the purpose! Are you free?
Only wait! only let me serve – deserve
Where you appoint and how you see the good!
I have the will – perhaps the power – at least
Means that have power against the world. For time –
Take my whole life for your experiment!
If you are bound – in marriage, say – why, still,
Still, sure, there's something for a friend to do,
Outside? A mere well-wisher, understand!
I'll sit, my life long, at your gate, you know,
Swing it wide open to let you and him
Pass freely, – and you need not look, much less
Fling me a "*Thank you – are you there, old friend?*"
Don't say that even: I should drop like shot!
So I feel now at least: some day, who knows?
After no end of weeks and months and years
You might smile "*I believe you did your best!*"

And that shall make my heart leap – leap such leap
As lands the feet in Heaven to wait you there!
Ah, there's just one thing more! How pale you look!
Why? Are you angry? If there's, after all,
Worst come to worst – if still there somehow be
The shame – I said was no shame, – none, I swear! –
In that case, if my hand and what it holds, –
My name, – might be your safeguard now – at once –
Why, here's the hand – you have the heart! Of course –
No cheat, no binding you, because I'm bound,
To let me off probation by one day,
Week, month, year, lifetime! Prove as you propose!
Here's the hand with the name to take or leave!
That's all – and no great piece of news, I hope!'

'Give me the hand, then!' she cries hastily.
'Quick, now! I hear his footstep!'

Hand in hand
The couple face him as he enters, stops
Short, stands surprised a moment, laughs away
Surprise, resumes the much-experienced man.

'So, you accept him?'

'Till us death do part!'

'No longer? Come, that's right and rational!
I fancied there was power in common sense,
But did not know it worked thus promptly. Well –
At last each understands the other, then?
Each drops disguise, then? So, at supper-time
These masquerading people doff their gear,
Grand Turk his pompous turban, Quakeress
Her stiff-starched bib and tucker, – make-believe
That only bothers when, ball-business done,
Nature demands champagne and *mayonnaise*.
Just so has each of us sage three abjured
His and her moral pet particular
Pretension to superiority,
And, cheek by jowl, we henceforth munch and joke!
Go, happy pair, paternally dismissed

To live and die together – for a month,
Discretion can award no more! Depart
From whatsoe'er the calm sweet solitude
Selected – Paris not improbably –
At month's end, when the honeycomb's left wax,
– You, daughter, with a pocketful of gold
Enough to find your village boys and girls
In duffel cloaks and hobnailed shoes from May
To – what's the phrase? – Christmas-come-never-mas!
You, son and heir of mine, shall reappear
Ere Spring-time, that's the ring-time, lose one leaf,
And – not without regretful smack of lip
The while you wipe it free of honey-smear –
Marry the cousin, play the magistrate,
Stand for the county, prove perfection's pink –
Master of hounds, gay-coated dine – nor die
Sooner than needs of gout, obesity,
And sons at Christ Church! As for me, – ah me,
I abdicate – retire on my success,
Four years well occupied in teaching youth
– My son and daughter the exemplary!
Time for me to retire now, having placed
Proud on their pedestal the pair: in turn,
Let them do homage to their master! You, –
Well, your flushed cheek and flashing eye proclaim
Sufficiently your gratitude: you paid
The *honorarium*, the ten thousand pounds
To purpose, did you not? I told you so!
And you, but, bless me, why so pale – so faint
At influx of good fortune? Certainly,
No matter how or why or whose the fault,
I save your life – save it, nor less nor more!
You blindly were resolved to welcome death
In that black boor-and-bumpkin-haunted hole
Of his, the prig with all the preachments! *You*
Installed as nurse and matron to the crones
And wenches, while there lay a world outside
Like Paris (which again I recommend)
In company and guidance of – first, this,
Then – all in good time – some new friend as fit –
What if I were to say, some fresh myself,
As I once figured? Each dog has his day,

And mine's at sunset: what should old dog do
But eye young litters' frisky puppyhood?
Oh I shall watch this beauty and this youth
Frisk it in brilliance! But don't fear! Discreet,
I shall pretend to no more recognize
My quondam pupils than the doctor nods
When certain old acquaintances may cross
His path in Park, or sit down prim beside
His plate at dinner-table: tip nor wink
Scares patients he has put, for reason good,
Under restriction, – maybe, talked sometimes
Of douche or horsewhip to, – for why? because
The gentleman would crazily declare
His best friend was – Iago! Ay, and worse –
The lady, all at once grown lunatic,
In suicidal monomania vowed,
To save her soul, she needs must starve herself!
They're cured now, both, and I tell nobody.
Why don't you speak? Nay, speechless, each of you
Can spare, – without unclasping plighted troth, –
At least one hand to shake! Left-hands will do –
Yours first, my daughter! Ah, it guards – it gripes
The precious Album fast – and prudently!
As well obliterate the record there
On page the last: allow me tear the leaf!
Pray, now! And afterward, to make amends,
What if all three of us contribute each
A line to that prelusive fragment, – help
The embarrassed bard who broke out to break down
Dumbfoundered at such unforeseen success?
"*Hail, calm acclivity, salubrious spot*"
You begin – *place aux dames!* I'll prompt you then!
"*Here do I take the good the gods allot!*"
Next you, Sir! What, still sulky? Sing, O Muse!
"*Here does my lord in full discharge his shot!*"
Now for the crowning flourish! mine shall be . . .'

'Nothing to match your first effusion, mar
What was, is, shall remain your masterpiece!
Authorship has the alteration-itch!
No, I protest against erasure. Read,
My friend!' (she gasps out). 'Read and quickly read

"*Before us death do part,*" what made you mine
And made me yours – the marriage-licence here!
Decide if he is like to mend the same!'

And so the lady, white to ghastliness,
Manages somehow to display the page
With left-hand only, while the right retains
The other hand, the young man's, – dreaming-drunk
He, with this drench of stupefying stuff,
Eyes wide, mouth open, – half the idiot's stare
And half the prophet's insight, – holding tight,
All the same, by his one fact in the world –
The lady's right-hand: he but seems to read –
Does not, for certain; yet, how understand
Unless he reads?

So, understand he does,
For certain. Slowly, word by word, *she* reads
Aloud that licence – or that warrant, say.

'"*One against two – and two that urge their odds*
To uttermost – I needs must try resource!
Madam, I laid me prostrate, bade you spurn
Body and soul: you spurned and safely spurned
So you had spared me the superfluous taunt
'Prostration means no power to stand erect,
Stand, trampling on who trampled – prostrate now!'
So, with my other fool-foe: I was fain
Let the boy touch me with the buttoned foil,
And him the infection gains, he too must needs
Catch up the butcher's cleaver. Be it so!
Since play turns earnest, here's my serious fence.
He loves you; he demands your love: both know
What love means in my language. Love him then!
Pursuant to a pact, love pays my debt:
Therefore, deliver me from him, thereby
Likewise delivering from me yourself!
For, hesitate – much more, refuse consent –
I tell the whole truth to your husband. Flat
Cards lie on table, in our gamester-phrase!
Consent – you stop my mouth, the only way."

'I did well, trusting instinct: knew your hand
Had never joined with his in fellowship
Over this pact of infamy. You known –
As he was known through every nerve of me.
Therefore I "*stopped his mouth the only way*"
But *my* way! none was left for you, my friend –
The loyal – near, the loved one! No – no – no!
Threaten? Chastise? The coward would but quail.
Conquer who can, the cunning of the snake!
Stamp out his slimy strength from tail to head,
And still you leave vibration of the tongue.
His malice had redoubled – not on me
Who, myself, choose my own refining fire –
But on poor unsuspicious innocence;
And, – victim, – to turn executioner
Also – that feat effected, forky tongue
Had done indeed its office! Once snake's "*mouth*"
Thus "*open*" – how could mortal "*stop it*"?'

'So!'

A tiger-flash – yell, spring, and scream: halloo!
Death's out and on him, has and holds him – ugh!
But *ne trucidet coram populo*
Juvenis senem! Right the Horatian rule!

There, see how soon a quiet comes to pass!

VIII

The youth is somehow by the lady's side.
His right-hand grasps her right-hand once again.
Both gaze on the dead body. Hers the word.

'And that was good but useless. Had I lived
The danger was to dread: but, dying now –
Himself would hardly become talkative,
Since talk no more means torture. Fools – what fools
These wicked men are! Had I borne four years,
Four years of weeks and months and days and nights,
Inured me to the consciousness of life
Coiled round by his life, with the tongue to ply, –
But that I bore about me, for prompt use

At urgent need, the thing that "*stops the mouth*"
And stays the venom? Since such need was now
Or never, – how should use not follow need?
Bear witness for me, I withdraw from life
By virtue of the licence – warrant, say,
That blackens yet this Album – white again,
Thanks still to my one friend who tears the page!
Now, let me write the line of supplement,
As counselled by my foe there: "*each a line!*"'

And she does falteringly write to end.

'*I die now through the villain who lies dead,*
Righteously slain. He would have outraged me,
So, my defender slew him. God protect
The right! Where wrong lay, I bear witness now.
Let man believe me, whose last breath is spent
In blessing my defender from my soul!'

And so ends the Inn Album.

As she dies,
Begins outside a voice that sounds like song,
And is indeed half song though meant for speech
Muttered in time to motion – stir of heart
That unsubduably must bubble forth
To match the fawn-step as it mounts the stair.

'All's ended and all's over! Verdict found
"*Not guilty*" – prisoner forthwith set free,
'Mid cheers the Court pretends to disregard!
Now Portia, now for Daniel, late severe,
At last appeased, benignant! "*This young man –*
Hem – has the young man's foibles but no fault.
He's virgin soil – a friend must cultivate.
I think no plant called 'love' grows wild – a friend
May introduce, and name the bloom, the fruit!"
Here somebody dares wave a handkerchief –
She'll want to hide her face with presently!
Good-bye then! "*Cigno fedel, cigno fedel,*
Addio!" Now, was ever such mistake –
Ever such foolish ugly omen? Pshaw!

Wagner, beside! "*Amo te solo, te*
Solo amai!" That's worth fifty such!
But, mum, the grave face at the opened door!'

And so the good gay girl, with eyes and cheeks
Diamond and damask, – cheeks so white erewhile
Because of a vague fancy, idle fear
Chased on reflection! – pausing, taps discreet;
And then, to give herself a countenance,
Before she comes upon the pair inside,
Loud – the oft-quoted, long-laughed-over line –
'"*Hail, calm acclivity, salubrious spot!*"
Open the door!'

No: let the curtain fall!

Pacchiarotto and How He Worked in Distemper et cetera

1876

Prologue

I

O the old wall here! How I could pass
  Life in a long Midsummer day,
My feet confined to a plot of grass,
  My eyes from a wall not once away!

II

And lush and lithe do the creepers clothe
  Yon wall I watch, with a wealth of green:
Its bald red bricks draped, nothing loth,
  In lappets of tangle they laugh between.

III

Now, what is it makes pulsate the robe?
  Why tremble the sprays? What life o'erbrims
The body, – the house, no eye can probe, –
  Divined as, beneath a robe, the limbs?

IV

And there again! But my heart may guess
  Who tripped behind; and she sang perhaps:
So, the old wall throbbed, and its life's excess
  Died out and away in the leafy wraps.

V

Wall upon wall are between us: life
  And song should away from heart to heart.
I – prison-bird, with a ruddy strife
  At breast, and a lip whence storm-notes start –

VI

Hold on, hope hard in the subtle thing
  That's spirit: though cloistered fast, soar free;
Account as wood, brick, stone, this ring
  Of the rueful neighbours, and – forth to thee!

Of Pacchiarotto, and How He Worked in Distemper

I

Query: was ever a quainter
Crotchet than this of the painter
Giacomo Pacchiarotto
Who took 'Reform' for his motto?

II

He, pupil of old Fungaio,
Is always confounded (heigho!)
With Pacchia, contemporaneous
No question, but how extraneous
In the grace of soul, the power
Of hand, – undoubted dower
Of Pacchia who decked (as *we* know,
My Kirkup!) San Bernardino,
Turning the small dark Oratory
To Siena's Art-laboratory,
As he made its straitness roomy
And glorified its gloomy,
With Bazzi and Beccafumi.
(Another heigho for Bazzi:
How people miscall him Razzi!)

III

This Painter was of opinion
Our earth should be his dominion
Whose Art could correct to pattern
What Nature had slurred – the slattern!
And since, beneath the heavens,
Things lay now at sixes and sevens,
Or, as he said, *sopra-sotto* –
Thought the painter Pacchiarotto
Things wanted reforming, therefore.
'Wanted it' – ay, but wherefore?
When earth held one so ready
As he to step forth, stand steady
In the middle of God's creation
And prove to demonstration
What the dark is, what the light is,

What the wrong is, what the righ is,
What the ugly, what the beautiful,
What the restive, what the dutiful,
In Mankind profuse around him?
Man, devil as now he found him,
Would presently soar up angel
At the summons of such evangel,
And owe – what would Man *not* owe
To the painter Pacchiarotto?
Ay, look to thy laurels, Giotto!

IV

But Man, he perceived, was stubborn,
Grew regular brute, once cub born;
And it struck him as expedient –
Ere he tried to make obedient
The wolf, fox, bear and monkey,
By piping advice in one key –
That his pipe should play a prelude
To something heaven-tinged not hell-hued,
Something not harsh but docile,
Man-liquid, not Man-fossil –
Not fact, in short, but fancy.
By a laudable necromancy
He would conjure up ghosts – a circle
Deprived of the means to work ill
Should his music prove distasteful
And pearls to the swine go wasteful.
To be rent of swine – that *was* hard!
With fancy he ran no hazard:
Fact might knock him o'er the mazzard.

V

So, the painter Pacchiarotto
Constructed himself a grotto
In the quarter of Stalloreggi –
As authors of note allege ye.
And on each of the whitewashed sides of it
He painted – (none far and wide so fit
As he to perform in fresco) –
He painted nor cried *quiesco*
Till he peopled its every square foot

With Man – from the Beggar barefoot
To the Noble in cap and feather:
All sorts and conditions together.
The Soldier in breastplate and helmet
Stood frowningly – hail fellow well met –
By the Priest armed with bell, book and candle.
Nor did he omit to handle
The Fair Sex, our brave distemperer:
Not merely King, Clown, Pope, Emperor –
He diversified too his Hades
Of all forms, pinched Labour and paid Ease,
With as mixed an assemblage of Ladies.

VI

Which work done, dry, – he rested him,
Cleaned pallet, washed brush, divested him
Of the apron that suits *frescanti*,
And, bonnet on ear stuck jaunty,
This hand upon hip well planted,
That, free to wave as it wanted,
He addressed in a choice oration
His folk of each name and nation,
Taught its duty to every station.
The Pope was declared an arrant
Impostor at once, I warrant.
The Emperor – truth might tax him
With ignorance of the maxim
'Shear sheep but nowise flay them!'
And the Vulgar that obey them,
The Ruled, well-matched with the Ruling,
They failed not of wholesome schooling
On their knavery and their fooling.
As for Art – where's decorum? Pooh-poohed it is
By Poets that plague us with lewd ditties,
And Painters that pester with nudities!

VII

Now, your rater and debater
Is balked by a mere spectator
Who simply stares and listens
Tongue-tied, while eye nor glistens
Nor brow grows hot and twitchy,

Nor mouth, for a combat itchy,
Quivers with some convincing
Reply – that sets him wincing?
Nay, rather – reply that furnishes
Your debater with just what burnishes
The crest of him, all one triumph,
As you see him rise, hear him cry 'Humph!
Convinced am I? This confutes me?
Receive the rejoinder that suits me!
Confutation of vassal for prince meet –
Wherein all the powers that convince meet,
And mash my opponent to mincemeat!'

VIII

So, off from his head flies the bonnet,
His hip loses hand planted on it,
While t'other hand, frequent in gesture,
Slinks modestly back beneath vesture,
As, – hop, skip and jump, – he's along with
Those weak ones he late proved so strong with!
Pope, Emperor, lo, he's beside them,
Friendly now, who late could not abide them,
King, Clown, Soldier, Priest, Noble, Burgess;
And his voice, that out-roared Boanerges,
How minikin-mildly it urges
In accents how gentled and gingered
Its word in defence of the injured!
'O call him not culprit, this Pontiff!
Be hard on this Kaiser ye won't if
Ye take into con-si-der-ation
What dangers attend elevation!
The Priest – who expects him to descant
On duty with more zeal and less cant?
He preaches but rubbish he's reared in.
The Soldier, grown deaf (by the mere din
Of battle) to mercy, learned tippling
And what not of vice while a stripling.
The Lawyer – his lies are conventional.
And as for the Poor Sort – why mention all
Obstructions that leave barred and bolted
Access to the brains of each dolt-head?'

IX

He ended, you wager? Not half! A bet?
Precedence to males in the alphabet!
Still, disposed of Man's A, B, C, there's X,
Y, Z, want assistance, – the Fair Sex!
How much may be said in excuse of
Those vanities – males see no use of –
From silk shoe on heel to laced poll's-hood!
What's their frailty beside our own falsehood?
The boldest, most brazen of . . . trumpets,
How kind can they be to their dumb pets!
Of their charms – how are most frank, how few venal!
While as for those charges of Juvenal –
Quae nemo dixisset in toto
Nisi (aedepol) ore illoto –
He dismissed every charge with an '*Apage!*'

X

Then, cocking (in Scotch phrase) his cap a-gee,
Right hand disengaged from the doublet
– Like landlord, in house he had sub-let
Resuming of guardianship gestion,
To call tenants' conduct in question –
Hop, skip, jump, to inside from outside
Of chamber, he lords, ladies, louts eyed
With such transformation of visage
As fitted the censor of this age.
No longer an advocate tepid
Of frailty, but champion intrepid
Of strength, not of falsehood but verity,
He, one after one, with asperity
Stripped bare all the cant-clothed abuses,
Disposed of sophistic excuses,
Forced folly each shift to abandon,
And left vice with no leg to stand on.
So crushing the force he exerted,
That Man at his foot lay converted!

XI

True – Man bred of paint-pot and mortar!
But why suppose folks of this sort are
More likely to hear and be tractable

Than folks all alive and, in fact, able
To testify promptly by action
Their ardour, and make satisfaction
For misdeeds *non verbis sed factis?*
'With folk all alive be my practice
Henceforward! O mortar, paint-pot O,
Farewell to ye!' cried Pacchiarotto,
'Let only occasion intérpose!'

XII

It did so: for, pat to the purpose
Through causes I need not examine,
There fell upon Siena a famine.
In vain did the magistrates busily
Seek succour, fetch grain out of Sicily,
Nay, throw mill and bakehouse wide open –
Such misery followed as no pen
Of mine shall depict ye. Faint, fainter
Waxed hope of relief: so, our painter,
Emboldened by triumph of recency,
How could he do other with decency
Than rush in this strait to the rescue,
Play schoolmaster, point as with fescue
To each and all slips in Man's spelling
The law of the land? – slips now telling
With monstrous effect on the city,
Whose magistrates moved him to pity
As, bound to read law to the letter,
They minded their hornbook no better.

XIII

I ought to have told you, at starting,
How certain, who itched to be carting
Abuses away clean and thorough
From Siena, both province and borough,
Had formed themselves into a company
Whose swallow could bolt in a lump any
Obstruction of scruple, provoking
The nicer throat's coughing and choking:
Fit Club, by as fit a name dignified
Of 'Freed Ones' – '*Bardotti*' – which signified
'Spare-Horses' that walk by the wagon

The team has to drudge for and drag on.
This notable club Pacchiarotto
Had joined long since, paid scot and lot to,
As free and accepted 'Bardotto.'
The Bailiwick watched with no quiet eye
The outrage thus done to society,
And noted the advent especially
Of Pacchiarotto their fresh ally.

XIV

These Spare-Horses forthwith assembled:
Neighed words whereat citizens trembled
As oft as the chiefs, in the Square by
The Duomo, proposed a way whereby
The city were cured of disaster.
'Just substitute servant for master,
Make Poverty Wealth and Wealth Poverty,
Unloose Man from overt and covert tie,
And straight out of social confusion
True Order would spring!' Brave illusion –
Aims heavenly attained by means earthy!

XV

Off to these at full speed rushed our worthy, –
Brain practised and tongue no less tutored,
In argument's armour accoutred, –
Sprang forth, mounted rostrum and essayed
Proposals like those to which 'Yes' said
So glibly each personage painted
O' the wall-side wherewith you're acquainted.
He harangued on the faults of the Bailiwick:
'Red soon were our State-candle's paly wick,
If wealth would become but interfluous,
Fill voids up with just the superfluous;
If ignorance gave way to knowledge
– Not pedantry picked up at college
From Doctors, Professors *et cetera* –
(*They* say: "*kai ta loipa*" – like better a
Long Greek string of *kappas, taus, lambdas,*
Tacked on to the tail of each damned ass) –
No knowledge we want of this quality,
But knowledge indeed – practicality

Through insight's fine universality!
If you shout "*Bailiffs, out on ye all! Fie,*
Thou Chief of our forces, Amalfi,
Who shieldest the rogue and the clotpoll!"
If you pounce on and poke out, with what pole
I leave ye to fancy, our Siena's
Beast-litter of sloths and hyenas –'
(Whoever to scan this is ill able
Forgets the town's name's a dissyllable)
'If, this done, ye did – as ye might – place
For once the right man in the right place,
If you listened to me . . .'

XVI

At which last 'If'
There flew at his throat like a mastiff
One Spare-Horse – another and another!
Such outbreak of tumult and pother,
Horse-faces a-laughing and fleering,
Horse-voices a-mocking and jeering,
Horse-hands raised to collar the caitiff
Whose impudence ventured the late 'If' –
That, had not fear sent Pacchiarotto
Off tramping, as fast as could trot toe,
Away from the scene of discomfiture –
Had he stood there stock-still in a dumb fit – sure
Am I he had paid in his person
Till his mother might fail to know her son,
Though she gazed on him never so wistful,
In the figure so tattered and tristful.
Each mouth full of curses, each fist full
Of cuffings – behold, Pacchiarotto,
The pass which thy project has got to,
Of trusting, nigh ashes still hot – tow!
(The paraphrase – which I much need – is
From Horace '*per ignes incedis.*')

XVII

Right and left did he dash helter-skelter
In agonized search of a shelter.
No purlieu so blocked and no alley
So blind as allowed him to rally

His spirits and see – nothing hampered
His steps if he trudged and not scampered
Up here and down there in a city
That's all ups and downs, more the pity
For folk who would outrun the constable.
At last he stopped short at the one stable
And sure place of refuge that's offered
Humanity. Lately was coffered
A corpse in its sepulchre, situate
By Saint John's Observance. 'Habituate
Thyself to the strangest of bedfellows,
And, kicked by the live, kiss the dead fellows!'
So Misery counselled the craven.
At once he crept safely to haven
Through a hole left unbricked in the structure
Ay, Misery, in have you tucked your
Poor client and left him conterminous
With – pah! – the thing fetid and verminous!
(I gladly would spare you the detail,
But History writes what I retail.)

XVIII

Two days did he groan in his domicile:
'Good Saints, set me free and I promise I'll
Abjure all ambition of preaching
Change, whether to minds touched by teaching
– The smooth folk of fancy, mere figments
Created by plaster and pigments, –
Or to minds that receive with such rudeness
Dissuasion from pride, greed and lewdness,
– The rough folk of fact, life's true specimens
Of mind – "*haud in posse sed esse mens*"
As it was, is, and shall be for ever
Despite of my utmost endeavour.
O live foes I thought to illumine,
Henceforth lie untroubled your gloom in!
I need my own light, every spark, as
I couch with this sole friend – a carcase!'

XIX

Two days thus he maundered and rambled;
Then, starved back to sanity, scrambled
From out his receptacle loathsome.
'A spectre!' – declared upon oath some
Who saw him emerge and (appalling
To mention) his garments a-crawling
With plagues far beyond the Egyptian.
He gained, in a state past description
A convent of monks, the Observancy.

XX

Thus far is a fact: I reserve fancy
For Fancy's more proper employment:
And now she waves wing with enjoyment,
To tell ye how preached the Superior
When somewhat our painter's exterior
Was sweetened. He needed (no mincing
The matter) much soaking and rincing,
Nay, rubbing with drugs odoriferous,
Till, rid of his garments pestiferous
And robed by the help of the Brotherhood
In odds and ends, – this gown and t'other hood, –
His empty inside first well-garnished, –
He delivered a tale round, unvarnished.

XXI

'Ah, Youth!' ran the Abbot's admonishment,
'Thine error scarce moves my astonishment.
For – why shall I shrink from asserting? –
Myself have had hopes of converting
The foolish to wisdom, till, sober,
My life found its May grow October.
I talked and I wrote, but, one morning,
Life's Autumn bore fruit in this warning:
"*Let tongue rest, and quiet thy quill be!*
Earth is earth and not heaven, and ne'er will be."
Man's work is to labour and leaven –
As best he may – earth here with heaven;
'Tis work for work's sake that he's needing:
Let him work on and on as if speeding
Work's end, but not dream of succeeding!

Because if success were intended,
Why, heaven would begin ere earth ended.
A Spare-Horse? Be rather a thill-horse,
Or – what's the plain truth – just a mill-horse!
Earth's a mill where we grind and wear mufflers:
A whip awaits shirkers and shufflers
Who slacken their pace, sick of lugging
At what don't advance for their tugging.
Though round goes the mill, we must still post
On and on as if moving the mill-post.
So, grind away, mouth-wise and pen-wise,
Do all that we can to make men wise!
And if men prefer to be foolish,
Ourselves have proved horse-like not mulish:
Sent grist, a good sackful, to hopper,
And worked as the Master thought proper.
Tongue I wag, pen I ply, who am Abbot;
Stick thou, Son, to daub-brush and dab-pot!
But, soft! I scratch hard on the scab hot?
Though cured of thy plague, there may linger
A pimple I fray with rough finger?
So soon could my homily transmute
Thy brass into gold? Why, the man's mute!'

XXII

'Ay, Father, I'm mute with admiring
How Nature's indulgence untiring
Still bids us turn deaf ear to Reason's
Best rhetoric – clutch at all seasons
And hold fast to what's proved untenable!
Thy maxim is – Man's not amenable
To argument: whereof by consequence –
Thine arguments reach me: a non-sequence!
Yet blush not discouraged, O Father!
I stand unconverted, the rather
That nowise I need a conversion.
No live man (I cap thy assertion)
By argument ever could take hold
Of me. 'Twas the dead thing, the clay-cold,
Which grinned "*Art thou so in a hurry*
That out of warm light thou must scurry
And join me down here in the dungeon

Because, above, one's Jack and one – John,
One's swift in the race, one – a hobbler,
One's a crowned king, and one – a capped cobbler,
Rich and poor, sage and fool, virtuous, vicious?
Why complain? Art thou so unsuspicious
That all's for an hour of essaying
Who's fit and who's unfit for playing
His part in the after-construction
– Heaven's Piece whereof Earth's the Induction?
Things rarely go smooth at Rehearsal.
Wait patient the change universal,
And act, and let act, in existence!
For, as thou art clapped hence or hissed hence,
Thou hast thy promotion or otherwise.
And why must wise thou have thy brother wise
Because in rehearsal thy cue be
To shine by the side of a booby?
No polishing garnet to ruby!
All's well that ends well – through Art's magic
Some end, whether comic or tragic,
The Artist has purposed, be certain!
Explained at the fall of the curtain –
In showing thy wisdom at odds with
That folly: he tries men and gods with
No problem for weak wits to solve meant,
But one worth such Author's evolvement.
So, back nor disturb play's production
By giving thy brother instruction
To throw up his fool's-part allotted!
Lest haply thyself prove besotted
When stript, for thy pains, of that costume
Of sage, which has bred the imposthume
I prick to relieve thee of, – Vanity!"

XXIII

'So, Father, behold me in sanity!
I'm back to the palette and mahlstick:
And as for Man – let each and all stick
To what was prescribed them at starting!
Once planted as fools – no departing
From folly one inch, *saeculorum*
In saecula! Pass me the jorum,

And push me the platter – my stomach
Retains, through its fasting, still some ache –
And then, with your kind *Benedicite*,
Good-bye!'

XXIV

I have told with simplicity
My tale, dropped those harsh analytics,
And tried to content you, my critics,
Who greeted my early uprising!
I knew you through all the disguising,
Droll dogs, as I jumped up, cried 'Heyday!
This Monday is – what else but May-day?
And these in the drabs, blues and yellows,
Are surely the privileged fellows.
So, saltbox and bones, tongs and bellows,'
(I threw up the window) 'your pleasure?'

XXV

Then he who directed the measure –
An old friend – put leg forward nimbly,
'We critics as sweeps out your chimbly!
Much soot to remove from your flue, sir!
Who spares coal in kitchen an't you, sir!
And neighbours complain it's no joke, sir,
– You ought to consume your own smoke, sir!'

XXVI

Ah, rogues, but my housemaid suspects you –
Is confident oft she detects you
In bringing more filth into my house
Than ever you found there! I'm pious
However: 'twas God made you dingy
And me – with no need to be stingy
Of soap, when 'tis sixpence the packet.
So, dance away, boys, dust my jacket,
Bang drum and blow fife – ay, and rattle
Your brushes, for that's half the battle!
Don't trample the grass, – hocus-pocus
With grime my Spring snowdrop and crocus, –
And, what with your rattling and tinkling,
Who knows but you give me an inkling

How music sounds, thanks to the jangle
Of regular drum and triangle?
Whereby, tap-tap, chink-chink, 'tis proven
I break rule as bad as Beethoven.
'That chord now – a groan or a grunt is't?
Schumann's self was no worse contrapuntist.
No ear! or if ear, so tough-gristled –
He thought that he sung while he whistled!'

XXVII

So, this time I whistle, not sing at all,
My story, the largess I fling at all
And every the rough there whose *aubade*
Did its best to amuse me, – nor *so* bad!
Take my thanks, pick up largess, and scamper
Off free, ere your mirth gets a damper!
You've Monday, your one day, your fun-day,
While mine is a year that's all Sunday.
I've seen you, times – who knows how many? –
Dance in here, strike up, play the zany,
Make mouths at the tenant, hoot warning
You'll find him decamped next May-morning;
Then scuttle away, glad to 'scape hence
With – kicks? no, but laughter and ha'pence!
Mine's freehold, by grace of the grand Lord
Who lets out the ground here, – my landlord:
To him I pay quit-rent – devotion;
Nor hence shall I budge, I've a notion,
Nay, here shall my whistling and singing
Set all his street's echoes a-ringing
Long after the last of your number
Has ceased my front-court to encumber
While, treading down rose and ranunculus,
You *Tommy-make-room-for-your-Uncle* us!
Troop, all of you – man or homunculus,
Quick march! for Xanthippe, my housemaid,
If once on your pates she a souse made
With what, pan or pot, bowl or *skoramis*
First comes to her hand – things were more amiss!
I would not for worlds be your place in –
Recipient of slops from the basin!
You, Jack-in-the-Green, leaf-and-twiggishness

Won't save a dry thread on your priggishness!
While as for Quilp-Hop-o'-my-thumb there,
Banjo-Byron that twangs the strum-strum there –
He'll think, as the pickle he curses,
I've discharged on his pate his own verses!
'Dwarfs are saucy,' says Dickens: so, sauced in
Your own sauce, . . .*

XXVIII

But, back to my Knight of the Pencil,
Dismissed to his fresco and stencil!
Whose story – begun with a chuckle,
And throughout timed by raps of the knuckle, –
To small enough purpose were studied
If it ends with crown cracked or nose bloodied.
Come, critics, – not shake hands, excuse me!
But – say have you grudged to amuse me
This once in the forty-and-over
Long years since you trampled my clover
And scared from my house-eaves each sparrow
I never once harmed by that arrow
Of song, *karterotaton belos*,
(Which Pindar declares the true *melos*)
I was forging and filing and finishing,
And no whit my labours diminishing
Because, though high up in a chamber
Where none of your kidney may clamber
Your hullabaloo would approach me?
Was it 'grammar' wherein you would 'coach' me –
You, – pacing in even that paddock
Of language allotted you *ad hoc*,
With a clog at your fetlocks, – you – scorners
Of me free of all its four corners?
Was it 'clearness of words which convey thought'?
Ay, if words never needed enswathe aught
But ignorance, impudence, envy
And malice – what word-swathe would then vie
With yours for a clearness crystalline?
But had you to put in one small line

*No, please! For
'Who would be satirical
On a thing so very small?' – PRINTER'S DEVIL.

Some thought big and bouncing – as noddle
Of goose, born to cackle and waddle
And bite at man's heel as goose-wont is,
Never felt plague its puny *os frontis* –
You'd know, as you hissed, spat and sputtered,
Clear cackle is easily uttered!

XXIX

Lo, I've laughed out my laugh on this mirth-day!
Beside, at week's end, dawns my birth-day,
That *hebdome, hieron emar* –
(More things in a day than you deem are!)
– *Tei gar Apollona chrusaora*
Egeinato Leto. So, grey or ray
Betide me, six days hence, I'm vexed here
By no sweep, that's certain, till next year!
'Vexed?' – roused from what else were insipid ease!
Leave snoring a-bed to Pheidippides!
We'll up and work! won't we, Euripides?

At the 'Mermaid'

The figure that thou here seest . . . Tut!
Was it for gentle Shakespeare put?
B. JONSON (*Adapted*)

I

I – 'Next Poet?' No, my hearties,
I nor am nor fain would be!
Choose your chiefs and pick your parties,
Not one soul revolt to me!
I, forsooth, sow song-sedition?
I, a schism in verse provoke?
I, blown up by bard's ambition,
Burst – your bubble-king? You joke.

II

Come, be grave! The sherris mantling
Still about each mouth, mayhap,
Breeds you insight – just a scantling –
Brings me truth out – just a scrap.

Look and tell me! Written, spoken,
   Here's my life-long work: and where
– Where's your warrant or my token
   I'm the dead king's son and heir?

III

Here's my work: does work discover –
   What was rest from work – my life?
Did I live man's hater, lover?
   Leave the world at peace, at strife?
Call earth ugliness or beauty?
   See things there in large or small?
Use to pay its Lord my duty?
   Use to own a lord at all?

IV

Blank of such a record, truly
   Here's the work I hand, this scroll,
Yours to take or leave; as duly,
   Mine remains the unproffered soul.
So much, no whit more, my debtors –
   How should one like me lay claim
To that largess elders, betters
   Sell you cheap their souls for – fame?

V

Which of you did I enable
   Once to slip inside my breast,
There to catalogue and label
   What I like least, what love best,
Hope and fear, believe and doubt of,
   Seek and shun, respect – deride?
Who has right to make a rout of
   Rarities he found inside?

VI

Rarities or, as he'd rather,
   Rubbish such as stocks his own:
Need and greed (O strange) the Father
   Fashioned not for him alone!
Whence – the comfort set a-strutting,
   Whence – the outcry 'Haste, behold!

Bard's breast open wide, past shutting,
  Shows what brass we took for gold!'

VII

Friends, I doubt not he'd display you
  Brass – myself call orichalc, –
Furnish much amusement; pray you
  Therefore, be content I balk
Him and you, and bar my portal!
  Here's my work outside: opine
What's inside me mean and mortal!
  Take your pleasure, leave me mine!

VIII

Which is – not to buy your laurel
  As last king did, nothing loth.
Tale adorned and pointed moral
  Gained him praise and pity both.
Out rushed sighs and groans by dozens,
  Forth by scores oaths, curses flew:
Proving you were cater-cousins,
  Kith and kindred, king and you!

IX

Whereas do I ne'er so little
  (Thanks to sherris) leave ajar
Bosom's gate – no jot nor tittle
  Grow we nearer than we are.
Sinning, sorrowing, despairing,
  Body-ruined, spirit-wrecked, –
Should I give my woes an airing, –
  Where's one plague that claims respect?

X

Have you found your life distasteful?
  My life did, and does, smack sweet.
Was your youth of pleasure wasteful?
  Mine I saved and hold complete.
Do your joys with age diminish?
  When mine fail me, I'll complain.
Must in death your daylight finish?
  My sun sets to rise again.

XI

What, like you, he proved – your Pilgrim –
   This our world a wilderness,
Earth still grey and heaven still grim,
   Not a hand there his might press,
Not a heart his own might throb to,
   Men all rogues and women – say,
Dolls which boys' heads duck and bob to,
   Grown folk drop or throw away?

XII

My experience being other,
   How should I contribute verse
Worthy of your king and brother?
   Balaam-like I bless, not curse.
I find earth not grey but rosy,
   Heaven not grim but fair of hue.
Do I stoop? I pluck a posy.
   Do I stand and stare? All's blue.

XIII

Doubtless I am pushed and shoved by
   Rogues and fools enough: the more
Good luck mine, I love, am loved by
   Some few honest to the core.
Scan the near high, scout the far low!
   'But the low come close:' what then?
Simpletons? My match is Marlowe;
   Sciolists? My mate is Ben.

XIV

Womankind – 'the cat-like nature,
   False and fickle, vain and weak' –
What of this sad nomenclature
   Suits my tongue, if I must speak?
Does the sex invite, repulse so,
   Tempt, betray, by fits and starts?
So becalm but to convulse so,
   Decking heads and breaking hearts?

XV
Well may you blaspheme at fortune!
I 'threw Venus' (Ben, expound!)
Never did I need importune
Her, of all the Olympian round.
Blessings on my benefactress!
Cursings suit – for aught I know –
Those who twitched her by the back tress,
Tugged and thought to turn her – so!

XVI
Therefore, since no leg to stand on
Thus I'm left with, – joy or grief
Be the issue, – I abandon
Hope or care you name me Chief!
Chief and king and Lord's anointed,
I? – who never once have wished
Death before the day appointed:
Lived and liked, not poohed and pished!

XVII
'Ah, but so I shall not enter,
Scroll in hand, the common heart –
Stopped at surface: since at centre
Song should reach *Welt-schmerz*, world-smart!'
'Enter in the heart?' Its shelly
Cuirass guard mine, fore and aft!
Such song 'enters in the belly
And is cast out in the draught.'

XVIII
Back then to our sherris-brewage!
'Kingship' quotha? I shall wait –
Waive the present time: some new age . . .
But let fools anticipate!
Meanwhile greet me – 'friend, good fellow,
Gentle Will,' my merry men!
As for making Envy yellow
With 'Next Poet' – (Manners, Ben!)

House

I

Shall I sonnet-sing you about myself?
  Do I live in a house you would like to see?
Is it scant of gear, has it store of pelf?
  'Unlock my heart with a sonnet-key?'

II

Invite the world, as my betters have done?
  'Take notice: this building remains on view,
Its suites of reception every one,
  Its private apartment and bedroom too;

III

'For a ticket, apply to the Publisher.'
  No: thanking the public, I must decline.
A peep through my window, if folk prefer;
  But, please you, no foot over threshold of mine!

IV

I have mixed with a crowd and heard free talk
  In a foreign land where an earthquake chanced:
And a house stood gaping, naught to balk
  Man's eye wherever he gazed or glanced.

V

The whole of the frontage shaven sheer,
  The inside gaped: exposed to day,
Right and wrong and common and queer,
  Bare, as the palm of your hand, it lay.

VI

The owner? Oh, he had been crushed, no doubt!
  'Odd tables and chairs for a man of wealth!
What a parcel of musty old books about!
  He smoked, – no wonder he lost his health!

VII
'I doubt if he bathed before he dressed.
   A brasier? – the pagan, he burned perfumes!
You see it is proved, what the neighbours guessed:
   His wife and himself had separate rooms.'

VIII
Friends, the goodman of the house at least
   Kept house to himself till an earthquake came:
'Tis the fall of its frontage permits you feast
   On the inside arrangement you praise or blame.

IX
Outside should suffice for evidence:
   And whoso desires to penetrate
Deeper, must dive by the spirit-sense –
   No optics like yours, at any rate!

X
'Hoity toity! A street to explore,
   Your house the exception! "*With this same key*
Shakespeare unlocked his heart," once more!'
   Did Shakespeare? If so, the less Shakespeare he!

Shop

I
So, friend, your shop was all your house!
   Its front, astonishing the street,
Invited view from man and mouse
   To what diversity of treat
   Behind its glass – the single sheet!

II
What gimcracks, genuine Japanese:
   Gape-jaw and goggle-eye, the frog;
Dragons, owls, monkeys, beetles, geese;
   Some crush-nosed human-hearted dog:
   Queer names, too, such a catalogue!

III

I thought 'And he who owns the wealth
Which blocks the window's vastitude,
– Ah, could I peep at him by stealth
Behind his ware, pass shop, intrude
On house itself, what scenes were viewed!

IV

'If wide and showy thus the shop,
What must the habitation prove?
The true house with no name a-top –
The mansion, distant one remove,
Once get him off his traffic-groove!

V

'Pictures he likes, or books perhaps;
And as for buying most and best,
Commend me to these City chaps!
Or else he's social, takes his rest
On Sundays, with a Lord for guest.

VI

'Some suburb-palace, parked about
And gated grandly, built last year:
The four-mile walk to keep off gout;
Or big seat sold by bankrupt peer:
But then he takes the rail, that's clear.

VII

'Or, stop! I wager, taste selects
Some out o' the way, some all-unknown
Retreat: the neighbourhood suspects
Little that he who rambles lone
Makes Rothschild tremble on his throne!'

VIII

Nowise! Nor Mayfair residence
Fit to receive and entertain, –
Nor Hampstead villa's kind defence
From noise and crowd, from dust and drain, –
Nor country-box was soul's domain!

IX

Nowise! At back of all that spread
  Of merchandise, woe's me, I find
A hole i' the wall where, heels by head,
  The owner couched, his ware behind,
  – In cupboard suited to his mind.

X

For why? He saw no use of life
  But, while he drove a roaring trade,
To chuckle 'Customers are rife!'
  To chafe 'So much hard cash outlaid
  Yet zero in my profits made!

XI

'This novelty costs pains, but – takes?
  Cumbers my counter! Stock no more!
This article, no such great shakes,
  Fizzes like wildfire? Underscore
  The cheap thing – thousands to the fore!'

XII

'Twas lodging best to live most nigh
  (Cramp, coffinlike as crib might be)
Receipt of Custom; ear and eye
  Wanted no outworld: 'Hear and see
  The bustle in the shop!' quoth he.

XIII

My fancy of a merchant-prince
  Was different. Through his wares we groped
Our darkling way to – not to mince
  The matter – no black den where moped
  The master if we interloped!

XIV

Shop was shop only: household-stuff?
  What did he want with comforts there?
'Walls, ceiling, floor, stay blank and rough,
  So goods on sale show rich and rare!
  "*Sell and scud home*" be shop's affair!'

XV

What might he deal in? Gems, suppose!
  Since somehow business must be done
At cost of trouble, – see, he throws
  You choice of jewels, everyone,
  Good, better, best, star, moon and sun!

XVI

Which lies within your power of purse?
  This ruby that would tip aright
Solomon's sceptre? Oh, your nurse
  Wants simply coral, the delight
  Of teething baby, – stuff to bite!

XVII

Howe'er your choice fell, straight you took
  Your purchase, prompt your money rang
On counter, – scarce the man forsook
  His study of the 'Times,' just swang
  Till-ward his hand that stopped the clang, –

XVIII

Then off made buyer with a prize,
  Then seller to his 'Times' returned
And so did day wear, wear, till eyes
  Brightened apace, for rest was earned:
  He locked door long ere candle burned.

XIX

And whither went he? Ask himself,
  Not me! To change of scene, I think.
Once sold the ware and pursed the pelf,
  Chaffer was scarce his meat and drink,
  Nor all his music – money-chink.

XX

Because a man has shop to mind
  In time and place, since flesh must live,
Needs spirit lack all life behind,
  All stray thoughts, fancies fugitive,
  All loves except what trade can give?

XXI

I want to know a butcher paints,
  A baker rhymes for his pursuit,
Candlestick-maker much acquaints
  His soul with song, or, haply mute,
  Blows out his brains upon the flute!

XXII

But – shop each day and all day long!
  Friend, your good angel slept, your star
Suffered eclipse, fate did you wrong!
  From where these sorts of treasures are,
  There should our hearts be – Christ, how far!

Pisgah-Sights. I

I

Over the ball of it,
  Peering and prying,
How I see all of it,
  Life there, outlying!
Roughness and smoothness,
  Shine and defilement,
Grace and uncouthness:
  One reconcilement.

II

Orbed as appointed,
  Sister with brother
Joins, ne'er disjointed
  One from the other.
All's lend-and-borrow;
  Good, see, wants evil,
Joy demands sorrow,
  Angel weds devil!

III

'Which things must – *why* be?'
  Vain our endeavour!
So shall things aye be

As they were ever.
'Such things should *so* be!'
Sage our desistence!
Rough-smooth let globe be,
Mixed – man's existence!

IV

Man – wise and foolish,
Lover and scorner,
Docile and mulish –
Keep each his corner!
Honey yet gall of it!
There's the life lying,
And I see all of it,
Only, I'm dying!

Pisgah-Sights. II

I

Could I but live again,
Twice my life over,
Would I once strive again?
Would not I cover
Quietly all of it –
Greed and ambition –
So, from the pall of it,
Pass to fruition?

II

'Soft!' I'd say, 'Soul mine!
Three-score and ten years,
Let the blind mole mine
Digging out deniers!
Let the dazed hawk soar,
Claim the sun's rights too!
Turf 'tis thy walk's o'er,
Foliage thy flight's to.'

III
Only a learner,
  Quick one or slow one,
Just a discerner,
  I would teach no one.
I am earth's native:
  No rearranging it!
I be creative,
  Chopping and changing it?

IV
March, men, my fellows!
  Those who, above me,
(Distance so mellows)
  Fancy you love me:
Those who, below me,
  (Distance makes great so)
Free to forego me,
  Fancy you hate so!

V
Praising, reviling,
  Worst head and best head,
Past me defiling,
  Never arrested,
Wanters, abounders,
  March, in gay mixture,
Men, my surrounders!
  I am the fixture.

VI
So shall I fear thee,
  Mightiness yonder!
Mock-sun – more near thee,
  What is to wonder?
So shall I love thee,
  Down in the dark, – lest
Glowworm I prove thee,
  Star that now sparklest!

Fears and Scruples

I

Here's my case. Of old I used to love him
   This same unseen friend, before I knew:
Dream there was none like him, none above him, –
   Wake to hope and trust my dream was true.

II

Loved I not his letters full of beauty?
   Not his actions famous far and wide?
Absent, he would know I vowed him duty;
   Present, he would find me at his side.

III

Pleasant fancy! for I had but letters,
   Only knew of actions by hearsay:
He himself was busied with my betters;
   What of that? My turn must come some day.

IV

'Some day' proving – no day! Here's the puzzle.
   Passed and passed my turn is. Why complain?
He's so busied! If I could but muzzle
   People's foolish mouths that give me pain!

V

'Letters?' (hear them!) 'You a judge of writing?
   Ask the experts! – How they shake the head
O'er these characters, your friend's inditing –
   Call them forgery from A to Z!

VI

'Actions? Where's your certain proof' (they bother)
   'He, of all you find so great and good,
He, he only, claims this, that, the other
   Action – claimed by men, a multitude?'

VII

I can simply wish I might refute you,
Wish my friend would, – by a word, a wink, –
Bid me stop that foolish mouth, – you brute you!
He keeps absent, – why, I cannot think.

VIII

Never mind! Though foolishness may flout me,
One thing's sure enough: 'tis neither frost,
No, nor fire, shall freeze or burn from out me
Thanks for truth – though falsehood, gained – though lost.

IX

All my days, I'll go the softlier, sadlier,
For that dream's sake! How forget the thrill
Through and through me as I thought 'The gladlier
Lives my friend because I love him still!'

X

Ah, but there's a menace someone utters!
'What and if your friend at home play tricks?
Peep at hide-and-seek behind the shutters?
Mean your eyes should pierce through solid bricks?

XI

'What and if he, frowning, wake you, dreamy?
Lay on you the blame that bricks – conceal?
Say "*At least I saw who did not see me,*
Does see now, and presently shall feel" ?'

XII

'Why, that makes your friend a monster!' say you:
'Had his house no window? At first nod,
Would you not have hailed him?' Hush, I pray you!
What if this friend happen to be – God?

Natural Magic

I

All I can say is – I saw it!
The room was as bare as your hand.
I locked in the swarth little lady, – I swear,
From the head to the foot of her – well, quite as bare!
'No Nautch shall cheat me,' said I, 'taking my stand
At this bolt which I draw!' And this bolt – I withdraw it,
And there laughs the lady, not bare, but embowered
With – who knows what verdure, o'erfruited, o'erflowered?
Impossible! Only – I saw it!

II

All I can sing is – I feel it!
This life was as blank as that room;
I let you pass in here. Precaution, indeed?
Walls, ceiling and floor, – not a chance for a weed!
Wide opens the entrance: where's cold now, where's gloom?
No May to sow seed here, no June to reveal it,
Behold you enshrined in these blooms of your bringing,
These fruits of your bearing – nay, birds of your winging!
A fairy-tale! Only – I feel it!

Magical Nature

I

Flower – I never fancied, jewel – I profess you!
Bright I see and soft I feel the outside of a flower.
Save but glow inside and – jewel, I should guess you,
Dim to sight and rough to touch: the glory is the dower.

II

You, forsooth, a flower? Nay, my love, a jewel –
Jewel at no mercy of a moment in your prime!
Time may fray the flower-face: kind be time or cruel,
Jewel, from each facet, flash your laugh at time!

Bifurcation

We were two lovers; let me lie by her,
My tomb beside her tomb. On hers inscribe –
'I loved him; but my reason bade prefer
Duty to love, reject the tempter's bribe
Of rose and lily when each path diverged,
And either I must pace to life's far end
As love should lead me, or, as duty urged,
Plod the worn causeway arm-in-arm with friend.
So, truth turned falsehood: "*How I loathe a flower,*
How prize the pavement!" still caressed his ear –
The deafish friend's – through life's day, hour by hour,
As he laughed (coughing) "*Ay, it would appear!*"
But deep within my heart of hearts there hid
Ever the confidence, amends for all,
That heaven repairs what wrong earth's journey did,
When love from life-long exile comes at call.
Duty and love, one broadway, were the best –
Who doubts? But one or other was to choose.
I chose the darkling half, and wait the rest
In that new world where light and darkness fuse.'

Inscribe on mine – 'I loved her: love's track lay
O'er sand and pebble, as all travellers know.
Duty led through a smiling country, gay
With greensward where the rose and lily blow.
"*Our roads are diverse: farewell, love!*" said she;
"*'Tis duty I abide by: homely sward*
And not the rock-rough picturesque for me!
Above, where both roads join, I wait reward.
Be you as constant to the path whereon
I leave you planted!" But man needs must move,
Keep moving – whither, when the star is gone
Whereby he steps secure nor strays from love?
No stone but I was tripped by, stumbling-block
But brought me to confusion. Where I fell,
There I lay flat, if moss disguised the rock,
Thence, if flint pierced, I rose and cried "*All's well!*
Duty be mine to tread in that high sphere
Where love from duty ne'er disparts, I trust,

And two halves make that whole, whereof – since here
One must suffice a man – why, this one must!"'

Inscribe each tomb thus: then, some sage acquaint
The simple – which holds sinner, which holds saint!

Numpholeptos

Still you stand, still you listen, still you smile!
Still melts your moonbeam through me, white awhile,
Softening, sweetening, till sweet and soft
Increase so round this heart of mine, that oft
I could believe your moonbeam-smile has past
The pallid limit, lies, transformed at last
To sunlight and salvation – warms the soul
It sweetens, softens! Would you pass that goal,
Gain love's birth at the limit's happier verge,
And, where an iridescence lurks, but urge
The hesitating pallor on to prime
Of dawn! – true blood-streaked, sun-warmth, action-time,
By heart-pulse ripened to a ruddy glow
Of gold above my clay – I scarce should know
From gold's self, thus suffused! For gold means love.
What means the sad slow silver smile above
My clay but pity, pardon? – at the best,
But acquiescence that I take my rest,
Contented to be clay, while in your heaven
The sun reserves love for the Spirit-Seven
Companioning God's throne they lamp before,
– Leaves earth a mute waste only wandered o'er
By that pale soft sweet disempassioned moon
Which smiles me slow forgiveness! Such the boon
I beg? Nay, dear, submit to this – just this
Supreme endeavour! As my lips now kiss
Your feet, my arms convulse your shrouding robe,
My eyes, acquainted with the dust, dare probe
Your eyes above for – what, if born, would blind
Mine with redundant bliss, as flash may find
The inert nerve, sting awake the palsied limb,

Bid with life's ecstasy sense overbrim
And suck back death in the resurging joy –
Love, the love whole and sole without alloy!

Vainly! The promise withers! I employ
Lips, arms, eyes, pray the prayer which finds the word,
Make the appeal which must be felt, not heard,
And none the more is changed your calm regard:
Rather, its sweet and soft grow harsh and hard –
Forbearance, then repulsion, then disdain.
Avert the rest! I rise, see! – make, again
Once more, the old departure for some track
Untried yet through a world which brings me back
Ever thus fruitlessly to find your feet,
To fix your eyes, to pray the soft and sweet
Which smile there – take from his new pilgrimage
Your outcast, once your inmate, and assuage
With love – not placid pardon now – his thirst
For a mere drop from out the ocean erst
He drank at! Well, the quest shall be renewed.
Fear nothing! Though I linger, unembued
With any drop, my lips thus close. I go!
So did I leave you, I have found you so,
And doubtlessly, if fated to return,
So shall my pleading persevere and earn
Pardon – not love – in that same smile, I learn,
And lose the meaning of, to learn once more,
Vainly!

What fairy track do I explore?
What magic hall return to, like the gem
Centuply-angled o'er a diadem?
You dwell there, hearted; from your midmost home
Rays forth – through that fantastic world I roam
Ever – from centre to circumference,
Shaft upon coloured shaft: this crimsons thence,
That purples out its precinct through the waste.
Surely I had your sanction when I faced,
Fared forth upon that untried yellow ray
Whence I retrack my steps? They end today
Where they began – before your feet, beneath

Your eyes, your smile: the blade is shut in sheath,
Fire quenched in flint; irradiation, late
Triumphant through the distance, finds its fate,
Merged in your blank pure soul, alike the source
And tomb of that prismatic glow: divorce
Absolute, all-conclusive! Forth I fared,
Treading the lambent flamelet: little cared
If now its flickering took the topaz tint,
If now my dull-caked path gave sulphury hint
Of subterranean rage – no stay nor stint
To yellow, since you sanctioned that I bathe,
Burnish me, soul and body, swim and swathe
In yellow license. Here I reek suffused
With crocus, saffron, orange, as I used
With scarlet, purple, every dye o' the bow
Born of the storm-cloud. As before, you show
Scarce recognition, no approval, some
Mistrust, more wonder at a man become
Monstrous in garb, nay – flesh disguised as well,
Through his adventure. Whatsoe'er befell,
I followed, whereso'er it wound, that vein
You authorized should leave your whiteness, stain
Earth's sombre stretch beyond your midmost place
Of vantage, – trode that tinct whereof the trace
On garb and flesh repel you! Yes, I plead
Your own permission – your command, indeed,
That who would worthily retain the love
Must share the knowledge shrined those eyes above,
Go boldly on adventure, break through bounds
O' the quintessential whiteness that surrounds
Your feet, obtain experience of each tinge
That bickers forth to broaden out, impinge
Plainer his foot its pathway all distinct
From every other. Ah, the wonder, linked
With fear, as exploration manifests
What agency it was first tipped the crests
Of unnamed wildflower, soon protruding grew
Portentous 'mid the sands, as when his hue
Betrays him and the burrowing snake gleams through;
Till, last . . . but why parade more shame and pain?
Are not the proofs upon me? Here again
I pass into your presence, I receive

Your smile of pity, pardon, and I leave ...
No, not this last of times I leave you, mute,
Submitted to my penance, so my foot
May yet again adventure, tread, from source
To issue, one more ray of rays which course
Each other, at your bidding, from the sphere
Silver and sweet, their birthplace, down that drear
Dark of the world, – you promise shall return
Your pilgrim jewelled as with drops o' the urn
The rainbow paints from, and no smatch at all
Of ghastliness at edge of some cloud-pall
Heaven cowers before, as earth awaits the fall
O' the bolt and flash of doom. Who trusts your word
Tries the adventure: and returns – absurd
As frightful – in that sulphur-steeped disguise
Mocking the priestly cloth-of-gold, sole prize
The arch-heretic was wont to bear away
Until he reached the burning. No, I say:
No fresh adventure! No more seeking love
At end of toil, and finding, calm above
My passion, the old statuesque regard,
The sad petrific smile!

O you – less hard
And hateful than mistaken and obtuse
Unreason of a she-intelligence!
You very woman with the pert pretence
To match the male achievement! Like enough!
Ay, you were easy victors, did the rough
Straightway efface itself to smooth, the gruff
Grind down and grow a whisper, – did man's truth
Subdue, for sake of chivalry and ruth,
Its rapier-edge to suit the bulrush-spear
Womanly falsehood fights with! O that ear
All fact pricks rudely, that thrice-superfine
Feminity of sense, with right divine
To waive all process, take result stain-free
From out the very muck wherein ...

Ah me!
The true slave's querulous outbreak! All the rest
Be resignation! Forth at your behest

I fare. Who knows but this – the crimson-quest –
May deepen to a sunrise, not decay
To that cold sad sweet smile? – which I obey.

Appearances

I

And so you found that poor room dull,
   Dark, hardly to your taste, my dear?
Its features seemed unbeautiful:
   But this I know – 'twas there, not here,
You plighted troth to me, the word
Which – ask that poor room how it heard!

II

And this rich room obtains your praise
   Unqualified, – so bright, so fair,
So all whereat perfection stays?
   Ay, but remember – here, not there,
The other word was spoken! Ask
This rich room how you dropped the mask!

Saint Martin's Summer

I

No protesting, dearest!
   Hardly kisses even!
      Don't we both know how it ends?
How the greenest leaf turns serest,
   Bluest outbreak – blankest heaven,
      Lovers – friends?

II

You would build a mansion,
   I would weave a bower
      – Want the heart for enterprise.
Walls admit of no expansion:
   Trellis-work may haply flower
      Twice the size.

III

What makes glad Life's Winter?
New buds, old blooms after.
Sad the sighing 'How suspect
Beams would ere mid-Autumn splinter,
Rooftree scarce support a rafter,
Walls lie wrecked?'

IV

You are young, my princess!
I am hardly older:
Yet – I steal a glance behind.
Dare I tell you what convinces
Timid me that you, if bolder,
Bold – are blind?

V

Where we plan our dwelling
Glooms a graveyard surely!
Headstone, footstone moss may drape, –
Name, date, violets hide from spelling, –
But, though corpses rot obscurely,
Ghosts escape.

VI

Ghosts! O breathing Beauty,
Give my frank word pardon!
What if I – somehow, somewhere –
Pledged my soul to endless duty
Many a time and oft? Be hard on
Love – laid there?

VII

Nay, blame grief that's fickle,
Time that proves a traitor,
Chance, change, all that purpose warps, –
Death who spares to thrust the sickle
Laid Love low, through flowers which later
Shroud the corpse!

VIII

And you, my winsome lady,
Whisper with like frankness!
Lies nothing buried long ago?
Are yon – which shimmer 'mid the shady
Where moss and violet run to rankness –
Tombs or no?

IX

Who taxes you with murder?
My hands are clean – or nearly!
Love being mortal needs must pass.
Repentance? Nothing were absurder.
Enough: we felt Love's loss severely;
Though now – alas!

X

Love's corpse lies quiet therefore,
Only Love's ghost plays truant,
And warns us have in wholesome awe
Durable mansionry; that's wherefore
I weave but trellis-work, pursuant
– Life, to law.

XI

The solid, not the fragile,
Tempts rain and hail and thunder.
If bower stand firm at Autumn's close,
Beyond my hope, – why, boughs were agile;
If bower fall flat, we scarce need wonder
Wreathing – rose!

XII

So, truce to the protesting,
So, muffled be the kisses!
For, would we but avow the truth,
Sober is genuine joy. No jesting!
Ask else Penelope, Ulysses –
Old in youth!

XIII

For why should ghosts feel angered?
  Let all their interference
    Be faint march-music in the air!
'Up! Join the rear of us the vanguard!
  Up, lovers, dead to all appearance,
    Laggard pair!'

XIV

The while you clasp me closer,
  The while I press you deeper,
    As safe we chuckle, – under breath,
Yet all the slyer, the jocoser, –
  'So, life can boast its day, like leap-year,
    Stolen from death!'

XV

Ah me – the sudden terror!
  Hence quick – avaunt, avoid me,
    You cheat, the ghostly flesh-disguised!
Nay, all the ghosts in one! Strange error!
  So, 'twas Death's self that clipped and coyed me,
    Loved – and lied!

XVI

Ay, dead loves are the potent!
  Like any cloud they used you,
    Mere semblance you, but substance they!
Build we no mansion, weave we no tent!
  Mere flesh – their spirit interfused you!
    Hence, I say!

XVII

All theirs, none yours the glamour!
  Theirs each low word that won me,
    Soft look that found me Love's, and left
What else but you – the tears and clamour
  That's all your very own! Undone me –
    Ghost-bereft!

Hervé Riel

I

On the sea and at the Hogue, sixteen hundred ninety-two,
  Did the English fight the French, – woe to France!
And, the thirty-first of May, helter-skelter through the blue,
Like a crowd of frightened porpoises a shoal of sharks pursue,
  Came crowding ship on ship to Saint-Malo on the Rance,
With the English fleet in view.

II

'Twas the squadron that escaped, with the victor in full chase;
  First and foremost of the drove, in his great ship, Damfreville;
    Close on him fled, great and small,
    Twenty-two good ships in all;
And they signalled to the place
'Help the winners of a race!
  Get us guidance, give us harbour, take us quick – or, quicker still,
  Here's the English can and will!'

III

Then the pilots of the place put out brisk and leapt on board;
  'Why, what hope or chance have ships like these to pass?' laughed they:
'Rocks to starboard, rocks to port, all the passage scarred and scored, –
Shall the "Formidable" here, with her twelve and eighty guns,
  Think to make the river-mouth by the single narrow way,
Trust to enter – where 'tis ticklish for a craft of twenty tons,
    And with flow at full beside?
    Now, 'tis slackest ebb of tide.
  Reach the mooring? Rather say,
While rock stands or water runs,
  Not a ship will leave the bay!'

IV

Then was called a council straight.
Brief and bitter the debate:
'Here's the English at our heels; would you have them take in tow

All that's left us of the fleet, linked together stern and bow,
For a prize to Plymouth Sound?
Better run the ships aground!'
(Ended Damfreville his speech).
'Not a minute more to wait!
Let the Captains all and each
Shove ashore, then blow up, burn the vessels on the beach!
France must undergo her fate.

V

'Give the word!' But no such word
Was ever spoke or heard;
For up stood, for out stepped, for in struck amid all these
– A Captain? A Lieutenant? A Mate – first, second, third?
No such man of mark, and meet
With his betters to compete!
But a simple Breton sailor pressed by Tourville for the fleet,
A poor coasting-pilot he, Hervé Riel the Croisickese.

VI

And 'What mockery or malice have we here?' cries Hervé Riel:
'Are you mad, you Malouins? Are you cowards, fools, or rogues?
Talk to me of rocks and shoals, me who took the soundings, tell
On my fingers every bank, every shallow, every swell
'Twixt the offing here and Grève where the river disembogues?
Are you bought by English gold? Is it love the lying's for?
Morn and eve, night and day,
Have I piloted your bay,
Entered free and anchored fast at the foot of Solidor.
Burn the fleet and ruin France? That were worse than fifty Hogues!
Sirs, they know I speak the truth! Sirs, believe me there's a way!
Only let me lead the line,
Have the biggest ship to steer,
Get this "Formidable" clear,
Make the others follow mine,
And I lead them, most and least, by a passage I know well,
Right to Solidor past Grève,
And there lay them safe and sound;

And if one ship misbehave, –
– Keel so much as grate the ground,
Why, I've nothing but my life, – here's my head!' cries Hervé Riel.

VII

Not a minute more to wait.
'Steer us in, then, small and great!
Take the helm, lead the line, save the squadron!' cried its chief.
Captains, give the sailor place!
He is Admiral, in brief.
Still the north-wind, by God's grace
See the noble fellow's face
As the big ship, with a bound,
Clears the entry like a hound,
Keeps the passage, as its inch of way were the wide sea's profound!
See, safe through shoal and rock,
How they follow in a flock,
Not a ship that misbehaves, not a keel that grates the ground,
Not a spar that comes to grief!
The peril, see, is past:
All are harboured to the last,
And just as Hervé Riel hollas 'Anchor!' – sure as fate,
Up the English come, – too late!

VIII

So, the storm subsides to calm:
They see the green trees wave
On the heights o'erlooking Grève.
Hearts that bled are stanched with balm.
'Just our rapture to enhance,
Let the English rake the bay,
Gnash their teeth and glare askance
As they cannonade away!
'Neath rampired Solidor pleasant riding on the Rance!'
How hope succeeds despair on each Captain's countenance!
Out burst all with one accord,
'This is Paradise for Hell!
Let France, let France's King
Thank the man that did the thing!'

What a shout, and all one word,
  'Hervé Riel!'
As he stepped in front once more,
  Not a symptom of surprise
  In the frank blue Breton eyes,
Just the same man as before.

IX

Then said Damfreville, 'My friend,
I must speak out at the end,
  Though I find the speaking hard.
Praise is deeper than the lips:
You have saved the King his ships,
  You must name your own reward.
'Faith, our sun was near eclipse!
Demand whate'er you will,
France remains your debtor still.
Ask to heart's content and have! or my name's not Damfreville.'

X

Then a beam of fun outbroke
On the bearded mouth that spoke,
As the honest heart laughed through
Those frank eyes of Breton blue:
'Since I needs must say my say,
  Since on board the duty's done,
  And from Malo Roads to Croisic Point, what is it but a run? –
Since 'tis ask and have, I may –
  Since the others go ashore –
Come! A good whole holiday!
  Leave to go and see my wife, whom I call the Belle Aurore!'
  That he asked and that he got, – nothing more.

XI

Name and deed alike are lost:
Not a pillar nor a post
  In his Croisic keeps alive the feat as it befell;
Not a head in white and black
On a single fishing-smack,
In memory of the man but for whom had gone to wrack
  All that France saved from the fight whence England bore the
    bell.

Go to Paris: rank on rank
  Search the heroes flung pell-mell
On the Louvre, face and flank!
  You shall look long enough ere you come to Hervé Riel.
So, for better and for worse,
Hervé Riel, accept my verse!
In my verse, Hervé Riel, do thou once more
Save the squadron, honour France, love thy wife the Belle
    Aurore!

A Forgiveness

I am indeed the personage you know.
As for my wife, – what happened long ago, –
You have a right to question me, as I
Am bound to answer.

('Son, a fit reply!'
The monk half spoke, half ground through his clenched teeth,
At the confession-grate I knelt beneath.)

Thus then all happened, Father! Power and place
I had as still I have. I ran life's race,
With the whole world to see, as only strains
His strength some athlete whose prodigious gains
Of good appal him: happy to excess, –
Work freely done should balance happiness
Fully enjoyed; and, since beneath my roof
Housed she who made home heaven, in heaven's behoof
I went forth every day, and all day long
Worked for the world. Look, how the labourer's song
Cheers him! Thus sang my soul, at each sharp throe
Of labouring flesh and blood – 'She loves me so!'

One day, perhaps such song so knit the nerve
That work grew play and vanished. 'I deserve
Haply my heaven an hour before the time!'
I laughed, as silverly the clockhouse-chime
Surprised me passing through the postern-gate
– Not the main entry where the menials wait

And wonder why the world's affairs allow
The master sudden leisure. That was how
I took the private garden-way for once.

Forth from the alcove, I saw start, ensconce
Himself behind the porphyry vase, a man.

My fancies in the natural order ran:
'A spy, – perhaps a foe in ambuscade, –
A thief, – more like, a sweetheart of some maid
Who pitched on the alcove for tryst perhaps.'

'Stand there!' I bid.

Whereat my man but wraps
His face the closelier with uplifted arm
Whereon the cloak lies, strikes in blind alarm
This and that pedestal as, – stretch and stoop, –
Now in, now out of sight, he thrids the group
Of statues, marble god and goddess ranged
Each side the pathway, till the gate's exchanged
For safety: one step thence, the street, you know!

Thus far I followed with my gaze. Then, slow,
Near on admiringly, I breathed again,
And – back to that last fancy of the train –
'A danger risked for hope of just a word
With – which of all my nest may be the bird
This poacher covets for her plumage, pray?
Carmen? Juana? Carmen seems too gay
For such adventure, while Juana's grave
– Would scorn the folly. I applaud the knave!
He had the eye, could single from my brood
His proper fledgeling!'

As I turned, there stood
In face of me, my wife stone-still stone-white.
Whether one bound had brought her, – at first sight
Of what she judged the encounter, sure to be
Next moment, of the venturous man and me, –
Brought her to clutch and keep me from my prey:
Whether impelled because her death no day

Could come so absolutely opportune
As now at joy's height, like a year in June
Stayed at the fall of its first ripened rose:
Or whether hungry for my hate – who knows? –
Eager to end an irksome lie, and taste
Our tingling true relation, hate embraced
By hate one naked moment: – anyhow
There stone-still stone-white stood my wife, but now
The woman who made heaven within my house.
Ay, she who faced me was my very spouse
As well as love – you are to recollect!

'Stay!' she said. 'Keep at least one soul unspecked
With crime, that's spotless hitherto – your own!
Kill me who court the blessing, who alone
Was, am, and shall be guilty, first to last!
The man lay helpless in the toils I cast
About him, helpless as the statue there
Against that strangling bell-flower's bondage: tear
Away and tread to dust the parasite,
But do the passive marble no despite!
I love him as I hate you. Kill me! Strike
At one blow both infinitudes alike
Out of existence – hate and love! Whence love?
That's safe inside my heart, nor will remove
For any searching of your steel, I think.
Whence hate? The secret lay on lip, at brink
Of speech, in one fierce tremble to escape,
At every form wherein your love took shape,
At each new provocation of your kiss.
Kill me!'

We went in.

Next day after this,
I felt as if the speech might come. I spoke –
Easily, after all.

'The lifted cloak
Was screen sufficient: I concern myself
Hardly with laying hands on who for pelf –
Whate'er the ignoble kind – may prowl and brave

Cuffing and kicking proper to a knave
Detected by my household's vigilance.
Enough of such! As for my love-romance –
I, like our good Hidalgo, rub my eyes
And wake and wonder how the film could rise
Which changed for me a barber's basin straight
Into – Mambrino's helm? I hesitate
Nowise to say – God's sacramental cup!
Why should I blame the brass which, burnished up,
Will blaze, to all but me, as good as gold?
To me – a warning I was overbold
In judging metals. The Hidalgo waked
Only to die, if I remember, – staked
His life upon the basin's worth, and lost:
While I confess torpidity at most
In here and there a limb; but, lame and halt,
Still should I work on, still repair my fault
Ere I took rest in death, – no fear at all!
Now, work – no word before the curtain fall!'

The 'curtain?' That of death on life, I meant:
My 'word,' permissible in death's event,
Would be – truth, soul to soul; for, otherwise,
Day by day, three years long, there had to rise
And, night by night, to fall upon our stage –
Ours, doomed to public play by heritage –
Another curtain, when the world, perforce
Our critical assembly, in due course
Came and went, witnessing, gave praise or blame
To art-mimetic. It had spoiled the game
If, suffered to set foot behind our scene,
The world had witnessed how stage-king and queen,
Gallant and lady, but a minute since
Enarming each the other, would evince
No sign of recognition as they took
His way and her way to whatever nook
Waited them in the darkness either side
Of that bright stage where lately groom and bride
Had fired the audience to a frenzy-fit
Of sympathetic rapture – every whit
Earned as the curtain fell on her and me,
– Actors. Three whole years, nothing was to see

But calm and concord; where a speech was due
There came the speech: when smiles were wanted too
Smiles were as ready. In a place like mine,
Where foreign and domestic cares combine,
There's audience every day and all day long;
But finally the last of the whole throng
Who linger lets one see his back. For her –
Why, liberty and liking: I aver,
Liking and liberty! For me – I breathed,
Let my face rest from every wrinkle wreathed
Smile-like about the mouth, unlearned my task
Of personation till next day bade mask,
And quietly betook me from that world
To the real world, not pageant: there unfurled
In work, its wings, my soul, the fretted power.
Three years I worked, each minute of each hour
Not claimed by acting: – work I may dispense
With talk about, since work in evidence,
Perhaps in history; who knows or cares?

After three years, this way, all unawares,
Our acting ended. She and I, at close
Of a loud night-feast, led, between two rows
Of bending male and female loyalty,
Our lord the king down staircase, while, held high
At arm's length did the twisted tapers' flare
Herald his passage from our palace, where
Such visiting left glory evermore.
Again the ascent in public, till at door
As we two stood by the saloon – now blank
And disencumbered of its guests – there sank
A whisper in my ear, so low and yet
So unmistakable!

'I half forget
The chamber you repair to, and I want
Occasion for one short word – if you grant
That grace – within a certain room you called
Our "Study," for you wrote there while I scrawled
Some paper full of faces for my sport.
That room I can remember. Just one short
Word with you there, for the remembrance' sake!'

'Follow me thither!' I replied.

We break
The gloom a little, as with guiding lamp
I lead the way, leave warmth and cheer, by damp
Blind disused serpentining ways afar
From where the habitable chambers are, –
Ascend, descend stairs tunnelled through the stone, –
Always in silence, – till I reach the lone
Chamber sepulchred for my very own
Out of the palace-quarry. When a boy,
Here was my fortress, stronghold from annoy,
Proof-positive of ownership; in youth
I garnered up my gleanings here – uncouth
But precious relics of vain hopes, vain fears;
Finally, this became in after years
My closet of entrenchment to withstand
Invasion of the foe on every hand –
The multifarious herd in bower and hall,
State-room, – rooms whatsoe'er the style, which call
On masters to be mindful that, before
Men, they must look like men and something more.
Here, – when our lord the king's bestowment ceased
To deck me on the day that, golden-fleeced,
I touched ambition's height, – 'twas here, released
From glory (always symbolled by a chain!)
No sooner was I privileged to gain
My secret domicile than glad I flung
That last toy on the table – gazed where hung
On hook my father's gift, the arquebus –
And asked myself 'Shall I envisage thus
The new prize and the old prize, when I reach
Another year's experience? – own that each
Equalled advantage – sportsman's – statesman's tool?
That brought me down an eagle, this – a fool!'

Into which room on entry, I set down
The lamp, and turning saw whose rustled gown
Had told me my wife followed, pace for pace.
Each of us looked the other in the face.
She spoke. 'Since I could die now . . .'

(To explain
Why that first struck me, know – not once again
Since the adventure at the porphyry's edge
Three years before, which sundered like a wedge
Her soul from mine, – though daily, smile to smile,
We stood before the public, – all the while
Not once had I distinguished, in that face
I paid observance to, the faintest trace
Of feature more than requisite for eyes
To do their duty by and recognize:
So did I force mine to obey my will
And pry no further. There exists such skill, –
Those know who need it. What physician shrinks
From needful contact with a corpse? He drinks
No plague so long as thirst for knowledge – not
An idler impulse – prompts inquiry. What,
And will you disbelieve in power to bid
Our spirit back to bounds, as though we chid
A child from scrutiny that's just and right
In manhood? Sense, not soul, accomplished sight,
Reported daily she it was – not how
Nor why a change had come to cheek and brow.)

'Since I could die now of the truth concealed,
Yet dare not, must not die – so seems revealed
The Virgin's mind to me – for death means peace,
Wherein no lawful part have I, whose lease
Of life and punishment the truth avowed
May haply lengthen, – let me push the shroud
Away, that steals to muffle ere is just
My penance-fire in snow! I dare – I must
Live, by avowal of the truth – this truth –
I loved you! Thanks for the fresh serpent's tooth
That, by a prompt new pang more exquisite
Than all preceding torture, proves me right!
I loved you yet I lost you! May I go
Burn to the ashes, now my shame you know?'

I think there never was such – how express? –
Horror coquetting with voluptuousness,
As in those arms of Eastern workmanship –
Yataghan, kandjar, things that rend and rip,

Gash rough, slash smooth, help hate so many ways,
Yet ever keep a beauty that betrays
Love still at work with the artificer
Throughout his quaint devising. Why prefer,
Except for love's sake, that a blade should writhe
And bicker like a flame? – now play the scythe
As if some broad neck tempted, – now contract
And needle off into a fineness lacked
For just that puncture which the heart demands?
Then, such adornment! Wherefore need our hands
Enclose not ivory alone, nor gold
Roughened for use, but jewels? Nay, behold!
Fancy my favourite – which I seem to grasp
While I describe the luxury. No asp
Is diapered more delicate round throat
Than this below the handle! These denote
– These mazy lines meandering, to end
Only in flesh they open – what intend
They else but water-purlings – pale contrast
With the life-crimson where they blend at last?
And mark the handle's dim pellucid green,
Carved, the hard jadestone, as you pinch a bean,
Into a sort of parrot-bird! He pecks
A grape-bunch; his two eyes are ruby-specks
Pure from the mine: seen this way, – glassy blank,
But turn them, – lo the inmost fire, that shrank
From sparkling, sends a red dart right to aim!
Why did I choose such toys? Perhaps the game
Of peaceful men is warlike, just as men
War-wearied get amusement from that pen
And paper we grow sick of – statesfolk tired
Of merely (when such measures are required)
Dealing out doom to people by three words,
A signature and seal: we play with swords
Suggestive of quick process. That is how
I came to like the toys described you now,
Store of which glittered on the walls and strewed
The table, even, while my wife pursued
Her purpose to its ending. 'Now you know
This shame, my three years' torture, let me go,
Burn to the very ashes! You – I lost,
Yet you – I loved!'

The thing I pity most
In men is – action prompted by surprise
Of anger: men? nay, bulls – whose onset lies
At instance of the firework and the goad!
Once the foe prostrate, – trampling once bestowed, –
Prompt follows placability, regret,
Atonement. Trust me, blood-warmth never yet
Betokened strong will! As no leap of pulse
Pricked me, that first time, so did none convulse
My veins at this occasion for resolve.
Had that devolved which did not then devolve
Upon me, I had done – what now to do
Was quietly apparent.

'Tell me who
The man was, crouching by the porphyry vase!'

'No, never! All was folly in his case,
All guilt in mine. I tempted, he complied.'

'And yet you loved me?'

'Loved you. Double-dyed
In folly and in guilt, I thought you gave
Your heart and soul away from me to slave
At statecraft. Since my right in you seemed lost,
I stung myself to teach you, to your cost,
What you rejected could be prized beyond
Life, heaven, by the first fool I threw a fond
Look on, a fatal word to.'

'And you still
Love me? Do I conjecture well or ill?'

'Conjecture – well or ill! I had three years
To spend in learning you.'

'We both are peers
In knowledge, therefore: since three years are spent
Ere thus much of yourself *I* learn – who went
Back to the house, that day, and brought my mind
To bear upon your action, uncombined

Motive from motive, till the dross, deprived
Of every purer particle, survived
At last in native simple hideousness,
Utter contemptibility, nor less
Nor more. Contemptibility – exempt
How could I, from its proper due – contempt?
I have too much despised you to divert
My life from its set course by help or hurt
Of your all-despicable life – perturb
The calm, I work in, by – men's mouths to curb,
Which at such news were clamorous enough –
Men's eyes to shut before my broidered stuff
With the huge hole there, my emblazoned wall
Blank where a scutcheon hung, – by, worse than all,
Each day's procession, my paraded life
Robbed and impoverished through the wanting wife
– Now that my life (which means – my work) was grown
Riches indeed! Once, just this worth alone
Seemed work to have, that profit gained thereby
Of good and praise would – how rewardingly! –
Fall at your feet, – a crown I hoped to cast
Before your love, my love should crown at last.
No love remaining to cast crown before,
My love stopped work now: but contempt the more
Impelled me task as ever head and hand,
Because the very fiends weave ropes of sand
Rather than taste pure hell in idleness.
Therefore I kept my memory down by stress
Of daily work I had no mind to stay
For the world's wonder at the wife away.
Oh, it was easy all of it, believe,
For I despised you! But your words retrieve
Importantly the past. No hate assumed
The mask of love at any time! There gloomed
A moment when love took hate's semblance, urged
By causes you declare; but love's self purged
Away a fancied wrong I did both loves
– Yours and my own: by no hate's help, it proves,
Purgation was attempted. Then, you rise
High by how many a grade! I did despise –
I do but hate you. Let hate's punishment
Replace contempt's! First step to which ascent –

Write down your own words I re-utter you!
"*I loved my husband and I hated – who*
He was, I took up as my first chance, mere
Mud-ball to fling and make love foul with!" Here
Lies paper!'

'Would my blood for ink suffice!'

'It may: this minion from a land of spice,
Silk, feather – every bird of jewelled breast –
This poignard's beauty, ne'er so lightly prest
Above your heart there...'

'Thus?'

'It flows, I see.
Dip there the point and write!'

'Dictate to me!
Nay, I remember.'

And she wrote the words.
I read them. Then – 'Since love, in you, affords
License for hate, in me, to quench (I say)
Contempt – why, hate itself has passed away
In vengeance – foreign to contempt. Depart
Peacefully to that death which Eastern art
Imbued this weapon with, if tales be true!
Love will succeed to hate. I pardon you –
Dead in our chamber!'

True as truth the tale.
She died ere morning; then, I saw how pale
Her cheek was ere it wore day's paint-disguise,
And what a hollow darkened 'neath her eyes,
Now that I used my own. She sleeps, as erst
Beloved, in this your church: ay, yours!

Immersed
In thought so deeply, Father? Sad, perhaps?
For whose sake, hers or mine or his who wraps
– Still plain I seem to see! – about his head

The idle cloak, – about his heart (instead
Of cuirass) some fond hope he may elude
My vengeance in the cloister's solitude?
Hardly, I think! As little helped his brow
The cloak then, Father – as your grate helps now!

Cenciaja

Ogni cencio vuol entrare in bucato. – *Italian Prover'*

May I print, Shelley, how it came to pass
That when your Beatrice seemed – by lapse
Of many a long month since her sentence fell –
Assured of pardon for the parricide, –
By intercession of staunch friends, or, say,
By certain pricks of conscience in the Pope
Conniver at Francesco Cenci's guilt, –
Suddenly all things changed and Clement grew
'Stern,' as you state, 'nor to be moved nor bent,
But said these three words coldly "*She must die*";
Subjoining "*Pardon? Paolo Santa Croce*
Murdered his mother also yestereve,
And he is fled: she shall not flee at least!"'
– So, to the letter, sentence was fulfilled?
Shelley, may I condense verbosity
That lies before me, into some few words
Of English, and illustrate your superb
Achievement by a rescued anecdote,
No great things, only new and true beside?
As if some mere familiar of a house
Should venture to accost the group at gaze
Before its Titian, famed the wide world through,
And supplement such pictured masterpiece
By whisper 'Searching in the archives here,
I found the reason of the Lady's fate,
And how by accident it came to pass
She wears the halo and displays the palm:
Who, haply, else had never suffered – no,
Nor graced our gallery, by consequence.'
Who loved the work would like the little news:

Who lauds your poem lends an ear to me
Relating how the penalty was paid
By one Marchese dell' Oriolo, called
Onofrio Santa Croce otherwise,
For his complicity in matricide
With Paolo his own brother, – he whose crime
And flight induced 'those three words – She must die.'
Thus I unroll you then the manuscript.

'God's justice' – (of the multiplicity
Of such communications extant still,
Recording, each, injustice done by God
In person of his Vicar-upon-earth,
Scarce one but leads off to the self-same tune) –
'God's justice, tardy though it prove perchance,
Rests never on the track until it reach
Delinquency. In proof I cite the case
Of Paolo Santa Croce.'

Many times
The youngster, – having been importunate
That Marchesine Costanza, who remained
His widowed mother, should supplant the heir
Her elder son, and substitute himself
In sole possession of her faculty, –
And meeting just as often with rebuff, –
Blinded by so exorbitant a lust
Of gold, the youngster straightway tasked his wits,
Casting about to kill the lady – thus.

He first, to cover his iniquity,
Writes to Onofrio Santa Croce, then
Authoritative lord, acquainting him
Their mother was contamination – wrought
Like hell-fire in the beauty of their House
By dissoluteness and abandonment
Of soul and body to impure delight.
Moreover, since she suffered from disease,
Those symptoms which her death made manifest
Hydroptic, he affirmed were fruits of sin
About to bring confusion and disgrace

Upon the ancient lineage and high fame
O' the family, when published. Duty bound,
He asked his brother – what a son should do?

Which when Marchese dell' Oriolo heard
By letter, being absent at his land
Oriolo, he made answer, this, no more:
'It must behove a son, – things haply so, –
To act as honour prompts a cavalier
And son, perform his duty to all three,
Mother and brothers' – here advice broke off.

By which advice informed and fortified,
As he professed himself – since bound by birth
To hear God's voice in primogeniture –
Paolo, who kept his mother company
In her domain Subiaco, straightway dared
His whole enormity of enterprise
And, falling on her, stabbed the lady dead;
Whose death demónstrated her innocence,
And happened, – by the way, – since Jesus Christ
Died to save man, just sixteen hundred years.
Costanza was of aspect beautiful
Exceedingly, and seemed, although in age
Sixty about, to far surpass her peers
The coetaneous dames, in youth and grace.

Done the misdeed, its author takes to flight,
Foiling thereby the justice of the world:
Not God's however, – God, be sure, knows well
The way to clutch a culprit. Witness here!
The present sinner, when he least expects,
Snug-cornered somewhere i' the Basilicate,
Stumbles upon his death by violence.
A man of blood assaults a man of blood
And slays him somehow. This was afterward:
Enough, he promptly met with his deserts,
And, ending thus, permits we end with him,
And push forthwith to this important point –
His matricide fell out, of all the days,
Precisely when the law-procedure closed

Respecting Count Francesco Cenci's death
Chargeable on his daughter, sons and wife.
'Thus patricide was matched with matricide,'
A poet not inelegantly rhymed:
Nay, fratricide – those Princes Massimi! –
Which so disturbed the spirit of the Pope
That all the likelihood Rome entertained
Of Beatrice's pardon vanished straight,
And she endured the piteous death.

Now see
The sequel – what effect commandment had
For strict inquiry into this last case,
When Cardinal Aldobrandini (great
His efficacy – nephew to the Pope)
Was bidden crush – ay, though his very hand
Got soil i' the act – crime spawning everywhere!
Because, when all endeavour had been used
To catch the aforesaid Paolo, all in vain –
'Make perquisition' quoth our Eminence,
'Throughout his now deserted domicile!
Ransack the palace, roof and floor, to find
If haply any scrap of writing, hid
In nook or corner, may convict – who knows? –
Brother Onofrio of intelligence
With brother Paolo, as in brotherhood
Is but too likely: crime spawns everywhere.'

And, every cranny searched accordingly,
There comes to light – O lynx-eyed Cardinal! –
Onofrio's unconsidered writing-scrap,
The letter in reply to Paolo's prayer,
The word of counsel that – things proving so,
Paolo should act the proper knightly part,
And do as was incumbent on a son,
A brother – and a man of birth, be sure!

Whereat immediately the officers
Proceeded to arrest Onofrio – found
At foot-ball, child's play, unaware of harm,
Safe with his friends, the Orsini, at their seat
Monte Giordano; as he left the house

He came upon the watch in wait for him
Set by the Barigel, – was caught and caged.

News of which capture being, that same hour,
Conveyed to Rome, forthwith our Eminence
Commands Taverna, Governor and Judge,
To have the process in especial care,
Be, first to last, not only president
In person, but inquisitor as well,
Nor trust the by-work to a substitute:
Bids him not, squeamish, keep the bench, but scrub
The floor of Justice, so to speak, – go try
His best in prison with the criminal:
Promising, as reward for by-work done
Fairly on all-fours, that, success obtained
And crime avowed, or such connivency
With crime as should procure a decent death –
Himself will humbly beg – which means, procure –
The Hat and Purple from his relative
The Pope, and so repay a diligence
Which, meritorious in the Cenci-case,
Mounts plainly here to Purple and the Hat.

Whereupon did my lord the Governor
So masterfully exercise the task
Enjoined him, that he, day by day, and week
By week, and month by month, from first to last
Toiled for the prize: now, punctual at his place,
Played Judge, and now, assiduous at his post,
Inquisitor – pressed cushion and scoured plank,
Early and late. Noon's fervour and night's chill,
Naught moved whom morn would, purpling, make amends!
So that observers laughed as, many a day,
He left home, in July when day is flame,
Posted to Tordinona-prison, plunged
Into a vault where daylong night is ice,
There passed his eight hours on a stretch, content,
Examining Onofrio: all the stress
Of all examination steadily
Converging into one pin-point, – he pushed
Tentative now of head and now of heart.
As when the nuthatch taps and tries the nut

This side and that side till the kernel sound, –
So did he press the sole and single point
– What was the very meaning of the phrase
'*Do as beseems an honoured cavalier*'?

Which one persistent question-torture, – plied
Day by day, week by week, and month by month,
Morn, noon and night, – fatigued away a mind
Grown imbecile by darkness, solitude,
And one vivacious memory gnawing there
As when a corpse is coffined with a snake:
– Fatigued Onofrio into what might seem
Admission that perchance his judgement groped
So blindly, feeling for an issue – aught
With semblance of an issue from the toils
Cast of a sudden round feet late so free,
He possibly might have envisaged, scarce
Recoiled from – even were the issue death
– Even her death whose life was death and worse!
Always provided that the charge of crime,
Each jot and tittle of the charge were true.
In such a sense, belike, he might advise
His brother to expurgate crime with . . . well,
With blood, if blood must follow on '*the course
Taken as might beseem a cavalier.*'

Whereupon process ended, and report
Was made without a minute of delay
To Clement who, because of those two crimes
O' the Massimi and Cenci flagrant late,
Must needs impatiently desire result.

Result obtained, he bade the Governor
Summon the Congregation and dispatch.
Summons made, sentence passed accordingly
– Death by beheading. When his death-decree
Was intimated to Onofrio, all
Man could do – that did he to save himself.
'Twas much, the having gained for his defence
The Advocate o' the Poor, with natural help
Of many noble friendly persons fain
To disengage a man of family,

So young too, from his grim entanglement:
But Cardinal Aldobrandini ruled
There must be no diversion of the law.
Justice is justice, and the magistrate
Bears not the sword in vain. Who sins must die.

So, the Marchese had his head cut off,
With Rome to see, a concourse infinite,
In Place Saint Angelo beside the Bridge:
Where, demonstrating magnanimity
Adequate to his birth and breed, – poor boy! –
He made the people the accustomed speech,
Exhorted them to true faith, honest works,
And special good behaviour as regards
A parent of no matter what the sex,
Bidding each son take warning from himself.
Truly, it was considered in the boy
Stark staring lunacy, no less, to snap
So plain a bait, be hooked and hauled ashore
By such an angler as the Cardinal!
Why make confession of his privity
To Paolo's enterprise? Mere sealing lips –
Or, better, saying 'When I counselled him
"*To do as might beseem a cavalier,*"
What could I mean but "*Hide our parent's shame*
As Christian ought, by aid of Holy Church!
Bury it in a convent – ay, beneath
Enough dotation to prevent its ghost
From troubling earth!"' Mere saying thus, – 'tis plain,
Not only were his life the recompense,
But he had manifestly proved himself
True Christian, and in lieu of punishment
Got praise of all men. So the populace.

Anyhow, when the Pope made promise good
(That of Aldobrandini, near and dear)
And gave Taverna, who had toiled so much,
A Cardinal's equipment, some such word
As this from mouth to ear went saucily:
'Taverna's cap is dyed in what he drew
From Santa Croce's veins!' So joked the world.

I add: Onofrio left one child behind,
A daughter named Valeria, dowered with grace
Abundantly of soul and body, doomed
To life the shorter for her father's fate.
By death of her, the Marquisate returned
To that Orsini House from whence it came:
Oriolo having passed as donative
To Santa Croce from their ancestors.

And no word more? By all means! Would you know
The authoritative answer, when folk urged
'What made Aldobrandini, hound-like staunch,
Hunt out of life a harmless simpleton?'
The answer was – 'Hatred implacable,
By reason they were rivals in their love.'
The Cardinal's desire was to a dame
Whose favour was Onofrio's. Pricked with pride,
The simpleton must ostentatiously
Display a ring, the Cardinal's love-gift,
Given to Onofrio as the lady's gage;
Which ring on finger, as he put forth hand
To draw a tapestry, the Cardinal
Saw and knew, gift and owner, old and young;
Whereon a fury entered him – the fire
He quenched with what could quench fire only – blood.
Nay, more: 'there want not who affirm to boot,
The unwise boy, a certain festal eve,
Feigned ignorance of who the wight might be
That pressed too closely on him with a crowd.
He struck the Cardinal a blow: and then,
To put a face upon the incident,
Dared next day, smug as ever, go pay court
I' the Cardinal's antechamber. Mark and mend,
Ye youth, by this example how may greed
Vainglorious operate in worldly souls!'

So ends the chronicler, beginning with
'God's justice, tardy though it prove perchance,
Rests never till it reach delinquency.'
Ay, or how otherwise had come to pass
That Victor rules, this present year, in Rome?

Filippo Baldinucci on the Privilege of Burial

A Reminiscence of A.D. 1676

I

'No, boy, we must not' – so began
  My Uncle (he's with God long since)
A-petting me, the good old man!
  'We must not' – and he seemed to wince,
And lost that laugh whereto had grown
  His chuckle at my piece of news,
How cleverly I aimed my stone –
  'I fear we must not pelt the Jews!

II

'When I was young indeed, – ah, faith
  Was young and strong in Florence too!
We Christians never dreamed of scathe
  Because we cursed or kicked the crew.
But now – well, well! The olive-crops
  Weighed double then, and Arno's pranks
Would always spare religious shops
  Whenever he o'erflowed his banks!

III

'I'll tell you' – and his eye regained
  Its twinkle – 'tell you something choice!
Something may help you keep unstained
  Your honest zeal to stop the voice
Of unbelief with stone-throw – spite
  Of laws, which modern fools enact,
That we must suffer Jews in sight
  Go wholly unmolested! Fact!

IV

'There was, then, in my youth, and yet
  Is, by our San Frediano, just
Below the Blessed Olivet,
  A wayside ground wherein they thrust
Their dead, – these Jews, – the more our shame!
  Except that, so they will but die,

Christians perchance incur no blame
  In giving hogs a hoist to sty.

V

'There, anyhow, Jews stow away
  Their dead; and, – such their insolence, –
Slink at odd times to sing and pray
  As Christians do – all make-pretence! –
Which wickedness they perpetrate
  Because they think no Christians see.
They reckoned here, at any rate,
  Without their host: ha, ha, he, he!

VI

'For, what should join their plot of ground
  But a good Farmer's Christian field?
The Jews had hedged their corner round
  With bramble-bush to keep concealed
Their doings: for the public road
  Ran betwixt this their ground and that
The Farmer's, where he ploughed and sowed,
  Grew corn for barn and grapes for vat.

VII

'So, properly to guard his store
  And gall the unbelievers too,
He builds a shrine and, what is more,
  Procures a painter whom I knew,
One Buti (he's with God) to paint
  A holy picture there – no less
Than Virgin Mary free from taint
  Borne to the sky by angels: yes!

VIII

'Which shrine he fixed, – who says him nay? –
  A-facing with its picture-side
Not, as you'd think, the public way,
  But just where sought these hounds to hide
Their carrion from that very truth
  Of Mary's triumph: not a hound
Could act his mummeries uncouth
  But Mary shamed the pack all round!

IX

'Now, if it was amusing, judge!
 – To see the company arrive,
Each Jew intent to end his trudge
 And take his pleasure (though alive)
With all his Jewish kith and kin
 Below ground, have his venom out,
Sharpen his wits for next day's sin,
 Curse Christians, and so home, no doubt!

X

'Whereas, each phyz upturned beholds
 Mary, I warrant, soaring brave!
And in a trice, beneath the folds
 Of filthy garb which gowns each knave,
Down drops it – there to hide grimace,
 Contortion of the mouth and nose
At finding Mary in the place
 They'd keep for Pilate, I suppose!

XI

'At last, they will not brook – not they! –
 Longer such outrage on their tribe:
So, in some hole and corner, lay
 Their heads together – how to bribe
The meritorious Farmer's self
 To straight undo his work, restore
Their chance to meet and muse on pelf –
 Pretending sorrow, as before!

XII

'Forthwith, a posse, if you please,
 Of Rabbi This and Rabbi That
Almost go down upon their knees
 To get him lay the picture flat.
The spokesman, eighty years of age,
 Grey as a badger, with a goat's
Not only beard but bleat, 'gins wage
 War with our Mary. Thus he dotes: –

XIII

'"*Friends, grant a grace! How Hebrews toil*
Through life in Florence – why relate
To those who lay the burden, spoil
Our paths of peace? We bear our fate.
But when with life the long toil ends,
Why must you – the expression craves
Pardon, but truth compels me, friends! –
Why must you plague us in our graves?

XIV

'"*Thoughtlessly plague, I would believe!*
For how can you – the lords of ease
By nurture, birthright – e'en conceive
Our luxury to lie with trees
And turf, – the cricket and the bird
Left for our last companionship:
No harsh deed, no unkindly word,
No frowning brow nor scornful lip!

XV

'"*Death's luxury, we now rehearse*
While, living, through your streets we fare
And take your hatred: nothing worse
Have we, once dead and safe, to bear!
So we refresh our souls, fulfil
Our works, our daily tasks; and thus
Gather you grain – earth's harvest – still
The wheat for you, the straw for us.

XVI

'"'What flouting in a face, what harm,
In just a lady borne from bier
By boys' heads, wings for leg and arm?'
You question. Friends, the harm is here –
That just when our last sigh is heaved,
And we would fain thank God and you
For labour done and peace achieved,
Back comes the Past in full review!

XVII
'"*At sight of just that simple flag,*
Starts the foe-feeling serpent-like
From slumber. Leave it lulled, nor drag –
Though fangless – forth, what needs must strike
When stricken sore, though stroke be vain
Against the mailed oppressor! Give
Play to our fancy that we gain
Life's rights when once we cease to live!

XVIII
'"*Thus much to courtesy, to kind,*
To conscience! Now to Florence folk!
There's core beneath this apple-rind,
Beneath this white-of-egg there's yolk!
Beneath this prayer to courtesy,
Kind, conscience – there's a sum to pouch!
How many ducats down will buy
Our shame's removal, sirs? Avouch!

XIX
'"*Removal, not destruction, sirs!*
Just turn your picture! Let it front
The public path! Or memory errs,
Or that same public path is wont
To witness many a chance befall
Of lust, theft, bloodshed – sins enough,
Wherein our Hebrew part is small.
Convert yourselves!" – he cut up rough.

XX
'Look you, how soon a service paid
Religion yields the servant fruit!
A prompt reply our Farmer made
So following: "*Sirs, to grant your suit*
Involves much danger! How? Transpose
Our Lady? Stop the chastisement,
All for your good, herself bestows?
What wonder if I grudge consent?

XXI

'" – *Yet grant it: since, what cash I take*
Is so much saved from wicked use.
We know you! And, for Mary's sake,
A hundred ducats shall induce
Concession to your prayer. One day
Suffices: Master Buti's brush
Turns Mary round the other way,
And deluges your side with slush.

XXII

'"*Down with the ducats therefore!*" Dump,
Dump, dump it falls, each counted piece,
Hard gold. Then out of door they stump,
These dogs, each brisk as with new lease
Of life, I warrant, – glad he'll die
Henceforward just as he may choose,
Be buried and in clover lie!
Well said Esaias – "*stiff-necked Jews!*"

XXIII

'Off posts without a minute's loss
Our Farmer, once the cash in poke
And summons Buti – ere its gloss
Have time to fade from off the joke –
To chop and change his work, undo
The done side, make the side, now blank,
Recipient of our Lady – who,
Displaced thus, had these dogs to thank!

XXIV

'Now, boy, you're hardly to instruct
In technicalities of Art!
My nephew's childhood sure has sucked
Along with mother's-milk some part
Of painter's-practice – learned, at least,
How expeditiously is plied
A work in fresco – never ceased
When once begun – a day, each side.

XXV

'So, Buti – (he's with God) – begins:
  First covers up the shrine all round
With hoarding; then, as like as twins,
  Paints, t'other side the burial-ground,
New Mary, every point the same;
  Next, sluices over, as agreed,
The old; and last – but, spoil the game
  By telling you? Not I, indeed!

XXVI

'Well, ere the week was half at end,
  Out came the object of this zeal,
This fine alacrity to spend
  Hard money for mere dead men's weal!
How think you? That old spokesman Jew
  Was High Priest, and he had a wife
As old, and she was dying too,
  And wished to end in peace her life!

XXVII

'And he must humour dying whims,
  And soothe her with the idle hope
They'd say their prayers and sing their hymns
  As if her husband were the Pope!
And she did die – believing just
  This privilege was purchased! Dead
In comfort through her foolish trust!
  "*Stiff-necked ones,*" well Esaias said!

XXVIII

'So, Sabbath morning, out of gate
  And on to way, what sees our arch
Good Farmer? Why, they hoist their freight –
  The corpse – on shoulder, and so, march!
"*Now for it, Buti!*" In the nick
  Of time 'tis pully-hauly, hence
With hoarding! O'er the wayside quick
  There's Mary plain in evidence!

XXIX

'And here's the convoy halting: right!
O they are bent on howling psalms
And growling prayers, when opposite!
And yet they glance, for all their qualms,
Approve that promptitude of his,
The Farmer's – duly at his post
To take due thanks from every phyz,
Sour smirk – nay, surly smile almost!

XXX

'Then earthward drops each brow again;
The solemn task's resumed; they reach
Their holy field – the unholy train:
Enter its precinct, all and each,
Wrapt somehow in their godless rites;
Till, rites at end, up-waking, lo
They lift their faces! What delights
The mourners as they turn to go?

XXXI

'Ha, ha, he, he! On just the side
They drew their purse-strings to make quit
Of Mary, – Christ the Crucified
Fronted them now – these biters bit!
Never was such a hiss and snort,
Such screwing nose and shooting lip!
Their purchase – honey in report –
Proved gall and verjuice at first sip!

XXXII

'Out they break, on they bustle, where,
A-top of wall, the Farmer waits
With Buti: never fun so rare!
The Farmer has the best: he rates
The rascal, as the old High Priest
Takes on himself to sermonize –
Nay, sneer "*We Jews supposed, at least,
Theft was a crime in Christian eyes!*"

XXXIII

'"*Theft?*" cries the Farmer. "*Eat your words!*
Show me what constitutes a breach
Of faith in aught was said or heard!
I promised you in plainest speech
I'd take the thing you count disgrace
And put it here – and here 'tis put!
Did you suppose I'd leave the place
Blank, therefore, just your rage to glut?

XXXIV

'"*I guess you dared not stipulate*
For such a damned impertinence!
So, quick, my greybeard, out of gate
And in at Ghetto! Haste you hence!
As long as I have house and land,
To spite you irreligious chaps
Here shall the Crucifixion stand –
Unless you down with cash, perhaps!"

XXXV

'So snickered he and Buti both.
The Jews said nothing, interchanged
A glance or two, renewed their oath
To keep ears stopped and hearts estranged
From grace, for all our Church can do;
Then off they scuttle: sullen jog
Homewards, against our Church to brew
Fresh mischief in their synagogue.

XXXVI

'But next day – see what happened, boy!
See why I bid you have a care
How you pelt Jews! The knaves employ
Such methods of revenge, forbear
No outrage on our faith, when free
To wreak their malice! Here they took
So base a method – plague o' me
If I record it in my Book!

XXXVII

'For, next day, while the Farmer sat
Laughing with Buti, in his shop,
At their successful joke, – rat-tat, –
Door opens, and they're like to drop
Down to the floor as in there stalks
A six-feet-high herculean-built
Young he-Jew with a beard that balks
Description. "*Help ere blood be spilt!*"

XXXVIII

– 'Screamed Buti: for he recognized
Whom but the son, no less no more,
Of that High Priest his work surprised
So pleasantly the day before!
Son of the mother, then, whereof
The bier he lent a shoulder to,
And made the moans about, dared scoff
At sober Christian grief – the Jew!

XXXIX

'"*Sirs, I salute you! Never rise!*
No apprehension!" (Buti, white
And trembling like a tub of size,
Had tried to smuggle out of sight
The picture's self – the thing in oils,
You know, from which a fresco's dashed
Which courage speeds while caution spoils)
"*Stay and be praised, sir, unabashed!*

XL

'"*Praised, – ay, and paid too: for I come*
To buy that very work of yours.
My poor abode, which boasts – well, some
Few specimens of Art, secures
Haply, a masterpiece indeed
If I should find my humble means
Suffice the outlay. So, proceed!
Propose – ere prudence intervenes!"

XLI

'On Buti, cowering like a child,
These words descended from aloft,
In tone so ominously mild,
With smile terrifically soft
To that degree – could Buti dare
(Poor fellow) use his brains, think twice?
He asked, thus taken unaware,
No more than just the proper price!

XLII

'"*Done!*" cries the monster. "*I disburse
Forthwith your moderate demand.
Count on my custom – if no worse
Your future work be, understand,
Than this I carry off! No aid!
My arm, sir, lacks nor bone nor thews:
The burden's easy, and we're made,
Easy or hard, to bear – we Jews!*"

XLIII

'Crossing himself at such escape,
Buti by turns the money eyes
And, timidly, the stalwart shape
Now moving doorwards; but, more wise,
The Farmer, – who, though dumb, this while
Had watched advantage, – straight conceived
A reason for that tone and smile
So mild and soft! The Jew – believed!

XLIV

'Mary in triumph borne to deck
A Hebrew household! Pictured where
No one was used to bend the neck
In praise or bow the knee in prayer!
Borne to that domicile by whom?
The son of the High Priest! Through what?
An insult done his mother's tomb!
Saul changed to Paul – the case came pat!

XLV

'"*Stay, dog-Jew . . . gentle sir, that is!*
Resolve me! Can it be, she crowned, –
Mary, by miracle, – Oh bliss! –
My present to your burial ground?
Certain, a ray of light has burst
Your veil of darkness! Had you else,
Only for Mary's sake, unpursed
So much hard money? Tell – oh, tell's!"

XLVI

'Round – like a serpent that we took
For worm and trod on – turns his bulk
About the Jew. First dreadful look
Sends Buti in a trice to skulk
Out of sight somewhere, safe – alack!
But our good Farmer faith made bold:
And firm (with Florence at his back)
He stood, while gruff the gutturals rolled –

XLVII

'"*Ay, sir, a miracle was worked,*
By quite another power, I trow,
Than ever yet in canvas lurked,
Or you would scarcely face me now!
A certain impulse did suggest
A certain grasp with this right-hand,
Which probably had put to rest
Our quarrel, – thus your throat once spanned!

XLVIII

'"*But I remembered me, subdued*
That impulse, and you face me still!
And soon a philosophic mood
Succeeding (hear it, if you will!)
Has altogether changed my views
Concerning Art. Blind prejudice!
Well may you Christians tax us Jews
With scrupulosity too nice!

XLIX

'"*For, don't I see, – let's issue join! –*
   Whenever I'm allowed pollute
(I – and my little bag of coin)
   Some Christian palace of repute, –
Don't I see stuck up everywhere
   Abundant proof that cultured taste
Has Beauty for its only care,
   And upon Truth no thought to waste?

L

'"'Jew, since it must be, take in pledge
   Of payment' – *so a Cardinal*
Has sighed to me as if a wedge
   Entered his heart – 'this best of all
My treasures!' *Leda, Ganymede*
   Or Antiope: swan, eagle, ape,
(Or what's the beast of what's the breed)
   And Jupiter in every shape!

LI

'"*Whereat if I presume to ask*
   'But, Eminence, though Titian's whisk
Of brush have well performed its task,
   How comes it these false godships frisk
In presence of – what yonder frame
   Pretends to image? Surely, odd
It seems, you let confront The Name
   Each beast the heathen called his god!'

LII

'"*Benignant smiles me pity straight*
   The Cardinal. ''Tis Truth, we prize!
Art's the sole question in debate!
   These subjects are so many lies.
We treat them with a proper scorn
   When we turn lies – called gods forsooth –
To lies' fit use, now Christ is born.
   Drawing and colouring are Truth.

LIII

"''Think you I honour lies so much
 As scruple to parade the charms
Of Leda – Titian, every touch –
 Because the thing within her arms
Means Jupiter who had the praise
 And prayer of a benighted world?
He would have mine too, if, in days
 Of light, I kept the canvas furled!'

LIV

'"*So ending, with some easy gibe.*
 What power has logic! I, at once,
Acknowledged error in our tribe
 So squeamish that, when friends ensconce
A pretty picture in its niche
 To do us honour, deck our graves,
We fret and fume and have an itch
 To strangle folk – ungrateful knaves!

LV

'"*No, sir! Be sure that – what's its style,*
 Your picture? – shall possess ungrudged
A place among my rank and file
 Of Ledas and what not – be judged
Just as a picture! and (because
 I fear me much I scarce have bought
A Titian) Master Buti's flaws
 Found there, will have the laugh flaws ought!"

LVI

'So, with a scowl, it darkens door –
 This bulk – no longer! Buti makes
Prompt glad re-entry; there's a score
 Of oaths, as the good Farmer wakes
From what must needs have been a trance,
 Or he had struck (he swears) to ground
The bold bad mouth that dared advance
 Such doctrine the reverse of sound!

LVII
'Was magic here? Most like! For, since,
Somehow our city's faith grows still
More and more lukewarm, and our Prince
Or loses heart or wants the will
To check increase of cold. 'Tis "*Live*
And let live! Languidly repress
The Dissident! In short, – contrive
Christians must bear with Jews: no less!"

LVIII
'The end seems, any Israelite
Wants any picture, – pishes, poohs,
Purchases, hangs it full in sight
In any chamber he may choose!
In Christ's crown, one more thorn we rue!
In Mary's bosom, one more sword!
No, boy, you must not pelt a Jew!
O Lord, how long? How long, O Lord?'

Epilogue

μεστοὶ . .
οἱ δ' ἀμφορῆς οἴνου μέλανος ἀνθοσμίου.

I
'The poets pour us wine –'
Said the dearest poet I ever knew,
Dearest and greatest and best to me.
You clamour athirst for poetry –
We pour. 'But when shall a vintage be'–
You cry – 'strong grape, squeezed gold from screw,
Yet sweet juice, flavoured flowery-fine?
That were indeed the wine!'

II
One pours your cup – stark strength,
Meat for a man; and you eye the pulp
Strained, turbid still, from the viscous blood
Of the snaky bough: and you grumble 'Good!

For it swells resolve, breeds hardihood;
   Dispatch it, then, in a single gulp!'
So, down, with a wry face, goes at length
The liquor: stuff for strength.

III

One pours your cup – sheer sweet,
   The fragrant fumes of a year condensed:
Suspicion of all that's ripe or rathe,
From the bud on branch to the grass in swathe.
'We suck mere milk of the seasons,' saith
   A curl of each nostril – 'dew, dispensed
Nowise for nerving man to feat:
Boys sip such honeyed sweet!'

IV

And thus who wants wine strong,
   Waves each sweet smell of the year away;
Who likes to swoon as the sweets suffuse
His brain with a mixture of beams and dews
Turned syrupy drink – rough strength eschews:
   'What though in our veins your wine-stock stay?
The lack of the bloom does our palate wrong.
Give us wine sweet, not strong!'

V

Yet wine is – some affirm –
   Prime wine is found in the world somewhere,
Of potable strength with sweet to match.
You double your heart its dose, yet catch –
As the draught descends – a violet-smatch,
   Softness – however it came there,
Through drops expressed by the fire and worm:
Strong sweet wine – some affirm.

VI

Body and bouquet both?
   'Tis easy to ticket a bottle so;
But what was the case in the cask, my friends?
Cask? Nay, the vat – where the maker mends
His strong with his sweet (you suppose) and blends
   His rough with his smooth, till none can know

How it comes you may tipple, nothing loth,
Body and bouquet both.

VII
'You' being just – the world.
No poets – who turn, themselves, the winch
Of the press; no critics – I'll even say,
(Being flustered and easy of faith today)
Who for love of the work have learned the way
Till themselves produce home-made, at a pinch:
No! You are the world, and wine ne'er purled
Except to please the world!

VIII
'For, oh the common heart!
And, ah the irremissible sin
Of poets who please themselves, not us!
Strong wine yet sweet wine pouring thus,
How please still – Pindar and Aeschylus! –
Drink – dipt into by the bearded chin
Alike and the bloomy lip – no part
Denied the common heart!

IX
'And might we get such grace,
And did you moderns but stock our vault
With the true half-brandy half-attar-gul,
How would seniors indulge at a hearty pull
While juniors tossed off their thimbleful!
Our Shakespeare and Milton escaped your fault,
So, they reign supreme o'er the weaker race
That wants the ancient grace!'

X
If I paid myself with words
(As the French say well) I were dupe indeed!
I were found in belief that you quaffed and bowsed
At your Shakespeare the whole day long, caroused
In your Milton pottle-deep nor drowsed
A moment of night – toped on, took heed
Of nothing like modern cream-and-curds.
Pay me with deeds, not words!

XI

For – see your cellarage!
  There are forty barrels with Shakespeare's brand.
Some five or six are abroach: the rest
Stand spigoted, fauceted. Try and test
What yourselves call best of the very best!
  How comes it that still untouched they stand?
Why don't you try tap, advance a stage
With the rest in cellarage?

XII

For – see your cellarage!
  There are four big butts of Milton's brew.
How comes it you make old drips and drops
Do duty, and there devotion stops?
Leave such an abyss of malt and hops
  Embellied in butts which bungs still glue?
You hate your bard! A fig for your rage!
Free him from cellarage!

XIII

'Tis said I brew stiff drink,
  But the deuce a flavour of grape is there.
Hardly a May-go-down, 'tis just
A sort of a gruff Go-down-it-must –
No Merry-go-down, no gracious gust
  Commingles the racy with Springtide's rare!
'What wonder,' say you 'that we cough, and blink
At Autumn's heady drink?'

XIV

Is it a fancy, friends?
  Mighty and mellow are never mixed,
Though mighty and mellow be born at once.
Sweet for the future, – strong for the nonce!
Stuff you should stow away, ensconce
  In the deep and dark, to be found fast-fixed
At the century's close: such time strength spends
A-sweetening for my friends!

XV

And then – why, what you quaff
  With a smack of lip and a cluck of tongue,
Is leakage and leavings – just what haps
From the tun some learned taster taps
With a promise 'Prepare your watery chaps!
  Here's properest wine for old and young!
Dispute its perfection – you make us laugh!
Have faith, give thanks, but – quaff!'

XVI

Leakage, I say, or – worse –
  Leavings suffice pot-valiant souls.
Somebody, brimful, long ago,
Frothed flagon he drained to the dregs; and lo,
Down whisker and beard what an overflow!
  Lick spilth that has trickled from classic jowls,
Sup the single scene, sip the only verse –
Old wine, not new and worse!

XVII

I grant you: worse by much!
  Renounce that new where you never gained
One glow at heart, one gleam at head,
And stick to the warrant of age instead!
No dwarf's-lap! Fatten, by giants fed!
  You fatten, with oceans of drink undrained?
You feed – who would choke did a cobweb smutch
The Age you love so much?

XVIII

A mine's beneath a moor:
  Acres of moor roof fathoms of mine
Which diamonds dot where you please to dig;
Yet who plies spade for the bright and big?
Your product is – truffles, you hunt with a pig!
  Since bright-and-big, when a man would dine,
Suits badly: and therefore the Koh-i-noor
May sleep in mine 'neath moor!

XIX

Wine, pulse in might from me!
It may never emerge in must from vat,
Never fill cask nor furnish can,
Never end sweet, which strong began –
God's gift to gladden the heart of man;
But spirit's at proof, I promise that!
No sparing of juice spoils what should be
Fit brewage – mine for me.

XX

Man's thoughts and loves and hates!
Earth is my vineyard, these grew there:
From grape of the ground, I made or marred
My vintage; easy the task or hard,
Who set it – his praise be my reward!
Earth's yield! Who yearn for the Dark Blue Sea's,
Let them 'lay, pray, bray' – the addle-pates!
Mine be Man's thoughts, loves, hates!

XXI

But someone says 'Good Sir!'
('Tis a worthy versed in what concerns
The making such labour turn out well)
'You don't suppose that the nosegay-smell
Needs always come from the grape? Each bell
At your foot, each bud that your culture spurns,
The very cowslip would act like myrrh
On the stiffest brew – good Sir!

XXII

'Cowslips, abundant birth
O'er meadow and hillside, vineyard too,
– Like a schoolboy's scrawlings in and out
Distasteful lesson-book – all about
Greece and Rome, victory and rout –
Love-verses instead of such vain ado!
So, fancies frolic it o'er the earth
Where thoughts have rightlier birth.

XXIII
'Nay, thoughtlings they themselves:
   Loves, hates – in little and less and least!
Thoughts? "*What is a man beside a mount!*"
Loves? "*Absent – poor lovers the minutes count!*"
Hates? "*Fie – Pope's letters to Martha Blount!*"
   These furnish a wine for a children's-feast:
Insipid to man, they suit the elves
Like thoughts, loves, hates themselves.'

XXIV
And, friends, beyond dispute
   I too have the cowslips dewy and dear.
Punctual as Springtide forth peep they:
I leave them to make my meadow gay.
But I ought to pluck and impound them, eh?
   Not let them alone, but deftly shear
And shred and reduce to – what may suit
Children, beyond dispute?

XXV
And, here's May-month, all bloom,
   All bounty: what if I sacrifice?
If I out with shears and shear, nor stop
Shearing till prostrate, lo, the crop?
And will you prefer it to ginger-pop
   When I've made you wine of the memories
Which leave as bare as a churchyard tomb
My meadow, late all bloom?

XXVI
Nay, what ingratitude
   Should I hesitate to amuse the wits
That have pulled so long at my flask, nor grudged
The headache that paid their pains, nor budged
From bunghole before they sighed and judged
   'Too rough for our taste, today, befits
The racy and right when the years conclude!'
Out on ingratitude!

XXVII

Grateful or ingrate – none,
    No cowslip of all my fairy crew
Shall help to concoct what makes you wink
And goes to your head till you think you think!
I like them alive: the printer's ink
    Would sensibly tell on the perfume too.
I may use up my nettles, ere I've done;
But of cowslips – friends get none!

XXVIII

Don't nettles make a broth
    Wholesome for blood grown lazy and thick?
Maws out of sorts make mouths out of taste.
My Thirty-four Port – no need to waste
On a tongue that's fur and a palate – paste!
    A magnum for friends who are sound! The sick –
I'll posset and cosset them, nothing loth,
Henceforward with nettle-broth!

La Saisiaz

1878

I

Good, to forgive;
   Best, to forget!
   Living, we fret;
Dying, we live.
Fretless and free,
   Soul, clap thy pinion!
   Earth have dominion,
Body, o'er thee!

II

Wander at will,
   Day after day, –
   Wander away,
Wandering still –
Soul that canst soar!
   Body may slumber:
   Body shall cumber
Soul-flight no more.

III

Waft of soul's wing!
   What lies above?
   Sunshine and Love,
Skyblue and Spring!
Body hides – where?
   Ferns of all feather,
   Mosses and heather,
Yours be the care!

La Saisiaz

A.E.S. 14 September 1877

Dared and done: at last I stand upon the summit, Dear and True!
Singly dared and done; the climbing both of us were bound to do.
Petty feat and yet prodigious: every side my glance was bent
O'er the grandeur and the beauty lavished through the whole ascent.
Ledge by ledge, out broke new marvels, now minute and now immense:
Earth's most exquisite disclosure, heaven's own God in evidence!
And no berry in its hiding, no blue space in its outspread,
Pleaded to escape my footstep, challenged my emerging head,
(As I climbed or paused from climbing, now o'erbranched by shrub and tree,
Now built round by rock and boulder, now at just a turn set free
Stationed face to face with – Nature? rather with Infinitude)
– No revealment of them all, as singly I my path pursued,
But a bitter touched its sweetness, for the thought stung 'Even so
Both of us had loved and wondered just the same, five days ago!'
Five short days, sufficient hardly to entice, from out its den
Splintered in the slab, this pink perfection of the cyclamen;
Scarce enough to heal and coat with amber gum the sloe-tree's gash,
Bronze the clustered wilding apple, redden ripe the mountain-ash:
Yet of might to place between us – Oh the barrier! Yon Profound
Shrinks beside it, proves a pin-point: barrier this, without a bound!

Boundless though it be, I reach you: somehow seem to have you here
– Who are there. Yes, there you dwell now, plain the four low walls appear;
Those are vineyards they enclose from; and the little spire which points
– That's Collonge, henceforth your dwelling. All the same, howe'er disjoints

Past from present, no less certain you are here, not there: have dared,
Done the feat of mountain-climbing, – five days since, we both prepared
Daring, doing, arm in arm, if other help should haply fail.
For you asked, as forth we sallied to see sunset from the vale,
'Why not try for once the mountain, – take a foretaste, snatch by stealth
Sight and sound, some unconsidered fragment of the hoarded wealth?
Six weeks at its base, yet never once have we together won
Sight or sound by honest climbing: let us two have dared and done
Just so much of twilight journey as may prove tomorrow's jaunt
Not the only mode of wayfare – wheeled to reach the eagle's haunt!'
So, we turned from the low grass-path you were pleased to call 'your own,'
Set our faces to the rose-bloom o'er the summit's front of stone
Where Salève obtains, from Jura and the sunken sun she hides,
Due return of blushing 'Good Night,' rosy as a borne-off bride's,
For his masculine 'Good Morrow' when, with sunrise still in hold,
Gay he hails her, and, magnific, thrilled her black length burns to gold.
Up and up we went, how careless – nay, how joyous! All was new,
All was strange. 'Call progress toilsome? that were just insulting you!
How the trees must temper noontide! Ah, the thicket's sudden break!
What will be the morning glory, when at dusk thus gleams the lake?
Light by light puts forth Geneva: what a land – and, of the land,
Can there be a lovelier station than this spot where now we stand?
Is it late, and wrong to linger? True, tomorrow makes amends.
Toilsome progress? child's play, call it – specially when one descends!
There, the dread descent is over – hardly our adventure, though!
Take the vale where late we left it, pace the grass-path, "mine," you know!

Proud completion of achievement!' And we paced it, praising still
That soft tread on velvet verdure as it wound through hill and hill;
And at very end there met us, coming from Collonge, the pair
– All our people of the Chalet – two, enough and none to spare.
So, we made for home together, and we reached it as the stars
One by one came lamping – chiefly that prepotency of Mars –
And your last word was 'I owe you this enjoyment!' – met with 'Nay:
With yourself it rests to have a month of morrows like today!'
Then the meal, with talk and laughter, and the news of that rare nook
Yet untroubled by the tourist, touched on by no travel-book,
All the same – though latent – patent, hybrid birth of land and sea,
And (our travelled friend assured you) – if such miracle might be –
Comparable for completeness of both blessings – all around
Nature, and, inside her circle, safety from world's sight and sound –
Comparable to our Saisiaz. 'Hold it fast and guard it well!
Go and see and vouch for certain, then come back and never tell
Living soul but us; and haply, prove our sky from cloud as clear,
There may we four meet, praise fortune just as now, another year!'

Thus you charged him on departure: not without the final charge
'Mind tomorrow's early meeting! We must leave our journey marge
Ample for the wayside wonders: there's the stoppage at the inn
Three-parts up the mountain, where the hardships of the track begin;
There's the convent worth a visit; but, the triumph crowning all –
There's Salève's own platform facing glory which strikes greatness small,
– Blanc, supreme above his earth-brood, needles red and white and green,
Horns of silver, fangs of crystal set on edge in his demesne.
So, some three weeks since, we saw them: so, tomorrow we intend

You shall see them likewise; therefore Good Night till tomorrow, friend!'
Last, the nothings that extinguish embers of a vivid day:
'What might be the Marshal's next move, what Gambetta's counter-play?'
Till the landing on the staircase saw escape the latest spark:
'Sleep you well!' 'Sleep but as well, you!' – lazy love quenched, all was dark.

Nothing dark next day at sundawn! Up I rose and forth I fared:
Took my plunge within the bath-pool, pacified the watch-dog scared,
Saw proceed the transmutation – Jura's black to one gold glow,
Trod your level path that let me drink the morning deep and slow,
Reached the little quarry – ravage recompensed by shrub and fern –
Till the overflowing ardours told me time was for return.
So, return I did, and gaily. But, for once, from no far mound
Waved salute a tall white figure. 'Has her sleep been so profound?
Foresight, rather, prudent saving strength for day's expenditure!
Ay, the chamber-window's open: out and on the terrace, sure!'

No, the terrace showed no figure, tall, white, leaning through the wreaths,
Tangle-twine of leaf and bloom that intercept the air one breathes,
Interpose between one's love and Nature's loving, hill and dale
Down to where the blue lake's wrinkle marks the river's inrush pale
– Mazy Arve: whereon no vessel but goes sliding white and plain,
Not a steamboat pants from harbour but one hears pulsate amain,
Past the city's congregated peace of homes and pomp of spires
– Man's mild protest that there's something more than Nature, man requires,
And that, useful as is Nature to attract the tourist's foot,
Quiet slow sure money-making proves the matter's very root, –
Need for body, – while the spirit also needs a comfort reached
By no help of lake or mountain, but the texts whence Calvin preached.

'Here's the veil withdrawn from landscape: up to Jura and beyond,
All awaits us ranged and ready; yet she violates the bond,
Neither leans nor looks nor listens: why is this?' A turn of eye
Took the whole sole answer, gave the undisputed reason 'why!'

This dread way you had your summons! No premonitory touch,
As you talked and laughed ('tis told me) scarce a minute ere the clutch
Captured you in cold forever. Cold? nay, warm you were as life
When I raised you, while the others used, in passionate poor strife,
All the means that seemed to promise any aid, and all in vain.
Gone you were, and I shall never see that earnest face again
Grow transparent, grow transfigured with the sudden light that leapt,
At the first word's provocation, from the heart-deeps where it slept.

Therefore, paying piteous duty, what seemed You have we consigned
Peacefully to – what I think were, of all earth-beds, to your mind
Most the choice for quiet, yonder: low walls stop the vines' approach,
Lovingly Salève protects you; village-sports will ne'er encroach
On the stranger lady's silence, whom friends bore so kind and well
Thither 'just for love's sake,' – such their own word was: and who can tell?
You supposed that few or none had known and loved you in the world:
May be! flower that's full-blown tempts the butterfly, not flower that's furled.
But more learned sense unlocked you, loosed the sheath and let expand
Bud to bell and outspread flower-shape at the least warm touch of hand
– Maybe, throb of heart, beneath which, – quickening farther than it knew, –
Treasure oft was disembosomed, scent all strange and unguessed hue.
Disembosomed, re-embosomed, – must one memory suffice,

Prove I knew an Alpine-rose which all beside named Edelweiss?

Rare thing, red or white, you rest now: two days slumbered through; and since
One day more will see me rid of this same scene whereat I wince,
Tetchy at all sights and sounds and pettish at each idle charm
Proffered me who pace now singly where we two went arm in arm, –
I have turned upon my weakness: asked 'And what, forsooth, prevents
That, this latest day allowed me, I fulfil of her intents
One she had the most at heart – that we should thus again survey
From Salève Mont Blanc together?' Therefore, – dared and done today
Climbing, – here I stand: but you – where?

If a spirit of the place
Broke the silence, bade me question, promised answer, – what disgrace
Did I stipulate 'Provided answer suit my hopes, not fears!'
Would I shrink to learn my life-time's limit – days, weeks, months or years?
Would I shirk assurance on each point whereat I can but guess –
'Does the soul survive the body? Is there God's self, no or yes?'
If I know my mood, 'twere constant – come in whatsoe'er uncouth
Shape it should, nay, formidable – so the answer were but truth.

Well, and wherefore shall it daunt me, when 'tis I myself am tasked,
When, by weakness weakness questioned, weakly answers – weakly asked?
Weakness never needs be falseness: truth is truth in each degree
– Thunderpealed by God to Nature, whispered by my soul to me.
Nay, the weakness turns to strength and triumphs in a truth beyond:
'Mine is but man's truest answer – how were it did God respond?'
I shall no more dare to mimic such response in futile speech,
Pass off human lisp as echo of the sphere-song out of reach,
Than, – because it well may happen yonder, where the far snows blanch

Mute Mont Blanc, that who stands near them sees and hears an avalanche, –
I shall pick a clod and throw, – cry 'Such the sight and such the sound!
What though I nor see nor hear them? Others do, the proofs abound!'
Can I make my eye an eagle's, sharpen ear to recognize
Sound o'er league and league of silence? Can I know, who but surmise?
If I dared no self-deception when, a week since, I and you
Walked and talked along the grass-path, passing lightly in review
What seemed hits and what seemed misses in a certain fence-play, – strife
Sundry minds of mark engaged in 'On the Soul and Future Life,' –
If I ventured estimating what was come of parried thrust,
Subtle stroke, and, rightly, wrongly, estimating could be just
– Just, though life so seemed abundant in the form which moved by mine,
I might well have played at feigning, fooling, – laughed 'What need opine
Pleasure must succeed to pleasure, else past pleasure turns to pain,
And this first life claims a second, else I count its good no gain?' –
Much less have I heart to palter when the matter to decide
Now becomes 'Was ending ending once and always, when you died?'
Did the face, the form I lifted as it lay, reveal the loss
Not alone of life but soul? A tribute to yon flowers and moss,
What of you remains beside? A memory! Easy to attest
'Certainly from out the world that one believes who knew her best
Such was good in her, such fair, which fair and good were great perchance
Had but fortune favoured, bidden each shy faculty advance;
After all – who knows another? Only as I know, I speak.'
So much of you lives within me while I live my year or week.
Then my fellow takes the tale up, not unwilling to aver
Duly in his turn 'I knew him best of all, as he knew her:
Such he was, and such he was not, and such other might have been

But that somehow every actor, somewhere in this earthly scene,
Fails.' And so both memories dwindle, yours and mine together linked,
Till there is but left for comfort, when the last spark proves extinct,
This – that somewhere new existence led by men and women new
Possibly attains perfection coveted by me and you;
While ourselves, the only witness to what work our life evolved,
Only to ourselves proposing problems proper to be solved
By ourselves alone, – who working ne'er shall know if work bear fruit
Others reap and garner, heedless how produced by stalk and root, –
We who, darkling, timed the day's birth, – struggling, testified to peace, –
Earned, by dint of failure, triumph, – we, creative thought, must cease
In created word, thought's echo, due to impulse long since sped!
Why repine? There's ever someone lives although ourselves be dead!

Well, what signifies repugnance? Truth is truth howe'er it strike.
Fair or foul the lot apportioned life on earth, we bear alike.
Stalwart body idly yoked to stunted spirit, powers, that fain
Else would soar, condemned to grovel, groundlings through the fleshly chain, –
Help that hinders, hindrance proved but help disguised when all too late, –
Hindrance is the fact acknowledged, howsoe'er explained as Fate,
Fortune, Providence: we bear, own life a burthen more or less.
Life thus owned unhappy, is there supplemental happiness
Possible and probable in life to come? or must we count
Life a curse and not a blessing, summed-up in its whole amount,
Help and hindrance, joy and sorrow?
Why should I want courage here?
I will ask and have an answer, – with no favour, with no fear, –
From myself. How much, how little, do I inwardly believe
True that controverted doctrine? Is it fact to which I cleave,
Is it fancy I but cherish, when I take upon my lips
Phrase the solemn Tuscan fashioned, and declare the soul's eclipse

Not the soul's extinction? take his 'I believe and I declare –
Certain am I – from this life I pass into a better, there
Where that lady lives of whom enamoured was my soul' – where this
Other lady, my companion dear and true, she also is?

I have questioned and am answered. Question, answer presuppose
Two points: that the thing itself which questions, answers, – *is*, it knows;
As it also knows the thing perceived outside itself, – a force
Actual ere its own beginning, operative through its course,
Unaffected by its end, – that this thing likewise needs must be;
Call this – God, then, call that – soul, and both – the only facts for me.
Prove them facts? that they o'erpass my power of proving, proves them such:
Fact it is I know I know not something which is fact as much.
What before caused all the causes, what effect of all effects
Haply follows, – these are fancy. Ask the rush if it suspects
Whence and how the stream which floats it had a rise, and where and how
Falls or flows on still! What answer makes the rush except that now
Certainly it floats and is, and, no less certain than itself,
Is the everyway external stream that now through shoal and shelf
Floats it onward, leaves it – may be – wrecked at last, or lands on shore
There to root again and grow and flourish stable evermore.
– May be! mere surmise not knowledge: much conjecture styled belief,
What the rush conceives the stream means through the voyage blind and brief.
Why, because I doubtless am, shall I as doubtless be? 'Because
God seems good and wise.' Yet under this our life's apparent laws
Reigns a wrong which, righted once, would give quite other laws to life.
'He seems potent.' Potent here, then: why are right and wrong at strife?

Has in life the wrong the better? Happily life ends so soon!
Right predominates in life? Then why two lives and double boon?
'Anyhow, we want it: wherefore want?' Because, without the want,
Life, now human, would be brutish: just that hope, however scant,
Makes the actual life worth leading; take the hope therein away,
All we have to do is surely not endure another day.
This life has its hopes for this life, hopes that promise joy: life done –
Out of all the hopes, how many had complete fulfilment? none.
'But the soul is not the body': and the breath is not the flute;
Both together make the music: either marred and all is mute.
Truce to such old sad contention whence, according as we shape
Most of hope or most of fear, we issue in a half-escape:
'We believe' is sighed. I take the cup of comfort proffered thus,
Taste and try each soft ingredient, sweet infusion, and discuss
What their blending may accomplish for the cure of doubt, till – slow,
Sorrowful, but how decided! needs must I o'erturn it – so!
Cause before, effect behind me – blanks! The midway point I am,
Caused, itself – itself efficient: in that narrow space must cram
All experience – out of which there crowds conjecture manifold,
But, as knowledge, this comes only – things may be as I behold,
Or may not be, but, without me and above me, things there are;
I myself am what I know not – ignorance which proves no bar
To the knowledge that I am, and, since I am, can recognize
What to me is pain and pleasure: this is sure, the rest – surmise.
If my fellows are or are not, what may please them and what pain, –
Mere surmise: my own experience – that is knowledge, once again!

I have lived, then, done and suffered, loved and hated, learnt and taught
This – there is no reconciling wisdom with a world distraught,
Goodness with triumphant evil, power with failure in the aim,
If – (to my own sense, remember! though none other feel the same!) –
If you bar me from assuming earth to be a pupil's place,

And life, time, – with all their chances, changes, – just probation-space,
Mine, for me. But those apparent other mortals – theirs, for them?
Knowledge stands on my experience: all outside its narrow hem,
Free surmise may sport and welcome! Pleasures, pains affect mankind
Just as they affect myself? Why, here's my neighbour colour-blind,
Eyes like mine to all appearance: 'green as grass' do I affirm?
'Red as grass' he contradicts me: which employs the proper term?
Were we two the earth's sole tenants, with no third for referee,
How should I distinguish? Just so, God must judge 'twixt man and me.
To each mortal peradventure earth becomes a new machine,
Pain and pleasure no more tally in our sense than red and green;
Still, without what seems such mortal's pleasure, pain, my life were lost
– Life, my whole sole chance to prove – although at man's apparent cost –
What is beauteous and what ugly, right to strive for, right to shun,
Fit to help and fit to hinder, – prove my forces everyone,
Good and evil, – learn life's lesson, hate of evil, love of good,
As 'tis set me, understand so much as may be understood –
Solve the problem: 'From thine apprehended scheme of things, deduce
Praise or blame of its contriver, shown a niggard or profuse
In each good or evil issue! nor miscalculate alike
Counting one the other in the final balance, which to strike,
Soul was born and life allotted: ay, the show of things unfurled
For thy summing-up and judgement, – thine, no other mortal's world!'
What though fancy scarce may grapple with the complex and immense
– 'His own world for every mortal?' Postulate omnipotence!
Limit power, and simple grows the complex: shrunk to atom size,
That which loomed immense to fancy low before my reason lies, –
I survey it and pronounce it work like other work: success

Here and there, the workman's glory, – here and there, his shame no less,
Failure as conspicuous. Taunt not 'Human work ape work divine?'
As the power, expect performance! God's be God's as mine is mine!
God whose power made man and made man's wants, and made, to meet those wants,
Heaven and earth which, through the body, prove the spirit's ministrants,
Excellently all, – did He lack power or was the will in fault
When He let blue heaven be shrouded o'er by vapours of the vault,
Gay earth drop her garlands shrivelled at the first infecting breath
Of the serpent pains which herald, swarming in, the dragon death?
What, no way but this that man may learn and lay to heart how rife
Life were with delights would only death allow their taste to life?
Must the rose sigh 'Pluck – I perish!' must the eve weep 'Gaze – I fade!'
– Every sweet warn ''Ware my bitter!' every shine bid 'Wait my shade'?
Can we love but on condition, that the thing we love must die?
Needs there groan a world in anguish just to teach us sympathy –
Multitudinously wretched that we, wretched too, may guess
What a preferable state were universal happiness?
Hardly do I so conceive the outcome of that power which went
To the making of the worm there in yon clod its tenement,
Any more than I distinguish aught of that which, wise and good,
Framed the leaf, its plain of pasture, dropped the dew, its fineless food.
Nay, were fancy fact, were earth and all it holds illusion mere,
Only a machine for teaching love and hate and hope and fear
To myself, the sole existence, single truth 'mid falsehood, – well!
If the harsh throes of the prelude die not off into the swell
Of that perfect piece they sting me to become a-strain for, – if
Roughness of the long rock-clamber lead not to the last of cliff,
First of level country where is sward my pilgrim-foot can prize, –
Plainlier! if this life's conception new life fail to realize, –
Though earth burst and proved a bubble glassing hues of hell, one huge

Reflex of the devil's doings – God's work by no subterfuge –
(So death's kindly touch informed me as it broke the glamour, gave
Soul and body both release from life's long nightmare in the grave)
Still, – with no more Nature, no more Man as riddle to be read,
Only my own joys and sorrows now to reckon real instead, –
I must say – or choke in silence – 'Howsoever came my fate,
Sorrow did and joy did nowise, – life well weighed, – preponderate.'
By necessity ordained thus? I shall bear as best I can;
By a cause all-good, all-wise, all-potent? No, as I am man!
Such were God: and was it goodness that the good within my range
Or had evil in admixture or grew evil's self by change?
Wisdom – that becoming wise meant making slow and sure advance
From a knowledge proved in error to acknowledged ignorance?
Power? 'tis just the main assumption reason most revolts at! power
Unavailing for bestowment on its creature of an hour,
Man, of so much proper action rightly aimed and reaching aim,
So much passion, – no defect there, no excess, but still the same, –
As what constitutes existence, pure perfection bright as brief
For yon worm, man's fellow-creature, on yon happier world – its leaf!
No, as I am man, I mourn the poverty I must impute:
Goodness, wisdom, power, all bounded, each a human attribute!

But, O world outspread beneath me! only for myself I speak,
Nowise dare to play the spokesman for my brothers strong and weak,
Full and empty, wise and foolish, good and bad, in every age,
Every clime, I turn my eyes from, as in one or other stage
Of a torture writhe they, Job-like couched on dung and crazed with blains
– Wherefore? whereto? ask the whirlwind what the dread voice thence explains!
I shall 'vindicate no way of God's to man,' nor stand apart,
'Laugh, be candid!' while I watch it traversing the human heart.
Traversed heart must tell its story uncommented on: no less
Mine results in 'Only grant a second life, I acquiesce

In this present life as failure, count misfortune's worst assaults
Triumph, not defeat, assured that loss so much the more exalts
Gain about to be.' For at what moment did I so advance
Near to knowledge as when frustrate of escape from ignorance?
Did not beauty prove most precious when its opposite obtained
Rule, and truth seem more than ever potent because falsehood reigned?
While for love – Oh how but, losing love, does whoso loves succeed
By the death-pang to the birth-throe – learning what is love indeed?
Only grant my soul may carry high through death her cup unspilled,
Brimming though it be with knowledge, life's loss drop by drop distilled,
I shall boast it mine – the balsam, bless each kindly wrench that wrung
From life's tree its inmost virtue, tapped the root whence pleasure sprung,
Barked the bole, and broke the bough, and bruised the berry, left all grace
Ashes in death's stern alembic, loosed elixir in its place!

Witness, Dear and True, how little I was 'ware of – not your worth
– That I knew, my heart assures me – but of what a shade on earth
Would the passage from my presence of the tall white figure throw
O'er the ways we walked together! Somewhat narrow, somewhat slow,
Used to seem the ways, the walking: narrow ways are well to tread
When there's moss beneath the footstep, honeysuckle overhead:
Walking slow to beating bosom surest solace soonest gives,
Liberates the brain o'erloaded – best of all restoratives.
Nay, do I forget the open vast where soon or late converged
Ways though winding? – world-wide heaven-high sea where music slept or surged
As the angel had ascendant, and Beethoven's Titan mace
Smote the immense to storm Mozart would by a finger's lifting chase?

Yes, I knew – but not with knowledge such as thrills me while I
view
Yonder precinct which henceforward holds and hides the
Dear and True.
Grant me (once again) assurance we shall each meet each some
day,
Walk – but with how bold a footstep! on a way – but what a way!
– Worst were best, defeat were triumph, utter loss were utmost
gain.
Can it be, and must, and will it?

Silence! Out of fact's domain,
Just surmise prepared to mutter hope, and also fear – dispute
Fact's inexorable ruling 'Outside fact, surmise be mute!'
Well!

Ay, well and best, if fact's self I may force the answer from!
'Tis surmise I stop the mouth of. Not above in yonder dome
All a rapture with its rose-glow, – not around, where pile and
peak
Strainingly await the sun's fall, – not beneath, where crickets
creak,
Birds assemble for their bed-time, soft the tree-top swell
subsides, –
No, nor yet within my deepest sentient self the knowledge hides.
Aspiration, reminiscence, plausibilities of trust
– Now the ready 'Man were wronged else,' now the rash 'and
God unjust' –
None of these I need. Take thou, my soul, thy solitary stand,
Umpire to the champions Fancy, Reason, as on either hand
Amicable war they wage and play the foe in thy behoof!
Fancy thrust and Reason parry! Thine the prize who stand aloof.

FANCY

I concede the thing refused: henceforth no certainty more plain
Than this mere surmise that after body dies soul lives again.
Two, the only facts acknowledged late, are now increased to
three –
God is, and the soul is, and, as certain, after death shall be.
Put this third to use in life, the time for using fact!

REASON

I do:
Find it promises advantage, coupled with the other two.
Life to come will be improvement on the life that's now; destroy
Body's thwartings, there's no longer screen betwixt soul and soul's joy.
Why should we expect new hindrance, novel tether? In this first
Life, I see the good of evil, why our world began at worst:
Since time means amelioration, tardily enough displayed,
Yet a mainly onward moving, never wholly retrograde.
We know more though we know little, we grow stronger though still weak,
Partly see though all too purblind, stammer though we cannot speak.
There is no such grudge in God as scared the ancient Greek, no fresh
Substitute of trap for dragnet, once a breakage in the mesh.
Dragons were, and serpents are, and blindworms will be: ne'er emerged
Any new-created python for man's plague since earth was purged.
Failing proof, then, of invented trouble to replace the old,
O'er this life the next presents advantage much and manifold:
Which advantage – in the absence of a fourth and farther fact
Now conceivably surmised, of harm to follow from the act –
I pronounce for man's obtaining at this moment. Why delay?
Is he happy? happiness will change: anticipate the day!
Is he sad? there's ready refuge: of all sadness death's prompt cure!
Is he both, in mingled measure? cease a burthen to endure!
Pains with sorry compensations, pleasures stinted in the dole,
Power that sinks and pettiness that soars, all halved and nothing whole,
Idle hopes that lure man onward, forced back by as idle fears –
What a load he stumbles under through his glad sad seventy years,
When a touch sets right the turmoil, lifts his spirit where, flesh-freed,
Knowledge shall be rightly named so, all that seems be truth indeed!

Grant his forces no accession, nay, no faculty's increase,
Only let what now exists continue, let him prove in peace
Power whereof the interrupted unperfected play enticed
Man through darkness, which to lighten any spark of hope sufficed, –
What shall then deter his dying out of darkness into light?
Death itself perchance, brief pain that's pang, condensed and infinite?
But at worst, he needs must brave it one day, while, at best, he laughs –
Drops a drop within his chalice, sleep not death his science quaffs!
Any moment claims more courage when, by crossing cold and gloom,
Manfully man quits discomfort, makes for the provided room
Where the old friends want their fellow, where the new acquaintance wait,
Probably for talk assembled, possibly to sup in state!
I affirm and re-affirm it therefore: only make as plain
As that man now lives, that, after dying, man will live again, –
Make as plain the absence, also, of a law to contravene
Voluntary passage from this life to that by change of scene, –
And I bid him – at suspicion of first cloud athwart his sky,
Flower's departure, frost's arrival – never hesitate, but die!

FANCY

Then I double my concession: grant, along with new life sure,
This same law found lacking now: ordain that, whether rich or poor
Present life is judged in aught man counts advantage – be it hope,
Be it fear that brightens, blackens most or least his horoscope, –
He, by absolute compulsion such as made him live at all,
Go on living to the fated end of life whate'er befall.
What though, as on earth he darkling grovels, man descry the sphere,
Next life's – call it, heaven of freedom, close above and crystal-clear?
He shall find – say, hell to punish who in aught curtails the term,

Fain would act the butterfly before he has played out the worm.
God, soul, earth, heaven, hell, – five facts now: what is to desiderate?

REASON

Nothing! Henceforth man's existence bows to the monition 'Wait!
Take the joys and bear the sorrows – neither with extreme concern!
Living here means nescience simply: 'tis next life that helps to learn.
Shut those eyes, next life will open, – stop those ears, next life will teach
Hearing's office, – close those lips, next life will give the power of speech!
Or, if action more amuse thee than the passive attitude,
Bravely bustle through thy being, busy thee for ill or good,
Reap this life's success or failure! Soon shall things be unperplexed
And the right and wrong, now tangled, lie unravelled in the next.'

FANCY

Not so fast! Still more concession! not alone do I declare
Life must needs be borne, – I also will that man become aware
Life has worth incalculable, every moment that he spends
So much gain or loss for that next life which on this life depends.
Good, done here, be there rewarded, – evil, worked here, there amerced!
Six facts now, and all established, plain to man the last as first.

REASON

There was good and evil, then, defined to man by this decree?
Was – for at its promulgation both alike have ceased to be.
Prior to this last announcement 'Certainly as God exists,
As He made man's soul, as soul is quenchless by the deathly mists,
Yet is, all the same, forbidden premature escape from time
To eternity's provided purer air and brighter clime, –
Just so certainly depends it on the use to which man turns
Earth, the good or evil done there, whether after death he earns
Life eternal, – heaven, the phrase be, or eternal death, – say, hell.
As his deeds, so proves his portion, doing ill or doing well!'
– Prior to this last announcement, earth was man's probation-place:
Liberty of doing evil gave his doing good a grace;
Once lay down the law, with Nature's simple 'Such effects succeed
Causes such, and heaven or hell depends upon man's earthly deed
Just as surely as depends the straight or else the crooked line
On his making point meet point or with or else without incline,'–
Thenceforth neither good nor evil does man, doing what he must.
Lay but down that law as stringent 'Wouldst thou live again, be just!'
As this other 'Wouldst thou live now, regularly draw thy breath!
For, suspend the operation, straight law's breach results in death –'
And (provided always, man, addressed this mode, be sound and sane)
Prompt and absolute obedience, never doubt, will law obtain!
Tell not me 'Look round us! nothing each side but acknowledged law,
Now styled God's – now, Nature's edict!' Where's obedience without flaw
Paid to either? What's the adage rife in man's mouth? Why, 'The best
I both see and praise, the worst I follow' – which, despite professed
Seeing, praising, all the same he follows, since he disbelieves

In the heart of him that edict which for truth his head receives.
There's evading and persuading and much making law amends
Somehow, there's the nice distinction 'twixt fast foes and faulty friends,
– Any consequence except inevitable death when 'Die,
Whoso breaks our law!' they publish, God and Nature equally.
Law that's kept or broken – subject to man's will and pleasure! Whence?
How comes law to bear eluding? Not because of impotence:
Certain laws exist already which to hear means to obey;
Therefore not without a purpose these man must, while those man may
Keep and, for the keeping, haply gain approval and reward.
Break through this last superstructure, all is empty air – no sward
Firm like my first fact to stand on 'God there is, and soul there is,'
And soul's earthly life-allotment: wherein, by hypothesis,
Soul is bound to pass probation, prove its powers, and exercise
Sense and thought on fact, and then, from fact educing fit surmise,
Ask itself, and of itself have solely answer, 'Does the scope
Earth affords of fact to judge by warrant future fear or hope?'

Thus have we come back full circle: fancy's footsteps one by one
Go their round conducting reason to the point where they begun,
Left where we were left so lately, Dear and True! When, half a week
Since, we walked and talked and thus I told you, how suffused a cheek
You had turned me had I sudden brought the blush into the smile
By some word like 'Idly argued! you know better all the while!'
Now, from me – Oh not a blush but, how much more, a joyous glow,
Laugh triumphant, would it strike did your 'Yes, better I do know'
Break, my warrant for assurance! which assurance may not be
If, supplanting hope, assurance needs must change this life to me.
So, I hope – no more than hope, but hope – no less than hope, because
I can fathom, by no plumb-line sunk in life's apparent laws,

How I may in any instance fix where change should meetly fall
Nor involve, by one revisal, abrogation of them all:
– Which again involves as utter change in life thus law-released,
Whence the good of goodness vanished when the ill of evil ceased.
Whereas, life and laws apparent re-instated, – all we know,
All we know not, – o'er our heaven again cloud closes, until, lo –
Hope the arrowy, just as constant, comes to pierce its gloom, compelled
By a power and by a purpose which, if no one else beheld,
I behold in life, so – hope!

Sad summing-up of all to say!
Athanasius contra mundum, why should he hope more than they?
So are men made notwithstanding, such magnetic virtue darts
From each head their fancy haloes to their unresisting hearts!

Here I stand, methinks a stone's throw from yon village I this morn
Traversed for the sake of looking one last look at its forlorn
Tenement's ignoble fortune: through a crevice, plain its floor
Piled with provender for cattle, while a dung-heap blocked the door.
In that squalid Bossex, under that obscene red roof, arose,
Like a fiery flying serpent from its egg, a soul – Rousseau's.
Turn thence! Is it Diodati joins the glimmer of the lake?
There I plucked a leaf, one week since, – ivy, plucked for Byron's sake.
Famed unfortunates! And yet, because of that phosphoric fame
Swathing blackness' self with brightness till putridity looked flame,
All the world was witched: and wherefore? what could lie beneath, allure
Heart of man to let corruption serve man's head as cynosure?
Was the magic in the dictum 'All that's good is gone and past;
Bad and worse still grows the present, and the worst of all comes last:
Which believe – for I believe it?' So preached one his gospel-news;
While melodious moaned the other 'Dying day with dolphin-hues!

Storm, for loveliness and darkness like a woman's eye! Ye mounts
Where I climb to 'scape my fellow, and thou sea wherein he counts
Not one inch of vile dominion! What were your especial worth
Failed ye to enforce the maxim "Of all objects found on earth
Man is meanest, much too honoured when compared with – what by odds
Beats him – any dog: so, let him go a-howling to his gods!"
Which believe – for I believe it!' such the comfort man received
Sadly since perforce he must: for why? the famous bard believed!

Fame! Then, give me fame, a moment! As I gather at a glance
Human glory after glory vivifying yon expanse,
Let me grasp them all together, hold on high and brandish well
Beacon-like above the rapt world ready, whether heaven or hell
Send the dazzling summons earthward, to submit itself the same,
Take on trust the hope or else despair flashed full on face by – Fame!
Thanks, thou pine-tree of Makistos, wide thy giant torch I wave!
Know ye whence I plucked the pillar, late with sky for architrave?
This the trunk, the central solid Knowledge, kindled core, began
Tugging earth-deeps, trying heaven-heights, rooted yonder at Lausanne.
This which flits and spits, the aspic, – sparkles in and out the boughs
Now, and now condensed, the python, coiling round and round allows
Scarce the bole its due effulgence, dulled by flake on flake of Wit –
Laughter so bejewels Learning, – what but Ferney nourished it?
Nay, nor fear – since every resin feeds the flame – that I dispense
With yon Bossex terebinth-tree's all-explosive Eloquence:
No, be sure! nor, any more than thy resplendency, Jean-Jacques,
Dare I want thine, Diodati! What though monkeys and macaques
Gibber 'Byron'? Byron's ivy rears a branch beyond the crew,
Green for ever, no deciduous trash macaques and monkeys chew!

As Rousseau, then, eloquent, as Byron prime in poet's power, –
Detonations, fulgurations, smiles – the rainbow, tears – the
showers, –
Lo, I lift the coruscating marvel – Fame! and, famed, declare
– Learned for the nonce as Gibbon, witty as wit's self Voltaire...
O the sorriest of conclusions to whatever man of sense
'Mid the millions stands the unit, takes no flare for evidence!
Yet the millions have their portion, live their calm or troublous
day,
Find significance in fireworks: so, by help of mine, they may
Confidently lay to heart and lock in head their life long – this:
'He there with the brand flamboyant, broad o'er night's forlorn
abyss,
Crowned by prose and verse; and wielding, with Wit's bauble,
Learning's rod...
Well? Why, he at least believed in Soul, was very sure of God.'

So the poor smile played, that evening: pallid smile long since
extinct
Here in London's mid-November! Not so loosely thoughts were
linked,
Six weeks since as I, descending in the sunset from Salève,
Found the chain, I seemed to forge there, flawless till it reached
your grave, –
Not so filmy was the texture, but I bore it in my breast
Safe thus far. And since I found a something in me would not
rest
Till I, link by link, unravelled any tangle of the chain,
– Here it lies, for much or little! I have lived all o'er again
That last pregnant hour: I saved it, just as I could save a root
Disinterred for re-interment when the time best helps to shoot.
Life is stocked with germs of torpid life; but may I never wake
Those of mine whose resurrection could not be without
earthquake!
Rest all such, unraised forever! Be this, sad yet sweet, the sole
Memory evoked from slumber! Least part this: then what the
whole?

The Two Poets of Croisic

1878

I

Such a starved bank of moss
   Till that May-morn,
Blue ran the flash across:
   Violets were born!

II

Sky – what a scowl of cloud
   Till, near and far,
Ray on ray split the shroud
   Splendid, a star!

III

World – how it walled about
   Life with disgrace
Till God's own smile came out:
   That was thy face!

The Two Poets of Croisic

I

'Fame!' Yes, I said it and you read it. First,
   Praise the good log-fire! Winter howls without.
Crowd closer, let us! Ha, the secret nursed
   Inside yon hollow, crusted roundabout
With copper where the clamp was, – how the burst
   Vindicates flame the stealthy feeder! Spout
Thy splendidest – a minute and no more?
So soon again all sobered as before?

II

Nay, for I need to see your face! One stroke
   Adroitly dealt, and lo, the pomp revealed!
Fire in his pandemonium, heart of oak
   Palatial, where he wrought the works concealed
Beneath the solid-seeming roof I broke,
   As redly up and out and off they reeled
Like disconcerted imps, those thousand sparks
From fire's slow tunnelling of vaults and arcs!

III

Up, out, and off, see! Were you never used, –
   You now, in childish days or rather nights, –
As I was, to watch sparks fly? not amused
   By that old nurse-taught game which gave the sprites
Each one his title and career, – confused
   Belief 'twas all long over with the flights
From earth to heaven of hero, sage and bard,
And bade them once more strive for Fame's award?

IV

New long bright life! and happy chance befell –
   That I know – when some prematurely lost
Child of disaster bore away the bell
   From some too-pampered son of fortune, crossed
Never before my chimney broke the spell!
   Octogenarian Keats gave up the ghost,
While – never mind Who was it cumbered earth –
Sank stifled, span-long brightness, in the birth.

V

Well, try a variation of the game!
  Our log is old ship-timber, broken bulk.
There's sea-brine spirits up the brimstone flame,
  That crimson-curly spiral proves the hulk
Was saturate with – ask the chloride's name
  From somebody who knows! I shall not sulk
If yonder greenish tonguelet licked from brass
Its life, I thought was fed on copperas.

VI

Anyhow, there they flutter! What may be
  The style and prowess of that purple one?
Who is the hero other eyes shall see
  Than yours and mine? That yellow, deep to dun –
Conjecture how the sage glows, whom not we
  But those unborn are to get warmth by! Son
O' the coal, – as Job and Hebrew name a spark, –
What bard, in thy red soaring, scares the dark?

VII

Oh and the lesser lights, the dearer still
  That they elude a vulgar eye, give ours
The glimpse repaying astronomic skill
  Which searched sky deeper, passed those patent powers
Constellate proudly, – swords, scrolls, harps, that fill
  The vulgar eye to surfeit, – found best flowers
Hid deepest in the dark, – named unplucked grace
Of soul, ungathered beauty, form or face!

VIII

Up with thee, mouldering ash men never knew,
  But I know! flash thou forth, and figure bold,
Calm and columnar as yon flame I view!
  Oh and I bid thee, – to whom fortune doled
Scantly all other gifts out – bicker blue,
  Beauty for all to see, zinc's uncontrolled
Flake-brilliance! Not my fault if these were shown,
Grandeur and beauty both, to me alone.

IX

No! as the first was boy's play, this proves mere
   Stripling's amusement: manhood's sport be grave!
Choose rather sparkles quenched in mid-career,
   Their boldness and their brightness could not save
(In some old night of time on some lone drear
   Sea-coast, monopolized by crag or cave)
– Save from ignoble exit into smoke,
Silence, oblivion, all death-damps that choke!

X

Launched by our ship-wood, float we, once adrift
   In fancy to that land-strip waters wash,
We both know well! Where uncouth tribes made shift
   Long since to just keep life in, billows dash
Nigh over folk who shudder at each lift
   Of the old tyrant tempest's whirlwind-lash
Though they have built the serviceable town
Tempests but tease now, billows drench, not drown.

XI

Croisic, the spit of sandy rock which juts
   Spitefully northward, bears nor tree nor shrub
To tempt the ocean, show what Guérande shuts
   Behind her, past wild Batz whose Saxons grub
The ground for crystals grown where ocean gluts
   Their promontory's breadth with salt: all stub
Of rock and stretch of sand, the land's last strife
To rescue a poor remnant for dear life.

XII

And what life! Here was, from the world to choose,
   The Druids' chosen chief of homes: they reared
– Only their women, – 'mid the slush and ooze
   Of yon low islet, – to their sun, revered
In strange stone guise, – a temple. May-dawn dews
   Saw the old structure levelled; when there peered
May's earliest eve-star, high and wide once more
Up towered the new pile perfect as before:

XIII

Seeing that priestesses – and all were such –
Unbuilt and then rebuilt it every May,
Each alike helping – well, if not too much!
For, 'mid their eagerness to outstrip day
And get work done, if any loosed her clutch
And let a single stone drop, straight a prey
Herself fell, torn to pieces, limb from limb,
By sisters in full chorus glad and grim.

XIV

And still so much remains of that grey cult,
That even now, of nights, do women steal
To the sole Menhir standing, and insult
The antagonistic church-spire by appeal
To power discrowned in vain, since each adult
Believes the gruesome thing she clasps may heal
Whatever plague no priestly help can cure:
Kiss but the cold stone, the event is sure!

XV

Nay more: on May-morns, that primeval rite
Of temple-building, with its punishment
For rash precipitation, lingers, spite
Of all remonstrance; vainly are they shent,
Those girls who form a ring and, dressed in white,
Dance round it, till some sister's strength be spent:
Touch but the Menhir, straight the rest turn roughs
From gentles, fall on her with fisticuffs.

XVI

Oh and, for their part, boys from door to door
Sing unintelligible words to tunes
As obsolete: 'scraps of Druidic lore,'
Sigh scholars, as each pale man importunes
Vainly the mumbling to speak plain once more.
Enough of this old worship, rounds and runes!
They serve my purpose, which is but to show
Croisic today and Croisic long ago.

XVII

What have we sailed to see, then, wafted there
By fancy from the log that ends its days
Of much adventure 'neath skies foul or fair,
On waters rough or smooth, in this good blaze
We two crouch round so closely, bidding care
Keep outside with the snow-storm? Something says
'Fit time for story-telling!' I begin –
Why not at Croisic, port we first put in?

XVIII

Anywhere serves: for point me out the place
Wherever man has made himself a home,
And there I find the story of our race
In little, just at Croisic as at Rome.
What matters the degree? the kind I trace.
Druids their temple, Christians have their dome:
So with mankind; and Croisic, I'll engage,
With Rome yields sort for sort, in age for age.

XIX

No doubt, men vastly differ: and we need
Some strange exceptional benevolence
Of nature's sunshine to develop seed
So well, in the less-favoured clime, that thence
We may discern how shrub means tree indeed
Though dwarfed till scarcely shrub in evidence.
Man in the ice-house or the hot-house ranks
With beasts or gods: stove-forced, give warmth the thanks!

XX

While, is there any ice-checked? Such shall learn
I am thankworthy, who propose to slake
His thirst for tasting how it feels to turn
Cedar from hyssop-on-the-wall. I wake
No memories of what is harsh and stern
In ancient Croisic-nature, much less rake
The ashes of her last warmth till out leaps
Live Hervé Riel, the single spark she keeps.

XXI

Take these two, see, each outbreak, – spirt and spirt
  Of fire from our brave billet's either edge
Which – call maternal Croisic ocean-girt!
  These two shall thoroughly redeem my pledge.
One flames fierce gules, its feebler rival – vert,
  Heralds would tell you: heroes, I allege,
They both were: soldiers, sailors, statesmen, priests,
Lawyers, physicians – guess what gods or beasts!

XXII

None of them all, but – poets, if you please!
  'What, even there, endowed with knack of rhyme,
Did two among the aborigines
  Of that rough region pass the ungracious time
Suiting, to rumble-tumble of the sea's,
  The songs forbidden a serener clime?
Or had they universal audience – that's
To say, the folk of Croisic, ay and Batz?'

XXIII

Open your ears! Each poet in his day
  Had such a mighty moment of success
As pinnacled him straight, in full display,
  For the whole world to worship – nothing less!
Was not the whole polite world Paris, pray?
  And did not Paris, for one moment – yes,
Worship these poet-flames, our red and green,
One at a time, a century between?

XXIV

And yet you never heard their names! Assist,
  Clio, Historic Muse, while I record
Great deeds! Let fact, not fancy, break the mist
  And bid each sun emerge, in turn play lord
Of day, one moment! Hear the annalist
  Tell a strange story, true to the least word!
At Croisic, sixteen hundred years and ten
Since Christ, forth flamed yon liquid ruby, then.

XXV

Know him henceforth as René Gentilhomme
  – Appropriate appellation! noble birth
And knightly blazon, the device wherefrom
  Was 'Better do than say'! In Croisic's dearth
Why prison his career while Christendom
  Lay open to reward acknowledged worth?
He therefore left it at the proper age
And got to be the Prince of Condé's page.

XXVI

Which Prince of Condé, whom men called 'The Duke,'
  – Failing the king, his cousin, of an heir,
(As one might hold would hap, without rebuke,
  Since Anne of Austria, all the world was 'ware,
Twenty-three years long sterile, scarce could look
  For issue) – failing Louis of so rare
A godsend, it was natural the Prince
Should hear men call him 'Next King' too, nor wince.

XXVII

Now, as this reasonable hope, by growth
  Of years, nay, tens of years, looked plump almost
To bursting, – would the brothers, childless both,
  Louis and Gaston, give but up the ghost –
Condé, called 'Duke' and 'Next King,' nothing loth
  Awaited his appointment to the post,
And wiled away the time, as best he might,
Till Providence should settle things aright.

XXVIII

So, at a certain pleasure-house, withdrawn
  From cities where a whisper breeds offence,
He sat him down to watch the streak of dawn
  Testify to first stir of Providence;
And, since dull country life makes courtiers yawn,
  There wanted not a poet to dispense
Song's remedy for spleen-fits all and some,
Which poet was Page René Gentilhomme.

XXIX

A poet born and bred, his very sire
  A poet also, author of a piece
Printed and published, 'Ladies – their attire':
  Therefore the son, just born at his decease,
Was bound to keep alive the sacred fire,
  And kept it, yielding moderate increase
Of songs and sonnets, madrigals, and much
Rhyming thought poetry and praised as such.

XXX

Rubbish unutterable (bear in mind!)
  Rubbish not wholly without value, though,
Being to compliment the Duke designed
  And bring the complimenter credit so, –
Pleasure with profit happily combined.
  Thus René Gentilhomme rhymed, rhymed till – lo,
This happened, as he sat in an alcove
Elaborating rhyme for 'love' – *not* 'dove.'

XXXI

He was alone: silence and solitude
  Befit the votary of the Muse. Around,
Nature – not our new picturesque and rude,
  But trim tree-cinctured stately garden-ground –
Breathed polish and politeness. All-imbued
  With these, he sat absorbed in one profound
Excogitation 'Were it best to hint
Or boldly boast "She loves me, – Araminte"?'

XXXII

When suddenly flashed lightning, searing sight
  Almost, so close to eyes; then, quick on flash,
Followed the thunder, splitting earth downright
  Where René sat a-rhyming: with huge crash
Of marble into atoms infinite –
  Marble which, stately, dared the world to dash
The stone-thing proud, high-pillared, from its place:
One flash, and dust was all that lay at base.

XXXIII

So, when the horrible confusion loosed
Its wrappage round his senses, and, with breath,
Seeing and hearing by degrees induced
Conviction what he felt was life, not death –
His fluttered faculties came back to roost
One after one, as fowls do: ay, beneath,
About his very feet there, lay in dust
Earthly presumption paid by heaven's disgust.

XXXIV

For, what might be the thunder-smitten thing
But, pillared high and proud, in marble guise,
A ducal crown – which meant 'Now Duke: Next, King'?
Since such the Prince was, not in his own eyes
Alone, but all the world's. Pebble from sling
Prostrates a giant; so can pulverize
Marble pretension – how much more, make moult
A peacock-prince his plume – God's thunderbolt.

XXXV

That was enough for René, that first fact
Thus flashed into him. Up he looked: all blue
And bright the sky above; earth firm, compact
Beneath his footing, lay apparent too;
Opposite stood the pillar: nothing lacked
There, but the Duke's crown: see, its fragments strew
The earth, – about his feet lie atoms fine
Where he sat nursing late his fourteenth line!

XXXVI

So, for the moment, all the universe
Being abolished, all 'twixt God and him, –
Earth's praise or blame, its blessing or its curse,
Of one and the same value, – to the brim
Flooded with truth for better or for worse, –
He pounces on the writing-paper, prim,
Keeping its place on table: not a dint
Nor speck had damaged 'Ode to Araminte.'

XXXVII

And over the neat crowquill calligraph
His pen goes blotting, blurring, as an ox
Tramples a flower-bed in a garden, – laugh
You may! – so does not he, whose quick heart knocks
Audibly at his breast: an epitaph
On earth's break-up, amid the falling rocks,
He might be penning in a wild dismay,
Caught with his work half-done on Judgement Day.

XXXVIII

And what is it so terribly he pens,
Ruining 'Cupid, Venus, wile and smile,
Hearts, darts,' and all his day's *divinior mens*
Judged necessary to a perfect style?
Little recks René, with a breast to cleanse,
Of Rhadamanthine law that reigned erewhile:
Brimful of truth, truth's outburst will convince
(Style or no style) who bears truth's brunt – the Prince.

XXXIX

'Condé, called "Duke," be called just "Duke," not more
To life's end! "Next King" thou forsooth wilt be?
Ay, when this bauble, as it decked before
Thy pillar, shall again, for France to see,
Take its proud station there! Let France adore
No longer an illusive mock-sun – thee –
But keep her homage for Sol's self, about
To rise and put pretenders to the rout!

XL

'What? France so God-abandoned that her root
Regal, though many a Spring it gave no sign,
Lacks power to make the bole, now branchless, shoot
Greenly as ever? Nature, though benign,
Thwarts ever the ambitious and astute.
In store for such is punishment condign:
Sure as thy Duke's crown to the earth was hurled,
So sure, next year, a Dauphin glads the world!'

XLI
Which penned – some forty lines to this effect –
Our René folds his paper, marches brave
Back to the mansion, luminous, erect,
Triumphant, an emancipated slave.
There stands the Prince. 'How now? My Duke's crown wrecked?
What may this mean?' The answer René gave
Was – handing him the verses, with the due
Incline of body: 'Sir, God's word to you!'

XLII
The Prince read, paled, was silent; all around,
The courtier-company, to whom he passed
The paper, read, in equal silence bound.
René grew also by degrees aghast
At his own fit of courage – palely found
Way of retreat from that pale presence: classed
Once more among the cony-kind. 'Oh, son,
It is a feeble folk!' saith Solomon.

XLIII
Vainly he apprehended evil: since,
When, at the year's end, even as foretold,
Forth came the Dauphin who discrowned the Prince
Of that long-craved mere visionary gold,
'Twas no fit time for envy to evince
Malice, be sure! The timidest grew bold:
Of all that courtier-company not one
But left the semblance for the actual sun.

XLIV
And all sorts and conditions that stood by
At René's burning moment, bright escape
Of soul, bore witness to the prophecy.
Which witness took the customary shape
Of verse; a score of poets in full cry
Hailed the inspired one. Nantes and Tours agape,
Soon Paris caught the infection; gaining strength,
How could it fail to reach the Court at length?

XLV

'O poet!' smiled King Louis, 'and besides,
  O prophet! Sure, by miracle announced,
My babe will prove a prodigy. Who chides
  Henceforth the unchilded monarch shall be trounced
For irreligion: since the fool derides
  Plain miracle by which this prophet pounced
Exactly on the moment I should lift
Like Simeon, in my arms, a babe, "God's gift!"

XLVI

'So call the boy! and call this bard and seer
  By a new title! him I raise to rank
Of "Royal Poet": poet without peer!
  Whose fellows only have themselves to thank
If humbly they must follow in the rear
  My René. He's the master: they must clank
Their chains of song, confessed his slaves; for why?
They poetize, while he can prophesy!'

XLVII

So said, so done; our René rose august,
  'The Royal Poet'; straightway put in type
His poem-prophecy, and (fair and just
  Procedure) added, – now that time was ripe
For proving friends did well his word to trust, –
  Those attestations, tuned to lyre or pipe,
Which friends broke out with when he dared foretell
The Dauphin's birth: friends trusted, and did well.

XLVIII

Moreover he got painted by Du Pré,
  Engraved by Daret also, and prefixed
The portrait to his book: a crown of bay
  Circled his brows, with rose and myrtle mixed;
And Latin verses, lovely in their way,
  Described him as 'the biforked hill betwixt:
Since he hath scaled Parnassus at one jump,
Joining the Delphic quill and Getic trump.'

XLIX

Whereof came . . . What, it lasts, our spirt, thus long
– The red fire? That's the reason must excuse
My letting flicker René's prophet-song
No longer; for its pertinacious hues
Must fade before its fellow joins the throng
Of sparks departed up the chimney, dues
To dark oblivion. At the word, it winks,
Rallies, relapses, dwindles, deathward sinks!

L

So does our poet. All this burst of fame,
Fury of favour, Royal Poetship,
Prophetship, book, verse, picture – thereof came
– Nothing! That's why I would not let outstrip
Red his green rival flamelet: just the same
Ending in smoke waits both! In vain we rip
The past, no further faintest trace remains
Of René to reward our pious pains.

LI

Somebody saw a portrait framed and glazed
At Croisic. 'Who may be this glorified
Mortal unheard-of hitherto?' amazed
That person asked the owner by his side,
Who proved as ignorant. The question raised
Provoked inquiry; key by key was tried
On Croisic's portrait-puzzle, till back flew
The wards at one key's touch, which key was – Who?

LII

The other famous poet! Wait thy turn,
Thou green, our red's competitor! Enough
Just now to note 'twas he that itched to learn
(A hundred years ago) how fate could puff
Heaven-high (a hundred years before) then spurn
To suds so big a bubble in some huff:
Since green too found red's portrait, – having heard
Hitherto of red's rare self not one word.

LIII

And he with zeal addressed him to the task
Of hunting out, by all and any means,
– Who might the brilliant bard be, born to bask
Butterfly-like in shine which kings and queens
And baby-dauphins shed? Much need to ask!
Is fame so fickle that what perks and preens
The eyed wing, one imperial minute, dips
Next sudden moment into blind eclipse?

LIV

After a vast expenditure of pains,
Our second poet found the prize he sought:
Urged in his search by something that restrains
From undue triumph famed ones who have fought,
Or simply, poetizing, taxed their brains:
Something that tells such – dear is triumph bought
If it means only basking in the midst
Of fame's brief sunshine, as thou, René, didst.

LV

For, what did searching find at last but this?
Quoth somebody 'I somehow somewhere seem
To think I heard one old De Chevaye is
Or was possessed of René's works!' which gleam
Of light from out the dark proved not amiss
To track, by correspondence on the theme;
And soon the twilight broadened into day,
For thus to question answered De Chevaye.

LVI

'True it is, I did once possess the works
You want account of – works – to call them so, –
Comprised in one small book: the volume lurks
(Some fifty leaves *in duodecimo*)
'Neath certain ashes which my soul it irks
Still to remember, because long ago
That and my other rare shelf-occupants
Perished by burning of my house at Nantes.

LVII

'Yet of that book one strange particular
Still stays in mind with me' – and thereupon
Followed the story. 'Few the poems are;
The book was two-thirds filled up with this one,
And sundry witnesses from near and far
That here at least was prophesying done
By prophet, so as to preclude all doubt,
Before the thing he prophesied about.'

LVIII

That's all he knew, and all the poet learned,
And all that you and I are like to hear
Of René; since not only book is burned
But memory extinguished, – nay, I fear,
Portrait is gone too: nowhere I discerned
A trace of it at Croisic. 'Must a tear
Needs fall for that?' you smile. 'How fortune fares
With such a mediocrity, who cares?'

LIX

Well, I care – intimately care to have
Experience how a human creature felt
In after-life, who bore the burden grave
Of certainly believing God had dealt
For once directly with him: did not rave
– A maniac, did not find his reason melt
– An idiot, but went on, in peace or strife,
The world's way, lived an ordinary life.

LX

How many problems that one fact would solve!
An ordinary soul, no more, no less,
About whose life earth's common sights revolve,
On whom is brought to bear, by thunder-stress,
This fact – God tasks him, and will not absolve
Task's negligent performer! Can you guess
How such a soul, – the task performed to point, –
Goes back to life nor finds things out of joint?

LXI

Does he stand stock-like henceforth? or proceed
  Dizzily, yet with course straightforward still,
Down-trampling vulgar hindrance? – as the reed
  Is crushed beneath its tramp when that blind will
Hatched in some old-world beast's brain bids it speed
  Where the sun wants brute-presence to fulfil
Life's purpose in a new far zone, ere ice
Enwomb the pasture-tract its fortalice.

LXII

I think no such direct plain truth consists
  With actual sense and thought and what they take
To be the solid walls of life: mere mists –
  How such would, at that truth's first piercing, break
Into the nullity they are! – slight lists
  Wherein the puppet-champions wage, for sake
Of some mock-mistress, mimic war: laid low
At trumpet-blast, there's shown the world, one foe!

LXIII

No, we must play the pageant out, observe
  The tourney-regulations, and regard
Success – to meet the blunted spear nor swerve,
  Failure – to break no bones yet fall on sward;
Must prove we have – not courage? well then, – nerve!
  And, at the day's end, boast the crown's award –
Be warranted as promising to wield
Weapons, no sham, in a true battle-field.

LXIV

Meantime, our simulated thunderclaps
  Which tell us counterfeited truths – these same
Are – sound, when music storms the soul, perhaps?
  – Sight, beauty, every dart of every aim
That touches just, then seems, by strange relapse,
  To fall effectless from the soul it came
As if to fix its own, but simply smote
And startled to vague beauty more remote?

LXV

So do we gain enough – yet not too much –
   Acquaintance with that outer element
Wherein there's operation (call it such!)
   Quite of another kind than we the pent
On earth are proper to receive. Our hutch
   Lights up at the least chink: let roof be rent –
How inmates huddle, blinded at first spasm,
Cognizant of the sun's self through the chasm!

LXVI

Therefore, who knows if this our René's quick
   Subsidence from as sudden noise and glare
Into oblivion was impolitic?
   No doubt his soul became at once aware
That, after prophecy, the rhyming-trick
   Is poor employment: human praises scare
Rather than soothe ears all a-tingle yet
With tones few hear and live, but none forget.

LXVII

There's our first famous poet. Step thou forth
   Second consummate songster! See, the tongue
Of fire that typifies thee, owns thy worth
   In yellow, purple mixed its green among,
No pure and simple resin from the North,
   But composite with virtues that belong
To Southern culture! Love not more than hate
Helped to a blaze . . . But I anticipate.

LXVIII

Prepare to witness a combustion rich
   And riotously splendid, far beyond
Poor René's lambent little streamer which
   Only played candle to a Court grown fond
By baby-birth: this soared to such a pitch,
   Alternately such colours doffed and donned,
That when I say it dazzled Paris – please
Know that it brought Voltaire upon his knees!

LXIX

Who did it, was a dapper gentleman,
  Paul Desforges Maillard, Croisickese by birth,
Whose birth that century ended which began
  By similar bestowment on our earth
Of the aforesaid René. Cease to scan
  The ways of Providence! See Croisic's dearth –
Not Paris in its plenitude – suffice
To furnish France with her best poet twice!

LXX

Till he was thirty years of age, the vein
  Poetic yielded rhyme by drops and spirts:
In verses of society had lain
  His talent chiefly; but the Muse asserts
Privilege most by treating with disdain
  Epics the bard mouths out, or odes he blurts
Spasmodically forth. Have people time
And patience nowadays for thought in rhyme?

LXXI

So, his achievements were the quatrain's inch
  Of homage, or at most the sonnet's ell
Of admiration: welded lines with clinch
  Of ending word and word, to every belle
In Croisic's bounds; these, brisk as any finch,
  He twittered till his fame had reached as well
Guérande as Batz; but there fame stopped, for – curse
On fortune – outside lay the universe!

LXXII

That's Paris. Well, – why not break bounds, and send
  Song onward till it echo at the gates
Of Paris whither all ambitions tend,
  And end too, seeing that success there sates
The soul which hungers most for fame? Why spend
  A minute in deciding, while, by Fate's
Decree, there happens to be just the prize
Proposed there, suiting souls that poetize?

LXXIII

A prize indeed, the Academy's own self
Proposes to what bard shall best indite
A piece describing how, through shoal and shelf,
The Art of Navigation, steered aright,
Has, in our last king's reign, – the lucky elf, –
Reached, one may say, Perfection's haven quite,
And there cast anchor. At a glance one sees
The subject's crowd of capabilities!

LXXIV

Neptune and Amphitrité! Thetis, who
Is either Tethys or as good – both tag!
Triton can shove along a vessel too:
It's Virgil! Then the winds that blow or lag, –
De Maille, Vendôme, Vermandois! Toulouse blew
Longest, we reckon: he must puff the flag
To fullest outflare; while our lacking nymph
Be Anne of Austria, Regent o'er the lymph!

LXXV

Promised, performed! Since *irritabilis gens*
Holds of the feverish impotence that strives
To stay an itch by prompt resource to pen's
Scratching itself on paper; placid lives,
Leisurely works mark the *divinior mens*:
Bees brood above the honey in their hives;
Gnats are the busy bustlers. Splash and scrawl, –
Completed lay thy piece, swift penman Paul!

LXXVI

To Paris with the product! This dispatched,
One had to wait the Forty's slow and sure
Verdict, as best one might. Our penman scratched
Away perforce the itch that knows no cure
But daily paper-friction: more than matched
His first feat by a second – tribute pure
And heartfelt to the Forty when their voice
Should peal with one accord 'Be Paul our choice!'

LXXVII

Scratch, scratch went much laudation of that sane
   And sound Tribunal, delegates august
Of Phoebus and the Muses' sacred train –
   Whom every poetaster tries to thrust
From where, high-throned, they dominate the Seine:
   Fruitless endeavour, – fail it shall and must!
Whereof in witness have not one and all
The Forty voices pealed 'Our Choice be Paul'?

LXXVIII

Thus Paul discounted his applause. Alack
   For human expectation! Scarcely ink
Was dry when, lo, the perfect piece came back
   Rejected, shamed! Some other poet's clink
'Thetis and Tethys' had seduced the pack
   Of pedants to declare perfection's pink
A singularly poor production. 'Whew!
The Forty are stark fools, I always knew.'

LXXIX

First fury over (for Paul's race – to-wit,
   Brain-vibrios – wriggle clear of protoplasm
Into minute life that's one fury-fit),
   'These fools shall find a bard's enthusiasm
Comports with what should counterbalance it –
   Some knowledge of the world! No doubt, orgasm
Effects the birth of verse which, born, demands
Prosaic ministration, swaddling-bands!

LXXX

'Verse must be cared for at this early stage,
   Handled, nay dandled even. I should play
Their game indeed if, till it grew of age,
   I meekly let these dotards frown away
My bantling from the rightful heritage
   Of smiles and kisses! Let the public say
If it be worthy praises or rebukes,
My poem, from these Forty old perukes!'

LXXXI

So, by a friend, who boasts himself in grace
With no less than the Chevalier La Roque, –
Eminent in those days for pride of place,
Seeing he had it in his power to block
The way or smooth the road to all the race
Of literators trudging up to knock
At Fame's exalted temple-door – for why?
He edited the Paris 'Mercury': –

LXXXII

By this friend's help the Chevalier receives
Paul's poem, prefaced by the due appeal
To Caesar from the Jews. As duly heaves
A sigh the Chevalier, about to deal
With case so customary – turns the leaves,
Finds nothing there to borrow, beg or steal –
Then brightens up the critic's brow deep-lined.
'The thing may be so cleverly declined!'

LXXXIII

Down to desk, out with paper, up with quill,
Dip and indite! 'Sir, gratitude immense
For this true draught from the Pierian rill!
Our Academic clodpoles must be dense
Indeed to stand unirrigated still.
No less, we critics dare not give offence
To grandees like the Forty: while we mock
We grin and bear. So, here's your piece! La Roque.'

LXXXIV

'There now!' cries Paul: 'the fellow can't avoid
Confessing that my piece deserves the palm;
And yet he dares not grant me space enjoyed
By every scribbler he permits embalm
His crambo in the Journal's corner! Cloyed
With stuff like theirs, no wonder if a qualm
Be caused by verse like mine: though that's no cause
For his defrauding me of just applause.

LXXXV

'Aha, he fears the Forty, this poltroon?
First let him fear *me!* Change smooth speech to rough!
I'll speak my mind out, show the fellow soon
Who is the foe to dread: insist enough
On my own merits till, as clear as noon,
He sees I am no man to take rebuff
As patiently as scribblers may and must!
Quick to the onslaught, out sword, cut and thrust!'

LXXXVI

And thereupon a fierce epistle flings
Its challenge in the critic's face. Alack!
Our bard mistakes his man! The gauntlet rings
On brazen visor proof against attack.
Prompt from his editorial throne up springs
The insulted magnate, and his mace falls, thwack,
On Paul's devoted brainpan, – quite away
From common courtesies of fencing-play!

LXXXVII

'Sir, will you have the truth? This piece of yours
Is simply execrable past belief.
I shrank from saying so; but, since naught cures
Conceit but truth, truth's at your service! Brief,
Just so long as "The Mercury" endures,
So long are you excluded by its Chief
From corner, nay, from cranny! Play the cock
O' the roost, henceforth, at Croisic!' wrote La Roque.

LXXXVIII

Paul yellowed, whitened, as his wrath from red
Waxed incandescent. Now, this man of rhyme
Was merely foolish, faulty in the head
Not heart of him: conceit's a venial crime.
'Oh by no means malicious!' cousins said:
Fussily feeble, – harmless all the time,
Piddling at so-called satire – well-advised,
He held in most awe whom he satirized.

LXXXIX

Accordingly his kith and kin – removed
  From emulation of the poet's gift
By power and will – these rather liked, nay, loved
  The man who gave his family a lift
Out of the Croisic level; 'disapproved
  Satire so trenchant.' Thus our poet sniffed
Home-incense, though too churlish to unlock
'The Mercury's' box of ointment was La Roque.

XC

But when Paul's visage grew from red to white,
  And from his lips a sort of mumbling fell
Of who was to be kicked, – 'And serve him right' –
  A gay voice interposed – 'did kicking well
Answer the purpose! Only – if I might
  Suggest as much – a far more potent spell
Lies in another kind of treatment. Oh,
Women are ready at resource, you know!

XCI

'Talent should minister to genius! Good:
  The proper and superior smile returns.
Hear me with patience! Have you understood
  The only method whereby genius earns
Fit guerdon nowadays? In knightly mood
  You entered lists with visor up; one learns
Too late that, had you mounted Roland's crest,
"Room!" they had roared – La Roque with all the rest!

XCII

'Why did you first of all transmit your piece
  To those same priggish Forty unprepared
Whether to rank you with the swans or geese
  By friendly intervention? If they dared
Count you a cackler, – wonders never cease!
  I think it still more wondrous that you bared
Your brow (my earlier image) as if praise
Were gained by simple fighting nowadays!

XCIII

'Your next step showed a touch of the true means
  Whereby desert is crowned: not force but wile
Came to the rescue. "Get behind the scenes!"
  Your friend advised: he writes, sets forth your style
And title, to such purpose intervenes
  That you get velvet-compliment three-pile;
And, though "The Mercury" said "nay," nor stock
Nor stone did his refusal prove La Roque.

XCIV

'Why must you needs revert to the high hand,
  Imperative procedure – what you call
"Taking on merit your exclusive stand"?
  Stand, with a vengeance! Soon you went to wall,
You and your merit! Only fools command
  When folk are free to disobey them, Paul!
You've learnt your lesson, found out what's o'clock,
By this uncivil answer of La Roque.

XCV

'Now let me counsel! Lay this piece on shelf
  – Masterpiece though it be! From out your desk
Hand me some lighter sample, verse the elf
  Cupid inspired you with, no god grotesque
Presiding o'er the Navy! I myself
  Hand-write what's legible yet picturesque;
I'll copy fair and femininely frock
Your poem masculine that courts La Roque!

XCVI

'Deïdamia he – Achilles thou!
  Ha, ha, these ancient stories come so apt!
My sex, my youth, my rank I next avow
  In a neat prayer for kind perusal. Sapped
I see the walls which stand so stoutly now!
  I see the toils about the game entrapped
By honest cunning! Chains of lady's-smock,
Not thorn and thistle, tether fast La Roque!'

XCVII

Now, who might be the speaker sweet and arch
   That laughed above Paul's shoulder as it heaved
With the indignant heart? – bade steal a march
   And not continue charging? Who conceived
This plan which set our Paul, like pea you parch
   On fire-shovel, skipping, of a load relieved,
From arm-chair moodiness to escritoire
Sacred to Phoebus and the tuneful choir?

XCVIII

Who but Paul's sister! named of course like him
   'Desforges'; but, mark you, in those days a queer
Custom obtained, – who knows whence grew the whim? –
   That people could not read their title clear
To reverence till their own true names, made dim
   By daily mouthing, pleased to disappear,
Replaced by brand-new bright ones: Arouet,
For instance, grew Voltaire; Desforges – Malcrais.

XCIX

'Demoiselle Malcrais de la Vigne' – because
   The family possessed at Brederac
A vineyard, – few grapes, many hips-and-haws, –
   Still a nice Breton name. As breast and back
Of this vivacious beauty gleamed through gauze,
   So did her sprightly nature nowise lack
Lustre when draped, the fashionable way,
In 'Malcrais de la Vigne' – more short, 'Malcrais.'

C

Out from Paul's escritoire behold escape
   The hoarded treasure! verse falls thick and fast,
Sonnets and songs of every size and shape.
   The lady ponders on her prize; at last
Selects one which – Oh angel and yet ape! –
   Her malice thinks is probably surpassed
In badness by no fellow of the flock,
Copies it fair, and 'Now for my La Roque!'

CI

So, to him goes, with the neat manuscript,
The soft petitionary letter. 'Grant
A fledgeling novice that with wing unclipt
She soar her little circuit, habitant
Of an old manor; buried in which crypt,
How can the youthful châtelaine but pant
For disemprisonment by one *ad hoc*
Appointed "Mercury's" Editor, La Roque?'

CII

'Twas an epistle that might move the Turk!
More certainly it moved our middle-aged
Pen-driver drudging at his weary work,
Raked the old ashes up and disengaged
The sparks of gallantry which always lurk
Somehow in literary breasts, assuaged
In no degree by compliments on style;
Are Forty wagging beards worth one girl's smile?

CIII

In trips the lady's poem, takes its place
Of honour in the gratified Gazette,
With due acknowledgement of power and grace;
Prognostication, too, that higher yet
The Breton Muse will soar: fresh youth, high race,
Beauty and wealth have amicably met
That Demoiselle Malcrais may fill the chair
Left vacant by the loss of Deshoulières.

CIV

'There!' cried the lively lady. 'Who was right –
You in the dumps, or I the merry maid
Who know a trick or two can baffle spite
Tenfold the force of this old fool's? Afraid
Of Editor La Roque? But come! next flight
Shall outsoar – Deshoulières alone? My blade,
Sappho herself shall you confess outstript!
Quick, Paul, another dose of manuscript!'

CV

And so, once well a-foot, advanced the game:
  More and more verses, corresponding gush
On gush of praise, till everywhere acclaim
  Rose to the pitch of uproar. 'Sappho? Tush!
Sure "Malcrais on her Parrot" puts to shame
  Deshoulières' pastoral, clay not worth a rush
Beside this find of treasure, gold in crock,
Unearthed in Brittany, – nay, ask La Roque!'

CVI

Such was the Paris tribute. 'Yes,' you sneer,
  'Ninnies stock Noodledom, but folk more sage
Resist contagious folly, never fear!'
  Do they? Permit me to detach one page
From the huge Album which from far and near
  Poetic praises blackened in a rage
Of rapture! and that page shall be – who stares
Confounded now, I ask you? – just Voltaire's!

CVII

Ay, sharpest shrewdest steel that ever stabbed
  To death Imposture through the armour-joints!
How did it happen that gross Humbug grabbed
  Thy weapons, gouged thine eyes out? Fate appoints
That pride shall have a fall, or I had blabbed
  Hardly that Humbug, whom thy soul aroints,
Could thus cross-buttock thee caught unawares,
And dismalest of tumbles proved – Voltaire's!

CVIII

See his epistle extant yet, wherewith
  'Henri' in verse and 'Charles' in prose he sent
To do her suit and service! Here's the pith
  Of half a dozen stanzas – stones which went
To build that simulated monolith –
  Sham love in due degree with homage blent
As sham – which in the vast of volumes scares
The traveller still: 'That stucco-heap – Voltaire's?'

CIX

'Oh thou, whose clarion-voice has overflown
The wilds to startle Paris that's one ear!
Thou who such strange capacity hast shown
For joining all that's grand with all that's dear,
Knowledge with power to please – Deshoulières grown
Learned as Dacier in thy person! mere
Weak fruit of idle hours, these crabs of mine
I dare lay at thy feet, O Muse divine!

CX

'Charles was my taskwork only; Henri trod
My hero erst; and now, my heroine – she
Shall be thyself! True – is it true, great God?
Certainly love henceforward must not be!
Yet all the crowd of Fine Arts fail – how odd! –
Tried turn by turn, to fill a void in me!
There's no replacing love with these, alas!
Yet all I can I do to prove no ass.

CXI

'I labour to amuse my freedom; but
Should any sweet young creature slavery preach,
And – borrowing thy vivacious charm, the slut! –
Make me, in thy engaging words, a speech,
Soon should I see myself in prison shut
With all imaginable pleasure.' Reach
The washhand-basin for admirers! There's
A stomach-moving tribute – and Voltaire's!

CXII

Suppose it a fantastic billet-doux,
Adulatory flourish, not worth frown!
What say you to the Fathers of Trévoux?
These in their Dictionary have her down
Under the heading 'Author': 'Malcrais, too,
Is "Author" of much verse that claims renown.'
While Jean-Baptiste Rousseau . . . but why proceed?
Enough of this – something too much, indeed!

CXIII

At last La Roque, unwilling to be left
  Behindhand in the rivalry, broke bounds
Of figurative passion; hilt and heft,
  Plunged his huge downright love through what surrounds
The literary female bosom; reft
  Away its veil of coy reserve with 'Zounds!
I love thee, Breton Beauty! All's no use!
Body and soul I love, – the big word's loose!'

CXIV

He's greatest now and to de-struc-ti-on
  Nearest. Attend the solemn word I quote,
O Paul! *There's no pause at per-fec-ti-on.*
  Thus knolls thy knell the Doctor's bronzèd throat!
Greatness a period hath, no sta-ti-on!
  Better and truer verse none ever wrote
(Despite the antique outstretched *a-i-on*)
Than thou, revered and magisterial Donne!

CXV

Flat on his face, La Roque, and, – pressed to heart
  His dexter hand, – Voltaire with bended knee!
Paul sat and sucked-in triumph; just apart
  Leaned over him his sister. 'Well!' smirks he,
And 'Well?' she answers, smiling – woman's art
  To let a man's own mouth, not hers, decree
What shall be next move which decides the game:
Success? She said so. Failure? His the blame.

CXVI

'Well!' this time forth affirmatively comes
  With smack of lip, and long-drawn sigh through teeth
Close clenched o'er satisfaction, as the gums
  Were tickled by a sweetmeat teased beneath
Palate by lubricating tongue: 'Well! crumbs
  Of comfort these, undoubtedly! no death
Likely from famine at Fame's feast! 'tis clear
I may put claim in for my pittance, Dear!

CXVII

'La Roque, Voltaire, my lovers! Then disguise
Has served its turn, grows idle; let it drop!
I shall to Paris, flaunt there in men's eyes
My proper manly garb and mount a-top
The pedestal that waits me, take the prize
Awarded Hercules. He threw a sop
To Cerberus who let him pass, you know,
Then, following, licked his heels: exactly so!

CXVIII

'I like the prospect – their astonishment,
Confusion: wounded vanity, no doubt,
Mixed motives; how I see the brows quick bent!
"What, sir, yourself, none other, brought about
This change of estimation? Phoebus sent
His shafts as from Diana?" Critic pout
Turns courtier smile: "Lo, him we took for her!
Pleasant mistake! You bear no malice, sir?"

CXIX

'Eh, my Diana?' But Diana kept
Smilingly silent with fixed needle-sharp
Much-meaning eyes that seemed to intercept
Paul's very thoughts ere they had time to warp
From earnest into sport the words they leapt
To life with – changed as when maltreated harp
Renders in tinkle what some player-prig
Means for a grave tune though it proves a jig.

CXX

'What, Paul, and are my pains thus thrown away,
My lessons end in loss?' at length fall slow
The pitying syllables, her lips allay
The satire of by keeping in full flow,
Above their coral reef, bright smiles at play:
'Can it be, Paul thus fails to rightly know
And altogether estimate applause
As just so many asinine hee-haws?

CXXI

'I thought to show you' . . . 'Show me,' Paul in-broke
'My poetry is rubbish, and the world
That rings with my renown a sorry joke!
What fairer test of worth than that, form furled,
I entered the arena? Yet you croak
Just as if Phoebé and not Phoebus hurled
The dart and struck the Python! What, he crawls
Humbly in dust before your feet, not Paul's?

CXXII

'Nay, 'tis no laughing matter though absurd
If there's an end of honesty on earth!
La Roque sends letters, lying every word!
Voltaire makes verse, and of himself makes mirth
To the remotest age! Rousseau's the third
Who, driven to despair amid such dearth
Of people that want praising, finds no one
More fit to praise than Paul the simpleton!

CXXIII

'Somebody says – if a man writes at all
It is to show the writer's kith and kin
He was unjustly thought a natural;
And truly, sister, I have yet to win
Your favourable word, it seems, for Paul
Whose poetry you count not worth a pin
Though well enough esteemed by these Voltaires,
Rousseaus and suchlike: let them quack, who cares?'

CXXIV

'– To Paris with you, Paul! Not one word's waste
Further: my scrupulosity was vain!
Go triumph! Be my foolish fears effaced
From memory's record! Go, to come again
With glory crowned, – by sister re-embraced,
Cured of that strange delusion of her brain
Which led her to suspect that Paris gloats
On male limbs mostly when in petticoats!'

CXXV

So laughed her last word, with the little touch
  Of malice proper to the outraged pride
Of any artist in a work too much
  Shorn of its merits. 'By all means be tried
The opposite procedure! Cast your crutch
  Away, no longer crippled, nor divide
The credit of your march to the World's Fair
With sister Cherry-cheeks who helped you there!'

CXXVI

Crippled, forsooth! what courser sprightlier pranced
  Paris-ward than did Paul? Nay, dreams lent wings:
He flew, or seemed to fly, by dreams entranced.
  Dreams? wide-awake realities: no things
Dreamed merely were the missives that advanced
  The claim of Malcrais to consort with kings
Crowned by Apollo – not to say with queens
Cinctured by Venus for Idalian scenes.

CXXVII

Soon he arrives, forthwith is found before
  The outer gate of glory. Bold tic-toc
Announces there's a giant at the door.
  'Ay, sir, here dwells the Chevalier La Roque.'
'Lackey! Malcrais, – mind, no word less nor more! –
  Desires his presence. I've unearthed the brock:
Now, to transfix him!' There stands Paul erect,
Inched out his uttermost, for more effect.

CXXVIII

A bustling entrance: 'Idol of my flame!
  Can it be that my heart attains at last
Its longing? that you stand, the very same
  As in my visions? . . . Ha! hey, how?' aghast
Stops short the rapture. 'Oh, my boy's to blame!
  You merely are the messenger! Too fast
My fancy rushed to a conclusion. Pooh!
Well, sir, the lady's substitute is – who?'

CXXIX

Then Paul's smirk grows inordinate. 'Shake hands!
  Friendship not love awaits you, master mine,
Though nor Malcrais nor any mistress stands
  To meet your ardour! So, you don't divine
Who wrote the verses wherewith ring the land's
  Whole length and breadth? Just he whereof no line
Had ever leave to blot your Journal – eh?
Paul Desforges Maillard – otherwise Malcrais!'

CXXX

And there the two stood, stare confronting smirk,
  Awhile uncertain which should yield the *pas*.
In vain the Chevalier beat brain for quirk
  To help in this conjuncture; at length 'Bah!
Boh! Since I've made myself a fool, why shirk
  The punishment of folly? Ha, ha, ha,
Let me return your handshake!' Comic sock
For tragic buskin prompt thus changed La Roque.

CXXXI

'I'm nobody – a wren-like journalist;
  You've flown at higher game and winged your bird,
The golden eagle! That's the grand acquist!
  Voltaire's sly Muse, the tiger-cat, has purred
Prettily round your feet; but if she missed
  Priority of stroking, soon were stirred
The dormant spit-fire. To Voltaire! away,
Paul Desforges Maillard, otherwise Malcrais!'

CXXXII

Whereupon, arm in arm, and head in air,
  The two begin their journey. Need I say,
La Roque had felt the talon of Voltaire,
  Had a long-standing little debt to pay,
And pounced, you may depend, on such a rare
  Occasion for its due discharge? So, gay
And grenadier-like, marching to assault,
They reach the enemy's abode, there halt.

CXXXIII

'I'll be announcer!' quoth La Roque: 'I know,
  Better than you, perhaps, my Breton bard,
How to procure an audience! He's not slow
  To smell a rat, this scamp Voltaire! Discard
The petticoats too soon, – you'll never show
  Your *haut-de-chausses* and all they've made or marred
In your true person. Here's his servant. Pray,
Will the great man see Demoiselle Malcrais?'

CXXXIV

Now, the great man was also, no whit less,
  The man of self-respect, – more great man he!
And bowed to social usage, dressed the dress,
  And decorated to the fit degree
His person; 'twas enough to bear the stress
  Of battle in the field, without, when free
From outside foes, inviting friends' attack
By – sword in hand? No, – ill-made coat on back!

CXXXV

And, since the announcement of his visitor
  Surprised him at his toilet, – never glass
Had such solicitation! 'Black, now – or
  Brown be the killing wig to wear? Alas,
Where's the rouge gone, this cheek were better for
  A tender touch of? Melted to a mass,
All my pomatum! There's at all events
A devil – for he's got among my scents!'

CXXXVI

So, 'barbered ten times o'er,' as Antony
  Paced to his Cleopatra, did at last
Voltaire proceed to the fair presence: high
  In colour, proud in port, as if a blast
Of trumpet bade the world 'Take note! draws nigh
  To Beauty, Power! Behold the Iconoclast,
The Poet, the Philosopher, the Rod
Of iron for imposture! Ah my God!'

CXXXVII

For there stands smirking Paul, and – what lights fierce
  The situation as with sulphur flash –
There grinning stands La Roque! No quarte-and-tierce
  Observes the grinning fencer, but, full dash
From breast to shoulderblade, the thrusts transpierce
  That armour against which so idly clash
The swords of priests and pedants! Victors there,
Two smirk and grin who have befooled – Voltaire!

CXXXVIII

A moment's horror; then quick turn-about
  On high-heeled shoe, – flurry of ruffles, flounce
Of wig-ties and of coat-tails, – and so out
  Of door banged wrathfully behind, goes – bounce –
Voltaire in tragic exit! vows, no doubt,
  Vengeance upon the couple. Did he trounce
Either, in point of fact? His anger's flash
Subsided if a culprit craved his cash.

CXXXIX

As for La Roque, he having laughed his laugh
  To heart's content, – the joke defunct at once,
Dead in the birth, you see, – its epitaph
  Was sober earnest. 'Well, sir, for the nonce,
You've gained the laurel; never hope to graff
  A second sprig of triumph there! Ensconce
Yourself again at Croisic: let it be
Enough you mastered both Voltaire and – me!

CXL

'Don't linger here in Paris to parade
  Your victory, and have the very boys
Point at you! "There's the little mouse which made
  Believe those two big lions that its noise,
Nibbling away behind the hedge, conveyed
  Intelligence that – portent which destroys
All courage in the lion's heart, with horn
That's fable – there lay couched the unicorn!"

CXLI

'Beware us, now we've found who fooled us! Quick
To cover! "In proportion to men's fright,
Expect their fright's revenge!" quoth politic
Old Machiavelli. As for me, – all's right:
I'm but a journalist. But no pin's prick
The tooth leaves when Voltaire is roused to bite!
So, keep your counsel, I advise! Adieu!
Good journey! Ha, ha, ha, Malcrais was – you!'

CXLII

'– Yes, I'm Malcrais, and somebody beside,
You snickering monkey!' thus winds up the tale
Our hero, safe at home, to that black-eyed
Cherry-cheeked sister, as she soothes the pale
Mortified poet. 'Let their worst be tried,
I'm their match henceforth – very man and male!
Don't talk to me of knocking-under! man
And male must end what petticoats began!

CXLIII

'How woman-like it is to apprehend
The world will eat its words! why, words transfixed
To stone, they stare at you in print, – at end,
Each writer's style and title! Choose betwixt
Fool and knave for his name, who should intend
To perpetrate a baseness so unmixed
With prospect of advantage! What is writ
Is writ: they've praised me, there's an end of it.

CXLIV

'No, Dear, allow me! I shall print these same
Pieces, with no omitted line, as Paul's.
Malcrais no longer, let me see folk blame
What they – praised simply? – placed on pedestals,
Each piece a statue in the House of Fame!
Fast will they stand there, though their presence galls
The envious crew: such show their teeth, perhaps
And snarl, but never bite! I know the chaps!'

CXLV

Oh Paul, oh piteously deluded! Pace
  Thy sad sterility of Croisic flats,
Watch, from their southern edge, the foamy race
  Of high-tide as it heaves the drowning mats
Of yellow-berried web-growth from their place,
  The rock-ridge, when, rolling as far as Batz,
One broadside crashes on it, and the crags,
That needle under, stream with weedy rags!

CXLVI

Or, if thou wilt, at inland Bergerac,
  Rude heritage but recognized domain,
Do as two here are doing: make hearth crack
  With logs until thy chimney roar again
Jolly with fire-glow! Let its angle lack
  No grace of Cherry-cheeks thy sister, fain
To do a sister's office and laugh smooth
Thy corrugated brow – that scowls forsooth!

CXLVII

Wherefore? Who does not know how these La Roques,
  Voltaires, can say and unsay, praise and blame,
Prove black white, white black, play at paradox
  And, when they seem to lose it, win the game?
Care not thou what this badger, and that fox,
  His fellow in rascality, call 'fame!'
Fiddlepin's end! Thou hadst it, – quack, quack, quack!
Have quietude from geese at Bergerac!

CXLVIII

Quietude! For, be very sure of this!
  A twelvemonth hence, and men shall know or care
As much for what today they clap or hiss
  As for the fashion of the wigs they wear,
Then wonder at. There's fame which, bale or bliss, –
  Got by no gracious word of great Voltaire
Or not-so-great La Roque, – is taken back
By neither, any more than Bergerac!

CXLIX

Too true! or rather, true as ought to be!
No more of Paul the man, Malcrais the maid,
Thenceforth for ever! One or two, I see,
Stuck by their poet: who the longest stayed
Was Jean-Baptiste Rousseau, and even he
Seemingly saddened as perforce he paid
A rhyming tribute 'After death, survive –
He hoped he should; and died while yet alive!'

CL

No, he hoped nothing of the kind, or held
His peace and died in silent good old age.
Him it was, curiosity impelled
To seek if there were extant still some page
Of his great predecessor, rat who belled
The cat once, and would never deign engage
In after-combat with mere mice, – saved from
More sonneteering, – René Gentilhomme.

CLI

Paul's story furnished forth that famous play
Of Piron's 'Métromanie': there you'll find
He's Francaleu, while Demoiselle Malcrais
Is Demoiselle No-end-of-names-behind!
As for Voltaire, he's Damis. Good and gay
The plot and dialogue, and all's designed
To spite Voltaire: at 'Something' such the laugh
Of simply 'Nothing!' (see his epitaph).

CLII

But truth, truth, that's the gold! and all the good
I find in fancy is, it serves to set
Gold's inmost glint free, gold which comes up rude
And rayless from the mine. All fume and fret
Of artistry beyond this point pursued
Brings out another sort of burnish: yet
Always the ingot has its very own
Value, a sparkle struck from truth alone.

CLIII

Now, take this sparkle and the other spirt
Of fitful flame, – twin births of our grey brand
That's sinking fast to ashes! I assert,
As sparkles want but fuel to expand
Into a conflagration no mere squirt
Will quench too quickly, so might Croisic strand,
Had Fortune pleased posterity to chowse,
Boast of her brace of beacons luminous.

CLIV

Did earlier Agamemnons lack their bard?
But later bards lacked Agamemnon too!
How often frustrate they of fame's award
Just because Fortune, as she listed, blew
Some slight bark's sails to bellying, mauled and marred
And forced to put about the First-rate! True,
Such tacks but for a time: still – small-craft ride
At anchor, rot while Beddoes breasts the tide!

CLV

Dear, shall I tell you? There's a simple test
Would serve, when people take on them to weigh
The worth of poets, 'Who was better, best,
This, that, the other bard?' (bards none gainsay
As good, observe! no matter for the rest)
'What quality preponderating may
Turn the scale as it trembles?' End the strife
By asking 'Which one led a happy life?'

CLVI

If one did, over his antagonist
That yelled or shrieked or sobbed or wept or wailed
Or simply had the dumps, – dispute who list, –
I count him victor. Where his fellow failed,
Mastered by his own means of might, – acquist
Of necessary sorrows, – he prevailed,
A strong since joyful man who stood distinct
Above slave-sorrows to his chariot linked.

CLVII

Was not his lot to feel more? What meant 'feel'
  Unless to suffer! Not, to see more? Sight –
What helped it but to watch the drunken reel
  Of vice and folly round him, left and right,
One dance of rogues and idiots! Not, to deal
  More with things lovely? What provoked the spite
Of filth incarnate, like the poet's need
Of other nutriment than strife and greed!

CLVIII

Who knows most, doubts most; entertaining hope,
  Means recognizing fear; the keener sense
Of all comprised within our actual scope
  Recoils from aught beyond earth's dim and dense.
Who, grown familiar with the sky, will grope
  Henceforward among groundlings? That's offence
Just as indubitably: stars abound
O'erhead, but then – what flowers make glad the ground!

CLIX

So, force is sorrow, and each sorrow, force:
  What then? since Swiftness gives the charioteer
The palm, his hope be in the vivid horse
  Whose neck God clothed with thunder, not the steer
Sluggish and safe! Yoke Hatred, Crime, Remorse,
  Despair: but ever 'mid the whirling fear,
Let, through the tumult, break the poet's face
Radiant, assured his wild slaves win the race!

CLX

Therefore I say . . . no, shall not say, but think,
  And save my breath for better purpose. White
From grey our log has burned to: just one blink
  That quivers, loth to leave it, as a sprite
The outworn body. Ere your eyelids' wink
  Punish who sealed so deep into the night
Your mouth up, for two poets dead so long, –
Here pleads a live pretender: right your wrong!

I

What a pretty tale you told me
   Once upon a time
– Said you found it somewhere (scold me!)
   Was it prose or was it rhyme,
Greek or Latin? Greek, you said,
While your shoulder propped my head.

II

Anyhow there's no forgetting
   This much if no more,
That a poet (pray, no petting!)
   Yes, a bard, sir, famed of yore,
Went where suchlike used to go,
Singing for a prize, you know.

III

Well, he had to sing, nor merely
   Sing but play the lyre;
Playing was important clearly
   Quite as singing: I desire,
Sir, you keep the fact in mind
For a purpose that's behind.

IV

There stood he, while deep attention
   Held the judges round,
– Judges able, I should mention,
   To detect the slightest sound
Sung or played amiss: such ears
Had old judges, it appears!

V

None the less he sang out boldly,
   Played in time and tune,
Till the judges, weighing coldly
   Each note's worth, seemed, late or soon,
Sure to smile 'In vain one tries
Picking faults out: take the prize!'

VI

When, a mischief! Were they seven
  Strings the lyre possessed?
Oh, and afterwards eleven,
  Thank you! Well, sir, – who had guessed
Such ill luck in store? – it happed
One of those same seven strings snapped.

VII

All was lost, then! No! a cricket
  (What 'cicada'? Pooh!)
– Some mad thing that left its thicket
  For mere love of music – flew
With its little heart on fire,
Lighted on the crippled lyre.

VIII

So that when (ah joy!) our singer
  For his truant string
Feels with disconcerted finger,
  What does cricket else but fling
Fiery heart forth, sound the note
Wanted by the throbbing throat?

IX

Ay and, ever to the ending,
  Cricket chirps at need,
Executes the hand's intending,
  Promptly, perfectly, – indeed
Saves the singer from defeat
With her chirrup low and sweet.

X

Till, at ending, all the judges
  Cry with one assent
'Take the prize – a prize who grudges
  Such a voice and instrument?
Why, we took your lyre for harp,
So it shrilled us forth F sharp!'

XI

Did the conqueror spurn the creature,
Once its service done?
That's no such uncommon feature
In the case when Music's son
Finds his Lotte's power too spent
For aiding soul-development.

XII

No! This other, on returning
Homeward, prize in hand,
Satisfied his bosom's yearning:
(Sir, I hope you understand!)
– Said 'Some record there must be
Of this cricket's help to me!'

XIII

So, he made himself a statue:
Marble stood, life-size;
On the lyre, he pointed at you
Perched his partner in the prize;
Never more apart you found
Her, he throned, from him, she crowned.

XIV

That's the tale: its application?
Somebody I know
Hopes one day for reputation
Through his poetry that's – Oh,
All so learned and so wise
And deserving of a prize!

XV

If he gains one, will some ticket,
When his statue's built,
Tell the gazer ''Twas a cricket
Helped my crippled lyre, whose lilt
Sweet and low, when strength usurped
Softness' place i' the scale, she chirped?

XVI

'For as victory was nighest,
While I sang and played, –
With my lyre at lowest, highest,
Right alike, – one string that made
"Love" sound soft was snapt in twain,
Never to be heard again, –

XVII

'Had not a kind cricket fluttered,
Perched upon the place
Vacant left, and duly uttered
"Love, Love, Love," whene'er the bass
Asked the treble to atone
For its somewhat sombre drone.'

XVIII

But you don't know music! Wherefore
Keep on casting pearls
To a – poet? All I care for
Is – to tell him that a girl's
'Love' comes aptly in when gruff
Grows his singing. (There, enough!)

Dramatic Idyls: First Series

1879

Martin Relph

My grandfather says he remembers he saw, when a youngster long ago,
On a bright May day, a strange old man, with a beard as white as snow,
Stand on the hill outside our town like a monument of woe,
And, striking his bare bald head the while, sob out the reason – so!

If I last as long as Methuselah I shall never forgive myself:
But – God forgive me, that I pray, unhappy Martin Relph,
As coward, coward I call him – him, yes, him! Away from me!
Get you behind the man I am now, you man that I used to be!

What can have sewed my mouth up, set me a-stare, all eyes, no tongue?
People have urged 'You visit a scare too hard on a lad so young!
You were taken aback, poor boy,' they urge, 'no time to regain your wits:
Besides it had maybe cost you life.' Ay, there is the cap which fits!

So, cap me, the coward, – thus! No fear! A cuff on the brow does good:
The feel of it hinders a worm inside which bores at the brain for food.
See now, there certainly seems excuse: for a moment, I trust, dear friends,
The fault was but folly, no fault of mine, or if mine, I have made amends!

For, every day that is first of May, on the hill-top, here stand I,
Martin Relph, and I strike my brow, and publish the reason why,
When there gathers a crowd to mock the fool. No fool, friends, since the bite
Of a worm inside is worse to bear: pray God I have balked him quite!

I'll tell you. Certainly much excuse! It came of the way they cooped

Us peasantry up in a ring just here, close huddling because tight-hooped
By the red-coats round us villagers all: they meant we should see the sight
And take the example, – see, not speak, for speech was the Captain's right.

'You clowns on the slope, beware!' cried he: 'This woman about to die
Gives by her fate fair warning to such acquaintance as play the spy.
Henceforth who meddle with matters of state above them perhaps will learn
That peasants should stick to their plough-tail, leave to the King the King's concern.

'Here's a quarrel that sets the land on fire, between King George and his foes:
What call has a man of your kind – much less, a woman – to interpose?
Yet you needs must be meddling, folk like you, not foes – so much the worse!
The many and loyal should keep themselves unmixed with the few perverse.

'Is the counsel hard to follow? I gave it you plainly a month ago,
And where was the good? The rebels have learned just all that they need to know.
Not a month since in we quietly marched: a week, and they had the news,
From a list complete of our rank and file to a note of our caps and shoes.

'All about all we did and all we were doing and like to do!
Only, I catch a letter by luck, and capture who wrote it, too.
Some of you men look black enough, but the milk-white face demure
Betokens the finger foul with ink: 'tis a woman who writes, be sure!

'Is it "Dearie, how much I miss your mouth!" – good natural stuff, she pens?

Some sprinkle of that, for a blind, of course: with talk about cocks and hens,
How "robin has built on the apple-tree, and our creeper which came to grief
Through the frost, we feared, is twining afresh round casement in famous leaf."

'But all for a blind! She soon glides frank into "Horrid the place is grown
With Officers here and Privates there, no nook we may call our own:
And Farmer Giles has a tribe to house, and lodging will be to seek
For the second Company sure to come ('tis whispered) on Monday week."

'And so to the end of the chapter! There! The murder, you see, was out:
Easy to guess how the change of mind in the rebels was brought about!
Safe in the trap would they now lie snug, had treachery made no sign:
But treachery meets a just reward, no matter if fools malign!

'That traitors had played us false, was proved – sent news which fell so pat:
And the murder was out – this letter of love, the sender of this sent that!
'Tis an ugly job, though, all the same – a hateful, to have to deal
With a case of the kind, when a woman's in fault: we soldiers need nerves of steel!

'So, I gave her a chance, dispatched post-haste a message to Vincent Parkes
Whom she wrote to; easy to find he was, since one of the King's own clerks,
Ay, kept by the King's own gold in the town close by where the rebels camp:
A sort of a lawyer, just the man to betray our sort – the scamp!

'"If her writing is simple and honest and only the lover-like stuff it looks,

And if you yourself are a loyalist, nor down in the rebels' books,
Come quick," said I, "and in person prove you are each of you clear of crime,
Or martial law must take its course: this day next week's the time!"

'Next week is now: does he come? Not he! Clean gone, our clerk, in a trice!
He has left his sweetheart here in the lurch: no need of a warning twice!
His own neck free, but his partner's fast in the noose still, here she stands
To pay for her fault. 'Tis an ugly job: but soldiers obey commands.

'And hearken wherefore I make a speech! Should any acquaintance share
The folly that led to the fault that is now to be punished, let fools beware!
Look black, if you please, but keep hands white: and, above all else, keep wives –
Or sweethearts or what they may be – from ink! Not a word now, on your lives!'

Black? but the Pit's own pitch was white to the Captain's face – the brute
With the bloated cheeks and the bulgy nose and the bloodshot eyes to suit!
He was muddled with wine, they say: more like, he was out of his wits with fear;
He had but a handful of men, that's true, – a riot might cost him dear.

And all that time stood Rosamund Page, with pinioned arms and face
Bandaged about, on the turf marked out for the party's firing-place.
I hope she was wholly with God: I hope 'twas His angel stretched a hand
To steady her so, like the shape of stone you see in our church-aisle stand.

I hope there was no vain fancy pierced the bandage to vex her eyes,
No face within which she missed without, no questions and no replies –
'Why did you leave me to die?' – 'Because . . .' Oh, fiends, too soon you grin
At merely a moment of hell, like that – such heaven as hell ended in!

Let mine end too! He gave the word, up went the guns in a line.
Those heaped on the hill were blind as dumb, – for, of all eyes, only mine
Looked over the heads of the foremost rank. Some fell on their knees in prayer,
Some sank to the earth, but all shut eyes, with a sole exception there.

That was myself, who had stolen up last, had sidled behind the group:
I am highest of all on the hill-top, there stand fixed while the others stoop!
From head to foot in a serpent's twine am I tightened: *I* touch ground?
No more than a gibbet's rigid corpse which the fetters rust around!

Can I speak, can I breathe, can I burst – aught else but see, see, only see?
And see I do – for there comes in sight – a man, it sure must be! –
Who staggeringly, stumblingly rises, falls, rises, at random flings his weight
On and on, anyhow onward – a man that's mad he arrives too late!

Else why does he wave a something white high-flourished above his head?
Why does not he call, cry, – curse the fool! – why throw up his arms instead?
O take this fist in your own face, fool! Why does not yourself shout 'Stay!
Here's a man comes rushing, might and main, with something he's mad to say'?

And a minute, only a moment, to have hell-fire boil up in your brain,
And ere you can judge things right, choose heaven, – time's over, repentance vain!
They level: a volley, a smoke and the clearing of smoke: I see no more
Of the man smoke hid, nor his frantic arms, nor the something white he bore.

But stretched on the field, some half-mile off, is an object. Surely dumb,
Deaf, blind were we struck, that nobody heard, not one of us saw him come!
Has he fainted through fright? One may well believe! What is it he holds so fast?
Turn him over, examine the face! Heyday! What, Vincent Parkes at last?

Dead! dead as she, by the self-same shot: one bullet has ended both,
Her in the body and him in the soul. They laugh at our plighted troth.
'Till death us do part?' Till death us do join past parting – that sounds like
Betrothal indeed! O Vincent Parkes, what need has my fist to strike?

I helped you: thus were you dead and wed: one bound, and your soul reached hers!
There is clenched in your hand the thing, signed, sealed, the paper which plain avers
She is innocent, innocent, plain as print, with the King's Arms broad engraved:
No one can hear, but if anyone high on the hill can see, she's saved!

And torn his garb and bloody his lips with heart-break – plain it grew
How the week's delay had been brought about: each guess at the end proved true.
It was hard to get at the folk in power: such waste of time! and then

Such pleading and praying, with, all the while, his lamb in the
lions' den!

And at length when he wrung their pardon out, no end to the
stupid forms –
The licence and leave: I make no doubt – what wonder if
passion warms
The pulse in a man if you play with his heart? – he was
something hasty in speech;
Anyhow, none would quicken the work: he had to beseech,
beseech!

And the thing once signed, sealed, safe in his grasp, – what
followed but fresh delays?
For the floods were out, he was forced to take such a roundabout
of ways!
And 'twas 'Halt there!' at every turn of the road, since he had to
cross the thick
Of the red-coats: what did they care for him and his 'Quick, for
God's sake, quick!'

Horse? but he had one: had it how long? till the first knave
smirked 'You brag
Yourself a friend of the King's? then lend to a King's friend
here your nag!'
Money to buy another? Why, piece by piece they plundered
him still,
With their 'Wait you must, – no help: if aught can help you, a
guinea will!'

And a borough there was – I forget the name – whose Mayor
must have the bench
Of Justices ranged to clear a doubt: for 'Vincent,' thinks he,
sounds French!
It well may have driven him daft, God knows! all man can
certainly know
Is – rushing and falling and rising, at last he arrived in a horror –
so!

When a word, cry, gasp, would have rescued both! Ay bite me!
The worm begins

At his work once more. Had cowardice proved – that only – my sin of sins!
Friends, look you here! Suppose . . . suppose . . . But mad I am, needs must be!
Judas the Damned would never have dared such a sin as I dream! For, see!

Suppose I had sneakingly loved her myself, my wretched self, and dreamed
In the heart of me 'She were better dead than happy and his!' – while gleamed
A light from hell as I spied the pair in a perfectest embrace,
He the saviour and she the saved, – bliss born of the very murder-place!

No! Say I was scared, friends! Call me fool and coward, but nothing worse!
Jeer at the fool and gibe at the coward! 'Twas ever the coward's curse
That fear breeds fancies in such: such take their shadow for substance still,
– A fiend at their back. I liked poor Parkes, – loved Vincent, if you will!

And her – why, I said 'Good morrow' to her, 'Good even,' and nothing more:
The neighbourly way! She was just to me as fifty had been before.
So, coward it is and coward shall be! There's a friend, now! Thanks! A drink
Of water I wanted: and now I can walk, get home by myself, I think.

Pheidippides

Χαίρετε, νικῶμεν.

First I salute this soil of the blessed, river and rock!
Gods of my birthplace, daemons and heroes, honour to all!
Then I name thee, claim thee for our patron, co-equal in praise
– Ay, with Zeus the Defender, with Her of the aegis and spear!
Also, ye of the bow and the buskin, praised be your peer,
Now, henceforth and forever, – O latest to whom I upraise
Hand and heart and voice! For Athens, leave pasture and flock!
Present to help, potent to save, Pan – patron I call!

Archons of Athens, topped by the tettix, see, I return!
See, 'tis myself here standing alive, no spectre that speaks!
Crowned with the myrtle, did you command me, Athens and
you,
'Run, Pheidippides, run and race, reach Sparta for aid!
Persia has come, we are here, where is She?' Your command I
obeyed,
Ran and raced: like stubble, some field which a fire runs through,
Was the space between city and city: two days, two nights did I
burn
Over the hills, under the dales, down pits and up peaks.

Into their midst I broke: breath served but for 'Persia has come!
Persia bids Athens proffer slaves'-tribute, water and earth;
Razed to the ground is Eretria – but Athens, shall Athens sink,
Drop into dust and die – the flower of Hellas utterly die,
Die, with the wide world spitting at Sparta, the stupid, the
stander-by?
Answer me quick, what help, what hand do you stretch o'er
destruction's brink?
How, – when? No care for my limbs! – there's lightning in all
and some –
Fresh and fit your message to bear, once lips give it birth!'

O my Athens – Sparta love thee? Did Sparta respond?
Every face of her leered in a furrow of envy, mistrust,
Malice, – each eye of her gave me its glitter of gratified hate!
Gravely they turned to take counsel, to cast for excuses. I stood

Quivering, – the limbs of me fretting as fire frets, an inch from dry wood:
'Persia has come, Athens asks aid, and still they debate?
Thunder, thou Zeus! Athene, are Spartans a quarry beyond
Swing of thy spear? Phoibos and Artemis, clang them "Ye must"!'

No bolt launched from Olumpos! Lo, their answer at last!
'Has Persia come, – does Athens ask aid, – may Sparta befriend?
Nowise precipitate judgement – too weighty the issue at stake!
Count we no time lost time which lags through respect to the Gods!
Ponder that precept of old, "No warfare, whatever the odds
In your favour, so long as the moon, half-orbed, is unable to take
Full-circle her state in the sky!" Already she rounds to it fast:
Athens must wait, patient as we – who judgement suspend.'

Athens, – except for that sparkle, – thy name, I had mouldered to ash!
That sent a blaze through my blood; off, off and away was I back,
– Not one word to waste, one look to lose on the false and the vile!
Yet 'O Gods of my land!' I cried, as each hillock and plain,
Wood and stream, I knew, I named, rushing past them again,
'Have ye kept faith, proved mindful of honours we paid you erewhile?
Vain was the filleted victim, the fulsome libation! Too rash
Love in its choice, paid you so largely service so slack!

'Oak and olive and bay, – I bid you cease to enwreathe
Brows made bold by your leaf! Fade at the Persian's foot,
You that, our patrons were pledged, should never adorn a slave!
Rather I hail thee, Parnes, – trust to thy wild waste tract!
Treeless, herbless, lifeless mountain! What matter if slacked
My speed may hardly be, for homage to crag and to cave
No deity deigns to drape with verdure? at least I can breathe,
Fear in thee no fraud from the blind, no lie from the mute!'

Such my cry as, rapid, I ran over Parnes' ridge;
Gully and gap I clambered and cleared till, sudden, a bar
Jutted, a stoppage of stone against me, blocking the way.
Right! for I minded the hollow to traverse, the fissure across:

'Where I could enter, there I depart by! Night in the fosse?
Athens to aid? Though the dive were through Erebos, thus I obey –
Out of the day dive, into the day as bravely arise! No bridge
Better!' – when – ha! what was it I came on, of wonders that are?

There, in the cool of a cleft, sat he – majestical Pan!
Ivy drooped wanton, kissed his head, moss cushioned his hoof:
All the great God was good in the eyes grave-kindly – the curl
Carved on the bearded cheek, amused at a mortal's awe,
As, under the human trunk, the goat-thighs grand I saw.
'Halt, Pheidippides!' – halt I did, my brain of a whirl:
'Hither to me! Why pale in my presence?' he gracious began:
'How is it, – Athens, only in Hellas, holds me aloof?

'Athens, she only, rears me no fane, makes me no feast!
Wherefore? Than I what godship to Athens more helpful of old?
Ay, and still, and forever her friend! Test Pan, trust me!
Go, bid Athens take heart, laugh Persia to scorn, have faith
In the temples and tombs! Go, say to Athens, "The Goat-God saith:
When Persia – so much as strews not the soil – is cast in the sea,
Then praise Pan who fought in the ranks with your most and least,
Goat-thigh to greaved-thigh, made one cause with the free and the bold!"

'Say Pan saith: "Let this, foreshowing the place, be the pledge!"'
(Gay, the liberal hand held out this herbage I bear
– Fennel – I grasped it a-tremble with dew – whatever it bode)
'While, as for thee . . .' But enough! He was gone. If I ran hitherto –
Be sure that, the rest of my journey, I ran no longer, but flew.
Parnes to Athens – earth no more, the air was my road:
Here am I back. Praise Pan, we stand no more on the razor's edge!
Pan for Athens, Pan for me! I too have a guerdon rare!

Then spoke Miltiades. 'And thee, best runner of Greece,
Whose limbs did duty indeed, – what gift is promised thyself?
Tell it us straightway, – Athens the mother demands of her son!'
Rosily blushed the youth: he paused: but, lifting at length
His eyes from the ground, it seemed as he gathered the rest of his strength
Into the utterance – 'Pan spoke thus: "For what thou hast done
Count on a worthy reward! Henceforth be allowed thee release
From the racer's toil, no vulgar reward in praise or in pelf!"

'I am bold to believe, Pan means reward the most to my mind!
Fight I shall, with our foremost, wherever this fennel may grow, –
Pound – Pan helping us – Persia to dust, and, under the deep,
Whelm her away for ever; and then, – no Athens to save, –
Marry a certain maid, I know keeps faith to the brave, –
Hie to my house and home: and, when my children shall creep
Close to my knees, – recount how the God was awful yet kind,
Promised their sire reward to the full – rewarding him – so!'

Unforeseeing one! Yes, he fought on the Marathon day:
So, when Persia was dust, all cried 'To Akropolis!
Run, Pheidippides, one race more! the meed is thy due!
"Athens is saved, thank Pan," go shout!' He flung down his shield,
Ran like fire once more: and the space 'twixt the Fennel-field
And Athens was stubble again, a field which a fire runs through,
Till in he broke: 'Rejoice, we conquer!' Like wine through clay,
Joy in his blood bursting his heart, he died – the bliss!

So, to this day, when friend meets friend, the word of salute
Is still 'Rejoice!' – his word which brought rejoicing indeed.
So is Pheidippides happy for ever, – the noble strong man
Who could race like a God, bear the face of a God, whom a God loved so well;
He saw the land saved he had helped to save, and was suffered to tell
Such tidings, yet never decline, but, gloriously as he began,
So to end gloriously – once to shout, thereafter be mute:
'Athens is saved!' – Pheidippides dies in the shout for his meed.

Halbert and Hob

Here is a thing that happened. Like wild beasts whelped, for den,
In a wild part of North England, there lived once two wild men
Inhabiting one homestead, neither a hovel nor hut,
Time out of mind their birthright: father and son, these – but –
Such a son, such a father! Most wildness by degrees
Softens away: yet, last of their line, the wildest and worst were these.

Criminals, then? Why, no: they did not murder and rob;
But, give them a word, they returned a blow – old Halbert as young Hob:
Harsh and fierce of word, rough and savage of deed,
Hated or feared the more – who knows? – the genuine wild-beast breed.

Thus were they found by the few sparse folk of the country-side;
But how fared each with other? E'en beasts couch, hide by hide,
In a growling, grudged agreement: so, father and son aye curled
The closelier up in their den because the last of their kind in the world.

Still, beast irks beast on occasion. One Christmas night of snow,
Came father and son to words – such words! more cruel because the blow
To crown each word was wanting, while taunt matched gibe, and curse
Competed with oath in wager, like pastime in hell, – nay, worse:
For pastime turned to earnest, as up there sprang at last
The son at the throat of the father, seized him and held him fast.

'Out of this house you go!' – (there followed a hideous oath) –
'This oven where now we bake, too hot to hold us both!
If there's snow outside, there's coolness: out with you, bide a spell
In the drift and save the sexton the charge of a parish shell!'

Now, the old trunk was tough, was solid as stump of oak
Untouched at the core by a thousand years: much less had its seventy broke

One whipcord nerve in the muscly mass from neck to shoulder-blade
Of the mountainous man, whereon his child's rash hand like a feather weighed.

Nevertheless at once did the mammoth shut his eyes,
Drop chin to breast, drop hands to sides, stand stiffened – arms and thighs
All of a piece – struck mute, much as a sentry stands,
Patient to take the enemy's fire: his captain so commands.

Whereat the son's wrath flew to fury at such sheer scorn
Of his puny strength by the giant eld thus acting the babe new-born:
And 'Neither will this turn serve!' yelled he. 'Out with you! Trundle, log!
If you cannot tramp and trudge like a man, try all-fours like a dog!'

Still the old man stood mute. So, logwise, – down to floor
Pulled from his fireside place, dragged on from hearth to door, –
Was he pushed, a very log, staircase along, until
A certain turn in the steps was reached, a yard from the house-door-sill.

Then the father opened eyes – each spark of their rage extinct, –
Temples, late black, dead-blanched, – right-hand with left-hand linked, –
He faced his son submissive; when slow the accents came,
They were strangely mild though his son's rash hand on his neck lay all the same.

'Hob, on just such a night of a Christmas long ago,
For such a cause, with such a gesture, did I drag – so –
My father down thus far: but, softening here, I heard
A voice in my heart, and stopped: you wait for an outer word.

'For your own sake, not mine, soften you too! Untrod
Leave this last step we reach, nor brave the finger of God!
I dared not pass its lifting: I did well. I nor blame
Nor praise you. I stopped here: and, Hob, do you the same!'

Straightway the son relaxed his hold of the father's throat.
They mounted, side by side, to the room again: no note
Took either of each, no sign made each to either: last
As first, in absolute silence, their Christmas-night they passed.

At dawn, the father sat on, dead, in the self-same place,
With an outburst blackening still the old bad fighting-face:
But the son crouched all a-tremble like any lamb new-yeaned.

When he went to the burial, someone's staff he borrowed – tottered and leaned.
But his lips were loose, not locked, – kept muttering, mumbling. 'There!
At his cursing and swearing!' the youngsters cried: but the elders thought 'In prayer.'
A boy threw stones: he picked them up and stored them in his vest.

So tottered, muttered, mumbled he, till he died, perhaps found rest.
'Is there a reason in nature for these hard hearts?' O Lear,
That a reason out of nature must turn them soft, seems clear!

Ivàn Ivànovitch

'They tell me, your carpenters,' quoth I to my friend the Russ,
'Make a simple hatchet serve as a tool-box serves with us.
Arm but each man with his axe, 'tis a hammer and saw and plane
And chisel, and – what know I else? We should imitate in vain
The mastery wherewithal, by a flourish of just the adze,
He cleaves, clamps, dovetails in, – no need of our nails and brads, –
The manageable pine: 'tis said he could shave himself
With the axe, – so all adroit, now a giant and now an elf,
Does he work and play at once!'
Quoth my friend the Russ to me,
'Ay, that and more beside on occasion! It scarce may be
You never heard tell a tale told children, time out of mind,
By father and mother and nurse, for a moral that's behind,
Which children quickly seize. If the incident happened at all,

We place it in Peter's time when hearts were great not small,
Germanized, Frenchified. I wager 'tis old to you
As the story of Adam and Eve, and possibly quite as true.'

In the deep of our land, 'tis said, a village from out the woods
Emerged on the great main-road 'twixt two great solitudes.
Through forestry right and left, black verst and verst of pine,
From village to village runs the road's long wide bare line.
Clearance and clearance break the else-unconquered growth
Of pine and all that breeds and broods there, leaving loth
Man's inch of masterdom, – spot of life, spirt of fire, –
To star the dark and dread, lest right and rule expire
Throughout the monstrous wild, a-hungered to resume
Its ancient sway, suck back the world into its womb:
Defrauded by man's craft which clove from North to South
This highway broad and straight e'en from the Neva's mouth
To Moscow's gates of gold. So, spot of life and spirt
Of fire aforesaid, burn, each village death-begirt
By wall and wall of pine – unprobed undreamed abyss.

Early one winter morn, in such a village as this,
Snow-whitened everywhere except the middle road
Ice-roughed by track of sledge, there worked by his abode
Ivàn Ivànovitch, the carpenter, employed
On a huge shipmast trunk; his axe now trimmed and toyed
With branch and twig, and now some chop athwart the bole
Changed bole to billets, bared at once the sap and soul.
About him, watched the work his neighbours sheepskin-clad;
Each bearded mouth puffed steam, each grey eye twinkled glad
To see the sturdy arm which, never stopping play,
Proved strong man's blood still boils, freeze winter as he may.

Sudden, a burst of bells. Out of the road, on edge
Of the hamlet – horse's hoofs galloping. 'How, a sledge?
What's here?' cried all as – in, up to the open space,
Work-yard and market-ground, folk's common meeting-place, –
Stumbled on, till he fell, in one last bound for life,
A horse: and, at his heels, a sledge held – 'Dmìtri's wife!
Back without Dmìtri too! and children – where are they?
Only a frozen corpse!'

They drew it forth: then – 'Nay,
Not dead, though like to die! Gone hence a month ago:
Home again, this rough jaunt – alone through night and snow –
What can the cause be? Hark – Droug, old horse, how he groans:
His day's done! Chafe away, keep chafing, for she moans:
She's coming to! Give here: see, motherkin, your friends!
Cheer up, all safe at home! Warm inside makes amends
For outside cold, – sup quick! Don't look as we were bears!
What is it startles you? What strange adventure stares
Up at us in your face? You know friends – which is which?
I'm Vàssili, he's Sergeì, Ivàn Ivànovitch ...'

At the word, the woman's eyes, slow-wandering till they neared
The blue eyes o'er the bush of honey-coloured beard,
Took in full light and sense and – torn to rags, some dream
Which hid the naked truth – O loud and long the scream
She gave, as if all power of voice within her throat
Poured itself wild away to waste in one dread note!
Then followed gasps and sobs, and then the steady flow
Of kindly tears: the brain was saved, a man might know.
Down fell her face upon the good friend's propping knee;
His broad hands smoothed her head, as fain to brush it free
From fancies, swarms that stung like bees unhived. He soothed –
'Loukèria, Loùscha!' – still he, fondling, smoothed and
smoothed.
At last her lips formed speech.

'Ivàn, dear – you indeed!
You, just the same dear you! While I ... O intercede,
Sweet Mother, with thy Son Almighty – let his might
Bring yesterday once more, undo all done last night!
But this time yesterday, Ivàn, I sat like you,
A child on either knee, and, dearer than the two,
A babe inside my arms, close to my heart – that's lost
In morsels o'er the snow! Father, Son, Holy Ghost,
Cannot you bring again my blessed yesterday?'

When no more tears would flow, she told her tale: this way.

'Maybe, a month ago, – was it not? – news came here,
They wanted, deeper down, good workmen fit to rear
A church and roof it in. "We'll go," my husband said:

"None understands like me to melt and mould their lead."
So, friends here helped us off – Ivàn, dear, you the first!
How gay we jingled forth, all five – (my heart will burst) –
While Dmìtri shook the reins, urged Droug upon his track!

'Well, soon the month ran out, we just were coming back,
When yesterday – behold, the village was on fire!
Fire ran from house to house. What help, as, nigh and nigher,
The flames came furious? "Haste," cried Dmìtri, "men must do
The little good man may: to sledge and in with you,
You and our three! We check the fire by laying flat
Each building in its path, – I needs must stay for that, –
But you . . . no time for talk! Wrap round you every rug,
Cover the couple close, – you'll have the babe to hug.
No care to guide old Droug, he knows his way, by guess,
Once start him on the road: but chirrup, none the less!
The snow lies glib as glass and hard as steel, and soon
You'll have rise, fine and full, a marvel of a moon.
Hold straight up, all the same, this lighted twist of pitch!
Once home and with our friend Ivàn Ivànovitch,
All's safe: I have my pay in pouch, all's right with me,
So I but find as safe you and our precious three!
Off, Droug!" – because the flames had reached us, and the men
Shouted "But lend a hand, Dmìtri – as good as ten!"

'So, in we bundled – I, and those God gave me once;
Old Droug, that's stiff at first, seemed youthful for the nonce:
He understood the case, galloping straight ahead.
Out came the moon: my twist soon dwindled, feebly red
In that unnatural day – yes, daylight, bred between
Moon-light and snow-light, lamped those grotto-depths which screen
Such devils from God's eye. Ah, pines, how straight you grow
Nor bend one pitying branch, true breed of brutal snow!
Some undergrowth had served to keep the devils blind
While we escaped outside their border!

'Was that – wind?
Anyhow, Droug starts, stops, back go his ears, he snuffs,
Snorts, – never such a snort! then plunges, knows the sough's
Only the wind: yet, no – our breath goes up too straight!
Still the low sound, – less low, loud, louder, at a rate

There's no mistaking more! Shall I lean out – look – learn
The truth whatever it be? Pad, pad! At last, I turn –

"'Tis the regular pad of the wolves in pursuit of the life in the sledge!
An army they are: close-packed they press like the thrust of a wedge:
They increase as they hunt: for I see, through the pine-trunks ranged each side,
Slip forth new fiend and fiend, make wider and still more wide
The four-footed steady advance. The foremost – none may pass:
They are elders and lead the line, eye and eye – green-glowing brass!
But a long way distant still. Droug, save us! He does his best:
Yet they gain on us, gain, till they reach, – one reaches . . . How utter the rest?
O that Satan-faced first of the band! How he lolls out the length of his tongue,
How he laughs and lets gleam his white teeth! He is on me, his paws pry among
The wraps and the rugs! O my pair, my twin-pigeons, lie still and seem dead!
Stepàn, he shall never have you for a meal, – here's your mother instead!
No, he will not be counselled – must cry, poor Stiòpka, so foolish! though first
Of my boy-brood, he was not the best: nay, neighbours have called him the worst:
He was puny, an undersized slip, – a darling to me, all the same!
But little there was to be praised in the boy, and a plenty to blame.
I loved him with heart and soul, yes – but, deal him a blow for a fault,
He would sulk for whole days. "Foolish boy! lie still or the villain will vault,
Will snatch you from over my head!" No use! he cries, screams, – who can hold
Fast a boy in a frenzy of fear! It follows – as I foretold!
The Satan-face snatched and snapped: I tugged, I tore – and then
His brother too needs must shriek! If one must go, 'tis men
The Tsar needs, so we hear, not ailing boys! Perhaps

My hands relaxed their grasp, got tangled in the wraps:
God, he was gone! I looked: there tumbled the cursed crew,
Each fighting for a share: too busy to pursue!
That's so far gain at least: Droug, gallop another verst
Or two, or three – God sends we beat them, arrive the first!
A mother who boasts two boys was ever accounted rich:
Some have not a boy: some have, but lose him, – God knows which
Is worse: how pitiful to see your weakling pine
And pale and pass away! Strong brats, this pair of mine!

'O misery! for while I settle to what near seems
Content, I am 'ware again of the tramp, and again there gleams –
Point and point – the line, eyes, levelled green brassy fire!
So soon is resumed your chase? Will nothing appease, naught tire
The furies? And yet I think – I am certain the race is slack,
And the numbers are nothing like. Not a quarter of the pack!
Feasters and those full-fed are staying behind ... Ah why?
We'll sorrow for that too soon! Now, – gallop, reach home, and die,
Nor ever again leave house, to trust our life in the trap
For life – we call a sledge! Teriòscha, in my lap!
Yes, I'll lie down upon you, tight-tie you with the strings
Here – of my heart! No fear, this time, your mother flings ...
Flings? I flung? Never! But think! – a woman, after all
Contending with a wolf! Save you I must and shall,
Terentiì!

'How now? What, you still head the race,
Your eyes and tongue and teeth crave fresh food, Satan-face?
There and there! Plain I struck green fire out! Flash again?
All a poor fist can do to damage eyes proves vain!
My fist – why not crunch that? He is wanton for ... O God,
Why give this wolf his taste? Common wolves scrape and prod
The earth till out they scratch some corpse – mere putrid flesh!
Why must this glutton leave the faded, choose the fresh?
Terentiì – God, feel! – his neck keeps fast thy bag
Of holy things, saints' bones, this Satan-face will drag
Forth, and devour along with him, our Pope declared
The relics were to save from danger!

'Spurned, not spared!
'Twas through my arms, crossed arms, he – nuzzling now with snout,
Now ripping, tooth and claw – plucked, pulled Terentiì out,
A prize indeed! I saw – how could I else but see? –
My precious one – I bit to hold back – pulled from me!
Up came the others, fell to dancing – did the imps! –
Skipped as they scampered round. There's one is grey, and limps:
Who knows but old bad Màrpha, – she always owed me spite
And envied me my births, – skulks out of doors at night
And turns into a wolf, and joins the sisterhood,
And laps the youthful life, then slinks from out the wood,
Squats down at door by dawn, spins there demure as erst
– No strength, old crone, – not she! – to crawl forth half a verst!

'Well, I escaped with one: 'twixt one and none there lies
The space 'twixt heaven and hell. And see, a rose-light dyes
The endmost snow: 'tis dawn, 'tis day, 'tis safe at home!
We have outwitted you! Ay, monsters, snarl and foam,
Fight each the other fiend, disputing for a share, –
Forgetful, in your greed, our finest off we bear,
Tough Droug and I, – my babe, my boy that shall be man,
My man that shall be more, do all a hunter can
To trace and follow and find and catch and crucify
Wolves, wolfkins, all your crew! A thousand deaths shall die
The whimperingest cub that ever squeezed the teat!
"Take that!" we'll stab you with, – "the tenderness we met
When, wretches, you danced round – not this, thank God – not this!
Hellhounds, we balk you!"

'But – Ah, God above! – Bliss, bliss –
Not the band, no! And yet – yes, for Droug knows him! One –
This only of them all has said "She saves a son!"
His fellows disbelieve such luck: but he believes,
He lets them pick the bones, laugh at him in their sleeves:
He's off and after us, – one speck, one spot, one ball
Grows bigger, bound on bound, – one wolf as good as all!
Oh but I know the trick! Have at the snaky tongue!
That's the right way with wolves! Go, tell your mates I wrung
The panting morsel out, left you to howl your worst!

Now for it – now! Ah me! I know him – thrice-accurst
Satan-face, – him to the end my foe!

'All fight's in vain:
This time the green brass points pierce to my very brain.
I fall – fall as I ought – quite on the babe I guard:
I overspread with flesh the whole of him. Too hard
To die this way, torn piecemeal? Move hence? Not I – one inch!
Gnaw through me, through and through: flat thus I lie nor
flinch!
O God, the feel of the fang furrowing my shoulder! – see!
It grinds – it grates the bone. O Kìrill under me,
Could I do more? Beside he knew wolf's way to win:
I clung, closed round like wax: yet in he wedged and in,
Past my neck, past my breasts, my heart, until . . . how feels
The onion-bulb your knife parts, pushing through its peels,
Till out you scoop its clove wherein lie stalk and leaf
And bloom and seed unborn?

'That slew me: yes, in brief,
I died then, dead I lay doubtlessly till Droug stopped
Here, I suppose. I come to life, I find me propped
Thus – how or when or why, – I know not. Tell me, friends,
All was a dream: laugh quick and say the nightmare ends!
Soon I shall find my house: 'tis over there: in proof,
Save for that chimney heaped with snow, you'd see the roof
Which holds my three – my two – my one – not one?

'Life's mixed
With misery, yet we live – must live. The Satan fixed
His face on mine so fast, I took its print as pitch
Takes what it cools beneath. Ivàn Ivànovitch,
'Tis you unharden me, you thaw, disperse the thing!
Only keep looking kind, the horror will not cling.
Your face smooths fast away each print of Satan. Tears
– What good they do! Life's sweet, and all its after-years,
Ivàn Ivànovitch, I owe you! Yours am I!
May God reward you, dear!'

Down she sank. Solemnly
Ivàn rose, raised his axe, – for fitly, as she knelt,
Her head lay: well-apart, each side, her arms hung, – dealt

Lightning-swift thunder-strong one blow – no need of more!
Headless she knelt on still: that pine was sound at core
(Neighbours were used to say) – cast-iron-kernelled – which
Taxed for a second stroke Ivàn Ivànovitch.

The man was scant of words as strokes. 'It had to be:
I could no other: God it was bade "Act for me!"'
Then stooping, peering round – what is it now he lacks?
A proper strip of bark wherewith to wipe his axe.
Which done, he turns, goes in, closes the door behind.
The others mute remain, watching the blood-snake wind
Into a hiding-place among the splinter-heaps.

At length, still mute, all move: one lifts, – from where it steeps
Redder each ruddy rag of pine, – the head: two more
Take up the dripping body: then, mute still as before,
Move in a sort of march, march on till marching ends
Opposite to the church; where halting, – who suspends,
By its long hair, the thing, deposits in its place
The piteous head: once more the body shows no trace
Of harm done: there lies whole the Loùscha, maid and wife
And mother, loved until this latest of her life.
Then all sit on the bank of snow which bounds a space
Kept free before the porch for judgement: just the place!

Presently all the souls, man, woman, child, which make
The village up, are found assembling for the sake
Of what is to be done. The very Jews are there:
A Gypsy-troop, though bound with horses for the Fair,
Squats with the rest. Each heart with its conception seethes
And simmers, but no tongue speaks: one may say, – none
breathes.

Anon from out the church totters the Pope – the priest –
Hardly alive, so old, a hundred years at least.
With him, the Commune's head, a hoary senior too,
Stàrosta, that's his style, – like Equity Judge with you, –
Natural Jurisconsult: then, fenced about with furs,
Pomeschìk, – Lord of the Land, who wields – and none demurs –
A power of life and death. They stoop, survey the corpse.

Then, straightened on his staff, the Stàrosta – the thorpe's
Sagaciousest old man – hears what you just have heard,
From Droug's first inrush, all, up to Ivàn's last word
'God bade me act for him: I dared not disobey!'

Silence – the Pomeschìk broke with 'A wild wrong way
Of righting wrong – if wrong there were, such wrath to rouse!
Why was not law observed? What article allows
Whoso may please to play the judge, and, judgement dealt,
Play executioner, as promptly as we pelt
To death, without appeal, the vermin whose sole fault
Has been – it dared to leave the darkness of its vault,
Intrude upon our day! Too sudden and too rash!
What was this woman's crime? Suppose the church should crash
Down where I stand, your lord: bound are my serfs to dare
Their utmost that I 'scape: yet, if the crashing scare
My children, – as you are, – if sons fly, one and all,
Leave father to his fate, – poor cowards though I call
The runaways, I pause before I claim their life
Because they prized it more than mine. I would each wife
Died for her husband's sake, each son to save his sire:
'Tis glory, I applaud – scarce duty, I require.
Ivàn Ivànovitch has done a deed that's named
Murder by law and me: who doubts, may speak unblamed!'

All turned to the old Pope. 'Ay, children, I am old –
How old, myself have got to know no longer. Rolled
Quite round, my orb of life, from infancy to age,
Seems passing back again to youth. A certain stage
At least I reach, or dream I reach, where I discern
Truer truths, laws behold more lawlike than we learn
When first we set our foot to tread the course I trod
With man to guide my steps: who leads me now is God.
"Your young men shall see visions": and in my youth I saw
And paid obedience to man's visionary law:
"Your old men shall dream dreams": and, in my age, a hand
Conducts me through the cloud round law to where I stand
Firm on its base, – know cause, who, before, knew effect.

'The world lies under me: and nowhere I detect
So great a gift as this – God's own – of human life.
"Shall the dead praise thee?" No! "The whole live world is rife,

God, with thy glory," rather! Life then, God's best of gifts,
For what shall man exchange? For life – when so he shifts
The weight and turns the scale, lets life for life restore
God's balance, sacrifice the less to gain the more,
Substitute – for low life, another's or his own –
Life large and liker God's who gave it: thus alone
May life extinguish life that life may trulier be!
How low this law descends on earth, is not for me
To trace: complexed becomes the simple, intricate
The plain, when I pursue law's winding. 'Tis the straight
Outflow of law I know and name: to law, the fount
Fresh from God's footstool, friends, follow while I remount.

'A mother bears a child: perfection is complete
So far in such a birth. Enabled to repeat
The miracle of life, – herself was born so just
A type of womankind, that God sees fit to trust
Her with the holy task of giving life in turn.
Crowned by this crowning pride, – how say you, should she spurn
Regality – discrowned, unchilded, by her choice
Of barrenness exchanged for fruit which made rejoice
Creation, though life's self were lost in giving birth
To life more fresh and fit to glorify God's earth?
How say you, should the hand God trusted with life's torch
Kindled to light the world – aware of sparks that scorch,
Let fall the same? Forsooth, her flesh a fire-flake stings
The mother drops the child! Among what monstrous things
Shall she be classed? Because of motherhood, each male
Yields to his partner place, sinks proudly in the scale:
His strength owned weakness, wit – folly, and courage – fear,
Beside the female proved male's mistress – only here.
The fox-dam, hunger-pined, will slay the felon sire
Who dares assault her whelp: the beaver, stretched on fire,
Will die without a groan: no pang avails to wrest
Her young from where they hide – her sanctuary breast.
What's here then? Answer me, thou dead one, as, I trow,
Standing at God's own bar, he bids thee answer now!
Thrice crowned wast thou – each crown of pride, a child – thy charge!
Where are they? Lost? Enough: no need that thou enlarge
On how or why the loss: life left to utter "lost"

Condemns itself beyond appeal. The soldier's post
Guards from the foe's attack the camp he sentinels:
That he no traitor proved, this and this only tells –
Over the corpse of him trod foe to foe's success.
Yet – one by one thy crowns torn from thee – thou no less
To scare the world, shame God, – livedst! I hold He saw
The unexampled sin, ordained the novel law,
Whereof first instrument was first intelligence
Found loyal here. I hold that, failing human sense,
The very earth had oped, sky fallen, to efface
Humanity's new wrong, motherhood's first disgrace.
Earth oped not, neither fell the sky, for prompt was found
A man and man enough, head-sober and heart-sound,
Ready to hear God's voice, resolute to obey.
Ivàn Ivànovitch, I hold, has done, this day,
No otherwise than did, in ages long ago,
Moses when he made known the purport of that flow
Of fire athwart the law's twain-tables! I proclaim
Ivàn Ivànovitch God's servant!'

At which name
Uprose that creepy whisper from out the crowd, is wont
To swell and surge and sink when fellow-men confront
A punishment that falls on fellow flesh and blood,
Appallingly beheld – shudderingly understood,
No less, to be the right, the just, the merciful.
'God's servant!' hissed the crowd.

When that Amen grew dull
And died away and left acquittal plain adjudged,
'Amen!' last sighed the lord. 'There's none shall say I grudged
Escape from punishment in such a novel case.
Deferring to old age and holy life, – be grace
Granted! say I. No less, scruples might shake a sense
Firmer than I boast mine. Law's law, and evidence
Of breach therein lies plain, – blood-red-bright, – all may see!
Yet all absolve the deed: absolved the deed must be!

'And next – as mercy rules the hour – methinks 'twere well
You signify forthwith its sentence, and dispel
The doubts and fears, I judge, which busy now the head

Law puts a halter round – a halo – you, instead!
Ivàn Ivànovitch – what think you he expects
Will follow from his feat? Go, tell him – law protects
Murder, for once: no need he longer keep behind
The Sacred Pictures – where skulks Innocence enshrined,
Or I mis-say! Go, some! You others, haste and hide
The dismal object there: get done, whate'er betide!'

So, while the youngers raised the corpse, the elders trooped
Silently to the house: where halting, someone stooped,
Listened beside the door; all there was silent too.
Then they held counsel; then pushed door and, passing through,
Stood in the murderer's presence.
                                                    Ivàn Ivànovitch
Knelt, building on the floor that Kremlin rare and rich
He deftly cut and carved on lazy winter nights.
Some five young faces watched, breathlessly, as, to rights,
Piece upon piece, he reared the fabric nigh complete.
Stèscha, Ivàn's old mother, sat spinning by the heat
Of the oven where his wife Kàtia stood baking bread.
Ivàn's self, as he turned his honey-coloured head,
Was just in act to drop, 'twixt fir-cones, – each a dome, –
The scooped-out yellow gourd presumably the home
Of Kolokol the Big: the bell, therein to hitch,
– An acorn-cup – was ready: Ivàn Ivànovitch
Turned with it in his mouth.

                                        They told him he was free
As air to walk abroad. 'How otherwise?' asked he.

Tray

Sing me a hero! Quench my thirst
Of soul, ye bards!
                                Quoth Bard the first:
'Sir Olaf, the good knight, did don
His helm and eke his habergeon . . .'
Sir Olaf and his bard —!

'That sin-scathed brow' (quoth Bard the second)
'That eye wide ope as though Fate beckoned
My hero to some steep, beneath
Which precipice smiled tempting death ...'
You too without your host have reckoned!

'A beggar-child' (let's hear this third!)
'Sat on a quay's edge: like a bird
Sang to herself at careless play,
And fell into the stream. "Dismay!
Help, you the standers-by!" None stirred.

'Bystanders reason, think of wives
And children ere they risk their lives.
Over the balustrade has bounced
A mere instinctive dog, and pounced
Plumb on the prize. "How well he dives!

'"Up he comes with the child, see, tight
In mouth, alive too, clutched from quite
A depth of ten feet – twelve, I bet!
Good dog! What, off again? There's yet
Another child to save? All right!

'"How strange we saw no other fall!
It's instinct in the animal.
Good dog! But he's a long while under:
If he got drowned I should not wonder –
Strong current, that against the wall!

'"Here he comes, holds in mouth this time
– What may the thing be? Well, that's prime!
Now, did you ever? Reason reigns
In man alone, since all Tray's pains
Have fished – the child's doll from the slime!"

'And so, amid the laughter gay,
Trotted my hero off, – old Tray, –
Till somebody, prerogatived
With reason, reasoned: "Why he dived,
His brain would show us, I should say.

'"John, go and catch – or, if needs be,
Purchase – that animal for me!
By vivisection, at expense
Of half-an-hour and eighteenpence,
How brain secretes dog's soul, we'll see!"'

Ned Bratts

'Twas Bedford Special Assize, one daft Midsummer's Day:
A broiling blasting June, – was never its like, men say.
Corn stood sheaf-ripe already, and trees looked yellow as that;
Ponds drained dust-dry, the cattle lay foaming around each flat.
Inside town, dogs went mad, and folk kept bibbing beer
While the parsons prayed for rain. 'Twas horrible, yes – but queer:
Queer – for the sun laughed gay, yet nobody moved a hand
To work one stroke at his trade: as given to understand
That all was come to a stop, work and such worldly ways,
And the world's old self about to end in a merry blaze.
Midsummer's Day moreover was the first of Bedford Fair,
With Bedford Town's tag-rag and bobtail a-bowsing there.

But the Court House, Quality crammed: through doors ope, windows wide,
High on the Bench you saw sit Lordships side by side.
There frowned Chief Justice Jukes, fumed learned Brother Small,
And fretted their fellow Judge: like threshers, one and all,
Of a reek with laying down the law in a furnace. Why?
Because their lungs breathed flame – the regular crowd forbye –
From gentry pouring in – quite a nosegay, to be sure!
How else could they pass the time, six mortal hours endure
Till night should extinguish day, when matters might haply mend?
Meanwhile no bad resource was – watching begin and end
Some trial for life and death, in a brisk five minutes' space,
And betting which knave would 'scape, which hang, from his sort of face.

So, their Lordships toiled and moiled, and a deal of work was done
(I warrant) to justify the mirth of the crazy sun,
As this and 'tother lout, struck dumb at the sudden show
Of red robes and white wigs, boggled nor answered 'Boh!'
When asked why he, Tom Styles, should not – because Jack Nokes
Had stolen the horse – be hanged: for Judges must have their jokes,
And louts must make allowance – let's say, for some blue fly
Which punctured a dewy scalp where the frizzles stuck awry –
Else Tom had fleered scot-free, so nearly over and done
Was the main of the job. Full-measure, the gentles enjoyed their fun,
As a twenty-five were tried, rank puritans caught at prayer
In a cow-house and laid by the heels, – have at 'em, devil may care! –
And ten were prescribed the whip, and ten a brand on the cheek,
And five a slit of the nose – just leaving enough to tweak.

Well, things at jolly high-tide, amusement steeped in fire,
While noon smote fierce the roof's red tiles to heart's desire,
The Court a-simmer with smoke, one ferment of oozy flesh,
One spirituous humming musk mount-mounting until its mesh
Entoiled all heads in a fluster, and Serjeant Postlethwayte
– Dashing the wig oblique as he mopped his oily pate –
Cried 'Silence, or I grow grease! No loophole lets in air?
Jurymen, – Guilty, Death! Gainsay me if you dare!'
– Things at this pitch, I say, – what hubbub without the doors?
What laughs, shrieks, hoots and yells, what rudest of uproars?

Bounce through the barrier throng a bulk comes rolling vast!
Thumps, kicks, – no manner of use! – spite of them rolls at last
Into the midst a ball which, bursting, brings to view
Publican Black Ned Bratts and Tabby his big wife too:
Both in a muck-sweat, both . . . were never such eyes uplift
At the sight of yawning hell, such nostrils – snouts that sniffed
Sulphur, such mouths a-gape ready to swallow flame!
Horrified, hideous, frank fiend-faces! yet, all the same,
Mixed with a certain . . . eh? how shall I dare style – mirth,
The desperate grin of the guess that, could they break from earth,

Heaven was above, and hell might rage in impotence
Below the saved, the saved!

'Confound you! (no offence!)
Out of our way, – push, wife! Yonder their Worships be!'
Ned Bratts has reached the bar, and 'Hey, my Lords,' roars he,
'A Jury of life and death, Judges the prime of the land,
Constables, javelineers, – all met, if I understand,
To decide so knotty a point as whether 'twas Jack or Joan
Robbed the henroost, pinched the pig, hit the "King's Arms" with a stone,
Dropped the baby down the well, left the tithesman in the lurch,
Or, three whole Sundays running, not once attended church!
What a pother – do these deserve the parish-stocks or whip,
More or less brow to brand, much or little nose to snip, –
When, in our Public, plain stand we – that's we stand here,
I and my Tab, brass-bold, brick-built of beef and beer,
– Do not we, slut? Step forth and show your beauty, jade!
Wife of my bosom – that's the word now! What a trade
We drove! None said us nay: nobody loved his life
So little as wag a tongue against us, – did they, wife?
Yet they knew us all the while, in their hearts, for what we are
– Worst couple, rogue and quean, unhanged – search near and far!
Eh, Tab? The pedlar, now – o'er his noggin – who warned a mate
To cut and run, nor risk his pack where its loss of weight
Was the least to dread, – aha, how we two laughed a-good
As, stealing round the midden, he came on where I stood
With billet poised and raised, – you, ready with the rope, –
Ah, but that's past, that's sin repented of, we hope!
Men knew us for that same, yet safe and sound stood we!
The lily-livered knaves knew too (I've balked a d—)
Our keeping the "Pied Bull" was just a mere pretence:
Too slow the pounds make food, drink, lodging, from out the pence!
There's not a stoppage to travel has chanced, this ten long year,
No break into hall or grange, no lifting of nag or steer,
Not a single roguery, from the clipping of a purse
To the cutting of a throat, but paid us toll. Od's curse!
When Gypsy Smouch made bold to cheat us of our due,
– Eh, Tab? the Squire's strong-box we helped the rascal to –

I think he pulled a face, next Sessions' swinging-time!
He danced the jig that needs no floor, – and, here's the prime,
'Twas Scroggs that houghed the mare! Ay, those were busy days!

'Well, there we flourished brave, like scripture-trees called bays,
Faring high, drinking hard, in money up to head
– Not to say, boots and shoes, when . . . Zounds, I nearly said –
Lord, to unlearn one's language! How shall we labour, wife?
Have you, fast hold, the Book? Grasp, grip it, for your life!
See, sirs, here's life, salvation! Here's – hold but out my breath –
When did I speak so long without once swearing? 'Sdeath,
No, nor unhelped by ale since man and boy! And yet
All yesterday I had to keep my whistle wet
While reading Tab this Book: book? don't say "book" – they're plays,
Songs, ballads and the like: here's no such strawy blaze,
But sky wide ope, sun, moon, and seven stars out full-flare!
Tab, help and tell! I'm hoarse. A mug! or – no, a prayer!
Dip for one out of the Book! Who wrote it in the Jail
– He plied his pen unhelped by beer, sirs, I'll be bail!

'I've got my second wind. In trundles she – that's Tab.
"Why, Gammer, what's come now, that – bobbing like a crab
On Yule-tide bowl – your head's a-work and both your eyes
Break loose? Afeard, you fool? As if the dead can rise!
Say – Bagman Dick was found last May with fuddling-cap
Stuffed in his mouth: to choke's a natural mishap!"
"Gaffer, be – blessed," cries she, "and Bagman Dick as well!
I, you, and he are damned: this Public is our hell:
We live in fire: live coals don't feel! – once quenched, they learn –
Cinders do, to what dust they moulder while they burn!"

'"If you don't speak straight out," says I – belike I swore –
"A knobstick, well you know the taste of, shall, once more,
Teach you to talk, my maid!" She ups with such a face,
Heart sunk inside me. "Well, pad on, my prate-apace!"

'"I've been about those laces we need for . . . never mind!
If henceforth they tie hands, 'tis mine they'll have to bind.
You know who makes them best – the Tinker in our cage,
Pulled-up for gospelling, twelve years ago: no age
To try another trade, – yet, so he scorned to take

Money he did not earn, he taught himself the make
Of laces, tagged and tough – Dick Bagman found them so!
Good customers were we! Well, last week, you must know,
His girl, – the blind young chit, who hawks about his wares, –
She takes it in her head to come no more – such airs
These hussies have! Yet, since we need a stoutish lace, –
'I'll to the gaol-bird father, abuse her to his face!'
So, first I filled a jug to give me heart, and then,
Primed to the proper pitch, I posted to their den –
Patmore – they style their prison! I tip the turnkey, catch
My heart up, fix my face, and fearless lift the latch –
Both arms a-kimbo, in bounce with a good round oath
Ready for rapping out: no 'Lawks' nor 'By my troth!'

'"There sat my man, the father. He looked up: what one feels
When heart that leapt to mouth drops down again to heels!
He raised his hand ... Hast seen, when drinking out the night,
And in, the day, earth grow another something quite
Under the sun's first stare? I stood a very stone.

'"'Woman!' (a fiery tear he put in every tone),
'How should my child frequent your house where lust is sport,
Violence – trade? Too true! I trust no vague report.
Her angel's hand, which stops the sight of sin, leaves clear
The other gate of sense, lets outrage through the ear.
What has she heard! – which, heard shall never be again.
Better lack food than feast, a Dives in the – wain
Or reign or train – of Charles!' (His language was not ours:
'Tis my belief, God spoke: no tinker has such powers).
'Bread, only bread they bring – my laces: if we broke
Your lump of leavened sin, the loaf's first crumb would choke!'

'"Down on my marrow-bones! Then all at once rose he:
His brown hair burst a-spread, his eyes were suns to see:
Up went his hands: 'Through flesh, I reach, I read thy soul!
So may some stricken tree look blasted, bough and bole,
Champed by the fire-tooth, charred without, and yet, thrice-
bound
With dreriment about, within may life be found,
A prisoned power to branch and blossom as before,
Could but the gardener cleave the cloister, reach the core,
Loosen the vital sap: yet where shall help be found?

Who says "How save it?" – nor "Why cumbers it the ground?"
Woman, that tree art thou! All sloughed about with scurf,
Thy stag-horns fright the sky, thy snake-roots sting the turf!
Drunkenness, wantonness, theft, murder gnash and gnarl
Thine outward, case thy soul with coating like the marle
Satan stamps flat upon each head beneath his hoof!
And how deliver such? The strong men keep aloof,
Lover and friend stand far, the mocking ones pass by,
Tophet gapes wide for prey: lost soul, despair and die!
What then? "Look unto me and be ye saved!" saith God:
"I strike the rock, outstreats the life-stream at my rod!
Be your sins scarlet, wool shall they seem like, – although
As crimson red, yet turn white as the driven snow!"'

'"There, there, there! All I seem to somehow understand
Is – that, if I reached home, 'twas through the guiding hand
Of his blind girl which led and led me through the streets
And out of town and up to door again. What greets
First thing my eye, as limbs recover from their swoon?
A book – this Book she gave at parting. 'Father's boon –
The Book he wrote: it reads as if he spoke himself:
He cannot preach in bonds, so, – take it down from shelf
When you want counsel, – think you hear his very voice!'

'"Wicked dear Husband, first despair and then rejoice!
Dear wicked Husband, waste no tick of moment more,
Be saved like me, bald trunk! There's greenness yet at core,
Sap under slough! Read, read!"

'Let me take breath, my lords!
I'd like to know, are these – hers, mine, or Bunyan's words?
I'm 'wildered – scarce with drink, – nowise with drink alone!
You'll say, with heat: but heat's no stuff to split a stone
Like this black boulder – this flint heart of mine: the Book –
That dealt the crashing blow! Sirs, here's the fist that shook
His beard till Wrestler Jem howled like a just-lugged bear!
You had brained me with a feather: at once I grew aware
Christmas was meant for me. A burden at your back,
Good Master Christmas? Nay, – yours was that Joseph's sack,
– Or whose it was, – which held the cup, – compared with mine!
Robbery loads my loins, perjury cracks my chine,

Adultery . . . nay, Tab, you pitched me as I flung!
One word, I'll up with fist . . . No, sweet spouse, hold your tongue!

'I'm hasting to the end. The Book, sirs – take and read!
You have my history in a nutshell, – ay, indeed!
It must off, my burden! See, – slack straps and into pit,
Roll, reach the bottom, rest, rot there – a plague on it!
For a mountain's sure to fall and bury Bedford Town,
"Destruction" – that's the name, and fire shall burn it down!
O 'scape the wrath in time! Time's now, if not too late.
How can I pilgrimage up to the wicket-gate?
Next comes Despond the slough: not that I fear to pull
Through mud, and dry my clothes at brave House Beautiful –
But it's late in the day, I reckon: had I left years ago
Town, wife, and children dear . . . Well, Christmas did, you know! –
Soon I had met in the valley and tried my cudgel's strength
On the enemy horned and winged, a-straddle across its length!
Have at his horns, thwick – thwack: they snap, see! Hoof and hoof –
Bang, break the fetlock-bones! For love's sake, keep aloof
Angels! I'm man and match, – this cudgel for my flail, –
To thresh him, hoofs and horns, bat's wing and serpent's tail!
A chance gone by! But then, what else does Hopeful ding
Into the deafest ear except – hope, hope's the thing?
Too late i' the day for me to thrid the windings: but
There's still a way to win the race by death's short cut!
Did Master Faithful need climb the Delightful Mounts?
No, straight to Vanity Fair, – a fair, by all accounts,
Such as is held outside, – lords, ladies, grand and gay, –
Says he in the face of them, just what you hear me say.
And the Judges brought him in guilty, and brought him out
To die in the market-place – Saint Peter's Green's about
The same thing: there they flogged, flayed, buffeted, lanced with knives,
Pricked him with swords, – I'll swear, he'd full a cat's nine lives, –
So to his end at last came Faithful, – ha, ha, he!
Who holds the highest card? for there stands hid, you see,
Behind the rabble-rout, a chariot, pair and all:
He's in, he's off, he's up, through clouds, at trumpet-call,

Carried the nearest way to Heaven-gate! Odds my life –
Has nobody a sword to spare? not even a knife?
Then hang me, draw and quarter! Tab – do the same by her!
O Master Worldly-Wiseman . . . that's Master Interpreter,
Take the will, not thc deed! Our gibbet's handy close:
Forestall Last Judgement-Day! Be kindly, not morose!
There wants no earthly judge-and-jurying: here we stand –
Sentence our guilty selves: so, hang us out of hand!
Make haste for pity's sake! A single moment's loss
Means – Satan's lord once more: his whisper shoots across
All singing in my heart, all praying in my brain,
"It comes of heat and beer!" – hark how he guffaws plain!
"Tomorrow you'll wake bright, and, in a safe skin, hug
Your sound selves, Tab and you, over a foaming jug!
You've had such qualms before, time out of mind!" He's right!
Did not we kick and cuff and curse away, that night
When home we blindly reeled and left poor humpback Joe
I' the lurch to pay for what . . somebody did, you know!
Both of us maundered then "Lame humpback, – never more
Will he come limping, drain his tankard at our door!
He'll swing, while – somebody . . ." Says Tab, "No, for I'll peach!"
"I'm for you, Tab," cries I, "there's rope enough for each!"
So blubbered we, and bussed, and went to bed upon
The grace of Tab's good thought: by morning, all was gone!
We laughed – "What's life to him, a cripple of no account?"
Oh, waves increase around – I feel them mount and mount!
Hang us! Tomorrow brings Tom Bearward with his bears:
One new black-muzzled brute beats Sackerson, he swears:
(Sackerson, for my money!) And, baiting o'er, the Brawl
They lead on Turner's Patch, – lads, lasses, up tails all, –
I'm i' the thick o' the throng! That means the Iron Cage,
– Means the Lost Man inside! Where's hope for such as wage
War against light? Light's left, light's here, I hold light still,
So does Tab – make but haste to hang us both! You will?'

I promise, when he stopped you might have heard a mouse
Squeak, such a death-like hush sealed up the old Mote House.
But when the mass of man sank meek upon his knees,
While Tab, alongside, wheezed a hoarse 'Do hang us, please!'
Why, then the waters rose, no eye but ran with tears,
Hearts heaved, heads thumped, until, paying all past arrears

Of pity and sorrow, at last a regular scream outbroke
Of triumph, joy and praise.

My Lord Chief Justice spoke,
First mopping brow and cheek, where still, for one that budged,
Another bead broke fresh: 'What Judge, that ever judged
Since first the world began, judged such a case as this?
Why, Master Bratts, long since, folk smelt you out, I wis!
I had my doubts, i' faith, each time you played the fox
Convicting geese of crime in yonder witness-box –
Yea, much did I misdoubt, the thief that stole her eggs
Was hardly goosey's self at Reynard's game, i' feggs!
Yet thus much was to praise – you spoke to point, direct –
Swore you heard, saw the theft: no jury could suspect –
Dared to suspect, – I'll say, – a spot in white so clear:
Goosey was throttled, true: but thereof godly fear
Came of example set, much as our laws intend;
And, though a fox confessed, you proved the Judge's friend.
What if I had my doubts? Suppose I gave them breath,
Brought you to bar: what work to do, ere "Guilty, Death," –
Had paid our pains! What heaps of witnesses to drag
From holes and corners, paid from out the County's bag!
Trial three dog-days long! *Amicus Curiae* – that's
Your title, no dispute – truth-telling Master Bratts!
Thank you, too, Mistress Tab! Why doubt one word you say?
Hanging you both deserve, hanged both shall be this day!
The tinker needs must be a proper man. I've heard
He lies in Gaol long since: if Quality's good word
Warrants me letting loose, – some householder, I mean –
Freeholder, better still, – I don't say but – between
Now and next Sessions . . . Well! Consider of his case,
I promise to, at least: we owe him so much grace.
Not that – no, God forbid! – I lean to think, as you,
The grace that such repent is any gaol-bird's due:
I rather see the fruit of twelve years' pious reign –
Astraea Redux, Charles restored his rights again!
– Of which, another time! I somehow feel a peace
Stealing across the world. May deeds like this increase!
So, Master Sheriff, stay that sentence I pronounced
On those two dozen odd: deserving to be trounced
Soundly, and yet . . . well, well, at all events dispatch
This pair of – shall I say, sinner-saints? – ere we catch

Their gaol-distemper too. Stop tears, or I'll indite
All weeping Bedfordshire for turning Bunyanite!'

So, forms were galloped through. If Justice, on the spur,
Proved somewhat expeditious, would Quality demur?
And happily hanged were they, – why lengthen out my tale? –
Where Bunyan's Statue stands facing where stood his Jail.

Dramatic Idyls: Second Series

1880

'You are sick, that's sure' – they say:
  'Sick of what?' – they disagree.
''Tis the brain' – thinks Doctor A;
  ''Tis the heart' – holds Doctor B;
'The liver – my life I'd lay!'
  'The lungs!' 'The lights!'
                                        Ah me!
  So ignorant of man's whole
Of bodily organs plain to see –
So sage and certain, frank and free,
About what's under lock and key –
  Man's soul!

Echetlos

Here is a story shall stir you! Stand up, Greeks dead and gone,
Who breasted, beat Barbarians, stemmed Persia rolling on,
Did the deed and saved the world, for the day was Marathon!

No man but did his manliest, kept rank and fought away
In his tribe and file: up, back, out, down – was the spear-arm
play:
Like a wind-whipt branchy wood, all spear-arms a-swing that
day!

But one man kept no rank and his sole arm plied no spear,
As a flashing came and went, and a form i' the van, the rear,
Brightened the battle up, for he blazed now there, now here.

Nor helmed nor shielded, he! but, a goat-skin all his wear,
Like a tiller of the soil, with a clown's limbs broad and bare,
Went he ploughing on and on: he pushed with a ploughman's
share.

Did the weak mid-line give way, as tunnies on whom the shark
Precipitates his bulk? Did the right-wing halt when, stark
On his heap of slain lay stretched Kallimachos Polemarch?

Did the steady phalanx falter? To the rescue, at the need,
The clown was ploughing Persia, clearing Greek earth of weed,
As he routed through the Sakian and rooted up the Mede.

But the deed done, battle won, – nowhere to be descried
On the meadow, by the stream, at the marsh, – look far and wide
From the foot of the mountain, no, to the last blood-plashed
seaside, –

Not anywhere on view blazed the large limbs thonged and brown,
Shearing and clearing still with the share before which – down
To the dust went Persia's pomp, as he ploughed for Greece, that
clown!

How spake the Oracle? 'Care for no name at all!
Say but just this: "We praise one helpful whom we call
The Holder of the Ploughshare." The great deed ne'er grows
small.'

Not the great name! Sing – woe for the great name Míltiadés
And its end at Paros isle! Woe for Themistokles
– Satrap in Sardis court! Name not the clown like these!

Clive

I and Clive were friends – and why not? Friends! I think you
laugh, my lad.
Clive it was gave England India, while your father gives – egad,
England nothing but the graceless boy who lures him on to
speak –
'Well, Sir, you and Clive were comrades –' with a tongue thrust
in your cheek!
Very true: in my eyes, your eyes, all the world's eyes, Clive was
man,
I was, am and ever shall be – mouse, nay, mouse of all its clan
Sorriest sample, if you take the kitchen's estimate for fame;
While the man Clive – he fought Plassy, spoiled the clever foreign
game,
Conquered and annexed and Englished!

Never mind! As o'er my punch
(You away) I sit of evenings, – silence, save for biscuit-crunch,
Black, unbroken, – thought grows busy, thrids each pathway of
old years,
Notes this forthright, that meander, till the long-past life appears
Like an outspread map of country plodded through, each mile
and rood,
Once, and well remembered still: I'm startled in my solitude
Ever and anon by – what's the sudden mocking light that breaks
On me as I slap the table till no rummer-glass but shakes
While I ask – aloud, I do believe, God help me! – 'Was it thus?
Can it be that so I faltered, stopped when just one step for us –'
(Us, – you were not born, I grant, but surely some day born
would be)

'– One bold step had gained a province' (figurative talk, you see)
'Got no end of wealth and honour, – yet I stood stock still no less?'
– 'For I was not Clive,' you comment: but it needs no Clive to guess
Wealth were handy, honour ticklish, did no writing on the wall
Warn me 'Trespasser, 'ware man-traps!' Him who braves that notice – call
Hero! none of such heroics suit myself who read plain words,
Doff my hat, and leap no barrier. Scripture says the land's the Lord's:
Louts then – what avail the thousand, noisy in a smock-frocked ring,
All-agog to have me trespass, clear the fence, be Clive their king?
Higher warrant must you show me ere I set one foot before
T'other in that dark direction, though I stand for evermore
Poor as Job and meek as Moses. Evermore? No! By-and-by
Job grows rich and Moses valiant, Clive turns out less wise than I.
Don't object 'Why call him friend, then?' Power is power, my boy, and still
Marks a man, – God's gift magnific, exercised for good or ill.
You've your boot now on my hearth-rug, tread what was a tiger's skin:
Rarely such a royal monster as I lodged the bullet in!
True, he murdered half a village, so his own death came to pass;
Still, for size and beauty, cunning, courage – ah, the brute he was!
Why, that Clive, – that youth, that greenhorn, that quill-driving clerk, in fine, –
He sustained a siege in Arcot... But the world knows! Pass the wine.

Where did I break off at? How bring Clive in? Oh, you mentioned 'fear'!
Just so: and, said I, that minds me of a story you shall hear.

We were friends then, Clive and I: so, when the clouds, about the orb
Late supreme, encroaching slowly, surely, threatened to absorb
Ray by ray its noontide brilliance, – friendship might, with steadier eye

Drawing near, bear what had burned else, now no blaze – all majesty.
Too much bee's-wing floats my figure? Well, suppose a castle's new:
None presume to climb its ramparts, none find foothold sure for shoe
'Twixt those squares and squares of granite plating the impervious pile
As his scale-mail's warty iron cuirasses a crocodile.
Reels that castle thunder-smitten, storm-dismantled? From without
Scrambling up by crack and crevice, every cockney prates about
Towers – the heap he kicks now! turrets – just the measure of his cane!
Will that do? Observe moreover – (same similitude again) –
Such a castle seldom crumbles by sheer stress of cannonade:
'Tis when foes are foiled and fighting's finished that vile rains invade,
Grass o'ergrows, o'ergrows till night-birds congregating find no holes
Fit to build in like the topmost sockets made for banner-poles.
So Clive crumbled slow in London – crashed at last.

A week before,
Dining with him, – after trying churchyard-chat of days of yore, –
Both of us stopped, tired as tombstones, head-piece, foot-piece, when they lean
Each to other, drowsed in fog-smoke, o'er a coffined Past between.
As I saw his head sink heavy, guessed the soul's extinguishment
By the glazing eyeball, noticed how the furtive fingers went
Where a drug-box skulked behind the honest liquor, – 'One more throw
Try for Clive!' thought I: 'Let's venture some good rattling question!' So –
'Come, Clive, tell us' – out I blurted – 'what to tell in turn, years hence,
When my boy – suppose I have one – asks me on what evidence
I maintain my friend of Plassy proved a warrior every whit
Worth your Alexanders, Caesars, Marlboroughs and – what said Pitt? –

Frederick the Fierce himself! Clive told me once' – I want to say –
'Which feat out of all those famous doings bore the bell away
– In his own calm estimation, mark you, not the mob's rough guess –
Which stood foremost as evincing what Clive called courageousness!
Come! what moment of the minute, what speck-centre in the wide
Circle of the action saw your mortal fairly deified?
(Let alone that filthy sleep-stuff, swallow bold this wholesome Port!)
If a friend has leave to question, – when were you most brave, in short?'

Up he arched his brows o' the instant – formidably Clive again.
'When was I most brave? I'd answer, were the instance half as plain
As another instance that's a brain-lodged crystal – curse it! – here
Freezing when my memory touches – ugh! – the time I felt most fear.
Ugh! I cannot say for certain if I showed fear – anyhow,
Fear I felt, and, very likely, shuddered, since I shiver now.'

'Fear!' smiled I. 'Well, that's the rarer: that's a specimen to seek,
Ticket up in one's museum, *Mind-Freaks, Lord Clive's Fear, Unique!*'

Down his brows dropped. On the table painfully he pored as though
Tracing, in the stains and streaks there, thoughts encrusted long ago.
When he spoke 'twas like a lawyer reading word by word some will,
Some blind jungle of a statement, – beating on and on until
Out there leaps fierce life to fight with.

'This fell in my factor-days.
Desk-drudge, slaving at Saint David's, one must game, or drink, or craze.

I chose gaming: and, – because your high-flown gamesters hardly take
Umbrage at a factor's elbow if the factor pays his stake, –
I was winked at in a circle where the company was choice,
Captain This and Major That, men high of colour, loud of voice,
Yet indulgent, condescending to the modest juvenile
Who not merely risked but lost his hard-earned guineas with a smile.

'Down I sat to cards, one evening, – had for my antagonist
Somebody whose name's a secret – you'll know why – so, if you list,
Call him Cock o' the Walk, my scarlet son of Mars from head to heel!
Play commenced: and, whether Cocky fancied that a clerk must feel
Quite sufficient honour came of bending over one green baize,
I the scribe with him the warrior, – guessed no penman dared to raise
Shadow of objection should the honour stay but playing end
More or less abruptly, – whether disinclined he grew to spend
Practice strictly scientific on a booby born to stare
At – not ask of – lace-and-ruffles if the hand they hide plays fair, –
Anyhow, I marked a movement when he bade me "Cut!"

'I rose.
"Such the new manoeuvre, Captain? I'm a novice: knowledge grows.
What, you force a card, you cheat, Sir?"

'Never did a thunder-clap
Cause emotion, startle Thyrsis locked with Chloe in his lap,
As my word and gesture (down I flung my cards to join the pack)
Fired the man of arms, whose visage, simply red before, turned black.

'When he found his voice, he stammered "That expression once again!"

'"Well, you forced a card and cheated!"

'"Possibly a factor's brain,
Busied with his all-important balance of accounts, may deem
Weighing words superfluous trouble: *cheat* to clerkly ears may seem
Just the joke for friends to venture: but we are not friends, you see!
When a gentleman is joked with, – if he's good at repartee,
He rejoins, as do I – Sirrah, on your knees, withdraw in full!
Beg my pardon, or be sure a kindly bullet through your skull
Lets in light and teaches manners to what brain it finds! Choose quick –
Have your life snuffed out or, kneeling, pray me trim yon candle-wick!"

'"Well, you cheated!"

'Then outbroke a howl from all the friends around.
To his feet sprang each in fury, fists were clenched and teeth were ground.
"End it! no time like the present! Captain, yours were our disgrace!
No delay, begin and finish! Stand back, leave the pair a space!
Let civilians be instructed: henceforth simply ply the pen,
Fly the sword! This clerk's no swordsman? Suit him with a pistol, then!
Even odds! A dozen paces 'twixt the most and least expert
Make a dwarf a giant's equal: nay, the dwarf, if he's alert,
Likelier hits the broader target!"

'Up we stood accordingly.
As they handed me the weapon, such was my soul's thirst to try
Then and there conclusions with this bully, tread on and stamp out
Every spark of his existence, that, – crept close to, curled about
By that toying tempting teasing fool-forefinger's middle joint, –
Don't you guess? – the trigger yielded. Gone my chance! and at the point
Of such prime success moreover: scarce an inch above his head
Went my ball to hit the wainscot. He was living, I was dead.

'Up he marched in flaming triumph – 'twas his right, mind! – up, within
Just an arm's length. "Now, my clerkling," chuckled Cocky with a grin
As the levelled piece quite touched me, "Now, Sir Counting-House, repeat
That expression which I told you proved bad manners! Did I cheat?"

'"Cheat you did, you knew you cheated, and, this moment, know as well.
As for me, my homely breeding bids you – fire and go to Hell!"

'Twice the muzzle touched my forehead. Heavy barrel, flurried wrist,
Either spoils a steady lifting. Thrice: then, "Laugh at Hell who list,
I can't! God's no fable either. Did this boy's eye wink once? No!
There's no standing him and Hell and God all three against me, – so,
I did cheat!"

'And down he threw the pistol, out rushed – by the door
Possibly, but, as for knowledge if by chimney, roof or floor,
He effected disappearance – I'll engage no glance was sent
That way by a single starer, such a blank astonishment
Swallowed up their senses: as for speaking – mute they stood as mice.

'Mute not long, though! Such reaction, such a hubbub in a trice!
"Rogue and rascal! Who'd have thought it? What's to be expected next,
When His Majesty's Commission serves a sharper as pretext
For . . . But where's the need of wasting time now? Naught requires delay:
Punishment the Service cries for: let disgrace be wiped away
Publicly, in good broad daylight! Resignation? No, indeed
Drum and fife must play the Rogue's March, rank and file be free to speed
Tardy marching on the rogue's part by appliance in the rear

– Kicks administered shall right this wronged civilian, – never fear,
Mister Clive, for – though a clerk – you bore yourself – suppose we say –
Just as would beseem a soldier!"

"'Gentlemen, attention – pray!
First, one word!"

'I passed each speaker severally in review.
When I had precise their number, names and styles, and fully knew
Over whom my supervision thenceforth must extend, – why, then –
'"Some five minutes since, my life lay – as you all saw, gentlemen –
At the mercy of your friend there. Not a single voice was raised
In arrest of judgement, not one tongue – before my powder blazed –
Ventured 'Can it be the youngster blundered, really seemed to mark
Some irregular proceeding? We conjecture in the dark,
Guess at random, – still, for sake of fair play – what if for a freak,
In a fit of absence, – such things have been! – if our friend proved weak
– What's the phrase? – corrected fortune! Look into the case, at least!'
Who dared interpose between the altar's victim and the priest?
Yet he spared me! You eleven! Whosoever, all or each,
To the disadvantage of the man who spared me, utters speech
– To his face, behind his back, – that speaker has to do with me:
Me who promise, if positions change and mine the chance should be,
Not to imitate your friend and waive advantage!"

'Twenty-five
Years ago this matter happened: and 'tis certain,' added Clive,
'Never, to my knowledge, did Sir Cocky have a single breath
Breathed against him: lips were closed throughout his life, or since his death,
For if he be dead or living I can tell no more than you.

All I know is – Cocky had one chance more; how he used it, – grew
Out of such unlucky habits, or relapsed, and back again
Brought the late-ejected devil with a score more in his train, –
That's for you to judge. Reprieval I procured, at any rate.
Ugh – the memory of that minute's fear makes gooseflesh rise! Why prate
Longer? You've my story, there's your instance: fear I did, you see!'

'Well' – I hardly kept from laughing – 'if I see it, thanks must be
Wholly to your Lordship's candour. Not that – in a common case –
When a bully caught at cheating thrusts a pistol in one's face,
I should underrate, believe me, such a trial to the nerve!
'Tis no joke, at one-and-twenty, for a youth to stand nor swerve.
Fear I naturally look for – unless, of all men alive,
I am forced to make exception when I come to Robert Clive.
Since at Arcot, Plassy, elsewhere, he and death – the whole world knows –
Came to somewhat closer quarters.'

Quarters? Had we come to blows,
Clive and I, you had not wondered – up he sprang so, out he rapped
Such a round of oaths – no matter! I'll endeavour to adapt
To our modern usage words he – well, 'twas friendly licence – flung
At me like so many fire-balls, fast as he could wag his tongue.

'You – a soldier? You – at Plassy? Yours the faculty to nick
Instantaneously occasion when your foe, if lightning-quick,
– At his mercy, at his malice, – has you, through some stupid inch
Undefended in your bulwark? Thus laid open, – not to flinch
– That needs courage, you'll concede me. Then, look here! Suppose the man,
Checking his advance, his weapon still extended, not a span
Distant from my temple, – curse him! – quietly had bade me "There!
Keep your life, calumniator! – worthless life I freely spare:
Mine you freely would have taken – murdered me and my good fame

Both at once – and all the better! Go, and thank your own bad aim
Which permits me to forgive you!" What if, with such words as these,
He had cast away his weapon? How should I have borne me, please?
Nay, I'll spare you pains and tell you. This, and only this, remained –
Pick his weapon up and use it on myself. I so had gained
Sleep the earlier, leaving England probably to pay on still
Rent and taxes for half India, tenant at the Frenchman's will.'

'Such the turn,' said I, 'the matter takes with you? Then I abate
– No, by not one jot nor tittle, – of your act my estimate.
Fear – I wish I could detect there: courage fronts me, plain enough –
Call it desperation, madness – never mind! for here's in rough
Why, had mine been such a trial, fear had overcome disgrace.
True, disgrace were hard to bear: but such a rush against God's face
– None of that for me, Lord Plassy, since I go to church at times,
Say the creed my mother taught me! Many years in foreign climes
Rub some marks away – not all, though! We poor sinners reach life's brink,
Overlook what rolls beneath it, recklessly enough, but think
There's advantage in what's left us – ground to stand on, time to call
"Lord, have mercy!" ere we topple over – do not leap, that's all!'

Oh, he made no answer, – re-absorbed into his cloud. I caught
Something like 'Yes – courage: only fools will call it fear.'

If aught
Comfort you, my great unhappy hero Clive, in that I heard,
Next week, how your own hand dealt you doom, and uttered just the word
'Fearfully courageous!' – this, be sure, and nothing else I groaned.
I'm no Clive, nor parson either: Clive's worst deed – we'll hope condoned.

Muléykeh

If a stranger passed the tent of Hóseyn, he cried 'A churl's!'
Or haply 'God help the man who has neither salt nor bread!'
– 'Nay,' would a friend exclaim, 'he needs nor pity nor scorn
More than who spends small thought on the shore-sand, picking pearls,
– Holds but in light esteem the seed-sort, bears instead
On his breast a moon-like prize, some orb which of night makes morn.

'What if no flocks and herds enrich the son of Sinán?
They went when his tribe was mulct, ten thousand camels the due,
Blood-value paid perforce for a murder done of old.
"God gave them, let them go! But never since time began,
Muléykeh, peerless mare, owned master the match of you,
And you are my prize, my Pearl: I laugh at men's land and gold!"

'So in the pride of his soul laughs Hóseyn – and right, I say.
Do the ten steeds run a race of glory? Outstripping all,
Ever Muléykeh stands first steed at the victor's staff.
Who started, the owner's hope, gets shamed and named, that day.
"Silence," or, last but one, is "The Cuffed," as we use to call
Whom the paddock's lord thrusts forth. Right, Hóseyn, I say, to laugh!'

'Boasts he Muléykeh the Pearl?' the stranger replies: 'Be sure
On him I waste nor scorn nor pity, but lavish both
On Duhl the son of Sheybán, who withers away in heart
For envy of Hóseyn's luck. Such sickness admits no cure.
A certain poet has sung, and sealed the same with an oath,
"For the vulgar – flocks and herds! The Pearl is a prize apart."'

Lo, Duhl the son of Sheybán comes riding to Hóseyn's tent,
And he casts his saddle down, and enters and 'Peace!' bids he.
'You are poor, I know the cause: my plenty shall mend the wrong.
'Tis said of your Pearl – the price of a hundred camels spent

In her purchase were scarce ill paid: such prudence is far from me
Who proffer a thousand. Speak! Long parley may last too long.'

Said Hóseyn 'You feed young beasts a many, of famous breed,
Slit-eared, unblemished, fat, true offspring of Múzennem:
There stumbles no weak-eyed she in the line as it climbs the hill.
But I love Muléykeh's face: her forefront whitens indeed
Like a yellowish wave's cream-crest. Your camels – go gaze on them!
Her fetlock is foam-splashed too. Myself am the richer still.'

A year goes by: lo, back to the tent again rides Duhl.
'You are open-hearted, ay – moist-handed, a very prince.
Why should I speak of sale? Be the mare your simple gift!
My son is pined to death for her beauty: my wife prompts "Fool,
Beg for his sake the Pearl! Be God the rewarder, since
God pays debts seven for one: who squanders on Him shows thrift."'

Said Hóseyn 'God gives each man one life, like a lamp, then gives
That lamp due measure of oil: lamp lighted – hold high, wave wide
Its comfort for others to share! once quench it, what help is left?
The oil of your lamp is your son: I shine while Muléykeh lives.
Would I beg your son to cheer my dark if Muléykeh died?
It is life against life: what good avails to the life-bereft?'

Another year, and – hist! What craft is it Duhl designs?
He alights not at the door of the tent as he did last time,
But, creeping behind, he gropes his stealthy way by the trench
Half-round till he finds the flap in the folding, for night combines
With the robber – and such is he: Duhl, covetous up to crime,
Must wring from Hóseyn's grasp the Pearl, by whatever the wrench.

'He was hunger-bitten, I heard: I tempted with half my store,
And a gibe was all my thanks. Is he generous like Spring dew?
Account the fault to me who chaffered with such an one!
He has killed, to feast chance comers, the creature he rode: nay, more –

For a couple of singing-girls his robe has he torn in two:
I will beg! Yet I nowise gained by the tale of my wife and son.

'I swear by the Holy House, my head will I never wash
Till I filch his Pearl away. Fair dealing I tried, then guile,
And now I resort to force. He said we must live or die:
Let him die, then, – let me live! Be bold – but not too rash!
I have found me a peeping-place: breast, bury your breathing while
I explore for myself! Now, breathe! He deceived me not, the spy!

'As he said – there lies in peace Hóseyn – how happy! Beside
Stands tethered the Pearl: thrice winds her headstall about his wrist:
'Tis therefore he sleeps so sound – the moon through the roof reveals.
And, loose on his left, stands too that other, known far and wide,
Buhéyseh, her sister born: fleet is she yet ever missed
The winning tail's fire-flash a-stream past the thunderous heels.

'No less she stands saddled and bridled, this second, in case some thief
Should enter and seize and fly with the first, as I mean to do.
What then? The Pearl is the Pearl: once mount her we both escape.'
Through the skirt-fold in glides Duhl, – so a serpent disturbs no leaf
In a bush as he parts the twigs entwining a nest: clean through,
He is noiselessly at his work: as he planned, he performs the rape.

He has set the tent-door wide, has buckled the girth, has clipped
The headstall away from the wrist he leaves thrice bound as before,
He springs on the Pearl, is launched on the desert like bolt from bow.
Up starts our plundered man: from his breast though the heart be ripped,
Yet his mind has the mastery: behold, in a minute more,
He is out and off and away on Buhéyseh, whose worth we know!

And Hóseyn – his blood turns flame, he has learned long since to ride,
And Buhéyseh does her part, – they gain – they are gaining fast
On the fugitive pair, and Duhl has Ed-Dárraj to cross and quit,
And to reach the ridge El-Sabán, – no safety till that be spied!
And Buhéyseh is, bound by bound, but a horse-length off at last,
For the Pearl has missed the tap of the heel, the touch of the bit.

She shortens her stride, she chafes at her rider the strange and queer:
Buhéyseh is mad with hope – beat sister she shall and must
Though Duhl, of the hand and heel so clumsy, she has to thank.
She is near now, nose by tail – they are neck by croup – joy! fear!
What folly makes Hóseyn shout 'Dog Duhl, Damned son of the Dust,
Touch the right ear and press with your foot my Pearl's left flank!'

And Duhl was wise at the word, and Muléykeh as prompt perceived
Who was urging redoubled pace, and to hear him was to obey,
And a leap indeed gave she, and evanished for evermore.
And Hóseyn looked one long last look as who, all bereaved,
Looks, fain to follow the dead so far as the living may:
Then he turned Buhéyseh's neck slow homeward, weeping sore.

And, lo, in the sunrise, still sat Hóseyn upon the ground
Weeping: and neighbours came, the tribesmen of Bénu-Asád
In the vale of green Er-Rass, and they questioned him of his grief;
And he told from first to last how, serpent-like, Duhl had wound
His way to the nest, and how Duhl rode like an ape, so bad!
And how Buhéyseh did wonders, yet Pearl remained with the thief.

And they jeered him, one and all: 'Poor Hóseyn is crazed past hope!
How else had he wrought himself his ruin, in fortune's spite?
To have simply held the tongue were a task for a boy or girl,
And here were Muléykeh again, the eyed like an antelope,

The child of his heart by day, the wife of his breast by night!' –
'And the beaten in speed!' wept Hóseyn: 'You never have loved my Pearl.'

Pietro of Abano

Petrus Aponensis – there was a magician!
When that strange adventure happened, which I mean to tell my hearers,
Nearly had he tried all trades – beside physician,
Architect, astronomer, astrologer, – or worse:
How else, as the old books warrant, was he able,
All at once, through all the world, to prove the promptest of appearers
Where was prince to cure, tower to build as high as Babel,
Star to name or sky-sign read, – yet pouch, for pains, a curse?

– Curse: for when a vagrant, – foot-sore, travel-tattered,
Now a young man, now an old man, Turk or Arab, Jew or Gypsy, –
Proffered folk in passing – O for pay, what mattered? –
'I'll be doctor, I'll play builder, star I'll name – sign read!'
Soon as prince was cured, tower built, and fate predicted,
'Who may you be?' came the question, when he answered '*Petrus ipse,*'
'Just as we divined!' cried folk – 'A wretch convicted
Long ago of dealing with the devil – you indeed!'

So, they cursed him roundly, all his labour's payment,
Motioned him – the convalescent prince would – to vacate the presence:
Babylonians plucked his beard and tore his raiment,
Drove him from that tower he built: while, had he peered at stars,
Town howled 'Stone the quack who styles our Dog-star – Sirius!'
Country yelled 'Aroint the churl who prophesies we take no pleasance
Under vine and fig-tree, since the year's delirious,
Bears no crop of any kind, – all through the planet Mars!'

Straightway would the whilom youngster grow a grisard,
Or, as case might hap, the hoary eld drop off and show a stripling.
Town and country groaned – indebted to a wizard!
'Curse – nay, kick and cuff him – fit requital of his pains!
Gratitude in word or deed were wasted truly!
Rather make the Church amends by crying out on, cramping, crippling
One who, on pretence of serving man, serves duly
Man's arch foe: not ours, be sure, but Satan's – his the gains!'

Peter grinned and bore it, such disgraceful usage:
Somehow, cuffs and kicks and curses seem ordained his like to suffer:
Prophet's pay with Christians, now as in the Jews' age,
Still is – stoning: so, he meekly took his wage and went,
– Safe again was found ensconced in those old quarters,
Padua's blackest blindest by-street, – none the worse, nay, somewhat tougher:
'Calculating,' quoth he, 'soon I join the martyrs,
Since, who magnify my lore on burning me are bent.'*
Therefore, on a certain evening, to his alley
Peter slunk, all bruised and broken, sore in body, sick in spirit,
Just escaped from Cairo where he launched a galley
Needing neither sails nor oars nor help of wind or tide,
– Needing but the fume of fire to set a-flying
Wheels like mad which whirled you quick – North, South, where'er you pleased require it, –
That is – would have done so had not priests come prying,
Broke his engine up and bastinadoed him beside.

* 'Studiando le mie cifre col compasso,
Rilevo che sarò presto sotterra,
Perchè del mio saper si fa gran chiasso,
E gl' ignoranti m' hanno mosso guerra.'

Said to have been found in a well at Abano in the last century. They were extemporaneously Englished thus: not as Father Prout chose to prefer them: –

Studying my ciphers with the compass,
I reckon – I soon shall be below-ground;
Because of my lore folk make great rumpus,
And war on myself makes each dull rogue round.

As he reached his lodging, stopped there unmolested,
(Neighbours feared him, urchins fled him, few were bold enough to follow)
While his fumbling fingers tried the lock and tested
Once again the queer key's virtue, oped the sullen door, –
Someone plucked his sleeve, cried 'Master, pray your pardon!
Grant a word to me who patient wait you in your archway's hollow!
Hard on you men's hearts are: be not your heart hard on
Me who kiss your garment's hem, O Lord of magic lore!

'Mage – say I, who no less, scorning tittle-tattle,
To the vulgar give no credence when they prate of Peter's magic,
Deem his art brews tempest, hurts the crops and cattle,
Hinders fowls from laying eggs and worms from spinning silk,
Rides upon a he-goat, mounts at need a broomstick:
While the price he pays for this (so turns to comic what was tragic)
Is – he may not drink – dreads like the Day of Doom's tick –
One poor drop of sustenance ordained mere men – that's milk!

'Tell such tales to Padua! Think me no such dullard!
Not from these benighted parts did I derive my breath and being!
I am from a land whose cloudless skies are coloured
Livelier, suns orb largelier, airs seem incense, – while, on earth –
What, instead of grass, our fingers and our thumbs cull,
Proves true moly! sounds and sights there help the body's hearing, seeing,
Till the soul grows godlike: brief, – you front no numbscull
Shaming by ineptitude the Greece that gave him birth!

'Mark within my eye its iris mystic-lettered –
That's my name! and note my ear – its swan-shaped cavity, my emblem!
Mine's the swan-like nature born to fly unfettered
Over land and sea in search of knowledge – food for song.
Art denied the vulgar! Geese grow fat on barley,
Swans require ethereal provend, undesirous to resemble 'em –
Soar to seek Apollo, – favoured with a parley
Such as, Master, you grant me – who will not hold you long.

'Leave to learn to sing – for that your swan petitions:
Master, who possess the secret, say not nay to such a suitor!
All I ask is – bless mine, purest of ambitions!
Grant me leave to make my kind wise, free, and happy! How?
Just by making me – as you are mine – their model!
Geese have goose-thoughts: make a swan their teacher first, then co-adjutor, –
Let him introduce swan-notions to each noddle, –
Geese will soon grow swans, and men become what I am now!

'That's the only magic – had but fools discernment,
Could they probe and pass into the solid through the soft and seeming!
Teach me such true magic – now and no adjournment!
Teach your art of making fools subserve the man of mind!
Magic is the power we men of mind should practise,
Draw fools to become our drudges, docile henceforth, never dreaming –
While they do our hests for fancied gain – the fact is
What they toil and moil to get proves falsehood: truth's behind!

'See now! you conceive some fabric – say, a mansion
Meet for monarch's pride and pleasure: this is truth – a thought has fired you,
Made you fain to give some cramped concept expansion,
Put your faculty to proof, fulfil your nature's task.
First you fascinate the monarch's self: he fancies
He it was devised the scheme you execute as he inspired you:
He in turn sets slaving insignificances
Toiling, moiling till your structure stands there – all you ask!

'Soon the monarch's known for what he was – a ninny:
Soon the rabble-rout leave labour, take their work-day wage and vanish:
Soon the late puffed bladder, pricked, shows lank and skinny –
"Who was its inflator?" ask we, "whose the giant lungs?"
Petri en pulmones! What though men prove ingrates?
Let them – so they stop at crucifixion – buffet, ban and banish!
Peter's power's apparent: human praise – its din grates
Harsh as blame on ear unused to aught save angels' tongues.

'Ay, there have been always, since our world existed,
Mages who possessed the secret – needed but to stand still, fix
eye
On the foolish mortal: straight was he enlisted
Soldier, scholar, servant, slave – no matter for the style!
Only through illusion; ever what seemed profit –
Love or lucre – justified obedience to the *Ipse dixi*:
Work done – palace reared from pavement up to soffit –
Was it strange if builders smelt out cheating all the while?

'Let them pelt and pound, bruise, bray you in a mortar!
What's the odds to you who seek reward of quite another nature?
You've enrolled your name where sages of your sort are,
– Michael of Constantinople, Hans of Halberstadt!
Nay and were you nameless, still you've your conviction
You it was and only you – what signifies the nomenclature? –
Ruled the world in fact, though how you ruled be fiction
Fit for fools: true wisdom's magic you – if e'er man – had't!

'But perhaps you ask me "Since each ignoramus
While he profits by such magic persecutes the benefactor,
What should I expect but – once I render famous
You as Michael, Hans and Peter – just one ingrate more?
If the vulgar prove thus, whatsoe'er the pelf be,
Pouched through my beneficence – and doom me dungeoned,
chained, or racked, or
Fairly burned outright – how grateful will yourself be
When, his secret gained, you match your – master just before?"

'That's where I await you! Please, revert a little!
What do folk report about you if not this – which, though
chimeric,
Still, as figurative, suits you to a tittle –
That, – although the elements obey your nod and wink,
Fades or flowers the herb you chance to smile or sigh at,
While your frown bids earth quake palled by obscuration
atmospheric, –
Brief, although through nature naught resists your *fiat*,
There's yet one poor substance mocks you – milk you may not
drink!

'Figurative language! Take my explanation!
Fame with fear, and hate with homage, these your art procures in plenty.
All's but daily dry bread: what makes moist thc ration?
Love, the milk that sweetens man his meal – alas, you lack:
I am he who, since he fears you not, can love you.
Love is born of heart not mind, *de corde natus haud de mente*;
Touch my heart and love's yours, sure as shines above you
Sun by day and star by night though earth should go to wrack!

'Stage by stage you lift me – kiss by kiss I hallow
Whose but your dear hand my helper, punctual as at each new impulse
I approach my aim? Shell chipped, the eaglet callow
Needs a parent's pinion-push to quit the eyrie's edge:
But once fairly launched forth, denizen of aether,
While each effort sunward bids the blood more freely through each limb pulse,
Sure the parent feels, as gay they soar together,
Fully are all pains repaid when love redeems its pledge!'

Then did Peter's tristful visage lighten somewhat,
Vent a watery smile as though inveterate mistrust were thawing.
'Well, who knows?' he slow broke silence. 'Mortals – come what
Come there may – are still the dupes of hope there's luck in store.
Many scholars seek me, promise mounts and marvels:
Here stand I to witness how they step 'twixt me and clapperclawing!
Dry bread, – that I've gained me: truly I should starve else:
But of milk, no drop was mine! Well, shuffle cards once more!'

At the word of promise thus implied, our stranger –
What can he but cast his arms, in rapture of embrace, round Peter?
'Hold! I choke!' the mage grunts. 'Shall I in the manger
Any longer play the dog? Approach, my calf, and feed!
Bene . . . won't you wait for grace?' But sudden incense
Wool-white, serpent-solid, curled up – perfume growing sweet and sweeter
Till it reached the young man's nose and seemed to win sense
Soul and all from out his brain through nostril: yes, indeed!

Presently the young man rubbed his eyes. 'Where am I?
Too much bother over books! Some reverie has proved amusing.
What did Peter prate of? 'Faith, my brow is clammy!
How my head throbs, how my heart thumps! Can it be I swooned?
Oh, I spoke my speech out – cribbed from Plato's tractate,
Dosed him with "the Fair and Good," swore – Dog of Egypt – I was choosing
Plato's way to serve men! What's the hour? Exact eight!
Home now, and tomorrow never mind how Plato mooned!

'Peter has the secret! Fair and Good are products
(So he said) of Foul and Evil: one must bring to pass the other.
Just as poisons grow drugs, steal through sundry odd ducts
Doctors name, and ultimately issue safe and changed.
You'd abolish poisons, treat disease with dainties
Such as suit the sound and sane? With all such kick-shaws vain you pother!
Arsenic's the stuff puts force into the faint eyes,
Opium sets the brain to rights – by cark and care deranged.

'What, he's safe within door? – would escape – no question –
Thanks, since thanks and more I owe, and mean to pay in time befitting.
What most presses now is – after night's digestion,
Peter, of thy precepts! – promptest practice of the same.
Let me see! The wise man, first of all, scorns riches:
But to scorn them must obtain them: none believes in his permitting
Gold to lie ungathered: who picks up, then pitches
Gold away – philosophizes: none disputes his claim.

'So with worldly honours: 'tis by abdicating,
Incontestably he proves he could have kept the crown discarded.
Sulla cuts a figure, leaving off dictating:
Simpletons laud private life? "The grapes are sour," laugh we.
So, again – but why continue? All's tumultuous
Here: my head's a-whirl with knowledge. Speedily shall be rewarded
He who taught me! Greeks prove ingrates? So insult you us?
When your teaching bears its first-fruits, Peter – wait and see!'

As the word, the deed proved; ere a brief year's passage,
Fop – that fool he made the jokes on – now he made the jokes
for, *gratis:*
Hunks – that hoarder, long left lonely in his crass age –
Found now one appreciative deferential friend:
Powder-paint-and-patch, Hag Jezebel – recovered,
Strange to say, the power to please, got courtship till she cried
Jam satis!
Fop be-flattered, Hunks be-friended, Hag be-lovered –
Nobody o'erlooked, save God – he soon attained his end.

As he lounged at ease one morning in his villa,
(Hag's the dowry) estimated (Hunks' bequest) his coin in coffer,
Mused on how a fool's good word (Fop's word) could fill a
Social circle with his praise, promote him man of mark, –
All at once – 'An old friend fain would see your Highness!'
There stood Peter, skeleton and scarecrow, plain writ
Phi-lo-so-pher
In the woe-worn face – for yellowness and dryness,
Parchment – with a pair of eyes – one hope their feeble spark.

'Did I counsel rightly? Have you, in accordance,
Prospered greatly, dear my pupil? Sure, at just the stage I find
you,
When your hand may draw me forth from the mad war-dance
Savages are leading round your master – down, not dead.
Padua wants to burn me: balk them, let me linger
Life out – rueful though its remnant – hid in some safe hole
behind you!
Prostrate here I lie: quick, help with but a finger
Lest I house in safety's self – a tombstone o'er my head!

'Lodging, bite and sup, with – now and then – a copper
– Alms for any poorer still, if such there be, – is all my asking.
Take me for your bedesman, – nay, if you think proper,
Menial merely, – such my perfect passion for repose!
Yes, from out your plenty Peter craves a pittance
– Leave to thaw his frozen hands before the fire whereat you're
basking!
Double though your debt were, grant this boon – remittance
He proclaims of obligation: 'tis himself that owes!'

'Venerated Master – can it be, such treatment
Learning meets with, magic fails to guard you from, by all appearance?
Strange! for, as you entered, – what the famous feat meant,
I was full of, – why you reared that fabric, Padua's boast.
Nowise for man's pride, man's pleasure, did you slyly
Raise it, but man's seat of rule whereby the world should soon have clearance
(Happy world) from such a rout as now so vilely
Handles you – and hampers me, for which I grieve the most.

'Since if it got wind you now were my familiar,
How could I protect you – nay, defend myself against the rabble?
Wait until the mob, now masters, willy-nilly are
Servants as they should be: then has gratitude full play!
Surely this experience shows how unbefitting
'Tis that minds like mine should rot in ease and plenty. Geese may gabble,
Gorge, and keep the ground: but swans are soon for quitting
Earthly fare – as fain would I, your swan, if taught the way.

'Teach me, then, to rule men, have them at my pleasure!
Solely for their good, of course, – impart a secret worth rewarding,
Since the proper life's-prize! Tantalus's treasure
Aught beside proves, vanishes and leaves no trace at all.
Wait awhile, nor press for payment prematurely!
Over-haste defrauds you. Thanks! since, – even while I speak, – discarding
Sloth and vain delights, I learn how – swiftly, surely –
Magic sways the sceptre, wears the crown and wields the ball!

'Gone again – what, is he? 'Faith, he's soon disposed of!
Peter's precepts work already, put within my lump their leaven!
Ay, we needs must don glove would we pluck the rose – doff
Silken garment would we climb the tree and take its fruit.
Why sharp thorn, rough rind? To keep unviolated
Either prize! We garland us, we mount from earth to feast in heaven,
Just because exist what once we estimated
Hindrances which, better taught, as helps we now compute.

'Foolishly I turned disgusted from my fellows!
Pits of ignorance – to fill, and heaps of prejudice – to level –
Multitudes in motley, whites and blacks and yellows –
What a hopeless task it seemed to discipline the host!
Now I see my error. Vices act like virtues
– Not alone because they guard – sharp thorns – the rose we first dishevel,
Not because they scrape, scratch – rough rind – through the dirt-shoes
Bare feet cling to bole with, while the half-mooned boot we boast.

'No, my aim is nobler, more disinterested!
Man shall keep what seemed to thwart him, since it proves his true assistance,
Leads to ascertaining which head is the best head,
Would he crown his body, rule its members – lawless else.
Ignorant the horse stares, by deficient vision
Takes a man to be a monster, lets him mount, then, twice the distance
Horse could trot unridden, gallops – dream Elysian! –
Dreaming that his dwarfish guide's a giant, – jockeys tell's.'

Brief, so worked the spell, he promptly had a riddance:
Heart and brain no longer felt the pricks which passed for conscience-scruples:
Free henceforth his feet, – *Per Bacco,* how they did dance
Merrily through lets and checks that stopped the way before!
Politics the prize now, – such adroit adviser,
Opportune suggester, with the tact that triples and quadruples
Merit in each measure, – never did the Kaiser
Boast a subject such a statesman, friend, and something more!

As he, up and down, one noonday, paced his closet
– Council o'er, each spark (his hint) blown flame, by colleagues' breath applauded,
Strokes of statecraft hailed with '*Salomo si nôsset!*'
(His the nostrum) – every throw for luck come double-six, –
As he, pacing, hugged himself in satisfaction,
Thump – the door went. 'What, the Kaiser? By none else were I defrauded
Thus of well-earned solace. Since 'tis fate's exaction, –
Enter, Liege my Lord! Ha, Peter, you here? *Teneor vix!*'

'Ah, Sir, none the less, contain you, nor wax irate!
You so lofty, I so lowly, – vast the space which yawns between us!
Still, methinks, you – more than ever – at a high rate
Needs must prize poor Peter's secret since it lifts you thus.
Grant me now the boon whereat before you boggled!
Ten long years your march has moved – one triumph – (though *e*'s short) – *hactēnus,*
While I down and down disastrously have joggled
Till I pitch against Death's door, the true *Nec Ultra Plus.*

'Years ago – some ten 'tis – since I sought for shelter,
Craved in your whole house a closet, out of all your means a comfort.
Now you soar above these: as is gold to spelter
So is power – you urged with reason – paramount to wealth.
Power you boast in plenty: let it grant me refuge!
Houseroom now is out of question: find for me some stronghold – some fort –
Privacy wherein, immured, shall this blind deaf huge
Monster of a mob let stay the soul I'd save by stealth!

'Ay, for all too much with magic have I tampered!
– Lost the world, and gained, I fear, a certain place I'm to describe loth!
Still, if prayer and fasting tame the pride long pampered,
Mercy may be mine: amendment never comes too late.
How can I amend beset by cursers, kickers?
Pluck this brand from out the burning! Once away, I take my Bible-oath,
Never more – so long as life's weak lamp-flame flickers –
No, not once I'll tease you, but in silence bear my fate!'

'Gently, good my Genius, Oracle unerring!
Strange now! can you guess on what – as in you peeped – it was I pondered?
You and I are both of one mind in preferring
Power to wealth, but – here's the point – what sort of power, I ask?
Ruling men is vulgar, easy and ignoble:
Rid yourself of conscience, quick you have at beck and call the fond herd.

But who wields the crozier, down may fling the crow-bill:
That's the power I covet now; soul's sway o'er souls – my task!

'"Well but," you object, "you have it, who by glamour
Dress up lies to look like truths, mask folly in the garb of reason:
Your soul acts on theirs, sure, when the people clamour,
Hold their peace, now fight now fondle, – earwigged through the brains."
Possibly! but still the operation's mundane,
Grosser than a taste demands which – craving manna – kecks at peason –
Power o'er men by wants material: why should one deign
Rule by sordid hopes and fears – a grunt for all one's pains?

'No, if men must praise me, let them praise to purpose!
Would we move the world, not earth but heaven must be our fulcrum – *pou sto!*
Thus I seek to move it: Master, why intérpose –
Balk my climbing close on what's the ladder's topmost round?
Statecraft 'tis I step from: when by priestcraft hoisted
Up to where my foot may touch the highest rung which fate allows toe,
Then indeed ask favour! On you shall be foisted
No excuse: I'll pay my debt, each penny of the pound!

'Ho, my knaves without there! Lead this worthy downstairs!
No farewell, good Paul – nay, Peter – what's your name remembered rightly?
Come, he's humble: out another would have flounced – airs
Suitors often give themselves when our sort bow them forth.
Did I touch his rags? He surely kept his distance:
Yet, there somehow passed to me from him – where'er the virtue might lie –
Something that inspires my soul – Oh, by assistance
Doubtlessly of Peter! – still, he's worth just what he's worth!

''Tis my own soul soars now: soaring – how? By crawling!
I'll to Rome, before Rome's feet the temporal-supreme lay prostrate!
"Hands" (I'll say) "proficient once in pulling, hauling
This and that way men as I was minded – feet now clasp!"
Ay, the Kaiser's self has wrung them in his fervour!

Now – they only sue to slave for Rome, nor at one doit the cost rate.
Rome's adopted child – no bone, no muscle, nerve or
Sinew of me but I'll strain, though out my life I gasp!'

As he stood one evening proudly – (he had traversed
Rome on horseback – peerless pageant! – claimed the Lateran as new Pope) –
Thinking 'All's attained now! Pontiff! Who could have erst
Dreamed of my advance so far when, some ten years ago,
I embraced devotion, grew from priest to bishop,
Gained the Purple, bribed the Conclave, got the Two-thirds, saw my coop ope,
Came out – what Rome hails me! O were there a wish-shop,
Not one wish more would I purchase – lord of all below!

'Ha! – who dares intrude now – puts aside the arras?
What, old Peter, here again, at such a time, in such a presence?
Satan sends this plague back merely to embarrass
Me who enter on my office – little needing you!
'Faith, I'm touched myself by age, but you look Tithon!
Were it vain to seek of you the sole prize left – rejuvenescence?
Well, since flesh is grass which Time must lay his scythe on,
Say your say and so depart and make no more ado!'

Peter faltered – coughing first by way of prologue –
'Holiness, your help comes late: a death at ninety little matters.
Padua, build poor Peter's pyre now, on log roll log,
Burn away – I've lived my day! Yet here's the sting in death –
I've an author's pride: I want my Book's survival:
See, I've hid it in my breast to warm me 'mid the rags and tatters!
Save it – tell next age your Master had no rival!
Scholar's debt discharged in full, be "Thanks" my latest breath!'

'Faugh, the frowsy bundle – scribblings harum-scarum
Scattered o'er a dozen sheepskins! What's the name of this farrago?
Ha – "*Conciliator Differentiarum*" –
Man and book may burn together, cause the world no loss!
Stop – what else? A tractate – eh, "*De Speciebus*

Ceremonialis Ma-gi-ae?" I dream sure! Hence, away, go,
Wizard, – quick avoid me! Vain you clasp my knee, buss
Hand that bears the Fisher's ring or foot that boasts the Cross!

'Help! The old magician clings like an octopus!
Ah, you rise now – fuming, fretting, frowning, if I read your features!
Frown, who cares? We're Pope – once Pope, you can't unpope us!
Good – you muster up a smile: that's better! Still so brisk?
All at once grown youthful? But the case is plain! Ass –
Here I dally with the fiend, yet know the Word – compels all creatures
Earthly, heavenly, hellish. *Apage, Sathanas!*
Dicam verbum Salomonis –' '– *dìcite!*' When – whisk! –

What was changed? The stranger gave his eyes a rubbing:
There smiled Peter's face turned back a moment at him o'er the shoulder,
As the black door shut, bang! 'So he 'scapes a drubbing!'
(Quoth a boy who, unespied, had stopped to hear the talk).
'That's the way to thank these wizards when they bid men
Benedicite! What ails you? You, a man, and yet no bolder?
Foreign Sir, you look but foolish!' '*Idmen, idmen!*'
Groaned the Greek. 'O Peter, cheese at last I know from chalk!'

Peter lived his life out, menaced yet no martyr,
Knew himself the mighty man he was – such knowledge all his guerdon,
Left the world a big book – people but in part err
When they style a true *Scientiae Com-pen-di-um:*
'*Admirationem incutit*' they sourly
Smile, as fast they shut the folio which myself was somehow spurred on
Once to ope: but love – life's milk which daily, hourly,
Blockheads lap – O Peter, still thy taste of love's to come!

Greek, was your ambition likewise doomed to failure?
True, I find no record you wore purple, walked with axe and fasces,
Played some antipope's part: still, friend, don't turn tail, you're
Certain, with but these two gifts, to gain earth's prize in time!

Cleverness uncurbed by conscience – if you ransacked
Peter's book you'd find no potent spell like these to rule the masses;
Nor should want example, had I not to transact
Other business. Go your ways, you'll thrive! So ends my rhyme.

When these parts Tiberius, – not yet Caesar, – travelled,
Passing Padua, he consulted Padua's Oracle of Geryon
(God three-headed, thrice wise) just to get unravelled
Certain tangles of his future. 'Fling at Abano
Golden dice,' it answered: 'dropt within the fount there,
Note what sum the pips present!' And still we see each die, the very one,
Turn up, through the crystal, – read the whole account there
Where 'tis told by Suetonius, – each its highest throw.

Scarce the sportive fancy-dice I fling show 'Venus':
Still – for love of that dear land which I so oft in dreams revisit –
I have – oh, not sung! but lilted (as – between us –
Grows my lazy custom) this its legend. What the lilt?

Doctor —

A Rabbi told me: On the day allowed
Satan for carping at God's rule, he came,
Fresh from our earth, to brave the angel-crowd.

'What is the fault now?' 'This I find to blame:
Many and various are the tongues below,
Yet all agree in one speech, all proclaim

'"Hell has no might to match what earth can show:
Death is the strongest-born of Hell, and yet
Stronger than Death is a Bad Wife, we know."

'Is it a wonder if I fume and fret –
Robbed of my rights, since Death am I, and mine
The style of Strongest? Men pay Nature's debt

'Because they must at my demand; decline
To pay it henceforth surely men will please,
Provided husbands with bad wives combine

'To baffle Death. Judge between me and these!'
'Thyself shalt judge. Descend to earth in shape
Of mortal, marry, drain from froth to lees

'The bitter draught, then see if thou escape
Concluding, with men sorrowful and sage,
A Bad Wife's strength Death's self in vain would ape!'

How Satan entered on his pilgrimage,
Conformed himself to earthly ordinance,
Wived and played husband well from youth to age

Intrepidly – I leave untold, advance
Through many a married year until I reach
A day when – of his father's countenance

The very image, like him too in speech
As well as thought and deed, – the union's fruit
Attained maturity. 'I needs must teach

'My son a trade: but trade, such son to suit,
Needs seeking after. He a man of war?
Too cowardly! A lawyer wins repute –

'Having to toil and moil, though – both which are
Beyond this sluggard. There's Divinity:
No, that's my own bread-winner – that be far

'From my poor offspring! Physic? Ha, we'll try
If this be practicable. Where's my wit?
Asleep? – since, now I come to think. . . . Ay, ay!

'Hither, my son! Exactly have I hit
On a profession for thee. *Medicus* –
Behold, thou art appointed! Yea, I spit

'Upon thine eyes, bestow a virtue thus
That henceforth not this human form I wear
Shalt thou perceive alone, but – one of us

'By privilege – thy fleshly sight shall bear
Me in my spirit-person as I walk
The world and take my prey appointed there.

'Doctor once dubbed – what ignorance shall balk
Thy march triumphant? Diagnose the gout
As cholic, and prescribe it cheese for chalk –

'No matter! All's one: cure shall come about
And win thee wealth – fees paid with such a roar
Of thanks and praise alike from lord and lout

'As never stunned man's ears on earth before.
"How may this be?" Why, that's my sceptic! Soon
Truth will corrupt thee, soon thou doubt'st no more!

'Why is it I bestow on thee the boon
Of recognizing me the while I go
Invisibly among men, morning, noon

'And night, from house to house, and – quick or slow –
Take my appointed prey? They summon thee
For help, suppose: obey the summons! so!

'Enter, look round! Where's Death? Know – I am he,
Satan who work all evil: I who bring
Pain to the patient in whate'er degree.

'I, then, am there: first glance thine eye shall fling
Will find me – whether distant or at hand,
As I am free to do my spiriting.

'At such mere first glance thou shalt understand
Wherefore I reach no higher up the room
Than door or window, when my form is scanned.

'Howe'er friends' faces please to gather gloom,
Bent o'er the sick, – howe'er himself desponds, –
In such case Death is not the sufferer's doom.

'Contrariwise, do friends rejoice my bonds
Are broken, does the captive in his turn
Crow "Life shall conquer"? Nip these foolish fronds

'Of hope a-sprout, if haply thou discern
Me at the head – my victim's head, be sure!
Forth now! This taught thee, little else to learn!'

And forth he went. Folk heard him ask demure
'How do you style this ailment? (There he peeps,
My father, through the arras!) Sirs, the cure

'Is plain as A. B. C.! Experience steeps
Blossoms of pennyroyal half an hour
In sherris. *Sumat!* – Lo, how sound he sleeps –

'The subject you presumed was past the power
Of Galen to relieve!' Or else 'How's this?
Why call for help so tardily? Clouds lour

'Portentously indeed, Sirs! (Naught's amiss:
He's at the bed-foot merely.) Still, the storm
May pass averted – not by quacks, I wis

'Like you, my masters! You, forsooth, perform
A miracle? Stand, sciolists, aside!
Blood, ne'er so cold, at ignorance grows warm!'

Which boasting by result was justified,
Big as might words be: whether drugged or left
Drugless, the patient always lived, not died.

Great the heir's gratitude, so nigh bereft
Of all he prized in this world: sweet the smile
Of disconcerted rivals: 'Cure? – say, theft

'From Nature in despite of Art – so style
This off-hand kill-or-cure work! You did much,
I had done more: folk cannot wait awhile!'

But did the case change? was it – 'Scarcely such
The symptoms as to warrant our recourse
To your skill, Doctor! Yet since just a touch

'Of pulse, a taste of breath, has all the force
With you of long investigation claimed
By others, – tracks an ailment to its source

'Intuitively, – may we ask unblamed
What from this pimple you prognosticate?'
'Death!' was the answer, as he saw and named

The coucher by the sick man's head. 'Too late
You send for my assistance. I am bold
Only by Nature's leave, and bow to Fate!

'Besides, you have my rivals: lavish gold!
How comfortably quick shall life depart
Cosseted by attentions manifold!

'One day, one hour ago, perchance my art
Had done some service. Since you have yourselves
Chosen – before the horse – to put the cart,

'Why, Sirs, the sooner that the sexton delves
Your patient's grave, the better! How you stare
– Shallow, for all the deep books on your shelves!

'Fare you well, fumblers!' Do I need declare
What name and fame, what riches recompensed
The Doctor's practice? Never anywhere

Such an adept as daily evidenced
Each new vaticination! Oh, not he
Like dolts who dallied with their scruples, fenced

With subterfuge, nor gave out frank and free
Something decisive! If he said 'I save
The patient,' saved he was: if 'Death will be

'His portion,' you might count him dead. Thus brave,
Behold our worthy, sans competitor
Throughout the country, on the architrave

Of Glory's temple golden-lettered for
Machaon *redivivus*! So, it fell
That, of a sudden, when the Emperor

Was smit by sore disease, I need not tell
If any other Doctor's aid was sought
To come and forthwith make the sick Prince well.

'He will reward thee as a monarch ought.
Not much imports the malady; but then,
He clings to life and cries like one distraught

'For thee – who, from a simple citizen,
Mayst look to rise in rank, – nay, haply wear
A medal with his portrait, – always when

'Recovery is quite accomplished. There!
Pass to the presence!' Hardly has he crossed
The chamber's threshold when he halts, aware

Of who stands sentry by the head. All's lost.
'Sire, naught avails my art: you near the goal,
And end the race by giving up the ghost.'

'How?' cried the monarch: 'Names upon your roll
Of half my subjects rescued by your skill –
Old and young, rich and poor – crowd cheek by jowl

'And yet no room for mine? Be saved I will!
Why else am I earth's foremost potentate?
Add me to these and take as fee your fill

'Of gold – that point admits of no debate
Between us: save me, as you can and must, –
Gold, till your gown's pouch cracks beneath the weight!'

This touched the Doctor. 'Truly a home-thrust,
Parent, you will not parry! Have I dared
Entreat that you forego the meal of dust

'– Man that is snake's meat – when I saw prepared
Your daily portion? Never! Just this once,
Go from his head, then, – let his life be spared!'

Whisper met whisper in the gruff response
'Fool, I must have my prey: no inch I budge
From where thou see'st me thus myself ensconce.'

'Ah,' moaned the sufferer, 'by thy look I judge
Wealth fails to tempt thee: what if honours prove
More efficacious? Naught to him I grudge

'Who saves me. Only keep my head above
The cloud that's creeping round it – I'll divide
My empire with thee! No? What's left but – love?

'Does love allure thee? Well then, take as bride
My only daughter, fair beyond belief!
Save me – tomorrow shall the knot be tied!'

'Father, you hear him! Respite ne'er so brief
Is all I beg: go now and come again
Next day, for aught I care: respect the grief

'Mine will be if thy first-born sues in vain!'
'Fool, I must have my prey!' was all he got
In answer. But a fancy crossed his brain.

'I have it! Sire, methinks a meteor shot
Just now across the heavens and neutralized
Jove's salutary influence: 'neath the blot

'Plumb are you placed now: well that I surmised
The cause of failure! Knaves, reverse the bed!'
'Stay!' groaned the monarch, 'I shall be capsized –

'Jolt – jolt – my heels uplift where late my head
Was lying – sure I'm turned right round at last!
What do you say now, Doctor?' Naught he said:

For why? With one brisk leap the Antic passed
From couch-foot back to pillow, – as before,
Lord of the situation. Long aghast

The Doctor gazed, then 'Yet one trial more
Is left me' inwardly he uttered. 'Shame
Upon thy flinty heart! Do I implore

'This trifling favour in the idle name
Of mercy to the moribund? I plead
The cause of all thou dost affect: my aim

'Befits my author! Why would I succeed?
Simply that by success I may promote
The growth of thy pet virtues – pride and greed.

'But keep thy favours! – curse thee! I devote
Henceforth my service to the other side.
No time to lose: the rattle's in his throat.

'So, – not to leave one last resource untried, –
Run to my house with all haste, somebody!
Bring me that knobstick thence, so often plied

'With profit by the astrologer – shall I
Disdain its help, the mystic Jacob's-Staff?
Sire, do but have the courage not to die

'Till this arrive! Let none of you dare laugh!
Though rugged its exterior, I have seen
That implement work wonders, send the chaff

'Quick and thick flying from the wheat – I mean,
By metaphor, a human sheaf it thrashed
Flail-like. Go fetch it! Or – a word between

'Just you and me, friend! – go bid, unabashed,
My mother, whom you'll find there, bring the stick
Herself – herself, mind!' Out the lackey dashed

Zealous upon the errand. Craft and trick
Are meat and drink to Satan: and he grinned
– How else? – at an excuse so politic

For failure: scarce would Jacob's-Staff rescind
Fate's firm decree! And ever as he neared
The agonizing one, his breath like wind

Froze to the marrow, while his eye-flash seared
Sense in the brain up: closelier and more close
Pressing his prey, when at the door appeared

– Who but his Wife the Bad? Whereof one dose,
One grain, one mite of the medicament,
Sufficed him. Up he sprang. One word, too gross

To soil my lips with, – and through ceiling went
Somehow the Husband. 'That a storm's dispersed
We know for certain by the sulphury scent!

'Hail to the Doctor! Who but one so versed
In all Dame Nature's secrets had prescribed
The staff thus opportunely? Style him first

'And foremost of physicians!' 'I've imbibed
Elixir surely,' smiled the prince, – 'have gained
New lease of life. Dear Doctor, how you bribed

'Death to forego me, boots not: you've obtained
My daughter and her dowry. Death, I've heard,
Was still on earth the strongest power that reigned,

'Except a Bad Wife!' Whereunto demurred
Nowise the Doctor, so refused the fee
– No dowry, no bad wife!

'You think absurd
This tale?' – the Rabbi added: 'True, our Talmud
Boasts sundry such: yet – have our elders erred
In thinking there's some water there, not all mud?'
I tell it, as the Rabbi told it me.

Pan and Luna

Si credere dignum est. – *Georgic.* iii. 390.

O worthy of belief I hold it was,
Virgil, your legend in those strange three lines!
No question, that adventure came to pass
One black night in Arcadia: yes, the pines,
Mountains and valleys mingling made one mass
Of black with void black heaven: the earth's confines,
The sky's embrace, – below, above, around,
All hardened into black without a bound.

Fill up a swart stone chalice to the brim
With fresh-squeezed yet fast-thickening poppy-juice:
See how the sluggish jelly, late a-swim,
Turns marble to the touch of who would loose
The solid smooth, grown jet from rim to rim,
By turning round the bowl! So night can fuse
Earth with her all-comprising sky. No less,
Light, the least spark, shows air and emptiness.

And thus it proved when – diving into space,
Stript of all vapour, from each web of mist
Utterly film-free – entered on her race
The naked Moon, full-orbed antagonist
Of night and dark, night's dowry: peak to base,
Upstarted mountains, and each valley, kissed
To sudden life, lay silver-bright: in air
Flew she revealed, Maid-Moon with limbs all bare.

Still as she fled, each depth – where refuge seemed –
Opening a lone pale chamber, left distinct
Those limbs: 'mid still-retreating blue, she teemed
Herself with whiteness, – virginal, uncinct
By any halo save what finely gleamed
To outline not disguise her: heaven was linked
In one accord with earth to quaff the joy,
Drain beauty to the dregs without alloy.

Whereof she grew aware. What help? When, lo,
A succourable cloud with sleep lay dense:
Some pine-tree-top had caught it sailing slow,
And tethered for a prize: in evidence
Captive lay fleece on fleece of piled-up snow
Drowsily patient: flake-heaped how or whence,
The structure of that succourable cloud,
What matter? Shamed she plunged into its shroud.

Orbed – so the woman-figure poets call
Because of rounds on rounds – that apple-shaped
Head which its hair binds close into a ball
Each side the curving ears – that pure undraped
Pout of the sister paps – that . . . Once for all,
Say – her consummate circle thus escaped

With its innumerous circlets, sank absorbed,
Safe in the cloud – O naked Moon full-orbed!

But what means this? The downy swathes combine,
Conglobe, the smothery coy-caressing stuff
Curdles about her! Vain each twist and twine
Those lithe limbs try, encroached on by a fluff
Fitting as close as fits the dented spine
Its flexile ivory outside-flesh: enough!
The plumy drifts contract, condense, constringe,
Till she is swallowed by the feathery springe.

As when a pearl slips lost in the thin foam
Churned on a sea-shore, and, o'er-frothed, conceits
Herself safe-housed in Amphitrite's dome, –
If, through the bladdery wave-worked yeast, she meets
What most she loathes and leaps from, – elf from gnome
No gladlier, – finds that safest of retreats
Bubble about a treacherous hand wide ope
To grasp her – (divers who pick pearls so grope) –

So lay this Maid-Moon clasped around and caught
By rough red Pan, the god of all that tract:
He it was schemed the snare thus subtly wrought
With simulated earth-breath, – wool-tufts packed
Into a billowy wrappage. Sheep far-sought
For spotless shearings yield such: take the fact
As learned Virgil gives it, – how the breed
Whitens itself for ever: yes, indeed!

If one forefather ram, though pure as chalk
From tinge on fleece, should still display a tongue
Black 'neath the beast's moist palate, prompt men balk
The propagating plague: he gets no young:
They rather slay him, – sell his hide to caulk
Ships with, first steeped in pitch, – nor hands are wrung
In sorrow for his fate: protected thus,
The purity we love is gained for us.

So did Girl-moon, by just her attribute
Of unmatched modesty betrayed, lie trapped,
Bruised to the breast of Pan, half-god half-brute,

Raked by his bristly boar-sward while he lapped
– Never say, kissed her! that were to pollute
Love's language – which moreover proves unapt
To tell how she recoiled – as who finds thorns
Where she sought flowers – when, feeling, she touched – horns!

Then – does the legend say? – first moon-eclipse
Happened, first swooning-fit which puzzled sore
The early sages? Is that why she dips
Into the dark, a minute and no more,
Only so long as serves her while she rips
The cloud's womb through and, faultless as before,
Pursues her way? No lesson for a maid
Left she, a maid herself thus trapped, betrayed?

Ha, Virgil? Tell the rest, you! 'To the deep
Of his domain the wildwood, Pan forthwith
Called her, and so she followed' – in her sleep,
Surely? – 'by no means spurning him.' The myth
Explain who may! Let all else go, I keep
– As of a ruin just a monolith –
Thus much, one verse of five words, each a boon:
Arcadia, night, a cloud, Pan, and the moon.

'Touch him ne'er so lightly, into song he broke:
Soil so quick-receptive, – not one feather-seed,
Not one flower-dust fell but straight its fall awoke
Vitalizing virtue: song would song succeed
Sudden as spontaneous – prove a poet-soul!'

Indeed?

Rock's the song-soil rather, surface hard and bare:
Sun and dew their mildness, storm and frost their rage
Vainly both expend, – few flowers awaken there:
Quiet in its cleft broods – what the after age
Knows and names a pine, a nation's heritage.

Jocoseria

1883

Wanting is – what?
Summer redundant,
Blueness abundant,
– Where is the blot?
Beamy the world, yet a blank all the same,
– Framework which waits for a picture to frame:
What of the leafage, what of the flower?
Roses embowering with naught they embower!
Come then, complete incompletion, O comer,
Pant through the blueness, perfect the summer!
Breathe but one breath
Rose-beauty above,
And all that was death
Grows life, grows love,
Grows love!

Donald

'Will you hear my story also,
  – Huge Sport, brave adventure in plenty?'
The boys were a band from Oxford,
  The oldest of whom was twenty.

The bothy we held carouse in
  Was bright with fire and candle;
Tale followed tale like a merry-go-round
  Whereof Sport turned the handle.

In our eyes and noses – turf-smoke:
  In our ears a tune from the trivet,
Whence 'Boiling, boiling,' the kettle sang,
  'And ready for fresh Glenlivet.'

So, feat capped feat, with a vengeance:
  Truths, though, – the lads were loyal:
'Grouse, five score brace to the bag!
  Deer, ten hours' stalk of the Royal!'

Of boasting, not one bit, boys!
  Only there seemed to settle
Somehow above your curly heads,
  – Plain through the singing kettle,

Palpable through the cloud,
  As each new-puffed Havana
Rewarded the teller's well-told tale, –
  This vaunt 'To Sport – Hosanna!

'Hunt, fish, shoot,
  Would a man fulfil life's duty!
Not to the bodily frame alone
  Does Sport give strength and beauty,

'But character gains in – courage?
  Ay, Sir, and much beside it!
You don't sport, more's the pity:
  You soon would find, if you tried it,

'Good sportsman means good fellow,
  Sound-hearted he, to the centre;
Your mealy-mouthed mild milksops
  – There's where the rot can enter!

'There's where the dirt will breed,
  The shabbiness Sport would banish!
Oh no, Sir, no! In your honoured case
  All such objections vanish.

''Tis known how hard you studied:
  A Double-First – what, the jigger!
Give me but half your Latin and Greek,
  I'll never again touch trigger!

'Still, tastes are tastes, allow me!
  Allow, too, where there's keenness
For Sport, there's little likelihood
  Of a man's displaying meanness!'

So, put on my mettle, I interposed.
  'Will you hear my story?' quoth I.
'Never mind how long since it happed,
  I sat, as we sit, in a bothy;

'With as merry a band of mates, too,
  Undergrads all on a level:
(One's a Bishop, one's gone to the Bench,
  And one's gone – well, to the Devil.)

'When, lo, a scratching and tapping!
  In hobbled a ghastly visitor.
Listen to just what he told us himself
  – No need of our playing inquisitor!'

Do you happen to know in Ross-shire
  Mount ... Ben ... but the name scarce matters:
Of the naked fact I am sure enough,
  Though I clothe it in rags and tatters.

You may recognize Ben by description;
Behind him – a moor's immenseness:
Up goes the middle mount of a range,
Fringed with its firs in denseness.

Rimming the edge, its fir-fringe, mind!
For an edge there is, though narrow;
From end to end of the range, a stripe
Of path runs straight as an arrow.

And the mountaineer who takes that path
Saves himself miles of journey
He has to plod if he crosses the moor
Through heather, peat and burnie.

But a mountaineer he needs must be,
For, look you, right in the middle
Projects bluff Ben – with an end in *ich* –
Why planted there, is a riddle:

Since all Ben's brothers little and big
Keep rank, set shoulder to shoulder,
And only this burliest out must bulge
Till it seems – to the beholder

From down in the gully, – as if Ben's breast,
To a sudden spike diminished,
Would signify to the boldest foot
'All further passage finished!'

Yet the mountaineer who sidles on
And on to the very bending,
Discovers, if heart and brain be proof,
No necessary ending.

Foot up, foot down, to the turn abrupt
Having trod, he, there arriving,
Finds – what he took for a point was breadth,
A mercy of Nature's contriving.

So, he rounds what, when 'tis reached, proves straight,
From one side gains the other:

The wee path widens – resume the march,
  And he foils you, Ben my brother!

But Donald – (that name, I hope, will do) –
  I wrong him if I call 'foiling'
The tramp of the callant, whistling the while
  As blithe as our kettle's boiling.

He had dared the danger from boyhood up,
  And now, – when perchance was waiting
A lass at the brig below, – 'twixt mount
  And moor would he stand debating?

Moreover this Donald was twenty-five,
  A glory of bone and muscle:
Did a fiend dispute the right of way,
  Donald would try a tussle.

Lightsomely marched he out of the broad
  On to the narrow and narrow;
A step more, rounding the angular rock,
  Reached the front straight as an arrow.

He stepped it, safe on the ledge he stood,
  When – whom found he full-facing?
What fellow in courage and wariness too,
  Had scouted ignoble pacing,

And left low safety to timid mates,
  And made for the dread dear danger,
And gained the height where – who could guess
  He would meet with a rival ranger?

'Twas a gold-red stag that stood and stared,
  Gigantic and magnific,
By the wonder – ay, and the peril – struck
  Intelligent and pacific:

For a red deer is no fallow deer
  Grown cowardly through park-feeding;
He batters you like a thunderbolt
  If you brave his haunts unheeding.

I doubt he could hardly perform *volte-face*
  Had valour advised discretion:
You may walk on a rope, but to turn on a rope
  No Blondin makes profession.

Yet Donald must turn, would pride permit,
  Though pride ill brooks retiring:
Each eyed each – mute man, motionless beast –
  Less fearing than admiring.

These are the moments when quite new sense,
  To meet some need as novel,
Springs up in the brain: it inspired resource:
  – 'Nor advance nor retreat but – grovel!'

And slowly, surely, never a whit
  Relaxing the steady tension
Of eye-stare which binds man to beast, –
  By an inch and inch declension,

Sank Donald sidewise down and down:
  Till flat, breast upwards, lying
At his six-foot length, no corpse more still,
  – 'If he cross me! The trick's worth trying.'

Minutes were an eternity;
  But a new sense was created
In the stag's brain too; he resolves! Slow, sure,
  With eye-stare unabated,

Feelingly he extends a foot
  Which tastes the way ere it touches
Earth's solid and just escapes man's soft,
  Nor hold of the same unclutches

Till its fellow foot, light as a feather whisk,
  Lands itself no less finely:
So a mother removes a fly from the face
  Of her babe asleep supinely.

And now 'tis the haunch and hind foot's turn
  – That's hard: can the beast quite raise it?

Yes, traversing half the prostrate length,
His hoof-tip does not graze it.

Just one more lift! But Donald, you see,
Was sportsman first, man after:
A fancy lightened his caution through,
– He well-nigh broke into laughter.

'It were nothing short of a miracle!
Unrivalled, unexampled –
All sporting feats with this feat matched
Were down and dead and trampled!'

The last of the legs as tenderly
Follows the rest: or never
Or now is the time! His knife in reach,
And his right-hand loose – how clever!

For this can stab up the stomach's soft,
While the left-hand grasps the pastern.
A rise on the elbow, and – now's the time
Or never: this turn's the last turn!

I shall dare to place myself by God
Who scanned – for He does – each feature
Of the face thrown up in appeal to Him
By the agonizing creature.

Nay, I hear plain words: 'Thy gift brings this!'
Up he sprang, back he staggered,
Over he fell, and with him our friend
– At following game no laggard.

Yet he was not dead when they picked next day
From the gully's depth the wreck of him;
His fall had been stayed by the stag beneath
Who cushioned and saved the neck of him.

But the rest of his body – why, doctors said,
Whatever could break was broken;
Legs, arms, ribs, all of him looked like a toast
In a tumbler of port-wine soaken.

'That your life is left you, thank the stag!'
  Said they when – the slow cure ended –
They opened the hospital door, and thence
  – Strapped, spliced, main fractures mended,

And minor damage left wisely alone, –
  Like an old shoe clouted and cobbled,
Out – what went in a Goliath well-nigh, –
  Some half of a David hobbled.

'You must ask an alms from house to house:
  Sell the stag's head for a bracket,
With its grand twelve tines – I'd buy it myself –
  And use the skin for a jacket!'

He was wiser, made both head and hide
  His win-penny: hands and knees on,
Would manage to crawl – poor crab – by the roads
  In the misty stalking-season.

And if he discovered a bothy like this,
  Why, harvest was sure: folk listened.
He told his tale to the lovers of Sport:
  Lips twitched, cheeks glowed, eyes glistened.

And when he had come to the close, and spread
  His spoils for the gazers' wonder,
With 'Gentlemen, here's the skull of the stag
  I was over, thank God, not under!' –

The company broke out in applause;
  'By Jingo, a lucky cripple!
Have a munch of grouse and a hunk of bread,
  And a tug, besides, at our tipple!'

And 'There's my pay for your pluck!' cried This,
  'And mine for your jolly story!'
Cried That, while T'other – but he was drunk –
  Hiccupped 'A trump, a Tory!'

I hope I gave twice as much as the rest;
For, as Homer would say, 'within gate
Though teeth kept tongue,' my whole soul growled
'Rightly rewarded, – Ingrate!'

Solomon and Balkis

Solomon King of the Jews and the Queen of Sheba, Balkis,
Talk on the ivory throne, and we well may conjecture their talk is
Solely of things sublime: why else has she sought Mount Zion,
Climbed the six golden steps, and sat betwixt lion and lion?

She proves him with hard questions: before she has reached the middle
He smiling supplies the end, straight solves them riddle by riddle;
Until, dead-beaten at last, there is left no spirit in her,
And thus would she close the game whereof she was first beginner:

'O wisest thou of the wise, world's marvel and well-nigh monster,
One crabbèd question more to construe or *vulgo* conster!
Who are those, of all mankind, a monarch of perfect wisdom
Should open to, when they knock at *spheteron do* – that's his dome?'

The King makes tart reply: 'Whom else but the wise his equals
Should he welcome with heart and voice? – since, king though he be, such weak walls
Of circumstance – power and pomp – divide souls each from other
That whoso proves kingly in craft I needs must acknowledge my brother.

'Come poet, come painter, come sculptor, come builder – whate'er his condition,
Is he prime in his art? We are peers! My insight has pierced the partition

And hails – for the poem, the picture, the statue, the building – my fellow!
Gold's gold though dim in the dust: court-polish soon turns it yellow.

'But tell me in turn, O thou to thy weakling sex superior,
That for knowledge hast travelled so far yet seemest no whit the wearier, –
Who are those, of all mankind, a queen like thyself, consummate
In wisdom, should call to her side with an affable "Up hither, come, mate!"'

'The Good are my mates – how else? Why doubt it?' the Queen upbridled:
'Sure even above the Wise, – or in travel my eyes have idled, –
I see the Good stand plain: be they rich, poor, shrewd or simple,
If Good they only are. . . . Permit me to drop my wimple!'

And in that bashful jerk of her body, she – peace, thou scoffer! –
Jostled the King's right-hand stretched courteously help to proffer,
And so disclosed a portent: all unaware the Prince eyed
The Ring which bore the Name – turned outside now from inside!

The truth-compelling Name! – and at once 'I greet the Wise – Oh,
Certainly welcome such to my court – with this proviso:
The building must be my temple, my person stand forth the statue,
The picture my portrait prove, and the poem my praise – you cat, you!'

But Solomon nonplussed? Nay! 'Be truthful in turn!' so bade he:
'See the Name, obey its hest!' And at once subjoins the lady
– 'Provided the Good are the young, men strong and tall and proper,
Such servants I straightway enlist, – which means . . .' but the blushes stop her.

'Ah, Soul,' the Monarch sighed, 'that wouldst soar yet ever crawlest,
How comes it thou canst discern the greatest yet choose the smallest,
Unless because heaven is far, where wings find fit expansion,
While creeping on all-fours suits, suffices the earthly mansion?

'Aspire to the Best! But which? There are Bests and Bests so many,
With a *habitat* each for each, earth's Best as much Best as any!
On Lebanon roots the cedar – soil lofty, yet stony and sandy –
While hyssop, of worth in its way, on the wall grows low but handy.

'Above may the Soul spread wing, spurn body and sense beneath her;
Below she must condescend to plodding unbuoyed by aether.
In heaven I yearn for knowledge, account all else inanity;
On earth I confess an itch for the praise of fools – that's Vanity.

'It is naught, it will go, it can never presume above to trouble me;
But here, – why, it toys and tickles and teases, howe'er I redouble me
In a doggedest of endeavours to play the indifferent. Therefore,
Suppose we resume discourse? Thou hast travelled thus far: but wherefore?

'Solely for Solomon's sake, to see whom earth styles Sagest?'
Through her blushes laughed the Queen. 'For the sake of a Sage? The gay jest!
On high, be communion with Mind – there, Body concerns not Balkis:
Down here, – do I make too bold? Sage Solomon, – one fool's small kiss!'

Cristina and Monaldeschi

Ah, but how each loved each, Marquis!
Here's the gallery they trod
Both together, he her god,
She his idol, – lend your rod,
Chamberlain! – ay, there they are – '*Quis*
Separabit?' – plain those two
Touching words come into view,
Apposite for me and you:

Since they witness to incessant
Love like ours: King Francis, he –
Diane the adored one, she –
Prototypes of you and me.
Everywhere is carved her Crescent
With his Salamander-sign –
Flame-fed creature: flame benign
To itself or, if malign,

Only to the meddling curious,
– So, be warned, Sir! Where's my head?
How it wanders! What I said
Merely meant – the creature, fed
Thus on flame, was scarce injurious
Save to fools who woke its ire,
Thinking fit to play with fire.
'Tis the Crescent you admire?

Then, be Diane! I'll be Francis.
Crescents change, – true! – wax and wane,
Woman-like: male hearts retain
Heat nor, once warm, cool again.
So, we figure – such our chance is –
I as man and you as . . . What?
Take offence? My Love forgot
He plays woman, I do not?

I – the woman? See my habit,
Ask my people! Anyhow,
Be we what we may, one vow

Binds us, male or female. Now, –
Stand, Sir! Read! '*Quis separabit?*'
Half a mile of pictured way
Past these palace-walls today
Traversed, this I came to say.

You must needs begin to love me;
First I hated, then, at best,
– Have it so! – I acquiesced;
Pure compassion did the rest.
From below thus raised above me,
Would you, step by step, descend,
Pity me, become my friend,
Like me, like less, loathe at end?

That's the ladder's round you rose by!
That – my own foot kicked away,
Having raised you: let it stay,
Serve you for retreating? Nay.
Close to me you climbed: as close by,
Keep your station, though the peak
Reached proves somewhat bare and bleak!
Woman's strong if man is weak.

Keep here, loving me forever!
Love's look, gesture, speech, I claim;
Act love, lie love, all the same –
Play as earnest were our game!
Lonely I stood long: 'twas clever
When you climbed, before men's eyes,
Spurned the earth and scaled the skies,
Gained my peak and grasped your prize.

Here you stood, then, to men's wonder;
Here you tire of standing? Kneel!
Cure what giddiness you feel,
This way! Do your senses reel?
Not unlikely! What rolls under?
Yawning death in yon abyss
Where the waters whirl and hiss
Round more frightful peaks than this.

Should my buffet dash you thither . . .
But be sage! No watery grave
Needs await you: seeming brave
Kneel on safe, dear timid slave!
You surmised, when you climbed hither,
Just as easy were retreat
Should you tire, conceive unmeet
Longer patience at my feet?

Me as standing, you as stooping, –
Who arranged for each the pose?
Lest men think us friends turned foes,
Keep the attitude you chose!
Men are used to this same grouping –
I and you like statues seen.
You and I, no third between,
Kneel and stand! That makes the scene.

Mar it – and one buffet . . . Pardon!
Needless warmth – wise words in waste!
'Twas prostration that replaced
Kneeling, then? A proof of taste.
Crouch, not kneel, while I mount guard on
Prostrate love – become no waif,
No estray to waves that chafe
Disappointed – love's so safe!

Waves that chafe? The idlest fancy!
Peaks that scare? I think we know
Walls enclose our sculpture: so
Grouped, we pose in Fontainebleau.
Up now! Wherefore hesitancy?
Arm in arm and cheek by cheek,
Laugh with me at waves and peak!
Silent still? Why, pictures speak.

See, where Juno strikes Ixion,
Primatice speaks plainly! Pooh –
Rather, Florentine Le Roux!
I've lost head for who is who –
So it swims and wanders! Fie on
What still proves me female! Here,

By the staircase! – for we near
That dark 'Gallery of the Deer.'

Look me in the eyes once! Steady!
Are you faithful now as erst
On that eve when we two first
Vowed at Avon, blessed and cursed
Faith and falsehood? Pale already?
Forward! Must my hand compel
Entrance – this way? Exit – well,
Somehow, somewhere. Who can tell?

What if to the self-same place in
Rustic Avon, at the door
Of the village church once more,
Where a tombstone paves the floor
By that holy-water basin
You appealed to – 'As, below,
This stone hides its corpse, e'en so
I your secrets hide'? What ho!

Friends, my four! You, Priest, confess him!
I have judged the culprit there:
Execute my sentence! Care
For no mail such cowards wear!
Done, Priest? Then, absolve and bless him!
Now – you three, stab thick and fast,
Deep and deeper! Dead at last?
Thanks, friends – Father, thanks! Aghast?

What one word of his confession
Would you tell me, though I lured
With that royal crown abjured
Just because its bars immured
Love too much? Love burst compression,
Fled free, finally confessed
All its secrets to that breast
Whence . . . let Avon tell the rest!

Mary Wollstonecraft and Fuseli

Oh but is it not hard, Dear?
  Mine are the nerves to quake at a mouse:
If a spider drops I shrink with fear:
  I should die outright in a haunted house;
While for you – did the danger dared bring help –
From a lion's den I could steal his whelp,
With a serpent round me, stand stock-still,
Go sleep in a churchyard, – so would will
Give me the power to dare and do
Valiantly – just for you!

Much amiss in the head, Dear,
  I toil at a language, tax my brain
Attempting to draw – the scratches here!
  I play, play, practise and all in vain:
But for you – if my triumph brought you pride,
I would grapple with Greek Plays till I died,
Paint a portrait of you – who can tell?
Work my fingers off for your 'Pretty well':
Language and painting and music too,
Easily done – for you!

Strong and fierce in the heart, Dear,
  With – more than a will – what seems a power
To pounce on my prey, love outbroke here
  In flame devouring and to devour.
Such love has laboured its best and worst
To win me a lover; yet, last as first,
I have not quickened his pulse one beat,
Fixed a moment's fancy, bitter or sweet:
Yet the strong fierce heart's love's labour's due,
Utterly lost, was – you!

Adam, Lilith, and Eve

One day it thundered and lightened.
Two women, fairly frightened,
Sank to their knees, transformed, transfixed,
At the feet of the man who sat betwixt;
And 'Mercy!' cried each – 'if I tell the truth
Of a passage in my youth!'

Said This: 'Do you mind the morning
I met your love with scorning?
As the worst of the venom left my lips,
I thought "If, despite this lie, he strips
The mask from my soul with a kiss – I crawl
His slave, – soul, body and all!"'

Said That: 'We stood to be married;
The priest, or someone, tarried;
"If Paradise-door prove locked?" smiled you.
I thought, as I nodded, smiling too,
"Did one, that's away, arrive – nor late
Nor soon should unlock Hell's gate!"'

It ceased to lighten and thunder.
Up started both in wonder,
Looked round and saw that the sky was clear,
Then laughed 'Confess you believed us, Dear!'
'I saw through the joke!' the man replied
They re-seated themselves beside.

Ixion

High in the dome, suspended, of Hell, sad triumph, behold us!
  Here the revenge of a God, there the amends of a Man.
Whirling forever in torment, flesh once mortal, immortal
  Made – for a purpose of hate – able to die and revive,
Pays to the uttermost pang, then, newly for payment replenished,
  Doles out – old yet young – agonies ever afresh;
Whence the result above me: torment is bridged by a rainbow, –

Tears, sweat, blood, – cach spasm, ghastly once, glorified now.
Wrung, by the rush of the wheel ordained my place of reposing,
Off in a sparklike spray, – flesh become vapour through pain, –
Flies the bestowment of Zeus, soul's vaunted bodily vesture,
Made that his feats observed gain the approval of Man, –
Flesh that hc fashioned with sense of the earth and the sky and the ocean,
Framed should pierce to the star, fitted to pore on the plant, –
All, for a purpose of hate, re-framed, re-fashioned, re-fitted
Till, consummate at length, – lo, the employment of sense!
Pain's mere minister now to the soul, once pledged to her pleasure –
Soul, if untrammelled by flesh, unapprehensive of pain!
Body, professed soul's slave, which serving beguiled and betrayed her,
Made things false seem true, cheated through eye and through ear,
Lured thus heart and brain to believe in the lying reported, –
Spurn but the traitorous slave, uttermost atom, away,
What should obstruct soul's rush on the real, the only apparent?
Say I have erred, – how else? Was I Ixion or Zeus?
Foiled by my senses I dreamed; I doubtless awaken in wonder:
This proves shine, that – shade? Good was the evil that seemed?
Shall I, with sight thus gained, by torture be taught I was blind once?
Sisuphos, teaches thy stone – Tantalos, teaches thy thirst
Aught which unaided sense, purged pure, less plainly demónstrates?
No, for the past was dream: now that the dreamers awake,
Sisuphos scouts low fraud, and to Tantalos treason is folly.
Ask of myself, whose form melts on the murderous wheel,
What is the sin which throe and throe prove sin to the sinner!
Say the false charge was true, – thus do I expiate, say,
Arrogant thought, word, deed, – mere man who conceited me godlike,
Sat beside Zeus, my friend – knelt before Heré, my love!
What were the need but of pitying power to touch and disperse it,
Film-work – eye's and ear's – all the distraction of sense?
How should the soul not see, not hear, – perceive and as plainly
Render, in thought, word, deed, back again truth – not a lie?

'Ay, but the pain is to punish thee!' Zeus, once more for a pastime,
Play the familiar, the frank! Speak and have speech in return!
I was of Thessaly king, there ruled and a people obeyed me:
Mine to establish the law, theirs to obey it or die:
Wherefore? Because of the good to the people, because of the honour
Thence accruing to me, king, the king's law was supreme.
What of the weakling, the ignorant criminal? Not who, excuseless,
Breaking my law braved death, knowing his deed and its due –
Nay, but the feeble and foolish, the poor transgressor, of purpose
No whit more than a tree, born to erectness of bole,
Palm or plane or pine, we laud if lofty, columnar –
Loathe if athwart, askew, – leave to the axe and the flame!
Where is the vision may penetrate earth and beholding acknowledge
Just one pebble at root ruined the straightness of stem?
Whose fine vigilance follows the sapling, accounts for the failure,
– Here blew wind, so it bent: there the snow lodged, so it broke?
Also the tooth of the beast, bird's bill, mere bite of the insect
Gnawed, gnarled, warped their worst: passive it lay to offence.
King – I was man, no more: what I recognized faulty I punished,
Laying it prone: be sure, more than a man had I proved,
Watch and ward o'er the sapling at birthtime had saved it, nor simply
Owned the distortion's excuse, – hindered it wholly: nay, more –
Even a man, as I sat in my place to do judgement, and pallid
Criminals passing to doom shuddered away at my foot,
Could I have probed through the face to the heart, read plain a repentance,
Crime confessed fools' play, virtue ascribed to the wise,
Had I not stayed the consignment to doom, not dealt the renewed ones
Life to retraverse the past, light to retrieve the misdeed?
Thus had I done, and thus to have done much more it behoves thee,
Zeus who madest man – flawless or faulty, thy work!
What if the charge were true, as thou mouthest, – Ixion the cherished

Minion of Zeus grew vain, vied with the godships and fell,
Forfeit through arrogance? Stranger! I clothed, with the grace of our human,
Inhumanity – gods, natures I likened to ours.
Man among men I had borne me till gods forsooth must regard me
– Nay, must approve, applaud, claim as a comrade at last.
Summoned to enter their circle, I sat – their equal, how other?
Love should be absolute love, faith is in fullness or naught.
'I am thy friend, be mine!' smiled Zeus: 'If Heré attract thee,'
Blushed the imperial cheek, 'then – as thy heart may suggest!'
Faith in me sprang to the faith, my love hailed love as its fellow,
'Zeus, we are friends – how fast! Heré, my heart for thy heart!'
Then broke smile into fury of frown, and the thunder of 'Hence, fool!'
Then through the kiss laughed scorn 'Limbs or a cloud was to clasp?'
Then from Olumpos to Erebos, then from the rapture to torment,
Then from the fellow of gods – misery's mate, to the man!
– Man henceforth and forever, who lent from the glow of his nature
Warmth to the cold, with light coloured the black and the blank.
So did a man conceive of your passion, you passion-protesters!
So did he trust, so love – being the truth of your lie!
You to aspire to be Man! Man made you who vainly would ape him:
You are the hollowness, he – filling you, falsifies void.
Even as – witness the emblem, Hell's sad triumph suspended,
Born of my tears, sweat, blood – bursting to vapour above –
Arching my torment, an iris ghostlike startles the darkness,
Cold white – jewelry quenched – justifies, glorifies pain.
Strive, mankind, though strife endure through endless obstruction,
Stage after stage, each rise marred by as certain a fall!
Baffled forever – yet never so baffled but, e'en in the baffling,
When Man's strength proves weak, checked in the body or soul –
Whatsoever the medium, flesh or essence, – Ixion's
Made for a purpose of hate, – clothing the entity Thou,

– Medium whence that entity strives for the Not-Thou beyond it,
Fire elemental, free, frame unencumbered, the All, –
Never so baffled but – when, on the verge of an alien existence,
Heartened to press, by pangs burst to the infinite Pure,
Nothing is reached but the ancient weakness still that arrests strength,
Circumambient still, still the poor human array,
Pride and revenge and hate and cruelty – all it has burst through,
Thought to escape, – fresh formed, found in the fashion it fled, –
Never so baffled but – when Man pays the price of endeavour,
Thunderstruck, downthrust, Tartaros-doomed to the wheel, –
Then, ay, then, from the tears and sweat and blood of his torment,
E'en from the triumph of Hell, up let him look and rejoice!
What is the influence, high o'er Hell, that turns to a rapture
Pain – and despair's murk mists blends in a rainbow of hope?
What is beyond the obstruction, stage by stage though it baffle?
Back must I fall, confess 'Ever the weakness I fled'?
No, for beyond, far, far is a Purity all-unobstructed!
Zeus was Zeus – not Man: wrecked by his weakness, I whirl.
Out of the wreck I rise – past Zeus to the Potency o'er him!
I – to have hailed him my friend! I – to have clasped her – my love!
Pallid birth of my pain, – where light, where light is, aspiring
Thither I rise, whilst thou – Zeus, keep the godship and sink!

Jochanan Hakkadosh

'This now, this other story makes amends
And justifies our Mishna,' quoth the Jew
Aforesaid. 'Tell it, learnedest of friends!'

A certain morn broke beautiful and blue
O'er Schiphaz city, bringing joy and mirth,
– So had ye deemed; while the reverse was true,

Since one small house there gave a sorrow birth
In such black sort that, to each faithful eye,
Midnight, not morning settled on the earth.

How else, when it grew certain thou wouldst die
Our much-enlightened master, Israel's prop,
Eximious Jochanan Ben Sabbathai?

Old, yea but, undiminished of a drop,
The vital essence pulsed through heart and brain;
Time left unsickled yet the plenteous crop

On poll and chin and cheek, whereof a skein
Handmaids might weave – hairs silk-soft, silver-white,
Such as the wool-plant's; none the less in vain

Had Physic striven her best against the spite
Of fell disease: the Rabbi must succumb;
And, round the couch whereon in piteous plight

He lay a-dying, scholars, – awe-struck, dumb
Throughout the night-watch, – roused themselves and spoke
One to the other: 'Ere death's touch benumb

'His active sense, – while yet 'neath Reason's yoke
Obedient toils his tongue, – befits we claim
The fruit of long experience, bid this oak

'Shed us an acorn which may, all the same,
Grow to a temple-pillar, – dear that day! –
When Israel's scattered seed finds place and name

'Among the envious nations. Lamp us, pray,
Thou the Enlightener! Partest hence in peace?
Hailest without regret – much less, dismay –

'The hour of thine approximate release
From fleshly bondage soul hath found obstruct?
Calmly envisagest the sure increase

'Of knowledge? Eden's tree must hold unplucked
Some apple, sure, has never tried thy tooth,
Juicy with sapience thou hast sought, not sucked?

'Say, does age acquiesce in vanished youth?
Still towers thy purity above – as erst –
Our pleasant follies? Be thy last word – truth!'

The Rabbi groaned; then, grimly, 'Last as first
The truth speak I – in boyhood who began
Striving to live an angel, and, amerced

'For such presumption, die now hardly man.
What have I proved of life? To live, indeed,
That much I learned: but here lies Jochanan

'More luckless than stood David when, to speed
His fighting with the Philistine, they brought
Saul's harness forth: whereat, "Alack, I need

'"Armour to arm me, but have never fought
With sword and spear, nor tried to manage shield,
Proving arms' use, as well-trained warrior ought.

'"Only a sling and pebbles can I wield!"
So he: while I, contrariwise, "No trick
Of weapon helpful on the battle-field

'"Comes unfamiliar to my theoric:
But, bid me put in practice what I know,
Give me a sword – it stings like Moses' stick,

'"A serpent I let drop apace." E'en so,
I, – able to comport me at each stage
Of human life as never here below

'Man played his part, – since mine the heritage
Of wisdom carried to that perfect pitch,
Ye rightly praise, – I, therefore, who, thus sage,

'Could sure act man triumphantly, enrich
Life's annals with example how I played
Lover, Bard, Soldier, Statist, – (all of which

'Parts in presentment failing, cries invade
The world's ear – "Ah, the Past, the pearl-gift thrown
To hogs, time's opportunity we made

'"So light of, only recognized when flown!
Had we been wise!") – in fine, I – wise enough, –
What profit brings me wisdom never shown

'Just when its showing would from each rebuff
Shelter weak virtue, threaten back to bounds
Encroaching vice, tread smooth each track too rough

'For youth's unsteady footstep, climb the rounds
Of life's long ladder, one by slippery one,
Yet make no stumble? Me hard fate confounds

'With that same crowd of wailers I outrun
By promising to teach another cry
Of more hilarious mood than theirs, the sun

'I look my last at is insulted by.
What cry, – ye ask? Give ear on every side!
Witness yon Lover! "How entrapped am I!

'"Methought, because a virgin's rose-lip vied
With ripe Khubbezleh's, needs must beauty mate
With meekness and discretion in a bride:

'"Bride she became to me who wail – too late –
Unwise I loved!" That's one cry. "Mind's my gift:
I might have loaded me with lore, full weight

'"Pressed down and running over at each rift
O' the brain-bag where the famished clung and fed.
I filled it with what rubbish! – would not sift

'"The wheat from chaff, sound grain from musty – shed
Poison abroad as oft as nutriment –
And sighing say but as my fellows said,

'"*Unwise I learned!*" That's two. "In dwarf's-play spent
Was giant's prowess: warrior all unversed
In war's right waging, I struck brand, was lent

'"For steel's fit service, on mere stone – and cursed
Alike the shocked limb and the shivered steel,
Seeing too late the blade's true use which erst

'"How was I blind to! My cry swells the peal –
Unwise I fought!" That's three. But wherefore waste
Breath on the wailings longer? Why reveal

'A root of bitterness whereof the taste
Is noisome to Humanity at large?
First we get Power, but Power absurdly placed

'In Folly's keeping, who resigns her charge
To Wisdom when all Power grows nothing worth:
Bones marrowless are mocked with helm and targe

'When, like your Master's, soon below the earth
With worms shall warfare only be. Farewell,
Children! I die a failure since my birth!'

'Not so!' arose a protest as, pell-mell,
They pattered from his chamber to the street,
Bent on a last resource. Our Targums tell

That such resource there is. Put case, there meet
The Nine Points of Perfection – rarest chance –
Within some saintly teacher whom the fleet

Years, in their blind implacable advance,
O'ertake before fit teaching born of these
Have magnified his scholars' countenance, –

If haply folk compassionating please
To render up – according to his store,
Each one – a portion of the life he sees

Hardly worth saving when 'tis set before
Earth's benefit should the Saint, Hakkadosh,
Favoured thereby, attain to full fourscore –

If such contribute (Scoffer, spare thy 'Bosh!')
A year, a month, a day, an hour – to eke
Life out, – in him away the gift shall wash

That much of ill-spent time recorded, streak
The twilight of the so-assisted sage
With a new sunrise: truth, though strange to speak!

Quick to the doorway, then, where youth and age,
All Israel, thronging, waited for the last
News of the loved one. ''Tis the final stage:

'Art's utmost done, the Rabbi's feet tread fast
The way of all flesh!' So announced that apt
Olive-branch Tsaddik: 'Yet, O Brethren, cast

'No eye to earthward! Look where heaven has clapped
Morning's extinguisher – yon ray-shot robe
Of sun-threads – on the constellation mapped

'And mentioned by our Elders, – yea, from Job
Down to Satam, – as figuring forth – what?
Perpend a mystery! Ye call it *Dob* –

'"The Bear": I trow, a wiser name than that
Were *Aish* – "The Bier": a corpse those four stars hold,
Which – are not those Three Daughters weeping at,

'*Banoth?* I judge so: list while I unfold
The reason. As in twice twelve hours this Bier
Goes and returns, about the East-cone rolled,

'So may a setting luminary here
Be rescued from extinction, rolled anew
Upon its track of labour, strong and clear,

'About the Pole – that Salem, every Jew
Helps to build up when thus he saves some Saint
Ordained its architect. Ye grasp the clue

'To all ye seek? The Rabbi's lamp-flame faint
Sinks: would ye raise it? Lend then life from yours,
Spare each his oil-drop! Do I need acquaint

'The Chosen how self-sacrifice ensures
Ten-fold requital? – urge ye emulate
The fame of those Old Just Ones death procures

'Such praise for, that 'tis now men's sole debate
Which of the Ten, who volunteered at Rome
To die for glory to our Race, was great

'Beyond his fellows? Was it thou – the comb
Of iron carded, flesh from bone, away,
While thy lips sputtered through their bloody foam

'Without a stoppage (O brave Akiba!)
"Hear, Israel, our Lord God is One"? Or thou,
Jischab? – who smiledst, burning, since there lay,

'Burning along with thee, our Law! I trow,
Such martyrdom might tax flesh to afford:
While that for which I make petition now,

'To what amounts it? Youngster, wilt thou hoard
Each minute of long years thou look'st to spend
In dalliance with thy spouse? Hast thou so soared,

'Singer of songs, all out of sight of friend
And teacher, warbling like a woodland bird,
There's left no Selah, 'twixt two psalms, to lend

'Our late-so-tuneful quirist? Thou, averred
The fighter born to plant our lion-flag
Once more on Zion's mount, – doth, all-unheard,

'My pleading fail to move thee? Toss some rag
Shall staunch our wound, some minute never missed
From swordsman's lustihood like thine! Wilt lag

'In liberal bestowment, show close fist
When open palm we look for, – thou, wide-known
For statecraft? whom, 'tis said, an if thou list,

'The Shah himself would seat beside his throne,
So valued were advice from thee' . . . But here
He stopped short: such a hubbub! Not alone

From those addressed, but, far as well as near,
The crowd broke into clamour: 'Mine, mine, mine –
Lop from my life the excrescence, never fear!

'At me thou lookedst, markedst me! Assign
To me that privilege of granting life –
Mine, mine!' Then he: 'Be patient! I combine

'The needful portions only, wage no strife
With Nature's law nor seek to lengthen out
The Rabbi's day unduly. 'Tis the knife

'I stop, – would cut its thread too short. About
As much as helps life last the proper term,
The appointed Fourscore, – that I crave, and scout

'A too-prolonged existence. Let the worm
Change at fit season to the butterfly!
And here a story strikes me, to confirm

'This judgement. Of our worthies, none ranks high
As Perida who kept the famous school:
None rivalled him in patience: none! For why?

'In lecturing it was his constant rule,
Whatever he expounded, to repeat
– Ay, and keep on repeating, lest some fool

'Should fail to understand him fully – (feat
Unparalleled, Uzzean!) – do ye mark? –
Five hundred times! So might he entrance beat

'For knowledge into howsoever dark
And dense the brain-pan. Yet it happed, at close
Of one especial lecture, not one spark

'Of light was found to have illumed the rows
Of pupils round their pedagogue. "What, still
Impenetrable to me? Then – here goes!"

'And for a second time he sets the rill
Of knowledge running, and five hundred times
More re-repeats the matter – and gains *nil.*

'Out broke a voice from heaven: "Thy patience climbs
Even thus high. Choose! Wilt thou, rather, quick
Ascend to bliss – or, since thy zeal sublimes

'"Such drudgery, will thy back still bear its crick,
Bent o'er thy class, – thy voice drone spite of drouth, –
Five hundred years more at thy desk wilt stick?"

'"To heaven with me!" was in the good man's mouth,
When all his scholars, – cruel-kind were they! –
Stopped utterance, from East, West, North and South,

'Rending the welkin with their shout of "Nay –
No heaven as yet for our instructor! Grant
Five hundred years on earth for Perida!"

'And so long did he keep instructing! Want
Our Master no such misery! I but take
Three months of life marítal. Ministrant

'Be thou of so much, Poet! Bold I make,
Swordsman, with thy frank offer! – and conclude,
Statist, with thine! One year, – ye will not shake

'My purpose to accept no more. So rude?
The very boys and girls, forsooth, must press
And proffer their addition? Thanks! The mood

'Is laudable, but I reject, no less,
One month, week, day of life more. Leave my gown,
Ye overbold ones! Your life's gift, you guess,

'Were good as any? Rudesby, get thee down!
Set my feet free, or fear my staff! Farewell,
Seniors and saviours, sharers of renown

'With Jochanan henceforward!' Straightway fell
Sleep on the sufferer; who awoke in health,
Hale everyway, so potent was the spell.

O the rare Spring-time! Who is he by stealth
Approaches Jochanan? – embowered that sits
Under his vine and figtree 'mid the wealth

Of garden-sights and sounds, since intermits
Never the turtle's coo, nor stays nor stints
The rose her smell. In homage that befits

The musing Master, Tsaddik, see, imprints
A kiss on the extended foot, low bends
Forehead to earth, then, all-obsequious, hints

'What if it should be time? A period ends –
That of the Lover's gift – his quarter-year
Of lustihood: 'tis just thou make amends,

'Return that loan with usury: so, here
Come I, of thy Disciples delegate,
Claiming our lesson from thee. Make appear

'Thy profit from experience! Plainly state
How men should Love!' Thus he: and to him thus
The Rabbi: 'Love, ye call it? – rather, Hate!

'What wouldst thou? Is it needful I discuss
Wherefore new sweet wine, poured in bottles caked
With old strong wine's deposit, offers us

'Spoilt liquor we recoil from, thirst-unslaked?
Like earth-smoke from a crevice, out there wound
Languors and yearnings: not a sense but ached

'Weighed on by fancied form and feature, sound
Of silver word and sight of sunny smile:
No beckoning of a flower-branch, no profound

'Purple of noon-oppression, no light wile
O' the West wind, but transformed itself till – brief –
Before me stood the fantasy ye style

'Youth's love, the joy that shall not come to grief,
Born to endure, eternal, unimpaired
By custom the accloyer, time the thief.

'Had Age's hard cold knowledge only spared
That ignorance of Youth! But now the dream,
Fresh as from Paradise, alighting fared

'As fares the pigeon, finding what may seem
Her nest's safe hollow holds a snake inside
Coiled to enclasp her. See, Eve stands supreme

'In youth and beauty! Take her for thy bride!
What Youth deemed crystal, Age finds out was dew
Morn set a-sparkle, but which noon quick dried

'While Youth bent gazing at its red and blue
Supposed perennial, – never dreamed the sun
Which kindled the display would quench it too.

'Graces of shape and colour – every one
With its appointed period of decay
When ripe to purpose! "Still, these dead and done,

'"Survives the woman-nature – the soft sway
Of undefinable omnipotence
O'er our strong male-stuff, we of Adam's clay."

'Ay, if my physics taught not why and whence
The attraction! Am I like the simple steer
Who, from his pasture lured inside the fence

'Where yoke and goad await him, holds that mere
Kindliness prompts extension of the hand
Hollowed for barley, which drew near and near

'His nose – in proof that, of the horned band,
The farmer best affected him? Beside,
Steer, since his calfhood, got to understand

'Farmers a many in the world so wide
Were ready with a handful just as choice
Or choicer – maize and cummin, treats untried.

'Shall I wed wife, and all my days rejoice
I gained the peacock? 'Las me, round I look,
And lo – "With me thou wouldst have blamed no voice

'"Like hers that daily deafens like a rook:
I am the phoenix!" – "I, the lark, the dove,
– The owl," for aught knows he who blindly took

'Peacock for partner, while the vale, the grove,
The plain held bird-mates in abundance. There!
Youth, try fresh capture! Age has found out Love

'Long ago. War seems better worth man's care.
But leave me! Disappointment finds a balm
Haply in slumber.' 'This first step o' the stair

'To knowledge fails me, but the victor's palm
Lies on the next to tempt him overleap
A stumbling-block. Experienced, gather calm,

'Thou excellence of Judah, cured by sleep
Which ushers in the Warrior, to replace
The Lover! At due season I shall reap

'Fruit of my planting!' So, with lengthened face,
Departed Tsaddik: and three moons more waxed
And waned, and not until the Summer-space

Waned likewise, any second visit taxed
The Rabbi's patience. But at three months' end,
Behold, supine beneath a rock, relaxed

The sage lay musing till the noon should spend
Its ardour. Up comes Tsaddik, who but he,
With 'Master, may I warn thee, nor offend,

'That time comes round again? We look to see
Sprout from the old branch – not the youngling twig –
But fruit of sycamine: deliver me,

'To share among my fellows, some plump fig,
Juicy as seedy! That same man of war,
Who, with a scantling of his store, made big

'Thy starveling nature, caused thee, safe from scar,
To share his gains by long acquaintanceship
With bump and bruise and all the knocks that are

'Of battle dowry, – he bids loose thy lip,
Explain the good of battle! Since thou know'st
Let us know likewise! Fast the moments slip,

'More need that we improve them!' – 'Ay, we boast,
We warriors in our youth, that with the sword
Man goes the swiftliest to the uttermost –

'Takes the straight way through lands yet unexplored
To absolute Right and Good, – may so obtain
God's glory and man's weal too long ignored,

'Too late attained by preachments all in vain –
The passive process. Knots get tangled worse
By toying with: does cut cord close again?

'Moreover there is blessing in the curse
Peace-praisers call war. What so sure evolves
All the capacities of soul, proves nurse

'Of that self-sacrifice in men which solves
The riddle – *Wherein differs Man from beast?*
Foxes boast cleverness and courage wolves:

'Nowhere but in mankind is found the least
Touch of an impulse "To our fellows – good
I' the highest! – not diminished but increased

'"By the condition plainly understood
– Such good shall be attained at price of hurt
I' the highest to ourselves!" Fine sparks, that brood

'Confusedly in Man, 'tis war bids spurt
Forth into flame: as fires the meteor-mass,
Whereof no particle but holds inert

'Some seed of light and heat, however crass
The enclosure, yet avails not to discharge
Its radiant birth before there come to pass

'Some push external, – strong to set at large
Those dormant fire-seeds, whirl them in a trice
Through heaven and light up earth from marge to marge:

'Since force by motion makes – what erst was ice –
Crash into fervency and so expire,
Because some Djinn has hit on a device

'For proving the full prettiness of fire!
Ay, thus we prattle – young: but old – why, first,
Where's that same Right and Good – (the wise inquire)

'So absolute, it warrants the outburst
Of blood, tears, all war's woeful consequence,
That comes of the fine flaring? Which plague cursed

'The more your benefited Man – offence,
Or what suppressed the offender? Say it did –
Show us the evil cured by violence,

'Submission cures not also! Lift the lid
From the maturing crucible, we find
Its slow sure coaxing-out of virtue, hid

'In that same meteor-mass, hath uncombined
Those particles and, yielding for result
Gold, not mere flame, by so much leaves behind

'The heroic product. E'en the simple cult
Of Edom's children wisely bids them turn
Cheek to the smiter with "*Sic Jesus vult.*"

'Say there's a tyrant by whose death we earn
Freedom, and justify a war to wage:
Good! – were we only able to discern

'Exactly how to reach and catch and cage
Him only and no innocent beside!
Whereas the folk whereon war wreaks its rage

'– How shared they his ill-doing? Far and wide
The victims of our warfare strew the plain,
Ten thousand dead, whereof not one but died

'In faith that vassals owed their suzerain
Life: therefore each paid tribute, – honest soul, –
To that same Right and Good ourselves are fain

'To call exclusively our end. From bole
(Since ye accept in me a sycamine)
Pluck, eat, digest a fable – yea, the sole

'Fig I afford you! "Dost thou dwarf my vine?"
(So did a certain husbandman address
The tree which faced his field), "Receive condign

'"Punishment, prompt removal by the stress
Of axe I forthwith lay unto thy root!"
Long did he hack and hew, the root no less

'As long defied him, for its tough strings shoot
As deep down as the boughs above aspire:
All that he did was – shake to the tree's foot

'Leafage and fruitage, things we most require
For shadow and refreshment: which good deed
Thoroughly done, behold the axe-haft tires

'His hand, and he desisting leaves unfreed
The vine he hacked and hewed for. Comes a frost,
One natural night's work, and there's little need

'Of hacking, hewing: lo, the tree's a ghost!
Perished it stares, black death from topmost bough
To farthest-reaching fibre! Shall I boast

'My rough work, – warfare, – helped more? Loving, now –
That, by comparison, seems wiser, since
The loving fool was able to avow

'He could effect his purpose, just evince
Love's willingness, – once 'ware of what she lacked,
His loved one, – to go work for that, nor wince

'At self-expenditure: he neither hacked
Nor hewed, but when the lady of his field
Required defence because the sun attacked,

'He, failing to obtain a fitter shield,
Would interpose his body, and so blaze,
Blest in the burning. Ah, were mine to wield

'The intellectual weapon – poet-lays, –
How preferably had I sung one song
Which . . . but my sadness sinks me: go your ways!

'I sleep out disappointment.' 'Come along,
Never lose heart! There's still as much again
Of our bestowment left to right the wrong

'Done by its earlier moiety – explain
Wherefore, who may! The Poet's mood comes next.
Was he not wishful the poetic vein

'Should pulse within him? Jochanan, thou reck'st
Little of what a generous flood shall soon
Float thy clogged spirit free and unperplexed

'Above dry dubitation! Song's the boon
Shall make amends for my untoward mistake
That Joshua-like thou couldst bid sun and moon –

'Fighter and Lover, – which for most men make
All they descry in heaven, – stand both stock-still
And lend assistance. Poet shalt thou wake!'

Autumn brings Tsaddik. 'Ay, there speeds the rill
Loaded with leaves: a scowling sky, beside:
The wind makes olive-trees up yonder hill

'Whiten and shudder – symptoms far and wide
Of gleaning-time's approach; and glean good store
May I presume to trust we shall, thou tried

'And ripe experimenter! Three months more
Have ministered to growth of Song: that graft
Into thy sterile stock has found at core

'Moisture, I warrant, hitherto unquaffed
By boughs, however florid, wanting sap
Of prose-experience which provides the draught

'Which song-sprouts, wanting, wither: vain we tap
A youngling stem all green and immature:
Experience must secrete the stuff, our hap

'Will be to quench Man's thirst with, glad and sure
That fancy wells up through corrective fact:
Missing which test of truth, though flowers allure

'The goodman's eye with promise, soon the pact
Is broken, and 'tis flowers, – mere words, – he finds
When things, – that's fruit, – he looked for. Well, once cracked

'The nut, how glad my tooth the kernel grinds!
Song may henceforth boast substance! Therefore, hail
Proser and poet, perfect in both kinds!

'Thou from whose eye hath dropped the envious scale
Which hides the truth of things and substitutes
Deceptive show, unaided optics fail

'To transpierce, – hast entrusted to the lute's
Soft but sure guardianship some unrevealed
Secret shall lift mankind above the brutes

'As only knowledge can?' 'A fount unsealed'
(Sighed Jochanan) 'should seek the heaven in leaps
To die in dew-gems – not find death, congealed

'By contact with the cavern's nether deeps,
Earth's secretest foundation where, enswathed
In dark and fear, primeval mystery sleeps –

'Petrific fount wherein my fancies bathed
And straight turned ice. My dreams of good and fair
In soaring upwards had dissolved, unscathed

'By any influence of the kindly air,
Singing, as each took flight, The Future – that's
Our destination, mists turn rainbows there,

'Which sink to fog, confounded in the flats
O' the Present! Day's the song-time for the lark,
Night for her music boasts but owls and bats.

'And what's the Past but night – the deep and dark
Ice-spring I speak of, corpse-thicked with its drowned
Dead fancies which no sooner touched the mark

'They aimed at – fact – than all at once they found
Their film-wings freeze, henceforth unfit to reach
And roll in aether, revel – robed and crowned

'As truths, confirmed by falsehood all and each –
Sovereign and absolute and ultimate!
Up with them, skyward, Youth, ere Age impeach

'Thy least of promises to reinstate
Adam in Eden! Sing on, ever sing,
Chirp till thou burst! – the fool cicada's fate,

'Who holds that after Summer next comes Spring,
Than Summer's self sun-warmed, spice-scented more.
Fighting was better! There, no fancy-fling

'Pitches you past the point was reached of yore
By Samsons, Abners, Joabs, Judases,
The mighty men of valour who, before

'Our little day, did wonders none profess
To doubt were fable and not fact, so trust
By fancy-flights to emulate much less.

'Were I a Statesman, now! Why, that were just
To pinnacle my soul, mankind above,
A-top the universe: no vulgar lust

'To gratify – fame, greed, at this remove
Looked down upon so far – or overlooked
So largely, rather – that mine eye should rove

'World-wide and rummage earth, the many-nooked,
Yet find no unit of the human flock
Caught straying but straight comes back hooked and crooked

'By the strong shepherd who, from out his stock
Of aids proceeds to treat each ailing fleece,
Here stimulate to growth, curtail and dock

'There, baldness or excrescence, – that, with grease,
This, with up-grubbing of the bristly patch
Born of the tick-bite. How supreme a peace

'Steals o'er the Statist, – while, in wit, a match
For shrewd Ahithophel, in wisdom . . . well,
His name escapes me – somebody, at watch

'And ward, the fellow of Ahithophel
In guidance of the Chosen!' – at which word
Eyes closed and fast asleep the Rabbi fell.

'Cold weather!' shivered Tsaddik. 'Yet the hoard
Of the sagacious ant shows garnered grain,
Ever abundant most when fields afford

'Least pasture, and alike disgrace the plain
Tall tree and lowly shrub. 'Tis so with us
Mortals: our age stores wealth ye seek in vain

'While busy youth culls just what we discuss
At leisure in the last days: and the last
Truly are these for Jochanan, whom thus

'I make one more appeal to! Thine amassed
Experience, now or never, let escape
Some portion of! For I perceive aghast

'The end approaches, while they jeer and jape,
These sons of Shimei: "Justify your boast!
What have ye gained from Death by twelve months' rape?"

'Statesman, what cure hast thou for – least and most –
Popular grievances? What nostrum, say,
Will make the Rich and Poor, expertly dosed,

'Forget disparity, bid each go gay
That, with his bauble, – with his burden, this?
Propose an alkahest shall melt away

'Men's lacquer, show by prompt analysis
Which is the metal, which the make-believe,
So that no longer brass shall find, gold miss

'Coinage and currency? Make haste, retrieve
The precious moments, Master!' Whereunto
There snarls an 'Ever laughing in thy sleeve,

'Pert Tsaddik? Youth indeed sees plain a clue
To guide man where life's wood is intricate:
How shall he fail to thrid its thickest through

'When every oak-trunk takes the eye? Elate
He goes from bole to brushwood, plunging finds –
Smothered in briars – that the small's the great!

'All men are men: I would all minds were minds!
Whereas 'tis just the many's mindless mass
That most needs helping: labourers and hinds

'We legislate for – not the cultured class
Which law-makes for itself nor needs the whip
And bridle, – proper help for mule and ass,

'Did the brutes know! In vain our statesmanship
Strives at contenting the rough multitude:
Still the ox cries "'Tis me thou shouldst equip

'"With equine trappings!" or, in humbler mood,
"Cribful of corn for me! and, as for work –
Adequate rumination o'er my food!"

'Better remain a Poet! Needs it irk
Such an one if light, kindled in his sphere,
Fail to transfuse the Mizraim cold and murk

'Round about Goshen? Though light disappear,
Shut inside, – temporary ignorance
Got outside of, lo, light emerging clear

'Shows each astonished starer the expanse
Of heaven made bright with knowledge! That's the way,
The only way – I see it at a glance –

'To legislate for earth! As poet. . . . Stay!
What is . . . I would that . . . were it . . . I had been . . .
O sudden change, as if my arid clay

'Burst into bloom! . . .' 'A change indeed, I ween,
And change the last!' sighed Tsaddik as he kissed
The closing eyelids. 'Just as those serene

'Princes of Night apprised me! Our acquist
Of life is spent, since corners only four
Hath Aisch, and each in turn was made desist

'In passage round the Pole (O Mishna's lore –
Little it profits here!) by strenuous tug
Of friends who eked out thus to full fourscore

'The Rabbi's years. I see each shoulder shrug!
What have we gained? Away the Bier may roll!
Tomorrow, when the Master's grave is dug,

'In with his body I may pitch the scroll
I hoped to glorify with, text and gloss,
My Science of Man's Life: one blank's the whole!

'Love, war, song, statesmanship – no gain, all loss,
The stars' bestowment! We on our return
Tomorrow merely find – not gold but dross,

'The body not the soul. Come, friends, we learn
At least thus much by our experiment –
That – that . . . well, find what, whom it may concern!'

But next day through the city rumours went
Of a new persecution; so, they fled
All Israel, each man, – this time, – from his tent,

Tsaddik among the foremost. When, the dread
Subsiding, Israel ventured back again
Some three months after, to the cave they sped

Where lay the Sage, – a reverential train!
Tsaddik first enters. 'What is this I view?
The Rabbi still alive? No stars remain

'Of Aisch to stop within their courses. True,
I mind me, certain gamesome boys must urge
Their offerings on me: can it be – one threw

'Life at him and it stuck? There needs the scourge
To teach that urchin manners! Prithee, grant
Forgiveness if we pretermit thy dirge

'Just to explain no friend was ministrant,
This time, of life to thee! Some jackanapes,
I gather, has presumed to foist his scant

'Scurvy unripe existence – wilding grapes
Grass-green and sorrel-sour – on that grand wine,
Mighty as mellow, which, so fancy shapes

'May fitly image forth this life of thine
Fed on the last low fattening lees – condensed
Elixir, no milk-mildness of the vine!

'Rightly with Tsaddik wert thou now incensed
Had he been witting of the mischief wrought
When, for elixir, verjuice he dispensed!'

And slowly woke, – like Shushan's flower besought
By over-curious handling to unloose
The curtained secrecy wherein she thought

Her captive bee, 'mid store of sweets to choose,
Would loll, in gold pavilioned lie unteased,
Sucking on, sated never, – whose, O whose

Might seem that countenance, uplift, all eased
Of old distraction and bewilderment,
Absurdly happy? 'How ye have appeased

'The strife within me, bred this whole content,
This utter acquiescence in my past,
Present and future life, – by whom was lent

'The power to work this miracle at last, –
Exceeds my guess. Though – *ignorance confirmed*
By knowledge sounds like paradox, I cast

'Vainly about to tell you – fitlier termed –
Of calm struck by encountering opposites,
Each nullifying either! Henceforth wormed

'From out my heart is every snake that bites
The dove that else would brood there: doubt, which kills
With hiss of "What if sorrows end delights?"

'Fear which stings ease with "Work the Master wills!"
Experience which coils round and strangles quick
Each hope with "Ask the Past if hoping skills

'"To work accomplishment, or proves a trick
Wiling thee to endeavour! Strive, fool, stop
Nowise, so live, so die – that's law! why kick

'"Against the pricks?" All out-wormed! Slumber, drop
Thy films once more and veil the bliss within!
Experience strangle hope? Hope waves a-top

'Her wings triumphant! Come what will, I win,
Whoever loses! Every dream's assured
Of soberest fulfilment. Where's a sin

'Except in doubting that the light, which lured
The unwary into darkness, meant no wrong
Had I but marched on bold, nor paused immured

'By mists I should have pressed through, passed along
My way henceforth rejoicing? Not the boy's
Passionate impulse he conceits so strong,

'Which, at first touch, truth, bubble-like, destroys, –
Not the man's slow conviction "Vanity
Of vanities – alike my griefs and joys!"

'Ice! – thawed (look up) each bird, each insect by –
(Look round) by all the plants that break in bloom,
(Look down) by every dead friend's memory

'That smiles "Am I the dust within my tomb?"
Not either, but both these – amalgam rare –
Mix in a product, not from Nature's womb,

'But stuff which He the Operant – who shall dare
Describe His operation? – strikes alive
And thaumaturgic. I nor know nor care

'How from this tohu-bohu – hopes which dive,
And fears which soar – faith, ruined through and through
By doubt, and doubt, faith treads to dust – revive

'In some surprising sort, – as see, they do! –
Not merely foes no longer but fast friends.
What does it mean unless – O strange and new

'Discovery! – this life proves a wine-press – blends
Evil and good, both fruits of Paradise,
Into a novel drink which – who intends

'To quaff, must bear a brain for ecstasies
Attempered, not this all-inadequate
Organ which, quivering within me, dies

'– Nay, lives! – what, how, – too soon, or else too late –
I was – I am . . .' ('He babbleth!' Tsaddik mused)
'O Thou Almighty who canst reinstate

'Truths in their primal clarity, confused
By man's perception, which is man's and made
To suit his service, – how, once disabused

'Of reason which sees light half shine half shade,
Because of flesh, the medium that adjusts
Purity to his visuals, both an aid

'And hindrance, – how to eyes earth's air encrusts,
When purged and perfect to receive truth's beam
Pouring itself on the new sense it trusts

'With all its plenitude of power, – how seem
The intricacies now, of shade and shine,
Oppugnant natures – Right and Wrong, we deem

'Irreconcilable? O eyes of mine,
Freed now of imperfection, ye avail
To see the whole sight, nor may uncombine

'Henceforth what, erst divided, caused you quail –
So huge the chasm between the false and true,
The dream and the reality! All hail,

'Day of my soul's deliverance – day the new,
The never-ending! What though every shape
Whereon I wreaked my yearning to pursue

'Even to success each semblance of escape
From my own bounded self to some all-fair
All-wise external fancy, proved a rape

'Like that old giant's, feigned of fools – on air,
Not solid flesh? How otherwise? To love –
That lesson was to learn not here – but there –

'On earth, not here! 'Tis there we learn, – there prove
Our parts upon the stuff we needs must spoil,
Striving at mastery, there bend above

'The spoiled clay potsherds, many a year of toil
Attests the potter tried his hand upon,
Till sudden he arose, wiped free from soil

'His hand, cried "So much for attempt – anon
Performance! Taught to mould the living vase,
What matter the cracked pitchers dead and gone?"

'Could I impart and could thy mind embrace
The secret, Tsaddik!' 'Secret none to me!'
Quoth Tsaddik, as the glory on the face

Of Jochanan was quenched. 'The truth I see
Of what that excellence of Judah wrote,
Doughty Halaphta. This a case must be

'Wherein, though the last breath have passed the throat,
So that "The man is dead" we may pronounce,
Yet is the Ruach – (thus do we denote

'The imparted Spirit) – in no haste to bounce
From its entrusted Body, – some three days
Lingers ere it relinquish to the pounce

'Of hawk-clawed Death his victim. Further says
Halaphta, "Instances have been, and yet
Again may be, when saints, whose earthly ways

‘“Tend to perfection, very nearly get
To heaven while still on earth: and, as a fine
Interval shows where waters pure have met

‘“Waves brackish, in a mixture, sweet with brine,
That's neither sea nor river but a taste
Of both – so meet the earthly and divine

‘“And each is either.” Thus I hold him graced –
Dying on earth, half inside and half out,
Wholly in heaven, who knows? My mind embraced

‘Thy secret, Jochanan, how dare I doubt?
Follow thy Ruach, let earth, all it can,
Keep of the leavings!’ Thus was brought about

The sepulture of Rabbi Jochanan:
Thou hast him, – sinner-saint, live-dead, boy-man, –
Schiphaz, on Bendimir, in Farzistan!

NOTE, – This story can have no better authority than that of the treatise, existing dispersedly in fragments of Rabbinical writing, משך של רבים בדים, from which I might have helped myself more liberally. Thus, instead of the simple reference to ‘Moses' stick,’ – but what if I make amends by attempting three illustrations, when some thirty might be composed on the same subject, equally justifying that pithy proverb ממשה עד משה לא קם כמשה.

I

Moses the Meek was thirty cubits high,
The staff he strode with – thirty cubits long:
And when he leapt, so muscular and strong
Was Moses that his leaping neared the sky
By thirty cubits more: we learn thereby
He reached full ninety cubits – am I wrong? –
When, in a fight slurred o'er by sacred song,
With staff outstretched he took a leap to try
The just dimensions of the giant Og.
And yet he barely touched – this marvel lacked
Posterity to crown earth's catalogue
Of marvels – barely touched – to be exact –
The giant's ankle-bone, remained a frog
That fain would match an ox in stature: fact!

II

And this same fact has met with unbelief!
  How saith a certain traveller? 'Young, I chanced
  To come upon an object – if thou canst,
Guess me its name and nature! 'Twas, in brief,
White, hard, round, hollow, of such length, in chief,
  – And this is what especially enhanced
  My wonder – that it seemed, as I advanced,
Never to end. Bind up within thy sheaf
Of marvels, this – Posterity! I walked
  From end to end, – four hours walked I, who go
A goodly pace, – and found – I have not balked
  Thine expectation, Stranger? Ay or No?
'Twas but Og's thigh-bone, all the while, I stalked
  Alongside of: respect to Moses, though!'

III

Og's thigh-bone – if ye deem its measure strange,
  Myself can witness to much length of shank
  Even in birds. Upon a water's bank
Once halting, I was minded to exchange
Noon heat for cool. Quoth I 'On many a grange
  I have seen storks perch – legs both long and lank:
  Yon stork's must touch the bottom of this tank,
Since on its top doth wet no plume derange
Of the smooth breast. I'll bathe there!' 'Do not so!'
  Warned me a voice from heaven. 'A man let drop
His axe into that shallow rivulet –
  As thou accountest – seventy years ago:
It fell and fell and still without a stop
  Keeps falling, nor has reached the bottom yet.'

Never the Time and the Place

Never the time and the place
  And the loved one all together!
This path – how soft to pace!
  This May – what magic weather!
Where is the loved one's face?
In a dream that loved one's face meets mine,
  But the house is narrow, the place is bleak
Where, outside, rain and wind combine
  With a furtive ear, if I strive to speak,
  With a hostile eye at my flushing cheek,
With a malice that marks each word, each sign!

O enemy sly and serpentine,
Uncoil thee from the waking man!
Do I hold the Past
Thus firm and fast
Yet doubt if the Future hold I can?
This path so soft to pace shall lead
Through the magic of May to herself indeed!
Or narrow if needs the house must be,
Outside are the storms and strangers: we –
Oh, close, safe, warm sleep I and she,
– I and she!

Pambo

Suppose that we part (work done, comes play)
With a grave tale told in crambo
– As our hearty sires were wont to say –
Whereof the hero is Pambo?

Do you happen to know who Pambo was?
Nor I – but this much have heard of him:
He entered one day a college-class,
And asked – was it so absurd of him? –

'May Pambo learn wisdom ere practise it?
In wisdom I fain would ground me:
Since wisdom is centred in Holy Writ,
Some psalm to the purpose expound me!'

'That psalm,' the Professor smiled, 'shall be
Untroubled by doubt which dirtieth
Pellucid streams when an ass like thee
Would drink there – the Nine-and-thirtieth.

'Verse first: *I said I will look to my ways*
That I with my tongue offend not.
How now? Why stare? Art struck in amaze?
Stop, stay! The smooth line hath an end knot!

'He's gone! – disgusted my text should prove
  Too easy to need explaining?
Had he waited, the blockhead might find I move
  To matter that pays remaining!'

Long years went by, when – 'Ha, who's this?
  Do I come on the restive scholar
I had driven to Wisdom's goal, I wis,
  But that he slipped the collar?

'What? Arms crossed, brow bent, thought-immersed?
  A student indeed! Why scruple
To own that the lesson proposed him first
  Scarce suited so apt a pupil?

'Come back! From the beggarly elements
  To a more recondite issue
We pass till we reach, at all events,
  Some point that may puzzle . . . Why "pish" you?'

From the ground looked piteous up the head:
  'Daily and nightly, Master,
Your pupil plods through that text you read,
  Yet gets on never the faster.

'At the self-same stand, – now old, then young!
  I will look to my ways – were doing
As easy as saying! – *that I with my tongue*
  Offend not – and 'scape pooh-poohing

'From sage and simple, doctor and dunce?
  Ah, nowise! Still doubts so muddy
The stream I would drink at once, – but once!
  That – thus I resume my study!'

    Brother, brother, I share the blame,
      Arcades sumus ambo!
    Darkling, I keep my sunrise-aim,
      Lack not the critic's flambeau,
    And *look to my ways*, yet, much the same,
      Offend with my tongue – like Pambo!

Ferishtah's Fancies

1884

'His genius was jocular, but, when disposed, he could be very serious.' – Article 'Shakespear,' JEREMY COLLIER'S *Historical &c. Dictionary*, 2nd edition, 1701.

'You, Sir, I entertain you for one of my Hundred; only, I do not like the fashion of your garments: you will say they are Persian: but let them be changed.' – *King Lear* III.6.

Prologue

Pray, Reader, have you eaten ortolans
    Ever in Italy?
Recall how cooks there cook them: for my plan's
    To – Lyre with Spit ally.
They pluck the birds, – some dozen luscious lumps,
    Or more or fewer, –
Then roast them, heads by heads and rumps by rumps,
    Stuck on a skewer.
But first, – and here's the point I fain would press, –
    Don't think I'm tattling! –
They interpose, to curb its lusciousness,
    – What, 'twixt each fatling?
First comes plain bread, crisp, brown, a toasted square:
    Then, a strong sage-leaf:
(So we find books with flowers dried here and there
    Lest leaf engage leaf.)
First, food – then, piquancy – and last of all
    Follows the thirdling:
Through wholesome hard, sharp soft, your tooth must bite
    Ere reach the birdling.
Now, were there only crust to crunch, you'd wince:
    Unpalatable!
Sage-leaf is bitter-pungent – so's a quince:
    Eat each who's able!
But through all three bite boldly – lo, the gust!
    Flavour – no fixture –
Flies, permeating flesh and leaf and crust
    In fine admixture.
So with your meal, my poem: masticate
    Sense, sight and song there!
Digest these, and I praise your peptics' state,
    Nothing found wrong there.
Whence springs my illustration who can tell?
    – The more surprising
That here eggs, milk, cheese, fruit suffice so well
    For gormandizing.
A fancy-freak by contrast born of thee,
    Delightful Gressoney!

Who laughest 'Take what is, trust what may be!'
That's Life's true lesson, – eh?

Maison Delapierre,
Gressoney Saint Jean, Val d'Aosta.
12 September 1883

The Eagle

Dervish – (though yet un-dervished, call him so
No less beforehand: while he drudged our way,
Other his worldly name was: when he wrote
Those versicles we Persians praise him for,
– True fairy-work – Ferishtah grew his style) –
Dervish Ferishtah walked the woods one eve,
And noted on a bough a raven's nest
Whereof each youngling gaped with callow beak
Widened by want; for why? beneath the tree
Dead lay the mother-bird. 'A piteous chance!
How shall they 'scape destruction?' sighed the sage
– Or sage about to be, though simple still.
Responsive to which doubt, sudden there swooped
An eagle downward, and behold he bore
(Great-hearted) in his talons flesh wherewith
He stayed their craving, then resought the sky.
'Ah, foolish, faithless me!' the observer smiled,
'Who toil and moil to eke out life, when lo
Providence cares for every hungry mouth!'
To profit by which lesson, home went he,
And certain days sat musing, – neither meat
Nor drink would purchase by his handiwork.
Then, – for his head swam and his limbs grew faint, –
Sleep overtook the unwise one, whom in dream
God thus admonished: 'Hast thou marked my deed?
Which part assigned by providence dost judge
Was meant for man's example? Should he play
The helpless weakling, or the helpful strength
That captures prey and saves the perishing?
Sluggard, arise: work, eat, then feed who lack!'

Waking, 'I have arisen, work I will,
Eat, and so following. Which lacks food the more,
Body or soul in me? I starve in soul:
So may mankind: and since men congregate
In towns, not woods, – to Ispahan forthwith!'

Round us the wild creatures, overhead the trees,
Underfoot the moss-tracks, – life and love with these!
I to wear a fawn-skin, thou to dress in flowers:
All the long lone Summer-day, that greenwood life of ours!

Rich-pavilioned, rather, – still the world without, –
Inside – gold-roofed silk-walled silence round about!
Queen it thou on purple, – I, at watch and ward
Couched beneath the columns, gaze, thy slave, love's guard!

So, for us no world? Let throngs press thee to me!
Up and down amid men, heart by heart fare we!
Welcome squalid vesture, harsh voice, hateful face!
God is soul, souls I and thou: with souls should souls have place.

The Melon-Seller

Going his rounds one day in Ispahan, –
Half-way on Dervishhood, not wholly there, –
Ferishtah, as he crossed a certain bridge,
Came startled on a well-remembered face.
'Can it be? What, turned melon-seller – thou?
Clad in such sordid garb, thy seat yon step
Where dogs brush by thee and express contempt?
Methinks, thy head-gear is some scooped-out gourd!
Nay, sunk to slicing up, for readier sale,
One fruit whereof the whole scarce feeds a swine?
Wast thou the Shah's Prime Minister, men saw
Ride on his right-hand while a trumpet blew
And Persia hailed the Favourite? Yea, twelve years
Are past, I judge, since that transcendency,
And thou didst peculate and art abased;
No less, twelve years since, thou didst hold in hand

Persia, couldst halve and quarter, mince its pulp
As pleased thee, and distribute – melon-like –
Portions to whoso played the parasite,
Or suck – thyself – each juicy morsel. How
Enormous thy abjection, – hell from heaven,
Made tenfold hell by contrast! Whisper me!
Dost thou curse God for granting twelve years' bliss
Only to prove this day's the direr lot?'

Whereon the beggar raised a brow, once more
Luminous and imperial, from the rags.
'Fool, does thy folly think my foolishness
Dwells rather on the fact that God appoints
A day of woe to the unworthy one,
Than that the unworthy one, by God's award,
Tasted joy twelve years long? Or buy a slice,
Or go to school!'

To school Ferishtah went;
And, schooling ended, passed from Ispahan
To Nishapur, that Elburz looks above
– Where they dig turquoise: there kept school himself,
The melon-seller's speech, his stock in trade.
Some say a certain Jew adduced the word
Out of their book, it sounds so much the same,
את־הטוב נקבל מאת האלהים
ואת־הרע לא נקבל: In Persian phrase,
'Shall we receive good at the hand of God
And evil not receive?' But great wits jump.

Wish no word unspoken, want no look away!
What if words were but mistake, and looks – too sudden, say!
Be unjust for once, Love! Bear it – well I may!

Do me justice always? Bid my heart – their shrine –
Render back its store of gifts, old looks and words of thine
– Oh, so all unjust – the less deserved, the more divine?

Shah Abbas

Anyhow, once full Dervish, youngsters came
To gather up his own words, 'neath a rock
Or else a palm, by pleasant Nishapur.

Said someone, as Ferishtah paused abrupt,
Reading a certain passage from the roll
Wherein is treated of Lord Ali's life:
'Master, explain this incongruity!
When I dared question "It is beautiful,
But is it true?" – thy answer was "In truth
Lives beauty." I persisting – "Beauty – yes,
In thy mind and in my mind, every mind
That apprehends: but outside – so to speak –
Did beauty live in deed as well as word,
Was this life lived, was this death died – not dreamed?"
"Many attested it for fact" saidst thou.
"Many!" but mark, Sir! Half as long ago
As such things were, – supposing that they were, –
Reigned great Shah Abbas: he too lived and died
– How say they? Why, so strong of arm, of foot
So swift, he stayed a lion in his leap
On a stag's haunch, – with one hand grasped the stag,
With one struck down the lion: yet, no less,
Himself, that same day, feasting after sport,
Perceived a spider drop into his wine,
Let fall the flagon, died of simple fear.
So all say, – so dost thou say?'

'Wherefore not?'
Ferishtah smiled: 'though strange, the story stands
Clear-chronicled: none tells it otherwise:
The fact's eye-witness bore the cup, beside.'

'And dost thou credit one cup-bearer's tale,
False, very like, and futile certainly,
Yet hesitate to trust what many tongues
Combine to testify was beautiful
In deed as well as word? No fool's report

Of lion, stag and spider, but immense
With meaning for mankind, – thy race, – thyself?'

Whereto the Dervish: 'First amend, my son,
Thy faulty nomenclature, call belief
Belief indeed, nor grace with such a name
The easy acquiescence of mankind
In matters nowise worth dispute, since life
Lasts merely the allotted moment. Lo –
That lion-stag-and-spider tale leaves fixed
The fact for us that somewhen Abbas reigned,
Died, somehow slain, – a useful registry, –
Which therefore we – "believe"? Stand forward, thou,
My Yakub, son of Yusuf, son of Zal!
I advertise thee that our liege, the Shah
Happily regnant, hath become assured,
By opportune discovery, that thy sires,
Son by the father upwards, track their line
To – whom but that same bearer of the cup
Whose inadvertency was chargeable
With what therefrom ensued, disgust and death
To Abbas Shah, the over-nice of soul?
Whence he appoints thee, – such his clemency, –
Not death, thy due, but just a double tax
To pay, on thy particular bed of reeds
Which flower into the brush that makes a broom
Fit to sweep ceilings clear of vermin. Sure,
Thou dost believe the story nor dispute
That punishment should signalize its truth?
Down therefore with some twelve dinars! Why start,
– The stag's way with the lion hard on haunch?
"Believe the story?" – how thy words throng fast! –
"Who saw this, heard this, said this, wrote down this,
That and the other circumstance to prove
So great a prodigy surprised the world?
Needs must thou prove me fable can be fact
Or ere thou coax one piece from out my pouch!"'

'There we agree, Sir: neither of us knows,
Neither accepts that tale on evidence
Worthy to warrant the large word – belief.
Now I get near thee! Why didst pause abrupt,

Disabled by emotion at a tale
Might match – be frank! – for credibility
The figment of the spider and the cup?
– To wit, thy roll's concerning Ali's life,
Unevidenced – thine own word! Little boots
Our sympathy with fiction! When I read
The annals and consider of Tahmasp
And that sweet sun-surpassing star his love,
I weep like a cut vine-twig, though aware
Zurah's sad fate is fiction, since the snake
He saw devour her, – how could such exist,
Having nine heads? No snake boasts more than three!
I weep, then laugh – both actions right alike.
But thou, Ferishtah, sapiency confessed,
When at the Day of Judgement God shall ask
"Didst thou believe?" – what wilt thou plead? Thy tears?
(Nay, they fell fast and stain the parchment still)
What if thy tears meant love? Love lacking ground
– Belief, – avails thee as it would avail
My own pretence to favour since, forsooth,
I loved the lady – I, who needs must laugh
To hear a snake boasts nine heads: they have three!'

'Thanks for the well-timed help that's born, behold,
Out of thy words, my son, – belief and love!
Hast heard of Ishak son of Absal? Ay,
The very same we heard of, ten years since,
Slain in the wars: he comes back safe and sound, –
Though twenty soldiers saw him die at Yezdt, –
Just as a single mule-and-baggage boy
Declared 'twas like he some day would, – for why?
The twenty soldiers lied, he saw him stout,
Cured of all wounds at once by smear of salve,
A Mubid's manufacture: such the tale.
Now, when his pair of sons were thus apprised
Effect was twofold on them. "Hail!" crowed This:
"Dearer the news than dayspring after night!
The cure-reporting youngster warrants me
Our father shall make glad our eyes once more,
For whom, had outpoured life of mine sufficed
To bring him back, free broached were every vein!"
"Avaunt, delusive tale-concocter, news

Cruel as meteor simulating dawn!"
Whimpered the other: "Who believes this boy
Must disbelieve his twenty seniors: no,
Return our father shall not! Might my death
Purchase his life, how promptly would the dole
Be paid as due!" Well, ten years pass, – aha,
Ishak is marching homeward, – doubts, not he,
Are dead and done with! So, our townsfolk straight
Must take on them to counsel. "Go thou gay,
Welcome thy father, thou of ready faith!
Hide thee, contrariwise, thou faithless one,
Expect paternal frowning, blame and blows!"
So do our townsfolk counsel: dost demur?'

'Ferishtah like those simpletons – at loss
In what is plain as pikestaff? Pish! Suppose
The trustful son had sighed "So much the worse!
Returning means – retaking heritage
Enjoyed these ten years, who should say me nay?"
How would such trust reward him? Trustlessness
– O' the other hand – were what procured most praise
To him who judged return impossible,
Yet hated heritage procured thereby.
A fool were Ishak if he failed to prize
Mere head's work less than heart's work: no fool he!'

'Is God less wise? Resume the roll!' They did.

You groped your way across my room i' the dear dark dead of night;
At each fresh step a stumble was: but, once your lamp alight,
Easy and plain you walked again: so soon all wrong grew right!

What lay on floor to trip your foot? Each object, late awry,
Looked fitly placed, nor proved offence to footing free – for why?
The lamp showed all, discordant late, grown simple symmetry.

Be love your light and trust your guide, with these explore my heart!
No obstacle to trip you then, strike hands and souls apart!
Since rooms and hearts are furnished so, – light shows you, – needs
love start?

The Family

A certain neighbour lying sick to death,
Ferishtah grieved beneath a palm-tree, whence
He rose at peace: whereat objected one
'Gudarz our friend gasps in extremity.
Sure, thou art ignorant how close at hand
Death presses, or the cloud, which fouled so late
Thy face, had deepened down not lightened off.'

'I judge there will be respite, for I prayed.'

'Sir, let me understand, of charity!
Yestereve, what was thine admonishment?
"All-wise, all-good, all-mighty – God is such!"
How then should man, the all-unworthy, dare
Propose to set aside a thing ordained?
To pray means – substitute man's will for God's:
Two best wills cannot be: by consequence,
What is man bound to but – assent, say I?
Rather to rapture of thanksgiving; since
That which seems worst to man to God is best,
So, because God ordains it, best to man.
Yet man – the foolish, weak and wicked – prays!
Urges "My best were better, didst Thou know"!'

'List to a tale. A worthy householder
Of Shiraz had three sons, beside a spouse
Whom, cutting gourds, a serpent bit, whereon
The offended limb swelled black from foot to fork.
The husband called in aid a leech renowned
World-wide, confessed the lord of surgery,
And bade him dictate – who forthwith declared
"Sole remedy is amputation." Straight
The husband sighed "Thou knowest: be it so!"
His three sons heard their mother sentenced: "Pause!"
Outbroke the elder: "Be precipitate
Nowise, I pray thee! Take some gentler way,
Thou sage of much resource! I will not doubt
But science still may save foot, leg and thigh!"
The next in age snapped petulant: "Too rash!

No reason for this maiming! What, Sir Leech,
Our parent limps henceforward while we leap?
Shame on thee! Save the limb thou must and shalt!"
"Shame on yourselves, ye bold ones!" followed up
The brisk third brother, youngest, pertest too:
"The leech knows all things, we are ignorant;
What he proposes, gratefully accept!
For me, had I some unguent bound to heal
Hurts in a twinkling, hardly would I dare
Essay its virtue and so cross the sage
By cure his skill pronounces folly. Quick!
No waiting longer! There the patient lies:
Out then with implements and operate!"'

'Ah, the young devil!'

'Why, his reason chimed
Right with the Hakim's.'

'Hakim's, ay – but chit's?
How? what the skilled eye saw and judged of weight
To overbear a heavy consequence,
That – shall a sciolist affect to see?
All he saw – that is, all such oaf should see,
Was just the mother's suffering.'

'In my tale,
Be God the Hakim: in the husband's case,
Call ready acquiescence – aptitude
Angelic, understanding swift and sure:
Call the first son – a wise humanity,
Slow to conceive but duteous to adopt:
See in the second son – humanity,
Wrong-headed yet right-hearted, rash but kind.
Last comes the cackler of the brood, our chit
Who, aping wisdom all beyond his years,
Thinks to discard humanity itself:
Fares like the beast which should affect to fly
Because a bird with wings may spurn the ground,
So, missing heaven and losing earth – drops how
But hell-ward? No, be man and nothing more –
Man who, as man conceiving, hopes and fears,

And craves and deprecates, and loves, and loathes,
And bids God help him, till death touch his eyes
And show God granted most, denying all.'

Man I am and man would be, Love – merest man and nothing more.
Bid me seem no other! Eagles boast of pinions – let them soar!
I may put forth angel's plumage, once unmanned, but not before.

Now on earth, to stand suffices, – nay, if kneeling serves, to kneel:
Here you front me, here I find the all of heaven that earth can feel:
Sense looks straight, – not over, under, – perfect sees beyond appeal.

Good you are and wise, full circle: what to me were more outside?
Wiser wisdom, better goodness? Ah, such want the angel's wide
Sense to take and hold and keep them! Mine at least has never tried.

The Sun

'And what might that bold man's announcement be' –
Ferishtah questioned – 'which so moved thine ire
That thou didst curse, nay, cuff and kick – in short,
Confute the announcer? Wipe those drops away
Which start afresh upon thy face at mere
Mention of such enormity: now, speak!'

'He scrupled not to say – (thou warrantest,
O patient Sir, that I unblamed repeat
Abominable words which blister tongue?)
God once assumed on earth a human shape:
(Lo, I have spitten!) Dared I ask the grace,
Fain would I hear, of thy subtility,
From out what hole in man's corrupted heart
Creeps such a maggot: fancies verminous
Breed in the clots there, but a monster born
Of pride and folly like this pest – thyself
Only canst trace to egg-shell it hath chipped.'

The sun rode high. 'During our ignorance' –
Began Ferishtah – 'folk esteemed as God
Yon orb: for argument, suppose him so, –

Be it the symbol, not the symbolized,
I and thou safelier take upon our lips.
Accordingly, yon orb that we adore
– What is he? Author of all light and life:
Such one must needs be somewhere: this is he.
Like what? If I may trust my human eyes,
A ball composed of spirit-fire, whence springs
– What, from this ball, my arms could circle round?
All I enjoy on earth. By consequence,
Inspiring me with – what? Why, love and praise.
I eat a palatable fig – there's love
In little: who first planted what I pluck,
Obtains my little praise, too: more of both
Keeps due proportion with more cause for each:
So, more and ever more, till most of all
Completes experience, and the orb, descried
Ultimate giver of all good, perforce
Gathers unto himself all love, all praise,
Is worshipped – which means loved and praised at height.
Back to the first good: 'twas the gardener gave
Occasion to my palate's pleasure: grace,
Plain on his part, demanded thanks on mine.
Go up above this giver, – step by step,
Gain a conception of what – (how and why,
Matters not now) – occasioned him to give,
Appointed him the gardener of the ground, –
I mount by just progression slow and sure
To some prime giver – here assumed yon orb –
Who takes my worship. Whom have I in mind,
Thus worshipping, unless a man, my like
Howe'er above me? Man, I say – how else,
I being man who worship? Here's my hand
Lifts first a mustard-seed, then weight on weight
Greater and ever greater, till at last
It lifts a melon, I suppose, then stops –
Hand-strength expended wholly: so, my love
First lauds the gardener for the fig his gift,
Then, looking higher, loves and lauds still more,
Who hires the ground, who owns the ground, Sheikh, Shah,
On and away, away and ever on,
Till, at the last, it loves and lauds the orb
Ultimate cause of all to laud and love.

Where is the break, the change of quality
In hand's power, soul's impulsion? Gift was grace,
The greatest as the smallest. Had I stopped
Anywhere in the scale, stayed love and praise
As so far only fit to follow gift,
Saying "I thanked the gardener for his fig,
But now that, lo, the Shah has filled my purse
With tomans which avail to purchase me
A fig-tree forest, shall I pay the same
With love and praise, the gardener's proper fee?"
Justly would whoso bears a brain object
"Giving is giving, gift claims gift's return,
Do thou thine own part, therefore: let the Shah
Ask more from who has more to pay." Perchance
He gave me from his treasure less by much
Than the soil's servant: let that be! My part
Is plain – to meet and match the gift and gift
With love and love, with praise and praise, till both
Cry "All of us is thine, we can no more!"
So shall I do man's utmost – man to man:
For as our liege the Shah's sublime estate
Merely enhaloes, leaves him man the same,
So must I count that orb I call a fire
(Keep to the language of our ignorance)
Something that's fire and more beside. Mere fire
– Is it a force which, giving, knows it gives,
And wherefore, so may look for love and praise
From me, fire's like so far, however less
In all beside? Prime cause this fire shall be,
Uncaused, all-causing: hence begin the gifts,
Thither must go my love and praise – to what?
Fire? Symbol fitly serves the symbolized
Herein, – that this same object of my thanks,
While to my mind nowise conceivable
Except as mind no less than fire, refutes
Next moment mind's conception: fire is fire –
While what I needs must thank, must needs include
Purpose with power, – humanity like mine,
Imagined, for the dear necessity,
One moment in an object which the next
Confesses unimaginable. Power!
– What need of will, then? naught opposes power:

Why, purpose? any change must be for worse:
And what occasion for beneficence
When all that is, so is and so must be?
Best being best now, change were for the worse.
Accordingly discard these qualities
Proper to imperfection, take for type
Mere fire, eject the man, retain the orb, –
The perfect and, so, inconceivable, –
And what remains to love and praise? A stone
Fair-coloured proves a solace to my eye,
Rolled by my tongue brings moisture curing drouth,
And struck by steel emits a useful spark:
Shall I return it thanks, the insentient thing?
No, – man once, man for ever – man in soul
As man in body: just as this can use
Its proper senses only, see and hear,
Taste, like or loathe according to its law
And not another creature's, – even so
Man's soul is moved by what, if it in turn
Must move, is kindred soul: receiving good
– Man's way – must make man's due acknowledgement,
No other, even while he reasons out
Plainly enough that, were the man unmanned,
Made angel of, angelic every way,
The love and praise that rightly seek and find
Their man-like object now, – instructed more,
Would go forth idly, air to emptiness.
Our human flower, sun-ripened, proffers scent
Though reason prove the sun lacks nose to feed
On what himself made grateful: flower and man,
Let each assume that scent and love alike
Being once born, must needs have use! Man's part
Is plain – to send love forth, – astray, perhaps:
No matter, he has done his part.'

'Wherefrom
What is to follow – if I take thy sense –
But that the sun – the inconceivable
Confessed by man – comprises, all the same,
Man's every-day conception of himself –
No less remaining unconceived!'

'Agreed!'

'Yet thou, insisting on the right of man
To feel as man, not otherwise, – man, bound
By man's conditions neither less nor more,
Obliged to estimate as fair or foul,
Right, wrong, good, evil, what man's faculty
Adjudges such, – how canst thou, – plainly bound
To take man's truth for truth and only truth, –
Dare to accept, in just one case, as truth
Falsehood confessed? Flesh simulating fire –
Our fellow-man whom we his fellows know
For dust – instinct with fire unknowable!
Where's thy man-needed truth – its proof, nay print
Of faintest passage on the tablets traced
By man, termed knowledge? 'Tis conceded thee,
We lack such fancied union – fire with flesh:
But even so, to lack is not to gain
Our lack's suppliance: where's the trace of such
Recorded?'

'What if such a tracing were?
If some strange story stood, – whate'er its worth, –
That the immensely yearned-for, once befell,
– The sun was flesh once? – (keep the figure!)'

'How?
An union inconceivable was fact?'

'Son, if the stranger have convinced himself
Fancy is fact – the sun, besides a fire,
Holds earthly substance somehow fire pervades
And yet consumes not, – earth, he understands,
With essence he remains a stranger to, –
Fitlier thou saidst "I stand appalled before
Conception unattainable by me
Who need it most" – than this – "What? boast he holds
Conviction where I see conviction's need,
Alas, – and nothing else? then what remains
But that I straightway curse, cuff, kick the fool!"'

Fire is in the flint: true, once a spark escapes,
Fire forgets the kinship, soars till fancy shapes
Some befitting cradle where the babe had birth –
Wholly heaven's the product, unallied to earth.
Splendours recognized as perfect in the star! –
In our flint their home was, housed as now they are.

Mihrab Shah

Quoth an inquirer, 'Praise the Merciful!
My thumb which yesterday a scorpion nipped –
(It swelled and blackened) – lo, is sound again!
By application of a virtuous root
The burning has abated: that is well:
But now methinks I have a mind to ask, –
Since this discomfort came of culling herbs
Nor meaning harm, – why needs a scorpion be?
Yea, there began, from when my thumb last throbbed,
Advance in question framing, till I asked
Wherefore should any evil hap to man –
From ache of flesh to agony of soul –
Since God's All-mercy mates All-potency?
Nay, why permits He evil to Himself –
Man's sin, accounted such? Suppose a world
Purged of all pain, with fit inhabitant –
Man pure of evil in thought, word and deed –
Were it not well? Then, wherefore otherwise?
Too good result? But He is wholly good!
Hard to effect? Ay, were He impotent!
Teach me, Ferishtah!'

Said the Dervish: 'Friend,
My chance, escaped today, was worse than thine:
I, as I woke this morning, raised my head,
Which never tumbled but stuck fast on neck.
Was not I glad and thankful!'

'How could head
Tumble from neck, unchopped – inform me first!
Unless we take Firdausi's tale for truth,
Who ever heard the like?'

'The like might hap
By natural law: I let my staff fall thus –
It goes to ground, I know not why. Suppose,
Whene'er my hold was loosed, it skyward sprang
As certainly, and all experience proved
That, just as staves when unsupported sink,
So, unconfined, they soar?'

'Let such be law –
Why, a new chapter of sad accidents
Were added to humanity's mischance,
No doubt at all, and as a man's false step
Now lays him prone on earth, contrariwise,
Removal from his shoulder of a weight
Might start him upwards to perdition. Ay!
But, since such law exists in just thy brain,
I shall not hesitate to doff my cap
For fear my head take flight.'

'Nor feel relief
Finding it firm on shoulder. Tell me, now!
What were the bond 'twixt man and man, dost judge,
Pain once abolished? Come, be true! Our Shah –
How stands he in thy favour? Why that shrug?
Is not he lord and ruler?'

'Easily!
His mother bore him, first of those four wives
Provided by his father, such his luck:
Since when his business simply was to breathe
And take each day's new bounty. There he stands –
Where else had I stood, were his birth-star mine?
No, to respect men's power, I needs must see
Men's bare hands seek, find, grasp and wield the sword
Nobody else can brandish! Bless his heart,
'Tis said, he scarcely counts his fingers right!'

'Well, then – his princely doles! from every feast
Off go the feasted with the dish they ate
And cup they drank from, – nay, a change besides
Of garments'...

'Sir, put case, for service done, –
Or best, for love's sake, – such and such a slave
Sold his allowance of sour lentil soup
To therewith purchase me a pipe-stick, – nay,
If he, by but one hour, cut short his sleep
To clout my shoe, – that were a sacrifice!'

'All praise his gracious bearing.'

'All praise mine –
Or would praise did they never make approach
Except on all-fours, crawling till I bade
"Now that with eyelids thou hast touched the earth,
Come close and have no fear, poor nothingness!"
What wonder that the lady-rose I woo
And palisade about from every wind,
Holds herself handsomely? The wilding, now,
Ruffled outside at pleasure of the blast,
That still lifts up with something of a smile
Its poor attempt at bloom'...

'A blameless life,
Where wrong might revel with impunity –
Remember that!'

'The falcon on his fist –
Reclaimed and trained and belled and beautified
Till she believes herself the Simorgh's match –
She only deigns destroy the antelope,
Stoops at no carrion-crow: thou marvellest?'

'So be it, then! He wakes no love in thee
For any one of divers attributes
Commonly deemed loveworthy. All the same,
I would he were not wasting, slow but sure,
With that internal ulcer'...

'Say'st thou so?
How should I guess? Alack, poor soul! But stay –
Sure in the reach of art some remedy
Must lie to hand: or if it lurk, – that leech

Of fame in Tebriz, why not seek his aid?
Couldst not thou, Dervish, counsel in the case?'

'My counsel might be – what imports a pang
The more or less, which puts an end to one
Odious in spite of every attribute
Commonly deemed loveworthy?'

'Attributes?
Faugh! – nay, Ferishtah, – 'tis an ulcer, think!
Attributes, quotha? Here's poor flesh and blood,
Like thine and mine and every man's, a prey
To hell-fire! Hast thou lost thy wits for once?'

'Friend, here they are to find and profit by!
Put pain from out the world, what room were left
For thanks to God, for love to Man? Why thanks, –
Except for some escape, whate'er the style,
From pain that might be, name it as thou mayst?
Why love, – when all thy kind, save me, suppose,
Thy father, and thy son, and . . . well, thy dog,
To eke the decent number out – we few
Who happen – like a handful of chance stars
From the unnumbered host – to shine o'erhead
And lend thee light, – our twinkle all thy store, –
We only take thy love! Mankind, forsooth?
Who sympathizes with their general joy
Foolish as undeserved? But pain – see God's
Wisdom at work! – man's heart is made to judge
Pain deserved nowhere by the common flesh
Our birthright, – bad and good deserve alike
No pain, to human apprehension! Lust,
Greed, cruelty, injustice, crave (we hold)
Due punishment from somebody, no doubt:
But ulcer in the midriff! that brings flesh
Triumphant from the bar whereto arraigned
Soul quakes with reason. In the eye of God
Pain may have purpose and be justified:
Man's sense avails to only see, in pain,
A hateful chance no man but would avert
Or, failing, needs must pity. Thanks to God

And love to man, – from man take these away,
And what is man worth? Therefore, Mihrab Shah,
Tax me my bread and salt twice over, claim
Laila my daughter for thy sport, – go on!
Slay my son's self, maintain thy poetry
Beats mine, – thou meritest a dozen deaths!
But – ulcer in the stomach, – ah, poor soul,
Try a fig-plaster: may it ease thy pangs!'

So, the head aches and the limbs are faint!
  Flesh is a burthen – even to you!
Can I force a smile with a fancy quaint?
  Why are my ailments none or few?

In the soul of me sits sluggishness:
  Body so strong and will so weak!
The slave stands fit for the labour – yes,
  But the master's mandate is still to seek.

You, now – what if the outside clay
  Helped, not hindered the inside flame?
My dim tomorrow – your plain today,
  Yours the achievement, mine the aim?

So were it rightly, so shall it be!
  Only, while earth we pace together
For the purpose apportioned you and me,
  Closer we tread for a common tether.

You shall sigh 'Wait for his sluggish soul!
  Shame he should lag, not lamed as I!'
May not I smile 'Ungained her goal:
  Body may reach her – by-and-by'?

A Camel-Driver

'How of his fate, the Pilgrims' soldier-guide
Condemned' (Ferishtah questioned), 'for he slew
The merchant whom he convoyed with his bales
– A special treachery?'

'Sir, the proofs were plain:
Justice was satisfied: between two boards
The rogue was sawn asunder, rightly served.'

'With all wise men's approval – mine at least.'

'Himself, indeed, confessed as much. "I die
Justly" (groaned he) "through over-greediness
Which tempted me to rob: but grieve the most
That he who quickened sin at slumber, – ay,
Prompted and pestered me till thought grew deed, –
The same is fled to Syria and is safe,
Laughing at me thus left to pay for both.
My comfort is that God reserves for him
Hell's hottest"...'

'Idle words.'

'Enlighten me!
Wherefore so idle? Punishment by man
Has thy assent, – the word is on thy lips.
By parity of reason, punishment
By God should likelier win thy thanks and praise.'

'Man acts as man must: God, as God beseems.
A camel-driver, when his beast will bite,
Thumps her athwart the muzzle: why?'

'How else
Instruct the creature – mouths should munch, not bite?'

'True, he is man, knows but man's trick to teach.
Suppose some plain word, told her first of all,
Had hindered any biting?'

'Find him such,
And fit the beast with understanding first!
No understanding animals like Rakhsh
Nowadays, Master! Till they breed on earth,
For teaching – blows must serve.'

'Who deals the blow –
What if by some rare method, – magic, say, –
He saw into the biter's very soul,
And knew the fault was so repented of
It could not happen twice?'

'That's something: still,
I hear, methinks, the driver say "No less
Take thy fault's due! Those long-necked sisters, see,
Lean all a-stretch to know if biting meets
Punishment or enjoys impunity.
For their sakes – thwack!"'

'The journey home at end,
The solitary beast safe-stabled now,
In comes the driver to avenge a wrong
Suffered from six months since, – apparently
With patience, nay, approval: when the jaws
Met i' the small of the arm, "Ha, Ladykin,
Still at thy frolics, girl of gold?" laughed he:
"Eat flesh? Rye-grass content thee rather with,
Whereof accept a bundle!" Now, – what change!
Laughter by no means! Now 'tis "Fiend, thy frisk
Was fit to find thee provender, didst judge?
Behold this red-hot twy-prong, thus I stick
To hiss i' the soft of thee!"'

'Behold? behold
A crazy noddle, rather! Sure the brute
Might wellnigh have plain speech coaxed out of tongue,
And grow as voluble as Rakhsh himself
At such mad outrage. "Could I take thy mind,
Guess thy desire? If biting was offence
Wherefore the rye-grass bundle, why each day's
Patting and petting, but to intimate
My playsomeness had pleased thee? Thou endowed
With reason, truly!"'

'Reason aims to raise
Some makeshift scaffold-vantage midway, whence
Man dares, for life's brief moment, peer below:
But ape omniscience? Nay! The ladder lent

To climb by, step and step, until we reach
The little foothold-rise allowed mankind
To mount on and thence guess the sun's survey –
Shall this avail to show us world-wide truth
Stretched for the sun's descrying? Reason bids
"Teach, Man, thy beast his duty first of all
Or last of all, with blows if blows must be, –
How else accomplish teaching?" Reason adds
"Before man's First, and after man's poor Last,
God operated and will operate."
– Process of which man merely knows this much, –
That nowise it resembles man's at all,
Teaching or punishing.'

'It follows, then,
That any malefactor I would smite
With God's allowance, God himself will spare
Presumably. No scapegrace? Then, rejoice
Thou snatch-grace safe in Syria!'

'Friend, such view
Is but man's wonderful and wide mistake.
Man lumps his kind i' the mass: God singles thence
Unit by unit. Thou and God exist –
So think! – for certain: think the mass – mankind –
Disparts, disperses, leaves thyself alone!
Ask thy lone soul what laws are plain to thee, –
Thee and no other, – stand or fall by them!
That is the part for thee: regard all else
For what it may be – Time's illusion. This
Be sure of – ignorance that sins, is safe.
No punishment like knowledge! Instance, now!
My father's choicest treasure was a book
Wherein he, day by day and year by year,
Recorded gains of wisdom for my sake
When I should grow to manhood. While a child,
Coming upon the casket where it lay
Unguarded, – what did I but toss the thing
Into a fire to make more flame therewith,
Meaning no harm? So acts man three-years old!
I grieve now at my loss by witlessness,
But guilt was none to punish. Man mature –

Each word of his I lightly held, each look
I turned from – wish that wished in vain – nay, will
That willed and yet went all to waste – 'tis these
Rankle like fire. Forgiveness? rather grant
Forgetfulness! The past is past and lost.
However near I stand in his regard,
So much the nearer had I stood by steps
Offered the feet which rashly spurned their help.
That I call Hell; why further punishment?'

When I vexed you and you chid me,
  And I owned my fault and turned
My cheek the way you bid me,
  And confessed the blow well earned, –

My comfort all the while was
  – Fault was faulty – near, not quite!
Do you wonder why the smile was?
  O'erpunished wrong grew right.

But faults you ne'er suspected,
  Nay, praised, no faults at all, –
Those would you had detected –
  Crushed eggs whence snakes could crawl!

Two Camels

Quoth one: 'Sir, solve a scruple! No true sage
I hear of, but instructs his scholar thus:
"Wouldst thou be wise? Then mortify thyself!
Balk of its craving every bestial sense!
Say 'If I relish melons – so do swine!
Horse, ass and mule consume their provender
Nor leave a pea-pod: fasting feeds the soul.'"
Thus they admonish: while thyself, I note,
Eatest thy ration with an appetite,
Nor fallest foul of whoso licks his lips
And sighs – "Well-saffroned was that barley soup!"
Can wisdom co-exist with – gorge-and-swill,

I say not, – simply sensual preference
For this or that fantastic meat and drink?
Moreover, wind blows sharper than its wont
This morning, and thou hast already donned
Thy sheepskin over-garment: sure the sage
Is busied with conceits that soar above
A petty change of season and its chance
Of causing ordinary flesh to sneeze?
I always thought, Sir'...

'Son,' Ferishtah said,
'Truth ought to seem as never thought before.
How if I give it birth in parable?
A neighbour owns two camels, beasts of price
And promise, destined each to go, next week,
Swiftly and surely with his merchandise
From Nishapur to Sebzevar, no truce
To tramp, but travel, spite of sands and drouth,
In days so many, lest they miss the Fair.
Each falls to meditation o'er his crib
Piled high with provender before the start.
Quoth this: "My soul is set on winning praise
From goodman lord and master, – hump to hoof,
I dedicate me to his service. How?
Grass, purslane, lupines and I know not what,
Crammed in my manger? Ha, I see – I see!
No, master, spare thy money! I shall trudge
The distance and yet cost thee not a doit
Beyond my supper on this mouldy bran."
"Be magnified, O master, for the meal
So opportunely liberal!" quoth that.
"What use of strength in me but to surmount
Sands and simooms, and bend beneath thy bales
No knee until I reach the glad bazaar?
Thus I do justice to thy fare: no sprig
Of toothsome chervil must I leave unchewed!
Too bitterly should I reproach myself
Did I sink down in sight of Sebzevar,
Remembering how the merest mouthful more
Had heartened me to manage yet a mile!"
And so it proved: the too-abstemious brute
Midway broke down, his pack rejoiced the thieves,

His carcass fed the vultures: not so he
The wisely thankful, who, good market-drudge,
Let down his lading in the market-place,
No damage to a single pack. Which beast,
Think ye, had praise and patting and a brand
Of good-and-faithful-servant fixed on flank?
So, with thy squeamish scruple. What imports
Fasting or feasting? Do thy day's work, dare
Refuse no help thereto, since help refused
Is hindrance sought and found. Win but the race –
Who shall object "He tossed three wine cups off,
And, just at starting, Lilith kissed his lips"?

'More soberly, – consider this, my Son!
Put case I never have myself enjoyed,
Known by experience what enjoyment means,
How shall I – share enjoyment? – no, indeed! –
Supply it to my fellows, – ignorant,
As so I should be of the thing they crave,
How it affects them, works for good or ill.
Style my enjoyment self-indulgence – sin –
Why should I labour to infect my kind
With sin's occasion, bid them too enjoy,
Who else might neither catch nor give again
Joy's plague, but live in righteous misery?
Just as I cannot, till myself convinced,
Impart conviction, so, to deal forth joy
Adroitly, needs must I know joy myself.
Renounce joy for my fellows' sake? That's joy
Beyond joy; but renounced for mine, not theirs?
Why, the physician called to help the sick,
Cries "Let me, first of all, discard my health!"
No, Son: the richness hearted in such joy
Is in the knowing what are gifts we give,
Not in a vain endeavour not to know!
Therefore, desire joy and thank God for it!
The Adversary said, – a Jew reports, –
החנם רא אזב אלהים:
In Persian phrase, "Does Job fear God for naught?"
Job's creatureship is not abjured, thou fool!
He nowise isolates himself and plays
The independent equal, owns no more

Than himself gave himself, so why thank God?
A proper speech were this מאלהים
"Equals we are, Job, labour for thyself,
Nor bid me help thee: bear, as best flesh may,
Pains I inflict not nor avail to cure:
Beg of me nothing thou thyself mayst win
By work, or waive with magnanimity,
Since we are peers acknowledged, – scarcely peers,
Had I implanted any want of thine
Only my power could meet and gratify."
No: rather hear, at man's indifference –
"Wherefore did I contrive for thee that ear
Hungry for music, and direct thine eye
To where I hold a seven-stringed instrument,
Unless I meant thee to beseech me play?"'

Once I saw a chemist take a pinch of powder
– Simple dust it seemed – and half-unstop a phial.
– Outdropped harmless dew. 'Mixed nothings make' – quoth he –
'Something!' So they did: a thunderclap, but louder –
Lightning-flash, but fiercer – put spectators' nerves to trial:
Sure enough, we learned what was, imagined what might be.

Had I no experience how a lip's mere tremble,
Look's half hesitation, cheek's just change of colour,
These effect a heartquake, – how should I conceive
What a heaven there may be? Let it but resemble
Earth myself have known! No bliss that's finer, fuller,
Only – bliss that lasts, they say, and fain would I believe.

Cherries

'What, I disturb thee at thy morning-meal:
Cherries so ripe already? Eat apace!
I recollect thy lesson yesterday.
Yet – thanks, Sir, for thy leave to interrupt' . . .

'Friend, I have finished my repast, thank God!'

'There now, thy thanks for breaking fast on fruit! –
Thanks being praise, or tantamount thereto.
Prithee consider, have not things degree,
Lofty and low? Are things not great and small,
Thence claiming praise and wonder more or less?
Shall we confuse them, with thy warrant too,
Whose doctrine otherwise begins and ends
With just this precept "Never faith enough
In man as weakness, God as potency"?
When I would pay soul's tribute to that same,
Why not look up in wonder, bid the stars
Attest my praise of the All-mighty One?
What are man's puny members and as mean
Requirements weighed with Star-King Mushtari?
There is the marvel!'

'Not to man – that's me.
List to what happened late, in fact or dream.
A certain stranger, bound from far away,
Still the Shah's subject, found himself before
Ispahan palace-gate. As duty bade,
He enters in the courts, will, if he may,
See so much glory as befits a slave
Who only comes, of mind to testify
How great and good is shown our lord the Shah.
In he walks, round he casts his eye about,
Looks up and down, admires to heart's content,
Ascends the gallery, tries door and door,
None says his reverence nay: peeps in at each,
Wonders at all the unimagined use,
Gold here and jewels there, – so vast, that hall –
So perfect yon pavilion! – lamps above
Bidding look up from luxuries below, –
Evermore wonder topping wonder, – last –
Sudden he comes upon a cosy nook,
A nest-like little chamber, with his name,
His own, yea, his and no mistake at all,
Plain o'er the entry: what, and he descries
Just those arrangements inside, – oh, the care! –
Suited to soul and body both, – so snug
The cushion – nay, the pipe-stand furnished so!
Whereat he cries aloud, – what think'st thou, Friend?

"That these my slippers should be just my choice,
Even to the colour that I most affect,
Is nothing: ah, that lamp, the central sun,
What must it light within its minaret
I scarce dare guess the good of! Who lives there?
That let me wonder at, – no slipper-toys
Meant for the foot, forsooth, which kicks them – thus!"

'Never enough faith in omnipotence, –
Never too much, by parity, of faith
In impuissance, man's – which turns to strength
When once acknowledged weakness every way.
How? Hear the teaching of another tale.

'Two men once owed the Shah a mighty sum
Beggars they both were: this one crossed his arms
And bowed his head, – "whereof," – sighed he, – "each hair
Proved it a jewel, how the host's amount
Were idly strewn for payment at thy feet!"
"Lord, here they lie, my havings poor and scant!
All of the berries on my currant-bush,
What roots of garlic have escaped the mice,
And some five pippins from the seedling tree, –
Would they were half-a-dozen! anyhow,
Accept my all, poor beggar that I am!"
"Received in full of all demands!" smiled back
The apportioner of every lot of ground
From inch to acre. Littleness of love
Befits the littleness of loving thing.
What if he boasted "Seeing I am great,
Great must my corresponding tribute be"?
Mushtari, – well, suppose him seven times seven
The sun's superior, proved so by some sage:
Am I that sage? To me his twinkle blue
Is all I know of him and thank him for,
And therefore I have put the same in verse –
"Like yon blue twinkle, twinks thine eye, my Love!"

'Neither shalt thou be troubled overmuch
Because thy offering, – littleness itself, –
Is lessened by admixture sad and strange
Of mere man's-motives, – praise with fear, and love

With looking after that same love's reward.
Alas, Friend, what was free from this alloy, –
Some smatch thereof, – in best and purest love
Proffered thy earthly father? Dust thou art,
Dust shalt be to the end. Thy father took
The dust, and kindly called the handful – gold,
Nor cared to count what sparkled here and there,
Sagely unanalytic. Thank, praise, love
(Sum up thus) for the lowest favours first,
The commonest of comforts! aught beside
Very omnipotence had overlooked
Such needs, arranging for thy little life.
Nor waste thy power of love in wonderment
At what thou wiselier lettest shine unsoiled
By breath of word. That this last cherry soothes
A roughness of my palate, that I know:
His maker knows why Mushtari was made.'

Verse-making was least of my virtues: I viewed with despair
Wealth that never yet was but might be – all that verse-making were
If the life would but lengthen to wish, let the mind be laid bare.
So I said 'To do little is bad, to do nothing is worse' –
    And made verse.

Love-making, – how simple a matter! No depths to explore,
No heights in a life to ascend! No disheartening Before,
No affrighting Hereafter, – love now will be love evermore.
So I felt 'To keep silence were folly': – all language above,
    I made love.

Plot-Culture

'Ay, but, Ferishtah,' – a disciple smirked, –
'That verse of thine "How twinks thine eye, my Love,
Blue as yon star-beam!" much arrides myself
Who haply may obtain a kiss therewith
This eve from Laila where the palms abound –
My youth, my warrant – so the palms be close!
Suppose when thou art earnest in discourse
Concerning high and holy things, – abrupt
I out with – "Laila's lip, how honey-sweet!" –

What say'st thou, were it scandalous or no?
I feel thy shoe sent flying at my mouth
For daring – prodigy of impudence –
Publish what, secret, were permissible.
Well, – one slide further in the imagined slough, –
Knee-deep therein, (respect thy reverence!) –
Suppose me well aware thy very self
Stooped prying through the palm-screen, while I dared
Solace me with caressings all the same?
Unutterable, nay – unthinkable,
Undreamable a deed of shame! Alack,
How will it fare shouldst thou impress on me
That certainly an Eye is over all
And each, to mark the minute's deed, word, thought,
As worthy of reward or punishment?
Shall I permit my sense an Eye-viewed shame,
Broad daylight perpetration, – so to speak, –
I had not dared to breathe within the Ear,
With black night's help about me? Yet I stand
A man, no monster, made of flesh not cloud:
Why made so, if my making prove offence
To Maker's eye and ear?'

'Thou wouldst not stand
Distinctly Man,' – Ferishtah made reply,
'Not the mere creature, – did no limit-line
Round thee about, apportion thee thy place
Clean-cut from out and off the illimitable, –
Minuteness severed from immensity.
All of thee for the Maker, – for thyself,
Workings inside the circle that evolve
Thine all, – the product of thy cultured plot.
So much of grain the ground's lord bids thee yield:
Bring sacks to granary in Autumn! spare
Daily intelligence of this manure,
That compost, how they tend to feed the soil:
There thou art master sole and absolute
– Only, remember doomsday! Twitt'st thou me
Because I turn away my outraged nose
Shouldst thou obtrude thereon a shovelful
Of fertilizing kisses? Since thy sire
Wills and obtains thy marriage with the maid,

Enough! Be reticent, I counsel thee,
Nor venture to acquaint him, point by point,
What he procures thee. Is he so obtuse?
Keep thy instruction to thyself! My ass –
Only from him expect acknowledgement
The while he champs my gift, a thistle-bunch,
How much he loves the largess: of his love
I only tolerate so much as tells
By wrinkling nose and inarticulate grunt,
The meal, that heartens him to do my work,
Tickles his palate as I meant it should.'

Not with my Soul, Love! – bid no Soul like mine
   Lap thee around nor leave the poor Sense room!
Soul, – travel-worn, toil-weary, – would confine
   Along with Soul, Soul's gains from glow and gloom,
Captures from soarings high and divings deep.
Spoil-laden Soul, how should such memories sleep?
Take Sense, too – let me love entire and whole –
      Not with my Soul!

Eyes shall meet eyes and find no eyes between,
   Lips feed on lips, no other lips to fear!
No past, no future – so thine arms but screen
   The present from surprise! not there, 'tis here –
Not then, 'tis now: – back, memories that intrude!
Make, Love, the universe our solitude,
And, over all the rest, oblivion roll –
      Sense quenching Soul!

A Pillar at Sebzevar

'Knowledge deposed, then!' – groaned whom that most grieved
As foolishest of all the company.
'What, knowledge, man's distinctive attribute,
He doffs that crown to emulate an ass
Because the unknowing long-ears loves at least
Husked lupines, and belike the feeder's self
– Whose purpose in the dole what ass divines?'

'Friend,' quoth Ferishtah, 'all I seem to know
Is – I know nothing save that love I can
Boundlessly, endlessly. My curls were crowned
In youth with knowledge, – off, alas, crown slipped
Next moment, pushed by better knowledge still
Which nowise proved more constant: gain, today,
Was toppling loss tomorrow, lay at last
– Knowledge, the golden? – lacquered ignorance!
As gain – mistrust it! Not as means to gain:
Lacquer we learn by: cast in fining-pot,
We learn, – when what seemed ore assayed proves dross, –
Surelier true gold's worth, guess how purity
I' the lode were precious could one light on ore
Clarified up to test of crucible.
The prize is in the process: knowledge means
Ever-renewed assurance by defeat
That victory is somehow still to reach,
But love is victory, the prize itself:
Love – trust to! Be rewarded for the trust
In trust's mere act. In love success is sure,
Attainment – no delusion, whatsoe'er
The prize be: apprehended as a prize,
A prize it is. Thy child as surely grasps
An orange as he fails to grasp the sun
Assumed his capture. What if soon he finds
The foolish fruit unworthy grasping? Joy
In shape and colour, – that was joy as true –
Worthy in its degree of love – as grasp
Of sun were, which had singed his hand beside.
What if he said the orange held no juice
Since it was not that sun he hoped to suck?
This constitutes the curse that spoils our life
And sets man maundering of his misery,
That there's no meanest atom he obtains
Of what he counts for knowledge but he cries
"Hold here, – I have the whole thing, – know, this time,
Nor need search farther!" Whereas, strew his path
With pleasures, and he scorns them while he stoops:
"This fitly call'st thou pleasure, pick up this
And praise it, truly? I reserve my thanks
For something more substantial." Fool not thus
In practising with life and its delights!

Enjoy the present gift, nor wait to know
The unknowable. Enough to say "I feel
Love's sure effect, and, being loved, must love
The love its cause behind, – I can and do!"
Nor turn to try thy brain-power on the fact,
(Apart from as it strikes thee, here and now –
Its how and why, i' the future and elsewhere)
Except to – yet once more, and ever again,
Confirm thee in thy utter ignorance:
Assured that, whatsoe'er the quality
Of love's cause, save that love was caused thereby,
This – nigh upon revealment as it seemed
A minute since – defies thy longing looks,
Withdrawn into the unknowable once more.
Wholly distrust thy knowledge, then, and trust
As wholly love allied to ignorance!
There lies thy truth and safety. Love is praise,
And praise is love! Refine the same, contrive
An intellectual tribute – ignorance
Appreciating ere approbative
Of knowledge that is infinite? With us
The small, who use the knowledge of our kind
Greater than we, more wisely ignorance
Restricts its apprehension, sees and knows
No more than brain accepts in faith of sight,
Takes first what comes first, only sure so far.
By Sebzevar a certain pillar stands
So aptly that its gnomon tells the hour;
What if the townsmen said "Before we thank
Who placed it, for his serviceable craft,
And go to dinner since its shade tells noon,
Needs must we have the craftsman's purpose clear
On half a hundred more recondite points
Than a mere summons to a vulgar meal!"
Better they say "How opportune the help!
Be loved and praised, thou kindly-hearted sage
Whom Hudhud taught, – the gracious spirit-bird, –
How to construct the pillar, teach the time!"
So let us say – not "Since we know, we love,"
But rather "Since we love, we know enough."
Perhaps the pillar by a spell controlled

Mushtari in his courses? Added grace
Surely I count it that the sage devised,
Beside celestial service, ministry
To all the land, by one sharp shade at noon
Falling as folk foresee. Once more then, Friend –
(What ever in those careless ears of thine
Withal I needs must round thee) – knowledge doubt
Even wherein it seems demonstrable!
Love, – in the claim for love, that's gratitude
For apprehended pleasure, nowise doubt!
Pay its due tribute, – sure that pleasure is,
While knowledge may be, at the most. See, now!
Eating my breakfast, I thanked God. – "For love
Shown in the cherries' flavour? Consecrate
So petty an example?" There's the fault!
We circumscribe omnipotence. Search sand
To unearth water: if first handful scooped
Yields thee a draught, what need of digging down
Full fifty fathoms deep to find a spring
Whereof the pulse might deluge half the land?
Drain the sufficient drop, and praise what checks
The drouth that glues thy tongue, – what more would help
A brimful cistern? Ask the cistern's boon
When thou wouldst solace camels: in thy case,
Relish the drop and love the lovable!'

'And what may be unlovable?'

'Why, hate!
If out of sand comes sand and naught but sand
Affect not to be quaffing at mirage,
Nor nickname pain as pleasure. That, belike,
Constitutes just the trial of thy wit
And worthiness to gain promotion, – hence,
Proves the true purpose of thine actual life.
Thy soul's environment of things perceived,
Things visible and things invisible,
Fact, fancy – all was purposed to evolve
This and this only – was thy wit of worth
To recognize the drop's use, love the same,
And loyally declare against mirage

Though all the world asseverated dust
Was good to drink? Say, "what made moist my lip,
That I acknowledged moisture": thou art saved!

'For why? The creature and creator stand
Rightly related so. Consider well!
Were knowledge all thy faculty, then God
Must be ignored: love gains him by first leap.
Frankly accept the creatureship: ask good
To love for: press bold to the tether's end
Allotted to this life's intelligence!
"So we offend?" Will it offend thyself
If, – impuissance praying potency, –
Thy child beseech that thou command the sun
Rise bright tomorrow – thou, he thinks supreme
In power and goodness, why shouldst thou refuse?
Afterward, when the child matures, perchance
The fault were greater if, with wit full-grown,
The stripling dared to ask for a dinar,
Than that the boy cried "Pluck Sitara down
And give her me to play with!" 'Tis for him
To have no bounds to his belief in thee:
For thee it also is to let her shine
Lustrous and lonely, so best serving him!'

Ask not one least word of praise!
  Words declare your eyes are bright?
What then meant that summer day's
Silence spent in one long gaze?
  Was my silence wrong or right?

Words of praise were all to seek!
  Face of you and form of you,
Did they find the praise so weak
When my lips just touched your cheek –
  Touch which let my soul come through?

A Bean-Stripe: also, Apple-Eating

'Look, I strew beans' . . .

(Ferishtah, we premise,
Strove this way with a scholar's cavilment
Who put the peevish question: 'Sir, be frank!
A good thing or a bad thing – Life is which?
Shine and shade, happiness and misery
Battle it out there: which force beats, I ask?
If I pick beans from out a bushelful –
This one, this other, – then demand of thee
What colour names each justly in the main, –
"Black" I expect, and "White" ensues reply:
No hesitation for what speck, spot, splash
Of either colour's opposite, intrudes
To modify thy judgement. Well, for beans
Substitute days, – show, ranged in order, Life –
Then, tell me its true colour! Time is short,
Life's days compose a span, – as brief be speech!
Black I pronounce for, like the Indian Sage, –
Black – present, past and future, interspersed
With blanks, no doubt, which simple folk style Good
Because not Evil: no, indeed? Forsooth
Black's shade on White is White too! What's the worst
Of Evil but that, past, it overshades
The else-exempted present? – memory,
We call the plague! "Nay, but our memory fades
And leaves the past unsullied!" Does it so?
Why, straight the purpose of such breathing-space,
Such respite from past ill, grows plain enough!
What follows on remembrance of the past?
Fear of the future! Life, from birth to death,
Means – either looking back on harm escaped,
Or looking forward to that harm's return
With tenfold power of harming. Black, not White,
Never the whole consummate quietude
Life should be, troubled by no fear! – nor hope –
I'll say, since lamplight dies in noontide, hope
Loses itself in certainty. Such lot
Man's might have been: I leave the consequence

To bolder critics of the Primal Cause;
Such am not I: but, man – as man I speak:
Black is the bean-throw: evil is the Life!')

'Look, I strew beans' – resumed Ferishtah – 'beans
Blackish and whitish; what they figure forth
Shall be man's sum of moments, bad and good,
That make up Life, – each moment when he feels
Pleasure or pain, his poorest fact of sense,
Consciousness anyhow: there's stand the first;
Whence next advance shall be from points to line,
Singulars to a series, parts to whole,
And moments to the Life. How look they now,
Viewed in the large, those little joys and griefs
Ranged duly all a-row at last, like beans
– These which I strew? This bean was white, this – black,
Set by itself, – but see if, good and bad
Each following either in companionship,
Black have not grown less black and white less white,
Till blackish seems but dun, and whitish – grey,
And the whole line turns – well, or black to thee
Or white belike to me – no matter which:
The main result is – both are modified
According to our eye's scope, power of range
Before and after. Black dost call this bean?
What, with a whiteness in its wake, which – see –
Suffuses half its neighbour? – and, in turn,
Lowers its pearliness late absolute,
Frowned upon by the jet which follows hard –
Else wholly white my bean were. Choose a joy!
Bettered it was by sorrow gone before,
And sobered somewhat by the shadowy sense
Of sorrow which came after or might come.
Joy, sorrow, – by precedence, subsequence –
Either on each, make fusion, mix in Life
That's both and neither wholly: grey or dun?
Dun thou decidest? grey prevails, say I:
Wherefore? Because my view is wide enough,
Reaches from first to last nor winks at all:
Motion achieves it: stop short – fast we stick, –
Probably at the bean that's blackest.

'Since –
Son, trust me, – this I know and only this –
I am in motion, and all things beside
That circle round my passage through their midst, –
Motionless, these are, as regarding me:
– Which means, myself I solely recognize.
They too may recognize themselves, not me,
For aught I know or care: but plain they serve
This, if no other purpose – stuff to try
And test my power upon of raying light
And lending hue to all things as I go
Moonlike through vapour. Mark the flying orb!
Think'st thou the halo, painted still afresh
At each new cloud-fleece pierced and passaged through,
This was and is and will be evermore
Coloured in permanence? The glory swims
Girdling the glory-giver, swallowed straight
By night's abysmal gloom, unglorified
Behind as erst before the advancer: gloom?
Faced by the onward-faring, see, succeeds
From the abandoned heaven a next surprise,
And where's the gloom now? – silver-smitten straight,
One glow and variegation! So with me,
Who move and make, – myself, – the black, the white,
The good, the bad, of life's environment.
Stand still! black stays black: start again! there's white
Asserts supremacy: the motion's all
That colours me my moment: seen as joy?
I have escaped from sorrow, or that was
Or might have been: as sorrow? – thence shall be
Escape as certain: white preceded black,
Black shall give way to white as duly, – so,
Deepest in black means white most imminent.
Stand still, – have no before, no after! – life
Proves death, existence grows impossible
To man like me. "What else is blessed sleep
But death, then?" Why, a rapture of release
From toil, – that's sleep's approach: as certainly,
The end of sleep means, toil is triumphed o'er:
These round the blank inconsciousness between
Brightness and brightness, either pushed to blaze
Just through that blank's interposition. Hence

The use of things external: man – that's I –
Practise thereon my power of casting light,
And calling substance, – when the light I cast
Breaks into colour, – by its proper name
– A truth and yet a falsity: black, white,
Names each bean taken from what lay so close
And threw such tint: pain might mean pain indeed
Seen in the passage past it, – pleasure prove
No mere delusion while I paused to look, –
Though what an idle fancy was that fear
Which overhung and hindered pleasure's hue!
While how, again, pain's shade enhanced the shine
Of pleasure, else no pleasure! Such effects
Came of such causes. Passage at an end, –
Past, present, future pains and pleasures fused
So that one glance may gather blacks and whites
Into a life-time, – like my bean-streak there,
Why, white they whirl into, not black – for me!'

'Ay, but for me? The indubitable blacks,
Immeasurable miseries, here, there
And everywhere i' the world – world outside thine
Paled off so opportunely, – body's plague,
Torment of soul, – where's found thy fellowship
With wide humanity all round about
Reeling beneath its burden? What's despair?
Behold that man, that woman, child – nay, brute!
Will any speck of white unblacken life
Splashed, splotched, dyed hell-deep now from end to end
For him or her or it – who knows? Not I!'

'Nor I, Son! "It" shall stand for bird, beast, fish,
Reptile, and insect even: take the last!
There's the palm-aphis, minute miracle
As wondrous every whit as thou or I:
Well, and his world's the palm-frond, there he's born,
Lives, breeds and dies in that circumference,
An inch of green for cradle, pasture-ground,
Purlieu and grave: the palm's use, ask of him!
"To furnish these," replies his wit: ask thine –
Who see the heaven above, the earth below,
Creation everywhere, – these, each and all

Claim certain recognition from the tree
For special service rendered branch and bole,
Top-tuft and tap-root: – for thyself, thus seen,
Palms furnish dates to eat, and leaves to shade,
– Maybe, thatch huts with, – have another use
Than strikes the aphis. So with me, my Son!
I know my own appointed patch i' the world,
What pleasures me or pains there: all outside –
How he, she, it, and even thou, Son, live,
Are pleased or pained, is past conjecture, once
I pry beneath the semblance, – all that's fit,
To practise with, – reach where the fact may lie
Fathom-deep lower. There's the first and last
Of my philosophy. Blacks blur thy white?
Not mine! The aphis feeds, nor finds his leaf
Untenable because a lance-thrust, nay,
Lightning strikes sere a moss-patch close beside,
Where certain other aphids live and love.
Restriction to his single inch of white,
That's law for him, the aphis: but for me,
The man, the larger-souled, beside my stretch
Of blacks and whites, I see a world of woe
All round about me: one such burst of black
Intolerable o'er the life I count
White in the main, and, yea – white's faintest trace
Were clean abolished once and evermore.
Thus fare my fellows, swallowed up in gloom
So far as I discern: how far is that?
God's care be God's! 'Tis mine – to boast no joy
Unsobered by such sorrows of my kind
As sully with their shade my life that shines.'

'Reflected possibilities of pain,
Forsooth, just chasten pleasure! Pain itself, –
Fact and not fancy, does not this affect
The general colour?'

'Here and there a touch
Taught me, betimes, the artifice of things –
That all about, external to myself,
Was meant to be suspected, – not revealed
Demonstrably a cheat, – but half seen through,

Lest white should rule unchecked along the line:
Therefore white may not triumph. All the same,
Of absolute and irretrievable
And all-subduing black, – black's soul of black
Beyond white's power to disintensify, –
Of that I saw no sample: such may wreck
My life and ruin my philosophy
Tomorrow, doubtless: hence the constant shade
Cast on life's shine, – the tremor that intrudes
When firmest seems my faith in white. Dost ask
"Who is Ferishtah, hitherto exempt
From black experience? Why, if God be just,
Were sundry fellow-mortals singled out
To undergo experience for his sake,
Just that the gift of pain, bestowed on them,
In him might temper to the due degree
Joy's else-excessive largess?" Why, indeed!
Back are we brought thus to the starting-point –
Man's impotency, God's omnipotence,
These stop my answer. Aphis that I am,
How leave my inch-allotment, pass at will
Into my fellow's liberty of range,
Enter into his sense of black and white,
As either, seen by me from outside, seems
Predominatingly the colour? Life,
Lived by my fellow, shall I pass into
And myself live there? No – no more than pass
From Persia, where in sun since birth I bask
Daily, to some ungracious land afar,
Told of by travellers, where the might of snow
Smothers up day, and fluids lose themselves
Frozen to marble. How I bear the sun,
Beat though he may unduly, that I know:
How blood once curdled ever creeps again,
Baffles conjecture: yet since people live
Somehow, resist a clime would conquer me,
Somehow provided for their sake must dawn
Compensative resource. "No sun, no grapes, –
Then, no subsistence!" – were it wisely said?
Or this well-reasoned – "Do I dare feel warmth
And please my palate here with Persia's vine,
Though, over-mounts, – to trust the traveller, –

Snow, feather thick, is falling while I feast?
What if the cruel winter force his way
Here also?" Son, the wise reply were this:
When cold from over-mounts spikes through and through
Blood, bone and marrow of Ferishtah, – then,
Time to look out for shelter – time, at least,
To wring the hands and cry "No shelter serves!"
Shelter, of some sort, no experienced chill
Warrants that I despair to find.'

'No less,
Doctors have differed here; thou say'st thy say;
Another man's experience masters thine,
Flat controverted by the sourly-Sage,
The Indian witness who, with faculty
Fine as Ferishtah's, found no white at all
Chequer the world's predominating black,
No good oust evil from supremacy,
So that Life's best was that it led to death.
How of his testimony?'

'Son, suppose
My camel told me: "Threescore days and ten
I traversed hill and dale, yet never found
Food to stop hunger, drink to stay my drouth;
Yet, here I stand alive, which take in proof
That to survive was found impossible!"
"Nay, rather take thou, non-surviving beast"
(Reply were prompt), "on flank this thwack of staff
Nowise affecting flesh that's dead and dry!
Thou wincest? Take correction twice, amend
Next time thy nomenclature! Call white – white!"
The sourly-Sage, for whom life's best was death,
Lived out his seventy years, looked hale, laughed loud,
Liked – above all – his dinner, – lied, in short.'

'Lied is a rough phrase: say he fell from truth
In climbing towards it! – sure less faulty so
Than had he sat him down and stayed content
With thy safe orthodoxy, "White, all white,
White everywhere for certain I should see
Did I but understand how white is black,

As clearer sense than mine would." Clearer sense, –
Whose may that be? Mere human eyes I boast,
And such distinguish colours in the main,
However any tongue, that's human too,
Please to report the matter. Dost thou blame
A soul that strives but to see plain, speak true,
Truth at all hazards? Oh, this false for real,
This emptiness which feigns solidity, –
Ever some grey that's white, and dun that's black, –
When shall we rest upon the thing itself
Not on its semblance? – Soul – too weak, forsooth,
To cope with fact – wants fiction everywhere!
Mine tires of falsehood: truth at any cost!'

'Take one and try conclusions – this, suppose!
God is all-good, all-wise, all-powerful: truth?
Take it and rest there. What is man? Not God:
None of these absolutes therefore, – yet himself,
A creature with a creature's qualities.
Make them agree, these two conceptions! Each
Abolishes the other. Is man weak,
Foolish and bad? He must be Ahriman,
Co-equal with an Ormuzd, Bad with Good,
Or else a thing made at the Prime Sole Will,
Doing a maker's pleasure – with results
Which – call, the wide world over, "what must be" –
But, from man's point of view, and only point
Possible to his powers, call – evidence
Of goodness, wisdom, strength? we mock ourselves
In all that's best of us, – man's blind but sure
Craving for these in very deed not word,
Reality and not illusion. Well, –
Since these nowhere exist – nor there where cause
Must have effect, nor here where craving means
Craving unfollowed by fit consequence
And full supply, aye sought for, never found –
These – what are they but man's own rule of right?
A scheme of goodness recognized by man,
Although by man unrealizable, –
Not God's with whom to will were to perform:
Nowise performed here, therefore never willed.
What follows but that God, who could the best,

Has willed the worst, – while man, with power to match
Will with performance, were deservedly
Hailed the supreme – provided . . . here's the touch
That breaks the bubble . . . this concept of man's
Were man's own work, his birth of heart and brain,
His native grace, no alien gift at all.
The bubble breaks here. Will of man create?
No more than this my hand which strewed the beans
Produced them also from its finger-tips.
Back goes creation to its source, source prime
And ultimate, the single and the sole.'

'How reconcile discordancy, – unite
Notion and notion – God that only can
Yet does not, – man that would indeed
But just as surely cannot, – both in one?
What help occurs to thy intelligence?'

'Ah, the beans, – or, – example better yet, –
A carpet-web I saw once leave the loom
And lie at gorgeous length in Ispahan!
The weaver plied his work with lengths of silk
Dyed each to match some jewel as it might,
And wove them, this by that. "How comes it, friend," –
(Quoth I) – "that while, apart, this fiery hue,
That watery dimness, either shocks the eye,
So blinding bright, or else offends again
By dullness, – yet the two, set each by each,
Somehow produce a colour born of both,
A medium profitable to the sight?"
"Such medium is the end whereat I aim," –
Answered my craftsman: "there's no single tinct
Would satisfy the eye's desire to taste
The secret of the diamond: join extremes,
Results a serviceable medium-ghost,
The diamond's simulation." Even so
I needs must blend the quality of man
With quality of God, and so assist
Mere human sight to understand my Life,
What is, what should be, – understand thereby
Wherefore I hate the first and love the last, –
Understand why things so present themselves

To me, placed here to prove I understand.
Thus, from beginning runs the chain to end,
And binds me plain enough. By consequence,
I bade thee tolerate, – not kick and cuff
The man who held that natures did in fact
Blend so, since so thyself must have them blend
In fancy, if it take a flight so far.'

'A power, confessed past knowledge, nay, past thought,
– Thus thought thus known!'

'To know of, think about –
Is all man's sum of faculty effects
When exercised on earth's least atom, Son!
What was, what is, what may such atom be?
No answer! Still, what seems it to man's sense?
An atom with some certain properties
Known about, thought of as occasion needs,
– Man's – but occasions of the universe?
Unthinkable, unknowable to man.
Yet, since to think and know fire through and through
Exceeds man, is the warmth of fire unknown,
Its uses – are they so unthinkable?
Pass from such obvious power to powers unseen,
Undreamed of save in their sure consequence:
Take that, we spoke of late, which draws to ground
The staff my hand lets fall: it draws, at least –
Thus much man thinks and knows, if nothing more.'

'Ay, but man puts no mind into such power!
He neither thanks it, when an apple drops,
Nor prays it spare his pate while underneath.
Does he thank Summer though it plumped the rind?
Why thank the other force – whate'er its name –
Which gave him teeth to bite and tongue to taste
And throat to let the pulp pass? Force and force,
No end of forces! Have they mind like man?'

'Suppose thou visit our lord Shalim-Shah,
Bringing thy tribute as appointed. "Here
Come I to pay my due!" Whereat one slave
Obsequious spreads a carpet for thy foot,

His fellow offers sweetmeats, while a third
Prepares a pipe: what thanks or praise have they?
Such as befit prompt service. Gratitude
Goes past them to the Shah whose gracious nod
Set all the sweet civility at work;
But for his ordinance, I much suspect,
My scholar had been left to cool his heels
Uncarpeted, or warm them – likelier still –
With bastinado for intrusion. Slaves
Needs must obey their master: "force and force,
No end of forces," act as bids some force
Supreme o'er all and each: where find that one?
How recognize him? Simply as thou didst
The Shah – by reasoning "Since I feel a debt,
Behoves me pay the same to one aware
I have my duty, he his privilege."
Didst thou expect the slave who charged thy pipe
Would serve as well to take thy tribute-bag
And save thee further trouble?'

'Be it so!
The sense within me that I owe a debt
Assures me – somewhere must be somebody
Ready to take his due. All comes to this –
Where due is, there acceptance follows: find
Him who accepts the due! and why look far?
Behold thy kindred compass thee about!
Ere thou wast born and after thou shalt die,
Heroic man stands forth as Shahan-Shah.
Rustem and Gew, Gudarz and all the rest,
How come they short of lordship that's to seek
Dead worthies! but men live undoubtedly
Gifted as Sindokht, sage Sulayman's match,
Valiant like Kawah: ay, and while earth lasts
Such heroes shall abound there – all for thee
Who profitest by all the present, past,
And future operation of thy race.
Why, then, o'erburdened with a debt of thanks,
Look wistful for some hand from out the clouds
To take it, when, all round, a multitude
Would ease thee in a trice?'

'Such tendered thanks
Would tumble back to who craved riddance, Son!
– Who but my sorry self? See! stars are out –
Stars which, unconscious of thy gaze beneath,
Go glorifying, and glorify thee too
– Those Seven Thrones, Zurah's beauty, weird Parwin!
Whether shall love and praise to stars be paid
Or – say – some Mubid who, for good to thee
Blind at thy birth, by magic all his own
Opened thine eyes, and gave the sightless sight,
Let the stars' glory enter? Say his charm
Worked while thyself lay sleeping: as he went
Thou wakedst: "What a novel sense have I!
Whom shall I love and praise?" "The stars, each orb
Thou standest rapt beneath," proposes one:
"Do not they live their life, and please themselves,
And so please thee? What more is requisite?"
Make thou this answer: "If indeed no mage
Opened my eyes and worked a miracle,
Then let the stars thank me who apprehend
That such an one is white, such other blue!
But for my apprehension both were blank.
Cannot I close my eyes and bid my brain
Make whites and blues, conceive without stars' help,
New qualities of colour? were my sight
Lost or misleading, would yon red – I judge
A ruby's benefaction – stand for aught
But green from vulgar glass? Myself appraise
Lustre and lustre; should I overlook
Fomalhaut and declare some fen-fire king,
Who shall correct me, lend me eyes he trusts
No more than I trust mine? My mage for me!
I never saw him: if he never was,
I am the arbitrator!" No, my Son!
Let us sink down to thy similitude:
I eat my apple, relish what is ripe –
The sunny side, admire its rarity
Since half the tribe is wrinkled, and the rest
Hide commonly a maggot in the core, –
And down Zerdusht goes with due smack of lips:
But – thank an apple? He who made my mouth
To masticate, my palate to approve,

My maw to further the concoction – Him
I thank, – but for whose work, the orchard's wealth
Might prove so many gall-nuts – stocks or stones
For aught that I should think, or know, or care.'

'Why from the world,' Ferishtah smiled, 'should thanks
Go to this work of mine? If worthy praise,
Praised let it be and welcome: as verse ranks,
So rate my verse: if good therein outweighs
Aught faulty judged, judge justly! Justice says:
Be just to fact, or blaming or approving:
But – generous? No, nor loving!

'Loving! what claim to love has work of mine?
Concede my life were emptied of its gains
To furnish forth and fill work's strict confine,
Who works so for the world's sake – he complains
With cause when hate, not love, rewards his pains.
I looked beyond the world for truth and beauty:
Sought, found and did my duty.'

Epilogue

Oh, Love – no, Love! All the noise below, Love,
Groanings all and moanings – none of Life I lose!
All of Life's a cry just of weariness and woe, Love –
'Hear at least, thou happy one!' How can I, Love, but choose?

Only, when I do hear, sudden circle round me
– Much as when the moon's might frees a space from cloud –
Iridescent splendours: gloom – would else confound me –
Barriered off and banished far – bright-edged the blackest shroud!

Thronging through the cloud-rift, whose are they, the faces
Faint revealed yet sure divined, the famous ones of old?
'What' – they smile – 'our names, our deeds so soon erases
Time upon his tablet where Life's glory lies enrolled?

'Was it for mere fool's-play, make-believe and mumming,
 So we battled it like men, not boylike sulked or whined?
Each of us heard clang God's "Come!" and each was coming:
 Soldiers all, to forward-face, not sneaks to lag behind!

'How of the field's fortune? That concerned our Leader!
 Led, we struck our stroke nor cared for doings left and right:
Each as on his sole head, failer or succeeder,
 Lay the blame or lit the praise: no care for cowards: fight!'

Then the cloud-rift broadens, spanning earth that's under
 Wide our world displays its worth, man's strife and strife's success:
All the good and beauty, wonder crowning wonder,
 Till my heart and soul applaud perfection, nothing less.

Only, at heart's utmost joy and triumph, terror
 Sudden turns the blood to ice: a chill wind disencharms
All the late enchantment! What if all be error –
 If the halo irised round my head were, Love, thine arms?

Palazzo Giustinian-Recanati, Venice.
1 December 1883

Parleyings with Certain People of Importance in Their Day:

to wit: BERNARD DE MANDEVILLE,
DANIEL BARTOLI,
CHRISTOPHER SMART,
GEORGE BUBB DODINGTON,
FRANCIS FURINI,
GERARD DE LAIRESSE,
and CHARLES AVISON.

Introduced by
A DIALOGUE BETWEEN APOLLO AND THE FATES;
concluded by
ANOTHER BETWEEN JOHN FUST AND HIS FRIENDS.

1887

IN MEMORIAM

J. MILSAND

OBIIT IV. SEPT. MDCCCLXXXVI

Absens absentem auditque videtque

Apollo and the Fates

A Prologue

(*Hymn. in Mercurium,* 559. *Eumenides,* 693–4, 697–8. *Alcestis,* 12, 33.)

APOLLO [*From above*]

Flame at my footfall, Parnassus! Apollo,
  Breaking a-blaze on thy topmost peak,
Burns thence, down to the depths – dread hollow –
  Haunt of the Dire Ones. Haste! They wreak
Wrath on Admetus whose respite I seek.

THE FATES [*Below. Darkness*]

Dragonwise couched in the womb of our Mother,
  Coiled at thy nourishing heart's core, Night!
Dominant Dreads, we, one by the other,
  Deal to each mortal his dole of light
On earth – the upper, the glad, the bright.

CLOTHO

Even so: thus from my loaded spindle
  Plucking a pinch of the fleece, lo, 'Birth'
Brays from my bronze lip: life I kindle:
  Look, 'tis a man! go, measure on earth
The minute thy portion, whatever its worth!

LACHESIS

Woe-purfled, weal-prankt, – if it speed, if it linger, –
  Life's substance and show are determined by me,
Who, meting out, mixing with sure thumb and finger,
  Lead life the due length: is all smoothness and glee,
All tangle and grief? Take the lot, my decree!

ATROPOS

– Which I make an end of: the smooth as the tangled
My shears cut asunder: each snap shrieks 'One more
Mortal makes sport for us Moirai who dangled
The puppet grotesquely till earth's solid floor
Proved film he fell through, lost in Naught as before.'

CLOTHO

I spin thee a thread. Live, Admetus! Produce him!

LACHESIS

Go, – brave, wise, good, happy! Now chequer the thread!
He is slaved for, yet loved by a god. I unloose him
A goddess-sent plague. He has conquered, is wed,
Men crown him, he stands at the height, –

ATROPOS

He is . . .

APOLLO [*Entering: Light*]

'Dead?'

Nay, swart spinsters! So I surprise you
Making and marring the fortunes of Man?
Huddling – no marvel, your enemy eyes you –
Head by head bat-like, blots under the ban
Of daylight earth's blessing since time began!

THE FATES

Back to thy blest earth, prying Apollo!
Shaft upon shaft transpierce with thy beams
Earth to the centre, – spare but this hollow
Hewn out of Night's heart, where our mystery seems
Mewed from day's malice: wake earth from her dreams!

APOLLO

Crones, 'tis your dusk selves I startle from slumber:
Day's god deposes you – queens Night-crowned!
– Plying your trade in a world ye encumber,
Fashioning Man's web of life – spun, wound,
Left the length ye allot till a clip strews the ground!

Behold I bid truce to your doleful amusement –
Annulled by a sunbeam!

THE FATES

Boy, are not we peers?

APOLLO

You with the spindle grant birth: whose inducement
But yours – with the niggardly digits – endears
To mankind chance and change, good and evil? Your shears . . .

ATROPOS

Ay, mine end the conflict: so much is no fable.
We spin, draw to length, cut asunder: what then?
So it was, and so is, and so shall be: art able
To alter life's law for ephemeral men?

APOLLO

Nor able nor willing. To threescore and ten

Extend but the years of Admetus! Disaster
O'ertook me, and, banished by Zeus, I became
A servant to one who forbore me though master:
True lovers were we. Discontinue your game,
Let him live whom I loved, then hate on, all the same!

THE FATES

And what if we granted – law-flouter, use-trampler –
His life at the suit of an upstart? Judge, thou –
Of joy were it fuller, of span because ampler?
For love's sake, not hate's, end Admetus – ay, now –
Not a grey hair on head, nor a wrinkle on brow!

For, boy, 'tis illusion: from thee comes a glimmer
Transforming to beauty life blank at the best.
Withdraw – and how looks life at worst, when to shimmer
Succeeds the sure shade, and Man's lot frowns – confessed
Mere blackness chance-brightened? Whereof shall attest

The truth this same mortal, the darling thou stylest,
Whom love would advantage, – eke out, day by day,
A life which 'tis solely thyself reconcilest
Thy friend to endure, – life with hope: take away
Hope's gleam from Admetus, he spurns it. For, say –

What's infancy? Ignorance, idleness, mischief:
Youth ripens to arrogance, foolishness, greed:
Age – impotence, churlishness, rancour: call *this* chief
Of boons for thy loved one? Much rather bid speed
Our function, let live whom thou hatest indeed!

Persuade thee, bright boy-thing! Our eld be instructive!

APOLLO

And certes youth owns the experience of age.
Ye hold then, grave seniors, my beams are productive
– They solely – of good that's mere semblance, engage
Man's eye – gilding evil, Man's true heritage?

THE FATES

So, even so! From without, – at due distance
If viewed, – set a-sparkle, reflecting thy rays, –
Life mimics the sun: but withdraw such assistance,
The counterfeit goes, the reality stays –
An ice-ball disguised as a fire-orb.

APOLLO

What craze

Possesses the fool then whose fancy conceits him
As happy?

THE FATES

Man happy?

APOLLO

If otherwise – solve
This doubt which besets me! What friend ever greets him
Except with 'Live long as the seasons revolve,'
Nót 'Death to thee straightway'? Your doctrines absolve

Such hailing from hatred: yet Man should know best.
He talks it, and glibly, as life were a load
Man fain would be rid of: when put to the test,
He whines 'Let it lie, leave me trudging the road
That is rugged so far, but methinks . . .'

THE FATES

Ay, 'tis owed

To that glamour of thine, he bethinks him 'Once past
The stony, some patch, nay, a smoothness of sward
Awaits my tired foot: life turns easy at last' –
Thy largess so lures him, he looks for reward
Of the labour and sorrow.

APOLLO

It seems, then – debarred

Of illusion – (I needs must acknowledge the plea)
Man desponds and despairs. Yet, – still further to draw
Due profit from counsel, – suppose there should be
Some power in himself, some compensative law
By virtue of which, independently . . .

THE FATES

Faugh!

Strength hid in the weakling!
What bowl-shape hast there,
Thus laughingly proffered? A gift to our shrine?
Thanks – worsted in argument! Not so? Declare
Its purpose!

APOLLO

I proffer earth's product, not mine.
Taste, try, and approve Man's invention of – WINE!

THE FATES

We feeding suck honeycombs.

APOLLO

Sustenance meagre!
Such fare breeds the fumes that show all things amiss.
Quaff wine, – how the spirits rise nimble and eager,
Unscale the dim eyes! To Man's cup grant one kiss
Of your lip, then allow – no enchantment like this!

CLOTHO

Unhook wings, unhood brows! Dost hearken?

LACHESIS

I listen:
I see – smell the food these fond mortals prefer
To our feast, the bee's bounty!

ATROPOS

The thing leaps! But – glisten
Its best, I withstand it – unless all concur
In adventure so novel.

APOLLO

Ye drink?

THE FATES

We demur.

APOLLO

Sweet Trine, be indulgent nor scout the contrivance
Of Man – Bacchus-prompted! The juice, I uphold,
Illuminates gloom without sunny connivance,
Turns fear into hope and makes cowardice bold, –
Touching all that is leadlike in life turns it gold!

THE FATES

Faith foolish as false!

APOLLO

But essay it, soft sisters!
Then mock as ye may. Lift the chalice to lip!
Good: thou next – and thou! Seems the web, to you twisters
Of life's yarn, so worthless?

CLOTHO

Who guessed that one sip
Would impart such a lightness of limb?

LACHESIS

I could skip

In a trice from the pied to the plain in my woof!
What parts each from either? A hair's breadth, no inch.
Once learn the right method of stepping aloof,
Though on black next foot falls, firm I fix it, nor flinch,
– Such my trust white succeeds!

ATROPOS

One could live – at a pinch!

APOLLO

What beldames? Earth's yield, by Man's skill, can effect
Such a cure of sick sense that ye spy the relation
Of evil to good? But drink deeper, correct
Blear sight more convincingly still! Take your station
Beside me, drain dregs! Now for edification!

Whose gift have ye gulped? Thank not me but my brother,
Blithe Bacchus, our youngest of godships. 'Twas he
Found all boons to all men, by one god or other
Already conceded, so judged there must be
New guerdon to grace the new advent, you see!

Else how would a claim to Man's homage arise?
The plan lay arranged of his mixed woe and weal,
So disposed – such Zeus' will – with design to make wise
The witless – that false things were mingled with real,
Good with bad: such the lot whereto law set the seal.

Now, human of instinct – since Semele's son,
Yet minded divinely – since fathered by Zeus,
With naught Bacchus tampered, undid not things done,
Owned wisdom anterior, would spare wont and use,
Yet change – without shock to old rule – introduce.

Regard how your cavern from crag-tip to base
Frowns sheer, height and depth adamantine, one death!
I rouse with a beam the whole rampart, displace
No splinter – yet see how my flambeau, beneath
And above, bids this gem wink, that crystal unsheath!

Withdraw beam – disclosure once more Night forbids you
Of spangle and sparkle – Day's chance-gift, surmised
Rock's permanent birthright: my potency rids you
No longer of darkness, yet light – recognized –
Proves darkness a mask: day lives on though disguised.

If Bacchus by wine's aid avail so to fluster
  Your sense, that life's fact grows from adverse and thwart
To helpful and kindly by means of a cluster –
  Mere hand-squeeze, earth's nature sublimed by Man's art –
Shall Bacchus claim thanks wherein Zeus has no part?

Zeus – wisdom anterior? No, maids, be admonished!
  If morn's touch at base worked such wonders, much more
Had noontide in absolute glory astonished
  Your den, filled a-top to o'erflowing. I pour
No such mad confusion. 'Tis Man's to explore

Up and down, inch by inch, with the taper his reason:
  No torch, it suffices – held deftly and straight.
Eyes, purblind at first, feel their way in due season,
  Accept good with bad, till unseemly debate
Turns concord – despair, acquiescence in fate.

Who works this but Zeus? Are not instinct and impulse,
  Not concept and incept his work through Man's soul
On Man's sense? Just as wine ere it reach brain must brim
      pulse,
  Zeus' flash stings the mind that speeds body to goal,
Bids pause at no part but press on, reach the whole.

For petty and poor is the part ye envisage
  When – (quaff away, cummers!) – ye view, last and first,
As evil Man's earthly existence. Come! *Is* age,
  Is infancy – manhood – so uninterspersed
With good – some faint sprinkle?

CLOTHO

I'd speak if I durst.

APOLLO

Draughts dregward loose tongue-tie.

LACHESIS

I'd see, did no web
Set eyes somehow winking.

APOLLO

Drains-deep lies their purge
– True collyrium!

ATROPOS

Words, surging at high-tide, soon ebb
From starved ears.

APOLLO

Drink but down to the source, they resurge.
Join hands! Yours and yours too! A dance or a dirge?

CHORUS

Quashed be our quarrel! Sourly and smilingly,
Bare and gowned, bleached limbs and browned,
Drive we a dance, three and one, reconcilingly,
Thanks to the cup where dissension is drowned,
Defeat proves triumphant and slavery crowned.

Infancy? What if the rose-streak of morning
Pale and depart in a passion of tears?
Once to have hoped is no matter for scorning!
Love once – e'en love's disappointment endears!
A minute's success pays the failure of years.

Manhood – the actual? Nay, praise the potential!
(Bound upon bound, foot it around!)
What *is*? No, what *may* be – sing! that's Man's essential!
(Ramp, tramp, stamp and compound
Fancy with fact – the lost secret is found!)

Age? Why, fear ends there: the contest concluded,
  Man *did* live his life, *did* escape from the fray:
Not scratchless but unscathed, he somehow eluded
  Each blow fortune dealt him, and conquers today:
Tomorrow – new chance and fresh strength, – might we say?

Laud then Man's life – no defeat but a triumph!
  [*Explosion from the earth's centre*]

CLOTHO

  Ha, loose hands!

LACHESIS

          I reel in a swound.

ATROPOS

Horror yawns under me, while from on high – humph!
  Lightnings astound, thunders resound,
Vault-roof reverberates, groans the ground! [*Silence*]

APOLLO

I acknowledge.

THE FATES

          Hence, trickster! Straight sobered are we!
  The portent assures 'twas our tongue spoke the truth,
Not thine. While the vapour encompassed us three
  We conceived and bore knowledge – a bantling uncouth,
Old brains shudder back from: so – take it, rash youth!

Lick the lump into shape till a cry comes!

APOLLO

          I hear.

THE FATES

Dumb music, dead eloquence! Say it, or sing!
What was quickened in us and thee also?

APOLLO

I fear.

THE FATES

Half female, half male – go, ambiguous thing!
While we speak – perchance sputter – pick up what we fling!

Known yet ignored, nor divined nor unguessed,
Such is Man's law of life. Do we strive to declare
What is ill, what is good in our spinning? Worst, best,
Change hues of a sudden: now here and now there
Flits the sign which decides: all about yet nowhere.

'Tis willed so, – that Man's life be lived, first to last,
Up and down, through and through, – not in portions, forsooth,
To pick and to choose from. Our shuttles fly fast,
Weave living, not life sole and whole: as age – youth,
So death completes living, shows life in its truth.

Man learningly lives: till death helps him – no lore!
It is doom and must be. Dost submit?

APOLLO

I assent –
Concede but Admetus! So much if no more
Of my prayer grant as peace-pledge! Be gracious though, blent,
Good and ill, love and hate streak your life-gift!

THE FATES

Content!

Such boon we accord in due measure. Life's term
We lengthen should any be moved for love's sake
To forego life's fulfilment, renounce in the germ
Fruit mature – bliss or woe – either infinite. Take
Or leave thy friend's lot: on his head be the stake!

APOLLO

On mine, griesly gammers! Admetus, I know thee!
Thou prizest the right these unwittingly give
Thy subjects to rush, pay obedience they owe thee!
Importunate one with another they strive
For the glory to die that their king may survive.

Friends rush: and who first in all Pherae appears
But thy father to serve as thy substitute?

CLOTHO

Bah!

APOLLO

Ye wince? Then his mother, well-stricken in years,
Advances her claim – or his wife –

LACHESIS

Tra-la-la!

APOLLO

But he spurns the exchange, rather dies!

ATROPOS

Ha, ha, ha!

[*Apollo ascends. Darkness*]

With Bernard de Mandeville

I

Ay, this same midnight, by this chair of mine,
Come and review thy counsels: art thou still
Staunch to their teaching? – not as fools opine
Its purport might be, but as subtler skill
Could, through turbidity, the loaded line
Of logic casting, sound deep, deeper, till
It touched a quietude and reached a shrine
And recognized harmoniously combine
Evil with good, and hailed truth's triumph – thine,
Sage dead long since, Bernard de Mandeville!

II

Only, 'tis no fresh knowledge that I crave,
Fuller truth yet, new gainings from the grave;
Here we alive must needs deal fairly, turn
To what account Man may Man's portion, learn
Man's proper play with truth in part, before
Entrusted with the whole. I ask no more
Than smiling witness that I do my best
With doubtful doctrine: afterward the rest!
So, silent face me while I think and speak!
A full disclosure? Such would outrage law.
Law deals the same with soul and body: seek
Full truth my soul may, when some babe, I saw
A new-born weakling, starts up strong – not weak –
Man every whit, absolved from earning awe,
Pride, rapture, if the soul attains to wreak
Its will on flesh, at last can thrust, lift, draw,
As mind bids muscle – mind which long has striven,
Painfully urging body's impotence
To effort whereby – once law's barrier riven,
Life's rule abolished – body might dispense
With infancy's probation, straight be given
– Not by foiled darings, fond attempts back-driven,
Fine faults of growth, brave sins which saint when shriven –
To stand full-statured in magnificence.

III

No: as with body so deals law with soul
That's stung to strength through weakness, strives for good
Through evil, – earth its race-ground, heaven its goal,
Presumably: so far I understood
Thy teaching long ago. But what means this
– Objected by a mouth which yesterday
Was magisterial in antithesis
To half the truths we hold, or trust we may,
Though tremblingly the while? 'No sign' – groaned he –
'No stirring of God's finger to denote
He wills that right should have supremacy
On earth, not wrong! How helpful could we quote
But one poor instance when he interposed
Promptly and surely and beyond mistake
Between oppression and its victim, closed
Accounts with sin for once, and bade us wake
From our long dream that justice bears no sword,
Or else forgets whereto its sharpness serves!
So might we safely mock at what unnerves
Faith now, be spared the sapping fear's increase
That haply evil's strife with good shall cease
Never on earth. Nay, after earth, comes peace
Born out of life-long battle? Man's lip curves
With scorn: there, also, what if justice swerves
From dealing doom, sets free by no swift stroke
Right fettered here by wrong, but leaves life's yoke –
Death should loose man from – fresh laid, past release?'

IV

Bernard de Mandeville, confute for me
This parlous friend who captured or set free
Thunderbolts at his pleasure, yet would draw
Back, panic-stricken by some puny straw
Thy gold-rimmed amber-headed cane had whisked
Out of his pathway if the object risked
Encounter, 'scaped thy kick from buckled shoe!
As when folk heard thee in old days pooh-pooh
Addison's tye-wig preachment, grant this friend –
(Whose groan I hear, with guffaw at the end
Disposing of mock-melancholy) – grant
His bilious mood one potion, ministrant

Of homely wisdom, healthy wit! For, hear!
'With power and will, let preference appear
By intervention ever and aye, help good
When evil's mastery is understood
In some plain outrage, and triumphant wrong
Tramples weak right to nothingness: nay, long
Ere such sad consummation brings despair
To right's adherents, ah, what help it were
If wrong lay strangled in the birth – each head
Of the hatched monster promptly crushed, instead
Of spared to gather venom! We require
No great experience that the inch-long worm,
Free of our heel, would grow to vomit fire,
And one day plague the world in dragon form.
So should wrong merely peep abroad to meet
Wrong's due quietus, leave our world's way safe
For honest walking.'

V

Sage, once more repeat
Instruction! 'Tis a sore to soothe not chafe.
Ah, Fabulist, what luck, could I contrive
To coax from thee another 'Grumbling Hive'!
My friend himself wrote fables short and sweet:
Ask him – 'Suppose the Gardener of Man's ground
Plants for a purpose, side by side with good,
Evil – (and that he does so – look around!
What does the field show?) – were it understood
That purposely the noxious plant was found
Vexing the virtuous, poison close to food,
If, at first stealing-forth of life in stalk
And leaflet-promise, quick his spud should balk
Evil from budding foliage, bearing fruit?
Such timely treatment of the offending root
Might strike the simple as wise husbandry,
But swift sure extirpation scarce would suit
Shrewder observers. Seed once sown thrives: why
Frustrate its product, miss the quality
Which sower binds himself to count upon?
Had seed fulfilled the destined purpose, gone
Unhindered up to harvest – what know I
But proof were gained that every growth of good

Sprang consequent on evil's neighbourhood?'
So said your shrewdness: true – so did not say
That other sort of theorists who held
Mere unintelligence prepared the way
For either seed's upsprouting: you repelled
Their notion that both kinds could sow themselves.
True! but admit 'tis understanding delves
And drops each germ, what else but folly thwarts
The doer's settled purpose? Let the sage
Concede a use to evil, though there starts
Full many a burgeon thence, to disengage
With thumb and finger lest it spoil the yield
Too much of good's main tribute! But our main
Tough-tendoned mandrake-monster – purge the field
Of him for once and all? It follows plain
Who set him there to grow beholds repealed
His primal law: his ordinance proves vain:
And what beseems a king who cannot reign,
But to drop sceptre valid arm should wield?

VI

'Still there's a parable' – retorts my friend –
'Shows agriculture with a difference!
What of the crop and weeds which solely blend
Because, once planted, none may pluck them thence?
The Gardener contrived thus? Vain pretence!
An enemy it was who unawares
Ruined the wheat by interspersing tares.
Where's our desiderated forethought? Where's
Knowledge, where power and will in evidence
'Tis Man's-play merely! Craft foils rectitude,
Malignity defeats beneficence.
And grant, at very last of all, the feud
'Twixt good and evil ends, strange thoughts intrude
Though good be garnered safely and good's foe
Bundled for burning. Thoughts steal: "even so –
Why grant tares leave to thus o'ertop, o'ertower
Their field-mate, boast the stalk and flaunt the flower,
Triumph one sunny minute? Knowledge, power
And will thus worked? Man's fancy makes the fault!
Man, with the narrow mind, must cram inside
His finite God's infinitude, – earth's vault

He bids comprise the heavenly far and wide,
Since Man may claim a right to understand
What passes understanding. So, succinct
And trimly set in order, to be scanned
And scrutinized, lo – the divine lies linked
Fast to the human, free to move as moves
Its proper match: awhile they keep the grooves,
Discreetly side by side together pace,
Till sudden comes a stumble incident
Likely enough to Man's weak-footed race,
And he discovers – wings in rudiment,
Such as he boasts, which full-grown, free-distent
Would lift him skyward, fail of flight while pent
Within humanity's restricted space.
Abjure each fond attempt to represent
The formless, the illimitable! Trace
No outline, try no hint of human face
Or form or hand!"'

VII

Friend, here's a tracing meant
To help a guess at truth you never knew.
Bend but those eyes now, using mind's eye too,
And note – sufficient for all purposes –
The ground-plan – map you long have yearned for – yes,
Made out in markings – more what artist can? –
Goethe's Estate in Weimar, – just a plan!
A. is the House, and B. the Garden-gate,
And C. the Grass-plot – you've the whole estate
Letter by letter, down to Y. the Pond,
And Z. the Pig-sty. Do you look beyond
The algebraic signs, and captious say
'Is A. the House? But where's the Roof to A.,
Where's Door, where's Window? Needs must House have such!'
Ay, that were folly. Why so very much
More foolish than our mortal purblind way
Of seeking in the symbol no mere point
To guide our gaze through what were else inane,
But things – their solid selves? 'Is, joint by joint,
Orion man-like, – as these dots explain
His constellation? Flesh composed of suns –
How can such be?' exclaim the simple ones.

Look through the sign to the thing signified –
Shown nowise, point by point at best descried,
Each an orb's topmost sparkle: all beside
Its shine is shadow: turn the orb one jot –
Up flies the new flash to reveal 'twas not
The whole sphere late flamboyant in your ken!

VIII

'What need of symbolizing? Fitlier men
Would take on tongue mere facts – few, faint and far,
Still facts not fancies: quite enough they are,
That Power, that Knowledge, and that Will, – add then
Immensity, Eternity: these jar
Nowise with our permitted thought and speech.
Why human attributes?'

A myth may teach:
Only, who better would expound it thus
Must be Euripides not Aeschylus.

IX

Boundingly up through Night's wall dense and dark,
Embattled crags and clouds, outbroke the Sun
Above the conscious earth, and one by one
Her heights and depths absorbed to the last spark
His fluid glory, from the far fine ridge
Of mountain-granite which, transformed to gold,
Laughed first the thanks back, to the vale's dusk fold
On fold of vapour-swathing, like a bridge
Shattered beneath some giant's stamp. Night wist
Her work done and betook herself in mist
To marsh and hollow there to bide her time
Blindly in acquiescence. Everywhere
Did earth acknowledge Sun's embrace sublime
Thrilling her to the heart of things: since there
No ore ran liquid, no spar branched anew,
No arrowy crystal gleamed, but straightway grew
Glad through the inrush – glad nor more nor less
Than, 'neath his gaze, forest and wilderness,
Hill, dale, land, sea, the whole vast stretch and spread,
The universal world of creatures bred
By Sun's munificence, alike gave praise –

All creatures but one only: gaze for gaze,
Joyless and thankless, who – all scowling can –
Protests against the innumerous praises? Man,
Sullen and silent.

Stand thou forth then, state
Thy wrong, thou sole aggrieved – disconsolate –
While every beast, bird, reptile, insect, gay
And glad acknowledges the bounteous day!

X

Man speaks now: 'What avails Sun's earth-felt thrill
To me? Sun penetrates the ore, the plant –
They feel and grow: perchance with subtler skill
He interfuses fly, worm, brute, until
Each favoured object pays life's ministrant
By pressing, in obedience to his will,
Up to completion of the task prescribed,
So stands and stays a type. Myself imbibed
Such influence also, stood and stand complete –
The perfect Man, – head, body, hands and feet,
True to the pattern: but does that suffice?
How of my superadded mind which needs
– Not to be, simply, but to do, and pleads
For – more than knowledge that by some device
Sun quickens matter: mind is nobly fain
To realize the marvel, make – for sense
As mind – the unseen visible, condense
– Myself – Sun's all-pervading influence
So as to serve the needs of mind, explain
What now perplexes. Let the oak increase
His corrugated strength on strength, the palm
Lift joint by joint her fan-fruit, ball and balm, –
Let the coiled serpent bask in bloated peace, –
The eagle, like some skyey derelict,
Drift in the blue, suspended, glorying, –
The lion lord it by the desert-spring, –
What know or care they of the power which pricked
Nothingness to perfection? I, instead,
When all-developed still am found a thing
All-incomplete: for what though flesh had force
Transcending theirs – hands able to unring

The tightened snake's coil, eyes that could outcourse
The eagle's soaring, voice whereat the king
Of carnage couched discrowned? Mind seeks to see,
Touch, understand, by mind inside of me,
The outside mind – whose quickening I attain
To recognize – I only. All in vain
Would mind address itself to render plain
The nature of the essence. Drag what lurks
Behind the operation – that which works
Latently everywhere by outward proof –
Drag that mind forth to face mine? No! aloof
I solely crave that one of all the beams
Which do Sun's work in darkness, at my will
Should operate – myself for once have skill
To realize the energy which streams
Flooding the universe. Above, around,
Beneath – why mocks that mind my own thus found
Simply of service, when the world grows dark,
To half-surmise – were Sun's use understood,
I might demónstrate him supplying food,
Warmth, life, no less the while? To grant one spark
Myself may deal with – make it thaw my blood
And prompt my steps, were truer to the mark
Of mind's requirement than a half-surmise
That somehow secretly is operant
A power all matter feels, mind only tries
To comprehend! Once more – no idle vaunt
"Man comprehends the Sun's self!" Mysteries
At source why probe into? Enough: display,
Make demonstrable, how, by night as day,
Earth's centre and sky's outspan, all's informed
Equally by Sun's efflux! – source from whence
If just one spark I drew, full evidence
Were mine of fire ineffably enthroned –
Sun's self made palpable to Man!'

XI

Thus moaned
Man till Prometheus helped him, – as we learn, –
Offered an artifice whereby he drew
Sun's rays into a focus, – plain and true,
The very Sun in little: made fire burn

And henceforth do Man service – glass-conglobed
Though to a pin-point circle – all the same
Comprising the Sun's self, but Sun disrobed
Of that else-unconceived essential flame
Borne by no naked sight. Shall mind's eye strive
Achingly to companion as it may
The supersubtle effluence, and contrive
To follow beam and beam upon their way
Hand-breadth by hand-breadth, till sense faint – confessed
Frustrate, eluded by unknown unguessed
Infinitude of action? Idle quest!
Rather ask aid from optics. Sense, descry
The spectrum – mind, infer immensity!
Little? In little, light, warmth, life are blessed –
Which, in the large, who sees to bless? Not I
More than yourself: so, good my friend, keep still
Trustful with – me? with thee, sage Mandeville!

*With Daniel Bartoli**

I

Don, the divinest women that have walked
Our world were scarce those saints of whom we talked.
My saint, for instance – worship if you will!
'Tis pity poets need historians' skill:
What legendary's worth a chronicle?

II

Come, now! A great lord once upon a time
Visited – oh a king, of kings the prime,
To sign a treaty such as never was:
For the king's minister had brought to pass
That this same duke – so style him – must engage
Two of his dukedoms as an heritage
After his death to this exorbitant

*A learned and ingenious writer. 'Fu Gesuita e Storico della Compagnia; onde scrisse lunghissime storie, le quali sarebbero lette se non fossero ripiene traboccanti di tutte le superstizioni . . . Egli vi ha ficcati dentro tanti miracoloni, che diviene una noia insopportabile a chiunque voglia leggere quelle storie: e anche a me, non mi bastò l'animo di proseguire molto avanti.' – ANGELO CERUTTI.

Craver of kingship. 'Let who lacks go scant,
Who owns much, give the more to!' Why rebuke?
So bids the devil, so obeys the duke.

III

Now, as it happened, at his sister's house
– Duchess herself – indeed the very spouse
Of the king's uncle, – while the deed of gift
Whereby our duke should cut his rights adrift
Was drawing, getting ripe to sign and seal –
What does the frozen heart but uncongeal
And, shaming his transcendent kin and kith,
Whom do the duke's eyes make acquaintance with?
A girl. 'What, sister, may this wonder be?'
'Nobody! Good as beautiful is she,
With gifts that match her goodness, no faint flaw
I' the white: she were the pearl you think you saw,
But that she is – what corresponds to white?
Some other stone, the true pearl's opposite,
As cheap as pearls are costly. She's – now, guess
Her parentage! Once – twice – thrice? Foiled, confess!
Drugs, duke, her father deals in – faugh, the scents! –
Manna and senna – such medicaments
For payment he compounds you. Stay – stay – stay!
I'll have no rude speech wrong her! Whither away,
The hot-head? Ah, the scapegrace! She deserves
Respect – compassion, rather! Right it serves
My folly, trusting secrets to a fool!
Already at it, is he? She keeps cool –
Helped by her fan's spread. Well, our state atones
For thus much licence, and words break no bones!'
(Hearts, though, sometimes.)

IV

Next morn 'twas 'Reason, rate,
Rave, sister, on till doomsday! Sure as fate,
I wed that woman – what a woman is
Now that I know, who never knew till this!'
So swore the duke. 'I wed her: once again –
Rave, rate, and reason – spend your breath in vain!'

V

At once was made a contract firm and fast,
Published the banns were, only marriage, last,
Required completion when the Church's rite
Should bless and bid depart, make happy quite
The coupled man and wife for evermore:
Which rite was soon to follow. Just before –
All things at all but end – the folk o' the bride
Flocked to a summons. Pomp the duke defied:
'Of ceremony – so much as empowers,
Naught that exceeds, suits best a tie like ours –'
He smiled – 'all else were mere futility.
We vow, God hears us: God and you and I –
Let the world keep at distance! This is why
We choose the simplest forms that serve to bind
Lover and lover of the human kind,
No care of what degree – of kings or clowns –
Come blood and breeding. Courtly smiles and frowns
Miss of their mark, would idly soothe or strike
My style and yours – in one style merged alike –
God's man and woman merely. Long ago
'Twas rounded in my ears "Duke, wherefore slow
To use a privilege? Needs must one who reigns
Pay reigning's due: since statecraft so ordains –
Wed for the commonweal's sake! law prescribes
One wife: but to submission licence bribes
Unruly nature: mistresses accept
– Well, at discretion!" Prove I so inept
A scholar, thus instructed? Dearest, be
Wife and all mistresses in one to me,
Now, henceforth, and forever!' So smiled he.

VI

Good: but the minister, the crafty one,
Got ear of what was doing – all but done –
Not sooner, though, than the king's very self,
Warned by the sister on how sheer a shelf
Royalty's ship was like to split. 'I bar
The abomination! Mix with muck my star?
Shall earth behold prodigiously enorbed
An upstart marsh-born meteor sun-absorbed?
Nuptial me no such nuptials!' 'Past dispute,

Majesty speaks with wisdom absolute,'
Admired the minister: 'yet, all the same,
I would we may not – while we play his game,
The ducal meteor's – also lose our own,
The solar monarch's: we relieve your throne
Of an ungracious presence, like enough:
Balked of his project he departs in huff,
And so cuts short – dare I remind the king? –
Our not so unsuccessful bargaining.
The contract for eventual heritage
Happens to *pari passu* reach the stage
Attained by just this other contract, – each
Unfixed by signature though fast in speech.
Off goes the duke in dudgeon – off withal
Go with him his two dukedoms past recall.
You save a fool from tasting folly's fruit,
Obtain small thanks thereby, and lose to boot
Sagacity's reward. The jest is grim:
The man will mulct you – for amercing him?
Nay, for . . . permit a poor similitude!
A witless wight in some fantastic mood
Would drown himself: you plunge into the wave,
Pluck forth the undeserving: he, you save,
Pulls you clean under also for your pains.
Sire, little need that I should tax my brains
To help your inspiration!' 'Let him sink!
Always contriving' – hints the royal wink –
'To keep ourselves dry while we claim his clothes.'

VII

Next day, the appointed day for plighting troths
At eve, – so little time to lose, you see,
Before the Church should weld indissolubly
Bond into bond, wed these who, side by side,
Sit each by other, bold groom, blushing bride, –
At the preliminary banquet, graced
By all the lady's kinsfolk come in haste
To share her triumph, – lo, a thunderclap!
'Who importunes now?' 'Such is my mishap –
In the king's name! No need that any stir
Except this lady!' bids the minister:
'With her I claim a word apart, no more:

For who gainsays – a guard is at the door.
Hold, duke! Submit you, lady, as I bow
To him whose mouthpiece speaks his pleasure now!
It well may happen I no whit arrest
Your marriage: be it so, – we hope the best!
By your leave, gentles! Lady, pray you, hence!
Duke, with my soul and body's deference!'

VIII

Doors shut, mouth opens and persuasion flows
Copiously forth. 'What flesh shall dare oppose
The king's command? The matter in debate
– How plain it is! Yourself shall arbitrate,
Determine. Since the duke affects to rate
His prize in you beyond all goods of earth,
Accounts as naught old gains of rank and birth,
Ancestral obligation, recent fame,
(We know his feats) – nay, ventures to disclaim
Our will and pleasure almost – by report –
Waives in your favour dukeliness, in short, –
We – ('tis the king speaks) – who might forthwith stay
Such suicidal purpose, brush away
A bad example shame would else record, –
Lean to indulgence rather. At his word
We take the duke: allow him to complete
The cession of his dukedoms, leave our feet
Their footstool when his own head, safe in vault,
Sleeps sound. Nay, would the duke repair his fault
Handsomely, and our forfeited esteem
Recover, – what if wisely he redeem
The past, – in earnest of good faith, at once
Give us such jurisdiction for the nonce
As may suffice – prevent occasion slip –
And constitute our actual ownership?
Concede this – straightway be the marriage blessed
By warrant of this paper! Things at rest,
This paper duly signed, down drops the bar,
Tomorrow you become – from what you are,
The druggist's daughter – not the duke's mere spouse,
But the king's own adopted: heart and house
Open to you – the idol of a court
"Which heaven might copy" – sing our poet-sort.

In this emergency, on you depends
The issue: plead what bliss the king intends!
Should the duke frown, should arguments and prayers
Nay, tears if need be, prove in vain, – who cares?
We leave the duke to his obduracy,
Companionless, – you, madam, follow me
Without, where divers of the body-guard
Wait signal to enforce the king's award
Of strict seclusion: over you at least
Vibratingly the sceptre threats increased
Precipitation! How avert its crash?'

IX

'Re-enter, sir! A hand that's calm, not rash,
Averts it!' quietly the lady said.
'Yourself shall witness.'
At the table's head
Where, 'mid the hushed guests, still the duke sat glued
In blank bewilderment, his spouse pursued
Her speech to end – syllabled quietude.

X

'Duke, I, your duchess of a day, could take
The hand you proffered me for love's sole sake,
Conscious my love matched yours; as you, myself
Would waive, when need were, all but love – from pelf
To potency. What fortune brings about
Haply in some far future, finds me out,
Faces me on a sudden here and now.
The better! Read – if beating heart allow –
Read this, and bid me rend to rags the shame!
I and your conscience – hear and grant our claim!
Never dare alienate God's gift you hold
Simply in trust for him! Choose muck for gold?
Could you so stumble in your choice, cajoled
By what I count my least of worthiness
– The youth, the beauty, – you renounce them – yes,
With all that's most too: love as well you lose,
Slain by what slays in you the honour! Choose!
Dear – yet my husband – dare I love you yet?'

XI

How the duke's wrath o'erboiled, – words, words and yet
More words, – I spare you such fool's fever-fret.
They were not of one sort at all, one size,
As souls go – he and she. 'Tis said, the eyes
Of all the lookers-on let tears fall fast.
The minister was mollified at last:
'Take a day, – two days even, ere through pride
You perish, – two days' counsel – then decide!'

XII

– 'If I shall save his honour and my soul?
Husband, – this one last time, – you tear the scroll?
Farewell, duke! Sir, I follow in your train!'

XIII

So she went forth: they never met again
The duke and she. The world paid compliment
(Is it worth noting?) when, next day, she sent
Certain gifts back – 'jewelry fit to deck
Whom you call wife.' I know not round what neck
They took to sparkling, in good time – weeks thence.

XIV

Of all which was the pleasant consequence,
So much and no more – that a fervid youth,
Big-hearted boy, – but ten years old, in truth, –
Laid this to heart and loved, as boyhood can,
The unduchessed lady: boy and lad grew man:
He loved as man perchance may: did meanwhile
Good soldier-service, managed to beguile
The years, no few, until he found a chance:
Then, as at trumpet-summons to advance,
Outbroke the love that stood at arms so long,
Brooked no withstanding longer. They were wed.
Whereon from camp and court alike he fled,
Renounced the sun-king, dropped off into night,
Evermore lost, a ruined satellite:
And, oh, the exquisite deliciousness
That lapped him in obscurity! You guess
Such joy is fugitive: she died full soon.
He did his best to die – as sun, so moon

Left him, turned dusk to darkness absolute.
Failing of death – why, saintship seemed to suit:
Yes, your sort, Don! He trembled on the verge
Of monkhood: trick of cowl and taste of scourge
He tried: then, kicked not at the pricks perverse,
But took again, for better or for worse,
The old way in the world, and, much the same
Man o' the outside, fairly played life's game.

XV

'Now, Saint Scholastica, what time she fared
In Paynimrie, behold, a lion glared
Right in her path! Her waist she promptly strips
Of girdle, binds his teeth within his lips,
And, leashed all lamblike, to the Soldan's court
Leads him.' Ay, many a legend of the sort
Do you praiseworthily authenticate:
Spare me the rest. This much of no debate
Admits: my lady flourished in grand days
When to be duchess was to dance the hays
Up, down, across the heaven amid its host:
While to be hailed the sun's own self almost –
So close the kinship – was – was –
Saint, for this,
Be yours the feet I stoop to – kneel and kiss!
So human? Then the mouth too, if you will!
Thanks to no legend but a chronicle.

XVI

One leans to like the duke, too: up we'll patch
Some sort of saintship for him – not to match
Hers – but man's best and woman's worst amount
So nearly to the same thing, that we count
In man a miracle of faithfulness
If, while unfaithful somewhat, he lay stress
On the main fact that love, when love indeed,
Is wholly solely love from first to last –
Truth – all the rest a lie. Too likely, fast
Enough that necklace went to grace the throat
– Let's say, of such a dancer as makes dote
The senses when the soul is satisfied –
Trogalia, say the Greeks – a sweetmeat tried

Approvingly by sated tongue and teeth,
Once body's proper meal consigned beneath
Such unconsidered munching.

XVII

Fancy's flight
Makes me a listener when, some sleepless night,
The duke reviewed his memories, and aghast
Found that the Present intercepts the Past
With such effect as when a cloud enwraps
The moon and, moon-suffused, plays moon perhaps
To who walks under, till comes, late or soon,
A stumble: up he looks, and lo, the moon
Calm, clear, convincingly herself once more!
How could he 'scape the cloud that thrust between
Him and effulgence? Speak, fool – duke, I mean!

XVIII

'Who bade you come, brisk-marching bold she-shape,
  A terror with those black-balled worlds of eyes,
That black hair bristling solid-built from nape
  To crown it coils about? O dread surmise!
Take, tread on, trample under past escape
  Your capture, spoil and trophy! Do – devise
Insults for one who, fallen once, ne'er shall rise!

'Mock on, triumphant o'er the prostrate shame!
  Laugh "Here lies he among the false to Love –
Love's loyal liegeman once: the very same
  Who, scorning his weak fellows, towered above
Inconstancy: yet why his faith defame?
  Our eagle's victor was at least no dove,
No dwarfish knight picked up our giant's glove –

'"When, putting prowess to the proof, faith urged
  Her champion to the challenge: had it chanced
That merely virtue, wisdom, beauty – merged
  All in one woman – merely these advanced
Their claim to conquest, – hardly had he purged
  His mind of memories, dearnesses enhanced
Rather than harmed by death, nor, disentranced,

'"Promptly had he abjured the old pretence
   To prove his kind's superior – first to last
Display erect on his heart's eminence
   An altar to the never-dying Past.
For such feat faith might boast fit play of fence
   And easily disarm the iconoclast
Called virtue, wisdom, beauty: impudence

'"Fought in their stead, and how could faith but fall?
   There came a bold she-shape brisk-marching, bent
No inch of her imperious stature, tall
   As some war-engine from whose top was sent
One shattering volley out of eye's black ball,
   And prone lay faith's defender!" Mockery spent?
Malice discharged in full? In that event,

'My queenly impudence, I cover close,
   I wrap me round with love of your black hair,
Black eyes, black every wicked inch of those
   Limbs' war-tower tallness: so much truth lives there
'Neath the dead heap of lies. And yet – who knows?
   What if such things are? No less, such things were.
Then was the man your match whom now you dare

'Treat as existent still. A second truth!
   They held – this heap of lies you rightly scorn –
A man who had approved himself in youth
   More than a match for – you? for sea-foam-born
Venus herself: you conquer him forsooth?
   'Tis me his ghost: he died since left and lorn,
As needs must Samson when his hair is shorn.

'Some day, and soon, be sure himself will rise,
   Called into life by her who long ago
Left his soul whiling time in flesh-disguise.
   Ghosts tired of waiting can play tricks, you know!
Tread, trample me – such sport we ghosts devise,
   Waiting the morn-star's reappearance – though
You think we vanish scared by the cock's crow.'

With Christopher Smart

I

It seems as if . . . or did the actual chance
Startle me and perplex? Let truth be said!
How might this happen? Dreaming, blindfold led
By visionary hand, did soul's advance
Precede my body's, gain inheritance
Of fact by fancy – so that when I read
At length with waking eyes your Song, instead
Of mere bewilderment, with me first glance
Was but full recognition that in trance
Or merely thought's adventure some old day
Of dim and done-with boyishness, or – well,
Why might it not have been, the miracle
Broke on me as I took my sober way
Through veritable regions of our earth
And made discovery, many a wondrous one?

II

Anyhow, fact or fancy, such its birth:
I was exploring some huge house, had gone
Through room and room complacently, no dearth
Anywhere of the signs of decent taste,
Adequate culture: wealth had run to waste
Nowise, nor penury was proved by stint:
All showed the Golden Mean without a hint
Of brave extravagance that breaks the rule.
The master of the mansion was no fool
Assuredly, no genius just as sure!
Safe mediocrity had scorned the lure
Of now too much and now too little cost,
And satisfied me sight was never lost
Of moderate design's accomplishment
In calm completeness. On and on I went,
With no more hope than fear of what came next,
Till lo, I push a door, sudden uplift
A hanging, enter, chance upon a shift
Indeed of scene! So – thus it is thou deck'st,
High heaven, our low earth's brick-and-mortar work?

III

It was the Chapel. That a star, from murk
Which hid, should flashingly emerge at last,
Were small surprise: but from broad day I passed
Into a presence that turned shine to shade.
There fronted me the Rafael Mother-Maid,
Never to whom knelt votarist in shrine
By Nature's bounty helped, by Art's divine
More varied – beauty with magnificence –
Than this: from floor to roof one evidence
Of how far earth may rival heaven. No niche
Where glory was not prisoned to enrich
Man's gaze with gold and gems, no space but glowed
With colour, gleamed with carving – hues which owed
Their outburst to a brush the painter fed
With rainbow-substance – rare shapes never wed
To actual flesh and blood, which, brain-born once,
Became the sculptor's dowry, Art's response
To earth's despair. And all seemed old yet new:
Youth, – in the marble's curve, the canvas' hue,
Apparent, – wanted not the crowning thrill
Of age the consecrator. Hands long still
Had worked here – could it be, what lent them skill
Retained a power to supervise, protect,
Enforce new lessons with the old, connect
Our life with theirs? No merely modern touch
Told me that here the artist, doing much,
Elsewhere did more, perchance does better, lives –
So needs must learn.

IV

Well, these provocatives
Having fulfilled their office, forth I went
Big with anticipation – well-nigh fear –
Of what next room and next for startled eyes
Might have in store, surprise beyond surprise.
Next room and next and next – what followed here?
Why, nothing! not one object to arrest
My passage – everywhere too manifest
The previous decent null and void of best
And worst, mere ordinary right and fit,

Calm commonplace which neither missed, nor hit
Inch-high, inch-low, the placid mark proposed.

V

Armed with this instance, have I diagnosed
Your case, my Christopher? The man was sound
And sane at starting: all at once the ground
Gave way beneath his step, a certain smoke
Curled up and caught him, or perhaps down broke
A fireball wrapping flesh and spirit both
In conflagration. Then – as heaven were loth
To linger – let earth understand too well
How heaven at need can operate – off fell
The flame-robe, and the untransfigured man
Resumed sobriety, – as he began,
So did he end nor alter pace, not he!

VI

Now, what I fain would know is – could it be
That he – whoe'er he was that furnished forth
The Chapel, making thus, from South to North,
Rafael touch Leighton, Michelagnolo
Join Watts – was found but once combining so
The elder and the younger, taking stand
On Art's supreme? And did yourself, who sang
A Song where flute-breath silvers trumpet-clang
And stations you for once on either hand
With Milton and with Keats, empowered to claim
Affinity on just one point – (or blame
Or praise my judgement, thus it fronts you full) –
Did you, like him, resume the void and null,
Subside to insignificance, – live, die
Proved both of you mere mortals who drew nigh
One moment – that, to Art's best hierarchy,
This, to the superhuman poet-pair?
What if, in one point only, then and there
The otherwise all-unapproachable
Allowed impingement? Does the sphere pretend
To span the cube's breadth, cover end to end
The plane with its embrace? No, surely! Still,
Contact is contact, sphere's touch no whit less
Than cube's superimposure. Such success

Befell Smart only out of throngs between
Milton and Keats that donned the singing-dress –
Smart, solely of such songmen, pierced the screen
'Twixt thing and word, lit language straight from soul, –
Left no fine film-flake on the naked coal
Live from the censer – shapely or uncouth,
Fire-suffused through and through, one blaze of truth
Undeadened by a lie, – (you have my mind) –
For, think! this blaze outleapt with black behind
And blank before, when Hayley and the rest...
But let the dead successors worst and best
Bury their dead: with life be my concern –
Yours with the fire-flame: what I fain would learn
Is just – (suppose me haply ignorant
Down to the common knowledge, doctors vaunt)
Just this – why only once the fire-flame was:
No matter if the marvel came to pass
The way folk judged – if power too long suppressed
Broke loose and maddened, as the vulgar guessed,
Or simply brain-disorder (doctors said)
A turmoil of the particles disturbed
Brain's workaday performance in your head,
Spurred spirit to wild action health had curbed:
And so verse issued in a cataract
Whence prose, before and after, unperturbed
Was wont to wend its way. Concede the fact
That here a poet was who always could –
Never before did – never after would –
Achieve the feat: how were such fact explained?

VII

Was it that when, by rarest chance, there fell
Disguise from Nature, so that Truth remained
Naked, and whoso saw for once could tell
Us others of her majesty and might
In large, her lovelinesses infinite
In little, – straight you used the power wherewith
Sense, penetrating as through rind to pith
Each object, thoroughly revealed might view
And comprehend the old things thus made new,
So that while eye saw, soul to tongue could trust
Thing which struck word out, and once more adjust

Real vision to right language, till heaven's vault
Pompous with sunset, storm-stirred sea's assault
On the swilled rock-ridge, earth's embosomed brood
Of tree and flower and weed, with all the life
That flies or swims or crawls, in peace or strife,
Above, below, – each had its note and name
For Man to know by, – Man who, now – the same
As erst in Eden, needs that all he sees
Be named him ere he note by what degrees
Of strength and beauty to its end Design
Ever thus operates – (your thought and mine,
No matter for the many dissident) –
So did you sing your Song, so truth found vent
In words for once with you?

VIII

Then – back was furled
The robe thus thrown aside, and straight the world
Darkened into the old oft-catalogued
Repository of things that sky, wave, land,
Or show or hide, clear late, accretion-clogged
Now, just as long ago, by tellings and
Re-tellings to satiety, which strike
Muffled upon the ear's drum. Very like
None was so startled as yourself when friends
Came, hailed your fast-returning wits: 'Health mends
Importantly, for – to be plain with you –
This scribble on the wall was done – in lieu
Of pen and paper – with – ha, ha! – your key
Denting it on the wainscot! Do you see
How wise our caution was? Thus much we stopped
Of babble that had else grown print: and lopped
From your trim bay-tree this unsightly bough –
Smart's who translated Horace! Write us now' . . .
Why, what Smart did write – never afterward
One line to show that he, who paced the sward,
Had reached the zenith from his madhouse cell.

IX

Was it because you judged (I know full well
You never had the fancy) – judged – as some –
That who makes poetry must reproduce

Thus ever and thus only, as they come,
Each strength, each beauty, everywhere diffuse
Throughout creation, so that eye and ear,
Seeing and hearing, straight shall recognize,
At touch of just a trait, the strength appear, –
Suggested by a line's lapse see arise
All evident the beauty, – fresh surprise
Startling at fresh achievement? 'So, indeed,
Wallows the whale's bulk in the waste of brine,
Nor otherwise its feather-tufts make fine
Wild Virgin's Bower when stars faint off to seed!'
(My prose – your poetry I dare not give,
Purpling too much my mere grey argument.)
– Was it because you judged – when fugitive
Was glory found, and wholly gone and spent
Such power of startling up deaf ear, blind eye,
At truth's appearance, – that you humbly bent
The head and, bidding vivid work good-bye,
Doffed lyric dress and trod the world once more
A drab-clothed decent proseman as before?
Strengths, beauties, by one word's flash thus laid bare
– That was effectual service: made aware
Of strengths and beauties, Man but hears the text,
Awaits your teaching. Nature? What comes next?
Why all the strength and beauty? – to be shown
Thus in one word's flash, thenceforth let alone
By Man who needs must deal with aught that's known
Never so lately and so little? Friend,
First give us knowledge, then appoint its use!
Strength, beauty are the means: ignore their end?
As well you stopped at proving how profuse
Stones, sticks, nay stubble lie to left and right
Ready to help the builder, – careless quite
If he should take, or leave the same to strew
Earth idly, – as by word's flash bring in view
Strength, beauty, then bid who beholds the same
Go on beholding. Why gains unemployed?
Nature was made to be by Man enjoyed
First; followed duly by enjoyment's fruit,
Instruction – haply leaving joy behind:
And you, the instructor, would you slack pursuit
Of the main prize, as poet help mankind

Just to enjoy, there leave them? Play the fool,
Abjuring a superior privilege?
Please simply when your function is to rule –
By thought incite to deed? From edge to edge
Of earth's round, strength and beauty everywhere
Pullulate – and must you particularize
All, each and every apparition? Spare
Yourself and us the trouble! Ears and eyes
Want so much strength and beauty, and no less
Nor more, to learn life's lesson by. Oh, yes –
The other method's favoured in our day!
The end ere the beginning: as you may,
Master the heavens before you study earth,
Make you familiar with the meteor's birth
Ere you descend to scrutinize the rose!
I say, o'erstep no least one of the rows
That lead man from the bottom where he plants
Foot first of all, to life's last ladder-top:
Arrived there, vain enough will seem the vaunts
Of those who say – 'We scale the skies, then drop
To earth – to find, how all things there are loth
To answer heavenly law: we understand
The meteor's course, and lo, the rose's growth –
How other than should be by law's command!'
Would not you tell such – 'Friends, beware lest fume
Offuscate sense: learn earth first ere presume
To teach heaven legislation. Law must be
Active in earth or nowhere: earth you see, –
Or there or not at all, Will, Power and Love
Admit discovery, – as below, above
Seek next law's confirmation! But reverse
The order, where's the wonder things grow worse
Than, by the law your fancy formulates,
They should be? Cease from anger at the fates
Which thwart themselves so madly. Live and learn,
Not first learn and then live, is our concern.'

With George Bubb Dodington

I

Ah, George Bubb Dodington Lord Melcombe, – no,
Yours was the wrong way! – always understand,
Supposing that permissibly you planned
How statesmanship – your trade – in outward show
Might figure as inspired by simple zeal
For serving country, king, and commonweal,
(Though service tire to death the body, tease
The soul from out an o'ertasked patriot-drudge)
And yet should prove zeal's outward show agrees
In all respects – right reason being judge –
With inward care that, while the statesman spends
Body and soul thus freely for the sake
Of public good, his private welfare take
No harm by such devotedness. Intends
Scripture aught else – let captious folk inquire –
Which teaches 'Labourers deserve their hire,
And who neglects his household bears the bell
Away of sinning from an infidel'?
Wiselier would fools that carp bestow a thought
How birds build nests; at outside, roughly wrought,
Twig knots with twig, loam plasters up each chink,
Leaving the inmate rudely lodged – you think?
Peep but inside! That specious rude-and-rough
Covers a domicile where downy fluff
Embeds the ease-deserving architect,
Who toiled and moiled not merely to effect
'Twixt sprig and spray a stop-gap in the teeth
Of wind and weather, guard what swung beneath
From upset only, but contrived himself
A snug interior, warm and soft and sleek.
Of what material? Oh, for that, you seek
How nature prompts each volatile! Thus – pelf
Smoothens the human mudlark's lodging, power
Demands some hardier wrappage to embrace
Robuster heart-beats: rock, not tree nor tower,
Contents the building eagle: rook shoves close
To brother rook on branch, while crow morose
Apart keeps balance perched on topmost bough.

No sort of bird but suits his taste somehow:
Nay, Darwin tells of such as love the bower –
His bower-birds opportunely yield us yet
The lacking instance when at loss to get
A feathered parallel to what we find
The secret motor of some mighty mind
That worked such wonders – all for vanity!
Worked them to haply figure in the eye
Of intimates as first of – doers' kind?
Actors', that work in earnest sportively,
Paid by a sourish smile. How says the Sage?
Birds born to strut prepare a platform-stage
With sparkling stones and speckled shells, all sorts
Of slimy rubbish, odds and ends and orts,
Whereon to pose and posture and engage
The priceless female simper.

II

I have gone
Thus into detail, George Bubb Dodington,
Lest, when I take you presently to task
For the wrong way of working, you should ask
'What fool conjectures that profession means
Performance? that who goes behind the scenes
Finds, – acting over, – still the soot-stuff screens
Othello's visage, still the self-same cloak's
Bugle-bright-blackness half reveals half chokes
Hamlet's emotion, as ten minutes since?'
No, each resumes his garb, stands – Moor or prince –
Decently draped: just so with statesmanship
All outside show, in short, is sham – why wince?
Concede me – while our parley lasts! You trip
Afterwards – lay but this to heart! (there lurks
Somewhere in all of us a lump which irks
Somewhat the sprightliest-scheming brain that's bent
On brave adventure, would but heart consent!)
– Here trip you, that – your aim allowed as right –
Your means thereto were wrong. Come, we, this night,
Profess one purpose, hold one principle,
Are at odds only as to – not the will
But way of winning solace for ourselves
– No matter if the ore for which zeal delves

Be gold or coprolite, while zeal's pretence
Is – we do good to men at – whose expense
But ours? who tire the body, tease the soul,
Simply that, running, we may reach fame's goal
And wreathe at last our brows with bay – the State's
Disinterested slaves, nay – please the Fates –
Saviours and nothing less: such lot has been!
Statesmanship triumphs pedestalled, serene, –
O happy consummation! – brought about
By managing with skill the rabble-rout
For which we labour (never mind the name –
People or populace, for praise or blame)
Making them understand – their heaven, their hell,
Their every hope and fear is ours as well.
Man's cause – what other can we have at heart?
Whence follows that the necessary part
High o'er Man's head we play, – and freelier breathe
Just that the multitude which gasps beneath
May reach the level where unstifled stand
Ourselves at vantage to put forth a hand,
Assist the prostrate public. 'Tis by right
Merely of such pretence, we reach the height
Where storms abound, to brave – nay, court their stress,
Though all too well aware – of pomp the less,
Of peace the more! But who are we, to spurn
For peace' sake, duty's pointing? Up, then – earn
Albeit no prize we may but martyrdom!
Now, such fit height to launch salvation from,
How get and gain? Since help must needs be craved
By would-be saviours of the else-unsaved,
How coax them to co-operate, lend a lift,
Kneel down and let us mount?

III

You say 'Make shift
By sham – the harsh word: preach and teach, persuade
Somehow the Public – not despising aid
Of salutary artifice – we seek
Solely their good: our strength would raise the weak,
Our cultivated knowledge supplement
Their rudeness, rawness: why to us were lent
Ability except to come in use?

Who loves his kind must by all means induce
That kind to let his love play freely, press
In Man's behalf to full performance!'

IV

Yes –
Yes, George, we know! – whereat they hear, believe,
And bend the knee, and on the neck receive
Who fawned and cringed to purpose? Not so, George!
Try simple falsehood on shrewd folk who forge
Lies of superior fashion day by day
And hour by hour? With craftsmen versed as they
What chance of competition when the tools
Only a novice wields? Are knaves such fools?
Disinterested patriots, spare your tongue
The tones thrice-silvery, cheek save smiles it flung
Pearl-like profuse to swine – a herd, whereof
No unit needs be taught, his neighbour's trough
Scarce holds for who but grunts and whines the husks
Due to a wrinkled snout that shows sharp tusks.
No animal – much less our lordly Man –
Obeys its like: with strength all rule began,
The stoutest awes the pasture. Soon succeeds
Discrimination, – nicer power Man needs
To rule him than is bred of bone and thew:
Intelligence must move strength's self. This too
Lasts but its time: the multitude at length
Looks inside for intelligence and strength
And finds them here and there to pick and choose:
'All at your service, mine, see!' Ay, but who's
My George, at this late day, to make his boast
'In strength, intelligence, I rule the roast,
Beat, all and some, the ungraced who crowd your ranks'?
'Oh, but I love, would lead you, gain your thanks
By unexampled yearning for Man's sake –
Passion that solely waits your help to take
Effect in action!' George, which one of us
But holds with his own heart communion thus:
'I am, if not of men the first and best,
Still – to receive enjoyment – properest:
Which since by force I cannot, nor by wit
Most likely – craft must serve in place of it.

Flatter, cajole! If so I bring within
My net the gains which wit and force should win,
What hinders?' 'Tis a trick we know of old:
Try, George, some other of tricks manifold!
The multitude means mass and mixture – right
Are mixtures simple, pray, or composite?
Dive into Man, your medley: see the waste!
Sloth-stifled genius, energy disgraced
By ignorance, high aims with sorry skill,
Will without means and means in want of will
– Sure we might fish, from out the mothers' sons
That welter thus, a dozen Dodingtons!
Why call up Dodington, and none beside,
To take his seat upon our backs and ride
As statesman conquering and to conquer? Well,
The last expedient, which must needs excel
Those old ones – this it is, – at any rate
Today's conception thus I formulate:
As simple force has been replaced, just so
Must simple wit be: men have got to know
Such wit as what you boast is nowise held
The wonder once it was, but, paralleled
Too plentifully, counts not, – puts to shame
Modest possessors like yourself who claim,
By virtue of it merely, power and place
– Which means the sweets of office. Since our race
Teems with the like of you, some special gift,
Your very own, must coax our hands to lift,
And backs to bear you: is it just and right
To privilege your nature?

V

'State things quite
Other than so' – make answer! 'I pretend
No such community with men. Perpend
My key to domination! Who would use
Man for his pleasure needs must introduce
The element that awes Man. Once for all,
His nature owns a Supernatural
In fact as well as phrase – which found must be
– Where, in this doubting age? Old mystery
Has served its turn – seen through and sent adrift

To nothingness: new wizard-craft makes shift
Nowadays shorn of help by robe and book, –
Otherwise, elsewhere, for success must look
Than chalked-ring, incantation-gibberish.
Somebody comes to conjure: that's he? Pish!
He's like the roomful of rapt gazers, – there's
No sort of difference in the garb he wears
From ordinary dressing, – gesture, speech,
Deportment, just like those of all and each
That eye their master of the minute. Stay!
What of the something – call it how you may –
Uncanny in the – quack? That's easy said!
Notice how the Professor turns no head
And yet takes cognizance of who accepts,
Denies, is puzzled as to the adept's
Supremacy, yields up or lies in wait
To trap the trickster! Doubtless, out of date
Are dealings with the devil: yet, the stir
Of mouth, its smile half smug half sinister,
Mock-modest boldness masked in diffidence, –
What if the man have – who knows how or whence? –
Confederate potency unguessed by us –
Prove no such cheat as he pretends?'

VI

Ay, thus
Had but my George played statesmanship's new card
That carries all! 'Since we' – avers the Bard –
'All of us have one human heart' – as good
As say – by all of us is understood
Right and wrong, true and false – in rough, at least,
We own a common conscience. God, man, beast –
How should we qualify the statesman-shape
I fancy standing with our world agape?
Disguise, flee, fight against with tooth and nail
The outrageous designation! 'Quack' men quail
Before? You see, a little year ago
They heard him thunder at the thing which, lo,
Today he vaunts for unscathed, while what erst
Heaven-high he lauded, lies hell-low, accursed!
And yet where's change? Who, awe-struck, cares to point
Critical finger at a dubious joint

In armour, true *aes triplex,* breast and back
Binding about, defiant of attack,
An imperturbability that's – well,
Or innocence or impudence – how tell
One from the other? Could ourselves broach lies,
Yet brave mankind with those unaltered eyes,
Those lips that keep the quietude of truth?
Dare we attempt the like? What quick uncouth
Disturbance of thy smug economy,
O coward visage! Straight would all descry
Back on the man's brow the boy's blush once more!
No: he goes deeper – could our sense explore –
Finds conscience beneath conscience such as ours.
Genius is not so rare, – prodigious powers –
Well, others boast such, – but a power like this
Mendacious intrepidity – *quid vis?*
Besides, imposture plays another game,
Admits of no diversion from its aim
Of captivating hearts, sets zeal a-flare
In every shape at every turn, – nowhere
Allows subsidence into ash. By stress
Of what does guile succeed but earnestness,
Earnest word, look and gesture? Touched with aught
But earnestness, the levity were fraught
With ruin to guile's film-work. Grave is guile;
Here no act wants its qualifying smile,
Its covert pleasantry to neutralize
The outward ardour. Can our chief despise
Even while most he seems to adulate?
As who should say 'What though it be my fate
To deal with fools? Among the crowd must lurk
Some few with faculty to judge my work
Spite of its way which suits, they understand,
The crass majority: – the Sacred Band,
No duping them forsooth!' So tells a touch
Of subintelligential nod and wink –
Turning foes friends. Coarse flattery moves the gorge:
Mine were the mode to awe the many, George!
They guess you half despise them while most bent
On demonstrating that your sole intent
Strives for their service. Sneer at them? Yourself
'Tis you disparage, – tricksy as an elf,

Scorning what most you strain to bring to pass,
Laughingly careless, – triply cased in brass, –
While pushing strenuous to the end in view.
What follows? Why, you formulate within
The vulgar headpiece this conception 'Win
A master-mind to serve us needs we must,
One who, from motives we but take on trust,
Acts strangelier – haply wiselier than we know –
Stronglier, for certain. Did he say "I throw
Aside my good for yours, in all I do
Care nothing for myself and all for you" –
We should both understand and disbelieve:
Said he "Your good I laugh at in my sleeve,
My own it is I solely labour at,
Pretending yours the while" – that, even that
We, understanding well, give credence to,
And so will none of it. But here 'tis through
Our recognition of his service, wage
Well earned by work, he mounts to such a stage
Above competitors as all save Bubb
Would agonize to keep. Yet, – here's the rub –
So slightly does he hold by our esteem
Which solely fixed him fast there, that we seem
Mocked every minute to our face, by gibe
And jest – scorn insuppressive: what ascribe
The rashness to? Our pay and praise to boot –
Do these avail him to tread underfoot
Something inside us all and each, that stands
Somehow instead of somewhat which commands
"Lie not"? Folk fear to jeopardize their soul,
Stumble at times, walk straight upon the whole, –
That's nature's simple instinct: what may be
The portent here, the influence such as we
Are strangers to?' –

VII

Exact the thing I call
Man's despot, just the Supernatural
Which, George, was wholly out of – far beyond
Your theory and practice. You had conned
But to reject the precept 'To succeed
In gratifying selfishness and greed,

Asseverate such qualities exist
Nowise within yourself! then make acquist
By all means, with no sort of fear!' Alack,
That well-worn lie is obsolete! Fall back
On still a working pretext – 'Hearth and Home,
The Altar, love of England, hate of Rome' –
That's serviceable lying – that perchance
Had screened you decently: but 'ware advance
By one step more in perspicacity
Of these our dupes! At length they get to see
As through the earlier, this the latter plea –
And find the greed and selfishness at source!
Ventum est ad triarios: last resource
Should be to what but – exquisite disguise
Disguise-abjuring, truth that looks like lies,
Frankness so sure to meet with unbelief?
Say – you hold in contempt – not them in chief –
But first and foremost your own self! No use
In men but to make sport for you, induce
The puppets now to dance, now stand stock-still,
Now knock their heads together, at your will
For will's sake only – while each plays his part
Submissive: why? through terror at the heart:
'Can it be – this bold man, whose hand we saw
Openly pull the wires, obeys some law
Quite above Man's – nay, God's?' On face fall they.
This was the secret missed, again I say,
Out of your power to grasp conception of,
Much less employ to purpose. Hence the scoff
That greets your very name folk see but one
Fool more, as well as knave, in Dodington.

With Francis Furini

I

Nay, *that*, Furini, never I at least
Mean to believe! What man you were I know,
While you walked Tuscan earth, a painter-priest,
Something about two hundred years ago.
Priest – you did duty punctual as the sun

That rose and set above Saint Sano's church,
Blessing Mugello: of your flock not one
But showed a whiter fleece because of smirch,
Your kind hands wiped it clear from: were they poor?
Bounty broke bread apace, – did marriage lag
For just the want of moneys that ensure
Fit hearth-and-home provision? – straight your bag
Unplumped itself, – reached hearts by way of palms
Goodwill's shake had but tickled. All about
Mugello valley, felt some parish qualms
At worship offered in bare walls without
The comfort of a picture? – prompt such need
Our painter would supply, and throngs to see
Witnessed that goodness – no unholy greed
Of gain – had coaxed from Don Furini – he
Whom princes might in vain implore to toil
For worldly profit – such a masterpiece.
Brief – priest, you poured profuse God's wine and oil
Praiseworthily, I know: shall praising cease
When, priestly vesture put aside, mere man,
You stand for judgement? Rather – what acclaim
– 'Good son, good brother, friend in whom we scan
No fault nor flaw' – salutes Furini's name,
The loving as the liberal! Enough:
Only to ope a lily, though for sake
Of setting free its scent, disturbs the rough
Loose gold about its anther. I shall take
No blame in one more blazon, last of all –
Good painter were you: if in very deed
I styled you great – what modern art dares call
My word in question? Let who will take heed
Of what he seeks and misses in your brain
To balance that precision of the brush
Your hand could ply so deftly: all in vain
Strives poet's power for outlet when the push
Is lost upon a barred and bolted gate
Of painter's impotency. Agnolo –
Thine were alike the head and hand, by fate
Doubly endowed! Who boasts head only – woe
To hand's presumption should brush emulate
Fancy's free passage by the pen, and show
Thought wrecked and ruined where the inexpert

Foolhardy fingers half grasped, half let go
Film-wings the poet's pen arrests unhurt!
No – painter such as that miraculous
Michael, who deems you? But the ample gift
Of gracing walls else blank of this our house
Of life with imagery, one bright drift
Poured forth by pencil, – man and woman mere,
Glorified till half owned for gods, – the dear
Fleshly perfection of the human shape, –
This was apportioned you whereby to praise
Heaven and bless earth. Who clumsily essays,
By slighting painter's craft, to prove the ape
Of poet's pen-creation, just betrays
Two-fold ineptitude.

II

By such sure ways
Do I return, Furini, to my first
And central confidence – that he I proved
Good priest, good man, good painter, and rehearsed
Praise upon praise to show – not simply loved
For virtue, but for wisdom honoured too
Needs must Furini be, – it follows – who
Shall undertake to breed in me belief
That, on his death-bed, weakness played the thief
With wisdom, folly ousted reason quite?
List to the chronicler! With main and might –
So fame runs – did the poor soul beg his friends
To buy and burn his hand-work, make amends
For having reproduced therein – (Ah me!
Sighs fame – that's friend Filippo) – nudity!
Yes, I assure you: he would paint – not men
Merely – a pardonable fault – but when
He had to deal with – oh, not mother Eve
Alone, permissibly in Paradise
Naked and unashamed, – but dared achieve
Dreadful distinction, at soul-safety's price
By also painting women – (why the need?)
Just as God made them: there, you have the truth!
Yes, rosed from top to toe in flush of youth,
One foot upon the moss-fringe, would some Nymph
Try, with its venturous fellow, if the lymph

Were chillier than the slab-stepped fountain-edge;
The while a-heap her garments on its ledge
Of boulder lay within hand's easy reach,
– No one least kid-skin cast around her! Speech
Shrinks from enumerating case and case
Of – were it but Diana at the chase,
With tunic tucked discreetly hunting-high!
No, some Queen Venus set our necks awry,
Turned faces from the painter's all-too-frank
Triumph of flesh! For – whom had he to thank
– This self-appointed nature-student? Whence
Picked he up practice? By what evidence
Did he unhandsomely become adept
In simulating bodies? How except
By actual sight of such? Himself confessed
The enormity: quoth Philip 'When I pressed
The painter to acknowledge his abuse
Of artistry else potent – what excuse
Made the infatuated man? I give
His very words: "Did you but know, as I,
– O scruple-splitting sickly-sensitive
Mild-moral-monger, what the agony
Of Art is ere Art satisfy herself
In imitating Nature – (Man, poor elf,
Striving to match the finger-mark of Him
The immeasurably matchless) – gay or grim,
Pray, would your smile be? Leave mere fools to tax
Art's high-strung brain's intentness as so lax
That, in its mid-throe, idle fancy sees
The moment for admittance!" Pleadings these –
Specious, I grant.' So adds, and seems to wince
Somewhat, our censor – but shall truth convince
Blockheads like Baldinucci?

III

I resume
My incredulity: your other kind
Of soul, Furini, never was so blind,
Even through death-mist, as to grope in gloom
For cheer beside a bonfire piled to turn
Ashes and dust all that your noble life
Did homage to life's Lord by, – bid them burn

– These Baldinucci blockheads – pictures rife
With record, in each rendered loveliness,
That one appreciative creature's debt
Of thanks to the Creator more or less,
Was paid according as heart's-will had met
Hand's-power in Art's endeavour to express
Heaven's most consummate of achievements, bless
Earth by a semblance of the seal God set
On woman his supremest work. I trust
Rather, Furini, dying breath had vent
In some fine fervour of thanksgiving just
For this – that soul and body's power you spent –
Agonized to adumbrate, trace in dust
That marvel which we dream the firmament
Copies in star-device when fancies stray
Outlining, orb by orb, Andromeda –
God's best of beauteous and magnificent
Revealed to earth – the naked female form.
Nay, I mistake not: wrath that's but lukewarm
Would boil indeed were such a critic styled
Himself an artist: artist! Ossa piled
Topping Olympus – the absurd which crowns
The extravagant – whereat one laughs, not frowns.
Paints he? One bids the poor pretender take
His sorry self, a trouble and disgrace,
From out the sacred presence, void the place
Artists claim only. What – not merely wake
Our pity that suppressed concupiscence –
A satyr masked as matron – makes pretence
To the coarse blue-fly's instinct – can perceive
No better reason why she should exist –
– God's lily-limbed and blush-rose-bosomed Eve –
Than as a hot-bed for the sensualist
To fly-blow with his fancies, make pure stuff
Breed him back filth – this were not crime enough?
But further – fly to style itself – nay, more –
To steal among the sacred ones, crouch down
Though but to where their garments sweep the floor –
– Still catching some faint sparkle from the crown
Crowning transcendent Michael, Leonard,
Rafael, – to sit beside the feet of such,
Unspurned because unnoticed, then reward

Their toleration – mercy overmuch –
By stealing from the throne-step to the fools
Curious outside the gateway, all-agape
To learn by what procedure, in the schools
Of Art, a merest man in outward shape
May learn to be Correggio! Old and young,
These learners got their lesson: Art was just
A safety-screen – (Art, which Correggio's tongue
Calls 'Virtue') – for a skulking vice: mere lust
Inspired the artist when his Night and Morn
Slept and awoke in marble on that edge
Of heaven above our awestruck earth: lust-born
His Eve low bending took the privilege
Of life from what our eyes saw – God's own palm
That put the flame forth – to the love and thanks
Of all creation save this recreant!

IV

Calm
Our phrase, Furini! Not the artist-ranks
Claim riddance of an interloper: no –
This Baldinucci did but grunt and sniff
Outside Art's pale – ay, grubbed, where pine-trees grow,
For pignuts only.

V

You the Sacred! If
Indeed on you has been bestowed the dower
Of Art in fullness, graced with head and hand,
Head – to look up not downwards, hand – of power
To make head's gain the portion of a world
Where else the uninstructed ones too sure
Would take all outside beauty – film that's furled
About a star – for the star's self, endure
No guidance to the central glory, – nay,
(Sadder) might apprehend the film was fog,
Or (worst) wish all but vapour well away,
And sky's pure product thickened from earth's bog –
Since so, nor seldom, have your worthiest failed
To trust their own soul's insight – why? except
For warning that the head of the adept
May too much prize the hand, work unassailed

By scruple of the better sense that finds
An orb within each halo, bids gross flesh
Free the fine spirit-pattern, nor enmesh
More than is meet a marvel custom blinds
Only the vulgar eye to. Now, less fear
That you, the foremost of Art's fellowship,
Will oft – will ever so offend! But – hip
And thigh – smite the Philistine! *You* – slunk here –
Connived at, by too easy tolerance,
Not to scrape palette simply or squeeze brush,
But dub your very self an Artist? Tush –
You, of the daubings, is it, dare advance
This doctrine that the Artist-mind must needs
Own to affinity with yours – confess
Provocative acquaintance, more or less,
With each impurely-peevish worm that breeds
Inside your brain's receptacle?

VI

Enough.
Who owns 'I dare not look on diadems
Without an itch to pick out, purloin gems
Others contentedly leave sparkling' – gruff
Answers the guard of the regalia: 'Why –
Consciously kleptomaniac – thrust yourself
Where your illicit craving after pelf
Is tempted most – in the King's treasury?
Go elsewhere! Sort with thieves, if thus you feel –
When folk clean-handed simply recognize
Treasure whereof the mere sight satisfies –
But straight your fingers are on itch to steal!
Hence with you!'
Pray, Furini!

VII

'Bounteous God,
Deviser and Dispenser of all gifts
To soul through sense, – in Art the soul uplifts
Man's best of thanks! What but Thy measuring-rod
Meted forth heaven and earth? more intimate,
Thy very hands were busied with the task
Of making, in this human shape, a mask –

A match for that divine. Shall love abate
Man's wonder? Nowise! True – true – all too true –
No gift but, in the very plenitude
Of its perfection, goes maimed, misconstrued
By wickedness or weakness: still, some few
Have grace to see Thy purpose, strength to mar
Thy work by no admixture of their own,
– Limn truth not falsehood, bid us love alone
The type untampered with, the naked star!'

VIII

And, prayer done, painter – what if you should preach?
Not as of old when playing pulpiteer
To simple-witted country folk, but here
In actual London try your powers of speech
On us the cultured, therefore sceptical –
What would you? For, suppose he has his word
In faith's behalf, no matter how absurd,
This painter-theologian? One and all
We lend an ear – nay, Science takes thereto –
Encourages the meanest who has racked
Nature until he gains from her some fact,
To state what truth is from his point of view,
Mere pin-point though it be: since many such
Conduce to make a whole, she bids our friend
Come forward unabashed and haply lend
His little life-experience to our much
Of modern knowledge. Since she so insists,
Up stands Furini.

IX

'Evolutionists!
At truth I glimpse from depths, you glance from heights,
Our stations for discovery opposites, –
How should ensue agreement? I explain:
'Tis the tip-top of things to which you strain
Your vision, until atoms, protoplasm,
And what and whence and how may be the spasm
Which sets all going, stop you: down perforce
Needs must your observation take its course,
Since there's no moving upwards: link by link
You drop to where the atoms somehow think,

Feel, know themselves to be: the world's begun,
Such as we recognize it. Have you done
Descending? Here's ourself, – Man, known today,
Duly evolved at last, – so far, you say,
The sum and seal of being's progress. Good!
Thus much at least is clearly understood –
Of power does Man possess no particle:
Of knowledge – just so much as shows that still
It ends in ignorance on every side:
But righteousness – ah, Man is deified
Thereby, for compensation! Make survey
Of Man's surroundings, try creation – nay,
Try emulation of the minimized
Minuteness fancy may conceive! Surprised
Reason becomes by two defeats for one –
Not only power at each phenomenon
Baffled, but knowledge also in default –
Asking what *is* minuteness – yonder vault
Speckled with suns, or this the millionth – thing,
How shall I call? – that on some insect's wing
Helps to make out in dyes the mimic star?
Weak, ignorant, accordingly we are:
What then? The worse for Nature! Where began
Righteousness, moral sense except in Man?
True, he makes nothing, understands no whit:
Had the initiator-spasm seen fit
Thus doubly to endow him, none the worse
And much the better were the universe.
What does Man see or feel or apprehend
Here, there, and everywhere, but faults to mend,
Omissions to supply, – one wide disease
Of things that are, which Man at once would ease
Had will but power and knowledge? failing both –
Things must take will for deed – Man, nowise loth,
Accepts pre-eminency: mere blind force –
Mere knowledge undirected in its course
By any care for what is made or marred
In either's operation – *these* award
The crown to? Rather let it deck thy brows,
Man, whom alone a righteousness endows
Would cure the wide world's ailing! Who disputes
Thy claim thereto? Had Spasm more attributes

Than power and knowledge in its gift, before
Man came to pass? The higher that we soar,
The less of moral sense like Man's we find:
No sign of such before, – what comes behind,
Who guesses? But until there crown our sight
The quite new – not the old mere infinite
Of changings, – some fresh kind of sun and moon, –
Then, not before, shall I expect a boon
Of intuition just as strange, which turns
Evil to good, and wrong to right, unlearns
All Man's experience learned since Man was he.
Accept in Man, advanced to this degree,
The Prime Mind, therefore! neither wise nor strong –
Whose fault? but were he both, then right, not wrong
As now, throughout the world were paramount
According to his will, – which I account
The qualifying faculty. He stands
Confessed supreme – the monarch whose commands
Could he enforce, how bettered were the world!
He's at the height this moment – to be hurled
Next moment to the bottom by rebound
Of his own peal of laughter. All around
Ignorance wraps him, – whence and how and why
Things are, – yet cloud breaks and lets blink the sky
Just overhead, not elsewhere! What assures
His optics that the very blue which lures
Comes not of black outside it, doubly dense?
Ignorance overwraps his moral sense,
Winds him about, relaxing, as it wraps,
So much and no more than lets through perhaps
The murmured knowledge – "Ignorance exists."

X

'I at the bottom, Evolutionists,
Advise beginning, rather. I profess
To know just one fact – my self-consciousness, –
'Twixt ignorance and ignorance enisled, –
Knowledge: before me was my Cause – that's styled
God: after, in due course succeeds the rest, –
All that my knowledge comprehends – at best –
At worst, conceives about in mild despair.
Light needs must touch on either darkness: where?

Knowledge so far impinges on the Cause
Before me, that I know – by certain laws
Wholly unknown, whate'er I apprehend
Within, without me, had its rise: thus blend
I, and all things perceived, in one Effect.
How far can knowledge any ray project
On what comes after me – the universe?
Well, my attempt to make the cloud disperse
Begins – not from above but underneath:
I climb, you soar, – who soars soon loses breath
And sinks, who climbs keeps one foot firm on fact
Ere hazarding the next step: soul's first act
(Call consciousness the soul – some name we need)
Getting itself aware, through stuff decreed
Thereto (so call the body) – who has stept
So far, there let him stand, become adept
In body ere he shift his station thence
One single hair's breadth. Do I make pretence
To teach, myself unskilled in learning? Lo,
My life's work! Let my pictures prove I know
Somewhat of what this fleshly frame of ours
Or is or should be, how the soul empowers
The body to reveal its every mood
Of love and hate, pour forth its plenitude
Of passion. If my hand attained to give
Thus permanence to truth else fugitive,
Did not I also fix each fleeting grace
Of form and feature – save the beauteous face –
Arrest decay in transitory might
Of bone and muscle – cause the world to bless
For ever each transcendent nakedness
Of man and woman? Were such feats achieved
By sloth, or strenuous labour unrelieved,
– Yet lavished vainly? Ask that underground
(So may I speak) of all on surface found
Of flesh-perfection! Depths on depths to probe
Of all-inventive artifice, disrobe
Marvel at hiding under marvel, pluck
Veil after veil from Nature – were the luck
Ours to surprise the secret men so name,
That still eludes the searcher – all the same,
Repays his search with still fresh proof – "Externe,

Not inmost, is the Cause, fool! Look and learn!"
Thus teach my hundred pictures: firm and fast
There did I plant my first foot. And the next?
Nowhere! 'Twas put forth and withdrawn, perplexed
At touch of what seemed stable and proved stuff
Such as the coloured clouds are: plain enough
There lay the outside universe: try Man –
My most immediate! and the dip began
From safe and solid into that profound
Of ignorance I tell you surges round
My rock-spit of self-knowledge. Well and ill,
Evil and good irreconcilable
Above, beneath, about my every side, –
How did this wild confusion far and wide
Tally with my experience when my stamp –
So far from stirring – struck out, each a lamp,
Spark after spark of truth from where I stood –
Pedestalled triumph? Evil there was good,
Want was the promise of supply, defect
Ensured completion, – where and when and how?
Leave that to the First Cause! Enough that now,
Here where I stand, this moment's me and mine,
Shows me what is, permits me to divine
What shall be. Wherefore? Nay, how otherwise?
Look at my pictures! What so glorifies
The body that the permeating soul
Finds there no particle elude control
Direct, or fail of duty, – most obscure
When most subservient? Did that Cause ensure
The soul such raptures as its fancy stings
Body to furnish when, uplift by wings
Of passion, here and now, it leaves the earth,
Loses itself above, where bliss has birth –
(Heaven, be the phrase) – did that same Cause contrive
Such solace for the body, soul must dive
At drop of fancy's pinion, condescend
To bury both alike on earth, our friend
And fellow, where minutely exquisite
Low lie the pleasures, now and here – no herb
But hides its marvel, peace no doubts perturb
In each small mystery of insect life –
– Shall the soul's Cause thus gift the soul, yet strife

Continue still of fears with hopes, – for why?
What if the Cause, whereof we now descry
So far the wonder-working, lack at last
Will, power, benevolence – a protoplast,
No consummator, sealing up the sum
Of all things, – past and present and to come
Perfection? No, I have no doubt at all!
There's my amount of knowledge – great or small,
Sufficient for my needs: for see! advance
Its light now on that depth of ignorance
I shrank before from – yonder where the world
Lies wreck-strewn, – evil towering, prone good – hurled
From pride of place, on every side. For me
(Patience, beseech you!) knowledge can but be
Of good by knowledge of good's opposite –
Evil, – since, to distinguish wrong from right,
Both must be known in each extreme, beside –
(Or what means knowledge – to aspire or bide
Content with half-attaining? Hardly so!)
Made to know on, know ever, I must know
All to be known at any halting-stage
Of my soul's progress, such as earth, where wage
War, just for soul's instruction, pain with joy,
Folly with wisdom, all that works annoy
With all that quiets and contents, – in brief,
Good strives with evil.

'Now then for relief,
Friends, of your patience kindly curbed so long.
"What?" snarl you, "Is the fool's conceit thus strong –
Must the whole outside world in soul and sense
Suffer, that he grow sage at its expense?"
By no means! 'Tis by merest touch of toe
I try – not trench on – ignorance, just know –
And so keep steady footing: how you fare,
Caught in the whirlpool – that's the Cause's care,
Strong, wise, good, – this I know at any rate
In my own self, – but how may operate
With you – strength, wisdom, goodness – no least blink
Of knowledge breaks the darkness round me. Think!
Could I see plain, be somehow certified
All was illusion, – evil far and wide

Was good disguised, – why, out with one huge wipe
Goes knowledge from me. Type needs antitype:
As night needs day, as shine needs shade, so good
Needs evil: how were pity understood
Unless by pain? Make evident that pain
Permissibly masks pleasure – you abstain
From outstretch of the finger-tip that saves
A drowning fly. Who proffers help of hand
To weak Andromeda exposed on strand
At mercy of the monster? Were all true,
Help were not wanting: "But 'tis false," cry you,
"Mere fancy-work of paint and brush!" No less,
Were mine the skill, the magic, to impress
Beholders with a confidence they saw
Life, – veritable flesh and blood in awe
Of just as true a sea-beast, – would they stare
Simply as now, or cry out, curse and swear,
Or call the gods to help, or catch up stick
And stone, according as their hearts were quick
Or sluggish? Well, some old artificer
Could do as much, – at least, so books aver, –
Able to make-believe, while I, poor wight,
Make-fancy, nothing more. Though wrong were right,
Could we but know – still wrong must needs seem wrong
To do right's service, prove men weak or strong,
Choosers of evil or of good. "No such
Illusion possible!" Ah, friends, you touch
Just here my solid standing-place amid
The wash and welter, whence all doubts are bid
Back to the ledge they break against in foam,
Futility: my soul, and my soul's home
This body, – how each operates on each,
And how things outside, fact or feigning, teach
What good is and what evil, – just the same,
Be feigning or be fact the teacher, – blame
Diffidence nowise if, from this I judge
My point of vantage, not an inch I budge.
All – for myself – seems ordered wise and well
Inside it, – what reigns outside, who can tell?
Contrariwise, who needs be told "The space
Which yields thee knowledge, – do its bounds embrace
Well-willing and wise-working, each at height?

Enough: beyond thee lies the infinite –
Back to thy circumscription!"

'Back indeed!
Ending where I began – thus: retrocede,
Who will, – what comes first, take first, I advise!
Acquaint you with the body ere your eyes
Look upward: this Andromeda of mine –
Gaze on the beauty, Art hangs out for sign
There's finer entertainment underneath.
Learn how they ministrate to life and death –
Those incommensurably marvellous
Contrivances which furnish forth the house
Where soul has sway! Though Master keep aloof,
Signs of His presence multiply from roof
To basement of the building. Look around,
Learn thoroughly, – no fear that you confound
Master with messuage! He's away, no doubt,
But what if, all at once, you come upon
A startling proof – not that the Master gone
Was present lately – but that something – whence
Light comes – has pushed Him into residence?
Was such the symbol's meaning, – old, uncouth –
That circle of the serpent, tail in mouth?
Only by looking low, ere looking high,
Comes penetration of the mystery.'

XI

Thanks! After sermonizing, psalmody!
Now praise with pencil, Painter! Fools attaint
Your fame, forsooth, because its power inclines
To livelier colours, more attractive lines
Than suit some orthodox sad sickly saint
– Grey male emaciation, haply streaked
Carmine by scourgings – or they want, far worse –
Some self-scathed woman, framed to bless not curse
Nature that loved the form whereon hate wreaked
The wrongs you see. No, rather paint some full
Benignancy, the first and foremost boon
Of youth, health, strength, – show beauty's May, ere June
Undo the bud's blush, leave a rose to cull
– No poppy, neither! yet less perfect-pure,

Divinely-precious with life's dew besprent.
Show saintliness that's simply innocent
Of guessing sinnership exists to cure
All in good time! In time let age advance
And teach that knowledge helps – not ignorance –
The healing of the nations. Let my spark
Quicken your tinder! Burn with – Joan of Arc!
Not at the end, nor midway when there grew
The brave delusions, when rare fancies flew
Before the eyes, and in the ears of her
Strange voices woke imperiously astir:
No, – paint the peasant girl all peasant-like,
Spirit and flesh – the hour about to strike
When this should be transfigured, that inflamed,
By heart's admonishing 'Thy country shamed,
Thy king shut out of all his realm except
One sorry corner!' and to life forth leapt
The indubitable lightning 'Can there be
Country and king's salvation – all through me?'
Memorize that burst's moment, Francis! Tush –
None of the nonsense-writing! Fitlier brush
Shall clear off fancy's film-work and let show
Not what the foolish feign but the wise know –
Ask Sainte-Beuve else! – or better, Quicherat,
The downright-digger into truth that's – Bah,
Bettered by fiction? Well, of fact thus much
Concerns you, that 'of prudishness no touch
From first to last defaced the maid; anon,
Camp-use compelling' – what says D'Alençon
Her fast friend? – 'though I saw while she undressed
How fair she was – especially her breast –
Never had I a wild thought!' – as indeed
I nowise doubt. Much less would she take heed –
When eve came, and the lake, the hills around
Were all one solitude and silence, – found
Barriered impenetrably safe about, –
Take heed of interloping eyes shut out,
But quietly permit the air imbibe
Her naked beauty till . . . but hear the scribe!
Now as she fain would bathe, one even-tide,
God's maid, this Joan, from the pool's edge she spied
The fair blue bird clowns call the Fisher-king:

And ''Las,' sighed she, 'my Liege is such a thing
As thou, lord but of one poor lonely place
Out of his whole wide France: were mine the grace
To set my Dauphin free as thou, blue bird!'
Properly Martin-fisher – that's the word,
Not yours nor mine: folk said the rustic oath
In common use with her was – 'By my troth'?
No, – 'By my Martin'! Paint this! Only, turn
Her face away – that face about to burn
Into an angel's when the time is ripe!
That task's beyond you. Finished, Francis? Wipe
Pencil, scrape palette, and retire content!
'*Omnia non omnibus*' – no harm is meant!

With Gerard de Lairesse

I

Ah, but – because you were struck blind, could bless
Your sense no longer with the actual view
Of man and woman, those fair forms you drew
In happier days so duteously and true, –
Must I account my Gerard de Lairesse
All sorrow-smitten? He was hindered too
– Was this no hardship? – from producing, plain
To us who still have eyes, the pageantry
Which passed and passed before his busy brain
And, captured on his canvas, showed our sky
Traversed by flying shapes, earth stocked with brood
Of monsters, – centaurs bestial, satyrs lewd, –
Not without much Olympian glory, shapes
Of god and goddess in their gay escapes
From the severe serene: or haply paced
The antique ways, god-counselled, nymph-embraced,
Some early human kingly personage.
Such wonders of the teeming poet's-age
Were still to be: nay, these indeed began –
Are not the pictures extant? – till the ban
Of blindness struck both palette from his thumb
And pencil from his finger.

II

Blind – not dumb,
Else, Gerard, were my inmost bowels stirred
With pity beyond pity: no, the word
Was left upon your unmolested lips:
Your mouth unsealed, despite of eyes' eclipse,
Talked all brain's yearning into birth. I lack
Somehow the heart to wish your practice back
Which boasted hand's achievement in a score
Of veritable pictures, less or more,
Still to be seen: myself have seen them, – moved
To pay due homage to the man I loved
Because of that prodigious book he wrote
On Artistry's Ideal, by taking note,
Making acquaintance with his artist-work.
So my youth's piety obtained success
Of all-too dubious sort: for, though it irk
To tell the issue, few or none would guess
From extant lines and colours, De Lairesse,
Your faculty, although each deftly-grouped
And aptly-ordered figure-piece was judged
Worthy a prince's purchase in its day.
Bearded experience bears not to be duped
Like boyish fancy: 'twas a boy that budged
No foot's breadth from your visioned steps away
The while that memorable 'Walk' he trudged
In your companionship, – the Book must say
Where, when and whither, – 'Walk,' come what come may,
No measurer of steps on this our globe
Shall ever match for marvels. Faustus' robe,
And Fortunatus' cap were gifts of price:
But – oh, your piece of sober sound advice
That artists should descry abundant worth
In trivial commonplace, nor groan at dearth
If fortune bade the painter's craft be plied
In vulgar town and country! Why despond
Because hemmed round by Dutch canals? Beyond
The ugly actual, lo, on every side
Imagination's limitless domain
Displayed a wealth of wondrous sounds and sights
Ripe to be realized by poet's brain
Acting on painter's brush! 'Ye doubt? Poor wights,

What if I set example, go before,
While you come after, and we both explore
Holland turned Dreamland, taking care to note
Objects whereto my pupils may devote
Attention with advantage?'

III

So commenced
That 'Walk' amid true wonders – none to you,
But huge to us ignobly common-sensed,
Purblind, while plain could proper optics view
In that old sepulchre by lightning split,
Whereof the lid bore carven, – any dolt
Imagines why, – Jove's very thunderbolt:
You who could straight perceive, by glance at it,
This tomb must needs be Phaeton's! In a trice,
Confirming that conjecture, close on hand,
Behold, half out, half in the ploughed-up sand,
A chariot-wheel explained its bolt-device:
What other than the Chariot of the Sun
Ever let drop the like? Consult the tome –*
I bid inglorious tarriers-at-home –
For greater still surprise the while that 'Walk'
Went on and on, to end as it begun,
Choke-full of chances, changes, every one
No whit less wondrous. What was there to balk
Us, who had eyes, from seeing? You with none
Missed not a marvel: wherefore? Let us talk.

IV

Say am I right? Your sealed sense moved your mind,
Free from obstruction, to compassionate
Art's power left powerless, and supply the blind
With fancies worth all facts denied by fate.
Mind could invent things, and to – take away,
At pleasure, leave out trifles mean and base
Which vex the sight that cannot say them nay
But, where mind plays the master, have no place.
And bent on banishing was mind, be sure,
All except beauty from its mustered tribe

*_The Art of Painting, &c._, by Gerard de Lairesse. Translated by J. F. Fritsch. 1778.

Of objects apparitional which lure
Painter to show and poet to describe –
That imagery of the antique song
Truer than truth's self. Fancy's rainbow-birth
Conceived 'mid clouds in Greece, could glance along
Your passage o'er Dutch veritable earth,
As with ourselves, who see, familiar throng
About our pacings men and women worth
Nowise a glance – so poets apprehend –
Since naught avails portraying them in verse:
While painters turn upon the heel, intend
To spare their work the critic's ready curse
Due to the daily and undignified.

V

I who myself contentedly abide
Awake, nor want the wings of dream, – who tramp
Earth's common surface, rough, smooth, dry or damp,
– I understand alternatives, no less
– Conceive your soul's leap, Gerard de Lairesse!
How were it could I mingle false with true,
Boast, with the sights I see, your vision too?
Advantage would it prove or detriment
If I saw double? Could I gaze intent
On Dryope plucking the blossoms red,
As you, whereat her lote-tree writhed and bled,
Yet lose no gain, no hard fast wide-awake
Having and holding nature for the sake
Of nature only – nymph and lote-tree thus
Gained by the loss of fruit not fabulous,
Apple of English homesteads, where I see
Nor seek more than crisp buds a struggling bee
Uncrumples, caught by sweet he clambers through?
Truly, a moot point: make it plain to me,
Who, bee-like, sate sense with the simply true,
Nor seek to heighten that sufficiency
By help of feignings proper to the page –
Earth's surface-blank whereon the elder age
Put colour, poetizing – poured rich life
On what were else a dead ground – nothingness –
Until the solitary world grew rife

With Joves and Junos, nymphs and satyrs. Yes,
The reason was, fancy composed the strife
'Twixt sense and soul: for sense, my De Lairesse,
Cannot content itself with outward things,
Mere beauty: soul must needs know whence there springs –
How, when and why – what sense but loves, nor lists
To know at all.

VI

Not one of man's acquists
Ought he resignedly to lose, methinks:
So, point me out which was it of the links
Snapt first, from out the chain which used to bind
Our earth to heaven, and yet for you, since blind,
Subsisted still efficient and intact?
Oh, we can fancy too! but somehow fact
Has got to – say, not so much push aside
Fancy, as to declare its place supplied
By fact unseen but no less fact the same,
Which mind bids sense accept. Is mind to blame,
Or sense, – does that usurp, this abdicate?
First of all, as you 'walked' – were it too late
For us to walk, if so we willed? Confess
We have the sober feet still, De Lairesse!
Why not the freakish brain too, that must needs
Supplement nature – not see flowers and weeds
Simply as such, but link with each and all
The ultimate perfection – what we call
Rightly enough the human shape divine?
The rose? No rose unless it disentwine
From Venus' wreath the while she bends to kiss
Her deathly love?

VII

Plain retrogression, this!
No, no: we poets go not back at all:
What you did we could do – from great to small
Sinking assuredly: if this world last
One moment longer when Man finds its Past
Exceed its Present – blame the Protoplast!
If we no longer see as you of old,

'Tis we see deeper. Progress for the bold!
You saw the body, 'tis the soul we see.
Try now! Bear witness while you walk with me,
I see as you: if we loose arms, stop pace,
'Tis that you stand still, I conclude the race
Without your company. Come, walk once more
The 'Walk': if I today as you of yore
See just like you the blind – then sight shall cry
– The whole long day quite gone through – victory!

VIII

Thunders on thunders, doubling and redoubling
Doom o'er the mountain, while a sharp white fire
Now shone, now sheared its rusty herbage, troubling
Hardly the fir-boles, now discharged its ire
Full where some pine-tree's solitary spire
Crashed down, defiant to the last: till – lo,
The motive of the malice! – all a-glow,
Circled with flame there yawned a sudden rift
I' the rock-face, and I saw a form erect
Front and defy the outrage, while – as checked,
Chidden, beside him dauntless in the drift –
Cowered a heapèd creature, wing and wing outspread
In deprecation o'er the crouching head
Still hungry for the feast foregone awhile.
O thou, of scorn's unconquerable smile,
Was it when this – Jove's feathered fury – slipped
Gore-glutted from the heart's core whence he ripped –
This eagle-hound – neither reproach nor prayer –
Baffled, in one more fierce attempt to tear
Fate's secret from thy safeguard, – was it then
That all these thunders rent earth, ruined air
To reach thee, pay thy patronage of men?
He thundered, – to withdraw, as beast to lair,
Before the triumph on thy pallid brow.
Gather the night again about thee now,
Hate on, love ever! Morn is breaking there –
The granite ridge pricks through the mist, turns gold
As wrong turns right. O laughters manifold
Of ocean's ripple at dull earth's despair!

IX

But morning's laugh sets all the crags alight
Above the baffled tempest: tree and tree
Stir themselves from the stupor of the night
And every strangled branch resumes its right
To breathe, shakes loose dark's clinging dregs, waves free
In dripping glory. Prone the runnels plunge,
While earth, distent with moisture like a sponge,
Smokes up, and leaves each plant its gem to see,
Each grass-blade's glory-glitter. Had I known
The torrent now turned river? – masterful
Making its rush o'er tumbled ravage – stone
And stub which barred the froths and foams: no bull
Ever broke bounds in formidable sport
More overwhelmingly, till lo, the spasm
Sets him to dare that last mad leap: report
Who may – his fortunes in the deathly chasm
That swallows him in silence! Rather turn
Whither, upon the upland, pedestalled
Into the broad day-splendour, whom discern
These eyes but thee, supreme one, rightly called
Moon-maid in heaven above and, here below,
Earth's huntress-queen? I note the garb succinct
Saving from smirch that purity of snow
From breast to knee – snow's self with just the tinct
Of the apple-blossom's heart-blush. Ah, the bow
Slack-strung her fingers grasp, where, ivory-linked
Horn curving blends with horn, a moonlike pair
Which mimic the brow's crescent sparkling so –
As if a star's live restless fragment winked
Proud yet repugnant, captive in such hair!
What hope along the hillside, what far bliss
Lets the crisp hair-plaits fall so low they kiss
Those lucid shoulders? Must a morn so blithe,
Needs have its sorrow when the twang and hiss
Tell that from out thy sheaf one shaft makes writhe
Its victim, thou unerring Artemis?
Why did the chamois stand so fair a mark
Arrested by the novel shape he dreamed
Was bred of liquid marble in the dark
Depths of the mountain's womb which ever teemed
With novel births of wonder? Not one spark

Of pity in that steel-grey glance which gleamed
At the poor hoof's protesting as it stamped
Idly the granite? Let me glide unseen
From thy proud presence: well mayst thou be queen
Of all those strange and sudden deaths which damped
So oft Love's torch and Hymen's taper lit
For happy marriage till the maidens paled
And perished on the temple-step, assailed
By – what except to envy must man's wit
Impute that sure implacable release
Of life from warmth and joy? But death means peace.

X

Noon is the conqueror, – not a spray, nor leaf,
Nor herb, nor blossom but has rendered up
Its morning dew: the valley seemed one cup
Of cloud-smoke, but the vapour's reign was brief,
Sun-smitten, see, it hangs – the filmy haze –
Grey-garmenting the herbless mountain-side,
To soothe the day's sharp glare: while far and wide
Above unclouded burns the sky, one blaze
With fierce immitigable blue, no bird
Ventures to spot by passage. E'en of peaks
Which still presume there, plain each pale point speaks
In wan transparency of waste incurred
By over-daring: far from me be such!
Deep in the hollow, rather, where combine
Tree, shrub and briar to roof with shade and cool
The remnant of some lily-strangled pool,
Edged round with mossy fringing soft and fine.
Smooth lie the bottom slabs, and overhead
Watch elder, bramble, rose, and service-tree
And one beneficent rich barberry
Jewelled all over with fruit-pendents red.
What have I seen! O Satyr, well I know
How sad thy case, and what a world of woe
Was hid by the brown visage furry-framed
Only for mirth: who otherwise could think –
Marking thy mouth gape still on laughter's brink,
Thine eyes a-swim with merriment unnamed
But haply guessed at by their furtive wink?
And all the while a heart was panting sick

Behind that shaggy bulwark of thy breast –
Passion it was that made those breath-bursts thick
I took for mirth subsiding into rest.
So, it was Lyda – she of all the train
Of forest-thridding nymphs, – 'twas only she
Turned from thy rustic homage in disdain,
Saw but that poor uncouth outside of thee,
And, from her circling sisters, mocked a pain
Echo had pitied – whom Pan loved in vain –
For she was wishful to partake thy glee,
Mimic thy mirth – who loved her not again,
Savage for Lyda's sake. She couches there –
Thy cruel beauty, slumberously laid
Supine on heaped-up beast-skins, unaware
Thy steps have traced her to the briery glade,
Thy greedy hands disclose the cradling lair,
Thy hot eyes reach and revel on the maid!

XI

Now, what should this be for? The sun's decline
Seems as he lingered lest he lose some act
Dread and decisive, some prodigious fact
Like thunder from the safe sky's sapphirine
About to alter earth's conditions, packed
With fate for nature's self that waits, aware
What mischief unsuspected in the air
Menaces momently a cataract.
Therefore it is that yonder space extends
Untrenched upon by any vagrant tree,
Shrub, weed well nigh; they keep their bounds, leave free
The platform for what actors? Foes or friends,
Here come they trooping silent: heaven suspends
Purpose the while they range themselves. I see!
Bent on a battle, two vast powers agree
This present and no after-contest ends
One or the other's grasp at rule in reach
Over the race of man – host fronting host,
As statue statue fronts – wrath-molten each,
Solidified by hate, – earth halved almost,
To close once more in chaos. Yet two shapes
Show prominent, each from the universe
Of minions round about him, that disperse

Like cloud-obstruction when a bolt escapes.
Who flames first? Macedonian is it thou?
Ay, and who fronts thee, King Darius, drapes
His form with purple, fillet-folds his brow.

XII

What, then the long day dies at last? Abrupt
The sun that seemed, in stooping, sure to melt
Our mountain ridge, is mastered: black the belt
Of westward crags, his gold could not corrupt,
Barriers again the valley, lets the flow
Of lavish glory waste itself away
– Whither? For new climes, fresh eyes breaks the day!
Night was not to be baffled. If the glow
Were all that's gone from us! Did clouds, afloat
So filmily but now, discard no rose,
Sombre throughout the fleeciness that grows
A sullen uniformity. I note
Rather displeasure, – in the overspread
Change from the swim of gold to one pale lead
Oppressive to malevolence, – than late
Those amorous yearnings when the aggregate
Of cloudlets pressed that each and all might sate
Its passion and partake in relics red
Of day's bequeathment: now, a frown instead
Estranges, and affrights who needs must fare
On and on till his journey ends: but where?
Caucasus? Lost now in the night. Away
And far enough lies that Arcadia.
The human heroes tread the world's dark way
No longer. Yet I dimly see almost –
Yes, for my last adventure! 'Tis a ghost.
So drops away the beauty! There he stands
Voiceless, scarce strives with deprecating hands.

XIII

Enough! Stop further fooling, De Lairesse!
My fault, not yours! Some fitter way express
Heart's satisfaction that the Past indeed
Is past, gives way before Life's best and last,
The all-including Future! What were life

Did soul stand still therein, forego her strife
Through the ambiguous Present to the goal
Of some all-reconciling Future? Soul,
Nothing has been which shall not bettered be
Hereafter, – leave the root, by law's decree
Whence springs the ultimate and perfect tree!
Busy thee with unearthing root? Nay, climb –
Quit trunk, branch, leaf and flower – reach, rest sublime
Where fruitage ripens in the blaze of day!
O'erlook, despise, forget, throw flower away,
Intent on progress? No whit more than stop
Ascent therewith to dally, screen the top
Sufficiency of yield by interposed
Twistwork bold foot gets free from. Wherefore glozed
The poets – 'Dream afresh old godlike shapes,
Recapture ancient fable that escapes,
Push back reality, repeople earth
With vanished falseness, recognize no worth
In fact new-born unless 'tis rendered back
Pallid by fancy, as the western rack
Of fading cloud bequeaths the lake some gleam
Of its gone glory!'

XIV

Let things be – not seem,
I counsel rather, – do, and nowise dream!
Earth's young significance is all to learn:
The dead Greek lore lies buried in the urn
Where who seeks fire finds ashes. Ghost, forsooth!
What was the best Greece babbled of as truth?
'A shade, a wretched nothing, – sad, thin, drear,
Cold, dark, it holds on to the lost loves here,
If hand have haply sprinkled o'er the dead
Three charitable dust-heaps, made mouth red
One moment by the sip of sacrifice:
Just so much comfort thaws the stubborn ice
Slow-thickening upward till it choke at length
The last faint flutter craving – not for strength,
Not beauty, not the riches and the rule
O'er men that made life life indeed.' Sad school
Was Hades! Gladly, – might the dead but slink

To life back, – to the dregs once more would drink
Each interloper, drain the humblest cup
Fate mixes for humanity.

XV

Cheer up, –
Be death with me, as with Achilles erst,
Of Man's calamities the last and worst:
Take it so! By proved potency that still
Makes perfect, be assured, come what come will,
What once lives never dies – what here attains
To a beginning, has no end, still gains
And never loses aught: when, where, and how –
Lies in Law's lap. What's death then? Even now
With so much knowledge is it hard to bear
Brief interposing ignorance? Is care
For a creation found at fault just there –
There where the heart breaks bond and outruns time,
To reach, not follow what shall be?

XVI

Here's rhyme
Such as one makes now, – say, when Spring repeats
That miracle the Greek Bard sadly greets:
'Spring for the tree and herb – no Spring for us!'
Let Spring come: why, a man salutes her thus:

Dance, yellows and whites and reds, –
Lead your gay orgy, leaves, stalks, heads
Astir with the wind in the tulip-beds!

There's sunshine; scarcely a wind at all
Disturbs starved grass and daisies small
On a certain mound by a churchyard wall.

Daisies and grass be my heart's bedfellows
On the mound wind spares and sunshine mellows:
Dance you, reds and whites and yellows!

With Charles Avison

I

How strange! – but, first of all, the little fact
Which led my fancy forth. This bitter morn
Showed me no object in the stretch forlorn
Of garden-ground beneath my window, backed
By yon worn wall wherefrom the creeper, tacked
To clothe its brickwork, hangs now, rent and racked
By five months' cruel winter, – showed no torn
And tattered ravage worse for eyes to see
Than just one ugly space of clearance, left
Bare even of the bones which used to be
Warm wrappage, safe embracement: this one cleft –
– O what a life and beauty filled it up
Startlingly, when methought the rude clay cup
Ran over with poured bright wine! 'Twas a bird
Breast-deep there, tugging at his prize, deterred
No whit by the fast-falling snow-flake: gain
Such prize my blackcap must by might and main –
The cloth-shred, still a-flutter from its nail
That fixed a spray once. Now, what told the tale
To thee, – no townsman but born orchard-thief, –
That here – surpassing moss-tuft, beard from sheaf
Of sun-scorched barley, horsehairs long and stout,
All proper country-pillage – here, no doubt,
Was just the scrap to steal should line thy nest
Superbly? Off he flew, his bill possessed
The booty sure to set his wife's each wing
Greenly a-quiver. How they climb and cling,
Hang parrot-wise to bough, these blackcaps! Strange
Seemed to a city-dweller that the finch
Should stray so far to forage: at a pinch,
Was not the fine wool's self within his range
– Filchings on every fence? But no: the need
Was of this rag of manufacture, spoiled
By art, and yet by nature near unsoiled,
New-suited to what scheming finch would breed
In comfort, this uncomfortable March.

II

Yet – by the first pink blossom on the larch! –
This was scarce stranger than that memory, –
In want of what should cheer the stay-at-home,
My soul, – must straight clap pinion, well nigh roam
A century back, nor once close plume, descry
The appropriate rag to plunder, till she pounced –
Pray, on what relic of a brain long still?
What old-world work proved forage for the bill
Of memory the far-flyer? 'March' announced,
I verily believe, the dead and gone
Name of a music-maker: one of such
In England as did little or did much,
But, doing, had their day once. Avison!
Singly and solely for an air of thine,
Bold-stepping 'March,' foot stept to ere my hand
Could stretch an octave, I o'erlooked the band
Of majesties familiar, to decline
On thee – not too conspicuous on the list
Of worthies who by help of pipe or wire
Expressed in sound rough rage or soft desire –
Thou, whilom of Newcastle organist!

III

So much could one – well, thinnish air effect!
Am I ungrateful? for, your March, styled 'Grand,'
Did veritably seem to grow, expand,
And greaten up to title as, unchecked,
Dream-marchers marched, kept marching, slow and sure,
In time, to tune, unchangeably the same,
From nowhere into nowhere, – out they came,
Onward they passed, and in they went. No lure
Of novel modulation pricked the flat
Forthright persisting melody, – no hint
That discord, sound asleep beneath the flint,
– Struck – might spring spark-like, claim due tit-for-tat,
Quenched in a concord. No! Yet, such the might
Of quietude's immutability,
That somehow coldness gathered warmth, well nigh
Quickened – which could not be! – grew burning-bright
With fife-shriek, cymbal-clash and trumpet-blare,
To drum-accentuation: pacing turned

Striding, and striding grew gigantic, spurned
At last the narrow space 'twixt earth and air,
So shook me back into my sober self.

IV

And where woke I? The March had set me down
There whence I plucked the measure, as his brown
Frayed flannel-bit my blackcap. Great John Relfe,
Master of mine, learned, redoubtable,
It little needed thy consummate skill
To fitly figure such a bass! The key
Was – should not memory play me false – well, C.
Ay, with the Greater Third, in Triple Time,
Three crotchets to a bar: no change, I grant,
Except from Tonic down to Dominant.
And yet – and yet – if I could put in rhyme
The manner of that marching! – which had stopped
– I wonder, where? – but that my weak self dropped
From out the ranks, to rub eyes disentranced
And feel that, after all the way advanced,
Back must I foot it, I and my compeers,
Only to reach, across a hundred years,
The bandsman Avison whose little book
And large tune thus had led me the long way
(As late a rag my blackcap) from today
And today's music-manufacture, – Brahms,
Wagner, Dvorak, Liszt, – to where – trumpets, shawms,
Show yourselves joyful! – Handel reigns – supreme?
By no means! Buononcini's work is theme
For fit laudation of the impartial few:
(We stand in England, mind you!) Fashion too
Favours Geminiani – of those choice
Concertos: nor there wants a certain voice
Raised in thy favour likewise, famed Pepusch
Dear to our great-grandfathers! In a bush
Of Doctor's wig, they prized thee timing beats
While Greenway trilled 'Alexis.' Such were feats
Of music in thy day – dispute who list –
Avison, of Newcastle organist!

V

And here's your music all alive once more –
As once it was alive, at least: just so
The figured worthies of a waxwork-show
Attest – such people, years and years ago,
Looked thus when outside death had life below,
– Could say 'We are now,' not 'We were of yore,'
– 'Feel how our pulses leap!' and not 'Explore –
Explain why quietude has settled o'er
Surface once all-awork!' Ay, such a 'Suite'
Roused heart to rapture, such a 'Fugue' would catch
Soul heavenwards up, when time was: why attach
Blame to exhausted faultlessness, no match
For fresh achievement? Feat once – ever feat!
How can completion grow still more complete?
Hear Avison! He tenders evidence
That music in his day as much absorbed
Heart and soul then as Wagner's music now.
Perfect from centre to circumference –
Orbed to the full can be but fully orbed:
And yet – and yet – whence comes it that 'O Thou' –
Sighed by the soul at eve to Hesperus –
Will not again take wing and fly away
(Since fatal Wagner fixed it fast for us)
In some unmodulated minor? Nay,
Even by Handel's help!

VI

I state it thus:
There is no truer truth obtainable
By Man than comes of music. 'Soul' – (accept
A word which vaguely names what no adept
In word-use fits and fixes so that still
Thing shall not slip word's fetter and remain
Innominate as first, yet, free again,
Is no less recognized the absolute
Fact underlying that same other fact
Concerning which no cavil can dispute
Our nomenclature when we call it 'Mind' –
Something not Matter) – 'Soul,' who seeks shall find
Distinct beneath that something. You exact
An illustrative image? This may suit.

VII

We see a work: the worker works behind,
Invisible himself. Suppose his act
Be to o'erarch a gulf: he digs, transports,
Shapes and, through enginery – all sizes, sorts,
Lays stone by stone until a floor compact
Proves our bridged causeway. So works Mind – by stress
Of faculty, with loose facts, more or less,
Builds up our solid knowledge: all the same,
Underneath rolls what Mind may hide not tame,
An element which works beyond our guess,
Soul, the unsounded sea – whose lift of surge,
Spite of all superstructure, lets emerge,
In flower and foam, Feeling from out the deeps
Mind arrogates no mastery upon –
Distinct indisputably. Has there gone
To dig up, drag forth, render smooth from rough
Mind's flooring, – operosity enough?
Still the successive labour of each inch,
Who lists may learn: from the last turn of winch
That let the polished slab-stone find its place,
To the first prod of pick-axe at the base
Of the unquarried mountain, – what was all
Mind's varied process except natural,
Nay, easy, even, to descry, describe,
After our fashion? 'So worked Mind: its tribe
Of senses ministrant above, below,
Far, near, or now or haply long ago
Brought to pass knowledge.' But Soul's sea, – drawn whence,
Fed how, forced whither, – by what evidence
Of ebb and flow, that's felt beneath the tread,
Soul has its course 'neath Mind's work overhead, –
Who tells of, tracks to source the founts of Soul?
Yet wherefore heaving sway and restless roll
This side and that, except to emulate
Stability above? To match and mate
Feeling with knowledge, – make as manifest
Soul's work as Mind's work, turbulence as rest,
Hates, loves, joys, woes, hopes, fears, that rise and sink
Ceaselessly, passion's transient flit and wink,
A ripple's tinting or a spume-sheet's spread
Whitening the wave, – to strike all this life dead,

Run mercury into a mould like lead,
And henceforth have the plain result to show –
How we Feel, hard and fast as what we Know –
This were the prize and is the puzzle! – which
Music essays to solve: and here's the hitch
That balks her of full triumph else to boast.

VIII

All Arts endeavour this, and she the most
Attains thereto, yet fails of touching: why?
Does Mind get Knowledge from Art's ministry?
What's known once is known ever: Arts arrange,
Dissociate, redistribute, interchange
Part with part, lengthen, broaden, high or deep
Construct their bravest, – still such pains produce
Change, not creation: simply what lay loose
At first lies firmly after, what design
Was faintly traced in hesitating line
Once on a time, grows firmly resolute
Henceforth and evermore. Now, could we shoot
Liquidity into a mould, – some way
Arrest Soul's evanescent moods, and keep
Unalterably still the forms that leap
To life for once by help of Art! – which yearns
To save its capture: Poetry discerns,
Painting is 'ware of passion's rise and fall,
Bursting, subsidence, intermixture – all
A-seethe within the gulf. Each Art a-strain
Would stay the apparition, – nor in vain:
The Poet's word-mesh, Painter's sure and swift
Colour-and-line-throw – proud the prize they lift!
Thus felt Man and thus looked Man, – passions caught
I' the midway swim of sea, – not much, if aught,
Of nether-brooding loves, hates, hopes and fears,
Enwombed past Art's disclosure. Fleet the years,
And still the Poet's page holds Helena
At gaze from topmost Troy – 'But where are they,
My brothers, in the armament I name
Hero by hero? Can it be that shame
For their lost sister holds them from the war?'
– Knowing not they already slept afar
Each of them in his own dear native land.

Still on the Painter's fresco, from the hand
Of God takes Eve the life-spark whereunto
She trembles up from nothingness. Outdo
Both of them, Music! Dredging deeper yet,
Drag into day, – by sound, thy master-net, –
The abysmal bottom-growth, ambiguous thing
Unbroken of a branch, palpitating
With limbs' play and life's semblance! There it lies,
Marvel and mystery, of mysteries
And marvels, most to love and laud thee for!
Save it from chance and change we most abhor!
Give momentary feeling permanence,
So that thy capture hold, a century hence,
Truth's very heart of truth as, safe today,
The Painter's Eve, the Poet's Helena,
Still rapturously bend, afar still throw
The wistful gaze! Thanks, Homer, Angelo!
Could Music rescue thus from Soul's profound,
Give feeling immortality by sound,
Then were she queenliest of Arts! Alas –
As well expect the rainbow not to pass!
'Praise "Radaminta" – love attains therein
To perfect utterance! Pity – what shall win
Thy secret like "Rinaldo"?' – so men said:
Once all was perfume – now, the flower is dead –
They spied tints, sparks have left the spar! Love, hate,
Joy, fear, survive, – alike importunate
As ever to go walk the world again,
Nor ghost-like pant for outlet all in vain
Till Music loose them, fit each filmily
With form enough to know and name it by
For any recognizer sure of ken
And sharp of ear, no grosser denizen
Of earth than needs be. Nor to such appeal
Is Music long obdurate: off they steal –
How gently, dawn-doomed phantoms! back come they
Full-blooded with new crimson of broad day –
Passion made palpable once more. Ye look
Your last on Handel? Gaze your first on Gluck!
Why wistful search, O waning ones, the chart
Of stars for you while Haydn, while Mozart
Occupies heaven? These also, fanned to fire,

Flamboyant wholly, – so perfections tire, –
Whiten to wanness, till . . . let others note
The ever-new invasion!

IX

I devote
Rather my modicum of parts to use
What power may yet avail to re-infuse
(In fancy, please you!) sleep that looks like death
With momentary liveliness, lend breath
To make the torpor half inhale. O Relfe,
An all-unworthy pupil, from the shelf
Of thy laboratory, dares unstop
Bottle, ope box, extract thence pinch and drop
Of dusts and dews a many thou didst shrine
Each in its right receptacle, assign
To each its proper office, letter large
Label and label, then with solemn charge,
Reviewing learnedly the list complete
Of chemical reactives, from thy feet
Push down the same to me, attent below,
Power in abundance: armed wherewith I go
To play the enlivener. Bring good antique stuff!
Was it alight once? Still lives spark enough
For breath to quicken, run the smouldering ash
Red right-through. What, 'stone-dead' were fools so rash
As style my Avison, because he lacked
Modern appliance, spread out phrase unracked
By modulations fit to make each hair
Stiffen upon his wig? See there – and there!
I sprinkle my reactives, pitch broadcast
Discords and resolutions, turn aghast
Melody's easy-going, jostle law
With licence, modulate (no Bach in awe),
Change enharmonically (Hudl to thank),
And lo, upstart the flamelets, – what was blank
Turns scarlet, purple, crimson! Straightway scanned
By eyes that like new lustre – Love once more
Yearns through the Largo, Hatred as before
Rages in the Rubato: e'en thy March,
My Avison, which, sooth to say – (ne'er arch
Eyebrows in anger!) – timed, in Georgian years

The step precise of British Grenadiers
To such a nicety, – if score I crowd,
If rhythm I break, if beats I vary, – tap
At bar's off-starting turns true thunder-clap,
Ever the pace augmented till – what's here?
Titanic striding toward Olympus!

X

                                        Fear
No such irreverent innovation! Still
Glide on, go rolling, water-like, at will –
Nay, were thy melody in monotone,
The due three-parts dispensed with!

XI

                                        This alone
Comes of my tiresome talking: Music's throne
Seats somebody whom somebody unseats,
And whom in turn – by who knows what new feats
Of strength, – shall somebody as sure push down,
Consign him dispossessed of sceptre, crown,
And orb imperial – whereto? – Never dream
That what once lived shall ever die! They seem
Dead – do they? lapsed things lost in limbo? Bring
Our life to kindle theirs, and straight each king
Starts, you shall see, stands up, from head to foot
No inch that is not Purcell! Wherefore? (Suit
Measure to subject, first – no marching on
Yet in thy bold C major, Avison,
As suited step a minute since: no: wait –
Into the minor key first modulate –
Gently with A, now – in the Lesser Third!)

XII

Of all the lamentable debts incurred
By Man through buying knowledge, this were worst:
That he should find his last gain prove his first
Was futile – merely nescience absolute,
Not knowledge in the bud which holds a fruit
Haply undreamed of in the soul's Spring-tide,
Pursed in the petals Summer opens wide,
And Autumn, withering, rounds to perfect ripe, –

Not this, – but ignorance, a blur to wipe
From human records, late it graced so much.
'Truth – this attainment? Ah, but such and such
Beliefs of yore seemed inexpugnable
When we attained them! E'en as they, so will
This their successor have the due morn, noon,
Evening and night – just as an old-world tune
Wears out and drops away, until who hears
Smilingly questions – "This it was brought tears
Once to all eyes, – this roused heart's rapture once?"
So will it be with truth that, for the nonce,
Styles itself truth perennial: 'ware its wile!
Knowledge turns nescience, – foremost on the file,
Simply proves first of our delusions.'

XIII

Now –
Blare it forth, bold C Major! Lift thy brow,
Man, the immortal, that wast never fooled
With gifts no gifts at all, nor ridiculed –
Man knowing – he who nothing knew! As Hope,
Fear, Joy, and Grief, – though ampler stretch and scope
They seek and find in novel rhythm, fresh phrase, –
Were equally existent in far days
Of Music's dim beginning – even so,
Truth was at full within thee long ago,
Alive as now it takes what latest shape
May startle thee by strangeness. Truths escape
Time's insufficient garniture: they fade,
They fall – those sheathings now grown sere, whose aid
Was infinite to truth they wrapped, saved fine
And free through March frost: May dews crystalline
Nourish truth merely, – does June boast the fruit
As – not new vesture merely but, to boot,
Novel creation? Soon shall fade and fall
Myth after myth – the husk-like lies I call
New truth's corolla-safeguard: Autumn comes,
So much the better!

XIV

Therefore – bang the drums,
Blow the trumpets, Avison! March-motive? that's
Truth which endures resetting. Sharps and flats,
Lavish at need, shall dance athwart thy score
When ophicleide and bombardon's uproar
Mate the approaching trample, even now
Big in the distance – or my ears deceive –
Of federated England, fitly weave
March-music for the Future!

XV

Or suppose
Back, and not forward, transformation goes?
Once more some sable-stoled procession – say,
From Little-ease to Tyburn – wends its way,
Out of the dungeon to the gallows-tree
Where heading, hacking, hanging is to be
Of half-a-dozen recusants – this day
Three hundred years ago! How duly drones
Elizabethan plain-song – dim antique
Grown clarion-clear the while I humbly wreak
A classic vengeance on thy March! It moans –
Larges and Longs and Breves displacing quite
Crotchet-and-quaver pertness – brushing bars
Aside and filling vacant sky with stars
Hidden till now that day returns to night.

XVI

Nor night nor day: one purpose move us both,
Be thy mood mine! As thou wast minded, Man's
The cause our music champions: I were loth
To think we cheered our troop to Preston Pans
Ignobly: back to times of England's best!
Parliament stands for privilege – life and limb
Guards Hollis, Haselrig, Strode, Hampden, Pym,
The famous Five. There's rumour of arrest.
Bring up the Train Bands, Southwark! They protest:
Shall we not all join chorus? Hark the hymn,
– Rough, rude, robustious – homely heart a-throb,
Harsh voice a-hallo, as beseems the mob!
How good is noise! what's silence but despair

Of making sound match gladness never there?
Give me some great glad 'subject,' glorious Bach,
Where cannon-roar not organ-peal we lack!
Join in, give voice robustious rude and rough, –
Avison helps – so heart lend noise enough!

Fife, trump, drum, sound! and singers then,
Marching, say 'Pym, the man of men!'
Up, heads, your proudest – out, throats, your loudest –
'Somerset's Pym!'

Strafford from the block, Eliot from the den,
Foes, friends, shout 'Pym, our citizen!'
Wail, the foes he quelled, – hail, the friends he held,
'Tavistock's Pym!'

Hearts prompt heads, hands that ply the pen
Teach babes unborn the where and when
– Tyrants, he braved them, – patriots, he saved them –
'Westminster's Pym!'

Fust and His Friends

An Epilogue

Inside the House of Fust, Mayence, 1457.

FIRST FRIEND

Up, up, up – next step of the staircase
Lands us, lo, at the chamber of dread!

SECOND FRIEND

Locked and barred?

THIRD FRIEND

Door open – the rare case!

FOURTH FRIEND

Ay, there he leans – lost wretch!

FIFTH FRIEND

His head
Sunk on his desk 'twixt his arms outspread!

SIXTH FRIEND

Hallo, – wake, man, ere God thunderstrike Mayence
– Mulct for thy sake who art Satan's, John Fust!
Satan installed here, God's rule in abeyance,
Mayence some morning may crumble to dust.
Answer our questions thou shalt and thou must!

SEVENTH FRIEND

Softly and fairly! Wherefore a-gloom?
 Greet us, thy gossipry, cousin and sib!
Raise the forlorn brow, Fust! Make room –
 Let daylight through arms which, enfolding thee, crib
From those clenchèd lids the comfort of sunshine!

FIRST FRIEND

So glib

Thy tongue slides to 'comfort' already? Not mine!
 Behoves us deal roundly: the wretch is distraught
– Too well I guess wherefore! Behoves a Divine
 – Such as I, by grace, boast me – to threaten one caught
In the enemy's toils, – setting 'comfort' at naught.

SECOND FRIEND

Nay, Brother, so hasty? I heard – nor long since –
 Of a certain Black Artsman who, – helplessly bound
By rash pact with Satan, – through paying – why mince
 The matter? – fit price to the Church, – safe and sound
Full a year after death in his grave-clothes was found.

Whereas 'tis notorious the Fiend claims his due
 During lifetime, – comes clawing, with talons a-flame,
The soul from the flesh-rags left smoking and blue:
 So it happed with John Faust; lest John Fust fare the same, –
Look up, I adjure thee by God's holy name!

For neighbours and friends – no foul hell-brood flock we!
 Saith Solomon 'Words of the wise are as goads':
Ours prick but to startle from torpor, set free
 Soul and sense from death's drowse.

FIRST FRIEND

And soul, wakened, unloads
Much sin by confession: no mere palinodes!

– 'I was youthful and wanton, am old yet no sage:
When angry I cursed, struck and slew: did I want?
Right and left did I rob: though no war I dared wage
With the Church (God forbid!) – harm her least ministrant –
Still I outraged all else. Now that strength is grown scant,

'I am probity's self' – no such bleatings as these!
But avowal of guilt so enormous, it balks
Tongue's telling. Yet penitence prompt may appease
God's wrath at thy bond with the Devil who stalks
– Strides hither to strangle thee!

FUST

Childhood so talks.

Not rare wit nor ripe age – ye boast them, my neighbours! –
Should lay such a charge on your townsman, this Fust
Who, known for a life spent in pleasures and labours
If freakish yet venial, could scarce be induced
To traffic with fiends.

FIRST FRIEND

So, my words have unloosed

A ply from those pale lips corrugate but now?

FUST

Lost count me, yet not as ye lean to surmise.

FIRST FRIEND

To surmise? to establish! Unbury that brow!
Look up, that thy judge may read clear in thine eyes!

SECOND FRIEND

By your leave, Brother Barnabite! Mine to advise!

– Who arraign thee, John Fust! What was bruited erewhile
  Now bellows through Mayence. All cry – thou hast trucked
Salvation away for lust's solace! Thy smile
  Takes its hue from hell's smoulder!

FUST

Too certain! I sucked
– Got drunk at the nipple of sense.

SECOND FRIEND

Thou hast ducked –

Art drowned there, say rather! Faugh – fleshly disport!
  How else but by help of Sir Belial didst win
That Venus-like lady, no drudge of thy sort
  Could lure to become his accomplice in sin?
Folk nicknamed her Helen of Troy!

FIRST FRIEND

Best begin

At the very beginning. Thy father, – all knew,
  A mere goldsmith ...

FUST

Who knew him, perchance may know this –
He dying left much gold and jewels no few:
  Whom these help to court with but seldom shall miss
The love of a leman: true witchcraft, I wis!

FIRST FRIEND

Dost flout me? 'Tis said, in debauchery's guild
  Admitted prime guttler and guzzler – O swine! –
To honour thy headship, those tosspots so swilled
  That out of their table there sprouted a vine
Whence each claimed a cluster, awaiting thy sign

To out knife, off mouthful: when – who could suppose
Such malice in magic? – each sot woke and found
Cold steel but an inch from the neighbour's red nose
He took for a grape-bunch!

FUST

Does that so astound
Sagacity such as ye boast, – who surround

Your mate with eyes staring, hairs standing erect
At his magical feats? Are good burghers unversed
In the humours of toping? Full oft, I suspect,
Ye, counting your fingers, call thumbkin their first,
And reckon a groat every guilder disbursed.

What marvel if wags, while the skinker fast brimmed
Their glass with rare tipple's enticement, should gloat
– Befooled and beflustered – through optics drink-dimmed –
On this draught and that, till each found in his throat
Our Rhenish smack rightly as Raphal? For, note –

They fancied – their fuddling deceived them so grossly –
That liquor sprang out of the table itself
Through gimlet-holes drilled there, – nor noticed how closely
The skinker kept plying my guests, from the shelf
O'er their heads, with the potable madness. No elf

Had need to persuade them a vine rose umbrageous,
Fruit-bearing, thirst-quenching! Enough! I confess
To many such fool-pranks, but none so outrageous
That Satan was called in to help me: excess
I own to, I grieve at – no more and no less.

SECOND FRIEND

Strange honours were heaped on thee – medal for breast,
Chain for neck, sword for thigh: not a lord of the land
But acknowledged thee peer! What ambition possessed
A goldsmith by trade, with craft's grime on his hand,
To seek such associates?

FUST

Spare taunts! Understand –

I submit me! Of vanities under the sun,
  Pride seized me at last as concupiscence first,
Crapulosity ever: true Fiends, every one,
  Haled this way and that my poor soul: thus amerced –
Forgive and forget me!

FIRST FRIEND

Had flesh sinned the worst,

Yet help were in counsel: the Church could absolve:
  But say not men truly thou barredst escape
By signing and sealing . . .

SECOND FRIEND

On me must devolve
  The task of extracting . . .

FIRST FRIEND

Shall Barnabites ape
Us Dominican experts?

SEVENTH FRIEND

Nay, Masters, – agape

When Hell yawns for a soul, 'tis myself claim the task
  Of extracting, by just one plain question, God's truth!
Where's Peter Genesheim thy partner? I ask
  Why, cloistered up still in thy room, the pale youth
Slaves tongue-tied – thy trade brooks no tattling forsooth!

No less he, thy *famulus,* suffers entrapping,
  Succumbs to good fellowship: barrel a-broach
Runs freely nor needs any subsequent tapping:
  Quoth Peter 'That room, none but I dare approach,
Holds secrets will help me to ride in my coach.'

He prattles, we profit: in brief, he assures
  Thou hast taught him to speak so that all men may hear
– Each alike, wide world over, Jews, Pagans, Turks, Moors,
  The same as we Christians – speech heard far and near
At one and the same magic moment!

FUST

That's clear!

Said he – how?

SEVENTH FRIEND

Is it like he was licensed to learn?
  Who doubts but thou dost this by aid of the Fiend?
Is it so? So it is, for thou smilest! Go, burn
  To ashes, since such proves thy portion, unscreened
By bell, book and candle! Yet lately I weened

Balm yet was in Gilead, – some healing in store
  For the friend of my bosom. Men said thou wast sunk
In a sudden despondency: not, as before,
  Fust gallant and gay with his pottle and punk,
But sober, sad, sick as one yesterday drunk!

FUST

Spare Fust, then, thus contrite! – who, youthful and healthy,
  Equipped for life's struggle with culture of mind,
Sound flesh and sane soul in coherence, born wealthy,
  Nay, wise – how he wasted endowment designed
For the glory of God and the good of mankind!

That much were misused such occasions of grace
  Ye well may upbraid him, who bows to the rod.
But this should bid anger to pity give place –
  He has turned from the wrong, in the right path to plod,
Makes amends to mankind and craves pardon of God.

Yea, friends, even now from my lips the '*Heureka* –
  Soul saved!' was nigh bursting – unduly elate!
Have I brought Man advantage, or hatched – so to speak – a
  Strange serpent, no cygnet? 'Tis this I debate
Within me. Forbear, and leave Fust to his fate!

FIRST FRIEND

So abject, late lofty? Methinks I spy respite.
  Make clean breast, discover what mysteries hide
In thy room there!

SECOND FRIEND

Ay, out with them! Do Satan despite!
  Remember what caused his undoing was pride!

FIRST FRIEND

Dumb devil! Remains one resource to be tried!

SECOND FRIEND

Exorcise!

SEVENTH FRIEND

Nay, first – is there any remembers
  In substance that potent '*Ne pulvis*' – a psalm
Whereof some live spark haply lurks 'mid the embers
  Which choke in my brain. Talk of 'Gilead and balm'?
I mind me, sung half through, this gave such a qualm

To Asmodeus inside of a Hussite, that, queasy,
  He broke forth in brimstone with curses. I'm strong
In – at least the commencement: the rest should go easy,
  Friends helping. '*Ne pulvis et ignis*' . . .

SIXTH FRIEND

All wrong!

FIFTH FRIEND

I've conned till I captured the whole.

SEVENTH FRIEND

Get along!

'Ne pulvis et cinis superbe te geras,
Nam fulmina' . . .

SIXTH FRIEND

Fiddlestick! Peace, dolts and dorrs!
Thus runs it *'Ne Numinis fulmina feras'* –
Then *'Hominis perfidi justa sunt sors*
Fulmen et grando et horrida mors.'

SEVENTH FRIEND

You blunder. *'Irati ne'* . . .

SIXTH FRIEND

Mind your own business!

FIFTH FRIEND

I do not so badly, who gained the monk's leave
To study an hour his choice parchment. A dizziness
May well have surprised me. No Christian dares thieve,
Or I scarce had returned him his treasure. These cleave:

'Nos pulvis et cinis, trementes, gementes,
Venimus' – some such word – *'ad te, Domine.*
Da lumen, juvamen, ut sancta sequentes
Cor . . . corda . . .' Plague take it!

SEVENTH FRIEND

– *'erecta sint spe'*:
Right text, ringing rhyme, and ripe Latin for me!

SIXTH FRIEND

A Canon's self wrote it me fair: I was tempted
To part with the sheepskin.

SEVENTH FRIEND

Didst grasp and let go
Such a godsend, thou Judas? My purse had been emptied
Ere part with the prize!

FUST

Do I dream? Say ye so?
Clouds break, then! Move, world! I have gained my '*Pou sto*'!

I am saved: Archimedes, salute me!

OMNES

Assistance!
Help, Angels! He summons . . . Aroint thee! – by name,
His familiar!

FUST

Approach!

OMNES

Devil, keep thy due distance!

FUST

Be tranquillized, townsmen! The knowledge ye claim
Behold, I prepare to impart. Praise or blame, –

Your blessing or banning whatever betide me,
At last I accept. The slow travail of years,
The long-teeming brain's birth – applaud me, deride me, –
At last claims revealment. Wait!

SEVENTH FRIEND

Wait till appears
Uncaged Archimedes cooped-up there?

SECOND FRIEND

Who fears?

Here's have at thee!

SEVENTH FRIEND

Correctly now! '*Pulvis et cinis*' . . .

FUST

The verse ye so value, it happens I hold
In my memory safe from *initium* to *finis*.
Word for word, I produce you the whole, plain enrolled,
Black letters, white paper – no scribe's red and gold!

OMNES

Aroint thee!

FUST

I go and return. [*He enters the inner room*]

FIRST FRIEND

Ay, 'tis '*ibis*'
No doubt: but as boldly '*redibis*' – who'll say?
I rather conjecture '*in Orco peribis!*'

SEVENTH FRIEND

Come, neighbours!

SIXTH FRIEND

I'm with you! Show courage and stay
Hell's outbreak? Sirs, cowardice here wins the day!

FIFTH FRIEND

What luck had that student of Bamberg who ventured
To peep in the cell where a wizard of note
Was busy in getting some black deed debentured
By Satan? In dog's guise there sprang at his throat
A flame-breathing fury. Fust favours, I note,

An ugly huge lurcher!

SEVENTH FRIEND

If I placed reliance
As thou, on the beads thou art telling so fast,
I'd risk just a peep through the keyhole.

SIXTH FRIEND

Appliance
Of ear might be safer. Five minutes are past.

OMNES

Saints, save us! The door is thrown open at last!

FUST [*re-enters, the door closing behind him*]

As I promised, behold I perform! Apprehend you
The object I offer is poison or pest?
Receive without harm from the hand I extend you
A gift that shall set every scruple at rest!
Shrink back from mere paper-strips? Try them and test!

Still hesitate? Myk, was it thou who lamentedst
Thy five wits clean failed thee to render aright
A poem read once and no more? – who repentedst
Vile pelf had induced thee to banish from sight
The characters none but our clerics indite?

Take and keep!

FIRST FRIEND

Blessed Mary and all Saints about her!

SECOND FRIEND

What imps deal so deftly, – five minutes suffice
To play thus the penman?

THIRD FRIEND

By Thomas the Doubter,
Five minutes, no more!

FOURTH FRIEND

Out on arts that entice
Such scribes to do homage!

FIFTH FRIEND

Stay! Once – and now twice –

Yea, a third time, my sharp eye completes the inspection
Of line after line, the whole series, and finds
Each letter join each – not a fault for detection!
Such upstrokes, such downstrokes, such strokes of all kinds
In the criss-cross, all perfect!

SIXTH FRIEND

There's nobody minds

His quill-craft with more of a conscience, o'erscratches
A sheepskin more nimbly and surely with ink,
Than Paul the Sub-Prior: here's paper that matches
His parchment with letter on letter, no link
Overleapt – underlost!

SEVENTH FRIEND

No erasure, I think –

No blot, I am certain!

FUST

Accept the new treasure!

SIXTH FRIEND

I remembered full half!

SEVENTH FRIEND

But who other than I
(Bear witness, bystanders!) when he broke the measure
Repaired fault with '*fulmen*'?

FUST

Put bickerings by!
Here's for thee – thee – and thee, too: at need a supply
[*distributing Proofs*]

For Mayence, though seventy times seven should muster!
How now? All so feeble of faith that no face
Which fronts me but whitens – or yellows, were juster?
Speak out lest I summon my Spirits!

OMNES

Grace – grace!
Call none of thy – helpmates! We'll answer apace!

My paper – and mine – and mine also – they vary
In nowise – agree in each tittle and jot!
Fust, how – why was this?

FUST

Shall such '*Cur*' miss a '*quare*'?
Within, there! Throw doors wide! Behold who complot
To abolish the scribe's work – blur, blunder and blot!
[*The doors open, and the Press is discovered in operation*]

Brave full-bodied birth of this brain that conceived thee
In splendour and music, – sustained the slow drag
Of the days stretched to years dim with doubt, – yet believed thee,
Had faith in thy first leap of life! Pulse might flag –
– Mine fluttered how faintly! – Arch-moment might lag

Its longest – I bided, made light of endurance,
Held hard by the hope of an advent which – dreamed,
Is done now: night yields to the dawn's reassurance:
I have thee – I hold thee – my fancy that seemed,
My fact that proves palpable! Ay, Sirs, I schemed

Completion that's fact: see this Engine – be witness
Yourselves of its working! Nay, handle my Types!
Each block bears a Letter: in order and fitness
I range them. Turn, Peter, the winch! See, it gripes
What's under! Let loose – draw! In regular stripes

Lies plain, at one pressure, your poem – touched, tinted,
Turned out tc perfection! The sheet, late a blank,
Filled – ready for reading, – not written but PRINTED!
Omniscient omnipotent God, Thee I thank,
Thee ever, Thee only! – Thy creature that shrank

From no task Thou, Creator, imposedst! Creation
Revealed me no object, from insect to Man,
But bore Thy hand's impress: earth glowed with salvation:
'Hast sinned? Be thou saved, Fust! Continue my plan,
Who spake and earth was: with my word things began.

'As sound so went forth, to the sight be extended
Word's mission henceforward! The task I assign,
Embrace – thy allegiance to evil is ended!
Have cheer, soul impregnate with purpose! Combine
Soul and body, give birth to my concept – called thine!

'Far and wide, North and South, East and West, have
  dominion
 O'er thought, wingèd wonder, O Word! Traverse world
In sun-flash and sphere-song! Each beat of thy pinion
 Bursts night, beckons day: once Truth's banner unfurled,
Where's Falsehood? Sun-smitten, to nothingness hurled!'

More humbly – so, friends, did my fault find redemption.
 I sinned, soul-entoiled by the tether of sense:
My captor reigned master: I plead no exemption
 From Satan's award to his servant: defence
From the fiery and final assault would be – whence?

By making – as man might – to truth restitution!
 Truth is God: trample lies and lies' father, God's foe!
Fix fact fast: truths change by an hour's revolution:
 What deed's very doer, unaided, can show
How 'twas done a year – month – week – day – minute ago?

At best, he relates it – another reports it –
 A third – nay, a thousandth records it: and still
Narration, tradition, no step but distorts it,
 As down from truth's height it goes sliding until
At the low level lie-mark it stops – whence no skill

Of the scribe, intervening too tardily, rescues
 – Once fallen – lost fact from lie's fate there. What scribe
– Eyes horny with poring, hands crippled with desk-use,
 Brains fretted by fancies – the volatile tribe
That tease weary watchers – can boast that no bribe

Shuts eye and frees hand and remits brain from toiling?
 Truth gained – can we stay, at whatever the stage,
Truth a-slide, – save her snow from its ultimate soiling
 In mire, – by some process, stamp promptly on page
Fact spoiled by pen's plodding, make truth heritage

Not merely of clerics, but poured out, full measure,
 On clowns – every mortal endowed with a mind?
Read, gentle and simple! Let labour win leisure
 At last to bid truth do all duty assigned,
Not pause at the noble but pass to the hind!

How bring to effect such swift sure simultaneous
  Unlimited multiplication? How spread
By an arm-sweep a hand-throw – no helping extraneous –
  Truth broadcast o'er Europe? 'The goldsmith,' I said,
'Graves limning on gold: why not letters on lead?'

So, Tuscan artificer, grudge not thy pardon
  To me who played false, made a furtive descent,
Found the sly secret workshop, – thy genius kept guard on
  Too slackly for once, – and surprised thee low-bent
O'er thy labour – some chalice thy tool would indent

With a certain free scroll-work framed round by a border
  Of foliage and fruitage: no scratching so fine,
No shading so shy but, in ordered disorder,
  Each flourish came clear, – unbewildered by shine,
On the gold, irretrievably right, lay each line.

How judge if thy hand worked thy will? By reviewing,
  Revising again and again, piece by piece,
Tool's performance, – this way, as I watched. 'Twas through glueing
  A paper-like film-stuff – thin, smooth, void of crease,
On each cut of the graver: press hard! at release,

No mark on the plate, but the paper showed double:
  His work might proceed: as he judged – space or speck
Up he filled, forth he flung – was relieved thus from trouble
  Lest wrong – once – were right never more: what could check
Advancement, completion? Thus lay at my beck –

At my call – triumph likewise! 'For,' cried I, 'what hinders
  That graving turns Printing? Stamp one word – not one
But fifty such, phoenix-like, spring from death's cinders, –
  Since death is word's doom, clerics hide from the sun
As some churl closets up this rare chalice.' Go, run

Thy race now, Fust's child! High, O Printing, and holy
  Thy mission! These types, see, I chop and I change
Till the words, every letter, a pageful, not slowly
  Yet surely lies fixed: last of all, I arrange
A paper beneath, stamp it, loosen it!

FIRST FRIEND

Strange!

SECOND FRIEND

How simple exceedingly!

FUST

Bustle, my Schoeffer!
Set type, – quick, Genesheim! Turn screw now!

THIRD FRIEND

Just that!

FOURTH FRIEND

And no such vast miracle!

FUST

'Plough with my heifer,
Ye find out my riddle,' quoth Samson, and pat
He speaks to the purpose. Grapes squeezed in the vat

Yield to sight and to taste what is simple – a liquid
Mere urchins may sip: but give time, let ferment –
You've wine, manhood's master! Well, *'rectius si quid*
Novistis im-per-ti-te!' Wait the event,
Then weigh the result! But whate'er Thy intent,

O Thou, the one force in the whole variation
Of visible nature, – at work – do I doubt? –
From Thy first to our last, in perpetual creation –
A film hides us from Thee – 'twixt inside and out,
A film, on this earth where Thou bringest about

New marvels, new forms of the glorious, the gracious,
We bow to, we bless for: no star bursts heaven's dome
But Thy finger impels it, no weed peeps audacious
Earth's clay-floor from out, but Thy finger makes room
For one world's-want the more in Thy Cosmos: presume

Shall Man, Microcosmos, to claim the conception
  Of grandeur, of beauty, in thought, word or deed?
I toiled, but Thy light on my dubiousest step shone:
  If I reach the glad goal, is it I who succeed
Who stumbled at starting tripped up by a reed,

Or Thou? Knowledge only and absolute, glory
  As utter be Thine who concedest a spark
Of Thy spheric perfection to earth's transitory
  Existences! Nothing that lives, but Thy mark
Gives law to – life's light: what is doomed to the dark?

Where's ignorance? Answer, creation! What height,
  What depth has escaped Thy commandment – to Know?
What birth in the ore-bed but answers aright
  Thy sting at its heart which impels – bids 'E'en so,
Not otherwise move or be motionless, – grow,

'Decline, disappear!' Is the plant in default
  How to bud, when to branch forth? The bird and the beast
– Do they doubt if their safety be found in assault
  Or escape? Worm or fly, of what atoms the least
But follows light's guidance, – will famish, not feast?

In such various degree, fly and worm, ore and plant,
  All know, none is witless: around each, a wall
Encloses the portion, or ample or scant,
  Of Knowledge: beyond which one hair's breadth, for all
Lies blank – not so much as a blackness – a pall

Some sense unimagined must penetrate: plain
  Is only old licence to stand, walk or sit,
Move so far and so wide in the narrow domain
  Allotted each nature for life's use: past it
How immensity spreads does he guess? Not a whit.

Does he care? Just as little. Without? No, within
  Concerns him: he Knows. Man Ignores – thanks to Thee
Who madest him know, but – in knowing – begin
  To know still new vastness of knowledge must be
Outside him – to enter, to traverse, in fee

Have and hold! 'Oh, Man's ignorance!' hear the fool whine!
How were it, for better or worse, didst thou grunt
Contented with sapience – the lot of the swine
Who knows he was born for just truffles to hunt? –
Monks' Paradise – '*Semper sint res uti sunt!*'

No, Man's the prerogative – knowledge once gained –
To ignore, – find new knowledge to press for, to swerve
In pursuit of, no, not for a moment: attained –
Why, onward through ignorance! Dare and deserve!
As still to its asymptote speedeth the curve,

So approximates Man – Thee, who, reachable not,
Hast formed him to yearningly follow Thy whole
Sole and single omniscience!
Such, friends, is my lot:
I am back with the world: one more step to the goal
Thanks for reaching I render – Fust's help to Man's soul!

Mere mechanical help? So the hand gives a toss
To the falcon, – aloft once, spread pinions and fly,
Beat air far and wide, up and down and across!
My Press strains a-tremble: whose masterful eye
Will be first, in new regions, new truth to descry?

Give chase, soul! Be sure each new capture consigned
To my Types will go forth to the world, like God's bread
– Miraculous food not for body but mind,
Truth's manna! How say you? Put case that, instead
Of old leasing and lies, we superiorly fed

These Heretics, Hussites...

FIRST FRIEND

First answer my query!
If saved, art thou happy?

FUST

I was and I am.

FIRST FRIEND

Thy visage confirms it: how comes, then, that – weary
And woe-begone late – was it show, was it sham? –
We found thee sunk thiswise?

SECOND FRIEND

– In need of the dram

From the flask which a provident neighbour might carry!

FUST

Ah, friends, the fresh triumph soon flickers, fast fades!
I hailed Word's dispersion: could heartleaps but tarry!
Through me does Print furnish Truth wings? The same aids
Cause Falsehood to range just as widely. What raids

On a region undreamed of does Printing enable
Truth's foe to effect! Printed leasing and lies
May speed to the world's farthest corner – gross fable
No less than pure fact – to impede, neutralize,
Abolish God's gift and Man's gain!

FIRST FRIEND

Dost surmise

What struck me at first blush? Our Beghards, Waldenses,
Jeronimites, Hussites – does one show his head,
Spout heresy now? Not a priest in his senses
Deigns answer mere speech, but piles faggots instead,
Refines as by fire, and, him silenced, all's said.

Whereas if in future I pen an opuscule
Defying retort, as of old when rash tongues
Were easy to tame, – straight some knave of the Huss-School
Prints answer forsooth! Stop invisible lungs?
The barrel of blasphemy broached once, who bungs?

SECOND FRIEND

Does my sermon, next Easter, meet fitting acceptance?
  Each captious disputative boy has his quirk
'*An cuique credendum sit?*' Well the Church kept '*ans*'
  In order till Fust set his engine at work!
What trash will come flying from Jew, Moor and Turk

When, goosequill, thy reign o'er the world is abolished!
  Goose – ominous name! With a goose woe began:
Quoth Huss – which means 'goose' in his idiom unpolished –
  'Ye burn now a Goose: there succeeds me a Swan
Ye shall find quench your fire!'

FUST

I foresee such a man.

Asolando : Fancies and Facts

1889

To Mrs Arthur Bronson

To whom but you, dear Friend, should I dedicate verses – some few written, all of them supervised, in the comfort of your presence, and with yet another experience of the gracious hospitality now bestowed on me since so many a year, – adding a charm even to my residences at Venice, and leaving me little regret for the surprise and delight at my visits to Asolo in bygone days?

I unite, you will see, the disconnected poems by a title-name popularly ascribed to the inventiveness of the ancient secretary of Queen Cornaro whose palace-tower still overlooks us: *Asolare* – 'to disport in the open air, amuse oneself at random.' The objection that such a word nowhere occurs in the works of the Cardinal is hardly important – Bembo was too thorough a purist to conserve in print a term which in talk he might possibly toy with: but the word is more likely derived from a Spanish source. I use it for love of the place, and in requital of your pleasant assurance that an early poem of mine first attracted you thither – where and elsewhere, at La Mura as Cà Alvisi, may all happiness attend you!

Gratefully and affectionately yours,

R. B.

Asolo: 15 October 1889

Prologue

'The Poet's age is sad: for why?
  In youth, the natural world could show
No common object but his eye
  At once involved with alien glow –
His own soul's iris-bow.

'And now a flower is just a flower:
  Man, bird, beast are but beast, bird, man –
Simply themselves, uncinct by dower
  Of dyes which, when life's day began,
Round each in glory ran.'

Friend, did you need an optic glass,
  Which were your choice? A lens to drape
In ruby, emerald, chrysopras,
  Each object – or reveal its shape
Clear outlined, past escape,

The naked very thing? – so clear
  That, when you had the chance to gaze,
You found its inmost self appear
  Through outer seeming – truth ablaze,
Not falsehood's fancy-haze?

How many a year, my Asolo,
  Since – one step just from sea to land –
I found you, loved yet feared you so –
  For natural objects seemed to stand
Palpably fire-clothed! No –

No mastery of mine o'er these!
  Terror with beauty, like the Bush
Burning but unconsumed. Bend knees,
  Drop eyes to earthward! Language? Tush!
Silence 'tis awe decrees.

And now? The lambent flame is – where?
  Lost from the naked world: earth, sky,
Hill, vale, tree, flower, – Italia's rare

O'er-running beauty crowds the eye –
But flame? The Bush is bare.

Hill, vale, tree, flower – they stand distinct,
Nature to know and name. What then?
A Voice spoke thence which straight unlinked
Fancy from fact: see, all's in ken:
Has once my eyelid winked?

No, for the purged ear apprehends
Earth's import, not the eye late dazed:
The Voice said 'Call my works thy friends!
At Nature dost thou shrink amazed?
God is it who transcends.'

Asolo: 6 September 1889

Rosny

Woe, he went galloping into the war,
Clara, Clara!
Let us two dream: shall he 'scape with a scar?
Scarcely disfigurement, rather a grace
Making for manhood which nowise we mar:
See, while I kiss it, the flush on his face –
Rosny, Rosny!

Light does he laugh: 'With your love in my soul' –
(Clara, Clara!)
'How could I other than – sound, safe and whole –
Cleave who opposed me asunder, yet stand
Scatheless beside you, as, touching love's goal,
Who won the race kneels, craves reward at your hand –
Rosny, Rosny?'

Ay, but if certain who envied should see!
Clara, Clara,
Certain who simper: 'The hero for me
Hardly of life were so chary as miss

Death – death and fame – that's love's guerdon when she
  Boasts, proud bereaved one, her choice fell on this
    Rosny, Rosny!'

So, – go on dreaming, – he lies 'mid a heap
    (Clara, Clara,)
Of the slain by his hand: what is death but a sleep?
  Dead, with my portrait displayed on his breast:
Love wrought his undoing: 'No prudence could keep
  The love-maddened wretch from his fate.' That is best,
    Rosny, Rosny!

Dubiety

I will be happy if but for once:
  Only help me, Autumn weather,
Me and my cares to screen, ensconce
  In luxury's sofa-lap of leather!

Sleep? Nay, comfort – with just a cloud
  Suffusing day too clear and bright:
Eve's essence, the single drop allowed
  To sully, like milk, Noon's water-white.

Let gauziness shade, not shroud, – adjust,
  Dim and not deaden, – somehow sheathe
Aught sharp in the rough world's busy thrust,
  If it reach me through dreaming's vapour-wreath.

Be life so, all things ever the same!
  For, what has disarmed the world? Outside,
Quiet and peace: inside, nor blame
  Nor want, nor wish whate'er betide.

What is it like that has happened before?
  A dream? No dream, more real by much.
A vision? But fanciful days of yore
  Brought many: mere musing seems not such.

Perhaps but a memory, after all!
 – Of what came once when a woman leant
To feel for my brow where her kiss might fall.
 Truth ever, truth only the excellent!

Now

Out of your whole life give but a moment!
All of your life that has gone before,
All to come after it, – so you ignore
So you make perfect the present, – condense,
In a rapture of rage, for perfection's endowment,
Thought and feeling and soul and sense –
Merged in a moment which gives me at last
You around me for once, you beneath me, above me –
Me – sure that despite of time future, time past, –
This tick of our life-time's one moment you love me!
How long such suspension may linger? Ah, Sweet –
The moment eternal – just that and no more –
When ecstasy's utmost we clutch at the core
While cheeks burn, arms open, eyes shut and lips meet!

Humility

What girl but, having gathered flowers,
Stript the beds and spoilt the bowers,
From the lapful light she carries
Drops a careless bud? – nor tarries
To regain the waif and stray:
'Store enough for home' – she'll say.

So say I too: give your lover
Heaps of loving – under, over,
Whelm him – make the one the wealthy!
Am I all so poor who – stealthy
Work it was! – picked up what fell:
Not the worst bud – who can tell?

Poetics

'So say the foolish!' Say the foolish so, Love?
'Flower she is, my rose' – or else 'My very swan is she' –
Or perhaps 'Yon maid-moon, blessing earth below, Love,
That art thou!' – to them, belike: no such vain words from me.

'Hush, rose, blush! no balm like breath,' I chide it:
'Bend thy neck its best, swan, – hers the whiter curve!'
Be the moon the moon: my Love I place beside it:
What is she? Her human self, – no lower word will serve.

Summum Bonum

All the breath and the bloom of the year in the bag of one bee:
All the wonder and wealth of the mine in the heart of one gem:
In the core of one pearl all the shade and the shine of the sea:
Breath and bloom, shade and shine, – wonder, wealth, and –
how far above them –
Truth, that's brighter than gem,
Trust, that's purer than pearl, –
Brightest truth, purest trust in the universe – all were for me
In the kiss of one girl.

A Pearl, A Girl

A simple ring with a single stone
To the vulgar eye no stone of price:
Whisper the right word, that alone –
Forth starts a sprite, like fire from ice,
And lo, you are lord (says an Eastern scroll)
Of heaven and earth, lord whole and sole
Through the power in a pearl.

A woman ('tis I this time that say)
With little the world counts worthy praise:
Utter the true word – out and away

Escapes her soul: I am wrapt in blaze,
Creation's lord, of heaven and earth
Lord whole and sole – by a minute's birth –
Through the love in a girl!

Speculative

Others may need new life in Heaven –
Man, Nature, Art – made new, assume!
Man with new mind old sense to leaven,
Nature – new light to clear old gloom,
Art that breaks bounds, gets soaring-room.

I shall pray: 'Fugitive as precious –
Minutes which passed, – return, remain!
Let earth's old life once more enmesh us,
You with old pleasure, me – old pain,
So we but meet nor part again!'

White Witchcraft

If you and I could change to beasts, what beast should either be?
Shall you and I play Jove for once? Turn fox then, I decree!
Shy wild sweet stealer of the grapes! Now do your worst on me!

And thus you think to spite your friend – turned loathsome? What, a toad?
So, all men shrink and shun me! Dear men, pursue your road!
Leave but my crevice in the stone, a reptile's fit abode!

Now say your worst, Canidia! 'He's loathsome, I allow:
There may or may not lurk a pearl beneath his puckered brow:
But see his eyes that follow mine – love lasts there, anyhow.'

Bad Dreams I

Last night I saw you in my sleep:
  And how your charm of face was changed!
I asked 'Some love, some faith you keep?'
  You answered 'Faith gone, love estranged.'

Whereat I woke – a twofold bliss:
  Waking was one, but next there came
This other: 'Though I felt, for this,
  My heart break, I loved on the same.'

Bad Dreams II

You in the flesh and here –
  Your very self! Now wait!
One word! May I hope or fear?
  Must I speak in love or hate?
Stay while I ruminate!

The fact and each circumstance
  Dare you disown? Not you!
That vast dome, that huge dance,
  And the gloom which overgrew
A – possibly festive crew!

For why should men dance at all –
  Why women – a crowd of both –
Unless they are gay? Strange ball –
  Hands and feet plighting troth,
Yet partners enforced and loth!

Of who danced there, no shape
  Did I recognize: thwart, perverse,
Each grasped each, past escape
  In a whirl or weary or worse:
Man's sneer met woman's curse,

While he and she toiled as if
  Their guardian set galley-slaves
To supple chained limbs grown stiff:
  Unmanacled trulls and knaves –
The lash for who misbehaves!

And a gloom was, all the while,
  Deeper and deeper yet
O'ergrowing the rank and file
  Of that army of haters – set
To mimic love's fever-fret.

By the wall-side close I crept,
  Avoiding the livid maze,
And, safely so far, outstepped
  On a chamber – a chapel, says
My memory or betrays –

Closet-like, kept aloof
  From unseemly witnessing
What sport made floor and roof
  Of the Devil's palace ring
While his Damned amused their king.

Ay, for a low lamp burned,
  And a silence lay about
What I, in the midst, discerned
  Though dimly till, past doubt,
'Twas a sort of throne stood out –

High seat with steps, at least:
  And the topmost step was filled
By – whom? What vestured priest?
  A stranger to me, – his guild,
His cult, unreconciled

To my knowledge how guild and cult
  Are clothed in this world of ours:
I pondered, but no result
  Came to – unless that Giaours
So worship the Lower Powers.

When suddenly who entered?
  Who knelt – did you guess I saw?
Who – raising that face where centred
  Allegiance to love and law
So lately – off-casting awe,

Down-treading reserve, away
  Thrusting respect . . . but mine
Stands firm – firm still shall stay!
  Ask Satan! for I decline
To tell – what I saw, in fine!

Yet here in the flesh you come –
  Your same self, form and face, –
In the eyes, mirth still at home!
  On the lips, that commonplace
Perfection of honest grace!

Yet your errand is – needs must be –
  To palliate – well, explain,
Expurgate in some degree
  Your soul of its ugly stain.
Oh, you – the good in grain –

How was it your white took tinge?
  'A mere dream' – never object!
Sleep leaves a door on hinge
  Whence soul, ere our flesh suspect,
Is off and away: detect

Her vagaries when loose, who can!
  Be she pranksome, be she prude,
Disguise with the day began:
  With the night – ah, what ensued
From draughts of a drink hell-brewed?

Then She: 'What a queer wild dream!
  And perhaps the best fun is –
Myself had its fellow – I seem
  Scarce awake from yet. 'Twas this –
Shall I tell you? First, a kiss!

'For the fault was just your own, –
'Tis myself expect apology:
You warned me to let alone
(Since our studies were mere philology)
That ticklish (you said) Anthology.

'So, I dreamed that I passed *exam*
Till a question posed me sore:
"Who translated this epigram
By – an author we best ignore?"
And I answered "Hannah More"!'

Bad Dreams III

This was my dream: I saw a Forest
Old as the earth, no track nor trace
Of unmade man. Thou, Soul, explorest –
Though in a trembling rapture – space
Immeasurable! Shrubs, turned trees,
Trees that touch heaven, support its frieze
Studded with sun and moon and star:
While – oh, the enormous growths that bar
Mine eye from penetrating past
Their tangled twine where lurks – nay, lives
Royally lone, some brute-type cast
I' the rough, time cancels, man forgives.

On, Soul! I saw a lucid City
Of architectural device
Every way perfect. Pause for pity,
Lightning! nor leave a cicatrice
On those bright marbles, dome and spire,
Structures palatial, – streets which mire
Dares not defile, paved all too fine
For human footstep's smirch, not thine –
Proud solitary traverser,
My Soul, of silent lengths of way –
With what ecstatic dread, aver,
Lest life start sanctioned by thy stay!

Ah, but the last sight was the hideous!
  A City, yes, – a Forest, true, –
But each devouring each. Perfidious
  Snake-plants had strangled what I knew
Was a pavilion once: each oak
Held on his horns some spoil he broke
By surreptitiously beneath
Upthrusting: pavements, as with teeth,
Griped huge weed widening crack and split
  In squares and circles stone-work erst.
Oh, Nature – good! Oh, Art – no whit
  Less worthy! Both in one – accurst!

Bad Dreams IV

It happened thus: my slab, though new,
  Was getting weather-stained, – beside,
Herbage, balm, peppermint o'ergrew
  Letter and letter: till you tried
Somewhat, the Name was scarce descried.

That strong stern man my lover came:
  – Was he my lover? Call him, pray,
My life's cold critic bent on blame
  Of all poor I could do or say
To make me worth his love one day –

One far day when, by diligent
  And dutiful amending faults,
Foibles, all weaknesses which went
  To challenge and excuse assaults
Of culture wronged by taste that halts –

Discrepancies should mar no plan
  Symmetric of the qualities
Claiming respect from – say – a man
  That's strong and stern. 'Once more he pries
Into me with those critic eyes!'

No question! so – 'Conclude, condemn
  Each failure my poor self avows!
Leave to its fate all you contemn!
  There's Solomon's selected spouse:
Earth needs must hold such maids – choose them!'

Why, he was weeping! Surely gone
  Sternness and strength: with eyes to ground
And voice a broken monotone –
  'Only be as you were! Abound
In foibles, faults, – laugh, robed and crowned

'As Folly's veriest queen, – care I
  One feather-fluff? Look pity, Love,
On prostrate me – your foot shall try
  This forehead's use – mount thence above,
And reach what Heaven you dignify!'

Now, what could bring such change about?
  The thought perplexed: till, following
His gaze upon the ground, – why, out
  Came all the secret! So, a thing
Thus simple has deposed my king!

For, spite of weeds that strove to spoil
  Plain reading on the lettered slab,
My name was clear enough – no soil
  Effaced the date when one chance stab
Of scorn . . . if only ghosts might blab!

Inapprehensiveness

We two stood simply friend-like side by side,
Viewing a twilight country far and wide,
Till she at length broke silence. 'How it towers
Yonder, the ruin o'er this vale of ours!
The West's faint flare behind it so relieves
Its rugged outline – sight perhaps deceives,
Or I could almost fancy that I see
A branch wave plain – belike some wind-sown tree

Chance-rooted where a missing turret was.
What would I give for the perspective glass
At home, to make out if 'tis really so!
Has Ruskin noticed here at Asolo
That certain weed-growths on the ravaged wall
Seem' . . . something that I could not say at all,
My thought being rather – as absorbed she sent
Look onward after look from eyes distent
With longing to reach Heaven's gate left ajar –
'Oh, fancies that might be, oh, facts that are!
What of a wilding? By you stands, and may
So stand unnoticed till the Judgement Day,
One who, if once aware that your regard
Claimed what his heart holds, – woke, as from its sward
The flower, the dormant passion, so to speak –
Then what a rush of life would startling wreak
Revenge on your inapprehensive stare
While, from the ruin and the West's faint flare,
You let your eyes meet mine, touch what you term
Quietude – that's an universe in germ –
The dormant passion needing but a look
To burst into immense life!'
'No, the book
Which noticed how the wall-growths wave' said she
'Was not by Ruskin.'
I said 'Vernon Lee?'

Which?

So, the three Court-ladies began
Their trial of who judged best
In esteeming the love of a man:
Who preferred with most reason was thereby confessed
Boy-Cupid's exemplary catcher and cager;
An Abbé crossed legs to decide on the wager.

First the Duchesse: 'Mine for me –
Who were it but God's for Him,
And the King's for – who but he?
Both faithful and loyal, one grace more shall brim

His cup with perfection: a lady's true lover,
He holds – save his God and his king – none above her.'

'I require' – outspoke the Marquise –
'Pure thoughts, ay, but also fine deeds:
Play the paladin must he, to please
My whim, and – to prove my knight's service exceeds
Your saint's and your loyalist's praying and kneeling –
Show wounds, each wide mouth to my mercy appealing.'

Then the Comtesse: 'My choice be a wretch,
Mere losel in body and soul,
Thrice accurst! What care I, so he stretch
Arms to me his sole saviour, love's ultimate goal,
Out of earth and men's noise – names of "infidel," "traitor,"
Cast up at him? Crown me, crown's adjudicator!'

And the Abbé uncrossed his legs,
Took snuff, a reflective pinch,
Broke silence: 'The question begs
Much pondering ere I pronounce. Shall I flinch?
The love which to one and one only has reference
Seems terribly like what perhaps gains God's preference.'

The Cardinal and the Dog

Crescenzio, the Pope's Legate at the High Council, Trent,
– Year Fifteen hundred twenty-two, March Twenty-five – intent
On writing letters to the Pope till late into the night,
Rose, weary, to refresh himself, and saw a monstrous sight:
(I give mine Author's very words: he penned, I re-indite.)

A black Dog of vast bigness, eyes flaming, ears that hung
Down to the very ground almost, into the chamber sprung
And made directly for him, and laid himself right under
The table where Crescenzio wrote – who called in fear and wonder
His servants in the ante-room, commanded everyone
To look for and find out the beast: but, looking, they found none.

The Cardinal fell melancholy, then sick, soon after died:
And at Verona, as he lay on his death-bed, he cried
Aloud to drive away the Dog that leapt on his bed-side.
Heaven keep us Protestants from harm: the rest . . . no ill betide!

The Pope and the Net

What, he on whom our voices unanimously ran,
Made Pope at our last Conclave? Full low his life began:
His father earned the daily bread as just a fisherman.

So much the more his boy minds book, gives proof of mother-wit,
Becomes first Deacon, and then Priest, then Bishop: see him sit
No less than Cardinal ere long, while no one cries 'Unfit!'

But someone smirks, some other smiles, jogs elbow and nods
head:
Each winks at each: ''I-faith, a rise! Saint Peter's net, instead
Of sword and keys, is come in vogue!' You think he blushes red?

Not he, of humble holy heart! 'Unworthy me!' he sighs:
'From fisher's drudge to Church's prince – it is indeed a rise:
So, here's my way to keep the fact for ever in my eyes!'

And straightway in his palace-hall, where commonly is set
Some coat-of-arms, some portraiture ancestral, lo, we met
His mean estate's reminder in his fisher-father's net!

Which step conciliates all and some, stops cavil in a trice:
'The humble holy heart that holds of new-born pride no spice!
He's just the saint to choose for Pope!' Each adds ''Tis my
advice.'

So, Pope he was: and when we flocked – its sacred slipper on –
To kiss his foot, we lifted eyes, alack the thing was gone –
That guarantee of lowlihead, – eclipsed that star which shone!

Each eyed his fellow, one and all kept silence. I cried 'Pish!
I'll make me spokesman for the rest, express the common wish.
Why, Father, is the net removed?' 'Son, it hath caught the fish.'

The Bean-Feast

He was the man – Pope Sixtus, that Fifth, that swineherd's son:
He knew the right thing, did it, and thanked God when 'twas done:
But of all he had to thank for, my fancy somehow leans
To thinking, what most moved him was a certain meal on beans.

For one day, as his wont was, in just enough disguise
As he went exploring wickedness, – to see with his own eyes
If law had due observance in the city's entrail dark
As well as where, i' the open, crime stood an obvious mark, –

He chanced, in a blind alley, on a tumble-down once house
Now hovel, vilest structure in Rome the ruinous:
And, as his tact impelled him, Sixtus adventured bold,
To learn how lowliest subjects bore hunger, toil, and cold.

There sat they at high-supper – man and wife, lad and lass,
Poor as you please but cleanly all and care-free: pain that was
– Forgotten, pain as sure to be let bide aloof its time, –
Mightily munched the brave ones – what mattered gloom or grime?

Said Sixtus 'Feast, my children! who works hard needs eat well.
I'm just a supervisor, would hear what you can tell.
Do any wrongs want righting? The Father tries his best,
But, since he's only mortal, sends such as I to test
The truth of all that's told him – how folk like you may fare:
Come! – only don't stop eating – when mouth has words to spare –

'You' – smiled he – 'play the spokesman, bell-wether of the flock!
Are times good, masters gentle? Your grievances unlock!
How of your work and wages? – pleasures, if such may be –
Pains, as such are for certain.' Thus smiling questioned he.

But somehow, spite of smiling, awe stole upon the group –
An inexpressible surmise: why should a priest thus stoop –
Pry into what concerned folk? Each visage fell. Aware,
Cries Sixtus interposing: 'Nay, children, have no care!

'Fear nothing! Who employs me requires the plain truth. Pelf
Beguiles who should inform me: so, I inform myself.
See!' And he threw his hood back, let the close vesture ope,
Showed face, and where on tippet the cross lay: 'twas the Pope.

Imagine the joyful wonder! 'How shall the like of us –
Poor souls – requite such blessing of our rude bean-feast?'
'Thus –
Thus amply!' laughed Pope Sixtus. 'I early rise, sleep late:
Who works may eat: they tempt me, your beans there: spare a plate!'

Down sat he on the door-step: 'twas they this time said grace:
He ate up the last mouthful, wiped lips, and then, with face
Turned heavenward, broke forth thankful: 'Not now, that earth obeys
Thy word in mine, that through me the peoples know Thy ways –
But that Thy care extendeth to Nature's homely wants,
And, while man's mind is strengthened, Thy goodness nowise scants
Man's body of its comfort, – that I whom kings and queens
Crouch to, pick crumbs from off my table, relish beans!
The thunders I but seem to launch, there plain Thy hand all see:
That I have appetite, digest, and thrive – that boon's for me.'

Muckle-Mouth Meg

Frowned the Laird on the Lord: 'So, red-handed I catch thee?
Death-doomed by our Law of the Border!
We've a gallows outside and a chiel to dispatch thee:
Who trespasses – hangs: all's in order.'

He met frown with smile, did the young English gallant:
Then the Laird's dame: 'Nay, Husband, I beg!
He's comely: be merciful! Grace for the callant
– If he marries our Muckle-mouth Meg!'

'No mile-wide-mouthed monster of yours do I marry:
Grant rather the gallows!' laughed he.
'Foul fare kith and kin of you – why do you tarry?'
'To tame your fierce temper!' quoth she.

'Shove him quick in the Hole, shut him fast for a week:
Cold, darkness and hunger work wonders:
Who lion-like roars now, mouse-fashion will squeak,
And "it rains" soon succeed to "it thunders."'

A week did he bide in the cold and the dark
– Not hunger: for duly at morning
In flitted a lass, and a voice like a lark
Chirped 'Muckle-mouth Meg still ye're scorning?

'Go hang, but here's parritch to hearten ye first!'
'Did Meg's muckle-mouth boast within some
Such music as yours, mine should match it or burst:
No frog-jaws! So tell folk, my Winsome!'

Soon week came to end, and, from Hole's door set wide,
Out he marched, and there waited the lassie:
'Yon gallows, or Muckle-mouth Meg for a bride!
Consider! Sky's blue and turf's grassy:

'Life's sweet: shall I say ye wed Muckle-mouth Meg?'
'Not I' quoth the stout heart: 'too eerie
The mouth that can swallow a bubblyjock's egg:
Shall I let it munch mine? Never, Dearie!'

'Not Muckle-mouth Meg? Wow, the obstinate man!
Perhaps he would rather wed me!'
'Ay, would he – with just for a dowry your can!'
'I'm Muckle-mouth Meg' chirruped she.

'Then so – so – so – so –' as he kissed her apace –
'Will I widen thee out till thou turnest
From Margaret Minnikin-mou', by God's grace,
To Muckle-mouth Meg in good earnest!'

Arcades Ambo

A: You blame me that I ran away?
Why, Sir, the enemy advanced:
Balls flew about, and – who can say

But one, if I stood firm, had glanced
In my direction? Cowardice?
I only know we don't live twice,
Therefore – shun death, is my advice.

B: Shun death at all risks? Well, at some!
True, I myself, Sir, though I scold
The cowardly, by no means come
Under reproof as overbold
– I, who would have no end of brutes
Cut up alive to guess what suits
My case and saves my toe from shoots.

The Lady and the Painter

SHE: Yet womanhood you reverence,
So you profess!
HE: With heart and soul.
SHE: Of which fact this is evidence!
To help Art-study, – for some dole
Of certain wretched shillings, – you
Induce a woman – virgin too –
To strip and stand stark-naked?
HE: True.

SHE: Nor feel you so degrade her?
HE: What
– (Excuse the interruption) – clings
Half-savage-like around your hat?
SHE: Ah, do they please you? Wild-bird-wings!
Next season, – Paris-prints assert, –
We must go feathered to the skirt:
My modiste keeps on the alert.

Owls, hawks, jays – swallows most approve...
HE: Dare I speak plainly?
SHE: Oh, I trust!
HE: Then, Lady Blanche, it less would move
In heart and soul of me disgust
Did you strip off those spoils you wear,

And stand – for thanks, not shillings – bare,
To help Art like my Model there.
She well knew what absolved her – praise
In me for God's surpassing good,
Who granted to my reverent gaze
A type of purest womanhood.
You – clothed with murder of His best
Of harmless beings – stand the test!
What is it *you* know?
SHE: That you jest!

Ponte dell' Angelo, Venice

Stop rowing! This one of our bye-canals
O'er a certain bridge you have to cross
That's named 'Of the Angel': listen why!
The name 'Of the Devil' too much appals
Venetian acquaintance, so – his the loss,
While the gain goes . . . look on high!

An angel visibly guards yon house:
Above each scutcheon – a pair – stands he,
Enfolds them with droop of either wing:
The family's fortune were perilous
Did he thence depart – you will soon agree,
If I hitch into verse the thing.

For, once on a time, this house belonged
To a lawyer of note, with law and to spare,
But also with overmuch lust of gain:
In the matter of law you were nowise wronged,
But alas for the lucre! He picked you bare
To the bone. Did folk complain?

'I exact' growled he 'work's rightful due:
'Tis folk seek me, not I seek them.
Advice at its price! They succeed or fail,
Get law in each case – and a lesson too:
Keep clear of the Courts – is advice *ad rem:*
They'll remember, I'll be bail!'

So, he pocketed fee without a qualm.
What reason for squeamishness? Labour done,
To play he betook him with lightened heart,
Ate, drank and made merry with song or psalm,
Since the yoke of the Church is an easy one –
Fits neck nor causes smart.

Brief: never was such an extortionate
Rascal – the word has escaped my teeth!
And yet – (all's down in a book no ass
Indited, believe me!) – this reprobate
Was punctual at prayer-time: gold lurked beneath
Alloy of the rankest brass.

For, play the extortioner as he might,
Fleece folk each day and all day long,
There was this redeeming circumstance:
He never lay down to sleep at night
But he put up a prayer first, brief yet strong,
'Our Lady avert mischance!'

Now it happened at close of a fructuous week,
'I must ask' quoth he 'some Saint to dine:
I want that widow well out of my ears
With her ailing and wailing. Who bade her seek
Redress at my hands? "She was wronged!" Folk whine
If to Law wrong right appears.

'Matteo da Bascio – he's my man!
No less than Chief of the Capucins:
His presence will surely suffumigate
My house – fools think lies under a ban
If somebody loses what somebody wins.
Hark, there he knocks at the grate!

'Come in, thou blessed of Mother Church!
I go and prepare – to bid, that is,
My trusty and diligent servitor
Get all things in readiness. Vain the search
Through Venice for one to compare with this
My model of ministrants: for –

'For – once again, nay, three times over,
My helpmate's an ape! so intelligent,
I train him to drudge at household work:
He toils and he moils, I live in clover:
Oh, you shall see! There's a goodly scent –
From his cooking or I'm a Turk!

'Scarce need to descend and supervise:
I'll do it, however: wait here awhile!'
So, down to the kitchen gaily scuttles
Our host, nor notes the alarmed surmise
Of the holy man. 'O depth of guile!
He blindly guzzles and guttles,

'While – who is it dresses the food and pours
The liquor? Some fiend – I make no doubt –
In likeness of – which of the loathly brutes?
An ape! Where hides he? No bull that gores,
No bear that hugs – 'tis the mock and flout
Of an ape, fiend's face that suits.

'So – out with thee, creature, wherever thou hidest!
I charge thee, by virtue of . . . right do I judge!
There skulks he perdue, crouching under the bed.
Well done! What, forsooth, in beast's shape thou confidest?
I know and would name thee but that I begrudge
Breath spent on such carrion. Instead –

'I adjure thee by –' 'Stay!' laughed the portent that rose
From floor up to ceiling: 'No need to adjure!
See Satan in person, late ape by command
Of Him thou adjurest in vain. A saint's nose
Scents brimstone though incense be burned for a lure.
Yet, hence! for I'm safe, understand!

''Tis my charge to convey to fit punishment's place
This lawyer, my liegeman, for cruelty wrought
On his clients, the widow and orphan, poor souls
He has plagued by exactions which proved law's disgrace,
Made equity void and to nothingness brought
God's pity. Fiends, on with fresh coals!'

'Stay!' nowise confounded, withstands Hell its match:
'How comes it, were truth in this story of thine,
God's punishment suffered a minute's delay?
Weeks, months have elapsed since thou squattedst at watch
For a spring on thy victim: what caused thee decline
Advantage till challenged today?'

'That challenge I meet with contempt,' quoth the fiend.
'Thus much I acknowledge: the man's armed in mail:
I wait till a joint's loose, then quick ply my claws.
Thy friend's one good custom – he knows not – has screened
His flesh hitherto from what else would assail:
At "Save me, Madonna!" I pause.

'That prayer did the losel but once pretermit,
My pounce were upon him. I keep me attent:
He's in safety but till he's caught napping. Enough!'
'Ay, enough!' smiles the saint – 'for the biter is bit,
The spy caught in somnolence. Vanish! I'm sent
To smooth up what fiends do in rough.'

'I vanish? Through wall or through roof?' the ripost
Grinned gaily. 'My orders were – "Leave not unharmed
The abode of this lawyer! Do damage to prove
'Twas for something thou quittedst the land of the lost –
To add to their number this unit!" Though charmed
From descent there, on earth that's above

'I may haply amerce him.' 'So do, and begone,
I command thee! For, look! Though there's doorway behind
And window before thee, go straight through the wall,
Leave a breach in the brickwork, a gap in the stone
For who passes to stare at!' 'Spare speech! I'm resigned:
Here goes!' roared the goblin, as all –

Wide bat-wings, spread arms and legs, tail out a-stream,
Crash obstacles went, right and left, as he soared
Or else sank, was clean gone through the hole anyhow.
The Saint returned thanks: then a satisfied gleam
On the bald polished pate showed that triumph was scored.
'To dinner with appetite now!'

Down he trips. 'In good time!' smirks the host. 'Didst thou
scent
Rich savour of roast meat? Where hides he, my ape?
Look alive, be alert! He's away to wash plates.
Sit down, Saint! What's here? Dost examine a rent
In the napkin thou twistest and twirlest? Agape . . .
Ha, blood is it drips nor abates

'From thy wringing a cloth, late was lavendered fair?
What means such a marvel?' 'Just this does it mean:
I convince and convict thee of sin!' answers straight
The Saint, wringing on, wringing ever – O rare! –
Blood – blood from a napery snow not more clean.
'A miracle shows thee thy state!

'See – blood thy extortions have wrung from the flesh
Of thy clients who, sheep-like, arrived to be shorn,
And left thee – or fleeced to the quick or so flayed
That, behold, their blood gurgles and grumbles afresh
To accuse thee! Ay, down on thy knees, get up sworn
To restore! Restitution once made,

'Sin no more! Dost thou promise? Absolved, then, arise!
Upstairs follow me! Art amazed at yon breach?
Who battered and shattered and scattered, escape
From thy purlieus obtaining? That Father of Lies
Thou wast wont to extol for his feats, all and each
The Devil's disguised as thine ape!'

Be sure that our lawyer was torn by remorse,
Shed tears in a flood, vowed and swore so to alter
His ways that how else could our Saint but declare
He was cleansed of past sin? 'For sin future – fare worse
Thou undoubtedly wilt,' warned the Saint, 'shouldst thou falter
One whit!' 'Oh, for that have no care!

'I am firm in my purposed amendment. But, prithee,
Must ever affront and affright me yon gap?
Who made it for exit may find it of use
For entrance as easy. If, down in his smithy
He forges me fetters – when heated, mayhap,
He'll up with an armful! Broke loose –

'How bar him out henceforth?' 'Judiciously urged!'
Was the good man's reply. 'How to balk him is plain.
There's nothing the Devil objects to so much,
So speedily flies from, as one of those purged
Of his presence, the angels who erst formed his train –
His, their emperor. Choose one of such!

'Get fashioned his likeness and set him on high
At back of the breach thus adroitly filled up:
Display him as guard of two scutcheons, thy arms:
I warrant no devil attempts to get by
And disturb thee so guarded. Eat, drink, dine and sup,
In thy rectitude, safe from alarms!'

So said and so done. See, the angel has place
Where the Devil had passage! All's down in a book.
Gainsay me? Consult it! Still faithless? Trust *me*?
Trust Father Boverio who gave me the case
In his Annals – gets of it, by hook or by crook,
Two confirmative witnesses: three

Are surely enough to establish an act:
And thereby we learn – would we ascertain truth –
To trust wise tradition which took, at the time,
Note that served till slow history ventured on fact,
Though folk have their fling at tradition forsooth!
Row, boys, fore and aft, rhyme and chime!

Beatrice Signorini

This strange thing happened to a painter once:
Viterbo boasts the man among her sons
Of note, I seem to think: his ready tool
Picked up its precepts in Cortona's school –
That's Pietro Berretini, whom they call
Cortona, these Italians: greatish-small,
Our painter was his pupil, by repute
His match if not his master absolute,
Though whether he spoiled fresco more or less,

And what's its fortune, scarce repays your guess
Still, for one circumstance, I save his name
– Francesco Romanelli: do the same!
He went to Rome and painted: there he knew
A wonder of a woman painting too –
For she, at least, was no Cortona's drudge:
Witness that ardent fancy-shape – I judge
A semblance of her soul – she called 'Desire'
With starry front for guide, where sits the fire
She left to brighten Buonarroti's house.
If you see Florence, pay that piece your vows,
Though blockhead Baldinucci's mind, imbued
With monkish morals, bade folk 'Drape the nude
And stop the scandal!' quoth the record prim
I borrow this of: hang his book and him!
At Rome, then, where these fated ones met first,
The blossom of his life had hardly burst
While hers was blooming at full beauty's stand:
No less Francesco – when half-ripe he scanned
Consummate Artemisia – grew one want
To have her his and make her ministrant
With every gift of body and of soul
To him. In vain. Her sphery self was whole –
Might only touch his orb at Art's sole point.
Suppose he could persuade her to enjoint
Her life – past, present, future – all in his
At Art's sole point by some explosive kiss
Of love through lips, would love's success defeat
Artistry's haunting curse – the Incomplete?
Artists no doubt they both were, – what beside
Was she? who, long had felt heart, soul spread wide
Her life out, knowing much and loving well,
On either side Art's narrow space where fell
Reflection from his own speck: but the germ
Of individual genius – what we term
The very self, the God-gift whence had grown
Heart's life and soul's life, – how make that his own?
Vainly his Art, reflected, smiled in small
On Art's one facet of her ampler ball;
The rest, touch-free, took in, gave back heaven, earth,
All where he was not. Hope, well-nigh ere birth
Came to Desire, died off all-unfulfilled.

'What though in Art I stand the abler-skilled,'
(So he conceited: mediocrity
Turns on itself the self-transforming eye)
'If only Art were suing, mine would plead
To purpose: man – by nature I exceed
Woman the bounded: but how much beside
She boasts, would sue in turn and be denied!
Love her? My own wife loves me in a sort
That suits us both: she takes the world's report
Of what my work is worth, and, for the rest,
Concedes that, while his consort keeps her nest,
The eagle soars a licensed vagrant, lives
A wide free life which she at least forgives –
Good Beatricé Signorini! Well
And wisely did I choose her. But the spell
To subjugate this Artemisia – where?
She passionless? – she resolute to care
Nowise beyond the plain sufficiency
Of fact that she is she and I am I
– Acknowledged arbitrator for us both
In her life as in mine which she were loth
Even to learn the laws of? No, and no,
Twenty times over! Ay, it must be so:
I for myself, alas!'
                                        Whereon, instead
Of the checked lover's-utterance – why, he said
– Leaning above her easel: 'Flesh is red'
(Or some such just remark) – 'by no means white
As Guido's practice teaches: you are right.'

Then came the better impulse: 'What if pride
Were wisely trampled on, whate'er betide?
If I grow hers, not mine – join lives, confuse
Bodies and spirits, gain not her but lose
Myself to Artemisia? That were love!
Of two souls – one must bend, one rule above:
If I crouch under proudly, lord turned slave,
Were it not worthier both than if she gave
Herself – in treason to herself – to me?'

And, all the while, he felt it could not be.
Such love were true love: love that way who can!

Someone that's born half woman not whole man:
For man, prescribed man better or man worse,
Why, whether microcosm or universe,
What law prevails alike through great and small,
The world and man – world's miniature we call?
Male is the master. 'That way' – smiled and sighed
Our true male estimator – 'puts her pride
My wife in making me the outlet whence
She learns all Heaven allows: 'tis my pretence
To paint: her lord should do what else but paint?
Do I break brushes, cloister me turned saint?
Then, best of all suits sanctity her spouse
Who acts for Heaven, allows and disallows
At pleasure, past appeal, the right, the wrong
In all things. That's my wife's way. But this strong
Confident Artemisia – an adept
In Art does she conceit herself? "Except
In just this instance," tell her, "no one draws
More rigidly observant of the laws
Of right design: yet here, – permit me hint, –
If the acromion had a deeper dint,
That shoulder were perfection." What surprise
– Nay scorn, shoots black fire from those startled eyes!
She to be lessoned in design forsooth!
I'm doomed and done for, since I spoke the truth.
Make my own work the subject of dispute –
Fails it of just perfection absolute
Somewhere? Those motors, flexors, – don't I know
Ser Santi, styled "Tirititototo
The pencil-prig," might blame them? Yet my wife –
Were he and his nicknamer brought to life,
Tito and Titian, to pronounce again –
Ask her who knows more – I or the great Twain
Our colourist and draughtsman!

'I help her,
Not she helps me; and neither shall demur
Because my portion is – ' he chose to think –
'Quite other than a woman's: I may drink
At many waters, must repose by none –
Rather arise and fare forth, having done
Duty to one new excellence the more,
Abler thereby, though impotent before

So much was gained of knowledge. Best depart
From this last lady I have learned by heart!'

Thus he concluded of himself – resigned
To play the man and master: 'Man boasts mind:
Woman, man's sport calls mistress, to the same
Does body's suit and service. Would she claim
– My placid Beatricé-wife – pretence
Even to blame her lord if, going hence,
He wistfully regards one whom – did fate
Concede – he might accept queen, abdicate
Kingship because of? – one of no meek sort
But masterful as he: man's match in short?
Oh, there's no secret I were best conceal!
Bicé shall know; and should a stray tear steal
From out the blue eye, stain the rose cheek – bah!
A smile, a word's gay reassurance – ah,
With kissing interspersed, – shall make amends,
Turn pain to pleasure.'
'What, in truth so ends
Abruptly, do you say, our intercourse?'
Next day, asked Artemisia: 'I'll divorce
Husband and wife no longer. Go your ways,
Leave Rome! Viterbo owns no equal, says
The byword, for fair women: you, no doubt,
May boast a paragon all specks without,
Using the painter's privilege to choose
Among what's rarest. Will your wife refuse
Acceptance from – no rival – of a gift?
You paint the human figure I make shift
Humbly to reproduce: but, in my hours
Of idlesse, what I fain would paint is – flowers.
Look now!'
She twitched aside a veiling cloth.
'Here is my keepsake – frame and picture both:
For see, the frame is all of flowers festooned
About an empty space, – left thus, to wound
No natural susceptibility:
How can I guess? 'Tis you must fill, not I,
The central space with – her whom you like best!
That is your business, mine has been the rest.
But judge!'

How judge them? Each of us, in flowers,
Chooses his love, allies it with past hours,
Old meetings, vanished forms and faces: no –
Here let each favourite unmolested blow
For one heart's homage, no tongue's banal praise,
Whether the rose appealingly bade 'Gaze
Your fill on me, sultana who dethrone
The gaudy tulip!' or 'twas 'Me alone
Rather do homage to, who lily am,
No unabashed rose!' 'Do I vainly cram
My cup with sweets, your jonquil?' 'Why forget
Vernal endearments with the violet?'
So they contested yet concerted, all
As one, to circle round about, enthral
Yet, self-forgetting, push to prominence
The midmost wonder, gained no matter whence.

There's a tale extant, in a book I conned
Long years ago, which treats of things beyond
The common, antique times and countries queer
And customs strange to match. ''Tis said, last year,'
(Recounts my author,) 'that the King had mind
To view his kingdom – guessed at from behind
A palace-window hitherto. Announced
No sooner was such purpose than 'twas pounced
Upon by all the ladies of the land –
Loyal but light of life: they formed a band
Of loveliest ones but lithest also, since
Proudly they all combined to bear their prince.
Backs joined to breasts, – arms, legs, – nay, ankles, wrists,
Hands, feet, I know not by what turns and twists,
So interwoven lay that you believed
'Twas one sole beast of burden which received
The monarch on its back, of breadth not scant,
Since fifty girls made one white elephant.
So with the fifty flowers which shapes and hues
Blent, as I tell, and made one fast yet loose
Mixture of beauties, composite, distinct
No less in each combining flower that linked
With flower to form a fit environment
For – whom might be the painter's heart's intent
Thus, in the midst enhaloed, to enshrine?

'This glory-guarded middle space – is mine?
For me to fill?'
'For you, my Friend! We part,
Never perchance to meet again. Your Art –
What if I mean it – so to speak – shall wed
My own, be witness of the life we led
When sometimes it has seemed our souls near found
Each one the other as its mate – unbound
Had yours been haply from the better choice
– Beautiful Bicé: 'tis the common voice,
The crowning verdict. Make whom you like best
Queen of the central space, and manifest
Your predilection for what flower beyond
All flowers finds favour with you. I am fond
Of – say – yon rose's rich predominance,
While you – what wonder? – more affect the glance
The gentler violet from its leafy screen
Ventures: so – choose your flower and paint your queen!'

Oh but the man was ready, head as hand,
Instructed and adroit. 'Just as you stand,
Stay and be made – would Nature but relent –
By Art immortal!'
Every implement
In tempting reach – a palette primed, each squeeze
Of oil-paint in its proper patch – with these,
Brushes, a veritable sheaf to grasp!
He worked as he had never dared.
'Unclasp
My Art from yours who can!' – he cried at length,
As down he threw the pencil – 'Grace from Strength
Dissociate, from your flowery fringe detach
My face of whom it frames, – the feat will match
With that of Time should Time from me extract
Your memory, Artemisia!' And in fact, –
What with the pricking impulse, sudden glow
Of soul – head, hand co-operated so
That face was worthy of its frame, 'tis said –
Perfect, suppose!
They parted. Soon instead
Of Rome was home, – of Artemisia – well,
The placid-perfect wife. And it befell

That after the first incontestably
Blessedest of all blisses (– wherefore try
Your patience with embracings and the rest
Due from Calypso's all-unwilling guest
To his Penelope?) – there somehow came
The coolness which as duly follows flame.
So, one day, 'What if we inspect the gifts
My Art has gained us?'
Now the wife uplifts
A casket-lid, now tries a medal's chain
Round her own lithe neck, fits a ring in vain
– Too loose on the fine finger, – vows and swears
The jewel with two pendent pearls like pears
Betters a lady's bosom – witness else!
And so forth, while Ulysses smiles.
'Such spells
Subdue such natures – sex must worship toys
– Trinkets and trash: yet, ah, quite other joys
Must stir from sleep the passionate abyss
Of – such an one as her I know – not this
My gentle consort with the milk for blood!
Why, did it chance that in a careless mood
(In those old days, gone – never to return –
When we talked – she to teach and I to learn)
I dropped a word, a hint which might imply
Consorts exist – how quick flashed fire from eye,
Brow blackened, lip was pinched by furious lip!
I needed no reminder of my slip:
One warning taught me wisdom. Whereas here ...
Aha, a sportive fancy! Eh, what fear
Of harm to follow? Just a whim indulged!

'My Beatricé, there's an undivulged
Surprise in store for you: the moment's fit
For letting loose a secret: out with it!
Tributes to worth, you rightly estimate
These gifts of Prince and Bishop, Church and State:
Yet, may I tell you? Tastes so disagree!
There's one gift, preciousest of all to me,
I doubt if you would value as well worth
The obvious sparkling gauds that men unearth

For toy-cult mainly of you womankind;
Such make you marvel, I concede: while blind
The sex proves to the greater marvel here
I veil to balk its envy. Be sincere!
Say, should you search creation far and wide,
Was ever face like this?'

He drew aside
The veil, displayed the flower-framed portrait kept
For private delectation.
No adept
In florist's lore more accurately named
And praised or, as appropriately, blamed
Specimen after specimen of skill,
Than Bicé. 'Rightly placed the daffodil –
Scarcely so right the blue germander. Grey
Good mouse-ear! Hardly your auricula
Is powdered white enough. It seems to me
Scarlet not crimson, that anemone:
But there's amends in the pink saxifrage.
O darling dear ones, let me disengage
You innocents from what your harmlessness
Clasps lovingly! Out thou from their caress,
Serpent!'
Whereat forth-flashing from her coils
On coils of hair, the *spilla* in its toils
Of yellow wealth, the dagger-plaything kept
To pin its plaits together, life-like leapt
And – woe to all inside the coronal!
Stab followed stab, – cut, slash, she ruined all
The masterpiece. Alack for eyes and mouth
And dimples and endearment – North and South,
East, West, the tatters in a fury flew:
There yawned the circlet. What remained to do?
She flung the weapon, and, with folded arms
And mien defiant of such low alarms
As death and doom beyond death, Bicé stood
Passively statuesque, in quietude
Awaiting judgement.
And out judgement burst
With frank unloading of love's laughter, first

Freed from its unsuspected source. Some throe
Must needs unlock love's prison-bars, let flow
The joyance.

'Then you ever were, still are,
And henceforth shall be – no occulted star
But my resplendent Bicé, sun-revealed,
Full-rondure! Woman-glory unconcealed,
So front me, find and claim and take your own –
My soul and body yours and yours alone,
As you are mine, mine wholly! Heart's love, take –
Use your possession – stab or stay at will
Here – hating, saving – woman with the skill
To make man beast or god!'

And so it proved:
For, as beseemed new godship, thus he loved,
Past power to change, until his dying-day, –
Good fellow! And I fain would hope – some say
Indeed for certain – that our painter's toils
At fresco-splashing, finer stroke in oils,
Were not so mediocre after all;
Perhaps the work appears unduly small
From having loomed too large in old esteem,
Patronized by late Papacy. I seem
Myself to have cast eyes on certain work
In sundry galleries, no judge needs shirk
From moderately praising. He designed
Correctly, nor in colour lagged behind
His age: but both in Florence and in Rome
The elder race so make themselves at home
That scarce we give a glance to ceilingfuls
Of such like as Francesco. Still, one culls
From out the heaped laudations of the time
The pretty incident I put in rhyme.

Flute-Music, with an Accompaniment

HE: Ah, the bird-like fluting
Through the ash-tops yonder –
Bullfinch-bubblings, soft sounds suiting
What sweet thoughts, I wonder?
Fine-pearled notes that surely
Gather, dewdrop-fashion,
Deep-down in some heart which purely
Secretes globuled passion –
Passion insuppressive –
Such is piped, for certain;
Love, no doubt, nay, love excessive
'Tis, your ash-tops curtain.

Would your ash-tops open
We might spy the player –
Seek and find some sense which no pen
Yet from singer, sayer,
Ever has extracted:
Never, to my knowledge,
Yet has pedantry enacted
That, in Cupid's College,
Just this variation
Of the old old yearning
Should by plain speech have salvation,
Yield new men new learning.

'Love!' but what love, nicely
New from old disparted,
Would the player teach precisely?
First of all, he started
In my brain Assurance –
Trust – entire Contentment –
Passion proved by much endurance;
Then came – not resentment,
No, but simply Sorrow:
What was seen had vanished:
Yesterday so blue! Tomorrow
Blank, all sunshine banished.

Hark! 'Tis Hope resurges,
Struggling through obstruction –
Forces a poor smile which verges
On Joy's introduction.
Now, perhaps, mere Musing:
'Holds earth such a wonder?
Fairy-mortal, soul-sense-fusing
Past thought's power to sunder!'
What? calm Acquiescence?
'Daisied turf gives room to
Trefoil, plucked once in her presence –
Growing by her tomb too!'

SHE: All's your fancy-spinning!
Here's the fact: a neighbour
Never-ending, still beginning,
Recreates his labour:
Deep o'er desk he drudges,
Adds, divides, subtracts and
Multiplies, until he judges
Noonday-hour's exact sand
Shows the hourglass emptied:
Then comes lawful leisure,
Minutes rare from toil exempted,
Fit to spend in pleasure.

Out then with – what treatise?
Youth's Complete Instructor
How to play the Flute. Quid petis?
Follow Youth's conductor
On and on, through *Easy,*
Up to *Harder, Hardest*
Flute-piece, till thou, flautist wheezy,
Possibly discardest
Tootlings hoarse and husky,
Mayst expend with courage
Breath – on tunes once bright now dusky –
Meant to cool thy porridge.

That's an air of Tulou's
He maltreats persistent,
Till as lief I'd hear some Zulu's

Bone-piped bag, breath-distent,
Madden native dances.
I'm the man's familiar:
Unexpectedness enhances
What your ear's auxiliar
– Fancy – finds suggestive.
Listen! That's *legato*
Rightly played, his fingers restive
Touch as if *staccato*.

HE: Ah, you trick-betrayer!
Telling tales, unwise one?
So the secret of the player
Was – he could surprise one
Well-nigh into trusting
Here was a musician
Skilled consummately, yet lusting
Through no vile ambition
After making capture
All the world, – rewarded
Amply by one stranger's rapture,
Common praise discarded.

So, without assistance
Such as music rightly
Needs and claims, – defying distance,
Overleaping lightly
Obstacles which hinder, –
He, for my approval,
All the same and all the kinder
Made mine what might move all
Earth to kneel adoring:
Took – while he piped Gounod's
Bit of passionate imploring –
Me for Juliet: who knows?

No! as you explain things,
All's mere repetition,
Practice-pother: of all vain things
Why waste pooh or pish on
Toilsome effort – never
Ending, still beginning –

After what should pay endeavour
  – Right-performance? winning
Weariness from you who,
  Ready to admire some
Owl's fresh hooting – Tu-whit, tu-who –
  Find stale thrush-songs tiresome.

SHE: Songs, Spring thought perfection,
  Summer criticizes:
What in May escaped detection,
  August, past surprises,
Notes, and names each blunder.
  You, the just-initiate,
Praise to heart's content (what wonder?)
  Tootings I hear vitiate
Romeo's serenading –
  I who, times full twenty,
Turned to ice – no ash-tops aiding –
  At his *caldamente*.

So, 'twas distance altered
  Sharps to flats? The missing
Bar when syncopation faltered
  (You thought – paused for kissing!)
Ash-tops too felonious
  Intercepted? Rather
Say – they well-nigh made euphonious
  Discord, helped to gather
Phrase, by phrase, turn patches
  Into simulated
Unity which botching matches, –
  Scraps redintegrated.

HE: Sweet, are you suggestive
  Of an old suspicion
Which has always found me restive
  To its admonition
When it ventured whisper
  'Fool, the strifes and struggles
Of your trembler – blusher – lisper
  Were so many juggles,

Tricks tried – oh, so often! –
Which once more do duty,
Find again a heart to soften,
Soul to snare with beauty.'

Birth-blush of the briar-rose,
Mist-bloom of the hedge-sloe,
Someone gains the prize: admire rose
Would he, when noon's wedge – slow –
Sure, has pushed, expanded
Rathe pink to raw redness?
Would he covet sloe when sanded
By road-dust to deadness?
So – restore their value!
Ply a water-sprinkle!
Then guess sloe is fingered, shall you?
Find in rose a wrinkle?

Here what played Aquarius?
Distance – ash-tops aiding,
Reconciled scraps else contrarious,
Brightened stuff fast fading.
Distance – call your shyness:
Was the fair one peevish?
Coyness softened out of slyness.
Was she cunning, thievish,
All-but-proved impostor?
Bear but one day's exile,
Ugly traits were wholly lost or
Screened by fancies flexile –

Ash-tops these, you take me?
Fancies' interference
Changed . . .
But since I sleep, don't wake me!
What if all's appearance?
Is not outside seeming
Real as substance inside?
Both are facts, so leave me dreaming:
If who loses wins I'd
Ever lose, – conjecture,

From one phrase trilled deftly,
All the piece. So, end your lecture,
Let who lied be left lie!

'Imperante Augusto Natus Est –'

What it was struck the terror into me?
This, Publius: closer! while we wait our turn
I'll tell you. Water's warm (they ring inside)
At the eighth hour, till when no use to bathe.

Here in the vestibule where now we sit,
One scarce stood yesterday, the throng was such
Of loyal gapers, folk all eye and ear
While Lucius Varius Rufus in their midst
Read out that long-planned late-completed piece,
His Panegyric on the Emperor.
'Nobody like him' little Flaccus laughed
'At leading forth an Epos with due pomp!
Only, when godlike Caesar swells the theme,
How should mere mortals hope to praise aright?
Tell me, thou offshoot of Etruscan kings!'
Whereat Maecenas smiling sighed assent.

I paid my quadrans, left the Thermae's roar
Of rapture as the poet asked 'What place
Among the godships Jove, for Caesar's sake,
Would bid its actual occupant vacate
In favour of the new divinity?'
And got the expected answer 'Yield thine own!' –
Jove thus dethroned, I somehow wanted air,
And found myself a-pacing street and street,
Letting the sunset, rosy over Rome,
Clear my head dizzy with the hubbub – say,
As if thought's dance therein had kicked up dust
By trampling on all else: the world lay prone,
As – poet-propped, in brave hexameters –
Their subject triumphed up from man to God.
Caius Octavius Caesar the August –
Where was escape from his prepotency?

I judge I may have passed – how many piles
Of structure dropt like doles from his free hand
To Rome on every side? Why, right and left,
For temples you've the Thundering Jupiter,
Avenging Mars, Apollo Palatine:
How count Piazza, Forum – there's a third
All but completed. You've the Theatre
Named of Marcellus – all his work, such work! –
One thought still ending, dominating all –
With warrant Varius sang 'Be Caesar God!'
By what a hold arrests he Fortune's wheel,
Obtaining and retaining heaven and earth
Through Fortune, if you like, but favour – no!
For the great deeds flashed by me, fast and thick
As stars which storm the sky on autumn nights –
Those conquests! but peace crowned them, – so, of peace!
Count up his titles only – these, in few –
Ten years Triumvir, Consul thirteen times,
Emperor, nay – the glory topping all –
Hailed Father of his Country, last and best
Of titles, by himself accepted so:
And why not? See but feats achieved in Rome –
Not to say, Italy – he planted there
Some thirty colonies – but Rome itself
All new-built, 'marble now, brick once,' he boasts:
This Portico, that Circus. Would you sail?
He has drained Tiber for you: would you walk?
He straightened out the long Flaminian Way.
Poor? Profit by his score of donatives!
Rich – that is, mirthful? Half-a-hundred games
Challenge your choice! There's Rome – for you and me
Only? The centre of the world besides!
For, look the wide world over, where ends Rome?
To sunrise? There's Euphrates – all between!
To sunset? Ocean and immensity:
North, – stare till Danube stops you: South, see Nile,
The Desert and the earth-upholding Mount.
Well may the poet-people each with each
Vie in his praise, our company of swans,
Virgil and Horace, singers – in their way –
Nearly as good as Varius, though less famed:
Well may they cry, 'No mortal, plainly God!'

Thus to myself myself said, while I walked:
Or would have said, could thought attain to speech,
Clean baffled by enormity of bliss
The while I strove to scale its heights and sound
Its depths – this masterdom o'er all the world
Of one who was but born, – like you, like me,
Like all the world he owns, – of flesh and blood.
But he – how grasp, how gauge his own conceit
Of bliss to me near inconceivable?
Or – since such flight too much makes reel the brain –
Let's sink – and so take refuge, as it were,
From life's excessive altitude – to life's
Breathable wayside shelter at its base!
If looms thus large this Caesar to myself
– Of senatorial rank and somebody –
How must he strike the vulgar nameless crowd,
Innumerous swarm that's nobody at all?
Why, – for an instance, – much as yon gold shape
Crowned, sceptred, on the temple opposite –
Fulgurant Jupiter – must daze the sense
Of – say, yon outcast begging from its step!
What, anti-Caesar, monarch in the mud,
As he is pinnacled above thy pate?
Ay, beg away! thy lot contrasts full well
With his whose bounty yields thee this support –
Our Holy and Inviolable One,
Caesar, whose bounty built the fane above!
Dost read my thought? Thy garb, alack, displays
Sore usage truly in each rent and stain –
Faugh! Wash though in Suburra! 'Ware the dogs
Who may not so disdain a meal on thee!
What, stretchest forth a palm to catch my alms?
Aha, why yes: I must appear – who knows? –
I, in my toga, to thy rags and thee –
Quaestor – nay, Aedile, Censor – Pol! perhaps
The very City-Praetor's noble self!
As to me Caesar, so to thee am I?
Good: nor in vain shall prove thy quest, poor rogue!
Hither – hold palm out – take this quarter-as!

And who did take it? As he raised his head,
(My gesture was a trifle – well, abrupt),

Back fell the broad flap of the peasant's-hat,
The homespun cloak that muffled half his cheek
Dropped somewhat, and I had a glimpse – just one!
One was enough. Whose – whose might be the face?
That unkempt careless hair – brown, yellowish –
Those sparkling eyes beneath their eyebrows' ridge
(Each meets each, and the hawk-nose rules between)
– That was enough, no glimpse was needed more!
And terrifyingly into my mind
Came that quick-hushed report was whispered us,
'They do say, once a year in sordid garb
He plays the mendicant, sits all day long,
Asking and taking alms of who may pass,
And so averting, if submission help,
Fate's envy, the dread chance and change of things
When Fortune – for a word, a look, a naught –
Turns spiteful and – the petted lioness –
Strikes with her sudden paw, and prone falls each
Who patted late her neck superiorly,
Or trifled with those claw-tips velvet-sheathed.'
'He's God!' shouts Lucius Varius Rufus: 'Man
And worms'-meat any moment!' mutters low
Some Power, admonishing the mortal-born.

Ay, do you mind? There's meaning in the fact
That whoso conquers, triumphs, enters Rome,
Climbing the Capitolian, soaring thus
To glory's summit, – Publius, do you mark –
Ever the same attendant who, behind,
Above the Conqueror's head supports the crown
All-too-demonstrative for human wear,
– One hand's employment – all the while reserves
Its fellow, backward flung, to point how, close
Appended from the car, beneath the foot
Of the up-borne exulting Conqueror,
Frown – half-descried – the instruments of shame,
The malefactor's due. Crown, now – Cross, when?

Who stands secure? Are even Gods so safe?
Jupiter that just now is dominant –
Are not there ancient dismal tales how once
A predecessor reigned ere Saturn came,

And who can say if Jupiter be last?
Was it for nothing the grey Sibyl wrote
'Caesar Augustus regnant, shall be born
In blind Judaea' – one to master him,
Him and the universe? An old-wife's tale?

Bath-drudge! Here, slave! No cheating! Our turn next.
No loitering, or be sure you taste the lash!
Two strigils, two oil-drippers, each a sponge!

Development

My Father was a scholar and knew Greek.
When I was five years old, I asked him once
'What do you read about?'
'The siege of Troy.'
'What is a siege and what is Troy?'
Whereat
He piled up chairs and tables for a town,
Set me a-top for Priam, called our cat
– Helen, enticed away from home (he said)
By wicked Paris, who couched somewhere close
Under the footstool, being cowardly,
But whom – since she was worth the pains, poor puss –
Towzer and Tray, – our dogs, the Atreidai, – sought
By taking Troy to get possession of
– Always when great Achilles ceased to sulk,
(My pony in the stable) – forth would prance
And put to flight Hector – our page-boy's self.
This taught me who was who and what was what:
So far I rightly understood the case
At five years old: a huge delight it proved
And still proves – thanks to that instructor sage
My Father, who knew better than turn straight
Learning's full flare on weak-eyed ignorance,
Or, worse yet, leave weak eyes to grow sand-blind,
Content with darkness and vacuity.

It happened, two or three years afterward,
That – I and playmates playing at Troy's Siege –
My Father came upon our make-believe.
'How would you like to read yourself the tale
Properly told, of which I gave you first
Merely such notion as a boy could bear?
Pope, now, would give you the precise account
Of what, some day, by dint of scholarship,
You'll hear – who knows? – from Homer's very mouth.
Learn Greek by all means, read the "Blind Old Man,
Sweetest of Singers" – *tuphlos* which means "blind,"
Hedistos which means "sweetest." Time enough!
Try, anyhow, to master him some day;
Until when, take what serves for substitute,
Read Pope, by all means!'
So I ran through Pope,
Enjoyed the tale – what history so true?
Also attacked my Primer, duly drudged,
Grew fitter thus for what was promised next –
The very thing itself, the actual words,
When I could turn – say, Buttmann to account.

Time passed, I ripened somewhat: one fine day,
'Quite ready for the Iliad, nothing less?
There's Heine, where the big books block the shelf:
Don't skip a word, thumb well the Lexicon!'

I thumbed well and skipped nowise till I learned
Who was who, what was what, from Homer's tongue,
And there an end of learning. Had you asked
The all-accomplished scholar, twelve years old,
'Who was it wrote the Iliad?' – what a laugh!
'Why, Homer, all the world knows: of his life
Doubtless some facts exist: it's everywhere:
We have not settled, though, his place of birth:
He begged, for certain, and was blind beside:
Seven cities claimed him – Scio, with best right,
Thinks Byron. What he wrote? Those Hymns we have.
Then there's the "Battle of the Frogs and Mice,"
That's all – unless they dig "Margites" up
(I'd like that) nothing more remains to know.'

Thus did youth spend a comfortable time;
Until – 'What's this the Germans say is fact
That Wolf found out first? It's unpleasant work
Their chop and change, unsettling one's belief:
All the same, while we live, we learn, that's sure.'
So, I bent brow o'er *Prolegomena*.

And, after Wolf, a dozen of his like
Proved there was never any Troy at all,
Neither Besiegers nor Besieged, – nay, worse, –
No actual Homer, no authentic text,
No warrant for the fiction I, as fact,
Had treasured in my heart and soul so long –
Ay, mark you! and as fact held still, still hold,
Spite of new knowledge, in my heart of hearts
And soul of souls, fact's essence freed and fixed
From accidental fancy's guardian sheath.
Assuredly thenceforward – thank my stars! –
However it got there, deprive who could –
Wring from the shrine my precious tenantry,
Helen, Ulysses, Hector and his Spouse,
Achilles and his Friend? – though Wolf – ah, Wolf!
Why must he needs come doubting, spoil a dream?

But then 'No dream's worth waking' – Browning says:
And here's the reason why I tell thus much.
I, now mature man, you anticipate,
May blame my Father justifiably
For letting me dream out my nonage thus,
And only by such slow and sure degrees
Permitting me to sift the grain from chaff,
Get truth and falsehood known and named as such.
Why did he ever let me dream at all,
Not bid me taste the story in its strength?
Suppose my childhood was scarce qualified
To rightly understand mythology,
Silence at least was in his power to keep:
I might have – somehow – correspondingly –
Well, who knows by what method, gained my gains,
Been taught, by forthrights not meanderings,
My aim should be to loathe, like Peleus' son,
A lie as Hell's Gate, love my wedded wife,

Like Hector, and so on with all the rest.
Could not I have excogitated this
Without believing such men really were?

That is – he might have put into my hand
The 'Ethics'? In translation, if you please,
Exact, no pretty lying that improves,
To suit the modern taste: no more, no less –
The 'Ethics': 'tis a treatise I find hard
To read aright now that my hair is grey,
And I can manage the original.
At five years old – how ill had fared its leaves!
Now, growing double o'er the Stagirite,
At least I soil no page with bread and milk,
Nor crumple, dogsear and deface – boys' way.

*Rephan**

How I lived, ere my human life began
In this world of yours, – like you, made man, –
When my home was the Star of my God Rephan?

Come then around me, close about,
World-weary earth-born ones! Darkest doubt
Or deepest despondency keeps you out?

Nowise! Before a word I speak,
Let my circle embrace your worn, your weak,
Brow-furrowed old age, youth's hollow cheek –

Diseased in the body, sick in soul,
Pinched poverty, satiate wealth, – your whole
Array of despairs! Have I read the roll?

All here? Attend, perpend! O Star
Of my God Rephan, what wonders are
In thy brilliance fugitive, faint and far!

*Suggested by a very early recollection of a prose story by the noble woman and imaginative writer, Jane Taylor, of Norwich.

Far from me, native to thy realm,
Who shared its perfections which o'erwhelm
Mind to conceive. Let drift the helm,

Let drive the sail, dare unconfined
Embark for the vastitude, O Mind,
Of an absolute bliss! Leave earth behind!

Here, by extremes, at a mean you guess:
There, all's at most – not more, not less:
Nowhere deficiency nor excess.

No want – whatever should be, is now:
No growth – that's change, and change comes – how
To royalty born with crown on brow?

Nothing begins – so needs to end:
Where fell it short at first? Extend
Only the same, no change can mend!

I use your language: mine – no word
Of its wealth would help who spoke, who heard,
To a gleam of intelligence. None preferred,

None felt distaste when better and worse
Were uncontrastable: bless or curse
What – in that uniform universe?

Can your world's phrase, your sense of things
Forth-figure the Star of my God? No springs,
No winters throughout its space. Time brings

No hope, no fear: as today, shall be
Tomorrow: advance or retreat need we
At our stand-still through eternity?

All happy: needs must we so have been,
Since who could be otherwise? All serene:
What dark was to banish, what light to screen?

Earth's rose is a bud that's checked or grows
As beams may encourage or blasts oppose:
Our lives leapt forth, each a full-orbed rose –

Each rose sole rose in a sphere that spread
Above and below and around – rose-red:
No fellowship, each for itself instead.

One better than I – would prove I lacked
Somewhat: one worse were a jarring fact
Disturbing my faultlessly exact.

How did it come to pass there lurked
Somehow a seed of change that worked
Obscure in my heart till perfection irked? –

Till out of its peace at length grew strife –
Hopes, fears, loves, hates, – obscurely rife, –
My life grown a-tremble to turn your life?

Was it Thou, above all lights that are,
Prime Potency, did Thy hand unbar
The prison-gate of Rephan my Star?

In me did such potency wake a pulse
Could trouble tranquillity that lulls
Not lashes inertion till throes convulse

Soul's quietude into discontent?
As when the completed rose bursts, rent
By ardours till forth from its orb are sent

New petals that mar – unmake the disc –
Spoil rondure: what in it ran brave risk,
Changed apathy's calm to strife, bright, brisk,

Pushed simple to compound, sprang and spread
Till, fresh-formed, faceted, floreted,
The flower that slept woke a star instead?

No mimic of Star Rephan! How long
I stagnated there where weak and strong,
The wise and the foolish, right and wrong,

Are merged alike in a neutral Best,
Can I tell? No more than at whose behest
The passion arose in my passive breast,

And I yearned for no sameness but difference
In thing and thing, that should shock my sense
With a want of worth in them all, and thence

Startle me up, by an Infinite
Discovered above and below me – height
And depth alike to attract my flight,

Repel my descent: by hate taught love.
Oh, gain were indeed to see above
Supremacy ever – to move, remove,

Not reach – aspire yet never attain
To the object aimed at! Scarce in vain, –
As each stage I left nor touched again.

To suffer, did pangs bring the loved one bliss,
Wring knowledge from ignorance, – just for this –
To add one drop to a love-abyss!

Enough: for you doubt, you hope, O men,
You fear, you agonize, die: what then?
Is an end to your life's work out of ken?

Have you no assurance that, earth at end,
Wrong will prove right? Who made shall mend
In the higher sphere to which yearnings tend?

Why should I speak? You divine the test.
When the trouble grew in my pregnant breast
A voice said 'So wouldst thou strive, not rest?

'Burn and not smoulder, win by worth,
Not rest content with a wealth that's dearth?
Thou art past Rephan, thy place be Earth!'

Reverie

I know there shall dawn a day
  – Is it here on homely earth?
Is it yonder, worlds away,
  Where the strange and new have birth,
That Power comes full in play?

Is it here, with grass about,
  Under befriending trees,
When shy buds venture out,
  And the air by mild degrees
Puts winter's death past doubt?

Is it up amid whirl and roar
  Of the elemental flame
Which star-flecks heaven's dark floor,
  That, new yet still the same,
Full in play comes Power once more?

Somewhere, below, above,
  Shall a day dawn – this I know –
When Power, which vainly strove
  My weakness to o'erthrow,
Shall triumph. I breathe, I move,

I truly am, at last!
  For a veil is rent between
Me and the truth which passed
  Fitful, half-guessed, half-seen,
Grasped at – not gained, held fast.

I for my race and me
  Shall apprehend life's law:
In the legend of man shall see
  Writ large what small I saw
In my life's tale: both agree.

As the record from youth to age
  Of my own, the single soul –
So the world's wide book: one page
  Deciphered explains the whole
Of our common heritage.

How but from near to far
  Should knowledge proceed, increase?
Try the clod ere test the star!
  Bring our inside strife to peace
Ere we wage, on the outside, war!

So, my annals thus begin:
  With body, to life awoke
Soul, the immortal twin
  Of body which bore soul's yoke
Since mortal and not akin.

By means of the flesh, grown fit,
  Mind, in surview of things,
Now soared, anon alit
  To treasure its gatherings
From the ranged expanse – to-wit,

Nature, – earth's, heaven's wide show
  Which taught all hope, all fear:
Acquainted with joy and woe,
  I could say 'Thus much is clear,
Doubt annulled thus much: I know.

'All is effect of cause:
  As it would, has willed and done
Power: and my mind's applause
  Goes, passing laws each one,
To Omnipotence, lord of laws.'

Head praises, but heart refrains
  From loving's acknowledgement.
Whole losses outweigh half-gains:
  Earth's good is with evil blent:
Good struggles but evil reigns.

Yet since Earth's good proved good –
  Incontrovertibly
Worth loving – I understood
  How evil – did mind descry
Power's object to end pursued –

Were haply as cloud across
  Good's orb, no orb itself:
Mere mind – were it found at loss
  Did it play the tricksy elf
And from life's gold purge the dross?

Power is known infinite:
  Good struggles to be – at best
Seems – scanned by the human sight,
  Tried by the senses' test –
Good palpably: but with right

Therefore to mind's award
  Of loving, as power claims praise?
Power – which finds naught too hard,
  Fulfilling itself all ways
Unchecked, unchanged: while barred,

Baffled, what good began
  Ends evil on every side.
To Power submissive man
  Breathes 'E'en as Thou art, abide!'
While to good 'Late-found, long-sought,

'Would Power to a plenitude
  But liberate, but enlarge
Good's strait confine, – renewed
  Were ever the heart's discharge
Of loving!' Else doubts intrude.

For you dominate, stars all!
  For a sense informs you – brute,
Bird, worm, fly, great and small,
  Each with your attribute
Or low or majestical!

Thou earth that embosomest
  Offspring of land and sea –
How thy hills first sank to rest,
  How thy vales bred herb and tree
Which dizen thy mother-breast –

Do I ask? 'Be ignorant
  Ever!' the answer clangs:
Whereas if I plead world's want,
  Soul's sorrows and body's pangs,
Play the human applicant, –

Is a remedy far to seek?
  I question and find response:
I – all men, strong or weak,
  Conceive and declare at once
For each want its cure. 'Power, speak

'Stop change, avert decay,
  Fix life fast, banish death,
Eclipse from the star bid stay,
  Abridge of no moment's breath
One creature! Hence, Night, hail, Day!'

What need to confess again
  No problem this to solve
By impotence? Power, once plain
  Proved Power, – let on Power devolve
Good's right to co-equal reign!

Past mind's conception – Power!
  Do I seek how star, earth, beast,
Bird, worm, fly, gained their dower
  For life's use, most and least?
Back from the search I cower.

Do I seek what heals all harm,
  Nay, hinders the harm at first,
Saves earth? Speak, Power, the charm!
  Keep the life there unamerced
By chance, change, death's alarm!

As promptly as mind conceives,
   Let Power in its turn declare
Some law which wrong retrieves,
   Abolishes everywhere
What thwarts, what irks, what grieves!

Never to be! and yet
   How easy it seems – to sense
Like man's – if somehow met
   Power with its match – immense
Love, limitless, unbeset

By hindrance on every side!
   Conjectured, nowise known,
Such may be: could man confide
   Such would match – were Love but shown
Stript of the veils that hide –

Power's self now manifest!
   So reads my record: thine,
O world, how runs it? Guessed
   Were the purport of that prime line,
Prophetic of all the rest!

'In a beginning God
   Made heaven and earth.' Forth flashed
Knowledge: from star to clod
   Man knew things: doubt abashed
Closed its long period.

Knowledge obtained Power praise.
   Had Good been manifest,
Broke out in cloudless blaze,
   Unchequered as unrepressed,
In all things Good at best –

Then praise – all praise, no blame –
   Had hailed the perfection. No!
As Power's display, the same
   Be Good's – praise forth shall flow
Unisonous in acclaim!

Even as the world its life,
So have I lived my own –
Power seen with Love at strife,
That sure, this dimly shown,
– Good rare and evil rife.

Whereof the effect be – faith
That, some far day, were found
Ripeness in things now rathe,
Wrong righted, each chain unbound,
Renewal born out of scathe.

Why faith – but to lift the load,
To leaven the lump, where lies
Mind prostrate through knowledge owed
To the loveless Power it tries
To withstand, how vain! In flowed

Ever resistless fact:
No more than the passive clay
Disputes the potter's act,
Could the whelmed mind disobey
Knowledge the cataract.

But, perfect in every part,
Has the potter's moulded shape,
Leap of man's quickened heart,
Throe of his thought's escape,
Stings of his soul which dart

Through the barrier of flesh, till keen
She climbs from the calm and clear,
Through turbidity all between,
From the known to the unknown here,
Heaven's 'Shall be,' from Earth's 'Has been'?

Then life is – to wake not sleep,
Rise and not rest, but press
From earth's level where blindly creep
Things perfected, more or less,
To the heaven's height, far and steep,

Where, amid what strifes and storms
May wait the adventurous quest,
Power is Love – transports, transforms
Who aspired from worst to best,
Sought the soul's world, spurned the worms'.

I have faith such end shall be:
From the first, Power was – I knew.
Life has made clear to me
That, strive but for closer view,
Love were as plain to see.

When see? When there dawns a day,
If not on the homely earth,
Then yonder, worlds away,
Where the strange and new have birth,
And Power comes full in play.

Epilogue

At the midnight in the silence of the sleep-time,
When you set your fancies free,
Will they pass to where – by death, fools think, imprisoned –
Low he lies who once so loved you, whom you loved so,
– Pity me?

Oh to love so, be so loved, yet so mistaken!
What had I on earth to do
With the slothful, with the mawkish, the unmanly?
Like the aimless, helpless, hopeless, did I drivel
– Being – who?

One who never turned his back but marched breast forward,
Never doubted clouds would break,
Never dreamed, though right were worsted, wrong would triumph,
Held we fall to rise, are baffled to fight better,
Sleep to wake.

No, at noonday in the bustle of man's work-time
  Greet the unseen with a cheer!
Bid him forward, breast and back as either should be,
'Strive and thrive!' cry 'Speed, – fight on, fare ever
    There as here!'

Poems uncollected by Browning, fugitives, and previously unpublished poems and fragments

[*Conclusion of a Compliment to the Captain*]

We boys are privates in our Regiment's ranks –
'Tis to our Captain that we all owe thanks!

The First-Born of Egypt

That night came on in Egypt with a step
So calmly stealing in the gorgeous train
Of sunset glories flooding the pale clouds
With liquid gold, until at length the glow
Sank to its shadowy impulse and soft sleep
Bent o'er the world to curtain it from life –
Vitality was hushed beneath her wing –
Pomp sought his couch of purple – care-worn grief
Flung slumber's mantle o'er him. At that hour
He in whose brain the burning fever fiend
Held revelry – his hot cheek turned awhile
Upon the cooler pillow. In his cell
The captive wrapped him in his squalid rags,
And sank amid his straw. Circean sleep!
Bathed in thine opiate dew, false hope vacates
Her seat in the sick soul, leaving awhile
Her dreamy fond imaginings – pale fear
His wild misgivings, and the warm life-springs
Flow in their wonted channels – and the train –
The harpy train of care, forsakes the heart.

Was it the passing sigh of the night wind
Or some lorn spirit's wail – that moaning cry
That struck the ear? – 'tis hushed – no! it swells on
On – as the thunder peal when it essays
To wreck the summer sky – that fearful shriek
Still it increases – 'tis the dolorous plaint,
The death cry of a nation –

It was a fearful thing – that hour of night -
I have seen many climes, but that dread hour
Hath left its burning impress on my soul

Never to be erased. Not the loud crash
When the shuddering forest swings to the red bolt,
Or march of the fell earthquake when it whelms
A city in its yawning gulf, could quell
That deep voice of despair. Pharaoh arose
Startled from slumber, and in anger sought
The reason of the mighty rushing throng
At that dark hour around the palace gates,
– And then he dashed his golden crown away
And tore his hair in frenzy when he knew
That Egypt's heir was dead – From every house,
The marbled mansion of regality
To the damp dungeon's walls – gay pleasure's seat
And poverty's bare hut, that cry was heard,
As guided by the Seraph's vengeful arm
The hand of death held on its withering course,
Blighting the hopes of thousands.

I sought the street to gaze upon the grief
Of congregated Egypt – there the slave
Stood by him late his master, for that hour
Made vain the world's distinctions – for could wealth
Or power arrest the woe? – Some were blue
As sculptured marble from the quarry late
Of whom the foot first in the floating dance,
The glowing cheek hued with the deepening flush
In the night revel – told the young and gay.
No kindly moisture dewed their stony eye,
Or damped their ghastly glare – for they felt not.
The chain of torpor bound around the heart
Had stifled it for ever. Tears stole down
The furrowed channels of those withered cheeks
Whose fount had long been chilled, but that night's terr
Had loosed the springs – for 'twas a fearful thing
To see a nation's hope so blasted. One
Pressed his dead child unto his heart – no spot
Of livid plague was nigh – no purple cloud
Of scathing fever – and he struck his brow
To rouse himself from that wild fantasy
Deeming it but a vision of the night.
I marked one old man with his only son
Lifeless within his arms – his withered hand

Wandering o'er the features of his child
Bidding him wake from that long dreary sleep,
And lead his old blind father from the crowd
To the green meadows – but he answered not;
And then the terrible truth flashed on his brain,
And when the throng rolled on some bade him rise
And cling not so unto the dead one there,
Nor voice nor look made answer – he was gone.
But one thought chained the powers of each mind
Amid that night's felt horror – each one owned
In silence the dread majesty – the might
Of Israel's God, whose red hand had avenged
His servants' cause so fearfully –

The Dance of Death

And as they footed it around,
They sang their triumphs o'er mankind!

de Stael

FEVER

Bow to me, bow to me;
Follow me in my burning breath,
Which brings as the simoom destruction and death.
My spirit lives in the hectic glow
When I bid the life streams tainted flow
In the fervid sun's deep brooding beam
When seething vapours in volumes steam,
And they fall – the young, the gay – as the flower
'Neath the fiery wind's destructive power.
This day I have gotten a noble prize –
There was one who saw the morning rise,
And watched fair Cynthia's golden streak
Kiss the misty mountain peak,
But I was there, and my poisonous flood
Envenomed the gush of the youth's warm blood.
They hastily bore him to his bed,
But o'er him Death his swart pennons spread:
The skillèd leech's art was vain,
Delirium revelled in each vein.
I marked each deathly change in him;

I watched each lustrous eye grow dim,
The purple cloud on his deep swollen brow,
The gathering death sweat's chilly flow,
The dull dense film obscure the eye,
Heard the last quick gasp and saw him die.

PESTILENCE

My spirit has passed on the lightning's wing
O'er city and land with its withering;
In the crowded street, in the flashing hall
My tramp has been heard: they are lonely all.
A nation has swept at my summons away
As mists before the glare of day.
See how proudly reigns my hand
In the blackening heaps on the surf-beat strand
Where the rank grass grows in deserted streets
Where the terrified stranger no passer meets
And all around the putrid air
Gleams lurid and red in Erinyes' stare
Where silence reigns, where late swelled the lute,
Thrilling lyre, mellifluous flute.
There if my prowess ye would know
Seek ye – and bow to your rival low.

AGUE

Bow to me, bow to me;
My influence is in the freezing deeps
Where the icy power of torpor sleeps,
Where the frigid waters flow
My marble chair is more cold below;
When the Grecian braved the Hellespont's flood
How did I curdle his fevered blood,
And sent his love in tumescent wave
To meet with her lover an early grave.
When Hellas' victor sought the rush
Of the river to lave in its cooling gush,
Did he not feel my iron clutch
When he fainted and sank at my algid touch?
These are the least of the trophies I claim –
Bow to me then, and own my fame.

MADNESS

Hear ye not the gloomy yelling
Or the tide of anguish swelling,
Hear ye the clank of fetter and chain,
Hear ye the wild cry of grief and pain,
Followed by the shuddering laugh
As when fiends the life-blood quaff?
See! see that band,
See how their bursting eyeballs gleam,
As the crocodiles' when crouched in the stream,
In India's sultry land.
Now they are seized in the rabies fell,
Hark! 'tis a shriek as from fiends of hell;
Now there is a plaining moan,
As the flow of the sullen river –
List! there is a hollow groan.
Doth it not make e'en *you* to shiver –
These are they struck of the barbs of my quiver.
Slaves before my haughty throne,
Bow then, bow to me alone.

CONSUMPTION

'Tis for me, 'tis for me;
Mine the prize of Death must be;
My spirit is o'er the young and gay
As on snowy wreaths in the bright noonday.
They wear a melting and vermeille flush
E'en while I bid their pulses hush,
Hueing o'er their dying brow
With the spring of health's best roseate glow
When the lover watches the full dark eye
Robed in tints of ianthine dye,
Beaming eloquent as to declare
The passions that deepen the glories there.
The frost in its tide of dazzling whiteness,
As Juno's brow of crystal brightness,
Such as the Grecian's hand could give
When he bade the sculptured marble 'live,'
The ruby suffusing the Hebe cheek,
The pulses that love and pleasure speak
Can his fond heart claim but another day,
And the loathsome worm on her form shall prey.

She is scathed as the tender flower,
When mildews o'er its chalice lour.
Tell me not of her balmy breath,
Its tide shall be shut in the fold of death;
Tell me not of her honied lip,
The reptile's fangs shall its fragrance sip.
Then will I say triumphantly
Bow to the deadliest – bow to me!

[*Epigram on School Days*]

Within those walls, and near that house of glass,
Did I three years of hapless childhood pass –
Damned undiluted misery it was!

Impromptu on Hearing a Sermon by the Rev. T. R— Pronounced 'Heavy'

... A *Heavy* Sermon! – Sure the error's great –
For not a word Tom uttered *had its weight.*

Sonnet

Eyes, calm beside thee, (Lady couldst thou know!)
   May turn away thick with fast-gathering tears:
I glance not where all gaze: thrilling and low
   Their passionate praises reach thee – my cheek wears
Alone no wonder when thou passest by;
Thy tremulous lids bent and suffused reply
To the irrepressible homage which doth glow
   On every lip but mine: if in thine ears
Their accents linger – and thou dost recall
   Me as I stood, still, guarded, very pale,
Beside each votarist whose lighted brow
Wore worship like an aureole, 'O'er them all
   My beauty,' thou wilt murmur, 'did prevail
Save that one only': – Lady couldst thou know!

[*Lines to the Memory of James Dow*]

Words we might else have been compelled to say
In silence to our hearts, great love, great praise,
Of thee, our father, have been freely said
By those whom none shall blame; and while thy life
Endures, a beauteous thing in their record,
We may desist; but thou art not alone:
A part of those thou lovedst here so well
Repose beside thee, and the Eyes that saw
Thy daily course of good could never see
The light their presence cast upon thy path:
Soft sanctuary-tapers of thy house
Close-curtained when the Priest came forth; on these
Let peace be, peace on thee our Mother too!
Serenest Spirit; do we vainly dream
Some portion of the constant joy you spread
Around you living, comforts even yet
The Child that never knew you, and the Girl
In whom your gentle soul seemed born again
To bless us longer? Peace like yours be ours
Till the same quiet home receive us all!

A Forest Thought

In far Esthonian solitudes
The parent-firs of future woods
Gracefully, airily spire at first
Up to the sky, by the soft sand nurst:
Self-sufficient are they, and strong
With outspread arms, broad, level and long;
But soon in the sunshine and the storm
They darken, changing fast their form –
Low boughs fall off, and in the bole
Each tree spends all its strenuous soul –
Till the builder gazes wistfully
Such noble ship-mast wood to see,
And cares not for its soberer hue,
Its rougher bark and leaves more few.

But just when beauty passes away
And you half regret it could not stay,
For all their sap and vigorous life, –
Under the shade, secured from strife
A seedling springs – the forest tree
In miniature, and again we see
The delicate leaves that will fade one day,
The fan-like shoots that will drop away,
The taper stem a breath could strain –
Which shall foil one day the hurricane:
We turn from this infant of the copse
To the parent-firs, – in their waving tops
To find some trace of the light green tuft
A breath could stir, – in the bole aloft
Column-like set against the sky,
The spire that flourished airily
And the marten bent as she rustled by.

So shall it be, dear Friends, when days
Pass, and in this fair child we trace
Goodness, full-formed in you, though dim
Faint-budding, just astir in him:
When rudiments of generous worth
And frankest love in him have birth,
We'll turn to love and worth full-grown,
And learn their fortune from your own.
Nor shall we vainly search to see
His gentleness – simplicity –
Not lost in your maturer grace –
Perfected, but not changing place.

May this grove be a charmed retreat . . .
May northern winds and savage sleet
Leave the good trees untouched, unshorn
A crowning pride of woods unborn:
And gracefully beneath their shield
May the seedling grow! All pleasures yield
Peace below and grace above,
The glancing squirrels' summer love
And the brood-song of the cushat-dove!

[*Transcriptions from the 'Anacreontea'*]

I. OF HIS LYRE; THAT IT WILL PLAY ONLY OF LOVE

I fain would sing of Cadmus king,
And fain of Atrean banqueting;
But still the harp through every string
Doth echo only love –
I brake the chord that erewhile sent
That note, and changed the instrument;
And how Alcides' labours went
I sang with fire, – but still the lyre
  Gave back the word of Love.
So farewell all heroical
Rare spirits!, for the lyre withal
  Can sound but only love.

II. TO HIS COMRADES, TO JUSTIFY HIMSELF IN DRINKING

The earth drinks herself dark with the fast-falling rain, –
And the roots of the trees drink her moisture again,
And the sea drinks the winds, till she welters aloud –
And the sun drinks the sea, till he sets in a cloud,
And the moon drinks the sun, till her circle is plain.
Then o wherefore, my friends, are ye angry and curst,
Because *I* too would drink, while the world is athirst?

III. BATHYLLUS' BEAUTY

In this shadow of Bathyllus
I will sit. The tree is fair
And hath shaken its smooth hair
From a branch of gentle bowing,
And Persuasion's fount doth fill us
With a murmur, near him flowing.
Who then, marking what is felt here,
Would pass by so sweet a shelter?

IV. TO HIMSELF, TO DROWN HIS CARES

When I drink the red red wine
  All my cares are sleeping –
What to me are thoughts that pine?
  What is moan and weeping?
I must die, whate'er I choose –
But why should life be turned from use?
  Drink we then the red red wine
    Bacchus hath in keeping!
  While we drink it, by that sign,
    All our cares are sleeping.

V. WINE THE POOR MAN'S WEALTH

Where Bacchus enters bright and bold
  The Cares are sleeping in a throng!
I seem to hold all Croesus' gold
  And choose to lift a noble song!
I lie on ground, with ivy crowned –
On all things with my soul I tread.
Take wines! For me, I drink instead!
  So fetch the goblet, boy of mine,
  For it is better, by this wine
  To be dead drunk than dead.

VI. CUPID BEAUTY'S SLAVE

O Love, the Muses bound him
And having brightly crowned him
  They gave him up for Beauty's slave.
Now Cytherea searches
With ransoms to repurchase
  And loose the chain of Love the slave.
But grant a freeing finger,
He will not go but linger –
  For Love hath learnt to be a slave.

VII. THE NEST OF LOVE

Thou indeed, little swallow,
A sweet yearly comer,
Art building a hollow
New nest every summer –
And then dost depart
Where no gazing can follow
Past Memphis, down Nile!
But Love all the while
Through the cold winter-weeks
Builds his nest in my heart.
As one passion takes flight
Another, oh swallow,
Is an egg warm and white,
And another is callow.
And all day and all night
Chirp the large gaping beaks!
And the loves who are older
Help the young and the poor loves,
And the young loves grown bolder
Increase as before loves –
Why what can be done?
If a noise comes from one,
Can I bear all this rout of a hundred and more loves?

VIII. TO A LADY, WITH AN OLD MAN'S LOVE-GIFT

Fly me not, fair creature,
  Though my locks are grey!
  Nor my love-vows cast away,
For thy flower of nature!
Let *these* garlands make thee sage!
  Twining as the truth is,
  Roses red as youth is,
With lilies white as age.

Sweetest, do not fly me
  Though my hair is grey,
Nor my love deny me

Though the flower of youthhood may
Bloom within thee fresh today!
Mark the garlands in our sight!
How with scarlet roses they
Entwine the lilies white.

IX. TO THE GRASSHOPPER

Blessing on thee, Grasshopper,
When upon the treetops fair
Thou dost sing as blithe as king
Drinking softly the small dew! –
For thine be all things which be new –
All things seen in open meadows,
All things brought from forest shadows!
And shepherds call thee sweetest one
Who dost harm in naught to none!
And mortals call thee precious comer,
And sweet prophet of the summer!
While the Muses do approve thee,
And their Phoebus, who doth love thee,
Did that fluted singing make thee!
Earthborn, wise . . . of slumberous fashion . . .
But sans body, blood, and passion,
For a god we almost take thee!

X. AGE AND MIRTH

I love to see a glad old man!
I love to see a young one dance –
Or even an old one, if he can.
Let him! Though white hairs perchance
Round his wrinkled brows be hung,
His foot shall prove his soul still young.

XI. THE POWER OF BEAUTY

Horns to bulls, gave nature,
Likewise hooves to horses:
Hares their footed swiftness,
Lions – teeth wide-yawning:
To the fishes – swimming,
To the birds their plume-play.
Women – no more had she!
What then? She gives Beauty.

[*'She was fifteen – had great eyes'*]

She was fifteen – had great eyes
Deep with dreams of paradise.
Not a paradise divine,
Nor Eve's Eden, nor yours, nor mine,
But the sort of thing made good
'Twixt warm weather and young blood.
As 'twixt sun and marsh the flies
Quicken in large companies,
'Twixt her fancies took its station,
Half corruption's half creation.
Yet she thought no harm, not she,
Meant no malice certainly,
Only she was weak and vain,
Lazy and afraid of pain:
Sat at open windows still
To watch the gold go up the hill,
Stood at open doors as still
To watch the gold come down the hill,
Lolled on couches with drawn-in
Feet, and knees to prop her chin,
Dreaming, dreaming – till one said,
'Get some work, thou idle head!'
Then she put out a white hand
Blandly to the basket-stand,
And you heard the stitches creep
Up the long hem, half asleep;

Little stitches with a murmur
Each one drawing past the former,
Till the staring face of Day
In the window paled away.

[*Aeschylus' Soliloquy*]

I am an old and solitary man,
And now at set of sun in Sicily
I sit down in the middle of this plain,
Which drives between the mountains and the sea
Its blank of nature. If a traveller came,
Seeing my bare bald skull and my still brows
And massive features coloured to a stone –
The tragic mask of a humanity
Whose part is played to an end, – he might mistake me
For some god Terminus set on these flats,
Or broken marble Faunus. Let it be.
Life has ebbed from me – I am on dry ground –
All sounds of life I held so thunderous sweet
Shade off to silence – all the perfect shapes,
Born of perception and men's images,
Which thronged against the outer rim of earth
And hung with floating faces over it,
Grow dim and dimmer – all the motions drawn
From Beauty in action which spun audibly
My brain round in a rapture, have grown still.
There's a gap 'twixt me and the life once mine,
Now others' and not mine, which now roars off
In gradual declination – till at last
I hear it in the distance droning small
Like a bee at sunset. Ay, and that bee's hum,
The buzzing fly, and mouthing of the grass
Cropped slowly near me by some straying sheep
Are strange to me with life – and separate from me
The outside of my being – I myself
Grow to the silence, fasten to the calm
Of inorganic nature . . . sky and rocks –
I shall pass on into their unity
When dying down into impersonal dusk.

Ah ha – these flats are wide!
The prophecy which said the house would fall
And thereby crush me, must bring down the sky,
The only roof above me where I sit,
Or ere it prove its oracle today.
Stand fast, ye pillars of the constant Heavens,
As Life doth in me – I who did not die
That day in Athens when the people's scorn
Hissed toward the sun as if to darken it,
Because my thoughts burned too much for the eyes
Over my head, because I spoke my Greek
Too deep down in my soul to suit their ears.
Who did not die to see the solemn vests
Of my white chorus round the thymele
Flutter like doves, and sweep back like a cloud
Before the shrill-lipped people . . . but stood calm
And cold, and felt the theatre wax hot
With mouthing whispers . . . the man Aeschylus
Is grey, I fancy – and his wrinkles ridge
The smoothest of his phrases – or the times
Have grown too polished for this old rough work –
We have no Sphinxes in the Parthenon
Nor any flints at Delphos – or, forsooth,
I think the Sphinxes wrote this Attic Greek –
Our Sophocles hath something more than this
Cast out on – their smile – I would not die
At this time by the crushing of a house
Who lived that Day out . . . I would go to death
With voluntary and majestic steps,
Jove thundering on the right hand. Let it be.

I am an old and solitary man.
Mine eyes feel dimly out the setting sun
Which drops its great red fruit of bitterness
Today as other days, as every day,
Within the patient waters. What do I say?
I whistle out my scorn against the sun
Who knelt his trilogy, morn, noon and night,
And set this tragic world against the sun –
Forgive me, great Apollo. – Bitter fruit
I think we never found that holy sun
Or ere with conjurations of our hands

Drove up the saltness of our hearts to it
A blessed fruit, a full Hesperian fruit
Which the fair sisters with their starry eyes
Did warm to scarlet bloom. O holy sun,
My eyes are weak and cannot hold thee round!
But in my large soul there is room for thee –
All human wrongs and shames cast out from it, –
And I invite thee, sun, to sphere thyself
In my large soul, and let my thoughts in white
Keep chorus round thy glory. Oh, the days
In which I sat upon Hymettus hill,
Ilissus seeming louder: and the groves
Of blessed olive, thinking of their use,
A little tunicked child, and felt my thoughts
Rise past the golden bees against thy face,
Great sun upon the sea. The City lay
Beneath me like an eaglet in an egg,
The beak and claws shut whitely up in calm –
And calm were the great waters – and the hills
Holding at arm's length their unmolten snows
Plunged in the light of Heaven, which trickled back
On all sides, a libation to the world.
There I sat, a child
Half hidden in purple thyme, with knees drawn up
By clasping of my little arms, and cheek
Laid slant across them with obtruded nose,
And full eyes gazing . . . ay, my eyes climbed up
Against the heated metal of thy shield,
Till their persistent look clove through the fire
And struck it into manyfolded fires,
And opened out the secret of the night,
Hid in the day-source Darkness mixed with light.
Then shot innumerous arrows in my eyes
From all sides of the Heavens – so blinding me –
As countless as the norland snowflakes fall
Before the north winds – rapid, wonderful,
Some shafts as bright as sunrays nine times drawn
Through the heart of the sun – some black as night in Hell –
All mixed, sharp, driven against me! And as I gazed
(For I gazed still) I saw the sea and earth
Leap up as wounded by the innumerous shafts,
And hurry round, and whirl into a blot

Across which evermore fell thick the shafts
As norland snow falls thick before the wind,
Until the northmen at the cavern's mouth
Can see no pinetree through. I could see naught,
No earth, no sea, no sky, no sun itself,
Only that arrowy rush of black and white
Across a surf of rainbows infinite
Drove piercing and blinding and astonishing;
And through it all Homerus, the blind man,
Did chant his vowelled music in my brain.
And then it was revealed, it was revealed,
That I should be a priest of the Unseen,
And build a bridge of sounds across the straight
From Heaven to earth, whence all the Gods might walk
Nor bend it with their soles.
And then I saw the Gods tread past me slow
From out the portals of the hungry dark,
And each one as he past breathed in my face
And made me greater. First old Saturn came,
Blind with eternal watches . . . calm and blind . . .
Then Zeus . . . his eagle blinking on his wrist
To his hands' rod of fires: in thunder-rolls
He glode on grandly – while the troop of Prayers
Buzzed dimly in the shadow of his light
With murmurous sounds, and poor beseeching tears.
And Neptune with beard and locks drawn straight
As seaweed – ay, and Pluto with his Dark
Cutting the dark as Lightning cuts the sun
Made individual by intensity.
And then Apollo trenching on the dusk
With a white glory, while the lute he bore
Struck on the air

[*Translation of Dante, 'Purgatory' V, 53–7*]

And sinners were we to the extreme hour;
Then, light from heaven fell, making us aware,
So that, repenting us and pardoned, out
Of life we passed to God, at peace with Him
Who fills the heart with yearning Him to see.

[*To Miss Unger*]

Dear Miss Unger,
You're young: but though younger
You ought to have known that one's ardour it damps,
To have to transmit you these valueless stamps.
The Postman will say, 'All you've done, Miss, is undone:
What goes on in Saint Frisco don't go here in London.'

The 'Moses' of Michael Angelo

And who is He that, sculptured in huge stone,
Sitteth a giant, where no works arrive
Of straining Art, and hath so prompt and live
The lips, I listen to their very tone?
Moses is He – Ay, that, makes clearly known
The chin's thick boast, and brow's prerogative
Of double ray: so did the mountain give
Back to the world that visage, God was grown
Great part of! Such was he when he suspended
Round him the sounding and vast waters; such
When he shut sea on sea o'er Mizraïm.
And ye, his hordes, a vile calf raised, and bended
The knee? This Image had ye raised, not much
Had been your error in adoring Him.

[*On Correggio*]

Could I, heart-broken, reach his place of birth
And stand before his Pictures – could I choose
But own at once 'the sovereign'st thing on earth
Is Parma-city for an inward bruise?'

Ben Karshook's Wisdom

I

'Would a man 'scape the rod?'
Rabbi Ben Karshook saith,
'See that he turn to God
The day before his death.'

'Ay, could a man inquire
When it shall come!' I say.
The Rabbi's eye shoots fire –
'Then let him turn today!'

II

Quoth a young Sadducee:
'Reader of many rolls,
Is it so certain we
Have, as they tell us, souls?'

'Son, there is no reply!'
The Rabbi bit his beard:
'Certain a soul have *I* –
We may have none,' he sneered.

Thus Karshook, the Hiram's-Hammer,
The Right-hand Temple-column,
Taught babes in grace their grammar,
And struck the simple, solemn.

[*A Variation on Lines of Landor*]

An Angel from his Paradise drove Adam:
From mine, a Devil drives me: *thank you, Madam!*

Very Original Poem, written with even a greater endeavour than ordinary after intelligibility, and hitherto only published on the first leaf of the author's son's account-book

'Twas a saying in use with the great Mr Lowndes,
Take all care of the pence and no care of the pounds;
For the pence may escape you like volatile elves,
While the slow solid pounds can take care of themselves.

On Being Defied to Express in a Hexameter: 'You Ought to Sit on the Safety-Valve'

Plane te valvam fas est pressisse salutis,
Aequum est te valvâque, salutis sede, locari;
Convenit in sellâ, valvâ residere salutis,
Omninoque salutis par considere valvâ;
Sedibus est justum valvae mansisse salutis,
Haesisse in valvâ te, sede salutis, oportet;
Est tibi valvis, inque salutis sede, sedendum;
Valvâ, sede salutiferâ super, assidet omnis
Qui discrimen adit, fortem quem numina servant:
Multiplicem versum tu mente, Robertule, figas!

[*Rhyme on Edward Burne-Jones*]

Don't play with sharp tools, these are edge 'uns,
   My Ned Jones!

[*Lines on Swinburne*]

      And now in turn see Swinburne bent
Above his favourite instrument –
      He strikes the trembling wire.
Let horn and flute at once be mute

Before the new lascivious lute,
Little man and great lyre –
I had him there! l-i-a-r!

[*Burlesque for Palgrave on the Pronunciation of 'Metamorphosis'*]

'Twas Goethe taught us all
By diagnosis,
That change in plants we call
Metamorphosis!

[*A Round Robin*]

Loch Luichart, Dingwall, N.B.

Dear Hosmer; or still dearer Hatty –
Mixture of *miele* and of *latte*,
So good and sweet and – somewhat fatty –

While linger still in Rome's old glory
When Scotland lies in cool before ye?
Make haste and come! – quoth Mr Story.

Sculpture is not a thing to sit to
In summertime; do find a fit toe
To kick the clay aside a bit – oh,
Yield to our prayers! quoth Mrs Ditto.

Give comfort to us poor and needy
Who, wanting you, are waiting greedy
Our meat and drink, yourself, quoth Edie.

Nay, though past clay, you chip the Parian,
Throw chisel down! quoth Lady Marian.

Be welcome, as to cow – the fodder-rick!
Excuse the simile! – quoth Sir Roderick.

Say not (in Scotch) 'in troth it canna be' –
But, honey, milk and, indeed, manna be!
Forgive a stranger! – Sarianna B.

Don't set an old acquaintance frowning,
But come and quickly! quoth R. Browning,
For since prodigious fault is found with you,
I – that is, Robin – must be Round with you.

P.S. Do wash your hands, or leave the dirt on,
But leave the tool as Gammer Gurton
Her needle lost, – Lady Ashburton
Thus ends this letter – ease my sick heart,
And come to my divine Loch Luichart!

W. W. Story, his mark X.
Emelyn Story,
Edith Marion Story,
M. Alford.
In order of infraposition
Signatures of
I am, Roderick Murchison,
Sarianna Browning,
Robert Browning,
L. Ashburton.

Helen's Tower

Ἑλένη ἐπὶ πύργῳ

Who hears of Helen's Tower, may dream perchance
How the Greek beauty from the Scaean gate
Gazed on old friends unanimous in hate,
Death-doomed because of her fair countenance.

Hearts would leap otherwise at thy advance,
Lady, to whom this Tower is consecrate!
Like hers, thy face once made all eyes elate,
Yet, unlike hers, was blessed by every glance.

The Tower of Hate is outworn, far and strange:
  A transitory shame of long ago,
  It dies into the sand from which it sprang;
But thine, Love's rock-built Tower, shall fear no change;
  God's self laid stable earth's foundations so,
  When all the morning stars together sang.

Mettle and Metal

Ay, Trochu, in Paris which Prussians environ,
  Has mettle, – but hardly the metal to win:
In vain you protest that 'the man is cast-iron' –
  These five months have taught me he's simply block-tin!

[*Lines for a Gift*]

The gift is small,
The love is all.

The Dogma Triumphant

Epigram on the Voluntary Imprisonment of the Pope as Proving His Infallibility

Dear Herries, let's hope, by impounding your Pope,
  We prove him infallible: *quare?*
Why, if he's in durance, who'll have the assurance
  To hint '*Papa potest errare?*'

[*Reflections on Reading a Life of Dickens*]

In Dickens, sure, philosophy was lacking,
  Since of calamities he counts the crowning
That, young, he had too much to do with Blacking.
  Old, he had not enough to do with ——————.

[*Rhyme for a Child Viewing a Naked Venus in a Painting of 'The Judgement of Paris'*]

He gazed and gazed and gazed and gazed,
Amazed, amazed, amazed, amazed.

[*Impromptu on Richard Wagner*]

Wagner gave six concerts: five
I have managed to survive.
He announces other two:
Stand these – hang me if I do!

[*On Benjamin Disraeli*]

We don't want to fight,
   By Jingo, if we do,
The head I'd like to punch
   Is Beaconsfield the Jew.

[*'Oh Love, Love'*]

I

Oh Love, Love, thou that from the eyes diffusest
Yearning, and on the soul sweet grace inducest –
Souls against whom thy hostile march is made –
Never to me be manifest in ire,
Nor, out of time and tune, my peace invade!
Since neither from the fire –
No, nor the stars – is launched a bolt more mighty
Than that of Aphrodité
Hurled from the hands of Love, the boy with Zeus for sire.

II

Idly, how idly, by the Alpheian river
And in the Pythian shrines of Phoebus, quiver
Blood-offerings from the bull, which Hellas heaps:
While Love we worship not – the Lord of men!
Worship not him, the very key who keeps
Of Aphrodité, when
She closes up her dearest chamber-portals:
– Love, when he comes to mortals,
Wide-wasting, through those deeps of woes beyond the deep!

[*'The blind man to the maiden said'*]

The blind man to the maiden said:
'O thou of hearts the truest,
Thy countenance is hid from me;
Let not my questions anger thee!
Speak, though in words the fewest!

'Tell me what kind of eyes are thine?
Dark eyes, or light ones rather?'
'My eyes are a decided brown
So much, at least – by looking down –
From the brook's glass I gather.'

'And is it red – thy little mouth?
That too the blind must care for!'
'Ah, I would tell that soon to thee,
Only – none yet has told it me.
I cannot answer, therefore!

'But dost thou ask what heart I have
There hesitate I never!
In thine own breast 'tis borne, and so
'Tis thine in weal and thine in woe
For life, for death, – thine ever!'

The Delivery to the Secular Arm: A Scene During the Existence of the Spanish Inquisition at Antwerp, 1570

Therefore the hand of God
Thy sentence with His finger
Hath written, and this tribunal
Consigneth it now straightway
Unto the secular arm.

[*'Thus I wrote in London, musing on my betters'*]

Thus I wrote in London, musing on my betters,
Poets dead and gone: and lo, the critics cried,
'Out on such a boast!' – as if I dreamed that fetters
Binding Dante, bind up – me! as if true pride
Were not also humble!
                                        So I smiled and sighed
As I oped your book in Venice this bright morning,
Sweet new friend of mine! and felt the clay or sand
– Whatsoe'er my soil be, – break – for praise or scorning –
Out in grateful fancies – weeds, but weeds expand
Almost into flowers – held by such a kindly hand!

Terse Verse –

being a contribution to Scottish anthology

Hail, ye hills and heaths of Ecclefechan!
Hail, ye banks and braes of Craigenputtock!
T. Carlyle was born in Ecclefechan,
Jane his wife was born in Craigenputtock:
She – a pearl where eye detect no speck can,
He – ordained to close with and cross-buttock
Cant, the giant – these, O Ecclefechan,
These your glories be, O Craigenputtock!

Gerousios Oinos

I dreamed there was once held a feast:
That lords assembled, most and least,
  And set them down to dine;
Till, eating ended – high of heart
Each guest, – the butler did his part,
  Poured out their proper wine.

Good tipple and of various growth
(You may believe without an oath)
  Glorified every glass:
All drank in honour of the host,
Then – high of heart, – rose least and most,
  And left the room – alas.

For in rushed straightway loon and lout,
Mere servingmen who skulked without:
  'Our masters turn their backs,
And now's the time to taste and try
What meat lords munch, – and, by and by,
  What wine they swill – best smacks.'

So said, so dine: first, hunger spends
Its rage on victual, odds and ends:
  But seeing that rage appeased,
'Now for the lords' wine,' all agree,
'Kept from the like of you and me!
  Wet whistles, chins once greased!

'How! not content with loading crop,
These lords have scarcely left a drop
  In every glass deep-drained!
The niggards mean our feast to prove
A horse-regale! But, one remove
  From wine is water stained.

'Fill up each glass with water! Get
Such flavour as may stick fast yet,
  Fancy shall do the rest!
Besides we boast our private flasks,

Good stiff mundungus, home-brewed casks
  Beating their bottled best!

'So here's your health to watered port!
Thanks: mine is sherry of a sort.
  Claret, though thinnish clear.
My Burgundy's the genuine stuff –
Bettered and bittered just enough
  By mixing it with beer.'

Oh, England (I awoke and laughed)
True wine thy lordly Poets quaffed,
  Yet left – for, what cared they! –
Each glass its heel-tap – flavouring sup
For flunkeys when, to liquor up,
  In swarmed – who, need I say!

[*Translation from Pindar's Seventh Olympian, Epode III*]

And to these Rhodians She, the Sharp-eyed One,
  Gave the supremacy to rule in Art,
  And, nobly-labouring, play the craftsman's part,
Beyond all dwellers underneath the sun.
So that the very ways by which ye pass
  Bore sculpture-living things that walk or creep,
  Like as the life: whence very high, and deep
Indeed, the glory of the Artist was.
For, in the well-instructed Artist, skill –
  However great – receives our greeting
As something greater still
  When unaccompanied by – cheating!

Classicality Applied to Tea-Dealing: A Fancy Inspired by Westbourne Grove

'Try our Hyson!'

When doctors with tirades on Tea affright us,
I think they miss a warning – and a nice one:
We've all heard talk of weeping Heraclitus:
Well, Heraclitus was the son of Hyson!

[*On Singers*]

All sorts of singers have this common vice:
To sing 'mid friends you have to ask them twice!
If you don't ask them, – that's another thing:
Until the judgement-day be sure they'll sing!

Goldoni

Goldoni, – good, gay, sunniest of souls, –
  Glassing half Venice in that verse of thine,
  What though it just reflect the shade and shine
Of common life, nor render as it rolls
Grandeur and gloom? Sufficient for thy scrolls
  Was Carnival: Parini's depths enshrine
  Secrets unsuited to that opaline
Surface of things which laughs along thy shoals.

There throng the People: how they come and go,
  Lisp the soft language, flaunt the bright garb, – see, –
On Piazza, Calle, under Portico,
  And over Bridge! Dear King of Comedy,
Be honoured! Thou who didst love Venice so, –
Venice, and we who love her, all love thee!

[*Rawdon Brown*]

'Tutti ga i so gusti e mi go i mii.'
(*Venetian saying*)

Sighed Rawdon Brown: 'Yes, I'm departing, Toni!
I needs must, just this once before I die,
Revisit England: *Anglus* Brown am I,
Although my heart's Venetian. Yes, old crony –
Venice and London – London's Death the Bony
Compared with Life – that's Venice! What a sky,
A sea, this morning! One last look! Good-bye,
Cà Pesaro! No lion – I'm a coney
To weep! I'm dazzled; 'tis that sun I view
Rippling the . . . the . . . Cospetto, Toni! Down
With carpet-bag and off with valise-straps!
Bella Venezia, non ti lascio più!'
Nor did Brown ever leave her; well, perhaps
Browning, next week, may find himself quite Brown!

[*Couplet for Furnivall on Two Publishers*]

The air one breathes with Smith may be the sharper:
But – save me from Scirocco's heat in Harper!

The Names

Shakespeare! – to such name's sounding, what succeeds
Fitly as silence? Falter forth the spell, –
Act follows word, the speaker knows full well,
Nor tampers with its magic more than needs.
Two names there are: That which the Hebrew reads
With his soul only; if from lips it fell,
Echo, back thundered by earth, heaven and hell,
Would own 'Thou didst create us!' Naught impedes
We voice the other name, man's most of might,
Awesomely, lovingly: let awe and love

Mutely await their working, leave to sight
  All of the issue as – below – above –
  Shakespeare's creation rises: one remove,
Though dread – this finite from that infinite.

The Founder of the Feast

(To Arthur Chappell)

'Enter my palace,' if a prince should say –
  'Feast with the Painters! See, in bounteous row,
  They range from Titian up to Angelo!'
Could we be silent at the rich survey?
A host so kindly, in as great a way
  Invites to banquet, substitutes for show
  Sound that's diviner still, and bids us know
Bach like Beethoven; are we thankless, pray?
  To him whose every guest not idly vaunts,
  'Sense has received the utmost Nature grants,
My cup was filled with rapture to the brim,
  When, night by night – ah, memory, how it haunts! –
  Music was poured by perfect ministrants,
By Hallé, Schumann, Piatti, Joachim.'

[*Folkestone Limerick*]

There was a sky-painter at Folkestone
Whose tone for the sky was egg-yolk's tone:
  This fanciful fellow
  Mistook blue for yellow
So – small was his fame out of Folkestone!

[*Conclusion of a Sonnet on 'Keely's Discovery'*]

All we can dream of loveliness within, –
  All ever hoped for by a will intense, –
  This shall one day be palpable to sense
And earth become to heaven akin.

Why I Am a Liberal

'Why?' Because all I haply can and do,
  All that I am now, all I hope to be, –
  Whence comes it save from fortune setting free
Body and soul the purpose to pursue,
God traced for both? If fetters, not a few,
  Of prejudice, convention, fall from me,
  These shall I bid men – each in his degree
Also God-guided – bear, and gaily too?

But little do or can the best of us:
  THAT LITTLE IS ACHIEVED THROUGH LIBERTY.
Who, then, dares hold – emancipated thus –
  His fellow shall continue bound? Not I,
Who live, love, labour freely, nor discuss
  A brother's right to freedom. That is 'Why.'

[*Lines for the Tomb of Levi Lincoln Thaxter*]

Thou, whom these eyes saw never, – say friends true
Who say my soul, helped onward by my song,
Though all unwittingly, has helped thee too?
I gave but of the little that I knew:
How were the gift requited, while along
Life's path I pace, couldst thou make weakness strong,
Help me with knowledge – for Life's Old, Death's New!

[*Impromptu Lines to Greet Marie Bancroft*]

Her advent was not hailed with shouts,
Nor banners, garlands, cymbals, drums;
The trees breathed gently sighs of love,
And whispered softly, 'Hush! she comes.'

Last Poem

I dined at Natorp's yester-eve:
And was it not a stab,
When he said 'She can't come. Don't grieve!
She dines with Mrs Gab.'

Epps

Asks anyone – 'Where's a tag for *steps*?'
I answer – 'Waiting its time
Till somebody versed in the English tongue
Shall start at the challenge, cry "Unsung
Till now, and all for want of a rhyme,
Is the prowess of Kentish Epps?"'

Two hundred and eighty years ago
Befell the siege of Ostend;
Epps soldiered it there: and, hew or hack
At his breast as the enemy might, his back
Got never a scratch: yet life must end
Somehow, – Epps ended – so!

He had lost an eye on the walls, look out
No longer could Epps: said he –
'Give me Saint George's cross – our flag
To carry: I can't see them – foes brag:
At all events they shall soon see me,
Knight and knave, lord and lout!'

'Epps got loose again!' yelped the curs:
  'At him – the blind side best!
Together as one – in a rush, on a heap,
Buffet the maimed old bull! Fame's cheap
  This morn for whoso has mind to wrest
Yon flag from his hold, win spurs!'

As a big wave bursts on a rock, broke they
  On bannerman Epps: as staunch
The drowned rock stands, but emerging feels
Weeds late on its head lie loose at its heels,
  So left bare, swirl – stript; root and branch,
Of his band stood Epps – laughed gay:

'I with my flag – that's well, no fear
  The colours stick to the staff:
But the staff 'tis a mere hand holds – lets fall
If there stab me or shoot one knave of them all:
  To hinder which game –' I hear Epps laugh –
'Stick, flag, to a new staff – here!'

And off in a trice from the staff that's wood,
  And on to a staff that's flesh,
Tears Epps and ties me tight round his breast
The flag in a red swathe: 'Here's the vest
  For my lifelong wear; at the foe afresh!
Staff, show flag's hardihood!'

Whereat, in a twinkling, man and horse
  Went down – one, two and three,
And how many more? But they shot and slashed:
Two bullets have riddled, two sword-blades gashed
  The staff through the flag, – leave free
To despoilers, – you think, – a corse?

No! Back from his slayers, staggeringly
  But, staff-like stout to the last,
Up to his mates – of the checked advance –
Reels Epps, his soul in his countenance,
  As he falters 'See! Flag to the staff sticks fast,
And, flag saved, staff may die!'

And die did Epps, with his English round:
Not so the fame of the feat:
For Donne and Dekker, brave poets and rare,
Gave it honour and praise: and I join the pair
With a heart that's loud though my voice compete
As a pipe with their trumpet-sound!

[*Lines for a Painting by Leighton*]

Yellow and pale as ripened corn
Which Autumn's kiss frees, – grain from sheath, –
Such was her hair, while her eyes beneath
Showed Spring's faint violets freshly born.

[*Suggestion for a Telegraphic Birthday Greeting*]

Bancroft, the message-bearing wire,
Which flashes my 'All hail' today,
Moves slowlier than the heart's desire
That what hand pens, tongue's self might say.

[*On Ignaz Moscheles*]

Hail to the man who upward strives
Ever in happy unconcern:
Whom neither blame nor praise contrives
From his own nature's path to turn.

On and still on, the journey went,
Yet has he kept us all in view –
Working in Age with Youth's intent,
In living – fresh, in loving – true.

[*Lines for the Jubilee Window*]

Fifty years' flight! Wherein should he rejoice
  Who hailed their birth, who as they die decays?
This – England echoes his attesting voice:
  'Wondrous and well – thanks, Ancient Thou of Days!'

[*'Sipping grog one day at sea'*]

Sipping grog one day at sea,
Says the Captain – 'Don't tell me!
Talk of "men's equality!"
T'ain't in nature: what's her rule?
Choose a crew, say – twelve about:
Why, before your first week's out
One they'll flatter, one they'll flout,
  One's their king and one's their fool!'
'What's the use' (says I) 'of rappin'
Nasty oaths out' (says I) 'Cap'n?
Here's my answer, "Does it happen
  That your crew cry, 'No such thing!'
You, the chap that knows, play Mummy
  For your father was a chummy . . .".'

Replies to Challenges to Rhyme

If ever you meet a rhinoceros
And a tree be in sight,
Climb quick! for his might
Is a match for the gods: he could toss Eros!

Hang your kickshaws and your made-dishes,
Give me bread and cheese and radishes –
Even stalish bread and baddish cheese.

You may at Pekin as at Poggibonsi,
Instead of tricksy priest, a dodgy bonze see.

Ah, massa, such a fiery oss
As him I rode at Timbuctoo!
Him would not suit a quiet boss!
Him kick, him rear, and him buck too!

Venus, sea froth's child,
Playing old gooseberry,
Marries Lord Rosebery
To Miss de Rothschild!

'Horns make the buck' cried rash Burdett;
And then used speech befitting Timbuctoo:
'I would the horns of the creature met
I' the belly o' the king and so made him buck too!'

[*Dialogue between Father and Daughter*]

F. Then, what do you say to the poem of Mizpah?
D. An out-and-out masterpiece – that's what it is, Pa!

[*Rhyming Exercises*]

He a recreant; in me a true knight thou dub'st, and
'On its own bottom let every tub stand.'

He for his volume meant
To get some emolument.

The Isle's Enchantress

Wind-wafted from the sunset, o'er the swell
  Of Summer's slumbrous sea, herself asleep,
Came shoreward, in her iridescent shell
  Cradled, the isle's enchantress. You who keep
A drowsy watch beside her – watch her well!

To Edward FitzGerald

I chanced upon a new book yesterday:
I opened it, and, where my finger lay
'Twixt page and uncut page, these words I read
– Some six or seven at most – and learned thereby
That you, FitzGerald, whom by ear and eye
She never knew, 'thanked God my wife was dead.'

Ay, dead! and were yourself alive, good Fitz,
How to return you thanks would task my wits:
Kicking you seems the common lot of curs –
While more appropriate greeting lends you grace:
Surely to spit there glorifies your face –
Spitting – from lips once sanctified by Hers.

Response to a Translation by Longfellow

What seems a soul where Love's outside the porch,
A house by night with neither fire nor torch.

[*Inscription for a Sketch*]

Here I'm gazing, wide awake,
Robert Browning, no mistake!

Notes

Browning's editions are often referred to in the notes by the dates of publication. Collected-edition references are:

1849	the two-volume *Poems*, Chapman & Hall, 1849
1863	the three-volume *The Political Works,* Chapman & Hall, 1863
1868	the six-volume *The Poetical Works,* Smith, Elder, 1868
1888	the sixteen-volume *The Poetical Works,* Smith, Elder, 1888–9 (the first impression of this edition)

Some secondary works are referred to by authors' or editors' surnames and short titles. Reference to the bibliography in 'Further Reading' should make these self-explanatory. Other abbreviations used are:

BIS	*Browning Institute Studies*
BNL	*Browning Newsletter*
BSN	*Browning Society Notes*
JEGP	*Journal of English and Germanic Philology*
MLN	*Modern Language Notes*
MLQ	*Modern Language Quarterly*
MLR	*Modern Language Review*
MP	*Modern Philology*
N&Q	*Notes and Queries*
OED	*Oxford English Dictionary*
PMLA	*Publications of the Modern Language Association*
PQ	*Philological Quarterly*
SBHC	*Studies in Browning and His Circle*
SP	*Studies in Philology*
TLS	*Times Literary Supplement*
TQ	*University of Toronto Quarterly*
VNL	*Victorian Newsletter*
VP	*Victorian Poetry*
VS	*Victorian Studies*

References to Shakespeare are to the Globe edition; to classical literature, normally to the Loeb edition; to *The Ring and the Book,* to the Penguin English Poets edition.

Fifine at the Fair

First published by Smith, Elder very early in June 1872; no second edition was called for. Revisions for *1888* were slight. The printers' *MS.* is in the Library of Balliol College. It has some messy stretches, interpolated passages and paste-ins, but is generally fairly clean, appearing to be a copy of an earlier draft. Its verse paragraphs are generally those of the printed poem, but the paragraph numbers were late additions to the *MS.* Within individual lines, extensive revisions were made in proof, affecting most lines in the poem, the revisions at that stage being very much more numerous than is usual even for Browning (for Browning's gratitude to Joseph Milsand, whose suggestions prompted many of the revisions, see Marie T. de S. Blanc, 'A French Friend of Browning – Joseph Milsand', *Scribner's Magazine* XX, 1896, 111). Browning's note in the *MS.* states that the poem was begun in December 1871 (the month in which *Prince Hohenstiel-Schwangau* was published), and finished on 11 May 1872. The latter date is, since the poem was published only three weeks later, in all probability that on which Browning finished with the proofs; the *MS.* was completed probably early in April, as Browning told Domett (*Diary,* 52–3). Browning had declared on 29 December 1871 that he was half-way through the poem, on 25 January 1872 that he had 'all but finished' it, and on 30 March that it was '*almost* done'.

In the *MS.* the Epilogue is followed by some lines in Greek from the *Choephori* (*Libation-Bearers*) of Aeschylus (816–18): 'by his mysterious utterance he bringeth darkness o'er men's eyes by night, and by day he is no whit clearer'. The quotation is dated 5 November 1872. A second quotation, written in later, is from the *Thesmophoriazusae* of Aristophanes (1128–31): 'What avails me? Shall I make a speech?/ His savage nature could not take it in./ True wit and wisdom were but labour lost/ On such a rude barbarian.' Browning had expected that readers would find the poem difficult: he told Domett in April that *Fifine* was 'the most metaphysical and boldest [poem] he had written since *Sordello*', and that he 'was very doubtful as to its reception'. On the title-page of the *MS.*, moreover, Browning quoted, in Greek, lines 11–13 of Pindar's *Olympian* 13: 'Fair is the tale I have to tell, and courage that maketh straight for the mark prompteth my tongue to speak; it is a hard struggle to quell one's inborn nature'; and also, from the *Acharnians* of Aristophanes, 488: 'Take courage! Forward! March! O well done, heart!' The exhortations give yet further evidence of the importance the poem had for Browning.

It was probably while on holiday in Brittany in the summer of 1865 that Browning saw the woman who suggested the Fifine of his poem at the Fair of Saint Gille. Browning took his motto from Molière's *Dom Juan* or *Le Festin de Pierre* (1665), but other than the name of Elvire and the reputation of his poem's speaker (who is, one assumes, Don Juan) for casuistry and profligacy, Browning took little else. *Fifine at the Fair* upset Rossetti enormously, the poet feeling that Browning had joined what he saw as the conspiracy against him, and W. C. DeVane, 'The Harlot and the Thoughtful Young Man', *SP* XXIX, 1932, 463–84, suggested that Rossetti had probably been right to see as a source of Browning's poem, and as an object of attack there, his own *Jenny*, which had been central in Robert Buchanan's attack on Rossetti's supposed sensuality, *The Fleshly School of Poetry* (October 1871).

In her *Life*, Mrs Orr had suggested that 'some leaven of bitterness' (282) working within Browning played its part in the bitterness and 'perplexing cynicism' of *Fifine at the Fair*, and W. O. Raymond, 'Browning's Dark Mood: A Study of *Fifine at the Fair*', *SP* XXXI, 1934, 578–99 (reprinted in *The Infinite Moment*, 105–28), stressed the probable biographical influence on the poem of the awkward situation that had developed between Browning and Lady Ashburton – on which, see T. L. Hood, 'Browning and Lady Ashburton', in *Letters*, 325–38. Hood's view, the traditional one, was that Browning had proposed to Lady Ashburton, but in such a manner that she had no choice but to refuse him, and that Browning was distressed deeply at what he regarded as a 'defection from constancy' in his relation with Mrs Browning. W. Whitla, 'Browning and the Ashburton Affair', *BSN* II, No. 2, 1972, 12–41, has argued impressively that in fact Lady Ashburton proposed to Browning; but at any rate there was a bitter row between the two, and the scars left on Browning may well have contributed to the mood of *Fifine*.

Fifine at the Fair remained one of Browning's least popular poems until fairly recently when it has attracted a good deal of interest and respect. J. T. Nettleship provided a useful summary in his essay in *Robert Browning: Essays and Thoughts*, John Lane, 1895, 221–67. Criticism includes: Cook, *Browning's Lyrics*, 115–22; Drew, *The Poetry of Browning*, 303–21; Irvine and Honan, *The Book, the Ring, and the Poet*, 462–70; J. L. Kendall, 'Browning's *Fifine at the Fair*: Meaning and Method', *VNL* 22, 1962, 16–18; Melchiori, 'Browning's Don Juan', *Browning's Poetry of Reticence*, 158–87; C. de L. Ryals, 'Browning's Amphibian: Don Juan at Home', *Essays in Criticism* XIX, 1969, 210–17; C. C. Watkins, 'The "Abstruser Themes" of Browning's *Fifine at the Fair*', *PMLA* LXXIV, 1959, 426–37.

[MOTTO]

The translation from Molière is Browning's.
6 *Attempts defence*] Falls to his fence *MS*.
7 *chap* jaw.
11 *erst* formerly (archaism).

PROLOGUE

Among other things, 'Amphibian' reflects Browning's new-found love of swimming.
16 *Like soul* The butterfly is a conventional artistic symbol for the soul.
58 *disport* relaxation (in this sense, an archaism).
73 *she* While there has been dispute as to the speaker of 'Amphibian', most readers take it that Browning speaks and that 'she' is the spirit of Mrs Browning.

FIFINE AT THE FAIR

10 *Pornic and Saint Gille* small Breton ports just south of the Loire. Browning spent some holidays in the area.
11 *parterre* level space with flower-beds in it.
12 *Bateleurs, baladines* entertainers at the Fair: jugglers and dancers.
14 *O pleasant land of France* quoting a song erroneously supposed to have been

sung by Mary Queen of Scots on leaving France. The French poet Béranger used the words as refrain for his song *Les Adieux de Marie Stuart.*

24 *Tricot* knitted material (the usage here is the earliest recorded in *OED*).

fines refines, thins.

27 *Perpend* ponder (archaism).

28 In Tennyson's *Holy Grail* (1869), as in Malory, Gawain's frivolousness denies him a vision of the Grail.

38 *Frenetic* frantic.

47 *losels* rascals (archaism).

53–5 the first of several triplets in the poem. Most of these triplets and the poem's two unrhymed lines result from manuscript interpolations or revisions (as here, where line 55 was added later).

90 *windlestraws* withered stalks of grass.

92 *blow-bell-down*] thistle-down *MS., 1872.* (*OED* records 'blow-ball': 'globular seeding head of the dandelion and allied plants', but not 'blow-bell'.)

102 *pique us* take pride in.

125 *Twin-headed Babe, and Human Nondescript* In 1803 at Bartholomew Fair, there were exhibited a two-headed calf and a monstrous fish called the 'Nondescript'. Alternatively, the line may refer to the original Siamese twins, Chang and Eng (1811–74), who, in 1869, had resumed exhibiting themselves in Europe; and to another nineteenth-century monster called 'Nondescript', a fake supposed to be a stuffed human head that was in fact the contorted face of a red howler monkey.

129 *Golden Fleece* The Order of the Golden Fleece was an Order of Knighthood instituted in 1430 by the Duke of Burgundy.

151 *swarth* swarthiness.

159 *bistre* brown.

163 *almandines* garnets of violet or purplish colour.

169 *quarte and tierce* fencing positions.

190 *flavorous* 'fragrant, odorous' (Johnson's *Dictionary*).

wot know (archaism).

202 *sick Louis* Louis XI ('Louis Onze' in line 205), French King 1461–83.

210 *Helen* Helen of Troy, given to Paris by her protectress, the goddess Aphrodite (Venus). W. Whitla suggests (private communication) that Browning's Helen and Cleopatra owe debts to Tennyson's *Dream of Fair Women.*

world's worst night and storm Browning is probably thinking of the Messenger's speech in the *Agamemnon* of Aeschylus, 636–80, and the storm that hit the fleet as the heroes returned from Troy.

211 *Lady Venus* a medievalism.

216 *Beldame* old woman.

225 *haught* haughty (archaism).

234 *pent-house* overhanging roof.

239 *Besprent* besprinkled (archaism).

246 *enough's a feast* 'enough is as good as a feast' (proverbial).

248 *bird* girl.

253 *imposes* places authoritatively.

259 *paragon* match.

262 *braving* challenging.

263 *blinking* turning the eyes away from (archaism).

her Helen of Troy.

263–4 *Troy-town beach/The purple prows of Greece* glancing allusion to 'Was this the face that launched a thousand ships ...' Rossetti's *Troy Town* (1870) is probably also in Browning's mind, especially since he suggested the subject to Rossetti (see Curle, *Robert Browning and Julia Wedgwood*, 78–9).

265 *seigneur* lord.

270 *Quality* people of high rank or social position (archaism, vulgar). Don Juan speaks sardonically.

275 *nice* discriminating, sensitive.

291 *quintal* a hundred pounds, or a hundredweight, or a hundred kilograms.

305 *certain myth* The myth as given here was used by Euripides in *Helen.*

mused mused over (the transitive verb is rare).

334 *extern* external.

335 *bodies show me minds* Browning is probably thinking of Plato, *Symposium* 210.

336 *the outward sign, the inward grace* 'an outward and visible sign of an inward and spiritual grace' (Catechism in *The Book of Common Prayer*).

348 *facette* facet (obsolete alternative English form, but also the French word).

358 *adamantine* in this context, 'magnetic'.

360 *beaks* prows.

362 *Asian* The point of the word here remains unexplained.

Ptolemaic witch Cleopatra, daughter of the Ptolemies.

366 *oriel* 'Sometimes vaguely put for *stained-glass*' (*OED*).

371 *lozenged* divided into diamond-shaped pieces.

374 *sherd* fragment.

375 *mope* one that mopes.

381 *Pariah* outcast (technically, low-caste Hindu of South India).

Nautch East-Indian dancing-girl.

439 *Three-times-three* For witches, three is a magic number.

445 *boots* use is it.

469 *graved* engraved.

482 *white-night* sleepless night (French *nuit blanche*).

483 *Solon* Athenian statesman and lawgiver; one of the Seven Sages of Greece.

485 *seemed her . . . meant her*] sounded . . . echoed *MS.*, *1872*.

486 *annoy, for cause – calm*] annoy could cause cold *MS.*, *1872*.

acquist acquisition (archaism).

501 *the fen-fire dancing*] brave Jack-o'-Lantern *MS.*

fen-fire a will of the wisp (ignis fatuus, jack o' lantern): flame-like phosphorescence over swampy ground.

504 *cribs* pilfers (colloquialism).

505 *squibs* fireworks.

507 *fizgig* light, frivolous woman.

513 *pride* object of pride.

518 *Rafael* painting by the great Italian artist (1483–1520).

524–5 *sell he must/His birthright for a mess of pottage* as Esau did (Genesis xxv 33).

551 *Doré* Gustave Doré (1833–83), fashionable illustrator and engraver.

556 *meet*] turn *MS.*, *1872*.

565 *this-day-year* a year ago.

566 *pochade* rough sketch (French; *OED* records only the usage here).

617 *me? I dare to ask*] me, – in tragic phrase *MS.* (The variant suggests a glancing allusion to Desdemona in the 'brothel' scene in *Othello* ['Unpin me here' – IV. 3. 35]; 'alabaster' in line 620 strengthens the allusion [V. 2. 7].)

622 one of the poem's two unrhymed lines.

638 *Bazzi* Sienese painter: Il Sodoma (*c.* 1477–1549).

Bazzi's] Razzi's *MS.*, *1872*. (For Browning's joke about the error, see 'Of Pacchiarotto', 18–19.)
639–40 *pillared cloud by day/And pillared fire by night* 'The Lord went before them by day in a pillar of a cloud, to lead them the way; and by night in a pillar of fire, to give them light; to go by day and night' (Exodus xiii 21).
641–4 Involved here is a particularly striking kind of modulation from minor to major. For technical details, see the note in the Florentine edition.
672 *deform* deformed (archaic adjectival usage).
684 *Ask Plato else* in part a referral to the authority, but with special reference to the *Symposium* and its views on love.
693 *fiat lux* 'let there be light' (Latin – Genesis i 3).
706 *Gérôme* fashionable French historical painter (1824–1904). Browning had met him in Paris in 1869.
720 *monadic* simple and unitary, but with potential.
724–7 *magic cup . . . Melpomene* The magic cup is Sir Joshua Reynolds's portrait of *Garrick between Tragedy and Comedy* (1762). In it David Garrick, the great actor, is pictured grinning at Melpomene, muse of Tragedy, but obviously more than content to be held by Thalia, muse of Comedy.
755 *Michelagnolo* Browning's standard spelling, the Tuscan one, for the great Italian painter and sculptor, the 'Master' of line 759 (1475–1564). In what follows Browning may have thought of the story of the statue of David, carved from a discarded block from which the sculptor realized the Idea implicit in it; more certainly, however, as W. Whitla suggests (private communication), he thought of the unfinished *Captives* (or *Slaves*) in Florence – the description comes closest to the block known as *The Awakening Giant*.
778–9 *daughter . . . Eidothée* 'Eidothea, daughter of mighty Proteus, the old man of the sea' (*Odyssey* IV, 365–6). Proteus, a minor sea-god, tended the seal-herds of Poseidon; another Proteus, often, as here, identified with the minor sea-god, was, as in the *Helen* of Euripides, the King of Egypt who cared for the real Helen until Menelaus reclaimed her.
781 *Mab* Don Juan's Mab is clearly Mercutio's sprite from *Romeo and Juliet* I. 4. 53–95.
instruct the Hero In *Odyssey* IV, Eidothea, favouring Menelaus, told him how to help himself and his comrades, held up by winds on the island of Pharos and suffering from hunger. He and three of his men were to surprise Proteus by disguising themselves as seals and holding him till he gave the required information.
784 *asleep beneath a rock* Proteus slept daily at midday in the shade of rocks.
785 *told their tale* counted his seals.
786 *fine fat seals with bitter breath* quoting *Odyssey* IV, 441–2.
793 *Emprise* enterprise.
796 *tool of triple tooth* sculptor's tool for rough work.
799 *pauls* obsolete Italian coins of little value.
816 *Conquering and to conquer* quoting Revelation vi 2.
859–71] *interpolated in MS* (858 and 872 rhyme).
861 *triple-tine* sculptor's tool for rough work.
894 *Heaven's face with flame*] Aspired to heaven *MS*.
903 *Glumdalclich* Glumdalclitch: the 'little nurse', forty feet tall, who cared for Gulliver in Brobdingnag.
905 Transliteration of Greek for 'God, men, or both together mixed' (Aeschylus, *Prometheus Bound,* 116) – Prometheus inquires about the Chorus, one composed of daughters of Ocean.

931 *bombèd* rounded, convex (*OED* calls the word rare in this sense, and cites only this example).

chrysopras golden-green precious stone.

935 *gastroknemian* of the chief muscle of the calf of the leg.

948 *thrid* thread (archaism).

957 *suspirative* sighing.

959 *pale* boundary. Here, the area in which perception of ultimates is limited by the senses.

968 *life's common chord* the level of ordinary life (compare 'Abt Vogler', 91).

975 *Sainte Marie* a hamlet two miles from Pornic, in which Browning stayed in 1862, 1863 and 1865.

976 *catch* see by an effort (*OED* 35).

980 *bead-blooms* that is, blooms like beads – of the camomile.

983 *camomile* aromatic creeping herb.

987 *Île Noirmoutier* The island is a few miles south-west of Pornic.

1046 *illude* deceive.

1049 *sowse* variant spelling of 'souse': with a sudden or deep plunge.

1050 *dowse* variant spelling of 'douse': plunge.

1105–6 *'howls' . . . to his gods* In Byron's *Childe Harold's Pilgrimage* IV, clxxx, Ocean sends man 'shivering in thy playful spray/And howling, to his Gods'.

1107 *Childishest childe* A 'childe' is a youth of gentle birth. Don Juan shares Browning's fondness for unusual superlatives.

1108 *Stay with the flat-fish, thou* 'In the Spectator which came yesterday, somebody repeated that foolish lie that I called Lord Byron "a flatfish" . . . I never said nor wrote a word against or about Byron's poetry or power in my life; but I did say, that, if he were in earnest and preferred being with the sea to associating with mankind, he would do well to stay with the sea's population; thereby simply taking him at his word, had it been honest' (Browning in a letter of 16 August 1873; see Hood, *Letters*, 159). Browning disliked what he saw as the hypocrisy and the anti-Christian philosophy of the famous address to Ocean ('Roll on, thou deep and dark blue Ocean – roll! . . .') in *Childe Harold's Pilgrimage* IV. For other examples of his antipathy, see *Sordello* VI, 1–7, and *Prince Hohenstiel-Schwangau,* 517–55. (Byron, of course, has his Don Juan figure.)

1115 *childishness* punning again on 'childe'.

1119–25 *taught . . . matched*] *MS. interpolation.*

1122 'Who hath measured the waters in the hollow of his hand' (Isaiah xl 12).

1125 *egged . . . bay* punning on both words.

1126 *there let him lay* quoting Byron's notorious solecism in *Childe Harold's Pilgrimage* IV, clxxx, but helping the joke by punning on 'lay'. By a happy accident, the pun, which needs the next line's opening to cement it, was momentarily concealed in both *1872* and *1888* since line 1126 ended a right-hand page.

1132 *beryl* transparent precious stone.

1133 *hair that*] wavelet *MS., 1872.*

1138] a good example of the fact that most of the poem's triplets result from later revisions in the *MS.* Browning had planned to delete this line, but changed his mind.

1147 *Thalassia* Thalassa (Greek for 'sea') was a Greek personification of the sea; presumably, Browning means a sea-nymph.

1148 *Triton* sea-god, son of Poseidon. He makes the sea roar by blowing through his conch.

1157 *Descents to Hell* Visits to the Underworld and discussions with spirits there are frequent in literature.

1188 *bubble-fish* Don Juan's name – not recorded in *OED* – for jellyfish.
1191 *globose* shaped like a globe ('now only in scientific use' – *OED*).
opaline opalescent, milky-blue.
1198 *but a tenth remained* A jellyfish is more than ninety per cent water.
1208 *fisher-bird that's king* kingfisher.
1213–18] *MS. interpolation.*
1215 *giving all and taking*] *MS. 1872*; taking all and giving *1888.*
1220 *seal* mark by a seal as.
1235 *snuff* detect or perceive by inhaling the odour (*OED* 4).
1245 *belled* bellowed.
1257 *loathlier* *OED* notes that 'loathly' was a rare word revived in the nineteenth century for literary usage; it does not, however, record Browning's comparative.
1280 *swell out your frog the right ox-size* In Aesop's fable, a frog trying to swell out to ox-size burst.
1285 *ramp* the act of ramping: raising the forelegs in the air.
1293–1319 *Art fain the fish to captivate . . . love at Taenarus* Arion, of Methymna in Lesbos, was a lyric poet and cithara player, and inventor of dithyrambic poetry. About 625 B.C. he lived at the Corinthian court of the tyrant Periander. Herodotus tells of his voyage when, threatened with murder, he played and sang, and then jumped into the sea. The dolphins were charmed by his music, and one of them carried him on its back to the port of Taenarus.
1305 *fret* ridge of metal across the fingerboard.
1309 *Orthian* Orthia was a Dorian goddess worshipped at Sparta as Artemis Orthia. Perhaps there is confusion of Arion with Orion – the latter lived with Artemis.
1316 *grim* grimness.
gulph gulf (obsolete form).
1318 *stems on* keeps on its course.
1322 *love-apple* The term is usually applied to the tomato.
1330 *god o' the grape* Dionysus (Bacchus).
1335 *animalcule* small animal.
1336 *blotch* 'a shapeless object' (*OED* 2b).
1340–44 *by strain . . . best pains*] *MS. interpolation.*
1347 *furify* 'to render furious' (*OED* 'very rare'). A nonce-word?
1348 *pismire* ant (obsolete or dialectal); the term is figuratively applied contemptuously to a person.
1351 *cuckoo-spits* Cuckoo-spit is the froth enclosing the larvae of insects on the leaves of plants. The usage here as a verb is probably unique.
1362 *self-centred* fixed, a centre around which other things move.
1395 *crank* liable to capsize.
1400 *firmland* solid land (*terra firma* – Latin).
1430 *tracklessness*] truculence *MS.* (Perhaps, since the *MS.* word is almost illegible, 'tracklessness' is a compositor's error.)
1431–41 The lines allude to Horace, *Odes* I, iii: 'To a Ship Bearing Vergil Over Seas'.
1431 *breast grew oak and triple brass* 'Oak and triple bronze must have girt the breast of him who first committed his frail bark to the angry sea' (Horace, *Odes* I, iii, 9–12).
1434–5 'Vain was the purpose of the god in severing the lands by the estranging main' (Horace, *Odes* I, iii, 21–3). Browning's phrasing may also be influenced by

Arnold's use of Horace in 'To Marguerite – Continued' (1852), 21–4: 'Who renders vain their deep desire? – /A God, a God their severance ruled!/And bade betwixt their shores to be/The unplumbed, salt, estranging sea.'

1441 *comfortable* reassuring (obsolete or archaic usage).

1446 *Attica* the district of Athens.

thrid thread (archaism).

1454 *Long Walls* the Walls connecting Athens with its port, Piraeus. The Spartans destroyed them in 404 B.C.

1461 *Iostephanos* 'the Violet-Crowned' – Pindar's famous epithet for Athens.

1462–71 *How quickly night comes ... ourselves are true* In thought, imagery and phrasing the lines are clearly influenced by Arnold's 'Dover Beach' (1867).

1465 *plash* splash.

1471 *A word, and I have done* Don Juan underestimates himself. Compare the title 'One Word More'.

1473 *express* positively.

1488 one of the two unrhymed lines in the poem.

1507 *excepted* exceptional.

1516 *threescore years and ten* 'The days of our years are threescore years and ten' (Psalm xc, 10).

1524 *A poet never dreams* 'The poet and the dreamer are distinct' (Keats, *The Fall of Hyperion*, 199).

1527 *mind, sound in a body sane* '*mens sana in corpore sano*': 'a sound mind in a sound body' (Juvenal, *Satires* X, 356).

1560 *four-cornered world* 'I saw four angels standing on the four corners of the earth' (Revelation vii 1).

1566–72 *no speech may evince ... puts poetry to shame* a frequent thought in Browning, always conscious of the inadequacies of language as a means of communicating truth.

1573 *record* italicized perhaps because the sense of setting down with an instrument of some kind was fairly new in 1872, but more probably because Don Juan is using the *English* word, the meaning of which is much more limited in French. See line 1585 also.

1584 *master of the spell* Don Juan may be thinking of Amphion, who built the walls of Thebes to his music.

1588 *Schumann's 'Carnaval'* a famous piece for the piano by the German romantic composer (1810–56).

1593 *spice-nut* gingerbread nut.

1597 *tricot* knitted sweater.

1599 *merceries* haberdasheries.

1618 *bespread* spread out.

1622 *board-head* head of the table.

1635 *gust* taste (Scotticism).

smack taste.

1662 *Columbine, Pantaloon* One of the pieces in *Carnaval* is called 'Pantalon and Columbine'.

1663 *She, toe-tips and staccato, – legato shakes his poll* In the piece ('Pantalon and Columbine'), she is represented in presto staccato passages, and he in slower legato passages.

poll head.

1664 *Fi la folle!* 'Fie on the madwoman!' (French).

1666 *Harlequin* One piece in *Carnaval* bears the name of the character who weds Columbine.
1671 *furled the films* wrapped the fine threads.
1672–3 *the sweet monotony of those/Three keys, flat, flat and flat, never a sharp at all* The 'three keys' are A flat, E flat and B flat (with their relative minors), varied only by brief excursions into D flat and B natural. The themes of *Carnaval* are based on a phrase of four notes, A (or A flat), E flat, C, B; in German these read A (or As), Es, C, H, spelling Asch, the town where Schumann's love lived. One consequence of this is a certain monotony of key not characteristic of Schumann.
1681 *tenths' and twelfths' unconscionable stretch* the stretch of the hand involved in playing notes in Schumann's music that are ten or twelve notes apart.
1686–7 *Mark's Church . . . Mark's Square* the Cathedral of Venice, and the Square on which it stands.
1688 *Procuratié-sides* The Procuratié are the arcades adjacent to the Cathedral, where the Church solicitors (*procuratori*) had their offices.
1691 *casqued* helmeted.
1695 *frontispiece* face (jocular).
1701 *chap* jaw.
1736 *simulacra* images, likenesses.
1738 *groundling* the ordinary person on the 'ground' or pit of a theatre.
1743–4 *lightlier . . . nearlier* The comparative forms here are very rare, perhaps unique.
1754 *checked* chequered.
1778 *case-hardened* hardened on the surface.
1793 *environment* surrounding.
1794 *strange orbs unearthed i' the Druid temple* 'Our Druids used to make balls for divining out of such *all-but-solid* gems with the central weakness – I have had them in my hand' (Browning to Elizabeth Barrett, 5 August 1846).
1795 *please*] lean *MS.*, *1872*.
1809 *composite* compound.
simple single uncompounded thing.
1835 *castellated* castle-like.
momently from moment to moment.
1844 *meseemed* it seemed to me (archaism).
1869 *baluster* a circular pillar – the usage here is somewhat unusual.
1883–4 *a frank farewell to what – we think – should be,/And . . . welcome what is* recalling the last two stanzas of Wordsworth's 'Elegiac Stanzas', with their 'farewell' to a deceptive ideal and 'welcome' of the real.
1888 *cirque* circle.
1912 *'Commercing with the skies'* Milton 'Il Penseroso', 39.
1915 *Domes* halls.
1926 *days are long i' the land* 'Honour thy father and thy mother: that thy days may be long upon the land which the Lord thy God giveth thee' (Exodus xx 12).
1942 *coign of vantage* *Macbeth* I. 6. 8.
1943 *house not made with hands* 2 Corinthians v 1.
1955 *fullness of the days* 'fulness of times' (Ephesians i 10).
1986 *raree-show* spectacular display.
1991 *seclude* prevent access to (obsolete usage).
2000 *the fine gold grew dim i' the temple* 'How is the gold become dim! how is the most fine gold changed!' (Lamentations iv 1).

2001 *brave* splendid.

abode Presumably the reference is to Solomon's temple with its pillars of brass.

2019 *turns blaze to black*] would turn to rest *MS., 1872.*

2045 *Druid monument* The monument is at Pornic. There is a granite dolmen, a sepulchre, with a passage about thirty feet long ending in a cross. Beside it is a menhir, a tall and formerly upright monumental stone.

2056 *sinister* on the left side, but inevitably suggesting 'foreboding' also.

2066–7 *from age/To age the same* perhaps reminiscent of 'To endless years the same' (Watts, 'O God, our help in ages past'), as are some of the following lines, which also recall Psalm xc, the psalm of which Watts's hymn is an adaptation.

2100 *run their rigs* played their pranks, or run riot (slang).

2109–15 *at bottom of the rungs ... earth to heaven* Genesis xxviii 12–18. J. M. Jephson, *Narrative of a Walking Tour in Brittany*, 1859, 199, describes the menhirs as 'analogous to the stone set up by Jason as an altar on which he poured oil'.

2130 *arch-word* prime or original word.

2131 *charactery* writing.

2162 *founderingly* probably a nonce-word; it is not recorded by *OED.*

2165 *Protoplast* the first creator.

2178 *triad* common-chord.

2188 *God, man, or both together mixed* Aeschylus, *Prometheus Bound,* 116. See 905n., and 907. With 2188–90, compare lines 905–9.

2195–9 *truth is forced ... prize the true* See lines 1505–9, on which this passage is a variation.

2197 *excepted* exceptional.

2210 The line from *Prometheus Bound* again (feminine forms in 905, neuter here).

2215 *Titan* Prometheus.

2216 *God, man, or mixture* *Prometheus Bound,* 116, again.

nymph The Chorus of *Prometheus Bound* is one of sea-nymphs.

2217–23 *From whom the clink ... friends we flock* Don Juan quotes from the first strophe of the opening Chorus of *Prometheus Bound.*

2225–6 *Three-formed Fate,/Moirai Trimorphoi* The English phrase translates the Greek one. In *Prometheus Bound,* 516, Prometheus tells the Chorus that the helm of Necessity is held by 'the threefold Fates and the unforgetting Furies' (Mrs Browning's translation).

2241–2 *makes the circuit just ... We end where we began* 'makes my circle just,/ And makes me end, where I begun' (Donne, 'A Valediction: forbidding Mourning', 35–6).

2244 *last is first* 'the last shall be first' (Matthew xix 30).

2256 *plumes up his will* 'plume up my will' (*Othello* I. 3. 349) – said by Iago.

2265 *bodies sprouted legs, through a desire to run* evolutionary theorizing, but Lamarckian rather than Darwinian.

2278–9 *such conclusion suits/Nowise the pride of man* The theories of Lamarck, with the importance they attached to will, gave man reason for pride; the theories of Darwin or of experience that make man passive rather than active in the evolutionary process make feelings of pride difficult.

2286 *love ends where love began* See line 2242.

2321 *stickle* strive, stand up.

2323 *bloomy* flowery (poeticism).

2330 *freak* vagary.

fret agitation (obsolete usage in this sense).

2347 *inconsciously* unconsciously (rare – the only adverbial usages recorded by *OED* are Browning's).

blank white or empty spot; see 2351n.

2351 *two silver whites* small French coins called *blancs* or *blanks* (see line 2347)? Or perhaps francs (also silver).

yellow double yolk double Louis d'or, or double Napoleon (forty francs) – both gold coins.

EPILOGUE

'The Householder' is reminiscent in some respects of Poe's 'The Raven' (1845).

30 *Affliction sore long time he bore . . . Till God did please to grant him ease* 'Instruction sore long time I bore,/And cramming was in vain;/Till heaven did please my woes to ease/With water on the brain' (Charles Kingsley, *The Water-Babies* [1863], viii).

32 *Love is all and Death is naught* Compare the epigraph, 12–14.

Red Cotton Night-Cap Country

First published by Smith, Elder early in May 1873. There was no second edition, and few changes were made for *1888* (the copy of *1873* that Browning used for preparing the text for *1888* and which provided the printers' copy is in the Berg Collection of the New York Public Library). The printers' manuscript is in the Library of Balliol College, and is clearly the first and last draft of the poem; it reveals that the division into four parts was a late idea. As is usual with Browning's later manuscripts, there are a considerable number of interpolations; the additions here are extensive in II, and even more so in III. Nevertheless, and despite the fact that Browning 'fiddles all the way' (1293) with the manuscript text, it is fairly clean. It bears an inscription in Greek on the title page in Browning's hand from Pindar's *Isthmian Ode* VIII, 13–14: 'it is better to look evermore at that which lieth before one's foot'. The manuscript dates the poem as begun on 1 December 1872 and finished on 23 January 1873.

At least three sets of proofs survive. The earliest of these (in the Berg Collection) has dates of late February (another partial set with the date 22 February 1873 is in the University of Texas). There are, however, very considerable differences between readings in this set of proofs and those in the manuscript, the implication being that the set is in fact the second set used by Browning; the differences are almost invariably within individual lines, but they affect more than half the lines in the poem. Another set of proofs, not seen for the present edition, was sold in November 1974; the printers' labels on it are dated 6 March 1873. A still later set, dated 15 March 1873, is also in the Berg Collection; it is called 'final proof' in an unidentified hand, but bears Browning's request for two more revises. It has extensive holograph revisions including the changes from the actual names of the true story on which Browning based his poem to those which appeared in the printed text. On the proofs and the revising, see L. L. Szladits, 'Browning's French Night-Cap', *Bulletin of the New York Public Library* LXI, 1957, 458–67.

The story Browning tells was one which he had encountered while staying near his French friend, Joseph Milsand, in 1870 and 1872, at Saint Aubin in Normandy, and which in August-September 1872 he pursued further. Helped by Milsand, he visited the poem's locations, caught sight of the heroine, read the court proceedings and newspaper accounts of them in the *Journal de Caen*, spoke to local people about the case, and arrived at his own interpretation of it (a set of working notes for the poem is in the Huntington Library). In a letter of 16 May 1889 to J. T. Nettleship, Browning wrote:

'I heard, first of all, the merest sketch of the story on the spot. Milsand told me that the owner of the house had destroyed himself from remorse at having behaved unfilially to his mother. In a subsequent visit (I paid one every year while Milsand lived there) he told me some other particulars, and they at once struck me as likely to have been occasioned by religious considerations as well as passionate woman-love, – and I concluded that there was no intention of committing suicide; and I said at once that I would myself treat the subject *just so.*

'Afterward he procured me the legal documents. I collected the accounts current among the people of the neighbourhood, inspected the house and grounds, and convinced myself that I had guessed rightly enough in every respect. Indeed the facts are so exactly put down, that, in order to avoid the possibility of prosecution for Libel – that is, telling the exact truth – I changed all the names of persons and places, as they stood in the original "Proofs," and gave them as they are to be found in Mrs Orr's Hand-book' (Hood, *Letters*, 309).

The dedication is not in the manuscript and was added in proof. Anne Thackeray (1837–1919), daughter of the novelist, was staying at Lion, about five miles away. She is the auditor of Browning's poem – later, after hostile reviews, she was not altogether happy about her association with it. As the poem states, she called the area 'White Cotton Night-Cap Country', and Browning changed her 'White' to 'Red' partly to point up the blood of his story. (For details of Browning's cottage and the country see Anne [Thackeray] Ritchie, *Records of Tennyson, Ruskin and Browning,* Macmillan, 1892, 222–33.)

For the red night-cap, Browning also owed a debt to Carlyle, whose symbol for revolutionary events it was throughout *The French Revolution* (1837) (on Browning's debts to Carlyle, see C. C. Watkins, 'Browning's "Red Cotton Night-Cap Country" and Carlyle', *VS* VII, 1964, 359–74). In the subtitle of his poem, 'Turf and Towers', Browning symbolizes the central conflict in his hero between the earthly and the heavenly, the senses and the soul, the heroine and the Virgin.

The protagonist of the poem was based on Antoine Mellerio (1827–70), a jeweller who, after leading a dissipated life for some years, had retired to Normandy with his mistress, had tried to commit suicide in Paris in 1867, had in another fit of remorse early in 1868 burned his hands off, and had finally killed himself on 13 April 1870 in a fall from a tower on his estate. His will, leaving everything, except for a life interest for his mistress, to the Church, had been contested by his relatives, but, after delays because of the Franco-Prussian War, the court at Caen upheld the will in a judgment of 9 July 1872 (an appeal against the decision was denied a year later). Though Browning's interest is essentially in his hero and his motives, the story is a grisly one, and perhaps it is mostly its sordidness that has led to the poem's having had few admirers and being but seldom read; some readers also find the tone, with its grotesque blend of savage humour, whimsical humour and intense seriousness, difficult to adjust to.

The materials excited Browning, as a letter to Isa Blagden of 19 September 1872, and a remark to Domett, show. In the former he speaks of 'a capital brand-new subject'; in the latter he said, 'I have got *such* a subject for a poem, if I could do justice to it.' Part of the reason for his excitement is unquestionably the parallels between the materials and the treatment of them in *The Ring and the Book* and *Red Cotton Night-Cap Country.*

While the poem was in press, Browning's publisher and the poet himself became worried about the possibility of a suit for libel, since the case over the hero's will had so recently been concluded. After advice from two lawyers, one the Attorney-General, Browning changed all the real proper names to fictitious ones (for letters on the subject, see DeVane and Knickerbocker, *New Letters,* 211–17). A list of these changes follows, with the line numbers being those of the poem's first references:

Line	Actual name	Name in *1873* and *1888*
9	Street of Peace	Place Vendôme
11	Mellerio, Brothers	The Firm-Miranda
41	Saint Aubin	Saint-Rambert
42	Lion, Lionesse	Joyeux, Joyous-Gard
82	Caen	Vire
422	Douvres	Londres
424	Dover	London
427	Courseulles (erroneously reported as 'Courcelle' by Mrs Orr)	La Roche
428	Bernières	Monlieu
430	Langrune	Villeneuve
	Luc	Pons
432	La Délivrande	La Ravissante
495	Bayeux	Raimbaux
499	Hugonin	Morillon
506	Bonnechose	Mirecourt
513	Mellerio	Miranda
522	Madrid	New York
614	Tailleville	Clairvaux
632	Turinese	Madrilene
638	Bény	Gonthier
643	Quai Voltaire	Quai Rousseau
645	Antoine	Léonce
1152	Italian	Castilian
1188	Dell Yvrande	Rare Vissante
1190	Regnobert	Aldabert
1194	Ragnebert	Eldobert
1204	Baudoin (Mrs Orr has 'Beaudoin')	Mailleville
1214	Quélen (Mrs Orr has 'Quelen')	Chaumont
1216	Talleyrand	Vertgalant
1513	Anna de Beaupré	Clara de Millefleurs
1519	Miromesnil Street	Coliseum Street
1659	Sophie Trayer (Mrs Orr has 'Mayer')	Lucie Steiner
1660	Lalory (Mrs Orr has 'Larocy')	Commercy
	Metz	Sierck
1667	Debacker	Muhlhausen
1691	Miranda di Mongino	Carlino Centofanti
1830	Italy	Portugal
1887	Alfred	Gustave
1911	Achille	Ulysse
2047	Mériel	Vaillant

Line	Actual name	Name in *1873* and *1888*
2251	Twenty-five	Thirty-three
2281	Pasquier	Beaumont
2508	Garges	Sceaux
3053	Jean de la Becquetière	Luc de la Maison Rouge
3054	Vire	Claise
3055	Anne	Maude
3077	Eliezer	Dionysius
3080	Elizabeth	Scolastica
3232	Thirteenth	Twentieth
3621	Picot	Fricquot

Furnivall reported that Browning toyed with the notion of restoring the real names in the final edition.

On the poem, see Mrs Orr, *Handbook*, 225–62. Critical material has recently become available: see Brendan Kenny, 'Browning as a Cultural Critic: *Red Cotton Night-Cap Country*', *BIS* VI, 1978, 137–60; C. de L. Ryals, 'Browning's *Red Cotton Night-Cap Country*', in W. P. Elledge and R. L. Hoffman (eds.), *Romantic and Victorian*, Fairleigh Dickinson University Press, 1971, 329–45; M. Siegchrist, 'Browning's *Red Cotton Night-Cap Country*: The Process of Imagination', *VP* XII, 1974, 137–52.

1 *fair friend* Anne Thackeray, later Lady Ritchie, to whom the poem is dedicated, and who is its auditor (1837–1919).
4 *champaign* the Campagna, countryside around Rome.
9 *Place Vendôme* fashionable Paris square. The store was actually in the Rue de la Paix nearby.
10 *Golconda* the Indian city famed for its diamonds.
20 *un-Murrayed* not recorded in Murray's guide-book.
21 *sea-coast-nook-ful* Browning's revenge on the French 'Norman bastards' of *Henry V* III. 5. 14 for calling England 'nook-shotten'?
25 *luzern* obsolete form of lucern(e): a clover-like plant.
36 *varech* seaweed.
42 *Joyous-Gard of yours* Anne Thackeray was staying at Lion (Joyous-Gard).
65 *ceiled* having a ceiling.
66 *suffer* allow.
72 *Corso* main street in Rome.
77–8 *Paris ... Versailles* After the Franco-Prussian War and the second siege of 1871, the Assembly remained at Versailles. With the new Constitution, it returned to Paris in 1875.
129 *posted*] pasted *MS*.
134 *Emperor* Napoleon III, exiled after the Franco-Prussian War, and dead in January 1873.
160 *idlesse* 'idleness, viewed in a poetic or romantic light' – *OED*.
idlesse stock our] pleasantness stock *MS*.
173 *cool comfort* 'cold comfort' (*King John* V. 7. 42).
180 *promise book*] tell me this *MS*.
194 *my ignorance*] impertinence *MS*.
194–243 The dissertation on nightcaps, as C. C. Watkins suggests (362), almost parodies the history of the sofa in Cowper's *The Task*.
199] Night's summons that the Day desist from din. *MS. first reading*.

247 *what a fiddle means* Browning began by using the exclamation, but is shifting to the noun.
250 *your Kensington* The Thackerays lived near Kensington Square, and Anne Thackeray's novel, *Old Kensington,* was appearing serially in *Cornhill Magazine.*
251 *special Fiddle-Show* current exhibition at the South Kensington Museum.
257 *Guarnerius* family of Italian violin-makers of the seventeenth and eighteenth centuries, from Cremona.
Straduarius the famous violin-maker from Cremona (1644–1737).
267 *Corelli* Italian composer and violinist (1653–1713).
268 *cushat-dove* ring-dove or wood-pigeon.
269] Most gentle Giga, sleepiest Saraband.' *MS.*
Giga the old Italian word for fiddler, and the Italian form of *gigue*: a lively piece of music (Corelli wrote one).
Saraband a slow stately Spanish dance or piece of music (Corelli wrote one).
270 *Paganini* the great Italian virtuoso violinist (1782–1840).
271 *tenuity* thinness.
282 *Pope* The poet Alexander Pope (1688–1744) was crippled, deformed and often ill. Even in society, he often wore a velvet cap that looked like a night-cap.
287 *Voltaire* The French writer (1694–1778) wore a velvet cap.
Hogarth The English satirical artist (1697–1764) wears a cap in his portraits.
288 *phyz* face (slang).
291 *Poor hectic Cowper* The English poet, William Cowper (1731–1800), was on the verge of madness or over it much of his life; in portraits he wears a hat.
sarsnet soft silky material.
296 *toilet* presumably in the obsolete sense of 'night-dress bag'? – see *OED* 1.
300–303 *French . . . 'Ninety-two* the story-book telling of the incident of 1792 is Carlyle's *The French Revolution.*
304 *Commune* the organization governing Paris.
308–14 *Louis . . . Cap of Freedom* The incident of 1792 is the incursion into the Tuileries of 20 June in which Louis XVI confronted the mob: 'His few National Grenadiers shuffle back with him, into the embrasure of a window: there he stands, with unimpeachable passivity, amid the shouldering and the braying; a spectacle to men. They hand him a red Cap of Liberty; he sets it quietly on his head, forgets it there . . . So stands Majesty in Red woollen Cap' (Carlyle, *The French Revolution* V, xii).
313 *Phrygian symbol* the cap of liberty, a red one (*bonnet-rouge*) adopted by the French revolutionists.
321 *did him stead* served him (obsolete usage).
324 *Corsican lieutenant* Napoleon Bonaparte. Carlyle's account of the storming of the Tuileries on 10 August 1872 includes: 'one strangest Patriot onlooker thinks that the Swiss, had they a commander, would beat. He is a man not unqualified to judge; the name of him Napoleon Bonaparte' (VI, vii).
327 *flags* flagstones.
canaille rabble.
328 *droll* buffoon.
336–7 *in cleric phrase/Quod semel, semper, et ubique* The Latin means: 'What once was, and is always, and everywhere.' 'In cleric phrase' either because Browning varies a saying of Saint Vincent of Lerins, or because of the prayer's 'as it was in the beginning, is now, and ever shall be'.
356 *Rahab-thread* the 'scarlet thread' which Joshua's spies gave Rahab to mark her window (Joshua ii 18).

361 *blank* vacant – and white.
364 *Octroi* officers collecting taxes on goods entering a town.
378 *Perks* holds up smartly.
393 *strain point* strain a point: go somewhat further than one technically should.
402 *musicalest* an unusual superlative, even by Browning's standards.
404 'though your sins be as scarlet, they shall be as white as snow; though they be red like crimson, they shall be as wool' (Isaiah i 18).
406 *Liebig* Justus, Baron von Liebig, German chemist (1833–73), improved methods of organic analysis (he died three weeks before Browning's poem appeared).
407 *prime* cover.
410 *ground* basic surface.
417 *thorpes* hamlets (archaism).
422–4 *mother-mouse . . . birth* 'The mountains are in labour, and a ridiculous mouse will be born' (Horace, *Art of Poetry,* 139).
425 *Conqueror* William I, the Conqueror, first Norman King of England (1066–87). Fear of a suit for libel led Browning to delete even 'the Conqueror' from the proofs, but he then decided to let it stand (he did the same thing with 'Normandy' earlier in the poem, and with 'Caen' later).
426 *pride* presumably a pride, epitomized in place-names, in the Norman influence on England resulting from the Conquest.
427 *La Roche*] Courseulle *MS.* (Browning meant 'Courseulles', and certainly not the 'Courcelle' of Mrs Orr's *Handbook.*)
432 *La Ravissante* Browning's name for the Church of Notre Dame de la Délivrande near Douvres. Its image of the Virgin was famous, and the place was a centre of pilgrimage and site of miraculous cures.
435 *safety-guards*] miracles *MS.*
437 *by crow-flight* in a straight line ('as the crow flies').
438 *Lourdes and La Salette* other French places of pilgrimage and miraculous cure.
441–2 *eschewed infallibility . . . compass-box* gave up the infallibility of monarchy for democracy with the French Revolution.
442 *vague*] mad *MS.*
444–5 *memorable day . . . For reinstatement of the misused Three* A marked revival of interest in religious matters was a feature of the time, and in 1872 there were mass pilgrimages to all three centres. La Délivrande was badly damaged after the Revolution, and for a while was used as a barn. Browning seems however to have more specific facts in mind; these remain unidentified.
448 *diligence* stagecoach.
464 *Alessandro Sforza* prince of the leading Milanese family (1409–73).
466 *poor Pope was in prison-house* After the loss of the Papal States in 1870, Pius IX, restricted to the Vatican, was known as 'the Prisoner in the Vatican'.
475 *colewort* cabbage or cabbage-like plant (archaism).
490 *offset* offshoot.
492 *Martinique* the department of France in the West Indies.
508 *strippage* 'branches stripped from trees' (*OED*, which calls the word rare, and cites only this example).
545 *Abaris* The priest of Apollo rode on a magic arrow.
556 *sage* It is doubtful that any individual is meant since the thought is frequent, and the expression here unmemorable. Watkins, however, suggests (364–5) Carlyle in *Sartor Resartus*: 'here or nowhere is thy Ideal . . . Fool! the Ideal is in thyself, the impediment too is in thyself.'

595 *diamond-necklace-dealing* alluding to the notorious scandal of 1784–6 in the French Court. Carlyle tells of it in *The Diamond Necklace* (1837).

610 *lucarnes* skylights or dormer windows.

616 *Abbey-for-the-Males* Abbaye aux Hommes, built by William the Conqueror in Caen. His original tomb there was destroyed and his bones scattered by the Calvinists (1572); and after his bones had been collected and reinterred, the second tomb was rifled at the time of the French Revolution.

622 *Red Cap* the cap of Liberty worn by the Revolutionists.

624 *National Domain* All Church holdings were nationalized in 1789.

627 *messuage* estate.

three-and-twenty years ago The fact is correct; Père Mellerio bought Tailleville in 1849.

630 *French phrase* that is, Père Miranda, Father Miranda.

632 *Madrilene* native of Madrid.

640 *demise* in 1860.

652 *branchage* a French word: 'branches in the mass' (*OED*, where the only examples cited are from Browning).

655 *Hey, presto, pass* a conjurer's command.

657 *à l'Anglaise* in the English manner.

compliment 'use ceremonious or adulatory language' (Johnson's *Dictionary*).

659 *Bosses* an unusual usage in a transferred sense from the protuberance on a shield.

660 *Lead*] Wind *MS.*, *1873*.

664 *Lead, lift*] Waft you *MS.*; Wind, waft *1873*.

666 *coquetry* 'attractive prettiness, winsomeness as the result of art' (*OED*, citing this usage in a transferred sense).

670 *lightsome*] pleasant *MS.*

672 *mansarde* curb – having two slopes, the lower steeper than the upper.

674 *brave* splendid.

696 *surprise* discover, come unexpectedly upon.

704 *Parc Anglais* English Park.

714 Alluding to the famous Paris street, the Champs Élysées (the Elysian Fields), and the Park, the Bois de Boulogne.

733 *a tragedy*] such element *MS.*

744 *regalized* made royal. A nonce-word in this sense? (*OED* describes as very rare, and cites in this sense only this example.)

745 *expounded* apparently used in the rare and obsolete sense, the etymological sense (Latin, *exponere*), of 'exposed to view' (*OED* 4)?

750 *stiver* coin of small value.

754 *arrow-flash* See line 545.

760 *restive prophet* Balaam (Numbers xxii–xxiii).

804 *sidelingly* side by side. A nonce-word? It is not recorded in *OED.*

814 *yet she begged and prayed*] therefore was it planned *MS.*

821 *your heroine*] this lady *MS.*

849 *out of mind as sight* varying the proverbial 'out of sight, out of mind'.

853 *impressment* used here with the sense of 'impression', a meaning for the 'rare' word not given in *OED.*

885 *suits* matches in colour (an obsolete usage).

888 *Châtelaine* lady of the manor.

897 *paled-off* with its boundaries marked.

930 *pranked* bedecked.
lazuli lapis lazuli, the blue stone.
951–2 *equalize . . . last as first* Matthew xx 1–16.
953] *not in MS.*
970 *doit* coin of little value.
971 *Peter-pence* funds contributed to the treasury of the Papacy.
981 *lorgnette* pair of glasses held in the hand, usually by a long handle.
983 *baignoire* theatre-box (first example cited by *OED*).
986 *parure* finery, ornament.
989 *fortune*] Tainville [*sic*] *MS.*
1006 *cul-de-sac* passage with one end blocked.
1017 *napery* household linen.
1018 *seize* apprehend.
1021 *laurustines* evergreen shrubs.
1025 *sinistrous* attended with misfortune.
coil used ambiguously: ado, and gathering in rings of rope.
1030 *at Vire they tried the case*] they tried the case at Caen *MS.* (The change avoids the unwanted rhyme – produced by the use of the pseudonym for Caen – of 'here', 'Vire'.)
1035 *cirque* circus.
1042 *Tuileries* the King's Palace in Paris, finally completely destroyed in 1871.
1074 *tessellated* patterned with small blocks of variously coloured material.
1076 *architrave* epistyle lowest part of an entablature, resting upon the top of the column.
1097 *Father Secchi* Jesuit and Italian astronomer (1818–78), director of a Rome observatory.
1117 *Idalian* Venus sometimes has the name Idalia, after the mountain-city Idalium in Cyprus sacred to her worship.
1118 *Victrix* 'Conqueror' (Latin).
1121 *Exalt* exalted (*OED*'s only examples are from Browning).
1171–2 *He stood impenetrably circuited,/Heaven-high*] It stood . . . the impenetrable circuit, high/As heaven *MS.*; Faith stood the impenetrable circuit, high/ As heaven *1873*.
1173 *sap* approaching a besieged place by covered trenches.
1185 *Delivering Virgin* the real name: La Délivrande.
1189 *erst* formerly (archaism).
1201 *Northmen's fury laid it low* in 830.
1202 *Not long* in fact, about 200 years.
1202–5 *an egregious sheep . . . Count of the country* The shepherd of Count Baudoin in the eleventh century 'perceived that one of his rams often retired from the flock and ran to a place near the pasture, there with its foot and its horns struck and scraped the earth, and then, being tired, lay down on the place where is now the image of the Virgin in the chapel of the Délivrande. This ram never ate, and yet it was the fattest of the flock. The count, thinking that this was a warning sent from heaven, went to the spot, together with the nobility, with a holy hermit, and with a great crowd of people who ran thither from surrounding places.

'He commanded that the trench which the ram had begun to make should be laid bare, and in it was found the image of Notre-Dame, more than eight hundred years old. This image was carried in solemn procession with universal joy by all the people into the church of Doûvres, but was soon taken back by an angel to the place where it had been found. Then the Count, understanding the Divine will, founded

and caused to be built on the spot the chapel, which now exists, and gave it to messieurs of Bayeux.' (From an account of 1642 as quoted in K. S. Macquoid, *Through Normandy*, Isbister, 1874.)
1214 *Chaumont* Quélen, Archbishop of Paris (1821–39).
1216 *Vertgalant* Talleyrand (1754–1838), the French statesman, notorious at times for his impiety, made his reconciliation with the Church two months before his death.
1223 *Voltaire* The eighteenth-century writer was a philosophical sceptic, the foe of organized religions, though not of religion.
1224 The line appears to be a quotation, which remains unidentified.
1231] *not in MS.*
1233] *not in MS.*
1234 *Rabelais* the fifteenth-century humanist and satirist.
1245 *acromia* outer extremities of the shoulder-blades.
1248 *meridional* southern.
1261 *Sganarelle* stock character in Molière, but Browning has in mind the superstitious pusillanimous valet of *Don Juan.*
1281] *not in MS.*
1286] Should let even you, dear thickhead, recognize *MS.*
1319 Latin: 'I have found my sheep which was lost' (Luke xv 6).
1336 *sciolist* one with only superficial knowledge.
1338–40 *Voltaire . . . significant* Voltaire died in pain, but not mad or raving despite strong legends. His death was precipitated by the tumultuous reception ('squibs and crackers') on his return to Paris from exile.
1361–7] *interpolated in MS.*
1363 *'Warrior to the wall!'* The march-tune remains unidentified.
1380 *rampired* protected with a rampart.
1393 *transitive* transitory (in this sense, obsolete and rare).
1404 *fowling* snaring.
1405 Birdbatting is 'performed by holding a large clap-net before a lanthorn, and at the same time beating the bushes' (Fielding, *Joseph Andrews* II, x). A *clapnet* can quickly be closed with a string.
1416 *teased* with the fibres pulled asunder.
1420 *contre-danse* country dance.
1424 *Winter-Garden* The Jardin d'Hiver (referred to in Browning's work-sheets) was an exceptionally fine pleasure-garden, roofed with glass, on the Champs Élysées.
Mabille The Jardin Mabille on the Avenue Montaigne had a ballroom popular with students, milliners, and young ladies of doubtful virtue.
1438 *The Varieties* the famous theatre, Les Variétés, on the Boulevard Montmartre, where the real Mellerio did in fact first see his lady.
1447 *polyanthus* flower related to the primrose.
1450 *captive*] bond slave *MS.*, *1873.*
1490 *falsish* described as rare by *OED*, which cites only this example.
1507 *ruddle* a red ochre used for marking sheep and colouring.
1513 *Clara de Millefleurs* 'Clara of the thousand flowers'.
1549] *not in MS.*
1578 *Court Guide* directory of nobility, gentry, and those presented at Court.
1594 *darlingly* a nonce-word.
1601 *Louis* twenty-franc piece.
1621 *cope* canopy, vault.

1626 *Favonian* gentle western (Favonius is the Roman name for Zephyrus).
1627 *warrants* guarantees security (*OED* 8 – 'rare').
Auster south or south-west wind.
1632 *elevate* elevated (poeticism).
1639 *pip* a disease in birds.
1649 *Houri* lady of the Mohammedan Paradise.
1654–7] *interpolated in MS.*
1664 *professed* made a profession of.
1687 *mazed* dazed (archaism).
1714 *chignon* nape of the neck.
1722 *dreadful cannonry* of the Crimean War.
1755 *throw first stone* 'He that is without sin among you, let him first cast a stone at her' (John viii 7).
1766 *aurorally* roseately, like the dawn.
1768 *fuliginous* sooty.
1770 *clout* cloth (archaism).
1772–3 *God's cloven tongues/Of fire* 'cloven tongues like as of fire' (Acts ii 3).
1777 *cupping-cloth* not in *OED*. Presumably a cloth used in 'cupping' – drawing blood to (and thus reddening) the skin.
1782–4] *interpolation in MS.*
1804–5 *straighten out/What's crooked* 'the crooked shall be made straight . . . And all flesh shall see the salvation of God' (Luke iii 5–6).
1841 *Aladdin's cave* the fabulous cave in which Aladdin found the lamp that did his bidding.
1877 *perdue* concealed.
1877–8] The lines are transposed in *MS.*
1879 *Deity-like from dusk machine* alluding to the '*deus ex machina*' (Latin: 'the god from the machine'): the providential saviour.
1898 *griffin* The mythical beast, a mixture of lion and eagle, guarded treasure.
1947] Could not the Tempter leave this ear alone? *MS.*
1950 *Magdalens* harlots (after Mary Magdalene of Mark xvi 9).
1956 *springe* snare.
2035 'give a kick to': *dare calci a* is Italian for 'kick'.
2049 *Dumas* the famous French novelist and dramatist (1803–70). His son, also Alexandre, was a well-known dramatist. Details of the testimonials here, like other details in the poem, are recorded in Browning's hand on sheets in the Huntington Library.
2054 *Bagatelle* eighteenth-century château on the edge of the Bois de Boulogne.
2055 *Hertford* the fourth Marquess of Hertford (1800–70), nicknamed 'Bagatelle' and owner of the property of that name.
hight named (archaism).
2071] *not in MS.*
2073–6] Politics? Spend his own life, so to save
The world of lives, each unit's particle
Of joy that's life, and lose the orb entire,
His own aforesaid! Artistry, perhaps? *MS.*
2081 *Artistry being*] Such life will be one *MS.*
2090] *artist-*] stormy *MS.*
2091] *not in MS.*
2096 *chace* obsolete form of 'chase'.

2100 *seigneur* lord.
2116] *not in MS.*
2120 *L'Ingegno* 'The Genius': Andrea Luigi of Assisi (1470–1556).
2129 *Boileau* French critic and poet (1636–1711).
2130 *devoir* respect.
2131 *Louis Quatorze* Louis XIV, King of France (1643–1715).
2132 *Pierre Corneille* the French heroic dramatist (1606–84).
2175 *dragon* Ladon was the dragon that guarded the Apples of the Hesperides.
2184 *October* in 1867.
2196 *quick* sensitive part.
2202 *Sardanapalus* last king of Assyria, famed in legend for his luxury and extravagance (seventh century B.C.).
2218 *Dalilah* Samson's mistress and betrayer.
2222–4 *that fool of Scripture . . . morning jollity* Luke xii 18–20.
2252 *bézique* card game.
2282 *mind* call to mind, remember.
2288 *Antony* Saint Antony of Egypt (*c.* 251–350) is said to have experienced every temptation the Devil could conceive of.
2299 *phlebotomize* let blood by opening a vein.
2303 *stuff* material for clothing.
2305] *not in MS.*
2308 *Unglossed* without its gloss (a neologism).
2329 *Words are but words and wind* 'Oaths are but words, and words but wind' (Butler, *Hudibras* II, i, 107 – and similarly elsewhere).
2358 *critical* precise.
2362 *concierge* janitor, porter.
2363 *seat* site.
2381–2] Let me explain a little. This good priest *MS.*
2393 *Miranda's life*] the last eight years *MS.*
2419] *not in MS.*
2431] *not in MS.*
2435 *besprent* strewed.
2446 *to point* to the smallest detail (archaism – *OED* D6b).
2459 Luke xv 6–7.
2537] Monsieur Antoine Mellerio, penitent *MS.*
2550 *inconsciously* unconsciously (rare).
2573 *broidery* embroidery (poeticism).
2590 *Burn, burn and purify my past* The actual words ('Brûle, brûle, disait-il, purifie mon passé'), according to evidence in court.
2593 *soul of tenfold strength* 'My strength is as the strength of ten,/Because my heart is pure' (Tennyson, 'Sir Galahad', 3–4).
2601 *phalanges* finger-bones.
2606–7, 2609–11] *MS. interpolations.*
2618 *febricity* state of being feverish (this is the only example cited in *OED*).
2627] *not in MS.*
2632 *ambrosial* ethereal.
2646 *and licked*] with feet *MS.*; and kicked *1873.*
2655 *Religio Medici* the title of Sir Thomas Browne's book (1642): Latin for 'A Doctor's Religion'.
2739] At taste of air prolonged, six hours for one *MS.*

2780 *rente* yearly income.
2791] *not in MS.*
2807 *dream-Château, in Spain* alluding to the expression 'Castles in Spain' – splendid day-dreams.
2808] A Branch is at Madrid, goes on the gold. *MS.*
2809 *man and man*] wolf and wolf *MS.*
2812] *not in MS.*
2823 *towers*] wall *MS., 1873.*
2864 *trine* group of three.
2886 *Neither to right hand nor to left* 'Turn not to the right hand nor to the left' (Proverbs iv 27).
2887 *guide* Joseph Milsand, Browning's French friend.
2893 *diamond* the 'Florentine' diamond – there are other versions of the legend here.
2895 *Navona* The Piazza Navona is a major square in central Rome.
2898 *ha'p'worth* halfpenny-worth.
2902 *orbit* eye.
2906 *Rouher* Eugène Rouher, French politician (1814–84), Premier 1863–9.
2908 *Ecumenical Assemblage* a council of Roman Catholic bishops in Rome. The twentieth Council, the Vatican Council, met in 1869–70.
2928 *crassitude* the state of being crass.
2932 *caoutchouc* india-rubber.
2945 *Milsand* Alongside the tribute to Milsand in the manuscript, Browning wrote, in Greek, lines from Euripides, *Rhesus*, 342–5: 'May Adrestea, daughter of Zeus, keep envy far from our lips. For I shall speak what I want in my heart to say.'
Milsand] O friend *MS., 1873.*
2945–6] *MS. interpolation.*
2974 *Demonstrate*] *MS., this edition*; Remonstrate *1873–88.* (The following 'to', and 'demonstration' in line 2963, make the *MS.* reading preferable.)
2986–3024] The paragraph is very heavily revised in the *MS.*
2996 *Stramonium* narcotic drug.
2997 *calomel* medicine used as a cathartic.
3005] Circumstance has ordained things otherwise *MS. first reading.*
3020–22 *drop by drop . . . let Gideon say* Judges vi 37–40.
3022 *by spoonfuls came*] came down to earth *MS., 1873.*
3039 *Fons et origo* 'the fount and origin' (Latin).
3051 *Perpend* consider (archaism).
3068 *Cistercian monk* not identified.
3078 *postulant* candidate for admission into a religious order.
3086–7 *What God hath joined/Let no man put asunder* 'What therefore God hath joined together, let not man put asunder' (Matthew xix 6; Mark x 9).
3089 *conceit* fancy.
3091–2 *oracles/Of God* Romans iii 2.
3151 *hopper* receiver through which materials pass to the mill.
3164 *Star of Sea* Stella Maris (Latin): the Virgin Mary.
3183] *not in MS.*
3193] *not in MS.*
3233 *'Seventy, – folly's year* The Franco-Prussian War broke out in 1870.
3238 *chose to ride* Mellerio called for his coach before ascending the belvedere.
3256 *tale* complete sum.

3268 *Ollivier* Émile Ollivier, Prime Minister of France at the time.
Roon Graf von Roon was Prussian Minister of War at the time.
3269 *Bismarck, Emperor . . . King* the Prime Minister of Prussia, Napoleon III of France, William I of Prussia.
3277–84 The passage is often quoted as central in Browning's aesthetic.
3287 *leaf* thin sheet of metal.
3313] *not in MS.*
3316 'all that is in the world, the lust of the flesh, and the lust of the eyes, and the pride of life, is not of the Father, but is of the world' (1 John ii 16).
3324 'No man can serve two masters' (Matthew vi 23).
3341 *I could not pluck my heart out* glancing at 'if thy right eye offend thee, pluck it out . . . for it is profitable for thee that one of thy members should perish, and not that thy whole body should be cast into hell' (Matthew v 29).
3355 *draff* dregs.
3362–85] The lines are heavily revised in *MS.*
3380 *move mountains* 'Faith will move mountains' (proverbial).
3383 *Miranda's method*] With me, the rule is *MS.*
3419 *out of nothing 'ex nihilo nihil fit'* ('out of nothing, nothing is made'); the idea that God made everything from nothing is traditional.
3419–20 'the Lord made heaven and earth, the sea, and all that in them is' (Fourth Commandment, Book of Common Prayer).
3422] *not in MS.*
3422 *minim* minute thing.
3432 *Here came Louis Onze* The French King made a pilgrimage to La Délivrande on 14 August 1443.
3436 *Commines* Philippe de Commines (*c.* 1447–1511), whose *Memoirs* focus on the reign of Louis XI.
3437 *Marie-Antoinette* Queen of Louis XVI; her visit to La Délivrande appears to be unhistorical.
3443–3450 Henri, Count of Chambord (1820–83), was son of the Duchess of Berry, and claimant to the French throne. The bouquet appears to be unhistorical.
3489 *At shilly-shally* irresolute.
3495] *not in MS.*
3496–3503 See 1202–5n.
3518, 3523, 3525, 3533] *not in MS.*
3547 *King of Italy* Victor Emmanuel took over Rome and completed his kingdom in 1870.
3548 *Legations* Papal provinces.
3552 *Henry* the Count of Chambord.
3553 *makes all things new* 'And he that sat upon the throne said, Behold, I make all things new' (Revelation xxi 5).
3555 *Alacoque* Margaret Mary (1647–90) French nun (canonized 1920), founder of the Order of the Sacred Heart.
3556 *Renan* Ernest Renan (1823–92), best known for his life of Jesus.
Veuillot Louis Veuillot (1813–83), writer on religion and history.
3558 *'The Universe'* the staunchly Roman Catholic journal edited by Veuillot. It had been suspended 1860–67.
3559–62] *MS. interpolation.*
3562 'old things are passed away; behold, all things are become new' (2 Corinthians v 17).

3568] *not in MS.*

3576–88] *MS. interpolation.*

3595 *gardener* His name was Richer. He heard the body hit the ground, but did not see the fall. He testified he thought the death accidental.

3596 *Dibbling* making holes in.

3608 *leap*] man *MS.*

3641] When bolt came captive upon prison-bars: *MS.*; When, bolt on prison-bars, a captive came *1873.*

3645] *not in MS.*

3668 *velleity* dream or wish, without accompanying action.

3680 *lignum vitae* Guaiacum wood is used for medicine.

3680–81 *grains/Of Paradise* aromatic drug.

3682 *rose of Jericho* Asiatic plant also known as the resurrection plant, and as Saint Mary's rose.

3683 *Holy-thorn* one of several plants supposed to have been used for Christ's crown of thorns.

passion-flower a flower so called because of the supposed resemblance of parts of it to elements in Christ's crucifixion.

3684 *smack* of the lips, in anticipation; or taste.

3688 *simples* plants or herbs used for medicinal purposes (archaism).

3690 *Monkshood* aconite, a poisonous plant used for medicine.

belladonna a poisonous plant used for medicine.

3730] *not in MS.*

3752 *ruddle* see 1507n.

3754 *goatly* described by *OED* as a nonce-word. Meaning 'goatish', it was used by Mrs Browning in the sonnet 'Flush or Faunus' (1850), 10. Goats are traditionally licentious.

3767 *topiary* trimming branches to give trees or shrubs ornamental qualities with artificial shapes.

3771 *cockney* pampered.

3773 *touchwood* the soft substance into which wood can be turned by the action of certain fungi.

3788 *mummeries* silly religious rituals.

3858 *scenical* theatrical.

3860] *not in MS.*

3884 *Christ's prime precept* Matthew xix 21.

3885 *craze* insane fancy.

3893 *Non compos mentis* Latin: 'not sound of mind'.

3895] *not in MS.*

3905–6] *not in MS.*

3915 *sheep lost* Matthew xviii 13–14.

3936–7] *not in MS.*

3939 *casts stone* John viii 7.

3958 *Siècle* a daily political newspaper.

3959 *Univers* see 3558n.

3962 *Schneider* Hortense Schneider, French actress and singer (1833–1920), a star after 1864.

3969–70] *not in MS.*

3977–9] Shall right the injured ones.
So, 'Cockatrice!' – *MS.*

3979 *Cockatrice* a fabulous monster. Figuratively, a treacherous mischief-maker.

3980 *Jezebel* Ahab's wife (2 Kings ix 30); a wicked painted woman.
Queen of the Camellias La Dame aux Camélias, heroine of the play by the younger Alexandre Dumas (1852), a beautiful courtesan who escapes to the country with her lover.
3985 *concurrence* competition (Gallicism).
3996 *one-eyed, in her French phrase, rules the blind* Behind the line is the frequently quoted and varied remark of Erasmus: 'In the kingdom of the blind the one-eyed man is king' ('En la terre des aveugles celui qui n'a qu'un œil y est roi'). Browning may also have had in mind *avoir de l'œil* – to look well, and *avoir l'œil* – to be on one's guard.
4012 *mew* cage.
4025 *Blake* a picture, relatively 'unfinished' in execution, by the English poet and painter.
Meissonier The French painter (1815–91) is noted for his attention to detail – Clara's portrait is 'finished'.
Meissonier] Gerard Dow *MS.*; Meissonnier [*sic*] *1873*.
4040 *Painted-peacock* a kind of butterfly.
4041 *Brimstone-wing* a kind of butterfly.
4049 *parterre* level space in a garden with various kinds of flower-beds.
4076 *Exposition* exhibition (Gallicism).
4080 *pendule* clock.
4081 *gimcrack* trumpery article.
Liszt Franz Liszt, Hungarian musician and pianist (1811–86).
4084 *fortune who assists the bold* Simonides, *Fragments* 94, quoted by Claudian, who called it Simonides' maxim; and often echoed.
4110 *throw* 'a twist of some fibre' (*OED*, which calls the sense rare, and cites only this example).
4116 *smoothening* The verb 'smoothen' was a favourite of Landor's.
4121 *nice* discriminating.
4123 *palmer-worm* a kind of caterpillar, hairy and destructive.
4124 *Ball in* gather itself into a ball.
4127 *scarabaeus* beetle; here the dung-beetle, representations of which were often used in Egypt for amulets.
4134 *midden* dunghill.
4137 *blotch* pustule.
4144 *thrum* short pieces of thread.
4195 *distemper* derangement of mind.
4205] *not in MS.*
4229 *How say you, friend?*] But story's done;/And – pardon granted for its length and breadth?/Tell me as homeward we retrace our steps! *Berg Collection proofs, first set.* (The addition is entered in Browning's hand, and the date 'August 1872' is appended; there was then to be a space, and then – instead of 'How say you, friend?' – an 'epilogue' was to begin 'Once more, and yet once more, we meet, fair friend!' The 'epilogue' was to be dated as the whole poem now is, the date of 23 January 1873 being first entered in the proof. The revisions are, except for the dates, cancelled in the same proof.)

Aristophanes' Apology

First published on 15 April 1875 by Smith, Elder. There was no independent second edition; indeed, copies of the first edition were still being advertised well after Browning's death. Browning revised the poem for *1888* somewhat more extensively than is usual with the later poems: five lines were added, and another one divided into two. In the printers' manuscript in the Library of Balliol College, many single lines and long passages are interpolated, and sections are heavily revised; most, at least, of the manuscript would appear to be the one and only draft of the poem. Browning's note states that the poem was begun about 11 August, and ended 7 November, 1874 at Mers, Picardy. The transcript of *Herakles* had, however, been written earlier; according to the manuscript it was completed on 17 June 1873. Other parts of the poem, notably 'Thamuris Marching', a version of the first line of which appears in Browning's notes for *Red Cotton Night-Cap Country,* may also have been written earlier and, like *Herakles*, incorporated into the manuscript.

As in *Balaustion's Adventure,* to which *Aristophanes' Apology* is a sequel, a 'transcript' of a play by Euripides is included; the *Herakles*, however, is a translation, not an adaptation, and is much less central and integrated in this poem than was *Alkestis* in *Balaustion's Adventure.* Euripides was Browning's favourite Greek dramatist, doubtless in part because of the obvious parallels between them. Browning appears to have studied Aristophanes intensively in 1873, and he was also steeped in much of the literature about the Greek dramatists. He is in part concerned here with defending Euripides against the kind of hostility rampant, for instance, in the strictures of A. W. von Schlegel (1767–1845) in *Lectures upon Dramatic Art and Literature* (of which a new edition was published in 1871). The immense erudition which seems to be displayed in *Aristophanes' Apology* in fact derives, essentially, from a few works. Among the more important of these are: Augustus Meineke's *Historia Critica Comicorum Graecorum,* the *Scholia in Aristophanem,* J. A. Symonds's *Studies of the Greek Poets* (First Series, 1873), and Plato's *Symposium.* For information about Greek food and drink, Browning is especially indebted to the *Deipnosophists* of Athenaeus, and for details about the fall of Athens, finally defeated by Sparta in 404 B.C., to Plutarch's *Life of Lysander* and to Thucydides. The major source, however, is the plays of Aristophanes themselves; the apology itself, which forms the bulk of the poem, is a patchwork of quotations and information from the plays and allusions to them, enriched by material drawn from the *Fragments,* the scholia and other sources. And while critics have tended to imply that Euripides is central in the poem, Aristophanes in fact is so – as with Blougram's monologue, 'Apology' is used ambiguously: 'All my roundabout/Ends at beginning, with my own defence' (2488–9). 'Indeed, I am no enemy of that Aristophanes – all on fire with invention, – and such music!', wrote Browning to Swinburne in 1881 (Hood, *Letters*, 193); and he told Carlyle: 'I felt in a manner bound to write it, so many blunders about Aristophanes afloat, even among the so-called learned' (W. Allingham, *A Diary*, Macmillan, 1907, 240). The poem's sources have been exhaustively dealt with in C. N. Jackson's 'Classical Elements in Browning's *Aristophanes' Apology*', *Harvard Studies in Classical Philology* XX, 1909, 15–73; T. L. Hood's compilation in the same journal, XXXIII, 1922, 78–180 (which has been separately reprinted): 'Browning's Ancient Classical Sources'; and F. M. Tisdel's 'Browning's *Aristophanes' Apology*', *University of Missouri Studies* II, 1927, 1–46. D. Smalley, 'A Parleying with Aristophanes', *PMLA* LV, 1940, 823–38, looks at the poem as a kind of Browning's *Poetics.*

Browning sets his poem in the spring of 405 B.C. (5368–70), framing the apology, the *Herakles*, and Balaustion's reply to Aristophanes, in the voyage from the fallen Athens to Rhodes of Balaustion and her husband. Balaustion recalls the previous spring when the apology was made. As the poem has it, Aristophanes was celebrating winning the comic prize with a second *Thesmophoriazusae* (*Priestesses of Demeter* – a lost play of which only fragments survive). His revels were interrupted by Sophocles with news of the death in Macedonia of Euripides; Aristophanes, somewhat sobered but still 'tolerably drunk', broke in on Balaustion and her husband as they were planning to read *Herakles* in tribute to their beloved dead dramatist. Browning handles chronology with poetic licence: among many instances, the first *Thesmophoriazusae* was first played in 411 (Browning makes it 407), Athens fell in 404 (Browning makes it 405).

Motto The Greek motto, reflecting Balaustion's attitude to the plays of Aristophanes, is an Aristophanic fragment. The English paraphrase is Browning's.
1 *Euthukles* Balaustion's husband. He followed her from Syracuse (see *Balaustion's Adventure*, 265–74).
4 *Athenai* Athens.
9 *Haides* Hades was god of the underworld, Hades.
11 *inarmed* clasped.
14 *sigh of soul escaped* alluding to the old belief that the soul leaves the body with the last breath.
17 *Olumpos* Mount Olympus in Thessaly, the abode of the gods.
18 *Akropolis* the citadel of Athens.
19 *Koré* 'Maid'; an Athenian name for Persephone, wife of Hades.
21 *unanimous* for 'unanimously' in the obsolete sense of 'conjointly'.
23 *glaucous* sea-green (the word comes from Greek, and illustrates Browning's extensive use in the poem of words derived from Greek).
24 *Glassing* mirroring.
27 *Multitudinously* 'the multitudinous seas' (*Macbeth* II. 2. 63).
29 *Attiké* Attica, the district in which Athens is situated.
32 *To* to the point of.
33 *hearted* fixed in the heart.
34 *Pallas* Pallas Athena, goddess of wisdom and deity of Athens.
35 *Helios* The cult of the sun-god was dominant in Rhodes, Balaustion's birthplace (the later Colossus of Rhodes was a statue of him). See 652–3 and note.
48 *'assert the wise'* a kind of classical tag (see also 58) used here with particular reference to a fragment of Philemon (see 5696).
50 *Philemon* New-Comedy poet, from Syracuse, rival of Menander and admirer of Euripides. The reference is an anachronism: he was born about forty years later. See 5692–5702.
51 *cark* worry (archaism).
53 *rose-smit earth* The Greek name of Rhodes means 'Isle of Roses'.
71 *Peiraius* the port of Athens, connected to it by the Long Walls. In his *Life of Lysander* Plutarch tells of the destruction of the Walls while flute-girls played their flutes. Balaustion speaks of the incident in detail near the end of the poem. (Browning's error in spelling the word as 'Peiraios' has been corrected throughout the text of the poem in this edition.)
76 *enginery* machinery.
79–80 *long double range/Themistoklean* Themistocles (*c.* 528–*c.* 462), the Athenian statesman, suggested the Long Walls.
82 *senseless* without senses.
89 *Dikast and heliast* judge and juror.
90 *sham-prophecy-retailer* translating words in *Birds*, 960, and *Peace*, 1047, 1094.

90–91 *scout/O' the customs* translating a word in *Frogs,* 363.
92 *Altar-scrap-snatcher* translating a word in *Knights,* 1358, and elsewhere in Aristophanes.
93 *Rivalities* rivalries.
Rivalities] Obscenities *MS.*
101 *kordax-step* dance of Old Comedy.
103 *Perikles* Pericles (*c.* 495–429) led Athens in its greatest days of glory.
104 'Who knows but that to live is to die, and to die is to live' (fragment of the lost *Phrixus* of Euripides).
106 *Prove thee Olympian* alluding to a famous passage in which Pericles is called Olympian in *Acharnians,* 530.
108 *spirit-place* In Plato's *Republic* the ideal city exists in Idea only; Balaustion conceives of the Idea in a new Athens. Compare *Fifine at the Fair,* 1454–5.
109 *Pheidias* Phidias (*c.* 499–*c.* 417), greatest of Athenian sculptors.
112 *Propulaia* The Propylaea is the famous gateway on the west of the Acropolis.
114 *Pnux* The Pnyx was the public place of assembly, to the west of the Acropolis.
Bema platform from which speeches were delivered at the Pnyx.
115 *Thunder and lighten thence a Hellas* In *Acharnians,* 531, Olympian Pericles 'Thundered and lightened, and confounded Hellas'. Hellas is the Greek name of Greece.
118 *Theatre* The Theatre of Dionysus was situated just south of the Acropolis.
119 *purple* Ancient Athenians wore purple mantles.
Staghunt-month March (with its festival of Artemis, goddess of hunting).
120 *Dionusia* festivals held in honour of Dionysus, when plays were performed.
122 *prize* At Greek theatre festivals, the dramatists competed for prizes.
128 *Hermippos* The Athenian comic poet accused the mistress of Pericles of impiety.
129 *Kratinos* Cratinus, comic dramatist, rival of Aristophanes, attacked Pericles and his friends, including Phidias.
130 *Eruxis* the name, in *Frogs,* of an ugly satirist. See also 1674.
131 *mop and mow* grimaces.
132–7 *There's a dog-faced dwarf . . . Zeus* In Lucian's *Deorum Concilium* X, 533, Momus says: 'but you, Egyptian dog's-face, . . . who are you, how came you to think that you may bark among the gods?'
132 *dog-faced dwarf* the Egyptian god, Anubis.
136 *dog-ape*] Platon *MS.* (The *MS.* name and line 367 indicate that Balaustion is referring here to the comic poet, Plato.)
137 *Momos* personification of fault-finding.
138–40 *Makaria . . . contention* Macaria is the self-sacrificing daughter of Heracles in the *Heraclidae* of Euripides; the quotation from her is of lines 593–6 in that play.
146–7] *not in MS., 1875.*
147 *Furies in the Oresteian song* The Furies haunted Orestes after he killed his mother, Clytemnestra. See the *Eumenides* (especially 46–59), third play in the Aeschylean trilogy, the *Oresteia.*
148 *wanting* lacking.
154 *prompt* readily rendered.
155 *pine, likelier die than if*] pine off far likelier than *MS., 1875.*
161 *Klutaimnestra* Clytemnestra, heroine of the *Agamemnon* of Aeschylus, murdered her husband, Agamemnon.

162 *Iokastê* Jocasta, mother and wife of Oedipus in *Oedipus Tyrannus* of Sophocles, hanged herself.

Medeia Medea, heroine of the *Medea* of Euripides, killed her own children.

163–6 *Small rebuked ... purify their tide* reflecting some conventional views about tragedy. Line 166 alludes to Aristotle's famous statement in the *Poetics* about *catharsis*, usually translated 'purgation' but sometimes 'purification'.

171 *Peplosed and kothorned* gowned and buskined.

173 *Choros* Balaustion imagines herself and her husband as playing the Chorus, commenting on the action in an Athenian tragedy.

175–6 *pity... terror* according to Aristotle, the emotions central to tragedy.

176–80 *Phrunichos ... not reform thyself* Phrynicus, Athenian tragic poet, produced his *Capture of Miletus* in 492, but he was fined and the play banned because the audience was moved to tears. The Persians had sacked Miletus in 494, and memories were fresh in the 'smart-place' (the place where one smarts or suffers).

185 *my first* the story of Balaustion's escape from the Syracusans in *Balaustion's Adventure*.

190 *the four* the four girls to whom Balaustion told her story in *Balaustion's Adventure* (see 4–5).

193 *Admetos* hero of *Alcestis*, the 'transcript' of which is included in *Balaustion's Adventure*.

195 *his friend* Heracles, who brings the dead wife of Admetus back alive to him in *Alcestis*.

197 *start* emerge into life.

199–202 There are echoes of *Frogs*, 244–9. The streamlet is the Ilissus.

200 *galingale* sedge.

202 *Baccheion* the Theatre of Dionysus (Bacchus) in Athens.

204 *boatman-spider* The boat-fly or water-boatman is an insect with two legs resembling oars.

205 *Lenaia* a Dionysiac festival, held early in the year, when plays were presented.

206 *Andromedê* The lost *Andromeda* of Euripides first appeared in 412.

207 *Kresphontes* The lost *Cresphontes* of Euripides first appeared about 421.

208 *Someone from Phokis* In his *Life of Lysander* Plutarch tells of an anonymous man from Phocis (in central Greece) who, when the Spartan forces were preparing to lay Athens waste after the Peloponnesian War, sang the first Chorus from the *Electra* of Euripides, and so moved his hearers that 'they felt it to be a cruel deed to destroy such a famous city which produced such poets'. Browning makes the 'someone' Balaustion's husband.

209 *temple-steps* Balaustion gave her version of the *Alcestis* on the steps of the Syracusan Temple of Heracles.

213–14 *trilogy ... Bacchai* The *Bacchae* of Euripides was probably composed in 407, and posthumously produced in or after 406, with the *Iphigenia in Aulis* and *Alcmaeon in Corinth*.

215 *teach the choros* Athenian tragic playwrights (see also 206–7) usually produced their own plays (comic playwrights did so less often).

tinged] taught *MS.*

217 *live*] new *MS.*, *1875*.

218 *new-born star*] star above *MS.*, *1875*.

222 *prore* prow.

227 *Amphitheos* a character in *Acharnians* (where see 51–2, 182–5).

230 *visitor* Aristophanes.

245 *tripod* oracle.

248 *Speak good words* translating a word in *Clouds*, 297.
251 *Aischulos* Aeschylus had died fifty years earlier.
261 *stade* stadium, an arena for athletics.
263 *diaulos* a double course: runners run to a goal, and then return to the starting-point (Euripides had been a leading athlete, and the image thus has special relevance).
hundred plays Euripides wrote about ninety plays.
267 *olive* The olive was sacred to Pallas Athena, goddess of Athens, and a symbol of peace for which Euripides had striven. A crown of olive was ancient Greece's highest honour for leading citizens, and the highest prize in the Olympic Games.
268 *Wiselier* Balaustion shares her creator's fondness for highly unusual comparatives and superlatives.
272 *idle poet* Euripides had a reputation for being anti-social; he participated less directly in civic affairs than many other artists.
275 *Antigoné* Probably first produced in 441, the play is generally regarded as one of the great Greek achievements.
278 *took on him command* In 440 Sophocles, as general, helped suppress the Samian revolt; tradition says he won the vote for general because of his *Antigone*.
283–6 *Cold hater . . . ten cities* Euripides was accused of misanthropy, and was said to have written much in a sea-cave on Salamis. He was devoted to reading.
286 *Shadow of an ass* See *Wasps*, 191. The reference is to Aesop's fable about the man who hired an ass, and who in the heat of the day sat down in its shadow, only to be told he had not paid for the shadow.
289 *final trilogy* an error resulting from a misinterpretation of the scholia: the three plays did not form a trilogy.
290 *Hupsipule, Phoinissai* The lost *Hypsipyle* and the *Phoenissae* were produced about 409.
Match] Strife *MS*.
290–92 *Match/Of Life . . . Zethos against Amphion* The allusion is to the lost *Antiope* (*c*. 408), the theme of which is suggested by surviving fragments. Zethus and Amphion, sons of Zeus and Antiope, were herdsman and musician respectively.
298 *youth's labour still*] such enterprise *MS*.; youth's enterprise *1873*.
302 *Macedonian Archelaos* Euripides went to the court of Archelaus in Macedonia in 408. There he wrote his last plays, died, and was buried at Arethusa.
306–7 Old *Lives* say that Euripides became a minister of Archelaus.
308–10 Euripides composed a play, not extant, in honour of Archelaus.
311 *phorminx* stringed instrument of the harp class.
312 *Alkmaion, maddened Pentheus*] *this edition*; 'Alkaion,' maddened 'Pentheus' *MS*., *1875–88*. Browning slips in making titles of what are obviously references to characters (compare 314), and in the former name. The lost *Alcmaeon of Corinth* was a play in the final trilogy of Euripides, written at the court of Archelaus; the trilogy also included the *Bacchae*, in which Pentheus is the leading character. The verb 'maddened' suggests the haunted turbulence and frenzy of the *Bacchae*.
314 *Iphigeneia* The *Iphigenia in Aulis, Bacchae,* and the lost *Alcmaeon of Corinth* formed the final trilogy of Euripides.
317 *Agathon* The Athenian tragic poet and friend of Euripides went to the court of Archelaus in 407.
319 *young Euripides* son of the playwright.
320 *Mounuchia* Munychia was the smallest of the three harbours of Athens.
320‸21] Five lines are cut out from the *MS*. here.
324 *their favourite* Aristophanes.

325 *City of Gapers* translating the epithet for Athens in *Acharnians,* 635, and elsewhere in Aristophanes.
328 *Glauketes . . . Morsimos* Glaucetes is a glutton (*Peace*, 1008). Morsimus was a poor tragic poet mentioned by Aristophanes, but Balaustion has almost certainly confused him with Morychus, the famous gourmet (*Peace*, 1008; and *Acharnians,* 887, where he is said to love Copaic eels).
329 *Kopaic* Lake Copaïs in Boeotia was famous for eels. For a passionate address to a Copaic eel, see *Acharnians,* 885–94.
330 *thousand drachmai* Drachmae were the standard Greek coins. Three drachmae is the price for a Copaic eel in *Acharnians,* 962. A thousand drachmae is the price for a small shark in the *Deipnosophists* of Athenaeus 7, 44, where Copaic eels are praised (7, 50).
331–2 Proper eel-cooking used 'salt, and marjoram and water'; foam-fish were parboiled with nettles, and then fried with nettles and herbs steeped in oil (*Deipnosophists* 7, 45 and 22).
333 *triremes* ships with three banks of oars.
334 *Arginousai* The Athenians won a naval victory over the Spartans near this group of islands off the west coast of Asia Minor in 406, but the Athenians executed six of their own commanders for failing to rescue crews of sinking ships in a storm.
336 *Mikon* Athenian fresco-painter (*Lysistrata,* 679).
336–7 *Thessalian mime . . . Lais* *Deipnosophists* 13, 86, tells of Thessalian dancing-women; the same work mentions Lais, the famous courtesan, and reports her death in Thessaly.
338 *Leogoras' blood-mare koppa-marked* Leogoras is an epicure (*Wasps*, 1269) and horse-owner (*Clouds,* 109). A horse branded with the koppa, symbol of Corinth, is referred to in *Clouds*, 23.
339 *talents* silver currency units. The horse was extremely valuable.
341 *choinix* transliteration of the Greek word for a *dry* measure (usually of corn).
Mendesian a good wine from Mende in Macedon.
348–50 The *Thesmophoriazusae* (*Priestesses of Demeter* or *Female Celebrators of the Feast*) was produced in 411; it is rich in parodies of Euripides. Browning changes its date to 407, and has it that the reworked play (of which in fact only fragments remain) was produced in 406 and won the prize denied Aristophanes for the original play. The autumn festival, the Thesmophoria, gives the play its title.
357–8 One legend is that women tore Euripides to pieces as he was going to visit one Craterus.
359 *loved by Sokrates* Euripides was a pupil of Socrates, who, though not fond of theatre, went to the plays of Euripides.
360–63 Old *Lives,* in which appear the names in 362, report that rival poets had the royal hounds turned on Euripides and that he was torn to pieces by them.
364 *Protagoras* Euripides was a pupil of the famous sophist.
365 *Phu* an Aristophanic exclamation: 'fie', 'faugh'.
Platon Plato ('Plato Comicus'), Athenian comic dramatist.
367 *hate our women* In his own time and among the Victorians, Euripides was reputed to be a misogynist.
371 *Arethousian Nikodikos' wife* The lady and her husband are mentioned in old *Lives.*
376 *The Festivals* play (*c.* 414) by Plato, the comic poet. A fragment mentions Euripides; and the scholia report the attack on him.
381 *assisted at* was present at.
383–4 *cuttlefish,/Or that seaweed-alphestes, scorpion-sort* The cuttlefish comes

from *Deipnosophists* 7, 123; in the same work (7, 15) is 'the fish that lives in seaweed, the alphestes, the scorpion also with its rosy meat'.

388 *Lusistraté* The *Lysistrata* (411) is generally regarded as the most obscene of the plays of Aristophanes.

401 *Kleons* Cleon, the notorious demagogue, vilified by Aristophanes in several plays (notably *Knights*), took leadership in Athens after the death of Pericles in 429. He was killed in 422.

409 *wine-lees* Actors in early comedy smeared their faces with wine lees. Aristophanes himself played the part of Cleon in *Knights* with his face thus smeared.

411 *Ashamed?*] Besides, *MS.*

Phuromachos 'we frail womankind/Must take the seats Phyromachus assigned us/. . . and not attract attention' (*Ecclesiazusae,* 21–3). The scholium says: 'Sphyromachus proposed a public resolution that the women and the men should sit apart.'

417 *Waves, said to wash pollution* Euripides, *Iphigenia in Tauris,* 1193.

420 *Phaidra* Phaedra is the heroine of the *Hippolytus* of Euripides; in love with her stepson, she committed suicide, her moral standards being somewhat different from those of the ladies in *Lysistrata.* See *Frogs*, 1043–4.

427 *him who charged this piece* Aristophanes attacked the presentation of Phaedra, in *Thesmophoriazusae* and *Frogs*.

431 *Scythian's whip* Scythian archers were policemen in Athens.

438 *Salabaccho* a courtesan twice alluded to by Aristophanes.

439 *Reconciliation* handmaid of Lysistrata; see *Lysistrata,* 1114. While it is generally held that no women appeared on the Greek stage, Browning clearly agrees with some scholars that they did appear occasionally in silent roles as dancers, musicians and so forth.

450 *Aristeides . . . Miltiades* Athenian statesman ('the Just') who fought at Marathon (died *c.* 463); and the victor of Marathon (died 489).

451 *golden tettix* The Athenians of older days wore golden grasshoppers in their hair (see *Knights*, 1331).

452 *Kleophon* Cleophon, violent Athenian demagogue in the later years of the Peloponnesian War.

460 *Euripides* Aristophanes made him a leading character in *Thesmophoriazusae.*

463 *his own depths*] excrement *MS. first reading*; his own filth *MS.*

466–8 If Balaustion has particular plays in mind, *Acharnians, Knights* and *Lysistrata* may be them.

467 *Pun-pelleted* Aristophanes used puns abundantly.

485–6 The opening of *Peace* is referred to: Trygaeus proposes to go to heaven on a huge dung-beetle.

488 *statue in the theatre* The Athenians erected one, next to that of Aeschylus.

489 *Bring the poet's body back* An Athenian petition that the ashes be returned was disregarded; Euripides was buried in Macedon.

491 *Alkamenes* eminent sculptor.

492 *seiren* The monument of Sophocles was said to include, as many ancient tombs did, the figure of a Siren.

meed not used in any sense given in *OED.* A problem, unsolved here.

493 *Thoukudides* Thucydides, the Athenian historian of the Peloponnesian War.

510 *pardon of Admetos* Balaustion and Browning are harder on Admetos than most readers.

514–15 *height o'er height/Ever surmounting, – destiny's decree* 'hard and harder, high and higher yet,/Truly this lot of mine is like to go' (*Balaustion's Adventure,* 1119–20).

524 Euripides forgets conveniently: it is not known who gained the prize.
532 *prologize* Balaustion introduces the *Herakles*.
533 *Eurustheus* Eurystheus, King of Argolis, laid the Twelve Labours on Heracles.
537 *triple-headed hound* Cerberus, guardian of Hades, dragged up to earth by Heracles.
539 *back – how should he come?* 'Is it you trust the sire of these, that's sunk/In Haides, will return? (3690–91).
540 *Lukos* Lycus, villain in *Heracles*, usurped the throne of Thebes, and threatened the family of Heracles in his absence.
541] Who in that prolonged absence, plain defeat *MS., 1875*.
543 *Megara* daughter of Creon, King of Thebes, and a character in *Heracles*. Creon gave her to Heracles after he had killed Erginus, to whom the Thebans had had to pay tribute.
545] Saw his occasion, seized the tempting prey, *MS., 1875*.
555] *not in MS., 1875*.
558 *Amphitruon* son of Alcaeus and grandson of Perseus; husband of Alcmena, the mother of Heracles. He speaks the prologue to *Heracles*.
562 *Komos* comus: revel.
564 *Phales, Iacchos* respectively, the phallus personified (see *Acharnians*, 263–79); and one of the Eleusinian deities (frequently identified with Bacchus, celebrated in a chorus – with Demeter and Persephone – in *Frogs*, 325–414).
567 *Jackdaw-song* Songs (*coronismata*) were sung on Rhodes, with collections taken up for the 'Jackdaw' (*Deipnosophists* 8, 59).
575 *Fifteen* Sophocles increased the size of the tragic Chorus to fifteen; in comedy, it numbered twenty-four; Browning may have slipped, or may be suggesting that the smaller Chorus is an economy made during the Peloponnesian War (see line 694).
576 *women's garb* The Chorus of the *Thesmophoriazusae* is made up of women.
577 *Three* By convention no more than three actors (apart from the Chorus and mute persons) could appear in a Greek tragedy at the time, but Aristophanic comedy often needs four actors.
577–9 *Mnesilochos . . . Toxotes . . . our Great and Dead* three leading characters in *Thesmophoriazusae*: a kinsman by marriage of Euripides, ('Archer') a Scythian policeman, and Euripides.
585–7 'it was decreed . . . that no woman should appear in public undressed, under the penalty of paying 1000 drachmas . . . a tablet, containing an account of the mulcts thus incurred, was publicly exposed in the Ceramicus upon a plane tree' (Potter, *Antiquities of Greece* II, 309).
588–9 *Elaphion . . . fawn-foot* Elaphion, assistant of Euripides in *Thesmophoriazusae*, was leader of the flute-players; for the dance alluded to, one performed to Persian music, see *Thesmophoriazusae*, 1172.
593 *Phaps* dove.
598 *Archon* The chief magistrate presided over the performances and over the celebratory dinner held after them.
601 *baldness* Aristophanes often alludes to his own baldness (see, for instance, *Knights*, 550).
606 *black*] *MS., 1875*; back *1888*.
614 *Hephaistos* Hephaestus, god of fire, patron of artists working in iron and metal.
615 *brother* Heracles.

625 *His either struggling handful* As a baby, Heracles held in either hand the two snakes sent by Hera to kill him, and killed them.
638 *Victory* statue of Pallas Athena in her temple on the Acropolis.
643 *Kallistion* transliteration of the Greek for 'fairest prize', or 'little Callisto' (an Arcadian nymph).
644 *Kubelion... Melittion* 'Blue-violet'... 'Little Honey'.
646 *Phibalion* 'Little Fig': Phibelian figs (from Phibalis, west of Attica) are referred to in *Acharnians,* 802.
647 *Korakinidion* 'Little black raven'.
648 *Nettarion, Phabion* 'Duckling', 'Little Dove'.
649 *Rhoidion* 'Rosie'.
650 *balsam-bloom* that is, 'Balsamion'. 'Balaustion', as is explained in *Balaustion's Adventure,* 207 (and in 5608 in this poem), means 'wild-pomegranate-flower'.
651 *me Rhodian* The Athenian citizenship of Aristophanes was often questioned. See 1904–8, 3236–8.
652–3 *if Helios wived,/As Pindaros sings somewhere* The allusion is to the *Olympian Odes* 7, 14 and 54–74, of Pindar (518–438), greatest of Greek lyric poets. See also lines 35–6 in *Aristophanes' Apology.*
660 *Pho* This 'Greek' exclamation appears to be Browning's invention.
662 *cheekband* See *Wasps,* 582. It is worn to support the cheeks in playing certain instruments.
663 *cuckoo-apple* the Greek word for 'plum' (presumably, in Greek lore, eating plums was supposed to render one dumb or foolish). The line is indebted to a Greek fragment.
664 *Thasian* a superior wine from Thasos, island in the northern Aegean.
665 *Threttanelo* sound imitative of the cithara: see *Plutus*, 290, 296.
666 *Neblaretai* a word Browning found in a one-word fragment from the lost *Banqueters* of Aristophanes; 'it concludes' (see C. Dahl, '*Neblaretai* and *Rattei* in Browning's *Aristophanes' Apology*', *MLN* LXXII, 1957, 271–3).
669 *By the cabbage* The exclamation occurs in *Deipnosophists* 9, 9.
670 *Chrusomelolonthion* The name, translated in the next line, comes from *Wasps,* 1341.
674 *Artamouxia tricks the Toxotes* In *Thesmophoriazusae,* in a burlesque of the rescue of Andromeda by Perseus in the final scene, Euripides is disguised as an old procuress in order to rescue Mnesilochus. He distracts the Scythian archer with a dancer (as Browning has it, Elaphion, Chrusomelolonthion-Phaps). He tells the archer that his name is Artamisia; the Scythian garbles it into 'Artamouxia' (1200–1201).
675 *Hermes* In *Thesmophoriazusae,* 1202, Euripides thanks Hermes for the successful deceit of the Scythian archer: Hermes was god of good luck.
lucky throw Aristophanes is probably metaphorical in speaking of a throw of the dice as determining that his play would be the last performed: the Archon probably decided the order.
676 *seven* During the Peloponnesian War, the regular ration of plays for a day was probably not seven but five: a tragic trilogy followed by a satyr-play and one comedy.
681 *goat's breakfast* a somewhat unappetizing one; see *Plutus*, 295, 313–14.
683 *forward to the crows* roughly, 'go to Hell'; a common Greek expression (see 1777, 2175, 3066, 5160).
689 *ivy* The ivy was sacred to Bacchus as the bay to Apollo; Aristophanes is wearing the victor's crown of ivy.

692 *Curtail expense* Budgets were in fact reduced in the later stages of the war.
693 *twenty-sixth* The Peloponnesian War began in 431.
696 *three-crest skull-caps, three days' salt-fish-slice* translating Aristophanic words in, for instance, *Birds*, 94, and *Acharnians,* 197 (three days' rations was the normal Athenian amount for an immediate expedition).
700 *Archinos and Agurrhios* The names of these legislators on comic performances come from the scholia and Meineke.
701 *Flay your dead dog* See *Lysistrata,* 158.
702 *loss of leather* See *Clouds,* 537, which makes clear that the leather made a phallus.
706 *Kudathenaian and Pandionid* the 'deme' and 'tribe' to which Aristophanes belonged.
711 *Step forward, strip for anapaests* translating *Acharnians,* 627. The traditional Greek comedy included, about the middle of the play, a choral interlude known as the parabasis ('step forward') in anapaestic metre. The chorus leader announced the beginning of the parabasis.
713 *tickling*] pelting *MS.*
714 *chick-peas ... plums* There are a number of references in the plays of Aristophanes to the throwing of such things into the audience.
718 *Choirilos* Like Phrynicus, Choerilus was an early tragic dramatist.
719 *goat-song* the literal meaning of 'tragedy'.
721–2 *Kratinos ... 'Clouds'* Cratinus, Athenian comic dramatist and a notorious toper, in extreme old age won the prize in 423, a year in which the *Clouds* of Aristophanes took third (and last) prize. The year before, in *Knights*, Aristophanes had called him senile.
725 *'Willow-wicker-flask'* the title (or a version of it) of the winning play of Cratinus in 423.
743 *Good Genius* the 'Happy Fortune' (Loeb translation) of, for instance, *Knights*, 85 and 106. Used again in 1351, 1353.
744 *unmixed* Greeks generally mixed water with wine.
750 The line echoes *Prometheus Bound* of Aeschylus, 89–90.
766 *accidents* non-essential characteristics.
768 *cinct* surrounded.
769 *satyr* woodland god or demon, part man, part animal. Satyrs attended upon Bacchus, and appeared in many Greek plays.
cranks humorous turns ('Quips, and cranks, and wanton wiles' – Milton, 'L'Allegro', 25).
boss and spike protective weapons of some kind (shield and lance?).
786–91 Reminiscent of several passages in *King Lear*.
792 *sagacious* perceptive.
794 *lyric shell or tragic barbiton* smaller or larger lyre.
795 *gauds* showy ceremonies.
796 *solace* enjoyment (*OED* 2); an obsolete usage.
803 *certes* certainly (an archaism).
813 *Tuphon ... mount* Zeus buried Typhon, the hundred-headed monster, under Mount Etna.
831 *comic visor* By the time of Aristophanes, comic actors generally wore masks.
845 *Sousarion* legendary founder of Greek comedy, said to have brought comedy from Megara to Attica about 470. That he ever existed is now thought doubtful.
846 *Megaric* of Megara, state west of Attica and south of Boeotia.
847 *Chionides* according to Aristotle, one of the two earliest Attic comic poets.

849 *sticking* moulding with a carpenter's plane (*OED* 18c).
853 *pashed* smashed.
869 *your*] late *MS., 1875.*
871 *so fast*] away *MS., 1875.*
880 *'Grasshoppers'* The play is a Browning invention. (The Florentine edition identified it as a lost play, and even 'found' a Greek title for it.)
881 *'Little-in-the-Fields'* conflation of two phrases for the Dionysiac Festival of December (*Acharnians*, 202 and 250).
886–7] The lines are transposed in *MS.* and *1875.*
901 *strength's a demiourgos*] Strength cries "Lay on, spare not!" *MS.*
demiourgos demiurge: Creator.
909 *Ameipsias* Athenian comic dramatist, rival of Aristophanes.
910 *Salaminian cave* a cave on Salamis (Euripides is said to have written in one).
912 *man and noise one*] transiency grow *MS.*
921] *not in MS., 1875.*
928] *not in MS., 1875.*
935 *of fancy sates my*] the Aristophanic *MS., 1875.*
937 *Iostephanos* 'the Violet-crowned': Aristophanes uses Pindar's famous epithet for Athens in, for instance, *Acharnians,* 637.
939 *O happy-maker*] Ever Athenai *MS.*
941–3 *Kleophon . . . Dekeleia* Decelea was an Attic deme friendly to Sparta, and strategically located. Led by Cleophon, the Athenians refused a Spartan peace offer in which the Spartans agreed even to withdraw from Decelea.
943 *Kleonumos* The butt of Athens and of Aristophanes, Cleonymus, a huge glutton and coward, threw away his shield at the Battle of Delium.
944 *threw away his shield* 'What is that brute which throws away its shield/Alike in air, in ocean, in the field?' (*Wasps*, 22–3). The riddle was well known; the answer is 'a serpent' (land and water snakes, and a constellation).
946 *Orestes* a footpad (see, for instance, *Birds*, 712, 1490–93).
948 *Melanthios* tragic dramatist attacked by Aristophanes for his gluttony among other things (see, for instance, *Peace*, 804–11).
951 *Set*] *MS., this edition*; Let *1875–88.*
958 *'Wasps'* the play of Aristophanes of 422 B.C.
963 *'Wine-lees-poet'* that is, comic poet (see 409 and note).
964 *Telekleides* Athenian comic dramatist.
965 *Murtilos, Hermippos* The brothers were Athenian comic dramatists.
966 *Eupolis* leading Athenian comic poet.
970–73 The information probably came from Meineke I, 538.
973 *phyz* face (humorous colloquialism); for daubing it, see 409n.
983 *Mullos . . . Euetes* reportedly, early writers of Athenian comedy.
987 *Morucheides-Surakosios* Morychides was Archon 440–39; Syracosius, 416–15.
988–91 Meineke refers to the laws, I, 40–43.
990 *Areopagite* member of the Council of Athens, the Areopagus. In the time of Aristophanes, it was a minor part of the judicial system.
996–1001 A tragic poet presented a trilogy of plays, and a fourth satyr-play ('the contemptuous fourth'), generally much lighter in tone. A comic poet presented only one play at the Festival.
1002–6 *Euripides . . . Satyr-play* Euripides had little use for the traditional satyr-play (which ultimately disappeared from the Greek stage): *Alcestis* was, in

fact, his fourth play in 438 B.C. Euripides wrote eight saytr-plays, not five, but Browning may have classified some of them differently.

1007 *trifle* spend frivolously (an obsolete usage).

1010 *Sokrates* The friend of Euripides was frequently attacked by the conservative Aristophanes.

'Life's not Life' Two fragments of Euripides include the saying. See the burlesques of Euripides in *Frogs*, 1082 and 1477.

1011 The line alludes to a famous line (612) in the *Hippolytus* of Euripides, hit at by Aristophanes in *Frogs*, 102–3 and 1471, and *Thesmophoriazusae,* 275–6.

1013 *head low and heels in heaven* Browning is indebted to the scholia on *Acharnians,* 399: Euripides wrote with his feet up.

1019 *my Comic lash*] the Comic Muse *MS*.

1022 *leek-and-onion-plait* an instrument of torture, rejected as too gentle, in *Frogs*, 621.

1023–5 In *Electra,* 520–78, Euripides clearly criticizes the recognition of Orestes by Electra in Aeschylus. By implication, Euripides might also be said to criticize the recognition in the *Electra* of Sophocles, which Browning may have thought of as preceding the play of Euripides.

1029 "The Birds" presented in 414 B.C.

1032 *gapers* See *Acharnians,* 635, and 325n.

1035 *must* new wine.

1036 *Fining* refining, purifying.

1042 *Alkibiades* Athenian leader in parts of the closing stages of the Peloponnesian War (he was twice in exile during these years).

1043 *Triphales . . . Trilophos* The former (*c*. 410?) is a lost play of Aristophanes; the title means 'the triple-phallused'. The lost play is thought to have attacked Alcibiades in its leading character, Triphales. 'Trilophos' means 'wearer of a three-crested helmet'; in the imaginary *Grasshoppers,* one gathers that Alcibiades as warrior was central.

1044–6 Alcibiades had great gifts, but lacked self-control, and never really did his gifts justice.

1047 *Tettix . . . Autochthon-brood* grasshoppers, native to the land. The grasshopper, symbolizing the closeness of the people to their native soil, was the symbol of old Athens.

1049 *emmet* ant (archaism).

1053 *Stagbeetle, huge Taügetan* A stagbeetle has mandibles like stag-horns; Taÿgetus is a mountain range west of Sparta. Stagbeetle represented Sparta in the 'play'. (*Peace* has a huge beetle in it.)

1056 *morbifies* makes diseased (the only example cited in *OED*).

1064 *Cockered no noddle up* did not coddle the mind (colloquial).

A, b, g the first three letters of the Greek alphabet.

1066–8 *Ruppapai . . . beneath* *Ruppapai* is the cry to which rowers kept time. See *Frogs*, 1073–5, where Aeschylus says that youngsters of his time knew nothing except to call for food, sing 'Ruppapai' as they rowed, and defecate on, and otherwise abuse, those below them in the boat.

1072–5 See *Clouds,* 973–6, 983.

1076–7 See *Clouds,* 1355, 1364–5.

1077 *romaunt* romance (an archaism).

1078 *Mitulené* Mytilene, chief city of Lesbos in the Aegean.

1080 *Oidipous* King of Thebes, who blinded himself in *Oedipus Tyrannus*.

1081 The nursery rhyme used here is 'The Man of Thessaly'.
1082 *Phaidras, Augês, Kanakês* Phaedra (in the *Hippolytus* of Euripides) fell in love with her stepson; Auge nearly married her son Telephus (*Telephus* is the title of a lost Euripides play, parodied in *Acharnians*); Canace committed incest with her brother.
1083 *tweedle* high-pitched.
1084 *Marathon* that is, the spirit that won the Battle.
1085 *Antistrophé* the second part (the 'turn-again') of the Chorus.
praise of Peace a constant Aristophanic theme.
1087 *Grub* uproot.
1088–9 *Romp with one's Thratta . . . bathing* translating *Peace*, 1138–9. 'Thratta' ('Thracian') is a stock name for a serving-girl.
1100 *None of the self-laudation* Aristophanes protests too much.
1109 *Aigina* Aristophanes was rumoured to have come from Aegina, the island near Athens.
1115 *Prutaneion* The Prytaneum was the City Hall in Athens; distinguished persons were entertained there at public expense (see *Frogs*, 761–4).
1120 *Ariphrades* an evil man, attacked in *Knights*, 1281–9.
1131 *Rural Dionusia* country festival held in December.
1133–4 *the Four – /Karkinos* Carcinus, comic dramatist, and his three dwarfish sons are attacked in *Peace*, 780–96, and in the conclusion of *Wasps*.
1139 That is, the fictitious play by Ameipsias beat the fictitious play by Aristophanes.
1143 *exomis* sleeveless vest, attire of slaves and labourers.
1148 *Parachoregema* subordinate Chorus.
1150–51 *Aristullos . . . rule the roast* Aristophanes used him, Meineke suggested, to represent Plato, and Browning accepts the suggestion. Browning sees the *Ecclesiazusae* as satirizing the treatment of women later recommended in Plato's *Republic*. Browning invents details for the second *Thesmophoriazusae*.
1152 *cribbed of* confined by.
1154 *Brave* bravo.
1156 *release* at the end of *Thesmophoriazusae*.
1157 *the old*] Skuthian *MS*.
1161 *Bald Bard's hetairai* the courtesans of Aristophanes.
1163 *Murrhiné, Akalanthis* names used by Aristophanes: Myrrhina is a character in *Lysistrata*; and Akalanthis ('Thistle-finch') is a name given to Artemis in *Birds*, 871–2.
1163–4 *beautiful/Their whole belongings* *Peace*, 524–6.
1168 *Kalligeneia* the third day of the Thesmophoria, the autumn festival in honour of Demeter.
1176 *choragos* chorus-leader.
mutes silent characters on the Greek stage.
1182 *Lusandros* Lysander was the Spartan admiral.
1183 *Euboia penitent* The island of Euboea, north of Attica, had revolted against Athens in 411.
1184 *Confederation* the Delian League or Confederacy: Athens and her allies.
1185–6 *The Great King's Eye . . . Kompolakuthes* conflating *Acharnians*, 91–2 and 589. Pseudartabas, ambassador of the Persian King, has a mask painted with one large eye.
1189 *Strattis* Athenian comic poet.
1191 *klepsudra* water-clock.

1191–3] Of the klepsudra sets resentment grave
Shaking our shark's-head fried in vinegar, *MS.*

1192–4 The dish owes much to Aristophanic recipes (see, for instance, *Birds,* 534–8, and *Plutus*, 720), and to Athenaeus, *Deipnosophists* 7, 44.

1193 *Sphettian* from the deme of Sphettus.

1194 *Silphion* plant used as relish.

1200 *Kleonclapper* Aristophanes clapped Cleon many times, especially in *Knights.*
erst formerly (an archaism). Cleon was killed in 422.

1205 *girl-voiced, crocus-vested Agathon* The adjectives are used of the reputedly effeminate Agathon in *Thesmophoriazusae,* 192 and 253. Agathon, fourth of Athenian tragic dramatists, followed Euripides to the court of Archelaus in 407.

1208 *Babaiax* exclamation of surprise (see, for instance, *Acharnians,* 64).

1211–21 *old pale-swathed majesty . . . ungarlanded* Sophocles died at the age of ninety in the year in which Aristophanes makes his apology. At the parade before the Great Dionysia in the spring of 406, he dressed his Chorus in black and left them ungarlanded in tribute to the dead Euripides.

1218 *Decent* becoming (an archaism).

1220 *Greater Feast* the Great or City Dionysia, when the major theatre contests were held.

1229 *dance*] his *MS.*

1232–41 An old *Life* has it that Heracles told Sophocles in a dream where a gold crown stolen from the Acropolis was hidden; Sophocles found it, and made it an offering to Heracles.

1239 *Medeia* the *Medea* of Euripides (431 B.C.).

1241 *Euphorion* The son of Aeschylus won the prize in 431, Sophocles was second, Euripides third.

1245–9 *Trugaios . . . out to sea* In *Peace* (421 B.C.), Trygeaus seeks to achieve peace. He speaks (697–9) of Sophocles as having become Simonides, a poet who loved money, and, using a Greek proverbial expression, adds that he is 'so old and sordid,/He'd put to sea upon a sieve for money'.

1250] *not in MS.*
Philonides. Kallistratos producers of several Aristophanes plays.

1251 *Retorts – "Mistake*] Quite otherwise *MS.*

1254 *Priest of Half-Hero Alkon* an error. Browning followed an emendation to an old *Life* of Sophocles.

1255 *Asklepios* Asclepius, son of Apollo, god of medicine, met with the old Sophocles, according to Plutarch, *Lives* I, 132.

1257 *Iophon* tragic dramatist, son of Sophocles. Legend has it that he tried to get control of his father's affairs, claiming that Sophocles was senile; Sophocles read a Chorus from his *Oedipus at Colonus* and persuaded the court otherwise.

1275 *hearted* fixed in the heart.

1294 *Ploutos* The first *Plutus*, a lost play, appeared in 408 (the second *Plutus* of 388 is extant).

1308–20] The lines are heavily revised in the *MS.*

1319 *Horses* alternative title for *Knights*.

1330 *'Antiope'* lost play of Euripides (*c.* 408 B.C.); the Antiope of the play was not the wife of Theseus, but the mother of Amphion and Zethus (see 290–92).

1331 *'Phoinissai'* The *Phoenissae* (*Phoenician Women*) is another late play of Euripides (*c.* 409).

1332–3 *'great and awful Victory/Accompany my life'* quoting the final lines of the

Phoenissae (and of two other Euripides plays), where they are not really part of the play but a prayer for victory in the dramatic contest.
1333 *Maketis* One old name for Macedonia was Macetia.
1337 *murk* dark.
1340 *Pentelikos* the mountain in Attica that provided the marble for the chief monuments of Athens.
1370 *ugsome* horrible (Scotticism).
1374 *Lift* lifted (obsolete usage).
1380 *Lamachos* In *Acharnians* (425 B.C.), Lamachus, the Athenian general later killed in the Athenian expedition, is a blusterer.
1382 *Philokleon* 'Cleon-lover', the central character of *Wasps*, a lover of jury service.
1384 *three-obol fee* Athenian jurymen got three obols a day (six obols make one drachma).
1385 *Paphlagonian* Paphlagon represents the demagogue Cleon in *Knights* (424 B.C.).
1387 *Pisthetairos, Strepsiades* central characters of *Birds* (414 B.C.) and *Clouds* (423 B.C.).
1412 *pure Hippolutos* victim of his stepmother's love in the *Hippolytus* of Euripides (428 B.C.).
1414 *Bellerophon* hero of a lost play of Euripides (Trygaeus on his dung-beetle in *Peace* burlesques Bellerophon on Pegasus).
1416 *Theseus* in the *Hippolytus*.
1424 *Love's overbrimming*] God's aspiration *MS.*
1426 *strait* limited.
1444 In *Iphigenia in Aulis,* 1212, Iphigenia wishes she could sing so as to cause rocks to move.
1453 *Faun* here, 'Satyr' (an anachronistic usage of a Roman word). Satyrs, goat-featured, attend Dionysus.
1456 *Nikias* the Athenian commander at Syracuse. Plutarch tells of his alarm at an eclipse, and of the repulsing of the Syracusan attack, but not of the mistake about the signal.
1461 *alalé* a victory whoop; see *Lysistrata,* 1291.
1470 *blended twain* Here, and at other places in the poem, Browning is clearly mindful of the opinion of Socrates, expressed to Agathon and Aristophanes in Plato's *Symposium*, that the tragic and the comic genius are identical. See 3440n.
1482 *Hermai* The Herms were pillars adorned with a head (usually of Hermes) and a phallus, and were erected at doorways and street corners. In 415 in Athens, they were mutilated, and the sacrilege greatly distressed Athenians. See *Lysistrata,* 1094.
1485 *homelier symbol* the phallus.
1487 *freak* capricious prank.
1499 *Evirate* castrate.
1501 *argute* shrewd.
1504–10 *if the tale be true . . . garden-chance* See lines 5325–36 for the 'tale'. Browning follows *Deipnosophists* 13, 45.
1506 *And questioned*] Demanded *MS.*, *1875*.
1558 *merely*] barely *MS.*, *1875*.
1559 *Sophroniskos' son* Socrates.
1561–2 *table-book and graver . . . psalterion* Dionysius, tyrant of Syracuse, bought

from the heirs of Euripides 'his psalterion, his tablet, and his graver' (ancient *Life*). See 3518–23, and 5686–91.

1561 *graver* tool for engraving.

1562 *psalterion* transliteration of the Greek word for 'psaltery', the ancient stringed instrument.

1569 *'Frenzied Hero'* The *Heracles* is often alluded to as *Furens* (after the sixteenth-century Aldine edition title); Browning's phrase translates 'Furens'.

1570 *pine-wood tablets . . . wax* common writing materials of the time.

1571 *Papuros* papyrus: writing paper, originally from Egypt.

1581 *Daimon* household deity.

1601‸2] Calmness supreme – Euripides is dead!' *MS. cancelled reading.* (The line, revised, was interpolated in the *MS.* to become 1605.)

1609 *Solon* Athenian legislator (*c.* 638–*c.* 558).

1610–11 possibly suggested by *Peace*, 647–56. Plutarch (*Lives* I, 188) mentions the law.

1612 *Elektra* See the *Electra* of Euripides, 900–902.

1622 *Olympiad* One Olympiad is four years.

1644] *not in MS.* (see 1078).

1670 *immerded* covered in dung.

1674 *Dogface Eruxis* The name appears in *Frogs*, 934, with the implication of ugliness; but Browning is almost certainly hitting at Alfred Austin, whose small stature he often ridiculed. See also 130.

1682] *not in MS.*

1682–5 The Giants revolted and tried to scale Olympus, but were thrown back by the gods and Heracles who hurled objects at them.

1691–1726 one sentence.

1719–20] Hating my hates, one false[, *MS.*] one true for both, –
Championed my cause – not flagellating foe *MS., 1875.*

1721 *rose and lily*] leeks and onions *MS.* (see 1022n.).

1722 *bowze* booze (colloquialism).

1734–9 In attacking Euripides, Aristophanes in his plays refers to his bookishness, his 'realistic' language, his mother's humble status (an invented one) as a market-gardener, and the role of Cephisophon in writing his plays and loving his wife (Cephisophon was a slave who probably helped with the music for the plays of Euripides). See, for instance, *Frogs*, 944.

1743 in *Wasps*. 838.

1752 *Wine-lees-song* translating the word used for 'comic play' in, for instance, *Acharnians*, 499 (see 963n.).

1775‸6] Either to fine, refine, turn faint, fall, freeze, *MS.* (The line is at the top of the *MS.* page, and may well have been inadvertently omitted.)

1812 *hunks* miser.

1814] *not in MS.*

1827 *ribroast* belabour with a cudgel.

scarify wound, make incisions. The images of bludgeon and rapier used here and elsewhere in the poem are commonplace in comic theory throughout history.

scarify] scorticate [*sic*] *MS.*

1833 *crabtree* Crabtree cudgels are common in literature.

1835 *stickled* strove.

1838 *As fig-leaf holds the fat-fry* taken from *Knights*, 954.

1843 *ellops* The word is obsolete, and the kind of fish meant is unknown.

1848 *shrewd* wicked (an obsolete usage).
1849 *sap* trench to approach a beseiged place.
1852 *Palaistra* Technically the 'palaestra' was a school for boys' physical training, or part of the Gymnasium used for wrestling, but Browning uses the word in its popular sense of 'Gymnasium', in the outer part of which teachers, especially sophists, presented their views.
1855 *the Cult* religion.
1859 *bray* pound into powder.
1860 *of proof* impenetrable (archaic usage).
1865 *in a sort* in a kind of way (see *OED* 21d – an archaic usage).
1874 *Whirligig* the Vortex (Socrates' substitute for Zeus) of *Clouds*, 380.
1884 *Glauketes* a glutton (*Peace*, 1006).
1885 *Chairephon* pupil of Socrates, silent character in *Wasps*, and referred to in *Clouds* and *Birds*.
1887 *I urged*] Staple *MS.*, *1875*.
1892 *Threttanelo, the Kuklops drunk* 'Threttanelo! Threttanelo!/And you, the Cyclops, will we find in dirty, drunken sleep reclined' (*Plutus*, 296–7). *Threttanelo* is a sound imitative of the cithara. The Cyclops are the one-eyed giants of Greek myth.
1900–1903 *Kleon ... Such other* Apparently Aristophanes attacked Cleon in the lost *Babylonians* in 426 B.C., and Cleon had arraigned him for defaming the State in the presence of strangers. Aristophanes gives details in *Acharnians*.
1904–5 *stranger, privileged/To act no play at all* The earliest plays of Aristophanes appear to have had others' names attached to them – perhaps in part because of doubts about his citizenship.
1906 *Kameirensian* of Camirus in Rhodes (Balaustion's home-town).
1907 *Lindian* Lindus was a city-state in Rhodes.
1908 *can't write Attic* an ironic statement. The plays of Aristophanes survived partly because of the purity of their language.
1914 *day-star* sun.
1915–16 *Aias ... seven times seven* Aias (Ajax) is the mighty Greek warrior of the *Iliad*, whose characteristic weapon is his shield, 'his tower-like shield of bronze, with seven-fold ox-hide' (*Iliad* VII, 219–20).
1923 *ramped* reared on hind legs.
1928 *Thearion* a baker, whose name survives only in fragments from lost plays of Aristophanes.
1932 *Kilikian* Cilicia is in southern Asia Minor.
1933 *San* dialect variant of 'sigma' (the Greek 's'). See *Clouds*, 122.
1934 *Menippos* Menippus was a horse-breeder and farmer (see *Birds*, 1293).
1935 *Kepphé* The lady apparently owes her existence to Browning.
1936 *Sporgilos* 'Clipper', a barber (*Birds*, 300).
1939 *Muse of Megara* Megaric comedy was thought crude and vulgar.
1940 *weasel-lap* presumably, by analogy with 'cat-lap': stuff fit for a weasel to drink.
1941 *marrow* marrow 'viewed as the seat of animal vitality and strength' (*OED* 2b).
Cheiron's hero-pap Chiron, friend of Heracles, was the wise medicine-man among the Centaurs, and instructed Achilles and other heroes.
1947 *Rocky Ones* The most ancient name of Athens was the Rocky Town; Aristophanes used the name in, for instance, *Birds*, 123.
1948 *mewls* baby-whinings.

1957 *in soak* becoming soaked.
1959 *Peparethian* a wine from the island east of Thessaly, referred to in a fragment of Aristophanes, and, along with Thasian, in *Deipnosophists* I, 52.
1978–9 *Hellas thundersmote/The Persian* at Marathon and Salamis especially.
1979–80 *had birth . . . at Salamis* Some old *Lives* record the legend.
1981 *Themistokles* commander of the Athenian fleet at Salamis.
1983 *Odusseus* Odysseus, hero of the *Odyssey*.
1987 *Theognis* elegiac poet of the late sixth century B.C.
1988 *Homeros* Traditionally, Homer flourished about 1000 B.C.
1991–5 In his *Life of Alcibiades* Plutarch reminded young men of their oath 'that they would account wheat and barley, and vines and olives, to be the limits of Attica; by which they were taught to claim a title to all land that was cultivated and productive'.
2004 *benignantest* Extraordinary superlatives are a Browning hallmark.
2005 *humanism* devotion to human interests.
2010 *Aphroditè* goddess of love, fertility and beauty (Venus).
2014–18 *Perikles . . . Promachos* Pericles entrusted Phidias with superintending work on the Acropolis. Part of this work was the sculptor's own colossal bronze statue of Athena Promachus. Money contributed by Athenian allies for military purposes was expended on the projects.
2019 *'Oresteia'* the tragic trilogy of Aeschylus.
2026 *gorcrow* carrion crow.
2028 *Kimon . . . Boulé* Cimon was the son of Miltiades, and a leading admiral and statesman. He was ostracized by the Boulé (the Athenian Council) in 461, but the line recalls days of Athenian glory.
2029–31 The 'crew' includes Socrates and Chaerephon; see *Clouds,* 102–4, 835–7.
2033 *"Wise men"* 'Sophists'.
Prodikos Prodicus of Ceos was a famous sophist; he is alluded to in *Clouds,* 361, and *Birds*, 692. His weakness is mentioned in Plato's *Morals* and *Protagoras*.
2035 *way Theseia . . . Tripods' way* The former appears not to have existed, though Browning is probably thinking of a street near the Theseum, north-west of the Acropolis. The latter street ran south and east of the Acropolis.
2036–8 Aristophanes often ridicules the Sophists' cosmological speculations.
2042–4 'Protagoras was the first person who asserted that in every question there were two sides to the argument exactly opposite to one another' (Diogenes Laertius IX, *Life of Protagoras,* 3).
2045 *kottabos* a Greek pastime, which involved throwing wine in a carefully prescribed manner from one container to another. For the 'last mode of playing', see 5100–5115.
2047 *Choes* 'The Jugs': the second day of the Anthesteria, the late-winter Athenian festival. See, for instance, *Acharnians,* 961.
2051–2 'I am not able to know whether they [the Gods] exist or whether they do not' (Diogenes Laertius IX, *Life of Protagoras,* 3).
2054–5 *Leda, as a swan,/Europa, as a bull* Zeus took the form of a swan when wooing Leda, and of a bull when wooing Europa.
2060 *Zeus . . . sieve* 'I had dreamed that the rain-water streamed from Zeus and his chamber-pot sieve' (*Clouds*, 373).
2061 *Theoros* a politician and perjurer (*Clouds,* 399), not hit by the thunderbolts of Zeus.
2063–4] Instruct your progeny what fools are you
For fearing Zeus, who is the atmosphere, *MS., 1875*.

2067–70 Aristophanes sounds rather like Browning's Caliban on the subject of the Quiet.
2071 See *Clouds*, 156–68, for discussion of the fascinating question.
2074 *hemlock . . . bull's blood* Hemlock is the poison, drunk, for instance, by Socrates. Themistocles is said to have poisoned himself with bull's blood (see *Knights*, 845, and *The Ring and the Book* XI, 2408–9).
2077 *Anaxagoras* The philosopher (500–428), teacher of Pericles, Socrates and Euripides, was the first to explain how eclipses occurred; he was imprisoned for impiety, but Pericles arranged his release.
2081 *Charon* the ferryman of the Styx in Hades.
2085 *Brilesian hollow* cave in Mount Brilessus (Pentelicus) in Attica – Mount Hymettus, more famous for its honey, was what Browning probably meant.
2086 *Bacchis* 'how sweet and pure was the nectar that distilled from her [Bacchis'] kisses!' (*Alciphron* 1, 38).
flavorous lip beats both] lip beats both, my boy *MS., 1875*.
2088 The fable has not been identified – perhaps Browning's own?
2093 *Spartanizes* The Spartans had a reputation for tough frugality.
frowns] prates *MS., 1875*.
2100 *Plataian* that is, prompt, generous, strong. The Boeotian city of Plataea sent 1,000 men to Marathon, and prompt help to Salamis.
2105 *Saperdion – the Empousa* respectively, a famous beauty and a frightful hobgoblin (see *Frogs*, 293, and *Ecclesiazusae*, 1056).
2112 *Muses' Bee, bay-bloom-fed Sophokles* Browning translates epithets from ancient *Lives*.
2113] *not in MS.*
2113 *Kimberic* cambric, transliteration of word in *Lysistrata*, 45, 52.
2114 *successor* Euripides. The criticisms implicit in the following passage are characteristically Aristophanic – and Victorian.
2117–19 See *Acharnians*, 410–13, and *Frogs*, 1063–4.
2123–4 *womankind . . . match the male* Even more than Aeschylus and Sophocles, Euripides presents powerful women in his plays.
2129–30 *I paint men as they are . . ./Not as they should be* 'Sophocles said that he drew men as they ought to be; Euripides, as they are' (Aristotle, *Poetics* XXV, 19).
2131 *Women and slaves* 'Even a woman may be good, and also a slave' (*Poetics* XV, 1).
2140 *"There are no Gods"* While the context suggests a quotation from the *Heracles*, the quotation is not in the play (or in Browning's translation of it). See 5710 and note.
2145 *roundabout* circuitous way (compare 'Martin Relph', 126).
2152 *A-sitting with my legs up* See 1013 and note.
2155 *Grace* There were three Graces (in Homer, two), personifications of gracefulness.
Furies the three Erinyes, avenging spirits.
2161 *enthusiastic* irrational, frenzied (the older sense of the word).
2164 *emballed* encompassed with a sphere.
2168 'Beauty is truth, truth beauty' (Keats, 'Ode on a Grecian Urn', 49).
2191 *shag-rag* shaggy, disreputable (compare *The Ring and the Book* V, 389).
2193 *Pity and terror* the emotions proper to tragedy in the *Poetics*.
2210 *Kuthereia* Cytherea: Aphrodite.
2215–20 See *Frogs*, 826–9.

2225 *plethron* 100 Greek feet.
2227–31 referring to the parody of the debate between Pheres and Admetus in *Clouds,* 1410–52.
2233–5 See *Frogs,* 1064–6.
2237 *Kresphontes* Cresphontes is the eponymous hero of a lost play (and great popular favourite) of Euripides.
2240 *chiton* the ancient Greek tunic.
2241 *pose* perplex. In *Clouds*, Strepsiades is anxious to learn arguments to help him avoid paying debts.
2243 *rarely gained a prize* Euripides gained only five victories, and one of them was posthumous.
2245 *Ions, Iophons* There is evidence that Euripides beat Ion and Iophon (he did so with *Hippolytus*) for the prize, but none that they ever beat him, though each did have a victorious year.
2254 *Euphorions* Euphorion, the son of Aeschylus, won four victories, one of them over Sophocles and Euripides in 431.
2266 *'Erechtheus'* a strongly patriotic lost play of Euripides.
2275 *Once again*] Look at me *MS.*
2293 *Mede* The Persians had taken over the Median Empire; here, as often, the word means 'Persian'.
2296 *Pound in their mortar Hellas* In *Peace* (259–300) the pestles (Cleon and the Spartan Brasides) used to pound up (foment) war seem to have disappeared.
2303 *tans hides* Aristophanes often alludes to Cleon's being a tanner.
2304 *Huperbolos* The Athenian demagogue, successor to Cleon, is referred to as Hyperbolus the Lampmaker in *Clouds,* 1065.
2305 *Eukrates . . . Lusikles* Athenian demagogues. Eucrates is named in *Knights,* 253, as a dealer in bran and by the scholia as the oakum-seller of 129; Lysicles, who married the mistress of the dead Pericles, is referred to in *Knights,* 132.
2306 *Kephalos* Cephalus was a demagogue and potter (see *Ecclesiazusae,* 248).
2307 *Diitriphes* maker of wicker flasks and demagogue. See *Birds*, 798–800, 1442.
2308 *Nausikudes* grain-dealer and demagogue (see *Ecclesiazusae,* 426).
2321–7 The references are to *Birds.* Cloudcuckooburg is the Utopia of the play, Hoopoe Triple-Crest (formerly King Tereus) is its king. The gods prepare to join it at the conclusion.
2331 *Palaistra-tool* See 1852n. Roughly, 'tool of a subtle intellect'.
2332–9 The reference is probably to the lost *Erechtheus.* Erechtheus was a legendary king of Athens. Amphictyon is a delegate to the Amphictyonic Council, which dealt with religious affairs in Greece. Phrixus, sung of in the Chorus, and eponymous hero of a lost Euripides play, rode the ram with the Golden Fleece.
2341–6 See Horace, *Satires* I, 8, 1–7.
2346 *Priapos* god of Procreation (and gardens); statues were often used as scarecrows.
2347] *not in MS.*
2352 *exomion* 'sleeveless coat'.
2367 *Phales Iacchos* Iacchus is here identified with Bacchus: 'Phallic Bacchus'.
2379 *heroize* play the hero.
2392–7 The *Cyclops* of Euripides (the only extant satyr-play).
2393 *grimly* The adjectival use is obsolete.
2399 *Droll* farcical composition.
2403 *Herakles drunk! From*] Content enough, from *MS.*

2413–14 The lines recall the ring image of *The Ring and the Book*.
2417 *Kallikratidas* Spartan admiral, drowned after defeat at the naval battle of Arginusae (406).
2419 *Theramenes* A captain at Arginusae, he was largely responsible for the trial and execution of the victorious Athenian commanders. A frequent turncoat and possible traitor, he was later executed.
2425 *Demos* In *Knights* (see 1321), old Demus ('the People') is boiled and made young again by the Sausage-Seller.
2429 *balsam* healing ointment (that is, he oozes health).
2441 *rouncey* riding horse (a spelling variant of an obsolete word).
2442 *sausage-selling snob* Cleon's replacement in *Knights* is a sausage-seller.
2443 *Alkibiades, come back* Alcibiades returned in triumph to Athens in 407.
2448 *chaunoprockt* nonce-word, transliterating the Greek for 'wide-breeched' (Loeb translation: 'nincompoop') in *Acharnians*, 104, 106.
2466‸7] By vaunting virtues latent in the slave,
The soldier, arts, trades, handicrafts alike; *cancelled MS. reading*.
2476 *degree* hierarchical order.
2481–6 *'Suppliants' . . . people* In the play of Euripides (*c.* 422 B.C.), 399–462, Theseus, king of Athens, fires up at the Theban herald, and lectures him on democracy.
2491 *exact* The word as an adverb is obsolete.
2496 *Kirké* Plato (Aristullus) is compared to Circe, the enchantress who turned the men of Odysseus into swine.
bewrays betrays (obsolete word).
2517 *word to you, the wise* 'A word to the wise [is sufficient]' (proverbial – Latin: *verbum* [*satis*] *sapienti*).
2536 *household drudge* Cephisophon. The following charges (and the one in 2535) are Aristophanic (see 1734–9n.).
2540 *scrub* drudge.
2549 See 1011 and note.
2574 *"slave, mere thrashing-block!"* In *Frogs*, 756.
2575 *very next of plays* Aristophanes launches into a summary of *Frogs* (405 B.C.), contaminated by details from *Plutus* (408 B.C. in its lost first version, 388 in its extant second one). In *Frogs* Dionysus, with his slave Xanthias, goes to Hades planning to bring back Euripides.
2602–6 *See Hermes . . . the longest* See 1482n.
2607 *craze* mania.
2608 *have up Hermes* call Hermes to account (Browning perhaps meant 'have at'). Hermes is not a character in *Frogs*, but figures as a butt in *Plutus*.
Karion the slave in Plutus, with a pun on 'Carian' (Carian slaves were reputed to be bad ones) and 'carrion' (see the motto of *Aristophanes' Apology*).
2613 *washing tripe in well-trough* Cario orders Hermes thus in *Plutus*, 1169.
2615–16 See 1255n.
2621 *memorize* make memorable.
2624–8 Cario describes the service in detail in *Plutus*, 653–747.
2625 *choused* cheated.
2626 *snake* traditionally associated with Asclepius.
snap seize quickly.
2627 The line translates *Plutus*, 680–81.
2633] *not in MS.*
2636 *saves his cash* See *Peace*, 699.

2638 *father* The father of Sophocles was, in fact, a wealthy industrialist.
2639–41 *queer captain . . . squadron's charge* Sophocles is not known to have won the prize with *Antigone* (*c*. 441 B.C.). See 278n.
2642–4 *son's help . . . property* See 1257n.
2662–8 See *Frogs*, 640–65, where Aeacus, slave of Pluto, is the Judge, and Dionysus and his slave are thrashed.
2693 *Kinesias* the feeble dithyrambic poet of *Clouds*, who longs to be a bird.
2700 *mint-perfumed* See *Ecclesiazusae*, 646–7, where the Greek word for 'mint' puns on that for 'dung'.
2705 *Aristonumos* comic playwright who attacked Aristophanes.
2706 *Sannurion* a comic playwright.
2707 See *Acharnians*, 598, where the three leaders of the expedition to Syracuse are called 'cuckoos'.
2708 *boil a stone* from *Wasps*, 208.
Rattei exclamation of dancers and revellers.
2717] But, in remembrance merely, makes less poor *MS., 1875*.
2718 *Each*] None, *MS., 1875*.
2719 *hind* farm labourer.
2729–30 *some rose was rifled . . . musk and myrrh* 'any nose/May ravage with impunity a rose:/Rifle a musk-pod and 'twill ache like yours!' (*Sordello* VI, 880–82).
2737–8 alluding to Aesop's fable of the lion and the mouse.
2791 *fly-flap* fly-swatter.
2822 *bell* cone or catkin? (In these senses, the word, according to *OED*, applies to hops, not trees.)
2838 *'Lemnians' . . . 'The Hours'* lost plays of Aristophanes.
2839 translating *Ecclesiazusae* (392 B.C.).
2840–44 *once a year . . . morrow-day* Compare *Imperante Augusto Natus Est* – (Browning learned from Suetonius that Augustus became a mendicant one day a year).
2849 *the sole unbarbarous land* the standard Greek view.
2861 *Kassiterides* 'Tin Islands': Cornwall and the Scilly Isles, and, by extension, the British Isles.
2864 *Zeuxis* leading Greek painter.
2912–14 The Olympic and Nemean Games honoured Zeus, the Pythian honoured Apollo, and the Isthmian honoured Poseidon.
2936–41 *The Banqueters* (427 B.C.) and *Babylonians* (426 B.C.) are lost plays of Aristophanes. 'Prometheus' is the *Prometheus Bound* (*c*. 470 B.C.), 'Oidipous' is the *Oedipus Tyrannus* (*c*. 430 B.C.), and 'Medeia' is the *Medea* (431 B.C.).
2945 *Plataia* The Persians were defeated near Plataea in 479.
2946–7 Balaustion refers to *Clouds* and *Acharnians*.
2963–78 Balaustion leans here on *Peace*, 738–64, and *Clouds*, 537–62.
2995 *litigation-itch* satirized in *Wasps*.
2996–7 *Withstand mob-rule . . . mob-favourites* especially in *Knights*, but generally everywhere in Aristophanes.
2998 *sophists* attacked especially in *Clouds*.
2999 *poets their accomplices* attacked especially in *Acharnians*, *Thesmophoriazusae* and *Frogs*.
3020–34 *Kresphontes* In lines 3021–34 Balaustion translates a fragment from the lost *Cresphontes* of Euripides.
3021–34] In all probability the lines were not originally written for *Aristophanes' Apology*; they are inserted in the *MS*. on paper different from that of the *MS*.

3043 *Kunthia* Artemis, called Cynthia from her birthplace, Mount Cynthus in Delos.
3044 Euripides presented his first play about ten years before Aristophanes was born, and had presented at least ten plays before Aristophanes produced his first.
3058 *What imbecile has dared*] Shall any sane man dare *MS.*
3067–70 See *Peace*, 447–53.
3074] *not in MS.*
3076 *skiadeion* umbrella.
3086 *and Huperbolos were shams*] stood abhorrent and accursed *MS.*; and Huperbolos accurst *1875*.
3087 *Nikias* Balaustion seems to be thinking more of Plutarch's Nicias than of Aristophanes'.
3089 *Choros crying 'Hence, impure!'* as in *Frogs*, 354, 369.
3102–3 In *Clouds* the Speculation-shop of Socrates is burned; Socrates was to have to take poison in 399 B.C.
3113 *exhibit Peace* in *Peace*.
3116–17 *Theoria ... Opora* 'Mayfair' and 'Harvest-home', attendants of Peace in *Peace*, 520–26. Silent characters, they represent the joys of games and abundant Autumn.
3133 *Acharnian charcoal* a major item in *Acharnians* (where the Chorus is made up of Acharnian charcoal-burners).
3134 *Kimmerian, Stugian* In Homer the Cimmerii live in perpetual darkness. Stygian: of Styx.
3140 *into privacy* that is, into returning to private life.
3142 *shoe-sole-shreds* Aristophanes frequently alludes to Cleon's being a tanner.
3165 *tunny* tuna.
3173–4 *Leonidas ... Thermopulai* The king of Sparta died with all his men at the pass of Thermopylae in 480 B.C.
3186–8 See 943n.
3187–9 *'Cake my buckler be ... Dikaiopolis!'* The words recall *Acharnians*, 1125–6. In *Acharnians* Dicaeopolis makes a personal peace with the Spartans.
3193] And shouts for can and smooth-sleeked dancing-girls! *MS.*
3203–9 *Philokleon turns Bdelukleon ... faugh!* In *Wasps*, Philocleon (Cleon-lover), lover of litigation, becomes more reasonable after discussion with his son Bdelycleon (Cleon-hater), but then misbehaves outrageously. The lines allude to several scenes in the play.
3214 *fribble* trifler.
3226 *stinging-nettle*] satire *MS.*
3227 *housebreaker*] infamous *MS.*
3228 *Fish-gorging* translating a word in *Peace*, 810.
midnight footpad translating a word in, for instance, *Frogs*, 773.
3236 *stranger* another allusion to the contemporary doubts that Aristophanes was an Athenian. See 1900–1907.
3240 *Kratinos helped* Aristophanes is said to have taken a scene in *Thesmophoriazusae* from Cratinus. Eupolis claimed to have collaborated in *Knights*.
3240–44 *Kleon's self ... privilege* See 1900–1907.
3252 *Logeion* the theatre-stage.
3253–4 *Perikles ... maids* See *Acharnians*, 523–7 (Balaustion errs slightly in her reference).
3264] (Translate – "His teaching is the bane of boys") *MS.*
3268–70] You never took the joke for earnest? sure? *MS.*

3273 *estray* stray.
3298 *Speculation-shop* translating a word coined by Aristophanes in *Clouds*, 94.
3299 *shop's master rose* At the performance of *Clouds* Socrates stood up in the audience so that it might see who was being attacked.
3301] *not in MS.*
3304 *unbadged* that is, without Athenian citizenship.
3307 *resumed mere auditor* In the lost *Banqueters* Aristophanes attacked Cleon; in *Acharnians* he commented on Cleon's wrath; in *Knights*, a year later, he vilified him. It is, however, *Peace*, 757–8 (presented after Cleon's death) that is alluded to in 3308–9. (In 1881 – see Hood, *Letters*, 193 – Browning wrote to Swinburne, 'I am confident that Euripides bore his fun and parodying good humouredly enough – as even Cleon did.')
3308 *Lamia* She had a woman's face and breasts, and a serpent's body.
3309 *Kukloboros* Cycloborus, an Attican hill-torrent. In *Acharnians*, 379–82, Aristophanes wrote: 'to the Council-house he haled me off,/And slanged, and lied, and slandered, and betongued me,/Roaring Cycloborus-wise; till I well nigh/Was done to death, bemiryslushified'.
camel-rest bowdlerizing 'camel-anus' in *Peace*, 758.
3313 *curious king* Dionysius of Syracuse, to whom Plato sent an Aristophanes play for its presentation of Athenian political life.
3317 *grig* grasshopper.
3350 *Kleon, dead enough* Cleon died in 422, but Balaustion alludes to plays presented before his death.
3352 *vinous dregs* Cratinus was a notorious and self-confessed drunkard.
3353 *'Bottle'* the play by the old Cratinus that won the prize in 423 (*Clouds* took third prize).
3374 *Magnes* early comic dramatist. *Knights*, 520–25, refers in an affectionate tone to his *Birds* and *Frogs* among other plays.
3375 *Archippos* comic playwright, noted for his puns.
Hegemon Hegemon of Thasos, comic playwright, noted for parodies of famous poems. See *Poetics* II. 5.
3378 Paraphrasing a fragment of Eupolis alluding to Socrates' stealing from Stesichorus – in his *Helen* (412 B.C.) Euripides relied heavily on the Stesichorean version of the story.
3380 *'Konnos'* The *Connus* of Ameipsias took second prize in 423 B.C. when *Clouds* was third.
3383 *Telekleides* Athenian comic playwright; surviving fragments attack Pericles and Cimon.
3386–90 See 1250n.
3393–5 *Morucheides . . . Kinesias* The names are those of archons named in the scholia as passing decrees about comic performances.
3400 *Krates* Crates, Athenian comic poet, cited by Aristotle (*Poetics* V) as advancing comic art and rejecting the personally satiric.
3400–3403] *not in MS.*
3402 *Pherekrates* Athenian comic playwright. Balaustion follows Meineke's characterization of him.
3409 *'Acharnes'* The *Acharnians* (425 B.C.) is the first extant play of Aristophanes. He was probably about twenty when he wrote it.
3429 *Bacchis* a courtesan.
3438–40] Himself unlicensing the lawlessness,
Re-ordinating outworn rule, and fresh

Flushing with lifeblood what is gross not strong,
Till Comedy and Tragedy combine, *MS.*

3440 'The genius of comedy was the same as that of tragedy, and ... the true artist in tragedy was an artist in comedy also' (Plato, *Symposium* – where Socrates, Agathon and Aristophanes discuss the topic).

3449 *Ilissos* The Ilissus river washes east and south Athens.

3477 *Triballos* The absurd Thracian deity of *Birds*, where he, Poseidon and Heracles compose the Olympic delegation to Cloudcuckooburg.

3500 *A story* The story that follows is certainly false but has a strong tradition. The son (3501) was Iophon; the Chorus spoken (3510–11) from *Oedipus at Colonus*, 668–719. Compare *Balaustion's Adventure*, 145, where the same Chorus is alluded to.

3516 *another "Herakles"* The *Heracles* was written much later than the *Alcestis* (transcribed in *Balaustion's Adventure*), in which Heracles figures prominently.

3519 *stulos* stylus (pen).

3521 *ode bewailing Age* See 4237–91.

3530 *Beating the god, affords such test* See *Frogs*, 640–65, where Dionysus and his slave are thrashed to determine which of them is the god.

3531–2 *rash hands ... prison-walls dispart* See Acts xii 1–9 (the delivery of Peter from prison). The allusion is clear and has interesting implications (compare 5663n.).

3533 *he fronts mad Pentheus* Dionysus confronts the threatening Pentheus, King of Thebes, in the *Bacchae* of Euripides; see the episodes beginning with lines 434 and 643.

3534] *not in MS.*

3534 *perfect piece* The same phrase is used of the *Alcestis* in *Balaustion's Adventure*, 226.

3535–7 *Zeus' Couchmate ... Herakles* Amphytrion's wife, Alcmena, was the mother of Heracles by Zeus. Amphytrion of Argos was the son of Alcaeus, son of Perseus, son of Zeus.

3538–41 Cadmus was the legendary founder of Thebes, capital of Boeotia. The Thebans sprang from dragon's teeth planted by Cadmus, who married the daughter of Ares, god of war.

3542 *Kreon* This early King of Thebes is often confused with the Creon, King of Corinth, who betrothed his daughter to Jason, and with the brother of Jocasta who succeeded Oedipus as King of Thebes.

3551–2 *Argos ... Kuklopian city* The Cyclops were the legendary founders of Argos.

3553 *Elektruon* Amphytrion accidentally killed his wife's father, Electryon, and fled Argos for Thebes, where Creon freed him from blood-guilt.

3556 *Eurustheus* the king of Argos who laid the Twelve Labours on Heracles.

3557 Awkwardly translated, the line alludes to Heracles' willingness to undertake to rid the world of monsters.

3559 *Heré* Hera, queen of the gods, always hated Heracles.

3561 *Tainaros* Taenarus: central peninsula of the southern Peloponnesus, and a town near the entrance to Hades.

3563 *three-shaped hound* Cerberus, the three-headed monster dog that guarded Hades. To bring it to earth was the last of the Labours.

3585 *domes* mansions, halls.

3591 *Minuai* Heracles defeated the Minyae people, and thus freed the Thebans from paying tribute to them.

3602 *Taphian town* Taphius, in the Ionian Sea, was the site of Amphitryon's vengeance on the slayers of his brothers-in-law.

3656 *swan-like power* In legend, the swan sings beautifully just before death.
3684 *Lukos* Lycus: his name means 'Wolf'.
3697 *marshy snake* Killing the Hydra of Lerna was one of the Labours.
3698 *Nemeian monster* Killing the Nemean lion was one of the Labours.
3725–9 alluding to the victory of Zeus over the Titans.
3730 Heracles fought with the Centaurs, half-men and half-horses, when attacked while visiting Pholus.
3731 *Pholoé* mountain between Arcadia and Elis in the Peloponnesus.
3734 *Dirphus, thy Abantid mother-town* Dirphus, a town that Heracles laid waste, on the island of Euboea, an old name for which was Abantis.
3799 *Helikon* mountain in Boeotia, sacred to the Muses.
Parnasos mountain range north of Delphi, sacred to Apollo and the Muses.
3923 *plectron* instrument for plucking the wires of such instruments as the lute (a transliteration of the Greek, the word in this form is not in *OED*).
3938 *lion-tenant* the Nemean lion.
3943 *Pencios* The Peneus is a river of Thessaly.
3946 *Pelion* mountain sacred to Zeus in northern Thessaly.
3947 *Homolé* mountain in Thessaly.
3951 *stag* The capturing of the Arcadian stag was one of the Labours.
3953 *goddess* Artemis, goddess of the hunt.
3954 *Oinoé* Oenoe, river in north-west Attica.
3955 *chariot-breed* Catching the man-eating horses of Diomede was one of the Labours.
3961 *Hebros* Thracian river.
3963 *Mukenaian tyrant* Eurystheus, King of Mycenae, who laid the Labours on Heracles.
3964 *Melian shore* The Gulf of Malis is in south-east Thessaly.
3965 *Amauros* The Anaurus is a stream in Thessaly.
3967 *Kuknos . . . Amphanaia* Cycnus was a son of Ares and a famous robber; Amphanae was a town in Thessaly.
3969 *the melodious maids* the Hesperides, who guarded the golden apples, which Heracles had to obtain as one of the Labours.
3972 *dragon* Ladon.
3979 *Atlas* The Titan, who held the world on his shoulders, owned the Garden of the Hesperides. Heracles tricked him into giving up three of the apples.
3981 *Amazons* To obtain the girdle of Hippolyta, queen of the Amazons, was one of the Labours.
3982 *Maiotis* Maeotis was an old name for the Sea of Azov.
3983 *Euxin* the Euxine Sea: the Black Sea.
3989] *not in MS.*
3995 *Erutheia* the island of Erytheia, south of Spain, home of Geryon; one of the Labours was to capture the oxen of the monster.
4040 *Pelasgia* Argolis.
4048 *Daidalos* Daedalus, the legendary great artificer.
4051 *Oichalia* Oechalia, town in Euboea.
4112 *propula* portals (transliteration of the Greek word).
4164 *Ismenos* the river flowing near Thebes.
4165 *Dirké* Dirce, fountain in Thebes, formerly the lady killed by Amphion and Zethus (see 3566).
4166 *incarnadined* 'The multitudinous seas incarnadine' (*Macbeth* II. 2. 63).
4210 *Orgies* the Eleusinian mysteries.

4212 *Chthonia* Demeter.
Hermion Harmonia, wife of Cadmus, daughter of Ares and Aphrodite.
4239 *Aitna* Etna, the mountain in Sicily.
4275 *Mnemosuné* Memory: Mother of the Muses.
4277 *tortoise-shell* lyre.
4278 *Bromios* Bacchus.
4282 *paian* paean: song of praise to Apollo.
Delian of Delos, the Aegean island on which Apollo was born.
4284 *Latona* mother of Apollo.
4359 *Acherontian* Acheron was one of the rivers of Hades.
4373 *Asopiad* The river-god Asopus had several famous daughters, including Aegina, Salamis and Ismene.
4376 *Puthios* Pythius: Apollo.
4379 *Spartan* The teeth Cadmus sowed, the 'Sown', were called the 'Sparti' (there is no connection here with the Peloponnesian city).
4391 *Plouton* Pluto: Hades.
4409 *Iris* messenger of the gods.
4458 *Keres, daughters of Tartaros* Tartarus is Hades or an even worse and lower region, where the goddesses are the daughters of Night.
4463 *Otototoi* transliteration of the Greek: 'Alas, alas'.
4483 *tympanies and the thyrsos* cymbals, and the staff of Bacchus.
4487 *pouring-out* libation.
4489 *I wis* I know (a pseudo-archaism).
4493 *Ai ai* woe, woe.
4503 *Pallas on the Titan* referring to the war of the Olympians against the Titans; the Titan alluded to is Enceladus.
4554 *Nisos' city* Megara, of which Nisus was the legendary king.
4559 *Isthmos* the Isthmus of Corinth.
4582 *outwinding* used here in a sense not given in *OED*: 'circling faster than'.
4592 *prevents him* anticipates him in action (an obsolete usage).
4629 *daughters of Danaos* Danaus had fifty daughters; they married the fifty sons of his brother. On the wedding-night, forty-nine of the daughters murdered their husbands. The fiftieth pair were the ancestors of the rulers of Argos.
4634 *Prokné's son* Procne cooked her son, Itylus or Itys, and served him as a dish to his father, Tereus. The story is frequent in poetry; hence the 'sacrifice to the Muses'.
4674 *bray*] break and bray *MS.*
4705 *Erinues* the Furies.
4706–13 Alcmena demanded of Amphitryon that he avenge the death of her brothers by sacking the Taphians' island city.
4737 *Sisupheian stone* the stone that Sisyphus in Hades continually rolled up a hill only to have it roll down again.
4738 *Demeter's sceptred maid* Persephone.
4750 *hap* happening.
4775 *begroan* The word is not recorded in *OED*.
4800 *Erechtheidai's town* Athens (after its legendary King, Erechtheus).
4826 *Phlegruia* Phlegra was the battle-ground of the Gods and the Giants.
4860 *sign'st* indicat'st.
4906–11 See the epigraph of *Prince Hohenstiel-Schwangau* for an abridged and different rendering.
4915 *accost* salutation.

4930 *Ixion* Zeus bound him to a wheel of fire in Hades (see Browning's poem of 1883).
4958 *Pallas' citadel* the Acropolis.
4963 *Knosian bull* the Minotaur of Cnossus. By slaying it, Theseus saved the seven youths and seven maidens of Athens who had been annually sacrificed to it.
4968–9] The lines are transposed in *MS.*
5072] *not in MS.* (where a line is left blank).
5081] *two lines in MS.*
5087 *Lachares* This Athenian sculptor appears to be Browning's invention (though he may have had in mind Leochares, the famous Athenian sculptor of the fourth century B.C. to whom the *Apollo Belvedere* has been attributed). Browning supported artists of his time, especially his son, who wished freedom to display nudes.
5126 another dig at Euripides' writing with his feet up (compare 1013, 2152).
5139] *not in MS.*
5145 *He* Shakespeare.
5146 *Tin-islands* the Cassiterides (see 2861n. and 5160): the British Isles.
5157 *rash he turns*] had I turned *MS.*
5163 *Thamuris* Thamyris was a Thracian bard who rashly challenged the Muses to a contest. They blinded him and made him forget his art.
5165–73 The details are from old *Lives.*
5166 *Poikilé* the Painted Colonnade of Athens.
5167 *Once and only once, trod stage* An exaggeration: Sophocles trod the stage at least twice. He gave up acting, however, because his voice was weak.
5170 *named* gave his name to. Sophocles, as Thamyris, played the lyre in the lost play.
5172–3 *Thamuris . . . case* That is, Sophocles was the model for a portrait of Thamyris in the Painted Colonnade.
5175 *'Rhesos'* The *Rhesus*, if it be by Euripides, is his earliest extant play. In it, the Muse, mother of the dead Rhesus, alludes to Thamyris (see *Rhesus*, 914–25).
Blind Bard Homer. *Rhesus* dramatizes *Iliad* X.
5188 *Thamuris marching* The song was probably not originally intended for *Aristophanes' Apology*. It is written on paper different from that of the manuscript, in which the poem's original title is scraped out and 'Thamuris song' substituted. Most of the lines introducing and following the song are pasted in to the manuscript, and a version of the poem's first line is in worksheets for *Red Cotton Night-Cap Country* that probably belong to 1872. Browning used hints from *Iliad* II, 594–600, and *Rhesus*. DeVane reports (*Handbook*, 384) the poet's fondness for reciting the poem in later years.
5191–6 See *Rhesus*, 921–5.
5192 *Eurutos* Eurytus, king of Oechalia in Euboea, father of Iole, whom Heracles loved.
5193 *Dorion* the place in Macedonia where Thamyris met the Muses.
5194 *Pangaios* mountain in Macedonia.
5200 *Balura – happier while its name was not* Influenced by Pausanias (4, 33) who explains the name as derived from the Greek word for 'throw away'; it was the river where Thamyris threw away his lyre in his blindness.
5210 *conclusive* concluding.
5220 *Pan* the goat-legged god of flocks and herds.
5246 *Homeros*] Pausanias *cancelled MS. reading* (see 5200n.).
5262 *Pieria* home of the Muses at the foot of Olympus.

5265] In *MS*. this line originally followed 5184.
5276 *'Prelude-Battle'* The *Proagon* of Aristophanes, of which fragments survive, attacked Euripides.
5277–8 *'Main-Fight' . . . Crown* *Frogs* (405 B.C.), in which Euripides, inevitably, fares badly in the Contest with Aeschylus.
5289–92 The posthumously presented *Bacchae* of Euripides is generally regarded as indeed a 'prodigy'.
5310] To rolls and peasoup and Oporia's [*sic*] breadth! *MS*.
5313–14] For the cup goes round,
And the cakes abound,
Slices of hare,
And eel-fry rare! *MS*.
5314 *spinks* chaffinches.
5316 *guttlings* gormandizings.
5317 *light Muse* Thalia ('luxuriant', 'blooming'), Muse of Comedy.
5318 *Melpomenê* Muse of Tragedy.
5319 *Amphion's part* The walls of Thebes rose to the music of Amphion's lyre.
5322–37] *a later addition to the MS*. (Many of the *MS*. interpolations involve precise and detailed material. The fact supports Browning's statement – see Hood, *Letters*, 208 – that he wrote the poem without subsidiary material available to him. It supports also DeVane's conjecture in *Handbook*, 376, that the poem was finished in London.)
5323 *story he referred to* See lines 1505–8.
5325–36 *Lais . . . thinks it so* translating the *Deipnosophists* of Athenaeus (13, 45). In the letter alluded to above (5322–37n.), Browning specifically mentions not having Athenaeus to hand.
5336 Quoted from the *Aeolus*, a lost play of Euripides (Browning corrects the misquotation of the line in *Deipnosophists*). Aristophanes parodied the line in *Frogs*, 1475.
5354 *lamping* shining.
5368–70 The lines date Balaustion's voyage and the final fall of Athens in the poem in 405 (not 406, the date on which scholarship has insisted). See also 5373n., 5383–4, 5642–51.
5372 *homicidal dragon-crop* The armed warriors that sprang from the dragons' teeth sown by Cadmus immediately fought among themselves until there survived only the five from whom the Thebans descended. The Thebans were among the Spartan allies who most vigorously pressed for the wasting of Athens after the Peloponnesian War.
5373 *Sophokles had dismissal* He died late in 406.
5374 *Happy as ever* as all reports agree; 'serene' is the characteristic epithet.
5375 *Plausive* applausive.
5376–81 *Iophon . . . ground* The play referred to is the *Oedipus at Colonus*, with which Sophocles posthumously won the prize. In fact it was first presented in 401 by the grandson of Sophocles, also named Sophocles; Balaustion anticipates the legend. In the play Oedipus experiences virtual apotheosis. The daughters of line 5381 are Ismene and Antigone.
5385 *promised 'Main-Fight'* See 5277.
5386–8 *Thasian . . . head* 'far surpassing all/Are those sweet flagons full of Thasian wine./Their fragrance long keeps lingering in the head,/Whilst all the rest evaporate and fade' (*Ecclesiazusae*, 1118–21).

5390 *Castalian* Castalia is the spring on Parnassus, sacred to Apollo and the Muses.

5396–5453 *Frogs* is described.

5411–12 *'He's all . . . neck!'* alluding to an Aristophanic fragment.

5412 *Chatterbox* Euripides. In *Frogs*, 842, Aeschylus calls Euripides 'chattery-babble-collector'.

5413 *'twisting words like wool'* alluding to an Aristophanic fragment.

5413–14 *usurped his seat/In Plouton's realm* Aeschylus occupies a seat beside Pluto in *Frogs*; he bequeaths it to Sophocles.

5414–15 *'the arch-rogue . . . altar-orts'* adaptation of *Frogs*, 1520–21. The phrasing recalls the 'snapper-up of unconsidered trifles', Autolycus (*The Winter's Tale* IV. 3. 26).

5414–16] In Plouton's realm – the rash Euripides. *MS.*

5415 *orts* leavings.

5420 *Mystics matched the Frogs* There are two Choruses in *Frogs,* one of initiates into the Mysteries, one of Frogs.

5425 *bits of tile* used in a Greek game (see 'tile', *OED* 4).

5430–31 See *Frogs,* 1200–1250, where repeated interjections by Aeschylus make an absurd recitation by Euripides even more absurd.

5433–4 See *Frogs,* 1402–6, where a line of Aeschylus referring to chariots outweighs one of Euripides referring to a mere club.

5435–6] And last, the younger rival improvised *MS.*

5437 *Triphales* The lost play, *Triphales,* of Aristophanes satirizes Alcibiades.

5439 *Pheidippides* the son, who is 'educated' in *Clouds.* In Browning's time it was thought that the character satirized Alcibiades.

5444–6 See *Frogs*, 1490–95. The Choir is the Chorus of Blessed Mystics (they had led good lives and been initiated into the Eleusinian mysteries).

5445 *prate-apace* chatterbox (compare 'Ned Bratts', 126).

5455 *prize* *Frogs* won the prize in 405 B.C.

5459 *Frogs croaked gay again* Most unusually, *Frogs* had a second performance, probably at the City Dionysia a few weeks after the first presentation at the Lenaea. Browning seemingly has it a year later, thus further confusing the chronology.

5460 *Elaphebolion-month* March, when the feast of the City Dionysia was held.

5461 *Aigispotamoi* At the Battle of Aegospotami in the Hellespont in 405 B.C. the last Athenian fleet was destroyed by Lysander, who then blockaded the Piraeus and forced Athens to surrender in the spring of 404 (Browning puts the surrender a year earlier).

5477 *helot* a Spartan serf.

5478–9 *'men . . . Socratize'* translating *Birds*, 1282–3.

5493 *Bakis* a famous Theban seer of legend.

5537 *depend* hang down.

5541 *Man of Phokis* See 208n.

5551–3 translating the *Electra* of Euripides, 167–9.

5566 *Tragic Two* Aeschylus and Sophocles.

5571–9 *Agamemnonian lady . . . King of Men* Electra was the daughter of Agamemnon, king of Mycenae, and Clytemnestra. Clytemnestra and her lover, Aegisthus, murdered Agamemnon; in the version of Euripides, Electra was then banished by Aegisthus and married off to a herdsman. Her brother Orestes found her, and the two planned revenge.

5576 *chares* chores. The word in this context was probably suggested by 'the

maid that milks/And does the meanest chares' (*Antony and Cleopatra* IV. 15. 75–6).
5587 *chaste Herdsman* In the *Electra* of Euripides, the marriage between the heroine and the herdsman is not consummated.
5589 *story's close* At the end of the Euripides play, a tearful Electra bids her city and countrymen farewell.
5592 *stranger* Orestes.
5600 *victim-queen* Clytemnestra.
5604–42] These lines are very heavily revised in *MS*.
5615–16 *doglike snatch/At aught still left dog* perhaps recalling Othello's epithet for Iago, 'Spartan dog' (V. 2. 361).
5622 *pinioned* shackled.
5632 *Kommos* lament (the Greek word means a beating of head and breast in lamentation): a feature of Greek tragedy in which character and Chorus lament alternately.
eleleleleu a tragic wail; see, for instance, *Prometheus Bound* of Aeschylus, 877.
5638 *Lakonians* Spartans (from Laconia, the district around Sparta).
5638–9 *crunched/Sea-urchin . . . coarse brutes* Athenaeus (*Deipnosophists* 3, 41) tells of a Spartan who, knowing no better, ate a sea-urchin whole.
5643 *Munuchion-month* April.
5663 *other earth, new heaven* 'For, behold, I create new heavens and a new earth: and the former shall not be remembered, nor come into mind' (Isaiah lxv 17); 'And I saw a new heaven and a new earth' (Revelation xxi 5).
5667 *saved his ship* by her version of *Alcestis* in *Balaustion's Adventure*.
5679–85 *He lies . . . black cold* 'In Macedonia, at the place where Euripides is buried, two streams approach from the right and left of his tomb, and unite. By one of these, travellers are in the habit of lying down and taking luncheon, because its water is good; but nobody goes near the stream on the other side of the tomb, because its water is said to be death-dealing' (Vitruvius 8, 3, 16). (Arethusa, the place where Euripides is buried, has no connection with the famous fountain of Syracuse.)
5686–91 See 1561–2 and note, and 3518–23. Browning adapts a passage from an old *Life*.
5692 *young Philemon* In 405 B.C. the real Philemon was about minus forty.
5695–7 translating a fragment of Philemon.
5710 *There are no gods* translating a fragment of Euripides.

The Inn Album

First published on 19 November 1875 by Smith, Elder, and serially in the *New York Times* of 14, 21 and 28 November 1875. Within three weeks 1,100 of the 2,000 copies printed had been sold, but no second edition was called for. The poem was but slightly revised for *1888*, and Mrs Orr errs in saying that 'important verbal corrections were made in *The Inn Album*' (*Life*, 379); no lines were added or deleted.

E. L. Cary (*Browning, Poet and Man*, Putnams, 1899, 204–5) says the plot was conceived and constructed in a morning, and according to Browning's note in the *MS*. the poem was begun on 1 June and finished on 1 August 1875. The manuscript, an obvious first and last copy, is fairly clean; the division into parts would seem from it to have been an afterthought. Browning told Domett on 9 December 1875 that he had originally intended a tragedy, but that he gave up the idea on hearing that Tennyson was writing *Queen Mary*. The poem remains, however, strongly dramatic in quality, and Browning called it 'a tragedy in a new style'.

The germ of the story is actual fact. In 1875 Browning said he had heard about the Baron de Ros (1792–1839) thirty years before, and DeVane argues convincingly (*Handbook*, 387–8) that he did so at Macready's theatre, to which Fanny Kemble submitted in December 1838 *An English Tragedy*, a play based upon the story of de Ros. Browning may also have known Bulwer-Lytton's *Paul Clifford* (1830), in which Henry Finish was modelled on de Ros. Browning's poem, however, builds on little more than an anecdote of an older roué, who, beaten in gambling by a younger man he had planned to fleece, offered him an abandoned mistress to induce him to postpone demand for payment; according to Furnivall (*N&Q* 5th series, V, 1876, 244–5) the lady in horror committed suicide. DeVane's suggestion that *The Inn Album* was influenced by the case of the Tichborne Claimant seems tenuous, despite Browning's keen interest in that case.

Reviewers, including Henry James (*The Nation* XXII, 20 January 1876, 49–50), were generally hostile, though Swinburne was one of a few who liked the 'new sensation novel': 'a fine study in the later manner of Balzac, and I always think the great English analyst greatest as he comes nearest in matter and procedure to the still greater Frenchman'. Of all Browning's poems *The Inn Album* is the most firmly rooted in Browning's own time and place by a host of topical allusions. Many of these are identified in A. B. Crowder, '*The Inn Album*: A Record of 1875', *BIS* II, 1974, 43–64, and C. C. Watkins, 'Robert Browning's "The Inn Album" and the Periodicals', *Victorian Periodicals Newsletter* VI, 1973, 11–17. Containing occasional useful information is J. M. Hitner, *Browning's Analysis of a Murder: A Case for "The Inn Album"*, Northern Michigan University Press, 1969. For criticism see: A. C. Bradley, 'Mr. Browning's *Inn Album*', *Macmillan's Magazine* XXXIII, 1876, 347–54; Drew, *Poetry of Browning*, 332–6; C. C. Watkins, 'Form and Sense in Browning's *The Inn Album*', *BIS* II, 1974, 65–76. DeVane, *Handbook*, 384–91 offers useful background information.

1 *Album* a kind of visitors' book.
11 *acclivity* ascending slope. The line, echoed through the poem, parodies eighteenth-century poetic diction.
12 *burn daylight* waste time. A proverbial expression, one used, for instance, by Mercutio to Romeo (I. 4. 43).
17 *neglects the form* a constant criticism of Browning.
18 *sense . . . sense*] thought . . . thought *MS. first reading.*
23 *Écarté . . . Blind Hookey* card games.
24 *Cutting-the-Pack* The player cutting the higher card wins the money.
31 *coign of vantage* *Macbeth* I. 6. 7.
35 *Sir Edwin's dripping stag* Reproductions of the fashionable Sir Edwin Landseer's *The Stag at Bay* (1846) sold widely in the Victorian period. The Royal Academy's Winter Exhibition of 1874 was devoted to Landseer (1802–73).
36 *couchant coast-guard creature* Landseer's *A Distinguished Member of the Humane Society* (1838) shows a faithful Newfoundland dog waiting to rescue distressed mariners. 'Couchant' (lying) is a heraldic term.
37 *Huguenot* *The Huguenot* (1852), famous painting by Millais (1829–96).
Light o' the World the painting (1853) by Holman Hunt (1827–1910).
39 *Salmo ferox* a stuffed salmon ('Salmon dauntless' – Latin).
65 *Place* that is, a country house of some elegance.
72 *Guillim* John Guillim (1565–1621), English antiquary, author of *A Display of Heraldrie* (1610).
77 *Corot* The French painter of 'tender sentiment' died on 22 February 1875.

79 *handsweep* not recorded in *OED*.
84 *pendent* hanging. Compare 'couchant' (36), another heraldic term.
96 *noisome-deep* injurious-deep – the candles have burned right down.
102 *satisfaction* pecuniary penalty.
108 *ask Colenso else* The Bishop of Natal in his *Critical Examination of the Pentateuch* (1862–79) pointed to Biblical mathematical impossibilities. He wrote books on algebra and trigonometry.
120 *Apollinaris* Apollinaris Natural Mineral Water, a new product, was first advertised in *The Times* on 3 June 1875.
132–4 *Three-two fives . . . noughts and fives* In a letter of 7 June 1887 Browning wrote: ' "Two fives, &c" are the expeditious way of adding up, *half to one's self* – the important business being to arrive at the *Total* – which is told out plainly' (T. J. Collins, 'Letters from Robert Browning To the Rev. J. D. Williams, 1874–1889', *BIS* IV, 1976, 46).
151 *Till death us twain do part* parodying the marriage service.
163 *Opera* The Opéra was completed in 1874. It became the major home of grand opera in the later nineteenth century.
164 *Salon* the annual Paris art exhibition of work by living artists.
china-sale Collecting china was all the rage in the 1870s; the word 'Chinamania' dates from 1875.
165 *Chantilly* the Paris race-track.
194 *Pisgah-view* Moses viewed the Promised Land from Mount Pisgah (Deuteronomy xxxiv 1–4).
210 *pass-book* bank-book.
pair hands (period slang).
238 *poke* bag or pocket.
240 *doit* trifling sum (from the almost valueless Dutch coin).
281–4 *free jackdaw . . . peacocks* alluding to Aesop's fable of the jay or jackdaw, who, decked out in peacock feathers, became ridiculous.
295 *Dalmatia* the region in the north-west of what is now Yugoslavia (the reference was perhaps suggested by pictures relating to the Emperor of Austria's tour in *Illustrated London News* of 15 May 1875 – see Crowder, 58).
302 *Ruskin* John Ruskin (1819–1900), acquaintance of Browning, writer, art critic, social reformer, philanthropist – and economist.
305 *Timon* the misanthropist of, say, Shakespeare's play.
310–25 mock-heroic bombast – as often in *The Inn Album*.
316 *one stone* fourteen pounds in weight.
318 *Rothschild* the wealthy banker (Browning's uncle worked for him), Member of Parliament, philanthropist (1808–79).
321 *hight* called (archaism).
325 *one more asteroid* Another was discovered in January 1875, but the discovery of new asteroids had become routine.
327 *Alfred's* a London club.
Istria area in the north-west of what is now Yugoslavia (see 295).
333 *Polo, Tent-pegging, Hurlingham, the Rink* Polo was introduced to England in 1869. Tent-pegging, a sport in which a galloping rider tries to pick up a tent-peg with his lance, was introduced to England on 29 May 1875 at Hurlingham, where a polo field had opened in 1874. The Rink was for roller-skating, a craze of the time (*OED*'s first citation of 'roller-skate' is of 1874).
338 *look* look to, 'prepare for receiving'.

339 *tails and tassels* The references are to clothing; the sense, roughly, is 'decorations', 'icing on the cake'. 'Tails' is perhaps a very early use of the slang expression for men's formal dress (Partridge dates the first use about 1880).

353 *Galopin* The race-horse won the Derby on 26 May 1875.

Gainsborough picture by Thomas Gainsborough (1727–88).

359 *phoenix* the fabulous bird of which only one exists at any one time.

362–3 *So endeth here/The morning's lesson* alluding to the clause used after the lesson is read in church.

366 *down-train* the train *from* London.

369 *farthing* then the smallest unit of currency: a quarter of a penny.

377 *clearing out* taking away all the cash of (slang; *OED*'s first recorded usage is 1850).

378 *cleaned* deprived of cash (slang – *OED* 4b).

379 *kennel* gaming-trough? the 'pot' or 'kitty' or 'pool'? (the word in the sense demanded here is not in *OED*, and Browning presumably uses a transitory slang-word). See A. B. Crowder, in *American Speech*, Spring–Summer 1972, 159–60.

flush full of money.

381 *blood from stone* The Older Man uses an abundance of trite phrases.

382–8 *You would hold your tongue ... "World"* Alluding to the Garrick Club quarrel. In 1858 Edmund Yates had published an account of Thackeray's private conversation at the Club. Dickens, who was Yates's adviser, and Thackeray became estranged as a result.

388 *"World"* a new society journal of the time, founded by Edmund Yates.

393 *Correggio's long-lost Leda* The painting alluded to, by the Italian artist (*c.* 1489–1534), was not long-lost in any obvious sense. The painting had been restored and the head repainted; just possibly Browning alludes to the restoration by Jacob Schlesinger (1792–1855) of the head of Leda, which had been cut out of the canvas by Louis d'Orléans, who thought it indecent.

397–8 *silk-purse ... sow-ear* 'You can't make a silk purse out of a sow's ear' (proverbial).

412 *pitched and tossed* gambled recklessly (from the gambling game 'pitch and toss').

413 *As* as if (a frequent sense in Browning).

Scotch-pebble agate.

418 *brilliant* diamond of the finest cut.

437–8 *money breed/Money* probably reminiscent of *Merchant of Venice* I. 3. 97–8. The play enjoyed a popular production in London in 1875.

443 *wind-egg* an egg without a shell or with a soft shell, but Browning is thinking of the legend behind the meaning that does not apply here: the legend that hens laying such eggs were, like the 'Thracian mares', impregnated by the wind.

446 *Mind your own –* The Older Man stifles 'business'.

475 Browning confessed to the error noted in the *Saturday Review* that a singular subject has a plural verb, but made no change for *1888*.

491 *Unlimited Loo* a card game. In 'limited loo' a player's contribution to the pot is limited to an agreed maximum amount, in 'unlimited loo' it is not.

499 *Gladstone, Carlyle, the Laureate* three Browning friends; the Liberal leader (temporarily in opposition in 1875, the year early in which he resigned as Liberal leader); the leading prose writer; Tennyson.

the Laureate] Kenealy *MS.* (Kenealy [1819–80] was the Tichborne Claimant's [Arthur Orton's] lawyer, and was in 1875 speaking on his behalf. He became a Member of Parliament 14 February 1875.)

523 *Rule Britannia* James Thomson's patriotic air (1740); its rousing music was written by Thomas Augustine Arne.
543 *Dizzy* Disraeli's nickname. In 1875 Disraeli was Prime Minister.
555–6 *lesson me/Over the knuckles* that is, teach me by rebuking (rap over the knuckles).
566 *Neither* The double negative was acceptable usage at the time.
576 *cut* passage.
616 *at twenty-one*] two years ago *MS.*
620 *middle age*] fifty years *MS.*
621 *four*] two *MS.* (similarly at other places in *MS.*).
631 *Ess or Psidium* two perfumes made by the same company. Ess Bouquet was a popular favourite, Psidium was a new product widely advertised in the spring of 1875.
661 *collecting-itch*] good books *MS.*
665 *Leporello-list* Leporello, servant of Don Giovanni in Mozart's opera, keeps a list of his master's conquests. There were two major productions of *Don Giovanni* in London in 1875.
692–3 *"a head reposed"/In French phrase* *à tête reposée*: at leisure.
700 *Long Vacation* English University phrase for the summer vacation, during which in theory undergraduates read widely.
801 *shaveling* contemptuous term for a tonsured ecclesiastic.
802 *Magdalen* harlot restored to purity, after the woman of Mark xvi 9, identified with the woman of Luke vii 37.
804 *"Loose hair and lifted eye," as someone says* 'Let then the Fair one beautifully cry,/In Magdalen's loose hair and lifted eye' (Pope, *To a Lady, Epistles to Several Persons* II, 11–12). In a letter of 7 June 1887, Browning wrote that 'the careless fellow was made purposely unsure in his quotations' (T. J. Collins, 'Letters from Robert Browning To the Rev. J. D. Williams, 1874–1889', *BIS* IV, 1976, 46).
805 *sneak*] snob *MS.*
807–8 *Finsbury/With Orton* Finsbury is a London constituency, Arthur Orton was the Tichborne Claimant convicted of perjury in February 1874. Four years after *The Inn Album* appeared, Orton was to be urged to run for Parliament as a means of getting free – presumably the suggestion had already been bruited before the poem was finished.
891–2 Cervantes, *Don Quixote* II, xlvii.
900 *Returned . . . for Westminster* that is, elected to Parliament.
902 *maiden-speech* first speech in Parliament.
903 that is, to become Conservative Prime Minister.
908 *Commemoration-week* week of high ceremony and festivity (Encaenia) at Oxford.
946 *Apollo Ball* an Oxford ball held by the Apollo University Lodge of Freemasons.
1043 *big and bony* fist.
1046 *blazon* coat of arms.
1049 *coward*] worship *MS.*
1085 *Barry* Sir Charles Barry (1795–1860), leading architect and designer of the Houses of Parliament.
1124 *Arctic expedition* In May and June 1875 ships left London on two Arctic expeditions that attracted much attention.
1160 *conceit* fancy.

1239–40 *Ach, mein Gott!/Sagen Sie* 'O, my God! Do you say'.
1241 *mit* with.
1242 *Raff* Joachim Raff (1822–82), German composer well-known in his time. A major event in musical circles in London in 1875 had been the first English performance of a symphony, *Im Walde,* by him.
1243 *Czerny* Karl Czerny (1791–1857), Austrian pianist, known for his technical studies for the piano.
1245 *Trollope* Anthony Trollope (1815–82), the English novelist.
1350] *not in MS.*
1379] *not in MS.*
1398 *should, silly-sooth,*] should snap his bait – *MS.*
1421 *perdue* hidden.
1487 *craze* insane fancy.
1534 *in petto* 'in the breast', 'undisclosed' (Italian).
1612 *Ritualists* The Ritualist movement within the Anglican Church wished a return to earlier Church rituals.
1613] *not in MS.;* printed as one line in *1875.*
1631 *mill-track blinked on* The image is that of a horse or mule hauling on a circular fixed and limited track that is only intermittently lit.
1691 *Bistre* brown pigment.
1735 *drenched* gave medicine to.
1736 *dub* beat with.
1740–42] That knows no waking as whatever want
Soothes the world-weary – there, no fault to find! *MS.*
1793] *not in MS.*
1823–4 especially reminiscent of 'A Grammarian's Funeral'.
1845 *Judas . . . Potter's Field* Judas Iscariot . . . the burial ground for strangers bought with Judas' thirty pieces of silver (Matthew xxvii 7).
1857 *Obeah-man* witch-doctor.
1876 *gauds* showy ceremonies.
1901 *priests*] books *MS.*
1918 *All's well that ends well* Shakespeare's play-title is proverbial.
1928 *stripes* lashings (archaism).
1946 *troublesomest* one of several unusual superlatives in the poem. There are, however, fewer of them than is normal in Browning.
2060 *Bismarck* The German Chancellor was sixty in 1875 and was being celebrated for bringing Germany together.
2068–9] The lady's proud pale queenliness of scorn
Buries with one red outbreak throat and brow – *MS., 1875.*
2107 parodying the marriage service.
2122 *Salvini* The leading Italian actor (1829–1916), an acquaintance of Browning's, had been playing Othello in London from April to July.
2125 *where's Iago* Carboni's Iago, contemporary reviewers agreed, was poor.
2131 *"Art means just art's concealment"* *'Ars est celare artem'* (Latin proverb).
2136 *worshipped you*] heard your lies *MS.*
2220 *emprison* obsolete form of 'imprison'.
2228–9 *bruise head/Ere he bruise heel* 'it shall bruise thy head, and thou shalt bruise his heel' (Genesis iii 15). The passage is but one instance of the pervasive imagery of the story of Adam and Eve in *The Inn Album.*
2231 *Tree of Life* Genesis ii 9.

2240 *interpellates* interrupts in action (obsolete usage).
2331 *Shut up* In the sense used here, the phrase was fairly new slang or colloquialism. *OED*'s first example is dated 1853.
2345 *the Club* The Club was founded in 1764 by Sir Joshua Reynolds and Dr Johnson. It was popular during the Victorian period.
"*sauter la coupe*" 'changing the turn-up card', a gaming term. De Ros was found guilty of cheating in this manner.
2346 *"cut"... "cut"* the cut of the card... broke off acquaintance with.
2349–50 *horse/They doctored at the Derby* In 1870 a horse called Macgregor was reportedly drugged in the Derby, one of England's major races.
2350 *doctored* doped. The slang dates from about 1860 (Partridge).
2379 *post you* expose you to ignominy by posting your name up at the Club together with the details.
2387 *wheal* ridge of flesh raised by a blow.
2408 *"boltsprit"* obsolete variant of 'bowsprit'.
2410 *Dared and done* The phrase and variations of it are extremely common in Browning. Browning seems to have taken it from Smart's *Song to David* (see J. C. Maxwell, 'Browning and Christopher Smart', *N&Q* new series VI, 1959, 449).
2418 *The Adversary* a frequent epithet for Satan.
2435 *kennel* gutter.
2446 *phyz* face (colloquialism).
2447 *couched it* removed the cataract from it – that is, cleared your sight (see *OED* 9b).
2525 *shaving-trick* If a clergyman 'so far yields to the dictates of nature and commonsense as to pitch his razors into the fire, and wear a beard, he is looked upon as a suspicious character, and perhaps has a bishop down on him' (anonymous pamphlet, *The Deficient Supply of Clergy*, 1863).
2526 *candle-crotchet* There was at the time continued controversy over such things as the presence, and right number if any, of candles in a church.
2546 *virtuousest* a characteristic Browning superlative, but here used uncharacteristically with a sense of its absurdity assisting the note of scorn.
2549 *Roman punch* a strong brew (a 1757 recipe calls for six lemon peels, a gallon of proof spirits, and two quarts of water).
2580 *Cape-side* this side of the Cape of Good Hope – that is, the west coast of Africa.
2591 *brave* splendid.
2620 *gold apple to my Hercules* One of the Twelve Labours of Hercules was to get some of the apples of the Hesperides.
2645 *undesecrate* The participial adjective is not in *OED*, which calls 'desecrate' as participial adjective rare and cites only the example from *Red Cotton Night-Cap Country*, 933 (in *1873* only).
2649 *when my prophet's rod became the snake* Moses' rod became a snake (Exodus iv 3).
2672 *"I was not my own"* 'ye are not your own' (1 Corinthians vi 19).
2673–4 *the eyes to see, the ears/To hear* 'blessed are your eyes, for they see: and your ears, for they hear' (Matthew xiii 16).
2687 *limes that make the College avenue* of Merton College, Oxford.
2699 *"Gods many and Lords many," says the Book* 'there be gods many, and lords many' (1 Corinthians viii 5).
2714–15 'Yet when the other far doth roam,/It leans, and hearkens after it,/And grows erect, as that comes home/... Thy firmness makes my circle just,/And makes

me end, where I begun' (Donne, 'A Valediction: forbidding Mourning', 29–32, 35–6). Compare *Fifine at the Fair*, 2241–2, 2286.

2728 *Sin no more* John v 14 and viii 11.

2805 *revealed* The religious undertones of the word in its context help to underline the parallels between the young man's sentiments here and those of Caponsacchi in *The Ring and the Book* about Pompilia.

2838 *drop like shot* The reference is to dropping molten lead into water to make shot for guns.

2861 *"Till us death do part!"* another reference to the marriage service.

2887 *Spring-time, that's the ring-time* 'Spring time, the only pretty ring time' (*As You Like It* V. 3. 20).

2894 *Christ Church* the Oxford college (the college of Browning's son).

2950 *place aux dames* French: 'Ladies first'.

3016^17] The white eyes uptwist – black the tongue protrudes! *cancelled MS. reading.*

3017–18 *ne trucidet coram populo/Juvenis senem* Latin: 'You will not let the young man slay the old man before the audience.' A variation on Horace's statement in the *Art of Poetry*, 185: 'Ne pueros coram populo Medea trucidet' ('You will not let Medea slay her boys before the audience').

3018 *Horatian rule* It is the standard classical rule about avoiding violence on stage. In commenting on Salvini's restraint in the production of *Othello* in the murder scene, two English journals had alluded to the rule in 1875.

3019^20] Four *MS.* lines were here deleted, and are illegible. There is fairly extensive *MS.* revision in the last few lines of the seventh section.

3041] *not in MS.*

3044–5 *God protect/The right* standard prayer in medieval combat and tournaments (see, for instance, 2 *Henry VI*, II. 3. 55).

3052 *unsubduably* a unique usage? The word is not recorded in *OED*.

3054–8 *Verdict . . . benignant* alluding to the trial scene (IV. 1) of *The Merchant of Venice*. The 'prisoner' there is Antonio. Portia is called a number of times a Daniel, the reference being to the Daniel of the Apocryphal Susannah. Ellen Terry's Portia in the 1875 London production was a triumph. On these and the following lines, see A. B. Crowder, 'A Note on Section VIII of Browning's *The Inn Album*', *SIB* I, 1973, 21–3.

3065–6 *"Cigno fedel, cigno fedel,/Addio!"* Italian translation of Lohengrin's farewell lines to the swan. The Royal Italian Opera had presented the first production of Wagner's *Lohengrin* in London in May 1875; another production followed in June. The response was most enthusiastic. The Wagner Society of London was founded in 1873.

3068–9 *"Amo te solo, te/Solo amai!"* an aria from Metastasio's *La Clemenza di Tito* (1743). 'Thee alone I love, thee alone have I loved.'

3075–8] The *MS* originally ended with line 3074; these lines are a later addition to the *MS*.

3079] *not in MS.*

Pacchiarotto and How He Worked in Distemper et cetera

The collection of nineteen heterogeneous poems called *Pacchiarotto and How He Worked in Distemper: With Other Poems* was published by Smith, Elder on 18 July 1876. The volume was not popular – except for 'Hervé Riel' its contents are still not well known – and no second edition was needed. The manuscript is in the

Balliol College Library: it has many interpolations and other revisions in the title poem but is otherwise generally fairly clean. There are few significant differences among *MS*,. *1876* and *1888*. Though the volume is the first of shorter poems since *Dramatis Personae* in 1864, only one poem, 'Hervé Riel', was definitely written before 1 February 1874, and most of the poems were written in 1876.

PROLOGUE

First published in *Pacchiarotto* on 18 July 1876. The text of *1888* is virtually identical. The date of composition is unknown, but the reference to 'creepers' in line 5 suggests that the poem was written not long before publication. Browning first called the poem 'Dedication', a better title perhaps, since the poem, referring as it does to Browning's love for his wife, is scarcely prelusive, though line 11 touches on the themes of 'House' and 'Shop', the 'storm-notes' of line 20 may be those in the title poem and the epilogue, and 'Numpholeptos' may refer to Browning's 'betrayal' of his dead wife.

5 *creepers* Browning alludes to a Virginia creeper that had grown into his study (see McAleer, *Learned Lady,* 49, 51).

OF PACCHIAROTTO, AND HOW HE WORKED IN DISTEMPER

The title poem was first published in *Pacchiarotto* on 18 July 1876; it is dated in *MS*. 15 April 1876, 1 May 1876. These are probably the dates between which it was composed, though Hood (*Letters*, 363) suggests that the poem originally ended with the 'Good-bye!' of line 456 on the first date, and that Browning added the following lines between then and 1 May. A letter of 25 May 1875 (Landis, *Letters*, 300) suggests that the poem may have been drafted a year or so earlier. Six lines and Browning's footnote were added in proof, but otherwise there are few differences among *MS*., *1876* and *1888*. The *MS*., described by the poet as 'the original copy', is heavily revised.

Browning here finally bursts out against the critics who over the years had generally given him far less than his due, who had subjected him to more than a modicum of abuse, and who had sometimes been deliberately dishonest (as was Alfred Austin in criticizing lines of Browning that he had himself altered so that they would be open to his criticism). As his special target, Browning selects Alfred Austin (1835–1913), who was to succeed Tennyson as Laureate in 1896. Austin was a politically active Tory, poetaster, devotee of Byron, and an asinine and abusive reviewer, whose review (1869) of Browning's achievement had enraged the poet and provides an important source for 'Of Pacchiarotto' (Austin's essay is reprinted in Litzinger and Smalley, *Browning: The Critical Heritage,* 339–53) – the volume in which Austin's essay was collected was withdrawn from circulation partly because it outraged Tennyson. Subsequent Austin comments had further infuriated Browning, who was like other poets of the period in finding Austin pestiferous. He thought him a 'filthy little snob' (McAleer, *Dearest Isa,* 332), complained of his lying 'for the malice rather than the fun of the thing' (Hood, *Letters*, 159), and remarked, 'whenever there is a funny piece of raving against me in a newspaper you may be sure my little bug of an Austin is biting his best' (Landis, *Letters*, 300). 'He has been flea-biting me', Browning wrote, 'for many years past in whatever rag of a newspaper he could hop into – which I should never have turned on my side to escape; but there was talk of "administering castigation to poor Mr Browning," which I have never brought myself to acquiesce in, even in metaphor ... I don't mind leaving on record that I had just that fancy about the people who "forty years long in the wilderness" criticized my works' (Griffin and Minchin, *Life*, 260). Browning had taken the odd shot at Austin in earlier poems (see *Balaustion's Adventure*, 306–35, and *Aristophanes' Apology*, 130–37, 1672–82), but here he really bombards him in a manner reminiscent in some respects of Aristophanes, and with rhymes of that Hudibrastic, Swiftian or Byronic kind of which Browning was so fond. For fuller background and information on the Austin–Browning antagonism, see Browning's letters to Isa Blagden of 22 March 1870 (McAleer, *Dearest Isa*, 332–3), Edmund Gosse of 19 August 1876 (Hood, *Letters*, 175–6), Mrs FitzGerald of 28 August 1876 (McAleer, *Learned Lady*, 36), and George Barrett of 25 May 1875 and 12 August 1876 (Landis, *Letters*, 300 and 303). See also W. L. Phelps, 'Robert Browning and Alfred Austin', *Yale Review* VII (1918), 580–91; Hood, *Letters*, 358–63; DeVane, *Handbook*, 394–8; and N. B. Crowell, *Alfred Austin, Victorian*, Weidenfeld & Nicolson, 1955, 107–21.

For a parallel to Austin, Browning chose another mediocre artist and failed politician, Jacopo Pacchiarotto (1474–1540) of Siena, a man of turbulent temperament who was, appropriately for Browning's purposes, almost unknown (his name does not appear in the current *Encyclopedia Britannica*, though in the ninth edition, 1875, Browning could have found virtually all the information he needed). Browning probably got his information, however, from a footnote to an 1855 edition of Vasari, and from Baldinucci, *Notizie de' Professori del Disegno*. Pacchiarotto engaged in a conspiracy in his native Siena in 1530, and in 1534 joined a revolutionary Club called the Bardotti. Forced to go into hiding in 1535, he spent two days in a church vault with a recent unsavoury corpse, and emerged covered with vermin to take refuge with monks. In 1539 he was exiled, but he returned to Siena and died there in 1540. Few of his works survive.

The poem's title offers yet another example of Browning's fondness for puns. To 'paint in distemper' (Italian: *pingere a tempere*) is to paint using colours mixed with some glutinous water-soluble substance, usually upon a ground of chalk or plaster mixed with gum. The word also means 'ill temper' (and perhaps also here, 'mental disorder').

The controversy around the poem after its appearance included the printing in the *Examiner* of 5 August 1876 of a poem of twenty-eight lines called 'To My Critics' and signed R— B—. Furnivall reprinted it (*Browning Society's Papers* I, 278) with a warning, 'that he never wrote it is certain. I only reprint it to stop any one else attributing it to him.' Crowell, Hood and McAleer (*Dearest Isa*, 334) assume Browning's authorship, and Pearsall (*Bibliography*, 25) thinks it probable. DeVane (*Handbook*, 560–61) does not agree, and neither, emphatically, does the present editor. On stylistic grounds alone, the lines would seem not to be Browning's but to be imitative of him, and they nowhere reach the standard – not Browning's highest – of *Pacchiarotto*. The verses can be found in Hood, *Letters*, 360.

3 *Giacomo* Most authorities call him Jacopo. Browning follows the name in the note to Vasari (1855).

4 *took 'Reform' for his motto* The painter engaged in political activity against the Sienese rulers. As satirist in his early verse, Austin played the role of reformer; in his preface to *The Season* (1861) he said that he wanted to correct the 'something in the world amiss', and the work's motto was Mill's sentence, 'The diseases of society can, no more than corporal maladies, be prevented or cured without being spoken about in plain language.'

5 *Fungaio* Bernardino Fungai (not 'Fungaio') (1460–1516) had a style which, like Pacchiarotto's, derived partly from Perugino; that he was Pacchiarotto's teacher appears to be Browning's idea.
7 *Pacchia* Girolamo del Pacchia (1477–?1540) was naturally confused with Pacchiarotto and for some time some of his paintings were attributed to the latter. He is now regarded as the better artist of the two.
12 *My Kirkup* Baron Seymour Kirkup (1788–1880), eccentric, art connoisseur, finder of Giotto's portrait of Dante, friend of the Brownings, student of the occult, Englishman resident in Florence, model for Hawthorne characters.
San Bernardino the Oratory in north-east Siena.
16 *gloomy* The word is not a noun, but for once becomes one.
17 *Bazzi* Giovanni Antonio Bazzi (Il Sodoma) (*c.* 1477–1549), one of the two leading Sienese painters.
Beccafumi Domenico di Pace Beccafumi (*c.* 1489–1551), the other of the two leading Sienese painters, admired by Vasari.
19 *people miscall him Razzi* as Browning did in the manuscript and first edition of *Fifine at the Fair*, 638. The error resulted from the misreading of a document.
22–3 *Art could correct . . . What Nature had slurred* The concept of art as tidying up Nature, patterning or methodizing it, is traditional, and was certainly accepted by Austin, who detested realism, and asked of Poetry 'Transfiguration of the Actual or Real into the Ideal at a lofty elevation'.
26 *sopra-sotto* 'topsy-turvy' (Italian).
44 *Giotto* the great Italian painter and architect (*c.* 1266–*c.* 1337).
49–50] The lines are transposed in *MS.*, *1876.*
60–61 *pearls to the swine . . . rent of swine* 'neither cast ye your pearls before swine, lest they trample them under their feet, and turn again and rend you' (Matthew vii 6).
63 *mazzard* head (jocular archaism).
66 *Stalloreggi* The name is in the footnote to Vasari (1855). One of Siena's main streets, south of the Cathedral is called Stalloreggi, but none of the city's seventeen quarters now bears the name.
71 *quiesco* 'I rest' (Italian).
78 *bell, book and candle* used in the ritual of excommunication.
80 *brave* splendid.
distemperer a nonce-word? *OED* calls it rare, and cites only this example.
85 *Which work done . . . he rested him* 'God ended his work which he had made; and he rested on the seventh day' (Genesis ii 2).
87 *frescanti* 'fresco-painters' (Italian).
93 *Taught its duty to*] On the duties of *MS.*, *1876.*
98 *Shear sheep but nowise flay them* 'It is the part of a good shepherd to shear the flock, not flay it' (Tiberius Caesar, second Roman Emperor).
103–5] *not in MS.*
119–22 Crowell (113) identifies the reference to Austin's 'My Satire and Its Censors' (1861), which had especially attacked his 'opponent', W. H. Dixon, editor of the *Athenaeum.* The journal had violently reviewed, anonymously Austin's first significant work, *The Season* (1861). Crowell points out that Austin had justified his poem's coarseness (and had made Browning angry) by appealing in a note to Mrs Browning's *Aurora Leigh*: 'Am I coarse?/Well, Love's coarse, Nature's coarse'.
123–35 Early on, Austin had given up satirizing the aristocracy and become a Tory.
127 *hop, skip and jump* alluding to Austin's strut, in part a result of his shortness,

and presumably in part a manifestation of his intense vanity. His walk drew the ridicule of others besides Browning, and helped to make him a cartoonist's delight.
132 *Boanerges* 'Sons of Thunder' (Mark iii 17), the brothers James and John, the apostles who wished to call down fire from heaven. Browning is almost certainly alluding to Austin's preface to *The Season*, where Austin remarks that the man who addresses the world 'in a whisper has no chance of being heard' and that 'language loud, strong, insolent' is needed.
133 *minikin* a diminutive creature. Austin was five feet tall.
137 *Kaiser* Correspondent for the *Standard*, Austin was the only Englishman in the Prussian headquarters during the Franco-Prussian War. He sided with the Prussians, entered Paris with them, and became a friend of Bismarck.
156 *poll's* head's ('not now in serious literary use' – *OED*).
158 *. . . trumpets* that is, strumpets.
161 *Juvenal* the Roman satirist (60–*c.*130) whose sixth satire, directed against women, strongly influenced Austin's attack on women and their licentiousness in *The Season.*
162–3 'which things nobody would have said entire except, indeed, from a filthy mouth' (Latin – Browning's, not Juvenal's).
164 *'Apage'* 'Begone' (Latin).
165 *cocking* turning up.
a-gee off the straight line (Scotticism).
168 *gestion* management.
190 *non verbis sed factis* 'not by words but by deeds' (Latin).
207 *fescue* pointer.
213 *hornbook* primer.
223 *Bardotti* the Sienese group of political reformers to which Pacchiarotto belonged. The name means 'Freed Ones' or 'Spare-Horses': horses that walk beside a wagon, not between the shafts.
227 *paid scot and lot to* settled with. The Bardotti had an initiation fee and subsequent monthly fees.
228 *Bardotto* singular of 'Bardotti'.
229 *Bailiwick* the city-government.
236 *Duomo* 'Cathedral' (Italian).
242 *Brave* splendid.
253 *interfluous* interfluent.
258 *kai ta loipa* the Greek equivalent to 'et cetera'.
259 *kappas, taus, lambdas* the Greek initial letters of the Greek equivalent of 'et cetera' – a standard abbreviation.
265 *Amalfi* the chief magistrate of Siena.
266 *clotpoll* blockhead.
278 *fleering* gibing.
293 *tow* flax-fibre.
295 *'per ignes incedis'* 'you tread over fires' (Horace, *Odes* II, i, 7, where the reading is actually *incedis per ignes*).
298 *purlieu* haunt.
309 *Saint John's Observance* The Basilica dell'Osservanza is to the north-east of Siena, the Church of San Giovanni in the centre of the city, beneath the Cathedral for which it serves as crypt. It was in the latter that the historical Pacchiarotto hid before taking refuge with the Observantine fathers. Otherwise, the statement of line 319 is correct.

329 *"haud in posse sed esse mens"* 'mind not as it might be, but as it is' (Latin). Probably a quotation from a scholastic philosopher, it remains unidentified.
330 'As it was in the beginning, is now, and ever shall be' (*Book of Common Prayer*).
342 *plagues . . . Egyptian* The plagues of Exodus viii–x are proverbial for their severity. For the plague of lice see viii 16–18.
344 *Observancy* The Observants (Friars Minor) are one of the three organizations of Franciscans.
351 *rincing* obsolete form of 'rinsing'.
357 *He delivered a tale round, unvarnished* 'I will a round unvarnished tale deliver' (*Othello* I. 3. 90).
358 *the Abbot's admonishment* The Abbot appears to be intimately familiar with Browning's poetry and many of its leading themes.
375 *thill-horse* a horse that works between the shafts of a wagon.
376–82 *mill-horse . . . mill-post* Compare *The Inn Album,* 1631.
387 *hopper* the receptacle receiving grain for a mill.
431 *All's well that ends well* Shakespeare's title is proverbial.
444 *imposthume* abscess, swelling.
447 *mahlstick* variant of 'maulstick': a light stick held in the left hand by painters as a support for the right hand.
451–2 *saeculorum/In saecula* 'forever and ever' (Latin).
452 *jorum* large drinking vessel.
455 *Benedicite* 'Blessings upon you' (a standard grace).
456 *I have told with simplicity/My tale, dropped those harsh analytics* 'He remains a mere analyst . . . [who writes] at least something very like poetry . . . [when] he is no longer Mr Browning "the dramatist, or, so to call him, analyst," but Mr Browning the man pure and simple' (Austin, in Litzinger and Smalley, *Browning: The Critical Heritage,* 345, 347).
462 *Monday . . . May-day* 1 May is a day of festival generally, and 'the day of the London chimney-sweepers' festival' (Brewer). In 1876 it fell on a Monday.
463 *these* chimney-sweeps.
  drabs] reds *MS.*
  drabs, blues and yellows the jacket-colours of leading journals of the day.
465 The sweeps are playing 'music'. The line is clarified by *OED*'s citation of Webster (1847–54): 'In burlesque music, the salt-box has been used like the marrow-bones, cleaver, tongs and poker, etc.'
469 *chimbly* dialectal variant of 'chimney'.
470–73] *MS. interpolation.* (Hood's statement in *Letters*, 363, that the lines are not in the *MS.* is erroneous.)
471 *an't* contraction for 'are not' and, illiterately (as here), 'is not'.
481 *dust my jacket* give me a good beating (colloquialism).
487–8 *you give me an inkling/How music sounds* Austin had written (Litzinger and Smalley, *Browning: The Critical Heritage,* 346–7), 'Mr Browning is both muddy and unmusical to the last degree. In fact, his style may fairly be described as the very incarnation of discordant obscurity.'
493 *Schumann* the German Romantic composer (1810–56).
  contrapuntist one skilled in counterpoint.
496 *not sing at all* 'He has no voice, and yet he wants to sing' (Austin, in Litzinger and Smalley, *Browning: The Critical Heritage,* 347).
498 *aubade* sunrise song.

501 *damper* a triple pun: (1) plate in a chimney to stop draughts, (2) something that dampens spirits, (3) piece of equipment to silence a musical instrument.
505 *zany* clown.
508 *scuttle* punning: (1) scurry, (2) receptacle for coal.
512 *quit-rent* a rent paid by a freeholder in lieu of services that might be required of him.
518 *ranunculus* a genus of plants, also called 'crowfoot', and including buttercups.
519 *Tommy-make-room-for-your-Uncle* alluding to a popular song of the time.
520 *homunculus* manikin.
521 *Xanthippe* The name of the wife of Socrates is proverbial for a shrew. One legend has it that after berating her husband, she emptied a vessel of dirty water over him; Socrates commented , 'After thunder, there generally follows rain.'
522 *souse* liquid used as a pickle (see line 531). Other apposite meanings, enriching the force of the word, are 'thump' (dialectal), dousing (dialectal), the swooping of a hawk on its prey.
523 *skoramis* transliteration of the Greek for 'chamber-pot' (Berdoe's note merits immortality: 'a vessel of dishonour'). Phelps's statement (585) that the word, and lines 523–4, do not appear in the *MS.* is erroneous, and his conjecture that Browning added material here because of some fresh impertinence by Austin is false. His imaginative statements have misled others, Hood and Crowell for instance.
527 *Jack-in-the-Green* a man or boy enclosed in a framework covered with leaves in the May-day sports of chimney-sweepers.
528 *a dry thread on*] from the pickle *MS.*
529 *Quilp* the evil dwarf of Dickens's *The Old Curiosity Shop.*
Quilp] my *MS.*
Hop-o'-my-thumb a dwarf, named in the anonymous *Taming of a Shrew* and probably identical with Tom Thumb. In his letter to Gosse of 19 August 1876, Browning claimed, absurdly, not to be aware of Austin's stature and to be using littleness only metaphorically. He refers to Austin's dishonesty in criticism, and goes on: 'If the "Examiner" can conceive of a gentler name than *littleness* for tricks of this kind persisted in up to the present time – *I* cannot. One particular piece of blackguardism headed "Men of Letters: R.B." – could only save its author from a kicking by the charitable hope that he was too small for that treatment. I never was unlucky enough to set eyes on the man: if he *is* physically as well as morally and intellectually a dwarf – you may be sure I should have considered him a pygmy had his stature been that of Goliath. But I really meant nothing except to enliven my visionary dance of chimney-sweeps by a grotesque monkey-image which had been thrusting itself upon my notice this long while: and it seems that one fillip more than avenges fifty flea-bites.'
530 *Banjo*] Quilp *MS.*
Banjo alluding in part to the chimney-sweep's blackness through the image of the negro minstrel.
Banjo-Byron In his early satire, Austin models himself in part on the Byron of *English Bards and Scotch Reviewers.* The modifier captures the thinner twanging of Austin as against Byron.
strum-strum 'a rude stringed instrument' (*OED*, which calls the word obsolete and rare. The latest usage cited by *OED* is dated 1728).
533 *'Dwarfs are saucy,' says Dickens* While Quilp's impudence is insisted on in *The Old Curiosity Shop,* the remark does not occur there. If Dickens said it, the location remains unidentified.

533–4 The lines glance at the proverbial 'What's sauce for the goose is sauce for the gander' (see lines 565–7). 'Austin' rhymes with 'sauced in'.

533–4] As if they should touch an utensil
Of mine – do the slops such immense ill! *MS.*

534n.] *not in MS.* It is curious that a year before the poem appeared Browning wrote to George Barrett (Landis, *Letters*, 300): ' "Dwarfs," Dickens tells us, "are mostly sarcy –" and if this particular Quilp gets any good, beside the penny-a-line, out of his "sarce," he has my full leave: but even dwarfs need not be blackguardly: and this one has a trick of "giving an instance of Mr Browning's unintelligible stuff" which he makes so indeed by altering my words to his own, – leaving out a whole line, for instance, and joining two broken ends! He did this in the "World" a fortnight ago. In the same article he said "my whole poem [*Aristophanes' Apology*] was a transcript from Jowett" – whom I have not seen these four years, and who never opened his mouth on that, or any other subject of the same sort, in his whole life: All this bug-juice from a creature I never saw in my life, and whose scribblings, except when they related to myself, I never read a line of! But – as the poet sings –

Who would be satirical
On a thing so very small?'

The letter is dated (and postmarked) 25 May 1875, and suggests that the poem or parts of it may have been drafted by that date. A printer's devil is the errand-boy in a printer's office. The couplet comes from 'Doctor Delaney's Villa', 3–4, formerly attributed to Swift, now generally thought to be by Thomas Sheridan. It is slightly misquoted.

535 *Knight* used jocularly, as often in such phrases denoting professions.

540 *crown cracked or nose bloodied* 'We must have bloody noses and cracked crowns' (1 *Henry IV* II. 3. 96).

543 *forty-and-over* in fact, forty-three.

547 *karterotaton belos* 'a shaft most mighty in strength' (Pindar, *Olympian Odes* I, 112; from the sentence Browning wrote on the fly-leaf of *The Old Yellow Book*).

548 *melos* 'mode'.

554 Browning's grammar had been criticized at times; see for instance *The Inn Album*, 475n.

556 *ad hoc* for this purpose only.

559 Austin had, like other critics, complained of Browning's obscurity. In his essay of 1869 he had, for instance, written: 'For poetic thought has its natural utterance or expression . . . poetic thought express[es] itself in a certain and inevitable kind and form of diction . . . Is the diction of poetry anything but diction that is at once clear' (Litzinger and Smalley, *Browning: The Critical Heritage*, 346).

565 *noddle* head (colloquialism).

565–70 Compare Browning's remark in a letter of 10 February 1887 (Hood, *Letters*, 261): 'I have had too long an experience of the inability of the human goose to do other than cackle when benevolent, and hiss when malicious; and no amount of goose criticism shall make me lift a heel at what waddles behind it.' Browning's pet geese, who died in 1876, were called 'Edinburgh' and 'Quarterly'.

568 *os frontis* 'forehead' (Latin).

572 *birth-day* 7 May. In 1876 it fell on a Sunday.

573 *hebdome, hieron emar* 'the seventh, the holy day' (Hesiod, *Works and Days*, 770).

575–6 *Tei . . . Leto* 'on which Leto bare Apollo with the blade of gold' (Hesiod, *Works and Days*, 771).

576 *grey or ray* that is, dismal or radiant.

579–81] *not in MS.*
580 *Pheidippides* The famous Greek runner had little time for snoring.
581 *Euripides* yet another example of Browning's feeling for, and identification with, the much-criticized playwright.

AT THE 'MERMAID'

First published in *Pacchiarotto* on 18 July 1876. The manuscript is clean, and it, *1876* and *1888* are virtually identical. The poem is dated 15 January 1876 in *MS*.

The Mermaid was the seventeenth-century tavern frequented by the leading actors and writers of the day, including, it seems probable and Browning assumes, Shakespeare, the speaker of this poem. The poem is closely related to the following 'House' and 'Shop', and is typical of Browning in its insistence on the separation of the poet's private and public life. DeVane (*Handbook*, 398–9) suggests an affinity also with the kind of criticism that lies behind the preceding poem, and quotes Austin's remark: 'The same coteries, and in many cases the very same people, who by dint of persistence imposed upon the unreflecting crowd the exaggerated estimate of Mr Tennyson . . . are now striving to induce them to abandon their idol and set up another. Where they have long put Mr Tennyson, they now want to place Mr Browning.' Austin's remark may have prompted Browning's poem, which is not to say, of course, that it is about Browning's refusal to replace Tennyson. The poem is characteristic of its author also in its optimism and its stress on the artist's need to be true to himself even at the expense of public approval.

Browning's epigraph adapts the opening line of Ben Jonson's 'To the Reader', printed in the First Folio (1623) opposite the portrait of Shakespeare. Jonson's whole poem is thematically relevant to Browning's, and Browning may have been influenced by its references to brass: 'This Figure, that thou here seest put,/It was for gentle Shakespeare cut,/Wherein the Graver had a strife/With Nature, to out-do the life:/O, could he but have drawn his wit/As well in brass, as he hath hit/His face, the Print would then surpass/All, that was ever writ in brass./But, since he cannot, Reader, look/Not on his Picture, but his Book.' Shakespeare was the model of the objective poet in Browning's essay on Shelley.

Motto 2 *Was*] *written in italics in MS.*
1 *Next Poet* Insofar as Browning is the speaker and specific reference is involved, the last poet is Tennyson. See headnote above. In 1869 Austin had written 'of certain critics who . . . having placed Mr Tennyson on a poetic pedestal considerably too high for him, are now beginning to waver in their extravagant creed, and are disposed to put him on one a trifle lower, placing Mr Browning there instead'. Insofar as Shakespeare is the speaker, the reader's temptation to look for parallels in Shakespeare's time and to think of the last poet as Marlowe yields little fruit – here, as elsewhere in the poem.
9 *sherris* as in Falstaff's praise of it, Shakespeare's word for 'sherry'.
mantling sparkling.
11 *scantling* small amount.
17 *discover* reveal (now a rare meaning).
34 *Once*] Sly *MS. first reading.*
39 *rout* probably 'collection' (*OED* 1c); possibly 'fuss' (*OED* 8b).
50 *orichalc* a yellow ore or alloy prized by the ancients. *OED* suggests that it was perhaps brass.
58 *last king* Insofar as Shakespeare is the speaker, the reference seems to lack

point. Insofar as Browning speaks, the reference – if consistency with 1 and 16 is desirable – is to Tennyson and *In Memoriam* (published just before Tennyson succeeded Wordsworth as Poet Laureate), a point that indicates strongly that to be over-specific, given Browning's respect for Tennyson, is to distort. Wordsworth is usually thought to be the point of reference, with critics seduced by sentiments in 'The Lost Leader'; but Byron (see line 81) is a more likely choice than Wordsworth.
59 *Tale adorned and pointed moral* 'To point a Moral, or adorn a Tale' (Johnson, *Vanity of Human Wishes*, 221).
63 *cater-cousins* good friends, on the best of terms (*Merchant of Venice* II. 2. 139).
81 *Pilgrim* The allusion is to the Byron of *Childe Harold's Pilgrimage*.
92 *Balaam-like I bless, not curse* Numbers xxiii 6–11.
103 *match* mate, companion (obsolete usage).
104 *Sciolists* people with superficial knowledge. Ben Jonson was indeed a man of learning.
114 *threw Venus* ambiguous: (1) made the best possible cast of the dice – three sixes; (2) overcame the goddess of erotic love, one of the Olympian circle.
132 *Welt-schmerz* 'world-smart', feeling of sentimental pessimism (German).
133 *shelly* shell-like.
138 *quotha* said he, forsooth (archaism, but used several times by Shakespeare).
143 *yellow* in colour symbolism, associated with envy and jealousy.

HOUSE

First published in *Pacchiarotto* on 18 July 1876. *MS.*, *1876* and *1888* are virtually identical. The poem is dated 1 February 1874 in the *MS.*

The poem is related to 'At the "Mermaid"' and, even more, 'Shop', and has Browning's characteristic stress on the separation of private and public lives. DeVane suggests (*Handbook*, 400–401) that Rossetti's sonnet sequence, *The House of Life* (1870), with its self-revelations, helped to impel this poem. Altick ('Memo to the Next Annotator of Browning', *VP* I, 1963, 67–8) suggests the supporting influence of Whittier's *My Namesake* (1857): 'Why should the stranger peer and pry/One's vacant house of life about;/And drag, for curious ear and eye,/His faults and follies out?/Why stuff, for fools to gaze upon,/With chaff of words the garb he wore.'

4 *Unlock my heart with a sonnet-key* See 38–9, and note.
29 *goodman* head of the household (archaism or Scotticism).
35 *spirit-sense* imagination.
38–9 *'With this same key/Shakespeare unlocked his heart'* 'With this key/Shakespeare unlocked his heart' (Wordsworth, 'Scorn Not the Sonnet', 2–3). The 'key' is the sonnet-form.

SHOP

First published in *Pacchiarotto* on 18 July 1876. There are a few differences between *MS.* and *1876*; *1876* and *1888* are virtually identical. The poem is dated 11 February 1874 in the *MS.*, ten days after 'House', to which it is a companion ,again stressing the right to a private life.
5 *sheet* pane.
6 *gimcracks* knick-knacks, trumpery articles.
6–10] *MS. interpolation.*

12 *vastitude* 'unusual largeness' (*OED*).
23 *City* London's financial centre.
City chaps businessmen (slang).
30 *takes the rail* takes the best place (from horse-racing).
35 *Rothschild* the leading banker (two of Browning's uncles worked for the house).
36–40] *MS. interpolation.*
36 *Mayfair* fashionable London area.
38 *Hampstead* middle-class area, then suburban, north-west of London.
40 *box* small house.
57 *Cramp* cramped.
66 *household stuff*] and plain enough *MS.*
67 *comforts*] gimcracks *MS.*
70 *scud* rush.
scud home] get done *MS.*
79 *coral* the Victorian equivalent of a modern teething-ring.
84 *Times* the London newspaper, *The Times.*
swang an obsolete form of 'swung', but here used as a vulgarism.
94 *Chaffer* bargaining.
101–3 *butcher . . . baker . . . Candlestick-maker* the three who went to sea in a tub in the nursery-rhyme 'Rub-a-dub-dub'.
109–10 'For where your treasure is, there will your heart be also' (Matthew vi 21).

PISGAH-SIGHTS. I

First published in *Pacchiarotto* on 18 July 1876 and reprinted unchanged in *1888.* The *MS.* text is virtually identical. The poem is dated 28 December 1875 in the *MS.* In the *Selections* of 1880 the 'Prologue' to *La Saisiaz* was called 'Pisgah-Sights. 3'. The old Moses viewed the Promised Land he was not to enter from the top of Mount Pisgah (Deuteronomy xxxiv 1–4).

PISGAH-SIGHTS. II

See the note above. This poem is dated 19 February 1876 in the *MS.*

10 'The days of our years are three-score years and ten' (Psalm xc, 10).
12 *deniers* very small sums (from the almost valueless French coin).
13 *dazed* dazzled from excess of light.

FEARS AND SCRUPLES

First published in *Pacchiarotto* on 18 July 1876. *MS.*, *1876* and *1888* are virtually identical. The poem is dated 26 February 1876 in the *MS.* The title is from Banquo's speech in *Macbeth* II. 3. 135: 'Fears and scruples shake us:/In the great hand of God I stand, and thence/Against the undivulged pretence I fight/Of treasonous malice.' In a letter to W. G. Kingsland, Browning wrote: 'Where there is a genuine love of the "letters" and "actions" of the invisible "friend," however these may be disadvantaged by an inability to meet the objections to their authenticity or historical value urged by "experts" who assume the privilege of learning over ignorance, it would indeed be a wrong to the wisdom and goodness of the "friend" if he were supposed capable of overlooking the actual "love" and only considering the "ignorance" which, failing to in any degree affect "love" is really the highest evidence that "love" exists. So I *meant*, whether the result be clear or no.'

33 Isaiah xxxviii 15.

NATURAL MAGIC

First published in *Pacchiarotto* on 18 July 1876. *MS.*, *1876* and *1888* are virtually identical. The poem is not dated in the *MS.*, but may have been written at the same time as its companion, 'Magical Nature'. DeVane (*Handbook*, 392) suggests that the poem may be left over from earlier, perhaps Italian, days, but also suggests (403) that the youthfulness is remarkable in a poet in his sixties. All but the title of the poem is pasted in to the *MS.*, where its appearance indicates it may have formed part of a longer poem.

5 *Nautch* East Indian dancing girl.

MAGICAL NATURE

First published in *Pacchiarotto* on 18 July 1876. *MS.*, *1876* and *1888* are virtually identical. The poem is dated 4 March 1876 in the *MS.* (for DeVane's datings, see the note above). All but the title of the poem is pasted in to the *MS.*, where its appearance indicates it may have formed part of a longer poem. The *MS.* is not cut from the same sheet as that used for its companion, 'Natural Magic'.

BIFURCATION

First published in *Pacchiarotto* on 18 July 1876. *MS.*, *1876* and *1888* are virtually identical. The clean *MS.* is dated 29 November 1875.

17 *broadway* wide open road.

NUMPHOLEPTOS

First published in *Pacchiarotto* on 18 July 1876. There are few differences in the readings of *MS.*, *1876* and *1888*. In the fairly clean *MS.*, the poem is dated 25 April 1876; the title, which means 'caught by a nymph', was originally in Greek. For his title and perhaps other elements, Browning is indebted to Plutarch, who explains the origin of the term in his *Life of Aristides* 11, 4, and who in his *Life of Numa Pompilius* 3, 7–4, 4, tells how Numa, after the death of his wife, had a celestial marriage with the goddess Egeria.

The poem puzzled the Browning Society as it has almost all readers. Asked by Furnivall to help out, Browning wrote that the key was in the title, and described the poem as 'an allegory ... of an impossible ideal object of love, accepted conventionally as such by a man who, all the while, cannot quite blind himself to the demonstrable fact that the possessor of knowledge and purity obtained without the natural consequences of obtaining them by achievement – not inheritance – such a being is imaginary, not real, a nymph and no woman: and only such an one would be ignorant of and surprised at the results of a lover's endeavour to emulate the qualities which the beloved is entitled to consider as pre-existent to earthly experience, and independent of its inevitable results.

'I had no particular woman in my mind; certainly never intended to personify wisdom, philosophy, or any other abstraction; and the orb, raying colour out of whiteness, was altogether a fancy of my own' (W. R. Nicoll and T. J. Wise, *Literary Anecdotes of the Nineteenth-Century* I, 497).

DeVane (*Handbook*, 405–6) approves the suggestion of Mrs Miller (*Robert Browning,* 259–61) that the poem has autobiographical roots, and that, despite Browning's statement that he had no particular woman in mind, the nymph is associated with Mrs Browning, and the speaker with the poet himself. The moon-imagery used elsewhere, notably in 'One Word More', with reference to Mrs Browning reappears here; and Mrs Miller reminds one of the relevant and famous remark from the poet's second letter to his future wife, 'You speak out, *you*, – I only make men and women speak – give you truth broken into prismatic hues, and fear the pure white light,' and associates it with the notable use of white and broken light in 'Numpholeptos'. The poem is thus seen as a veiled record of a moment of revolt against Browning's devotion to his wife's memory.

20 *Spirit-Seven* 'The "seven spirits" are in the Apocalypse, also in Coleridge and Byron: a common image' (Browning to Furnivall). 'There were seven lamps of fire burning before the throne, which are the seven Spirits of God' (Revelation iv 5).
21 *lamp* shine.
34 *Love, the love whole and sole*] Browning wrote to Gosse (25 July 1876) that the 'line should run: "So grant me – love – whole, sole," *etc.*' (Hood, *Letters*, 174), but made no change for *1888*.
49 *erst* formerly (archaism).
51 *unembued* obsolete variant of 'unimbued'.
60 *Centuply* a hundred-fold.
61 *hearted* at the heart.
73 *blank* white.
84 *bow* rainbow. Compare 'Deaf and Dumb', 1–4.
93 *trode* trod (archaism).
101 *bickers* flashes (poeticism).
121 *smatch* tincture.
133 *petrific* turning into stone (rare).
134 the only unrhymed line in the poem.

APPEARANCES

First published in *Pacchiarotto* on 18 July 1876. *MS.*, *1876* and *1888* have few differences. The *MS.* is dated 6 April 1876.

6 *it*] I *MS.*
12 *you*] he *MS. first reading.*

SAINT MARTIN'S SUMMER

First published in *Pacchiarotto* on 18 July 1876. *MS.* and *1876* are almost identical. Browning made no revisions for *1888*. The poem is dated 27 March 1876 in *MS.*

The title ('Indian Summer' is the North-American equivalent phrase) alludes to the period during which a kind of second summer often briefly occurs (9 October to 11 November), and is used here with reference to the second love of the poem (in a letter of 7 October 1882, Browning was to write: 'This fine summer of Saint Martin does indeed cast the other half of his charitable cloak around us' – Hood, *Letters*, 212). Most scholars have agreed that the poem stems from Browning's stormy relation with Lady Ashburton after the proposal, one usually dated in 1869 (see Hood, *Letters*, 325–38; and W. Whitla, 'Browning and the Ashburton Affair', *BSN* II, No. 2, 1972, 12–41). On this poem's relation to the Ashburton affair, see K. L. Knickerbocker, 'An Echo from Browning's Second Courtship', *SP* XXXII, 1935, 120–24, where it is suggested that the poem 'represents the arguments with which the poet may actually have confronted the importunate Lady Ashburton, or it may simply represent arguments which occurred to him later, alone' (121). On the poem – and for a suggestion that its speaker and Browning's Don Juan have something in common – see Drew, *Poetry of Browning*, 87–93.

7–9 Browning told Lady Ashburton that his 'heart was buried in Florence, and the attractiveness of a marriage with her lay in its advantage to Pen' (Hudson, *Browning to His American Friends*, 170–71).
29 *obscurely* inconspicuously.
34 *Pledged my soul to endless duty* Compare 'Numpholeptos', especially 148–52.
35 *Many a time and oft* *Merchant of Venice* I. 3. 107.
46 *shady* not recorded as a noun in *OED*.
50 *My hands are clean – or nearly* Writing to Isa Blagden (19 August 1871), Browning remarked, just before noting that his son was going to Lady Ashburton's, 'I shall wash my hands clean in a minute, before I see her [his wife], as I trust to do' (McAleer, *Dearest Isa*, 365).
71 *Penelope, Ulysses* heroine and hero, wife and husband, of the *Odyssey*.
72 *Old*] that is, wise.
79 *closer*] closelier *MS.*
80 *deeper*] deeplier *MS.*
82 *jocoser*] jocoselier *MS.*
89 *clipped* hugged (archaism).
coyed caressed.
94 *Build we no mansion* Compare 7, and 'Build thee more stately mansions, O my soul' (O. W. Holmes, *The Chambered Nautilus*, 1858, 29).

HERVÉ RIEL

First published on 28 February 1871 in *Cornhill Magazine* XXIII, March 1871, 257–60, and reprinted in *Pacchiarotto* on 18 July 1876. The original *MS.* is in the Pierpont Morgan Library. In the *MS.* of *Pacchiarotto* the copy for the poem is clearly Browning's transcription of the original printers' *MS.* (he had requested it be returned to him) or of the *Cornhill* publication. The Morgan *MS.* is very rough, and obviously not the printers' *MS.*; and the punctuation was radically revised before the poem appeared in *Cornhill Magazine*. In both *MSS.* and in *Cornhill*, the place and date are given as Croisic and 30 September 1867, at which time Browning was holidaying in Brittany. Browning generally disliked publishing in magazines, and had turned down an earlier request by *Cornhill* for 'Hervé Riel', but the poet sold it to his publisher, George Smith, for one hundred guineas, which were donated to the starving French under siege in Paris. See the letter of 4 February 1871 in Orr, *Life*, 278–9, in which the poet remarks: 'I fancy this is a case [cause?] in which one may handsomely puff one's own ware, and I venture to call my verses good for once.' Browning made no verbal revisions for *1876* or *1888*.

The Battle of La Hogue (named from the Cape in north-west Normandy) in May 1692 between a French fleet and a combined English–Dutch fleet was the decisive naval battle of the War of the Grand Alliance. Hervé Riel (1654–1729) saved the French surviving ships as told in the poem; his reward was an absolute discharge as he requested, not one day's leave – Browning admitted his error when Furnivall discovered it (see two letters of December 1881 in Hood, *Letters*, 206–7). The main source was a guidebook, *Notes sur le Croisic,* first published at Nantes in 1842 by one Caillo jeune; the present editor owns the *MS*. (part of lot 198 at the 1913 sale) of notes from this work in Sarianna Browning's hand. To this *MS*. is appended in the poet's hand a transcript from a hitherto unidentified minor source for the poem, a passage from Alexis Rochon's *Voyage à Madagascar* [1791], II, 38, where reference is made to the paucity of historical record for the feat. Browning found an extract from this work in a volume that was to be his chief source, a hitherto unidentified one, for *The Two Poets of Croisic*: Gustave Grandpré's *Promenade au Croisic* III (1828, 186). Riel was almost unknown until Browning celebrated his exploit in this, one of the better-known and most-loved poems, and the statue to the sailor from Le Croisic erected in his home-town on 17 March 1913 is a direct result of the poem.

5 *Saint-Malo* port at the mouth of the Rance river in northern Brittany.
8 *Damfreville* captain of the largest French ship, the *Formidable*.
17] *not in Morgan MS*. The line was possibly influenced by conflated memories of Tennyson's 'Charge of the Light Brigade' and 'The Lotus Eaters' ('Cannon to right of them,/Cannon to left of them', 18–19; 'Rolled to starboard, rolled to larboard, when the surge was seething free', 151).
18 *twelve and eighty* literally rendering the French *quatre-vingt-douze*.
30 *Plymouth Sound* the famous inlet and roadstead between Devon and Cornwall in south-west England.
43 *Tourville* Admiral of the French Fleet.
44 *Croisickese* a native of Croisic, in southern Brittany near the mouth of the Loire.
46 *Malouins* natives of Saint-Malo.
47 *rocks and shoals*] Malo harbour *Morgan MS*.
tell count.
49 *offing* off-shore position beyond the anchoring ground.
Grève the treacherous strand of the Bay of Mont-Saint-Michel.
disembogues flows out at the mouth.
53 *Solidor* fourteenth-century lookout-tower of the Rance estuary.
92 *rampired* ramparted (archaism). The ramparts were restored in the nineteenth century.
124 *Belle Aurore* 'Beautiful Dawn' (the name is historical).
129 *head* figurehead.
132 *bore the bell* came off best (like the leading sheep or bell-wether).
135 *Louvre* the art museum of Paris.

A FORGIVENESS

First published in *Pacchiarotto* on 18 July 1876. *MS.*, *1876* and *1888* are almost identical. The poem is dated 5 February 1876 in the *MS.*, which is very clean and appears to be a fair copy. In the *MS.* table of contents, the poem is called 'Komm Spanisch!' (Flemish, 'How Spanish!'), and the same title appears before the poem but is there followed by '(Egmont)'. The significance of 'Egmont' remains undetermined, and no source for the poem has been found, though the Egmonts were a great Flemish family. The family's most famous member, Lamoral, Count of Egmont (1522–68), the hero of Goethe's tragedy, was a knight of the Golden Fleece (see line 195) brutally beheaded by the Spanish, to whose increasingly authoritarian rule in the Netherlands and Flanders he had become strongly opposed, but he is clearly not the model for Browning's speaker. It is just possible that the projected reference to Egmont was to offer a reminder of the appalling injustice meted out by the Spanish to Egmont as a parallel to that of the poem's Spanish speaker to his wife.

In a letter of 15 March 1885, Browning chose 'A Forgiveness' as the narrative among the four poems of moderate length to represent him fairly (Hood, *Letters*, 235).

14 *behoof* a misuse of the word for 'behalf'.
29 *porphyry* beautiful hard rock.
38 *thrids* threads (archaism).
76 *bell-flower* campanula.
97 *Hidalgo* Don Quixote.
99–100 *barber's basin . . . Mambrino's helm* In *Don Quixote* I, xxi, and some later chapters, the confused hero thinks a copper barber's basin is the golden helmet of Mambrino, the pagan King of old romance.
105–7 *The Hidalgo waked . . . and lost* When Don Quixote comes to see things as they are and not as he has imagined them to be, life loses its savour and he soon dies.
126 *enarming* variant of 'inarming': embracing.
183 *annoy* annoyance (poeticism).
195 *golden-fleeced* that is, admitted to the Spanish order of knighthood.
201 *arquebus* old kind of portable firearm (the word in Flemish and German meant 'hook-gun', and a misunderstanding by Browning may have led to the 'hook' earlier in the line).
242 *serpent's tooth* normally associated, though not here, with ingratitude (*King Lear* I. 4.310).
249 *arms of Eastern workmanship* Browning had such a collection bequeathed to him.
250 *Yataghan, kandjar* Moslem sword, eastern dagger (variant of 'khanjar').
256 *bicker* gleam (poeticism).
258 *needle* As a verb in the sense demanded here, the word is not recorded in *OED*.
265 *diapered* diversified and adorned with a pattern.
269 *purlings* decorative twisting cords.
271 *handle* The hilt described is that of a Sind peshkabz owned by Browning (*The Browning Collections*, lot 1297).
281 *statesfolk* persons of great state or position.
295 *instance* instigation.
338 *wanting* lacking.

348 *ropes of sand* proverbial for weak links.
378 *has passed*] should pass *MS.*
387 *erst* formerly (archaism).

CENCIAJA

First published in *Pacchiarotto* on 18 July 1876. There are a few minor differences between *MS.* (which is very clean) and *1876*, and even fewer between *1876* and *1888*. The poem is dated 28 April 1876 in the *MS.*

The title and motto are explained by Browning in a letter of 27 July 1876: ' "aia" is generally an accumulative yet depreciative termination: "Cenciaia" – a bundle of rags: a trifle. The proverb means "every poor creature will be for pressing into the company of his betters," and I used it to deprecate the notion that I intended anything of the kind' (Hood, *Letters*, 174). The title also puns on the title of Shelley's play, *The Cenci* (1819), which dramatizes the story of Count Francesco Cenci (called by Landor 'the wickedest man on record'), whose murder in 1599 was planned by his daughter Beatrice, his son and his wife, all of whom were executed a year later despite the extraordinary evil of the Count, the provocation for the deed, and public sympathy. Browning's poem offers a kind of footnote to help explain the motive of Pope Clement VIII for refusing clemency to the Cencis. Browning commented (see Hood, *Letters*, 176–7) on his source for the poem, somewhat misleadingly. K. L. Knickerbocker, 'Browning's *Cenciaja*', *SP* XIII, 1934, 390–400, demonstrates that the main source was a manuscript in the British Museum and that Browning followed it so closely that many lines of his poem are virtual translation of the document dealing with the case he treats of (the article prints the passages from the poem beside the manuscript passages to which they are indebted). A few details may come from another manuscript, some come from Shelley's play, and Browning's chief modification is in the blackening of Cardinal Aldobrandini. Knickerbocker's judgement is that 'Browning here places an almost air-tight restraint on his imagination' (400). The poem is generally regarded as what Browning called it: a trifle, or what Knickerbocker calls it: a 'filler'.

1 *print, Shelley*] tell, Poet *MS.*
7 In Shelley's version of the story, Count Cenci had bought from the Pope pardons for his crimes.
8 *Clement* Pope Clement VIII (1592–1605).
9 'The Pope is stern; not to be moved or bent' (*Cenci* V. 4. 1).
10 'And said these three words, coldly: "They must die" ' (*Cenci* V. 4. 14).
11–13 'And he replied: "Paolo Santa Croce
Murdered his mother yester evening,
And he is fled" ' (*Cenci* V. 4. 18–20).
'Pardon?' and *'she shall not flee at least!'* are not in Shelley's play.
15 *I condense verbosity*] I translate a manuscript *MS.*
22 *Titian* not a reference to a painting by the Venetian of Beatrice Cenci; Titian died before she was born.
82 *Subiaco* town east of Rome.
97 *Basilicate* region in southern Italy.
110 *Massimi* The fratricide is referred to in Browning's main source.
119 *Was bidden*] Saw need to *MS.*
142 *Orsini* one of the most powerful of Roman families.
143 *Monte Giordano* in Rome, site of the Orsini home.

145 *Barigel* the Chief Constable.
152 *by-work* 'accessory and subsidiary work' (*OED* 2, where the word in this sense is thought to be obsolete, and the last recorded usage is dated 1601).
158 *connivency* connivence (archaism).
161 *The Hat and Purple* of the Cardinalate.
163–4] Notable in the Cenci-trial too,
But here . . . Enough! The Purple and the Hat! *MS.*
176 *Tordinona-prison* on the Tiber, opposite Castel Sant'Angelo.
220 *Advocate o' the Poor* court-appointed defence lawyer.
227 *Bears not the sword in vain* 'the minister of God . . . beareth not the sword in vain' (Romans xiii 4).

Who sins must die 'the soul that sinneth, it shall die' (Ezekiel xviii 4); 'the wages of sin is death' (Romans vi 23).
229–30] The lines are transposed in *MS.*, *1876*.
230 *Place Saint Angelo beside the Bridge* The Castle, the neighbouring Piazza and the adjacent Bridge are all named after Saint Angelo: 'the proper head-and-hanging-place/On bridge-foot close by Castle Angelo' (*The Ring and the Book* I, 350–51).
239 *snap* seize quickly.
242 *privity* being privy.
249 *dotation* endowment.
260 *cap is dyed* A Cardinal's cap is red.
279–82 *ring . . . tapestry* In the main source, the ring is a diamond, and the tapestry-episode does not exist.
288 *wight* creature (archaism).
300 *Victor* Victor Emmanuel II (1820–78), first king of united Italy.

FILIPPO BALDINUCCI ON THE PRIVILEGE OF BURIAL

First published in *Pacchiarotto* on 18 July 1876. There are a few minor differences between *MS.*, *1876* and *1888*. The poem is dated 19 May 1876 in the fairly clean *MS.*, and was written hurriedly while the earlier poems were being printed – the title does not appear in the *MS.* table of contents.

The *Notizie de' Professori del Disegno* (six volumes, 1681–1728) of Filippo Baldinucci (1624–96), the speaker of this poem, was a frequent Browning source (see DeVane, *Browning's Parleyings*, 167–212). Browning, however, thought him stupid and bigoted, and attacks him here and in his 'Parleying with Francis Furini'. The particular source for the present poem is Baldinucci's life of Lodovico Buti, a minor Florentine artist (*c.* 1560–*c.* 1603), that includes a story (III, 422) which Browning gives a bicentenary retelling. (A translation of the story is in G. W. Cooke, *Guide-Book to the Poetic and Dramatic Works of Robert Browning*, Houghton-Mifflin, 1901, 139–42.) Browning adds to the story his own invented revenge on Buti.

Speakers in the poem are quoted at several removes, and the handling of quotation marks became complicated for Browning who tried using inverted commas in unusual ways, and who found himself in the *MS.* unable to follow his own highly complex instructions to the printers for their use. The text of the present edition modifies Browning's quotation marks considerably, and tries to follow accepted practices.

14 *Arno* the river flowing through Florence.
26 *San Frediano* a gate of Florence.

27 *Blessed Olivet* Monte Oliveto.
63 *mummeries* The word is often applied to religious rituals regarded as ridiculous.
73 *phyz* face (colloquialism).
74 *brave* splendid.
113–14] *Ours – for, while living, we rehearse*
Dying, as through your streets we fare MS.
122 *from bier*] aloft *MS., 1876.*
152 *cut up rough* became angry (colloquialism).
176 *Esaias* variant of Isaiah.
stiff-necked Jews The Jews are described by the Lord as 'stiff-necked' (Exodus, Deuteronomy and Acts), but not by Isaiah. In Isaiah xlviii 4, however, 'thy neck is an iron sinew'.
178 *poke* bag or pocket (archaism).
187–8 *sucked/Along with mother's-milk* 'sucked in such doctrines with his mother's milk' (G. P. R. James, *The Convict*, 1847, II, 50).
206 *High Priest* 'It was remarked I mistook a Rabbi for a High Priest! This comes of forgetting that one writes dramatically. The speaker, Baldinucci, is a typically ignorant Tuscan, and makes the gross mistake already noted in Arbuthnot's *Martinus Scriblerus* – of whom it is said, at the very beginning: "Those who had never seen a Jesuit took him for one, while others thought him rather to be some High Priest of the Jews." Somebody objected to a Jewish burying-ground being in the neighbourhood of any habitation, but Baldinucci tells the story, and describes the locality as he knew it – and I follow him, of course' (Browning to Furnivall – Hood, *Letters*, 287).
222 *pully-hauly* pulling and hauling.
244 *biters bit* proverbial.
248 *verjuice* sour juice of unripe fruit.
287–8 *plague o' me/If I record it* He did not record it; the record is Browning's.
352 *Saul changed to Paul* referring to the miraculous conversion of the persecutor Saul into the Christian Saint Paul.
354 *crowned*] crowns *MS., 1876.*
359 *unpursed*] disbursed *MS., 1876.*
370 *trow* suppose (archaism).
397–400 *Leda . . . shape* Jupiter loved Leda, queen of Sparta; Ganymede, the Trojan boy; and Antiope, daughter of Asopus; and in approaching them he adopted the forms of a swan, an eagle and a satyr.
402 *Titian* the sixteenth-century Venetian painter.
405–8 Many orthodox Jews do not actually name God.
464 *O Lord, how long? How long, O Lord?* 'Then said I, Lord, how long?' (Isaiah vi 11); 'How long, O Lord, holy and true, dost thou not judge and avenge our blood on them that dwell on the earth?' (Revelation vi 10).

EPILOGUE

First published in *Pacchiarotto* on 18 July 1876. There are a few minor differences between *MS., 1876* and *1888*. The poem is dated 24 April 1876 in the *MS.*, and had as its original title with the poem and in the table of contents 'Cowslip Wine'. The Greek motto is from the *Plutus* of Aristophanes, 807–8: 'casks full of red and fragrant wine'. The poem offers an important statement on Browning's art. On it see Drew, *Poetry of Browning*, 51–3.

1 *'The poets pour us wine'* 'And the poets poured us wine' (Elizabeth Barrett, *Wine of Cyprus*, 168).
6 *screw* of the wine-press.
19 *rathe* early (poeticism).
37 *smatch* tincture.
38] *not in MS., 1876.*
52–3] The lines are transposed in *MS.*
55 *purled* rippled.
63 *bloomy* bloom-coloured.
67 *attar-gul* essence of roses.
73–4 *paid myself with words/(As the French say well)* The French phrase *se payer de mots* (literally, 'to pay oneself with words') means 'to be the dupe of empty words'.
75 *bowsed* drunk.
77 *pottle* an old two-quart measure.
78 *toped* drank largely (archaism or poeticism).
82 *forty* thirty-seven plays, the sonnets, *Venus and Adonis, Rape of Lucrece.*
90 *four Paradise Lost, Paradise Regained, Samson Agonistes* and, probably, *Comus.*
94 *Embellied* not recorded in *OED* (nor is 'Imbellied').
117 *chaps* jowls.
124 *Frothed* made to froth? (a meaning not given in *OED*).
126 *spilth* what has spilled.
133 *lap* drink (slang).
135 *smutch* smudge.
143 *Koh-i-noor* the huge Indian diamond presented to Victoria in 1849.
146 *must* new wine.
150 *at proof* as it should be.
158 *Dark Blue Sea's* 'Roll on, thou deep and dark blue Ocean, roll!' (Byron, *Childe Harold's Pilgrimage* IV, clxxix). See also line 154. This stanza is the only one in the 'Epilogue' in which line 2 does not rhyme with line 6. The 'these grew there' of 154 suggests that a rhyme might have been originally intended, but that a syntactical reversal occurred which Browning failed to notice in the *1876* and never corrected.
159 *Let them 'lay, pray, bray'* Hitting at Byron's notorious solecism in *Childe Harold's Pilgrimage* IV, clxxx: 'there let him lay'. The whole passage annoyed Browning – see *Fifine at the Fair*, 1108n. and 1126n.
addle-pates muddle-headed ones.
167 *cowslip* a weed the blossoms of which are used for wine.
177 *thoughtlings* insignificant thoughts.
181 *Martha Blount* the lifelong friend of Alexander Pope to whom he wrote and dedicated epistles.
220 *Thirty-four Port* that is, port of fine quality, put up in 1834.
221 *fur* a coating on the tongue resulting from some kinds of disease.
222 *magnum* two-quart bottle.

La Saisiaz

First published in a volume entitled *La Saisiaz: The Two Poets of Croisic:* on 15 May 1878 by Smith, Elder, seven months after *The Agamemnon of Aeschylus.* It was well reviewed, but no second edition was called for; the volume was still being advertised after Browning's death. The volume bore a simple dedication to Mrs Sutherland Orr, which was dropped, probably inadvertently, in *1888*; Mrs Orr, sister of Frederic Leighton, and Browning's close friend and admirer, was later to write her *Handbook* and *Life*. The *MS.* of *La Saisiaz* is in the Library of Balliol College. It is a fair copy, is exceptionally clean, and is, like the first edition, dated 9 November 1877. Between *MS.* and *1878* Browning made a few minor changes; between *1878* and *1888* there are a very few punctuation revisions but only one trifling verbal change.

The meaning of the title (or what Browning thought or knew he meant by it) is not known (see P. Honan in *BNL* 5, 1970, 29–30). Mrs Orr (*Handbook*, 188) says the title is 'Savoyard for "The Sun"'; but Honan presents evidence that it is Savoyard patois for 'fissure' or 'rock-cleft', and suggests the metaphorical appropriateness of such a meaning for the poem. It is at any rate the name of the chalet, a few miles south of Geneva, in which Browning, his sister and Miss Anne Egerton Smith were staying when, early in the morning of 14 September 1877, Browning found the body of his old friend, the suddenness of her death intensifying the force of his grief (see Browning's letter of 15 September in *New Letters*, 240–41). Five days later Browning climbed the neighbouring mountain, La Salève, which he and Miss Smith had planned to climb on the day she died. *La Saisiaz* is largely, then, prompted by the experience of her death, and in a letter of 30 January 1880 to J. D. Williams, Browning described the death as 'the only one relating to a personal experience (at least, *directly*) in all my books. I could not tell the incidents of that memorable week more faithfully in prose and as an accurate account of what happened: and they impressed me so much that I could proceed to nothing else till I had in some way put it all on paper. There was much more to say, – but what *is* said is strictly true' (T. J. Collins, 'Letters from Robert Browning To the Rev. J. D. Williams, 1874–1889', *BIS* IV, 1976, 14). Behind the poem, too, are the religious speculations that had nerved many of Browning's poems, and discussions between Browning and Miss Smith about articles in the new journal, *The Nineteenth Century*, in the summer and autumn of 1877, and especially in the September issue with its symposium on eschatology. Though the poem leaves aside, like many other Browning poems, the answers of Christian Revelation to the problems it raises, *La Saisiaz* is a major document for the poet's religious beliefs, the more so because he speaks here more directly than usual. The metre is that of Tennyson's *Locksley Hall*.

On the poem see DeVane, *Handbook*, 421–3 (and the note to DeVane's treatment: H. N. Fairchild, '*La Saisiaz* and *The Nineteenth Century*', *MP* XLVIII, 1950, 104–11). Two critical essays are Drew, *Poetry of Browning*, 157–66; and F. E. L. Priestley, 'A Reading of *La Saisiaz*', *TQ* XXV, 1955, 47–59 (reprinted in Drew, *Robert Browning*, 242–56).

[PROLOGUE:] *'Good, to forgive'*

1–5 'Oh, – "good to forgive – best to forget" – only means the feeling on a review of a life's "fret," as it dwindles into insignificancy before an opening prospect of a new and – so far as the old is concerned – a "fretless" existence' (Browning in a letter of 30 January 1880 – T. J. Collins, 'Letters from Robert Browning To the Rev. J. D. Williams, 1874–1889', *BIS* IV, 1976, 14).

LA SAISIAZ

1 *Dared and done* a favourite phrase of Browning, who seems to have taken it from the last line of Smart's *Song to David* (see J. C. Maxwell, 'Browning and Christopher Smart', *N&Q* new series VI, 1959, 449). Compare 25–7, 32, 138.
7 *outspread* 'Rich outspreads of the vineyards and the corn' (Mrs Browning, *Aurora Leigh* VII, 444).
24 *Collonge* Miss Smith was buried in the churchyard in the nearby town of Collonges.
37 *Jura* mountain range in eastern France and western Switzerland. As the context makes clear, the mountains are to the west of La Salève. For photographs of the poem's locale, see Griffin and Minchin, *Life*, 263–4.
40 *magnific* magnificent (literary archaism).
44 *lake* Lake Geneva.
53 *the pair* Sarianna Browning and their friend, Gustave Dourlans.
56 *lamping* shining.
Mars the planet.
59 *rare nook* a place recommended by Dourlans as superior to La Salève.
69 *him* Dourlans had agreed to climb La Salève with Miss Smith and Browning.
75 *Blanc* Mont Blanc. The great mountain is about fifty miles south-east of La Salève.
77 *some three weeks since* on 28 August. Browning writes of the excursion in a letter of 30 August (McAleer, *Learned Lady*, 47).
80 *Marshal* Marie Edmé Patrice de MacMahon, Marshal of France, and President of the French Republic (1873–9).
Gambetta Léon Gambetta (1838–82), architect of the constitution of the Third Republic, and opponent of MacMahon.
88 *ardours* flames.
92 *terrace* balcony, veranda.
97 *Arve* The river flows at the foot of La Salève.
99 *city* Geneva.
100 Browning is probably thinking of *Childe Harold's Pilgrimage* III, lxxxv–cix, where Byron is stimulated by Lake Geneva and its surroundings into expressing preferences for Nature over the world of Man.
102 *Quiet slow sure money-making* In a letter of 30 August 1877 (McAleer, *Learned Lady*, 46), Browning writes of the peasantry as ignoble and absorbed in money-grubbing, and without the 'universal presence of Love' which Byron found (in *Childe Harold's Pilgrimage* III).
104 *Calvin* The French theologian made Geneva the focal point of the Reformation.
116 *first word's provocation* Genesis i 3.
provocation summons (obsolete usage in the Latin sense of the word).
130 *Edelweiss* Alpine plant with white flowers. In his *Thoreau* (1862), Emerson had remarked that the name meant 'Noble Purity'.
154 *sphere-song* alluding to the Ptolemaic concept of the music of the spheres.
163–4 Browning alludes to the discussions in *The Nineteenth Century*, and especially to Frederic Harrison's two-part article in the June and July numbers (1877), 'The Soul and Future Life'. Harrison's title was picked up in the September and October issues as topic for a 'modern symposium'.
187 *This – that somewhere*] That already *MS*.

196 probably a sarcastic comment on the positivist conception of immortality, one in which the individual lives on in effects on others' lives. Harrison had presented the conception in *The Nineteenth Century*.

212 *solemn Tuscan* Dante.

213–15 *'I believe ... my soul'* In a letter of 11 May 1876 Browning wrote: 'Dante wrote what I will transcribe from my wife's Testament, wherein I recorded it fourteen years ago, "Thus I believe, thus I affirm, thus I am certain it is, that from this life I shall pass to another better, there, where that lady lives of whom my soul was enamoured" ' (Hood, *Letters*, 172). The lines are from *Convivio* II, 9.

215 *that lady* Dante's Beatrice, Browning's Elizabeth.

218 glancing at Descartes' 'Cogito, ergo sum': 'I think, therefore I am'.

218 *is*] is itself *MS.*; is [no italics] *1878*.

242 *brutish* 'the life of man, solitary, poor, nasty, brutish, and short' (Hobbes, *Leviathan* I, xiii).

266 *wisdom*] Wisdom *MS.*

267 *power*] Power *MS.*

282 *to prove*] of learning *MS.*

318 *fineless* unlimited (*OED* calls the word 'rare').

327 *glassing* mirroring.

334 *Sorrow did and joy did nowise*] Sorrows did and joys did never *MS.*

334 The line, divorced from context, is often used to rebut over-simple notions of the 'optimistic' Browning.

335 *necessity*] Necessity *MS.*

336 *cause*] Cause *MS.*

353 *Job-like . . . blains* Job ii 7–8.

blains boils.

354 *whirlwind what the dread voice thence explains* Job xxxviii–xlii, where God's voice rebukes Job from the whirlwind.

355 *'vindicate no way of God's to man'* 'justify the ways of God to men' (*Paradise Lost* I, 26); 'vindicate the ways of God to man' (Pope, *Essay on Man* I, 16).

372 *alembic* apparatus for distilling.

elixir quintessence or soul of a thing; also the essence that can give eternal life.

403 *behoof* a misuse of the word for 'behalf' (compare 'A Forgiveness', 14).

527 *half*] not *MS.*

546 *Athanasius contra mundum* 'Athanasius against the world' (Latin). 'The whole world against Athanasius' (Hooker, *Laws of Ecclesiastical Polity* V, xlii); 'In the Nicene Council [325] he was almost the only high ecclesiastic who stood firm against the Arians . . . *Athanasius contra mundum*; a proverb which . . . sets forth the claims of individual . . . judgement' (A. P. Stanley, *History of the Eastern Church* VII, 234).

553 *Bossex* At Bossey (not 'Bossex'), near Geneva, Rousseau spent part of his childhood.

555–6 *Diodati . . . Byron's sake* a villa two miles from Geneva, where Byron wrote part of *Childe Harold's Pilgrimage* in 1816.

561–3 *'All that's good is gone . . . I believe it'* summarizing an aspect of Rousseau's thought.

564 *Dying day with dolphin hues* 'parting day/Dies like the dolphin, whom each pang imbues/With a new colour' (Byron, *Childe Harold's Pilgrimage* IV, xxix).

565 *Storm, for loveliness and darkness like a woman's eye* 'storm, and darkness, ye are wondrous strong,/Yet lovely in your strength, as is the light/Of a dark eye in woman' (Byron, *Childe Harold's Pilgrimage* III, xcii).

565–6 *Ye mounts/Where I climb to 'scape my fellow* typically Byronic – see, for instances, *Childe Harold's Pilgrimage* III, xiii, xlv, lxxii.
566–7 *thou sea wherein he counts/Not one inch of vile dominion* 'Roll on, thou deep and dark blue Ocean – roll!/Ten thousand fleets sweep over thee in vain;/Man marks the earth with ruin – his control/Stops with the shore' (Byron, *Childe Harold's Pilgrimage* IV, clxxix).
569–70 *Man is meanest . . . let him go a-howling to his gods* alluding generally to the apostrophe to Ocean in *Childe Harold's Pilgrimage* IV, clxxix–clxxxiv, and especially to clxxx: 'howling, to his Gods'. Compare *Fifine at the Fair*, 1105–6, and 1108n.
577 *earthward*] downward *MS.*, *1878*.
579 *pine-tree of Makistos* See Browning's translation of the *Agamemnon*, 310. The pine on Mount Macistus on the island of Euboea was one of the beacons which flashed the news to Greece of the sack of Troy.
580 *architrave* epistyle: support resting on top of a column (archaism).
582 *Lausanne* the Swiss city on the north shore of Lake Geneva, where Edward Gibbon completed his *Decline and Fall*.
583 *aspic* asp (the form is used mainly in poetry).
583–4 *aspic . . . python* 'the subtle little serpent, known as the asp or aspic, and the huge king of snakes, the python, symbolize here the insinuating brilliancy of Wit which Voltaire supplies to the imagined torch, and they picture, also, both the snapping of fire in the boughs of a pine-tree and the whirls of flame round its trunk almost hiding the solid glowing core of fire representing the pillar of solid learning Gibbon furnishes to the torch' (Florentine edition).
586 *Ferney* the site of Voltaire's estate near Geneva.
587–94] *MS. interpolation.*
588 *terebinth* turpentine.
590 *Diodati* Byron (see 555–6n.). In *Childe Harold's Pilgrimage* III, lxxvii–lxxxi, civ–cvii, Byron associates Rousseau, Gibbon and Voltaire with the landscape around Geneva (the landscape also has associations with Shelley; the omission of reference to him in *La Saisiaz* may be significant). Byron's three 'Mortals . . . sought and found, by dangerous roads,/A path to perpetuity of fame' (cv).
macaques species of monkeys.
594 *fulgurations* lightning-like flashes.
602 *flamboyant* wavy, suggesting the outline of a flame.
604 *he* Berdoe (*Browning Cyclopaedia*, 252) identifies the 'he' as Voltaire, and says the notion that Browning is referring to himself is 'preposterous'. Berdoe – as is his wont – errs: the 'he' is Browning.
614 *re-interment* planting again (not burial again).

The Two Poets of Croisic

First published in the volume entitled *La Saisiaz: The Two Poets of Croisic:* on 15 May 1878 by Smith, Elder. The *MS.* of *The Two Poets* is in the Library of Balliol College; it is messy, and would appear to be the first and last copy of the poem. It is heavily revised throughout, except for the epilogue, which was not originally intended for *The Two Poets*. There are only very minor differences between *MS.*, *1878* and *1888*. According to the *MS.* the poem was begun the day after Browning finished *La Saisiaz*: Browning's note states that the poem was begun on Saturday, 10 November, and ended 8 December 1877. The prologue is undated, and the epilogue is dated 15 January 1878. There are only two links of significance between

La Saisiaz and *The Two Poets*: Miss Anne Egerton Smith, whose sudden death prompted the former poem, spent several weeks with Browning and his sister at Le Croisic in the late summer of 1867, and both poems comment on the fleetingness of fame.

Browning spent parts of the summers of 1866 and 1867 at Le Croisic, the small fishing-port in south-west Brittany to the north-west of the mouth of the Loire, and had celebrated one of its sons in 'Hervé Riel'. Here he celebrates two others, his main source being not Caillo jeune's *Notes sur Le Croisic* (as stated by DeVane, *Handbook*, 425), but Gustave Grandpré's *Promenade au Croisic* III (Paris, Corbet, 1828), a volume also used for a source of 'Hervé Riel' (the present editor owns a *MS*. mainly in the hand of Sarianna Browning but with notes by the poet, which makes the debt to Grandpré clear). Of the first poet treated, little more is known than is told in the poem: René Gentilhomme was born in 1610, and became page and poet to Henry, Prince of Condé (1588–1646), who was expected to succeed Louis XIII as King of France. In 1637 Gentilhomme predicted the birth of the future Louis XIV, and when in 1638 his prophecy was proved accurate, he was made 'Royal Poet' by Louis XIII. The second poet is better known. Paul Desforges-Maillard (1699–1772) was involved in a hoax that provided the source for Alexis Piron's play, *La Métromanie* (1738), a play Browning may have known though he gives no details other than those in his source. Desforges-Maillard sent poems to the editor of the *Mercure*, De La Roque, in the hand of his sister and under the name of Mlle Malcrais de la Vigne. De La Roque waxed enthusiastic and expressed love for the imaginary lady, and Voltaire praised her highly. The *Poésies* of the lady appeared in 1735 and attracted much attention until the hoax was revealed. The author published three more works under his own name, but had no further success. Browning's poem has not lacked readers, but there is virtually no criticism on it. It uses *ottava rima* as its verse form, and is, in other respects also, one of the most Byronic of Browning's poems.

[PROLOGUE:] '*Such a starved bank of moss*'

DeVane (*Handbook*, 424) suggests that the poem was written to Mrs Browning.

2 *May-morn* Browning's first meeting with Elizabeth Barrett was in the afternoon of 20 May 1845.

THE TWO POETS OF CROISIC

2 *log-fire* One perhaps recalls the shipwreck-wood fire of 'By the Fireside' in 'James Lee's Wife', set in nearby Pornic.

11 *pandemonium* the devils' palace in Hell.

27–8 *bore away the bell/From* triumphed over.

30 *Octogenarian Keats* Keats died at the age of twenty-four.

32 *span-long* brief.

40 *copperas* a metal protosulphate.

46–7 *Son/O' the coal, – as Job and Hebrew name a spark* See Job v 7 and Isaiah l 11, where the word 'sparks' is the Hebrew 'sons of the coal' (or flame).

53 *Constellate* cluster together.

61 *bicker* gleam.

74 *land-strip* The peninsula on which Le Croisic stands is also called Le Croisic.

83–4 *what Guérande shuts/Behind her* The little town and former capital of Brittany, a few miles north-east of Le Croisic, has, behind it, protected countryside and farmland.

84 *Batz* inland village just east of Le Croisic.

Saxons Le Croisic was founded by the Saxons. Murray's Guides refer to the men of Batz as 'evident Saxons'.

84–5 *grub/The ground for crystals* Around Le Croisic are salt-marshes, from which Browning watched workers gathering and preparing salt.

92 *islet* Sène, associated with many legends of the Druids, the Celtic priests and medicine-men. Compare Arnold's 'Stanzas from Carnac' (1867), and the references in *Fifine at the Fair* to the memorials near Pornic. The whole area has many remains, thought to be of Druid origin in Browning's time.

107 *Menhir* a large monumental stone. The particular one referred to is about half a mile north-west of the church.

116 *shent* reproved.

156 *Cedar from hyssop-on-the-wall* 'from the cedar tree that is in Lebanon even unto the hyssop that springeth out of the wall' (1 Kings iv 33); 'hyssop' is used figuratively as the type of a low plant.

160 *Hervé Riel* the Le Croisic sailor, hero of Browning's poem, who saved a French fleet in 1692.

162 *billet* firewood.

165 *gules . . . vert* the heraldic colours of red and green.

185 *Assist* 'be present' (Gallicism).

186 *Clio* Browning invokes the Muse of History, one of the nine Muses.

196 *'Better do than say'* According to Browning's source, the motto *Mieux faire que dire* appeared on Gentilhomme's arms on the du Pré portrait alluded to in line 377.

203 *hap* happen (archaism).

204 *Anne of Austria* The Spanish princess (1601–66) married Louis XIII in 1615.

212 *Gaston* younger brother of Louis XIII, and Duke of Orleans.

225–8 *his very sire . . . just born at his decease* Browning's notes, appended to his sister's transcript, refer to 'Lespine (René Thimothée) Gentilhomme du Croisic, mort dit-on en 1610: auteur d'un petit poème de la *Parure des Dames*. Père de René-' ('Lespine [René Thimothée] Gentilhomme of Le Croisic, who is said to have died in 1610: author of a short poem on ladies' attire. Father of René . . .').

240 *Love . . . dove* Compare 'Too Late', 90, and 'Dîs Aliter Visum', 63.

249–320 Browning expands on his source, which says of Gentilhomme's prophecy: 'Il la fit à l'occasion du tonnerre qui venait écraser une couronne ducale, placée sur le pilier de l'escalier du jardin de cette maison, duquel accident il tirait dans ses vers un augure, qu'il regardait comme certain, de la naissance d'un dauphin.' ('He made it [the prophecy] on an occasion when a thunderstorm had just destroyed a ducal wreath placed on the pillar of a garden stairway at the house in question; in his verses, he interpreted this accident as an omen, which he considered reliable, of the birth of a dauphin.')

299 *divinior mens* 'more divine thought', 'inspiration' (Latin). Sarianna Browning's transcript from Grandpré refers to 'la fureur poétique, ou plutôt prophétique' ('poetic or, rather, prophetic frenzy') that possessed Gentilhomme.

302 *Rhadamanthine* extremely rigorous (Rhadamanthus was an inflexible judge in Hades).

321 *some forty lines* 'une pièce d'environ quarante vers' (Sarianna Browning's transcript from Grandpré).

335 *cony-kind* rabbit-kind – that is, timorous.

336 *It is a feeble folk* 'The conies are but a feeble folk' (Proverbs xxx 26).
344 *sun* Louis XIV was known as the Sun King.
360 *Simeon* son of Jacob and Leah (Genesis xxix 33).
363 *'Royal Poet'* Sarianna Browning's transcript of Grandpré: 'il parait que cette prédiction avait procuré à l'auteur le nom de poète royal' ('it appears that this prediction had secured for the author the name of royal poet').
377 *Du Pré* Guillaume du Pré, sculptor and medallion-maker (1574–1647).
378 *Daret* Picrre Daret, engraver (1604–78). Sarianna Browning's transcript refers to a 1637 Daret engraving of a du Pré representation of René.
381–4 *Latin verses . . . Getic trump* Sarianna Browning's transcript includes an epigram attributed to 'J. Leocheus [John Leech, seventeenth-century poet] *Scotus eloquentiae et philo. professor*': 'Aspicis effigiem vatis spirantis in aere,/Qui junxit Geticae Delphica plectra tubae/Sic oculos, sic ille humeros sic *Nobilis* ora,/Unum defuerat, dulciùs ille canit.' ('You see the image of a poet breathing in bronze,/Who has joined Delphic quill with Getic trumpet/So *celebrated* for his eyes, shoulders and face,/ [But] one thing was lacking, the other sings more sweetly.')
382 *biforked hill* Parnassus, sacred to the Muses and Apollo, has two peaks. To scale the mountain is to write poetry.
384 *Delphic quill* that is, the Classical artistic genius.
Getic trump 'Getic' has been used loosely for 'Gothic' – 'Gothic trumpet', in context, means Romantic artistic genius.
392 *deathward*] dwindling *MS.*; dwindles, *1878*.
397] Strontion his rival René – just the same *MS*.
401 *Somebody* Gustave Grandpré records seeing the portrait in the home of a gentleman whose name he does not give, and who replied to Grandpré's inquiry 'qu'il l'ignorait complètement' ('that he was completely unaware of it').
409–56 *The other famous poet . . . he prophesied about* based on the following passage from Sarianna Browning's transcript: 'Desforges fit de vains efforts pour se procurer ses oeuvres; on lui dit pourtant que M. de Chevaye, auditeur à la chambre des comptes de Bretagne, en possédait un exemplaire. Il lui écrivit pour le lui demander. Voici la réponse de M. de Chevaye. "J'ai eu dans mon cabinet les poésies de René Gentilhomme, mais elles ont été enveloppés dans l'incendie de ma maison à Nantes, avec une grande quantité de livres rares . . ."' ('Desforges tried in vain to procure his works; however, he was told that a Monsieur de Chevaye, a commissioner in the Brittany Audit Court, owned a copy. He wrote and asked him for it. Here is Monsieur de Chevaye's reply: "I did have the poems of René Gentilhomme in my study, but they, along with a large quantity of rare books, perished when my house in Nantes was destroyed by fire . . ."')
444 *in duodecimo* The book is formed from sheets divided into twelve leaves.
468–9 *believing God had dealt/For once directly with him* Browning's interest here is paralleled by his interest in Christopher Smart in the *Parleyings*.
488 *fortalice* small fort.
555–6 *In verses of society had lain/His talent chiefly* Sarianna Browning's transcript records that Desforges-Maillard 's'était fait une sorte de réputation dans sa jeunesse, en composant des couplets de circonstance et de petits vers de société' ('had achieved a reputation of sorts in his youth by composing occasional couplets and short society verses').
559 *Spasmodically* punning (1) by fits and starts; (2) like members of the Spasmodic School of poetry: the group including Bailey (1816–1902), Dobell (1824–74) and Alexander Smith (1830–67).
562 *ell* Technically, the English ell is forty-five inches.

577 *prize* The 1730 prize topic was 'Les progrès de l'art de la navigation sous Louis XIV' ('Advancements in the Art of Navigation under Louis XIV').

Academy The French Academy was founded by Richelieu in 1635.

585 *Neptune and Amphitrité* God of the Sea (Poseidon) and his wife.

586 *Tethys* one of the first twelve Titans, wife of Oceanus.

tag serve as a tag.

587 *Triton* sea deity, son of Neptune and Amphitrite, messenger and trumpeter of Neptune.

588 *It's Virgil* In the *Aeneid*, Neptune and Triton and others helped to save the fleet of Aeneas.

589 Named are prominent aristocrats of the day.

593 *irritabilis gens* 'the sensitive tribe' (of poets: Horace, *Epistles* II, ii, 102).

602 *the Forty* the French Academy (with its membership of forty).

611 *Phoebus* Apollo, god of poetry.

613 *Seine* the river on which Paris stands.

620 *clink* jingle.

626 *vibrios* species of bacteria.

637 *bantling* small child.

646 *literators* literary men (French: *littérateurs*).

650–51 *appeal/To Caesar from the Jews* Saint Paul's appeal (Acts xxv 10–11).

659 *Pierian rill* haunt of the Muses on Mount Olympus.

669 *crambo* contemptible rhyme.

727 *Roland* the greatest of Charlemagne's knights, and hero of romance.

761 *Deïdamia* daughter of Lycomedes, seduced by Achilles while the Greek warrior was disguised as a girl.

767 *lady's-smock* cuckooflower.

775 *escritoire* writing-desk.

786 *Brederac* identified by Cooke, *Guide-Book,* and by the Florentine edition as a Brittany village; the present editor has found no record of it except as the name of Desforges-Maillard's estate in Browning's main source.

797 *angel and yet ape* 'Is man an ape or an angel?' (Disraeli in a speech of 1864).

807 *ad hoc* 'for this purpose' (Latin).

809 *Turk* traditionally savage and barbarous.

824 *Deshoulières* the woman poet from Paris (1638–94).

831 *Sappho* the great woman poet of the sixth century B.C.

854 *aroints* drives away with an execration (*OED* points out that the word is used as an inflected verb by the Brownings – and apparently by no one else).

855 *cross-buttock* to throw over the hip in a special way in wrestling.

858 Voltaire sent the imaginary lady copies of his epic poem, *La Henriade* (1728), and of his prose history, *Histoire de Charles XII* (1731). See too his poem, 'Épître à une dame ou soi-disant telle' (1732), which Browning translates in lines 865–86 (Voltaire's lines are in Sarianna Browning's transcript from Grandpré).

870 *Dacier* André Dacier (1651–1722) was the learned philologist, but the reference may be to his wife (1651–1720), who translated Homer.

874 *erst* formerly (archaism).

891–2 *fathers of Trévoux . . . Dictionary* The famous *Dictionary* was published by the Jesuits at Trévoux, near Bourg, between 1704 and 1771. The details about the entry come from Grandpré.

895 *Jean-Baptiste Rousseau* the lyric poet (1671–1741) – not *the* Rousseau.

903–4 adapting the actual words, given in Sarianna Browning's transcript as: 'Je vous aime, ma chère Bretonne; pardonnez cet aveu, mais le mot est lâche.' ('I love you, dear lass of Brittany; forgive my boldness, but I can't restrain my tongue.')

905–12 Browning admired John Donne, and often echoed him, in a century in which his reputation was not as high as it is now. In an unpublished letter of 4 February 1883 (in the Huntington Library) he asked Furnivall: 'Was there ever a more lovely line, to eye and ear, written than Donne's

And like the tender stalk at whose end stands
The woodbine quivering, are her arms and hands.

One follows up the stalk on to the final flower.' (Donne's lines are from 'Elegy 8', 27–8.) The lines cited here (905–9) are from Donne's 'The Progress of the Soul', 338–40: ' 'Tis greatest now, and to destruction/Nearest; there's no pause at perfection./Greatness a period hath, but hath no station.' In 911 Browning glances sardonically at the old *-tion* endings, pronounced as two syllables.

914 *dexter* right (used especially in heraldry).

933 *prize* The prize awarded Hercules for completing the Twelve Labours was immortality.

934–6 *He threw a sop . . . exactly so* not, in fact, exactly so – Paul's knowledge is shaky. It was the Sibyl (*Aeneid* VI) who threw the sop to the three-headed monstrous dog that guarded Hades; Hercules dragged him up to earth as the last of his Labours. The heel-licking is romantically Desforgian but not classical: Cerberus did not enjoy the experience.

942 *Diana* goddess of hunting.

966 *Phoebé* another name for Diana.

966–7 *Phoebus . . . Python* Apollo slew the mighty monster at Delphi.

977–9 *Somebody says . . . natural* If the person and saying exist, they remain unidentified.

1008 *Idalian* The city and mountain of Idalium in Cyprus were sacred to Venus.

1014 *brock* badger.

1034 *yield the pas* The French idiom *céder le pas* (literally, 'to yield the step') means 'to give precedence'.

1039–40 *Comic sock . . . tragic buskin* the light shoe worn by actors in comedy in Greece and Rome, and the boot reaching to the knee worn by actors in tragedy.

1041 *wren* one of the smallest of birds.

1043 *acquist* thing acquired.

1062 *haut-de-chausses* breeches.

1081 *'barbered ten times o'er'* *Antony and Cleopatra* II. 2. 229.

1091 *quarte-and-tierce* fencing positions.

1122–4 *In proportion . . . Machiavelli* The quotation, if it is one, remains unidentified.

1133 *Mortified* vexed.

1152 *chaps* punning: fellows, and jaws.

1161 *Bergerac* town in south-west France.

1165 *angle* nook.

1175 *Fiddlepin* not in *OED*.

1191–2 *'After death survive . . . and died while yet alive!'* adapting Jean-Baptiste Rousseau, *Épigrammes* XXII, 3–4: 'Après sa mort, il crut vivre/Et mourut de son vivant' ('He thought that after death he'd live,/And died from too much living'). The lines are quoted in Browning's worksheets for the poem.

1197–8 *rat who belled/The cat once* alluding to the fable in which a mouse suggested that the cat should have a warning bell round its neck to warn mice of its approach, but others wondered who would bell it. Thus to bell the cat is to risk oneself for others (as Gentilhomme did in making his prophecy).

1208 *see his epitaph* 'Here lies one who was nothing' ('Ci-gît qui ne fut rien') – Piron's epitaph, cited by Voltaire in *La Vanité* as happy, and worthy of Piron's tomb.

1209–16 clearly recalling the ring-image of *The Ring and the Book*.

1223 *chowse* trick.

1226 *later bards lacked Agamemnon too* Besides the obvious meaning, Browning is probably also alluding to the hostile reception of his transcript of the *Agamemnon* published in 1877.

1232 *Beddoes* Thomas Lovell Beddoes (1803–49) was admired by Browning, who, had he been elected Professor of Poetry at Oxford, would have devoted his inaugural lecture to Beddoes. In 1872 Browning inherited Beddoes's papers.

1275 *blink* spark.

[EPILOGUE:] *'What a pretty tale you told me'*

First published in *La Saisiaz: The Two Poets of Croisic:* on 15 May 1878. In the manuscript the poem's original title of 'Eunomos of Locri' is deleted, and the 'epilogue' in *MS.* and *1878* is dated 15 January 1878. *MS.*, *1878* and *1888* are virtually identical. In the *Selections* of 1880 the poem was printed under the title 'A Tale'.

The poem is based on a story told often in classical times, the particular source being the poem by Paulus Silentiarius in the *Greek Anthology* VI, 54: 'To Lycorean Apollo doth Locrian Eunomus dedicate the brazen cicada, in memory of his contest for the crown. The contest was in lyre-playing, and opposite him stood his competitor, Parthis. But when the Locrian shell rang to the stroke of the plectrum, the string cracked with a hoarse cry. But before the running melody could go lame, a cicada landed on the lyre chirping tenderly and caught up the vanishing note of the chord, adapting to the fashion of our playing its wild music that used to echo in the woods. Therefore, divine son of Leto, doth he honour thee with the gift of thy cicada, perching the brazen songster upon thy lyre.'

31–3 *seven . . . eleven.* The traditional lyre had seven strings; how many strings it ultimately had is not known, but there are old references to citharas of eleven strings.

65 *Lotte* heroine of Goethe's *Sorrows of Young Werther*.

104 *casting pearls* 'neither cast ye your pearls before swine' (Matthew vii 6).

Dramatic Idyls, First Series

The six poems of *Dramatic Idyls* were first published by Smith, Elder on 28 April 1879. The volume was well received, and, for the first time since *Balaustion's Adventure*, a second edition was called for. This appeared in 1882 with the expanded title *Dramatic Idyls, First Series,* the second-series volume having appeared in the interval. The *MS.* is in the Library of Balliol College; it is exceptionally clean, and is obviously a fair copy. There are very few variants among *MS.*, *1879*, *1882* and *1888*. It is probable that most or all of the volume was composed in the second half of 1878. DeVane, whose comments on textual matters on the *Dramatic Idyls* are unreliable, remarks incorrectly (*Handbook*, 428–9) that the *MS.* shows signs of rough usage, and is ledi nto improbable speculation because Browning made use of post-office sticky tape.

The title suggests links between the new volume and some earlier volumes, though the narrative element is generally somewhat stronger than in *Dramatic Lyrics, Dramatic Romances* and *Dramatis Personae,* and the doctrinal and dramatic interest somewhat less. The title also inevitably forces comparisons with Tennyson's idyls and idylls – as Tennyson himself realized in regretting that Browning had appropriated what he thought of as his own word. Browning's idyls are obviously very different from Tennyson's, about which Browning had privately been rather critical. Browning himself described what he meant by the term in a letter of 7 October 1889: 'a succinct little story complete in itself; not necessarily concerning pastoral matters, by any means, though from the prevalency of such topics in the idyls of Theocritus, such is the general notion. These of mine are called "Dramatic" because the story is told by some actor in it, not by the poet himself. The subjects are sombre enough, with the exception of the Greek one; and are all in rhymed verse; this last is a metre of my own' (W. M[eynell]., 'The Detachment of Browning', *Athenaeum*, 4 January 1890, 18–19).

As DeVane points out, the metres (that of 'Tray' excepted) approximate those of Greek idyls; and besides the measure of formal unity in the volume, there is also some kind of thematic unity in the stress on conscience and remorse. John Woolford (*BSN* VI, No. 2, 1976, 19–28) suggests 'that the collection is concerned with the role of extreme experience . . . in human life'.

MARTIN RELPH

First published in *Dramatic Idyls* 28 April 1879. *MS., 1879, 1882* and *1888* are virtually identical. The poem was probably written in the autumn of 1878.

The source has not been identified. Mrs Orr (*Handbook*, 309–10) remarked, 'It embodies a vague remembrance of something read by Mr Browning when he was himself a boy,' and DeVane (*Handbook*, 432) thought the story was an incident in the Forty-Five, the rebellion led by Bonnie Prince Charlie in 1745. In an unpublished letter of 4 December 1885 in the Armstrong Browning Library, however, Browning wrote that he transferred to England an incident from the American Revolution in a tale read perhaps fifty years before, that the incident was in all probability not historical, and that he himself invented the 'motive' of the poem in the role played by Martin Relph. The 'motive' would seem to owe something to the compulsion of Coleridge's Ancient Mariner to find in telling his story an outlet for his remorse.

5 *Methuselah* He died at the age of 969 (Genesis v 27).
12 *the cap which fits* the remark which applies (alluding to the expression 'If the cap fits, wear it').
17 *first of May* traditionally a festive and celebratory day.
29 *King George* any one of the three Georges, but George II if the background be the Forty-Five, George III if Browning kept to the time of the original tale.
126 *roundabout* indirect way.

PHEIDIPPIDES

First published in *Dramatic Idyls* on 28 April 1879. In *1882* one line was added and two other lines were revised, in *1888* another phrase was reworked, and after

Browning's death (a unique instance) line 62 was added. The poem was probably written in the second half of 1878.

The stories were well known of the run of Pheidippides to Sparta and of his meeting with Pan, and of the run from the Battle of Marathon in 490 with the runner expiring with news of the victory. Herodotus provides the details of the run to Sparta and the meeting with Pan (VI, 105–6), and Lucian identified the Marathon runner as Pheidippides (or Philippides) and gave him his dying words, 'Rejoice, we conquer,' which Browning used for the poem's motto (*Pro lapsu inter salutandum* 3, 727–8). Browning is apparently the first writer to combine the two stories. He may also have made some use of Pausanias and Plutarch. See J. W. Cunliffe, 'Browning and the Marathon Race', *PMLA* XXIV, 1909, 154–63.

2 *daemons* guardian spirits.
4 *Her of the aegis and spear* Pallas Athene, represented with shield and spear, the deity of Athens.
5 *ye of the bow and the buskin* Artemis, goddess of hunting, and of the moon.
6 *latest* Herodotus (II, 145) says that Pan was among the most recent of the gods.
8 *Pan* god of flocks and shepherds, and of the countryside, part man and part goat.
9 *Archons* Magistrates.
tettix Ancient Athenians wore badges representing grasshoppers, symbolic of Athens and the relation between its people and the ground from which they sprang.
11 *myrtle* sometimes used for crowns for heroes.
15 *two days, two nights* According to Herodotus, he reached Sparta (about 140 miles away) the next day after leaving Athens.
18 Persia had asked for the water and earth, symbolic of submission, in 493 (Herodotus VI, 48–9).
19 *Eretria* city on the island of Euboea.
25 *Did Sparta respond?* Pheidippides is less charitable to the Spartans than are Herodotus and most historians.
31 *Zeus* The king of the gods on Olympus was rather given to hurling thunderbolts.
32 *Phoibos* Apollo (twin-brother of Artemis).
47 *filleted victim* beast decked out for sacrifice.
fulsome abundant.
49 *Oak* sometimes regarded as sacred to thunder. A crown of oak-leaves is sometimes symbolic of courage.
olive sacred to Pallas Athene; a crown of olive was a reward for distinguished civic service.
bay sacred to Apollo. A wreath of it protected against thunder and lightning, and a crown of bay (or laurel) symbolized victory.
52 *Parnes* Herodotus had the meeting near Mount Parthenium in Arcadia. Parnes is an Attic mountain and well out of the way – the change, involving their meeting in Attica, may well have been deliberate.
61 *fosse* ditch.
62] *Cambridge edition (1895 printing only), Florentine and Centenary editions; not in MS., 1879–88.* DeVane (*Handbook*, 433) states that the line was first published in the Cambridge edition according to the poet's instructions.
Erebos Hades, or a place of darkness on the way to Hades.
70–75 Pan 'called him by his name, and bade him ask the Athenians "wherefore they neglected him so entirely, when he was kindly disposed towards them, and had

often helped them in times past, and would do so again in times to come?" ' (Herodotus). Pan's subsequent remarks are Browning's invention.

75 *Test Pan, trust me*] Put Pan to the test *MS., 1879–82*.

79 *fought in the ranks* Legend had it that Pan fought at Marathon.

83] – Fennel, whatever it bode – I grasped it a-tremble with dew) *MS., 1879*.

fennel 'Marathon' means 'fennel-field'; Pan's pledge is Browning's invention.

86] *not in MS., 1879*.

87 *razor's edge* originally a Greek idiom.

88 *I too have a guerdon rare*] myself have a guerdon too *MS., 1879* (see Hood, *Letters*, 189, and the note).

89 *Miltiades* Athenian general at Marathon.

101 *maid* addition to the sources.

109 *Fennel-field* the literal meaning of 'Marathon'.

111–14 *'Rejoice, we conquer!' . . . the word of salute/Is still 'Rejoice!'* 'Philippides, the one who acted as courier, is said to have used it first in our sense when he brought the news of victory from Marathon and addressed the magistrates in session when they were anxious how the battle had ended; "Joy to you, we've won," he said, and there and then he died, breathing his last breath with that "Joy to you" ' (Lucian – Loeb translation).

HALBERT AND HOB

First published in *Dramatic Idyls* on 28 April 1879. Browning made minor changes for *1882*; it and *1888* are almost identical. The poem was probably written in the second half of 1878.

The basis for the poem is in the *Ethics* of Aristotle: 'Take for instance the man who defended himself on the charge of striking his father by saying "yes, but *he* struck *his* father, and *he* struck *his*, and" (pointing to his child) "this boy will strike *me* when he is a man; it runs in the family"; or the man who when he was being dragged along by his son bade him stop at the doorway, since he himself had dragged his father only as far as that' (VII, 6, 2). The story is also told elsewhere.

13 *aye*] lay *MS., 1879*; ay *1882*.

24 *shell* wooden coffin.

34 *eld* of the olden time (archaism and poeticism).

45 *Hob, on just such*] Halbert, on such *MS., 1879*.

52 *and, Hob*] Halbert *MS., 1879*.

60 *yeaned* born (archaism, dialectal).

66 'Is there any cause in nature that makes these hard hearts?' (*Lear* III. 6. 82).

IVÀN IVÀNOVITCH

First published in *Dramatic Idyls* on 28 April 1879. *MS., 1879, 1882* and *1888* are virtually identical. The poem was written in Switzerland, while Browning and his sister were staying in the village of Splügen near the Italian border (18 August–23 September 1878). The poem probably owes something to Browning's visit to Russia in 1834, but the particular probable source is not a Russian one but an anonymous book of 1855, *An Englishwoman in Russia* (174–5) – see DeVane, *Handbook*, 438–9, for the anecdote. Browning modified the story in a few fairly minor respects. The Russian accents and some other details are not always accurate, though Browning asked a Russian lady in Venice about the names he had used in the poem very shortly after writing it.

The poem has been among the more popular of Browning's later works, and has provoked considerable disagreement about the moral issues posed. Tennyson thought the woman right; most readers have thought her wrong, without necessarily condoning Ivàn's justice. On the poem see P. Drew, '"The Raw Material of Moral Sentiment": Another View of "Ivàn Ivànovitch"', *BSN* V, No. 2, 1975, 3–6; E. W. Slinn, 'The Judgement of Instinct in "Ivàn Ivànovitch"', *BSN* IV, No. 1, 1974, 3–9.

14–15 *Peter's time . . . Frenchified* Peter the Great (1672–1725) opened Russia up to European, and especially French, influence.
19 *forestry* a vast extent of trees.
verst about two thirds of a mile.
28 *highway broad and straight* Browning may have thought of the story of Tsar Nicholas, who insisted that the railway between Saint Petersburg and Moscow should be dead straight.
Neva's mouth The river empties into the Gulf of Finland at Leningrad (then Saint Petersburg).
35 *Ivàn Ivànovitch* roughly equivalent to Jack Jackson.
38 *billets* firewood.
53 *Droug* Russian for 'Friend'.
55 *motherkin* the Russian *matushka*, affectionate diminutive of *mat* (mother).
60 *Vàssili* more properly, Vasìli – there are other similar inaccuracies.
101 *glib* in the rare (and dialectal) sense of 'smooth and slippery'.
114 *lamped* lighting as with a lamp.
133 *Satan-faced* Russians thought wolves reincarnations of Satan's witches.
135 *pigeons* The diminutive of the word for 'pigeon' was the most frequent form of endearment in Russian.
137 *Stiòpka* diminutive of Stèpan.
166 *Teriòscha* diminutive of Terentiì.
181 *Pope* priest.
193 *erst* formerly (archaism).
197 *endmost* furthest (*OED* calls the word rare).
205 *whimperingest* Browning's fondness for unusual superlatives remained with him throughout his career.
243 *unharden* *OED* records no example between 1611 and this; the word is presumably rare.
282 *Stàrosta* Elder, the leader of the Commune.
283 *Jurisconsult* Master of Jurisprudence.
284 *Pomeschìk* the leading landowner in the area.
286 *thorpe* village (archaism).
309 *old Pope* reminiscent of the Pope of *The Ring and the Book*. In Browning's source (and analogues to it) the case is decided by the Tsar.
317–19 *Your young men . . . dream dreams* 'your old men shall dream dreams, your young men shall see visions' (Joel ii 28, quoted in Acts ii 17).
324 *"Shall the dead praise thee?"* 'shall the dead arise and praise thee' (Psalm lxxxviii, 10).
324–5 *"The whole live world is rife,/God, with thy glory"* echoing many Biblical statements – for instance, 'the whole earth is full of his glory' (Isaiah vi 3).
359 *trow* believe (archaism).

380–81 *Moses . . . twain-tables* Deuteronomy x 4–5.
412 *Kremlin* the Moscow fortress and palace.
421 *Kolokol* the huge bell of the Kremlin.

TRAY

First published in *Dramatic Idyls* on 28 April 1879. *MS.* and all texts are virtually identical. The poem was probably written late in 1878.

A vice-president of the Victoria Society for the Protection of Animals, Browning was an ardent anti-vivisectionist (a watered-down law against vivisection had been passed in 1876) – compare 'Arcades Ambo' in *Asolando.* Mrs Orr (*Handbook,* 313) says the poem is based on an incident seen and reported by a friend of Browning in Paris. C. R. Tracy, 'The Source and Meaning of Browning's *Tray*', *PMLA* LV, 1940, 615–17, shows that the poem is influenced by Frederic Harrison's contribution to the symposium in *The Nineteenth Century* on 'The Soul and Future Life' that had also influenced *La Saisiaz.* Drew, *Poetry of Browning,* 53–4, sees the poem as a burlesque of the melodramatic heroics of Morris and Byron, and certainly the dog's reticence contrasts with the absence of it in many traditional heroes of poetry. In 'Development', 11, Browning gives Tray as the name of one of the family dogs in his childhood; the famous Tray is the 'poor dog' of Thomas Campbell's 'The Harper' (1799).

2 *Bard the first* Clearly William Morris is glanced at. His *Sigurd the Volsung* had appeared in 1876, and Browning briefly here touches on Morris's medievalizing, his use of archaisms, his interest in saga.
4 *His helm and eke his habergeon* his helmet and also his sleeveless coat of mail.
6 *Bard the second* clearly the Byron of *Childe Harold's Pilgrimage.*

NED BRATTS

First published in *Dramatic Idyls* on 28 April 1879. Two lines were added in *1882* and a footnote was cancelled in *1888*; there are otherwise few differences between the *MS.* and all texts. The poem was written mainly in Switzerland, while Browning and his sister were staying in Splügen near the Italian border (18 August–23 September 1878) – 'Ivàn Ivànovitch' and perhaps other Dramatic Idyls were written during the same period. As DeVane (*Handbook,* 442) points out, however, Browning probably added material upon his return to London in November.

In a letter to Furnivall of 11 March 1882, Browning wrote: 'The story of "Old Tod," as told in Bunyan's "Life and Death of Mr Badman," was distinctly in my mind when I wrote *Ned Bratts* – at the Splügen, without reference to what I had read when quite a boy' (Hood, *Letters,* 209). Bunyan wrote: 'At a Summer Assizes holden at *Hartfort,* while the Judge was sitting upon the Bench, comes this old Tod into the Court, cloathed in green Suit, with his Leathern Girdle in his hand, his Bosom open, and all on a dung sweat, as if he had run for his Life; and being come in, he spake aloud as follows: *My Lord, said he, Here is the veryest Rogue that breaths upon the face of the earth. I have been a Thief from a Child: When I was but a little one, I gave myself to rob Orchards, and to do other such like wicked things, and I have continued a Thief ever since. My Lord, there has not been a Robbery committed thus many years, within so many miles of this place, but I have either been at it, or privy to it.*

'The Judge thought the fellow was mad, but after some conference with some of the Justices, they agreed to Indict him; and so they did of several felonious Actions; to all which he heartily confessed Guilty, and so was hanged with his Wife at the same time.'

The story is, however, really only part of the foundation of Browning's. The poet treats fact freely, moving, for instance, the scene of the incident from Hertford to Bedford, the county town west of Cambridge and about fifty miles north of London, where John Bunyan was in prison from November 1660–March 1672. He sets his action in midsummer 1672, by which time Bunyan was in fact out of gaol, and his eldest daughter, the blind Mary, was dead. Historically, too, the book Bunyan gave Bratts could not have been *Pilgrim's Progress,* which was published only in 1678 (until 1885 it was believed that Bunyan wrote his masterpiece in Bedford Gaol before his release in 1672; then, until fairly recently, it was thought to have been written in 1675–6 when Bunyan was again incarcerated; now it is thought to have been largely a product of the first imprisonment). Moreover, of course, Browning invented the connection between Ned Bratts's confession and Bunyan's influence. *Pilgrim's Progress* is a major source for the poem, being frequently alluded to. Browning probably used the biographies of Bunyan by Southey and Macaulay. On the poem, see Burrows, *Browning the Poet*, 258–64, and R. E. Gridley in *BSN* VI, No. 1, 1976, 10–16. In the following notes, *Pilgrim's Progress* is cited from R. Sharrock's edition (Penguin).

5 *bibbing* drinking.
12 *tag-rag and bobtail* riff-raff.
bowsing boozing.
13 *Quality* The vulgar dialectal word for people of high social position is here used rather sardonically.
17 *Of a reek* steaming (generally a northern usage).
18 *forbye* besides (a northern usage or archaism).
32 *frizzles* short crisp curls.
33 *fleered* laughed impudently.
34 *main* main part.
43 *Serjeant* member of a superior order of barristers from which were chosen common-law judges.
52 *Tabby* Tabitha.
53 *muck-sweat* profuse sweat (Bunyan's 'dung sweat').
64 *javelineers* javelin-men: judges' escorts at assizes (Browning's is the only usage in this sense recorded in *OED*).
67 *tithesman* The form is not recorded in *OED*.
71 *Public* public house ('pub').
82 *midden* manure pile (dialectal).
83 *billet* wooden club.
92 *Od's* a minced form of 'God's', very common in the seventeenth century.
96 *danced the jig that needs no floor* adapting proverbial expressions – for instance, 'dance the Tyburn jig' and 'dance upon nothing'.
97 *houghed* hamstrung.
98 *brave, like scripture-trees called bays* 'I have seen the wicked in great power, and spreading himself like a green bay tree' (Psalm xxxvii 35).
100 *Zounds* euphemism for 'God's wounds'.
102 *the Book* *Pilgrim's Progress.*
104 *'Sdeath* euphemism for 'God's death'.
106 *whistle wet* To wet one's whistle is to have a drink.

108 *strawy* worthless as straw.
114 *Gammer* rustic title for an old woman.
crab crab-apple.
117 *fuddling-cap* drinking-cap (to fuddle one's cap is to get drunk).
119 *Gaffer* rustic title for an old man.
124 *knobstick* knobbed stick.
126 *prate-apace* chatterbox.
129 *Tinker* Bunyan was a tinker, and was arrested for preaching near Bedford, and gaoled when he refused to promise not to preach. He supported himself and his family while he was in gaol by making laces.
141 *Patmore* Legend has it that Bunyan was gaoled in the town gaol on Bedford Bridge, but he was in fact a prisoner of the county gaol.
156–7 *Dives . . . Charles* Dives is the name traditionally given (as in *Pilgrim's Progress*, 63) to the rich man (Latin, *dives*) of Luke xvi 19. A *wain* is a wagon – but Charles's Wain is another name for the constellation of seven stars of the Great Bear. As a Puritan, Bunyan had fought against the Royalists; his imprisonment followed shortly after the Restoration of the monarchy and the return of Charles II (1660–85).
161 *Down on my marrow-bones* 'Down on your marrow-bones' ('Down on your knees') is a gentle way of telling a person to beg pardon.
168 *cloister* in the archaic or obsolete sense of 'enclosed space'.
170 *"Why cumbers it the ground?"* 'cut it down; why cumbereth it the ground' (Luke xiii 7).
171 *sloughed* recalling Bunyan's Slough of Despond.
172 *stag-horns* 'the bare upper branches of a tree' (*OED*, which calls the usage here a nonce-use).
174 *marle* soil (but associated with Hell through Milton's use of the word in *Paradise Lost* I, 296).
178 *Tophet* the Biblical valley of burning, symbolic of Hell (Isaiah xxx 33; *Paradise Lost* I, 404). Christian in *Pilgrim's Progress* (40) fears he will fall into Tophet.
179 *"Look unto me and be ye saved!"* quoting Isaiah xlv 22.
180 'thou [Moses] shalt smite the rock, and there shall come water out of it' (Exodus xvii 6); 'Moses lifted up his hand, and with his rod he smote the rock twice: and the water came out abundantly' (Numbers xx 11).
180] In *1879* and *1882* (not in *MS.*) there was a footnote to the line:

They did not eat
His flesh, nor suck those oils which thence outstreat.
Donne's *Progress of the Soul*, line 344.

(The lines come from the stanza following that quoted in *The Two Poets of Croisic*, 905–9.)
180 *outstreats* out flows (*OED* calls the word rare and obsolete, and cites only the Donne and Browning examples). The Florentine edition errs in stating that the word occurs in *Pilgrim's Progress*.
181–2 *Be your sins scarlet . . . driven snow* 'though your sins be as scarlet, they shall be as white as snow; though they be red like crimson, they shall be as wool' (Isaiah i 18); 'driven snow' is a cliché.
193 *tick* instant (colloquialism). The usage here is the earliest in this sense recorded by *OED*.
201 *lugged* baited.
203 *Christmas* error for 'Christian'. DeVane (*Handbook*, 442) errs in stating

that the most notable change made for *1888* was the substitution of 'Christian' for 'Christmas': the word was 'Christmas' in *MS*. and all texts.

burden at your back 'I fear that this burden that is upon my back will sink me lower than the grave; and I shall fall into Tophet' (Christian to Evangelist, *Pilgrim's Progress*, 40).

204–5 *Joseph's sack . . . the cup* 'the cup was found in Benjamin's sack' (Genesis xliv 12).

211 *slack straps* 'Must here the burden fall from off my back?/Must here the strings that bound it to me, crack?' (*Pilgrim's Progress*, 70).

213 *mountain* Mount Sinai, which Christian fears will fall on his head, and from which flashes of fire come (51).

214 *"Destruction"* the city that Christian flees in *Pilgrim's Progress*, and which, Christian is informed, 'will be burned with fire from Heaven' (39).

215 *'scape the wrath in time* 'Fly from the wrath to come' was written on the scroll given Christian by Evangelist (41).

216 *wicket-gate* the 'strait gate' of Matthew vii 13 whither Evangelist directs Christian to receive instructions (41).

217 *Despond the slough* Christian and Pliable fall into the Slough of Despond, and Pliable gives up (45).

218 *House Beautiful* Christian reaches the palace (78) designed 'for the relief and security of pilgrims'.

220 *Christmas did* Christian left his beloved wife and four children behind in the City of Destruction.

222 *enemy horned and winged* Apollyon, whom Christian meets in the Valley of Humiliation and who figures also in 'Childe Roland'. Bratts's imagination adds details to Bunyan's story.

227 *Hopeful* Christian meets Hopeful (135) shortly after Faithful is killed.

229 *thrid* thread (archaism).

231 *Master Faithful* Christian's companion for much of his journey (101–34).

Delightful Mounts the Delectable Mountains ('Immanuel's Land'), which Christian saw (88) from the House Beautiful.

232 *Vanity Fair* Christian and Faithful come to Vanity-Fair (124), and Faithful is killed there.

236 *Saint Peter's Green* in Bedford.

237–8 *they flogged . . . swords* 'they scourged him, then they buffeted him, then they lanced his flesh with knives; after that they stoned him with stones, then pricked him with their swords' (134).

241–3 *Behind the rabble-rout . . . Heaven-gate* 'there stood behind the multitude a chariot and a couple of horses, waiting for Faithful, who . . . was taken up into it, and straightway was carried up through the clouds, with sound of trumpet, the nearest way to the Celestial Gate' (134).

243 *Odds my life* an exclamatory formula common in the seventeenth century, using the minced form of 'God's'.

246 *Master Worldly-Wiseman* Christian meets him early on his journey (49). (It seems clear that Bratts has not finished *Pilgrim's Progress*.)

Master Interpreter Christian comes to his house (59) and has pictures interpreted for him.

247 *Take the will, not the deed* proverbial.

249 *here we stand* 'Here I stand; I can do no otherwise. God help me. Amen!' (Luther at the Diet of Worms).

263 *peach* inform (slang).

270 *Sackerson* The bear's name comes from *Merry Wives* I. 1. 307.
271 *Brawl* kind of dance.
273–5 *Iron Cage ... War against light* While with Interpreter, Christian meets (65) in the Iron Cage of Despair the man who was 'once a fair and flourishing professor' but who, having 'sinned against the light of the word', is given over to despair.
278 *Mote* the eminence on which the Court House stood.
288 *I wis* I know (pseudo-archaism).
289–90 *fox/Convicting geese* 'To set the fox to keep the geese' is proverbial, but Browning may have had in mind Thomas Fuller's 'A Fox should not be of the Jury at a Goose's trial' (*Gnomologia,* 116).
292 *Reynard* the traditional name in fable for a fox.
i' feggs i' faith (*OED* does not record Browning's spelling 'feggs').
303 *dog-days* days of great heat.
Amicus Curiae 'friend of the court' – Latin (a legal term for one who offers advice to a court).
307 *proper* admirable (archaism in this sense).
316 *Astraea Redux* 'Justice Restored' (Latin) – with the Restoration.
325 *on the spur* in utmost haste.
325–6] *not in MS., 1879.*
328 *Bunyan's Statue* The statue by Sir Joseph Boehm (1834–90) was given to the town by the Duke of Bedford in 1874.

Dramatic Idyls, Second Series

The *Second Series* of *Dramatic Idyls* was published on 15 June 1880 by Smith, Elder. The volume was clearly designed to capitalize on the success of the *Dramatic Idyls* of the year before, but it was not well received, and no second edition was needed. The very clean *MS.* is in the Library of Balliol College. For *1880* Browning made many revisions in proof but almost all of them are trifling, and there are virtually no significant differences among *MS., 1880* and *1888*. With the possible exceptions of the prologue and epilogue, the poems were written between 20 January and 19 April 1880.

[PROLOGUE:] '"*You are sick, that's sure," – they say*'

First published in *Dramatic Idyls, Second Series* on 15 June 1880, and reprinted without substantive change in *1888*. The poem is not dated in the *MS.*, but was probably written to introduce the volume, and its and Browning's interest in man's soul, in March or April 1880.

ECHETLOS

First published in *Dramatic Idyls, Second Series* on 15 June 1880, and reprinted with only trifling changes in *1888*. The poem is unique, or virtually so, in that *MS.* and *1880* readings are absolutely identical. In the *MS.* the poem is dated 2 February 1880.

Like 'Pheidippides', to which this poem is an obvious companion, 'Echetlos' celebrates a hero of the Battle of Marathon in 490, when the Athenians and Plataeans 'saved the world'. The hero's name means 'holder of the ploughshare'. The main source is Pausanias (*Description of Greece* I, 32): 'And it chanced, as they say, in the battle that a man of rustic appearance and dress appeared, who slew many of the Persians with a ploughshare, and vanished after the fight: and when the Athenians made inquiry of the oracle, the god gave no other answer, but bade them honour the hero Echetlus.' Browning also derived information from Herodotus, about the battle (VI, 109–14) and about Miltiades (VI, 132–6). Sir Sidney Colvin records ('Some Personal Recollections', *Scribner's Magazine* LXVII, 1920, 79) that Browning read the poem with 'his foot stamping vigorously in time'.

2 *Barbarians* For ancient Greeks, the term meant all non-Greeks.
11 *clown* peasant.
12 *share* ploughshare.
13 *weak mid-line* At Marathon the Persians broke through the weaker middle of the Greek lines, but were then massacred by the Greeks on the flanks.
15 *Kallimachos Polemarch* Callimachus, the Athenian war minister (Polemarch), was killed at Marathon. He commanded the right wing, and died well.
18 *Sakian ... Mede* The Sakae were a Scythian tribe, the Medes an Asiatic people closely associated with the Persians.
21 *plashed* spattered.
25 *Oracle* that of Apollo, at Delphi.
28–9 *Míltiadés ... Paros* The Greek commander at Marathon was wounded at Paros a year later, and died of his wound after being accused of treason.
29–30 *Themistokles/ – Satrap in Sardis court* The Athenian statesman and general defeated the Persians at Salamis in 480. Later accused of treason, he was exiled and became provincial governor (satrap) for the Persians of Sardis, capital of Lydia in Asia Minor.

CLIVE

First published in *Dramatic Idyls, Second Series* on 15 June 1880, and reprinted with a few trivial changes in *1888*. The poem is dated 27 February 1880 in the *MS*.

Shortly after his marriage, Browning first heard the story of Clive's duel; in writing the poem he made use of John Malcolm's *Life of Robert, Lord Clive* (1836), and of Macaulay's review essay of that book (1840). He adds the frame, the hypotheses about what Clive would have done had the opponent spared him and maintained his innocence, and the confession of cheating (though Browning said he thought he had Macaulay's authority for the confession). On the rather confused question of the sources, see Horsman, *Diary of Alfred Domett*, 237–8; DeVane, *Handbook*, 448–50; T. J. Collins, 'The Sources of Browning's "Clive": New Evidence', *BNL* 3, 1969, 3–8; L. Stevenson, 'The Source for "Clive"', *BNL* 4, 1970, 40–41, and Collins's reply, 41–2.

Browning chose 'Clive' as an example of the 'Idyllic (in the Greek sense)' as one of the four poems of moderate length to represent him fairly (see Hood, *Letters*, 235). It is the best known of the poems of its volume. On it see R. Felgar, 'Browning's Narrative Technique in "Clive"', *BSN* IV, No. 3, 1974, 10–16; H. Ward, 'Moral Irony in Browning's "Clive"', *BSN* IV, No. 3, 1974, 16–23; and M. Siegchrist, 'Narrative Obtuseness in Browning's "Clive"', *SIB* III, No. 1, 1975, 53–60.

2 *Clive it was gave England India* His brilliant military victories over French and various Indian forces made him the hero of British India, and political and administrative success followed. On returning to England in 1767, he was accused

of accepting large presents; after a long investigation he was acquitted. He committed suicide in 1774.

8 *Plassy* the battle of 1757 in which Clive won north-east India for Britain. The name is usually spelled 'Plassey'.

11 *thrids* threads (archaism).

12 *this forthright, that meander* 'Through forthrights and meanders' (*Tempest* III. 3. 3). A *forthright* is a straight course, a *meander* a winding one.

13 *rood* a measure of six to eight yards.

16 *rummer-glass* a kind of large drinking glass.

27 *smock-frocked* wearing loose-fitting farm-labourer's cloaks.

34 *magnific* magnificent (a literary usage).

39 *greenhorn* novice.

quill-driving clerk Clive went to India as a clerk with the East India Company in 1743, but joined the military service a year later.

40 *Arcot* Clive established his reputation in 1751 by capturing and holding the city of Madras.

47 *bee's-wing* old port with bee's-wing: the crust that develops in old port.

59 *Clive crumbled slow in London – crashed* Worn out by the long investigation of charges against him, and an opium addict in failing health, Clive committed suicide in 1774.

70 *Pitt* Sir William Pitt in a speech in the House of Commons compared Clive to the greatest of generals.

72 *bore the bell* came first.

88 *encrusted*] entrusted *MS.*

91 *factor* company-clerk.

92 *Saint David's* fort near Madras.

craze go mad.

101 *Cock o' the Walk* the leading bully.

Mars Roman god of war.

111 *force* To force a card is to fix things so that another, supposed to have free choice of where to pick or cut a card, is in fact compelled to take or cut a certain card. Browning's usage here is the first recorded in *OED.*

112 *Thyrsis . . . Chloe* classical names for pastoral lovers.

142 *clerkling* young clerk.

Cocky with] he with such *MS.*

145–6 Malcolm quotes Clive as saying: 'Fire, and be d——d . . . I said you cheated: I say so still, and I will never pay you.'

147 *flurried* agitated.

151 *I did cheat* The confession is not in the sources.

162 *Rogue's March* the tune played when a soldier is drummed out of a regiment.

183 *Twenty-five* in fact, twenty-eight.

229 *Lord Plassy* Clive's title.

MULÉYKEH

First published in *Dramatic Idyls, Second Series* on 15 June 1880, and reprinted without substantive change in *1888*. Several revisions were made in proof from the exceptionally clean *MS.*, where the poem is dated 22 February 1880. Browning's specific source for the traditional Bedouin legend was probably R. Springfield's *The Horse and His Rider; or Sketches and Anecdotes of the Noble Quadruped* (1847),

199–201 (see DeVane, *Handbook,* 451–2). Some of the names, details and accentings are Browning's.

1 *Hóseyn* The name means 'horse-busy'.
12 *Pearl* Muléykeh is in fact the diminutive for 'queen'.
21 *Duhl* The name means 'dwarfish'.
57 *chaffered* haggled.
61 *Holy House* Mahommed's family.
68 *headstall* part of the halter or bridle that fits round the head.
90 *tap of the heel, the touch of the bit* 'Every Bedouin trains the animals he rides to obey some sign of this kind, to which he has recourse only on urgent occasions, and which he makes a close secret' (Springfield). In Springfield's version of the tale, the secret signs were a pinch on the right ear, and 'a touch with the heel' (see 96).
90 *heel*] spur *MS.*
104 *Bénu-Asád* The name means 'sons of the lion'.
114 *speed!' wept*] race!' said *MS.*

PIETRO OF ABANO

First published in *Dramatic Idyls, Second Series* on 15 June 1880, and reprinted with a few trifling revisions in *1888*. There were many revisions in proof from the *MS.*, which is clean but has itself the odd change. The *MS.* is dated 20 January 1880, but the date occurs after line 416, where, it would appear, Browning originally thought of the poem as ending; the addition is not dated.

Browning referred to Pietro of Abano in a letter to Miss Barrett of 8 February 1846 (Kintner, *Letters* I, 443–4): 'Poor dear wonderful persecuted Pietro d'Abano wrote this quatrain on the people's plaguing him about his mathematical studies and wanting to burn him – he helped to build Padua Cathedral, wrote a Treatise on Magic still extant, and passes for a conjuror in his country to this day – when there is a storm the mothers tell the children that he is in the air; his pact with the evil one obliged him to drink no *milk*; no natural human food! You know Tieck's novel about him? [1825, a translation appeared in *Blackwood's* in 1839]. Well, this quatrain is said, I believe truly, to have been discovered in a well near Padua some fifty years ago.' Browning then quoted the quatrain in Italian, and his own translation of it (see Browning's note to line 40).

Browning probably first became acquainted with Pietro on his first visit to Italy in 1838, and his visits to Italy of 1878 and 1879 may have stimulated further interest. For his facts, he went to the *Biographie Universelle* (of which he had made such extensive use in his youth). Pietro (*c.* 1250–*c.* 1316) came from the village of Abano near Padua, and studied medicine at Padua, Greek at Constantinople, and philosophy at Paris. He became Professor of Medicine at Padua, where he also had a great reputation as a magician. This involved him with the Inquisition, and just before his death he was sentenced to burning. He was supposed to have fainted on seeing milk or cheese.

Browning combines details about Pietro with a Spanish medieval story which gave the details for the Greek's involvement with Pietro. The story was told by Don Juan Manuel in 1335 in *Libro de Patronio* or *El Conde Lucanor,* translated by James York as *Count Lucanor; or, the Fifty Pleasant Stories of Patronio* (1868), where the Dean of Santiago provides the model for Browning's Greek. In the twelfth of the tales, the Dean of Santiago is, he believes, helped by a magician, Don Illan, to become bishop, then cardinal, then Pope. He is ungrateful, and wakes to find he has been dreaming under Don Illan's influence. It may be that Browning heard the story from an acquaintance, Connop Thirlwall. The music with which the poem concludes seems to be Browning's own.

1 *Petrus Aponensis* 'Peter of Abano' (Latin).
7 *high as Babel* The Tower of Babel was to 'reach unto heaven' (Genesis xi 4).
14 *Petrus ipse* 'Peter himself' (Latin).
21 *Dog-star – Sirius* the popular name and the astronomer's name for the brightest star.
22 *Aroint* drive away with an execration (*OED* indicates that only the Brownings used the word as a verb; compare *Two Poets of Croisic,* 156).
pleasance pleasure (poeticism).
24 *Mars* The planet's influence has traditionally been destructive.
25 *whilom* former (archaism).
grisard grey-haired man (described by *OED* as rare, Browning's here being the only substantive usage recorded).
26 *eld* old man (poeticism).
33 *grinned and bore* proverbial.
40n. The Italian stanza was quoted by Browning in his letter to Miss Barrett of 8 February 1846. His translation there differs slightly from the one here. For Miss Barrett's translation, see Kintner, *Letters* I, 444, and for yet another slightly different Browning version see Browning's letter to Furnivall of 21 October 1881 (Hood, *Letters*, 201). Father Prout (Rev. Francis W. Mahoney) became much attached to the Brownings in Florence. The version he preferred is given in his *Reliques* (4): 'Studying my cyphers with the compass,/I find I shall soon be under the daisy;/ Because of my lore, folks make such a rumpus,/That every dull dog is thereat *unaisy*.'
48 *bastinadoed* thrashed (archaism).
52 *sullen* stubborn, moving sluggishly.
56 *garment's hem, O Lord* Matthew ix 20; xiv 36.
63 *tick* instant.
70 *moly* the fabulous herb that protected Odysseus against Circe.
71 *numbscull* variant spelling of 'numskull'.
73 *within my eye its iris mystic-lettered* Browning said 'there was an old superstition that, if you look into the iris of a man's eye, you see the letters of his name, or the word telling his fate'.
74 *my ear – its swan-shaped cavity, my emblem* 'showing the gift for leadership' (Florentine edition).
78 *provend* provender (obsolete).
79 *Apollo* Legend has it that his soul passed into the swan.
87 *noddle* head (colloquialism).
88 *Geese will soon grow swans* The opposition of the two birds is traditional as in the saying 'all your swans are geese'.
95 *hests* behests (archaism).
101 *fascinate* cast a spell over.
109 *Petri en pulmones* 'Lo, the lungs of Peter' (Latin).
118 *Ipse dixi* 'Myself have spoken' (Latin).
121 *bray* crush to powder.
124 *Michael of Constantinople* Michael VIII, Byzantine Emperor (1261–82), distinguished for his learning.
Hans of Halberstadt presumably the magician of *Transcendentalism,* the reference being anachronistic.

150 *de corde natus haud de mente* 'born of heart not mind' (Latin).
154 *punctual* attentive to duty (archaism).
161 *tristful* sad (archaism).
166 *clapperclawing* abuse.
168 *shuffle cards* manipulate matters.
171–2 *manger . . . dog* A person who will not let another use what he himself does not need is known as a dog in the manger after the fable of the dog who would not allow the ox near the hay.
173 *Bene . . .* the first syllables of the grace ('Bless you') that is concluded in 408.
181 *Plato's tractate* *The Republic.*
182 *the Fair and Good* two of the Platonic triad of the Beautiful, the True and the Good.

Dog of Egypt perhaps Anubis, the dog-faced god of Egypt (Florentine edition, which claims, wrongly, that sagacity was his especial quality), the equivalent of Hermes. Perhaps a meaningless oath. Perhaps Thoth, Egyptian god of magicians and wisdom, often identified with Hermes in Egypt, where his images are often dog-featured (or Browning may have erred, or the Greek may be following traditional conjurer's practice and reversing the word 'God').
183 *Exact* The usage as an adverb is an obsolete one.
192 *cark* anxiety (archaism).
203 *Sulla* The brutal Roman general (138–78 B.C.) retired in 79 B.C.
204 *"The grapes are sour"* In Aesop's fable, from which the expression 'sour grapes' comes, the fox disparaged the grapes beyond its reach as sour.
211 *Hunks* miser.
213 *Jezebel* the wife of Ahab (2 Kings ix 30) whose name typifies wicked painted women.
214 *Jam satis* 'enough now' (Latin).
235 *bedesman* obsolete spelling of 'beadsman', used here in the obsolete sense of 'humble servant'.
244 *fabric* probably the Palazzo della Ragione (1306), where Giotto's paintings were based on Pietro's instructions.
249 *familiar* close friend, evil spirit or demon, member of the household (all meanings are appropriate here).
259–60 *Tantalus's treasure . . . vanishes* Tantalus was tortured in Hades by having food and drink just out of reach.
266 *lump their leaven* 'a little leaven leaveneth the whole lump' (1 Corinthians v 6).
280 *half-mooned boot* the boot with turned-up toe of the upper classes.
287 *Elysian* heavenly.
291 *Per Bacco* 'by Bacchus' (Italian).
299 *'Salomo si nôsset'* 'had Solomon known this' (Latin).
300 *nostrum*] hazard *MS.*
304 *'Teneor vix'* 'I can scarcely contain myself' (Latin).
309 *boggled* demurred.
310 *hactēnus* 'hitherto' (Latin: the 'e' *is* short).
312 *Nec Ultra Plus* 'no farther' (Latin): the inscription on the Pillars of Hercules, the end of the world.
315 *spelter* zinc.
322 *Lost the world, and gained* 'what shall it profit a man, if he shall gain the whole world, and lose his own soul' (Mark viii 36).

326 *Pluck this brand from out the burning* 'ye were as a firebrand plucked out of the burning' (Amos iv 11).

335 *crozier* pastoral staff of a bishop.

crow-bill forceps for extracting objects from wounds.

340 *earwigged* Earwigs are fabled to enter the ears and pierce the brain; Browning's usage here is a nonce-use (*OED*, which defines the word: '?Having a "maggot" or craze in one's brain').

342 *manna* food from heaven (Exodus xvi 15).

kecks at rejects with loathing, retches at.

peason obsolete form of 'pease', the earlier form of 'peas'.

346 *move the world . . . fulcrum* Archimedes is said to have remarked: 'Give me but one firm spot on which to stand, and I will move the earth.'

pou sto 'on which to stand' (Greek, from the quotation above).

366 *doit* a trifling sum (from the small Dutch coin).

370 *Lateran* The Lateran Basilica is the cathedral of Rome, the Pope's church, and the senior Church of the Roman Catholic Church.

371 *erst* formerly (archaism).

374 *the Purple* the rank of Cardinal.

the Conclave . . . the Two-thirds Ten days after the death of a Pope, the College of Cardinals meets in conclave to elect a new Pope. A two-thirds majority is required.

coop the cell to which a Cardinal is assigned during the Conclave.

381 *Tithon* The goddess of the dawn fell in love with him and granted him immortality but forgot to ask for eternal youth, so that he withered away. He is the speaker of Tennyson's famous poem.

383 *flesh is grass* 'All flesh is grass, and all the goodliness thereof is as the flower of the field' (Isaiah xl 6).

388 *sting in death* 'The sting of death is sin' (1 Corinthians xv 56).

394 *farrago* hotchpotch.

395 *"Conciliator Differentiarum"* Pietro's best known work (1472): ('Conciliator of Differences' – Latin).

397–8 *"De Speciebus/Ceremonialis Ma-gi-ae"* an invented work, 'Of Kinds of Magic Ceremonial' (Latin).

400 *Fisher's ring* the seal-ring with which the Pope is invested at his election, bearing a device of Saint Peter fishing.

foot that boasts the Cross The Pope's slipper has a cross worked on it.

407–8 *'Apage, Sathanas!/Dicam verbum Salomonis'* 'Begone, Satan! I shall speak the expression of Solomon' (Latin).

408 *'– dicite'* the conclusion of the grace begun in 173.

414 *Benedicite* 'Bless you' (Latin).

415 *Foreign*] Learned *MS.*

'Idmen, idmen' 'we know, we know' (Greek).

420 *Scientiae Com-pen-di-um* 'Digest of Knowledge' (Latin).

421 *'Admirationem incutit'* 'It inspires admiration' (Latin).

426 *fasces* rods bound round an axe, emblematic of power.

433 *Tiberius* He became second Roman Emperor in A.D. 14.

434 *Geryon* The monster slain by Heracles had three heads and three bodies.

439 *crystal* the clear water.

440 *Suetonius* The source for the last stanza is the life of Tiberius (14) by the Roman historian and biographer (*c.* 69–*c.* 140) in his *Lives of the Caesars.*

440–41 *highest throw . . . 'Venus'* Suetonius says that the highest numbers came up; 'Venus' (compare 'At the "Mermaid"', 114) is triple-six, or otherwise the highest possible throw of the dice.

444 *lilt* The following lilt is patterned on the metre of four lines of the poem. That Browning had adopted the custom of lilting out his metres is apparently true.

DOCTOR —

First published in *Dramatic Idyls, Second Series* on 15 June 1880. The clean *MS.* is dated 10 March 1880. Between it and *1880* there are a number of fairly trifling changes; a few further insignificant revisions were made for *1888*.

No written source has been identified, but the poem is probably based on Jewish folk-lore, developing the text of Ecclesiastes vii 26: 'And I find more bitter than death the woman, whose heart is snares and nets, and her hands as bands: whoso pleaseth God shall escape from her; but the sinner shall be taken by her.' The proverb derived from the text is given in line 9: 'Stronger than Death is a Bad Wife'.

1 *day allowed* Job i 6, ii 1.
41 *Medicus* 'Physician' (Latin).
47–8 *walk/The world* Job i 7, ii 1.
86 *pennyroyal* a kind of mint often used in medicine.
87 *sherris* archaic form of 'sherry'.
Sumat 'Let him take it' (Latin).
89 *Galen* the Greek medical authority of the second century.
93 *wis* know (pseudo-archaism).
95 *sciolists* possessors of superficial knowledge.
96] At ignorance blood, ne'er so cold, grows warm!' *MS.*, *1880*.
123 To put the cart before the horse is proverbial.
131 *vaticination* prognostication.
140 *Machaon redivivus* 'Machaon brought back to life' (Latin). Machaon, the son of Asclepius, was a famous Greek physician killed in the Trojan War.
143 *Doctor's aid*] aid than this *MS.*
168 *meal of dust* Genesis iii 14.
199 *Antic* performer playing a grotesque part.
216 *knobstick* a stick with a knob at the end.
218 *Jacob's-Staff* a pilgrim's staff (after the apostle James).
248 *Elixir* a potion that would supposedly prolong life indefinitely.
250 *boots* matters.
256 *Talmud* the work based on scriptures that collects Jewish laws and doctrines, and is next in spiritual significance for Jews to the Bible.
257 *Boasts*] Have *MS.*

PAN AND LUNA

First published in *Dramatic Idyls, Second Series* on 15 June 1880. The clean *MS.* is dated 9 April 1880; several minor changes were made in proof; *1880* and *1888* are almost identical.

The poem, one of the most Keatsian of Browning's works, owes much to Vergil's third *Georgic* besides the motto, 'If it is worthy of belief', alluded to in the first line; the myth it expresses 'explains' the first eclipse of the moon by reference to the love of Pan (god of flocks and shepherds, half-man and half-goat) and Luna (Artemis, goddess of the moon). The 'strange three lines' from which the motto comes are the crucial ones for 'Pan and Luna': "'Twas with gift of such snowy wool, if we may trust the tale, that Pan, Arcadia's god, charmed and beguiled thee, O Moon, calling thee to the depths of the woods; nor didst thou scorn his call' (391–3). Browning made some other use of material from the third *Georgic* also.

Notably different in kind from other dramatic idyls, 'Pan and Luna' is frequently fancied to have biographical significance, especially since the moon and Mrs Browning are so often associated in Browning's verse, and since Mrs Browning had dealt with Pan; but DeVane's suggestion (*Handbook*, 457) that the poem may possibly try to recapture the brief rapture of Browning's life with his wife seems over-imaginative, and has strange implications for Browning's image of himself. Two studies of the poem are: D. S. Hair, 'Browning's "Pan and Luna": An Experiment in Idyl', *BSN* IV, No. 2, 1974, 3–8; W. D. Shaw, 'Mystification and Mystery: Browning's "Pan and Luna"', *BSN* IV, No. 2, 1974, 9–12.

4 *Arcadia* region in the Peloponnesus, home of Pan, and associated with pastoral life.
27 *teemed* plumped (a slightly unusual reflexive use of the verb, not precisely covered in *OED*).
28 *uncinct* uncircled.
34 *succourable* affording succour (archaism).
39] *MS. interpolation.*
47 *innumerous* innumerable (poeticism).
50 *Conglobe* gather into a globe.
54 *flexile* supple (*OED* describes the word as somewhat rare).
55 *constringe* become dense (the only intransitive usage recorded in *OED*).
56 *springe* snare.
58 *conceits* fancies.
59 *Amphitrite's dome* the sea. Amphitrite was the wife of the sea-god, Poseidon.
60 *bladdery* abounding in bladders ('with bladdery seaweed strewed' – Coleridge, 'To a Lady' ii).
62–3 *that safest of retreats/Bubble about*] *MS. interpolation.*
69–80 *Sheep far-sought ... gained for us* 'If wool be your care, first clear away the prickly growth of burs and caltrops; shun rich pastures, and from the first choose flocks with white, soft fleeces. But the ram, however white be his fleece, if he have but a black tongue under his moist palate, cast out, lest with dusky spots he tarnish the coats of the new-born lambs; and look about for another in your teeming field' (Vergil, *Georgics* III, 384–90).
82 *modesty betrayed* In Vergil, Luna is very willing. See 97–100.
84 *sward* skin (the word is usually used with reference to pork rind).
97–100 adapting and commenting on the three lines (391–3) quoted in the head-note above.

[EPILOGUE:] '"*Touch him ne'er so lightly ...*"'

First published in *Dramatic Idyls, Second Series* on 15 June 1880, and reprinted unchanged in *1888*. The clean *MS.* and *1880* are almost identical. The lines are not dated in the *MS.*, but the poem probably belongs to April or May 1880.

The poem is clearly an important statement about the art of poetry as Browning saw it in 1880, and the statement is perhaps especially interesting if set against

'Transcendentalism' of 1855. Specific identifications of the two poets of the poem were made; in a 'sequel', Browning identified the second poet as Dante and denied that he had meant himself (see 'Thus I wrote in London, musing on my betters . . .'). If specific identification be appropriate, the two poets may well be the earlier Browning and the later one.

Jocoseria

The ten poems in *Jocoseria* were first published – after a gap between volumes of almost three years – on 9 March 1883 by Smith, Elder. The printers' *MS.* is in the Library of Balliol College. It is exceptionally clean and is clearly a fair copy, except for 'Jochanan Hakkadosh', parts at least of which would appear to be first and last draft. The volume is probably the least carefully printed of all Browning first editions. A second edition was needed almost immediately, and a third edition appeared in 1885; both are mere reprints of the first edition and have no textual significance.

Only one poem in the volume is dated, 'Jochanan Hakkadosh' (22 December 1882). Browning wrote on 24 November 1881 (Hood, *Letters*, 204) that he had written a poem or two for another volume, but on 12 December 1881 (Hood, *Letters*, 206) he said that he had nothing designed or accomplished. 'Donald' seems to belong to the autumn of 1882, and it is a reasonable guess that all or virtually all of the volume belongs to the last few months of 1882. The *MS.* went to the printers on 9 January 1883.

The title, as Browning pointed out in a letter of 10 March 1883 (Hood, *Letters*, 214), came from Otto Melander's *Jocoseria* (1597), a collection of jokes and anecdotes that in his note to *Paracelsus* Browning had called 'rubbish'. Browning's recognition that his volume mingles the jocose and the serious and that it lacks any real unity is explicit in a letter of 9 January 1883 (Hood, *Letters*, 213): 'It is a collection of things grav*ish* and gay*ish* – hence the title *Jocoseria* – which is Batavian Latin, I think. There are some eleven of these pieces . . . May some morsels of this Olla Podrida take your taste!' One of the eleven pieces was dropped: 'Gerousios Oinos', which, evidence in the *MS.* indicates, was to have preceded 'Pambo'; Browning presumably omitted it because of the offence it might have created. The comparative carelessness of the proof-reading, most uncharacteristic of Browning, and the title suggest a certain diffidence on Browning's part about the collection; so does his comment (Hood, *Letters*, 218) on the volume's having 'had the usual luck of the little-deserving'.

'WANTING IS – WHAT?'

First published in *Jocoseria* on 9 March 1883, where it was entitled 'Wanting Is – What?' In *1888* the title was dropped, the poem thus becoming prefatory to the volume; one verbal change was made, and the indentation was revised to give the poem the appearance of a cross, an appearance that implies that heavenly (rather than earthly) love is what perfects imperfection. *MS.* and *1883* are identical except for a capital letter. The date of composition is unknown, but was probably late in 1882.

The lyric is well known and much parodied. W. R. Hancock's parody begins: 'Browning is – what?/Riddle redundant,/Baldness abundant,/Sense, who can spot?' Swinburne's begins: 'Wanting is – all,/Jargon abundant,/Verbiage redundant,/ Sputter and squall.'

4 *blot*] spot *MS.*, *1883*. In a letter of 26 July 1883 Browning wrote: 'I accept thankfully your "blot" – which means exactly what it should – instead of "spot" – which was ambiguous' (T. J. Collins, 'Letters from Robert Browning To the Rev. J. D. Williams, 1874–1889', *BIS* IV, 1976, 30).
9 *comer* Christ? The New Testament often refers to the Lord as him 'that cometh' or 'is to come'.

DONALD

First published in *Jocoseria* on 9 March 1883, and reprinted virtually without change in *1888*. Differences between *MS.* and *1883* are trifling.

A letter dates the poem in August 1882, Browning writing of 'an old peculiarity in my mental digestion – a long and obscure process. There comes up unexpectedly some subject for poetry, which has been dormant, and apparently dead, for perhaps dozens of years. A month since I wrote a poem of some two hundred lines about a story I heard more than forty years ago, and never dreamed of trying to repeat, wondering how it had so long escaped me; and so it has been with my best things' (quoted by K. de K. Bronson, 'Browning in Venice', *Century Magazine* LXIII, 1902, 574–5). Mrs Orr (*Handbook*, 322) says that the story was told to Browning by one who heard it from the participant himself, and in a letter of 11 January 1884 (T. J. Collins, 'Letters from Robert Browning To the Rev. J. D. Williams, 1874–1889', *BIS* IV, 1976, 34), Browning says the anecdote was told him by one who saw no harm in the 'sporting adventure'. The story was, however, told in *The Keepsake* of 1832 by Scott, who claimed to have heard the tale as a boy from its participant Duncan. Scott is more sympathetic to the stalker than Browning, who hated hunting (his son liked it) and cruelty to animals generally, and whose details differ in some respects from Scott's and induce greater sympathy for the deer.

5 *bothy* hut or cottage.
10 *trivet* support for kettle or pot.
12 *Glenlivet* a fine Scotch whisky.
16 *Royal* a fine stag.
42 *Double-First* at Oxford, a first-class degree in two subjects instead of the regular one.
61 *Ross-shire* the mountainous county towards the north of Scotland.
62 *Mount . . . Ben* The Englishman feels after the Scottish word for 'Mount'.
76 *burnie* small burn (Scotticism).
79 *end in ich* as often in Gaelic.
102 *foiling* trampling.
107 *brig* a Scottish form of 'bridge'.
126 *magnific* magnificent (literary archaism).
129 *fallow* pale-brown or reddish-yellow.
133 *volte-face* about-turn.
136 *Blondin* The French tightrope-walker (1829–97) had settled in England soon after crossing Niagara Falls in 1859.
206 *clouted* patched up.
210 *bracket* bragget: a drink made of honey and ale (Scotticism).
214 *win-penny* that which wins a penny.
227 *bread,*] *MS.*, *1883*; *not in 1888*.
228 *tipple* drink (colloquialism).
234 *gate*] *Florentine and this edition*; grate *MS.*, *1883–88* ('the sense, the rhyme

the adaptation from Homer – all combines to reveal not only the verbal slip, but the poet's intention' – *Florentine edition*). Compare 'Ponte dell' Angelo, Venice', 54n.

234–5 *'within gate . . . teeth kept tongue'* that is, 'I kept silent'. Homer is fond of the epic periphrasis (see *Odyssey* I, 64, for instance) in which the teeth become a fence or wall sheltering the tongue.

SOLOMON AND BALKIS

First published in *Jocoseria* on 9 March 1883 and reprinted without verbal change in *1888*. There are only few and trifling differences between *MS.* and *1883*. The date of writing is unknown, but was probably in the latter months of 1882.

Accounts of the visit of the Queen of Sheba to Solomon appear in 1 Kings x 1–13 and 2 Chronicles ix 1–12. Many legends were built on the Biblical foundations, and most of Browning's embellishments are to be found in the Talmud. The same story is treated in FitzGerald's translation of Jami's *Salaman and Absal* (1856), where avarice rather than vanity is Solomon's motive.

1 *Balkis* She is nameless in the Bible, but is 'Balkis' in some Arabic legends.
2 *ivory throne* 1 Kings x 18; 2 Chronicles ix 17.
3 *Mount Zion* that is, Jerusalem. The Temple was on Mount Moriah.
4 *six golden steps . . . lion and lion* 1 Kings x 18–19; 2 Chronicles ix 17–18.
5 *proves* tests.
7 *there is left no spirit in her* 'there was no more spirit in her' (1 Kings x 5; 2 Chronicles ix 4).
10 *vulgo* 'popularly' (Latin).
conster the old spelling of 'construe'; the word was pronounced 'conster' until well on in the nineteenth century.
12 *spheteron do* 'his dome' (Greek).
28 *wimple* veil or hood.
32 *Ring which bore the Name* The powers of Solomon's ring (as in 'Abt Vogler') are famous: the Name is the ineffable one of the Lord.
38 *hest* behest (archaism).
47 *On Lebanon roots the cedar* The cedars of Lebanon are often referred to in the Bible; they were used for Solomon's Temple.
48 Solomon 'spake of trees, from the cedar tree that is in Lebanon even unto the hyssop that springeth out of the wall' (1 Kings iv 33).

CRISTINA AND MONALDESCHI

First published in *Jocoseria* on 9 March 1883. One minor verbal change excepted, *MS.*, *1883* and *1888* are verbally identical. The date of writing is unknown, but was probably in the last half of 1882.

Christina (1626–89) abdicated after ten years as Queen of Sweden in 1654. In 1657–8 she stayed in the Royal Palace of Fontainebleau, south-east of Paris, and there, on the afternoon of 10 November 1657, she had her Master of the Horse, the Marquis Gian Rinaldi Monaldeschi, executed for treason. He had almost certainly been the Queen's lover, but Browning departs from history – which he treats generally in the poem with considerable licence – to make the execution more an act of private vengeance and less one of state justice than in all probability it was.

The Brownings' friend Anna Jameson had treated Christina in her *Memoirs of*

Celebrated Female Sovereigns (1832), and Browning may also have seen a Balliol prize essay of 1880 by A. H. Hardinge, and the *Relation* dealing with the execution published by the Queen's own Court. A summary of fact and fancy on the poem and guides to it are offered in C. N. Wenger, 'Clio's Rights in Poetry: Browning's *Cristina and Monaldeschi*', *PMLA* LX, 1945, 256–70.

2 *gallery* the Gallery of Diana of Poitiers in the Royal Palace.
5–6 *'Quis/Separabit?'* 'Who will separate?' (Latin).
10–11 *King Francis ... Diane* Diane de Poitiers was the mistress of Henry II, son of Francis I, and French king (1547–59). Legends, almost certainly untrue, have it that she was also involved with Francis, king 1515–47.
13 *Crescent* The moon is the emblem of Diana (Diana was goddess of the moon).
14 *Salamander-sign* the sign of Francis I: a salamander in the midst of flames. The mythical salamanders lived in flames but did not eat them, despite the 'Flame-fed' of 15.
95 *estray* stray.
96 *love's*] you *MS.*; love *1883*.
105 *Juno strikes Ixion* Ixion tried to make love to the Queen of the Gods, and was for his temerity bound to a wheel of fire in Hades. See Browning's poem in *Jocoseria*.
106 *Primatice* the French name of Francesco Primaticcio (1504–70), who painted many frescoes at Fontainebleau.
107 *Florentine Le Roux* 'Rosso Fiorentino' (1495–1540) worked with Primaticcio at Fontainebleau.
112 *'Gallery of the Deer'* Galerie des Cerfs, in which Monaldeschi was killed.
114 *erst* formerly (archaism).
116 *Avon* a village near the Royal Palace.
129 *Priest* Father le Bel, Prior of the Maturins, tried to intercede for Monaldeschi's life.
132 *mail* Since Monaldeschi was wearing mail, Christina's three soldiers had to behead him. The historical Christina was not present at the killing.
144 *Avon* Monaldeschi is buried in the Church there.

MARY WOLLSTONECRAFT AND FUSELI

First published in *Jocoseria* on 9 March 1883, and reprinted without change in *1888*. *MS.* and *1883* are virtually identical. The poem was probably written in the latter months of 1882.

Mary Wollstonecraft (1759–97), author of *Vindication of the Rights of Women*, married William Godwin in 1797 and died the same year at the birth of her daughter, Mary, who was to marry Shelley. Browning owned John Knowles's *Life and Writings of Fuseli* (1831) and may have used it as a source for Mary Wollstonecraft's unrequited passion for Henry Fuseli, the celebrated artist (1741–1825), but chronology makes impossible DeVane's curious suggestion (*Handbook*, 467) that he may have been led to it by *The Life, Letters and Literary Remains of Edward Bulwer, Lord Lytton* (1883). Knowles's view – and that in Browning's poem – of the relation between Fuseli and Mary Wollstonecraft is not accepted; it is generally thought that they were close friends only.

ADAM, LILITH, AND EVE

First published in *Jocoseria* on 9 March 1883, and reprinted with only one punctuation change in *1888*. *MS.* and *1883* are almost identical. The poem was probably written in the latter months of 1882.

The names may well have been designed to suggest the timelessness of the poem's theme. Talmudic legend gave Adam an earlier wife, Lilith (the accounts in Genesis i 27 and ii 22 of the creation of woman appearing to be contradictory).

7 *mind* remember (archaism).

IXION

First published in *Jocoseria* on 9 March 1883, and reprinted almost without change in *1888*. Several revisions were made in proof for *1883*, but none is of much significance. The poem probably belongs to the latter months of 1882.

Ixion was a bad King of Thessaly, named as the first murderer by Aeschylus. He killed his father-in-law brutally and earned men's opprobrium. Zeus took pity on him and purified him in Olympus. But Ixion fell in love with Hera, Queen of the Gods, and tried to seduce her. Zeus thwarted him by making a cloud that looked like Hera; on it Ixion fathered the Centaurs. Zeus punished him by having him bound to a rotating wheel of fire in Hades. Browning omits reference to Ixion's evil acts and makes his attempt to seduce Hera a matter of weakness merely. Ixion becomes sympathetic and Zeus the villain, and the poem a kind of attack on a Christian doctrine that Browning did not accept: that of eternal punishment or, perhaps more properly, on the inadequacy of a religion that holds such a doctrine. Or is there perhaps some irony in Ixion's protests? The metre of the poem is the classical elegaic. The poem is often judged the best in *Jocoseria*.

8 *Tears, sweat, blood* ''tis in vain to dew, or mollify/It [the world] with thy tears, or sweat, or blood' (Donne, *An Anatomy of the World*, 430–31).
28 *Sisuphos* Sisyphus, like Ixion and Tantalus, was subjected to unusually severe punishment in Hades: forever to roll a stone up a hill, only to have it roll down again.
Tantalos Zeus punished Tantalus by standing him in Hades up to his neck in water which receded when he tried to drink, and by having food always just out of his reach.
35 *thought, word, deed* 'We acknowledge and bewail our manifold sins and wickedness . . . By thought, word and deed, Against thy Divine Majesty, Provoking most justly thy wrath and indignation against us' (General Confession, Book of Common Prayer).
conceited fancied.
44 *obey*] perform *MS.*
85 *Olumpos* Mount Olympus, home of the gods.
Erebos here, Hades.
92 *falsifies* gives a false account of.
95 *iris* rainbow (traditionally associated with hope). See 116.
97 *mankind*] my kind *MS.*, *1883*.
112 *Tartaros* the lowest region of Hades.
121 *past Zeus to the Potency* as Caliban moves past Setebos to the Quiet.
124 *godship*] weakness *MS.*

JOCHANAN HAKKADOSH

First published in *Jocoseria* on 9 March 1883, and reprinted in *1888* with several verbal changes (the list in DeVane, *Handbook,* 471, is misleading since it includes fewer than half of the lines affected). The *MS.* is far from clean, and at least large parts of it are clearly both first and final draft. Though no lines were added or deleted, revisions in proof were unusually extensive, affecting scores of lines. The original *MS.* title was 'Hagadosch Jochanan', revised in *MS.* to 'Hakkadosch Jochanan'; the final spelling change was made in proof, and the two names were there transposed at the suggestion, through a friend, of Joseph Jacobs, a Jew. The proof-reading for *1888* was, by Browning's normal standards, careless, and it seems reasonable to assume that Browning found the work as verbose as most readers have done.

The *MS.* dates the work 22 December 1882. The note and the three sonnets follow the date, and DeVane (*Handbook*, 470) thinks they were written soon afterwards; the *MS.* however makes it clear that the three sonnets were not originally written for 'Jochanan Hakkadosh', and they may well have been composed before it.

Browning knew little Hebrew, but his interest in rabbinical lore is reflected in other poems also (see J. Berlin-Lieberman, *Robert Browning and Hebraism,* Azriel, 1934, and for 'Jochanan Hakkadosh' pages 54–76 especially). 'The whole story', wrote Browning on 10 April 1883 (Hood, *Letters*, 216–17), 'is a fiction of my own, with just this foundation, that the old Rabbins fancied that *earnest wishing* might add to a valued life.' The story told here is essentially Browning's own invention despite the deliberate mystification of the note at the end where the bad Hebrew of the title of the supposed Hebrew source is meant to mean 'A Pack of Many Lies', and where the 'pithy proverb' translates oracularly as 'From Moses to Moses arose none like to Moses'. The poem nevertheless includes elements from Jewish lore and legend. 'Hakkadosh' means 'the Holy' ('Jochanan' is 'John'), and one prototype is the Rabbi Jehudah I Hannasi, who was given the name 'Hakkadosh'. The central figure is, Berlin-Lieberman suggested, a composite of three models, another being Jochanan ben Nappcha, and the third, Jochanan ben Sakkai (teacher of the model for 'Ben Karshook's Wisdom'). The last was reputed to have lived 120 years, with his life extended by the contributions of others. The story of Rabbi Perida comes from *Travels of Rabbi Benjamin . . . of Tudela* in a translation by R. Gerrans (1784); Browning told the story to Julia Wedgwood (Curle, *Robert Browning and Julia Wedgwood,* 61–2) in 1864.

The poem is little known or read, but has some interest as an expression of many of Browning's most characteristic religious themes.

2 *Mishna* 'Doctrine' (Hebrew): the collection of basic precepts forming the foundation of the Talmud.

2–3 *the Jew/Aforesaid* Jochanan Hakkadosh: Jehudah I was the reputed writer or transcriber of the Mishna in the second century.

5 *Schiphaz* Shiraz, city in south-west Persia (see 801).

12 *Eximious* eminent (*OED* describes the word as rare, and notes that the few nineteenth-century usages 'are humorously bombastic or pedantic'). Compare *The Ring and the Book* IX, 109.

Jochanan Ben Sabbathai The name is Browning's invention.

16 *poll* crown of the head.

18 *wool-plant* *OED* suggests the mullein, and cites only this usage of the word.

41 *erst* formerly (archaism).

49–55 *stood David . . . can I wield* 'And Saul armed David with his armour, and he put an helmet of brass upon his head; also he armed him with a coat of mail. And David girded his sword upon his armour, and he assayed to go; for he had not proved it. And David said unto Saul, I cannot go with these; for I have not proved them. And David put them off him. And he took his staff in his hand, and chose him five smooth stones out of the brook, and put them in a shepherd's bag which he had, even in a scrip; and his sling was in his hand' (1 Samuel xvii 38–40).
60–61 *Moses' stick,/' "A serpent I let drop apace,"* See Browning's note at the end of the poem. See also Exodus iv 2–4, where Moses' rod becomes a serpent and then a rod again.
66 *rightly praise*] all avow *MS.*
67 *Could sure*] Needs must *MS.*
71–2 *pearl-gift thrown/To hogs* perhaps glancing at 'neither cast ye your pearls before swine' (Matthew vii 6).
89 *Khubbezleh* The name is Browning's invention, but 'Khubezza' is Arabic for 'mallow', and mallows have rose-coloured flowers.
97 *musty*] blemished *MS.*
103 *steel's fit*] woodland *MS.*
109 *root of bitterness* 'Looking diligently lest any man fail of the grace of God; lest any root of bitterness springing up trouble you, and thereby many be defiled' (Hebrews xii 15).
120 *Targums* versions of the Old Testament in Aramaic.
122 *Nine Points of Perfection* the nine regulations for the better guidance of Judaism reputedly introduced by Rabbi Jochanan ben Sakkai.
143 *The way of all flesh* the traditional misquotation of Joshua xxiii 14 and 1 Kings ii 2.
144 *Olive-branch* The Talmud often compares pious men to olives and olive-branches.
Tsaddik Browning's invention; his name means 'righteous'.
149 *Satam* not identified. A Browning error or invention apparently.
150 *Perpend* ponder (archaism).
150–51 *Dob –/' "The Bear"* 'Dob' is Hebrew for 'Bear' (the constellation).
151 *trow* suppose (archaism).
152 *Aish – "The Bier"* 'Aisch' is Hebrew for 'Bier': the Great Bear.
four stars those forming the pot of the dipper.
153–4 *Three Daughters . . . Banoth* 'Banoth' is Hebrew for 'Daughters': the three stars in the handle of the dipper.
156 *East-cone* Pole-star.
159 *strong*] fresh *MS.*
160 *Salem* Hebrew for 'Peace', used for Jerusalem as in Psalm lxxvi 2, and associated here with the New Jerusalem.
166 *Chosen*] faithful *MS.*
168 *Old Just Ones* ten legendary second-century Jewish martyrs under the Emperor Hadrian. They had defied Roman law and continued to teach Jewish law.
175 *Akiba* one of the ten martyrs. He was combed to death with an iron comb while repeating a declaration of God's unity.
177 *Jischab* Browning's error for Joshobeb or Yeshebab, another of the ten martyrs. Browning gives him the death of another martyr, Hanina ben Teradian, who was burned at the stake while wrapped in a scroll of the Law.
185 *teacher*] master *MS.*
186 *Selah* The meaning of the Hebrew word is unknown. It occurs in the

Psalms as, seemingly, a musical or liturgical direction (see, for instance, Psalm lxvii 1).
187 *quirist* The form is not recorded in *OED*, where even 'choirist' is described as rare.
188 *lion* the emblem of the tribe of Judah.
189 *Zion's mount* in Jerusalem.
195 *an if thou list* and if it pleases you (archaism).
196 *Shah* King (of Persia, in which the poem is set).
208 *cut its thread* In Greek mythology, the oldest of the Fates, Atropos, cuts the thread of (ends) life.
210 *appointed Fourscore* 'The days of our years are threescore years and ten; and if by reason of strength they be fourscore years, yet is their strength labour and sorrow; for it is soon cut off, and we fly away' (Psalm xc 10).
215 *Perida* In a letter of 19 August 1864 Browning quotes the story from the translation of R. Gerrans of *Travels of Rabbi Benjamin, Son of Jonah of Tudela*, 1784 (Curle, *Robert Browning and Julia Wedgwood*, 61–2): 'Rabbi Perida took such great care of his scholars, who from appearances were as promising as my own, that he made it a general rule to read and explain the same thing four hundred times over: but such was his fortune, that on a particular occasion, one of his hopeful pupils, either through stupidity or inattention, was at the end of the lecture as wise as he was at the beginning: whereupon the Rabbi gave a specimen of his patience by repeating the same lecture over four hundred times more. At this, a voice was heard from heaven, to the following purpose, "Perida, either live four hundred years, or obtain innocence and eternal life for thee and thy posterity!" Perida without hesitation chose the latter: but his scholars, out of cruel kindness, cried "No, no, no – but four hundred years for Perida!" Their request was granted: he lived four hundred years: and if he was a schoolmaster all the time, I heartily pity him.' The story is in the Talmud.

221 *Uzzean* Job, pattern of all patience, was from Uz (Job i 1).
222 *Five hundred* four hundred in the source.
224 *happed* chanced (archaism).
226 *illumed* poetical shortening of 'illumined'.
227 *pupils* one pupil in the source.
236 *drouth* variant of 'drought'.
239 *cruel-kind* 'cruel-kindness' in the source.
241 *welkin* firmament (poeticism).
256 *Rudesby* disorderly fellow (archaism).
263–4 *sits/Under his vine and figtree* 'they shall sit every man under his vine and under his fig tree' (Micah iv 4 – Micah is describing the joy of the Restoration).
294 *accloyer* oppressor (the word is not recorded in *OED*, which describes the verb 'accloy' as obsolete or archaic).
303 *quick*] has *MS.*, *1883*.
321] This steer, since calfhood, gets to understand *MS.*; Steer, long since calfhood, got to understand *1883*.
324 *cummin* a fennel-like plant.
326 *'Las* aphetic form of 'alas'.
339] The stumbling-block experience. Gather calm, *MS.*; A stumbling-block experience. Gather calm, *1883*.
354 *sycamine* mulberry (archaism); used by Browning to mean a kind of fig-tree, from the Hebrew from which the word 'sycamine' derives.

357 *scantling* small part.
386 *fires*] *MS., this edition*; fares *1883–8*.
395 *fervency* glowing or burning heat (*OED* 1 – now rare).
396 *Djinn* Arabian demon.
402 *plague cursed*] amerced *MS*.
408 *virtue* particular good quality.
413 *Edom's children* Christians (Edom is the Talmudic name for Rome or Christianity).
413–14 *turn/Cheek to the smiter* 'whosoever shall smite thee on thy right cheek, turn to him the other also' (Matthew v 39).
"*Sic Jesus vult*" 'Thus Jesus wishes' (Latin).
427 *call*] claim *MS., 1883*.
446 *stares*] *MS., this edition*; starves *1883–8*.
474–7 *Joshua-like . . . lend assistance* Joshua x 12–13.
488 *florid,*] blossomed – *MS*.
490 *Which*] Mere *MS., 1883*.
492 *secrete*] *MS., 1883, this edition*; secret *1888*.
hap luck (archaism).
495 *Missing*] Wanting *MS*.
496 *goodman* good man (obsolete usage).
501 *Proser and poet*] Rabbi, prose-poet *MS*.
502 *eye hath dropped the envious scale* 'there fell from his eyes as it had been scales' (Acts ix 18 – the conversion of Saul).
envious that may be envied.
509 *Sighed Jochanan*] Replied the sage *MS*.
514 *Petrific* having the quality of petrifying (rare).
522 *boasts*] has *MS*.
524 *thicked* covered (variant spelling of 'theeked' – Scotticism).
525 *Dead*] Fallen *MS*.
539 *Samsons, Abners, Joabs, Judases* all great leaders of the Jews: respectively, the Philistines' foe (Judges xiii-xvi); the captain of Saul's armies (1 Samuel xiv 50); the commander of David's armies (2 Samuel viii 16); the fourth son of Jacob ('Judas' is the Greek form of 'Juda(h)') and founder of the tribe of Judah (Genesis xlix 8).
554 *proceeds to*] should wisely *MS*.
560 *Ahithophel* Absalom's fellow-conspirator against David (2 Samuel xvi 20–23) counselled like 'the oracle of God'.
570 *stores*] has *MS*.
578 *Shimei* the Benjamite who cursed David (2 Samuel xvi 5–14).
585 *alkahest* the 'universal solvent' of the alchemists.
585] Propose a remedy to rub away *MS*.
594 *thickest*] To emend to 'thickets' is tempting, especially since Browning's proof-reading of the poem did not meet his usual standards. However *MS., 1883* and *1888* all have the satisfactory 'thickest'.
599] Unluckily 'tis just the mindless mass *MS*.
600 *hinds* farm labourers.
612 *Mizraim* 'Egypt' (Hebrew).
613 *Goshen* area in Egypt occupied by the Israelites (Genesis xlv 10).
614] Inside, – contemporaneous ignorance *MS*.
622 *ween* suppose (archaism).
635 *glorify with,*] blacken with both *MS*. (revision removed an unfortunate ambiguity).

653 *mind me* remember (archaism).
666 *milk-*] mere *MS.* (the whole stanza was extensively revised in proof).
668 *witting* aware (obsolete usage).
669 *verjuice* the acid juice of unripe fruit.
670 *Shushan* 'Lily' (Hebrew).
693 *skills* avails (archaism).
695 *Wiling* inducing.
696–7 *kick/Against the pricks* Acts ix 5, xxvi 14.
702 *Where's a*] There's no *MS., 1883.*
704 *darkness, meant*] dark had done *MS.*; darkness, did *1883.*
708 *conceits* fancies.
710 *slow*] cold *MS.*
710–11 *Vanity/Of vanities* Ecclesiastes i 2.
720 *thaumaturgic* wonder-working.
721 *tohu-bohu* chaos (Hebrew – the 'without form and void' of Genesis i 2).
741 *visuals* visual rays.
746] Then, the intricacies of shade and shine, *MS., 1883.*
759–60 *rape . . . on air* alluding to the myth of Ixion who made love to a cloud believing it to be Hera (see Browning's 'Ixion').
768 *wiped*] *not in MS.*
769 *His hand, cried*] Wipes hand, cries *MS.*
777 *Halaphta* the name of several Talmudic teachers.
must] may *MS.*
780 *Ruach* 'the imparted Spirit' (the 'breath' of Genesis ii 7).
782 *three days* Talmudic scholars believe that the soul hangs over the dead body for three days before giving up and going to Heaven. (For Browning's opinion of the belief of some reviewers that Jochanan was revived by a blood transfusion, see Hood, *Letters*, 216).
801 *Bendimir* The Bundamir river flows to the east of Shiraz.
Farzistan region in south-west Persia.

NOTE

The title of the imaginary treatise cited in Browning's note in Hebrew is meant to mean 'A Collection of Many Lies' (Browning's Hebrew actually means 'A crime attracts many lies' and is grammatically incomplete). Moses' stick is referred to in line 60. The 'pithy proverb' means 'From Moses to Moses arose none like to Moses'. It is a well-known Jewish saying, which Browning probably took from a book in his library, J. P. Baratier's *Rabbi Benjamin* (1734). The second Moses referred to is Moses Maimonides or Moses ben Maimon, the great Hebrew scholar (1135–1204).

Rabbinical legend made Og a very big giant indeed, several miles tall. In the Bible, Og King of Bashan had a huge bed (Deuteronomy iii 11); Moses was able to kill him on the way to the Promised Land because Og got tangled up in a mountain he planned to throw at the Israelites. Browning's sonnets are based squarely on Talmudic legends.

I. 1 *Moses the Meek* 'the man Moses was very meek, above all the men which were upon the face of the earth' (Numbers xii 3).
thirty cubits An English cubit of eighteen inches approximates other kinds of

cubit. Moses' size varies from legend to legend; Browning's dimensions are on the generous side.
I. 7 *slurred o'er* passed over lightly.
I. 9 *just* exact.
I. 13–14 *frog/That fain would match an ox* alluding to Aesop's fable, in which a frog burst while trying to blow itself up to ox-size.
II. 13 *Og's thigh-bone* a favourite subject of the legends. In one version a grave-digger pursued a stag three miles inside Og's thigh-bone.

NEVER THE TIME AND THE PLACE

First published in *Jocoseria* on 9 March 1883. The *MS.*, *1883* and *1888* are identical except in indentation; the *MS.* has no title. The date of composition is unknown, but May 1882 is a reasonable guess. The loved one is obviously Mrs Browning. On the poem, see F. Kaplan, 'Death and Lovely Song: Browning's "Never the Time and the Place"', *BSN* V, No. 2, 1975, 17–21.

PAMBO

First published in *Jocoseria* on 9 March 1883. A few minor revisions were made in proof; there are no verbal differences between *1883* and *1888*. The date of composition is unknown, but a date late in 1882 is probable.

The source is Wanley's *Wonders of the Little World* III, iv: 'Pambo came to a Learned Man, and desired him to teach him some Psalm, he began to read unto him the thirty ninth, and the first Verse, which is: "I said I will look to my ways, that I offend not with my Tongue." Pambo shut the Book and took his leave saying he would go learn that point: And having absented himself for some Months, he was demanded by his Teacher, when he would go forward: he answered that he had not yet learn'd his old Lesson, to speak in such a manner as not to offend with his Tongue.' Browning may also have consulted the *Ecclesiastical History* of Socrates (IV, xxiii).

2 *crambo* contemptible rhyme.
17–18 'I said, I will take heed to my ways, that I sin not with my tongue' (Psalm xxxix 1). Browning follows Wanley's form (see above).
27 *wis* know (pseudo-archaism).
47] The stream I am fain to drink at once, *MS.*
50 *Arcades sumus ambo* 'We are both Arcadians' (Vergil, *Eclogues* VII, 4: 'Arcades ambo').
52 *flambeau* torch.

Ferishtah's Fancies

Published by Smith, Elder on 21 November 1884. Two more editions were needed in 1885, one in January, one later in the year. Each of these editions has minor textual significance: both add two lines to 'The Melon-Seller', and the third edition (not the second as DeVane erroneously states in *Handbook*, 475n.) contains corrections to Browning's Hebrew, including some suggested by C. J. Lyall in a letter of 13 December 1884 (see A. J. Armstrong, ed., *Intimate Glimpses from Browning's Letter File*, Baylor University's Browning Interests VIII, 1934, 100–101). There are other minor changes among the three editions, and another handful for *1888*, but DeVane's reference to a 'considerable number' of revisions is misleading. The *MS.* is in the Library of Balliol College; most of it is fair copy and very clean. It has some interesting revisions, and a few minor revisions were made in proof, where, also, some of the titles were changed (DeVane's statement that the new titles came when Browning was three-quarters done is puzzling, since the new titles do not appear in the *MS.*). The *MS.* suggests that some sections may possibly have been reordered. Balliol College also owns Mrs Orr's copy of what is almost certainly a binding of the final revises for *1884* with some Browning notes presumably designed for her guidance in preparing the second edition of her *Handbook,* which appeared early in 1886 (Browning's notes, previously unpublished, are printed in the notes below).

The Prologue and Epilogue are dated 12 September and 1 December 1883, and much of the volume seems, from dates and other evidence in the *MS.*, to have been written between these dates. DeVane suggests (*Handbook,* 475, 478) that Browning may have had the 'The Eagle' with him when he arrived at Gressoney Saint Jean, from which the Prologue is dated, but with the possible exception of that section it is doubtful that the poem was begun until September 1883. It is probable that by the end of that month Browning had finished the poem through to the end of 'A Camel-Driver' and begun 'Two Camels', and that he then laid it aside for a while. Except for the Epilogue (dated 1 December and perhaps not originally intended for *Ferishtah's Fancies*), it would seem that Browning took the work up again shortly before 15 January 1884 and that he had completed the blank-verse sections, save for some later additions notably to the final one, by the end of January or early in February. Most of the intercalary songs were probably written somewhat later. Mrs Orr says (*Life*, 362) she thinks the lyrics were written on consecutive days, but this is not true for all of them at least. In an unpublished letter of 14 February 1884 (in the Huntington Library) Browning wrote of a poem made up of twelve poems with lyrical prologue and epilogue, but makes no reference to the lyrics. Smith, Elder delayed publication presumably so as to take advantage of Christmas sales and to avoid interference with sales of *Jocoseria*, but also because of negotiations for publication in the United States.

Ferishtah's Fancies clearly relates in various ways to 'Jochanan Hakkadosh', which may have prompted Browning to further religious poems with Persian setting. Mrs Orr says (*Handbook,* 331): 'The idea of "Ferishtah's Fancies" grew out of a fable by Pilpay, which Mr Browning read when a boy. He lately put this into verse; and it then occurred to him to make the poem the beginning of a series, in which the Dervish, who is first introduced as a learner, should reappear in the character of a teacher.' She is here building on Browning's note (*Orr copy*, 7): 'This ['The Eagle'] is from Pilpay's Fables: I read it when a boy and lately put it into verse: then it occurred to [me] to make the Dervish one Ferishtah, and t[he] poem the beginning of a series' – in a note to 'The Eagle', 5, in *Orr copy* Browning indicated that 'Ferishtah' meant 'Fairy'. DeVane notes (*Handbook*, 476) that the edition of *The Fables of Pilpay* that the boy Browning used was probably an 1818 selection. Pilpay (Bidpai) is the supposed author of the *Panchatantra,* probably compiled before A.D. 500, the main collection of beast fables (in prose interspersed with aphoristic verses) in Sanskrit literature; *The Fables of Bidpai* (or *Pilpay*) is the title of the Arabic version. In *Ferishtah's Fancies,* only 'The Eagle' derives directly from it. The other materials are in the main Browning's inventions. For local colour, DeVane suggests, Browning used Helen Zimmern's *The Epic of Kings, Stories Retold from Firdusi* (1882) – Miss Zimmern, a friend of Browning, gave him a copy of the book in which her preface specifically thanks him for encouragement. DeVane points out (*Handbook*, 477) that many of the Persian references occur in the last hundred lines of 'A Bean-Stripe: also, Apple-Eating'; these lines were almost certainly composed after all other blank-verse sections of the poem.

Ferishtah's Fancies, though most readers have found Browning neglecting the kind of aesthetic he advocated in 'Transcendentalism', is important as a fairly direct statement of the poet's mature religious beliefs. As the epigraph from *Lear* suggests, Browning did not pretend that Ferishtah was more than a transparent disguise for himself; in a letter of October 1884, the poet said his friend should not 'suppose there is more than a thin disguise of a few Persian names and allusions. There was no such person as Ferishtah; and the stories are all inventions. The Hebrew quotations are put in for a purpose, as a direct acknowledgement that certain doctrines may be found in the Old Book which the Concocters of Novel Schemes of Morality put forth as discoveries of their own' (W. R. Nicoll and T. J. Wise, *Literary Anecdotes of the Nineteenth Century* I, 471).

PROLOGUE

The very clean *MS.* and all texts are virtually identical. The prologue is dated 12 September 1883 in *MS.* and text.

1 *ortolans* species of bunting; a delicacy in parts of Europe.
12 *fatling* 'young animal fattened for slaughter' (*OED* cites only animals, not birds) – Browning's usage seems somewhat unorthodox.
16 *leaf* in two senses: of a book, of a plant.
18 *thirdling* 'a nonce-word' (*OED*).
20 *birdling* The first usage cited in *OED* is Mrs Browning's in 1856.
31 *peptics* digestive organs (humorous usage).
38 *Gressoney* town in the Alps in north-west Italy, a few miles south of Mount Rosa. Browning spent September and the last half of August there in 1883.

THE EAGLE

The very clean *MS.* and all texts are virtually identical. Browning may well have written the poem, undated in *MS.*, before leaving England for Italy. As Browning indicated, the story came from *The Fables of Pilpay* (II, iii: 'The Dervise, The Falcon, and the Raven'), where there is only one young raven and no dead mother. The Creator in it says to the Dervise: 'If thou wouldst imitate any one of the birds thou hast seen to my glory, use the talents I have given thee, and imitate the Falcon that feeds the Raven, and not the Raven that lies a sluggard in his nest, and expects his food from another.'

1 *Dervish* a Mohammedan friar.
5 In *Orr copy*, Browning wrote: 'Ferishtah = Fairy'.
35 *Ispahan* famed city in central Persia.

THE MELON-SELLER

The very clean *MS.* and all texts are almost identical except for the translation of the Hebrew added in the second edition, and revisions to the Hebrew made in the third edition. The poem is undated in *MS.*, but probably belongs to September 1883.

In *Orr copy*, 9, Browning noted: 'This incident I read of in a letter from the "Times" correspondent many years ago,' and he had told the story to Miss Barrett in his letter of 6 August 1846 (Kintner, *Letters* II, 939), also referring to *The Times*. Kintner failed to find any such letter (940), but notes that the use of the story in *Ferishtah's Fancies* is 'the most notable' indication that Browning re-read the love-letters later in life.

11 *Shah* 'King' (Persian).
34 *Nishapur* small city in north-east Persia, birthplace of Omar Khayyam, near some noted turquoise mines.
Elburz mountain range in northern Persia, to the west of Nishapur.
37–8 The question of the authorship and sources of Job is vexed.
39–40 On the Hebrew, Browning noted in *Orr copy*: 'This, written with the Points which I have subjoined, would be pronounced thus, – making a tolerable verse and a half.

Ĕth-hăttōv n'quăbbēl mēēth hā Ĕlōhīm
v'ĕth-hārā lō n'quăbbēl?

Shall we receive good at the hand of God and shall we not receive evil?' In the third edition, Browning made three revisions in the Hebrew to make the pointing consistent.
40–42 *In Persian phrase . . . great wits jump.*] But great wits jump. *MS., 1884.*
41–2 'shall we receive good at the hand of God, and shall we not receive evil' (Job ii 10).
42 *jump* agree completely.

SHAH ABBAS

All texts are virtually identical, and there were few changes in proof. The poem is undated in the very clean *MS.*, but probably belongs to September 1883. The title in *MS.* is '3. Belief'.

4 *abrupt*] awhile *MS.*
6 *Lord Ali* husband of Mohammed's daughter Fatima.
18 In *Orr copy*, 14, Browning noted: 'Invented'. Browning's figure is not the famous Abbas the Great, Shah 1587–1628.
47 *Yakub* another imaginary character.
48 *advertise* notify.
54] With that offence wherefrom came death-disgust *MS.*
79 *boots* avails.
81 *Tahmasp*] *1885(3), 1888*; Thamasp *MS., 1884, 1885(2)* – C. J. Lyall suggested the change. In *Orr copy* Browning noted 'Invented'.
84 *Zurah* an invented character.
99 *Ishak* In *Orr copy* Browning noted 'Invented'.
102 *Yezdt* city in central Persia.
107 *Mubid* magician, sage.

THE FAMILY

All texts are virtually identical; there were a very few revisions in proof from the very clean *MS*. The poem probably belongs to September 1883. The *MS* title is '4. The Father's Family'.

2 *grieved*] sat *MS.*
3 *at peace*] and smiled *MS.*
22 *tale* In *Orr copy* Browning noted 'Invented'.
23 *Shiraz* city in south-west Persia (the Schiphaz of 'Jochanan Hakkadosh').
51 *Hakim* C. J. Lyall pointed out to Browning that the accent required by the metre made the word mean 'Ruler' whereas Browning wanted the word for 'physician'. Browning made no change, this being the only failure to follow up Lyall's suggestions.
54 *sciolist* one with superficial knowledge.
60 *a wise*] dutiful *MS.*
62 *son* –] – rude *MS.*
63 *rash but kind*] reason's type *MS.*
64 *chit*] fool *MS.*

'MAN I AM AND MAN WOULD BE ...'

DeVane suggests (*Handbook*, 482) that the lyric may be Browning's protest at the adulation of Mrs Bloomfield-Moore in the Summer of 1884.

1 *Love* –] weak *MS.*

THE SUN

MS. and all editions differ only slightly. The clean *MS.* is undated, but it suggests that the poems in *Ferishtah's Fancies* up to and including 'The Sun' were written in the order of their printing. September 1883 is the probable date. The title in the *MS.* is '5. Incarnation'.

70 *tomans* Persian gold coins.
104 *naught*] *1885(2), 1885(3), 1888*; what *MS., 1884.*
149 *plainly*] thiswise *MS., 1884, 1885(2), 1885 (3).*

'FIRE IS IN THE FLINT ...'

The lyric inevitably recalls Wordsworth's *Immortality Ode* and Plato, as well as *Timon of Athens* I. 1. 22–3: 'The fire i' the flint/Shows not till it be struck.'

MIHRAB SHAH

MS. and all editions differ only slightly (though more than indicated in DeVane's inaccurate statement in *Handbook*, 483). The *MS.* is fairly clean until the last few lines which are heavily, and interestingly, revised. The page numbering of the *MS.* indicates that possibly 'Mihrab Shah' stood later in the poem than it now stands. The *MS.* title is '6. Pain'. DeVane (*Handbook*, 483) errs in saying the poem is undated. It is dated 20 September 1883 in the *MS.* after line 130, lines 131–6 being added later.

17 *thought, word and deed* 'our manifold sins and wickedness, Which we from time to time most grievously have committed, By thought, word, and deed' (General Confession, Book of Common Prayer).

27 *Firdausi* the leading Persian poet (*c.* 940–1020), author of the Persian epic, *Shah Namah.*

Firdausi] Firdusi *MS., 1884, 1885(2)* – the change was suggested by C. J. Lyall.

46 *Shah*] Khan *MS.*

66 *clout* nail.

81 *Simorgh* In *Orr copy* Browning noted: 'Fabulous creature in Persian mythology'. It is a huge, rational, talking, aged bird.

match] mate *MS., 1884.*

92 *Tebriz* city in north-west Persia.

99 *quotha* indeed, forsooth (archaism).

119 *Lust*] Scorn *MS. first reading.*

120–21] Hate, any human punishment you please! *MS. first reading.*

123–4] Straight to a level: in the eyes of God *MS. first reading.*

124 *eye*] eyes *MS., 1884, 1885(2), 1885(3).*

125–6] Pain has a purpose and is justified:
Our eyes are only made to see, in pain, *MS. first reading.*

130 *Therefore, Mihrab Shah,*] Let pain continue then! *MS. first reading* (the poem originally ended with this line).

Mihrab Shah In *Orr copy* Browning noted: 'Invention'.

Shah] Khan *MS.*

131–6] *added later to MS.*

132 *sport*] slave *MS.*

133 *poetry*] Rhuibayat *MS. first reading* (the Persian word means 'quatrains', but Browning can hardly but have thought of FitzGerald's poem, so markedly different from his own).

A CAMEL-DRIVER

There are a few differences among the texts, none of much significance. *MS.* and *1884* are very close, but a few changes were made in proof. The poem is dated (before its lyric) 23 September 1883 in the *MS.*, three days after 'Mihrab Shah'; pagination in the *MS.* also indicates that the poem was composed immediately after 'Mihrab Shah'. Browning noted in *Orr copy* that the tale was 'invented'. Browning never accepted the doctrine of eternal punishment.

29 *Rakhsh*] Ruksh *MS., 1884, 1885(2)* – the change was suggested by C. J. Lyall. In *Orr copy* Browning noted: 'Rustum's Horse, in the "Shah Nemeh"'. Arnold's spelling in 'Sohrab and Rustum' was 'Ruksh'.

51 *twy-prong, thus*] implement *MS.*

53 *noddle* head (jocular).

81 *snatch-grace* perhaps a Browning coinage; this is *OED*'s only example of the combination.

TWO CAMELS

The various printings are very close in their readings, and differences are fairly trivial. The *MS.* is messy. The *MS.* shows that the poem originally ended with line 64, and that it was written to follow 'A Camel-Driver'. It also shows that it was the last section begun at Gressoney. DeVane (*Handbook*, 485) errs in saying that the *MS.* is undated; it is dated September 1883–15 January 1884 in the *MS.* after line 64 – Browning cancelled the dating, presumably when he added to the poem in

MS. – so that the poem was begun in Italy and finished in England. Browning was no ascetic.

18 *conceits* imaginings.
27 *Sebzevar*] Sebzevah *MS., 1884, 1885(2)* – the change was suggested by C. J. Lyall. Sebsevar (Sabzawar, Sabsevar) is a town in north-east Persia, sixty-odd miles west of Nishapur.
35 *purslane* low succulent herb.
38 *doit* trifling sum (after the small Dutch coin).
43 *simooms* hot, dry sand-winds.
48 *Sebzevar*] Khelib walls *MS.*; Sebzevah *1884, 1885(2)*.
58 *good-and-faithful-servant* 'Well done, thou good and faithful servant' (Matthew xxv 21).
64] With this line the poem originally ended in the *MS.*
88 *Adversary* Satan.
89 'Doth Job fear God for nought?' (Job i 9). In *Orr copy* Browning noted: 'Pronounced Hăchīnnām yārē Īyōv Ĕlohim? "Does Job serve [*sic*] God for naught?"' (This edition prints the correct Hebrew of *MS., 1884, 1885*; in *1888* there were three changes, presumably misprints.)
93–5] The independent equal: throws away
What himself gave himself, so his to give!
A proper rule for you and me, that same! *MS.*
95 In *Orr copy* Browning annotated the Hebrew: 'Mē Ĕlōhīm "From God"'. He corrected the Hebrew for *1885(3)*.
107 *seven-stringed instrument* lyre.

'ONCE I SAW A CHEMIST . . .'

8 *just* 'that just is or takes place' (*OED* 12: a nonce-use).

CHERRIES

The readings of *MS.* and all texts are almost identical. The *MS.* title is '9. Gratitude'. The *MS.* pagination shows that the poem was written to take the place it occupies in *Ferishtah's Fancies.* The poem is dated 15 January in the *MS.*, the same terminal date given for 'Two Camels'.

2 *Eat*] Champ *MS.*
19 *Mushtari* In *Orr copy* Browning noted: 'The planet Jupiter'.
58 *the Shah*] our Khan *MS.*
88–9 *Dust . . . the end* 'dust thou art, and unto dust shalt thou return' (Genesis iii 19).

PLOT-CULTURE

The *MS.* and all texts are very close in their readings except that the lyric ('Not with my Soul, Love! . . .') does not appear in the *MS.* The section was numbered 10 in *MS.*, but the title there (one of about eight letters) has been heavily erased. The poem is dated 17 January 1884 in the *MS.*, two days after 'Cherries'; the lyric was the last part written of *Ferishtah's Fancies,* and almost certainly belongs to early September 1884.

3 *arrides* pleases (obsolete – *OED*'s last recorded usage is from 1823).
49 *maid*] slut *MS.*

'NOT WITH MY SOUL, LOVE! ...'

The lyric is not in the *MS.*, where Browning noted 'Leave room for a small poem's insertion here'. The poem was almost certainly written fairly early in September 1884. Mrs Bloomfield-Moore, an American friend and admirer with whom Browning stayed in Saint Moritz in September, remarked to him on being called back to America: 'Remember, I have loved you with the best and most enduring love – Soul-love' (C. J. B-M., 'Robert Browning', *Lippincott's Magazine* XLV, 1890, 690; see also Miller, *Robert Browning,* 268–9). Browning's poem replies to her remark, and protests against her adulatory Platonic love.

13 *memories* probably of Mrs Browning.

A PILLAR AT SEBZEVAR

There are few differences between the readings of the clean *MS.* and the various texts. The *MS.* title is '11. A Pillar at Khorosan'. The poem is undated, but the *MS.* suggests it was written after 'Plot-Culture' at a fairly late stage. The superiority of love to knowledge is nowhere urged more strongly by Browning than here.

17 *fining-pot* refining-pot.
71 *use*] thank *MS., 1884, 1885(2), 1885(3).*
76] A certain pillar stands by Khorosan *MS.*; A certain pillar stands by Sebzevah *1884, 1885(2)*; A certain pillar stands by Sebzevar *1885(3).*
77 *gnomon* pillar.
86 *Hudhud* In *Orr copy* Browning noted: 'Fabulous bird of Solomon'.
146 *dinar* a Persian coin.
147 *Sitara* In *Orr copy* Browning noted: 'Persian for "*a star*" '.

A BEAN-STRIPE: ALSO, APPLE-EATING

There are few differences between the readings of the fairly clean *MS.* and all printings. The *MS.* title is '12. A Bean-Stripe'. The poem originally ended with line 364; the evidence provided by *MS.* and *1884* indicates, very clearly, that lines 365–478 were added at a very late stage, and certainly after the first set of proofs. DeVane's conjecture that most of the poem was written in Venice seems most unlikely; the undated *MS.* suggests that the poem was written after 'A Pillar at Sebzevar', probably in late January or early February 1884.

2 *cavilment* The word is not recorded in *OED* – presumably a Browning coinage.
17 *Indian Sage* Buddha.
45 *fact of sense*] primal fact *MS.*
65 *jet* glossy black.
95 *erst* formerly (archaism).
116 *inconsciousness* unconsciousness (*OED* records 'inconscious' and – from Browning only – 'inconsciously', but not 'inconsciousness').
150 *aphis* minute insect, destructive of vegetation.
155 *Purlieu* haunt.

202 *disintensify* the only usage cited in *OED*.
239 *over-mounts* 'beyond the mountains' (*OED*). Compare *Sordello* III, 476.
251 *sourly-Sage* Buddha (see 17).
275 *for*] be *MS.*, *1884*.
297 *Ahriman* the leader of Evil in Zoroastrianism and Persian thought.
298 *an Ormuzd*] the Maker *MS.*
Ormuzd the leader of Good in Zoroastrianism and Persian thought.
329–33] In *MS.* and *1884* the lines are part of the preceding speech of Ferishtah.
354 *my Life*] the world *MS.*
365–478] *a later addition to the MS.*
391 *Shalim-Shah* In *Orr copy* Browning emended the name to 'Shahin', and noted: 'Persian for "King of Kings" '. The reading remained constant despite the revision in 421 (see note).
403 *bastinado* a whack, especially on the soles (archaism).
421 *Shahan-Shah*] Shalim-Shah *MS.*, *1884*, *1885(2)* – the revision was suggested by C. J. Lyall, but Browning left the form unrevised in 391.
422–6 *Rustem . . . Kawah* In *Orr copy* Browning noted: 'Heroes in the "Shah Nemah" '.
438 In *Orr copy* Browning noted: 'Ursa Major, Venus, Pleiades'.
440 *Mubid* Mage.
462 *Fomalhaut* bright star in the Southern Fish.
472 *Zerdusht* In *Orr copy* Browning noted: 'Zoroaster'.
477 *gall-nuts* galls resembling nuts.

'WHY FROM THE WORLD . . .'

The *MS.* suggests that the lyric may have been included with *Ferishtah's Fancies* at a very late stage.

8 *work*] verse *MS.*

EPILOGUE

The very clean *MS.* and all texts are virtually identical. The Epilogue, much the best known part of *Ferishtah's Fancies* because of the chill of its final stanza, is dated 1 December 1883 in *MS.* and all texts. The palace was that of Mrs Bronson, Browning's friend, with whom he was staying. There is nothing to suggest that the Epilogue was originally intended for *Ferishtah's Fancies.* It is probably addressed to Mrs Browning.

Parleyings with Certain People of Importance in Their Day

Published on 28 January 1887 by Smith, Elder. No second edition was needed. The very clean *MS.* is in the Library of Balliol College. It is obviously a fair copy, except for parts of the 'Parleying with Gerard de Lairesse', which appear to be the only drafts. The readings of *MS.* and *1887* are unusually close, and only a very few minor changes were made in proof. In the *MS.* each part is separately paginated, and it is clear that Browning reordered some of the parts. Revisions for *1888* were very few and minor. The volume was dedicated to Joseph Milsand, to whom *Sordello* had been dedicated in *1863*, and who had died on 4 September 1886.

The title owes a debt to Dante. In 'One Word More' (1855), 46, Browning had quoted from the *Vita Nuova*, xxxv: 'Certain people of importance'. Browning's addition implies their later obscurity and also, perhaps, that they have outlived their importance to Browning himself.

Except for the 'Parleying with Francis Furini', which is dated 30 September 1886 in the *MS.*, the date of no part is known. It seems clear that the poem was begun in 1885, and what seems to be the first extant reference to the work is in a letter of 7 September 1887 (see Hood, *Letters*, 239). The Prologue, which DeVane suggests was stimulated by Milsand's death, may have been the last part written. The *Parleyings* was completed in the autumn of 1886.

Mrs Orr's treatment of the *Parleyings* in her *Handbook*, 339–61, is important, partly because it is based on conversations with Browning. Mrs Orr begins: 'This volume occupies, even more than its predecessor, a distinctive position in Mr Browning's work. It does not discard his old dramatic methods, but in a manner it inverts them; Mr Browning has summoned his group of men not for the sake of drawing their portraits, but that they might help to draw his own. It seems as if the accumulated convictions which find vent in the "parleyings" could no longer endure even the form of dramatic disguise; and they appear in them in all the force of direct reiterated statement, and all the freshness of novel points of view. And the portrait is in some degree a biography; it is full of reminiscences. The "people" with whom Mr Browning parleys, important in their own day, virtually unknown in ours, are with one exception his old familiar friends: men whose works connect themselves with the intellectual sympathies and the imaginative pleasures of his earliest youth.' Browning addresses Bernard de Mandeville, as he might address any other of his listeners, 'Silent face me while I think and speak'; and the poem is unusually direct and personal for Browning – even the prologue and epilogue while 'both dramatic and fanciful', are, as Mrs Orr says (*Handbook*, 340), 'scarcely less expressive of the author's mental personality than the body of the work'. W. C. DeVane's study of *Browning's Parleyings*, Yale University Press, 1927, is subtitled *The Autobiography of a Mind*, and DeVane noted that the work involved seven of Browning's main interests: philosophy, history, poetry, politics, painting, the classics and music; the scheme may be a trifle forced, but is suggestive, and DeVane's work is generally regarded as an indispensable aid with the *Parleyings*.

The poem baffled Browning's contemporaries and parts of it are still difficult, even for those equipped with the general knowledge of Browning's work which the poet seems to presuppose. DeVane's full-length treatment is helpful, and so is his unusually full handling in his *Handbook*, 490–524. Introductions in the Florentine edition are useful. Illuminating recent studies are by Ryals, *Browning's Later Poetry*, 201–26, and Mark Siegchrist, 'Type Needs Antitype: The Structure of Browning's *Parleyings*', *VNL* L, 1976, 1–10.

APOLLO AND THE FATES: A PROLOGUE

The *MS.*, *1887* and *1888* are virtually identical. DeVane's suggestion that the poem was written soon after Milsand's death seems most reasonable. The Prologue may be the last section composed of the *Parleyings*.

Browning was of course intimately familiar with the *Alcestis* of Euripides, which he had adapted in *Balaustion's Adventure*. In his head-note to the poem Browning indicates his debt especially to lines 12 and 33 of the play. The first line is in Apollo's statement: 'The son of Pheres; him I snatched from death,/Cozening the Fates: the Sisters promised me – /"Admetus shall escape the imminent death/If he for ransom gives another life"' (11–14). The second line is in the question to Apollo:

'Did this not suffice thee, to thwart that doom/Of Admetus, when, all by thy cunning beguiled/Were the Fates?' (32–4). Browning refers also to a passage from the Homeric *Hymn to Mercury* (558–60), which speaks of the Fates: 'From their home they fly now here, now there, feeding on honeycomb and bringing all things to pass. And when they are inspired through yellow honey, they are willing to speak truth.' The two passages cited from the *Eumenides* of Aeschylus are from comments of the Chorus of Furies to Apollo: 'Such was thy style of action also in the house of Pheres, when thou didst move the Fates to make mortals free from death', and 'Thou it was in truth who didst beguile with wine those ancient goddesses and thus abolish the dispensations of eld' (723–4 and 737–8 in the Loeb Classical Library version).

Apollo is the sun-god and the god of poetry, and the wine of the prologue clearly represents the imagination under the influence of which the three gloomy Fates (Moirai) of classical myth become transformed. Clotho, carrying the spindle, presides over birth, and spins the thread of life; Lachesis, carrying a globe or scroll, determines its length; and Atropos, eldest of the three, carries the shears and cuts the thread.

The Prologue introduces such themes in the *Parleyings* as the value of imagination in seeing life as essentially good, the mixture of good and evil in life, men's struggles upwards. As DeVane has pointed out, it balances the Epilogue, celebrating the birth of the imagination as the latter celebrates the birth of the means of disseminating its products widely.

1 *Parnassus* the mountain, sacred to the Muses and to Apollo and Dionysus, on whose slopes Delphi is set.
4 *Dire Ones* the Fates.
5 *Admetus* hero of the *Alcestis* of Euripides, king of Pherae, husband of Alcestis who volunteered to die in his place.
6–7 *Mother ... Night* 'Mother' is metaphorical; the Fates were traditionally daughters of Themis by Zeus.
16 *Woe-purfled, weal-prankt* Woe and weal are traditional opposites; 'purfled' means 'fringed' or 'embroidered', 'prankt' means 'decorated'.
28 *slaved for, yet loved by a god* Zeus punished Apollo by making him herdsman to Admetus; Admetus treated him well, and Apollo loved him.
29 *goddess-sent plague* Admetus forgot to sacrifice to Artemis at his bridal-feast, and found his bridal-chamber full of serpents. In the original legend this portended his imminent death, averted by Apollo's winning over the Fates (as in this prologue).
45 *clip* clipping.
49 *digits* in two senses: numbers (of years), and fingers.
58 *forbore* showed mercy or indulgence to (described by *OED* as a rare sense).
81 *eld* age (obsolete usage).
82 *certes* certainly (poeticism).
91 *conceits him* imagines himself.
102 *stony* not recorded as a noun in *OED*.
116 *suck honeycombs* See the Homeric *Hymn to Mercury*, 559.
127 *Bacchus* god of wine (Dionysus).
147 *youngest* Bacchus is post-Homeric, and the last god to enter Olympus.
156 *Semele* The daughter of Cadmus and Harmonia, she saw Zeus and burned up. Zeus snatched the unborn Dionysus from her body and hid him in his thigh.
164 *flambeau* torch.
173 *cluster* bunch of grapes.

187 *incept* not recorded as a noun by *OED*.
192 *cummers* old gossips.
196 *dregward* not in *OED*; presumably a nonce-word.
198 *collyrium* remedy for eye disorders.
222 *swound* swoon (archaism).
229 *bantling* brat, bastard.
256 *griesly* obsolete form of 'grisly'.
gammers rustic title for old women.
258–65 *subjects to rush ... dies* Only Alcestis is willing to die to save Admetus, and he agrees to her death.

WITH BERNARD DE MANDEVILLE

There are only a few insignificant differences among *MS.*, *1887* and *1888*. The poem's date is unknown, but its position in the *Parleyings* and thematic similarity to A Bean-Stripe: also, Apple-Eating' make a dating in the autumn of 1885 a reasonable one.

Bernard de Mandeville (1670–1733) was a Dutch physician who settled in England and who is remembered for *The Fable of the Bees: Or, Private Vices, Publick Benefits,* a book that had several printings in the eighteenth century. An early version appeared in 1705, and an enlarged one in 1714; two chapters were added in 1723, and a 'Vindication' was added in 1724 when the book found its final form. Browning was given his copy of the 1795 edition in 1833, just after he had finished *Pauline.* Browning seems to have misunderstood the book, about the intention and meaning of which there is still disagreement, its ironies being complex. Essentially, however, a book which held that self-seeking is the foundation of a good society and which is extremely cynical about human nature was ironically taken by Browning as a work that squared with his own convictions. Mrs Orr notes (345) that Mandeville defends the morality of his purpose 'in successive additions to the work, asserting and reasserting, by statement and illustration, that his object has been to expose the vices inherent to human society – in no sense to justify them; and Mr Browning fully accepts the vindication and even regards it as superfluous. He sees nothing, either in the fable itself or the commentary first attached to it, which may not equally be covered by the Christian doctrine of original sin, or the philosophic acceptance of evil as a necessary concomitant, or condition, of good: and finds fresh guarantees for a sound moral intention in the bright humour and sound practical sense in which the book abounds.'

Browning used, or rather misused, Mandeville to challenge the pessimism of Carlyle whose mouth 'Was magisterial in antithesis/To half the truths we hold'. Browning's old friend had died in 1881. Browning here sums up his own religious views on good and evil, the role of doubt, the inadequacy of intellect and the importance of heart in reaching 'truth'. For a discussion that sees the poem's three characters as three parts of Browning's personality, see M. E. Cox, 'With Bernard de Mandeville', *West Virginia University Philological Papers* XIII, 1961, 31–6. It is DeVane's view that Browning relied on his memories of *The Fable of the Bees* from over fifty years before, and that he consulted for the poem only the 'Preface' and 'Vindication' of Mandeville's work.

33 *brave* splendid.
saint used absolutely and in a rare sense to mean 'become regarded as saintly' (see *OED* 3).

40 *mouth* that of Thomas Carlyle (1795–1881).
63 *parlous* probably in the sense of 'risky to deal with'.
67 *object*] upstart *MS*.
70 *Addison's tye-wig preachment* Joseph Addison (1672–1719), writer and orthodox thinker. A 'tye-wig' is a wig in which the hair is tied behind the head with a ribbon – it is used here attributively as equivalent to 'conservative'. A 'preachment' is a wearisome discourse, a contemptible sermon. Mandeville was reported by Johnson in his *Life of Addison* to have thought Addison a parson in a tye-wig.
93 *'Grumbling Hive'* The title of the first version of Mandeville's book was *The Grumbling Hive: Or, Knaves Turn'd Honest.*
102 *spud* digging implement.
123 *burgeon* young shoot (poeticism).
126 *mandrake* mandragora, a poisonous plant.
176 *Weimar* The city in central Germany was Goethe's base from 1775 to his death in 1832.
189 *Orion* The constellation is represented pictorially as a warrior.
206 *Euripides not Aeschylus* because the former's handling was untraditional. Browning had dedicated his *Agamemnon of Aeschylus* to Carlyle.
215 *wist* knew (pseudo-archaism).
221 *spar* crystalline mineral.
230 *innumerous* innumerable (poeticism).
294 *display*] my play *MS*.
301 *Prometheus* He stole fire from heaven and gave it to man. That he made fire using a lens is Browning's invention.
305 *conglobed* formed into a globe.

WITH DANIEL BARTOLI

Differences among *MS.*, *1887* and *1888* are few and insignificant. The two names of the original person addressed (a doctor of some kind, see 239n.) have been heavily erased in the *MS*. DeVane suggests that the person may have been Nathaniel Wanley, whose *Wonders of the Little World* (1678) strongly influenced the young Browning. DeVane suggests that the poem belongs to the early summer of 1886, but since his only reason, obscured though it is by his phrasing, for the suggestion is that Lady Ashburton is alluded to in the 'Parleying' and in a letter of June 1886, it seems more reasonable to assume, given the *MS*. numbering of later sections of the *Parleyings,* that the poem was written after 'Bernard de Mandeville' and that it probably belongs to the autumn or early winter of 1885.

Daniel Bartoli was an Italian Jesuit historian (1609–85). Browning had acquired his *De' Simboli Trasportati al Morale* in 1830 in the edition of his own Italian tutor, Angelo Cerutti, whom Browning quotes in his note to the poem: 'He was a Jesuit and historian of the Society; wherefore he wrote very long stories, which would be read if they were not overflowing with every superstition . . . He threw in so many little miracles, which became an intolerable nuisance to whomsoever wished to read these stories: even I did not have enough heart to push very much ahead.' The work had been important to the young Browning for purposes of learning Italian, but Bartoli's moralizing clearly struck him as intolerable. In the 'Parleying', very different from the others – and not only in being the only narrative one – Bartoli is used merely as a point of departure as Browning turns from his kind of tale (though saints' legends are, rather strangely, not part of Bartoli's stock in trade) to one of his own, one about an unacknowledged but very true saint. This poem reminds one of Browning's 'The Glove' (1845), and DeVane argues that that poem and the play *Colombe's Birthday* (1844) owe debts to the main source for this 'Parleying', the *Mémoires* of the Marquis de Lassay (1756). Browning may also have drawn details rom the *Biographie Universelle* and Sainte-Beuve's *Causerie* on de Lassay (see V. Cook, 'Browning's "Parley" and de Lassay's "Mémoire"', *MLN* LIX, 1944, 553–6; and R. P. Felgar, 'Several Misconceptions about Browning's Sources for the "Parleying with Daniel Bartoli"', *BNL*, No. 8, 1972, 49–52).

In de Lassay's story, set in the reign of Louis XIV (1643–1715), the heroine is Marianne Pajot, who is about to marry the Duke of Lorraine. Just before the marriage, the King's minister forbids the wedding unless the Duke will assign his lands to France as he had previously agreed to do. Marianne will not allow the Duke's or her own honour to be impugned by his signing any such agreement, and the marriage does not occur. Marianne is admired by a youth, de Lassay himself, who later marries her; when she dies, he is for some time desolate. Browning adds to the story his own account of the Duke's future, married to a woman of doubtful reputation, but faithful to Marianne after his fashion.

The story has obvious autobiographical elements. DeVane suggests that the model for Browning's heroine here – as elsewhere – is in part his wife, and that in some measure Browning is the young man of 'The Glove' and this 'Parleying', who understands the motives of the lady who withdraws from the world, who marries her and lives happily to her death, after which he is for some time forlorn but ultimately recovers and rejoins society. The bold 'she-shape' (287) of the poem's concluding stanzas is almost certainly a close relative of Lady Ashburton, with whom Browning's relation in the years 1869–71 had been unhappy, affecting, it is generally agreed, such poems as *Fifine at the Fair* and 'Saint Martin's Summer'.

1 *Don*] Sir *MS. first reading.*
7 *king* Louis XIV.
11 *Two of his dukedoms* The detail is not in the *Mémoires,* but is in Sainte-Beuve and the *Biographie.*
32 *Drugs . . . her father deals in* The information is not in the *Mémoires,* but is in Sainte-Beuve and the *Biographie.*
33 *Manna and senna* a vegetable juice used as a gentle laxative, and cassia leaflets used as cathartics and emetics.
41 *words break no bones* 'Sticks and stones will break my bones,/But names [or 'words'] will never hurt me' (traditional folk-phrase).
91 *solar monarch* Sun King (compare 231).
97 *pari passu* 'with equal step' (Latin).
201 *yet my*] late my *MS. first reading*; still my *MS.*
221 *ten years old* thus in Sainte-Beuve, but not in *Mémoires* (where he is fifteen) or in *Biographie.*
229 *They were wed* Browning omits the fact that de Lassay was a widower.
236 *moon* often associated with Mrs Browning in her husband's verse.
239 *Don*] Doctor *MS. first reading*; Daniel *MS.*
241 *kicked not at the pricks* 'to kick against the pricks' (Acts ix 5; xxvi 14).
245–50 *Saint Scholastica . . . Leads him* Neither the saint nor the story is in Bartoli – the whole thing is apparently Browning's invention, a sample of the kind of tale to which Browning objects and which he associates with Bartoli somewhat arbitrarily, since in fact Bartoli did not tell saints' tales. Saint Scholastica (fifth century) was sister to Saint Benedict. DeVane suggests that Browning may have

chosen her because 'scholastic' hits at Bartoli's pedantry, and because it is a rank in the Jesuit order. *Paynimrie* is 'Heathen Land'.

254 *dance the hays* perform winding movements.

273 *Trogalia* 'sweetmeats'.

280–81 *cloud . . . moon* to some extent, Lady Ashburton and Mrs Browning.

287–342] The lines are pasted in to the *MS.*, and may well have not been written originally for inclusion here.

332–3 *sea-foam-born/Venus* In one tradition, the goddess of sensual love was born from the sea-foam.

335 *Samson when his hair is shorn* Judges xvi 19.

340–42 *ghosts . . . scared by the cock's crow* a traditional belief, as in *Hamlet* I. 2. 218–19.

WITH CHRISTOPHER SMART

The *MS.*, *1887* and *1888* are almost identical. In a letter to J. T. Nettleship of 21 August 1889, Browning revised a 'faulty passage' (87–103); the revisions have been incorporated in the present text as Browning indicated he wished to incorporate them in his next text (see R. M. Spence in *N&Q*, ninth series V, 1900, 124; and P. Kelley and R. Hudson in *N&Q*, new series XVII, 1970, 22–3). In the *MS.* the title page was numbered IV but is corrected to III. A dating of late 1885 seems probable.

The English poet Christopher Smart (1722–71) was best known for his fits of madness and for his poem, *Song to David* (1763), which, tradition has it, he wrote in whole or part with a key on the wainscot of the cell in which he was confined in a madhouse in 1763. Browning seems to have first read the poem in an edition of 1827, and he alludes to Smart in *Paracelsus* I, 770–74. He reread the poem late in 1844 or early in 1845, and used it in 'Saul'. It profoundly affected him; he knew it by heart. DeVane asserts that Browning uses Smart, who saw earth's glories and thanked God, to attack doctrines of art for art's sake and to offer a contrast with Swinburne and other late contemporaries of Browning. It should perhaps be noted that Smart's great 'Jubilate Agno' was not known to Browning; it was first published in 1939.

76–7 *sound/And sane at starting* not factually true. Browning unhistorically confines Smart's madness to the one time during which he composed his *Song to David.* Compare 84–6.

90 *Leighton* Frederic Leighton (1830–96), painter and sculptor, Browning's friend, brother of Mrs Orr, President of the Royal Academy.

91 *Watts* G. F. Watts, English painter and sculptor (1817–1904).

93] *letter to Nettleship, this edition*; On Art's supreme – or that yourself who sang *MS.*, *1887*, *1888*.

99 *Did you, like him,*] *letter to Nettleship, this edition*; How came it you *MS.*, *1887*, *1888*.

101 *both of you*] *letter to Nettleship, this edition*; plainly two *MS.*, *1887*, *1888*.

111 *Smart only* Browning goes beyond even William Rossetti's view that the *Song to David* is 'the only great *accomplished* poem of the last century'.

115–16 *naked coal/Live from the censer* alluding to the coal of Isaiah vi 6.

120 *Hayley* William Hayley (1745–1820), English poet and biographer.

121–2 *let the dead . . . Bury their dead* Matthew viii 22.

148 *the old things thus made new* 'Behold I make all things new. And he said unto me, Write: for these words are true and faithful' (Revelation xxi 5).
152 *Pompous* full of pomp.
158 *erst* formerly (archaism).
158–9 *all that he sees/Be named* Genesis ii 19–20.
179–80 *lopped . . . this unsightly bough* In the 1791 edition of Smart's works, *Song to David* was deliberately omitted.
180 *bay-tree* sacred to Apollo, god of poetry.
181 *translated Horace* Browning had been given a copy of what was probably the verse translation in 1824. Smart's prose translation belongs to 1756, his verse one to 1767.
187–95 *who makes poetry must reproduce . . . fresh achievement* Compare 'Fra Lippo Lippi', 296–306.
195–8 not Smart's, but a Browning attempt to capture Smart characteristics.
198 *Virgin's Bower* a kind of clematis.
stars open corollas (of the flowers).
faint die (rare sense).
231 *a superior*] the instructor's *MS.*
255 *Offuscate* rare form of 'obfuscate'.
264 *Live and learn* proverbial.

WITH GEORGE BUBB DODINGTON

Differences between *MS.*, *1887* and *1888* are few and trivial. The *MS.* title page is numbered VI, corrected to IV. The title in the *MS.* was originally longer, but what was probably 'Lord Melcombe' is heavily erased. The date is unknown, but the spring of 1886 seems a reasonable assumption, especially since Browning acquired a copy of Dodington's *Diary* on 20 January 1886.

George Bubb, later George Bubb Dodington, made Baron Melcombe a year before his death (1691–1762), was, by general agreement, intelligent, knowledgeable, vain, treacherous, self-seeking, obsequious, snobbish, tasteless, obese and wealthy. He became a Member of Parliament in 1715 and remained one till defeated in 1754. He was generally despised by the right people, including Pope, who used him as part-model for Bufo in 'Epistle to Doctor Arbuthnot', 229–44. Dodington's *Diary* (1784) was in Browning's library – Browning had read it as a young man – and Browning was especially indebted to H. P. Wyndham's 'Preface' for his information. He also made use of the *Works* of Sir Charles Hanbury Williams (1822), annotated by Horace Walpole, which included satirical verses on Dodington.

As DeVane points out, the real Dodington was knave, but no fool, and Browning has otherwise engaged in distortion – in, for instance, making the electoral system closer to that of his own time than to Dodington's. He did so to attack Disraeli (1804–81), Conservative leader, and Prime Minister 1867–8 and 1874–80. Browning detested Disraeli, not least because of what he saw as Disraeli's deviousness. It is Disraeli, not Dodington, who is the poem's central figure. Browning had said he would 'give it him one of these days' (Allingham, *Diary*, 246), and here Disraeli has his day.

10 *right reason* that is, reason operating on the level of grace, not nature.
16 *Labourers deserve their hire* 'the labourer is worthy of his hire' (Luke x 7).
17 *bears the bell* wins the prize.

17–18 'But if any provide not for his own, and specially for those of his own house, he hath denied the faith, and is worse than an infidel' (1 Timothy v 8).
32 *volatile* bird.
40 *Darwin* The great biologist writes of bower-birds in *The Descent of Man* (1871).
41 *bower-birds* Australian species of starling. They build bowers as places of resort, and decorate them with such things as shells and bones.
52 *orts* refuse.
53 *engage* secure.
67 *trip* detect in an inaccuracy.
72 *trip* make a mistake.
78 *coprolite* stony fossil of animal excrement.
80 *tease* irritate, chafe.
82 *bay* symbolic of victory.
130 *Pearl-like profuse to swine* 'neither cast ye your pearls before swine, lest they trample them under their feet, and turn again and rend you' (Matthew vii 6).
170 *conquering and to conquer* quoting Revelation vi 2.
187 *Perpend* ponder.
219–20 *Since we ... have one human heart* Florentine edition and DeVane suggest: 'One touch of nature makes the whole world kin' (*Troilus and Cressida* III. 3. 175). Perhaps, rather, Wordsworth's 'Thanks to the human heart by which we live' ('Immortality Ode', 202).
234 *aes triplex* 'triple brass' (Horace, *Odes* I, iii, 9).
249 *quid vis?* 'what do you want?' (Latin).
261 *chief* a common Tory name for Disraeli.
267 *Sacred Band* the body of 300 choice Thebans who fought Sparta in the fourth century B.C.
277 *triply cased in brass* see 234, and note.
283–4 *stranglier . . . wiselier . . . Stronglier* Browning maintained his fondness for comparatives unusual even by the standards of his time to the end of his career.
300 *insuppressive* unsuppressible ('rare' – *OED*).
309–10 *Exact . . . Supernatural* a central motif in *The Return of the Druses* (1843), and prominent elsewhere in Browning.
310 *despot* in the older sense of 'master' or 'lord', often with a suggestion of deity.
316 *acquist* acquisition.
327 *Ventum est ad triarios* 'It has come to the third rank' (Latin). The expression was proverbial. The third rank being the reserve, the expression means 'We are at our last resource.'

WITH FRANCIS FURINI

1887 and *1888* are virtually identical. The parleying was more extensively revised in proof than any other part, especially in the later pages. The title-page number III is corrected to V in the *MS.*, which dates the poem 30 September 1886. It was among the last parts of the *Parleyings* to be written.

Francesco Furini (*c.* 1600–1649) was an obscure Florentine painter of nudes, who was a priest for the last years of his life. He was a most attractive person, especially noted for his generosity. Rumour had it that he asked on his deathbed that his paintings be burned. Browning first saw his paintings during his years in Florence, and of the seven men parleyed with, Furini is the only one who did not influence the young Browning (and the only one who was not a writer).

Browning's main source was Baldinucci's life of Furini in his *Notizie de' Professori del Disegno,* often used elsewhere by Browning (see DeVane, *Browning's Parleyings,* 167–81, for a slightly exaggerated account of Baldinucci's influence). Browning quarrels here, as in 'Filippo Baldinucci on the Privilege of Burial' (1876), with the Italian writer, differing from him in his conception of Furini, and attacking him for his narrowness over Furini's nudes. Browning is here coming to the defence of his son's nudes, which had been objected to by the treasurer of the Royal Academy, J. C. Horsley, in 1885 and 1886. In 1884 Horsley refused to show a Pen Browning nude sculpture of Dryope, and in 1886 he had attacked his portrait of *Joan of Arc and the Kingfisher* for which Browning wrote an accompanying motto, included as lines 601–7 of this Parleying.

Furini was first painter, then priest. In the second part of his poem (the least unified of the *Parleyings*), Browning, who knew little about evolutionary theory, attacks the evolutionists of his day for – as he saw it – degrading the image of man and for the inadequacy of their conception of God. The two themes come together in the image of Andromeda, a subject in a Furini painting, the figure who had always loomed so large in Browning's imagination and poetry – and life, even before her appearance in *Pauline.* The nude Andromeda of Furini here becomes symbolic of Browning and his faith, standing in a sea of doubt, waiting for rescue.

4 *about two hundred years ago* Furini died in 1649.
6 *Saint Sano's church* Furini moved to his church, San Ansano, in Mugello, a region near Florence, about 1633.
42 *Agnolo* Michel Agnolo (Michelangelo).
71 *chronicler* Filippo Baldinucci.
92 *Diana* Browning's son painted the Roman goddess of the hunt.
141 *Andromeda* The northern constellation is named after the maiden rescued by Perseus from the rock to which she had been bound as food for a monster.
145–6 *critic . . . artist* Both Baldinucci and Horsley were artists.
146–7 *Ossa piled/Topping Olympus* The Titans piled Mount Ossa on Mount Pelion (or vice versa) and (in some versions of the legend) put them on Mount Olympus in their effort to reach the Olympic gods. 'To pile Ossa on Pelion' is proverbial for adding embarrassment to embarrassment, or difficulty to difficulty.
154 *satyr masked as matron* Satyrs are the hairy goat-men of classical myth, known for their lasciviousness. Horsley had attacked the nude in art in *The Times,* 20–25 May 1885; his letter of 20 May was signed 'A British Matron'.
165 *Leonard* Leonardo da Vinci.
173 *Correggio* the Italian painter (*c.* 1489–1534).
175–6 *Art, which Correggio's tongue/Calls 'Virtue'* The present editor cannot supply the needed annotation.
177 *Night and Morn* Michelangelo's statues in the Medici chapel of San Lorenzo in Florence. Both are female.
180 *His Eve* Michelangelo's *Creation of Eve,* on the ceiling of the Sistine Chapel.
208 *Now, less fear*] Little fear *MS., 1887.*
210–11 *hip/And thigh – smite the Philistine* Samson 'smote them [the Philistines] hip and thigh with a great slaughter' (Judges xv 8).
235–6 *Thy measuring-rod/Meted forth heaven and earth* Isaiah xl 12; Revelation xxi 15; Exodus xl.
385 *save* DeVane (*Browning's Parleyings,* 208n.) interprets the word as meaning 'except'. It seems, however, rather to mean here 'preserve'. See, however, line 614.
399 *Externe* outside (poeticism).

446 *sealing up the sum* 'Thou sealest up the sum, full of wisdom, and perfect in beauty' (Ezekiel xxviii 12).
490] To my Andromeda you see on strand *MS.*
493 *Mere fancy-work*] Furini's work *MS.*
501 *old artificer* Zeuxis. The Greek painter of the fifth century B.C. became legendary for his verisimilitude.
519] Nay, nor a hair's breadth: all is wise and well *MS.*
531] Go inside and get knowledge. *MS. first reading.*
532 *ministrate* *OED* calls the verb obsolete, and cites only this intransitive usage. The previous transitive usage recorded is in Bailey's *Dictionary* (1727).
539 *messuage* dwelling.
545 *That circle of the serpent, tail in mouth* symbol of Deity or Eternity (the serpent, says Plutarch, 'feeds upon its own body; even so all things spring from God, and will be resolved into deity again').
554] Carmine by drops disciplinary, – worse – *MS.*
562 *besprent* besprinkled.
576] Yet neither yet so moved by country shamed *MS.*
585 *Sainte-Beuve* the French historian and critic (1804–69).
Quicherat Jules Quicherat edited the five volumes of papers on Joan's trial (1841–9).
588–93 *'of prudishness . . . wild thought'* In a letter of 12 May 1886 Browning wrote: 'I am ashamed at the objection taken by some of the critics to the Eve-like simplicity of Pen's peasant-girl, who before going on to saintliness (which the Church still withholds from her) was satisfied with the proverbially next step to it – cleanliness. If they knew anything of Joan's habits even when advanced in her saintly career, they would remember she was no prude by any means. Her favoured young cavalier, the Duc d'Alençon, mentions that he had frequently seen her undress, and that "aliquando videbat ejus mammas quae pulchrae erant" ["sometimes he saw her breasts which were very beautiful"] – in his very words' (Hood, *Letters,* 247). The poem's quotations from d'Alençon, the Duke who was Joan's friend and chronicler, are in Quicherat, *Procès* . . . IV, 4–5.
600 *scribe* Browning himself. Lines 601–7 were the motto for the portrait by Pen Browning of Joan preparing to bathe (1886). They were printed by mistake in *New Poems* (1914) and the Macmillan edition (1915) as previously unpublished, from another *MS.*, with a few trivial variants, under the title 'Joan of Arc and the Kingfisher'.
604 *'Las* aphetic form of 'Alas'.
614 *That task's beyond you* The clause perhaps supports DeVane's reading of 385 in which he sees Browning as criticizing Furini's skill with faces.
616 *Omnia non omnibus* 'All things are not for all people' (Latin).
no harm is meant echoing the letters in *The Times* of 20 and 21 May 1885.

WITH GERARD DE LAIRESSE

1887 and *1888* are virtually identical. Browning made a few revisions from the *MS.* in proof. In the *MS.* the poem was originally numbered V. The condition of the *MS.* suggests that there was no other draft of the Parleying. The date is unknown, but the summer or early autumn of 1886 seems probable.

Gerard de Lairesse was a Dutch artist (1641–1711) who became a writer on art when he went blind, and whose influence on Browning's landscapes, notably in

'Childe Roland' and in this Parleying, is very strong. Browning saw his paintings, ones based on classical themes but usually set in Dutch surroundings, in the Dulwich Art Gallery as a boy, and he read de Lairesse's treatise, *The Art of Painting in All Its Branches* in the translation of J. F. Fritsch (1778). In 1874 Browning wrote in his copy: 'I read this book more often and with greater delight when I was a child than any other: and still remember the main of it most gratefully for the good I seem to have got from the prints and the wonderful text.' De Lairesse was regarded in his own time as a great painter, a 'second Raphael', but Browning shared the general opinion that the painting was of little value. Ironically the writer's reputation outlived the artist's. De Lairesse spoke for the superiority of the ancients to the moderns. Browning saw himself among his contemporary poets as the one who had been most ruthlessly 'modern', and Matthew Arnold, whose 'Preface' of 1853 had urged writers to use materials and principles from the past, and who had himself used them, is the poet for whom de Lairesse acts as surrogate – Browning had quoted from the 'Preface' with approval perhaps more apparent than real in his preface to the *Agamemnon of Aeschylus.*

To Browning, as 'Old Pictures in Florence' and 'Cleon' and this Parleying show, the Greek ideal was limited beside the Christian one, largely because with Christianity had come belief in immortality. See DeVane, 'Browning and the Spirit of Greece', in H. Davis and others (eds.), *Nineteenth-Century Studies,* Cornell University Press, 1940, 179–98.

46 *Walk* In *The Art of Painting* VI, xvi–xvii, de Lairesse goes on an imaginary walk to show the ideal and the horrible in landscape.
50 *Faustus' robe* the magic cloak with which he could fly.
51 *Fortunatus' cap* The hero of medieval legend had a wishing-cap.
75 *Phaeton* He insisted on driving the Chariot of the Sun one day. He drove so dangerously that Zeus (Jove) killed him with a thunderbolt. De Lairesse described what he took to be Phaeton's grave in *The Art of Painting,* 255.
88 *sealed sense* referring to his blindness.
120 *Dryope* She plucked some lotus blossoms, and then saw blood flowing from the tree, which was really the nymph Lotis. Dryope herself became a tree. De Lairesse dealt with the story in *The Art of Painting,* 239–40.
121 *lote* anglicized form of 'lotus' (archaism).
163–5 *rose . . . deathly love* The Adonis flower was the rose, once white, reddened by the blood of Venus, pricked by a thorn as she rushed to help her dying love, Adonis.
165] Deathly Adonis!
Rag-wort – *MS.*
166–80] *MS. interpolation.*
170 *Protoplast* Creator.
172 *Progress for the bold!*] Let the truth be told – *MS.*
179] When you declare you're blind – why, then, I'll cry *MS.*
189 *form erect* that of Prometheus, chained to a rock in the Caucasus, where a vulture ate his constantly renewed liver. DeVane and the Florentine edition think Browning's picture is influenced by Mrs Browning's translation of the *Prometheus Bound* of Aeschylus.
207–9] *MS. interpolation.*
230 *Moon-maid* Diana (Artemis), goddess of the moon and hunting, patroness of unmarried girls.
239 *repugnant* resisting.

255 *strange and sudden deaths* like those of the children of Niobe or of Iphigeneia. To get near or to anger Artemis was, in many legends, somewhat dangerous.
256 *Hymen* god of marriage.
283 *Satyr* Satyrs were hairy goat-men, generally lascivious, and often attendant upon Dionysus. In the account of Moschus, one fell in love with the girl Lyda. Browning's source is probably Shelley's translation from the Greek of Moschus, 'Pan Echo, and the Satyr'.
295 *thridding* threading (archaism).
299 *Echo* The nymph had an unrequited love for the satyr that loved Lyda. Pan, in turn, loved Echo, but the god of flocks and forests was also unlucky.
302 *couches*] *MS., 1887, this edition*; crouches *1888.*
307‸8] About six lines have here been presumably deleted by cutting the *MS.* page – the passage may have been rather lurid.
315 *momently* at every moment.
332 *Macedonian* Alexander the Great.
333 *Darius* Darius III, King of Persia, conquered by Alexander.
356 *Caucasus*] Olympus *MS. first reading.*
357 *Arcadia* the region in the Peloponnesus where Pan lived, and which was a setting for pastoral.
381 *Twistwork* not recorded in *OED.*
382–9 *'Dream afresh . . . gone glory'* a palpable hit at Arnold's 'Preface' of 1853.
409 *Achilles* In *Odyssey* XI, 489–91, the Greek hero in Hades says he would rather be humble among the living than king of the dead.
424 *'Spring for the tree and herb – no Spring for us'* The line is very typical of pastoral elegy, but appears not to be a quotation. The suggestion of Homer's *Iliad* by DeVane and Florentine edition is most unlikely.
426–34] First published, with different punctuation but no verbal variants, entitled 'Spring Song', on page 1 of *The New Amphion* ('The Book of the Edinburgh University Union Fancy Fair'), 1886.

WITH CHARLES AVISON

There are a very few trivial differences between *MS., 1887* and *1888.* The opening passage suggests a dating of March or April 1886.

Music was always most important to Browning, and he here deals with his thoughts and feelings about it. Charles Avison was a Newcastle organist (*c.* 1710–70). Browning's father owned a *MS.* copy of Avison's *Grand March,* alluded to in the Parleying and printed at its end. The Browning library also had Avison's book, *Essay on Musical Expression* (1752), from which Browning had learned much and which he used in writing this poem.

DeVane notes that Browning's poems on music are inevitably melancholic, and that they are so because the poet, while feeling that music can plumb deeper than any art and that there is something miraculous about it, recognizes too how fleeting is its spiritual exploration – and, in this poem also, how fleeting is one particular kind or ideal of music in its history. DeVane notes too that it is characteristic of Browning that as he plays or hears music, crowd scenes fill his imagination, as they had, for instance, in 'A Toccata of Galuppi's'.

17 *blackcap* a kind of small warbler.
27 *Greenly* vigorously.

51 *'March'* Griffin and Minchin report (*Life*, 15–16): 'one of his earliest memories was of her [his mother] playing Avison's once popular Grand March in C Major'.
57 *whilom* once upon a time (archaism).
61 *greaten* expand (archaism).
68–9 *flint . . . spark-like* Shakespeare's lines from *Timon of Athens* seem to have lodged firmly in Browning's imagination: 'The fire i' the flint/Shows not till it be struck' (I. I. 22–3).
73 *Quickened* came to life.
81 *John Relfe* Browning's music-master, indebted to Abbé Vogler, organist and musical theorist.
84 *figure such a bass* provide the figures (numerals), a kind of musical shorthand used to indicate an appropriate bass line. Relfe was a master of counterpoint and the 'figured bass'.
86 *Greater Third* Major Third: an interval of four semitones. In other words, the piece is in the key of C Major.
87–8 *no change . . . Dominant* The music, that is, is simple and straightforward. The change from Tonic down to Dominant is the simplest change in the succession of chords.
99 *Brahms* the German composer (1833–97).
100 *Wagner, Dvorak, Liszt* the German composer (1813–83), the Czech composer (1841–1904), the Hungarian pianist and composer (1811–86).
shawms medieval instruments of the oboe class.
101 *Handel* The German composer settled in England (1685–1759).
102 *Buononcini* Giovanni Battista Buononcini (1670–1747), associate, and later for a time rival, of Handel. His best success came in London.
104 *We stand in England* The allusion seems to be to the well-known tradition of standing as Handel's 'Hallelujah Chorus' in the *Messiah* is sung (the tradition going back to the first London performance of 23 March 1743). The point, presumably, is that Handel *is* supreme.
105 *Geminiani* Francesco Geminiani, the Italian composer and violinist (1687–1762) spent time in London, where Avison was his pupil. Avison thought him greater than Handel.
107 *Pepusch* Dr John Christopher Pepusch (1667–1752), organist, composer, theorist and music teacher, settled in London. He is best known for choosing and arranging the music for *The Beggar's Opera*.
108 *bush* that is, a bushy head of hair.
110 *Greenway* not identified. DeVane (*Browning's Parleyings*, 257) suggests, unconvincingly, Maurice Greene (1696–1755), acquainted with the circle of musicians named by Browning.
'Alexis' cantata by Pepusch (*c.* 1716), well known till the 1840s.
111 *list* wishes (archaism).
132–5 *'O Thou' . . . Wagner fixed it fast* referring to the song to the evening star in Wagner's *Tannhauser* (1845).
136 *unmodulated minor* a minor key without a move to a concluding major chord. Until about 1750 it was thought to be unsuitable to end on a minor chord; compositions concluded with a 'Tierce de Picardie', a major chord.
143 *Innominate* not named.
154 *enginery* machinery.
167 *operosity* laboriousness.
225–31 Browning refers to and paraphrases the passage that Ruskin thought repre-

sented the highest level in poetry (*Modern Painters* III, xii): Helen's words from *Iliad* III, 235–44.

227 *brothers* Castor and Pollux.

232 *Painter's fresco* Michelangelo's *Creation of Eve* on the ceiling of the Sistine Chapel.

253 "*Radaminta*" an error for *Radamisto,* Handel's opera (1720) in which a man sings for the wife he thinks dead.

255 "*Rinaldo*" Handel opera (1711).

257 *spar* crystalline mineral.

263 *ken* mental perception.

270 *Gluck* the Bavarian composer (1714–87). 'The current [operatic] repertory begins . . . with a composer who boldly dared to return to dramatic truth – Gluck' (*Oxford Companion to Music*).

272 *Haydn* Austrian composer (1732–1809), 'Father of the Symphony', and founder of modern chamber music and instrumental music.

Mozart The art of Mozart (1756–91) was founded on that of Haydn.

274 *Flamboyant* flamingly coloured.

290 *reactives* reagents ('rare' – *OED*).

301 *broadcast* widely scattered.

303 *easy-going* not recorded as a noun in *OED*.

304 *Bach* The German composer (1685–1750) wrote according to strict laws different from those that developed in modern laws of modulation.

305 *Change enharmonically* Enharmonic change takes advantage 'of the fact that the same notes can be called by different names, which lead different ways, and . . . into unexpected keys' (*Grove*).

Hudl J. J. Hudl, an obscure German musician, composed a book on modulation (1802).

309 *Largo* a very slow tempo.

310 *Rubato* a bending of tempo within a given passage for purposes of expression.

312 *Georgian years* the years, ending in 1830, when England was ruled by kings named George.

313 *British Grenadiers* the famous Regiment.

333 *Purcell* The English composer and organist (*c.* 1659–95) influenced Handel.

338 *A* the relative minor key to the key of C Major (that is, the minor key which has the same key signature as the key of C Major).

Lesser Third Minor Third: an interval of three semitones.

382 *motive* 'The briefest intelligible and self-existent melodic or rhythmic unit' (*Oxford Companion*).

385 *ophicleide and bombardon* Both are powerful brass instruments.

392 *Little-ease* dungeon in the Tower of London.

Tyburn the site of London's gallows, and the regular place of execution until 1783.

400 *Larges . . . Longs . . . Breves* descriptive terms for notes of longer duration than the shorter crotchets and quavers of 401.

404] We'll neither: one intent shall move us both, *MS*.

406] Champion we some great cause! for I were loth *MS*.

407 *Preston Pans* site of the battle in Scotland north of Newcastle in 1745 in which the royal forces were beaten by Prince Charles Edward and his Highlanders.

410–11 *Hollis . . . The famous Five* The five named are the five members of the Long Parliament whom Charles I tried to arrest in 1642; all were leading Parliamentarians. One is reminded of Browning's play *Strafford* (1837) and his 'Cavalier Tunes' (1842).

412 *Train Bands* local militia.

Southwark metropolitan borough in south London.

418 *'subject'* theme or principal phrase.

423 *Pym* John Pym (1583–1643), Parliamentary leader. In Browning's *Strafford* he is the antagonist who loves Strafford but seeks his death.

425 *Somerset* the county in which Pym was born.

426 *Strafford* hero of Browning's play; the King's Minister, executed in 1641.

Eliot Sir John Eliot (1592–1632) opposed the policies of Charles I and died in the Tower.

429 *Tavistock* Pym was Member of Parliament for Tavistock in Devon.

433 *Westminster* the site of the Houses of Parliament.

FUST AND HIS FRIENDS: AN EPILOGUE

MS., *1887* and *1888* vary only slightly. The word 'Epilogue' was cancelled in the *MS.* and did not appear in *1887*. The poem is undated in the *MS.*, but it probably was written in the autumn of 1886, near or at the end of the period of composition of the *Parleyings*.

The episode is Browning's invention. Johann Fust (*c.* 1400–66) was a banker of Mainz, in south-west Germany (called in the poem as it often was by its French name of Mayence). He advanced money to Gutenberg to explore his invention of printing, and sued Gutenberg to get his money back. He may have taken Gutenberg's equipment from him, but at any rate he and his future son-in-law, Peter Schoeffer, printed the first book with a complete date, a Psalter, on 14 August 1457. Browning sets his scene on the evening of the day, and gives Fust the credit for inventing printing. Browning gets history wrong, but his misconceptions were common at the time.

Johann Fust and Johann Faust were not related, let alone the same person. The two however had been often identified as one and the same, and Browning has strong – though erroneous – backing for using material from the Faust legend, and especially from Goethe. He may also, as DeVane suggests, have been indebted to Defoe who, in his *Political and Modern History of the Devil* (1726), has learned Divines convinced that 'poor Faustus (who was indeed nothing but a mere printer), dealt with the Devil'.

The epilogue has several points in common with the prologue and, as DeVane suggests, celebrates the means of disseminating the products of the imagination.

12 *gossipry* relative.

sib relative.

32 *'Words of the wise are as goads'* quoting Ecclesiastes xii 11.

35 *palinodes* recantations.

55 *Barnabite* The Barnabites were a religious order.

61 *disport* amusement (archaism).

62 *Belial* Satan.

65 *Helen of Troy* Faust marries Helen in Part II of Goethe's play; she is the paramour of Faustus in Marlowe's.

70 *leman* paramour.

wis know (pseudo-archaism).

72 *guttler* glutton.
74 *out of their table there sprouted a vine* as in the first part of *Faust* in Auerbach's cellar in Leipzig.
75 *cluster* bunch of grapes.
83 *humours* vagaries.
85 *groat . . . guilder* silver coin . . . gold coin.
86 *skinker* tapster (archaism).
90 *Rhenish . . . Raphal* kinds of wine.
92 *liquor sprang out of the table* It did so earlier in the scene in *Faust* in Auerbach's cellar.
101 *Strange honours were heaped on thee* in *Faust* II.
104 *goldsmith* Johann's brother and father were goldsmiths.
108 *Crapulosity* apparently a nonce-word. It is not in *OED*.
113 *signing and sealing* a compact with the Devil.
118 *Peter Genesheim* Peter Schoeffer of Gernsheim [*sic*] (town south-east of Mainz).
121 *famulus* 'servant' (Latin).
135 *bell, book and candle* used in the ritual of excommunication.
weened thought (archaism).
136 *Balm yet was in Gilead* 'Is there no balm in Gilead?' (Jeremiah viii 22).
139 *pottle* drink.
punk prostitute (archaism).
151 *Heureka* The 'I have found it' of Archimedes, now used to indicate surprised joy at a discovery. *OED* remarks that the correct spelling, 'Heureka', is rare.
153 *Have*] *Have* [italics] *MS., 1887.*
162 *'Ne pulvis'* The Latin in the passages that follow is often curious, often almost meaningless, often ungrammatical. The meaning is not important; essentially the 'friends' are trying to recall the formulae for exorcism and making a hash of it. 'Ne' here is an error for 'Nos': the Latin means roughly 'Don't let dust'.
166 *Asmodeus* evil demon in the Apocryphal Book of Tobit.
Hussite a heretical follower of John Huss, burned in 1415.
169 *'Ne pulvis et ignis'* He still has it wrong; his Latin means roughly 'Don't let dust and fire'.
171–2 *'Ne pulvis . . . fulmina'* roughly, 'Don't let dust and ash make yourself proud,/For thunderbolts.'
172 *dorrs* buzzing insects.
173 *'Ne Numinis fulmina feras'* 'Don't bear God's thunderbolts.'
174–4 *'Hominis . . . mors'* 'Of a treacherous man just are the lot,/Thunder and hail and dreadful death.'
176 *'Irati ne'* 'angry lest'.
181–4 *'Nos . . . corda'* 'We dust and ashes, trembling, groaning, come . . . to you, Lord. Give light, help, in order that followers of the sacred heart . . .'
184 *'erecta sint spe'* 'may be upright in hope'.
190 *'Pou sto'* 'a place to stand on' (Greek). Archimedes said he could move the world if he had a place to stand on.
192 *Aroint thee* avaunt.
193 *familiar* close associate.
201 *'Pulvis et cinis'* 'dust and ashes'.
203 *initium* to *finis* 'beginning to end'.
206 *'ibis'* 'you will go'.
207 *'redibis'* 'you will return'.

208 *'in Orco peribis'* 'you will perish in Hell'.
211 *Bamberg* Bavarian city (a famous Bible was printed there in 1460).
216 *lurcher* mongrel.
233 *Thomas the Doubter* the apostle who doubted (John xx 25).
240 *criss-cross* alphabet.
249 *'fulmen'* 'thunderbolt'. See 172, where Seventh Friend erred.
251 *seventy times seven* Matthew xviii 22.
258 *'Cur' miss a 'quare'* 'Why' miss a 'wherefore' (and 'dog' miss a 'quarry').
285 Genesis i 6; John i 1.
302 *lies' father* Satan is the 'Father of Lies'.
322 *clowns* peasants.
325 *hind* farm labourer.
353 *phoenix* the unique bird that springs from the ashes of the former phoenix.
363–4 *'Plough with my heifer,/Ye find out my riddle,' quoth Samson* 'If ye had not plowed with my heifer, ye had not found out my riddle' (Judges xiv 18).
368–9 *'rectius si quid/Novistis im-per-ti-te'* 'If you've known anything better, im-part it' (Latin).
385] *not in MS.*
420 *'Semper sint res uti sunt'* 'May things always be as they are' (Latin).
425 *asymptote* line which approaches nearer and nearer a given curve, but does not touch it.
439 *manna* the miraculous food provided for the Children of Israel (Exodus xvi 14).
455 *Dost surmise*] *not in MS.*
456 *Beghards* herctical vowless monastic fraternities.
Waldenses heretical religious sect that ultimately associated itself with the Protestant Reformation.
457 *Jeronimites* Hieronymites, medieval order of hermits (not heretical).
461 *opuscule* small work.
468 *'An cuique credendum sit'* 'Should anyone believe' (Latin).
474–5 'It is thus that you silence the goose, but a hundred years hence there will arise a swan whose singing ye shall not be able to silence' (attributed to John Huss, whose name means 'Goose', as he was burned at the stake). The 'swan' and 'man' are Luther.

Asolando

Browning's final volume was published by Smith, Elder on 12 December 1889, the volume being postdated 1890, as with many other nineteenth-century books published late in the year. Browning, who had received advance copies, heard of its success later in the day, and died late in the evening at Venice. *Asolando* went through nine more editions in following months, and in 1894 it was included in the seventeenth volume of the *Poetical Works,* edited by E. Berdoe. No reprints have any textual authority, and the copy-text for the present edition is therefore the first edition. The exceptionally clean and careful *MS.* is a fair copy, made at Asolo in September–October 1889. Browning had wanted it to go to Balliol College, but his son held on to it, and it was sold in 1913 at the Sotheby sale and is now in the Pierpont Morgan Library in New York, together with a set of proofs (the final, and probably only, set) with the poet's revisions and corrections, which were made in Venice in November 1889. The Morgan Library also has a copy of the printed text in which the title page is dated, probably uniquely, 1889.

A few of the poems in the *MS.* are dated, and those dates and other evidence strongly suggest that all the poems, excepting only 'The Cardinal and the Dog' (1840?), were products of the poet's last two years or so of life, that the bulk of the volume belongs to the first nine months of 1889, and that some verses were written within two months of publication. In a letter of 15 October 1889 (DeVane and Knickerbocker, *New Letters*, 384), Browning refers to a few poems as having been written in Asolo, and all of them 'revised and copied'; the volume's dedication of the same date refers to 'some few [verses] written, all of them supervised' in Asolo; and in a letter of 14 October 1889 he writes of his thirty pieces: 'not a few written, and all supervised, in this lovely Asolo, – my spot of predilection in the whole world, I think' (T. J. Collins, 'Letters from Robert Browning To the Rev. J. D. Williams, 1874–1889', *BIS* IV, 1976, 56). He posted the *MS.* from Asolo on 15 October 1889.

In July 1889 Browning said that his title was to be *A New Series of Jocoseria,* but he changed his mind about it, probably while staying near Mrs Katherine C. Bronson, his American friend, and her home, La Mura, in Asolo (see Mrs Bronson's 'Browning in Asolo', in *Century Magazine* LIX, 1900, 920–31) – Mrs Bronson's home in Venice, Cà Alvisi, is also alluded to in the dedication to her. In the dedication, Browning explains that his title-name is 'popularly ascribed to the inventiveness of the ancient secretary of Queen Cornaro whose palace-tower still overlooks us: *Asolare* – "to disport in the open air, amuse oneself at random." The objection that such a word nowhere occurs in the works of the Cardinal is hardly important – Bembo was too thorough a purist to conserve in print a term which in talk he might possibly toy with: but the word is more likely derived from a Spanish source.' Browning's title, like that of *Jocoseria,* is another punning one. Asolo Browning did indeed love; he called it 'the most beautiful spot I ever was privileged to see' (*New Letters,* 383), and had loved it since first seeing it, more than fifty years before, in 1838; *Pippa Passes* is set there, and Browning's son was to live and die there after his father's death. The Queen Cornaro of the dedication, alluded to in *Pippa Passes* II, 258, was Caterina Cornaro (*c.* 1454–1510), former Venetian Queen of Cyprus, who set up court in Asolo after abdicating in Cyprus. Her minister, Cardinal Pietro Bembo (1470–1547), the distinguished humanist, and historian of Venice, alluded to in *The Ring and the Book* VI, 1666, wrote dialogues on love which were called *Gli Asolani* (1505) after their setting (Browning owned a copy of a 1554 edition).

The poems are, as Browning says in the dedication, 'disconnected', and the volume neither aims at unity nor achieves it. The subtitle, *Fancies and Facts,* does however suggest a dominant theme in the volume – and indeed in Browning's works as a whole, where not only the words but the concepts they embody are so frequently opposed. Among Browning's works, *Jocoseria* is the nearest thing to *Asolando* in kind (though in quality *Asolando* is much superior). Readers have generally agreed that Browning's final volume is among the fresher and more youthful parts of his achievement.

PROLOGUE

First published in *Asolando,* where it is dated (as it is in *MS.*) 6 September 1889 from Asolo, shortly after Browning had arrived there. He had visited Asolo in 1838 and 1878. In a letter of 14 October 1889 Browning wrote: 'it is a strange experience that the impression I had in my first visit to this delightful place near fifty years ago . . . – strange that this impression of beauty should be confirmed if not heightened' (T. J. Collins, 'Letters from Robert Browning To the Rev. J. D. Williams',

BIS IV, 1976, 55–6). The poem inevitably reminds one of 'Tintern Abbey' and the 'Immortality Ode', and takes its place in a tradition of nineteenth-century poetry dealing with the theme of the loss of poetic vision and the compensating gain. In opposing fancy and fact (see, especially, 39) the poem is prelusive to its volume with its subtitle of *Fancies and Facts*.

4 *alien glow* Compare the 'celestial light' of the opening of Wordsworth's 'Immortality Ode': 'There was a time when meadow, grove, and stream,/The earth, and every common sight,/To me did seem/Apparelled in celestial light,/The glory and the freshness of a dream.'
5 *iris-bow* rainbow (Iris was goddess of the rainbow).
5–6 *iris-bow./And now a flower* The second verse-paragraph of the 'Immortality Ode' begins: 'The Rainbow comes and goes,/And lovely is the Rose' (10–11).
8 *uncinct* uncircled.
10 *glory* 'splendour' and 'halo'.
13 *chrysopras* golden-green precious stone.
22 *one step just from sea to land* Asolo is an easy journey from the port of Venice, thirty-odd miles away.
27–8 *Bush/Burning but unconsumed* 'And the angel of the Lord appeared unto him in a flame of fire out of the midst of a bush: and he looked, and, behold, the bush burned with fire, and the bush was not consumed' (Exodus iii 2). (The Voice of God then addresses Moses from the bush.)
39 *ken* sight.
44 *Nature*] nature *MS*. (revision made in proofs).

ROSNY

First published in *Asolando*. Mrs Orr (*Life*, 379) says it was written in December 1887; Miss Whiting (*The Brownings*, 267) says January 1888; it is undated in the *MS*. The titular hero is Maximilien de Béthune, Duke of Sully (1560–1641), known until 1606 as the Baron de Rosny, Rosny being the name of the chateau near Mantes, west of Paris, where the Duke was born. In the Battle of Ivry, just south of Mantes, he was wounded in 1590. The speaker, Clara, appears to be Browning's invention.

DUBIETY

First published in *Asolando*. The poem is undated in the *MS*., but seems to belong to the group of poems written at Asolo in September–October 1889. The 'woman' of 22 is presumably Mrs Browning. Here fact is superior to fancy.

12 *dreaming's*] dream's *MS*. (revised in proof).

NOW

First published in *Asolando*. DeVane (*Handbook*, 529) reports a *MS*. dated January 1888 (not seen for this edition). In the *MS*. of *Asolando*, the poem is undated. The motif of the 'infinite moment' is frequent in Browning.

HUMILITY

First published in *Asolando*; it is undated in the *MS*.

POETICS

First published in *Asolando*; it is undated in the *MS.*

SUMMUM BONUM

First published in *Asolando*; it is undated in the *MS.* The title means 'The Highest Good' (Latin). A debt to the second stanza of Jonson's 'Have you seen but a bright lily grow' from *The Devil is an Ass* II, vi, has been suggested (H. F. Brown in *Spectator*, 6 August 1921).

A PEARL, A GIRL

First published in *Asolando*; it is undated in the *MS.* The ring recalls the magical ring of Solomon in 'Abt Vogler' and 'Solomon and Balkis'.

SPECULATIVE

First published in *Asolando*; it is undated in the *MS.* The poem may refer to the poet's wish to be reunited with his wife.

WHITE WITCHCRAFT

First published in *Asolando.* The poem is undated in the *MS.* Mrs Orr (*Life*, 379) says the poem was suggested by a letter from a friend in the summer of 1888 which spoke of the huge number of toads in the Channel Islands. DeVane suggests (*Handbook*, 531) that the poem belongs to the autumn of 1888 when Browning had met a fox at Primiero in the Dolomites. The title refers to witchcraft that practises only white magic, in which the Devil is not invoked.

2 *play Jove* Jove frequently disguised himself as an animal.
3 *stealer of the grapes* In The Song of Solomon ii 15, foxes spoil the vines for the tender grapes. The fable of Aesop about the fox and the grapes seems inappropriate as a point of reference here.
7 *Canidia* Horace's name for a sorceress in *Epodes* V and XVII. In V she uses as a poison the 'gore of a loathsome toad'; in XVII Canidia will use her magic only to increase the love of the aged decrepit Horace.
8 *pearl beneath his puckered brow* The toad traditionally (as in *As You Like It* II. 1. 13–14) wears a jewel in its head.

BAD DREAMS

The four rather obscure poems published first in *Asolando* under the title 'Bad Dreams' are undated in the *MS.* Mrs Orr (*Life*, 379) thinks that two or three of them were written in the winter of 1887–8. Mrs Bloomfield-Moore, Browning's American friend, remarked that 'Bad Dreams' was a poem 'no one can understand so well as myself' (quoted by Miller, *Robert Browning*, 268), but the implications of the remark are not clear.

32 *trulls* strumpets.
62 *Giaours* infidels.

108 *Hannah More* author, bluestocking, moralist, philanthropist (1745–1833).
124 *cicatrice* scar.
142 *erst* formerly (archaism).

INAPPREHENSIVENESS

First published in *Asolando.* The *MS.* is undated, but the poem surely belongs to Browning's visit to Mrs Bronson in Asolo in September–October 1889. In a letter of 8 October 1889 Browning said he found the Turret (the Asolo castle) 'rather the worse for careful weeding' (McAleer, *Learned Lady,* 202), with which one may compare line 13 here. The poem may well record a real experience with Mrs Bronson, as Mrs Miller suggests (*Robert Browning,* 277–8).

12 *Ruskin* The great writer (1819–1900) had been publishing his autobiography, *Praeterita,* at intervals between 1885 and 1889.
32 *Vernon Lee* pseudonym of Violet Paget (1856–1935), essayist and novelist.

WHICH?

First published in *Asolando.* The *MS.* is undated, and DeVane's reason for suggesting the probability of 1888 (*Handbook*, 534) is unconvincing.

15 *paladin* knightly hero.
20 *losel* worthless person (archaism).

THE CARDINAL AND THE DOG

First published in *Asolando.* The poem was written, probably in 1840, for Willie Macready, oldest son of the actor, to illustrate (the illustrations are in the Armstrong Browning Library – see *BNL*, No. 3, 1969, 34–5, 42). (Later, Browning gave the boy 'The Pied Piper' to illustrate.) In *The Bookman* XLII, May 1912, 68, there is a facsimile version of the poem in the hand of Browning's father; DeVane believes (*Handbook,* 535) that the text is the poet's earlier draft. That it was the version given to Willie Macready is suggested by the fact that lines 5 and 15 do not appear in it. The original version divided the lines in two, and had the date (line 2) right: 1552. The source was Wanley's *Wonders of the Little World* (611): 'Crescentius the Popes Legate at the Council of Trent 1552. March 25. was busie writing of Letters to the Pope till it was far in the night, whence rising to refresh himself, he saw a black Dog of a vast bigness, flaming eyes, ears that hung down almost to the ground enter the room, which came directly towards him, and laid himself down under the table. Frighted at the sight, he called his Servants in the Antichamber, commanded them to look for the Dog, but they could find none. The Cardinal fell melancholy, thence sick, and died at Verona: on his death-bed he cryed out to drive away the Dog that leaped upon his bed.' Crescenzio was President of the Council of Trent considering the question of Protestantism, about which the Cardinal was inflexible. In March 1552 he was ill and tired when, as the legend – probably Protestant – has it, he saw the traditional harbinger of death; he died 1 June 1552 at Verona, fancy having become fact.

THE POPE AND THE NET

First published in *Asolando*. The *MS*. is undated and the date uncertain, but the poem was probably written in 1888 or 1889. No Pope since Saint Peter has been a fisherman or a son of one, and the story is probably Browning's, though the mock-humility may well have derived from Gregorio Leti's *Life of Pope Sixtus the Fifth*. Sixtus (1585–90), of humble birth and the hero of 'The Bean-Feast', was extremely weak and decrepit until the moment he was elected Pope, and fancy gave way to fact.

2 *Conclave* the gathering to elect a new Pope.
8 *Saint Peter's net* Peter was a fisherman.
9 *sword and keys* Papal insignia (John xviii 10; Matthew xvi 19 – Peter's sword and the Keys of the Kingdom).
19 *sacred slipper* the Papal slipper, which has a cross embroidered on it.

THE BEAN-FEAST

First published in *Asolando*. The *MS*. is undated; the poem probably belongs to 1888 or 1889. Browning seems to have founded his story on one about Sixtus V (Pope 1585–90), perhaps the model also for the preceding poem, in a translation (1754) of Leti's *Life of Pope Sixtus the Fifth*: 'Another time, as he pass'd through the city, seeing the gates of that Convent open, he suddenly got out of his chariot, and went into the Porter's lodge, where he found the Porter, who was a Lay-brother, eating a plate of beans with oil poured over them. As the meanness of the repast put him in mind of his former condition [Sixtus had been a swineherd], he took a wooden spoon, and sitting down close to the porter, on a stair-case, first ate one platter full with him and then another, to the great surprise of those that were with him: After he had thank'd the Lay-brother for his entertainment, he turn'd to his attendants, and said, "We shall live two years longer for this; for we have eat with an appetite, and without fear or suspicion." And then, lifting up his eyes to Heaven, said, "The Lord be prais'd for permitting a Pope, once in his life, to make a meal in peace and quietness" ' (299).

34 *tippet* a band worn by priests around the neck, with the two ends hanging in front.

MUCKLE-MOUTH MEG

First published in *Asolando*. The *MS*. is undated, but the poem probably belongs about June 1889: an unpublished letter to Browning in the *MS*. of *Asolando* shows he had told the story himself a few days or so before 19 July 1889. The story (involving an ugly Meg with, indeed, a huge mouth) is well known, and deals with ancestors of Sir Walter Scott, who himself told the story in *Tales of a Grandfather* XXXVII; Lockhart also told it in his *Life of Sir Walter Scott*. Browning himself said that he thought the incident legendary, not historical, and that he got it from Jowett, who got it from Lady Stewart (*Diary of Miss Evelyn Barclay, Baylor University Browning Interests*, Fifth series, 1932, 35–6). 'Muckle' is a Scotticism, and means 'huge'. The English lord was called William Scott, and the Scottish laird was Sir Gideon Murray of Elibank. In this poem, ugly fancy gives way to fair fact.

3 *chiel* fellow (Scotticism).
7 *callant* lad (Scotticism).

16 *'it rains' soon succeed to 'it thunders'* Browning may have had in mind the comment attributed to Socrates after his wife had first scolded him and then doused him with dirty water: 'After thunder, there generally follows rain.'
21 *parritch* porridge (Scotticism).
31 *bubblyjock* turkey-cock (Scotticism).
35 *just for a dowry your can* In Scott's telling of the story, the lady was 'without any tocher' (without dowry).
can power (Scotticism).
39 *Minnikin* diminutive (also a playful and endearing term for a female).

ARCADES AMBO

First published in *Asolando*. The *MS.* is undated, but the poem probably belongs to 1888 or 1889 (DeVane suggests 27 August 1889, on which date Browning gave his support to an anti-vivisectionist hospital – *Handbook,* 539). The title comes from Vergil, *Eclogues* VII, 4, to which Browning had alluded in 'Pambo', 50, and which means 'Both Arcadians', and by modern extension, 'two people of similar tastes or habits'. Browning was an anti-vivisectionist; compare 'Tray'.

14 *shoots* twinges.

THE LADY AND THE PAINTER

First published in *Asolando*. The *MS.* is undated, but the poem was composed on a drive from Bassano to Asolo in September or October 1889. Mrs Bronson asked him what had inspired it, and Browning replied: 'Well, . . . the birds twittering in the trees suggested it to me. You know I don't like women to wear those wings in their bonnets' (Katherine C. Bronson, 'Browning in Asolo', *Century Magazine* LIX, 1900, 923). Browning had earlier, notably in 'With Francis Furini', attacked those who objected to nudes in art, and he was always a friend of animals and birds.

PONTE DELL'ANGELO, VENICE

First published in *Asolando*. The poem is dated 9 January 1889 in the *MS*. Browning had stayed with Mrs Bronson in Venice in November–December 1888, and had burrowed in Tassini's *Curiosità Veneziane* (1863), a book explaining the origins of the names of bridges and streets in Venice and detailing histories and legends of its palaces. There he found a story of 1552 in Tassini's account of the Ponte dell' Angelo (Bridge of the Angel) – for a translation, see DeVane, *Handbook,* 541–2. Tassini led Browning to the *Annales* (1632–9) of Father Boverio (1568–1638), historian of the Capuchins, alluded to in lines 184–5. He heard the legend also from Mrs Bronson's gondolier, Luigi (see K. de K. Bronson, 'Browning in Venice', *Century Magazine,* LXIII, 1902, 579).

12 *hitch into verse* 'Slides into verse, and hitches into rhyme' (Pope, *Horatian Satires* II, i, 79). Compare *The Ring and the Book* VIII, 149, and *Prince Hohenstiel-Schwangau,* 544.
19] The line provides a particularly good example of the fact that Browning controlled his own punctuation. The printers added commas before 'growled' and after 'he' to the readings in the *MS.*; in proof Browning deleted these commas.
23 *ad rem* 'to the point' (Latin).

28 *Ate, drank and made merry* Ecclesiastes viii 15; Luke xii 19.
32 *the word has escaped my teeth* a frequent Homeric formula – see, for example, *Odyssey* I, 64.
43 *fructuous* fruitful, profitable.
49 *Matteo da Bascio* He was in fact the founder of the order of friars known as the Capuchin (founded 1525–8).
51 *suffumigate* the word, described as 'very rare' by *OED*, means 'fumigate from below'; Browning appears to use it as a synonym for 'fumigate'.
54 *grate*] gate *MS.* (revised to 'grate' in proof) – compare this edition's emendation in 'Donald', 234.
72 *guttles* gormandizes.
75 *loathly* loathsome (poeticism).
81 *perdue* hidden.
109 *losel* worthless fellow (archaism).
112 *biter is bit* proverbial.
151 *Sin no more* John v 14; viii 11.
154 *purlieus* haunts.
Father of Lies Satan.
173 *erst* formerly (archaism).

BEATRICE SIGNORINI

First published in *Asolando.* Mrs Orr (*Life*, 379) says the poem was written early in 1888, and Whiting (*The Brownings,* 267) agrees; but the *MS.* is dated 23 April 1889.

The materials come from accounts in that important source for Browning, Filippo Baldinucci's *Notizie de' Professori del Disegno*: those of Francesco Romanelli (1617–62) and Artemisia Gentileschi (1597–*c.*1652), the latter account providing the particular story told in 'Beatrice Signorini' (for a translation of the relevant pages, see DeVane, *Handbook*, 544). Romanelli and his wife Beatrice Signorini seem to have been most attractive people. Artemisia Gentileschi is better known. She specialized in portraits, nudes and flowers. Her father, Orazio Gentileschi, is also well known; both spent time in England.

Browning told Evelyn Barclay that he thought 'Beatrice Signorini' the best poem in *Asolando*. The relevance of the volume's subtitle to the poem is apparent.

2 *Viterbo* Romanelli's birthplace is about forty miles north-west of Rome.
4 *Cortona* town in Tuscany.
5–6 *Pietro Berretini . . . Cortona* Pietro Berrettini da Cortona (1596–1669), painter and architect.
17–24 *'Desire' . . . hang his book and him* Baldinucci writes of the Gentileschi picture of the nude *Desire* painted to commemorate the achievements of Michelangelo Buonarroti. Baldinucci records that he suggested the nakedness be covered, and it was. Browning valued the nude in art.
26–7 *The blossom . . . blooming* Gentileschi was twenty years older than Romanelli. Browning omits the fact she was married.
38 *Artistry's haunting curse – the Incomplete* a characteristic Browning theme, the curse being seen generally as a blessing.
53 *conceited* fancied.
79 *Guido* Gentileschi studied under Guido Reni (1575–1642), the Bolognese painter.
111 *acromion* outer extremity of the shoulder blade.

118 *motors, flexors* muscles.
119 *Ser Santi* Santi di Tito (1536–1603), Tuscan artist, was given his nickname by Titian.
122 *Titian* the greatest Venetian artist (*c.* 1490–1576).
145 *Bicé* abbreviation of Beatricé.
159 *paint the human figure* Romanelli did not paint nudes, and thus drew Baldinucci's praise for avoiding obscenity.
161 *idlesse* idleness viewed romantically (archaism).
flowers Historically, fruit was Gentileschi's speciality.
186 *book* not identified, though it sounds like Wanley.
198–203 Browning seems to refer 'to a fairly common type of Mogul picture showing individuals intertwined to make up animals and so on' (M. Peckham, in *BNL*, No. 7, 1971, 45).
251–2 *Calypso . . . Penelope* The 'guest' is Ulysses, whom Romanelli painted. Penelope was his wife, Calypso the nymph who detained him.
268–9] *a late addition to the MS.*
299 *mouse-ear* probably the blue forget-me-not.
auricula kind of primula.
302 *pink saxifrage* Beatrice and Browning were probably thinking of the white saxifrage.
307 *spilla* 'pin' (Italian). In the source Romanelli is absent when Beatrice destroys the portrait.
325 *occulted* hidden.

FLUTE-MUSIC, WITH AN ACCOMPANIMENT

First published in *Asolando*. The poem was dated by Mrs Orr (*Life*, 379) in January 1888, and Miss Whiting (*The Brownings*, 269) attributes it to early 1888. In the *MS.* the date has been heavily deleted, but while the day and month are illegible, the year is clearly 1889. The indications of speaker were not in *MS.* and were added in proof. Fact and fancy are clearly opposed in the poem.

9 *insuppressive* insuppressible ('very rare' – *OED*).
47 *Trefoil* clover.
63 *Quid petis* 'What do you seek' (Latin).
71–2 *Breath . . . porridge* 'To keep one's breath to cool one's porridge' is proverbial.
73 *Tulou* Jean-Louis Tulou (1786–1865), leading French flautist, and composer for the flute.
78 *familiar* close acquaintance.
82–4 *legato . . . staccato* opposites, the former with a smooth connection between the notes, the latter with breaks between notes.
93 *capture*] *this edition*; captive *MS.*, *1889*. (The rhyme is needed. Fairly clearly, Browning's transcription of his draft was inaccurate.)
106 *Gounod* Charles Gounod, French composer (1818–93), wrote a *Romeo and Juliet* (1867).
132 *caldamente* 'with warmth' (musical).
162 *Rathe* early.
169 *Aquarius* the constellation ('Water-bearer') associated with rainy weather.
180 *flexile* flexible.

'IMPERANTE AUGUSTO NATUS EST–'

First published in *Asolando*. The *MS*. is undated; the poem probably belongs to 1888 or 1889.

With its interest in the Christian impact on the classical world, the work is a kind of companion to 'An Epistle . . . of Karshish' and 'Cleon'. This poem is set in 2 B.C. The title means 'He was born, Augustus regnant', the 'He' being Christ. Augustus is Octavius Caesar (63 B.C.–A.D. 14), first Roman Emperor. The poem's main source is the life of Augustus in *The Lives of the Caesars* (*c*. 121) of Suetonius, and most of the poem's mass of detail comes from that work: the buildings and other public works, the physical appearance of the Emperor and his annual begging, and so on. The senator who speaks and the Publius spoken to are Browning's inventions.

8 *Lucius Varius Rufus* Augustan poet of importance in his day (*c*. 74–14 B.C.), author of a *Panegyric*, not extant, on Augustus. His appearing is an anachronism.
11 *little Flaccus* Horatius Flaccus (Horace), who was short and fat. Another anachronism; Horace's dates are 65–8 B.C.
12 *Epos* epic.
15 *offshoot of Etruscan kings* Leading Roman families liked to trace their ancestry back to the Etruscans, the most significant people in Italy until the ascendancy of Rome.
16 *Maecenas* friend and counsellor of Augustus, Vergil's patron, plutocrat, friend of Varius and Horace. He died in 8 B.C.
17 *quadrans* a small coin, the price of a bath in Horace.
Thermae baths. The huge major community centre.
21 *new divinity* 'Augustus' means 'Consecrated in the Augury'; the Emperor was afforded divine honours.
34–69 The details are from Suetonius.
40 *Marcellus* nephew of Augustus (42–23 B.C.).
52 *Father of his Country* Augustus became *pater patriae* in 2 B.C.
56 *thirty* twenty-eight in Suetonius.
57 *'marble now, brick once'* Suetonius says of Rome that Augustus 'could justly boast that he had found it built of brick and left it in marble'.
69 *earth-upholding Mount* Mount Atlas in north-west Africa. Atlas, the Titan, held the heavens on his shoulders.
73 *Nearly as good as Varius* Varius Rufus was highly acclaimed. His works have perished, and he is best known as the editor of Vergil's *Aeneid*.
82 *conceit* conception.
91 *Innumerous* innumerable (poeticism).
94 *Fulgurant* flashing like lightning.
104 *Suburra* Subura: valley and district in Rome, notorious for dirt, bustle and shady morality.
109–10 *Quaestor . . . Aedile, Censor . . . Praetor* city officers.
Pol by Pollux; truly.
113 *quarter-as* small coin; same as quadrans (17).
120–22 Suetonius notes the tawny hair, the 'clear bright eyes', the eyebrows that meet, and a nose which 'projected a little at top and then bent slightly inward'.
126–30 'It was likewise because of a dream that every year on an appointed day he begged alms of the people, holding out his open hand to have pennies dropped into it' (Suetonius, XCI).

139–51 In a Triumph, a victorious general rode to the Temple of Jupiter on the Capitoline Hill. An attendant slave, whose presence was in part designed to avert the evil eye, held a gold crown of Jupiter over the triumphator's head (for which, in fact, it was too heavy). Further to ward off the evil eye, a scourge, bell and amulet (*fascinum*) were attached to the chariot.
155 *predecessor* Cronus.
157 *grey Sibyl* probably the Erythraean Sibyl. In the *Sibylline Oracles* III, 55–60, and VIII, 211, the coming of a Messiah is prophesied.
163 *strigils* scrapers for use in baths.
oil-drippers Romans oiled their skin after a bath.

DEVELOPMENT

First published in *Asolando*. The poem is undated in the *MS.*, but probably belongs to 1888 or 1889.

The account of Browning's education in Homer is essentially accurate, though Sarianna Browning denied that it was specifically so. Browning was always devoted to Homer, but the poem is 'about' much more than reading Homer, alluding as it does to the Biblical (as well as classical) Higher Criticism and its 'unsettling one's belief' (65), and reminding one of much in 'A Death in the Desert', especially in its stress on the need to conceive of man as developing animal; and again bearing on educational theory, on the theme of 'Transcendentalism', and on the relation of fiction and fancy to fact (see, especially, 72–7) in a way that recalls Browning statements in *The Ring and the Book* in particular.

6 *Priam* king of Troy.
7–8 *Helen . . . Paris* Paris, son of Priam, abducted Helen, wife of Menelaus, and precipitated the Trojan War.
11 *Atreidai* sons of Atreus: Menelaus, and Agamemnon, king of Mycenae.
13 *Achilles* The greatest Greek warrior sulks in his tent through much of the *Iliad*.
15 *Hector* the greatest Trojan warrior, killed by Achilles after the death of his friend, Patroclus, drove him into action again.
30 *Pope* Alexander Pope's translation of the *Iliad* appeared 1715–20.
43 *Buttmann* Philipp Karl Buttmann (1764–1829), German scholar and author of a Greek Grammar.
46 *Heine* Christian Gottlob Heyne (1729–1812), editor of a standard *Iliad* (1802).
57 *Seven cities* traditionally, 'Seven wealthy towns contend for Homer dead,/ Through which the living Homer begg'd his bread' (Thomas Seward, *On Homer*, 1738).
57–8 *Scio . . . Thinks Byron* Scio is one of the traditional seven cities. In *The Bride of Abydos* II, 27, Byron refers to the 'blind old man of Scio's rocky isle'.
58 *Hymns* The *Homeric Hymns* are now known not to be by Homer.
59 *"Battle of the Frogs and Mice"* mock-heroic Greek poem, involving burlesques of the *Iliad*, at one time attributed to Homer.
60 *dig "Margites" up* The lost Greek comic poem was thought by Aristotle to be Homer's.
64 *Wolf* Friedrich August Wolf (1759–1824), author of the *Prolegomena in Homerum* I (1795), argued that the *Iliad* and *Odyssey* were handed down in an oral tradition and that multiple authorship was involved.
81 *Spouse* Andromache.

82 *Friend* Patroclus.
84 *Browning*] someone *MS. first reading.*
99 *forthrights* straight courses (archaism).
forthrights not meanderings 'forthrights and meanders' (*Tempest* III. 3. 3).
100 *Peleus' son* Achilles. The unconventional reference to his loathing a lie is presumably to his resentment at Agamemnon's breach of faith in depriving him of Briseis.
106 *'Ethics'* Aristotle's *Nicomachean Ethics.*
113 *Stagirite* Aristotle, born at Stagira.

REPHAN

First published in *Asolando*. Undated in the *MS.*, the poem probably belongs to 1888 or 1889.

The title comes from Acts vii 43, with its reference to 'the star of your god Remphan' ('Rephan' in the Roman version). The name, there that of a false god, seems to mean 'Saturn'. The source for the poem, as Browning indicates in his note, is a story of Jane Taylor (of Ongar, not Norwich – Browning was probably thinking of William Taylor of Norwich). Jane Taylor (1783–1824), author of 'Twinkle, twinkle, little star', wrote 'How It Strikes a Stranger' (in *Contributions of Q. Q.*, 1824), which suggested this poem and the title of 'How It Strikes a Contemporary'. Browning gives the name to the star from which the stranger comes, and shifts the emphasis of the story by focusing on the perfection (which, as usual in Browning, is really no perfection at all) of Rephan, something that Miss Taylor had left to implication, her focus having been on the stranger's obsession with earning immortality. For further details of the source, see DeVane, *Handbook*, 550–51. On Browning's conclusion, DeVane suggests the influence of Herbert's conclusion to 'The Pulley'.

13 *perpend* ponder (archaism).
20 *vastitude* vast space.
49 *Each rose sole rose*] Nay, rose the sole *MS.* (revised in proof).
74 *floreted* made up of little flowers (into a compound flower).
97–102] Enough, for you know, you hope, ye men,
You fear, you agonize here: what then?
Is an end to your love's work out of ken?

Have you no assurance that, at end,
Wrong will be right? Who made shall mend
In the higher sphere to which longings tend? *MS.* (revised in proof).
99 *ken* sight.

REVERIE

First published in *Asolando*. The *MS.* date was erased. DeVane (*Handbook*, 552) thinks it looks like 14 October 1889 – the day before Browning posted his *MS.*; the present editor thinks it looks like 14 February 1889. On the poem see Drew, *Poetry of Browning*, 170–74.

The poem reminds one of much in Browning's thought, especially perhaps of much in 'Rabbi Ben Ezra'. The temptation to see the poem as intended as a kind of last testament on subjects of central import in Browning's philosophy is irresistible.

64 *Earth's*] All *MS.* (revised in proof).
105 *dizen* adorn.
134 *unamerced* unpunished.
156–7 'In the beginning God created the heaven and the earth' (Genesis i 1).
167 *hailed the*] equalled *MS.* (revised in proof).
178 *rathe* poeticism for 'early' (here with the sense of 'unripe').
180 *scathe* injury.
182 *leaven the lump* 1 Corinthians v 6.
187–8 *clay . . . potter's act* 'we are the clay, and thou our potter' (Isaiah lxiv 8). Reminders of 'Rabbi Ben Ezra' are especially strong here.
189 *whelmed* overwhelmed.
194 *Throe*] Glory *MS.* (revised in proof).

EPILOGUE

First published in *Asolando*. The poem is undated. It presumably belongs to 1888 or 1889, and has all the markings of a final testament about Browning's feelings. The *Pall Mall Gazette* of 1 February 1890 records that 'one evening, just before his death-illness, the poet was reading this [the third stanza] from a proof to his daughter-in-law and sister. He said: "It almost sounds like bragging to say this, and as if I ought to cancel it; but it's the simple truth; and as it's true, it shall stand."'

3 *fools*] you *MS. first reading.*
11 *marched*] put *MS. first reading.*

Poems uncollected by Browning, fugitives, and previously unpublished poems and fragments

The verses printed here, in an order designed to approximate that of composition, include lines printed at various periods of Browning's life over a period of nearly seventy years. Most of them are trivial, but some are of real quality: 'Aeschylus' Soliloquy', 'Helen's Tower', 'To Edward FitzGerald', for example. Some are fun: 'On Correggio', 'Impromptu on Richard Wagner', 'Terse Verse'. Others, while fairly powerless as poetry, throw light on more important aspects of Browning's achievement: some of the childhood verses, or 'Why I am a Liberal'.

Some verses, as stated in the Preface, remain to be collected. Some verses that have been attributed to Browning are here excluded. Among them are: (a) a couplet, almost certainly not Browning's, which has been reputed to be Browning's first poem, recited before he could read (Griffin and Minchin, *Life*, 30): 'Good people all who wish to see/A boy take physic, look at me'; (b) 'On Louvel's Reply' (by Browning's father); (c) two poems in Domett's volume of 1833 that Domett attributes to a friend: 'The Voice of the Pestilence' and 'Night: A Fragment'; (d) 'A Miniature' (in fact, by Mrs Watts-Jones); (e) 'To My Critics' (judged by DeVane and the present editor not to be Browning's): see the note to 'Of Pacchiarotto'; (f) a quatrain attributed to Browning and said to be in his hand and from the Flower Collection in G. Michelmore's Catalogue 21: 'And who is the bard/With his sad locks flowing?/Alfred! – on whom/To write we're going!'; (g) a couplet parodying

Watts 'told to' Sarianna by her brother, and printed in *Works and Days from the Journal of Michael Field,* John Murray, 1933, 209.

Most of the verses that follow have been previously published but not previously collected. Wherever possible, the texts printed here are based on manuscripts.

Some previously unpublished verses were published in *Cornhill Magazine* and in *New Poems* (1914), after the *MSS.* had become available at the Sotheby, Wilkinson and Hodge sale in May 1913. W. Whitla printed and edited six fugitives in *Six Stray Verses,* privately printed in an edition of twenty at Oxford, 1966; three of these and one other appeared in *N&Q*, new series XXI, 1974, 448–53. Also important is the gathering and editing of P. Honan in 'The Texts of Fifteen Fugitives by Robert Browning', *VP* V, 1967, 157–69 (of the items about which he says 'more information is needed', A and B are in the Armstrong Browning Library of Baylor University – the present editor may not print them; C and D have not been located; and E is by Mrs Watts-Jones, not Browning).

[CONCLUSION OF A COMPLIMENT TO THE CAPTAIN]

First published in Griffin and Minchin, *Life*, 29, and composed about 1821. The lines are recorded in Alfred Domett's *Diary* (ed. E. A. Horsman, 1953), 73. Domett says that Browning told him that, at the age of eight or nine, 'he made a copy of verses, which he remembered to this day and "great *bosh* they were", intended to ingratiate himself with the Master', Reverend Thomas Ready, of the school in Peckham that Browning attended. Browning quoted the two lines as the conclusion. The lines have not previously been collected.

THE FIRST-BORN OF EGYPT

First published by Bertram Dobell in January 1914 in *Cornhill Magazine* XXXVI, 1914, 4–5; and reprinted in *New Poems,* 1914, 3–7, and collected in the Macmillan edition (1915). The text is doubtless hopelessly corrupt; the present one is based on the *Cornhill* printing and on the copy of a letter from Sarah Flower transcribing the poem in the hand of Bertram Dobell which is now in the Library of the University of Toronto.

The poem is one of two survivors from the volume *Incondita* that Browning put together at the age of fourteen, hoping for publication. Like 'The Dance of Death', the poem probably dates from 1826. Unable to find a publisher, Browning apparently destroyed the *MS.* However, his friend, Sarah Flower, had transcribed the poems into an album (later destroyed), and sent a copy of the poem and 'The Dance of Death' in a letter of 31 May 1827 to her guardian W. J. Fox. The letter survived to provide Dobell with the text he used in 1914.

The poem's source is Exodus xi 4–10, xii 1–33.

14 *Circean sleep* Circe was the sorceress, skilled with drugs, who turned the men of Odysseus into swine.

20 *harpy* the winged monster of classical myth that contaminated anything that came near it.

THE DANCE OF DEATH

First published by Bertram Dobell in January 1914 in *Cornhill Magazine* XXXVI, 1914, 6–8, and reprinted in *New Poems,* 1914, 8–12, and collected in the Macmillan edition (1915). The present text is based on the *Cornhill* one with the odd reading from the copy of Sarah Flower's letter transcribing the poem, which is in the hand of Bertram Dobell, and is now in the Library of the University of Toronto. The poem probably dates from 1826, and was preserved by Sarah Flower's letter of 31 May 1827 – see the note to the preceding poem.

It is often said to be indebted to Coleridge's 'Fire, Famine and Slaughter'. The motto attributed to Mme de Staël (1766–1817) has not been located.

3 *simoom* hot sand-wind.
12 *Cynthia* Artemis (Diana), goddess of the moon.
37 *Erinyes* Furies.
47 *Grecian* Leander, drowned while swimming the Hellespont to visit Hero, who then drowned herself.
54 *algid* chilly (especially of the chill of ague).
65 *crocodiles'*] *Dobell transcript*; tiger's *all texts.*
stream] *Dobell transcript*; jungle's lair *all texts.*
85 *ianthine* violet-coloured.
89 *Juno* wife of Jupiter and queen of the gods.
90 *Grecian* Pygmalion fell in love with his ivory statue, which came alive as Galatea and loved him.
92 *Hebe* The daughter of the king and queen of the gods could restore youth and vigour.
96 *scathed* injured (archaism, Scotticism).

[EPIGRAM ON SCHOOL DAYS]

First published in 1953 in E. A. Horsman's edition of *The Diary of Alfred Domett*, 74. In his entry for 7 February 1873 Domett wrote: 'Browning made some remark expressive of the digust with which he always thought of the place [the Ready school at Peckham], and added, "I made an epigram one day upon it." As far as I remember it was to the following effect (the last line I know word for word)' – Domett goes on to cite the lines, noting that Browning used a 'suddenly deepened tone' for the last line. The text is clearly unlikely to be accurate, especially since Domett is recalling lines recited 'once in the days of our early acquaintance' from over thirty years earlier, remembered in turn, Domett reports, by Browning from some earlier period. The lines, which have not hitherto been collected, probably date from about 1827.

1 *those*] *British Library transcript, this edition*; these *Diary.*
house of glass The school had a garden and greenhouse attached to it.
2 *three* Domett puts a question mark after the word. Browning attended school in Peckham for about five years.

IMPROMPTU ON HEARING A SERMON BY THE REV. T. R— PRONOUNCED 'HEAVY'

First published in 1891 in Orr, *Life*, 56; the epigram was written in March 1833, the date of the letter of Browning to W. J. Fox (now in the Huntington Library) in which the lines appear, and from which the present text is printed. The lines have not hitherto been collected. The Rev. Thomas Ready was the Master of Browning's school at Peckham.

SONNET

['Eyes, calm beside thee, (Lady couldst thou know!)']

First published in *The Monthly Repository,* new series VIII, October 1834, 712. It was signed 'Z.' as were some other poems of Browning published about the same time, and was dated 17 August 1834. It has frequently been reprinted and collected. Griffin and Minchin, *Life*, 309, suggest that the sonnet was addressed to Eliza Flower, Browning's friend, perhaps the model for Pauline, and the ward of W. J. Fox, editor of *The Monthly Repository.*

[LINES TO THE MEMORY OF JAMES DOW]

The poem first appeared upon the gravestone of James Dow, M.D. (1776–9 October 1832) in the additional burying-ground of Saint Mary's Church, Barnsley, Yorkshire, source of the text printed here. In its present form, the poem was first published by E. G. Bayford in *N&Q* CXCIII, 1948, 248–9. A version of the poem was printed from the *MS.* in the hand of Sarianna Browning (now in the University of Toronto Library) in *Cornhill Magazine* XXXVI, February 1914, 145, by F. G. Kenyon, who included it the same year in *New Poems,* 30. That version, collected in the Macmillan edition (1915), uses the first person singular instead of the first person plural, and is six lines shorter; it appeared as 'Lines to the Memory of His Parents' (1866), and was thought to be prompted by the death of Browning's father. The title used in the present edition is that suggested by DeVane, *Handbook,* 556. In its proper form, the poem has not hitherto been collected.

DeVane dates the lines in 1832, but J. Maynard (*VP* XIV, 1976, 67–9) has shown that it is altogether likely that they date in fact from 1836 or early 1837. They were requested by William Alexander Dow, a lawyer to whose son Browning became godfather late in 1837 (see notes to 'A Forest Thought'). Macready recorded in his *Diary* for 20 March 1837: 'Browning related an amusing story of his [Dow's] application to him for an epitaph on his father – to which, when Browning had promised it, he added his mother, her [in fact, Dow's] sister, and an infant two years old; and subsequently, on receiving the report of the marble-mason of Barnsley, wished two more lines to be added to the complete epitaph as the stone would hold two more!'

1 *we* William Alexander Dow and Margaret Dow, children of James Dow.
7–10] They lie beside thee whom thou lovedst most; *Toronto MS*; They lay beside thee whom thou lovest most; *Cornhill*; They lie beside thee whom thou lovest most; *New Poems.*
13 *Mother* Sarah Dow (1775–1828).
14–16] *not in MS., Cornhill, New Poems.*
17 *Child that never knew you* Edward James Dow died in 1810 before he was ten months old.
Girl Sarah Helen Dow (1805–22).
18 *soul*] souls *Toronto MS., Cornhill, New Poems.*
19–20] Perhaps a later addition as suggested by Macready's diary entry.

A FOREST THOUGHT

First published in *Country Life* XVII, 10 June 1905, 797, with a facsimile of part of the *MS.*; and often reprinted and collected. There is a *MS.* in the hand of Sarianna

Browning in the Library of the University of Toronto, which includes the note: 'Written and inscribed to W. A. and A. D. by their sincere friend R. B.' The *MS.* s dated 4 November 1837, when Browning was godfather to the eldest son of his friend William Alexander Dow (see note to ['Lines to the Memory of James Dow']). The introduction to the poem in *Country Life* states: 'On returning to the house after the christening, Browning went into a room by himself and there wrote the poem and handed it to the parents.' The poem seems clearly to include memories of Browning's journey to Saint Petersburg in March–April 1834.

50 *grace*] *Toronto MS., this edition*; peace *all texts.*
52 *cushat-dove* wood-pigeon or ring-dove.

[TRANSCRIPTIONS FROM THE 'ANACREONTEA']

Of the eleven 'transcriptions', the first ten have not previously been printed, while the eleventh was first printed in 1936 in the Catalogue for Sale 4249 (the H. B. Smith Collection) of the American Art Association–Anderson Galleries. None of the verses has previously been collected.

The first ten of these transcriptions appear in Browning's hand in a *MS.* in the Houghton Library of Harvard University (MS Eng 865), in what is obviously a fair copy, one made in the tiny handwriting that Browning sometimes affected; a few words are difficult to read, and the occasional punctuation mark needs to be supplied. In the Houghton *MS.* each of the translations is preceded by the Greek first line of the verses being translated (at the end of the *MS.*, Browning notes 'Transcribed from Anacreon'). In the Sotheby sale of 1913, Lot 187 included a *MS.* of 'You ought to sit on the safety-valve', the draft of 'She was fifteen – had great eyes', and 'translations of songs or epigrams from Anacreon'.

The date of Browning's translations is unknown, but it seems reasonable to attribute them to 1845: (a) they are the kind of verses that a young lover would find congenial; (b) the handwriting and the spellings of Greek names are those of the younger Browning; (c) in [IX], 15, the *MS.* has the two-dot ellipsis characteristic of the young Browning; (d) both Browning and Elizabeth Barrett were steeped in the *Anacreontics*: Browning's father reportedly used the songs as lullabies for his young son (*Catalogue ... of the late R. W. B. Browning ...* sold by James Tregaskis, London, 9 June 1913, 8), and Browning retained his father's copy of the *Odes* (Lot 333 of *The Browning Collections*), while Miss Barrett had also been brought up on Anacreon (see, for instance, her letters of 1828 and 1832 in B. P. McCarthy, ed. *Elizabeth Barrett to Mr. Boyd,* John Murray, 1955, 52 and 161–2, where she writes, of verses later translated by Browning [II and IX]; and her translation of Anacreon in F. G. Kenyon, ed., *Letters of Elizabeth Barrett Browning,* Smith, Elder, 1897, I, 263). Doubtless the *Anacreontea* were discussed during the courtship at Wimpole Street: writing to Miss Barrett on 31 March 1845, Browning alludes to Anacreon and to contemporary scholarship, which was then showing that the verses attributed to the Ionian poet (sixth century B.C.) were in fact products of several centuries.

The lyrics of Anacreon and his imitators have strongly influenced English literature and have often been translated, by Cowley and Herrick among others. The skilful verse translations of J. M. Edmonds in the Loeb Classical Library (1931) help to measure the competence of Browning's rather freer and lengthier transcriptions. The titles of the present edition are the Loeb titles (with one exception, [IX], where Edmonds translates 'cricket' rather than 'grasshopper').

[I]: 23c among the Loeb *Anacreontea*.
1–2 *I fain . . . banqueting* that is, the poet would fain sing of heroic subjects. Cadmus was the legendary founder of Thebes, and Agamemnon and Menelaus were sons (or grandsons) of Atreus, king of Argos, whose most celebrated banquet was that in which he served his brother Thyestes with the flesh of his children.
5–6] I changed the chord from its intent,
I took a whole new instrument *MS. alternative reading.*
(*Intent* has its literal meaning of 'a stretching out'.)
7 *Alcides* Heracles, stepson of Amphitryon, son of Alcaeus.
[II]: 21 among the Loeb *Anacreontea*. 'Is not the prototype of Shelley's poem ['Love's Philosophy'] to be found in Anacreon's ode, beginning 'Η γη μελαινα πινει –, where, because the trees drink the earth, and the sea drinks the rivers, and the sun drinks the sea, and the moon drinks the sun, the poet considers it quite allowable to drink too?' (*Elizabeth Barrett to Mr. Boyd,* 52).
3 The *MS.* is annotated by Browning: 'Marcus Antoninus Lib. X cap. 21.' There Marcus Aurelius attributes to a poet a roughly similar sentiment.
[III]: 18b among the Loeb *Anacreontea*.
1 *Bathyllus* a Samian youth whom Anacreon loved.
[IV]: 45 among the Loeb *Anacreontea*.
8 *Bacchus* Dionysus, god of wine.
[V]: 48 among the Loeb *Anacreontea*.
3 *Croesus* The Lydian king (sixth century B.C.) was famous for his wealth.
6 *soul* punning on 'sole'.
7 *wines*] The reading is doubtful.
[VI]: 19 among the Loeb *Anacreontea*.
1 *Love* Cupid, the Greek Eros, god of love.
4 *Cytherea* Aphrodite (Venus), goddess of erotic love.
[VII]: 25b among the Loeb *Anacreontea*.
7 *Memphis* the fabulous city of ancient Egypt.
[VIII]: 51 among the Loeb *Anacreontea*.
[IX]: 34 among the Loeb *Anacreontea* (where the title is 'To the Cricket').
13 *Phoebus* Apollo, god of music among other things, and associated with the nine Muses.
[X]: 39 among the Loeb *Anacreontea*.
[XI]: 24 among the Loeb *Anacreontea*. The verses are not in the Houghton *MS.*; the text here is that of the American Art Association catalogue.

['SHE WAS FIFTEEN – HAD GREAT EYES']

Except for the first two lines (printed in *The Browning Collections,* 1913) and the first four lines (printed in 1916 on page 18 of R. H. Dodd's catalogue of Brownings items), these verses have not been previously published. The untitled and unsigned *MS.* was sold in 1913 (part of lot 187) and is in the Pierpont Morgan Library in New York City. It is written in the miniature handwriting that Browning sometimes affected, and some words are difficult to read. It is characteristic of Browning only in that it is – like many of his works – uncharacteristic of him, but the natural assumption that the lines are his is strengthened by the facts that the lines are obviously hurriedly dashed off (with minimal punctuation, as usual in early Browning drafts), and that in lines 16 and 18 the first reading of *sun* has been revised to *gold*, and in 18 *go* has been changed to *come*. The date is unknown, and the *MS.* paper is not watermarked. It is remotely possible that Miss Barrett may have suggested the young lady of the poem, but at any rate the lines seem early or reasonably so. A dating about 1845 seems as likely as any.

[AESCHYLUS' SOLILOQUY]

This impressive fragment was first published in November 1913 in *Cornhill Magazine* XXXV, 1913, 577–81; and was included in *New Poems*, 1914, 61–7, and collected in the Macmillan edition (1915). The *MS.*, which was sold in 1913 and is in the British Library, includes uncancelled variant readings, is rather rough and thinly punctuated, and is often difficult to read. The present text is printed from the *MS.*; most of the punctuation has been supplied, and choices have been made of uncancelled variant readings.

In the catalogue for the 1913 sale (lot 188) it was suggested that the soliloquy had been intended for *Aristophanes' Apology*, but the suggestion has nothing to commend it. The *MS.* is untitled, and the present title is Kenyon's ('Aeschylus Soliloquizes' – balancing 'Artemis Prologizes' – might be better). The *MS.* is undated; DeVane suggests (*Handbook*, 570) that the poem belongs to late February or March 1845 when Miss Barrett and Browning were strongly interested in *Prometheus Bound*. The maturity of the writing makes it improbable that it could have been written much before that, and its manner seems more akin to that of parts of *Dramatic Lyrics*, *Dramatic Romances* and *Men and Women* than to later work. The paper on which it is written is not like that of most of the later work either.

It is somewhat puzzling that a potentially fine poem was left incomplete in rough draft; unlikely is the very tentative suggestion of DeVane (*Handbook*, 570) that the difficulty of rendering the catastrophe may account for the poem's incompleteness. The sources are Plutarch's *Cimon* VIII, 9–11, and the *Vita* of Aeschylus: 'Some say that he went away to Hiero because he was unpopular at Athens, having been beaten by the young Sophocles . . . But some say that the bringing in of the chorus scattered about at the performance of the *Eumenides* so frightened the public that some were struck dumb, and some miscarried. Coming then to Sicily . . . living three years more, being aged, he met his end thus. An eagle having seized a tortoise, not knowing how to get at his prey, went to drop it on the rocks to break the shell, but it being dropped on the poet, killed him. It had been prophesied, "A blow from heaven will kill you."'

1 *old* Aeschylus was probably about sixty-nine.
10 *Terminus* boundary-mark.
11 *Faunus* Roman form of Pan.
15 *images*] images (imagery?) [*sic*] *MS., Cornhill, New Poems.*
41 *people's scorn* In *Cimon* VIII, 9–11, Plutarch tells of the victory (468) of Sophocles, who had just produced his first plays, over Aeschylus, as a result of which, Plutarch says, the angry Aeschylus left Athens for Sicily. See also the note from the *Vita* above.
45 *ears*] *MS., this edition*; case *all texts.*
47 *chorus* Aeschylus is presumably thinking of the fear induced by his Chorus in the *Eumenides* of 458 B.C., just before he left Athens.
thymele the altar of Dionysus in the centre of the Orchestra in the ancient Greek theatre.
70 *knelt*] *MS., this edition*; knell *all texts.*
72 *Apollo* god of the sun and poetry.
76 *Hesperian fruit* golden apple from the mythical Garden of the Hesperides.

85 *Hymettus* mountain near Athens, famous for its honey.
86 *Ilissus* river near Athens.
107 *innumerous* innumerable (poeticism).
118 *wind,*] wind (?flakes fall) [*sic*] *MS., Cornhill, New Poems.*
124 *piercing*] {piercing?? / pressing?} [*sic*] *MS., Cornhill, New Poems.*
132–48 perhaps influenced by the procession at the beginning of Keats's *Hyperion.*
135 *Saturn* identified with Cronos (Time), Titan, father of Zeus.
137 *eagle* the Bird of Jove to the Romans.
139 *glode* obsolete and Spenserian past tense of 'glide'.
140 *shadow*] {mist / shadow} [*sic*] *MS., Cornhill, New Poems.*
142 *Neptune* god of the sea.
143 *Pluto* god of the underworld.
146 *trenching* encroaching.

[TRANSLATION OF DANTE, 'PURGATORY' V, 53–7]

First published in 1899 in *The Letters of Robert Browning and Elizabeth Barrett Barrett* I, 348. The letter of 21 December 1845 is in Kintner, *Letters* I, where the lines appear on page 336. The *MS.* is in the Library of Wellesley College. The lines have not previously been collected.

In the letter, Browning speaks of setting about reconsidering *Sordello*, and remarks: 'yesterday I was reading the "Purgatorio" and the first speech of the group of which Sordello makes one struck me with a new significance, as well describing the man and his purpose and fate in my own poem – see; one of the burthened, contorted souls tells Virgil and Dante –'. Browning goes on to quote *Purgatorio* v, 52–7. He then adds, introducing his translation, 'Which is just my Sordello's story . . . could I "*do*" it off hand, I wonder –'.

[TO MISS UNGER]

First published in 1900 in *A Catalogue of the Printed Books, Manuscripts Autograph Letters Etc. Collected Since the Printing of the First Catalogue in 1886 by the Late Frederick Locker Lampson,* Charles Whittingham & Co. at the Chiswick Press, 1900, 49. The lines, according to the note in this *Appendix to the Rowfant Library,* were 'inserted' in Browning's autograph in a copy of the edition of *Christmas-Eve and Easter-Day.* The lines were first reprinted by W. Whitla under the title 'To Miss Unger' in *Six Stray Verses,* 1966, and were again reprinted by him under the title '[Lines to Miss Unger]' in *N&Q*, new series XXI, 1974, 448. Whitla dates the lines 1850, but the date remains uncertain and the present editor's guess is that they are later; the lines were 'inserted', not 'written', in Locker-Lampson's copy of Browning's volume, and the reference in the *Catalogue* to the poem 'written in Florence in 1850' is, despite Whitla, surely to *Christmas-Eve and Easter-Day.* Miss Unger, otherwise unidentified, had presumably written to Browning from San Francisco and sent US stamps for his reply.

5 *done . . . is undone* As Whitla suggests, the phrasing recalls Donne's playing with his name in 'A Hymn to God the Father', and in 'John Donne, Anne Donne, undone'.

THE 'MOSES' OF MICHAEL ANGELO

First published in September 1914 in *Cornhill Magazine* XXXVII, 1914, 289; it was reprinted in *New Poems*, 1914, 26, and collected in the Macmillan edition. The *MS*. is in the Library of the University of Toronto; it is dated from Siena, 27 September 1850, is 'Given to Ba "for love's sake" ', and is said to be 'From Zappi'. Browning's sonnet translates that of the minor Italian poet Giambattista Felice Zappi (1667–1719). The statue is in San Pietro in Vincoli, Rome. According to Vasari, 'there was no other work to be seen, antique or modern, which could rival it'.

7–8 *the mountain give/Back to the world that visage* 'when Moses came down from mount Sinai with the two tables of testimony in Moses' hand, when he came down from the mount, that Moses wist not that the skin of his face shone while he talked with him' (Exodus xxxiv 29).
9–11 *he suspended ... Mizraïm* Exodus xiv 21–9. 'Mizraïm' is Hebrew for 'Egypt'.
12 *vile calf raised* Exodus xxxii 4.

[ON CORREGGIO]

First printed in Sotheby's auction catalogue (lot 26) for the sale of 10 December 1913, and edited and reprinted by W. Whitla in *Six Stray Verses*, 1966, and *N&Q*, new series XXI, 1974, 449. The lines are thus introduced in a letter from Browning to Mrs Jameson (1794–1860), the art writer and friend of the Brownings: 'At which of the Colnaghi's [art galleries] can one see the Correggio you spoke of one evening at Carlyle's? I am just now hungry for his pictures, and mean whenever I am sore at heart to go and get well before the great cupola at – but why not versify, since that, or something like it, is my trade?' The 'great cupola' is that of the Cathedral of Parma; it is decorated with Correggio's famous *Assumption of the Virgin*. The lines, Whitla suggests, belong probably to the summer of 1851, when the Brownings were in London, on the way to which they had visited Parma in June and seen the cupola there. Browning often refers to Correggio (*c*. 1489–1534), and seems to have been especially fond of him.

1 *place of birth* Correggio, after which Antonio Allegri is named, is a town in north-central Italy near Parma.
3–4 *'the sovereign'st thing on earth/Is Parma-city for an inward bruise'* a punning variation on 'the sovereign'st thing on earth/Was parmaceti for an inward bruise' (1 *Henry IV* I. 3. 58–9). 'Parmaceti' is a popular corruption of 'spermaceti', a fatty substance from the sperm whale used in medicines.

BEN KARSHOOK'S WISDOM

First published in the annual, *The Keepsake*, 1856, edited by a friend of Browning. Browning himself did not collect the work, but it has otherwise been often reprinted and collected. The poem was dated from Rome, 27 April 1854.

In a letter of 15 September 1881 to Furnivall, Browning comments on the error in 'One Word More', 136, where he had included Karshook rather than Karshish as a character in *Men and Women*, and adds, '*Karshook* (*Hebrew*: a Thistle) just belongs to the snarling verses I remember to have written but forget for whom' (Hood, *Letters*, 196) – 'Karshook' does not, in fact, mean a thistle.

Browning's character is based on the 'severe and domineering' Rabbi Eliezer ben Hyrkanos, a noted teacher around A.D. 100 (see J. Berlin-Lieberman, *Robert Browning and Hebraism,* Azriel, 1934, 30-35). In *MLN* LXIX, 1954, 569-72, C. Dahl suggested that the source for the second part is a story about the artist Fuseli, included in John Knowles, *The Life and Writings of Henry Fuseli* I, 1831, 391.

1-4 Berlin-Lieberman suggests the influence of 'Repent one day before thy death' (Pirke Aboth I, 15).
5-8 Berlin-Lieberman suggests the influence of Talmud Tract. Sabbath 153a: 'His [the Rabbi's] disciples once asked him: "But can a man know on what day he will die?" "All the more reason", replied Rabbi E. [Eliezer], "why he should repent today, lest he die tomorrow. Thus all his days will be spent in repentance".'
17 *Hiram* the 'worker in brass' who made the pillars for Solomon's Temple (1 Kings vii 13-22).
18 *The Right-hand Temple-column* Berlin-Lieberman cites from the Talmud (Tract. Ber. fol. 28b): 'Light of Israel, the right hand pillar, strong hammer'.

[A VARIATION ON LINES OF LANDOR]

The lines were first published as Landor's in 1900 in M. E. Grant Duff, *Notes from a Diary 1886-1888*, John Murray, 1900, and have taken their place in his works under the title '[Paradise Lost]'. They have not been collected in Browning editions. The scrap with the holograph *MS.*, initialled by Browning, is in the Boston Public Library along with lines in Landor's hand which Browning reworked: 'Out of his Paradise an Angel drove/Adam, a Devil now drives me from mine', and with a copy, made by Kate Field, of a letter to her from the Brownings dated from Siena 21 August 1859. The poet Walter Savage Landor (1775-1864), eighty-four at the time of the squib, and notorious for his domestic upheavals, had been driven from his home by his wife in the summer of 1859 and had turned to the Brownings for help. They had arranged for him a cottage near theirs at Siena, and there they, and sometimes Kate Field, cared for him. Miss Field (1838-96), the young American writer, was universally loved, and the Brownings and Landor adored her. She collected autographs, and Browning obviously enclosed his scrap and Landor's for her album. In Browning's part of the letter to her of 21 August 1859, he says: 'Mr Landor's last in his domestic misadventure. It seemed perfect as far as it goes but my wife fancied *rhymes* would have beseemed so short a composition and I tried my hand accordingly. Between ourselves I think my arrangement the happier of the two - for the Devil's name is Legion in this business - wife, daughter and sons emulating each other in all that entitles people to the horrible epithet - and, you will see, I take Mrs L. by the horns.'

VERY ORIGINAL POEM ...

The poem, with its lengthy title, was first published in September 1966 by G. Monteiro in *N&Q*, new series XIII, 1966, 340. Monteiro found the lines among the Theodore F. Dwight papers in the Archives of the Massachusetts Historical Society. The poem is signed, and is dated at London, 8 March 1864, the day before the fifteenth birthday of Browning's son. The *MS.* includes Browning's note on Lowndes: 'A famous accountant in Queen Anne's time'. Another *MS.* is in the Armstrong Browning Library of Baylor University. It has several variants and a different title and is dated 10 April 1884 – the present editor may not reproduce it. The poem has not previously been collected.

The source, noted by Monteiro, is, in all probability, Lord Chesterfield's letter of 5 February 1750: 'Old Mr [William] Lowndes, the famous Secretary of the Treasury in the reigns of King William, Queen Anne, and King George the First, used to say, "Take care of the pence, and the pounds will take care of themselves." To this maxim, which he not only preached but practised, his two grandsons at this time owe the very considerable fortunes that he left them.' Lowndes's dates are 1652–1724.

ON BEING DEFIED TO EXPRESS IN A HEXAMETER: 'YOU OUGHT TO SIT ON THE SAFETY-VALVE'

First published in September 1914 in *Cornhill Magazine* XXXVII, 1914, 289. The lines were reprinted in *New Poems,* 1914, 29, and collected in the Macmillan edition. Who defied Browning is unknown; the *MS.* was found among the papers of Browning's publisher and friend, George Smith, and is now in the University of Toronto Library. It is dated 22 February 1866. Another *MS.* (part of lot 187 at the Sotheby sale in 1913), in which the last line does not appear, is in the Pierpont Morgan Library in New York City. Entitled 'Plane te valvam' it is an earlier draft and a note at the end has a variant of the final title.

In lines 1–7 Browning meets the challenge in each line. The Latin of lines 8–10 means: 'On the valve, the safety-bearing seat, sits everyone who is approaching danger, everyone whom the heavenly powers keep strong. Do you, my little Robert, imprint on your mind, this complicated verse.' The accents used by Browning indicate long ablatives rather than short nominatives.

9–10] Cui prudentia adest, numina quemque tegunt. *Morgan MS.*

[RHYME ON EDWARD BURNE-JONES]

First published in 1907 in William Allingham's *Diary*, 151, as a Browning improvisation of 21 April 1867, a day when Allingham had lunch with Browning and his sister. The lines have not previously been collected. The title is Honan's.

The Pre-Raphaelite painter Edward Burne-Jones (1833–98) was known as Ned Jones to his friends, and was an acquaintance of Browning. The impromptu reminds one of Browning's fondness for finding impossible rhymes.

[LINES ON SWINBURNE]

First published in 1974 by R. Secor, in *SIB* II, No. 2, 1974, 58–60. The lines have not previously been collected. They are in the papers of Violet Hunt, used for *The Wife of Rossetti* (1932), in the Library of Cornell University, and appear to have come from some papers of William Allingham. His *Diary* (Macmillan, 1907), 173, records for 8 February 1868 a luncheon with Browning, and the Hunt papers quote the lines on Swinburne as part of the conversation. Browning remarked, 'When I came to "fluteplayers" [Tennyson] and then "hornblowers" [Browning] I made an epigram' – the lines on Swinburne follow. Secor points out that Browning was alluding to Swinburne's review of Arnold in the *Fortnightly Review* for 16 October 1867, 422, where he praises Arnold for his 'triumph of the lyre; and he has had to refashion it for himself among a nation and in an age of fluteplayers and horn-blowers' (422). In referring to Swinburne's 'lascivious lute' (5), Browning alludes to Swinburne's *Poems and Ballads* of 1866 which had created a sensation.

5 *lascivious lute* 'the lascivious pleasing of a lute' (*Richard III* I. i. 14).
7 *l-i-a-r*] *this edition*; l-y-r-e *Hunt papers*; l-y-a-r *Secor emendation.*

[BURLESQUE FOR PALGRAVE ON THE PRONUNCIATION OF 'METAMORPHOSIS']

First published by Francis Turner Palgrave in the *Athenaeum,* 3559, for 11 January 1896, 52, where Palgrave (1824–97), best known for his anthology *The Golden Treasury,* printed a letter from Browning to himself of 1 April 1869 which includes the lines. Browning described the versicle as 'a burlesque with metre to match'. The lines, not previously collected, were reprinted in Hood, *Letters*, 130–31; the present title is Honan's. Palgrave had remonstrated with Browning very shortly before on the quantity assigned by Browning to the word *metamorphosis* in *The Ring and the Book* X, 1615. Browning changed the *1869* reading, 'The immeasurable metamorphosis', to 'Metamorphosis the immeasurable' in *1872*. In the revised line there, as in the fourth line here, Browning meets Palgrave's objection that 'the penultimate syllable ... is long in Greek', despite his own feeling, expressed in the letter, that the word is naturally difficult to get into serious heroic measure and that it is a naturalized word. Goethe (1749–1832) did research in biological morphology, and Browning's statement about the German writer here is in fact correct.

[A ROUND ROBIN]

First published in Cornelia Carr, *Harriet Hosmer: Letters and Memories,* Moffatt, Yard, 1912, 275–6, together with Miss Hosmer's reply. Mrs Carr printed the lines from a letter to her from Miss Hosmer of September 1869. The poem was reprinted in *New Poems,* 1914, 31–2, and collected in the Macmillan edition.

Hatty Hosmer (1830–1908) was an American sculptress whom the Brownings had known in Rome, and the lines were sent to her there from a house-party at the estate of Lady Ashburton in Ross-shire, Scotland. The lines are dated 5 September 1869. While there are eight signatories to the poem, it reads throughout very much like Browning's, and Miss Hosmer says it was Browning's in her letter to Mrs Carr. A Round Robin is a petition or protest signed in a circular form so that no name heads the list.

2 *miele ... latte* 'honey' ... 'milk' (Italian).
6 *Story* William Wetmore Story (1819–95), American sculptor. The Brownings met him and his wife in Rome, and they became close friends. Their daughter Edith ('Edie') was born in 1844.
14 *Parian* of the island of Paros, one of the Cyclades in the Aegean, long famous for its white marble for sculptures.
15 *Lady Marian* Lady Marian Alford (1817–88), artist, author and patron, had met the Brownings in Rome in 1860.
17 *Sir Roderick* Sir Roderick Impey Murchison (1792–1871), noted British geologist.
19 *manna* divine food – after that miraculously supplied to the Children of Israel in the wilderness (Exodus xvi 14).

24 *Round* plain-spoken.
26 *Gammer Gurton* The plot of the 'second English comedy' in verse (*Gammer Gurton's Needle*, acted 1566) involves the loss of the heroine's needle.
27 *Lady Ashburton* Lady Louisa Ashburton (1827–1903), who figures prominently in Browning's biography and poetry as the lady to whom, it is generally thought, he proposed, probably in 1869.

HELEN'S TOWER

First printed privately in a pamphlet with Tennyson's poem of the same title and other material. It was first published in the *Pall Mall Gazette*, 28 December 1883, after Browning had heard that Tennyson proposed to make his poem public. The most admired of Browning's sonnets has been often reprinted and collected. The Greek motto means 'Helen on the tower', and refers to *Iliad* III, 153–4. The *MS.* (in the Houghton Library) is dated 26 April 1870; the tower was christened on 20 November 1870.

The sonnet was written at the request of the Marquis of Dufferin who in 1861 built a tower at Clandeboye, Ireland, honouring his mother, Helen, Lady Dufferin and Countess of Gifford (1807–67). In an unpublished letter of 24 December 1883 to Furnivall in the Folger Library, Browning says, 'There was no compliment in what I said about the singularly love-inducing lady.'

2 *Scaean gate* In *Iliad* III, 145, Helen comes to this gate of Troy and its tower where Priam and the Trojan elders are in conference.
13 Job xxxviii 4–6.
14 'the morning stars sang together, and all the sons of God shouted for joy' (Job xxxviii 7).

METTLE AND METAL

First published in 1974 in W. Irvine and P. Honan, *The Book, the Ring, and the Poet*, 457. The *MS.*, dated 30 April 1871, dates the poem at the end of January 1871, and is in the Armstrong Browning Library of Baylor University. The lines have not hitherto been collected. They were written for Lady Charlemont. Paris surrendered to the Prussians on 28 January 1871.

1 *Trochu* Louis Jules Trochu (1815–96), French general and military governor of Paris, was much criticized for his conduct of its defence in the Franco-Prussian War.

[LINES FOR A GIFT]

First published in 1952 by Betty Miller in her *Robert Browning*, 253. Mrs Miller quotes the lines from a letter of 31 March 1871 to the small daughter of Lady Ashburton, to whom Browning sent a copy of the secondary source for *The Ring and the Book*. The lines have not previously been collected.

THE DOGMA TRIUMPHANT

First published in 1914 in *New Poems*, 73. The lines, signed Italia, were collected in the Macmillan edition. The *MS.* was sold at the Sotheby sale (lot 178) in 1913.

The lines were probably written late in 1870 or early in 1871. On 18 July 1870 the doctrine of Papal infallibility had been promulgated. Late in the year, Italian forces occupied Rome, which in 1871 became the new capital of Italy. Pius IX refused to recognize his loss of temporal power and became 'the Prisoner in the Vatican'. Herries has not been identified.

2 *quare* 'why' (Latin).
4 *Papa potest errare* 'The Pope can err' (Latin).

[REFLECTIONS ON READING A LIFE OF DICKENS]

First published in 1905 in Lady Dilke [E. F. G. Pattison], *The Book of the Spiritual Life. With a Memoir of the Author by the Rt. Hon. Sir Charles W. Dilke, Bt., M.P.*, John Murray, 1905, 38. The lines were reprinted by W. H. G. Armytage in *TQ* XXI, 1952, 181. The verses have not been previously collected; Honan printed them under the title '[Quatrain for Mrs. Pattison on Charles Dickens]'. The lines are included in a letter (now in the British Library) to Mrs Emily Pattison (perhaps model for Dorothea in *Middlemarch*) of 27 December 1871, and are in this edition printed from that letter, in which Browning led up to his lines thus: 'We are all reading the Life of Dickens and admiring his sensitiveness at having brushed shoes and trimmed gallipots in his early days, when, – did he see with the eyes of certain of his sagest friends, – it was the best education imaginable for the likes of him. Shall I versify?'

Browning knew Dickens by 2 January 1838, and they met several times in the 1860s. The new *Life* to which Browning refers is that of John Forster, the first volume of which, just published when Browning read it, revealed for the first time the twelve-year-old's traumatic experiences in 1824 in the blacking warehouse in which he was an apprentice.

[RHYME FOR A CHILD VIEWING A NAKED VENUS IN A PAINTING OF 'THE JUDGEMENT OF PARIS']

First published by Laura Troubridge in *Memories and Reflections*, Heinemann, 1925, 45. The lines have not previously been collected. Lady Troubridge records visiting the Grosvenor Gallery with G. F. Watts when she was twelve (thus dating the lines about 1872), and meeting Browning before a *Judgement of Paris* in which Venus was in an 'entirely undraped condition'. Browning remarked, 'Well, let us make a funny rhyme about it, shall we?' and improvised the lines. Honan's title (162) is '[*Rhyme for a Child on a Painting of Venus and Paris*]'.

[IMPROMPTU ON RICHARD WAGNER]

First printed in the American Art Association Catalogue for the sale of 16 December 1929, lot 3, which reports the lines as being in Browning's hand and as dated 21 May 1877. As Honan remarks, reprinting and editing the lines (163), the location of the *MS.* is unknown, but the date, content and style suggest the lines' authenticity. Honan entitled the poem '[*Quatrain on Richard Wagner*]'. The lines have not previously been collected.

[ON BENJAMIN DISRAELI]

First published in Lucy Masterman's edition of *Mary Gladstone (Mrs. Drew): Her Diaries and Letters,* Methuen, 1930, 135. The lines were reprinted and edited by W. Whitla in *Six Stray Verses,* 1966, and by J. McNally, 'Two Small Verses of Browning', *VP* IX, 1971, 338–41. The title given here is Whitla's. The lines have not previously been collected.

Mary Gladstone, who found Browning 'refreshing' on the Eastern question, records in her *Diary* for 4 April 1878 a large breakfast at the Gladstones' including Browning, Tennyson and Burne-Jones among others. Browning ended the conversation on the Eastern question with his impromptu. McNally notes (339) that on the same day that Browning delivered his impromptu, Disraeli referred to Browning in a letter as a 'noisy, conceited poet'. Browning disliked Disraeli (Lord Beaconsfield) intensely, as instanced by the 'Parleying with George Bubb Dodington'. The anti-Semitism of the versicle is most uncharacteristic of Browning.

Browning's poem is based on the refrain of the 1878 music-hall song by G. W. Hunt: 'We don't want to fight, yet by Jingo, if we do,/We've got the ships, we've got the men, and got the money too!' Disraeli's policy of sending a British fleet into Turkish waters to resist the advance of Russia came to be known as a 'Jingo' policy.

['OH LOVE, LOVE']

First published by Professor J. P. Mahaffy in his *Euripides,* Macmillan, 1879, 116. The poem has been frequently reprinted and collected. The lines translate the first strophe and antistrophe in a Chorus from the *Hippolytus* of Euripides (525–44). Mahaffy introduced Browning's lines by quoting the Greek, and adding: 'Mr Browning has honoured me (Dec. 18, 1878) with the following translation of these stanzas, so that the general reader may not miss the meaning or the spirit of the ode. The English metre, though not a strict reproduction, gives an excellent idea of the original' (115–16).

8 *Aphroditê* goddess of erotic love.
9 *boy* Eros, god of love.
10 *Alpheian river* The Alphaeus river is in the Peloponnesus.
11 *Pythian shrines of Phoebus* the temple of Apollo at Delphi.

['THE BLIND MAN TO THE MAIDEN SAID']

First published in Clara Bell's translation of a sentimental romance by Wilhelmine von Hillern, *The Hour Will Come, A Tale of an Alpine Cloister,* Sampson Low, Marston, 1879, II, 174. The lines were annotated: 'The translator is indebted for these verses to the kindness of a friend.' The lines have frequently been reprinted and collected, though Browning did not collect them. In a letter to Furnivall of 10 April 1883 Browning wrote: 'I did indeed translate that little song for Mrs Bell, never dreaming anybody would suppose there was "another hand" in her work. See now! I should have thought it very mean had I told anybody "that's mine!", and she herself unnecessarily tells it – from sheer honesty, I have no doubt, on somebody observing "what, you versify?" ' (Hood, *Letters*, 216). The lines in the novel are sung by Beata to the blind Donatus, who has asked her about her appearance.

THE DELIVERY TO THE SECULAR ARM: A SCENE DURING THE EXISTENCE OF THE SPANISH INQUISITION AT ANTWERP, 1570

First published in *New Poems,* 1914, 69, under the title 'A Scene in the Building of the Inquisitors at Antwerp', and collected in the Macmillan edition. A *MS.* of the lines together with Browning's transcript of lines of Calderón which he translates is in the Armstrong Browning Library of Baylor University, and is dated 28 July 1880. There is another *MS.* with the same date in the Library of Yale University from which DeVane and Knickerbocker (*New Letters,* 256) printed the Calderón and Browning lines. DeVane clearly forgot the printing in his curious note five years later in *Handbook*, 573.

The translation was made for a motto for a picture by Browning's son, showing a girl being handed over for execution.

['THUS I WROTE IN LONDON, MUSING ON MY BETTERS']

First published in the *Century Magazine* XXV, November 1882, 160, and often reprinted and collected. The lines were written impromptu in Venice in the album of Miss Edith Longfellow, daughter of the poet, on 14 October 1880. They are in the same form as the epilogue to *Dramatic Idyls, Second Series*, 'Touch him ne'er so lightly', and they comment on it, Browning claiming here that he was not praising himself, as some readers had urged, but Dante. Browning was annoyed at the lines' being published. In an unpublished letter of 9 December 1882 in the Huntington Library, Browning remonstrates with Furnivall, asking him not to publish 'that little friendly scribble', and saying that the original poem 'is *spoiled* by this excrescence'. To Furnivall's reply that Browning's note had come too late (the poem was printed in *Browning Society's Papers* I, 48), Browning replied in another unpublished letter on 13 December 1882 that he relied on Furnivall to prevent the poem's being stereotyped.

TERSE VERSE

First published by Hallam, Lord Tennyson in 1897 in his *Tennyson: A Memoir by His Son* II, 230; the lines have not hitherto been collected. The undated holograph *MS.* from which the present text is printed is in the Tennyson Research Centre in the City Library, Lincoln. Lord Tennyson dated the poem 1875–9. Honan (160–61) suggests December 1865, when Jane Carlyle was still alive (she died in April 1866), noting that Browning saw the Tennysons that month when Carlyle was being congratulated on his seventieth birthday. The lines appear, however, between letters dated 24 November 1880 and 13 March 1883 in an album of letters (probably compiled by the poet?), which are arranged chronologically with only one or two minor slips. The present editor's guess is that the poem probably belongs about 1882, after Carlyle's death in 1881. In printing the lines, Lord Tennyson remarked that they were produced impromptu for Tennyson's amusement. They provide one of several examples of Browning's enjoying the challenge of finding impossible rhymes – here, for the birthplaces of the Carlyles.

6 *cross-buttock* to throw over the hip in a special way in wrestling. Browning used the word in *The Two Poets of Croisic,* 855, also.

GEROUSIOS OINOS

First published in April 1914 in *Cornhill Magazine* XXXVI, 1914, 575–6, and reprinted in *New Poems,* 1914, 46–8, and collected in the Macmillan edition. A proof of the poem turned up at the Sotheby sale in 1913. It had been intended for *Jocoseria,* but was excluded, presumably because Browning thought it might offend his contemporary poets, for whose verse in his later years he generally found little use. The poem probably dates from 1882. The title transliterates the Greek from *Iliad* IV, 259, and means 'Wine of the Elders'.

29 *regale* feast.
35 *mundungus* refuse (obsolete).
46 *heel-tap* the liquor left in a glass after drinking.

[TRANSLATION FROM PINDAR'S SEVENTH OLYMPIAN, EPODE III]

First published in *New Poems,* 1914, 40, and collected in the Macmillan edition. The *MS.* dated 10 January 1884 [*sic* – Browning's error for 1883] is in the Armstrong Browning Library of Baylor University. Browning sent a copy of the lines, with different punctuation but no verbal variants, in a letter to his friend J. D. Williams of 10 March 1883 (Hood, *Letters,* 214), where Browning introduces the lines, 'Just after the termination of the "Belt Trial", I was looking into Pindar, and came upon the 3[d] Epode of his seventh Olympian. I made this rough translation at once – to match the Judge's quotation from Aristotle.' The translation is loose, and the final lines are adaptation rather than translation.

The *MS.* was written, it seems from a letter of 14 January 1883 (in *New Poems,* 39–40), to be sent to the *Pall Mall Gazette,* but neither letter nor translation was apparently sent. Browning's translation was prompted by a noted legal case of 1882 when R. C. Belt, a sculptor, sued Sir Charles Bennet Lawes for calling his own certain pieces of sculpture that were not entirely his own. He won the case before Baron Huddleston, who, leaning on Aristotle for support, suggested that a Middlesex jury was as good a judge of Art as a Royal Academician.

1 *Rhodians* Rhodes was a centre of art from very early times.
Sharp-eyed One Athena, goddess of wisdom.
6 *sculpture-living things* Legend had it that Rhodians tied their statues' feet together to prevent their running away.

CLASSICALITY APPLIED TO TEA-DEALING: A FANCY INSPIRED BY WESTBOURNE GROVE

The lines have not previously been published. The *MS.* is in the Houghton Library of Harvard College, on paper embossed with the address (11 Kensington Park Gardens) of Frederic Leighton, and is dated 'Tea-time', 11 June 1883. The envelope is addressed to Miss Hood at 10 Kensington Park Gardens, a street close to the street, Westbourne Grove, of the title. Another version of the lines (which the present editor is not permitted to quote) is in the Armstrong Browning Library of Baylor University, on the same sheet (written for an album) as a squib on Andrea del Sarto's *Jupiter and Leda.* This other *MS.* is dated 6 February 1834 and is entitled 'On the deleterious effects of tea' (see Sotheby's catalogue for the sale of

20 July 1954, lot 434). It would seem that nearly fifty years after composing the lines, Browning recalled them as a *jeu d'esprit* to be sent to a neighbour of Leighton. The Baylor version, besides its different title, has a motto and minor variants.

Heraclitus (*c.* 535–*c.* 474 B.C.), son of Hyson or Heracion, was the Greek philosopher of Ephesus, known as the 'weeping philosopher' because of his focus on the fleetingness of life. Hyson is also a species of Chinese green tea, and Browning's context suggests he is thinking of the so-called 'young Hyson' which means 'before the rains'. The poem is, the present editor hopes, the only one of Browning's demanding a knowledge of Chinese for full understanding.

[ON SINGERS]

First published in the *Pall Mall Gazette,* 13 December 1883, with an inaccurate report of the origin. The lines were reprinted in 1884 in the *Browning Society's Papers* I, 99, and in *New Poems,* 1914, 45, and were collected in the Macmillan edition. They are edited by W. Whitla in *Six Stray Verses.* The *MS.* is in the Armstrong Browning Library.

The lines were translated impromptu on 10 July 1883 in the album of Felix Moscheles, the artist and Browning's friend, where Sir James Ingham had inscribed the first three lines of Horace, *Satires* I, iii. When Browning saw the lines, 'he took up a pen and wrote without pausing to think', Moscheles reports in his *Fragments of an Autobiography,* Nisbet, 1899, 340.

1 *sorts of singers*] *MS., Fragments, Six Stray Verses*; singers, trust me, *Pall Mall Gazette, New Poems, Macmillan edition.*

GOLDONI

First published in England in the *Pall Mall Gazette,* 8 December 1883. Browning himself did not collect the poem, but it has often been reprinted and collected. The *MS.*, from which the text of the present edition is printed, is in the Casa Goldoni in Venice.

The poem was written hurriedly on 27 November 1883 in Venice, while, Mrs Orr says (*Life*, 339), a messenger waited for it, Browning having been asked for a contribution to an album to which leading men of letters in Italy contributed in connection with the unveiling of a monument to Goldoni in Venice. Carlo Goldoni (1707–93) is Italy's most famous writer of stage comedy. Strongly influenced by Molière, he wrote well over 100 plays.

5 *scrolls*] *MS., this edition*; shoals *all texts.*
6 *Parini* Giuseppe Parini (1729–99), Italian poet.
8 *shoals*] *MS., this edition*; scrolls *all texts.*
11 *Calle* narrow Venetian street.

[RAWDON BROWN]

First published in February 1884 in the *Century Magazine* XXVII, 1884, 640. Browning did not collect the sonnet, but it has often been reprinted and collected. The *MS.* is in the Carl H. Pforzheimer Library in New York City. The poem is dated 28 November 1883.

The poem was written at the request of Mrs Arthur Bronson, Browning's American friend to whom he dedicated *Asolando*, and with whom he spent time in Asolo and Venice. The introductory statement to the poem in *Century Magazine* includes the information that 'Mr Rawdon Brown, an Englishman of culture well known by visitors in Venice, died in that city in the summer of 1883. He went to Venice for a short visit, with a definite object in view, and ended by staying forty years.' '*Anglus* Brown am I,/Although my heart's Venetian' was used on Brown's tomb. The sonnet's motto means, 'Everyone follows his taste, and I follow mine.'

1 *Sighed*] Quoth *MS. first reading.*
Toni Brown's gondolier and attendant.
3 *Anglus* English.
8 *Cà Pesaro* major Palace on the Grand Canal.
coney rabbit.
10 *Cospetto* 'Good Heavens'.
12 'Beautiful Venice, I no longer abandon you.'
14 *quite*] grown *MS.*
quite Brown that is, unable to leave Venice for England (he left on 8 December).

[COUPLET FOR FURNIVALL ON TWO PUBLISHERS]

First published in 1933 by T. L. Hood in *Letters*, 226, where the lines occur in a letter to Furnivall of 17 February 1884. They were reprinted and edited by Honan (163–4); they have not hitherto been collected. The title is Honan's.

In the letter Browning asks Furnivall to decline the 'surprising proposal' of an American lady who had, it appears, offered to intervene with Harper's to publish Browning, but on condition that they saw his work before agreeing to publish it, a condition unacceptable to Browning whose stipulation with Smith, Elder, his own publishers, was that they – even his friend George Smith – were not to read his works until they were in corrected proofs.

2 *Scirocco* Sirocco, a hot and blighting Mediterranean wind.

THE NAMES

First published 29 May 1884 as the first contribution to *Shaksperean Show Book* [*sic*], a booklet printed for the Shakespearean Show held 29–31 May in the Albert Hall in aid of the Chelsea Hospital for Women – among other contributors were Tennyson and Wilde. The poem was published the same day in the *Pall Mall Gazette*, and has often been reprinted and collected. An autographed proofsheet with Browning's revisions is in the Folger Library. The poem is dated 12 March 1884. In an unpublished letter to Furnivall of 27 March 1884, in the Huntington Library, Browning says: 'I indited a sonnet for the Fair – too hastily perhaps, but it may do.'

The poem alludes to the fact that many Jews believe it wrong to speak the name of God.

THE FOUNDER OF THE FEAST

First printed in the *World* for 16 April 1884. The poem has often been reprinted and collected. At the Sotheby sale in 1913, a clipping of the poem from the *World* with Browning's revisions was sold; the revisions turned a fifteen-line poem into a sonnet. The lines were dated 5 April 1884. The *MS.* is in the Beinecke Library of Yale University.

At the request of Joseph Joachim, the lines were contributed to an album presented to Arthur Chappell (1834–1904), music publisher and organizer of the Popular Concerts at Saint James's Hall, which Browning frequently and lovingly attended.

5 *so*] as *MS.*, *World.*
9] Thanks, then, to Arthur Chappell, – thanks to him/Whose every guest henceforth not idly vaunts *MS.*; Thanks then to Arthur Chappell, thanks to him/Whose every guest henceforth not idly vaunts *World.*
14 The four named were all frequent and distinguished performers at the Popular Concerts: Sir Charles Hallé (1819–95), conductor and pianist; Clara Josephine Schumann (1819–96), pianist, widow of the composer; Alfredo Carlo Piatti (1822–1901), noted violoncellist; Joseph Joachim (1831–1907), noted Hungarian violinist, and a Browning acquaintance.

[FOLKESTONE LIMERICK]

First published by E. C. McAleer in 1966 in *Learned Lady,* 180, from a Browning letter of 26 April 1884 (now in the Carl H. Pforzheimer Library), where it is untitled. The limerick (Browning's only one?) has not been reprinted or collected. The letter makes clear that Browning is replying to remarks of Mrs FitzGerald: 'As to the rhyme for Folkestone, I am forced to say there is an *l.* in that word which sounds in the ear and should appear to the eye, – and it is absent from "joke's tone": my example would therefore run thus –', at which point Browning gives his lines rhyming on the Kentish port.

[CONCLUSION OF A SONNET ON 'KEELY'S DISCOVERY']

First published in 1890 by Browning's friend, Mrs C. J. Bloomfield-Moore of Philadelphia, in *Lippincott's Magazine* XLV, 1890, 686. The lines were written at Christmas 1884, which Mrs Bloomfield-Moore spent in London. She remarks: 'One Christmas evening when we were amusing ourselves by giving Mr Browning subjects and rhymes for sonnets, I gave the rhymes, and "Keely's Discovery" as the subject. Much more expeditiously than I had written down the rhymes to which he was to confine himself in its composition, he wrote the sonnet. The time will come when the world will look upon this sonnet as an inspired prophecy, the closing lines of which are as follows' – she then quotes the last four lines.

John Ernst Worrell Keely (1827–98) announced his discovery of a new physical force in 1873. In 1874 he exhibited the 'Keely Motor' operated by this force. Mrs Bloomfield-Moore financed the 'discovery' (an imposture using compressed air) for several years.

WHY I AM A LIBERAL

First published in 1885 in a collection of statements edited by Andrew Reid, *Why I Am a Liberal, Being Definitions by the Best Minds of the Liberal Party,* Cassell, 1885, 11. The sonnet has often been reprinted and collected. Browning's statement led all the rest, appearing immediately before Gladstone's. Browning always regarded himself as a liberal.

[LINES FOR THE TOMB OF LEVI LINCOLN THAXTER]

First published in *Poet Lore* I, August 1889, 398, and reprinted in Mrs Orr's *Life*, 1891, 353. The lines have often been reprinted and collected. There are *MSS.*, both dated 19 April 1885, in the Huntington and Balliol College Libraries; and the letter including the lines to Thaxter's son, who had requested an inscription for the boulder above his father's grave on the Maine coast, is in the Pierpont Morgan Library. Thaxter (1824–84) was an admirer of Browning and gave readings from his works. He was the husband of the poet Celia Laighton Thaxter. Maria S. Porter, in her privately printed *Recollections* . . ., 1893, 49, quotes Browning as saying 'my friends in Britain . . . regarded Mr Levi Thaxter as the best reader and interpreter of my poems you have had there [in the U S]'.

[IMPROMPTU LINES TO GREET MARIE BANCROFT]

First published in Marie and Squire Bancroft, *The Bancrofts: Recollections of Sixty Years,* John Murray, 1909, 396. Bancroft introduces the quatrain thus: 'At a Richmond dinner he [Browning] greeted my wife's appearance on the terrace of the Star and Garter with this impromptu – which, let me add, may be very imperfect, as it was hurriedly written down on a *menu* card' (395–6). The actress and actor, acquaintances of Browning, retired as theatrical managers in 1885, and Honan (164) suggests the date as a likely one for the impromptu. Bancroft quotes two Browning letters (395), the first of which is dated 29 June 1885, and which may possibly refer to the Richmond dinner that provided the occasion for the lines. The versicle has not been collected; the title is Honan's.

LAST POEM

The lines have not been previously published. The *MS.* is in the Carl H. Pforzheimer Library in New York City in an undated letter from Browning to 'Dear Friend' accepting an invitation to dinner on Pen's behalf and his own, and wishing the friend's husband well. The lady whose absence, as the title implies, threatened Browning's life, and Mrs Gab will probably remain for ever unidentified. Gustav Natorp (1836–?) became a sculptor late in life; in 1888 he exhibited at the Royal Academy a bronze figure of Browning. The date of the lines is unknown. Browning knew Natorp well from 1879 on. The Warwick Crescent address on the letter indicates a date before July 1887.

EPPS

The first and last stanzas were first printed in *The Browning Collections* (lot 196). The whole poem was first published in October 1913 in *Cornhill Magazine* XXXV, 1913, 433–5. The poem was reprinted in *New Poems,* 1914, 56–9, and collected in the Macmillan edition. The *MS.*, which includes uncancelled variants of some readings, is in the Berg Collection of the New York Public Library. It is dated 6 January 1886.

Epps was the maiden name of two of Browning's friends, Mrs Edmund Gosse and Lady Alma Tadema, and Browning wrote the poem for them, unaware though they were of their Kentish ancestor, who was reportedly killed at the siege of Ostend, 1601–4. The source is a note in A. B. Grosart's edition of Donne (1872) to what Grosart called 'Satire VI (To Sir Nicholas Smyth)', a poem not now attributed to Donne but generally assigned to Sir John Roe. Lines 26–7 refer to Epps, 'like Epps it often wars,/And still is hurt'; Grosart's note identifies the Epps with a character in Dekker's *Knight's Conjuring,* viii (there seem to be no grounds for the identification). Grosart's note is given in DeVane, *Handbook*, 569; Browning follows his source closely. Gosse reports that Browning did not treat his verses 'as a serious specimen of his poetic art' (*New Poems,* 56).

6 *Kentish*] William *MS. first reading.*

13 *He had lost an eye on the walls* 'He lost an eye on the walls' (Grosart's note).

22 *maimed old*] *MS., this edition*; old maiméd *all texts.*

30 *band*] $\left\{\begin{array}{l}\text{band}\\ \text{company}\end{array}\right\}$ *MS., all texts.*

39 *ties me tight round*] *MS.?, this edition*; $\left\{\begin{array}{l}\text{ties}\\ \text{binds}\end{array}\right\}$ me $\left\{\begin{array}{l}\text{round}\\ \text{tight}\end{array}\right\}$ about *all texts.*

42 *Staff, show flag's*] *MS. second reading, this edition*; Flag, help staff's *MS. first reading*; Flagstaff, show your *all texts.*

46 *bullets*] $\left\{\begin{array}{l}\text{bullets}\\ \text{balls}\end{array}\right\}$ *MS., all texts.*

46–7 *Two bullets . . . flag* 'he was twice shot, and twice run through the body, yet wold not surrender his hold' (Grosart's note).

47 *leave*] $\left\{\begin{array}{l}\text{leave}\\ \text{left}\end{array}\right\}$ *MS., all texts.*

59 *a heart*] *MS., this edition*; heart *MS. first reading, all texts.*

[LINES FOR A PAINTING BY LEIGHTON]

First ascribed to Browning and published by Ernest Rhys, *Sir Frederic Leighton,* George Bell, 1895, 71. The lines were reprinted, with incorrect punctuation, in Hood, *Letters*, 368, in a note in which Hood erroneously refers to these lines instead of Browning's 'Eurydice to Orpheus'. That they are Browning's lines, Hood suggests, is probable (167), that they are almost certainly his is suggested by the holograph *MS.*, now in the Huntington Library, from which the text of the present edition is printed, and which was quoted in *The Browning Collections* (lot 192). There Browning has indicated in Latin that the lines are of uncertain authorship, but, as indicated by analogy with his own lines which he signed 'Felix Moscheles' (see the note to 'The Isle's Enchantress'), that is in all probability part of a game Browning played in developing mottos for friends' pictures ('Eurydice to Orpheus', also written for a Leighton picture, was called 'a fragment', and its author was unidentified). The lines, which have not been previously collected, were written for a 'picture of a little girl with golden hair and pale blue eyes', which Frederic Leighton, Browning's friend and President of the Royal Academy, painted probably in 1887.

[SUGGESTION FOR A TELEGRAPHIC BIRTHDAY GREETING]

First published by Browning's friend, Mrs C. J. Bloomfield-Moore, in May 1890, in *Lippincott's Magazine* XLV, 1890, 686. The lines were reprinted with the erroneous and misleading title of 'Reply to a Telegraphic Greeting' in *New Poems,* 1914,

70, and the Macmillan edition. The lines were written at the request of Mrs Bloomfield-Moore for a telegram to the American historian, George Bancroft (1800–91) to congratulate him on his eighty-seventh birthday (3 October) in 1887. Mrs Bloomfield-Moore says that the lines were written impromptu 'almost as quick as thought', but M. A. DeWolfe Howe in his *Life and Letters of George Bancroft*, 1908, II, 309, says that Browning sent the lines with a note: 'I enclose a short metre with a view to saving your charges for the cable dispatch!' That Howe's version is correct is supported by an unpublished letter of 26 September 1887 in the Carl H. Pforzheimer Library, in which Browning says he will provide at least a quatrain in honour of Mr Bancroft's birthday.

2 *my 'All Hail'*] *this edition*; all my hail *Lippincott's*; thy 'All Hail' *New Poems.*
3 *the*] my *New Poems.*
4] That, half what pen writes, tongue might say. *New Poems.*

[ON IGNAZ MOSCHELES]

First published in 1888 in *Letters of Felix Mendelssohn to Ignaz and Charlotte Moscheles*, Trübner, 1888, 21 and 246. That volume was edited and translated by Felix Moscheles, who reprinted the lines in his *Fragments of an Autobiography*, Nisbet, 1899, 30–31. A copy of the poem appeared in *The Browning Collections* (lot 192). The lines were reprinted in DeVane and Knickerbocker, *New Letters*, 353, in the text of a letter of 30 November 1887 from Browning to Felix Moscheles (now in the Library of Yale University), and incorrectly stated there to be a free translation of Horace, *Sermones* I, ii, 11. The lines were edited by W. Whitla in *Six Stray Verses*, 1966, under the title 'To Ignaz Moscheles'; he also printed them under the title '[*Stanzas to Ignaz Moscheles*]' in *N&Q*, new series XXI, 1974, 450. The lines were reprinted as recently discovered and hitherto unpublished in *The Times Higher Education Supplement*, 26 January 1973, 4. The lines have not hitherto been collected.

The verses were written late in November 1887. They translate lines of the German poet and diplomat, Karl Klingeman (1798–1862), which had been written for birthday celebrations on 30 May of Ignaz Moscheles (1794–1870) in 1832 (the first stanza) and 1844 (the second stanza). The German verses are in the *Letters of Felix Mendelssohn* (illustrations 3 and 27). Browning made a number of copies (with minor variants) of his letter to Moscheles including the lines.

Ignaz Moscheles was a pianist and composer, and friend of Beethoven. His son Felix painted Browning's portrait and became his friend, and Browning's translation was an answer to his request for one.

As Whitla points out, the verses remind one of the final stanzas of the 'Epilogue' to *Asolando*.

7 *intent*] content *Letters of Felix Mendelssohn.*

[LINES FOR THE JUBILEE WINDOW]

First published in the *Pall Mall Gazette*, 4 January 1888, 10. The lines have often been collected and reprinted; they were edited by Whitla in *N&Q*, new series XXI, 1974, 451–2. The lines were requested by Browning's friend, F. W. Farrar, Archdeacon of Westminster, on 17 December 1887 for a window, picturing the Queen and celebrating her Jubilee, in Saint Margaret's Church, Westminster (the window was destroyed by German bombing in the Second World War). Browning's lines in his reply to Farrar's request are dated 18 December 1887. The *MS.* is in the Armstrong Browning Library of Baylor University.

Browning's intense concern over punctuation is nicely illustrated by the fact that 'the glass painters made a slight error in punctuation in fixing the lines in the window. Mr Browning pointed out the mistake with some vexation, and the glass was altered at his own request' (*Pall Mall Gazette,* 31 December 1889).

The lines were parodied and heavily criticized by Browning's contemporaries. DeVane entitles them 'Jubilee Memorial Lines', and Whitla, 'Quatrain for the Jubilee Window'.

['SIPPING GROG ONE DAY AT SEA']

The lines have not previously been published. They are in the Berg Collection of the New York Public Library, and are in Browning's later handwriting. The hasty draft is unsigned and undated. The poem is clearly going nowhere, and peters out with a fifteenth illegible line. A dating of about 1888 seems reasonable.

REPLIES TO CHALLENGES TO RHYME

The first of these replies was first published in 1897 in slightly different form by Hallam, Lord Tennyson in *Alfred Lord Tennyson: A Memoir* II, 230, in a section covering the years 1875–9. The fourth was first printed in *The Browning Collections,* where lot 189 consisted of a single sheet with the 'Replies'. The others were first published with the group of six in *New Poems,* 1914, 71–2, and were collected in the Macmillan edition. The *Memoir* introduces Browning's quatrain thus: 'They [Tennyson and Browning] would laugh heartily together at Browning's faculty for absurd and abstruse rhymes. I remember a dinner where Jebb, Miss Thackeray, and Browning were present. Browning said he thought that he could make a rhyme for every word in the English language. We gave him "rhinoceros". Without a pause he said' – the lines follow. As DeVane (*Handbook,* 575) says, only the fifth of the 'Replies' can be dated precisely, but an unfortunate misprint gives a date wrong by nine years. Hannah de Rothschild married Lord Rosebery in 1878.

I. There is a manuscript of these lines in the hand of Emily Tennyson in the Tennyson Research Centre in Lincoln.
1 *If ever you meet*] *New Poems*; O, if you should see *Memoir.*
4 *could*] *New Poems*; can *Memoir.*
Eros god of love.
II. A scrap of paper in the Armstrong Browning Library of Baylor University, printed in 1913 (item 478) in the sales catalogue of Bertram Dobell, *Browning Memorials,* gives the rhymes for the lines here: 'Made dishes – raddishes – baddish cheese'. A kickshaw is a fancy cookery dish; made-dishes are dishes made of several ingredients.
III. 1 *Poggibonsi* town in Tuscany.
2 *bonze* European term for Japanese Buddhist clergy.
V. 1 *Venus* The goddess of erotic love is often reputed to have been born from sea-foam.
2 *Playing old gooseberry* To play gooseberry is to act as chaperone, or to be an unwanted third when lovers are together.
3 *Rosebery* Archibald Philip Primrose, fifth Earl of Rosebery, Liberal politician

and historian and later briefly Prime Minister (1847–1929). In 1878 he married Hannah, child of the leading banking family.

[DIALOGUE BETWEEN FATHER AND DAUGHTER]

First published in *New Poems,* 1914, 72, and collected in the Macmillan edition. The date is not known. *Mizpah*, Hebrew for 'watch-tower' (Genesis xxxi 49), is several times a place of meeting in the Bible.

[RHYMING EXERCISES]

First printed in 1913 in the sales catalogue of Bertram Dobell (item 478). The scraps of paper on which Browning wrote these lines and others are in the Armstrong Browning Library of Baylor University. The date of the lines, not previously collected, is unknown.

THE ISLE'S ENCHANTRESS

First published in the *Pall Mall Gazette,* 26 March 1889. The lines were reprinted in Felix Moscheles, *Fragments of an Autobiography*, Nisbet, 1899, 336, and in *New Poems,* 1914, 60; they were collected in the Macmillan edition. The *MS.* is in the Berg Collection of the New York Public Library.

The painter Felix Moscheles (1833–1917) had painted a Browning portrait in 1884, and Browning used subsequently to visit his studio. Moscheles records in his *Fragments of an Autobiography*, 335–6, that, early in 1889, he was seeking a title for a 'shell-picture' he was working on, and that Browning suggested 'Why not call it *more shells* by *Moscheles*?' Other suggested lines seeming inadequate, Moscheles suggested some invented lines attributed to an invented name such as 'Grelice di Napoli', and gave Browning a suggestion to work from: 'And as I walked along those lovely shores, and breathed the air of balmy climes, I waking dreamt of living forms that wedded opalescent shells; of peace, and rest, and blissful harmonies'. Browning replied the next day with an early draft, signed 'Felix Moscheles': 'And as I wandered by the happy shores/And breathed the sunset air of balmy climes,/I waking dreamt of some transcendent shape,/A woman's – framed by opalescent shells,/Peacefully lulled by Nature's harmonies.' 'A day or two later' 'The Isle's Enchantress' was posted (the postmark is 7 March 1889) as a substitute for Browning's earlier version (printed by Honan, 164, under the title '[Variation on a Description by Moscheles for "The Isle's Enchantress"]'). Whitla also printed the lines (both versions) in *Six Stray Verses.* It was Moscheles who sent the lines to the *Pall Mall Gazette*; his painting was rejected by the Grosvenor Gallery (see Hood, *Letters,* 280).

3 *Came*] *MS.*; Come *Pall Mall Gazette, New Poems.*

TO EDWARD FITZGERALD

First published in the *Athenaeum*, 13 July 1889, 64. The poem has frequently been reprinted and collected. It was written on 8 July 1889.

The lines were prompted by Browning's reading – as the book flipped open in a friend's garden – a remark of FitzGerald's in W. Aldis Wright's newly published edition, *Letters and Literary Remains of Edward FitzGerald,* Macmillan, 1889, I, 280–81: 'Mrs Browning's Death is rather a relief to me, I must say: no more Aurora Leighs, thank God! A woman of real Genius, I know: but what is the upshot of it all? She and her Sex had better mind the Kitchen and their Children; and perhaps the Poor: except in such things as little Novels, they only devote themselves to what Men do much better, leaving that which Men do worse or not at all.' Browning, shocked and irate, sent the lines to the *Athenaeum* 8 July; the next day he wrote to one of the editors, Norman MacColl (see Hood, *Letters*, 311), asking that if the lines were unsuitable they be returned to him 'for publication elsewhere. Remember I never saw the man, nor did my wife ever know of his existence.' It is said that MacColl later delayed opening a telegram from Browning asking that the lines not be published until it was 'too late'. The *Athenaeum* printed Wright's letter of apology on 20 July. Browning's fury at the comment of FitzGerald (1809–81) is recorded in other letters (see Hood, *Letters*, 311–14, 317; Landis, *Letters of the Brownings,* 330–31; and, especially, a full and moving letter to Lady Tennyson of 21 July 1889, first published by C. Ricks, *TLS*, 3 June 1965, and included in Collins, *The Brownings to the Tennysons*, 48–50).

The incident may well have hastened Browning's death. 'Rabbi Ben Ezra' and 'Mihrab Shah' record fairly indirectly Browning's antipathy to FitzGerald's verse.

[RESPONSE TO A TRANSLATION BY LONGFELLOW]

First printed by Maria S. Porter, *Recollections of Louisa May Alcott, John Greenleaf Whittier, and Robert Browning,* Boston (privately printed), 1893, 57. The Boston lady collected autographs, and met Browning a few times in the summer of 1889. Browning saw two Italian lines in the album in Longfellow's hand together with the poet's translation of them: 'Che sembra mi alma, doves amor non stanze,/Casa di notte, senza foco, o face.' 'The soul, where love abideth not, resembles/A house by night, without or fire or torch.' Maria Porter reports: 'When he caught sight of Longfellow's lines, he exclaimed, "Longfellow didn't make the rhyme. I'll try my hand at it." And as quick as thought wrote [Browning's lines are quoted]. Saying gleefully, "I've done it: there's my rhyme!"' Honan reports (166) that in the album the Browning lines are dated 30 July 1889; they are undated in the *Recollections.* Honan, most unusually, errs (166n.) in saying that there is a facsimile of Longfellow's and Browning's entries on page 48; only Longfellow's appears there. The title is Honan's. The Italian lines have not been traced to a source. Browning's lines have not hitherto been collected.

[INSCRIPTION FOR A SKETCH]

The lines appear on a pencil sketch by C. D. Giles (1857–1941) in the Armstrong Browning Library of Baylor University (the sketch and lines are reproduced in *BNL*, No. 3, 1969, 36, with a note by J. Herring on pages 43–4). The sketch was first published by W. M. Rossetti in the *Magazine of Art* XIII, April 1890, 266. Browning dated the lines on the sketch 24 November 1889. The lines have not hitherto been collected.

They are probably Browning's last composition. Evelyn Barclay (who became Mrs C. D. Giles in 1891) recorded in her *Diary* for 26 November (dating the event two days later than Browning, but she often errs in detail): 'That afternoon Mr

Giles was sketching. Mr Browning said, "Come now, Giles, do me." In a few minutes he had done a pencil sketch . . . That evening I asked him to write his name below it, which he did' – Miss Barclay goes on to quote the lines (*Diary of Miss Evelyn Barclay*, Baylor University Browning Interests, Fifth Series, 1932, 7). Giles himself said the sketch was made in the evening.

Index of Titles

Index of First Lines